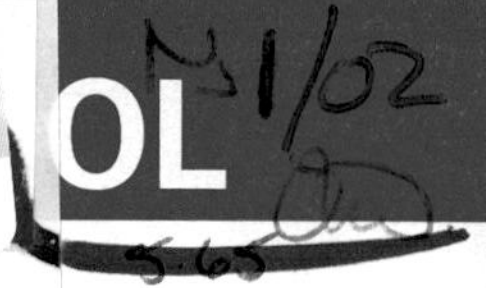

Key to Map Pages	2 - 3
Large Scale City Centre	4 - 5
Map Pages	6 - 175
Index to Streets, Towns, Villages and selected Places of Interest	176 - 262
Index to Hospitals and Hospices	263-264

REFERENCE

- Motorway — M57
- A Road — A580
  - Proposed
- B Road — B5202
- Dual Carriageway
- One-way Street — Traffic flow on A Roads is indicated by a heavy line on the driver's left. All one-way streets are shown on Large Scale Pages 4-5
- Restricted Access
- Pedestrianized Road
- Track & Footpath
- Railway — Level Crossing, Station, Tunnel
- Built-up Area — STONE ST.
- Local Authority Boundary
- Postcode Boundary
- Map Continuation — 18; Large Scale 4
- Car Park (selected)
- Church or Chapel
- Fire Station
- Hospital
- House Numbers — A & B Roads only — 18, 25
- Information Centre
- National Grid Reference — 335
- Police Station
- Post Office
- Toilet
  - with facilities for the Disabled
- Educational Establishment
- Hospital or Hospice
- Industrial Building
- Leisure or Recreational Facility
- Place of Interest
- Public Building
- Shopping Centre or Market
- Other Selected Buildings

SCALE

Map Pages 6-175
1:15840 4 inches to 1 mile
0 — ¼ Mile
0 — 250 Metres
6.31cm to 1km 10.16cm to 1 mile

Map Pages 4-5
1:10560 6 inches to 1 mile
0 — ⅛ — ¼ Mile
0 — 100 — 200 — 300 Metres
9.46cm to 1km 15.24cm to 1 mile

Head Office:
Fairfield Road, Borough Green, Sevenoaks, Kent TN15 8PP
Tel: 01732 781000 (General Enquiries & Trade Sales)
Showrooms:
44 Gray's Inn Road, London WC1X 8HX
Tel: 020 7440 9500 (Retail Sales)
www.a-zmaps.co.uk

Edition 3 2000 Edition 3a 2001 (part revision)

KEY TO MAP PAGES

Formby
A5147
B5195
B5195
Aug
A565
R. Alt
Hightown
B5193
Ince
Blundell
Homer Green
Lydiate
6 7
MAGHULL
Little
Crosby
8 9
Lunt
Sefton
10 11
Thornton
12 13
Netherton
LIVERPOOL
BAY
Crosby Channel
CROSBY
16 17
Waterloo
Great
Crosby
Buckley
Hill
18 19
Litherland
7
20 21
Aintree
Seaforth
32 33
BOOTLE
Orrell
34 35
Fazakerley
36 37
Walton
LARGE SCALE
4 5
LIVERPOOL
CITY CENTRE
50 51
New Brighton
52 53
Kirkdale
54 55
56 57
Anfield
Everton
Egremont
(Kingsway)
LIVERPOOL
WALLASEY
Liscard
70 71
72 1 73
74 75
76 77
78 79
Leasowe
Meols
Moreton
Seacombe
Mersey
Tunnels
90 91
HOYLAKE
2
Bidston
Upton
Claughton
(Queensway)
Wavertree
92 93
Greasby
94 95
96 97
BIRKENHEAD
98 99
Toxteth
100 101
Sefton
Park
Newton
112 113
West
Grange
Kirby
Frankby
114 115
Woodchurch
116 3 117
M53
Oxton
Tranmere
118 119
Prenton
Rock
Ferry
120 121
New
Ferry
Dingle
Mossley
Hill
122 123
Aigburth
Caldy
134 135
Irby
Thurstaston
136 137
Pensby
Thingwall
138 139
Barnston
Storeton
BEBINGTON
140 141
4
142 143
Port
Sunlight
RIVER
MERSEY
Spital
Bromborough
HESWALL
156 157
158 159
Gayton
160 161
Thornton
Hough
162 163
Brookhurst
Eastham
Ferry
Eastham
RIVER DEE
(AFON DYFRDWY)
Gayton
Sands
B5135
B5151
170 171
5
6
7
8
M53
Holywell
Bank
Parkgate
NESTON
Willaston
Little
Sutton
B5133
B5134
A540
Little
Neston
ENGLAND
WALES
A550
A41
B5132

SCALE
0 1 2 Miles
0 1 2 3 Kilometres

Burton
Ledsham

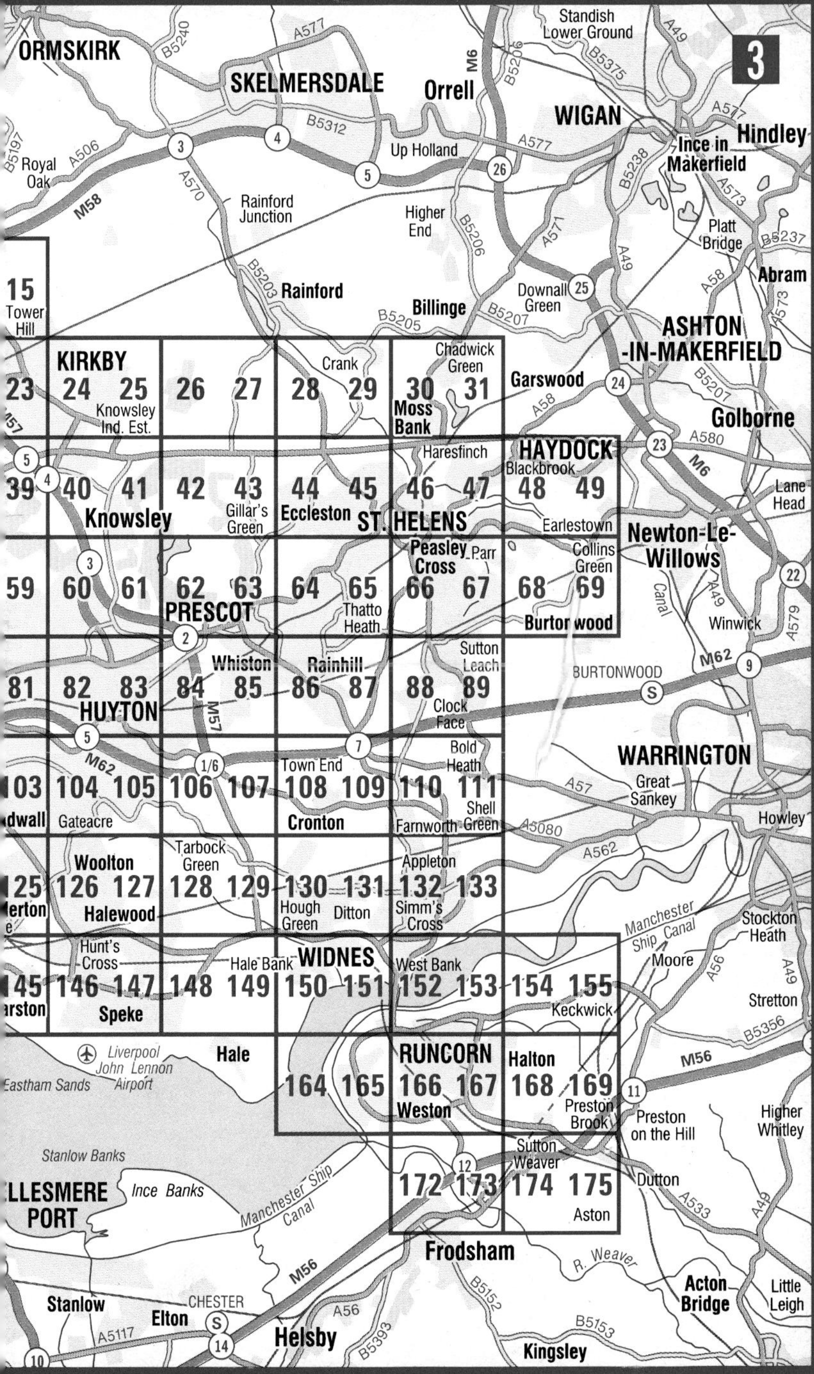

Standish
Lower Ground
A577
A49
ORMSKIRK
B5240
M6
B5206
B5375
SKELMERSDALE
Orrell
WIGAN
A577
B5312
Hindley
3
4
A577
Ince in
Makerfield
B5197
Royal
Oak
A506
Up Holland
5
26
B5238
A573
A570
M58
Rainford
Junction
Higher
End
B5206
A571
Platt
Bridge
B5237
A49
B5203
Rainford
Billinge
Downall
Green
25
A58
Abram
A573
15
Tower
Hill
B5205
B5207
ASHTON
-IN-MAKERFIELD
KIRKBY
Crank
Chadwick
Green
Garswood
24
B5207
23 24 25 26 27 28 29 30 31
Knowsley
Ind. Est.
Moss
Bank
A58
Golborne
M57
Haresfinch
HAYDOCK
23
A580
5
Blackbrook
M6
39 4 40 41 42 43 44 45 46 47 48 49
Lane
Head
Knowsley
Gillar's
Green
Eccleston
ST. HELENS
Earlestown
Newton-Le-
Willows
Peasley
Cross
Parr
Collins
Green
3
59 60 61 62 63 64 65 66 67 68 69
Canal
A49
22
PRESCOT
Thatto
Heath
Burtonwood
Winwick
A579
2
Sutton
Leach
Whiston
Rainhill
BURTONWOOD
M62
9
81 82 83 84 85 86 87 88 89
S
HUYTON
M57
Clock
Face
5
7
Bold
Heath
WARRINGTON
M62
1/6
Town End
103 104 105 106 107 108 109 110 111
A57
Great
Sankey
dwall
Gateacre
Cronton
Farnworth
Shell
Green
A5080
Howley
Tarbock
Green
A562
Woolton
Appleton
125 126 127 128 129 130 131 132 133
erton
Halewood
Hough
Green
Ditton
Simm's
Cross
Manchester
Ship Canal
Stockton
Heath
Hunt's
Cross
Hale Bank
WIDNES
West Bank
Moore
A56
A49
145 146 147 148 149 150 151 152 153 154 155
arston
Speke
Keckwick
Stretton
B5356
Liverpool
John Lennon
Airport
Hale
RUNCORN
Halton
M56
Eastham Sands
164 165 166 167 168 169
11
Weston
Preston
Brook
Preston
on the Hill
Higher
Whitley
Stanlow Banks
Sutton
Weaver
12
172 173 174 175
Dutton
LLESMERE
PORT
Ince Banks
Manchester Ship
Canal
A533
A49
Aston
Frodsham
R. Weaver
M56
B5152
Acton
Bridge
Little
Leigh
Stanlow
CHESTER
Elton
S
A56
B5153
A5117
14
Helsby
B5393
Kingsley
10

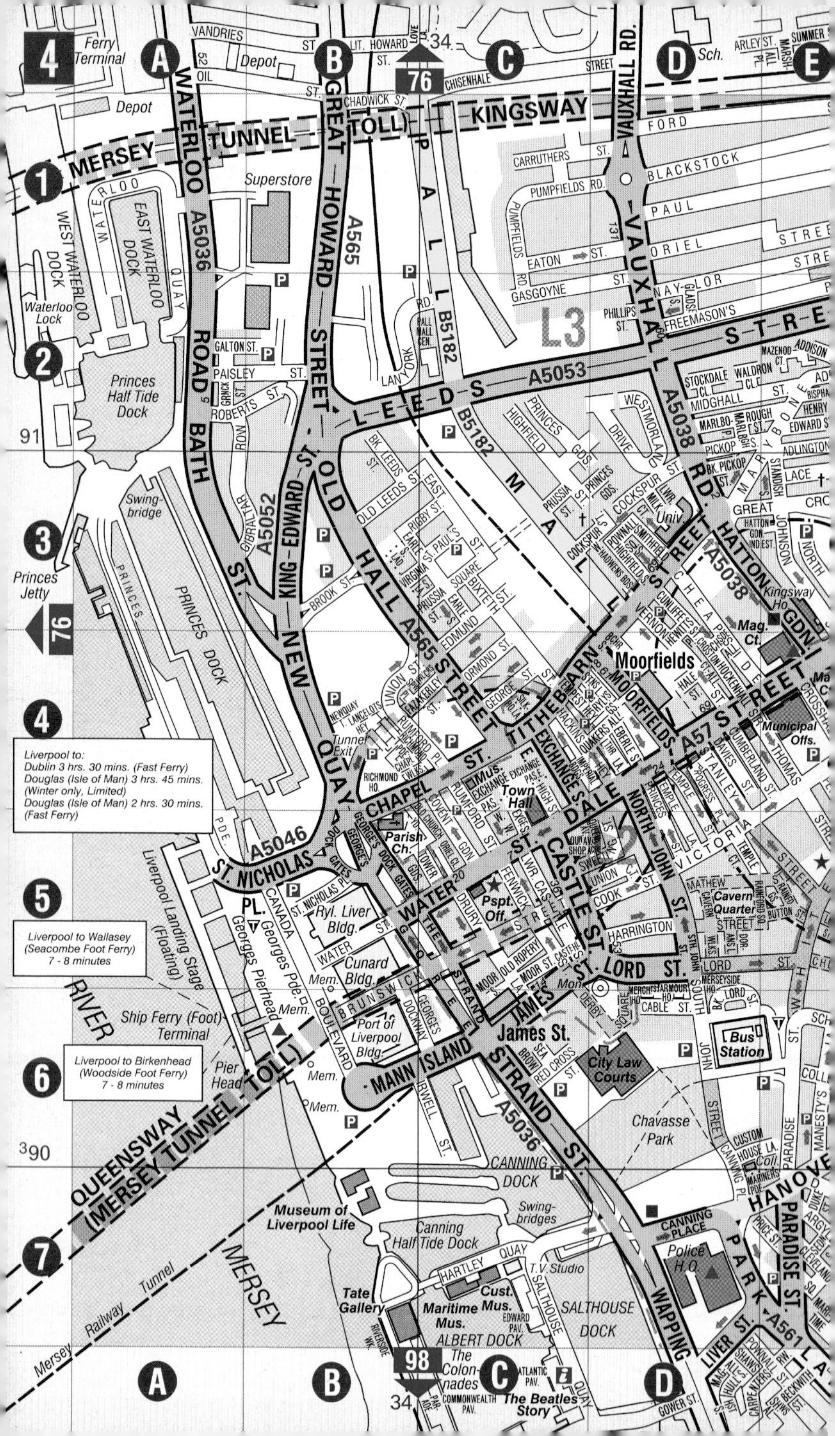

Ferry Terminal
Depot
MERSEY TUNNEL (TOLL)
KINGSWAY
WATERLOO ROAD
A5036
GREAT HOWARD STREET
A565
VAUXHALL RD.
Sch.
76
CHISENHALE
ST.
LIT. HOWARD
VANDRIES ST.
OIL ST.
CHADWICK ST.
FORD
CARRUTHERS ST.
BLACKSTOCK
PUMPFIELDS RD.
PAUL
STREET
ORIEL
EATON ST.
GASGOYNE ST.
NAYLOR
PHILLIPS ST.
FREEMASON'S
L3
Superstore
WATERLOO
WEST WATERLOO DOCK
EAST WATERLOO DOCK
QUAY
Waterloo Lock
Princes Half Tide Dock
PALL MALL
B5182
GALTON ST.
PAISLEY ST.
ROBERTS ST.
LEEDS STREET
A5053
WESTMORLAND DRIVE
HIGHFIELD
PRINCES GDS.
A5038
MIDGHALL
STOCKDALE CL.
WALDRON CL.
MAZENOD CT.
ADDISON
MARYBONE
PICKOP
ADLINGTON
LACE
GREAT
HATTON GDN.
Kingsway Ho.
91
BATH ST.
A5052
GIBRALTAR ROW
KING EDWARD ST.
OLD HALL STREET
A565
OLD LEEDS ST.
EAST ST.
RIGBY ST.
ST. PAUL'S SQUARE
BIXTETH ST.
BROOK ST.
MAL
COCKSPUR ST.
PRUSSIA ST.
Univ.
Swing-bridge
PRINCES DOCK
PRINCES
Princes Jetty
76
CHEAPSIDE
VERNON ST.
Mag. Ct.
Moorfields
TITHEBARN ST.
MOORFIELDS
A57
STREET
Municipal Offs.
HACKINS HEY
EXCHANGE ST. E.
UNION ST.
NEW QUAY
Tunnel Exit
RICHMOND HO.
CHAPEL ST.
Mus.
Town Hall
DALE ST.
NORTH JOHN ST.
VICTORIA STREET
TEMPLE CT.
CUMBERLAND ST.
STANLEY ST.
Liverpool to:
Dublin 3 hrs. 30 mins. (Fast Ferry)
Douglas (Isle of Man) 3 hrs. 45 mins. (Winter only, Limited)
Douglas (Isle of Man) 2 hrs. 30 mins. (Fast Ferry)
A5046
ST. NICHOLAS PL.
Parish Ch.
WATER ST.
CASTLE ST.
Pspt. Off.
DRURY LA.
FENWICK ST.
COOK ST.
HARRINGTON ST.
MATHEW STREET
Cavern Quarter
LORD ST.
Liverpool Landing Stage (Floating)
Georges Pierhead
CANADA BOULEVARD
Georges Pde.
Ryl. Liver Bldg.
Cunard Bldg.
Mem.
BRUNSWICK ST.
Port of Liverpool Bldg.
JAMES ST.
James St.
STRAND ST.
MOOR ST.
Mon.
DERBY SQUARE
CABLE ST.
Bus Station
Liverpool to Wallasey (Seacombe Foot Ferry) 7 - 8 minutes
RIVER
Ship Ferry (Foot) Terminal
Pier Head
Liverpool to Birkenhead (Woodside Foot Ferry) 7 - 8 minutes
MANN ISLAND
City Law Courts
SEA BROW
RED CROSS ST.
Chavasse Park
JOHN STREET
CANNING PL.
CUSTOM HOUSE LA.
PARADISE
HANOVER
390
QUEENSWAY (MERSEY TUNNEL (TOLL))
A5036
CANNING DOCK
IRWELL ST.
Museum of Liverpool Life
Swing-bridges
Canning Half Tide Dock
CANNING PLACE
Police H.Q.
PARK LA.
PARADISE ST.
A561
MERSEY
Mersey Railway Tunnel
HARTLEY QUAY
T.V. Studio
Cust. Mus.
Tate Gallery
Maritime Mus.
SALTHOUSE DOCK
SALTHOUSE QUAY
WAPPING
ALBERT DOCK
EDWARD PAV.
LIVER ST.
The Colonnades
98
ATLANTIC PAV.
The Beatles Story
COMMONWEALTH PAV.
GOWER ST.
34
A
B
C
D
E
1
2
3
4
5
6
7

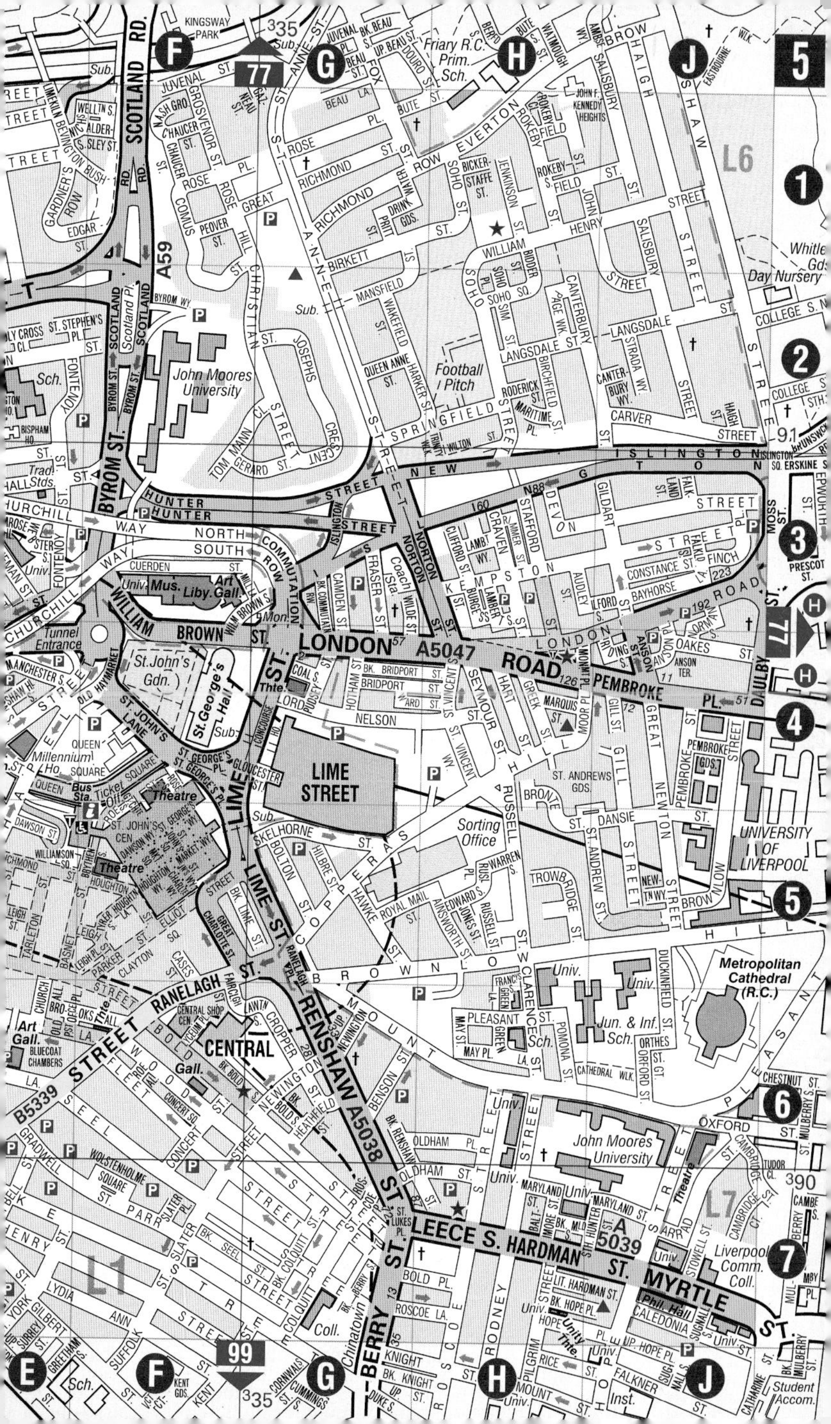
5
F
G
H
J
E
1
2
3
4
5
6
7
77
99
335
390
L6
L1
L7
KINGSWAY PARK
SCOTLAND RD.
JUVENAL ST.
NASH GRO.
GROSVENOR ST.
CHAUCER ST.
ROSE PL.
COMUS ST.
PEOVER ST.
GREAT ST.
CHRISTIAN ST.
ROSE PL.
RICHMOND ROW
RICHMOND ST.
BIRKETT ST.
MANSFIELD ST.
WAKEFIELD ST.
QUEEN ANNE ST.
HARKER ST.
ST. ANNE ST.
FOX ST.
BEAU LA.
BUTE ST.
EVERTON ROW
Friary R.C. Prim. Sch.
SALISBURY ST.
HAIGH ST.
SHAW ST.
JOHN F. KENNEDY HEIGHTS
ROKEBY ST.
BICKERSTAFFE ST.
JENKINSON ST.
HENRY ST.
WILLIAM HENRY ST.
SOHO ST.
SOHO SQ.
CANTERBURY ST.
LANGSDALE ST.
STRADA WY.
Football Pitch
SPRINGFIELD
RODERICK ST.
BIRCHFIELD ST.
MARITIME PL.
CARVER STREET
COLLEGE ST. N.
COLLEGE ST.
Whitley Gdns.
Day Nursery
ISLINGTON
ISLINGTON SQ.
ERSKINE ST.
EPWORTH ST.
MOSS ST.
PRESCOT ST.
NEW ISLINGTON
GILDART ST.
DEVON ST.
FALKLAND ST.
STAFFORD ST.
CRAVEN ST.
CLIFFORD ST.
LAMBT WY.
KEMPSTON ST.
CONSTANCE ST.
BAYHORSE LA.
FINCH PL.
AUDLEY ST.
LONDON ROAD
A5047
PEMBROKE PL.
DAULBY ST.
ANSON ST.
OAKES ST.
ANSON TER.
NORTON ST.
COACH STA.
WILDE ST.
FRASER ST.
CAMDEN ST.
BK. COMMUTATION RW
COMMUTATION ROW
HUNTER STREET
ISLINGTON STREET
SCOTLAND PL.
BYROM ST.
BYROM WY.
John Moores University
ST. JOSEPHS CRES.
TOM MANN CL.
GERARD ST.
CHURCHILL WAY NORTH
CHURCHILL WAY SOUTH
CUERDEN ST.
Univ. Mus. Liby. Art Gall.
WILLIAM BROWN ST.
Tunnel Entrance
St. John's Gdn.
St. George's Hall
LIME ST.
LIME STREET
Thte.
COAL S.
LORD NELSON ST.
BRIDPORT ST.
BK. BRIDPORT ST.
HOTHAM ST.
ST. VINCENT ST.
SEYMOUR ST.
HART ST.
GREEK ST.
MARQUIS ST.
MOOR PL.
GILL ST.
GREAT NEWTON ST.
PEMBROKE ST.
PEMBROKE GDNS.
ST. ANDREWS GDS.
BRONTE ST.
DANSIE ST.
ST. ANDREW ST.
RUSSELL ST.
Sorting Office
TROWBRIDGE ST.
NEWTON WY.
BROWNLOW HILL
UNIVERSITY OF LIVERPOOL
SKELHORNE ST.
BOLTON ST.
HILBRE ST.
COPPERAS HILL
HAWKE ST.
ROYAL MAIL ST.
AINSWORTH ST.
EDWARD S.
JONES ST.
WARREN S.
BROWNLOW ST.
Metropolitan Cathedral (R.C.)
DUCKINFIELD ST.
CLARENCE ST.
POMONA ST.
Univ.
Jun. & Inf. Sch.
PLEASANT ST.
MAY PL.
CATHEDRAL WLK.
ORFORD ST.
MOUNT PLEASANT
CHESTNUT ST.
OXFORD ST.
CAMBRIDGE ST.
TUDOR CL.
MULBERRY S.
QUEEN SQUARE
Millennium Ho.
Bus Sta.
Ticket Off.
ST. JOHN'S LANE
ST. GEORGE'S PL.
GLOUCESTER ST.
Theatre
ST. JOHN'S CEN.
DAWSON ST.
WILLIAMSON SQ.
HOUGHTON ST.
ELLIOT ST.
CLAYTON SQ.
GREAT CHARLOTTE ST.
BK. LIME ST.
RANELAGH ST.
CASES ST.
PARKER ST.
LEIGH ST.
TARLETON ST.
BASNETT ST.
CHURCH ST.
Art Gall.
BLUECOAT CHAMBERS
RANELAGH STREET
CENTRAL
CENTRAL SHOP CEN.
LYCEUM PL.
BOLD ST.
FLEET ST.
WOOD ST.
CONCERT SQ.
CONCERT ST.
SEEL ST.
B5339
GRADWELL ST.
WOLSTENHOLME SQUARE
PARR ST.
SLATER ST.
BK. SEEL ST.
HENRY ST.
LYDIA ANN ST.
GILBERT ST.
YORK ST.
SURREY ST.
SUFFOLK ST.
GREETHAM S.
KENT ST.
KENT GDS.
Sch.
Gall.
NEWINGTON
CROPPER ST.
RENSHAW A5038
BENSON ST.
BK. RENSHAW
OLDHAM PL.
OLDHAM ST.
ST. LUKES PL.
LEECE S.
HARDMAN ST.
A5039
MYRTLE ST.
MARYLAND ST.
HUNTER ST.
BALTIMORE ST.
LIT. HARDMAN ST.
BK. HOPE PL.
HOPE PL.
UP. HOPE PL.
Unity Thte.
Phil. Hall
CALEDONIA ST.
SUGNALL ST.
FALKNER ST.
Inst.
PILGRIM ST.
RICE ST.
MOUNT ST.
RODNEY ST.
ROSCOE ST.
BERRY ST.
BOLD PL.
ROSCOE LA.
KNIGHT ST.
BK. KNIGHT ST.
DUKE S.
Chinatown
COLQUITT ST.
BK. COLQUITT ST.
Coll.
CORNWALLIS ST.
CUMMINGS S.
Liverpool Comm. Coll.
Theatre
STOWELL ST.
CATHARINE ST.
BK. MULBERRY ST.
Student Accom.
CAMBRIDGE CT.
Sub.
P

6
A
B
C
336
37
405
04
03
1
2
3
4
5
Lydiate
Lydiate Hall Farm
War Meml.
Nursery
Abbey View
Hill Top Poultry Farm
Lydiate Hill Bridge
SOUTHPORT ROAD
STATION ROAD
Ryecrofts Farm
Hall
The Thorns
Lollies Bridge
Cherry Tree Farm
Pye's Farm
Moss Hall
Jacks Bridge
ACRES LANE
PUNNELL'S LANE
Pilling Lane Farm
PILLING LANE
Gore Ho. Fm.
CARR LA.
Gore Lodge
ALT CAR LANE
Meadow View Farm
Berry's Farm
Bridge Farm
Lydiate Bridge
Lydiate House
GORE HOUSES
LEEDS AND LIVERPOOL CANAL
SANDY LANE
SANDHURST WAY
BIRCHFIELD WAY
SILVER BIRCH WAY
MOSS
A5147
CHARLES
MANION AV.
MANION CL.
Tennis Court
Rec. Grd.
Nurseries
WELD BLUNDELL AV.
KINGSLEY RD.
BLACKHURST CL.
NURSERY
Jun. & Inf. Schs.
LAMBSHEAR LA.
Lydiate Prim. Sch.
HAIGH CRESCENT
COPPULL RD.
BARNIES
MARSHALL'S CL.
THE FIELDINGS
THE MOORINGS
HERONS CT.
MALLARD HO.
Gore Ho. Cottages
Crisp's Farm
Old Gore House Farm
Upper Gore Farm
BELLS LANE
Fir Grove
Maghull Brook
Football Grd.
HAVEN WLK.
HIGHBANKS
NEDENS GR.
LIVERPOOL ROAD
WEST LANCASHIRE
SEFTON
GREEN LANE
Maukin Farm
Peel Farm
PEEL COTTAGE
St. John Bosco R.C. Prim. Sch.
Prim. Sch.
Comm. Cen.
RIGBY
CRAWFD AV.
TURNBRIDGE RD.
GREENBANK
HICKSON AV.
GORDON AV.
GRANVILLE AV.
THE ROUND
Playground
WEST MEADE
MEADE
WESTWAY
B5422
CORNMILL LODGE
MILTON WAY
EMPRESS CL.
GLEBE CL.
GREEN LA.
SHOP
Shaw's Turn Bridge
PARKFIELD GRO.
HOMEFIELD
NORTH ROAD
12
A
B
C
336
37

7
AUGHTON
Brookfields Green
Moss Side
L39
L31
D
E
F
1
2
3
4
5
13
38
39
405
04
03
Hollin House Farm
Sudell Lane
Sudell Bridge
Pye's Cottages
Beaconsfield Farm
St. Michael Rd.
Old Rectory
Church Lane
Holt Coppice
Smithy Lane Farm
Swan Fm.
Smithy Lane
Swan Lane
Back Lane
Pygon's Hill
Pygon's Hill House
Pygon's Hill Farm
Sewage Works
Brook
Home Farm
High House Farm
Elmsfield Pk
Riding School
Brookfield Lane
Brookfield House
Rose Hill Farm
Rose Hill
Pygon's Farm
Rose Mount Nurseries
Football Field
West Lancashire
Sefton
Springfield Road
Cockbeck Bridge
Butcher's Lane
Nell's La.
Aughton Chase Riding Centre
Northway Nurseries
Track
Cycle
Robbin's Bridge
Moss Lane Farm
Moss House Farm
Brookfields Farm
Northway
A59
Road
235
156
Oakfield House
Highway Farm
Old La.
Mill House Farm
Holtgreen Nurseries
Spring Farm
Mill Villas
Aspinwall House
Elm House
Lane
St. Thomas C. of E. Prim. Sch.
B5407
Oakhill Farm
Kenyons Lane
Heskin Cl.
Bowl. Green
Oakhill Cott. La.
Ridgeway
Ridgeway Park
Alexander Drive
Park Av.
Park Drive
Millbank Farm
Maghull Brook
Marlbgh Av.
Runnymede
Seymour Dr.
Aragon Cl.
The Boleyn
Byron Road
Highgate Rd.
Fawcett
The Cleves
Kenyon's Lodge
Millbank Cotts.
Millbank
Maghull Smallholdings Estate
Wynnstay Av.
Merrilox
Withens
Northway Prim. Sch.
Lathom
Croxteth Cl.
Rufford Drive
Scarsbrk Cl.
Play. Field
Oakhill Cl.
Park Lane
Dodd's Lane
Dodd's Farm
Moss Lane
Brock Av.
Gilpin Av.
Lowther Av.
Wenning Av.
Ribble Av.
Wasdale Avenue
Yarrow Av.
Derwent Cl.
Kelbeck Cl.
Watton Avenue
Beck Cl.
Parkbourn Sq
Parkbourn Dr.
Moss Side Fm.
Trent Drive
Roedean Cl.
275
Sandford Dri.
Leighton Av.
Howells Cl.
Playgrd.
Ennerdale Av.
Hawkshead Cl.
Keswick Cl.
Eskdale
Kendal
Ravenglass Av.
Grasmere Rd.
Coniston Rd.
Ambleside
Langdale Dri.
Penrith
Cartmel
Patterdale Cres.
Lune Av.
Troutbeck Av.
Calder
Hindburn
Duddon
Hodder Av.
Douglas Drive
Mersey
Sudell Av.
Avenue
Bridge Fm. Dri.
Thirlmere
Lake M.
Windermere
Tebay Cl.
Ulverston Cl.
Drive
Haweswater Gro.
Eastway
Deyes
School Lane
A5147
East Way
North-way
Hunt Rd.
Hillary Cr.
Scott Cl.
Tensing
Buttermere Cl.
Beechwood Ct.
Orchard
Maghull Country Club
Foxhouse La.
Moss Dr.
Green Heys Dr.
Heskin Dr.
Highfield Pk.
Highfield
The Poplars
Playing Field
Deyes High Sch.
Swim. Pool
Ten. Cts.
Haymans Grn.
Sandiways
Bluestone La.
Ten. Ct.
Glenn Park
Longfold
Penfold
Cl.

8
A
B
C
1
2
3
4
5
MARSTON RD.
ELVINGTON
MAY FAIR CL.
330
31
02
01
400
Playing Fields
Flea Moss Wood
MOSS
GORSEY LANE
Sniggery Farm
L38
Woodham Knoll
Old Sniggery
Far Moss Pool
Sniggery Wood
ACKERS
DIBB
WEST LANCASHIRE GOLF COURSE
PLAYING FIELD
Club House
Hall Road
Merrilocks Plantation
SPINNEY CRES.
PADDOCK CL.
ST. ANDREWS ROAD
ST. ANDREWS DR.
EAST MANOR RD.
SUNNINGDALE DR.
PRESTWICK DRI.
ROEHAMPTON DRI.
MERRI WOOD
FAR MOSS ROAD
HALL ROAD WEST
BURBO BANK ROAD NORTH
WARD RD.
RICHARD
LINKSIDE CT.
DRUMMOND RD.
MARGARET RD.
THE SERPENTINE NORTH
HALLTNE CL.
MERRILOCKS GREEN
MERRILOCKS
DOWHILLS PARK
DOWHILLS DRI.
DOWHILLS
Football Ground
ST. MICHAEL'S ROAD
ST. MICHAEL'S RD.
ST. ANTHONY'S
Games Ground
ESHE ROAD
ESHE ROAD NORTH
COLLEGE ROAD
CAMBRIDGE ROAD
BERWICK
ENNISMORE
SHERWOOD RD.
BERKELEY RD.
INGLE GREEN
FOUNTAIN CT.
THE SERPENTINE
PARK
WARREN
Blundellsands Park
CRESCENT RD.
BIRKENSHAW AV.
LYNTON CT
HAMILTON CT.
LINVILLE AV.
CLEMENTS
16
DRIVE
ROAD
LINDEN AV.
AVENUE NORTH
BRONSHILL CT.
OSBERT RD.

9
D
E
F
32
33
West Lo
Pav.
The Round House
MOOR LANE INCE
A565
INCE BLUNDELL PARK
MOSS WOOD
Long Wood
PARK WALL ROAD
Lion Cottage
Border Plantation
02
B5193
Trap Plantation
LANE
Delph Farm
DELPH ROAD
St. Mary's R.C. Prim. Sch.
Sunnyfields
Bens Gorse
THORNTON WOOD
BACK LANE
Kennel Plantation
Crosby Hall
Church Wood
Bens Gorse Belt
Well Farm
Little Crosby
LITTLE CROSBY ROAD
White House Farm
Model Farm
The Vista
Moor Hey Plantation
Cottage Farm
VIRGIN'S LANE
10
LITTLE HEYS LA.
INCE
WOODLAND VW.
BURYING GROUND PLANTATION
L23
Crab Wood
Holy Family High Sch.
Moor Park
Sports Ground
Pav.
Ronald House School
Sports Grd.
WOODEND AV.
LONGFIELD
MILL CL.
BARNCROFT PL.
OAKLANDS AVENUE
HALSALL CL.
VILLIERS
CHESTNUT AV.
SYCAMORE AV.
BEECH PK.
BEECH AV.
ELM AV.
EDGEMOOR
THORNFIELD
Tithebarn
WILLOW WAY
MAYFAIR AV.
MANOR AV.
ILFORD AV.
KAIGH AV.
MOORLAND AV.
PARK AV.
ESPLEN AV.
POPLAR AV.
CHESTERFIELD
MOOR COPPICE
THE STABLES
MILLCROFT
GREENWAY
MORET CL.
MOOR A565
FOREFIELD
MOOR CL.
BRENTWOOD AV.
CHETWOOD AV.
WINDMILL AV.
St. Luke's Halswell Sch.
FAIRWAYS
AVENUE
DE VILLIERS AV.
MILLER AV.
ROAD
MAUNDERS CT.
ROSEMOOR
MOORFIELD
ELMWOOD AV.
HIGHFIELD GR.
THE BYPASS
GREAT CROSBY
MOOR DRIVE
THE BYWAY
WEST MOOR DR.
SOUTH MOOR
NORTHERN RD.
OLD FARM RD.
TITHE RD.
CHARMALUE AV.
ROWENA CL.
MOOR CL.
HILLCREST RD.
LUPTON DRIVE
NEWBOROUGH AV.
400
CAMBRIDGE AVE
VICTORIA ROAD
ISLINGTON
LIVERPOOL ROAD
17
ASCOT PARK
MOORSIDE
Forefield Jun. Sch.
1
2
3
4
5

Pav.
33
A
B
C
34
INCE BLUNDELL PARK
Hunt's Brook Farm
Red Brick House
The Laurels
EAST LANE
BROAD LA.
Broad Farm
Stanley Cotts.
Holly Farm
Homer Green
LUNT LANE
ROAD
WALL
PARK
Brook
Hunt's
MOOR LANE
INCE
Long Wood
1
Lion Cottage
Border Plantation
02
Homer Green Farm
LANE
Wrak's Farm
Holly Farm
LONG
GATES
A565
LANE
2
THORNTON WOOD
BACK LANE
9
LITTLE HEYS LA.
Hospice
INCE
SOUTHPORT ROAD
PARK DR.
WOODLAND VW.
DRIVE
BRENDA CRES.
SEFTON
Moor Hey Plantation
3
Cottage Farm
VIRGIN'S
L23
Thornton Lodge
Thornton
Orchard House
BACK LA.
BACK LANE
ROTHWELLS LA.
HOLGATE PK.
HOLGATE
PARK VW.
The Elms
Crematorium
Cemetery
01
BROOK RD.
ROAD
CHELLOW DENE
QUARRY RD.
GREEN LA.
LYDIATE
HARTDALE RD.
ST.
Lib.
MOORLANDS RD.
NORTHWICH CL.
WESTBOURNE AV.
RAKES
LANE
Holy Family R.C. High Sch.
THE CRES.
4
WATER
HALIFAX
MIDGLEY GRN.
PHILLIPS CL.
CRESCENT
COLES CRES.
Prim. Sch.
LYDIATE PK.
GEORGE MOORE CT.
HEDGECROFT
MASEFIELD
A5207
Rec. Grd.
Sports Grd.
A565
LANE
THORNFIELD RD.
RONALDSWAY
WHINFIELD
WHITE MEADOW DR.
SORANY CL.
EDGE
RD.
STANNYFIELD
BRETLANDS RD.
SAFFRON MS.
JUNIPER GDNS.
ELMSFIELD RD.
HEATHER WAY
BLAKEFIELD RD.
NEWFIELD CL.
ROAD
LANE
Maddox Cottages
CHESTNUT AV.
SYCAMORE AV.
BEECH PK.
BEECH AV.
ELM
AVENUE
EDGEMOOR
MORET CL.
LARCHFIELD
AMAURY RD.
RADBURN
ST. WILLIAM
GREEN CROFT
CARAWAY CL.
TANHOUSE
FIELD WLK.
HUMPHREYS HEY
Thornton Hall
RUNNELL'S
Tithebarn
MERIBEL
THE STABLES
MILLCROFT
LINK AV.
GORSE
FIELD AV.
HEY RD.
Prim. Sch.
Tan House Farm
Windles Green
MOOR
5
MOOR COPPICE
CHESTERFIELD
GREENWAY
DRIVE
DRI.
EDGEMOOR
FERN
STILE HEY
LOWER HEY
RD.
Newfield Sch.
CONEY CRES.
ROAD
DRUMMOND
MOOR CL.
BRENTWOOD AV.
CHETWOOD
FOREFIELD
HIGH-FIELD GR.
MAUNDERS CT.
ELMWOOD AV.
ROSEMOOR
MOORFIELD
CRANFIELD RD.
Playing Fields
AMAURY
SEVEN ACRE RD.
DRIVE
Sports Ground
400
TITHEBARN RD.
CHARMALUE AV.
ROWENA CL.
ROAD
MOORSIDE CL.
HILLCREST
RD.
LUPTON DRIVE
Tennis Courts
Chesterfield Sch.
18
ROAD
EDGEMOOR CL.
LANE
Edge Farm
34
33
LA.
Forefield Jun. Sch.
NEWBOROUGH
HURST RD.
ROAD
AVE.
VALLEY CL.
TRAWDEN WAY

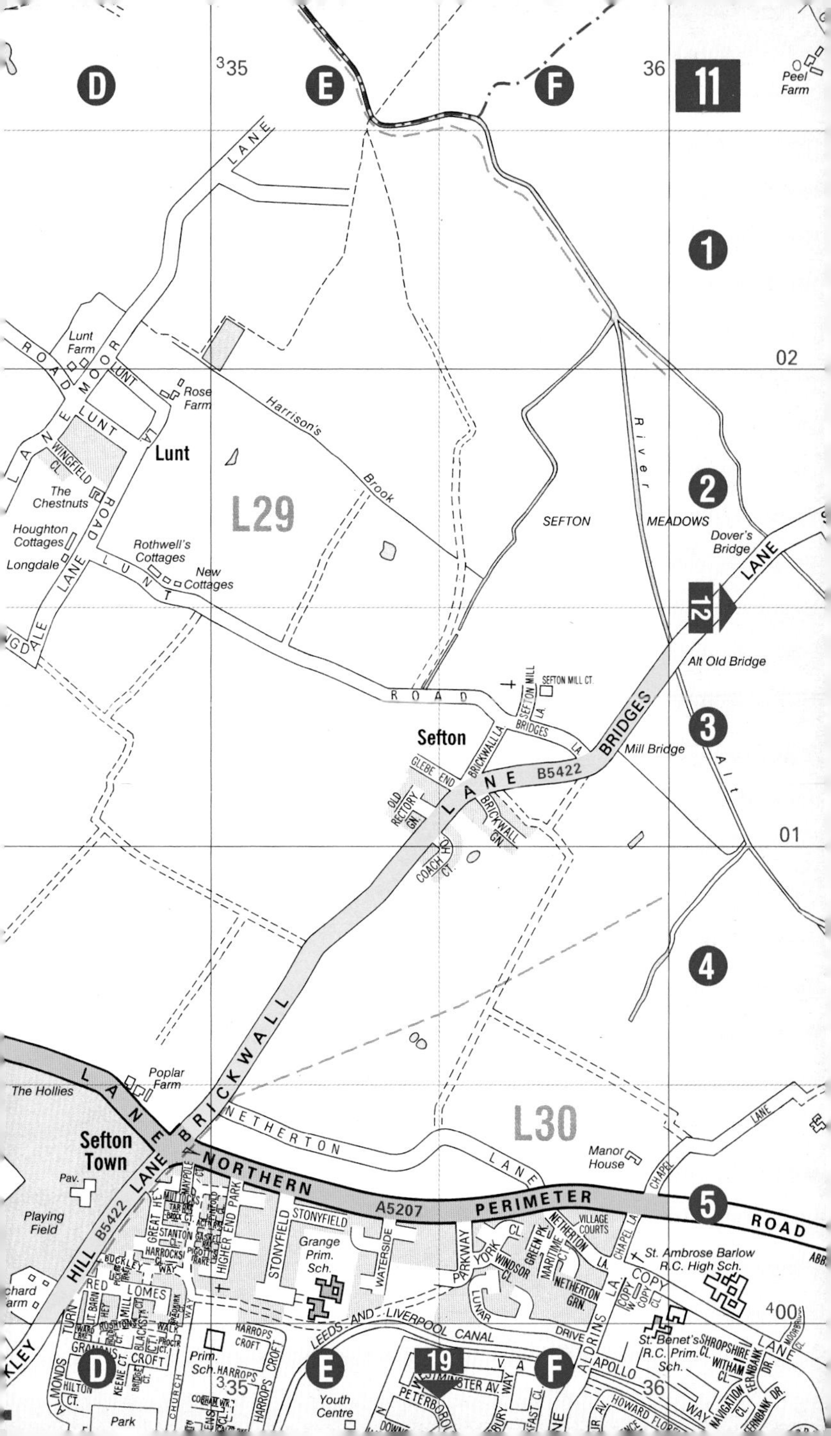
11
D
E
F
335
36
Peel Farm
1
2
3
4
5
02
01
400
Lunt Farm
MOOR
ROAD
LUNT
Rose Farm
LA.
LANE
WINGFIELD CL.
Lunt
The Chestnuts
Houghton Cottages
Longdale
ROAD
LANE
Rothwell's Cottages
New Cottages
LUNT
ROAD
Harrison's Brook
L29
SEFTON
MEADOWS
River
Alt
Dover's Bridge
LANE
12
Alt Old Bridge
SEFTON MILL LA.
SEFTON MILL CT.
BRIDGES LA.
BRIDGES
Mill Bridge
Sefton
GLEBE END
BRICKWALL LA.
LANE
B5422
OLD RECTORY GN.
BRICKWALL GN.
COACH HO. CT.
BRICKWALL
Poplar Farm
The Hollies
LANE
Sefton Town
NETHERTON
LANE
L30
Manor House
CHAPEL
LANE
NORTHERN
A5207
PERIMETER
ROAD
Pav.
Playing Field
B5422
HILL
LANE
MAYPOLE
MUTTOCKS
STANTON
HARROCKS
GREAT HEY
PINFOLD
PIGOTTS
HIGHER END PARK
STONYFIELD
STONYFIELD
Grange Prim. Sch.
WATERSIDE
PARKWAY
YORK
CL.
WINDSOR CL.
GREEN PK.
MARITIME CT.
NETHERTON LA.
VILLAGE COURTS
CHAPEL LA.
NETHERTON GRN.
St. Ambrose Barlow R.C. High Sch.
COPY LA.
COPY CL.
ALDRINS LA.
LUNAR
DRIVE
LEEDS AND LIVERPOOL CANAL
HARROPS CROFT
Prim. Sch.
CHURCH
BUCKLEY
RED LOMES
MILL
CROFT
KEENE CT.
HILTON CT.
ALMONDS TURN
Park
Youth Centre
19
WESTMINSTER AV.
PETERBOROUGH
APOLLO WAY
St. Benet's R.C. Prim. Sch.
SHROPSHIRE CL.
WITHAM CL.
NAVIGATION CL.
FERNBANK DR.
HOWARD FLOREY
Orchard Farm
COBHAM WK.

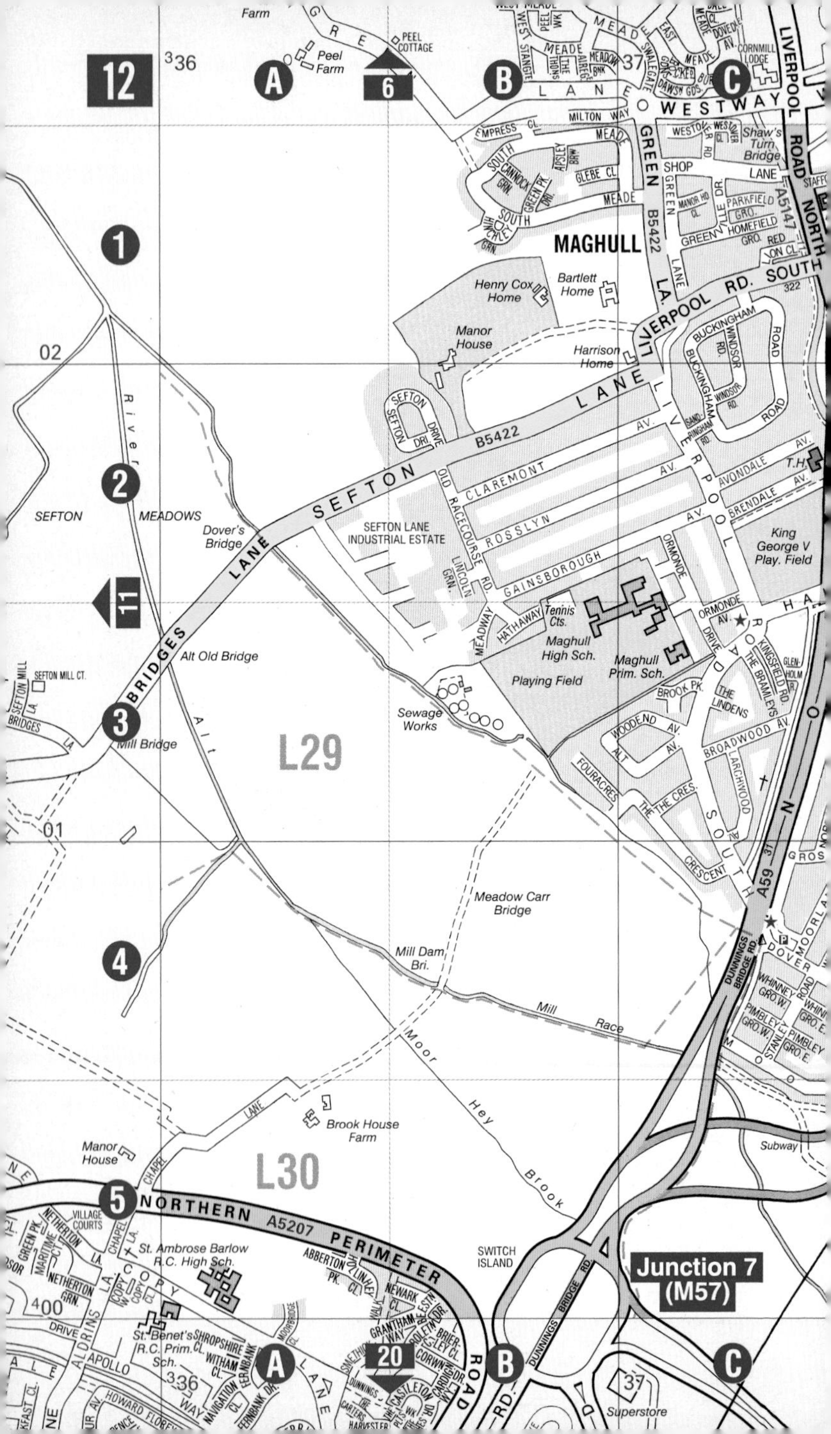

Farm
Peel Farm
PEEL COTTAGE
6
A
B
C
MAGHULL
WESTWAY
LIVERPOOL ROAD NORTH
A5147
GREEN LA.
B5422
MILTON WAY
EMPRESS CL.
MEADE
GLEBE CL.
SOUTH MEADE
Shaw's Turn Bridge
SHOP LANE
PARKFIELD GRO.
HOMEFIELD GRO.
GREENVILLE DR.
Henry Cox Home
Bartlett Home
Manor House
Harrison Home
LIVERPOOL RD. SOUTH
BUCKINGHAM RD.
WINDSOR RD.
SEFTON LANE
B5422
SEFTON DRIVE
CLAREMONT AV.
ROSSLYN AV.
GAINSBOROUGH RD.
AVONDALE AV.
BRENDALE AV.
King George V Play. Field
SEFTON LANE INDUSTRIAL ESTATE
OLD RACECOURSE RD.
ORMONDE AV.
ORMONDE DRIVE
MEADWAY
HATHAWAY
Tennis Cts.
Maghull High Sch.
Maghull Prim. Sch.
Playing Field
Sewage Works
BROOK PK.
THE LINDENS
THE BRAMLEYS
KINGSFIELD RD.
WOODEND AV.
ALT AV.
BROADWOOD AV.
FOURACRES
THE CRES.
LARCHWOOD AV.
SOUTH CRESCENT
A59
02
01
1
2
3
4
5
11
SEFTON
MEADOWS
River Alt
Dover's Bridge
BRIDGES LANE
Alt Old Bridge
SEFTON MILL CT.
SEFTON MILL LA.
Mill Bridge
L29
Meadow Carr Bridge
Mill Dam Bri.
Mill Race
Moor Hey Brook
DUNNINGS BRIDGE RD.
DOVER RD.
WHINNEY GRO. W.
PIMBLEY GRO. W.
Brook House Farm
Manor House
CHAPEL LANE
L30
NORTHERN A5207 PERIMETER ROAD
SWITCH ISLAND
Subway
Junction 7 (M57)
St. Ambrose Barlow R.C. High Sch.
St. Benet's R.C. Prim. Sch.
COPY LANE
NETHERTON LA.
NETHERTON GRN.
VILLAGE COURTS
ALDRINS LA.
APOLLO WAY
NAVIGATION CL.
FERNBANK DR.
20
Superstore
336
337
400

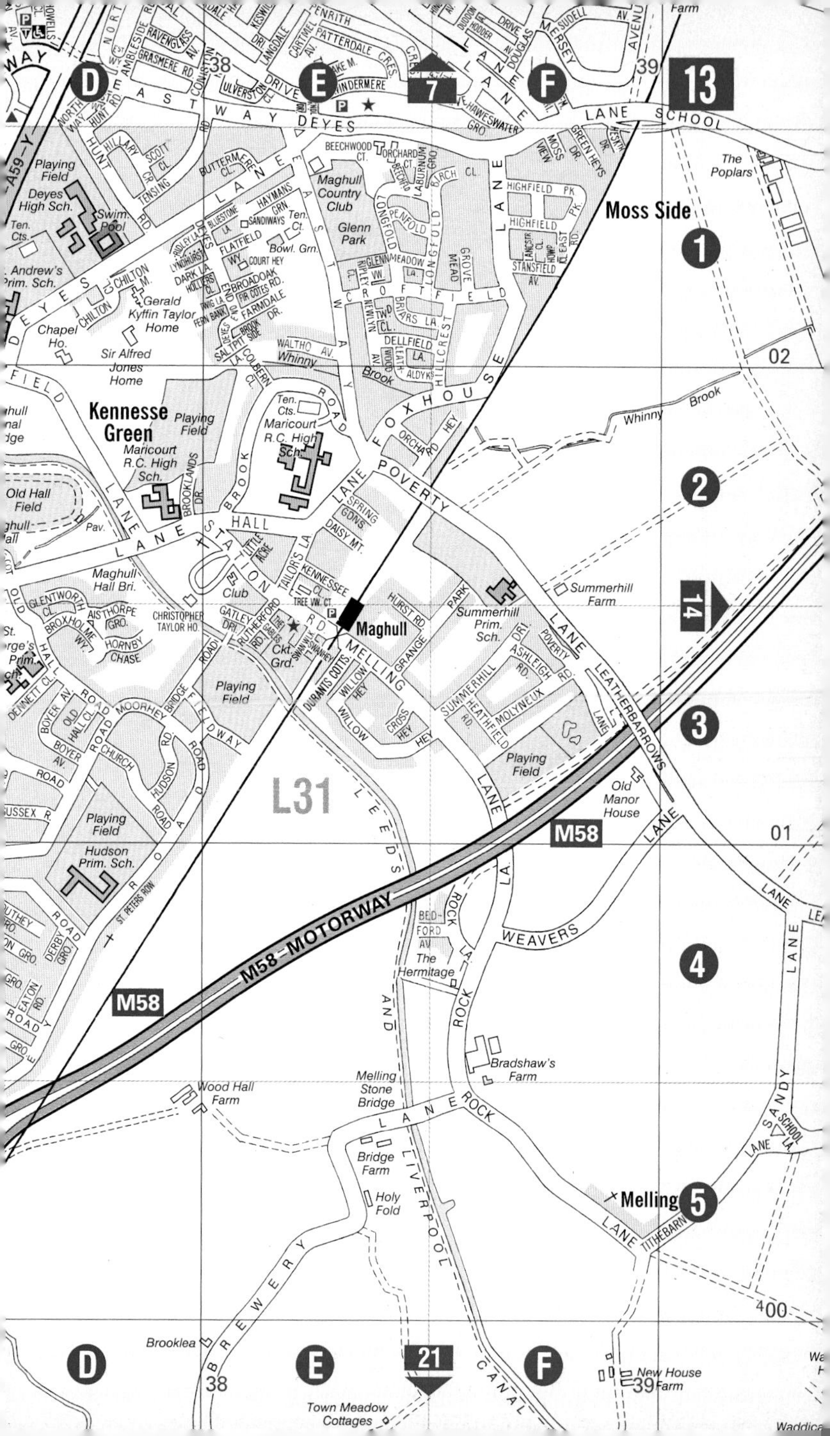

D
E
F
7
14
21
1
2
3
4
5
38
39
02
01
400
Moss Side
Kennesse Green
Maghull
Melling
L31
M58
M58-MOTORWAY
A59
EASTWAY
DEYES LANE
SCHOOL LANE
DEYES LANE
WINDERMERE DRIVE
ULVERSTON
PATTERDALE CRES.
PENRITH
CARTMEL AV.
LANGDALE DRI.
KESWICK
CONISTON AV.
AMBLESIDE RD.
RAVENGLASS
GRASMERE RD.
NORTHWAY
WEST HUNT RD.
HUNT RD.
HILLARY
SCOTT CL.
TENSING
BUTTERMERE CL.
HAYMANS GRN.
SANDIWAYS
BLUESTONE LA.
FLATFIELD WY.
COURT HEY
BROADOAK
FIR COTES RD.
FARMDALE DR.
DARK LA.
LYNDHURST
BROOK
SALTPIT SIDE
FERN BANK
COLBERN CL.
WALTHO AV.
Whinny Brook
EASTWAY
BEECHWOOD CT.
ORCHARD CT.
LABURNUM GRO.
BIRCH CL.
LONGFOLD
LONGFOLD
PENFOLD
GLENNMEADOW
CROFTFIELD
RIPLEY
NEWLYN AV.
BRIARS LA.
DELLFIELD LA.
HILLCREST
ALDYKS
GROVE MEAD
HIGHFIELD PK.
HIGHFIELD
STANSFIELD AV.
MOSS VIEW
GREENHEYS DR.
HESKETH DR.
DOUGLAS
MERSEY
SUDELL AV.
DUDDON
HODDER
DRIVE
HAWESWATER GRO.
FOXHOUSE LANE
ORCHARD HEY
POVERTY LANE
SPRING GDNS.
DAISY MT.
KENNESSEE CL.
TREE VW. CT.
TAILOR'S LA
LITTLE ACRE
HALL LANE
STATION RD.
BROOKLANDS DR.
BROOK ROAD
Maghull Country Club
Glenn Park
Ten. Cts.
Ten. Ct.
Bowl. Grn.
Playing Field
Deyes High Sch.
Swim. Pool
Ten. Cts.
St. Andrew's Prim. Sch.
Chapel Ho.
Gerald Kyffin Taylor Home
Sir Alfred Jones Home
CHILTON
CHILTON CL.
CHILTON M.
Maricourt R.C. High Sch.
Maricourt R.C. High Sch.
Old Hall Field
Pav.
Maghull Hall Bri.
Club
CHRISTOPHER TAYLOR HO.
GLENTWORTH CL.
BROXHOLME WY.
AISTHORPE GRO.
HORNBY CHASE
GATLEY DRI.
RUTHERFORD RD.
THE GABLES
SWAN WALK
SWANHEY
Ckt. Grd.
DURANTS COTTS.
MELLING RD.
WILLOW HEY
WILLOW HEY
CROSS HEY
GRANGE
HURST RD.
PARK
Summerhill Prim. Sch.
Summerhill Farm
SUMMERHILL DRI.
ASHLEIGH RD.
HEATHFIELD RD.
MOLYNEUX
POVERTY LANE
LEATHERBARROWS LANE
Playing Field
Old Manor House
DENNETT CL.
BOYER AV.
OLD HALL CL.
HALL ROAD
MOORHEY ROAD
CHURCH ROAD
HUDSON RD.
HUDSON ROAD
BRIDGE FIELDWAY
Playing Field
Playing Field
Hudson Prim. Sch.
SUSSEX R.
ROAD
ST. PETERS ROW
DERBY GRO.
EATON RD.
LEEDS AND LIVERPOOL CANAL
BED-FORD AV.
The Hermitage
ROCK LA.
WEAVERS LANE
ROCK LANE
Bradshaw's Farm
Melling Stone Bridge
Wood Hall Farm
LANE
Bridge Farm
Holy Fold
BREWERY
Brooklea
Town Meadow Cottages
New House Farm
SANDY LANE
SCHOOL LA.
TITHEBARN LANE
LANE
The Poplars
Whinny Brook
Farm

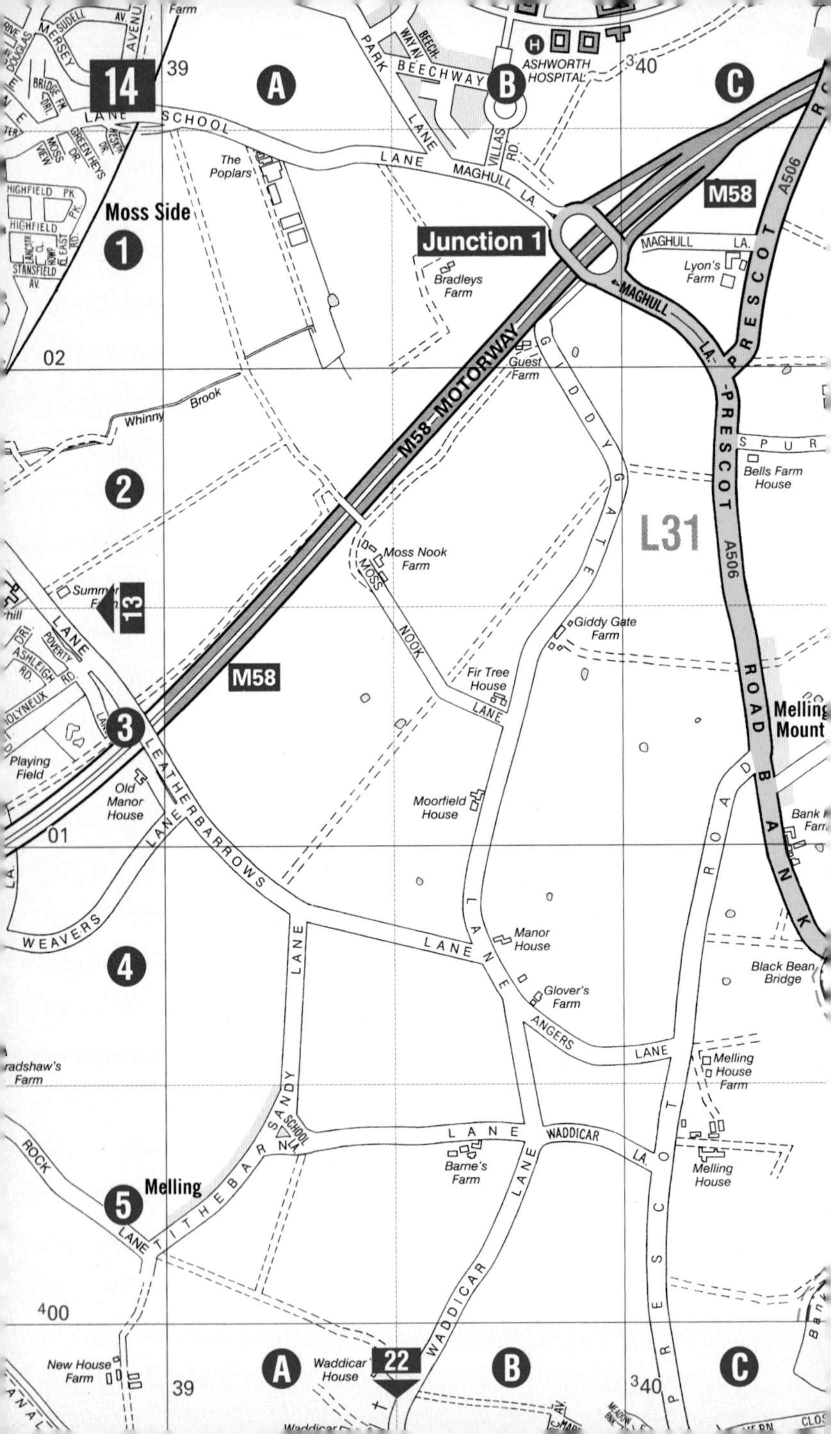

14
Moss Side
Junction 1
M58–MOTORWAY
M58
ASHWORTH HOSPITAL
The Poplars
Bradleys Farm
Guest Farm
Lyon's Farm
Whinny Brook
Moss Nook Farm
Summer Farm
13
Giddy Gate Farm
Fir Tree House
Bells Farm House
L31
Melling Mount
Playing Field
Old Manor House
Moorfield House
Manor House
Glover's Farm
Black Bean Bridge
Melling House Farm
Melling House
Barne's Farm
Melling
New House Farm
Waddicar House
22
SCHOOL LANE
MAGHULL LA.
PARK LANE
BEECHWAY
VILLAS RD.
MAGHULL LA.
PRESCOT RD.
A506
SPUR
GIDDY GATE LANE
MOSS NOOK LANE
LEATHERBARROWS LANE
WEAVERS LANE
SANDY LANE
LANE ANGERS LANE
WADDICAR LA.
WADDICAR LANE
TITHEBARN LANE
ROCK LANE
PRESCOT ROAD
BANK ROAD
SCHOOL LA.
POVERTY LANE
ASHLEIGH RD.
MOLYNEUX RD.
HIGHFIELD PK.
HIGHFIELD
STANSFIELD AV.
MERSEY
SUDELL AV.
DOUGLAS
BRIDGE FM DRI.
GREEN HEYS DR.
MOSS VIEW
39
340
400
02
01

15
Cunscough Hall
Big Wood
Outlet Farm
New House
SEFTON
WEST LANCASHIRE
Hesketh's Farm
Depot (disused)
Simonswood Brook
Moss Cottage
Meadow View
Simonswood Hall
Shacklady's Plantation
Little Dale Farm
Sandhole Cotts.
Gate House Bridge
L33
Tower Hill
Ravenscroft Prim. Sch.
Eastcroft Prim. Sch.
Comm. Cen.
Club
Prim. Sch. Support Cen.
Overdale Prim. Sch.
Tanpit
MOORFIELD SHOP. CEN
St. Peter & St. Paul R.C. Prim. Sch.
SEFTON
KNOWSLEY
STOPGATE LA.
PINGWOOD LANE
DALE LA.
SHEVINGTON'S LANE
A506
23

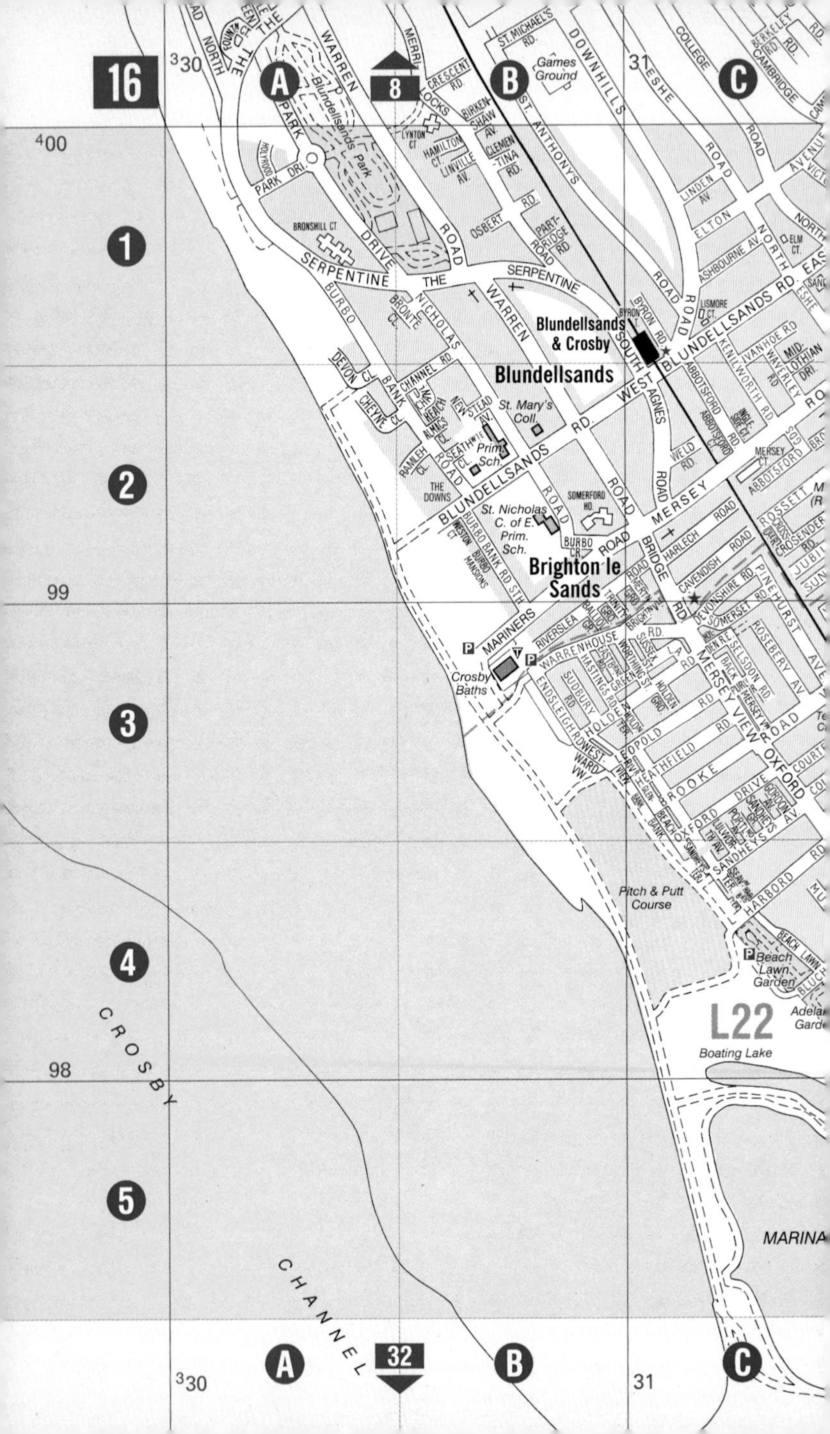

16
8
32
A
B
C
1
2
3
4
5
330
31
400
99
98
Blundellsands Park
Games Ground
Blundellsands & Crosby
Blundellsands
St. Mary's Coll.
Prim. Sch.
St. Nicholas C. of E. Prim. Sch.
Brighton le Sands
Crosby Baths
Pitch & Putt Course
Beach Lawn Garden
L22
Boating Lake
MARINA
CROSBY
CHANNEL
THE SERPENTINE
SERPENTINE
PARK DRI.
WARREN ROAD
WARREN
DOWNHILLS ROAD
ST. ANTHONYS ROAD
COLLEGE ROAD
ESHE ROAD
BLUNDELLSANDS RD. EAST
BLUNDELLSANDS RD. WEST
BLUNDELLSANDS ROAD
SOUTH ROAD
AGNES ROAD
MERSEY ROAD
BRIDGE RD.
NICHOLAS RD.
BURBO BANK RD. STH.
MARINERS ROAD
MERSEY VIEW
OXFORD ROAD
OXFORD DRIVE
SANDHEYS AV.
HARBORD
HARLECH ROAD
CAVENDISH ROAD
DEVONSHIRE RD.
PINEHURST AVE.
ROSEBERY AV.
SELSDON RD.
ROOKE
HEATHFIELD RD.
LEOPOLD RD.
HOLDEN
ENDSLEIGH RD.
WARRENHOUSE
RIVERSLEA
SUDBURY RD.
WESTWARD VW.
LINDEN AV.
ELTON
ASHBOURNE AV.
KENILWORTH RD.
IVANHOE RD.
WAVERLEY RD.
ABBOTSFORD RD.
WELD RD.
SOMERFORD HO.
BRONSHILL CT.
HOLYROOD
OSBERT RD.
PARTRIDGE RD.
CLEMENTINA RD.
BIRKENSHAW AV.
LINVILLE AV.
HAMILTON CT.
LYNTON CT.
CRESCENT RD.
ST. MICHAEL'S RD.
CAMBRIDGE RD.
BERKELEY RD.
BURBO BANK
DEVON CL.
CHEYNE CL.
CHANNEL RD.
NEWSTEAD AV.
RAMLEH CL.
THE DOWNS
BURBO MANSIONS
WESTON CT.
BURBO CR.
ROSSETT
CROSENDEN RD.
MERSEY CT.
ABBOTSFORD GDS.
LISMORE CT.
ELM CT.
BYRON RD.
MIDLOTHIAN DRI.

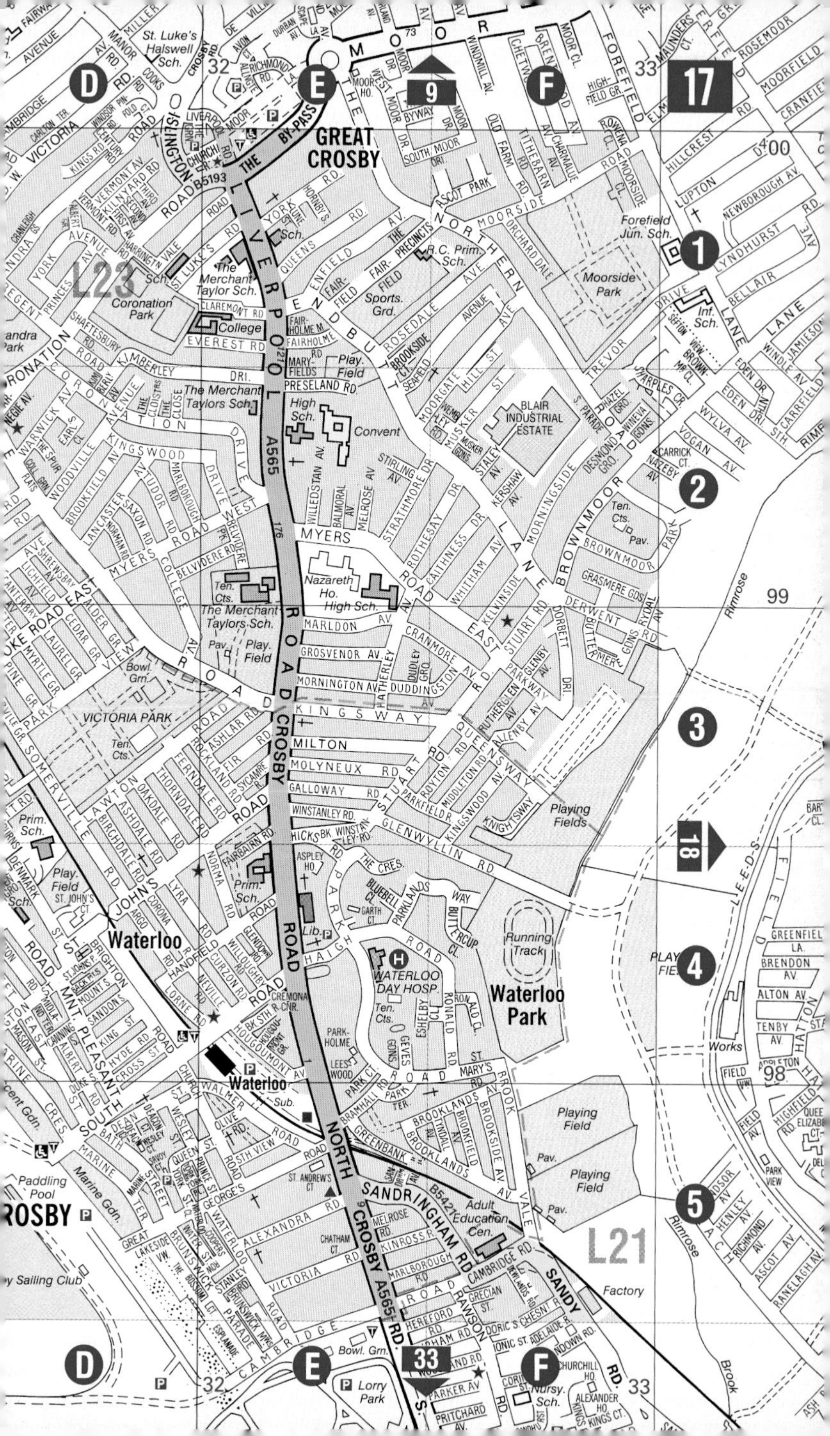

17
9
18
33
D
E
F
1
2
3
4
5
32
33
99
98
L23
L21
GREAT CROSBY
Waterloo
Waterloo Park
ROSBY
MOOR
THE BY-PASS
LIVERPOOL ROAD
CROSBY ROAD NORTH
A565
B5193
B5421
ISLINGTON
VICTORIA ROAD
CORONATION DRIVE
COLLEGE ROAD
MYERS ROAD EAST
MYERS ROAD WEST
ENDBUTT LANE
NORTHERN
MOORSIDE ROAD
FOREFIELD LANE
BROWNMOOR LANE
KINGSWAY
MILTON
MOLYNEUX RD.
GALLOWAY RD.
WINSTANLEY RD.
GLENWYLLIN RD.
QUEENSWAY
STUART RD.
HAIGH RD.
SANDRINGHAM RD.
SOUTH RD.
CAMBRIDGE RD.
ALEXANDRA RD.
VICTORIA RD.
MARINE CRES.
SANDY RD.
St. Luke's Halswell Sch.
The Merchant Taylor Sch.
The Merchant Taylors Sch.
College
Coronation Park
R.C. Prim. Sch.
Sports. Grd.
High Sch.
Convent
BLAIR INDUSTRIAL ESTATE
Moorside Park
Forefield Jun. Sch.
Inf. Sch.
Nazareth Ho. High Sch.
VICTORIA PARK
Play. Field
Ten. Cts.
Playing Fields
Running Track
WATERLOO DAY HOSP.
Lib.
Prim. Sch.
Playing Field
Adult Education Cen.
Factory
Works
Rimrose Brook
Paddling Pool
Marine Gdn.
Sailing Club
Lorry Park
Bowl. Grn.
St. Nursy. Sch.
Sub.

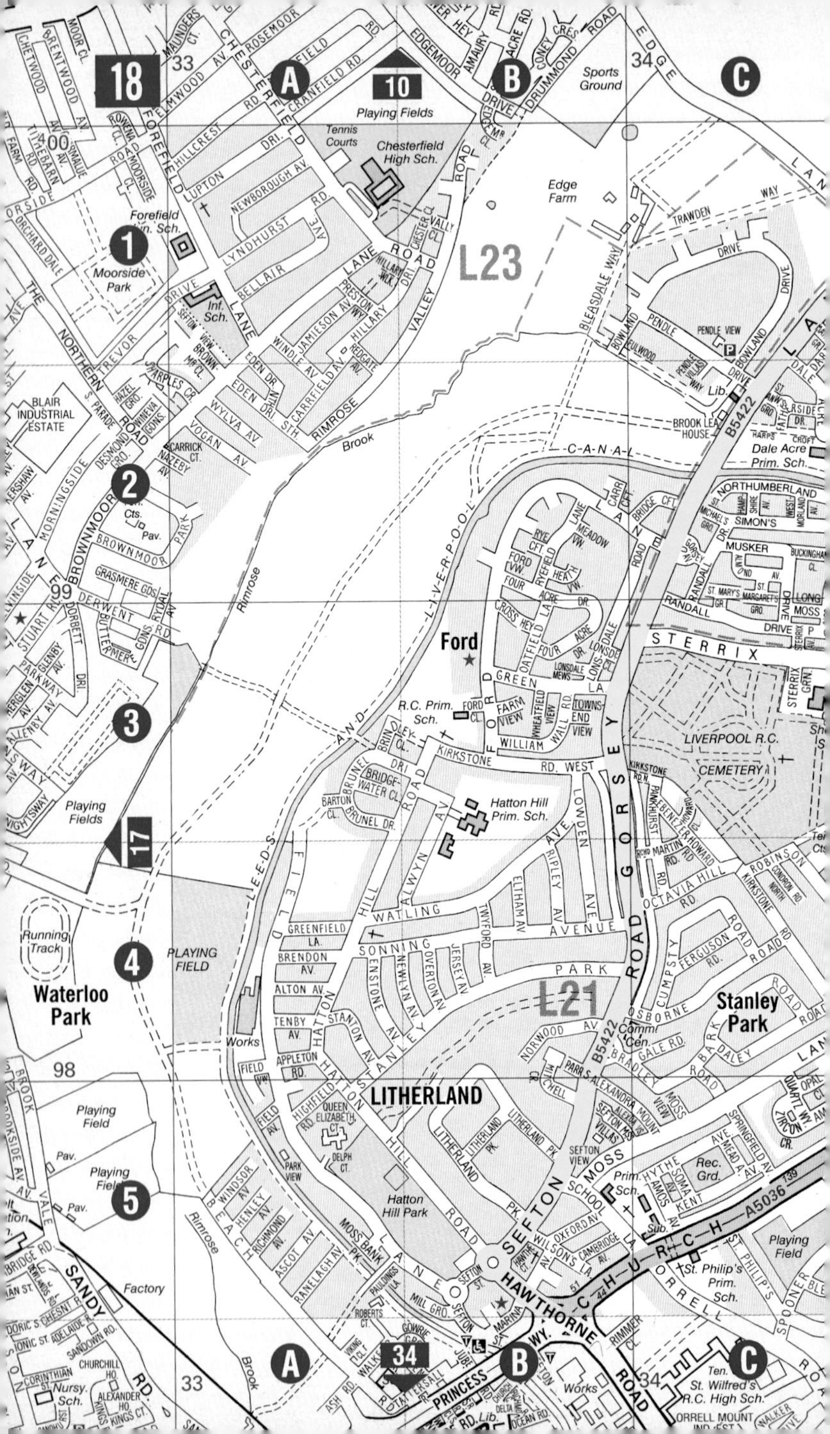

18
10
17
34
A
B
C
1
2
3
4
5
33
34
400
99
98
L23
L21
Playing Fields
Tennis Courts
Chesterfield High Sch.
Sports Ground
Edge Farm
Forefield Jun. Sch.
Moorside Park
Inf. Sch.
BLAIR INDUSTRIAL ESTATE
Brook
Rimrose
CANAL
LIVERPOOL AND LEEDS
Ford
R.C. Prim. Sch.
Hatton Hill Prim. Sch.
LIVERPOOL R.C. CEMETERY
Dale Acre Prim. Sch.
BROOK LEA HOUSE
Lib.
B5422
Running Track
PLAYING FIELD
Waterloo Park
Works
LITHERLAND
Hatton Hill Park
Stanley Park
Comm. Cen.
Rec. Grd.
Playing Field
St. Philip's Prim. Sch.
A5036
HAWTHORNE ROAD
SEFTON
CHURCH
Factory
Pav.
Nursy. Sch.
St. Wilfred's R.C. High Sch.
ORRELL MOUNT IND. EST.
CHESTERFIELD
FOREFIELD LANE
EDGEMOOR DRIVE
DRUMMOND ROAD
NORTHERN ROAD
BROWNMOOR LANE
RIMROSE VALLEY ROAD
BLEASDALE WAY
GORSEY ROAD
STERRIX LANE
KIRKSTONE RD. WEST
HATTON HILL ROAD
WATLING AVENUE
SONNING AV.
PARK AVENUE
STANLEY ROAD
LITHERLAND ROAD
SEFTON ROAD
MOSS LANE
OCTAVIA HILL RD.
SANDY ROAD
PRINCESS WY.
ORRELL LANE
RIMMER CL.

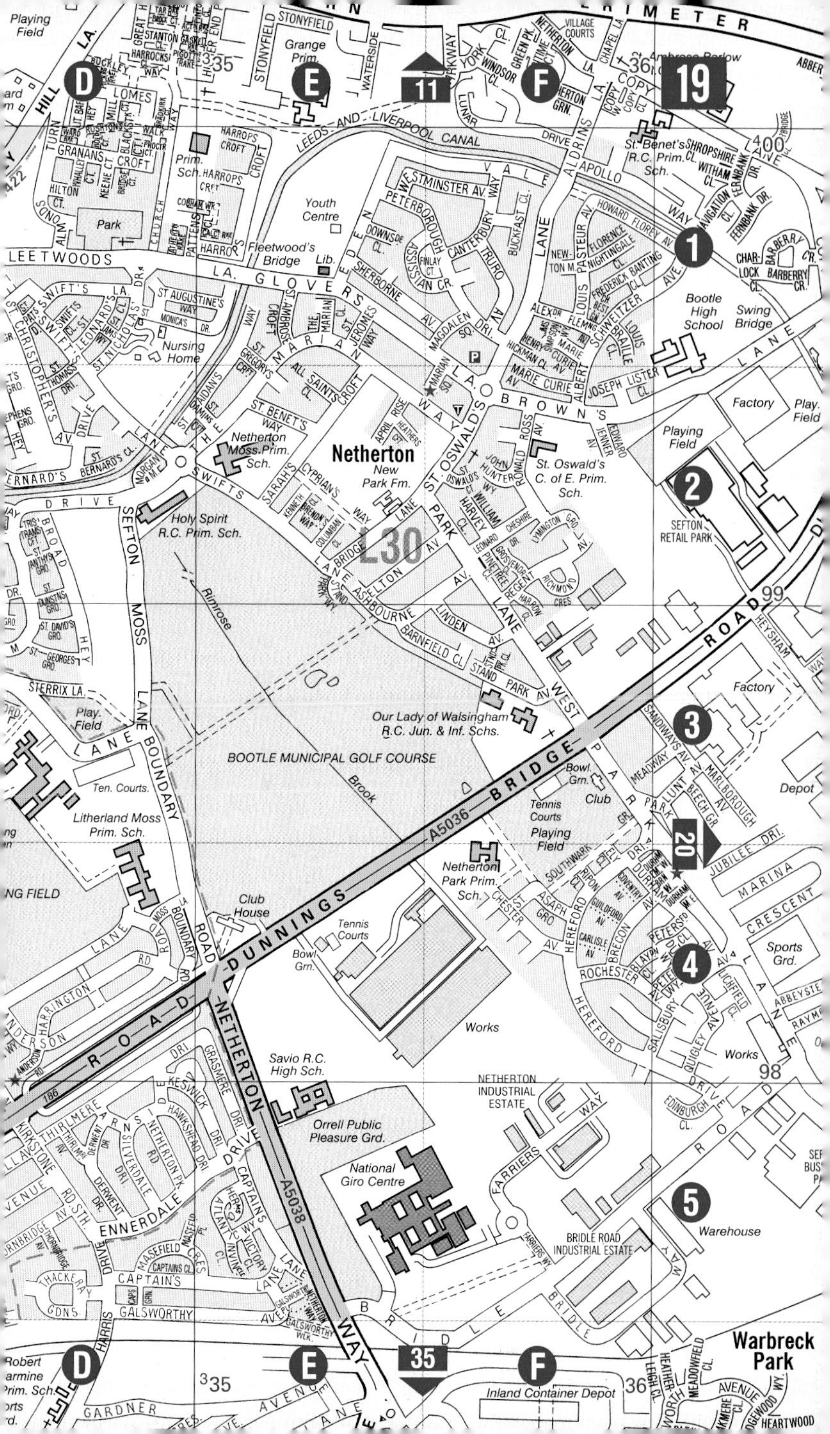

19
11
20
35
D
E
F
1
2
3
4
5
L30
Netherton
New Park Fm.
Playing Field
Stonyfield
Grange Prim.
Waterside
Leeds and Liverpool Canal
Village Courts
Netherton Grn.
St. Benet's R.C. Prim. Sch.
Youth Centre
Fleetwood's Bridge
Lib.
Prim. Sch.
Park
Nursing Home
Netherton Moss Prim. Sch.
Holy Spirit R.C. Prim. Sch.
Bootle High School
Swing Bridge
Factory
Play. Field
Playing Field
Sefton Retail Park
St. Oswald's C. of E. Prim. Sch.
Our Lady of Walsingham R.C. Jun. & Inf. Schs.
Bootle Municipal Golf Course
Rimrose Brook
Litherland Moss Prim. Sch.
Ten. Courts.
Club House
Bowl. Grn.
Club
Tennis Courts
Playing Field
Netherton Park Prim. Sch.
Works
Depot
Sports Grd.
Savio R.C. High Sch.
Orrell Public Pleasure Grd.
National Giro Centre
Netherton Industrial Estate
Bridle Road Industrial Estate
Warehouse
Warbreck Park
Inland Container Depot
Dunnings Bridge Road
A5036
Netherton Way
A5038
Bridle Road
Leeds and Liverpool Canal
Glovers La.
Fleetwoods La.
Browns La.
St. Oswald's La.
Park La.
Park La. West
Sefton Drive
Moss Lane
Boundary Lane
Apollo Way
Aldrins La.
Marian Way
Marina Crescent
Jubilee Dri.
Heysham Rd.
Sandways Av.
Hereford Dri.
Rochester Av.
Edinburgh Cl.
Farriers Way
Ennerdale Rd.
Captains La.
Galsworthy Ave.
Harris Dr.
Gardner Av.
Thirlmere Av.
Kirkstone Rd.
Harrington Rd.
Anderson Rd.
Sterrix La.
Robert Carmine Prim. Sch.
335
36
400
99
98
186

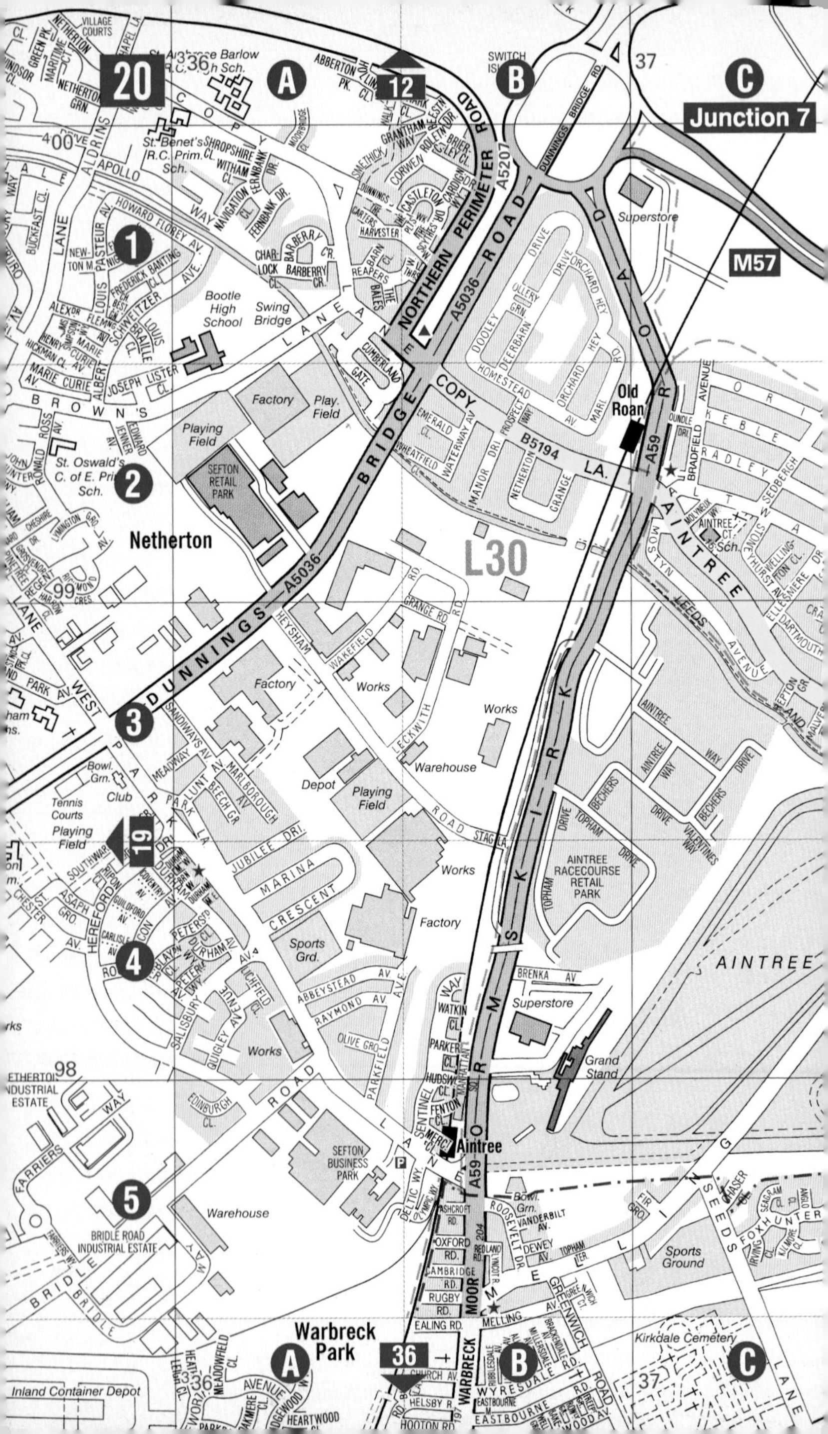
A
B
C
12
36
19
Junction 7
M57
1
2
3
4
5
Netherton
L30
AINTREE
Warbreck Park
Aintree
Old Roan
Superstore
Bootle High School
Swing Bridge
St. Benet's R.C. Prim. Sch.
St. Oswald's C. of E. Prim. Sch.
SEFTON RETAIL PARK
SEFTON BUSINESS PARK
AINTREE RACECOURSE RETAIL PARK
BRIDLE ROAD INDUSTRIAL ESTATE
Inland Container Depot
Kirkdale Cemetery
Grand Stand
Factory
Works
Warehouse
Depot
Playing Field
Play. Field
Sports Grd.
Sports Ground
Tennis Courts
Bowl. Grn.
Club
NORTHERN PERIMETER ROAD
A5207
A5036
DUNNINGS BRIDGE ROAD
BRIDGE
DUNNINGS
ORMSKIRK ROAD
A59
B5194
COPY LA.
BROWN'S LANE
APOLLO WAY
HOWARD FLOREY AV.
ALDRINS LANE
LOUIS PASTEUR AV.
SCHWEITZER AVE.
JOSEPH LISTER CL.
MARIE CURIE AV.
HENRY CURIE
LOUIS BRAILLE CL.
FREDERICK BANTING CL.
WEST PARK AV.
PARK LA.
MARINA CRESCENT
JUBILEE DRI.
STAG LA.
HEYSHAM ROAD
WAKEFIELD RD.
GRANGE RD.
LECKWITH
MARLBOROUGH AV.
SANDIWAYS AV.
MEADWAY
LUNT AV.
BEECH GR.
HEREFORD
SOUTHWARK
DURHAM AV.
ABBEYSTEAD AV.
RAYMOND AV.
OLIVE GRO.
PARKFIELD AVE.
SALISBURY AV.
QUIGLEY AVENUE
LICHFIELD
EDINBURGH CL.
FARRIERS WAY
BRIDLE ROAD
MELLING ROAD
MOOR LANE
WARBRECK MOOR
SENTINEL WY.
DELTIC WY.
ROOSEVELT DR.
VANDERBILT AV.
DEWEY AV.
TOPHAM TER.
GREENWICH ROAD
SEEDS LANE
FOXHUNTER DR.
AINTREE WAY
BECHERS DRIVE
VALENTINES WAY
TOPHAM DRIVE
LEEDS AVENUE
AINTREE LANE
ORCHARD HEY
HOMESTEAD AV.
MARL RD.
DOOLEY DRIVE
DEERBARN
MANOR DRI.
NETHERTON GRANGE
WATERWAY AV
EMERALD CL.
WHEATFIELD CL.
CUMBERLAND GATE
BRADFIELD AVENUE
KEBLE
RADLEY
SEDBERGH
ORIEL
AINTREE CT. Sch.
WELLINGTON CL.
ELLESMERE DR.
DARTMOUTH
ASHCROFT RD.
OXFORD RD.
CAMBRIDGE RD.
RUGBY RD.
EALING RD.
CHURCH AV.
HELSBY RD.
HOOTON RD.
WYRESDALE RD.
EASTBOURNE RD.
MEADOWFIELD CL.
HEARTWOOD
AVENUE
98
99
400
336
37
197
204

21
D
E
F
13
22
37
38
39
400
99
98
Fold
LANE
TITH
Brooklea
BREWERY
New House
Farm
Town Meadow
Cottages
Carr
Cottage
Waddicar
Farm
Holmes
Bridge
LEEDS AND LIVERPOOL CANAL
Brooklands
Farm
L31
Aintree Hall
Farm
M57 MOTORWAY
M57
Holy Rosary
R.C. Prim.
Sch.
Ledsons
Bridge
Aintree
SPENCERS LANE
Bull Bridge
Works
River Alt
Weir
Mill
Farm
Library
Tennis
Court
Pav.
Playing Field
B5194
LANE
SCHOOL LA.
WANGO
B5192
CANAL
Handcock's
Bridge
RACE COURSE
L9
L10
Stand
Becher's Brook
LIVERPOOL
GOLF
AINTREE LANE
White
Thorn Sch.
Redbridge
High
Sch.
Meadow
Bank
Sch.
SEFTON
LIVERPOOL
SIGNAL WORKS
Playing
Fields
Recreation
Ground
Newhall
Swim. Pool
Fazakerley
Sports Cen.
Educ.
Cen.
Fazakerley
Playing
Fields
Fazakerley
High Sch.
JOSEPH
MORGAN
HEIGHTS
Fazakerley
LONGMOOR LANE
GREYSTONE RD.
Lib.
COPPLE
MOOR

14
38
21
A
B
C
1
2
3
4
5
39
340
400
99
98
L31
L10
New House Farm
Waddicar House
Waddicar Farm
James Bridge
CANAL
SPENCER'S LANE
Ledsons Bridge
Works
Waddicar
Melling Prim. Sch.
Kirkby Park
Kirkby
Westvale
Westvale Prim. Sch.
Recreation Ground
Adventure Playgrd.
M57
M57 MOTORWAY
KNOWSLEY
SEFTON
Weir
Alt
LIVERPOOL MUNICIPAL GOLF COURSE
River Alt
Knowsley Sports Club
Club House
Junction 6
Kirkby Stadium
Kirkby Sports Cen.
Comm. Cen.
PRESCOT ROAD
GLOVERS BROW
WADDICAR LANE
WHITEFIELD DRIVE
WHITEFIELD RD.
AINTREE LANE
VALLEY ROAD
A506
MOOR LA.
INGOE LA.
OXTON CL.
BURTONS LA.
Burton's Bridge
Brook
Kirkby
Knowsley Brook
White Thorn Sch.
Redbridge High Sch.
Meadow Bank Sch.
Fazakerley Playing Fields
Educ. Cen.
JOSEPH MORGAN HEIGHTS
LONGMOOR LANE
Lib.
Fazakerley High Sch.
HAVEN ROAD
FIELD LANE
COPPLE
MALVERN
PENNINE
CHILTERN DR.
MOUNT RD.
NORTH PARK
SOUTH PARK ROAD
PARKWAY WEST
PARKWAY EAST
STATION RD.
STUART RD.
ANDREW AV.
BEECH AV.
HAYES CRES.
RAINBOW DRIVE
AMANDA WAY
HOULSTON RD.
MELVERLEY RD.
COPTHORNE RD.
HESKETH RD.
TILSTON RD.
MERCER RD.
DENVER ROAD
ELSTEAD RD.
BOLTON AV.
ALVANLEY RD.
DELAWARE CRESCENT
KIRKBY ROW
WILLIAM ROAD
STANTON RD.
LINGTREE RD.
PENLEY CR.
SOUTHNEY CL.
PICKWORTH WY.
SATINWOOD CRES.
HICKORY GRO.
BROOKBANK CT.
ALT SIDE CT.
BECK CL.
MEADOW BROOK CL.
GREENBANK DR.
MOOR CT.
EDGEMOOR DRI.
DRAKE

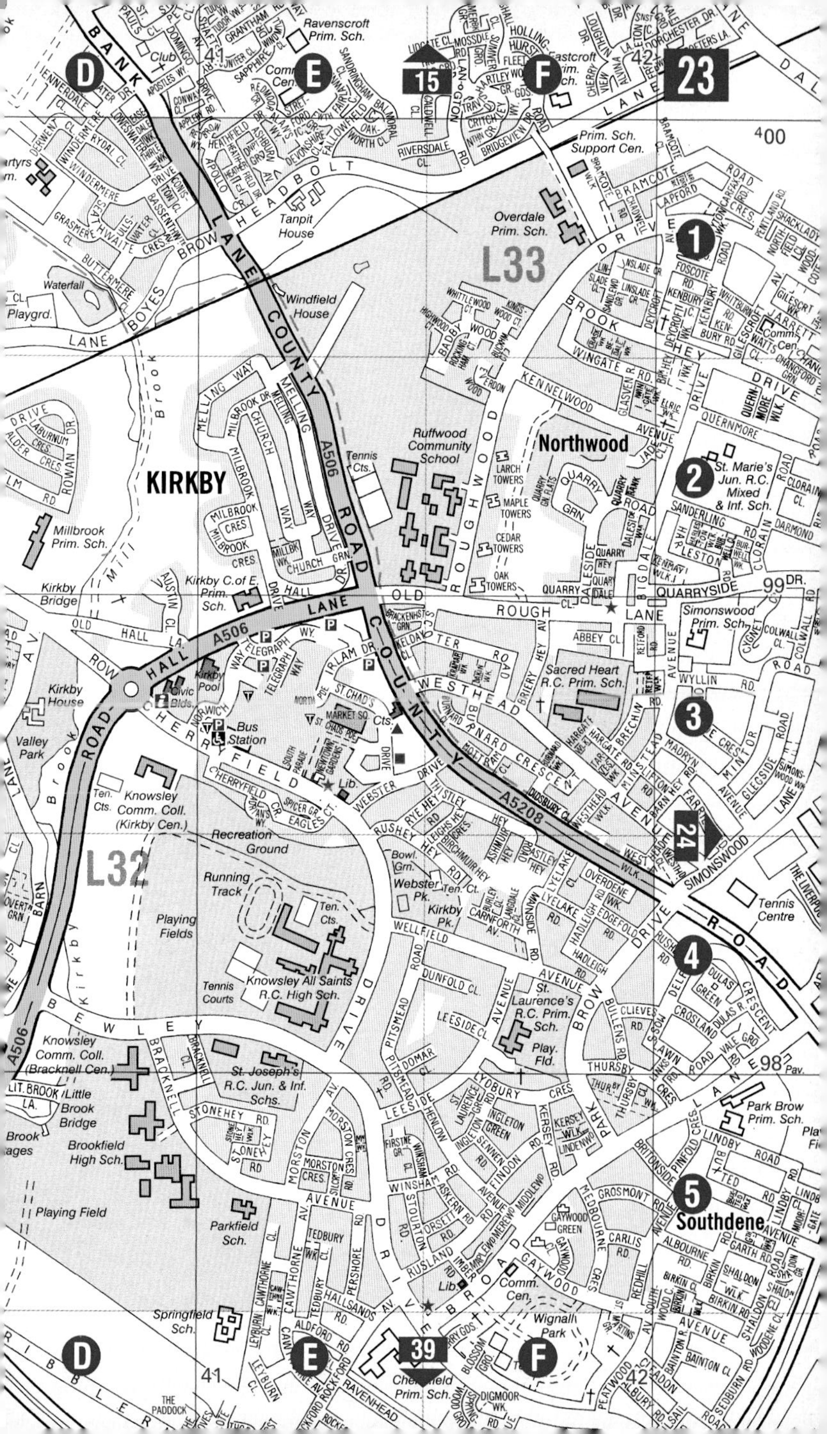
23
15
39
24
D
E
F
1
2
3
4
5
41
42
400
99
98
L33
L32
KIRKBY
Northwood
Southdene
Ravenscroft Prim. Sch.
Eastcroft Prim. Sch.
Prim. Sch. Support Cen.
Overdale Prim. Sch.
Tanpit House
Windfield House
Waterfall
Playgrd.
Club
Ruffwood Community School
Tennis Cts.
LARCH TOWERS
MAPLE TOWERS
CEDAR TOWERS
OAK TOWERS
St. Marie's Jun. R.C. Mixed & Inf. Sch.
Simonswood Prim. Sch.
Sacred Heart R.C. Prim. Sch.
Millbrook Prim. Sch.
Kirkby C.of E. Prim. Sch.
Kirkby Bridge
Kirkby House
Valley Park
Kirkby Pool
Civic Blds.
Bus Station
Lib.
Cts.
Knowsley Comm. Coll. (Kirkby Cen.)
Ten. Cts.
Recreation Ground
Running Track
Playing Fields
Tennis Courts
Knowsley All Saints R.C. High Sch.
Bowl. Grn.
Webster Pk.
Kirkby Pk.
Tennis Centre
St. Laurence's R.C. Prim. Sch.
Play. Fld.
Knowsley Comm. Coll. (Bracknell Cen.)
Little Brook Bridge
Brookfield High Sch.
St. Joseph's R.C. Jun. & Inf. Schs.
Parkfield Sch.
Playing Field
Springfield Sch.
Comm. Cen.
Wignall Park
Park Brow Prim. Sch.
Cherryfield Prim. Sch.
COUNTY ROAD
A506
A5208
HALL LANE
OLD HALL LANE
ROUGH LANE
BROOK HEY DRIVE
KENNELWOOD AVENUE
QUARRY ROAD
QUARRYSIDE DR.
SIMONSWOOD LANE
WESTHEAD AVENUE
BEWLEY DRIVE
BROAD LANE
MOORGATE AVENUE
ROUGHWOOD DRIVE
MELLING WAY
MILLBROOK LANE
CHERRYFIELD DRIVE
WEBSTER DRIVE
WELLFIELD AVENUE
BROW
PARK BROW DRIVE
BOYES BROW
HEADBOLT LANE
BANK LANE
RIBBLER LANE
ROWAN DR.
BARNARD CRESCENT
LINDBY ROAD
TIRRELL AVENUE

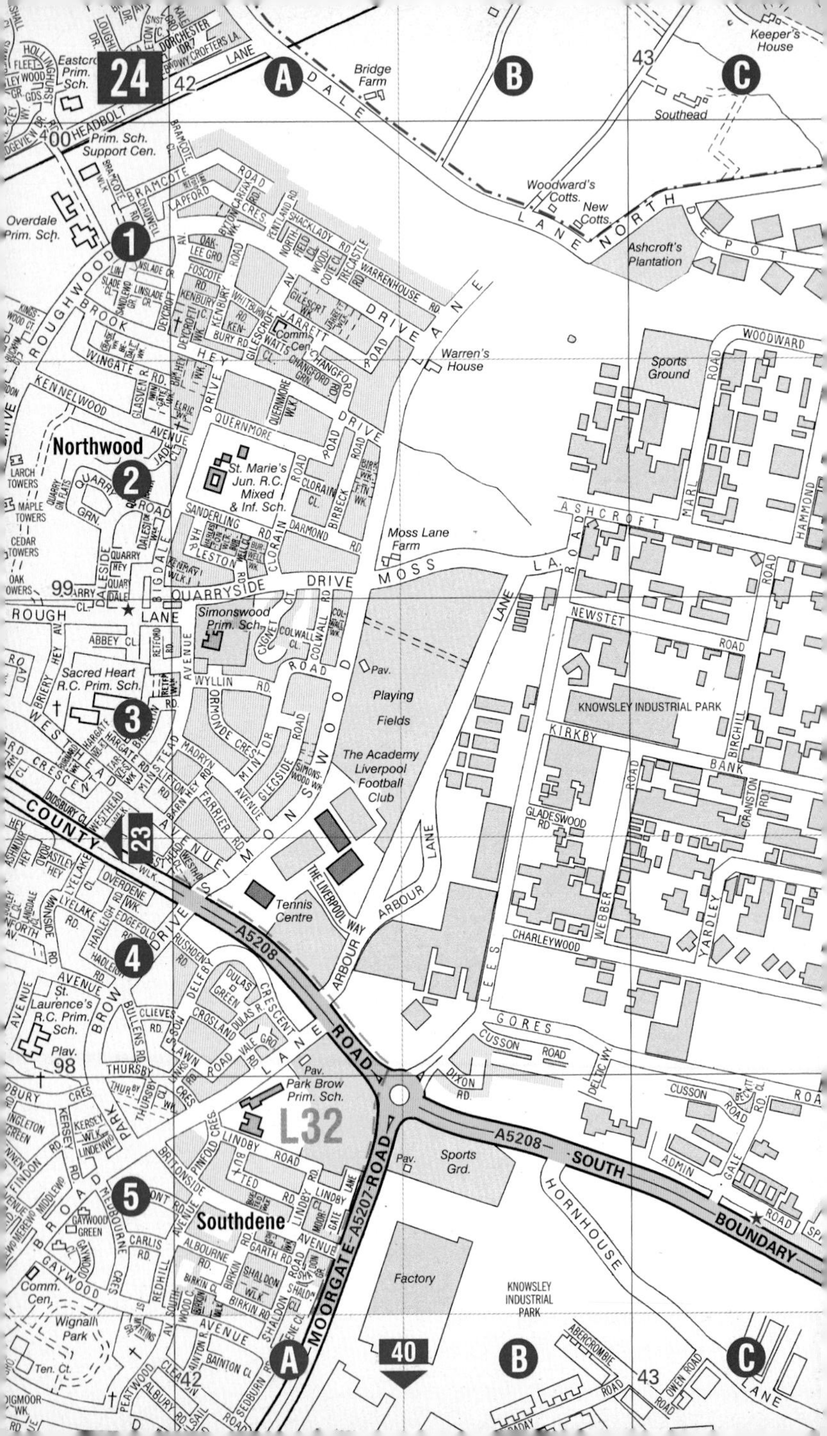
Northwood
Southdene
KNOWSLEY INDUSTRIAL PARK
L32
A5208
COUNTY ROAD
SOUTH BOUNDARY ROAD
MOORGATE ROAD
A5207
St. Marie's Jun. R.C. Mixed & Inf. Sch.
Simonswood Prim. Sch.
Sacred Heart R.C. Prim. Sch.
St. Laurence's R.C. Prim. Sch.
Park Brow Prim. Sch.
Overdale Prim. Sch.
Playing Fields
The Academy Liverpool Football Club
Tennis Centre
Moss Lane Farm
Warren's House
Ashcroft's Plantation
Woodward's Cotts.
New Cotts.
Southead
Keeper's House
Bridge Farm
Sports Ground
Factory
Wignall Park
23
40

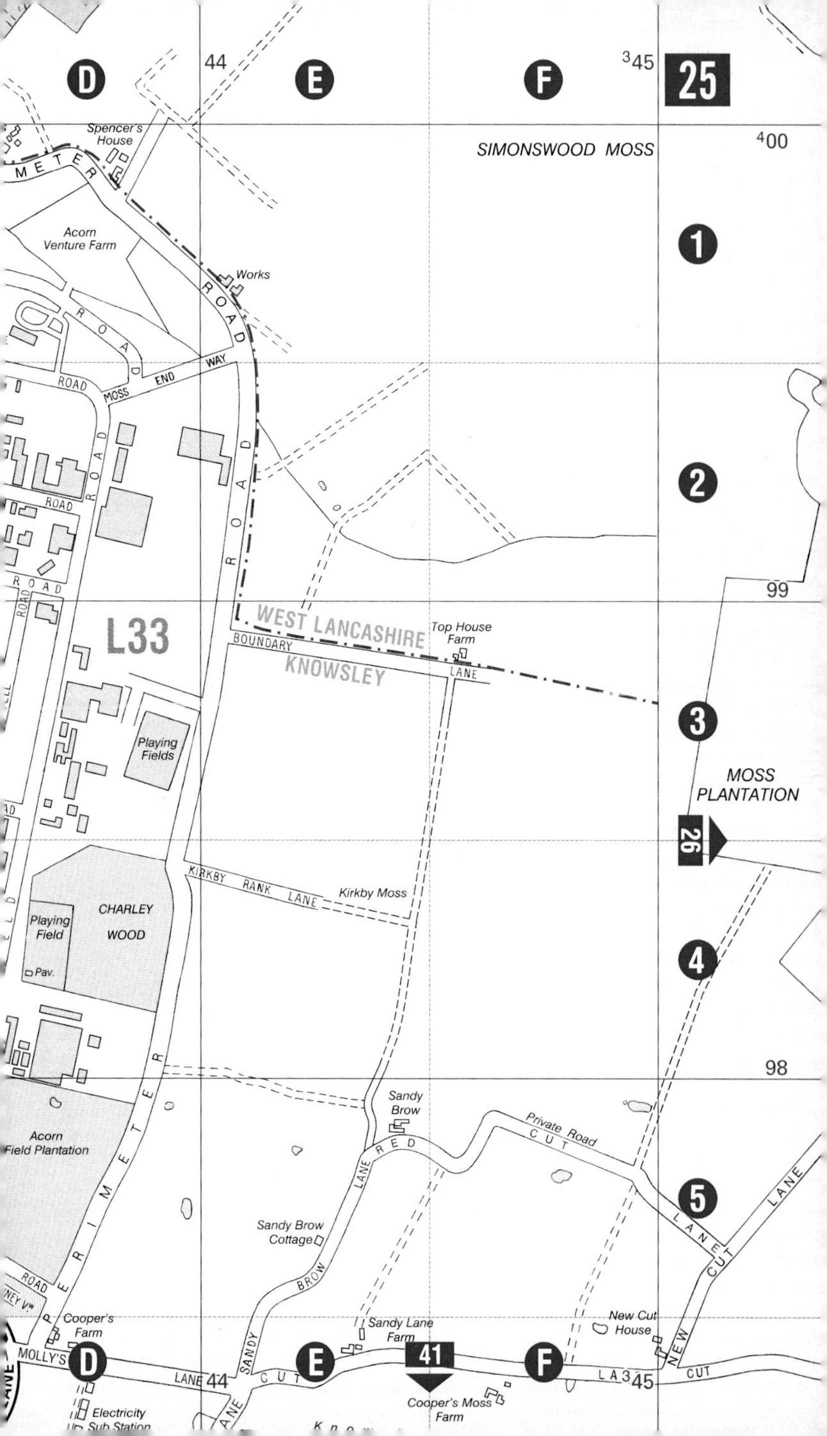
D
E
F
44
345
400
SIMONSWOOD MOSS
Spencer's House
Acorn Venture Farm
Works
ROAD
MOSS END WAY
L33
WEST LANCASHIRE
KNOWSLEY
BOUNDARY LANE
Top House Farm
99
Playing Fields
MOSS PLANTATION
26
KIRKBY RANK LANE
Kirkby Moss
CHARLEY WOOD
Playing Field
Pav.
98
Acorn Field Plantation
PERIMETER ROAD
Sandy Brow
RED LANE
Private Road
CUT
Sandy Brow Cottage
BROW
Cooper's Farm
Sandy Lane Farm
New Cut House
NEW CUT LANE
MOLLY'S LANE
41
SANDY
CUT
Cooper's Moss Farm
Electricity Sub Station

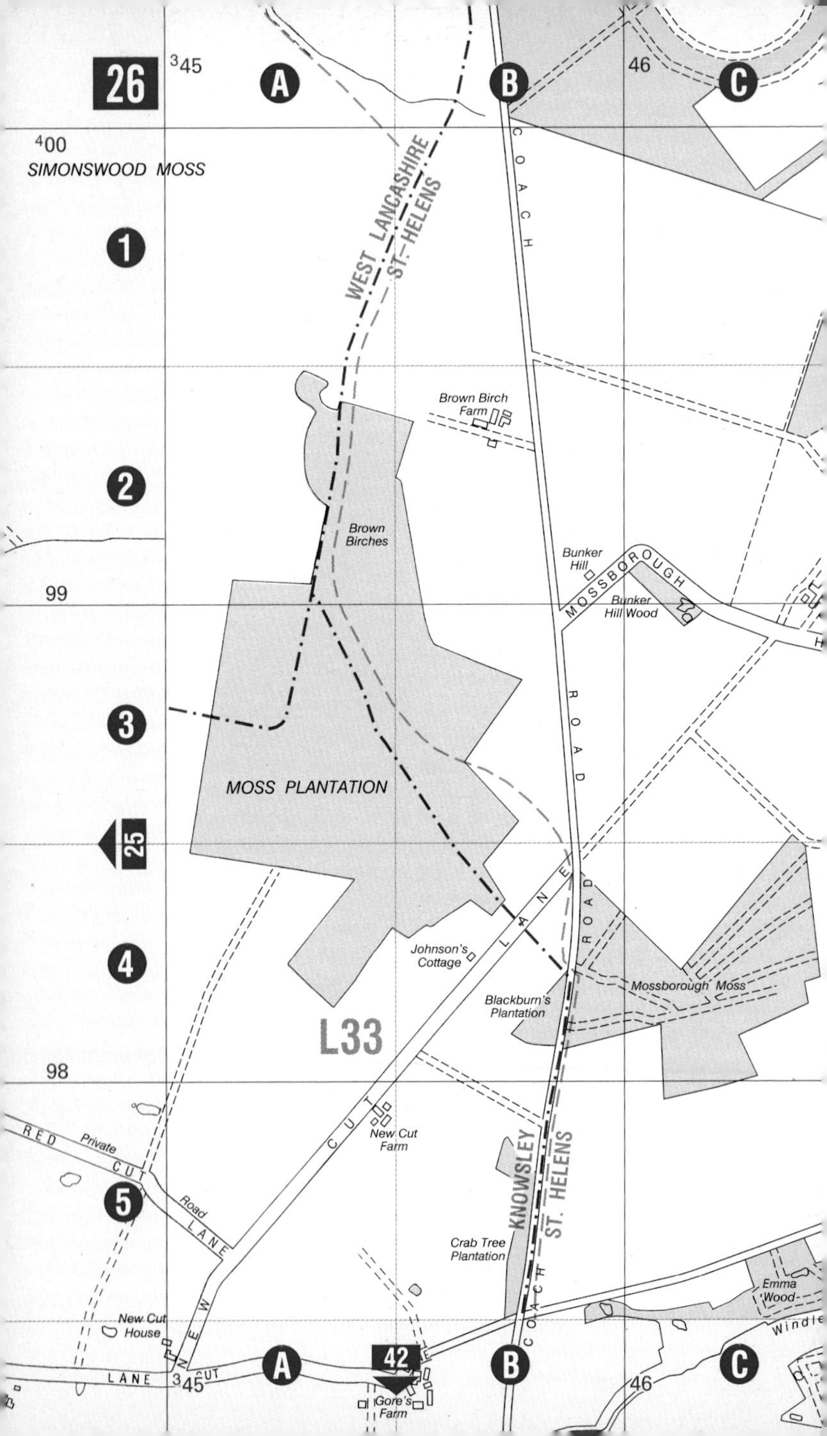

345
A
B
C
46
400
SIMONSWOOD MOSS
1
2
3
4
5
WEST LANCASHIRE
ST. HELENS
COACH
Brown Birch Farm
Brown Birches
Bunker Hill
MOSSBOROUGH
Bunker Hill Wood
99
ROAD
MOSS PLANTATION
25
LANE
ROAD
Johnson's Cottage
Blackburn's Plantation
Mossborough Moss
L33
98
RED
Private
CUT
Road
LANE
CUT
New Cut Farm
KNOWSLEY
ST. HELENS
Crab Tree Plantation
Emma Wood
Windle
NEW
New Cut House
LANE
CUT
345
42
Gore's Farm
COACH
46

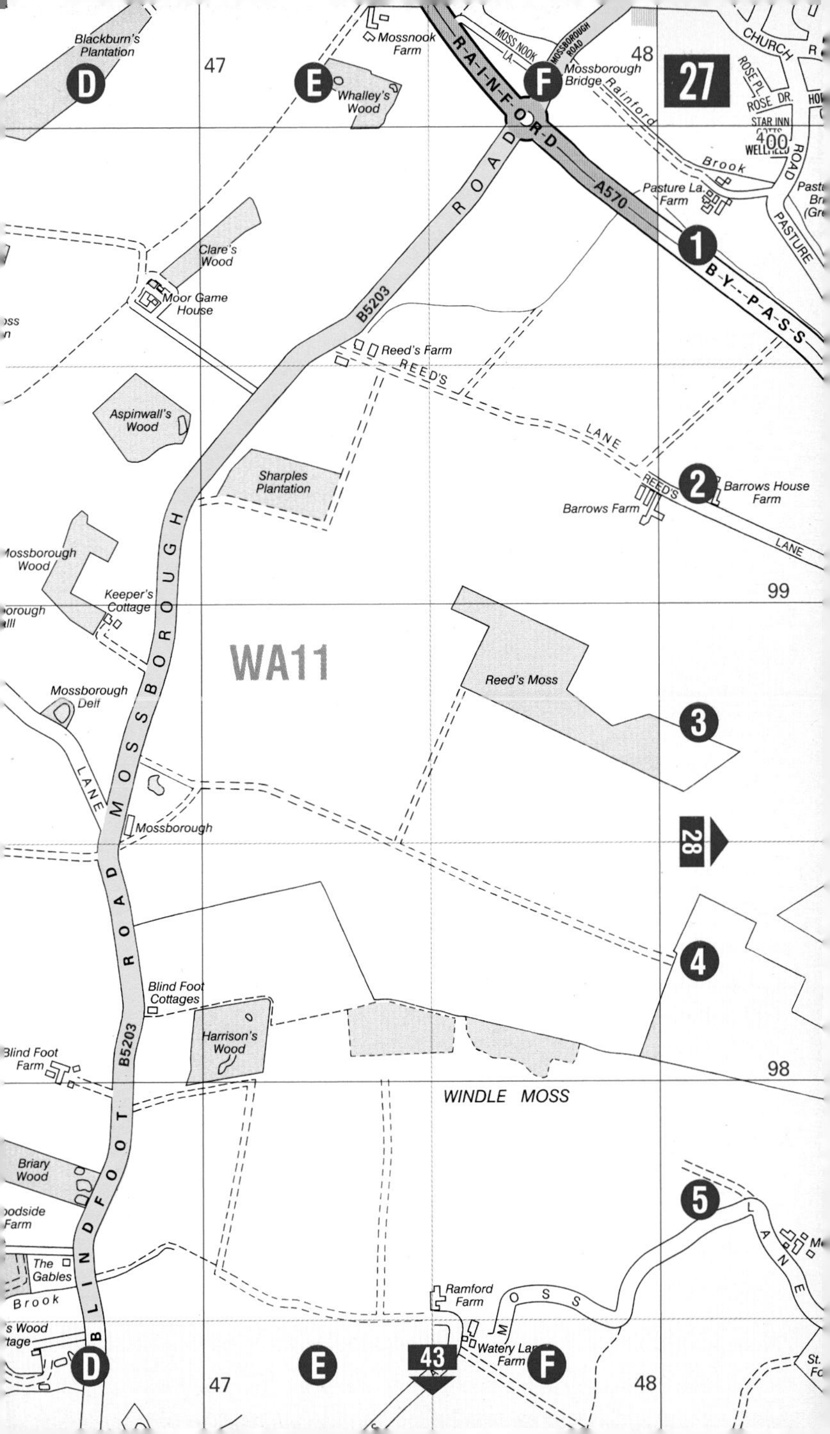

27
28
43
D
E
F
47
48
99
98
1
2
3
4
5
WA11
Blackburn's Plantation
Mossnook Farm
Whalley's Wood
MOSS NOOK LA.
MOSSBOROUGH ROAD
Mossborough Bridge
RAINFORD ROAD
Rainford Brook
CHURCH
ROSE PL.
ROSE DR.
STAR INN COTTS.
WELLFIELD
ROAD
Pasture La. Farm
PASTURE
A570
BY-PASS
Clare's Wood
Moor Game House
B5203
Reed's Farm
REED'S LANE
Aspinwall's Wood
Sharples Plantation
Barrows House Farm
Barrows Farm
Mossborough Wood
Keeper's Cottage
Reed's Moss
Mossborough Delf
LANE
MOSSBOROUGH ROAD
Mossborough
Blind Foot Cottages
Harrison's Wood
Blind Foot Farm
WINDLE MOSS
Briary Wood
BLINDFOOT ROAD
The Gables
Brook
Ramford Farm
MOSS LANE
Watery Lane Farm

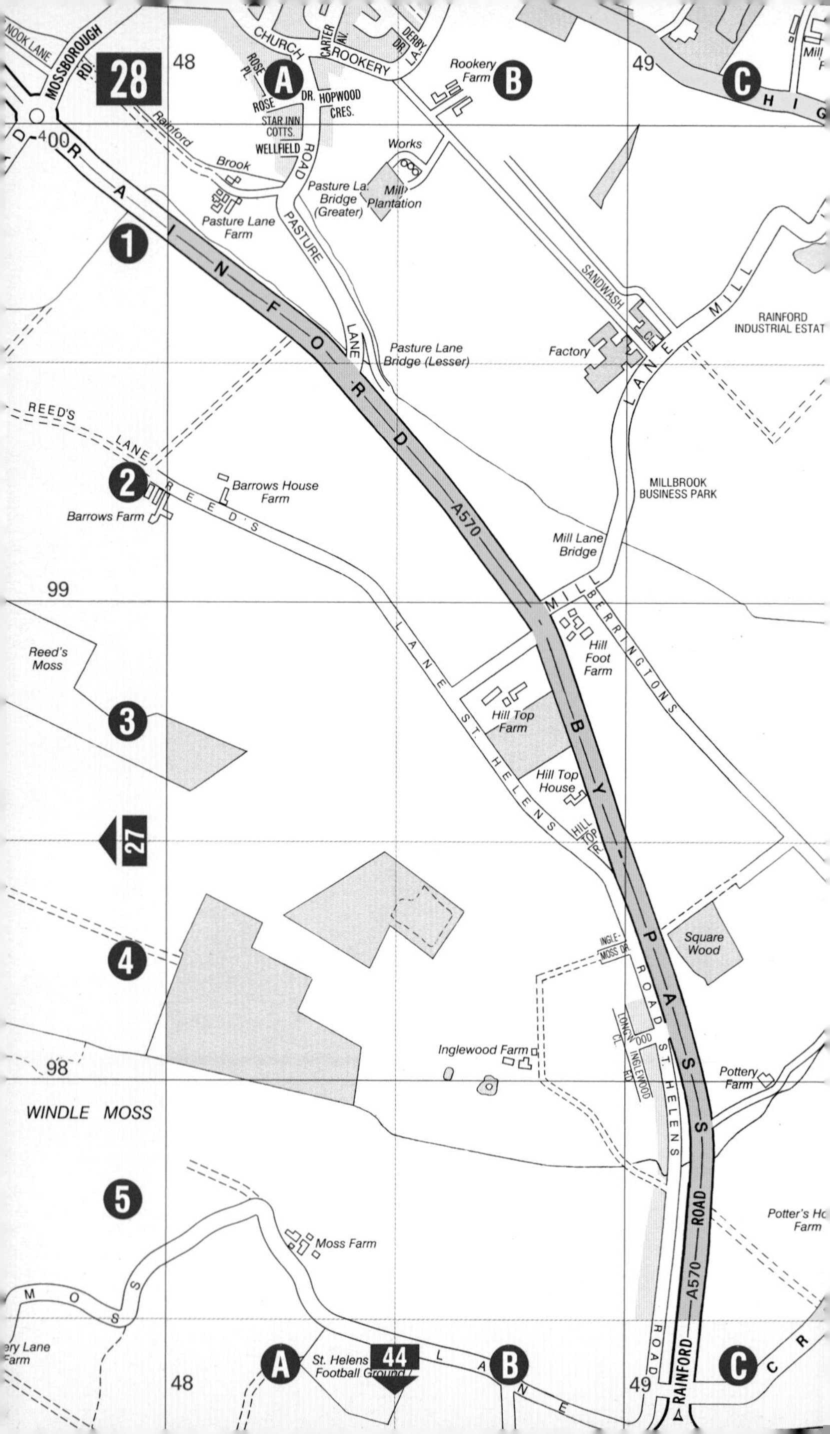

28
48
49
99
98
NOOK LANE
MOSSBOROUGH RD.
CHURCH
CARTER AV.
ROOKERY
DERBY DR.
LA.
ROSE PL.
ROSE DR.
HOPWOOD CRES.
STAR INN COTTS.
WELLFIELD
ROAD
Rookery Farm
Rainford
Brook
Works
Pasture La. Bridge (Greater)
Mill Plantation
Pasture Lane Farm
PASTURE
LANE
RAINFORD
A570
SANDWASH CL.
MILL LANE
RAINFORD INDUSTRIAL ESTAT
Factory
Pasture Lane Bridge (Lesser)
REED'S LANE
Barrows House Farm
Barrows Farm
MILLBROOK BUSINESS PARK
Mill Lane Bridge
MILL
BERRINGTONS
Reed's Moss
Hill Foot Farm
Hill Top Farm
Hill Top House
ST. HELENS LANE
HILL TOP R.
BY-PASS
27
INGLE-MOSS DR.
Square Wood
LONGWOOD CL.
INGLEWOOD RD.
Inglewood Farm
ST. HELENS ROAD
Pottery Farm
WINDLE MOSS
ROAD
Potter's Ho Farm
Moss Farm
MOSS
ery Lane Farm
St. Helens Football Ground
44
LANE
RAINFORD

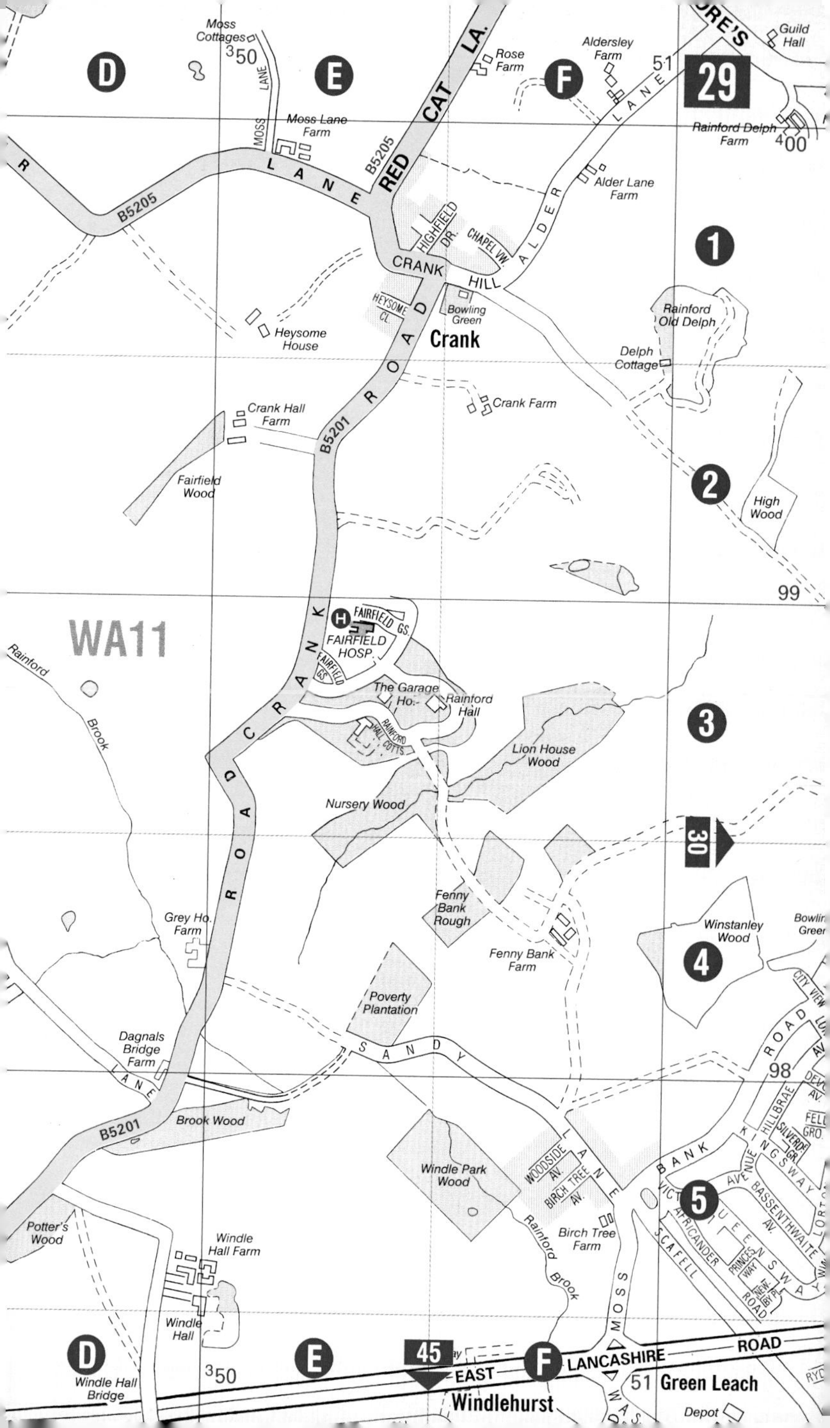

29
Moss Cottages
Moss Lane Farm
Rose Farm
Aldersley Farm
Guild Hall
Rainford Delph Farm
Alder Lane Farm
RED CAT LA.
B5205
LANE
HIGHFIELD DR.
CHAPEL VW.
ALDER
CRANK
HILL
HEYSOME CL.
Bowling Green
Crank
Heysome House
Rainford Old Delph
Delph Cottage
Crank Farm
Crank Hall Farm
CRANK ROAD
B5201
Fairfield Wood
High Wood
WA11
Rainford Brook
FAIRFIELD GS.
FAIRFIELD HOSP.
The Garage Ho.
Rainford Hall
RAINFORD HALL COTTS.
Lion House Wood
Nursery Wood
30
Fenny Bank Rough
Fenny Bank Farm
Winstanley Wood
Grey Ho. Farm
Poverty Plantation
Dagnals Bridge Farm
SANDY LANE
Brook Wood
Windle Park Wood
WOODSIDE AV.
BIRCH TREE AV.
Birch Tree Farm
BANK ROAD
VICTORIA AVENUE
AFRICANDER
SCAFELL
PRINCES WAY
QUEENSWAY
KINGSWAY
BASSENTHWAITE AV.
HILLBRAE
CITY VIEW
Potter's Wood
Windle Hall Farm
Windle Hall
Windle Hall Bridge
45
EAST LANCASHIRE ROAD
MOSS
Green Leach
Windlehurst
Depot

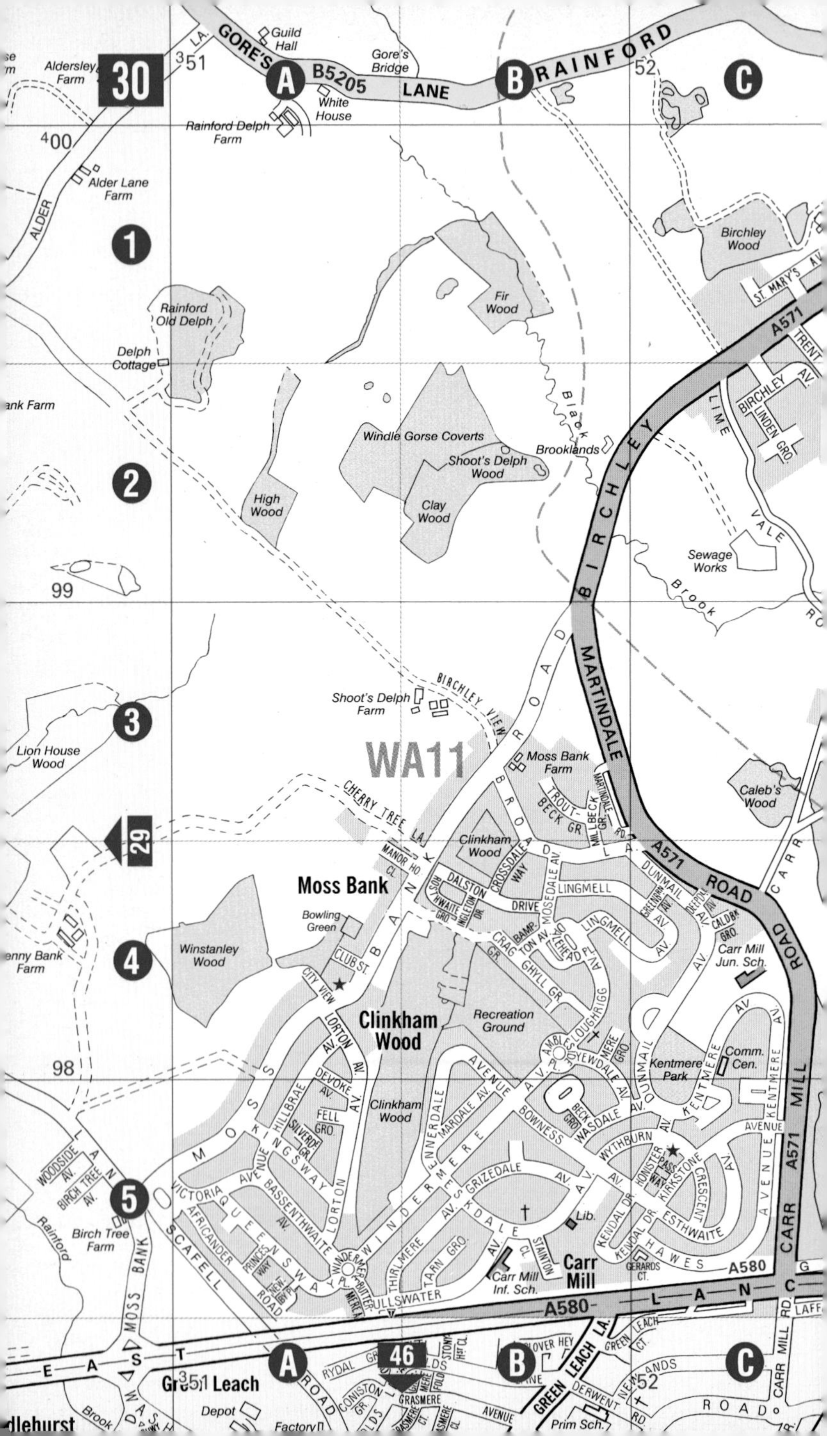
30
Aldersley Farm
Guild Hall
GORE'S LANE
B5205
RAINFORD
Gore's Bridge
White House
Rainford Delph Farm
Alder Lane Farm
ALDER LA.
Birchley Wood
Rainford Old Delph
Fir Wood
Delph Cottage
Windle Gorse Coverts
Shoot's Delph Wood
Brooklands
Black Brook
High Wood
Clay Wood
Sewage Works
BIRCHLEY ROAD
MARTINDALE ROAD
A571
Shoot's Delph Farm
BIRCHLEY VIEW
Lion House Wood
WA11
Moss Bank Farm
Caleb's Wood
CHERRY TREE LA.
29
Clinkham Wood
Moss Bank
Bowling Green
Winstanley Wood
Recreation Ground
Carr Mill Jun. Sch.
Kentmere Park
Comm. Cen.
98
99
Rainford Brook
Birch Tree Farm
Carr Mill Inf. Sch.
Lib.
Carr Mill
A580
EAST LANCS ROAD
46
Green Leach
Depot
Factory
Prim Sch.
CARR MILL ROAD
GREEN LEACH LA.
A
B
C
1
2
3
4
5
51
52

Billinge
Billinge Lane Farm
Black Hurst Hall
Ashfield Farm
Billinge Chapel End Prim. Sch.
Nugent House Sch.
Playing Field
WN5
Barrows Farm
CHADWICK GREEN
Charity Farm
ARCH LA.
Mine
Goft Hey Wood
Brown Heath Nook
WN4
Hollin Hey House
Hollin Hey Farm
Carter's Fold Farm
Old Garswood Park
Deer House Farm
Crock Hey Wood
Carr Mill Dam
Old Garswood Hall Farm
Old Garswood Hall Farm
Waggon Road Plantation
Ash Wood
Glass House Close Wood
Works
A580
Stanley Bank Wood
(PROPOSED)
LIVERPOOL ROAD
GARSWOOD ROAD
MAIN ST.
A571
CARR MILL ROAD
OLD ROAD
WOOD ROAD
HIRE ROAD
53
54
400
99
98

47

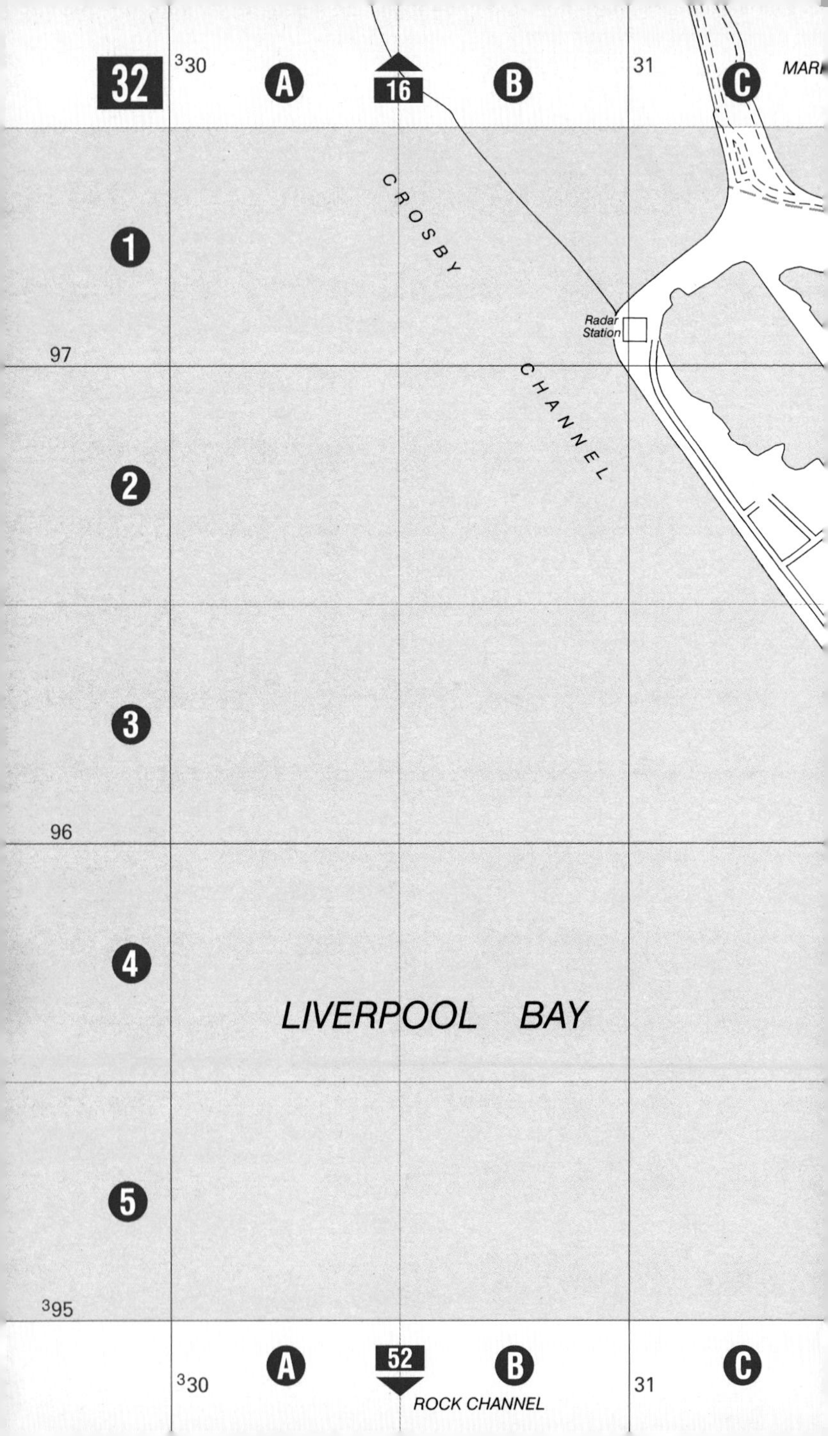

330
A
16
B
31
C
MAR
1
CROSBY
Radar Station
97
CHANNEL
2
3
96
4
LIVERPOOL BAY
5
395
A
52
B
C
330
31
ROCK CHANNEL

33
D
E
F
17
L22
SEAFORTH NATURE RESERVE
Lorry Park
Seaforth
Depots
Lorry Park
Trailer Park
PORT OF LIVERPOOL EURO RAIL TERMINAL
L21
Travelling Crane
SEAFORTH CONTAINER PORT
Container Stacking Area
Graving Dock
Branch Dock (No2)
Gladstone Dock
Branch Dock (No1)
Customs Offices
Customs Office
L20
Lighthouse
Hornby Dock
Branch Dock (No3)
Branch Dock (No2)
Alexandra Dock
Branch Dock (No. 1)
Timber Yards
Works
Factory
Adult Education Cen.
CROSBY ROAD SOUTH
A565
PRINCESS A5036
SANDY ROAD
B5421
CAMBRIDGE ROAD
KNOWSLEY RD.
RIMROSE ROAD
GROVE ST.
CHURCH ROAD
REGENT ROAD
SEAFORTH NATURE RESERVE
Nursy. Sch.
Lib.
Prim. Sch.
34
53
32
33
1
2
3
4
5

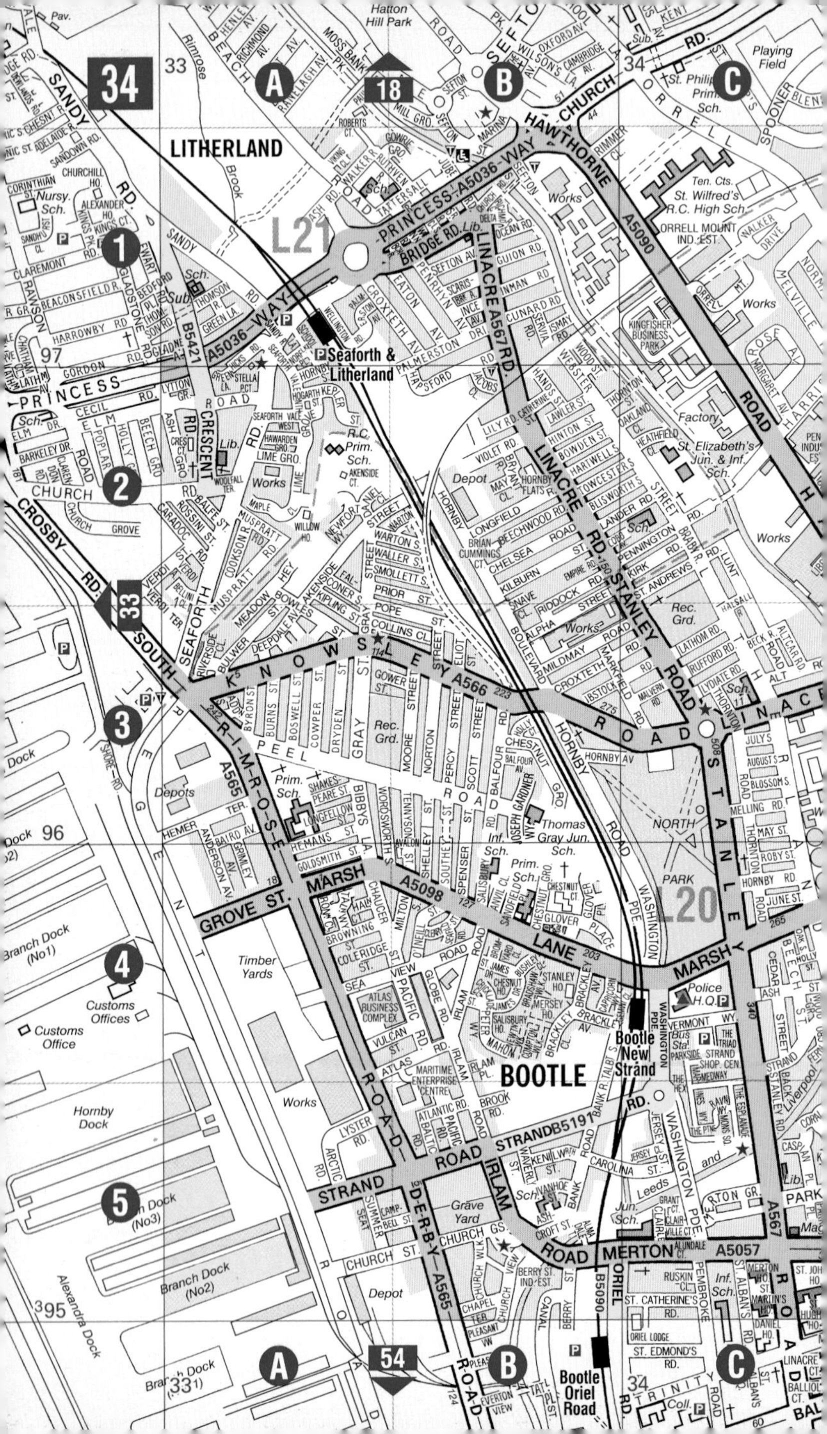
34
33
18
33
54
A
B
C
1
2
3
4
5
97
96
95
34
LITHERLAND
BOOTLE
L21
L20
Hatton Hill Park
Seaforth & Litherland
Bootle New Strand
Bootle Oriel Road
PRINCESS WAY A5036
HAWTHORNE ROAD A5090
LINACRE RD. A567
STANLEY RD.
KNOWSLEY ROAD A566
LINACRE ROAD
RIMROSE ROAD A565
DERBY ROAD A565
CROSBY RD. SOUTH
MARSH LANE A5098
STRAND ROAD B5191
MERTON ROAD A5057
ORIEL RD. B5090
SANDY RD.
CHURCH RD.
CHURCH GROVE
SEAFORTH RD.
CRESCENT RD.
B5421
GROVE ST.
IRLAM RD.
WASHINGTON PDE.
HORNBY BOULEVARD
ORRELL RD.
PEEL ROAD
GORDON AV.
PRINCESS RD.
Rimrose Brook
Hornby Dock
Branch Dock (No1)
Branch Dock (No2)
Branch Dock (No3)
Alexandra Dock
Customs Offices
Customs Office
Timber Yards
Works
Depot
Depots
Grave Yard
NORTH PARK
Police H.Q.
St. Wilfred's R.C. High Sch.
St. Elizabeth's Jun. & Inf. Sch.
Thomas Gray Jun. Sch.
ORRELL MOUNT IND. EST.
KINGFISHER BUSINESS PARK
ATLAS BUSINESS COMPLEX
MARITIME ENTERPRISE CENTRE
STRAND SHOP. CEN.
BERRY ST. IND. EST.
Playing Field
Rec. Grd.
Factory

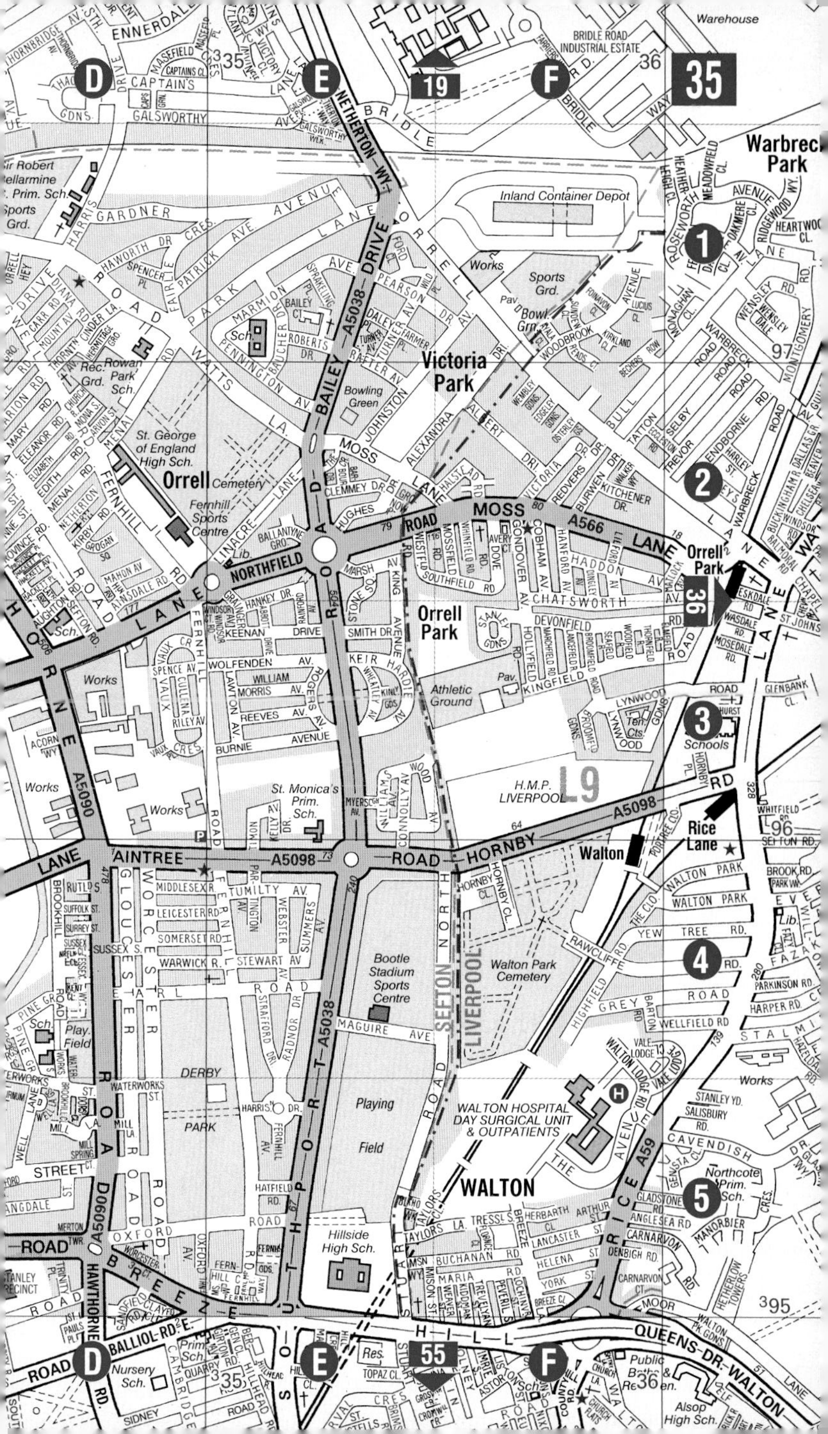
D
E
F
19
Warehouse
BRIDLE ROAD INDUSTRIAL ESTATE
36
ENNERDALE
335
MASEFIELD
CAPTAINS CL.
CAPTAIN'S
GALSWORTHY
NETHERTON WY.
BRIDLE
BRIDLE WAY
Warbreck Park
Inland Container Depot
Sir Robert Bellarmine Prim. Sch.
Sports Grd.
GARDNER
AVENUE
HARRIS
ROSEWORTH
MEADOWFIELD CL.
AVENUE
RIDGEWOOD WY.
HEARTWOOD CL.
1
HAWORTH DR
SPENCER PL.
PATRICK
FAIRLIE
PARK
LANE
ORRELL
Works
Sports Grd.
Pav.
Bowl. Grn.
WOODBROOK
KIRKLAND CL.
MONAGHAN CL.
WENSLEY RD.
WENSLEYDALE
MONTGOMERY
97
MARMION
Sch.
BAILEY CL.
PEARSON
DALEY PL.
ROBERTS DR.
PENNINGTON AV.
FARMER PL.
RAFTER AV.
Victoria Park
Rowan Park Sch.
Rec. Grd.
WATTS LA.
Bowling Green
JOHNSTON
ALEXANDRA
ALBERT
WARBRECK
SELBY
TATTON
TREVOR
ENDBORNE RD.
2
St. George of England High Sch.
Orrell
Cemetery
MOSS LANE
CLEMMEY DR
HUGHES
BAILEY DRIVE
A5038
Fernhill Sports Centre
VICTORIA DRI.
REDVERS DR.
BURWEN DR.
KITCHENER DR.
WARBRECK
MOSS
A566
LANE
ROAD
79
80
18
NORTHFIELD
LINACRE LANE
BALLANTYNE GRO.
Lib.
Orrell Park
36
MARSH AV.
STONE SQ.
KING AVENUE
MOSSFIELD RD.
WHINFIELD RD.
SOUTHFIELD RD
AVERY CT.
DOVE
GONDOVER AV.
COBHAM AV.
HANFORD AV.
HADDON
CHATSWORTH
Orrell Park
STANLEY GDNS.
DEVONFIELD
ESKDALE RD.
WASDALE RD.
MOSEDALE RD.
ST. JOHNS
HORNE
506
ROAD
LANE
177
AINSDALE RD.
MAHON AV
GROGAN SQ.
KIRBY RD.
NETHERTON RD.
MENAI
FERNHILL RD
HANKEY DR.
KEENAN DRIVE
RAINFORD
SMITH DR
WOLFENDEN AV.
WILLIAM
MORRIS AV.
REEVES AV.
BURNIE AVENUE
ROGERS AV.
KEIR HARDIE AV.
SPENCE AV
VAUX CRES.
CULLENA
RILEY AV.
KINGFIELD
Athletic Ground
Pav.
LYNWOOD
Ten. Cts.
BROOMFIELD GDNS.
3
Schools
HORNBY PL.
ROAD
GLENBANK CL.
Works
ACORN WY.
A5090
Works
St. Monica's Prim. Sch.
H.M.P. LIVERPOOL
L9
RD
328
Works
WILLIAMS AV.
CONNOLLY AV
WOOD AV.
A5098
64
Rice Lane
WHITFIELD
96
SEFTON RD.
Walton
LANE
AINTREE
A5098
73
ROAD
HORNBY
HORNBY CL.
WALTON PARK
BROOK RD
478
RUTLAND
SUFFOLK ST.
SURREY ST.
SUSSEX S.
GLOUCESTER
WORCESTER
MIDDLESEX R.
TUMILTY AV.
LEICESTER RD
SOMERSET RD
WARWICK R.
STEWART AV
WEBSTER
SUMMERS AV.
FERNHILL
ROAD
240
RAWCLIFFE
YEW TREE RD.
4
Lib.
Bootle Stadium Sports Centre
Walton Park Cemetery
SEFTON
LIVERPOOL
NORTH
HIGHFIELD
GREY ROAD
BARTON
WELLFIELD RD
PARKINSON RD.
HARPER RD.
280
FAZAKERLEY
PINE GR.
Sch.
Play. Field
WATERWORKS
WATERWORKS ST.
DERBY
PARK
MAGUIRE AVE
STRATFORD DR.
RADNOR DR
VALE LODGE
WALTON LODGE RD
139
Works
STANLEY YD.
SALISBURY RD.
CAVENDISH
MILL LA.
MILL
WELL LANE
STREET
HARRIS DR.
FERNHILL AV.
Playing Field
WALTON HOSPITAL DAY SURGICAL UNIT & OUTPATIENTS
THE AVENUE
RICE
A59
Northcote Prim. Sch.
5
MANORBIER
LANGDALE
HATFIELD RD.
ROAD
WALTON
TAYLORS LA.
TRESSELL
HERBARTH CL.
ARTHUR ST.
GLADSTONE RD.
ANGLESEA RD
CARNARVON
MERTON
ROAD
A5090
OXFORD
OXFORD AV.
BUCHANAN RD.
LANCASTER
HELENA
DENBIGH RD.
CARNARVON CT.
HETHERLOW TOWERS
TWR
TRINITY PL.
HAWTHORNE
BREEZE
Hillside High Sch.
MARIA RD.
YORK
BREEZE CL.
STANLEY PRECINCT
ROAD
SANDFIELD
STUART
395
MOOR
BALLIOL RD. E.
HILL
QUEENS-DR.-WALTON
WALTON PK. GDNS.
LANE
Res.
55
ROAD
D
E
F
Nursery Sch.
Prim. Sch.
35
TOPAZ CL.
CL.
Sch.
Public Baths & Rec. Gdn.
36
COUNTY RD.
Alsop High Sch.
RD.
SIDNEY
CAMBRIDGE
ROAD
CRES

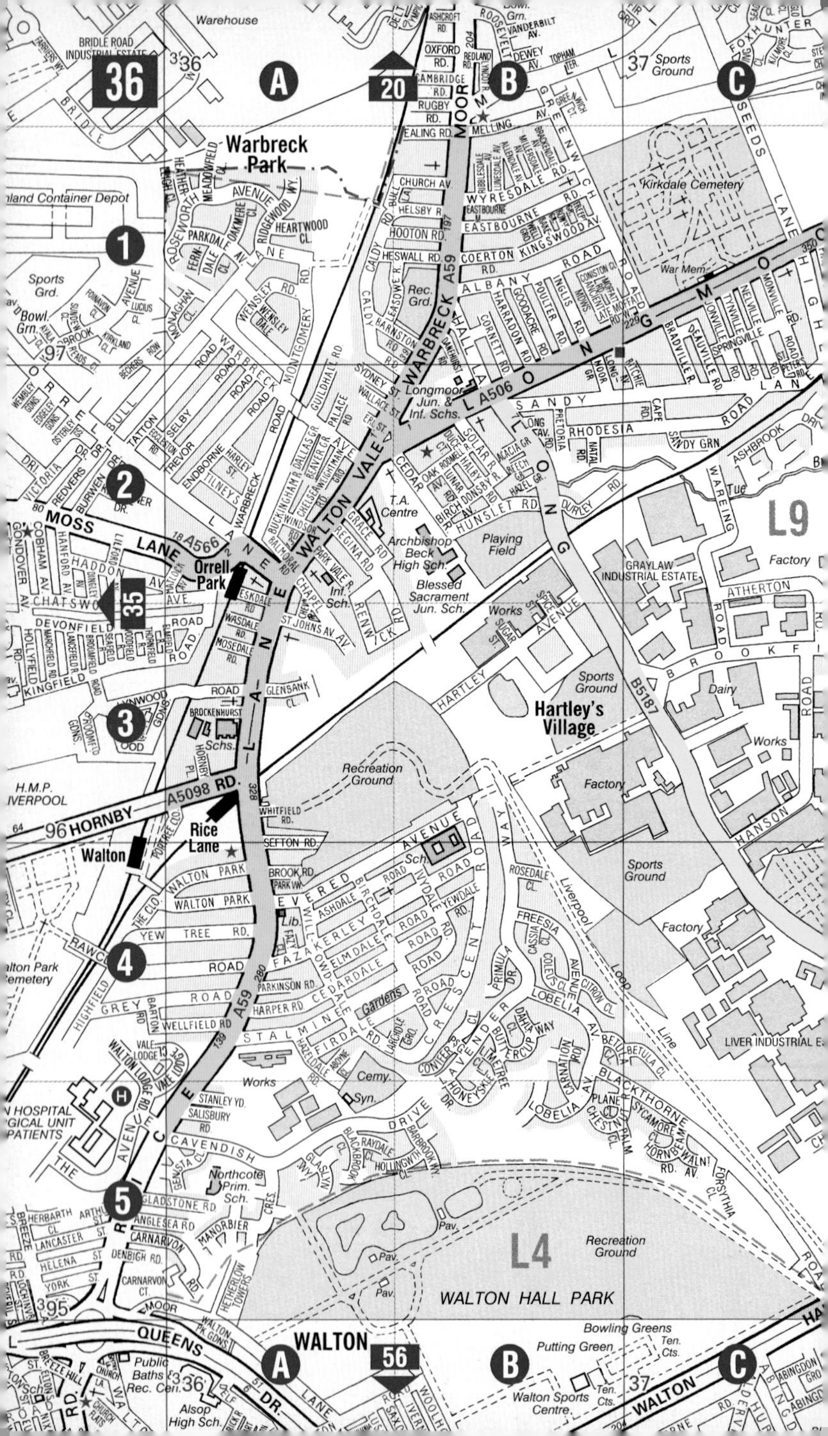

36
20
35
56
A
B
C
1
2
3
4
5
L9
L4
Warehouse
BRIDLE ROAD INDUSTRIAL ESTATE
Warbreck Park
Inland Container Depot
Sports Grd.
Bowl. Grn.
Kirkdale Cemetery
Sports Ground
War Mem.
Rec. Grd.
Longmoor Jun. & Inf. Schs.
T.A. Centre
Archbishop Beck High Sch.
Blessed Sacrament Jun. Sch.
Playing Field
Inf. Sch.
Works
GRAYLAW INDUSTRIAL ESTATE
Factory
Dairy
Hartley's Village
Orrell Park
Recreation Ground
Rice Lane
Walton
H.M.P. LIVERPOOL
Schs.
Lib.
Sch.
Gardens
Cemy.
Syn.
Northcote Prim. Sch.
LIVER INDUSTRIAL ESTATE
Liverpool Loop Line
WALTON HALL PARK
Pav.
Bowling Greens
Putting Green
Ten. Cts.
Walton Sports Centre
WALTON
Public Baths & Rec. Cen.
Alsop High Sch.
WALTON VALE A59
WARBRECK MOOR A59
RICE LANE A59
LONGMOOR LANE A506
LONG LANE B5187
MOSS LANE A566
HORNBY RD. A5098
QUEENS DR.
ORRELL LANE
WARBRECK AVENUE
MONTGOMERY RD.
SANDY ROAD
RHODESIA RD.
HARTLEY AVENUE
BROOKFIELD ROAD
ATHERTON RD.
HANSON RD.
WALTON PARK
YEW TREE RD.
EVERED AVENUE
FAZAKERLEY ROAD
CAVENDISH DRIVE
STALMINE RD.
CRESCENT ROAD
BLACKTHORNE RD.
LOBELIA AV.
GREENWICH ROAD
ALBANY ROAD
EASTBOURNE RD.
WYRESDALE RD.
MELLING AV.
HIGHFIELD RD.
GREY ROAD

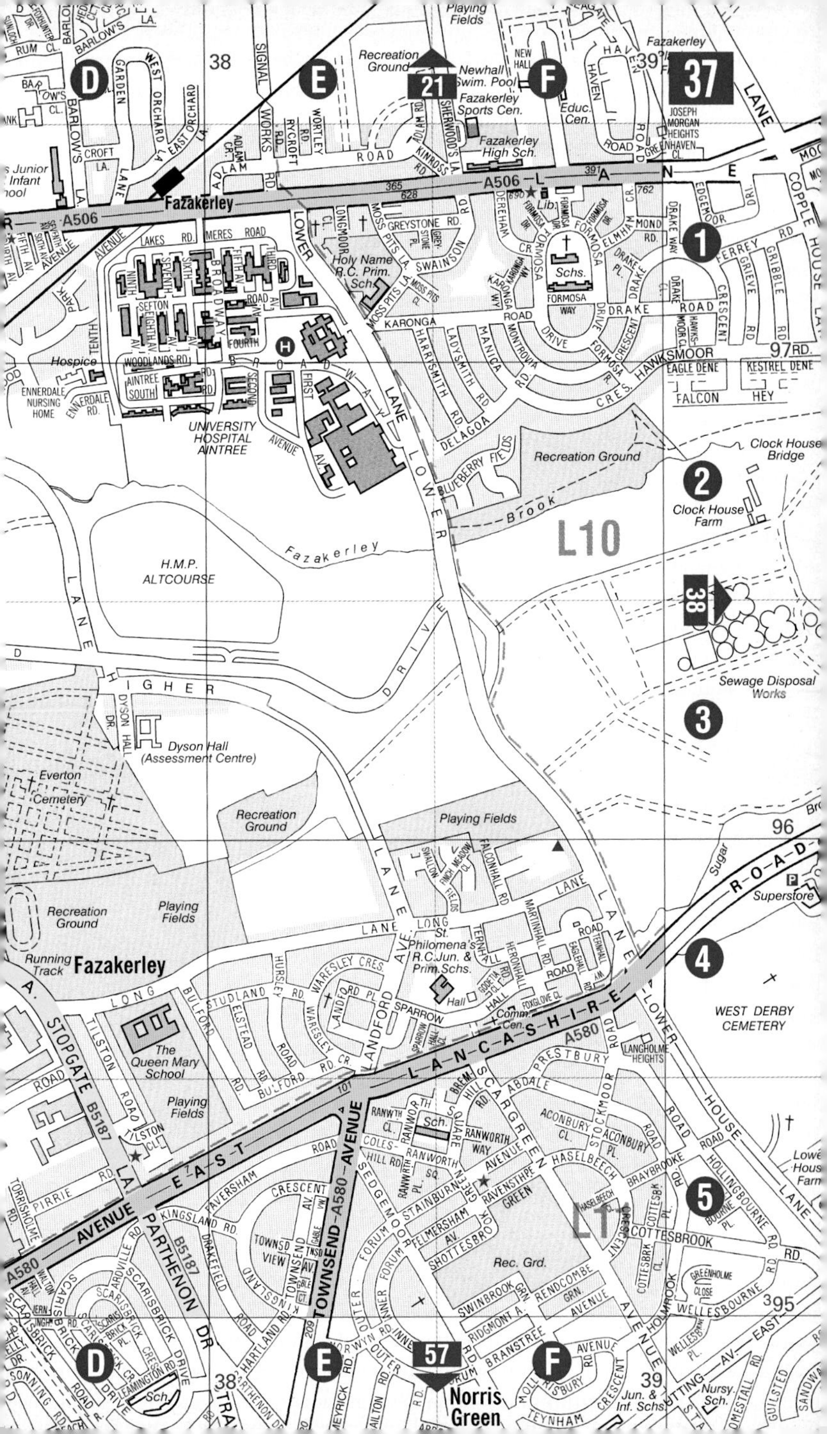

37
Fazakerley
A506
LANE
LOWER LANE
UNIVERSITY HOSPITAL AINTREE
H.M.P. ALTCOURSE
Fazakerley Brook
L10
L11
Recreation Ground
Newhall Swim. Pool
Fazakerley Sports Cen.
Fazakerley High Sch.
Educ. Cen.
Joseph Morgan Heights
Holy Name R.C. Prim. Sch.
Lib.
Schs.
Hospice
Ennerdale Nursing Home
Clock House Bridge
Clock House Farm
Sewage Disposal Works
Playing Fields
HIGHER LANE
DRIVE
Dyson Hall (Assessment Centre)
Everton Cemetery
Running Track
St. Philomena's R.C. Jun. & Prim. Schs.
Hall
Comm. Cen.
Superstore
WEST DERBY CEMETERY
EAST LANCASHIRE ROAD
A580
The Queen Mary School
STOPGATE LA.
B5187
PARTHENON DR
TOWNSEND AVENUE
Sch.
Rec. Grd.
Lower House Farm
COTTESBROOK
WELLESBOURNE
HOLMROOK AVENUE
LONG LANE
Norris Green
Jun. & Inf. Schs.
Nursy. Sch.
21
38
57
D
E
F
1
2
3
4
5
38
39
97
96
395

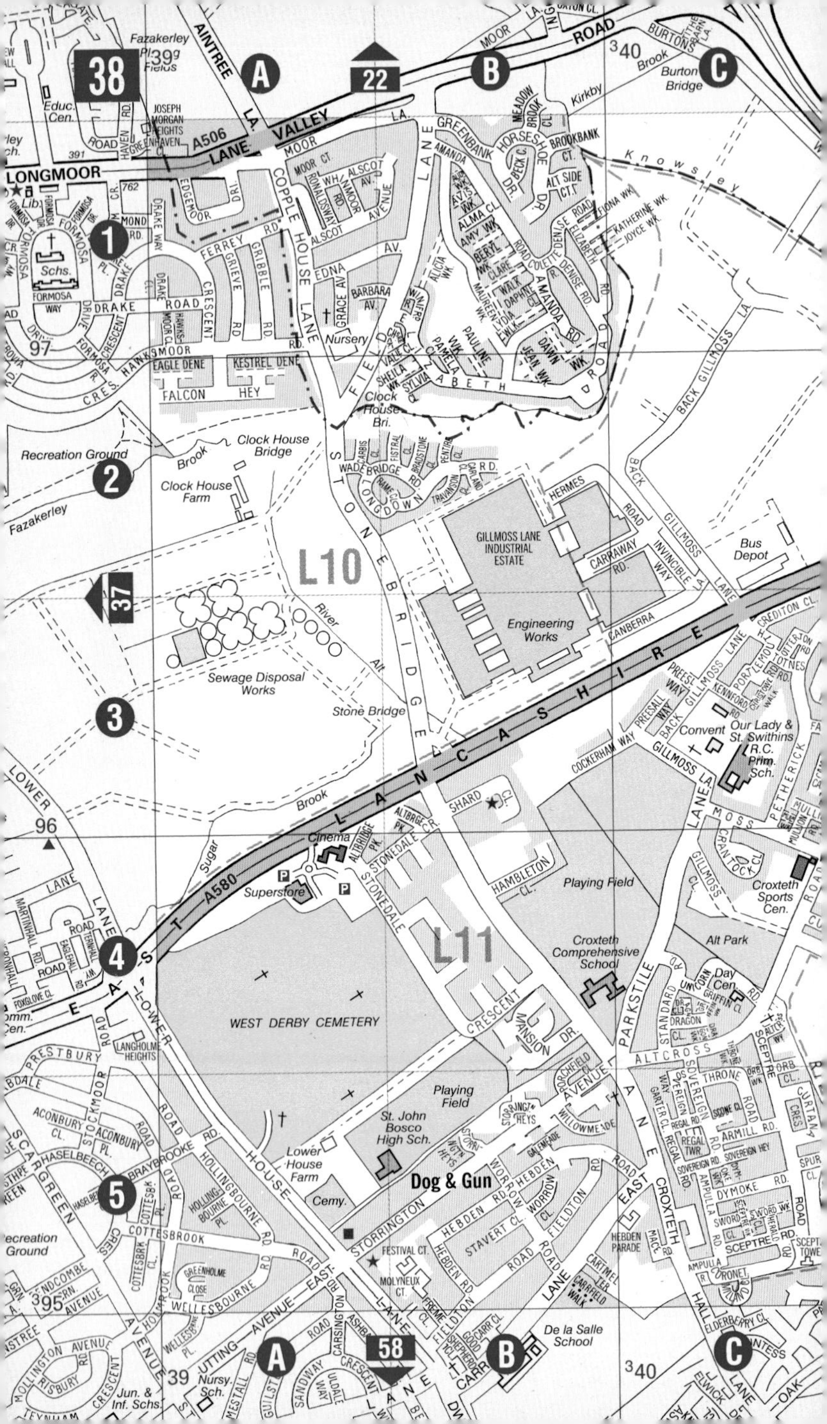

38
22
37
58
A
B
C
1
2
3
4
5
339
340
391
762
97
96
395
Fazakerley Fields
AINTREE LA.
MOOR LA.
ROAD
A506
LANE VALLEY
LONGMOOR
Lib.
Educ. Cen.
Schs.
JOSEPH MORGAN HEIGHTS
GREENHAVEN CL.
HAVEN RD.
FORMOSA
FORMOSA DR.
FORMOSA PL.
FORMOSA WAY
FORMOSA DRIVE
DRAKE ROAD
DRAKE WAY
DRAKE CL.
DRAKE PL.
FERREY RD.
GRIEVE RD.
GRIBBLE RD.
EDGEMOOR DRI.
CRESCENT
HAWKSMOOR RD.
EAGLE DENE
KESTREL DENE
FALCON HEY
HAWKSMOOR CRES.
MOOR CT.
RONALDSWAY
WHINMOOR RD.
ALSCOT AV.
ALSCOT AVENUE
COPPLE HOUSE LANE
EDNA AV.
GRACE AV.
BARBARA AV.
Nursery
FIELD LANE
GREENBANK LANE
AMANDA RD.
MEADOW BROOK CL.
HORSESHOE DR.
BECK CL.
BROOKBANK CT.
ALT SIDE CT.
ALMA CL.
AMY WK.
BERYL WK.
CLARE WK.
DAPHNE CL.
LYDIA WK.
EWLA WK.
ALICIA WK.
MAUREEN WK.
COLETTE RD.
DENISE ROAD
DENISE RD.
ELIZABETH
FIONA WK.
KATHERINE WK.
JOYCE WK.
WINIFRED
SHEILA WK.
SYLVIA CL.
PAMELA WK.
PAULINE WK.
JEAN WK.
DAWN WK.
ELIZABETH ROAD
Kirkby
Brook
Burton Bridge
BURTONS WAY
TITHE BARN LA.
Knowsley
Clock House Bri.
Recreation Ground
Brook
Clock House Bridge
Clock House Farm
Fazakerley
STONEBRIDGE LANE
CARBIS CL.
FISTRAL CL.
BRADSTONE CL.
PENTIRE CL.
WADEBRIDGE RD.
LONGDOWN
TRAVANSON CL.
CARLAND RD.
L10
GILLMOSS LANE INDUSTRIAL ESTATE
HERMES ROAD
CARRAWAY RD.
INVINCIBLE WAY
CANBERRA
Engineering Works
BACK GILLMOSS LA.
BACK GILLMOSS LANE
Bus Depot
GILLMOSS LANE
River Alt
Sewage Disposal Works
Stone Bridge
EAST LANCASHIRE ROAD
A580
CREDITON CL.
OTTERTON CL.
TOTNES RD.
PORTLEMOUTH RD.
KENNFORD RD.
PREESALL WAY
COCKERHAM WAY
Convent
Our Lady & St. Swithins R.C. Prim. Sch.
GILLMOSS LA.
PETHERICK
MOSS LANE
CRANTOCK CL.
Croxteth Sports Cen.
Brook
Sugar
Cinema
ALTBRIDGE PK.
ALTBRIDGE CR.
STONEDALE CR.
STONEDALE
Superstore
SHARD CL.
HAMBLETON CL.
Playing Field
L11
Croxteth Comprehensive School
Alt Park
PARKSTILE RD.
UNICORN
Day Cen.
GRIFFIN CL.
DRAGON CL.
STANDARD RD.
ALTCROSS
ALTCROSS RD.
SCEPTRE RD.
THRONE ROAD
ORB WK.
ORB CL.
CURTANA CRES.
SOVEREIGN
SOVEREIGN RD.
SOVEREIGN HEY
SCONE CL.
ARMILL RD.
GARTER CL.
REGAL RD.
REGAL TWR.
AMPULLA RD.
DYMOKE RD.
SWORD WK.
SWORD CL.
SCEPTRE RD.
CORONET RD.
ELDERBERRY CL.
HALL LANE
COUNTESS
ELWICK
LOWER LANE
MARTINHALL RD.
EAGLEHALL RD.
TERMHALL RD.
FOXGLOVE CL.
Comm. Cen.
WEST DERBY CEMETERY
CRESCENT
MANSION DR.
PORCHFIELD CL.
AVENUE
WILLOWMEADE
STORRINGTON HEYS
GALEMEADE
HEBDEN
WORROW CL.
WORROW ROAD
FIELDTON RD.
EAST LANE
CROXTETH
HEBDEN PARADE
MACE RD.
CARTMEL TER.
CARRFIELD WALK
Playing Field
St. John Bosco High Sch.
Lower House Farm
Cemy.
Dog & Gun
STORRINGTON AVENUE
FESTIVAL CT.
MOLYNEUX CT.
HEBDEN RD.
STAVERT CL.
FREME CL.
FIELDTON
SHEPHERD CL.
GOOD CARR CL.
CARR LANE
De la Salle School
LOWER HOUSE LANE
LANGHOLME HEIGHTS
PRESTBURY
ACONBURY CL.
ACONBURY PL.
STOCKMOOR ROAD
HASELBEECH
SCARGREEN AVENUE
BRAYBROOKE RD.
HOLLINGBOURNE ROAD
HOLLINGBOURNE PL.
COTTESBROOK ROAD
COTTESBROOK PL.
COTTESBRK. CL.
GREENHOLME CLOSE
WELLESBOURNE ROAD
WELLESBOURNE PL.
HOMBROOK
Recreation Ground
MOLLINGTON AVENUE
RISBURY
UTTING AVENUE EAST
CARSINGTON ROAD
ASHBOURNE
SANDWAY CRESCENT
ULDALE WAY
GUILSTED RD.
MESTALL RD.
Nursy. Sch.
Jun. & Inf. Schs.
TEYNHAM

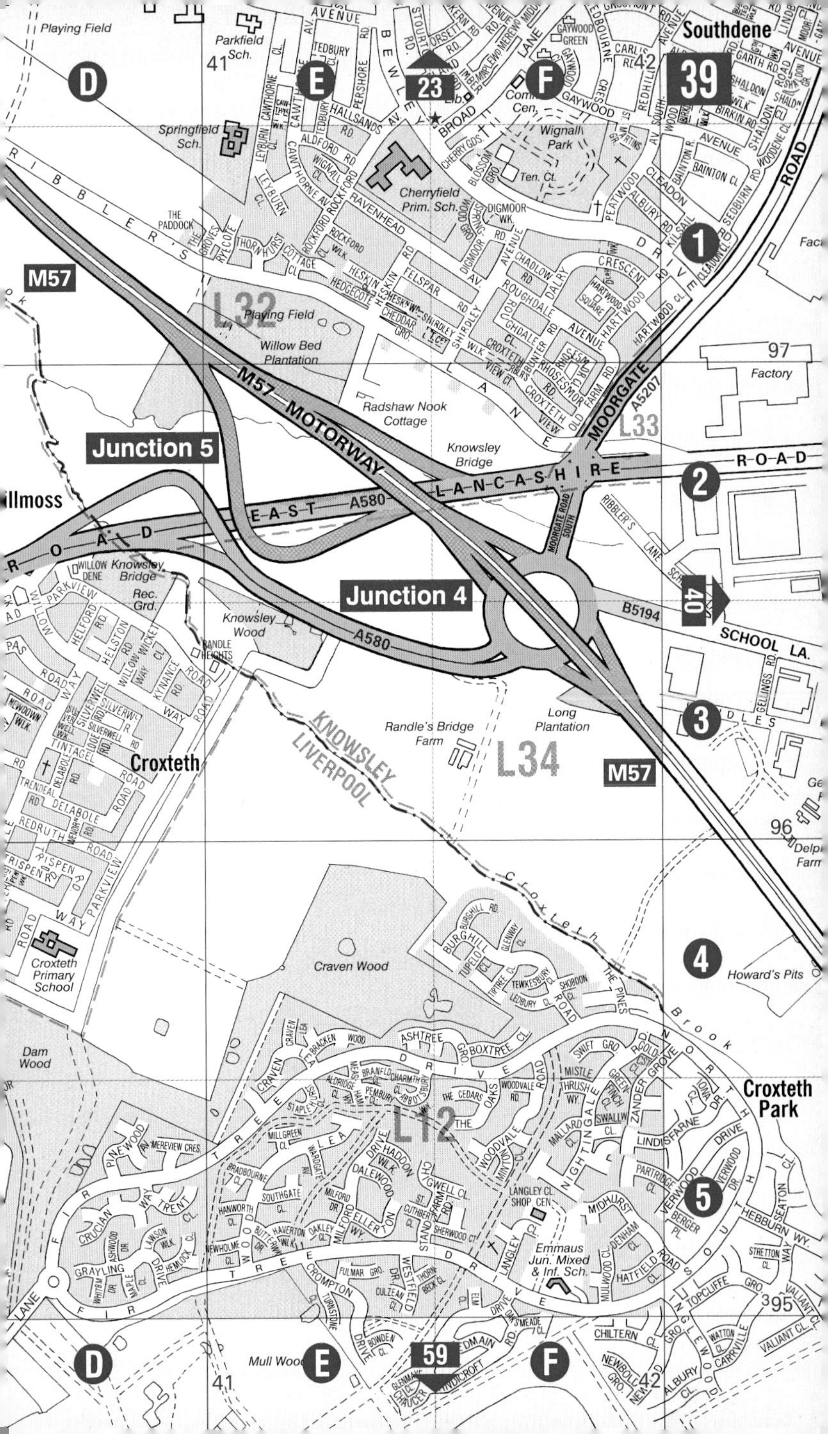

39
Southdene
23
40
59
D
E
F
1
2
3
4
5
41
42
97
96
395
Playing Field
Parkfield Sch.
Springfield Sch.
Cherryfield Prim. Sch.
Comm. Cen.
Wignall Park
Ten. Ct.
Lib.
AVENUE
TEDBURY
PERSHORE RD.
HALLSANDS AV.
ALDFORD RD.
WIGNALL CL.
ROCKFORD
RAVENHEAD
BEWLEY
BROAD
LANE
GAYWOOD GREEN
GAYWOOD
CARLIS
REDHILL
SOUTHWOOD
BAINTON CL.
SEDBURN RD.
SHALDON
BIRKIN RD.
WOODENE CL.
ROAD
CLEADON
ALBURY
PEATWOOD
KILSAIL
DRIVE
CRESCENT
DALRY
CHADLOW RD.
ROUGHDALE
AVENUE
HARTWOOD SQUARE
HARTWOOD
RHOSESMOR
CROXTETH VIEW
OLD FARM RD.
MOORGATE
A5207
CHERRY GDS.
BLOSSOM GRO.
DIGMOOR WK.
DIGMOOR RD.
SPRINGWOOD GRO.
HESKIN
FELSPAR
HEDGECOTE
CHEDDAR GRO.
SHIRDLEY
COTTAGE CL.
THORNHURST
RYECOTE
THE GROVES
THE PADDOCK
LEYBURN
CAWTHORNE
RIBBLER'S
L32
L33
L34
L12
M57
M57 MOTORWAY
Playing Field
Willow Bed Plantation
Radshaw Nook Cottage
Knowsley Bridge
Factory
Fac
Junction 5
Junction 4
EAST LANCASHIRE ROAD
A580
MOORGATE ROAD SOUTH
RIBBLER'S LANE
B5194
SCHOOL LA.
GELLINGS RD.
llmoss
WILLOW DENE
Knowsley Bridge
Rec. Grd.
Knowsley Wood
RANDLE HEIGHTS
PARKVIEW
WILLOW
HELFORD RD.
HELSTON RD.
WILLOW WICKET WAY
KYNANCE RD.
SILVERWELL
TINTAGEL
DELABOLE RD.
TRENDEAL RD.
REDRUTH
TRISPEN RD.
Croxteth
Croxteth Primary School
KNOWSLEY
LIVERPOOL
Randle's Bridge Farm
Long Plantation
Delph Farm
Croxteth Brook
Howard's Pits
Craven Wood
BURGHILL RD.
TUPELO CL.
GLENWAY
TEWKESBURY CL.
LEDBURY CL.
SHOBDON
THE PINES
Dam Wood
CRAVEN
BRACKEN WOOD
ASHTREE GRO.
BOXTREE CL.
DRIVE
SWIFT GRO.
MISTLE THRUSH WY.
FINCH
SWALLOW CL.
ZANDER GROVE
IONA
NORTH
Croxteth Park
LINDISFARNE
DRIVE
VERWOOD DR.
PARTRIDGE CL.
NIGHTINGALE
MALLARD CL.
MINTON
WOODVALE
THE CEDARS
OAKS
THE
STAPLEHURST
ALDRIDGE CL.
PEMBURY CL.
CHARMOUTH
ABBOTSBURY
MILLGREEN CL.
LEA
PINEWOOD AV.
MEREVIEW CRES.
TRENT CL.
FIR TREE
BRADBOURNE CL.
SOUTHGATE CL.
HADDON WLK.
DALEWOOD
GWELL CL.
ST. CUTHBERTS CL.
FARM RD.
SHERWOOD CT.
LANGLEY CL.
LANGLEY CL. SHOP. CEN.
Emmaus Jun. Mixed & Inf. Sch.
MIDHURST
DENHAM CL.
HATFIELD
MULWOOD CL.
HANWORTH CL.
HAVERTON WLK.
OAKLEY CL.
MILFORD DR.
ELLERTON WY.
NEWHOLME CL.
CRUCIAN
WAY
LAWSON WLK.
HEMLOCK CL.
GRAYLING DRIVE
ASHWOOD DR.
MAPLE CL.
CROMPTON
FULMAR GRO.
CULZEAN CL.
WESTFIELD DR.
TURNSTONE
BOWDEN CL.
ELM
OAK'S MEADE CL.
HEBBURN WY.
SEATON CL.
BERGER PL.
STRETTON CL.
TOPCLIFFE GRO.
VALIANT CL.
WATTON CL.
CARRVILLE
CHILTERN CL.
NEWBOLD GRO.
ALBURY CL.
INGLEWOOD
LANE
Mull Wood
CHAUCER

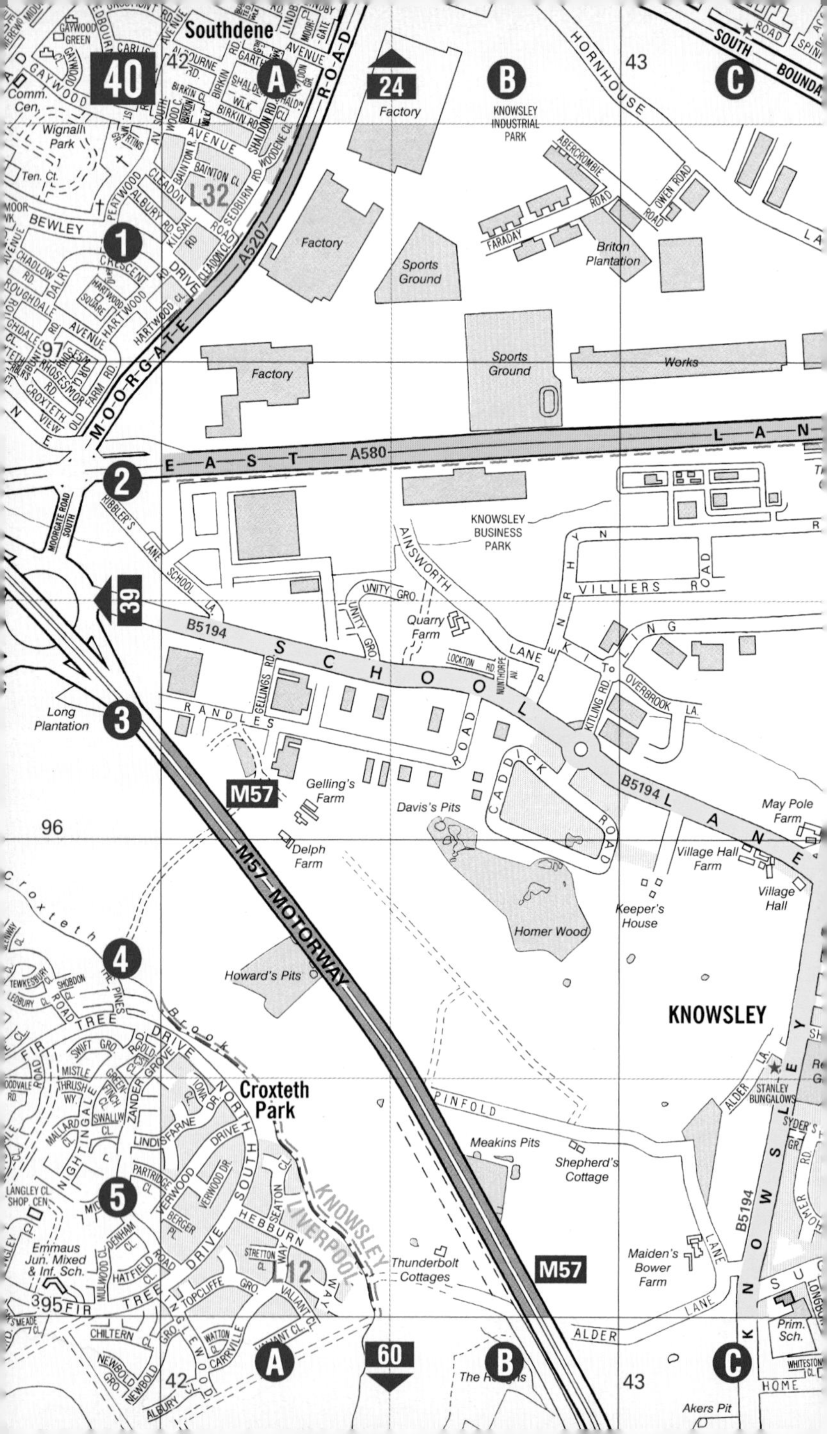

40
Southdene
Knowsley Industrial Park
Factory
Sports Ground
Works
Briton Plantation
East Lane A580
Knowsley Business Park
School Lane B5194
Quarry Farm
Gelling's Farm
Davis's Pits
Delph Farm
Long Plantation
M57 Motorway
Howard's Pits
Homer Wood
Keeper's House
Village Hall Farm
Village Hall
May Pole Farm
KNOWSLEY
Stanley Bungalows
Croxteth Park
Meakins Pits
Shepherd's Cottage
Thunderbolt Cottages
Maiden's Bower Farm
Emmaus Jun. Mixed & Inf. Sch.
Prim. Sch.
The Roughs
Akers Pit
Knowsley Lane B5194
Moorgate Road A5207
Alder Lane
Pinfold
Wignall Park
L32
L12
24
39
60

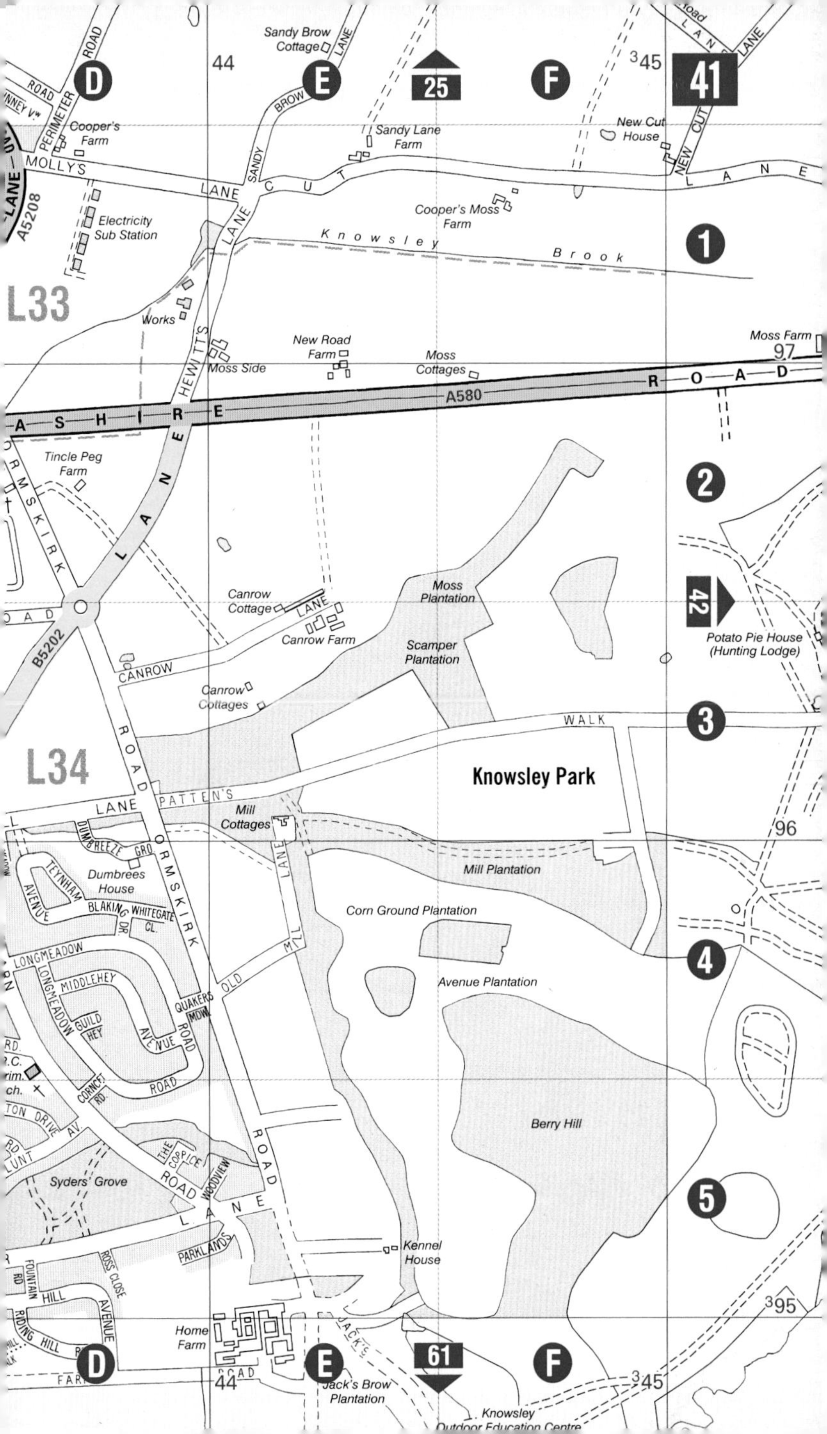

41
25
42
61
D
E
F
1
2
3
4
5
44
345
97
96
395
L33
L34
Sandy Brow Cottage
Cooper's Farm
Sandy Lane Farm
New Cut House
Molly's Lane
Cut Lane
New Cut Lane
A5208
Electricity Sub Station
Cooper's Moss Farm
Knowsley Brook
Works
New Road Farm
Moss Side
Moss Cottages
Moss Farm
Hewitt's Lane
Sandy Lane
Perimeter Road
Brow Lane
A580
Lancashire Road
Tincle Peg Farm
Ormskirk Road
B5202
Canrow Cottage
Canrow Lane
Canrow Farm
Moss Plantation
Scamper Plantation
Potato Pie House (Hunting Lodge)
Canrow Cottages
Walk
Knowsley Park
Patten's Lane
Mill Cottages
Mill Lane
Old Mill Lane
Dumbreeze Gro
Dumbrees House
Teynham Avenue
Blaking Dr.
Whitegate Cl.
Mill Plantation
Corn Ground Plantation
Longmeadow
Middlehey Avenue
Guild Hey
Quakers Mow
Quakers Road
Avenue Plantation
Cornfield Rd.
R.C. Prim. Sch.
Berry Hill
The Coppice
Woodview
Road Lane
Syders' Grove
Parklands
Ross Close
Fountain Rd
Hill Avenue
Riding Hill Rd
Kennel House
Home Farm
Jack's Brow
Farm Road
Jack's Brow Plantation
Knowsley Outdoor Education Centre

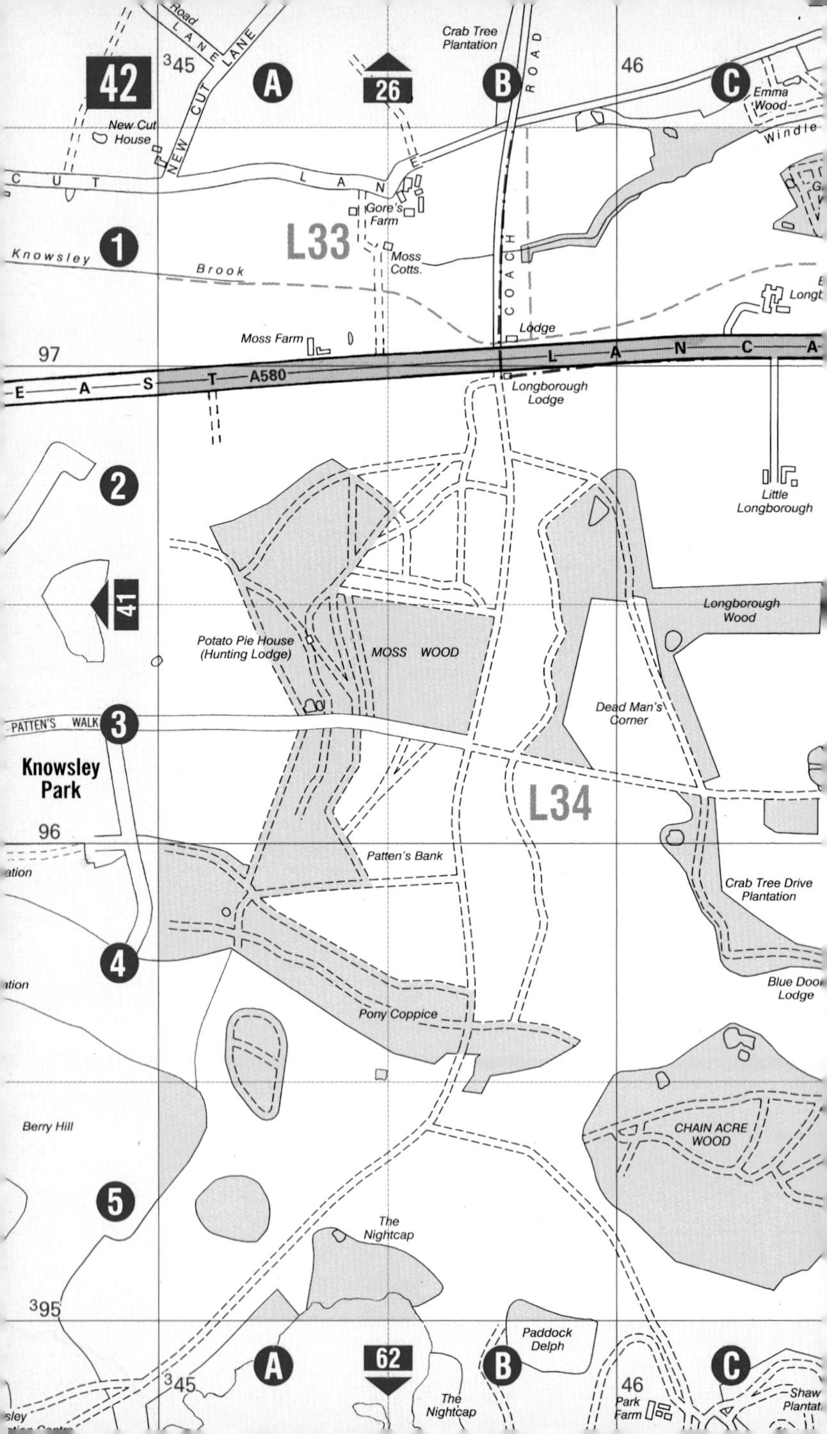

42
26
41
62
A
B
C
1
2
3
4
5
345
46
97
96
395
Crab Tree Plantation
New Cut House
NEW CUT LANE
CUT LANE
COACH ROAD
Emma Wood
Windle
Gore's Farm
L33
Moss Cotts.
Knowsley Brook
Lodge
Moss Farm
EAST LANCASHIRE
A580
Longborough Lodge
Little Longborough
Longborough Wood
Potato Pie House (Hunting Lodge)
MOSS WOOD
Dead Man's Corner
PATTEN'S WALK
Knowsley Park
L34
Patten's Bank
Crab Tree Drive Plantation
Blue Door Lodge
Pony Coppice
Berry Hill
CHAIN ACRE WOOD
The Nightcap
Paddock Delph
Park Farm
Shaw Plantat

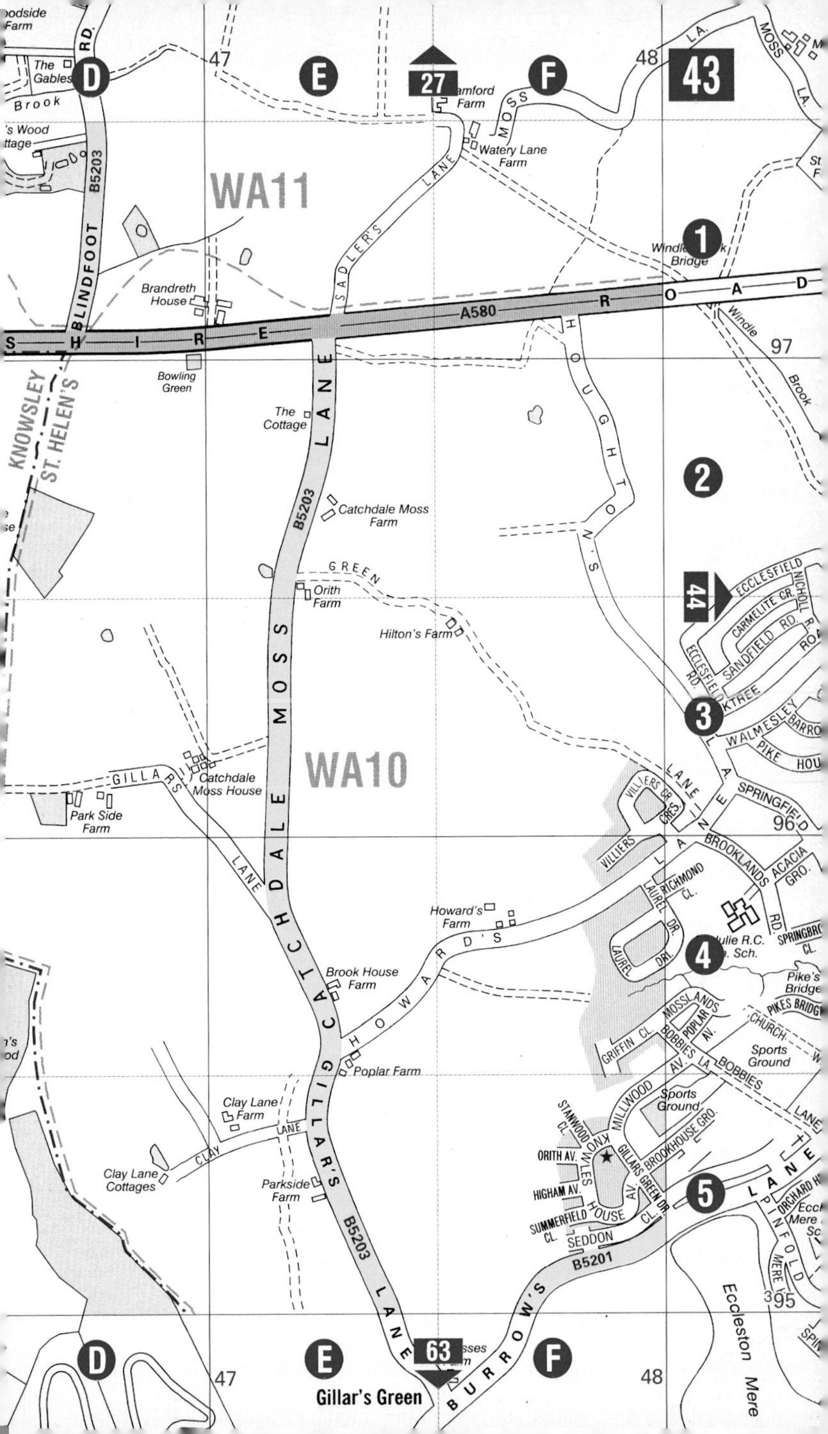
43
27
44
63
WA11
WA10
A580
B5203
B5201
SHIRE ROAD
BLINDFOOT RD.
SADLER'S LANE
MOSS LA.
CATCHDALE MOSS LANE
GILLAR'S LANE
HOWARD'S LANE
HOUGHTON'S LANE
CLAY LANE
BURROW'S LANE
KNOWSLEY
ST. HELEN'S
Brandreth House
Bowling Green
The Cottage
Catchdale Moss Farm
Orith Farm
Hilton's Farm
Catchdale Moss House
Park Side Farm
Howard's Farm
Brook House Farm
Poplar Farm
Clay Lane Farm
Clay Lane Cottages
Parkside Farm
Watery Lane Farm
The Gables
Brook
Windle Brook
Bridge
Sports Ground
Pike's Bridge
Eccleston Mere
Gillar's Green
47
48
97
96
395

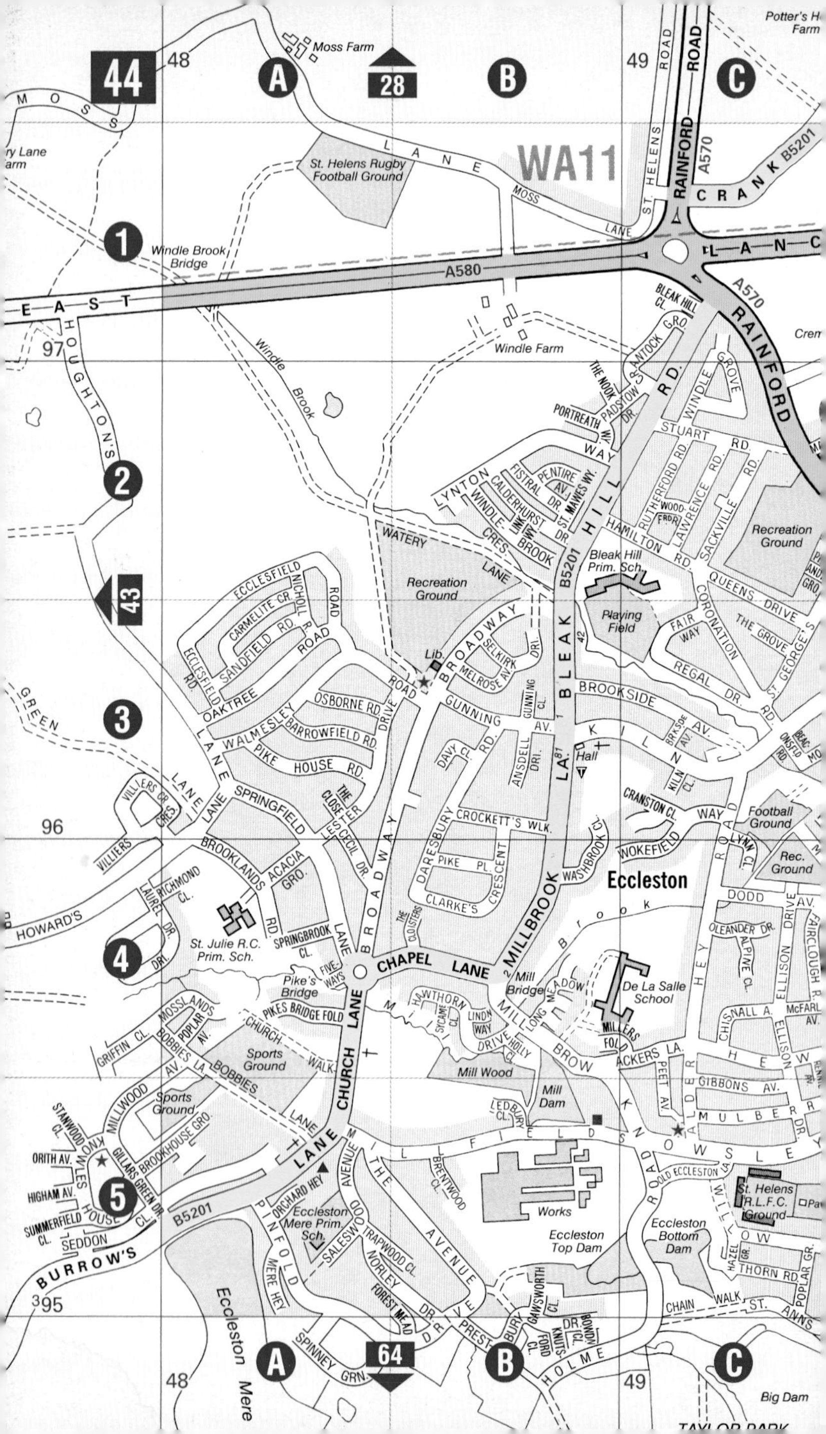
44
28
43
64
A
B
C
1
2
3
4
5
48
49
97
96
395
WA11
Moss Farm
Potter's H
Farm
MOSS LANE
St. Helens Rugby Football Ground
Windle Brook Bridge
EAST LANCS
A580
ST. HELENS ROAD
RAINFORD ROAD
A570
CRANK B5201
Windle Farm
Windle Brook
HOUGHTON'S
BLEAK HILL CL.
BLEAK HILL RD.
QUANTOCK GRO.
THE NOOK
PADSTOW DR.
PORTREATH WY.
WAY
WINDLE GROVE
STUART RD.
LYNTON
FISTRAL DR.
PENTIRE AV.
CALDERHURST DR.
ST. MAWES WY.
WINDLE BROOK
LINK WY.
CRES.
RUTHERFORD RD.
WOOD FRDR.
LAWRENCE RD.
SACKVILLE RD.
HAMILTON RD.
Recreation Ground
WATERY LANE
Recreation Ground
Bleak Hill Prim. Sch.
QUEENS DRIVE
B5201
BLEAK LA.
Playing Field
FAIR WAY
CORONATION
THE GROVE
ST. GEORGE'S RD.
REGAL DR.
ECCLESFIELD
NICHOLL R.
ROAD
CARMELITE CR.
SANDFIELD RD.
ROAD
ECCLESFIELD RD.
Lib.
BROADWAY
SELKIRK
MELROSE AV.
DRI.
GUNNING CL.
BROOKSIDE AV.
OAKTREE
OSBORNE RD.
DRIVE
ROAD
GUNNING AV.
WALMESLEY
BARROWFIELD RD.
KILN
BRKSDE AV.
GREEN LANE
PIKE HOUSE RD.
DAVY CL.
RD.
ANSDELL DRI.
Hall
KILN CL.
VILLIERS CR.
CRES.
SPRINGFIELD LANE
THE CLOSE
LESTER
CRANSTON CL.
WAY
Football Ground
VILLIERS
BROOKLANDS
ACACIA GRO.
CECIL DR.
DARESBURY
CROCKETT'S WLK.
PIKE PL.
CRESCENT
WASHBROOK CL.
WOKEFIELD
ROAD
LYNN CL.
Rec. Ground
Eccleston
HOWARD'S
RICHMOND CL.
LAUREL DR.
DRI.
St. Julie R.C. Prim. Sch.
RD.
SPRINGBROOK CL.
LANE
THE CLOISTERS
CLARKE'S
MILLBROOK
DODD AV.
Brook
OLEANDER DR.
ALPINE CL.
ELLISON DRIVE
FAIRCLOUGH R.
FIVE-WAYS
CHAPEL LANE
Pike's Bridge
Mill Bridge
MEADOW
De La Salle School
HAWTHORN
SYCAMORE CL.
LINDN WAY
DRIVE
HOLLY CL.
LONG
MILLERS FOLD
HEY
MOSSLANDS
POPLAR AV.
PIKES BRIDGE FOLD
CHURCH WALK
CHURCH LANE
MILL BROW
ACKERS LA.
CHISNALL A.
McFARL AV.
GRIFFIN CL.
BOBBIES LA.
BOBBIES LANE
Sports Ground
Mill Wood
Mill Dam
PEET AV.
ALDER
GIBBONS AV.
MILLWOOD AV.
Sports Ground
LEDBURY CL.
MULBERRY DR.
STANWOOD CL.
KNOWLES
MILLFIELDS
KNOWSLEY
ORITH AV.
GILLARS GREEN DR.
BROOKHOUSE GRO.
LANE
AVENUE
THE AVENUE
BRENTWOOD CL.
ROAD
OLD ECCLESTON LA.
HIGHAM AV.
HOUSE
ORCHARD HEY
Works
St. Helens R.L.F.C. Ground
SUMMERFIELD CL.
SEDDON CL.
B5201
Eccleston Mere Prim. Sch.
SALESWOOD
TRAPWOOD CL.
NORLEY
Eccleston Top Dam
Eccleston Bottom Dam
HAZEL GR.
THORN RD.
POPLAR GR.
BURROW'S
PINFOLD
MERE HEY
FOREST MEAD
DR.
GAWSWORTH CL.
BOWDN CL.
KNUTS-FORD CL.
DR.
CHAIN WALK
ST. ANNS
Eccleston Mere
SPINNEY GRN.
DRIVE
PRESTBURY
HOLME
Big Dam
TAYLOR PARK

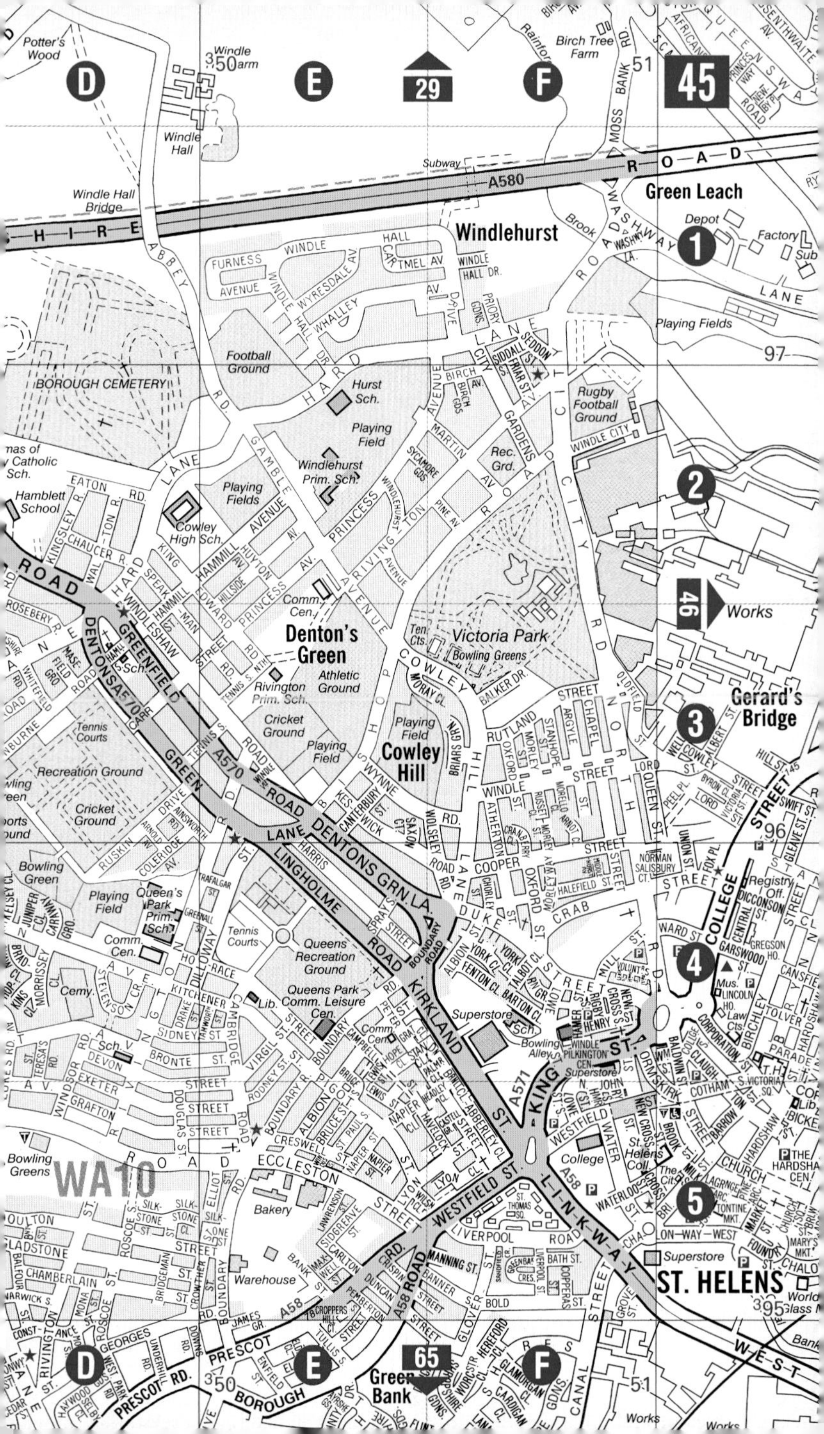
45
29
46
65
D
E
F
1
2
3
4
5
Potter's Wood
Windle Farm
350
Birch Tree Farm
51
Windle Hall
Subway
A580
R O A D
S H I R E
Windle Hall Bridge
Green Leach
Depot
Factory
Sub
Windlehurst
Brook
WASHWAY LANE
Playing Fields
97
BOROUGH CEMETERY
Football Ground
Hurst Sch.
Playing Field
Windlehurst Prim. Sch.
Rugby Football Ground
Rec. Grd.
Playing Fields
Cowley High Sch.
Hamblett School
Denton's Green
Victoria Park
Bowling Greens
Athletic Ground
Rivington Prim. Sch.
Cricket Ground
Playing Field
Cowley Hill
Works
Gerard's Bridge
Tennis Courts
Recreation Ground
Cricket Ground
Bowling Green
Playing Field
Queen's Park Prim. Sch.
Comm. Cen.
Cemy.
Tennis Courts
Queens Recreation Ground
Queens Park Comm. Leisure Cen.
Lib.
Superstore
Bowling Alley
College
St. Helens Coll.
Registry Off.
Mus.
Law Cts.
Bowling Greens
WA10
Bakery
Warehouse
Superstore
ST. HELENS
World Glass
395
96
145
Green Bank
350
51
WINDLE CITY
HARD LANE
CITY ROAD
NORTH ROAD
DENTONS GRN. LA.
LINGHOLME ROAD
KIRKLAND ST.
A570
A571
A58
KING ST.
LINKWAY
WEST
COLLEGE STREET
CORPORATION ST.
ECCLESTON STREET
WESTFIELD ST.
LIVERPOOL ROAD
PRESCOT RD.
BOROUGH
CANAL STREET
DUKE ST.
COOPER ST.
CRAB ST.
WINDLE ST.
BOUNDARY ROAD
GREENFIELD ROAD
DENTONS GREEN LANE
WINDLESHAW RD.
ABBEY RD.
MOSS BANK RD.

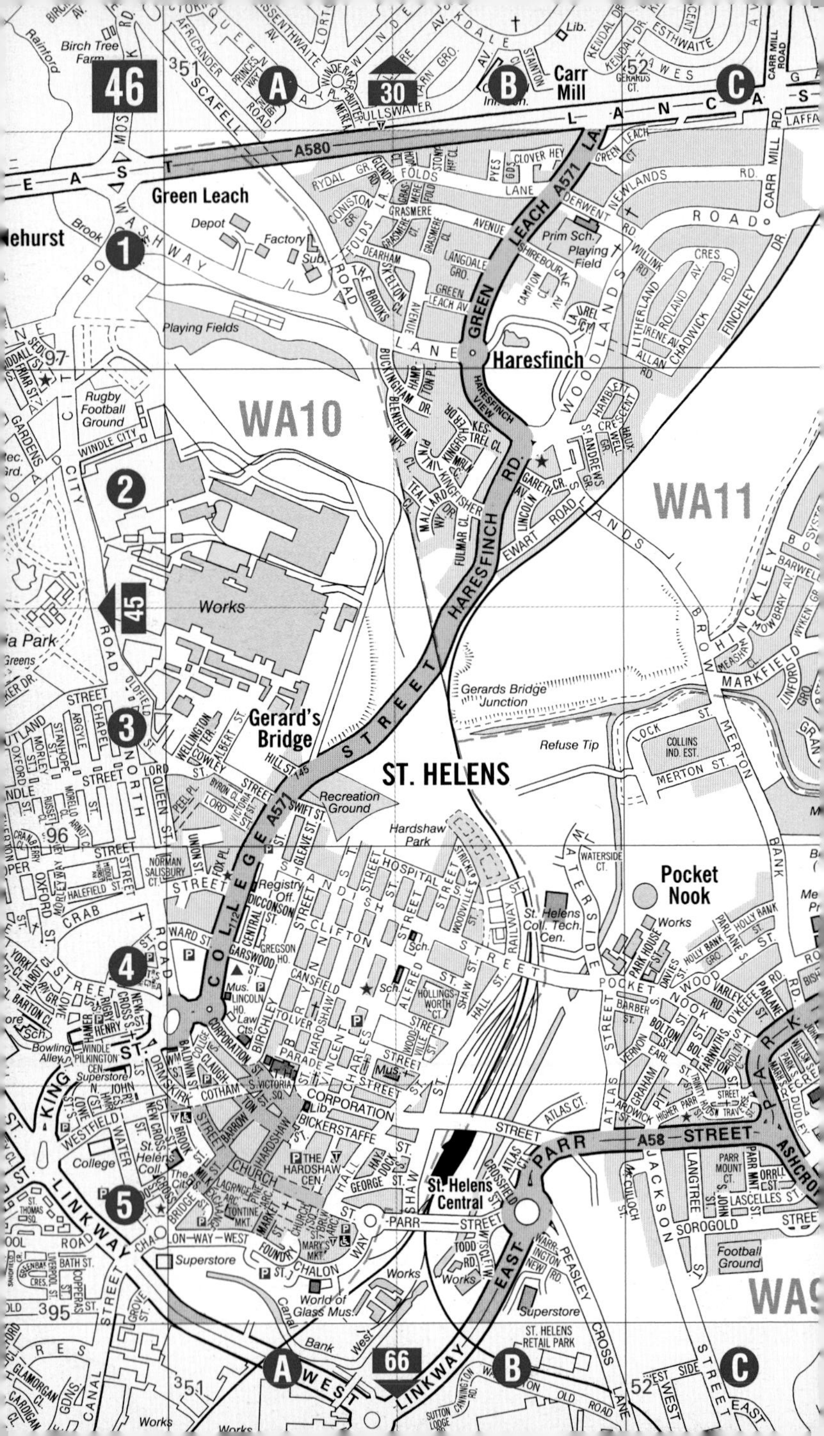
30
45
66
A
B
C
1
2
3
4
5
351
352
395
396
397
Birch Tree Farm
Rainford
Carr Mill
Green Leach
Haresfinch
WA10
WA11
WA9
Gerard's Bridge
ST. HELENS
Pocket Nook
Playing Fields
Rugby Football Ground
Works
Depot
Factory
Prim Sch.
Playing Field
Gerards Bridge Junction
Refuse Tip
Recreation Ground
Hardshaw Park
COLLINS IND. EST.
St. Helens Coll. Tech. Cen.
Registry Off.
Mus.
Law Cts.
Lib.
Sch.
Bowling Alley
Superstore
College
St. Helens Coll.
THE HARDSHAW CEN.
St. Helens Central
World of Glass Mus.
ST. HELENS RETAIL PARK
Football Ground
EAST LANCASHIRE ROAD
A580
A571
A58
GREEN LEACH LANE
HARESFINCH ROAD
HARESFINCH VIEW
COLLEGE STREET
NORTH ROAD
CITY ROAD
WINDLE CITY
WASHWAY ROAD
FOLDS LANE
FOLDS ROAD
NEWLANDS RD.
CARR MILL ROAD
DERWENT RD.
WOODLANDS RD.
EWART ROAD
HINCKLEY RD.
MARKFIELD
MERTON BANK
MERTON ST.
LOCK ST.
HOSPITAL STREET
STANDISH STREET
CLIFTON STREET
SHAW STREET
POCKET NOOK STREET
ATLAS STREET
PARR STREET
CORPORATION STREET
BICKERSTAFFE STREET
CHURCH STREET
ORMSKIRK STREET
KING STREET
LINKWAY
LINKWAY WEST
LINKWAY EAST
CHALON WAY WEST
CHALON WAY
PEASLEY CROSS LANE
JACKSON ST.
WARRINGTON NEW RD.
WARRINGTON OLD ROAD
WEST SIDE
EAST ST.
ASHCROFT
CRAB STREET
DUKE STREET
BOLTON ST.
ROLAND AV.
CHADWICK RD.
FINCHLEY DR.
LITHERLAND CRES
SCAFELL ROAD
WINDERMERE
ULLSWATER
CONISTON GR.
GRASMERE AVENUE
LANGDALE GRO.
GREEN LEACH AV.
BUCKINGHAM DR.
BLENHEIM WY.
KINGFISHER DR.
FULMAR CL.
MALLARD WY.
ST. ANDREWS GR.
GARETH CR.
LINCOLN AV.
WATERSIDE
PARR MOUNT CT.
LASCELLES ST.
SOROGOLD STREET
LANGTREE
FOUNDRY
HALL ST.
Canal

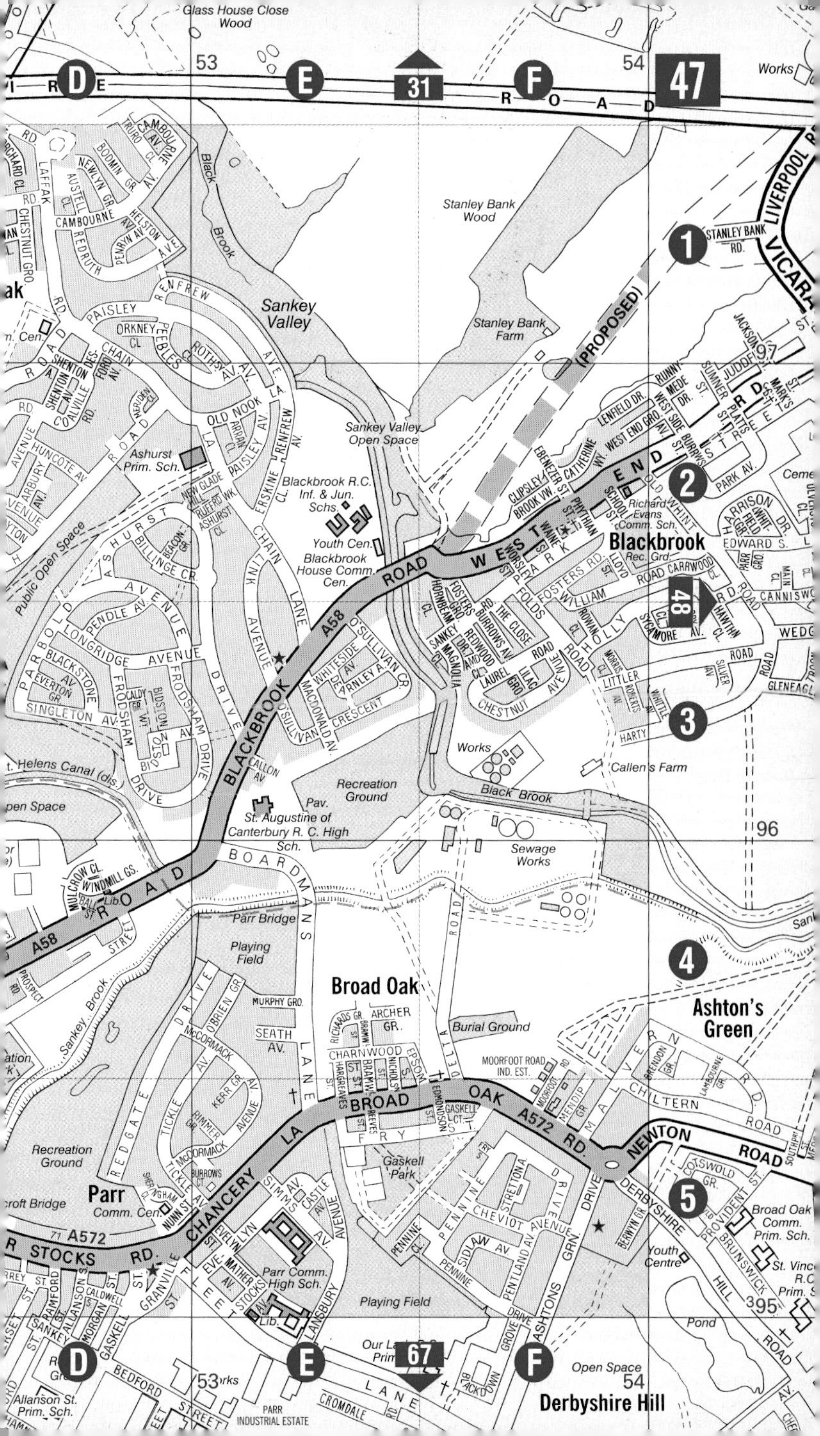

Glass House Close Wood
53
54
31
Works
Stanley Bank Wood
Black Brook
Sankey Valley
Stanley Bank Farm
(PROPOSED)
STANLEY BANK RD.
LIVERPOOL
VICARAGE
Sankey Valley Open Space
Ashurst Prim. Sch.
Blackbrook R.C. Inf. & Jun. Schs.
Youth Cen.
Blackbrook House Comm. Cen.
Blackbrook
Rec. Grd.
Richard Evans Comm. Sch.
WEST END ROAD
BLACKBROOK ROAD
A58
48
Public Open Space
St. Helens Canal (dis.)
Open Space
Recreation Ground
Pav.
St. Augustine of Canterbury R.C. High Sch.
Works
Callen's Farm
Black Brook
Sewage Works
96
Parr Bridge
Playing Field
Sankey Brook
Broad Oak
Burial Ground
MOORFOOT ROAD IND. EST.
Ashton's Green
BROAD OAK A572 RD.
NEWTON ROAD
CHANCERY LA
Recreation Ground
Parr
Parr Comm. Cen.
A572
STOCKS RD.
Gaskell Park
Parr Comm. High Sch.
Playing Field
Youth Centre
Broad Oak Comm. Prim. Sch.
St. Vinc R.C. Prim. S
395
Pond
67
Open Space
Derbyshire Hill
Allanson St. Prim. Sch.
PARR INDUSTRIAL ESTATE

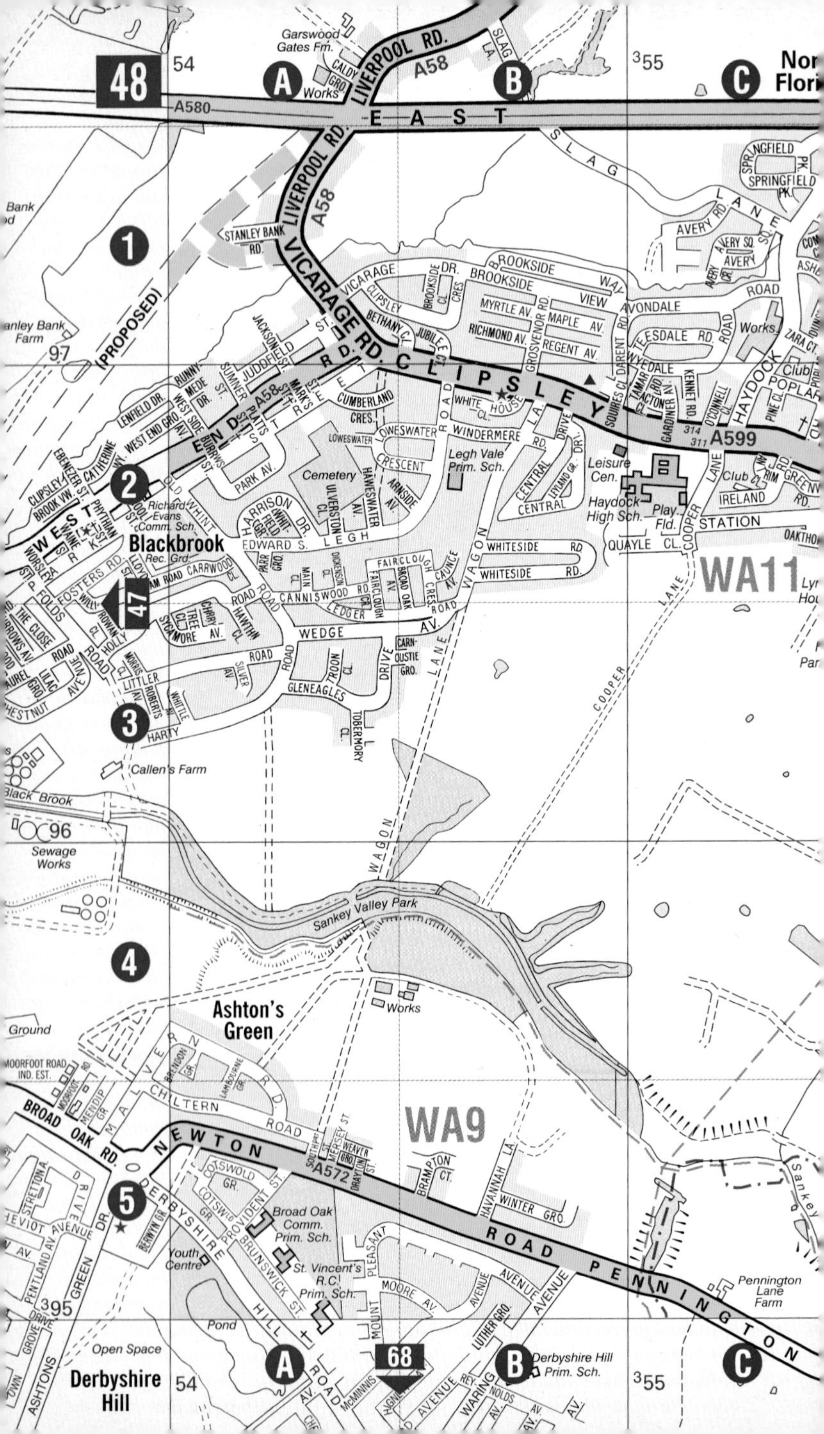

48
54
355
Nor
Flori
Garswood Gates Fm.
Works
LIVERPOOL RD.
A58
A580
EAST
SLAG LANE
SPRINGFIELD PK.
AVERY RD.
AVERY SQ.
STANLEY BANK RD.
VICARAGE RD.
(PROPOSED)
Stanley Bank Farm
BROOKSIDE
BROOKSIDE WAY
MYRTLE AV.
MAPLE AV.
RICHMOND AV.
REGENT AV.
GROSVENOR RD.
AVONDALE ROAD
TEESDALE RD.
WYEDALE
DARENT RD.
KENNET RD.
HAYDOCK
POPLAR
CLIPSLEY
A599
WEST END RD.
JUDDFIELD ST.
CUMBERLAND CRES.
LOWESWATER CRESCENT
WINDERMERE
Legh Vale Prim. Sch.
Cemetery
Leisure Cen.
Haydock High Sch.
Play. Fld.
CENTRAL DRIVE
STATION
IRELAND RD.
QUAYLE CL.
COOPER LANE
WA11
Blackbrook
Rec. Grd.
Richard Evans Comm. Sch.
WHITESIDE RD.
WAGON LANE
CANNISWOOD RD.
LEDGER ROAD
WEDGE AV.
47
CARRWOOD
HAWTHORN CL.
SYCAMORE AV.
GLENEAGLES
TOBERMORY CL.
HARTY
Callen's Farm
Black Brook
96
Sewage Works
Sankey Valley Park
Works
Ashton's Green
MOORFOOT ROAD IND. EST.
CHILTERN ROAD
MALVERN RD.
WA9
BROAD OAK RD.
NEWTON ROAD
A572
PENNINGTON
Broad Oak Comm. Prim. Sch.
St. Vincent's R.C. Prim. Sch.
Youth Centre
DERBYSHIRE HILL
Pond
Open Space
Derbyshire Hill
Derbyshire Hill Prim. Sch.
Pennington Lane Farm
Sankey
68
395

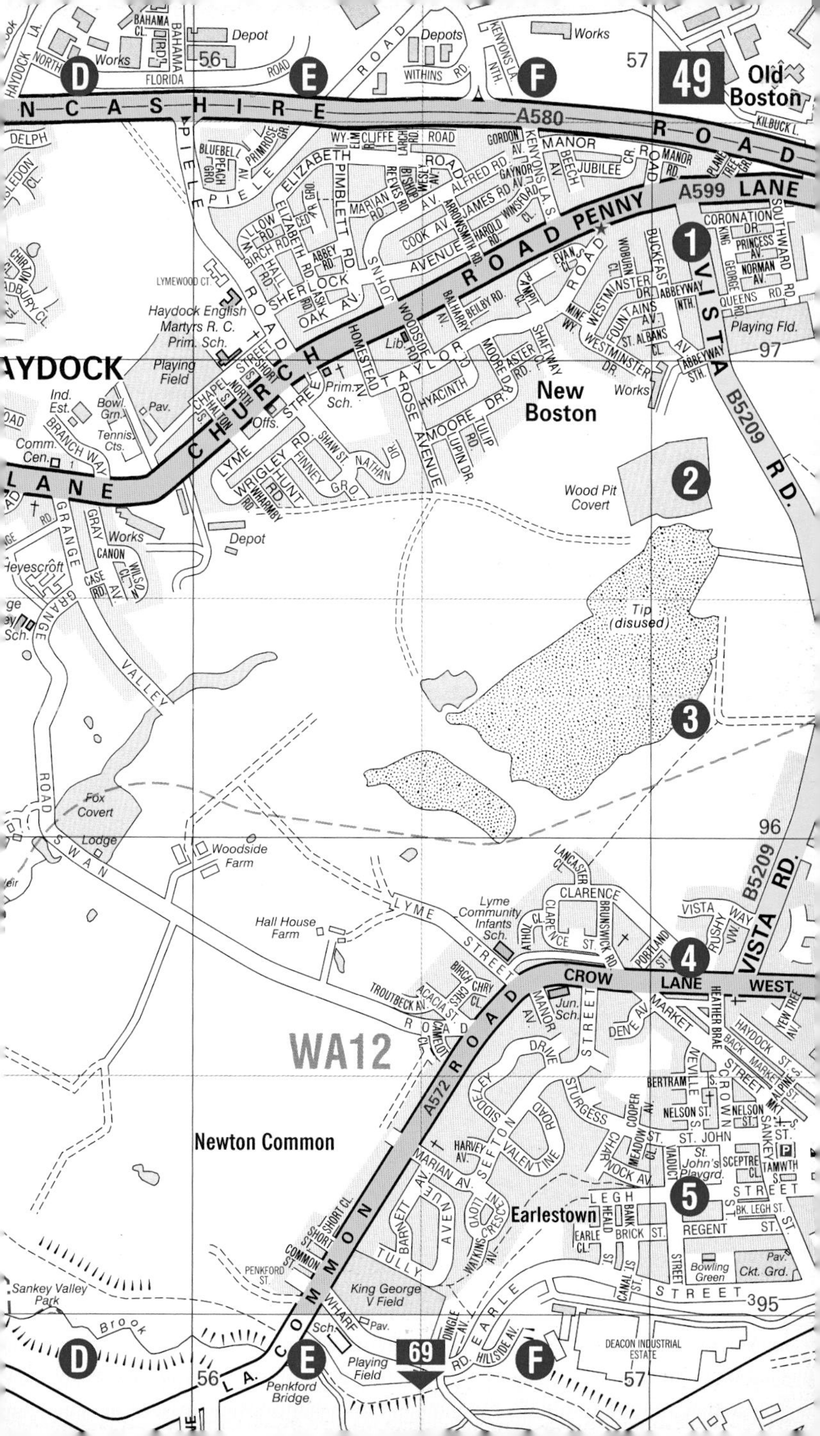
49
Old Boston
Haydock
New Boston
Newton Common
Earlestown
WA12
LANCASHIRE ROAD
A580
PENNY LANE
A599
CHURCH ROAD
VISTA ROAD
B5209
CROW LANE WEST
A572
COMMON ROAD
Wood Pit Covert
Tip (disused)
Fox Covert
Woodside Farm
Hall House Farm
Lyme Community Infants Sch.
Haydock English Martyrs R. C. Prim. Sch.
King George V Field
Deacon Industrial Estate
Sankey Valley Park
Penkford Bridge
Playing Field
Bowling Green
Ckt. Grd.
St. John's Playgrd.
Works
Depot
Depots
69
56
57
96
97
395

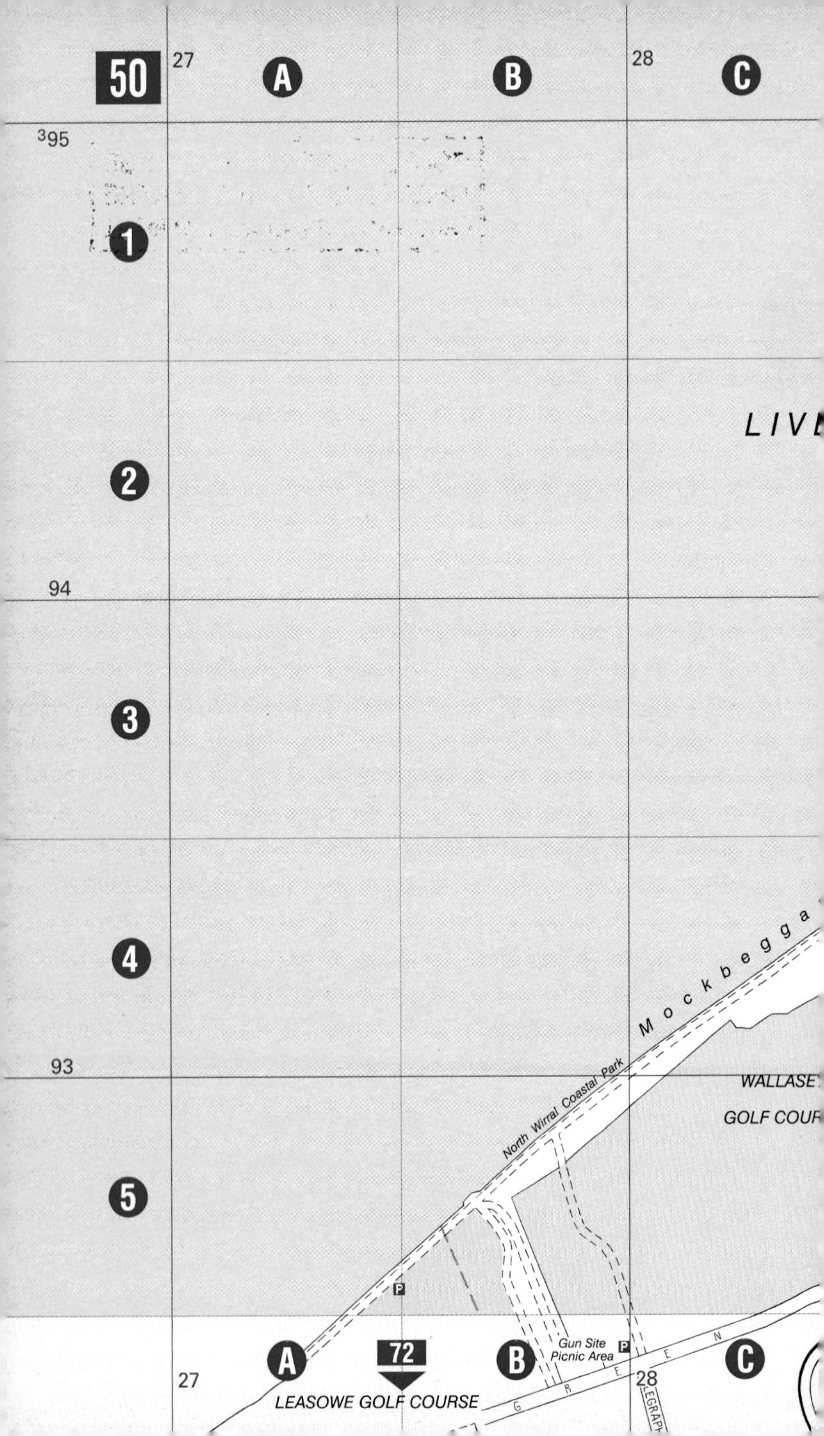
27
A
B
28
C
395
1
2
LIV
94
3
4
Mockbegga
93
North Wirral Coastal Park
WALLASE
GOLF COUR
5
P
72
Gun Site
Picnic Area
P
27
28
LEASOWE GOLF COURSE
GREEN

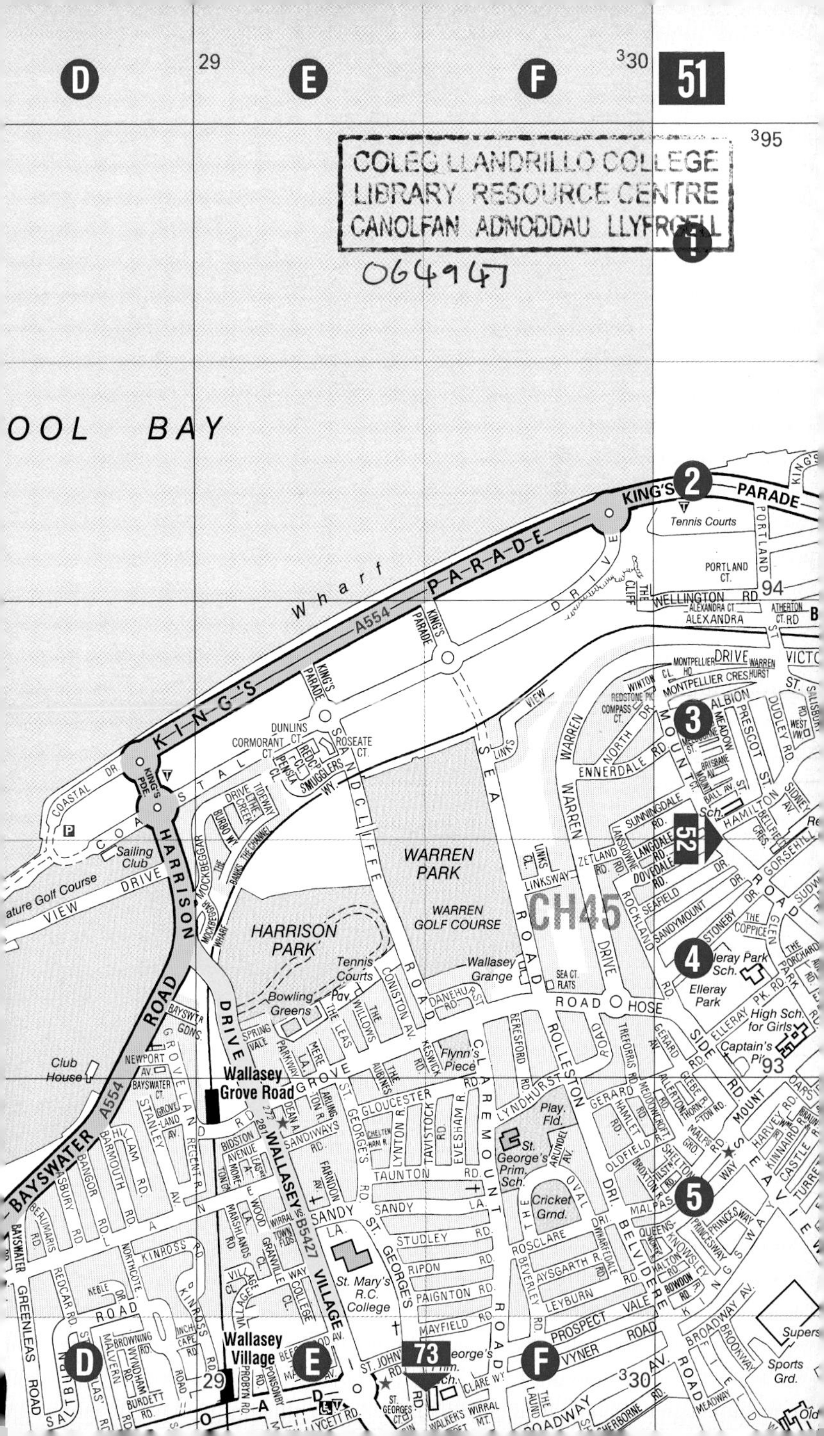

51
D
E
F
29
330
395
94
93
OOL BAY
Wharf
KING'S PARADE
A554
COASTAL DR.
VIEW DRIVE
Sailing Club
HARRISON DRIVE
HARRISON ROAD
HARRISON PARK
WARREN PARK
WARREN GOLF COURSE
Tennis Courts
Bowling Greens
Pav.
Wallasey Grange
SANDCLIFFE ROAD
SEA ROAD
WARREN DRIVE
CLIFF DRIVE
CH45
Club House
BAYSWATER ROAD
Wallasey Grove Road
WALLASEY VILLAGE
B5427
GROVE RD.
SANDY LA.
ST. GEORGE'S RD.
CLAREMOUNT ROAD
ROLLESTON DRI.
BELVIDERE RD.
St. George's Prim. Sch.
Play. Fld.
Cricket Grnd.
St. Mary's R.C. College
Flynn's Piece
HOSE SIDE RD.
Elleray Park Sch.
Elleray Park
High Sch. for Girls
Captain's Pit
KINGS WAY
MOUNT RD.
Wallasey Village
Sports Grd.
VYNER ROAD
PROSPECT VALE
52
73
2
3
4
5

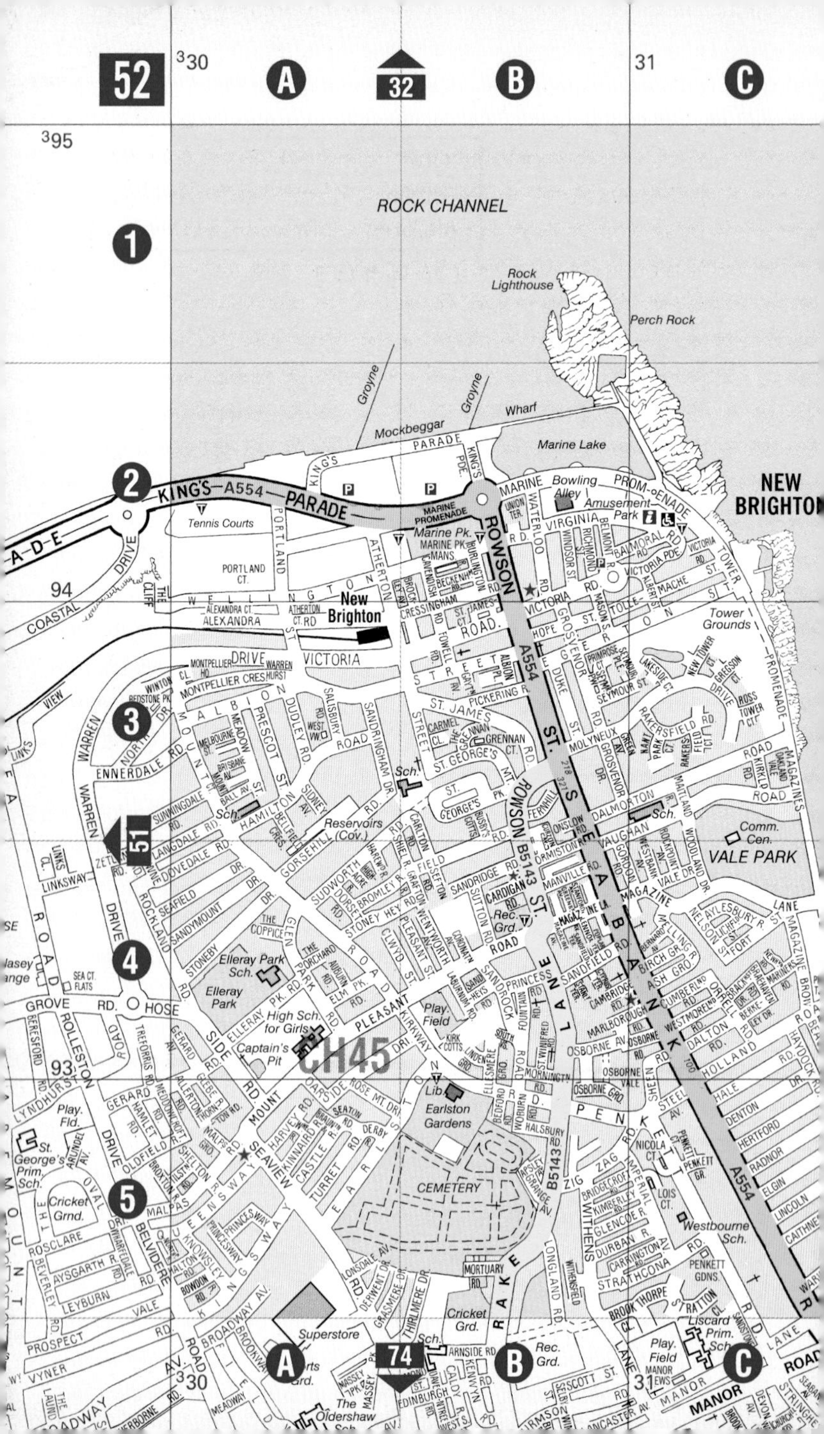
330
A
32
B
31
C
395
ROCK CHANNEL
1
Rock Lighthouse
Perch Rock
Groyne
Groyne
Wharf
Mockbeggar
Marine Lake
NEW BRIGHTON
2
KING'S PARADE A554
Tennis Courts
PORTLAND CT.
MARINE PROMENADE
Marine Pk.
MARINE PK. MANS.
Bowling Alley
Amusement Park
VIRGINIA RD.
WATERLOO RD.
94
COASTAL DRIVE
WELLINGTON RD.
ALEXANDRA RD.
New Brighton
VICTORIA RD.
TOWER PROMENADE
Tower Grounds
MONTPELLIER DRIVE
MONTPELLIER CRES
3
WARREN DRIVE
ENNERDALE RD.
MOUNT RD.
PRESCOT ST.
DUDLEY RD.
SANDRINGHAM DR.
ST. JAMES RD.
ST. GEORGE'S MT.
ROWSON ST.
A554
MOLYNEUX DR.
GROSVENOR RD.
RAKERSFIELD RD.
MAGAZINES RD.
Comm. Cen.
VALE PARK
51
Sch.
Reservoirs (Cov.)
GORSEHILL RD.
SANDRIDGE RD.
ROWSON B5143 ST.
MAGAZINE LANE
Rec. Grd.
CARDIGAN RD.
4
Elleray Park Sch.
Elleray Park
GROVE RD.
HOSE SIDE RD.
High Sch. for Girls
Captain's Pit
PLEASANT ST.
Play. Field
CH45
93
Lib.
Earlston Gardens
EARLSTON RD.
SEAVIEW RD.
LYNDHURST RD.
Play. Fld.
St. George's Prim. Sch.
5
Cricket Grnd.
QUEENSWAY
KINGSWAY
CEMETERY
MORTUARY RD.
RAKE LANE
ZIG ZAG RD.
PENKETT RD.
Westbourne Sch.
A554
HOLLAND RD.
MANOR RD.
Superstore
Sch.
74
Cricket Grd.
Rec. Grd.
Play. Field
Liscard Prim. Sch.
The Oldershaw Sch.
MANOR

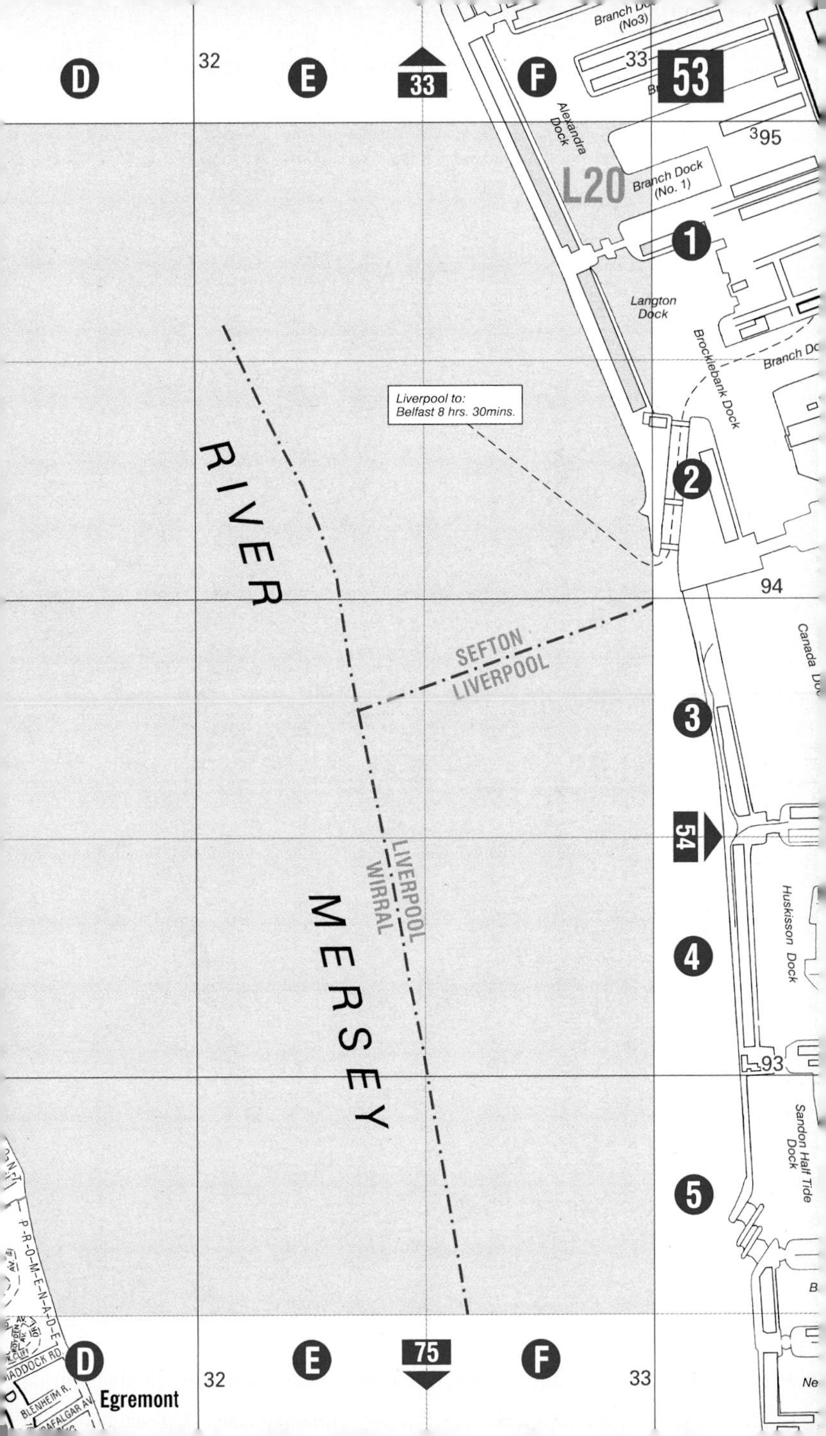

D
E
F
32
33
53
Branch Dock (No3)
Alexandra Dock
395
L20
Branch Dock (No. 1)
1
Langton Dock
Brocklebank Dock
Branch Dock
Liverpool to:
Belfast 8 hrs. 30mins.
2
RIVER
94
Canada Dock
SEFTON
LIVERPOOL
3
54
LIVERPOOL
WIRRAL
MERSEY
Huskisson Dock
4
93
Sandon Half Tide Dock
5
PROMENADE
BLENHEIM R.
Egremont
D
E
75
F
32
33

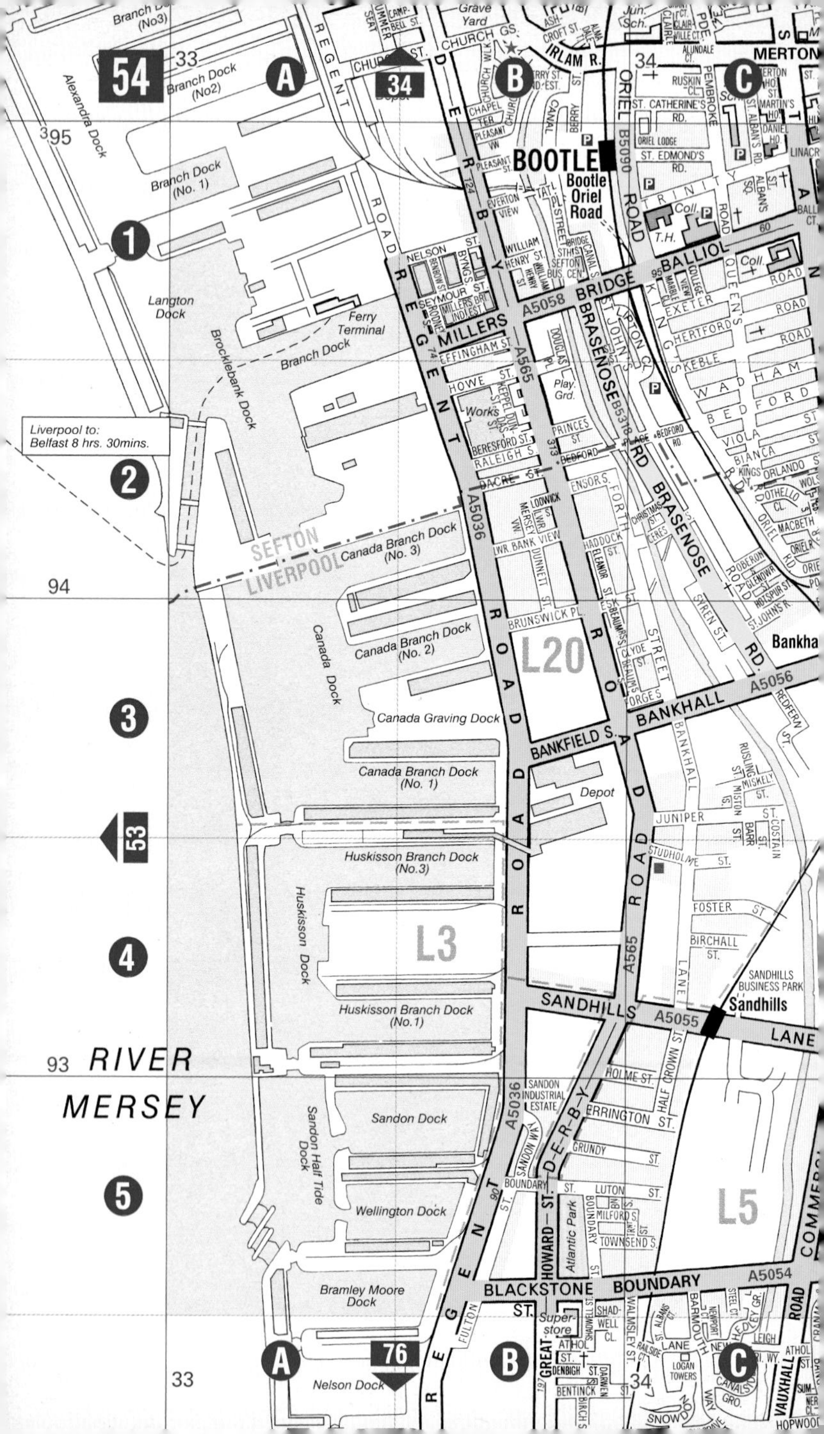

54
Branch Dock (No3)
Branch Dock (No2)
Alexandra Dock
Branch Dock (No. 1)
Langton Dock
Brocklebank Dock
Branch Dock
Ferry Terminal
Liverpool to:
Belfast 8 hrs. 30mins.
SEFTON
LIVERPOOL
Canada Branch Dock (No. 3)
Canada Branch Dock (No. 2)
Canada Dock
Canada Graving Dock
Canada Branch Dock (No. 1)
Huskisson Branch Dock (No.3)
Huskisson Dock
Huskisson Branch Dock (No.1)
L3
RIVER
MERSEY
Sandon Dock
Sandon Half Tide Dock
Wellington Dock
Bramley Moore Dock
Nelson Dock
53
34
76
REGENT ROAD
DERBY ROAD
BOOTLE
Bootle Oriel Road
ORIEL ROAD
B5090
BALLIOL
BRIDGE
A5058
A565
A5036
BRASENOSE RD
MILLERS
Works
Play. Grd.
L20
BANKHALL
A5056
BANKFIELD S.
Depot
SANDHILLS
A5055
LANE
Sandhills
SANDHILLS BUSINESS PARK
L5
SANDON INDUSTRIAL ESTATE
Atlantic Park
BLACKSTONE
BOUNDARY
A5054
GREAT HOWARD ST.
Superstore
VAUXHALL ROAD
COMMERC
MERTON
IRLAM R.
T.H.
Coll.
Bankha

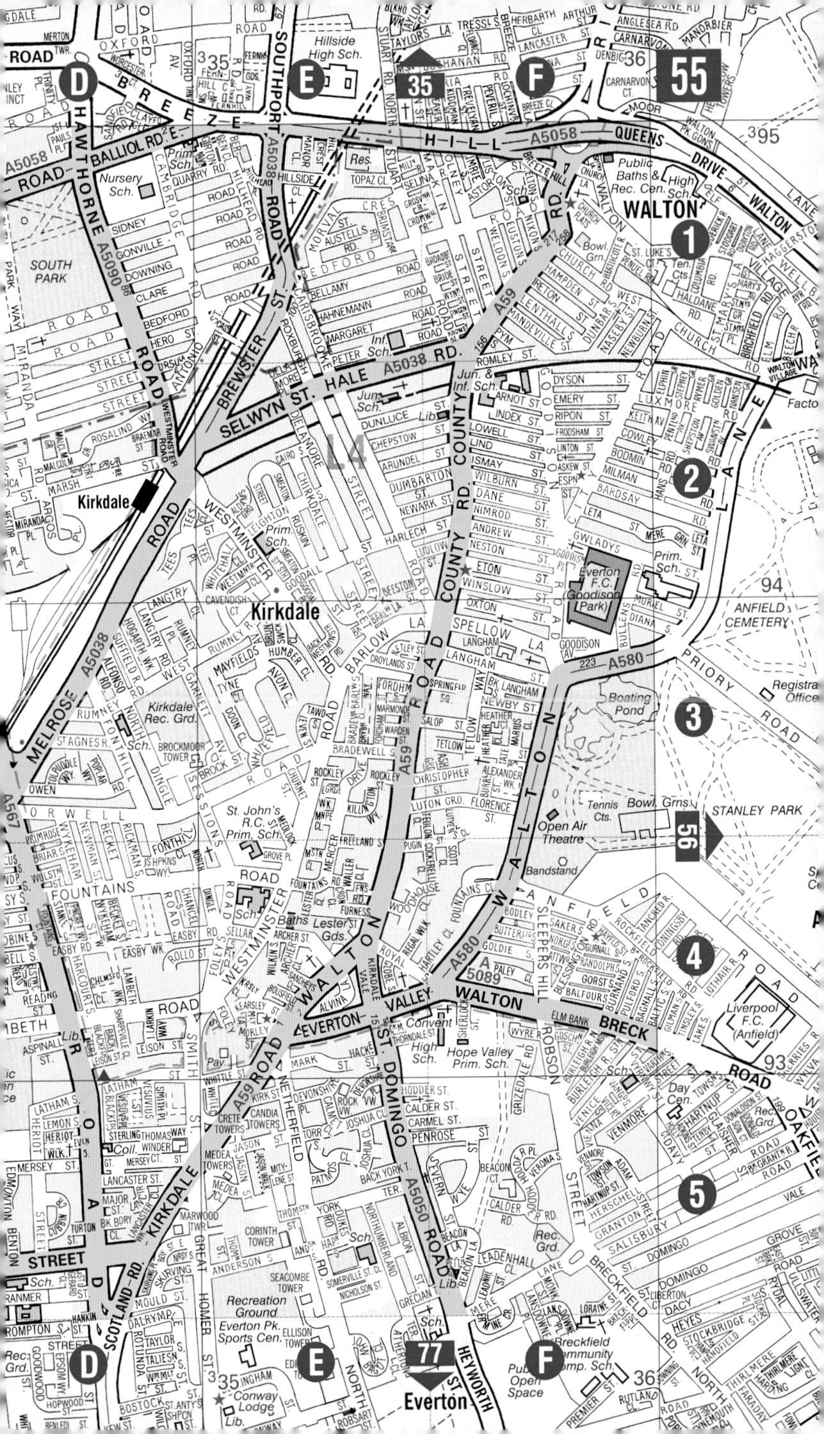

55
35
56
77
Everton
D
E
F
1
2
3
4
5
35
36
395
94
93
L4
WALTON
Kirkdale
Kirkdale
SOUTH PARK
STANLEY PARK
ANFIELD CEMETERY
Everton F.C. (Goodison Park)
Liverpool F.C. (Anfield)
Hillside High Sch.
Nursery Sch.
Public Baths & Rec. Cen.
High Sch.
Prim. Sch.
Jun. Sch.
Inf. Sch.
Jun. & Inf. Sch.
Lib.
Boating Pond
Tennis Cts.
Bowl. Grns
Open Air Theatre
Bandstand
Registrar Office
Factory
Kirkdale Rec. Grd.
St. John's R.C. Prim. Sch.
Convent High Sch.
Hope Valley Prim. Sch.
Day Cen.
Rec. Grd.
Recreation Ground
Everton Pk. Sports Cen.
Conway Lodge
Breckfield Community Comp. Sch.
Public Open Space
Lester Gds.
Baths
Coll.
Bowl. Grn.
Ten. Cts.
A5058
A5038
A5090
A59
A580
A5089
A5050
A567
BREEZE HILL
QUEENS DRIVE
WALTON LANE
HAWTHORNE ROAD
BALLIOL RD.
SOUTHPORT ROAD
STUART RD. NORTH
WALTON PK. GDNS
WALTON VILLAGE
CHURCH RD. WEST
COUNTY RD.
GOODISON ROAD
BREWSTER ST.
SELWYN ST.
HALE RD.
WESTMINSTER ROAD
STANLEY ROAD
MELROSE ROAD
KIRKDALE RD.
SCOTLAND RD.
WALTON ROAD
EVERTON VALLEY
WALTON BRECK ROAD
ANFIELD ROAD
PRIORY ROAD
ST. DOMINGO ROAD
ST. DOMINGO VALE
ST. DOMINGO GROVE
NETHERFIELD RD.
HEYWORTH ST.
BRECKFIELD RD. NORTH
GREAT HOMER ST.
SMITH ST.
BARLOW LA.
SPELLOW LA.
LANGHAM ST.
FOUNTAINS RD.
ORWELL RD.
OXFORD RD.
CAMBRIDGE RD.
SIDNEY RD.
GONVILLE RD.
DOWNING RD.
CLARE RD.
BEDFORD RD.
HERO ST.
BELLAMY RD.
HAHNEMANN RD.
MARGARET RD.
PETER RD.
DUNLUCE ST.
CHEPSTOW ST.
ARUNDEL ST.
DUMBARTON ST.
NEWARK ST.
HARLECH ST.
LUDLOW ST.
DYSON ST.
EMERY ST.
RIPON ST.
FRODSHAM ST.
LINTON ST.
ASKEW ST.
LOWELL ST.
LIND ST.
ISMAY ST.
WILBURN ST.
DANE ST.
NIMROD ST.
ANDREW ST.
NESTON ST.
ETON ST.
WINSLOW ST.
OXTON ST.
GWLADYS ST.
BULLENS RD.
MURIEL ST.
DIANA ST.
LUXMORE RD.
COWLEY RD.
BODMIN RD.
MILMAN RD.
BARDSAY RD.
LETA ST.
MERE GRN
ROMLEY ST.
CHURCH RD.
HALDANE RD.
CARNARVON RD.
ANGLESEA RD.
MANORBIER
LANCASTER ST.
TAYLORS LA.
BUCHANAN RD.
TOPAZ CL.
HILLSIDE CL.
MORVAL CRES.
ST. AUSTELLS RD.
ROXBURGH
CARISBROOKE
WESTMINSTER CL.
GOODALL ST.
CAVENDISH
HUMBER CL.
MAYFIELDS
AVON CL.
TYNE
DOON CL.
WHITEFIELD RD.
RUMNEY RD. WEST
LANGTRY RD.
GARNETT AV.
SESSIONS RD.
DINGLE
FONTHILL
NORTH
BROCK ST.
BROCKMOOR TOWER
ALFONSO RD.
MIRANDA RD.
ARGOS PL.
MARSH ST.
ROSALIND WY.
BRAEMAR ST.
MALCOLM
OWEN RD.
POPLAR WY.
TOLPUDDLE WY.
ST. AGNES R.
WYKEHAM ST.
NEWMAN ST.
BECKET ST.
RICKMAN ST.
PRIMROSE
BRIAR ST.
FOUNTAINS CL.
EASBY RD
EASBY WK.
ROLLO ST.
LAMBETH RD.
LEISON ST.
LATHAM ST.
LEMON ST.
HERIOT ST.
MERSEY ST.
LANCASTER ST.
MAJOR ST.
TURNTON
STERLING WAY
THOMAS WINDER CT.
VESUVIUS ST.
CRETE TOWERS
MEDEA TOWERS
CANDIA TOWERS
JASON ST.
DEVONSHIRE
ROCK VW.
JOSHUA CL.
HODDER ST.
CALDER ST.
CARMEL ST.
PENROSE ST.
BACK YORK T.
NORTHUMBERLAND
ALBION ST.
SEVERN ST.
WYE ST.
BEACON LA.
LEADENHALL CL.
CORINTH TOWER
SEACOMBE TOWER
ANDERSON S.
MOULD ST.
DALRYMPLE ST.
TAYLOR ST.
ROTUNDA ST.
TALIESN ST.
BOSTOCK ST.
ELLISON TOWER
GRECIAN ST.
JOHN BAGOT CL.
ATHERTON ST.
LANSDOWNE PL.
LORAINE ST.
PREMIER ST.
RUTLAND CL.
HEYES ST.
DACY ST.
STOCKBRIDGE ST.
HANDFIELD ST.
THIRLMERE RD.
FARADAY ST.
HARDING ST.
SALISBURY RD.
GRANTON RD.
HERSCHELL ST.
VENMORE ST.
VIENNA ST.
VENICE ST.
BURLEIGH RD.
HARTNUP ST.
CLAISHER ST.
TOWSON ST.
OAKFIELD RD.
ROBSON ST.
GRIZEDALE RD.
WYRE RD.
ELM BANK
SLEEPERS HILL
BLESSINGTON RD.
RANDOLPH S.
GORST S.
BALFOUR S.
BURNAND S.
PULFORD S.
BAGNALL S.
BALTIC S.
TINSLEY S.
LOTHAIR R.
CONINGSBY R.
ROCKFIELD R.
TANCRED R.
SAKER S.
BODLEY S.
BUTTERFIELD S.
GOLDIE S.
PALEY CL.
HARTLEY CL
REGAL WLK.
WOODHOUSE CL.
ROYAL ST.
LUTON GRO.
FLORENCE ST.
ALEXANDER WK.
TATE ST.
CHRISTOPHER ST.
TETLOW ST.
SALOP ST.
NEWBY ST.
HEATHER ST.
BK. LANGHAM ST.
SPRINGFIELD SQ.
FORDHAM
MARMONDE ST.
WARDEN ST.
BRADEWELL S.
ROCKLEY ST.
KILLINGTON WY.
FREELAND ST.
MERCER
FURNESS
WOODHOUSE CL.
FOLEY ST.
SELLAR ST.
ARCHER ST.
WILKIN S.
KEARSLEY ST.
MORLEY ST.
ALVINA LA.
KIRKDALE VALE
MARK ST.
HACKET
Sch.
Lib.
Pav.

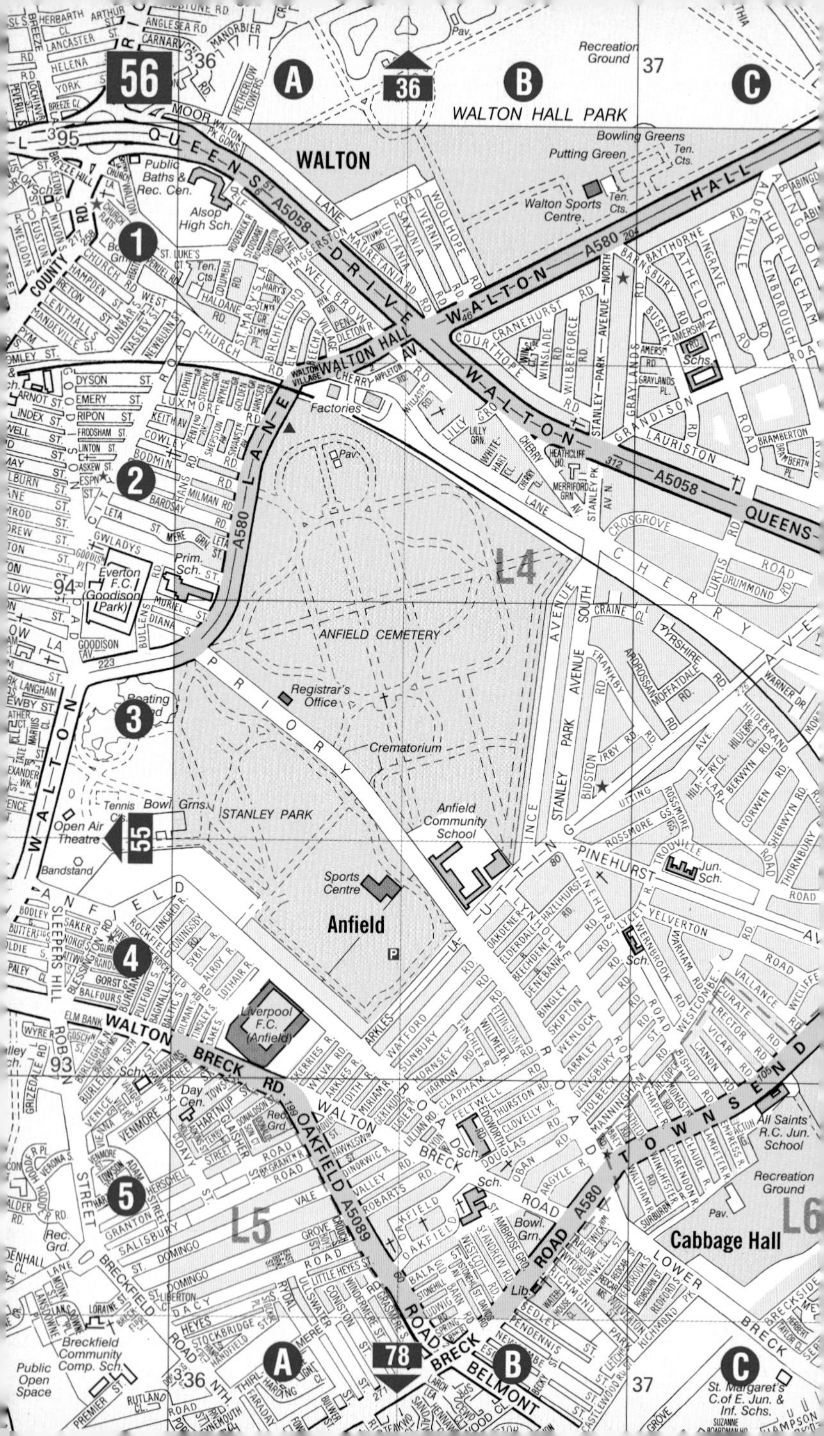

56
36
78
55
A
B
C
1
2
3
4
5
36
37
WALTON
WALTON HALL PARK
Recreation Ground
Bowling Greens
Putting Green
Ten. Cts.
Walton Sports Centre
QUEENS DRIVE
A5058
WALTON HALL AV.
A580
WALTON LANE
WALTON VILLAGE
Factories
Public Baths & Rec. Cen.
Alsop High Sch.
COUNTY RD.
CHURCH RD.
Everton F.C. (Goodison Park)
GOODISON RD.
GOODISON AV.
Prim. Sch.
L4
ANFIELD CEMETERY
Registrar's Office
Crematorium
PRIORY RD.
STANLEY PARK
Boating Lake
Tennis Cts.
Bowl Grns.
Open Air Theatre
Bandstand
Sports Centre
Anfield
P
Anfield Community School
Liverpool F.C. (Anfield)
CHERRY LANE
UTTING AVENUE
STANLEY PARK AVENUE SOUTH
STANLEY PARK AVENUE NORTH
PINEHURST AV.
Jun. Sch.
BRECK RD.
OAKFIELD RD.
A5089
TOWNSEND LANE
All Saints' R.C. Jun. School
Recreation Ground
Cabbage Hall
L6
L5
LOWER BRECK RD.
BELMONT RD.
Breckfield Community Comp. Sch.
Public Open Space
St. Margaret's C.of E. Jun. & Inf. Schs.
Day Cen.
Rec. Grd.
Lib.
Bowl. Grn.
Pav.
WALTON BRECK RD.
SLEEPERS HILL
WALTON ROAD
ANFIELD RD.
BRECKFIELD RD. NTH.

57
37
58
79
D
E
F
1
2
3
4
5
38
39
95
94
93
L11
L12
L13
Norris Green
Clubmoor
Tue Brook
Recreation Ground
Norris Green Park
Superstore
Rec. Grd.
Playing Field
Cricket & Tennis Grd.
Larkhill Estate Gardens
Gardens
Lib.
T.A. Cen.
William Roberts Rec. Cen.
Broadway Market
Broad Sq. Jun. & Inf. Schs.
Acorn Nursy. Sch.
Roscoe Jun. & Inf. Schs.
Jun. & Inf. Schs.
Nursy. Sch.
Monksdown Jun. Sch.
Pavilion Sports Centre
Tennis Cts.
West Derby Sch.
West Derby School
Liverpool Community College
Peter Lloyd
Lister Drive Jun. & Inf. Schs.
Cemy.
Schs.
Sch.
Liverpool Loop Line
A580
A5058
A5049
B5187
QUEENS DRIVE
WALTON LANE
WALTON HALL AVENUE
TOWNSEND AVENUE
MUIRHEAD AVENUE
MUIRHEAD AVENUE EAST
STRAWBERRY RD.
PARTHENON DR
PARTHENON DRI.
UTTING AVENUE
CARR LANE EAST
BROAD LANE
LORENZO DRI.
LORENZO DRIVE
WEST DERBY RD.
MILL BANK
SANDY LANE
SCARISBRICK DRIVE
SCARISBRICK ROAD
LEAMINGTON RD
FAIRFAX DRIVE
MALMESBURY RD.
MILDMAY RD.
FRAMPTON ROAD
LAMBOURNE ROAD
KNIGHTON RD.
DANEVILLE RD.
HARTLAND RD.
KINGSLAND RD.
NORWYN RD.
INNER FORUM
OUTER FORUM
FORUM RD.
SEDGEMOOR
SWINBROOK GRN.
RIDGMONT A.
BRANSTREE AVENUE
MOLLINGTON AVENUE
RISBURY
TEYNHAM CRESCENT
ABBOTSFORD ROAD
MEYRICK RD.
RAILTON RD.
NETHERWOOD RD.
COLMORE RD.
FAIRMEAD RD.
FRANKEL RD.
WANDSWORTH ROAD
PARKHURST RD.
SCARSDALE RD.
PORCHESTER RD.
SETTRINGTON RD.
LEWISHAM RD.
NORRIS GREEN CRESCENT
THORNHOLME CRES.
OXENHOLME CRES.
GLASSONBY
DEANSCALES ROAD
RUSHMERE RD.
ELLERGREEN RD.
BELGREEN RD.
STALISFIELD AVE.
BRANTHWAITE CRESCENT
HEATHWAITE CRES.
GAYHURST
SWALLOW
WINSKILL
LEWISHAM RD.
BERKESWELL
MONKSDOWN RD.
COTTESBROOK
WELLESBOURNE RD.
HOLMROOK AVENUE
SCARGREEN AVENUE
FELMERSHAM AV.
HOMESTALL RD.
GUILSTED
BROADWAY
BRIDGEWAY
BACK BROADWAY
NEW HALL LA.
WAPSHARE ROAD
LOWERSON CRESCENT
DURRANT RD.
HAWKER ROAD
CAVAN ROAD
KILREA RD.
KILREA ROAD
FERGUSON RD.
ASSER RD.
BELLAIRS RD.
MONASH RD.
BIRDWOOD RD.
ALTHAM RD.
AGAR ROAD
MORNINGSIDE
MORNINGSIDE VIEW
CIRCULAR RD.
BROAD SQUARE
BROAD VIEW
RICHARD KELLY DRIVE
NORMANDALE
BRAYFIELD RD.
FLEMINGTON
GARSFIELD
SANDYVILLE ROAD
LANGLAND CL.
KINMEL CL.
SANDEMAN RD.
ALLEYNE RD.
BYNG RD.
GRENFELL
GATCLIFF RD.
EASTMAN RD.
LARKHILL LANE
MALLESON RD.
MAIDEN LANE
LISBURN LANE
ADSHEAD ROAD
CULME ROAD
HALSEY CRESCENT
CLINTON PL.
THREE BUTT LANE
TOLLERTON
LIDDELL
EATON ROAD
WESTCLIFFE RD.
ALMOND'S
HORNSPIT
EDDISBURY
NORTH
BROWNING RD.
HEWITSON RD.
MAXWELL RD.
BORELLA ROAD
SANDY GRO.
MARLOWE
DELAMAIN
MEADE RD.
ACHESON
BALLANTYNE
SANDRINGHAM RD.
VICTORIA
MARLBOROUGH
PORTRUSH ST.
CRAIGS RD.
WINDSOR
BIRKDALE CL.
ELLERSLIE
BUCKINGHAM ROAD
DORSET ROAD
CHESTER RD.
CLIFTON RD.
OSBORNE RD.
GORSEBURN
FAIRBURN
ESKBURN
DEANSBURN
CRAIGBURN
BANKBURN
AUBURN
BANKFIELD ROAD
HUGHENDEN RD.
UPPINGHAM
QUARRY
DERBY

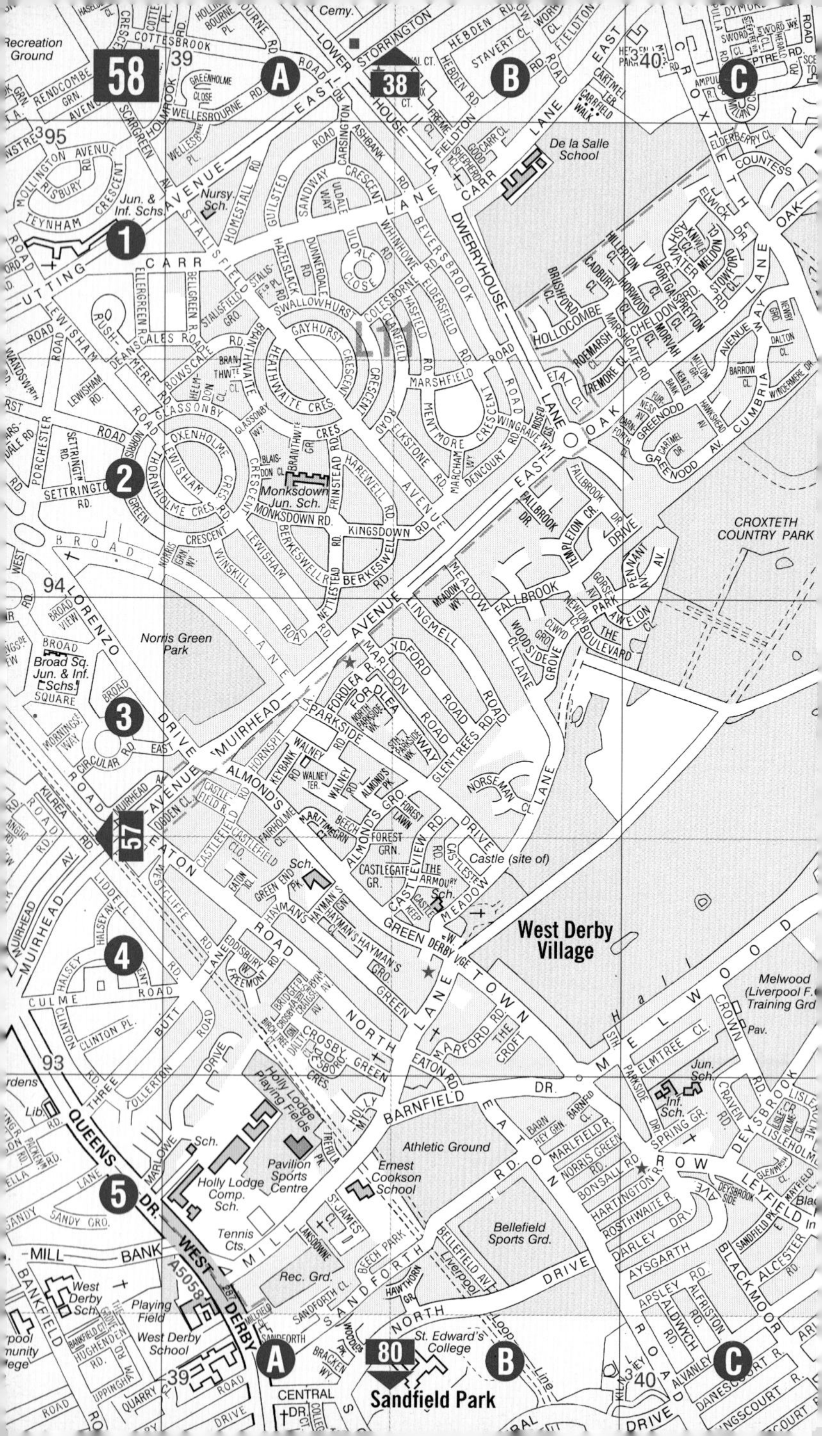

58
38
57
80
A
B
C
1
2
3
4
5
39
40
95
94
93
L11
Recreation Ground
Cemy.
LOWER
HOUSE
STORRINGTON
EAST
DWERRYHOUSE
LANE
CARR
UTTING
AVENUE
De la Salle School
Nursy. Sch.
Jun. & Inf. Schs.
Monksdown Jun. Sch.
CROXTETH COUNTRY PARK
Norris Green Park
Broad Sq. Jun. & Inf. Schs.
West Derby Village
Castle (site of)
Melwood (Liverpool F.C. Training Grd)
Pav.
Holly Lodge Playing Fields
Pavilion Sports Centre
Holly Lodge Comp. Sch.
Tennis Cts.
Rec. Grd.
Athletic Ground
Ernest Cookson School
Bellefield Sports Grd.
St. Edward's College
Sandfield Park
West Derby Sch.
Playing Field
West Derby School
Inf. Sch.
Jun. Sch.
Sch.
QUEENS DR.
WEST DERBY
A5058
MILL BANK
MUIRHEAD AVENUE
MUIRHEAD AVENUE EAST
LORENZO DRIVE
BROAD LANE
EAST LANCASHIRE ROAD
EATON ROAD
MILL LANE
NORTH DRIVE
SANDFORTH
BARNFIELD DR.
ROW
DEYSBROOK
LEYFIELD
BLACKMOOR
TOWN
HALEWOOD
MEADOW LANE
ALMOND'S GREEN
HAYMAN'S GREEN
LISTER DRIVE
CROXTETH
OAK LANE
COUNTESS
CUMBRIA WAY
AVENUE
LISLEHOLME
Loop Line
Liverpool

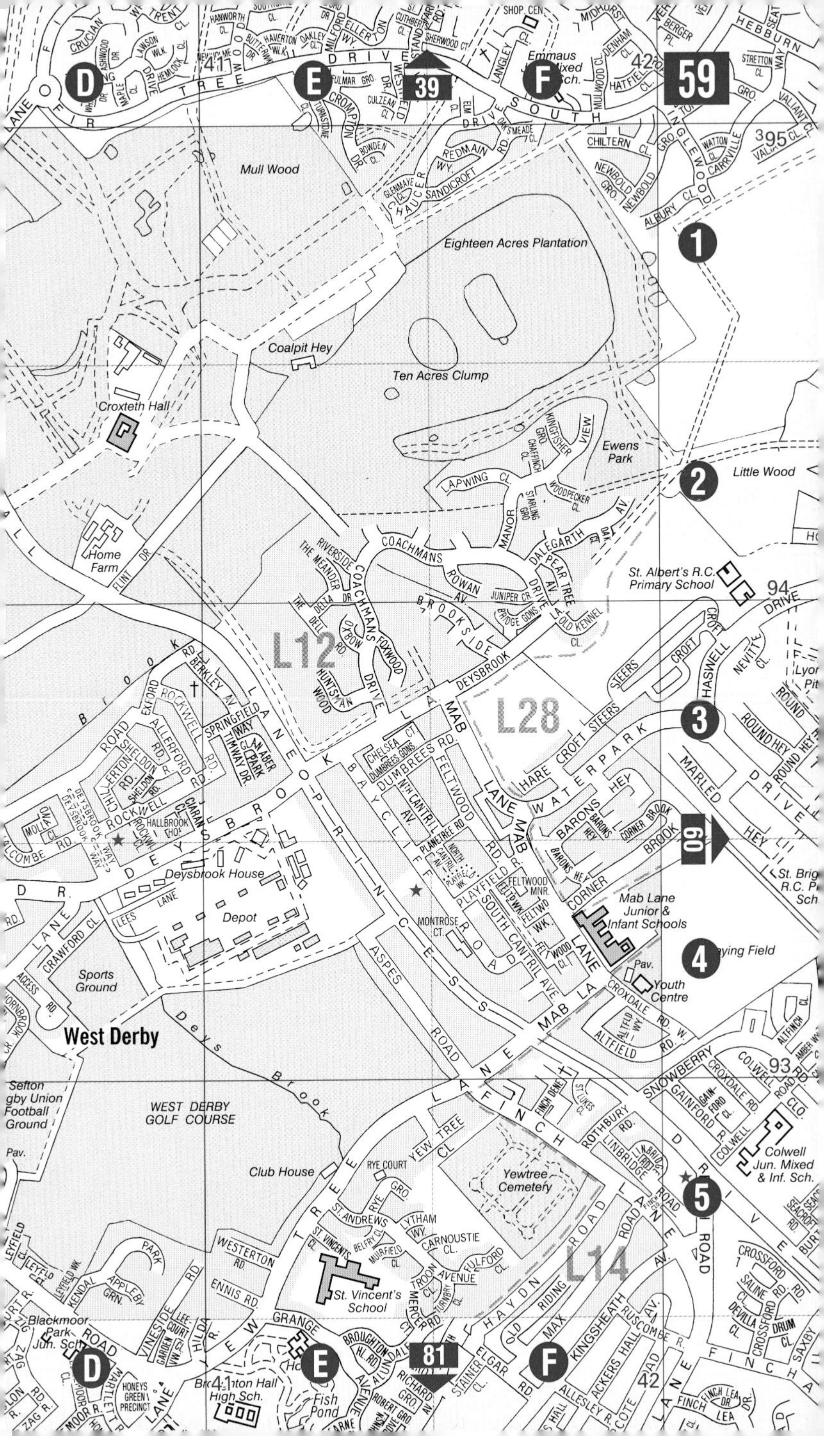
39
60
81
D
E
F
1
2
3
4
5
41
42
395
94
93
L12
L28
L14
Mull Wood
Eighteen Acres Plantation
Coalpit Hey
Ten Acres Clump
Croxteth Hall
Home Farm
Ewens Park
Little Wood
St. Albert's R.C. Primary School
Emmaus Jun. Mixed Sch.
Deysbrook House
Depot
Sports Ground
West Derby
Sefton Rugby Union Football Ground
Pav.
WEST DERBY GOLF COURSE
Club House
Yewtree Cemetery
St. Vincent's School
Mab Lane Junior & Infant Schools
Playing Field
Pav.
Youth Centre
Colwell Jun. Mixed & Inf. Sch.
Blackmoor Park Jun. Sch.
Broughton Hall High Sch.
Fish Pond
FIR TREE DRIVE
DRIVE SOUTH
DEYSBROOK LANE
PRINCESS DRIVE
MAB LANE
FINCH LANE
FINCH LANE
WATERPARK DRIVE
MARLED HEY
ROUND HEY
SNOWBERRY ROAD
YEW TREE CL.
ASPES ROAD
BAYCLIFF ROAD
SOUTH CANTRIL AVE.
FELTWOOD RD.
DUMBREES RD.
COACHMANS DRIVE
BROOKSIDE AV.
DALEGARTH AV.
MANOR DRIVE
LAPWING CL.
KINGFISHER GRO.
CHAFFINCH CL.
WOODPECKER CL.
STARLING GRO.
HARE CROFT
STEERS CROFT
HASWELL DRIVE
NEVITTE CL.
BARONS HEY
CORNER BROOK
CROXDALE RD. W.
ALTFIELD RD.
ROTHBURY RD.
LINBRIDGE RD.
GAINFORD RD.
COLWELL RD.
HAYDN ROAD
OLD RIDING
MAX RD.
KINGSHEATH AV.
ACKERS HALL AV.
RUSCOMBE R.
ELGAR RD.
GRANGE AVENUE
BROUGHTON HL. RD.
RICHARD GRO.
TROON CL.
MERCER RD.
CARNOUSTIE CL.
FULFORD CL.
LYTHAM WY.
ST. ANDREWS
ST. VINCENTS CL.
RYE COURT
RYE GRO.
WESTERTON RD.
ENNIS RD.
KENDAL
APPLEBY GRN.
PARK
VINESIDE
HILDA
CRAWFORD CL.
LEES LANE
ROCKWELL RD.
SPRINGFIELD WAY
TIMWAY DR.
ALLERFORD RD.
SHELDON RD.
CHILLERTON RD.
BERKLEY AV.
EXFORD
FLINT DR.
Brook
Deys Brook
CHILTERN CL.
NEWBOLD GRO.
INGLEWOOD
ALBURY CL.
CARRVILLE
WATTON CL.
REDMAIN WY.
SANDICROFT RD.
CHAUCER
CROMPTON DR.
BOWDEN CL.
CULZEAN CL.
FULMAR GRO.
WESTFIELD DR.
LANGLEY CL.
MULWOOD CL.
HATFIELD CL.
DENHAM CL.
MIDHURST
BERGER PL.
HEBBURN WAY
STRETTON CL.
CRUCIAN
ASHWOOD DR.
MAPLE CL.
LAWSON WLK.
HEMLOCK CL.
TRENT CL.
HANWORTH CL.
HAVERTON WLK.
OAKLEY WY.
MILFORD DR.
ELLERTON
SHERWOOD CT.
SHOP. CEN.
CROSSFORD RD.
SALINE RD.
DEVILLA CL.
DRUM CL.
SAXBY
FINCH LEA DR.
ALLESLEY R.
ST. LUKES
FINCH DENE
MONTROSE CT.
PLAYFIELD RD.
HALLBROOK HO.
CIARAN CL.
ACCESS RD.
JUNIPER CR.
BRIDGE GDNS.
OLD KENNEL CL.
PEAR TREE AV.
ROWAN AV.
RIVERSIDE
THE MEANDER
DELTA DR.
THE DELL
OXBOW RD.
FOXWOOD
HUNTSMAN WOOD
CHELSEA CT.
DUMBREES GDNS.
PLANETREE RD.
NTH. CANTRIL AV.
ALTFIELD WY.
COLWELL CL.
GAINFORD CL.
CROXDALE RD.
St. Brigid's R.C. P. Sch.

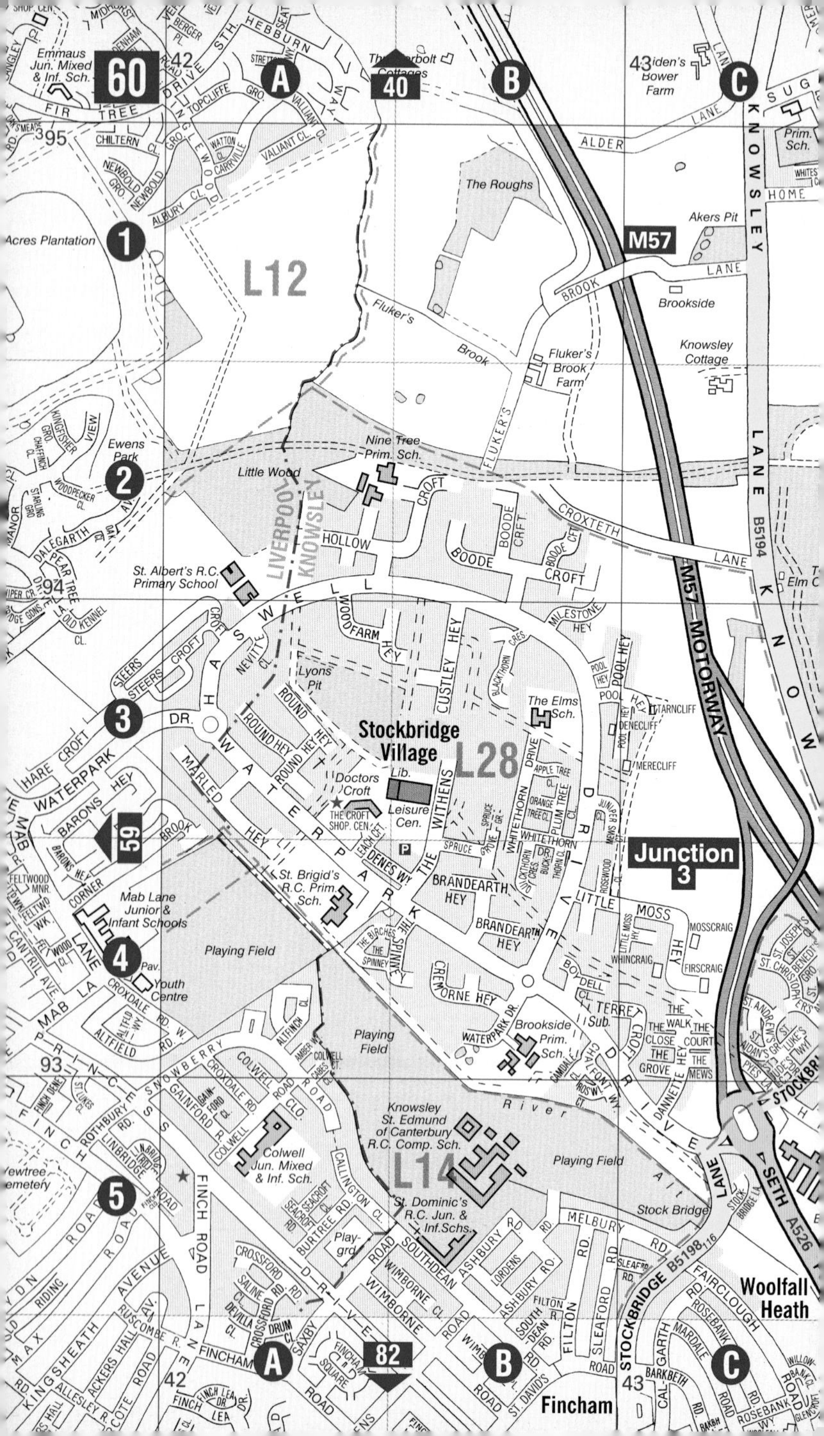
60
A
B
C
40
Emmaus Jun. Mixed & Inf. Sch.
Fir Tree Drive
Topcliffe Gro.
Chiltern Cl.
Newbold Gro.
Albury Cl.
Valiant Cl.
Carrville
Watton Cl.
Hebburn
Thunderbolt Cottages
Aiden's Bower Farm
Alder Lane
Prim. Sch.
Home
Acres Plantation
L12
The Roughs
Akers Pit
M57
Brook Lane
Brookside
Fluker's Brook
Fluker's Brook Farm
Knowsley Cottage
Knowsley Lane
B5194
Ewens Park
Kingfisher Gro.
Chaffinch Cl.
View
Woodpecker Cl.
Starling Gro.
Dalegarth
Pear Tree
Manor
Little Wood
Nine Tree Prim. Sch.
Liverpool
Knowsley
Croft
Hollow
Boode Croft
Croxteth Lane
Elm Cl.
St. Albert's R.C. Primary School
Haswell
Old Kennel Cl.
Woodfarm Hey
Custley Hey
Blackthorn Cres.
Milestone Hey
Pool Hey
M57 Motorway
Steers Croft
Nevitte Cl.
Lyons Pit
Round Hey
The Elms Sch.
Starncliff
Denecliff
Merecliff
Hare Croft
Waterpark Dr.
Stockbridge Village
L28
Lib.
Leisure Cen.
Doctors Croft
The Croft Shop. Cen.
Leach Cft.
Marled Hey
Barons Hey
Brook
59
The Withens
Apple Tree Cl.
Orange Tree Cl.
Plum Tree Cl.
Whitethorn Drive
Juniper Mews
Spruce Grove
Junction 3
Feltwood Mnr.
Feltwood Wk.
Corner
Mab Lane Junior & Infant Schools
St. Brigid's R.C. Prim. Sch.
Denes Wy.
Brandearth Hey
Little Moss Hey
Mosscraig
Whincraig
Firscraig
The Birches
The Spinney
Cantril Ave.
Wood Cl.
Lane
Playing Field
Pav.
Youth Centre
Cremorne Hey
Boydell Cl.
Terret Croft
Sub.
The Walk
The Close
The Court
The Grove
The Mews
Dannette Hey
Mab La.
Croxdale Rd. W.
Altfield Rd.
Altfinch Cl.
Colwell Ct.
Waterpark Dr.
Brookside Prim. Sch.
Chalfont Wy.
St. Joseph's
St. Benedict's Gro.
St. Christopher's
St. Andrew's Gro.
St. Luke's
St. Aidan's Gro.
Pyes La.
Stockbridge
93
Snowberry
Croxdale Rd.
Colwell Road
Gainford Rd.
Gainford Cl.
Colwell
Clo.
Amber Wy.
Cabes Ct.
River Alt
Prince's
Finch Dene
St. Lukes
Rothbury Rd.
Linbridge Road
Colwell Jun. Mixed & Inf. Sch.
Knowsley St. Edmund of Canterbury R.C. Comp. Sch.
L14
Playing Field
Stock Bridge
Seth
A526
Yewtree Cemetery
5
Finch Road
Callington Cl.
Seacroft Cl.
Seacroft Rd.
Burtree Rd.
Play-grd.
St. Dominic's R.C. Jun. & Inf. Schs.
Southdean Road
Ashbury Rd.
Melbury Rd.
Stockbridge B5198
Stockbridge La.
Sleaford Rd.
Fairclough
Woolfall Heath
Riding
Avenue
Max
Kingsheath
Ackers Hall Av.
Ruscombe R.
Lane
Crossford Rd.
Saline Cl.
Devilla Cl.
Crossford
Drum Cl.
Drive
Wimborne Cl.
Wimborne Road
Lordens
Filton Rd.
South Dean Rd.
Sleaford Road
Rosebank Rd.
Mardale
Garth
Cal.
Barkbeth Rd.
Willow Bank Cl.
Road
Fincham
Saxby
Fincham Square
82
42
43
Allesley R.
Cote
Finch Lea Dr.
St. David's
Fincham
Rosebank Wy.
Glencroft
1
2
3
4
94
95

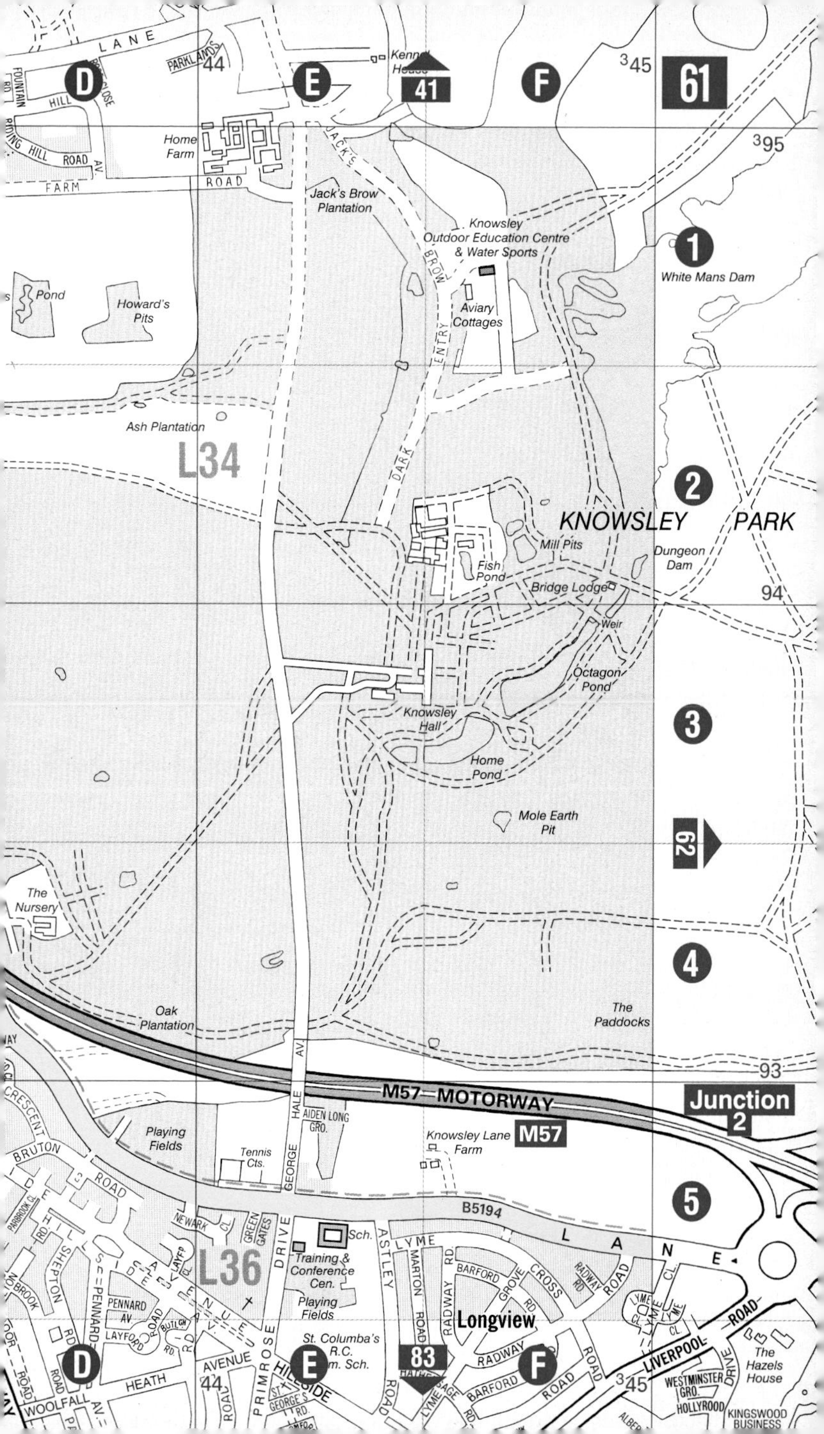

LANE
PARKLANDS
FOUNTAIN RD.
HILL
CLOSE
RIDING HILL ROAD
AV.
FARM
ROAD
Home Farm
Kennel House
41
Jack's Brow Plantation
JACK'S
BROW
DARK
ENTRY
Knowsley Outdoor Education Centre & Water Sports
Aviary Cottages
White Mans Dam
Pond
Howard's Pits
Ash Plantation
L34
KNOWSLEY PARK
Mill Pits
Fish Pond
Dungeon Dam
Bridge Lodge
Weir
Octagon Pond
Knowsley Hall
Home Pond
Mole Earth Pit
62
The Nursery
Oak Plantation
The Paddocks
M57 MOTORWAY
Junction 2
M57
HALE AV.
GEORGE
AIDEN LONG GRO.
Playing Fields
Tennis Cts.
Knowsley Lane Farm
CRESCENT
BRUTON ROAD
PARBROOK CL.
SHEPTON RD
PENNARD AV
LAYFORD
ROAD
BROOK
B5194
LANE
NEWARK CL.
GREEN GATES
L36
DRIVE
PRIMROSE
Sch.
Training & Conference Cen.
Playing Fields
ASTLEY
LYME
MARTON ROAD
RADWAY
BARFORD
GROVE RD
CROSS
RADWAY RD
ROAD
LYME CL.
CL
Longview
St. Columba's R.C. Jun. Sch.
83
HILLSIDE
ST. GEORGE'S RD.
AVENUE
HEATH
WOOLFALL AV.
LIVERPOOL ROAD
WESTMINSTER GRO.
HOLLYROOD
DRIVE
The Hazels House
KINGSWOOD BUSINESS
44
345
395
94
93

The Nightcap
42
A
B
C
Paddock Delph
Park Farm
The Nightcap
White Man's Dam
Garden Wood
KNOWSLEY SAFARI PARK
Hag Brow
KNOWSLEY PARK
Mill Pits
Dungeon Dam
Weir
Octagon Pond
Mizzy Dam
Mizzy Plantations
Mole Earth Pit
61
Riding Hill
Parkside
Safari Park Entrance
A58
The Paddocks
Tennis Cts.
Knowsley Prescot School
The Paddocks
Prescot Brook
PRESCOT
Prescot Nursery
PADDOCK ROAD
M57 MOTORWAY
Junction 2
KNOWSLEY LANE
B5194
A57
M57
B5199 LANE
L36
LIVERPOOL ROAD
Longview
Brook Bridge
LIVERPOOL RD. WEST B5200
DERBY
A57
MANCHESTER
SOUTH AVENUE
CENTRAL AVENUE
King George V Mem. Playing Field
84
HUYTON
CARR
WOOD LA
KINGSWOOD BUSINESS
HOLLYROOD
MINSTER
Cemetery
NORRIS RD.
PRESTON

D
E
F
47
48
43
85
64
1
2
3
4
5
395
94
93
WA10
L34
L35
Gillar's Green
GILLAR'S LANE
B5203
B5201
Burgesses Farm
Trap Wood
Eccleston Mere
SUMMERFIELD CL.
HOUSE
SEDDON
PINFOLD
MERE HEY
SPINNEY
Burrow's Lane Farm
Mere View Farm
Trapwood Cottage
Trap Lodge
KNOWSLEY
ST. HELENS
Ivy House
Roughley's Brow Farm
Sale's Wood
Gorse Plantation
Cricket Ground
No. 4 RESERVOIR
No. 3 RESERVOIR
No. 2 Reservoir
No. 1 Reservoir
BURROW'S
Roughley's Brow House
Keeper's House
Yates Plantation
House
Eccleston Nursery
Valencia Farm
VALENCIA GR.
FERN GDNS.
NEW RD.
A58
ROAD
ST. HELENS
BY-PASS
PARK AVENUE
WEST CL.
EAST CL.
CENTRAL
Recreation Ground
Our Lady's R.C. Prim. Sch.
LLOYD
BELVEDERE CL.
CANTERBURY CL.
CHAPMAN GR.
HAMNETT RD.
FLETCHER AV.
LAWLER GRO.
ST. JAMES' RD.
THE GREEN
HILARY CLO.
ALBANY AVENUE
ELM
GROVE
THE WOODLANDS
FOREST CL.
THE PADDOCK
INGLEHOLME GDNS.
Eccleston Lane Ends Prim. Sch.
Evelyn Prim. Sch.
Tennis Cts.
BEECH AV.
HEATH CL.
Eccleston Park
GORSEY
GROVE
AVENUE
HOLME CL.
MIDDLEHURST CL.
Football Grd.
HALSALL ST.
MOSS
EVANS
WARD ST.
CROSS
ROWSONS
GROSVENOR
OLD
B5201
LANE
FAIRHOLME
CROFT
AVENUE
Eccles
PORTICO CT.
PORTICO AV.
GEORGIAN CL.
PLUM TREE CL.
PORTICO LA.
Portico Lodge
THE GABLES
BROOM CL.
ALDER ROAD
ALDER CL.
RYDAL AV.
GRASMERE AV.
CONISTON AV.
DERWENT AV.
LAUREL RD.
HAWTHORN RD.
CLIFTON-VILLE RD.
GREENWOOD CL.
EVELYN AV.
Works
COLUMBIA RD.
QUEENS RD.
ALBANY RD.
MARYVILLE RD.
Prescot Prim. Sch.
Playing Field
OLIVER LYME RD.
BRETHERTON
LAVENDER CR.
FAIRHURST TER.
SUTHERLAND RD.
HUNTER CT.
DERBY SQ.
WARRINGTON
ST. HELENS RD.
A57
ST.
ACKERS
CYPRUS
ASPINALL ST.
LEYLAND
ECCLESTON
PRESCOT CEN.
Civic Hall
BEACONS-FIELD
HOUGHTON ST.
KEMBLE
B5200 STREET
WILLIAMS
CHESTER ST.
STATION
COOK S.
KING ST.
PRESCOT
SCOTCHBARN
Scotchbarn Pool
LACEY RD.
LANE
SCOTCHBARN
SINCLAIR CL.
AVENUE
GRAY'S AVE
VINING
FORD
SUNDALE
McVINNIE RD.
DELPH LANE
HONEYBOURNE DR.
WATLING
TWO BUTT
LITCHBOROUGH GRO.
Sports Gr.
Prescot Leisure Centre
SINCLAIR
ROAD
Ten. Cts.
ROAD

64
44
86
63
Eccleston Mere
Eccleston Mere Prim. Sch.
Eccleston Top Dam
Eccleston Bottom Dam
Works
Big Dam
TAYLOR PARK
Little Dam
GRANGE PARK GOLF COURSE
Spring Pit
Recreation Ground
WA10
Club House
Carmel College
Mere View Farm
Sale's Wood
Gorse Plantation
Cricket Ground
L34
Valencia Farm
ST. HELENS ROAD
PRESCOT ROAD
A58
Grange Park
Broadway Comm. Leisure Cen.
Broadway Comm. High Sch.
Pav.
Eccleston Pk. Trad. Cen.
Portico
Eccleston Park
Playing Fields
Willowbrook Hospice
L35
Public Open Space
Portico Lodge
ST. HELENS
KNOWSLEY
Farm Annexe
Knowsley St. Edmund Arrowsmith R.C. Comp. Sch.
Ten. Cts.
Tennis Cts.
RAINHILL ROAD
B5413
PINFOLD
PRESTBURY DRIVE
HOLME ROAD
CHAIN WALK
FRECKLETON RD.
MITCHELL RD.
LESLIE
BROADWAY
SPRINGFIELD ROAD
SCHOLES LANE
SCHOLES PARK
UPLAND
MAIN AVENUE
AUSTIN AV.
CUMBERLAND AV.
PORTICO LA.
DELPH LA.
OLD ROAD
GROVE AVENUE
CENTRAL AVENUE
PARK AVENUE
TWO BUTT LA.
SCOTCHBARN LA.
McVINNIE RD.
WEDGEWOOD GARDENS
Eccleston Park

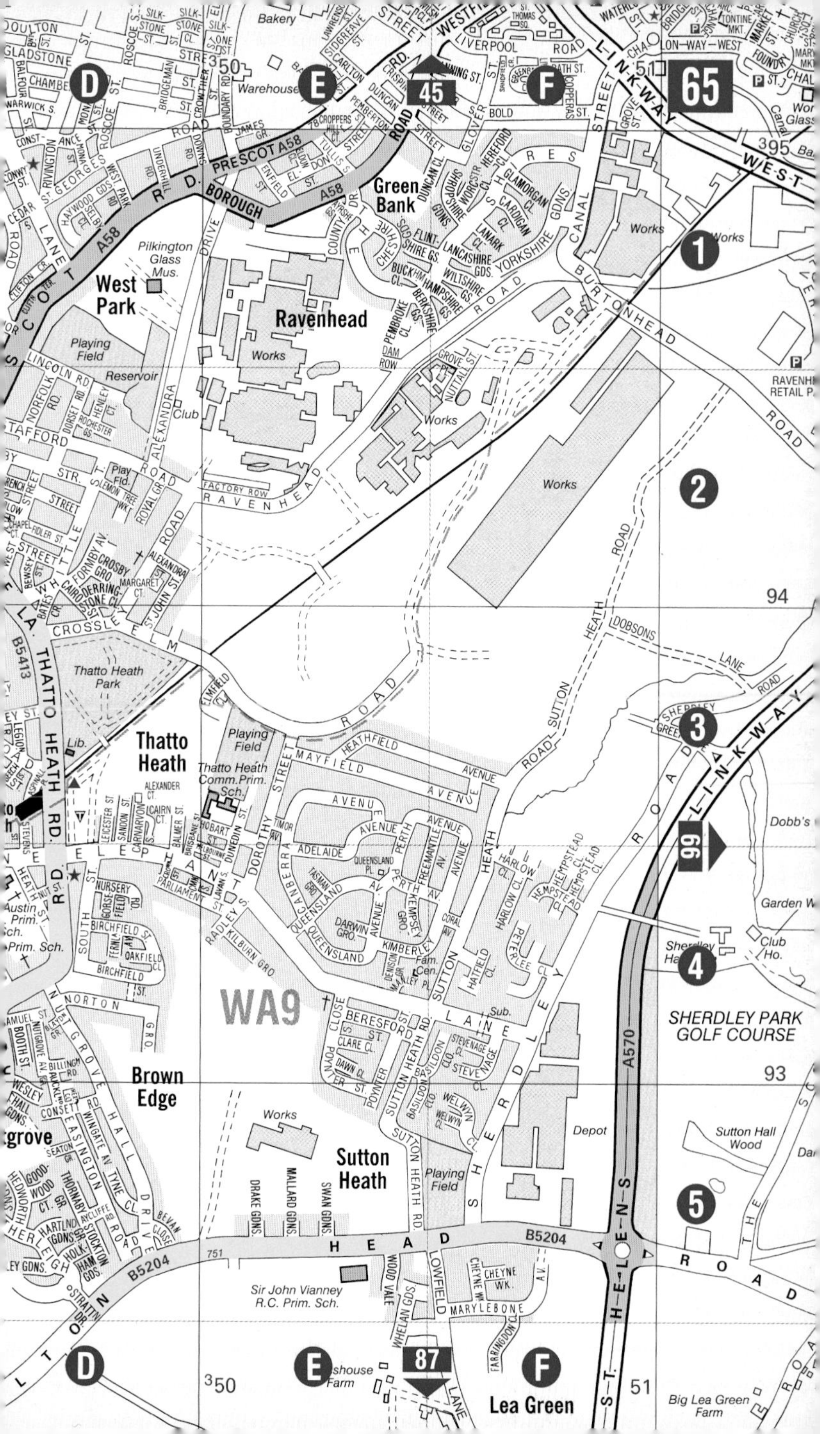
65
45
99
87
D
E
F
1
2
3
4
5
West Park
Ravenhead
Green Bank
Thatto Heath
Brown Edge
Sutton Heath
Lea Green
WA9
SHERDLEY PARK GOLF COURSE
Sutton Hall Wood
Pilkington Glass Mus.
Thatto Heath Park
Playing Field
Reservoir
Works
Depot
Thatto Heath Comm.Prim. Sch.
Sir John Vianney R.C. Prim. Sch.
Sherdley Hall
Club Ho.
Big Lea Green Farm
LINKWAY
LINKWAY WEST
PRESCOT RD.
BOROUGH ROAD
THATTO HEATH RD.
ELEPHANT LANE
ELTON HEAD ROAD
SHERDLEY ROAD
SUTTON HEATH ROAD
BURTONHEAD ROAD
RAVENHEAD ROAD
ELM ROAD
ALEXANDRA ROAD
A58
A570
B5204
B5413
350
51
94
93

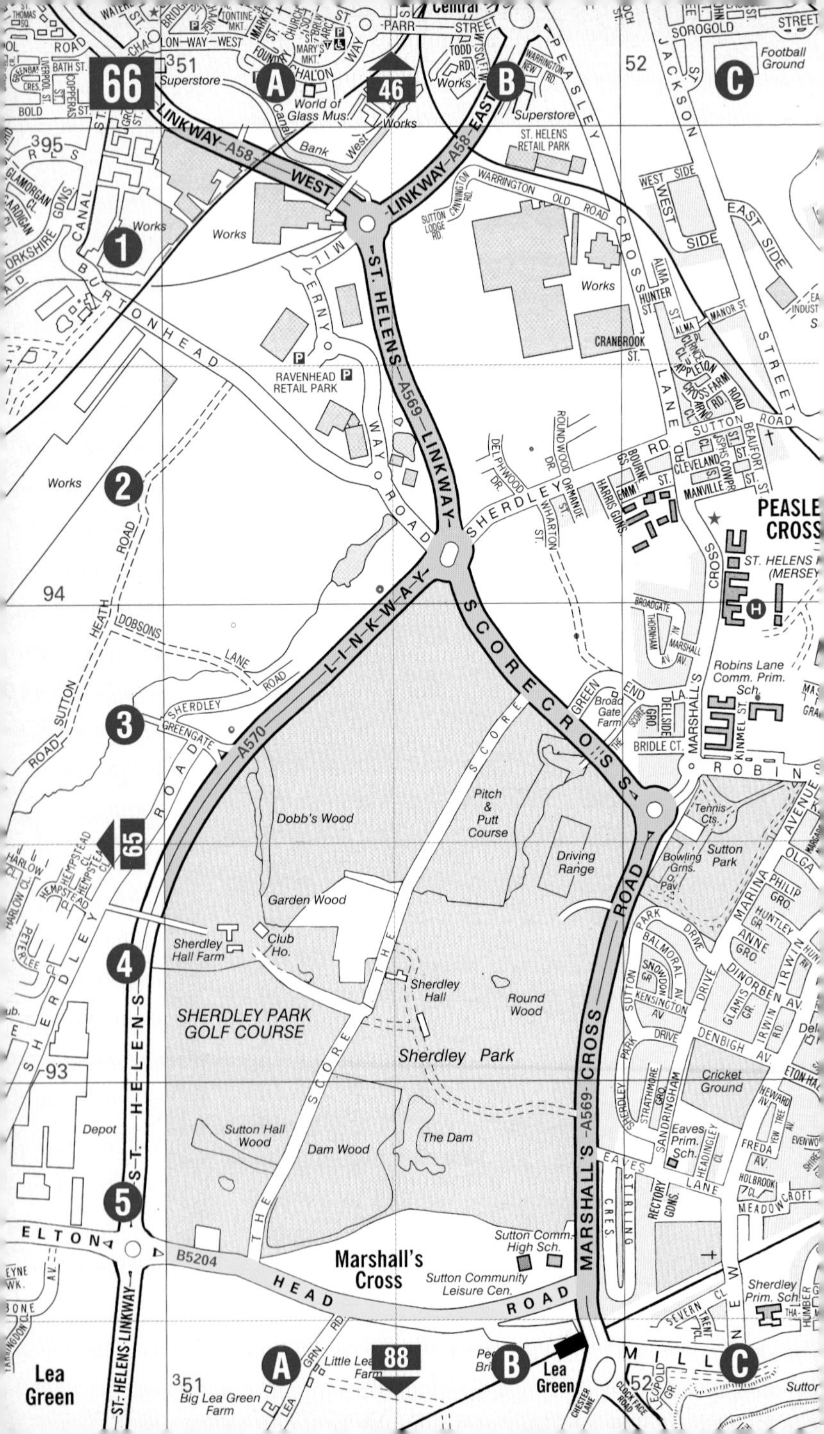
66
46
65
88
A
B
C
1
2
3
4
5
LINKWAY-A58-WEST
LINKWAY-A58-EAST
ST. HELENS-A569-LINKWAY
LINKWAY-A570
SCORECROSS
MARSHALL'S-A569-CROSS ROAD
ST. HELENS LINKWAY
ELTON HEAD ROAD
B5204
Superstore
World of Glass Mus.
Works
ST. HELENS RETAIL PARK
RAVENHEAD RETAIL PARK
Football Ground
WARRINGTON OLD ROAD
PEASLEY CROSS
ST. HELENS
Robins Lane Comm. Prim. Sch.
SHERDLEY PARK GOLF COURSE
Sherdley Park
Sherdley Hall Farm
Club Ho.
Sherdley Hall
Dobb's Wood
Garden Wood
Pitch & Putt Course
Driving Range
Round Wood
Sutton Hall Wood
Dam Wood
The Dam
Sutton Park
Tennis Cts.
Bowling Grns.
Pav.
Cricket Ground
Eaves Prim. Sch.
Sutton Comm. High Sch.
Sutton Community Leisure Cen.
Marshall's Cross
Sherdley Prim. Sch.
Depot
Lea Green
Big Lea Green Farm
Little Lea Farm
BURTONHEAD ROAD
SUTTON HEATH ROAD
DOBSONS LANE ROAD
SHERDLEY ROAD
SHERDLEY ROAD
THE SCORE
JACKSON ST.
PEASLEY CROSS LANE
SUTTON ROAD
ROBINS LANE
MILL LANE
EAVES LANE
52
94
93
351
395

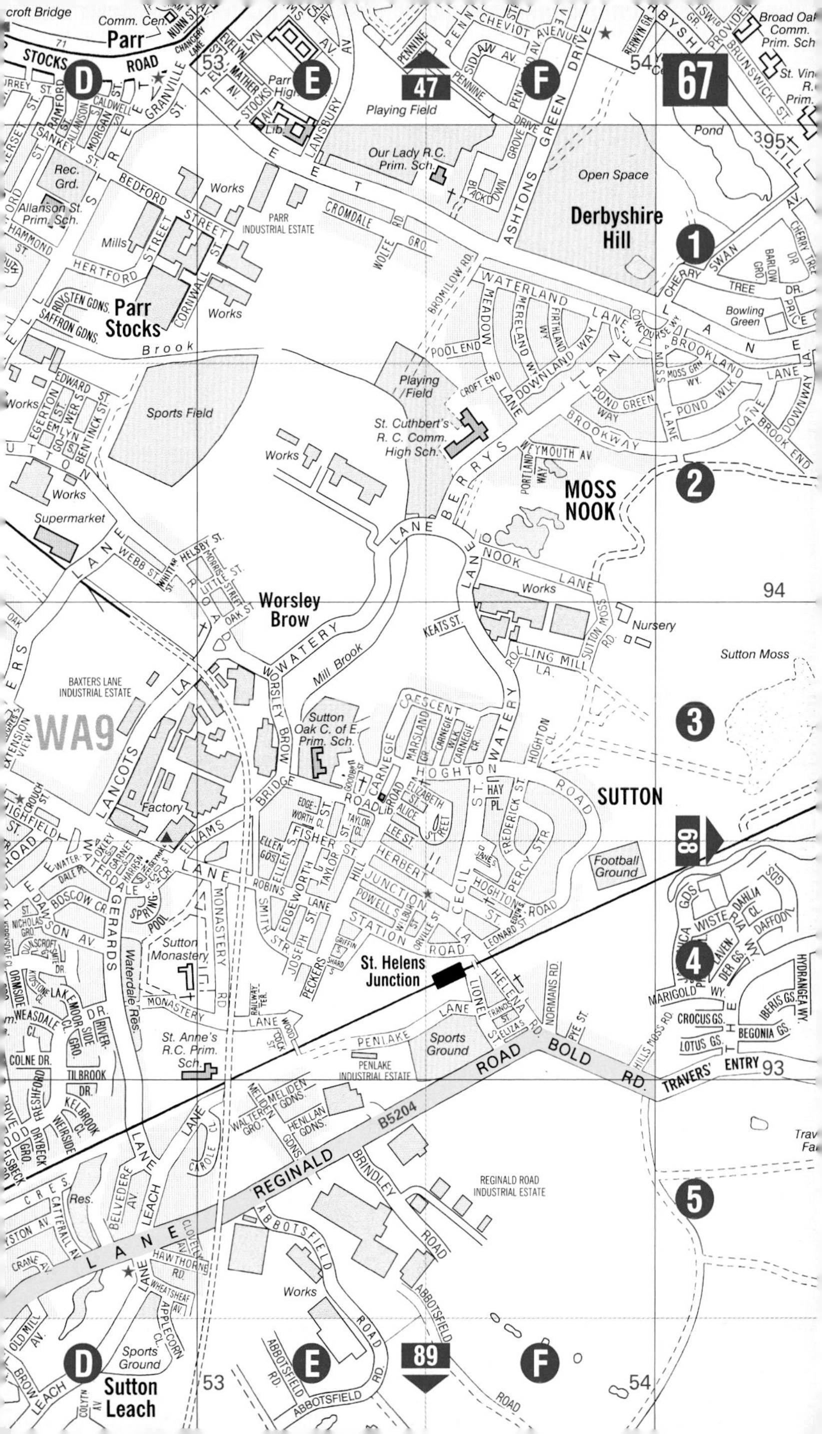

67
47
89
89
Parr
Parr Stocks
Derbyshire Hill
Moss Nook
Worsley Brow
Sutton
St. Helens Junction
Sutton Leach
WA9
Open Space
Playing Field
Our Lady R.C. Prim. Sch.
Parr Industrial Estate
St. Cuthbert's R.C. Comm. High Sch.
Sports Field
Works
Supermarket
Baxters Lane Industrial Estate
Sutton Oak C. of E. Prim. Sch.
Factory
Sutton Monastery
Waterdale Res.
St. Anne's R.C. Prim. Sch.
Sports Ground
Penlake Industrial Estate
Football Ground
Reginald Road Industrial Estate
Sutton Moss
Nursery
Bowling Green
Rec. Grd.
Allanson St. Prim. Sch.
Mills
Pond
Broad Oak Comm. Prim. Sch.
Stocks Road
Reginald Road
Bold Rd.
B5204
Travers' Entry
Berrys Lane
Watery Lane
Lancots La.
Derbyshire Hill Road
Nook Lane
Waterland Lane
Brookland Lane
Herbert St.
Junction La.
Station Road
Monastery Lane
Abbotsfield Road
Brindley Rd.
Penlake Lane
Robins Lane
Ellams Lane
Worsley Brow
Mill Brook
Brook
53
54
93
94
395
D
E
F
1
2
3
4
5

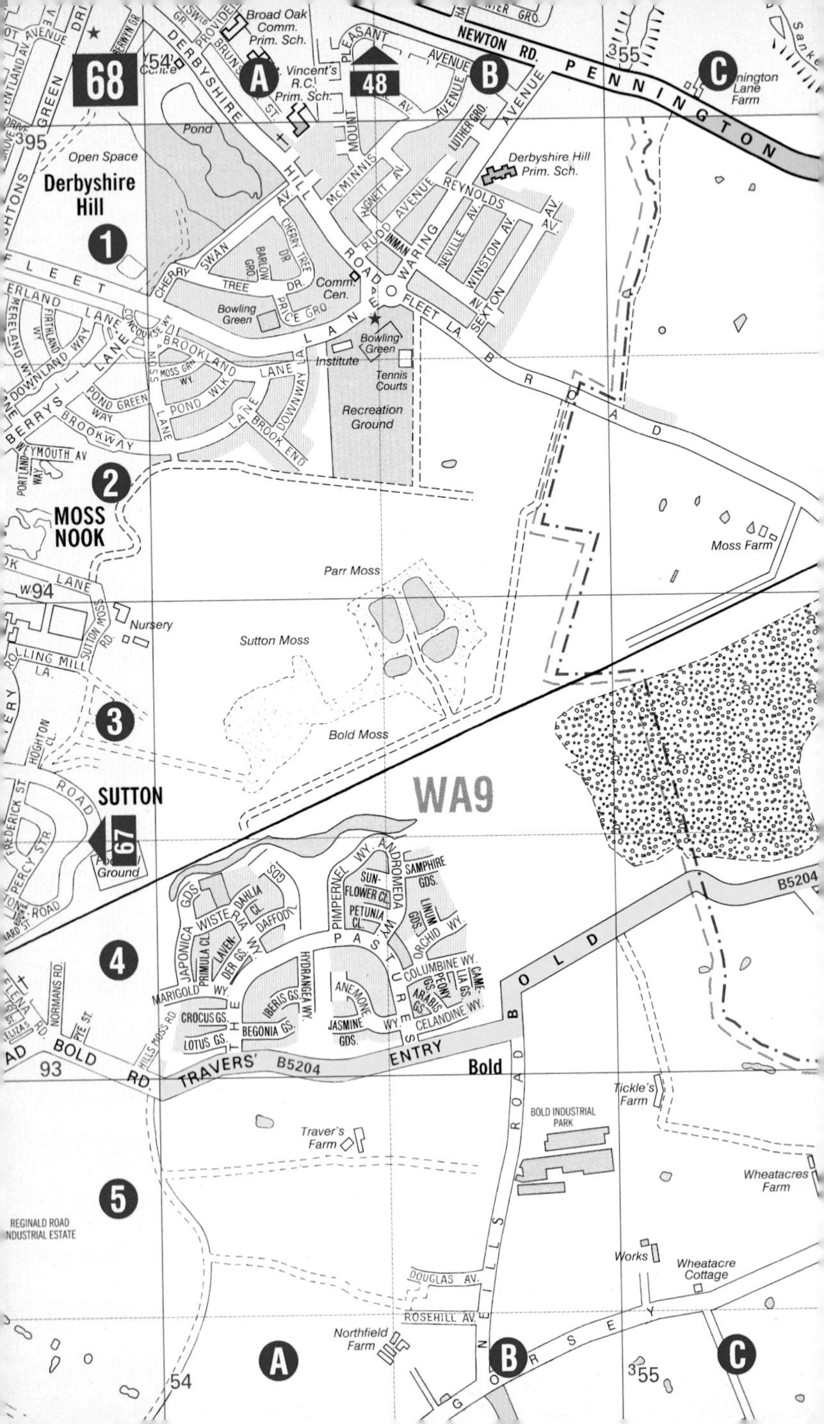

68
48
67
A
B
C
1
2
3
4
5
395
94
93
354
355
54
55
Derbyshire Hill
MOSS NOOK
SUTTON
Bold
WA9
Broad Oak Comm. Prim. Sch.
St. Vincent's R.C. Prim. Sch.
Derbyshire Hill Prim. Sch.
Pennington Lane Farm
NEWTON RD.
PENNINGTON
PLEASANT
AVENUE
MOUNT
DERBYSHIRE
HILL ROAD
PROVIDENCE
BRUNSWICK ST.
LUTHER GRO.
McMINNIS
HIGNETT AV.
RUDD AVENUE
REYNOLDS AV.
WARING AV.
INMAN
NEVILLE AV.
WINSTON AV.
SEXTON AV.
Pond
Open Space
GREEN
Y.M.C.A. Centre
FLEET LANE
FLEET LA.
BROAD
CHERRY TREE DR.
SWAN AV.
BARLOW GRO.
PRICE GRO.
Comm. Cen.
Bowling Green
Institute
Tennis Courts
Recreation Ground
ERLAND
MERELAND WY.
FIRTHLAND WY.
DOWNLAND WAY
CONCOURSE WY.
BROOKLAND LANE
MOSS GRN. WY.
MOSS LANE
POND GREEN WAY
POND WLK.
LANE
DOWNWAY LA.
BROOK END
BROOKWAY
BERRYS LANE
WEYMOUTH AV.
PORTLAND WAY
Moss Farm
Parr Moss
Sutton Moss
Bold Moss
Nursery
SUTTON MOSS RD.
ROLLING MILL LA.
HOGHTON CL.
ROAD
FREDERICK ST.
PERCY STR.
Football Ground
NORMANS RD.
PYE ST.
ELIZAS
BOLD RD.
HILLS MOSS RD.
TRAVERS' ENTRY
B5204
BOLD ROAD
JAPONICA GDS.
WISTERIA WY.
DAHLIA CL.
DAFFODIL
PRIMULA CL.
LAVENDER GS.
MARIGOLD WY.
CROCUS GS.
LOTUS GS.
BEGONIA GS.
IBERIS GS.
HYDRANGEA WY.
PIMPERNEL WY.
ANDROMEDA
SUNFLOWER CL.
PETUNIA CL.
SAMPHIRE GDS.
LINUM GDS.
ORCHID WY.
PASTURES
COLUMBINE WY.
CAMELIA GS.
PEONY GS.
ARABIS GS.
CELANDINE WY.
ANEMONE
JASMINE GDS.
Traver's Farm
Tickle's Farm
BOLD INDUSTRIAL PARK
Wheatacres Farm
REGINALD ROAD INDUSTRIAL ESTATE
NEILLS ROAD
Works
Wheatacre Cottage
DOUGLAS AV.
ROSEHILL AV.
Northfield Farm
GORSEY

69
Earlestown
49
D
E
F
56
57
95
94
93
1
2
3
4
5
WA12
WA5
Sankey Valley Park
Brook
A572
COMMON LANE
PENKFORD LANE
B5204
Penkford Bridge
PENKFORD ST.
SHORT ST.
SHORT CL.
WHARF ROAD
Sch.
Pav.
Playing Field
King George V Field
BARNETT AVENUE
LLOYD
WATKINS AV.
DINGLE AV.
EARLE ROAD
HILLSIDE AV.
LEGH
HEALD
BANK ST.
BRICK ST.
EARLE CL.
CANAL ST.
REGENT ST.
BK. LEGH ST.
Ckt. Grd.
STREET
DEACON INDUSTRIAL ESTATE
JUNCTION LA.
SANKEY VALLEY INDUSTRIAL ESTATE
SANKEY VALLEY PK.
Sankey Viaduct
Mill Farm
BRADLEY LANE
Bradley Lock
Park Brow Plantation
Bradlegh Wood
Collins Green Farm
Rose Villa
THATCHERS MOUNT
Collins Green
ALBERT TERRACE
BACK PENNY LANE
PENNY LANE
RAILWAY VW.
WINWICK VW.
COLLINS GREEN LANE
Hillside
White House Farm
Burtonwood Brewery
Yew Tree Farm
BACK LANE
FORSHAW'S LA.
PHIPPS' LANE
LUMBER LANE
Higher Farm
Works
Bradlegh Old Hall
Moat
HALL LANE
Boarded Barn Farm
Mill Farm Cottage
Derby Farm
Burtonwood Prim. Sch.
GREEN LANE
BURTONWOOD
WINSFORD DR.
BURTONWOOD INDUSTRIAL ESTATE
SUNNINGDALE CL.
SUNNINGDALE ROAD
ALDRIDGE CL.
MELROSE AVE.
MELROSE AV.
EASTWOOD RD.
CHEDDAR GRO.
BAKEWELL RD.
BAKEWELL CL.
FIR TREE LA.
Vicarage
ALDER LA.
PINEWOOD RD.
SHAFTSBURY WAY
DRI.
CAMBOURNE
ARNCLIFFE DR.
EPWORTH CL.
ROXBORO' CL.
ROAD
COLNE RD.
KAREN CL.
BROOKVALE CL.
DORCHESTER WY.
ARUNDEL CL.
WEYMOUTH WY.
EXMOUTH WY.
SHERBOURNE WY.
WARRINGTON
ST. HELENS
Haley Head Farm
Phipps' Bridge
Government Offices
Phipps' Brook
CHAPEL LANE
KINNOCK PK.
Recreation Ground
CLAY LANE
MERCER ST.
FAIRCLOUGH ST.
JACKSON ST.
MILNTHORPE RD.
Prim. Sch.
SHERWOOD CRES.
Lib.
Cemy.
SEDGEWICK CR.
WEBB DR.
NORCOTT DR.
KILSHAW RD.
PERRINS RD.
KNIGHT RD.
HERBERT ST.
HAWKSHEAD ROAD
ALMOND DRI.
SPURLING RD.
GLEAVE CL.
GREEN JONES BROW
Green Jones Br.
Community Centre
BARN LA.
Primrose Hill Farm
FARMER'S LA.
Tan House Farm
TAN HOUSE LA.
Lymedene
ACTON RD.
ROAD NORTH
GRIFFIN CL.
HALEY RD.
MITCHELL AV.
SOUTH
Ashton's Farm
Clay Lane Farm
Old Lodge Farm

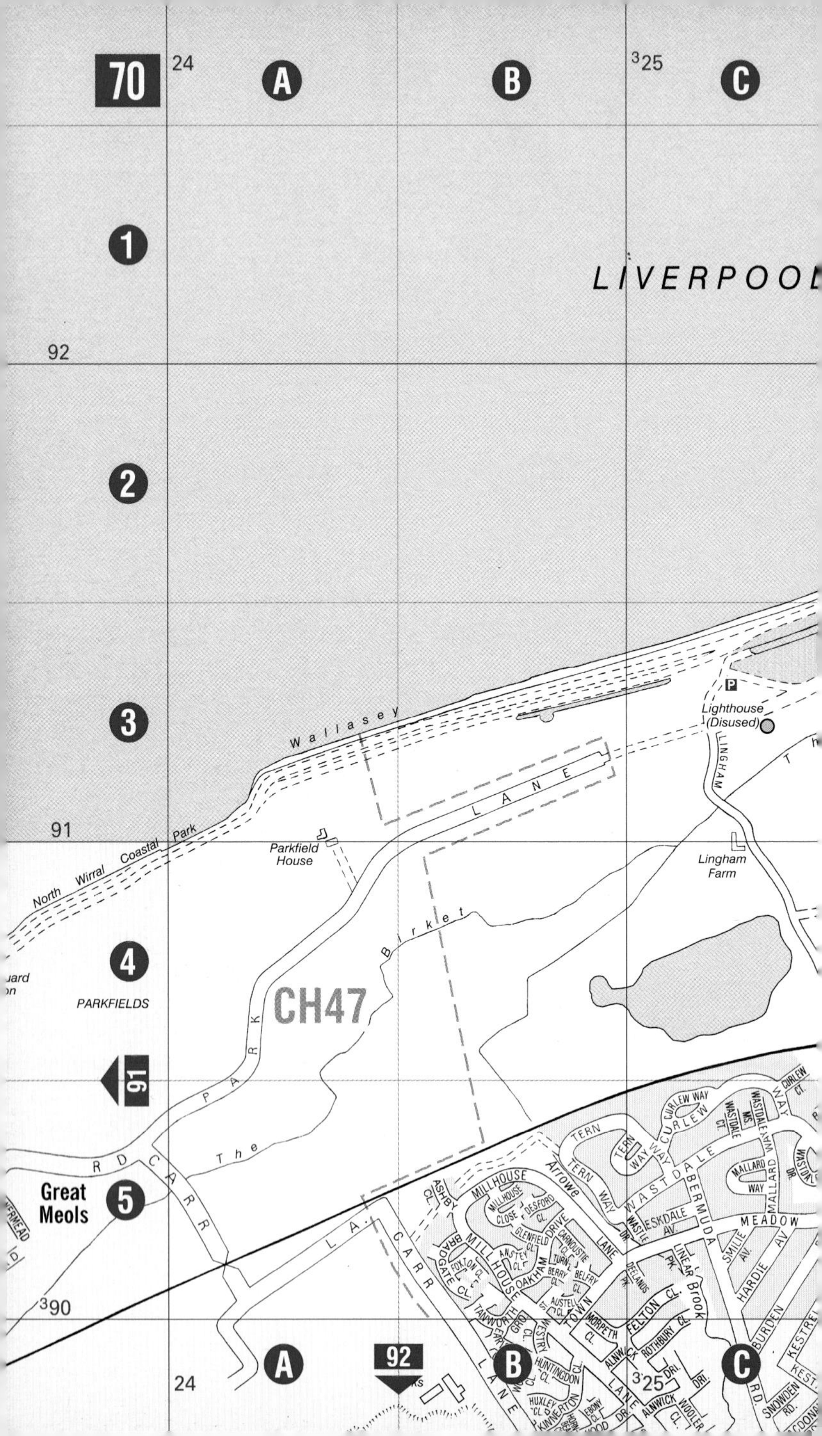

24
A
B
325
C
1
LIVERPOOL
92
2
3
Wallasey
LANE
Lighthouse (Disused)
LINGHAM
91
North Wirral Coastal Park
Parkfield House
Lingham Farm
Birket
4
PARKFIELDS
CH47
PARK
91
The
RD
CARR
Great Meols
5
LA.
CARR
MILLHOUSE
Arrowe
TERN
TERN WAY
CURLEW WAY
WASTDALE
BERMUDA
MEADOW
MALLARD
ESKDALE AV.
SMILIE AV.
HARDIE AV.
BURDEN
OAKHAM
TOWN
MORPETH CL.
FELTON CL.
ROTHBURY CL.
Brook
390
A
92
B
24
325
C
ALNWICK
LANE

BAY
Club House
LEASOWE GOLF COURSE
Leasowe
Leasowe Castle
Moreton Common
Coastal Park
Wirral Christian Cen.
Rugby Football Grounds
Playing Fields
Castleway Prim. Sch.
Rec. Grd.
CH46
Playing Field
Birket
Works
Factory
Golf Driving Range
Pasture Rd. Bridge
Moreton
Eastway Prim. Sch.
Prim. Sch.
Clare Mount School
Fender Farm
Lingham Prim. Sch.
Running Track
Comm. Cen.
Lib.
Wimbrick Hey Assess. Unit
LEASOWE ROAD
A551
PASTURE ROAD
A553
HOYLAKE ROAD
PASTURE AVENUE
DITTON LANE
FENDER LANE
BIRKET AVENUE
TWICKENHAM DR.
BLACKHEATH DR.
MORETON

72
93

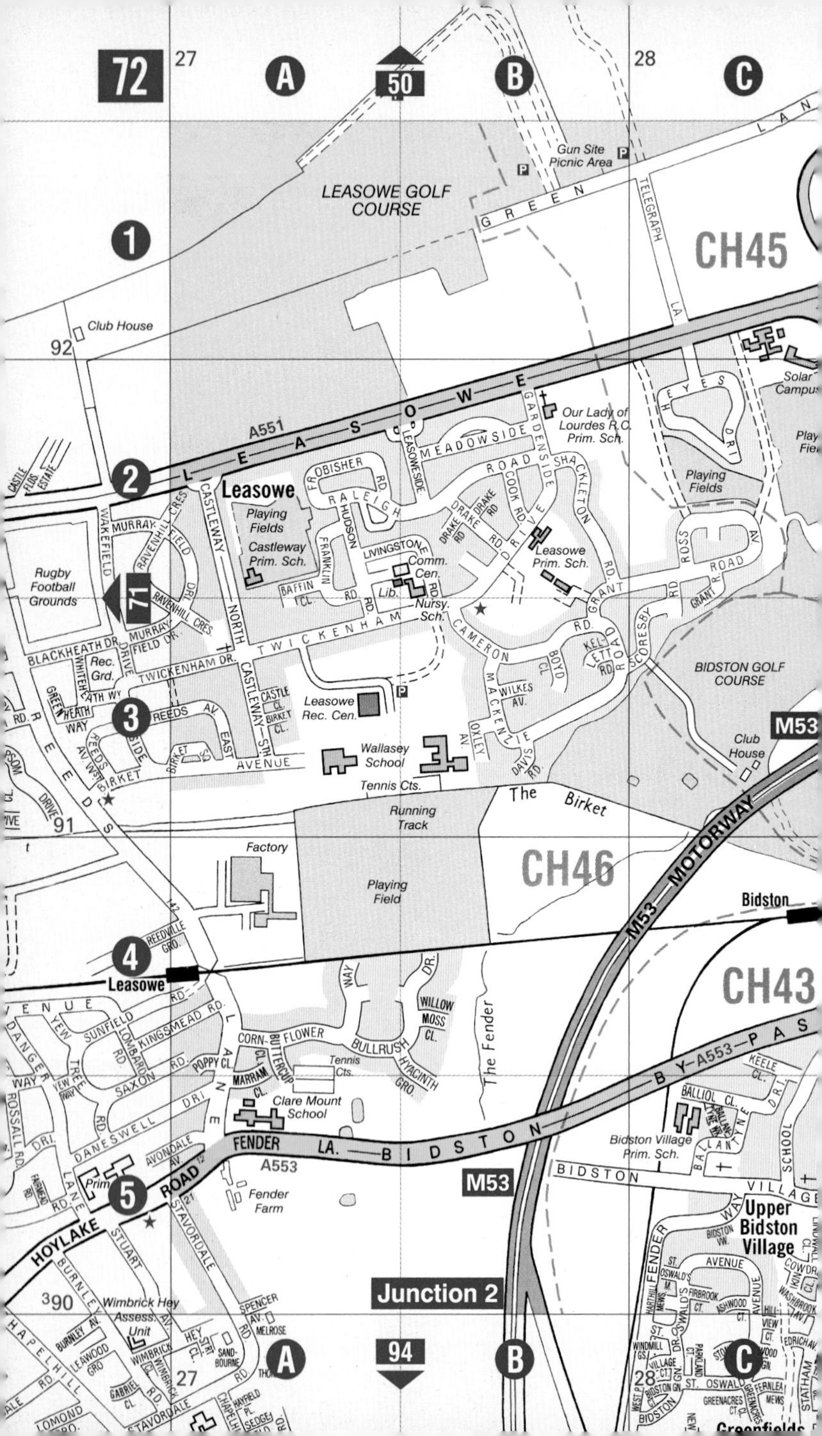
LEASOWE GOLF COURSE
Gun Site Picnic Area
Club House
Leasowe
Playing Fields
Castleway Prim. Sch.
Rugby Football Grounds
Our Lady of Lourdes R.C. Prim. Sch.
Playing Fields
Solar Campus
Comm. Cen.
Lib.
Nursy. Sch.
Leasowe Prim. Sch.
Rec. Grd.
Leasowe Rec. Cen.
Wallasey School
Tennis Cts.
Running Track
The Birket
BIDSTON GOLF COURSE
Club House
Factory
Playing Field
CH45
CH46
CH43
Bidston
Leasowe
M53 MOTORWAY
The Fender
Clare Mount School
Tennis Cts.
Fender Farm
Bidston Village Prim. Sch.
Upper Bidston Village
Wimbrick Hey Assess. Unit
Junction 2
A551
A553
LEASOWE
BIDSTON BY-PASS
HOYLAKE ROAD
FENDER LA.
Greenfields

50
71
94

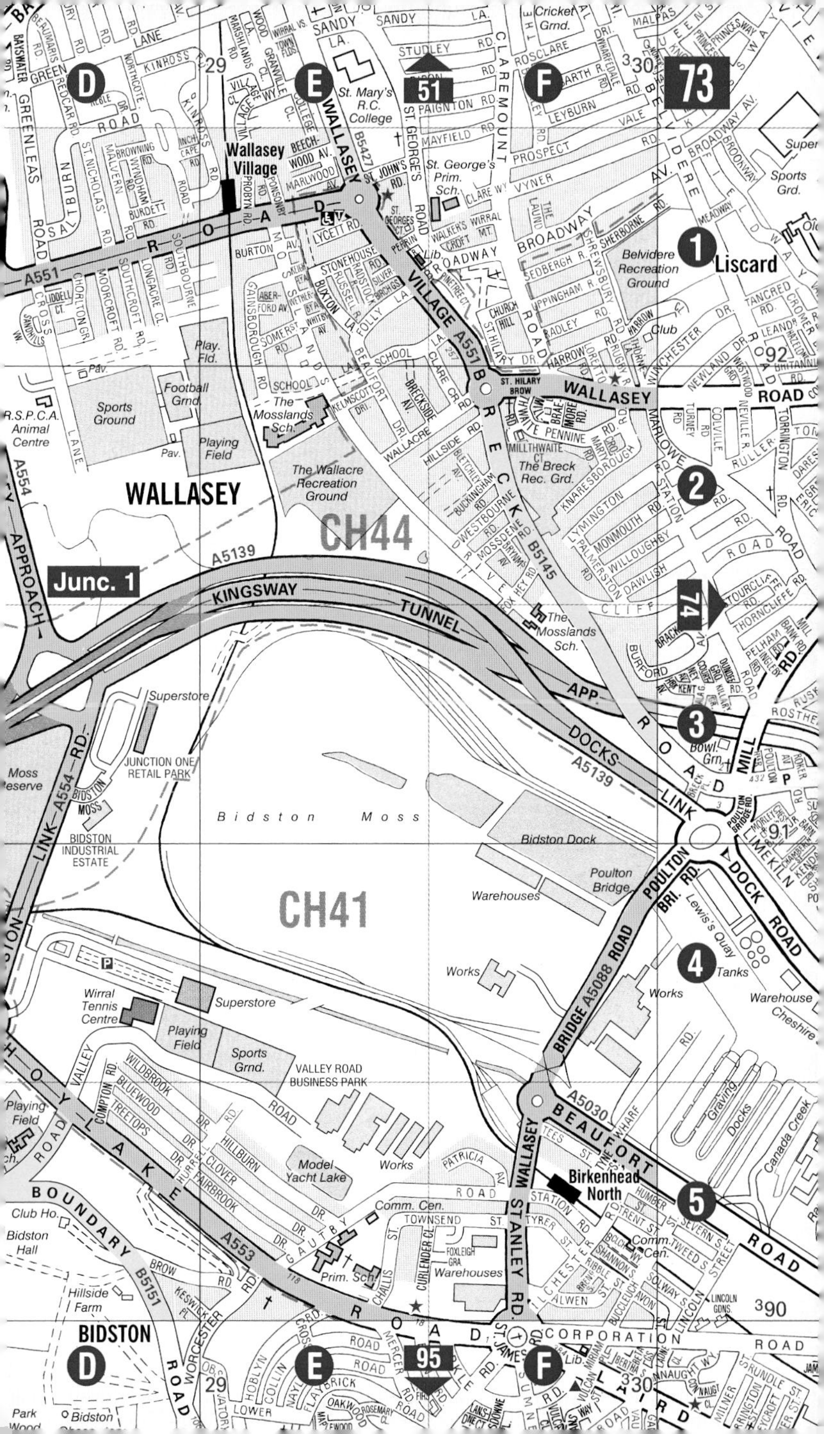
73
51
74
95
D
E
F
1
2
3
4
5
29
330
390
Wallasey Village
Liscard
WALLASEY
BIDSTON
CH44
CH41
Junc. 1
St. Mary's R.C. College
St. George's Prim. Sch.
Belvidere Recreation Ground
Sports Grd.
Club
R.S.P.C.A. Animal Centre
Sports Ground
Football Grnd.
Play. Fld.
Playing Field
Pav.
The Mosslands Sch.
The Wallacre Recreation Ground
The Breck Rec. Grd.
KINGSWAY
TUNNEL
APP.
DOCKS
LINK
A5139
A551
A554
A553
A5088
A5030
B5427
B5145
B5151
Superstore
JUNCTION ONE RETAIL PARK
Moss Reserve
BIDSTON INDUSTRIAL ESTATE
Bidston Moss
Bidston Dock
Poulton Bridge
Warehouses
Works
Lewis's Quay
Tanks
Warehouse
Cheshire
Graving Docks
Canada Creek
Wirral Tennis Centre
Playing Field
Sports Grnd.
VALLEY ROAD BUSINESS PARK
Model Yacht Lake
Comm. Cen.
Prim. Sch.
Birkenhead North
Club Ho.
Bidston Hall
Hillside Farm
Park Wood
Bow. Grn.
Cricket Grnd.
WALLASEY ROAD
WALLASEY VILLAGE
BRECK ROAD
ST. HILARY BROW
CLAREMOUNT ROAD
BROADWAY
BROADWAY AV.
BELVIDERE ROAD
LINK A554 RD.
BIDSTON MOSS
APPROACH
BIDSTON LINK
POULTON BRIDGE ROAD
DOCK ROAD
BEAUFORT ROAD
WALLASEY BRIDGE ROAD
STANLEY RD.
HOYLAKE ROAD
BOUNDARY ROAD
VALLEY ROAD
CORPORATION ROAD
STATION RD
TOWNSEND ST.
GAUTBY
PATRICIA AV
SANDY LA.
STUDLEY RD.
PAIGNTON RD.
MAYFIELD RD.
PROSPECT VALE
VYNER
LEYBURN
ROSCLARE
MALPAS
KINROSS
GREENLEAS
SALTBURN ROAD
ST. NICHOLAS RD.
MALVERN RD.
BURDETT RD.
LONGACRE CL.
SOUTHCROFT RD.
MOORCROFT RD.
CHORLTON GR.
SOUTHBOURNE
BURTON AV.
GAINSBOROUGH RD.
LYCETT RD.
MOSSLANDS
STONEHOUSE
BUXTON LA.
FOLLY LA.
SCHOOL LA.
BEAUFORT DRI.
BRECKSIDE AV.
CLARE CR.
WALLACRE DRI.
HILLSIDE RD.
BUCKINGHAM
WESTBOURNE RD.
MOSSDENE RD.
FOX HEY RD.
PENNINE
MILLTHWAITE CT.
KNARESBOROUGH
LYMINGTON
MONMOUTH RD.
WILLOUGHBY
PALMERSTON
DAWLISH
STATION RD.
MARLOWE
TURNEY RD.
COLVILLE RD.
NEVILLE R.
TORRINGTON
RULLER
CLIFF
TOURCLIFFE
THORNCLIFFE RD.
BURFORD
PELHAM
INGLEBY
MILL RD.
ROSTHER
POULTON
LIMEKILN
WINCHESTER DR.
NEWLAND DR.
TANCRED RD.
HARROW
SHREWSBURY
SEDBERGH R.
SHERBORNE
UPPINGHAM R.
RADLEY
CHURCH HILL
ST. HILARY DR.
WILDBROOK
BLUEWOOD
TREETOPS
COMPTON RD.
HILLBURN
CLOVER
FAIRBROOK
DR.
BROW
KESWICK PL.
WORCESTER
ST. JAMES RD.
LAIRD
CHALLIS ST.
CURLENDER CL.
TEES ST.
TYNE ST.
HUMBER
TRENT ST.
TWEED S
SEVERN S
SOLWAY S
AVON
BUCCLEUCH
RIBBLE
SHANNON S
ILCHESTER
ALWEN
LINCOLN GDNS.
WHARF
HOBLYN
COLLIN
FLAYBRICK
OAKWOOD
ROSEMARY
MERCER
LOWER
Lib.

A
B
C
52
73
91
96
1
2
3
4
5
CH45
CH44
CH41
Liscard
Poulton
Wallasey
Birkenhead North
Cricket Grnd.
Superstore
Sports Grd.
Cricket Grd.
Rec. Grd.
Play. Field
Liscard Prim. Sch.
Westbourne Sch.
The Oldershaw Sch.
Belvidere Recreation Ground
Club
The Breck Rec. Grd.
The Mosslands Sch.
Victoria Central Hospital
Park Prim. Sch.
Cricket Ground
Football Ground
Central Park
Bowling Greens
Recreation Ground
Bowl. Grn.
Neighbourhood Resource Centre
Nursy. Sch.
Poulton Bridge
Bidston Dock
Lewis's Quay
Tanks
Warehouse
Cheshire's Quay
Works
Gas Works
Victoria Park
Uveco Bus. Cen.
Sheds
Gallagher Ind. Est.
Wirral Business Centre
Graving Docks
Canada Creek
West Float
Rank's Creek
Gillbrook Basin
Cavendish Wharf
Duke St. Wharf
Jetty
Comm. Cen.
Lib.
Odyssey Centre
A551
A5088
A5027
A5139
A5030
B5143
B5142
B5145
Broadway
Broadway Av.
Belvidere Rd.
Kingsway
Seaview Rd.
Seabank Rd.
Rake La.
Manor Rd.
Manor La.
Liscard Village
Liscard Rd.
Liscard Cr.
Wallasey Rd.
Mill La.
Woodstock Rd.
Oxton Rd.
Poulton Rd.
Gorsey La.
Breck Rd.
Docks Link
Dock Rd.
Poulton Bridge Rd.
Bridge Rd.
Beaufort Rd.
Tunnel Approach
Gorsedale Rd.
Wallasey Bridge Rd.
Duke St.
Corporation Rd.
Cleveland St.
Laird St.
Stanley Rd.
Claremount Rd.
Cliff Rd.
Lowe Rd.
Torrington Rd.
Grosvenor St.
Central Park Av.
Canterbury Rd.
Hampstead Rd.
Serpentine Rd.
Oxford Rd.
Trafalgar Rd.

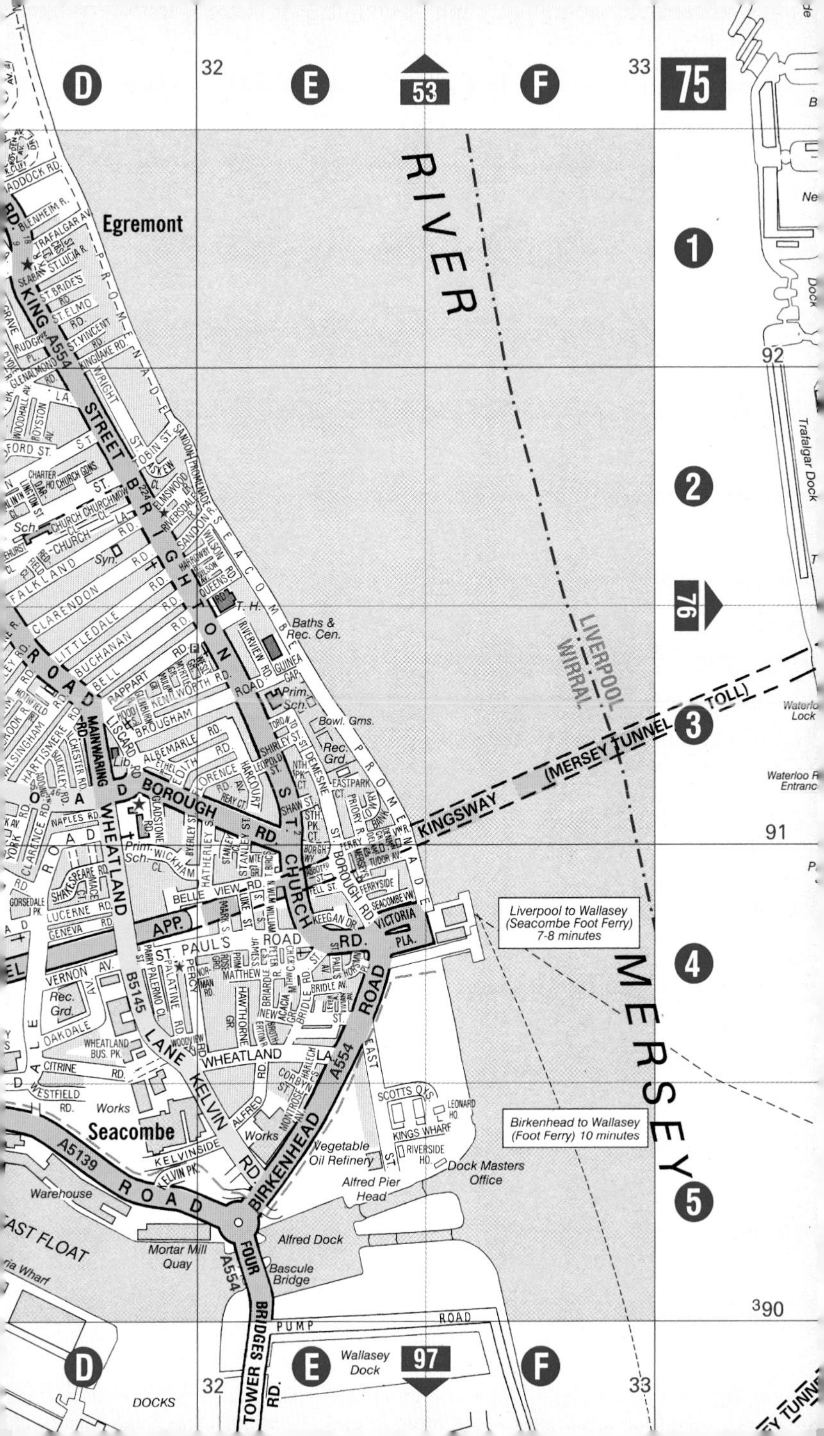
75
D
E
F
32
33
53
97
76
1
2
3
4
5
92
91
390
RIVER
MERSEY
Egremont
Seacombe
LIVERPOOL
WIRRAL
KINGSWAY (MERSEY TUNNEL TOLL)
Liverpool to Wallasey
(Seacombe Foot Ferry)
7-8 minutes
Birkenhead to Wallasey
(Foot Ferry) 10 minutes
KING STREET
A554
BRIGHTON ST.
SEACOMBE PROMENADE
BOROUGH RD.
WHEATLAND LANE
B5145
KELVIN RD.
BIRKENHEAD ROAD
A5139 ROAD
FOUR BRIDGES
TOWER BRIDGES RD.
ST. PAUL'S ROAD
VICTORIA PLA.
CHURCH RD.
LISCARD RD.
MAINWARING RD.
BELLE VIEW RD.
GENEVA RD.
LUCERNE RD.
VERNON AV.
OAKDALE
CITRINE RD.
WESTFIELD RD.
KELVINSIDE
KELVIN PK.
ALFRED RD.
CORBYN ST.
MONTROSE AV.
HAWTHORNE GR.
BRIDLE RD.
SCOTTS QYS.
KINGS WHARF
RIVERSIDE HO.
LEONARD HO.
EAST ST.
Baths &
Rec. Cen.
Bowl. Grns.
Rec. Grd.
Prim. Sch.
Lib.
Syn.
Sch.
T. H.
Works
Warehouse
Vegetable
Oil Refinery
Dock Masters
Office
Alfred Pier
Head
Alfred Dock
Mortar Mill
Quay
Bascule
Bridge
Wallasey
Dock
PUMP ROAD
EAST FLOAT
DOCKS
WHEATLAND BUS. PK.
Trafalgar Dock
Waterloo
Lock
Waterloo
Entranc
FALKLAND
CLARENDON
LITTLEDALE
BUCHANAN
BELL
BROUGHAM
ALBEMARLE RD.
KENILWORTH RD.
RIVERVIEW RD.
GUINEA GAP
EASTPARK CT.
FERRYSIDE
SEACOMBE VW.
KEEGAN DR.
SHAKESPEARE RD.
NAPLES RD.
GLADSTONE RD.
WICKHAM CL.
HATHERLEY ST.
STANLEY ST.
TRAFALGAR AV.
BLENHEIM R.
ST. VINCENT RD.
KINGLAKE RD.
WRIGHT ST.
TOBIN ST.
SANDON PROMENADE
ELMSWOOD
RIVERSDALE R.
CHURCH GDNS.
ROYSTON AV.
GORSEDALE PK.
PALATINE RD.
PALERMO CL.
PERCY

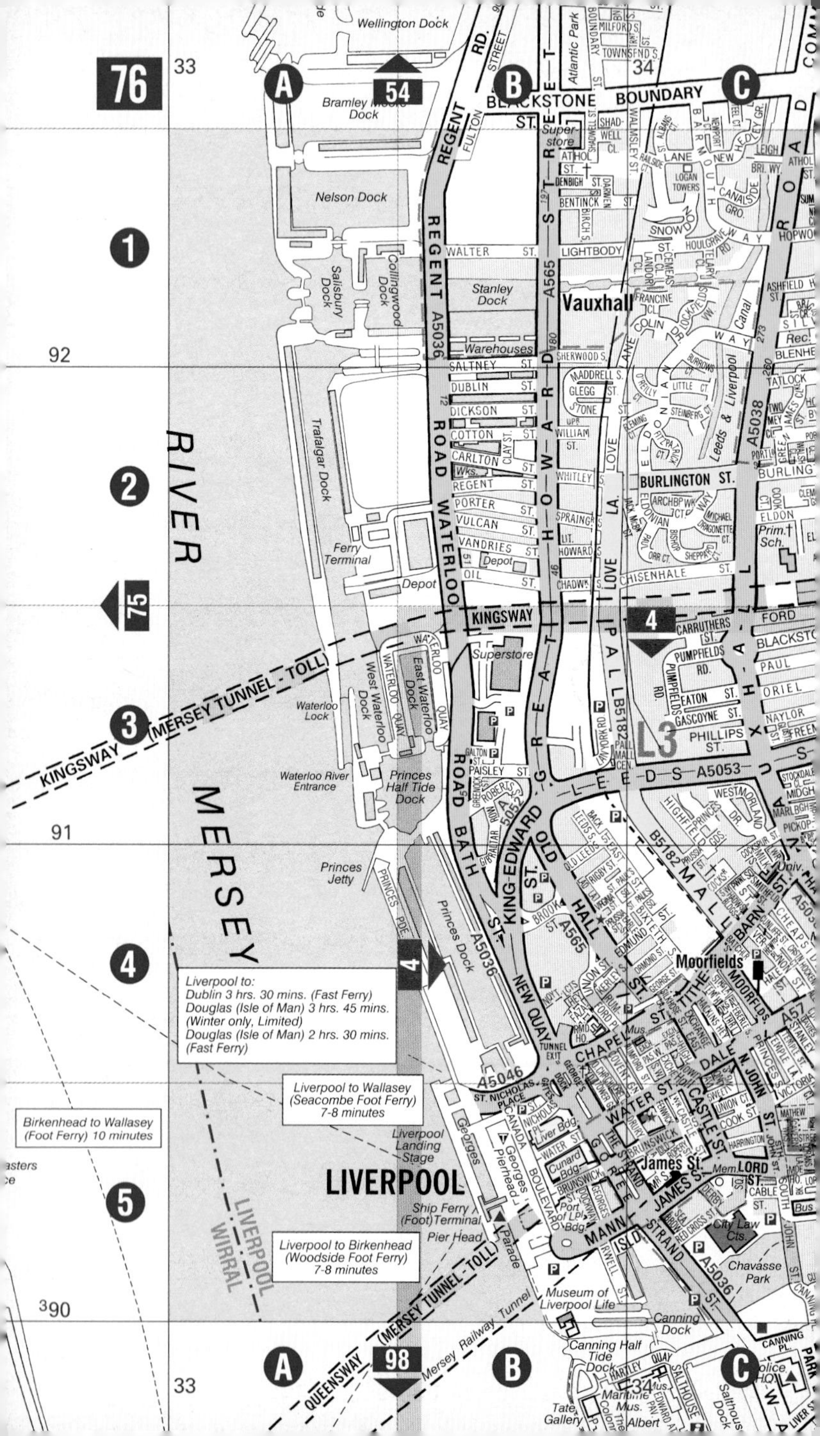

Wellington Dock
54
Bramley Moore Dock
Nelson Dock
Salisbury Dock
Collingwood Dock
Stanley Dock
Warehouses
Trafalgar Dock
Ferry Terminal
Depot
RIVER MERSEY
75
KINGSWAY (MERSEY TUNNEL - TOLL)
Waterloo Lock
West Waterloo Dock
East Waterloo Dock
Waterloo River Entrance
Princes Half Tide Dock
Princes Jetty
Princes Dock
Liverpool to:
Dublin 3 hrs. 30 mins. (Fast Ferry)
Douglas (Isle of Man) 3 hrs. 45 mins. (Winter only, Limited)
Douglas (Isle of Man) 2 hrs. 30 mins. (Fast Ferry)
Liverpool to Wallasey (Seacombe Foot Ferry) 7-8 minutes
Birkenhead to Wallasey (Foot Ferry) 10 minutes
Liverpool Landing Stage
LIVERPOOL
Ship Ferry (Foot) Terminal
Pier Head
Liverpool to Birkenhead (Woodside Foot Ferry) 7-8 minutes
LIVERPOOL
WIRRAL
QUEENSWAY (MERSEY TUNNEL - TOLL)
Mersey Railway Tunnel
98
REGENT RD.
REGENT ROAD A5036
WATERLOO ROAD
BATH ROAD
BLACKSTONE ST.
BOUNDARY
GREAT HOWARD STREET A565
Vauxhall
Atlantic Park
KINGSWAY
Superstore
LOVE LA.
BURLINGTON ST.
Leeds & Liverpool Canal
A5038
PALL MALL B5182
L3
LEEDS ST. A5053
KING EDWARD ST.
OLD HALL ST.
NEW QUAY
A5046
CHAPEL ST.
TITHEBARN ST.
Moorfields
DALE ST.
WATER ST.
CASTLE ST.
NORTH JOHN ST.
James St.
LORD ST.
CANADA BOULEVARD
Georges Pierhead
STRAND
A5036
City Law Cts.
Chavasse Park
Museum of Liverpool Life
Canning Dock
Canning Half Tide Dock
Salthouse Dock
Tate Gallery
Maritime Mus.
Albert
Police H.Q.
A
B
C
1
2
3
4
5
33
34
92
91
390

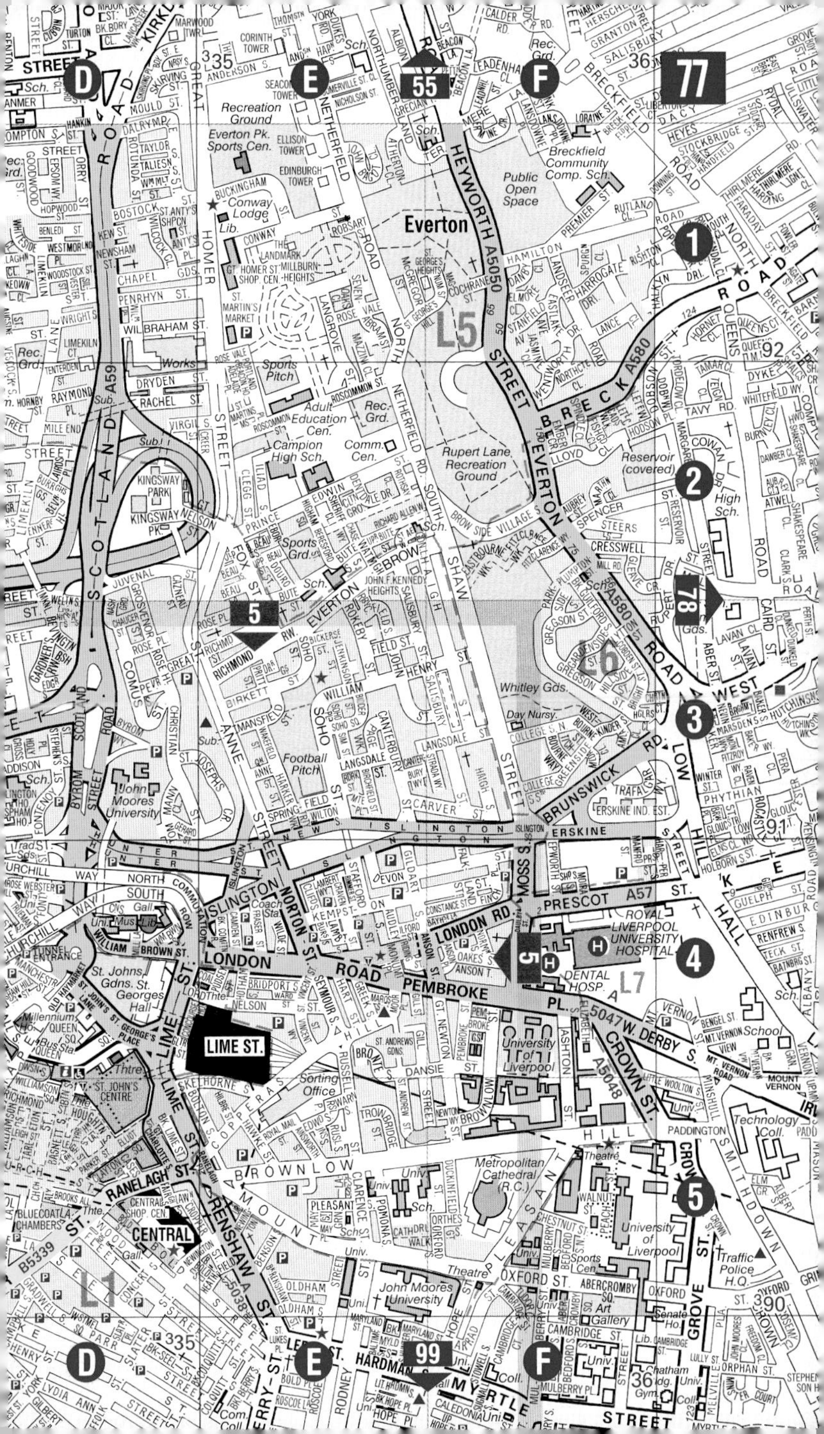
D
E
F
55
Everton
L5
L6
L7
L1
5
78
99
1
2
3
4
5
Recreation Ground
Everton Pk. Sports Cen.
Conway Lodge
Breckfield Community Comp. Sch.
Public Open Space
HEYWORTH A5050
NETHERFIELD
GREAT HOMER STREET
SCOTLAND ROAD A59
Rupert Lane Recreation Ground
Reservoir (covered)
High Sch.
Sports Pitch
Adult Education Cen.
Campion High Sch.
Comm. Cen.
KINGSWAY PARK
BRECK A580
EVERTON
SHAW
Sports Grd.
JOHN F. KENNEDY HEIGHTS
Whitley Gds.
Day Nursy.
Football Pitch
John Moores University
ERSKINE IND. EST.
BRUNSWICK RD.
NEW ISLINGTON
PRESCOT A57 ST.
ROYAL LIVERPOOL UNIVERSITY HOSPITAL
DENTAL HOSP.
LONDON ROAD
PEMBROKE PL.
W. DERBY S.
CROWN ST.
University of Liverpool
LIME ST.
St. Johns Gdns.
St. Georges Hall
Bus Sta.
ST. JOHN'S CENTRE
Sorting Office
Metropolitan Cathedral (R.C.)
Technology Coll.
MOUNT VERNON
BROWNLOW
MOUNT PLEASANT
RANELAGH ST.
CENTRAL
CENTRAL SHOP. CEN.
RENSHAW ST.
BLUECOAT CHAMBERS
Traffic Police H.Q.
OXFORD ST.
Art Gallery
Senate Ho.
HARDMAN ST.
MYRTLE STREET
Chatham Bldg.

78
56
77
100
A
B
C
1
2
3
4
5
L5
L6
L7
Cabbage Hall
Breckfield Community Comp. Sch.
Public Open Space
St. Margaret's C.of E. Jun. & Inf. Schs.
Newsham Ho.
THE MALL
Jun. & Inf. Sch.
Rec. Grd.
Reservoir (covered)
High Sch.
Factory
St. Michael's R.C. Prim. Sch.
Grant Gds.
Whitley Gds.
Day Nursy.
ERSKINE IND. EST.
Kensington
Resr. (covered)
Kensington Gdns.
Bowling Greens
Lib.
Cemy.
ROYAL LIVERPOOL UNIVERSITY HOSPITAL
DENTAL HOSP.
University of Liverpool
Technology Coll.
School
Theatre
Traffic Police H.Q.
Sports Cen.
Art Gallery
Edge Hill
WAVERTREE SHOPPING CENTRE
Edge Hill
Depots
Botanic Garden
Comm. Cen.
Schs.
BELMONT ROAD
A5089 ROAD
ROCKY
BRECK ROAD
WEST DERBY ROAD
A5049
A580
EVERTON
LOW HILL
KENSINGTON
A57
PRESCOT ST.
BRUNSWICK RD.
HALL LANE
B5340
W. DERBY S.
EDGE LANE
A5047
MOUNT VERNON
IRVINE ST.
CROWN ST.
A5048
SMITHDOWN
WAVERTREE
DURNING ROAD
HOLT ROAD
B5173
B5178
SHEIL ROAD
B5188
GARDNER
HAMPSTEAD
MOLYNEUX
OXFORD ST.
ABERCROMBY SQ.
CAMBRIDGE ST.
MULBERRY
90
91
92
36
37
50

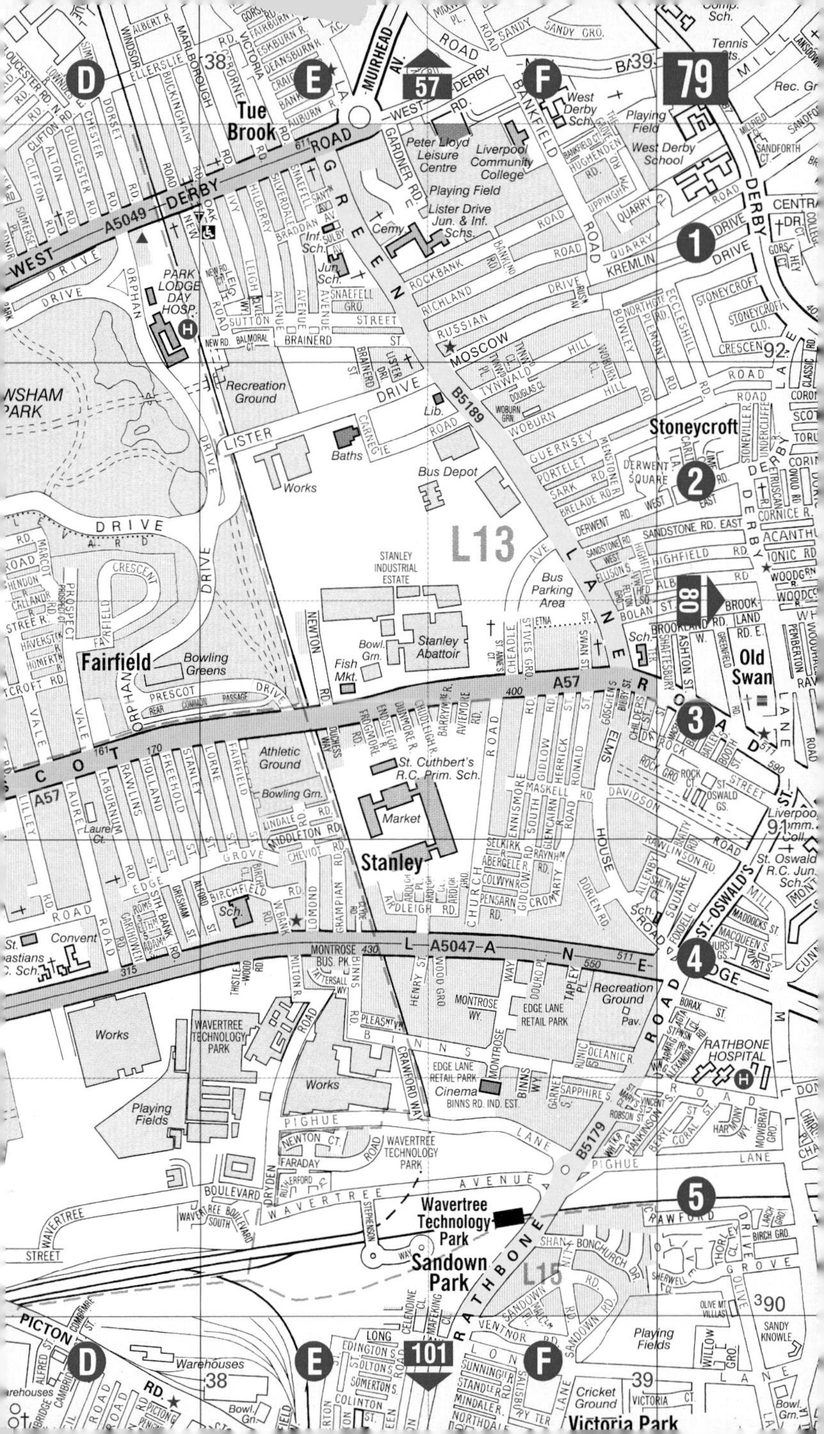

79
57
80
101
D
E
F
D
E
F
1
2
3
4
5
38
39
Tue Brook
WEST DERBY ROAD
A5049
GREEN LANE
B5189
Peter Lloyd Leisure Centre
Liverpool Community College
Playing Field
Lister Drive Jun. & Inf. Schs.
Cemy.
West Derby Sch.
West Derby School
Playing Field
PARK LODGE DAY HOSP.
Recreation Ground
LISTER DRIVE
Baths
Lib.
Works
Bus Depot
L13
STANLEY INDUSTRIAL ESTATE
Bus Parking Area
Stanley Abattoir
Bowl. Grn.
Fish Mkt.
Stoneycroft
Old Swan
Fairfield
Bowling Greens
PRESCOT DRIVE
PRESCOT ROAD
A57
Athletic Ground
Bowling Grn.
St. Cuthbert's R.C. Prim. Sch.
Market
Stanley
Laurel Ct.
Convent
St. Sebastians R.C. Sch.
EDGE LANE
A5047
MONTROSE BUS. PK
MONTROSE WY.
EDGE LANE RETAIL PARK
Recreation Ground
Pav.
RATHBONE HOSPITAL
St. Oswald R.C. Jun. Sch.
ST. OSWALD'S ST.
Works
WAVERTREE TECHNOLOGY PARK
Works
Playing Fields
Cinema
BINNS RD. IND. EST.
PIGHUE LANE
B5179
WAVERTREE AVENUE
BOULEVARD
Wavertree Technology Park
Sandown Park
RATHBONE ROAD
L15
Playing Fields
Cricket Ground
Victoria Park
Warehouses
PICTON RD.
Bowl. Grn.

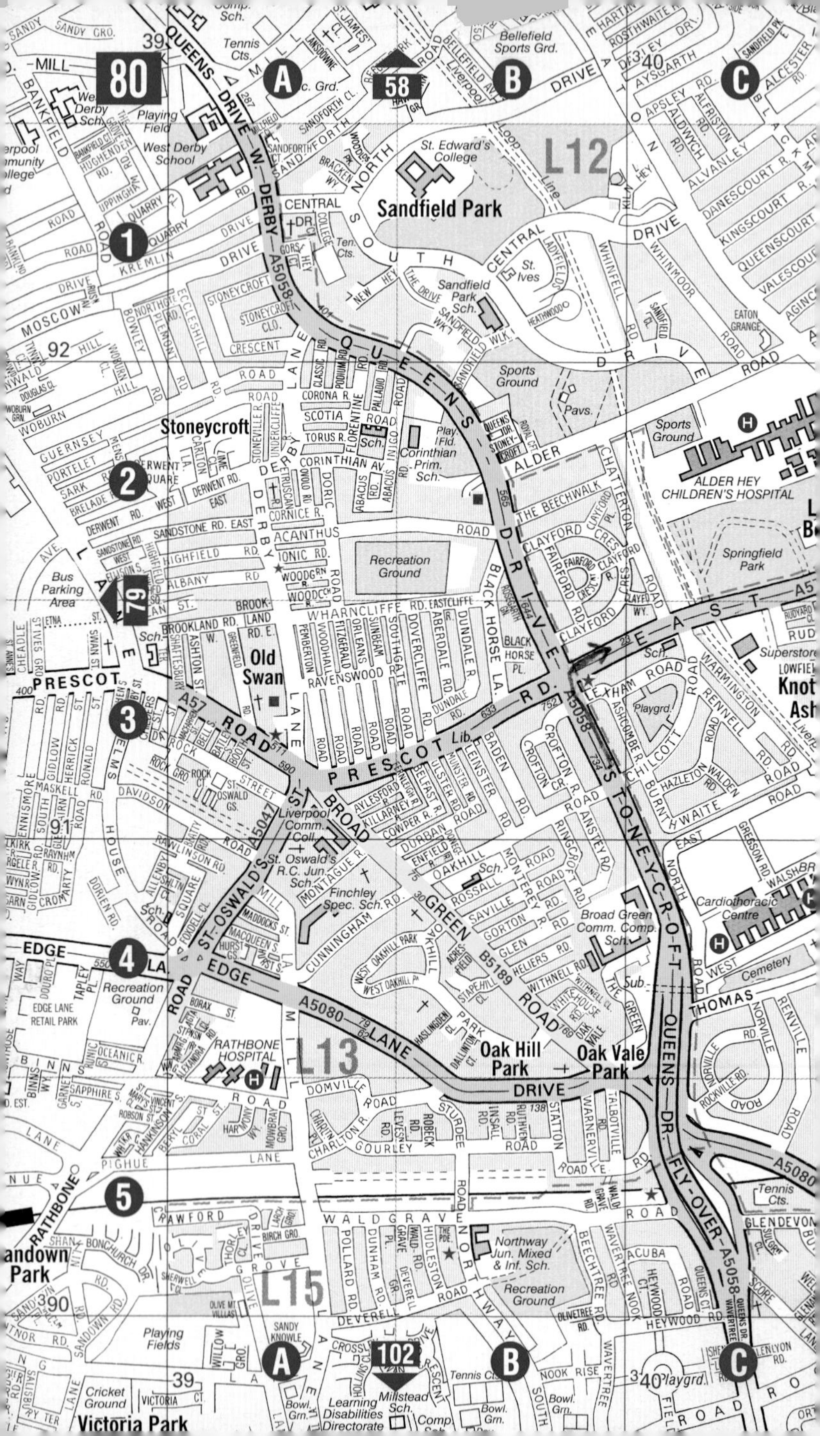

80
58
79
102
A
B
C
1
2
3
4
5
39
40
92
91
90
L12
L13
L15
Sandfield Park
St. Edward's College
West Derby School
West Derby Sch.
Playing Field
Bellefield Sports Grd.
Tennis Cts.
Sandfield Park Sch.
St. Ives
Sports Ground
Pavs.
ALDER HEY CHILDREN'S HOSPITAL
Springfield Park
Stoneycroft
Old Swan
Recreation Ground
Corinthian Prim. Sch.
Bus Parking Area
Liverpool Comm. Coll.
St. Oswald's R.C. Jun. Sch.
Finchley Spec. Sch.
Broad Green Comm. Comp. Sch.
Cardiothoracic Centre
Cemetery
Oak Hill Park
Oak Vale Park
RATHBONE HOSPITAL
EDGE LANE RETAIL PARK
Northway Jun. Mixed & Inf. Sch.
Sandown Park
Playing Fields
Cricket Ground
Victoria Park
Learning Disabilities Directorate
Millstead Sch.
Knotty Ash
Superstore
QUEENS DRIVE
WEST DERBY A5058
PRESCOT ROAD
A57
EAST PRESCOT RD.
STONEYCROFT
QUEENS DR. FLY-OVER A5058
EDGE LANE
A5080
DRIVE
BROAD GREEN ROAD
B5189
ST. OSWALD'S ST.
A5047
DERBY LANE
BLACK HORSE LA.
ALDER ROAD
MILL LANE
WALDGRAVE ROAD
NORTHWAY
THOMAS LANE
RATHBONE ROAD

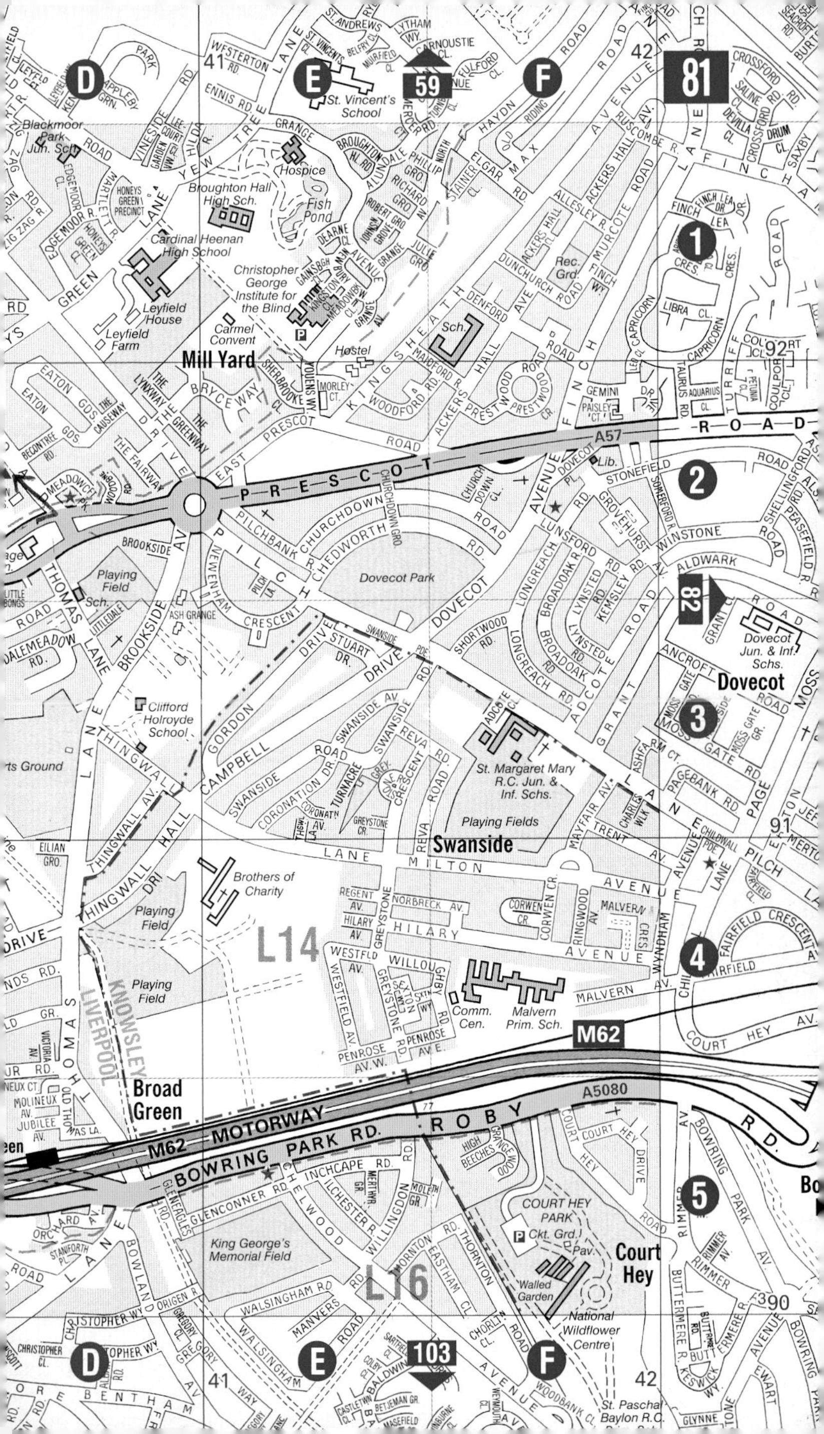

81
59
82
103
D
E
F
1
2
3
4
5
41
42
91
92
390
St. Vincent's School
Hospice
Broughton Hall High Sch.
Fish Pond
Cardinal Heenan High School
Christopher George Institute for the Blind
Leyfield House
Leyfield Farm
Carmel Convent
Mill Yard
Hostel
Blackmoor Park Jun. Sch.
Rec. Grd.
Sch.
Lib.
Dovecot Park
Playing Field
Dovecot Jun. & Inf. Schs.
Dovecot
Clifford Holroyde School
St. Margaret Mary R.C. Jun. & Inf. Schs.
Playing Fields
Swanside
Brothers of Charity
L14
Comm. Cen.
Malvern Prim. Sch.
M62
A57
A5080
Broad Green
LIVERPOOL
KNOWSLEY
M62 MOTORWAY
BOWRING PARK RD.
ROBY RD.
King George's Memorial Field
L16
COURT HEY PARK
Ckt. Grd.
Pav.
Court Hey
Walled Garden
National Wildflower Centre
St. Paschal Baylon R.C.
PRESCOT ROAD
EAST PRESCOT ROAD
PILCH LANE
DOVECOT AVENUE
KINGSHEATH AV.
FINCH LANE
THOMAS LANE
BROOKSIDE AV.
GREEN LANE
YEW TREE LANE
MAX ROAD
HALL LANE
MILTON AVENUE
HILARY AVENUE
MALVERN AV.
COURT HEY AV.

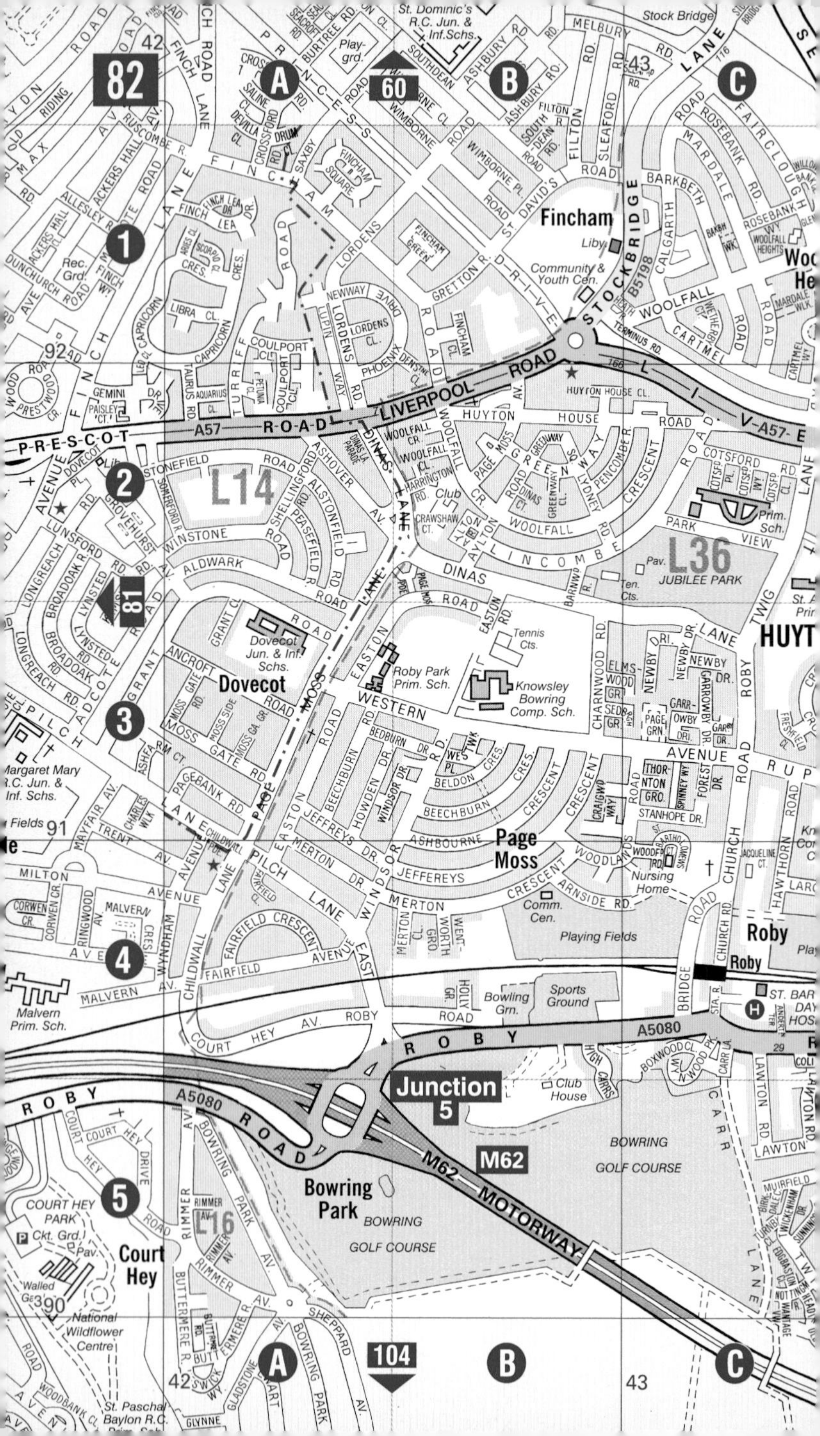

82
60
104
81
A
B
C
1
2
3
4
5
42
43
91
92
90
L14
L36
L16
Fincham
Dovecot
Page Moss
Roby
Court Hey
Bowring Park
HUYT
St. Dominic's R.C. Jun. & Inf. Schs.
Stock Bridge
Play-grd.
Rec. Grd.
Liby.
Community & Youth Cen.
Dovecot Jun. & Inf. Schs.
Roby Park Prim. Sch.
Knowsley Bowring Comp. Sch.
Tennis Cts.
Ten. Cts.
Pav.
JUBILEE PARK
Prim. Sch.
Club
Margaret Mary R.C. Jun. & Inf. Schs.
Fields
Malvern Prim. Sch.
Nursing Home
Comm. Cen.
Playing Fields
Bowling Grn.
Sports Ground
Club House
Junction 5
M62
M62 MOTORWAY
BOWRING GOLF COURSE
COURT HEY PARK
Ckt. Grd.
Walled Gdn.
National Wildflower Centre
St. Paschal Baylon R.C. Prim. Sch.
ST. BAR DAY HOS
A57
A5080
B5198
LIVERPOOL ROAD
PRESCOT ROAD
ROBY ROAD
STOCKBRIDGE LANE
PRINCESS DRIVE
FINCH LANE
FINCHAM ROAD
ST. DAVID'S ROAD
MELBURY RD.
ASHBURY RD.
WIMBORNE ROAD
WIMBORNE PL.
SOUTHDEAN RD.
FILTON ROAD
SLEAFORD RD.
ROSEBANK ROAD
FAIRCLOUGH RD.
MARDALE ROAD
BARKBETH ROAD
CALGARTH RD.
WOOLFALL HEIGHTS
WOOLFALL CR.
CARTMEL
TERMINUS RD.
LORDENS ROAD
LORDENS CL.
NEWWAY
LUPIN
PHOENIX
DENSTONE CL.
GRETTON RD.
FINCHAM SQUARE
FINCHAM GREEN
SAXBY
CROSSFORD RD.
DRUM CL.
SALINE CL.
DEVILLA CL.
BURTREE RD.
COULPORT CL.
TURRIFF ROAD
TAURUS RD.
AQUARIUS CL.
PETUNIA CL.
CAPRICORN CRES.
LIBRA CL.
SCORPIO CL.
ARIES CL.
FINCH LEA DR.
GEMINI DR.
PAISLEY CT.
PRESTWOOD CR.
ACKERS HALL AV.
ALLESLEY RD.
DUNCHURCH ROAD
RUSCOMBE R.
MAX ROAD
RIDING
STONEFIELD ROAD
SOMERFORD R.
WINSTONE ROAD
ALDWARK ROAD
SHELLINGFORD RD.
ALSTONFIELD RD
PEASEFIELD RD.
ASHOVER AV.
DINAS LANE
DINAS ROAD
HUYTON HOUSE ROAD
HUYTON HOUSE CL.
WOOLFALL CRESCENT
WOOLFALL CL.
HARRINGTON RD.
CRAWSHAW CT.
AYLTON RD.
PAGE MOSS ROAD
GREENWAY
LYDNEY RD.
PENCOMBE R.
LINCOMBE ROAD
COTSFORD RD.
PARK VIEW
TWIG LANE
BARNWOOD R.
DOVECOT AVENUE
DOVECOT PL.
GROVEHURST
LUNSFORD RD.
BROADOAK RD.
LONGREACH RD.
LYNSTED RD.
ADCOTE RD.
GRANT ROAD
GRANT CL.
ANCROFT ROAD
MOSS GATE RD.
MOSS SIDE
MOSS GATE GR.
PAGE MOSS LANE
EASTON ROAD
WESTERN AVENUE
BEDBURN DR.
BEECHBURN CRES.
HOWDEN DR.
WINDSOR DR.
BELDON CRES.
ASHBOURNE CRESCENT
JEFFREYS DR.
JEFFEREYS CRESCENT
MERTON DR.
WOODLANDS RD.
ARNSIDE RD.
CHARNWOOD RD.
ELMSWOOD GR.
NEWBY DRI.
NEWBY DR.
GARROWBY DR.
THORNTON GRO.
SPINNEY WY
FOREST DR.
STANHOPE DR.
CRAIGWD WAY
CHURCH ROAD
CHURCH RD.
BRIDGE ROAD
HAWTHORN ROAD
JACQUELINE CT.
RUPERT
FRESHFIELD
PILCH LANE
PILCH LANE EAST
ASHFARM CT.
PAGEBANK RD.
CHILDWALL LANE
CHILDWALL AVENUE
MAYFAIR AV.
TRENT AV.
MILTON AVENUE
CORWEN CR.
RINGWOOD AV.
MALVERN CRES.
MALVERN AV.
WYNDHAM AV.
FAIRFIELD CRESCENT
FAIRFIELD AVENUE
MERTON GRO.
WENTWORTH GRO.
HOLLY GR.
COURT HEY AV.
COURT HEY DRIVE
COURT HEY ROAD
BOXWOOD CL.
HIGH CARRS
CARR LANE
LAWTON RD.
MUIRFIELD CL.
TWICKENHAM
EDGBASTON
WANTAGE VW.
BOWRING PARK AV.
RIMMER AV.
BUTTERMERE R.
SHEPPARD AV.
GLADSTONE
GLYNNE
WOODBANK CL.

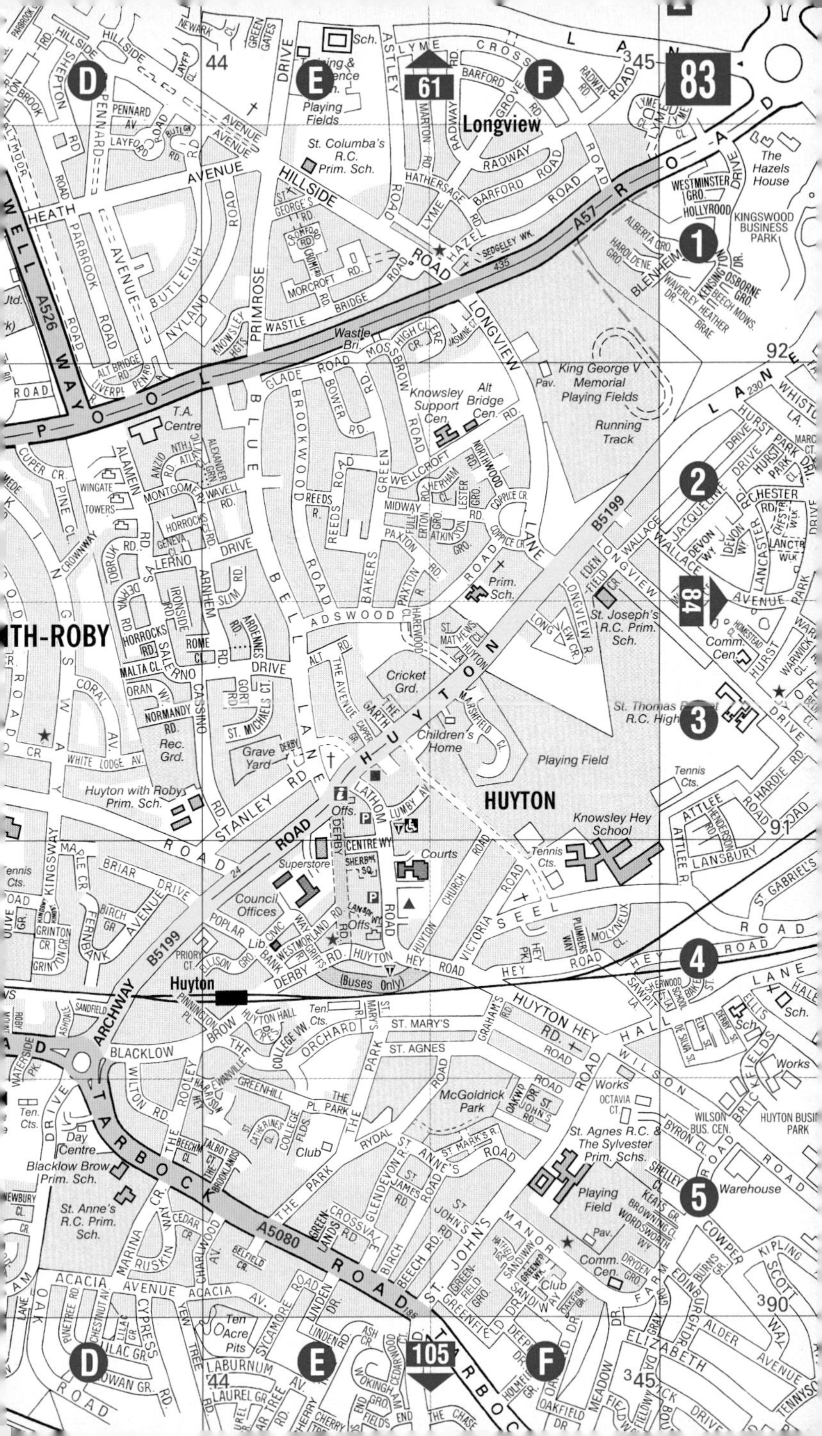
61
84
105
D
E
F
1
2
3
4
5
44
345
92
91
390
Longview
HUYTON
TH-ROBY
Huyton
The Hazels House
KINGSWOOD BUSINESS PARK
King George V Memorial Playing Fields
Running Track
Knowsley Support Cen.
Alt Bridge Cen.
St. Columba's R.C. Prim. Sch.
St. Joseph's R.C. Prim. Sch.
St. Thomas Becket R.C. High
Knowsley Hey School
Huyton with Roby Prim. Sch.
Council Offices
Superstore
Courts
McGoldrick Park
St. Agnes R.C. & The Sylvester Prim. Schs.
Blacklow Brow Prim. Sch.
St. Anne's R.C. Prim. Sch.
Ten Acre Pits
HUYTON BUSINESS PARK
WILSON BUS. CEN.
A57
A526
B5199
A5080
POOL ROAD
HUYTON LANE
TARBOCK ROAD
LONGVIEW LANE
BLUE BELL LANE
ARCHWAY
STANLEY ROAD
SEEL ROAD
HUYTON HEY ROAD
HUYTON HALL ROAD
WILSON ROAD
ACACIA AVENUE

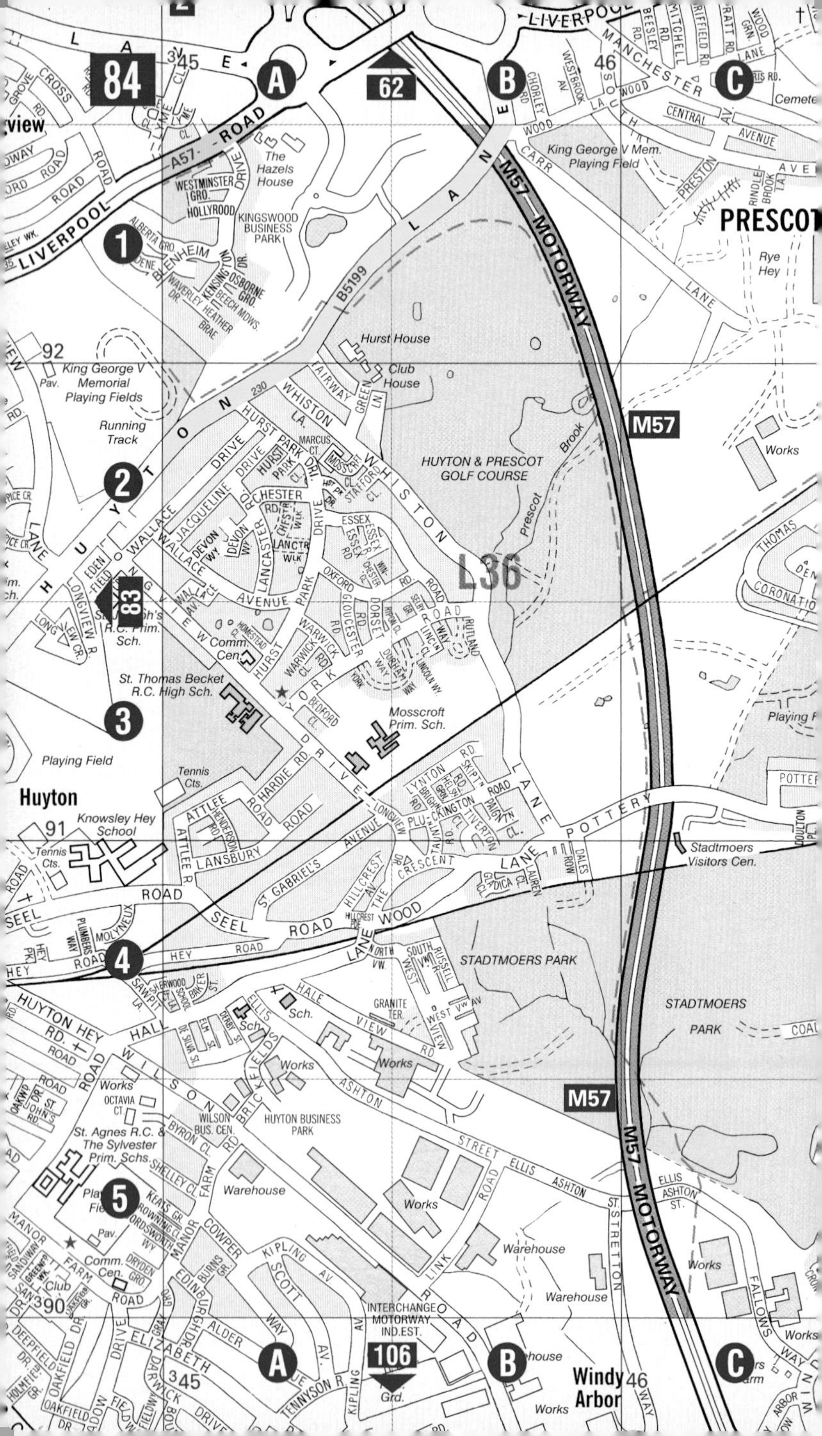

A
B
C
62
LIVERPOOL
MANCHESTER
A57 ROAD
LIVERPOOL ROAD
The Hazels House
KINGSWOOD BUSINESS PARK
WESTMINSTER GRO.
HOLLYROOD
BLENHEIM
KENSINGTON DR.
OSBORNE GRO.
BEECH MDWS.
HEATHER BRAE
WAVERLEY DR.
WOOD LANE
CARR LANE
B5199
King George V Mem. Playing Field
CENTRAL AVENUE
PRESTON AVE
PRESCOT
Rye Hey
M57 MOTORWAY
M57
Hurst House
Club House
King George V Memorial Playing Fields
Pav.
Running Track
HUYTON LANE
HUYTON & PRESCOT GOLF COURSE
Prescot Brook
WHISTON LA.
FAIRWAY
HURST PARK DRI.
JACQUELINE DRIVE
WALLACE DRIVE
WALLACE AVENUE
LANCASTER RD.
CHESTER RD.
ESSEX RD.
OXFORD RD.
DORSET RD.
GLOUCESTER RD.
WARWICK RD.
YORK WAY
DURHAM WAY
RUTLAND
L36
83
LONGVIEW DRIVE
LONGVIEW CR.
Comm. Cen.
St. Thomas Becket R.C. High Sch.
Mosscroft Prim. Sch.
Works
THOMAS
CORONATION
Playing Field
Tennis Cts.
Huyton
Knowsley Hey School
ATTLEE ROAD
HARDIE RD.
LANSBURY AVENUE
ST. GABRIEL'S AVENUE
HILLCREST AV.
THE CRESCENT
POTTERY LANE
Stadtmoers Visitors Cen.
SEEL ROAD
WOOD LANE
HEY ROAD
STADTMOERS PARK
HUYTON HEY RD.
HALL LANE
WILSON ROAD
HALE VIEW RD.
GRANITE TER.
Sch.
ASHTON STREET
ELLIS ASHTON ST.
HUYTON BUSINESS PARK
WILSON BUS. CEN.
St. Agnes R.C. & The Sylvester Prim. Schs.
Warehouse
Works
LINK ROAD
STRETTON WAY
MANOR FARM ROAD
COWPER WAY
KIPLING AV.
SCOTT AV.
INTERCHANGE MOTORWAY IND.EST.
106
ELIZABETH DRIVE
Windy Arbor
FALLOWS WAY
90
91
92
345
46

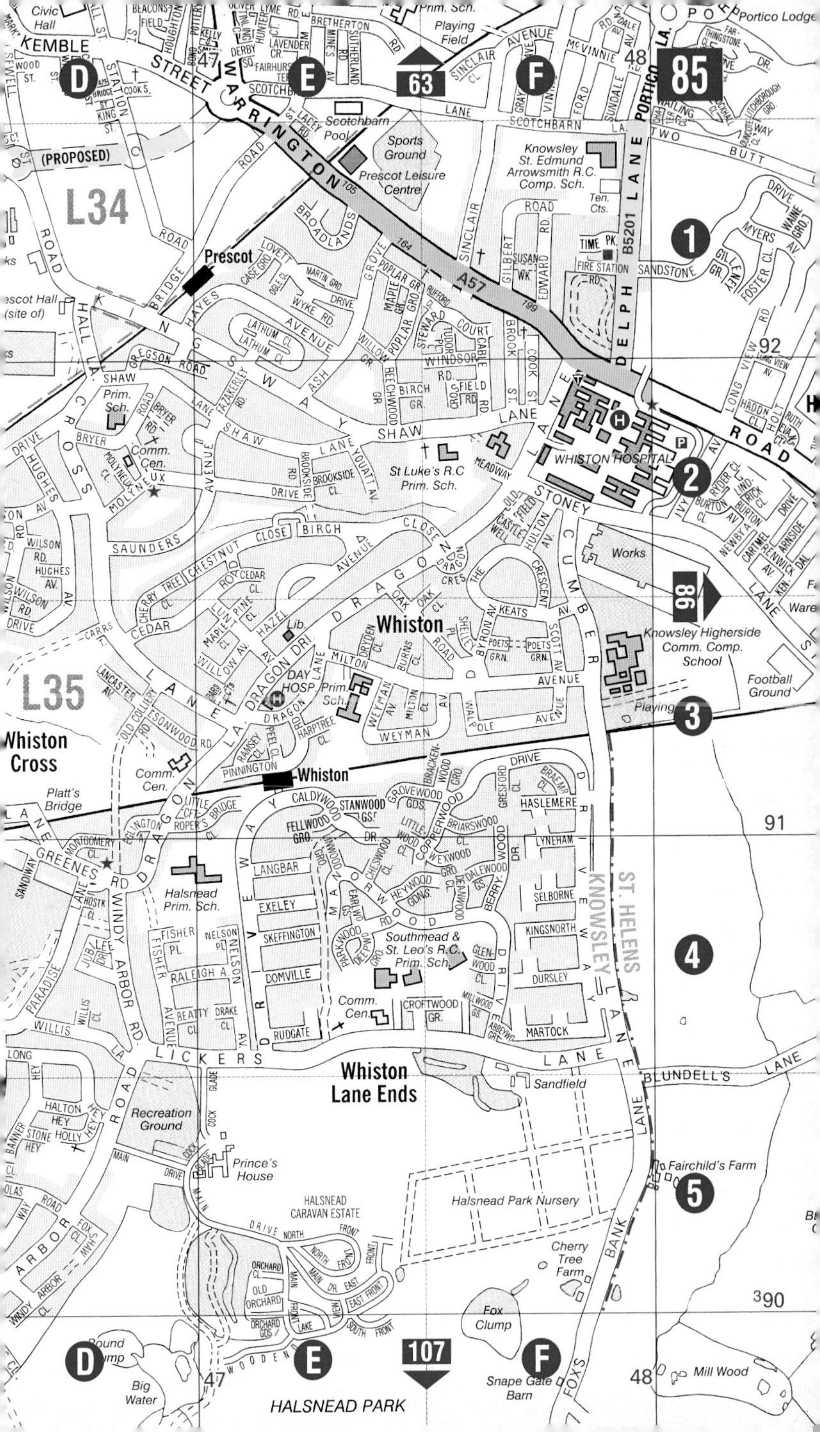

85
63
98
107
D
E
F
1
2
3
4
5
L34
L35
47
48
92
91
390
Civic Hall
KEMBLE
Portico Lodge
Playing Field
Prim. Sch.
WARRINGTON
STREET
SCOTCHBARN LANE
Scotchbarn Pool
Sports Ground
Prescot Leisure Centre
(PROPOSED)
Knowsley St. Edmund Arrowsmith R.C. Comp. Sch.
Ten. Cts.
PORTICO LA.
DELPH LANE
B5201
TWO BUTT
A57
Prescot
Prescot Hall (site of)
KINGSWAY
HALL LA.
CROSS
FIRE STATION
TIME PK.
SANDSTONE
SHAW LANE
BROADLANDS
Shaw Prim. Sch.
Comm. Cen.
WHISTON HOSPITAL
St Luke's R.C Prim. Sch.
MOLYNEUX
STONEY
WARRINGTON ROAD
SAUNDERS
Works
CUMBER
DRAGON
Whiston
Lib.
Knowsley Higherside Comm. Comp. School
Football Ground
DAY HOSP.
Prim. Sch.
CARRS LANE
Whiston Cross
Platt's Bridge
Playing
Whiston
Halsnead Prim. Sch.
GREENES RD.
WINDY ARBOR RD.
KNOWSLEY
ST. HELENS
Southmead & St. Leo's R.C. Prim. Sch.
Comm. Cen.
LICKERS LANE
Whiston Lane Ends
Sandfield
BLUNDELL'S LANE
Recreation Ground
Prince's House
HALSNEAD CARAVAN ESTATE
Halsnead Park Nursery
Fairchild's Farm
Cherry Tree Farm
Fox Clump
Round Clump
Big Water
Snape Gate Barn
Mill Wood
HALSNEAD PARK
FOXS BANK LANE

86
64
85
108
A
B
C
1
2
3
4
5
48
49
Portico Lodge
PORTICO LA.
SCOTCHBARN LA.
Knowsley St. Edmund Arrowsmith R.C. Comp. Sch.
Ten. Cts.
TWO BUTT LANE
Farm Annexe
B5413 ROAD
MARTLEW DAY HOSP.
Hanging Farm
WEDGEWOOD
CHURCHILL GDNS.
DELPH LANE
FIRE STATION RD.
SANDSTONE
MYERS AV.
DRIVE
LONGTON LANE
SANDHURST ROAD
LONG VIEW AV.
COUNCIL ST.
Holt
Recreation Ground
Longton Lane Community Prim. Sch.
ST. WINIFRED RD.
AMANDA
STAPLETON
KING EDWARD CL.
WHISTON HOSPITAL
A57
WARRINGTON
STONEY LANE
CUMBER LANE
Works
Factory
Warehouse
Knowsley Higherside Comm. Comp. School
Playing Field
Football Ground
Fishpond Farm
KNOWSLEY
ST. HELENS
Rec. Grd.
Rainhill
RAINHILL RD.
RAINHILL
B5413
VINCENT RD.
WARBURTON HEY
ELLABY RD.
Cedric Ho
RITHERUP
VICTORIA TER.
St. Ann's C. of E. Prim. Sch.
Mus.
Lib.
THE PRIORY
TRENT CL.
SEVERN RD.
CALDER
LOWTHER DRIVE
HEYES MOUNT
MARIAN DR.
LANE VIEW
MILL LANE
L35
Blundell's Hill
Blundell's Hill Farm
BLUNDELL'S LANE
Club House
Blundell's Hill Wood
Willis Hall Farm
Dean's Farm
BLUNDELLS HILL GOLF COURSE
CRONTON LANE
WA8
Sandfield
Fairchild's Farm
Park Nursery
Cherry Tree Farm
390
BANK LANE
FOXS BANK
Mill Wood
Rainhill Hall Farm
Sandy Carr Farm
The Rough
HALL LANE
ASHTON
HASLEMERE
SELBORNE
KINGSNORTH
DURSLEY
MARTOCK
RIVER WAY
91
92

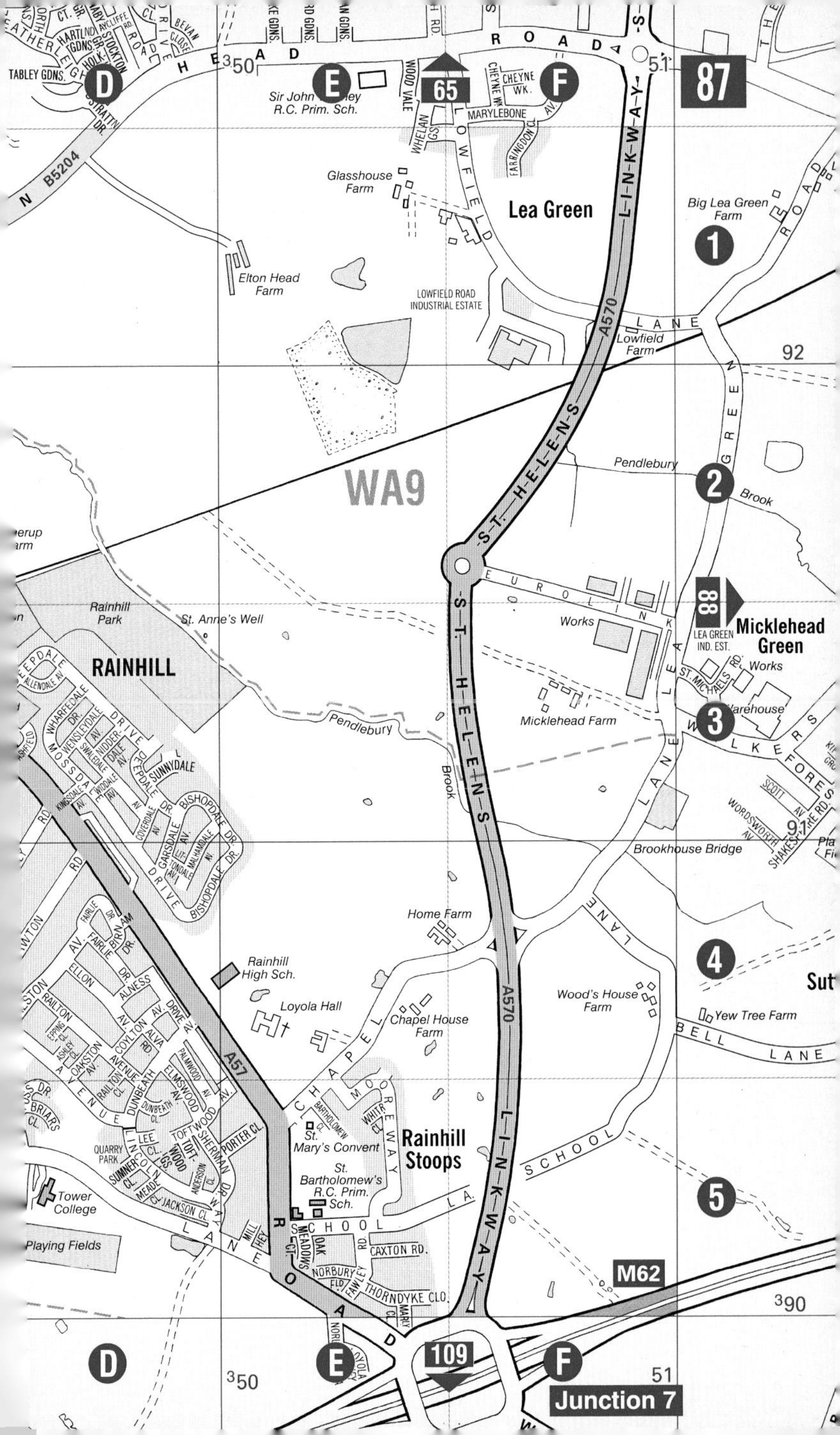

87
65
88
109
Junction 7
M62
A570
A57
B5204
WA9
Lea Green
RAINHILL
Rainhill Stoops
Micklehead Green
ELTON HEAD ROAD
ST. HELENS LINKWAY
TABLEY GDNS.
STRATTON DR.
WOOD VALE
CHEYNE WK.
MARYLEBONE AV.
FARRINGDON CL.
WHELAN GS.
LOWFIELD
Sir John Fisher R.C. Prim. Sch.
Glasshouse Farm
Elton Head Farm
LOWFIELD ROAD INDUSTRIAL ESTATE
Lowfield Farm
LANE
Big Lea Green Farm
LEA GREEN ROAD
Pendlebury Brook
EUROLINK
Works
LEA GREEN IND. EST.
ST. MICHAELS RD.
Warehouse
WALKERS LANE
FORREST
SCOTT AV.
WORDSWORTH AV.
SHAKESPEARE RD.
Micklehead Farm
Rainhill Park
St. Anne's Well
Brookhouse Bridge
Home Farm
Rainhill High Sch.
Loyola Hall
Chapel House Farm
CHAPEL LANE
Wood's House Farm
Yew Tree Farm
BELL LANE
SCHOOL LANE
St. Mary's Convent
St. Bartholomew's R.C. Prim. Sch.
MOOREWAY
WHITBY CL.
SCHOOL LA.
MEADOWS
OAK RD.
CAXTON RD.
NORBURY AV.
FAWLEY
THORNDYKE CLO.
MARY CL.
Tower College
Playing Fields
LANE
MILL HEY
PORTER CL.
SHERIDAN DR.
TOFTWOOD
JACKSON CL.
SUMNER CL.
LINCOLN
QUARRY PARK
WHARFEDALE DR.
WENSLEYDALE AV.
DEEPDALE DR.
SUNNYDALE
BISHOPDALE DR.
GARSDALE AV.
COVERDALE AV.
RAILTON AV.
COYLTON AV.
ELLON
FAIRLIE DR.
BIRNAM DR.
ALNESS
DUNBEATH
ELMSWOOD AV.
OAKSTON AVENUE
A570
350
51
92
91
390
D
E
F
1
2
3
4
5

88
66
87
110
Marshall's Cross
Lea Green
Micklehead Green
Sutton Manor
L35
Junction 7
M62
M62 MOTORWAY
ELTON
HEAD ROAD
MARSHALL'S CROSS RD.
LINKWAY
ST. HELENS LINKWAY
MILL LANE
CLOCK LANE
CHESTER LANE
B5419
B5204
A569
LEA GREEN
WALKERS LANE
CHAPEL LANE
BELL LANE
SCHOOL LANE
UNION BANK LANE
JUBITS LANE
GARTON ST.
PARKSIDE AV.
FOUR ACRE LANE
FOREST RD.
Sutton Comm. High Sch.
Sutton Comm. Leisure Cen.
Peet's Bridge
Little Lea Green Farm
Big Lea Green Farm
Lowfield Farm
Works
Pendlebury Brook
LEA GREEN INDUSTRIAL ESTATE
Warehouse
Micklehead Farm
Brookhouse Bridge
Playing Field
Prim. Sch.
King George's Field
Pav.
Shop. Cen.
Lib.
Comm. Cen.
St. Theresa's R.C. Prim. Sch.
St. Theresa's Church Hall
Vicarage
Wood's House Farm
Yew Tree Farm
Bowling Green
Football Field
Sidney Farm
Union Bank Farm
A
B
C
1
2
3
4
5
351
52
92
91
390

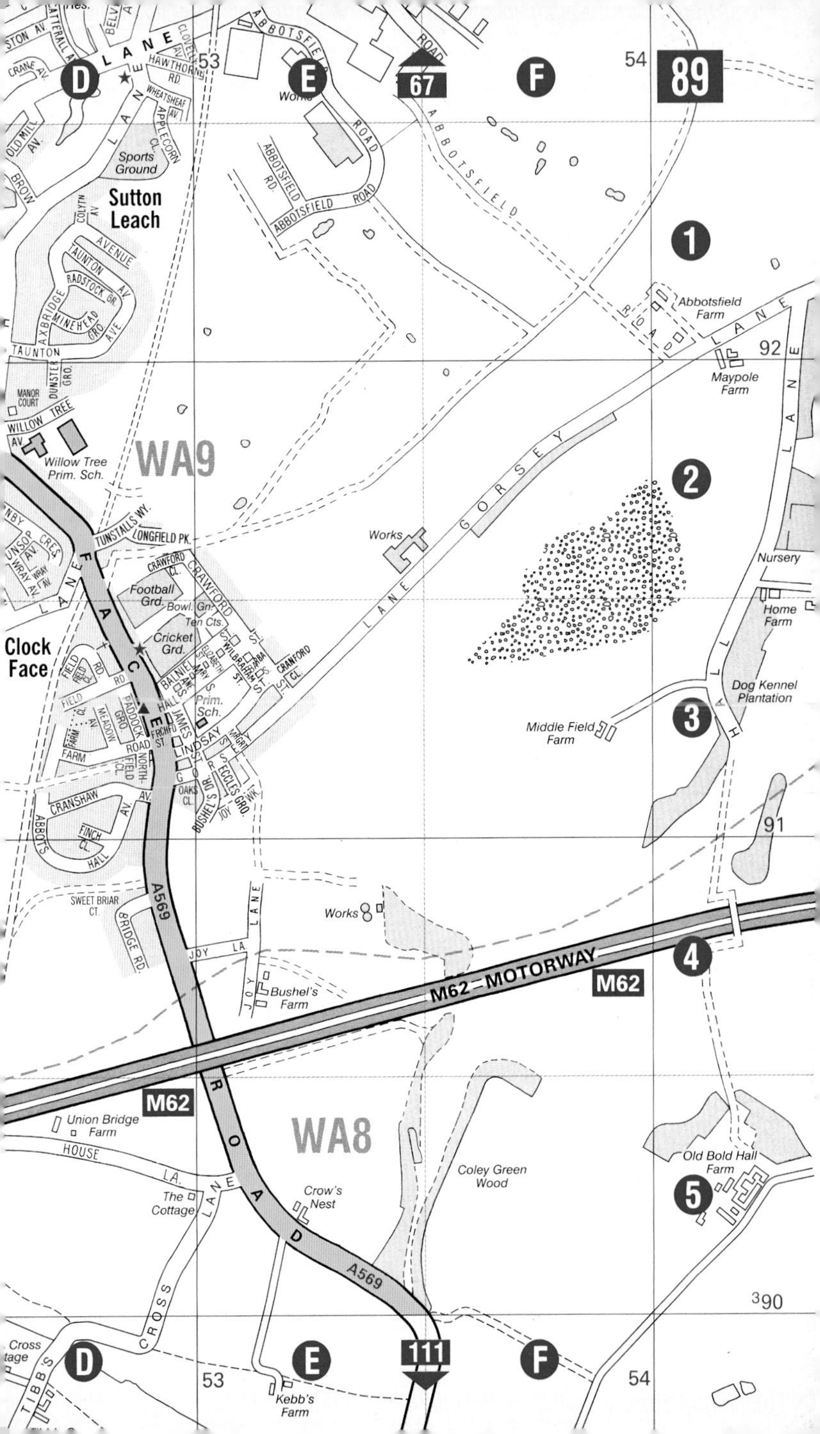
Sutton Leach
Clock Face
WA9
WA8
M62 – MOTORWAY
M62
A569
FACE ROAD
GORSEY LANE
ABBOTSFIELD ROAD
HALL LANE
Sports Ground
Willow Tree Prim. Sch.
Football Grd.
Bowl. Gn.
Ten Cts.
Cricket Grd.
Prim. Sch.
Works
Abbotsfield Farm
Maypole Farm
Nursery
Home Farm
Dog Kennel Plantation
Middle Field Farm
Bushel's Farm
Union Bridge Farm
The Cottage
Crow's Nest
Coley Green Wood
Old Bold Hall Farm
Kebb's Farm
HOUSE LA.
CROSS LANE
JOY LANE
JOY LA.
TIBB'S
Cross tage
SWEET BRIAR CT.
BRIDGE RD.
CRANSHAW AV.
FINCH HALL CL.
ABBOTS
LINDSAY ST.
CRAWFORD ST.
CRANFORD CL.
TUNSTALLS WY.
LONGFIELD PK.
TAUNTON AVENUE
RADSTOCK GR.
MINEHEAD GRO.
AXBRIDGE AV.
DUNSTER GRO.
MANOR COURT
WILLOW TREE AV.
COLYTN
HAWTHORNE RD.
WHEATSHEAF AV.
APPLECORN CL.
CLOVELLY AV.
OLD MILL AV.
BROW
CRANE AV.
LANE
53
54
92
91
390
67
111
D
E
F
1
2
3
4
5

LIVERPOOL BAY
HOYLAKE
Model Boating Pond
Jetty
Lifeboat Station
PROMENADE
PARADE
NORTH PARADE
MEOLS
HOYLE RD.
DENESHEY RD.
SAXON RD.
Putting Grn.
QUEENS PARK
Bowl. Grn.
HOYLAKE COTTAGE HOSPITAL
WYNSTAY RD.
GARDEN HEY
CLYDESDALE RD.
DOVEDALE RD.
AVONDALE RD.
FERNDALE RD.
TRINITY RD.
CHAPEL RD.
MANOR RD.
NEWTON RD.
SANDRINGHAM CL.
CARLTON
WAVERLEY RD.
Prim. Sch.
Lib.
Manor
Football Ground
Sports Ground
HARRINGTON AV.
HADFIELD AV.
MELROSE AV.
ALDERLEY RD.
CABLE RD.
GROVE RD.
LAKE RD.
NORTH RD.
MARKET ST.
A553
GROSVENOR RD.
PROCTOR RD.
CARR LANE IND. EST.
CARR LANE
Rec. Grd.
T.A. Centre
Club House
HOYLAKE MUNICIPAL GOLF COURSE
Hoylake
STATION
T.H.
MONTROSE CT.
ROSECROFT CT.
GAP
LIGHTHOUSE
KINGS GAP
VALENTIA RD.
MARINE
QUEEN'S RD.
WARREN RD.
CURZON RD.
COURTENAY RD.
ST. MARGARET'S RD.
PENRHOS RD.
BARTON CL.
BARTON ROAD
BEACH
CORONATION RD.
STANLEY ROAD
ROYAL LIVERPOOL GOLF COURSE
Club House
MEOLS DRIVE
A540
DRUMMOND
MORPETH RD.
EDWARD RD.
YEOMAN COTTS.
GEORGE RD.
CARSTHORNE RD.
CARHAM
Sports Grd.
112

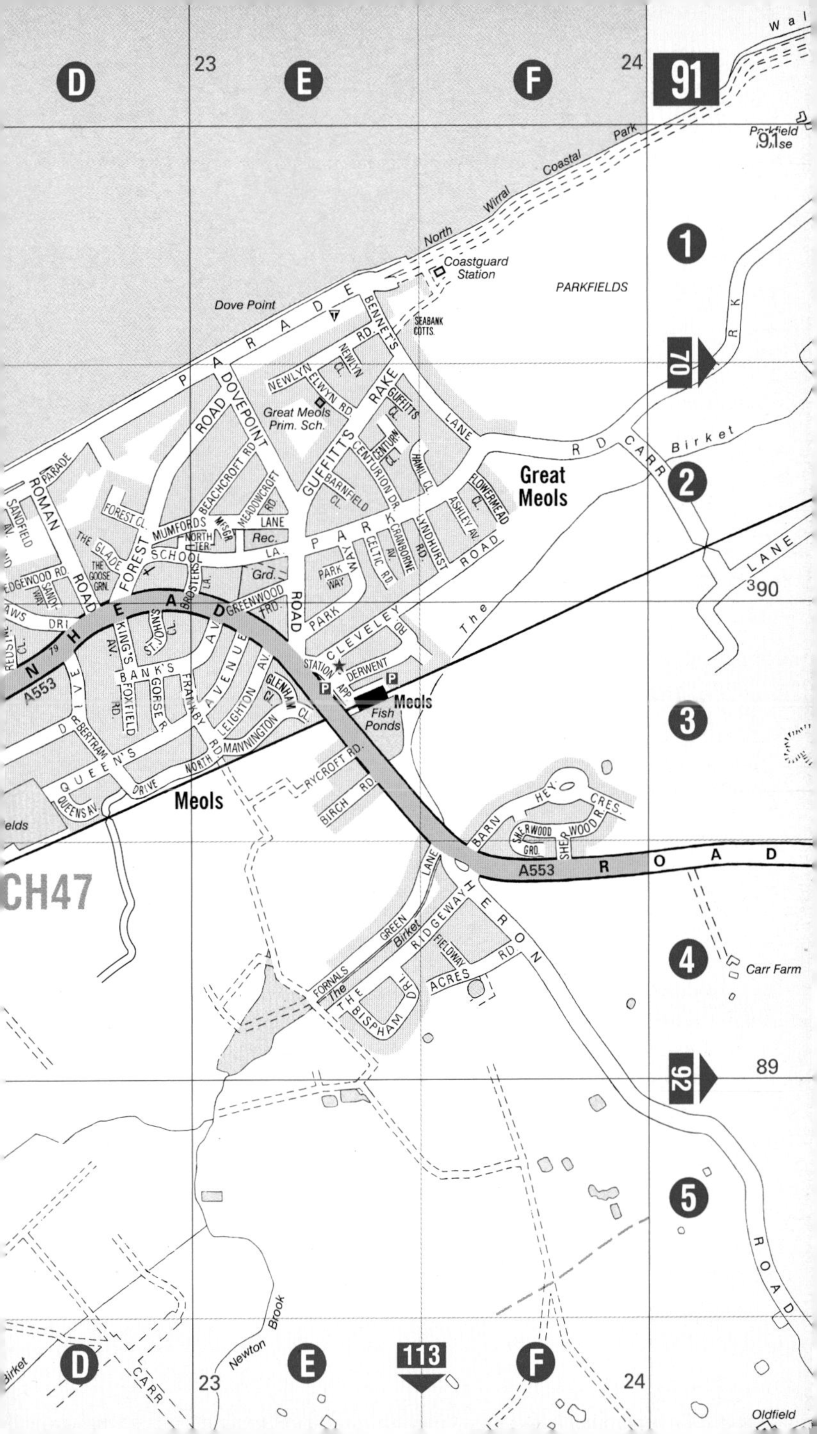
D
E
F
23
24
Wal
Parkfield
North Wirral Coastal Park
Coastguard Station
PARKFIELDS
Dove Point
PARADE
BENNETS
SEABANK COTTS.
NEWLYN RD.
NEWLYN CL.
ELWYN RD
Great Meols Prim. Sch.
RAKE
GUFFITTS CL.
GUFFITTS
CENTURION CL.
CENTURION DR.
HAMIL CL.
BARNFIELD CL.
LANE
CARR
Birket
Great Meols
FLOWERMEAD CL.
ASHLEY AV.
LYNDHURST RD.
CRANBORNE AV.
CELTIC RD.
PARK WAY
ROAD
DOVEPOINT ROAD
BEACHCROFT RD.
MEADOWCROFT RD.
ROMAN ROAD
PARADE
SANDFIELD AV.
FOREST CL.
MUMFORDS
NORTH TER.
MEADOW LANE
Rec.
SCHOOL LA.
Grd.
THE GLADE
THE GOOSE GRN.
FOREST
BROSTERS LA.
GREENWOOD RD.
EDGEWOOD RD.
SANDY WAY
DR.
CLEVELEY RD.
DERWENT
STATION APP.
Meols
Fish Ponds
The
390
HEAD
ST. JOHNS CL.
KING'S AV.
BANK'S
FOXFIELD RD.
GORSE R.
FRANKBY AV.
AVENUE
LEIGHTON AV.
GLENHAM CL.
CL.
MANNINGTON
NORTH RD.
A553
DRIVE
BERTRAM
QUEEN'S DRIVE
QUEENS AV.
Meols
RYCROFT RD.
BIRCH RD.
BARN HEY CRES.
SHERWOOD GRO.
SHERWOOD R.
ROAD
CH47
LANE
GREEN
The Birket
RIDGEWAY
FIELDWAY
ACRES RD
HERON
FORNALS
THE BISPHAM DRI.
Carr Farm
89
Newton Brook
CARR
Birket
ROAD
Oldfield
1
2
3
4
5
70
92
113

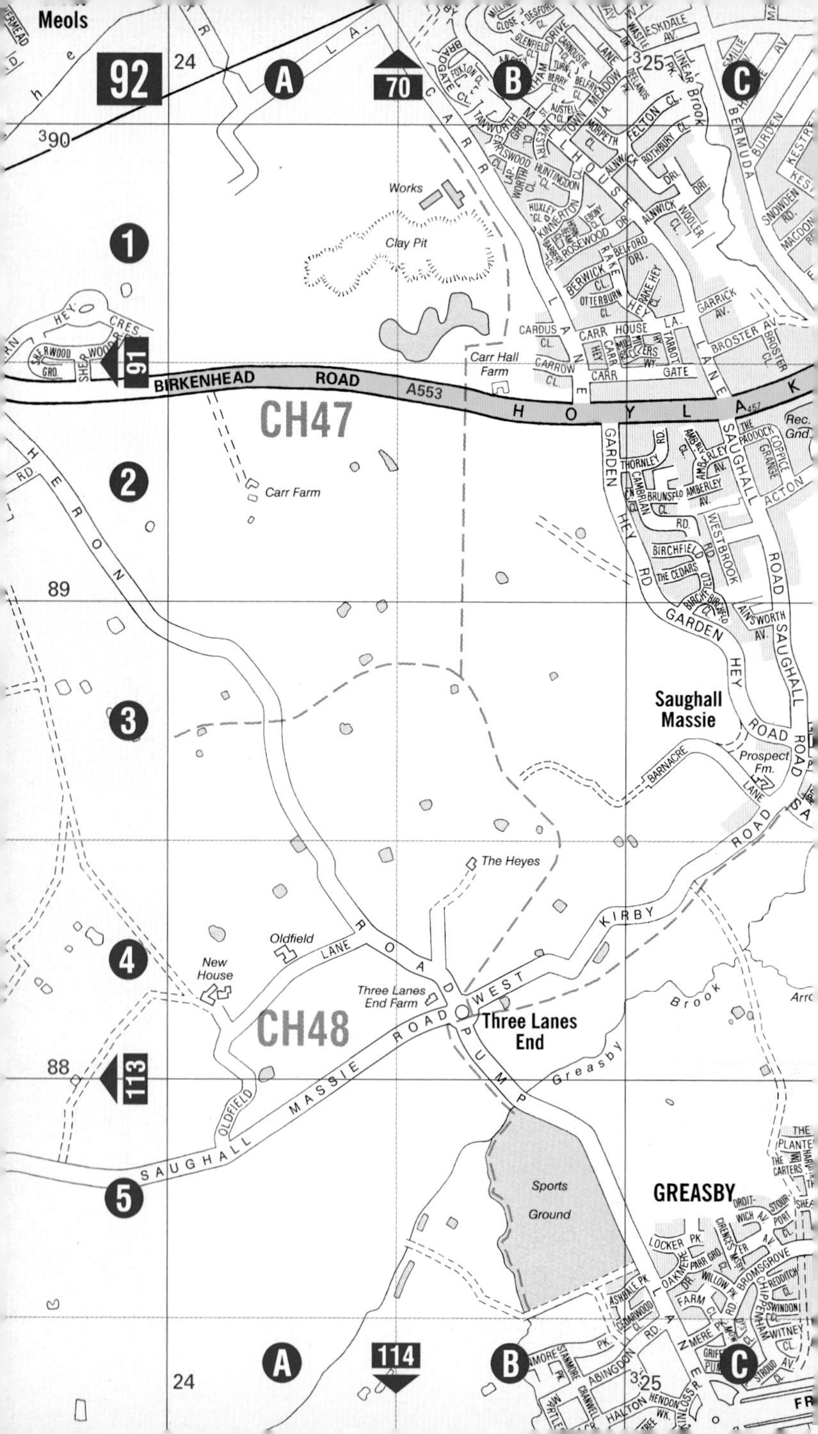
Meols
24
A
70
B
3 25
C
390
1
2
3
4
5
89
88
Works
Clay Pit
Carr Hall Farm
Carr Farm
BIRKENHEAD ROAD
A553
HOYLAKE
CH47
CH48
CARR LANE
CARR HOUSE LA.
CARR GATE
CARDUS CL.
CARROW CL.
ALNWICK DRI.
MORPETH LA.
FELTON CL.
ROTHBURY CL.
WOOLER CL.
ROSEWOOD DR.
BELFORD DRI.
BERWICK CL.
OTTERBURN CL.
RAKE HEY
GARRICK AV.
BROSTER AV.
BERMUDA
BURDEN
SNOWDEN RD.
ESKDALE AV.
LINEAR PK.
HOUSE
MEADOW
LANE
HUNTINGDON CL.
KINNERTON CL.
HUXLEY CL.
TANWORTH GRO.
BRADGATE CL.
GLENFIELD DRIVE
SHERWOOD GRO.
HEY CRES.
HERON RD
GARDEN HEY RD
SAUGHALL ROAD
THORNLEY RD.
AMBERLEY AV.
CAMBRIAN CL.
BRUNSFIELD CL.
WESTBROOK RD.
BIRCHFIELD
THE CEDARS
AINSWORTH AV.
THE PADDOCK
COPPICE GRANGE
ACTON
Rec. Gnd.
Saughall Massie
BARNACRE LANE
Prospect Fm.
The Heyes
Oldfield
OLDFIELD LANE
New House
Three Lanes End Farm
Three Lanes End
WEST KIRBY ROAD
POOL LANE
SAUGHALL MASSIE ROAD
OLDFIELD
Greasby Brook
Sports Ground
GREASBY
LOCKER PK.
OAKMERE DR.
PARR GRO.
WILLOW PK.
BROMSGROVE
CHIPPENHAM
REDDITCH
SWINDON CL.
WITNEY CL.
STROUD AV.
FARM CL.
ASHDALE PK.
CEDARWOOD CL.
ABINGDON RD.
STANMORE PK.
CRANWELL
HALTON
HENDON WK.
KINLOSS R.
MERE PK.
DROITWICH AV.
STOURPORT CL.
CIRENCESTER AV.
THE PLANTERS
THE CARTERS
91
113
114
A
B
C
24
3 25

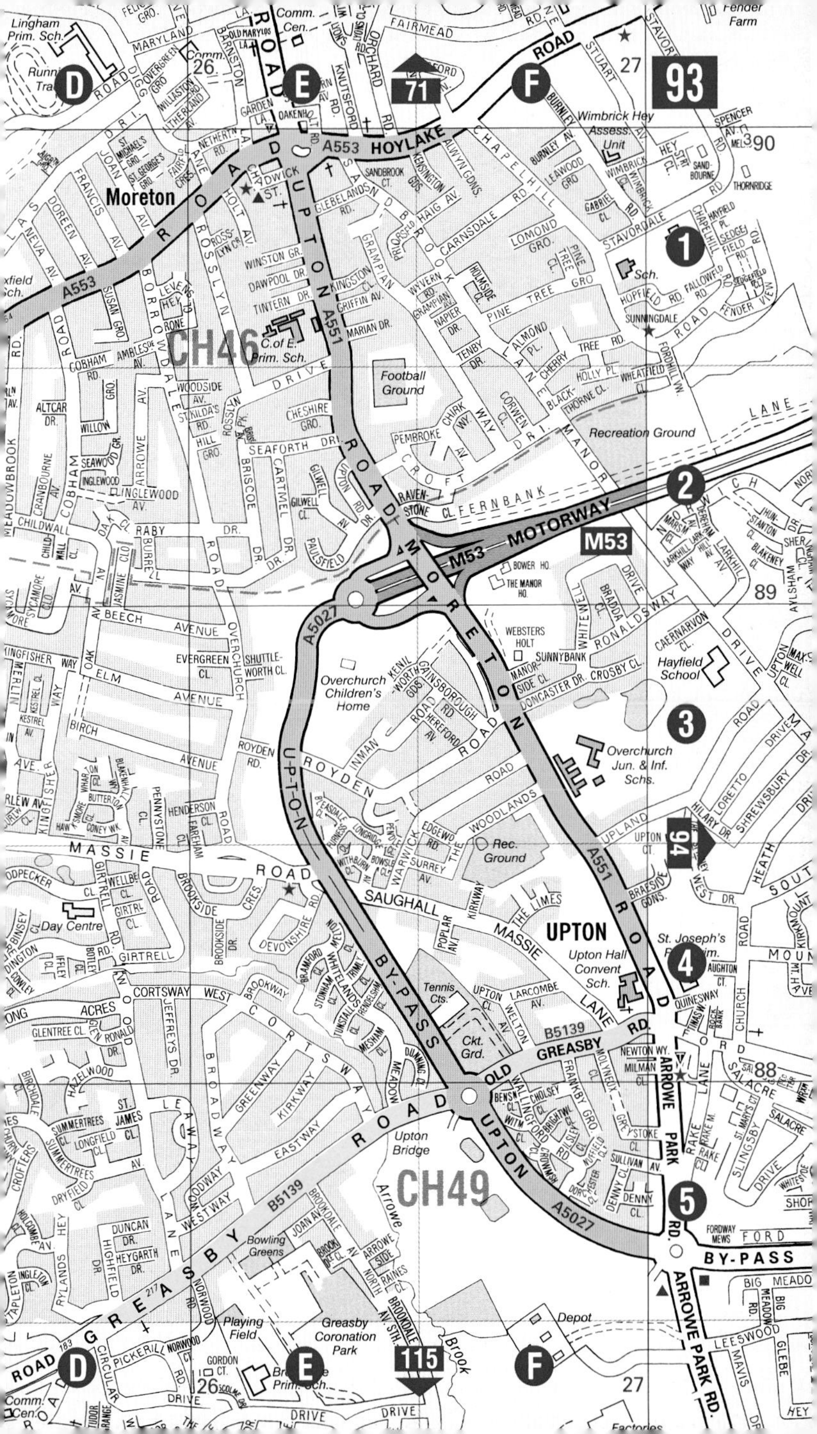

Lingham Prim. Sch.
Fender Farm
Comm. Cen.
FAIRMEAD
MARYLAND
BARNSTON
KNUTSFORD
ORCHARD
ROAD
STUART
STAVORDALE
26
27
71
D
E
F
HOYLAKE
A553
Wimbrick Hey Assess. Unit
BURNLEY
WIMBRICK
CHAPELHILL
THORNRIDGE
390
Moreton
UPTON
A551
SANDBROOK CT.
KENSINGTON
ALWYN GDNS.
GLEBELANDS RD.
HAIG AV.
CARNSDALE RD.
LOMOND GRO.
PINE TREE GRO
HOLMSIDE CL.
GRAMPIAN
WINSTON GR.
DAWPOOL DR.
TINTERN DR.
KINGSTON
GRIFFIN AV.
MARIAN DR.
C.of E. Prim. Sch.
CH46
Football Ground
ALMOND PL.
CHERRY TREE RD.
HOLLY PL.
WHEATFIELD
BLACKTHORNE CL.
Sch.
HOPFIELD RD.
FALLOWFIELD
SUNNINGDALE
FORDHILL
FENDER VIEW
1
2
3
4
5
LANE
Recreation Ground
MANOR
DRIVE
TENBY DR.
NAPIER DR.
CORWEN CL.
PEMBROKE
CHIRK WY.
CROFT
SEAFORTH DR.
CHESHIRE GRO.
FERNBANK
RAVENSTONE CL.
MOTORWAY
M53
NORWICH
LARKHILL
BOWER HO.
THE MANOR HO.
89
RONALDSWAY
BRADDA
WHITEWELL
CAERNARVON CL.
Hayfield School
WEBSTERS HOLT
SUNNYBANK
MANORSIDE CL.
DONCASTER DR.
CROSBY CL.
Overchurch Jun. & Inf. Schs.
A5027
Overchurch Children's Home
GAINSBOROUGH RD.
HEREFORD AV.
INMAN
ROYDEN
THE WOODLANDS
Rec. Ground
UPLAND
UPTON CT.
94
LORETTO
SHREWSBURY
HILARY DR.
WEST DR.
HEATH
BRAESIDE GDNS.
St. Joseph's Prim.
Upton Hall Convent Sch.
SAUGHALL MASSIE LANE
THE LIMES
POPLAR AV.
KIRKWAY
SURREY AV.
WARWICK
EDGEWD RD.
Tennis Cts.
Ckt. Grd.
LARCOMBE AV.
WELTON
B5139
GREASBY RD.
OLD
NEWTON WY.
MILMAN CL.
ARROWE PARK
QUINESWAY
ROCK BANK
CHURCH
LANE
88
SALACRE
RAKE LANE
SLINGSBY DRIVE
BY-PASS
UPTON
UPTON-BY-PASS
CH49
Upton Bridge
Arrowe Brook
FRANKBY GRO.
WALLINGFORD
CHOLSEY
MOLYNEUX
GREYSTOKE CL.
SULLIVAN AV.
DENNY CL.
FORDWAY MEWS
FORD
ARROWE PARK RD.
BIG MEADOW
LEESWOOD
MAVIS
GLEBE
Depot
Factories
MASSIE ROAD
BROOKSIDE
DEVONSHIRE RD.
Day Centre
GIRTRELL
CORTSWAY WEST
ACRES
GLENTREE CL.
BROADWAY
GREENWAY
KIRKWAY
EASTWAY
LEAWAY
WESTWAY
WOODWAY
GREASBY
ROAD
Bowling Greens
Playing Field
Greasby Coronation Park
BROOKDALE
ARROWE SIDE
115
NORWOOD
PICKERILL
CIRCULAR
GORDON CT.
Prim. Sch.
DRIVE
Comm. Cen.
HEYGARTH DR.
DUNCAN DR.
HIGHFIELD
RYLANDS HEY
SUMMERTREES
LONGFIELD
ST. JAMES CL.
HAZELWOOD
BEECH AVENUE
ELM AVENUE
BIRCH AVENUE
EVERGREEN CL.
SHUTTLEWORTH CL.
OVERCHURCH
ROYDEN RD.
HENDERSON CL.
PENNYSTONE
FAREHAM
KINGFISHER WAY
MERLIN
KESTREL AV.
OAK
CHILDWALL
RABY DR.
BURREL
CARTMEL DR.
BRISCOE DR.
MEADOWBROOK
CRANBOURNE AV.
COBHAM
ARROWE
INGLEWOOD AV.
ALTCAR DR.
WILLOW
BORROWDALE
ROSSLYN
A553
SUSAN GRO.
DOREEN AV.
FRANCIS AV.
NEVA AV.

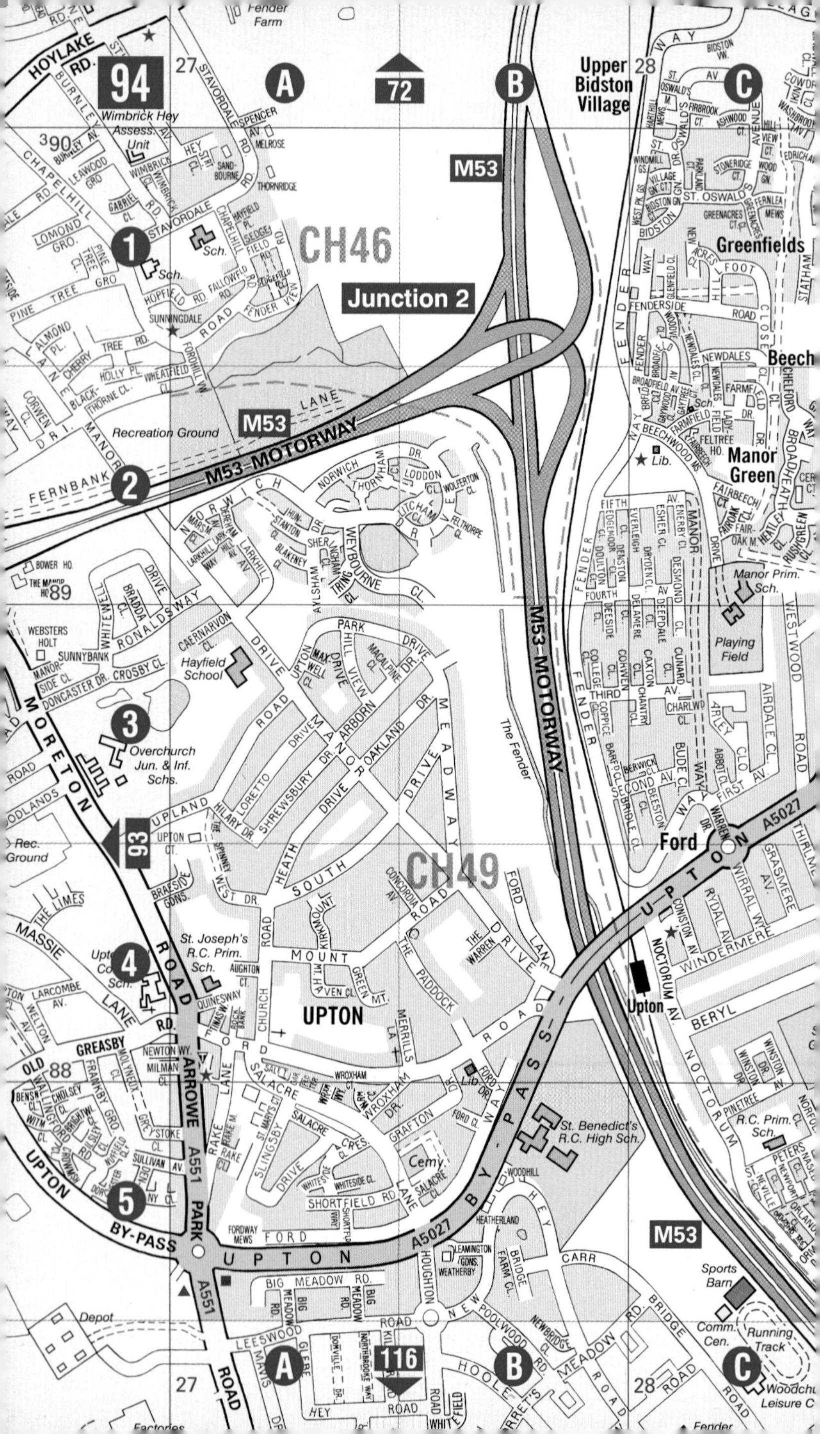

94
72
93
116
A
B
C
27
28
90
89
88
1
2
3
4
5
Fender Farm
HOYLAKE RD.
Wimbrick Hey Assess. Unit
Upper Bidston Village
CH46
CH49
Junction 2
M53
M53-MOTORWAY
Greenfields
Beechwood
Manor Green
Recreation Ground
FERNBANK
MANOR DRIVE
LANE
STAVORDALE RD.
SPENCER AV.
MELROSE
THORNRIDGE
HEY CL.
SANDBOURNE
CHAPELHILL RD.
LOMOND GRO.
PINE TREE GRO
HOPFIELD RD.
FALLOWFIELD RD.
FENDER VIEW
SUNNINGDALE
FORDHILL VW.
ALMOND PL.
CHERRY TREE RD.
HOLLY PL.
WHEATFIELD
BLACKTHORNE CL.
CORWEN CL.
BURNLEY AV.
LEAWOOD GRO
GABRIEL CL.
WIMBRICK CL.
Sch.
NORWICH DRIVE
WEYBOURNE CL.
THORNHAM
LODDON CL.
WOLFERTON CL.
LITCHAM CL.
FELTHORPE CL.
HUNSTANTON CL.
BLAKENEY CL.
SHERINGHAM CL.
TRING CL.
AYLSHAM DR.
DEREHAM
MARSH
LARKHILL AV.
LARKHILL WAY
BOWER HO.
THE MANOR HO.
WHITEWELL DRIVE
BRADDA CL.
RONALDSWAY
CAERNARVON CL.
Hayfield School
WEBSTERS HOLT
SUNNYBANK
MANORSIDE CL.
DONCASTER DR.
CROSBY CL.
MORETON ROAD
Overchurch Jun. & Inf. Schs.
UPLAND
UPTON CT.
HILARY DR.
LORETTO DRIVE
SHREWSBURY DR.
MANOR ROAD
ARBORN DR.
OAKLAND DR.
MEADWAY
PARK DRIVE
HILL VIEW DRIVE
MAXWELL CL.
MACALPINE CL.
UPTON PARK DRIVE
HEATH ROAD
SOUTH DRIVE
THE SPINNEY
WEST DR.
BRAESIDE GDNS.
Rec. Ground
THE LIMES
MASSIE LANE
LARCOMBE AV.
WELTON AV.
St. Joseph's R.C. Prim. Sch.
AUGHTON CT.
QUINESWAY
KIRKMOUNT
CONCORDIA AV.
ROAD
MOUNT
MT. HAVEN CL.
GREEN MT.
THE PADDOCK
THE WARREN
FORD DRIVE
FORD LANE
MERRILLS LA.
UPTON
CHURCH ROAD
ROCK BANK
GREASBY RD.
NEWTON WY.
MILMAN CL.
MOLYNEUX
FRANKBY GRO.
OLD
WALLINGFORD RD.
CHOLSEY
BENSON CL.
GREYSTOKE CL.
SULLIVAN AV.
ARROWE PARK ROAD
A551
RAKE LANE
RAKE M.
SALACRE
WROXHAM DR.
WROXHAM CT.
SLINGSBY DRIVE
SALACRE CRES.
GRAFTON
WHITESIDE CL.
SHORTFIELD RD.
SALACRE LANE
Cemy.
Lib.
FORD CL.
FORDWAY MEWS
FORD
UPTON BY-PASS
A5027
St. Benedict's R.C. High Sch.
WOODHILL
HEATHERLAND
LEAMINGTON GDNS.
WEATHERBY
BRIDGE FARM CL.
HEY
CARR
HOUGHTON
BIG MEADOW RD.
MEADOW RD.
Depot
LEESWOOD
ST. MARY'S
GLEBE
DOMVILLE DR.
NORTHBROOKE WAY
KILN
NEW ROAD
POOLWOOD RD.
NEWBRIDGE CL.
MEADOW ROAD
BRIDGE ROAD
HOOLE ROAD
WHITEFIELD
Factories
The Fender
M53-MOTORWAY
FENDER WAY
FENDER LANE
ST. OSWALD'S
BIDSTON VW.
FIRBROOK CT.
ASHWOOD CT.
HILLVIEW CT.
STONERIDGE CT.
WOOD GN.
FERNLEA MEWS
GREENACRES CT.
HILLFOOT CLOSE
FENDERSIDE ROAD
NEWDALES CL.
FARMFIELD DR.
LADYFIELD
FELTREE HO.
BEECHWOOD MS.
FAIRBEECH CT.
FAIROAK CL.
HEATLEY CL.
BROADHEATH AV.
CHELFORD CL.
Lib.
FIFTH AV.
FOURTH AV.
THIRD AV.
SECOND AV.
FIRST AV.
ESHER CL.
DENSTON CL.
DRYDEN CL.
DESMOND CL.
DOULTON CL.
DEESIDE CL.
DELAMERE CL.
DEEPDALE CL.
CAXTON CL.
CUNARD CL.
COLLEGE CL.
CORWEN CL.
CHANTRY CL.
CHARLWD CL.
COPPICE CL.
BARFORD CL.
BERWICK CL.
BUDE CL.
BEESTON CL.
BRIDLE CL.
ABBOT CL.
ARLEY CLO.
AIRDALE CL.
WESTWOOD ROAD
Manor Prim. Sch.
Playing Field
WARREN WAY
Ford
UPTON ROAD
GRASMERE AV.
THIRLMERE
RYDAL AV.
WIRRAL WY.
CONISTON AV.
WINDERMERE
NOCTORUM AV.
Upton
BERYL
NOCTORUM
WINSTON DR.
WINSTON AV.
PINETREE CL.
R.C. Prim. Sch.
PETERS
ST. NEVILLE
NEWPORT CL.
ORLANDO
Sports Barn
Comm. Cen.
Running Track
Woodchurch Leisure C.
Fender

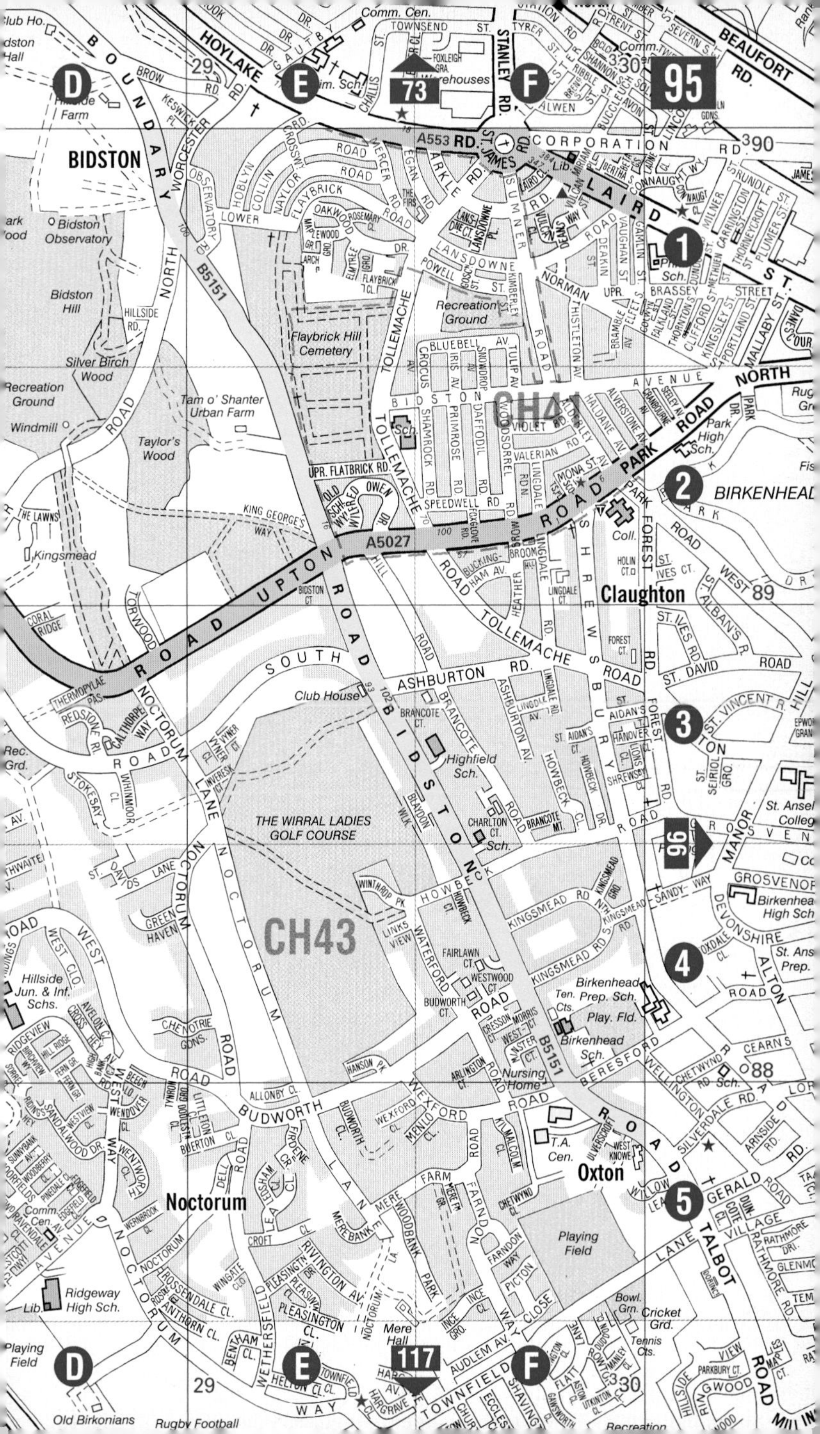
95
73
96
117
BIDSTON
Bidston Observatory
Bidston Hill
Silver Birch Wood
Recreation Ground
Windmill
Tam o' Shanter Urban Farm
Taylor's Wood
Kingsmead
Flaybrick Hill Cemetery
CH41
CH43
BIRKENHEAD
Claughton
Oxton
Noctorum
THE WIRRAL LADIES GOLF COURSE
Highfield Sch.
Birkenhead Prep. Sch.
Birkenhead Sch.
Birkenhead High Sch.
St. Anselm College
Park High Sch.
Ridgeway High Sch.
Hillside Jun. & Inf. Schs.
Playing Field
Bowl. Grn.
Cricket Grd.
Tennis Cts.
Mere Hall
Nursing Home
T.A. Cen.
Club House
Old Birkonians
Rugby Football
HOYLAKE RD.
BOUNDARY RD.
A553 RD.
CORPORATION RD.
BEAUFORT RD.
LAIRD ST.
UPTON ROAD
A5027
PARK ROAD NORTH
BIDSTON ROAD
B5151
TOLLEMACHE ROAD
SOUTH ROAD
NOCTORUM LANE
NOCTORUM ROAD
BUDWORTH ROAD
SHREWSBURY RD.
FOREST RD.
TALBOT ROAD
GROSVENOR
DEVONSHIRE
BIDSTON AVENUE
ASHBURTON RD.
KINGSMEAD RD.
WEST ROAD
NOCTORUM AVENUE
TOWNFIELD WAY
29
330
390
89
88
D
E
F
1
2
3
4
5

96
74
118
95
A
B
C
1
2
3
4
5
Gillbrook Basin
Cavendish Wharf
Duke St. Wharf
Jetty
BEAUFORT RD.
A5030
B5146
CORPORATION ROAD
CORPORATION RD.
CLEVELAND ST.
DUKE ST.
ODYSSEY CENTRE
STANLEY RD.
ILCHESTER RD.
ST. JAMES
Lib.
LAIRD STREET
A553
SUMNER RD.
LANSDOWNE PL.
NORMAN ST.
Prim. Sch.
Bus Depot
JAMESBROOK CL.
BRASSEY STREET
UPR. BRASSEY ST.
Kilgarth Sch.
OLD BIDSTON RD.
BECKWITH ST.
Birkenhead Park
PARK RD. NORTH
NORTH RD.
A5027
PARK ROAD NORTH
AVENUE
Rugby Grd.
Tennis Courts
Bowling Greens
Fish Pond
BIRKENHEAD PARK
PARK DRIVE
CAVENDISH DRIVE
Park High Sch.
MONA ST.
UPTON RD.
Coll.
PARK FOREST
Claughton
WEST PARK RD.
ASHVILLE RD.
DRIVE
Playing Fields
Sports Grd.
Cricket Ground
Pav.
T.A. Cen.
The Laurels
Park High School
PARK ROAD SOUTH
EAST
CLAUGHTON
TOLLEMACHE ROAD
SHREWSBURY RD.
FOREST RD.
ST. DAVID ROAD
EGERTON ROAD
ST. VINCENT R.
HILL
ORD.
EPWORTH GRANGE
CANNON HL.
CANNON MT.
St. Anselm's College
ST. ANDREW'S RD.
SLATEY ROAD
GRANGE ROAD
GROSVENOR ROAD
Playing Fld.
Convent
Spts. Cen.
CH43
Birkenhead High Sch.
DEVONSHIRE PL.
DEVONSHIRE ROAD
St. Anselm's Prep. Sch.
ALTON RD.
MANOR HILL
PALM GROVE
EUSTON GROVE
GRANGE MT.
WESTBOURNE ROAD
OXTON ROAD
BALLS RD. E.
Mus.
HOWBECK RD.
KINGSMEAD RD.
BIDSTON ROAD
Birkenhead Prep. Sch.
Birkenhead Sch.
Nurs. Home
BERESFORD ROAD
WELLINGTON RD.
SHREWSBURY RD.
LORNE RD.
MATHER ROAD
BALL'S ROAD
PALM HILL
CHRISTCHURCH RD.
KINGS MT.
A552
BOROUGH ROAD
Sch.
HOSP.
MOUNT ROAD
VICTORIA MT.
CLAUGHTON FIRS
Oxton
T.A. Cen.
Playing Field
TALBOT ROAD
B5151
GERALD ROAD
VILLAGE ROAD
Bowl. Gm.
Cricket Grd.
Tennis Cts.
KINGSLAND RD.
CARLTON RD.
Prim. Sch.
Wirral Metro. Coll.
WOODCHURCH ROAD
INGESTRE RD.
Prep. Sch.
FERNLEIGH
HIGHGREEN

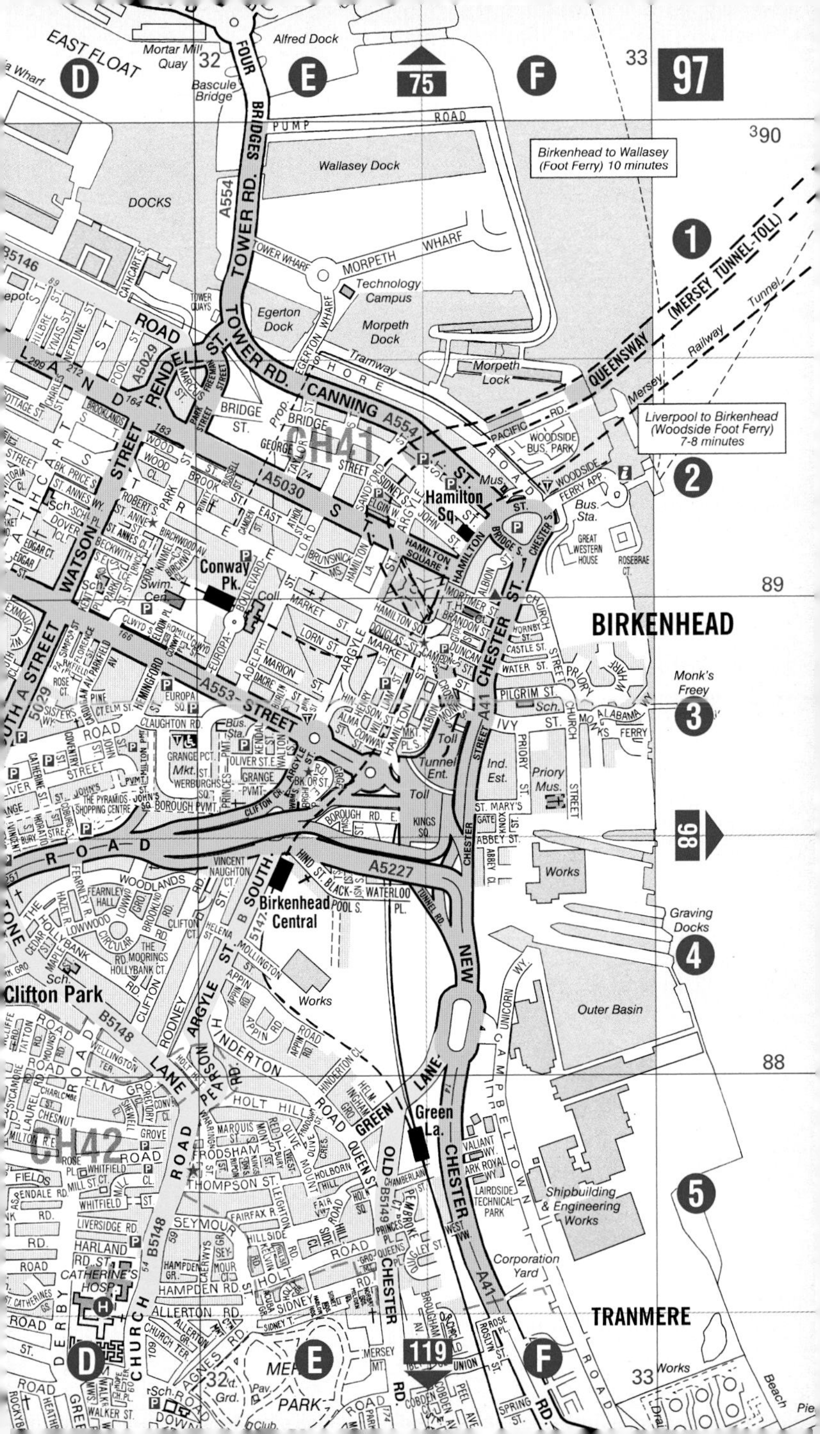
EAST FLOAT
Mortar Mill Quay
Alfred Dock
Bascule Bridge
FOUR BRIDGES
75
PUMP ROAD
Wallasey Dock
DOCKS
Birkenhead to Wallasey (Foot Ferry) 10 minutes
TOWER RD.
MORPETH WHARF
Technology Campus
Egerton Dock
Morpeth Dock
Morpeth Lock
QUEENSWAY (MERSEY TUNNEL-TOLL)
Mersey Railway Tunnel
Liverpool to Birkenhead (Woodside Foot Ferry) 7-8 minutes
CANNING ST.
CH41
WOODSIDE BUS. PARK
WOODSIDE FERRY APP.
Bus Sta.
GREAT WESTERN HOUSE
ROSEBRAE CT.
Hamilton Sq.
HAMILTON SQUARE
Conway Pk.
BIRKENHEAD
Monk's Ferry
Priory Mus.
Ind. Est.
Tunnel Ent.
Toll
KINGS SQ.
98
Works
Graving Docks
Outer Basin
Birkenhead Central
Clifton Park
Green La.
CH42
Shipbuilding & Engineering Works
LAIRDSIDE TECHNICAL PARK
Corporation Yard
TRANMERE
ST. CATHERINE'S HOSP.
119
Beach
A554
A5030
A553
A5227
A41
A5029
B5148
B5149
B5146

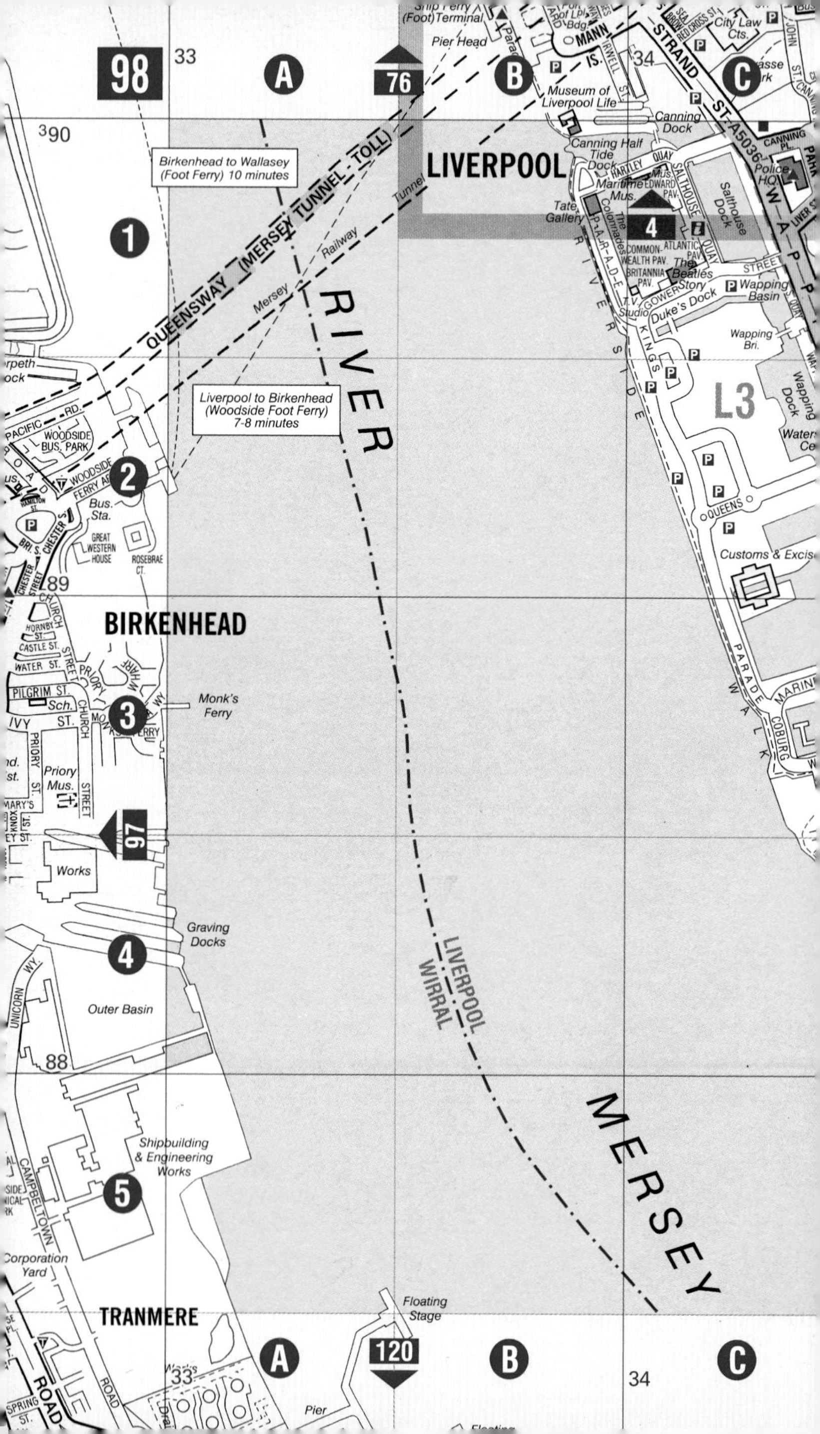

98
33
A
76
B
C
34
Pier Head
STRAND
City Law Cts.
Museum of Liverpool Life
Canning Dock
Canning Half Tide Dock
LIVERPOOL
Birkenhead to Wallasey (Foot Ferry) 10 minutes
QUEENSWAY (MERSEY TUNNEL - TOLL)
Mersey Railway Tunnel
HARTLEY QUAY
Maritime Mus.
Tate Gallery
The Colonnades
4
Salthouse Dock
SALTHOUSE QUAY
COMMON-WEALTH PAV.
ATLANTIC PAV.
BRITANNIA PAV.
The Beatles Story
Wapping Basin
GOWER ST.
Duke's Dock
T.V. Studio
RIVERSIDE
KINGS PARADE
Wapping Bri.
Wapping Dock
L3
1
RIVER
Liverpool to Birkenhead (Woodside Foot Ferry) 7-8 minutes
PACIFIC RD.
WOODSIDE BUS. PARK
WOODSIDE FERRY APP.
2
Bus. Sta.
GREAT WESTERN HOUSE
ROSEBRAE CT.
HAMILTON ST.
CHESTER ST.
QUEENS
Customs & Excise
89
BIRKENHEAD
HORNBY ST.
CASTLE ST.
WATER ST.
CHURCH STREET
PRIORY
PILGRIM ST.
Sch.
IVY ST.
3
Monk's Ferry
PRIORY ST.
Priory Mus.
PARADE
COBURG
WALK
97
Works
Graving Docks
4
UNICORN WY.
Outer Basin
LIVERPOOL
WIRRAL
88
MERSEY
Shipbuilding & Engineering Works
CAMPBELTOWN
5
Corporation Yard
TRANMERE
Floating Stage
A
120
B
C
33
34
Pier
ROAD
SPRING ST.

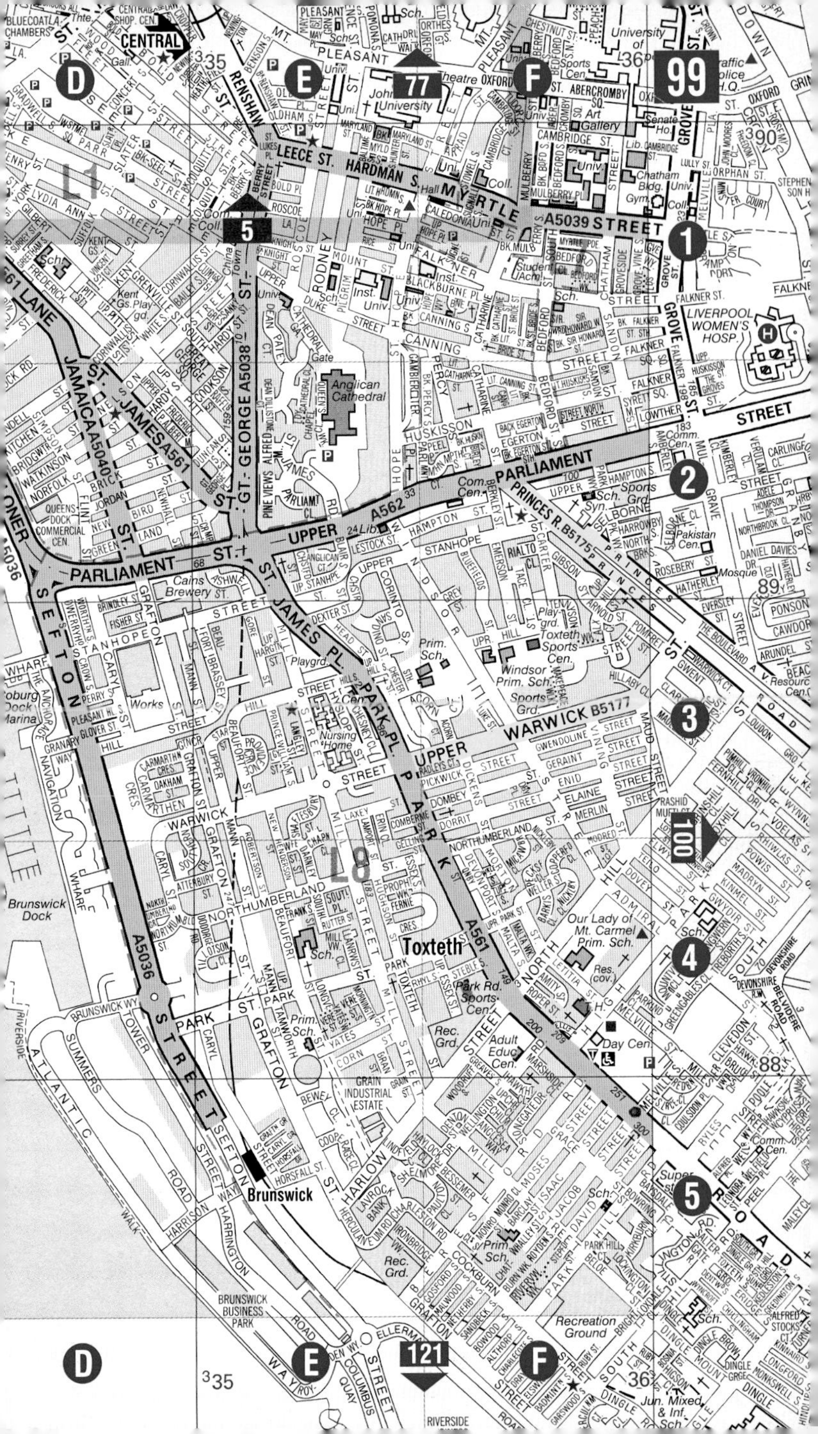

99
77
5
100
121
D
E
F
1
2
3
4
5
CENTRAL
L1
L8
335
3 35
36
390
89
88
RENSHAW ST.
LEECE ST.
HARDMAN S.
MYRTLE
A5039 STREET
University of
Traffic Police H.Q.
OXFORD
ABERCROMBY SQ.
Art Gallery
Senate Ho.
CAMBRIDGE ST.
Chatham Bldg.
Univ.
Gym.
Coll.
FALKNER ST.
LIVERPOOL WOMEN'S HOSP.
GROVE
CATHARINE
CANNING
HUSKISSON
EGERTON
PERCY
Anglican Cathedral
GT. GEORGE A5038 ST.
ST. JAMES A561
JAMAICA A5040
PARLIAMENT ST.
UPPER PARLIAMENT
A562
PRINCES R. B5175
PRINCES
THE BOULEVARD
Cains Brewery
STANHOPE
ST. JAMES PL.
PARK PL.
PARK
A561
UPPER WARWICK B5177
WINDSOR
Windsor Prim. Sch.
Toxteth Sports Cen.
Nursing Home
SEFTON
A5036
SEFTON STREET
Brunswick Dock
Coburg Dock Marina
NAVIGATION
WHARF
Toxteth
Park Rd. Sports Cen.
Rec. Grd.
Adult Educ. Cen.
Day Cen.
Our Lady of Mt. Carmel Prim. Sch.
GRAIN INDUSTRIAL ESTATE
Brunswick
BRUNSWICK BUSINESS PARK
ATLANTIC
WALK
HARRINGTON
HARRISON
Recreation Ground
DINGLE
SOUTH
Jun. Mixed & Inf. Sch.
RIVERSIDE
ELLERMAN
COLUMBUS QUAY
Mosque
Pakistan Cen.
Resource Cen.
Comm. Cen.
Super store
ROAD

100
78
99
122
A
B
C
1
2
3
4
5
36
37
88
89
90
L7
L8
University of Liverpool
Traffic Police H.Q.
OXFORD ST.
Art Gallery
Senate Ho.
CAMBRIDGE ST.
Chatham Bldg.
Gym.
Coll.
MYRTLE ST.
GROVE STREET
A5048
Edge Hill
WAVERTREE SHOPPING CENTRE
Depots
Public Open Space
LIVERPOOL WOMEN'S HOSP.
PARLIAMENT STREET
A562
SMITHDOWN ROAD
SMITHDOWN LANE
UPPER PARLIAMENT ST.
PRINCES RD.
PRINCES AVENUE
B5175
B5174
B5173
B5342
TUNNEL B5173
LODGE LANE
KINGSLEY ROAD
GRANBY STREET
MULGRAVE ST.
UPPER STANHOPE ST.
Pakistan Cen.
Mosque
Play Field
Tiber St. Jun. & Inf. Schs.
Princes Park
PRINCES PARK
CROXTETH ROAD
CROXTETH GROVE
SEFTON PARK ROAD
SEFTON DRI.
MANDELA COURT
DEVONWALL GARDENS
SUNNYSIDE
CAVENDISH GDNS.
Bowling Grns.
Tennis Court
The Lake
Bellerive High Sch.
The Belvedere School
The Belvedere Sch.
DEVONSHIRE RD.
BELVIDERE RD.
ULLET ROAD
ALEXANDRA HOUSE
ALEXANDRA GREEN
AIGBURTH ROAD
A561
AIGBURTH DRIVE
Running Track
Monument
Tennis Cts.
Putting Grn.
Bowling Grns.
Toxteth Sports Cen.
Windsor Prim. Sch.
Sports Grd.
Our Lady of Mt. Carmel Prim. Sch.
Day Cen.
Adult Educ. Cen.
Super-store
PARK ROAD
Recreation Ground
Comp. Sch.
THE TURNER HOME
Playing Field
Rec. Grd.
Jun. Mixed & Inf. Sch.
MANOR HOUSE
ALEXANDRA PK.
SERVITE HO.
ST. PETER'S CT.
T.A. Cen.
CLIN.
LIVINGSTON DR.
Lib.

101
79
102
123
Wavertree Technology Park
Sandown Park
Victoria Park
Wavertree
Sefton Park
SEFTON PARK
Mossley Hill
Greenbank Park
L15
L17
L18
D
E
F
1
2
3
4
5
38
39
88
89
PICTON ROAD
B5178
WELLINGTON ROAD
RATHBONE ROAD
B5179
HIGH STREET
SMITHDOWN ROAD
B5342
A562
QUEENS DRIVE
A5058
MOSSLEY HILL
GREENBANK LANE
NORTH MOSSLEY HILL ROAD
PENNY LANE
CHURCH RD. NORTH
CHURCH ROAD
ALLERTON ROAD
DOVEDALE RD.
BRIARDALE RD.
CROXTETH DRIVE
AIGBURTH VALE
IBBOTSON'S LANE
ELMSLEY ROAD
ROSE LANE
LONG LANE
GAINSBOROUGH RD.
GRANT AV.
CRAWFORD AV.
Warehouses
Cricket Ground
Playing Fields
Athletics Centre
Athletics Track
Tennis Centre
Tennis Cts.
All Weather Pitch
Bowling Greens
Picton Sports Cen.
Wavertree Trading Estate
The Royal Sch. for the Blind
Blue Coat School Playing Fields
The Blue Coat School
The York Centre
Bellerive High Sch.
Penny Lane Neighbourhood Centre
Dovedale Jun. & Inf. Schs.
Liverpool College Playing Fields
Liverpool Coll. (Up. Sch.)
All Weather Sports Pitches
Liverpool College (Lwr. Sch.)
St. Anthony of Padua R.C. Jun. & Inf. Sch.
Mossley Hill Hospital
Nursing Home
Rathbone Ho.
Greenbank Ho.
Roscoe & Gladstone Hall
Derby & Rathbone Hall
Westfield
Parkside Halls of Residence
Sports Grd.
Palm House
Pavilions

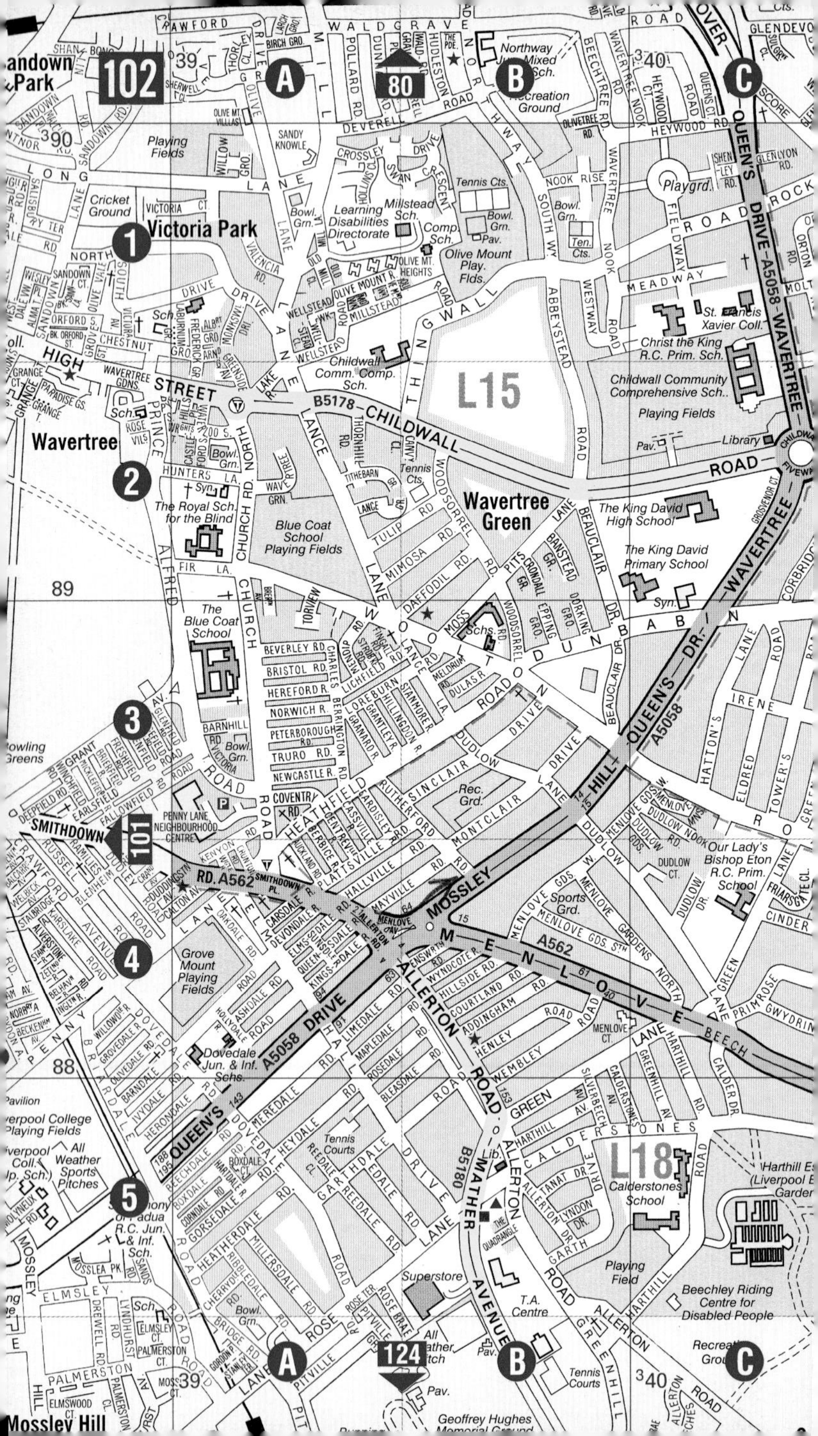
102
Sandown Park
Victoria Park
Wavertree
Wavertree Green
L15
L18
Mossley Hill
Playing Fields
Cricket Ground
Learning Disabilities Directorate
Millstead Sch.
Comp. Sch.
Olive Mount Play. Flds.
Northway Jun. Mixed Sch.
Recreation Ground
Tennis Cts.
Bowl. Grn.
Playgrd.
St. Francis Xavier Coll.
Christ the King R.C. Prim. Sch.
Childwall Community Comprehensive Sch.
Childwall Comm. Comp. Sch.
Library
The Royal Sch. for the Blind
Blue Coat School Playing Fields
The Blue Coat School
The King David High School
The King David Primary School
Penny Lane Neighbourhood Centre
Grove Mount Playing Fields
Rec. Grd.
Sports Grd.
Our Lady's Bishop Eton R.C. Prim. School
Dovedale Jun. & Inf. Schs.
Liverpool College Playing Fields
All Weather Sports Pitches
Tennis Courts
Calderstones School
Playing Field
Superstore
T.A. Centre
Beechley Riding Centre for Disabled People
Geoffrey Hughes Memorial Ground
HIGH STREET
B5178 CHILDWALL ROAD
QUEEN'S DRIVE A5058 WAVERTREE
QUEEN'S DRIVE A5058
SMITHDOWN RD. A562
MENLOVE AVENUE A562
ALLERTON ROAD
B5180 MATHER AVENUE
MOSSLEY HILL
WOOLTON ROAD
DUNBABIN ROAD
PENNY LANE
CHURCH ROAD
THINGWALL LANE
LANCE LANE
80
101
124
39
340
89
88
A
B
C
1
2
3
4
5

103
81
104
125
D
E
F
1
2
3
4
5
41
42
88
89
390
Court Hey
COURT HEY PARK
Ckt. Grd.
Pav.
King George's Memorial Field
National Wildflower Centre
St. Paschal Baylon R.C. Prim. Sch.
Ten. Cts.
Bowling Grn.
Rudston Jun.& Inf. Sch.
B5178
CHILDWALL VALLEY
Pavilion
Public Open Space
Playing Field
Score Lane Gardens
CHILDWALL
Craighurst Primary Sch.
Abbots Lea School
L16
L25
The Grounds
Childwall College of Further Education
Alderman John Village Garden
GATEACRE SHOP. CEN.
Liverpool Hope University College
Sports Ground
Childwall C.of E. Primary Sch.
Playing Fields
Childwall Woods
Gateacre School
Playing Field
Black Wood
409
479
Woolton Park
High Lee Sports Ground
St. Francis Xaviers College
Harold Magnay School Play. Fld.
Abbots Lea School
Lower Lee Sch.
Play. Field
Knolle Park
Palmerston Sch.
Strawberry Fields
Woolton Hill
Reynolds Park
Tennis Courts
Recreation Ground
A562
WOOLTON ROAD
WOOLTON HILL RD.
BEACONSFIELD ROAD
CHURCH ROAD
QUEENS DRIVE
GATEACRE PARK DRIVE
HARTSBOURNE AVENUE
CHILDWALL ABBEY ROAD
CHILDWALL PRIORY RD.
SCORE LANE
BARNHAM DR.
GATEACRE BROW
CHILDWALL PARK AVENUE
COUNTISBURY DRIVE
WELL LANE
BALDWIN AV.
WALSINGHAM ROAD
MANVERS ROAD
CHRISTOPHER WY.
BOWLAND
ORCHARD AV.
GLADSTONE RD.
EDENHURST
SANDBROOK RD.
CRANWELL ROAD
QUICKSWOOD DR.
ROCKBOURNE
DOWNHAM WAY
BLACKWOOD AV.
WOOD VIEW RD.
CUCKOO LANE
GRANGE LANE
DRUIDS' CROSS
DRUIDSVILLE RD.
HORNBY LANE
GIPSY LANE
ALDBOURNE AVE
DUNSDON RD.

104
82
103
126
A
B
C
1
2
3
4
5
42
43
89
88
390
409
479
L16
L25
M62
B5178
B5171
COURT HEY PARK
Ckt. Grd.
Pav.
Walled Garden
National Wildflower Centre
Park
BOWRING GOLF COURSE
RIMMER AV.
RIMMER AV.
ROAD
BUTTERMERE R.
BUTTERMERE RD.
BUTTERMERE R.
KESWICK WY.
GLYNNE GR.
GLADSTONE
EWART RD.
AVENUE
BOWRING PARK AV.
SHEPPARD AVENUE
EDENHURST AVENUE
St. Paschal Baylon R.C. Sch.
ST. PASCHAL BAYLON BLVD.
WOODBANK CL.
AVENUE
PEACEHAVEN CL.
HARWICH GR.
CHILDWALL
Ten. Cts.
Pav.
Sports Ground
Bowling Grn.
Public Open Space
SANDBROOK RD.
VALLEY
JACKSONS POND DR.
HARTSBOURNE
WELLGREEN ROAD
NAPPS WY.
HILDWALL HTS.
DRONFIELD WY.
LWR. FARM RD.
MARCHWD WAY
DEEPDALE RD.
CRAIGHURST RD.
CRANWELL ROAD
Craighurst Primary Sch.
KNOWSLEY
LIVERPOOL
SARUM RD.
SHREWTON RD.
DAMERHAM CFT.
ACRES CL.
ELMHURST
DAMERHAM MS.
CLOVERDALE RD.
DAUNTSEY BW.
DAUNTSEY MEWS
DALEBROOK CL.
CROSS ACRE RD.
ROAD
CORNWOOD CL.
COLTON
HEADBOURNE CL.
WELL
GATEACRE
AVENUE
LYNDENE RD.
CRANWELL RD.
TALGARTH WY.
HARTOPP RD.
MILDENHALL
MURRAYFIELD
MERIDEN
MARLBRK
ROAD
AVENUE
CHILDWALL
RIMMERBROOK
FARMBROOK
KENTON CL.
ROADWATER CL.
STAPLETON
DORSET
MADEIRA DRIVE
GENOA CL.
ECCLES DR.
VIENNESE RD.
SIMNEL CL.
TRELWNY
DORCHESTER ROAD
MAYFORD CL.
Joseph Williams Prim. & Wheatmill Spec. Sch.
NAYLORSFIELD
NAYLORSFIELD DR.
ST. CYRILS CL.
SOUTHBROOK WAY
WOODGATE
SILVERBK
FARMVIEW
Sch.
Alderman John Village Garden
ESCOR RD.
HAYLES CL.
HARTSBOURNE
HAVELEIGH
HASLEMERE
CHISLEHURST
THURNE WY.
GREEN
GORSEY COP WY.
GORSEY COP RD.
MALLTON WK.
HATHAWAY
HATHAWAY CL.
Playing Fields
Our Lady of the Assumption R.C. Jun. & Inf. Schs.
HEDGEFIELD RD.
ABBEYVALE
STAPLEFORD DRI.
WAYS
CROSS
LANE
GATEACRE SHOP. CEN.
LEYBOURNE CL.
LEYBOURNE GRN.
LEYBOURNE GRO.
ROAD
CRANLEIGH PL.
CRANLEIGH RD.
CAPSTICK CR.
COCKSHEAD RD.
COCKSHEAD WAY
AVENUE
BELLE VALE SHOPPING CENTRE
Swim. Pool
ROAD
Belle Vale Park
LEE PARK
WESTB
PARK
PEARCE CL.
QUICKSWOOD DR.
DOWNHAM CL.
DOWNHAM WAY
HEATH CL.
QUICKSWOOD
ACRESGATE CT.
ELMSFIELD CL.
GRANGE
GRANGEMEADOW RD.
BARNMEADOW RD.
SPRINGMEADOW RD.
STATION
WYNER RD. NORTH
WYNER RD. SOUTH
BEECHURST CL.
LINESIDE CL.
HARTSBOURNE AV.
BESFORD
HERDMAN CL.
BESFORD HOUSE
WAMBO LA.
CHURCHFIELD RD.
LENTON RD.
HEATH HEY
Gateacre School
Playing Field
GRANGESIDE
WAY
ROAD
Gateacre
LARCHWOOD CL.
OAKWOOD CL.
Belle Vale Jun. & Inf. Sch.
BESFORD R.
CHURCH COTTS.
BARDON CL.
ROCKBNE WY.
CUCKOO NOOK
FIELDFARE CL.
DRIVE
ROCKBOURNE GRN.
REDWING LA.
LANE
BEECHURST RD.
OAKHURST CL.
SOUTH STN.
GORSEWOOD
GORSEWOOD GR.
REDWOOD CL.
GORSEDD
ROAD
Yth. Cen.
ST. STEPHENS CL.
VICARAGE CL.
ADSTONE RD.
MARSHE
WOOLTON
WOOD VIEW RD.
WILLOW GN.
LYNTON GN.
SISKIN GRN.
PEACOCK GRN.
CUCKOO CL.
CUCKOO LANE
MEADOW DR.
Oakfield Cen.
OAKFIELD AVE.
MT. MERRION
THE PADDOCK
ASHURST CL.
EAGLEHURST ROAD
BELLE VUE RD.
Liverpool
VALE
JONES FARM RD.
WIDMORE RD.
WOODLEE RD.
PARK
ROSEHILL CT.
ROAD
HILLSIDE
GRANGE WEINT
GRANGE RISE
GATEACRE CT.
CHARTMOUNT WAY
SOUTH STATION RD.
KILLESTER RD.
LEE
RINGWAY
BEECHILL CL.
FORDCOMBE RD.
CHARDSTOCK DR.
KINGS
GREENDALE
Woolton Park
BOWER
ROAD
ROSE BROW
GATEACRE BROW
BELLE
YORK COTTS.
LANE
Rec. Grd.
Loop
Line
VALE
MARTLAND R.
FRITH RD.
ROAD
HALEWOOD
ROAD
WOOLTON HILL ROAD
Play. Fld.
Knolle Park
CHURCH
COURTENAY RD.
PARKWOOD RD.
WINHILL
WOOLTON
RUNNYMEDE CL.
ACREFIELD RD.
DALEMS
SANDFIELD
LWR. SDFD R.
Nursery
HALEWOOD CL.
HOLLYMEAD CL.
THORNSIDE WK.
ELM HO.
THE NOOK
Corporation Depot
BARONCROFT RD.
Woolton Hill
Reynolds Park
Tennis Courts
GLENVILLE CL.
HUNTS
HOLLYTREE
ROAD
TURNERS CT.
DEE HO.
WEAVER HO.
RIBBLE HO.
RIBBLE ROAD
RIVER WEAVER CT.
DEE CT.
THE RIDGE
WOOLTON PK. CL.
LONGWORTH WAY
GLENACRES
RESERVOIR
ROAD
CRESTO
ORIENT DRI.
DRIVE CROSS
MEADOW
KNOTTY M.

105
83
106
127
D
E
F
1
2
3
4
5
344
345
390
89
88
L36
L35
L27
St. Anne's R.C. Prim. Sch.
MARINA
RUSKIN
CEDAR CR.
CHARLWOOD
BELFIELD CR.
ACACIA AVENUE
PINETREE
CHESTNUT AV.
LILAC GR.
CYPRESS
ROWAN GR.
ROAD
OAK DRIVE
Ten Acre Pits
SYCAMORE RD.
LABURNUM AV.
LAUREL GR.
PEAR TREE RD.
YEW TREE RD.
WILLOW AV.
CHERRY TREE RD.
LINDEN DR.
ASH CR.
WOKINGHAM GRO.
CEDARWOOD CL.
FIELDS END
SILVERDALE CL.
HILL RD.
THE CHASE
GREENLANDS
CROSSVALE RD.
BIRCH
TARBOCK RD.
ST. JOHN'S RD.
GREENFIELD GRO.
SANDIWAY
MANOR FARM ROAD
Field
Pav.
Comm. Cen.
DEEPFIELD DR.
HOLMEFIELD GR.
OAKFIELD DR.
OAKFIELD DRIVE
MEADOW FIELDWAY
ELIZABETH
DARWICK DR.
BOUNDARY DR.
ALDER AVENUE
SCOTT
KIPLING
TENNYSON ROAD
MANLEY RD.
LOGWOOD
ROAD
COWPER
M62 MOTORWAY
A5080
HUYTON BROOK
BIGLANDS DRIVE
BELL CL.
CHALLOW CL.
BARKER CL.
SPENCER CL.
RICKMAN WY.
CORNEL WAY
MALLOW WAY
CAMPION WAY
LANE
BARDLEY
HAWKE GN.
RICHMOND WY.
CRINGLES
Wheathill Farm
NAYLOR'S ROAD
WHEAT
HOLT LANE
Club House
CHILDWALL GOLF COURSE
CONEY
Holt Hall (Adult Training Centre)
Sewage Works
NAYLORS
CALDWAY
HOLT LANE
BRUEN CL.
PAVELEY BANK
WHEATHILLS IND. EST.
Sub.
CRANBRY
SULLINGTON DR.
CLEMATIS
CLOUDBY CL.
LYDIETH
PINEWOOD CL.
DIGNUM
DAMSON
EVERGREEN CL.
ROSESIDE DR.
LAURUS CL.
DRIVE
KENWOOD CL.
SKELLINGTON
FOLD
Netherley Bridge
NETHERLEY ROAD
Yew Tree Farm
WHITEFIELD
RUSHLAKE DR.
TUFFINS CORNER
Public Open Space
LODGE GRO.
CRABTREE
BRAMLEY CL.
CRISPIN RD.
LINDEN
GARDEN LODGE GR.
RUSSET CL.
GATESIDE CL.
St. Gregory's R.C. Jun. Mixed & Inf. Sch.
MIDDLEMASS HEY
VETCH HEY
BROWNBILL BANK
Norman Pannell Prim. Sch.
B5178
CALDWAY
ROAD
WOOD
Netherley Brook
Lib.
Thtre.
Lee Manor High School
Lee Manor Sports Cen.
Club House
Playing Field
FULMAR CL.
WHEATEAR CL.
DUNLIN CL.
SHEARWATER CL.
STONECHAT CL.
PARKVIEW DRIVE
BRITTARGE BROW
FERN CL.
TUDOR HOUSE
LINGFORD CL.
LANGSHAW LEA
SHERFORD CL.
SHARWOOD RD.
BEESANDS
Cross Farm Junior Mixed & Infant School
TOTHALE TURN
WINSTER DRIVE
ULVERSTON LAWN
EGREMONT RD.
KIRKBRIDE LN.
APPLEBY RD.
LAKESIDE LAWN
HEYSHAM RD.
MARDALE RD.
RIDSDALE LAWN
Mill Bridge Farm
Mill Brook
EE PARK
F COURSE
Works
North End Cottages
LANE
44

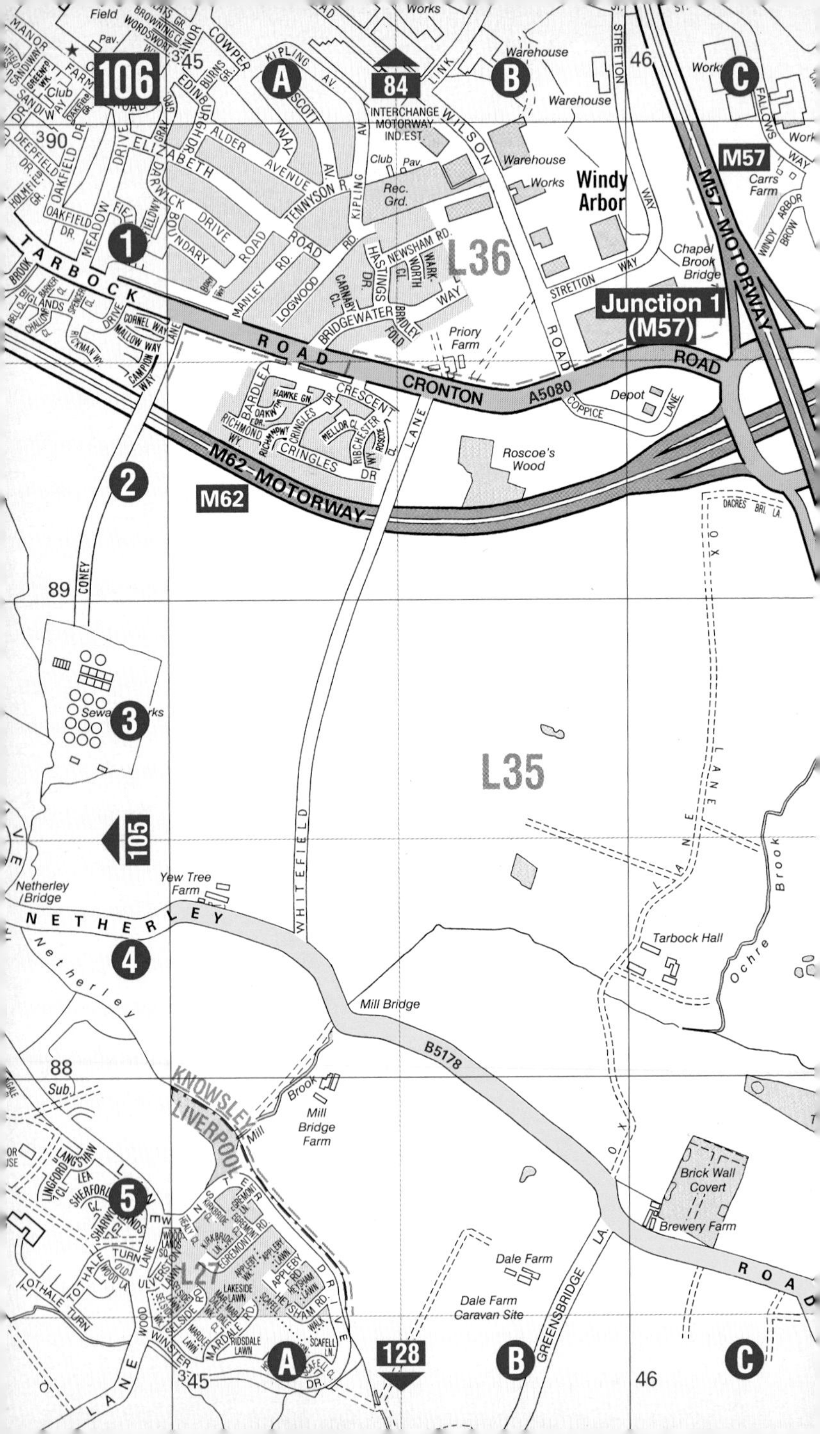
106
84
105
128
A
B
C
1
2
3
4
5
L36
L35
L27
Windy Arbor
Junction 1 (M57)
M57
M57 MOTORWAY
M62
M62 MOTORWAY
TARBOCK ROAD
CRONTON ROAD
A5080
NETHERLEY
B5178
ROAD
INTERCHANGE MOTORWAY IND. EST.
Warehouse
Works
Rec. Grd.
Club
Pav.
Priory Farm
Depot
Roscoe's Wood
Chapel Brook Bridge
Carrs Farm
Yew Tree Farm
Netherley Bridge
Sewage Works
Mill Bridge
Mill Bridge Farm
Tarbock Hall
Brick Wall Covert
Brewery Farm
Dale Farm
Dale Farm Caravan Site
Ochre Brook
KNOWSLEY
LIVERPOOL
WHITEFIELD LANE
CONEY LANE
OX LANE
GREENSBRIDGE LA.
STRETTON WAY
STRETTON ROAD
WILSON ROAD
KIPLING AV.
TENNYSON R.
ALDER AVENUE
ELIZABETH
DARWICK DRIVE
BOUNDARY
MANLEY RD.
LOGWOOD ROAD
HASTINGS DR.
NEWSHAM RD.
BRIDGEWATER
BRADLEY FOLD
BARDLEY CRESCENT
CRINGLES DR.
RICHMOND WY.
RIBCHESTER DR.
HAWKE GN.
MELLOR CL.
COPPICE LANE
CORNEL WAY
MALLOW WAY
CAMPION WAY
BIGLANDS DRIVE
OAKFIELD DR.
MEADOW
DEEPFIELD DR.
HOLMFIELD GR.
EDINBURGH RD.
COWPER
SCOTT
MANOR FARM ROAD
Field
Club
DACRES BRI. LA.
WINDY ARBOR BROW
FALLOWS WAY
Sub.
LANGSHAW
SHERFORD CL.
LINGFORD CL.
TOTHALE TURN
WOOD LANE
ULVERSTON LAWN
WINSTER
EGREMONT RD.
APPLEBY LAWN
HEYSHAM RD.
LAKESIDE LAWN
RIDSDALE LAWN
SCAFELL LN.
DRIVE
Mill
Brook
88
89
90
45
46

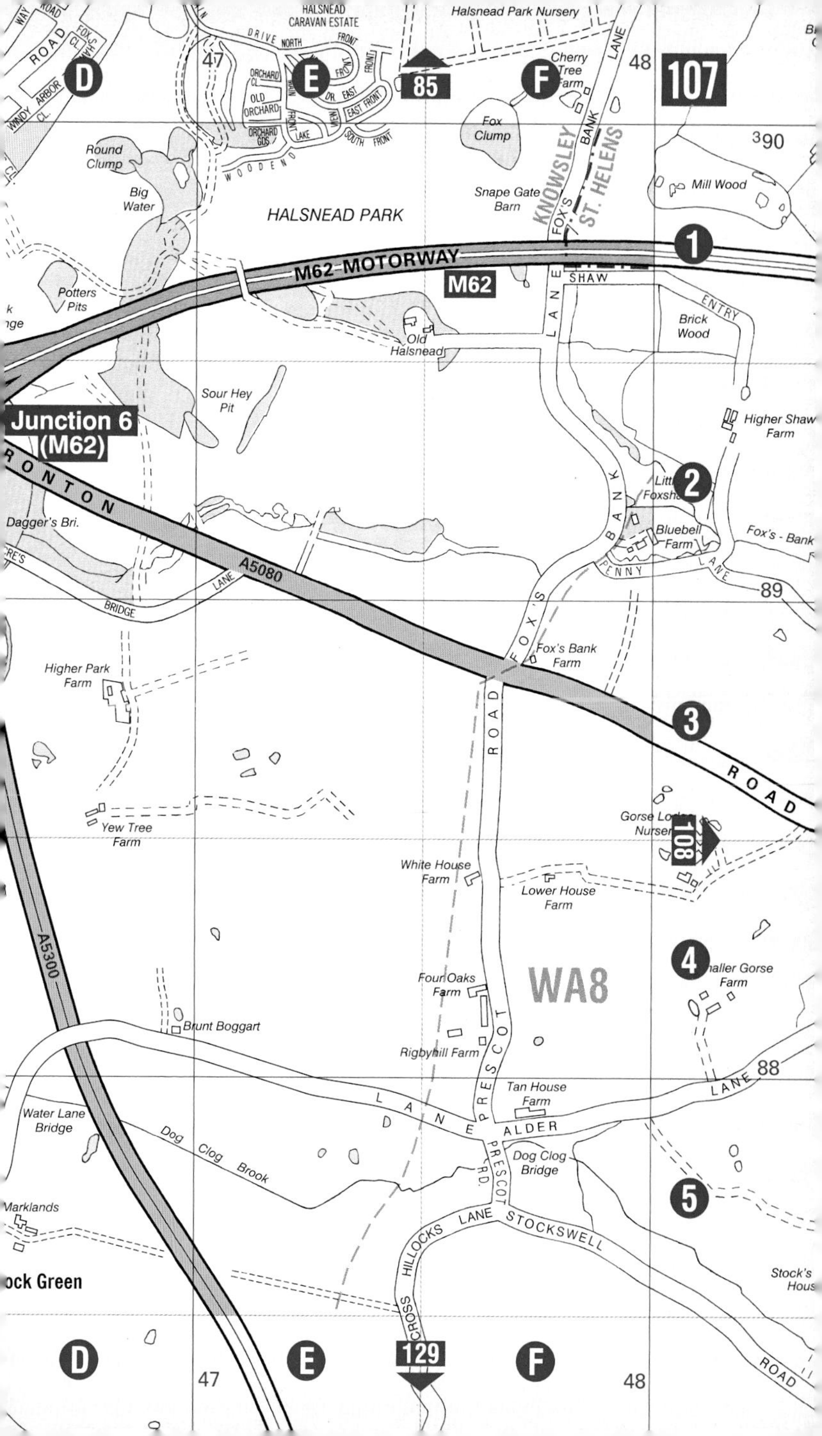

107
HALSNEAD CARAVAN ESTATE
Halsnead Park Nursery
85
Cherry Tree Farm
Fox Clump
KNOWSLEY LANE
FOX'S BANK
ST. HELENS
Round Clump
Big Water
HALSNEAD PARK
Snape Gate Barn
Mill Wood
M62 MOTORWAY
M62
SHAW ENTRY
Brick Wood
Potters Pits
Old Halsnead
Sour Hey Pit
Junction 6 (M62)
Higher Shaw Farm
RONTON ROAD
Little Foxshaw
Bluebell Farm
Fox's Bank
PENNY LANE
Dagger's Bri.
A5080
BRIDGE LANE
Fox's Bank Farm
Higher Park Farm
PRESCOT ROAD
Gorse Lodge Nursery
108
Yew Tree Farm
White House Farm
Lower House Farm
A5300
Four Oaks Farm
WA8
Smaller Gorse Farm
Brunt Boggart
Rigbyhill Farm
Tan House Farm
ALDER LANE
Water Lane Bridge
Dog Clog Brook
Dog Clog Bridge
PRESCOT RD.
Marklands
HILLOCKS LANE
STOCKSWELL ROAD
CROSS
Stock's House
Bold Heath Green
129
D
E
F
47
48
390
89
88
1
2
3
4
5

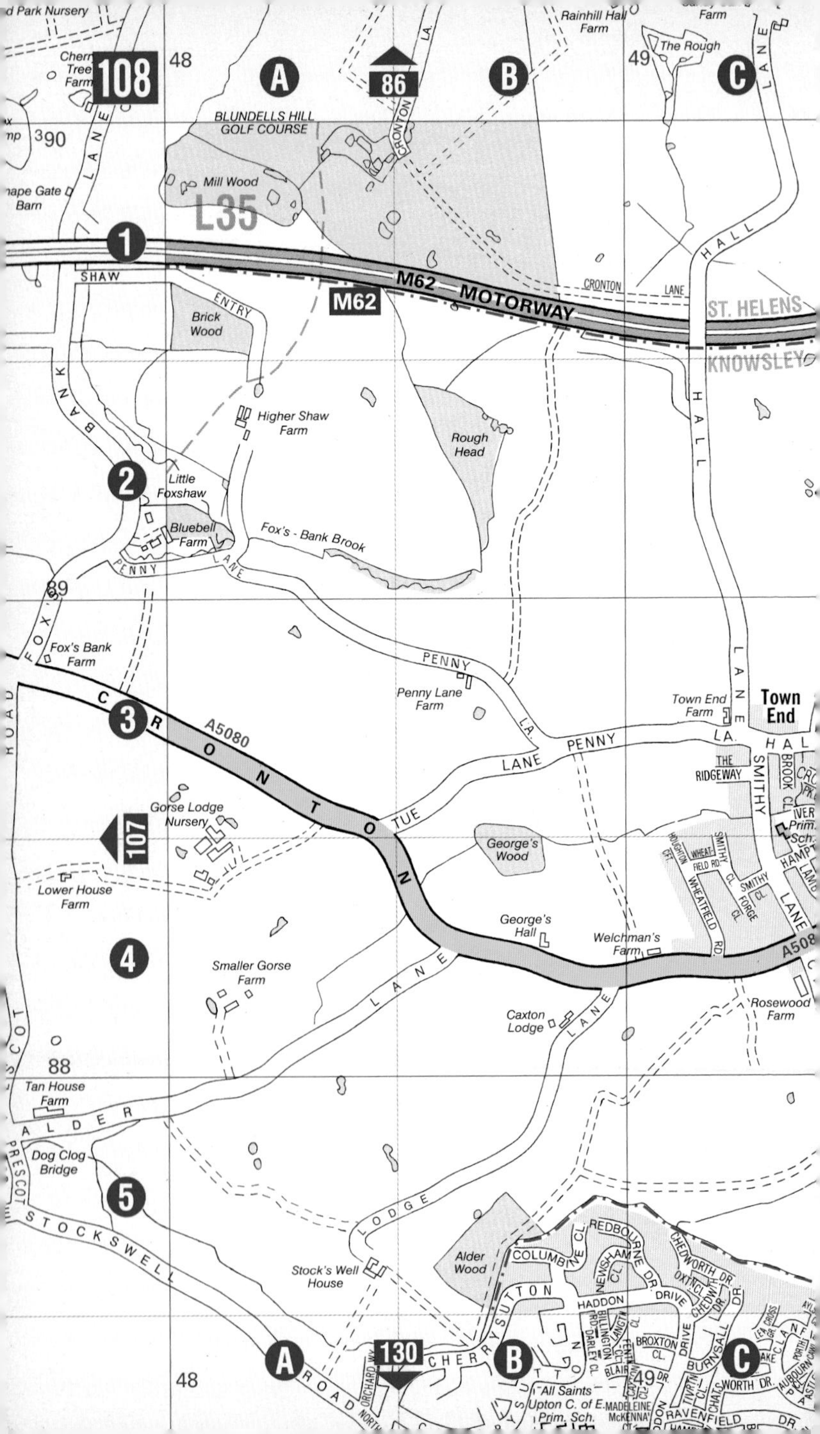
108
48
A
86
B
49
C
BLUNDELLS HILL GOLF COURSE
Mill Wood
L35
1
M62 MOTORWAY
M62
ST. HELENS
KNOWSLEY
Brick Wood
Higher Shaw Farm
Rough Head
2
Little Foxshaw
Bluebell Farm
Fox's - Bank Brook
89
Fox's Bank Farm
Penny Lane Farm
Town End Farm
Town End
3
A5080
CRONTON
Gorse Lodge Nursery
107
George's Wood
Lower House Farm
George's Hall
Welchman's Farm
4
Smaller Gorse Farm
Caxton Lodge
Rosewood Farm
88
Tan House Farm
Dog Clog Bridge
5
Alder Wood
Stock's Well House
A
130
B
48
49
C
All Saints Upton C. of E. Prim. Sch.
Rainhill Hall Farm
The Rough
Cherry Tree Farm
Park Nursery
Snape Gate Barn
390

109
87
110
131
Junction 7
M62
M62 MOTORWAY
WARRINGTON ROAD
A57
WIDNES EASTERN BY-PASS
A557
ST. HELENS
HALTON
KNOWSLEY
WA8
CRONTON ROAD
A5080
LUNT'S HEATH RD.
NORLAND'S LANE
WILMERE LANE
BIRCHFIELD ROAD
SANDY LANE
UPTON LANE
OLD UPTON LANE
Sandhill Farm
Rainhill Place Farm
Fairview House
PLAYING FIELDS
THE NORLANDS
Nursing Home
Norlands House
Visitor Centre
PEX HILL
Cronton Wood
The Grange
Widnes Sixth Form College
Community Centre
R.C. Prim. Sch.
Rock House
Upton Lodge
Upton House
Upton Rocks
Linacre House
Rec. Ground
Pavs.
Crematorium
SCHOOL LA
CAXTON RD.
THORNDYKE CLO.
ST. HELENS LINKWAY
ROUNDABOUT LA.
MILL LANE
STRATTON PARK
TYNWALD CRES.
HILL VIEW
COWAN WAY
TUSON DR.
TUSON DRIVE
LINDEN WAY
INGHAM RD.
BRIDLE PATH
BUCKINGHAM DR.
CORONER'S LA
CLARENCE AV.
HOLYROOD AV.
MONICA DR.
SANDRINGHAM R.
WINDSOR R.
BALMORAL RD.
UPTON PARK
GATE
NEW BARNET
WHITSTABLE CT.
LESSINGHAM ROAD
GRANGE WAY
CORNERHOUSE LANE
College
Playing Fields
D
E
F
1
2
3
4
5
350
390
51
89
88
50

M62 MOTORWAY
Junction 7
88
109
132
UNION BANK LANE
Union Bank Farm
JUBITS LANE B5419
WARRINGTON ROAD A57
Rainhill Place Farm
Wilmere House
Old Brook Hall
Upper Bank Farm Cottage
WIDNES EASTERN BY-PASS A557
A557
Fairview House
PLAYING FIELDS
WILMERE LANE B5419
WA8
Cranshaw Hall
CRANSHAW LA.
THE NORLANDS Nursing Home
Glebe Farm
LUNT'S HEATH ROAD A5080
CRONTON LA.
BIRCHFIELD ROAD B5419
Lunt's Bridge Farm
BOLD IND. EST.
Sports Grd.
Lunts Heath Prim. Sch.
Grave Yard
Lunts Heath
Rec. Ground
Farnworth C. of E. Prim. Sch.
Cricket Ground
Works
Upton Rocks
Crematorium
FARNWORTH ST.
PIT LANE
DERBY ROAD
UPTON LANE
BRIDLE PATH
CORONER'S LANE
GLEBE LANE

Cottage
Nest
Farm
D
E
F
53
54
89
390
CLOCK FACE ROAD
A569
CROSS LANE
Cross
Tibb's Cross Farm
Kebb's Farm
Eccles Plantation
Club House
MERSEY VALLEY GOLF COURSE
1
2
3
4
5
Nursery Farm
Holly House
SCHOOL LA.
A57
Bold Heath Plantation
Heath Side
FERNDALE CL.
LANE
Liverpool Road Nursery
Bold Heath Farm
Works
ROAD
Bold Heath
SANDY LA.
ENTRY LANE
Hayfield Farm
ST. HELENS
LANE
MILL GREEN
Mill Green Farm
SOUTH LANE
SOUTH LA.
South Lane Farm
88
A5080
ROAD FARNWORTH ROAD
Rose Farm
Boundary Farm
Abbey Farm
Pendlebury Farm
LANE
CEDARDALE PK.
Barrow's Green
GREEN
DAFFODIL CL.
SNOWBERRY CL.
WEATES CLOSE
DYKIN CL.
WHALLEY GRO.
SCHOOL WY.
Moorfield Prim. Sch.
NURSERY CL.
Youth Centre
BARROWS
Wood End Farm
ELTHAM CL.
MITHRIL CL.
BELGRAVE CL.
SHEVINGTON
FAIRBURN
RIBBLE CL.
HUMBER CL.
CROSS GATES
AVEBURY
133

90
134
HOYLAKE MUNICIPAL GOLF COURSE
ROYAL LIVERPOOL GOLF COURSE
CH47
WEST KIRBY
West Kirby
MEOLS DRIVE
GRANGE ROAD
A540
B5141
BANKS ROAD
GREENBANK LANE
LANG LANE
BLACK HORSE
COLUMN ROAD
VILLAGE ROAD
CHURCH ROAD
RECTORY RD.
SANDY LANE
CALDY ROAD
SOUTH PARADE
HILBRE ROAD
DEE LANE
West Kirby Marine Lake
(Wirral Sailing School)
Club House
Playing Field
Football Ground
Grange Hill
War Mem.
Cemetery
Ashton Park
Comm. Cen.
Prim. Sch.
Avalon Prep. Sch.
Tell's Tower
Gilroy Nature Pa
W.Kirby Grammar Sch. for Girls
T.A. Centre

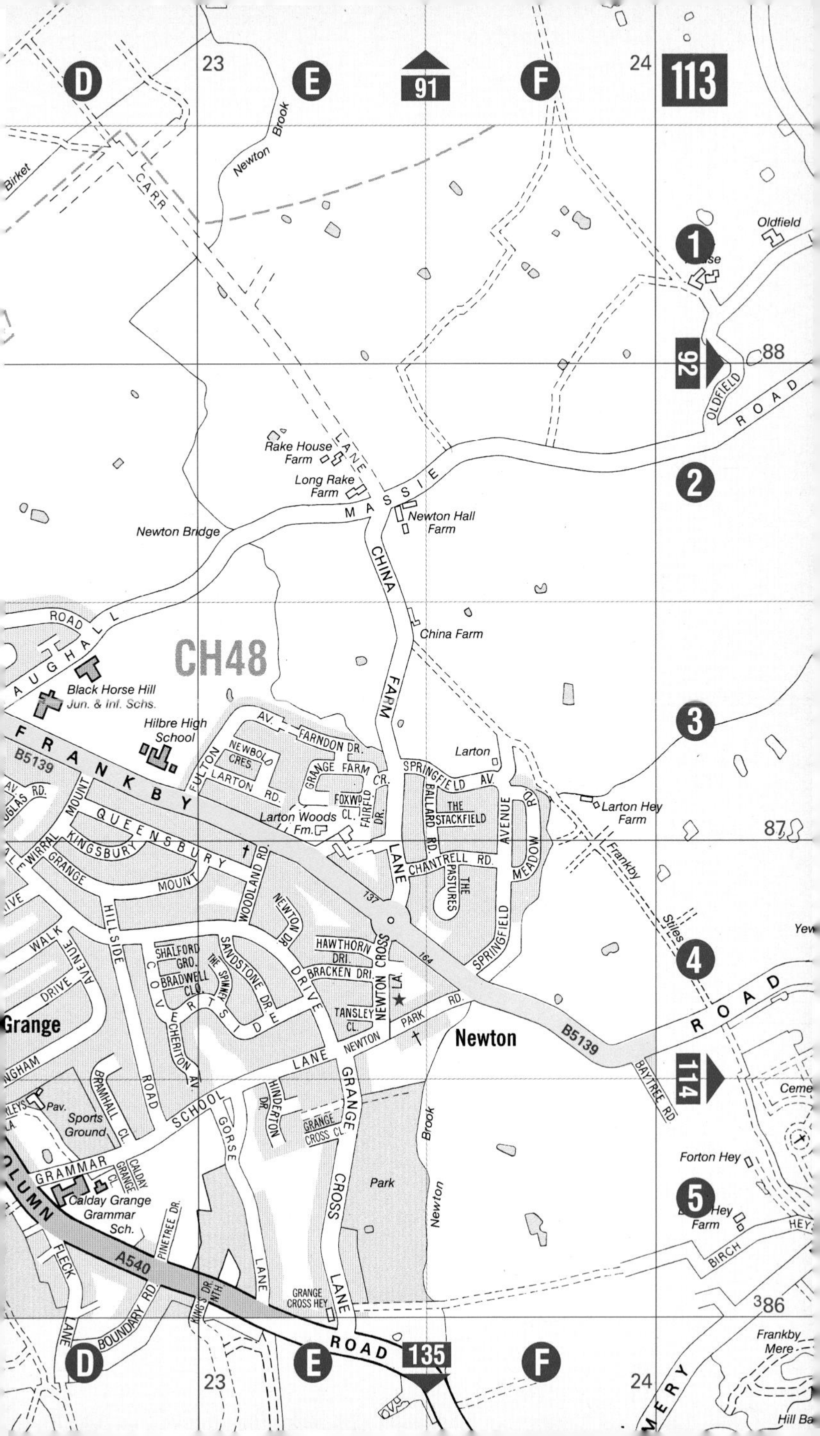

91
D
E
F
23
24
Newton Brook
Birket
CARR
LANE
Oldfield
Rake House Farm
Long Rake Farm
MASSIE
ROAD
OLDFIELD
92
88
Newton Hall Farm
Newton Bridge
CHINA
FARM
China Farm
CH48
AUGHALL
Black Horse Hill Jun. & Inf. Schs.
Hilbre High School
FRANKBY
B5139
FULTON
AV.
FARNDON DR.
NEWBOLD CRES.
LARTON RD.
GRANGE FARM CR.
FOXWD. CL.
FAIRFIELD DR.
Larton Woods Fm.
Larton
SPRINGFIELD AV.
BALLARD RD.
THE STACKFIELD
AVENUE
MEADOW
Larton Hey Farm
87
Frankby
Stiles
MOUNT
QUEENSBURY
KINGSBURY
WIRRAL
GRANGE
HILLSIDE
WOODLAND RD.
NEWTON DR.
LANE
CHANTRELL RD.
THE PASTURES
SPRINGFIELD
137
164
HAWTHORN DRI.
BRACKEN DRI.
NEWTON CROSS LA.
TANSLEY CL.
PARK RD.
NEWTON
Newton
B5139
ROAD
BAYTREE RD.
114
WALK
AVENUE
DRIVE
SHALFORD GRO.
BRADWELL CLO.
THE SPINNEY
SANDSTONE DR.
COVERTSIDE
CHERITON AV.
DRIVE
Grange
SCHOOL LANE
HINDERTON DR.
GRANGE CROSS CL.
GORSE
LANE
GRANGE CROSS LANE
Brook
Newton
Park
Pav.
Sports Ground
BRAMHALL CL.
ROAD
GRAMMAR
CALDAY GRANGE CL.
Calday Grange Grammar Sch.
PINETREE DR.
COLUMN
A540
FLECK
LANE
BOUNDARY RD.
KING'S DR. NTH.
GRANGE CROSS HEY
ROAD
135
Forton Hey
Hey Farm
BIRCH
HEY
386
Frankby Mere
MERY
Yew
Ceme
Hill Ba

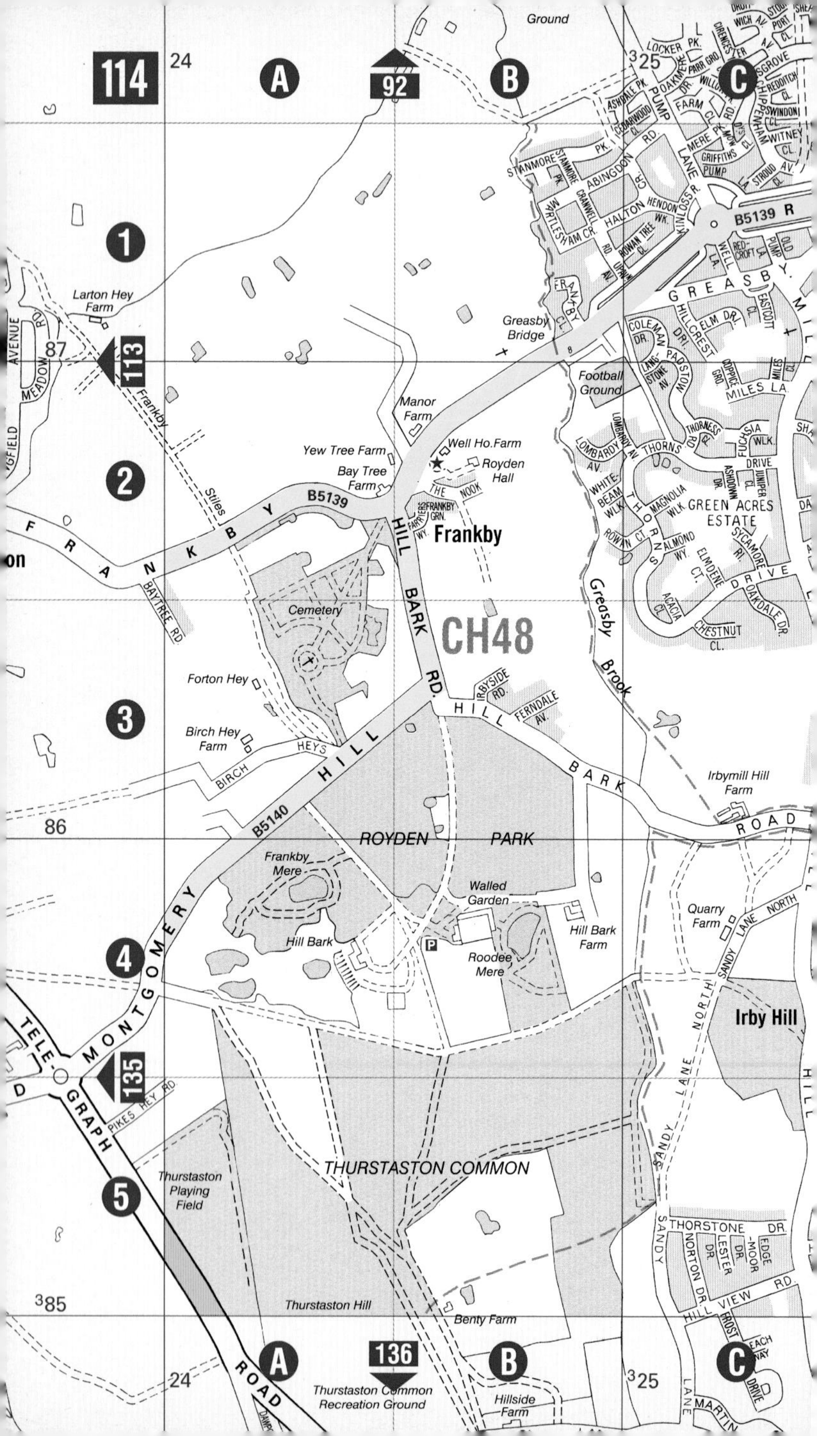

114
24
A
92
B
C
Ground
3 25
LOCKER PK.
CIRENCESTER AV.
WICH AV.
STOCKPORT CL.
SHEA
ASHDALE PK.
PUMP
OAKMERE DR.
PARR GRO.
WILLOW
SGROVE
CHIPPENHAM
REDDITCH CL.
SWINDON CL.
WITNEY CL.
CEDARWOOD CL.
FARM CL.
MERE PK.
GRIFFITHS CL.
STROUD AV.
ABINGDON RD.
PK.
LANE
STANMORE
STANMORE PK.
CRANWELL
MARTLESHAM CR.
HALTON
HENDON WK.
KINLOSS R.
B5139 R
ROWAN TREE CL.
UPAVON AV.
RD.
WELL LA.
REDCROFT
PUMP LA.
OLD
GREASBY
MILL
FRANKBY CL.
EASTCOTT CL.
HILLCREST DRI.
ELM DRI.
COLEMAN DR.
PADSTOW
LANGSTONE AV.
COPPICE GRO.
MILES CL.
MILES LA.
1
Larton Hey Farm
Greasby Bridge
AVENUE
MEADOW RD.
87
113
GFIELD
Frankby
Football Ground
Manor Farm
LOMBARDY AV.
THORNS
THORNESS CL.
FUCHSIA WLK.
DRIVE
SHA
Yew Tree Farm
Well Ho.Farm
Royden Hall
2
Bay Tree Farm
THE NOOK
WHITEBEAM WLK.
MAGNOLIA WLK.
GREEN ACRES ESTATE
ASHDOWN DR.
JUNIPER CL.
Stiles
B5139
FRANKBY GRN.
FARRIERS WY.
Frankby
HILL BARK RD.
ROWAN CT.
ALMOND WY.
ELMDENE CT.
SYCAMORE RI.
DRIVE
on
FRANKBY
BAYTREE RD.
Cemetery
CH48
Greasby Brook
ACACIA CL.
CHESTNUT CL.
OAKDALE DR.
Forton Hey
IRBYSIDE RD.
FERNDALE AV.
3
HILL BARK
Birch Hey Farm
BIRCH HEYS
HILL
Irbymill Hill Farm
ROAD
86
B5140
ROYDEN PARK
Frankby Mere
Walled Garden
Quarry Farm
SANDY LANE NORTH
MONTGOMERY
Hill Bark
P
Roodee Mere
Hill Bark Farm
4
NORTH
Irby Hill
TELEGRAPH
135
PIKES HEY RD.
D
SANDY LANE
HILL
THURSTASTON COMMON
5
Thurstaston Playing Field
SANDY
THORSTONE DR.
NORTON DR.
LESTER DR.
EDGEMOOR DR.
HILL VIEW RD.
3 85
Thurstaston Hill
Benty Farm
FROST
BEACH WAY
A
136
B
C
24
ROAD
Thurstaston Common Recreation Ground
Hillside Farm
3 25
LANE
DRIVE
MARTIN

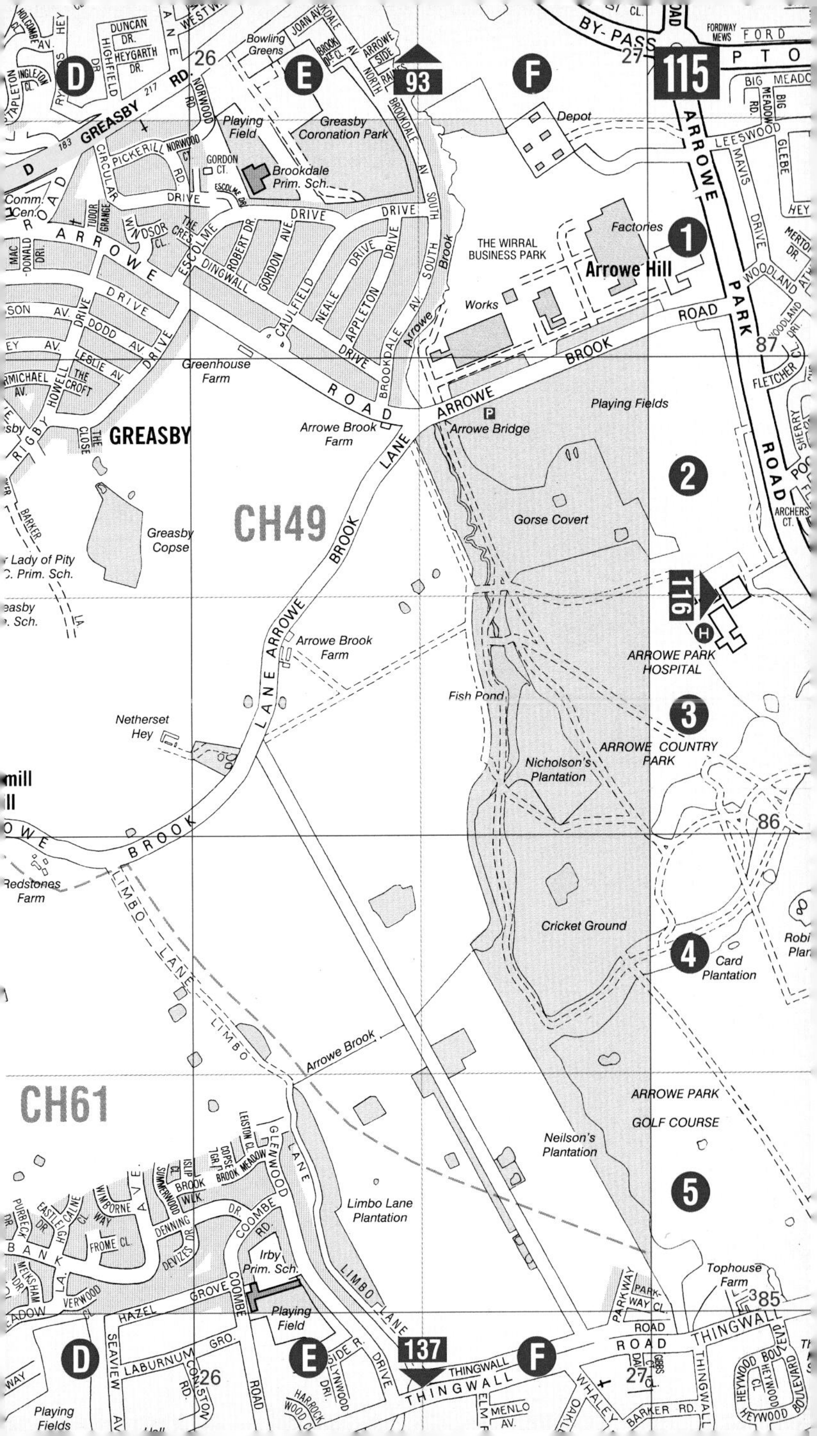
93
137
116
GREASBY
CH49
CH61
Arrowe Hill
THE WIRRAL BUSINESS PARK
Factories
Depot
Works
Greasby Coronation Park
Brookdale Prim. Sch.
Playing Field
Bowling Greens
Greenhouse Farm
Arrowe Brook Farm
Arrowe Bridge
Playing Fields
Gorse Covert
Greasby Copse
ARROWE PARK HOSPITAL
ARROWE COUNTRY PARK
Fish Pond
Nicholson's Plantation
Netherset Hey
Cricket Ground
Card Plantation
Arrowe Brook
ARROWE PARK GOLF COURSE
Neilson's Plantation
Limbo Lane Plantation
Irby Prim. Sch.
Tophouse Farm
Redstones Farm
ARROWE BROOK ROAD
ARROWE BROOK LANE
ARROWE PARK ROAD
GREASBY RD.
THINGWALL ROAD
LIMBO LANE
BY-PASS

116
UPTON
BY-PASS
FORD
FORDWAY MEWS
A
B
C
94
MEADOW RD.
BIG MEADOW RD.
CARR
28
27
HEATHERLAND
LEAMINGTON GDNS.
WEATHERBY
HEY
NEW
Depot
LEESWOOD
ROAD
MAVIS DRIVE
GLEBE
DOMVILLE DR.
NORTHBROOKE WAY
KILN ROAD
HOUGHTON
POOLWOOD RD.
NEWBRIDGE CL.
MEADOW
RD.
HOOLE
ORRET'S
HEY ROAD
WHITEFIELD CL.
Comm. Cen.
Running Track
Woodchurch Leisure C
BRIDGE
Factories
THE WIRRAL BUSINESS PARK
1
Arrowe Hill
ARROWE
A551
MERTON DR.
ATHERTON DR.
Arrowe Hill Prim. Sch.
DOLLEY CT.
FERNY BROW
FLAMBARDS
Fender Prim. Sch.
SELBOURNE CL.
CHEVERTON CL.
BRACKENDALE
PEMBERTON
WOODLAND
LOWER GRN
WOODLAND DRI.
ROAD
BROOK
87
ARROWE
FLETCHER CL.
CHESHIRE ACRE
GREENWOOD RD.
THE MEADOW
HUDDLESTON CL.
WOOD
MEADOW RD.
Playing Fields
Bridge
PARK
SHERRY LANE
DRUIDS WAY
POOL LA.
POOL
MEADOW
CALDWELL DRIVE
GRASS WOOD RD.
GANNEY'S
ACKERS
SPRINGFIELD CL.
2
Gorse Covert
YEWTREE CL.
NANTWICH CL.
ARCHERS WAY
Sch.
CHURCH LANE
CRESCENT
HOME
Woodchurch
FARM
Lib.
RD.
ARCHERS CT.
FLEET
GOODAKRS MDW.
TROUTBECK CL.
CROFT
ELTHAM
ELTHAM CLO.
ROBIN WAY
SCHOOLFIELD
SCHOOLFIELD CL.
SANDFIELD RD.
115
CHILDWALL
CREWE GRN
GREEN ROAD
CHURCH
SANDFIELD RD.
FIELD
ROAD
ACKERS RD.
ARROWE PARK HOSPITAL
BEECHWOOD CT.
CHURCHWOOD CT.
MARITIME CT.
WOODVALE CT.
COMMON
WOODCHURCH
A552
CH49
LANDICAN
3
ARROWE COUNTRY PARK
Nicholson's Plantation
Bowling Greens
Ten. Cts.
86
Miniature Golf Course
Landican Cemetery
Cricket Ground
4
Robinson's Plantation
Card Plantation
Club House
WOODCHURCH LA.
Landica
Home Farm
ROAD
Old Hall Farm
ARROWE PARK GOLF COURSE
Neilson's Plantation
5
Nursery
LANDICAN
B5138
EAST
CH61
Tophouse Farm
385
PARKWAY
PARKWAY CL.
ROAD
THINGWALL RD.
PENSBY RD.
TORRINGTON
TORRINGTON GDNS.
BARNSTON
A551
The Farm
THINGWALL
RICHMOND WAY
HAZELDENE AV.
138
Thingwall Prim. & Stanley Schs.
BEVERLEY GDNS.
DRIVE
GALLOPERS LA.
WHALEY
DANE CL.
BARKER RD.
HEYWOOD CL.
HEYWOOD BOULEVARD
OAKLE
MENLO AV.

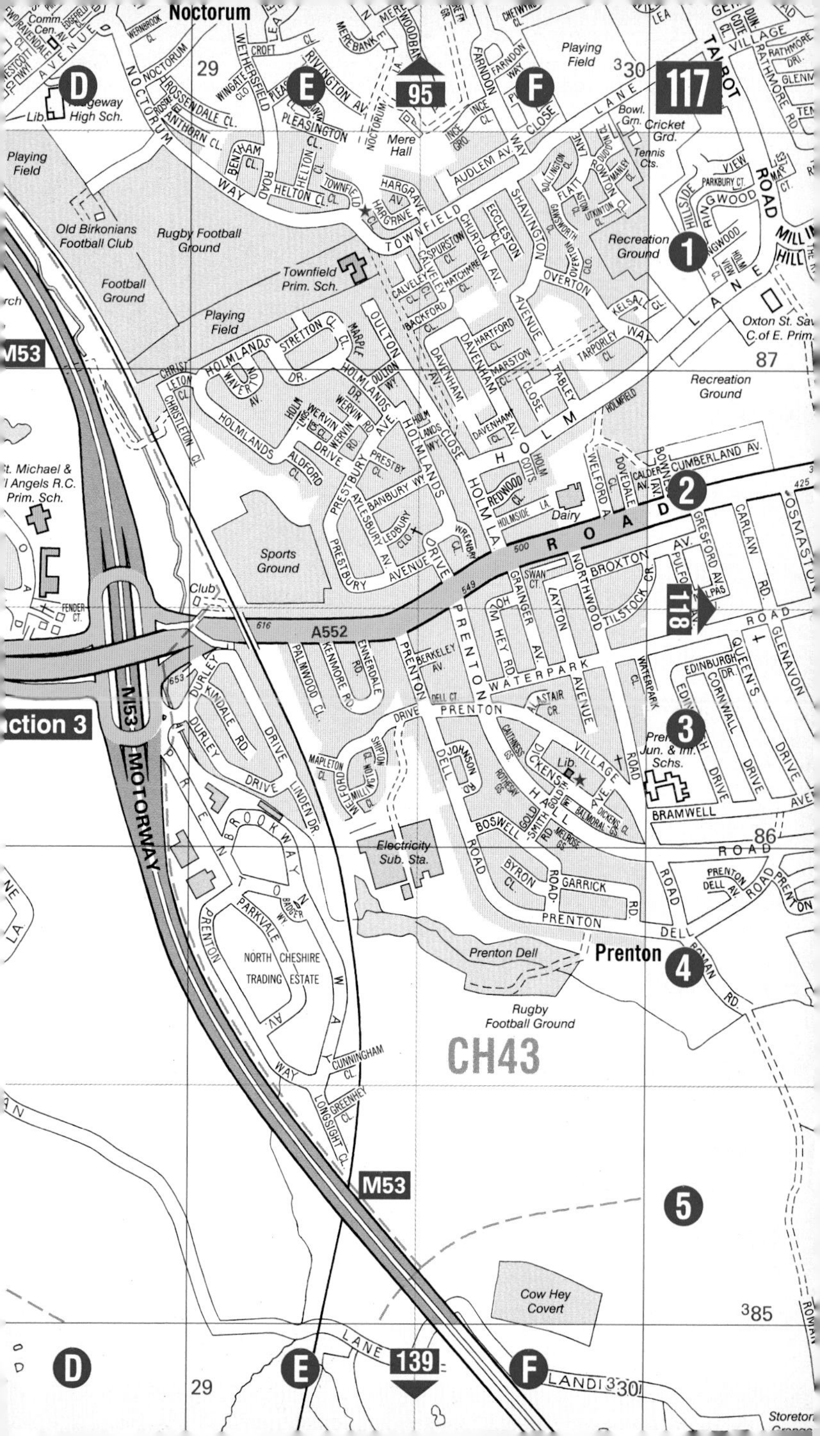

117
Noctorum
D
E
F
29
330
95
Ridgeway High Sch.
Lib.
Playing Field
Old Birkonians Football Club
Rugby Football Ground
Football Ground
Townfield Prim. Sch.
Playing Field
Mere Hall
Bowl. Grn.
Cricket Grd.
Tennis Cts.
Recreation Ground
Oxton St. Saviour C.of E. Prim.
87
Recreation Ground
1
2
3
4
5
M53
St. Michael & All Angels R.C. Prim. Sch.
Sports Ground
Club
A552
118
Section 3
M53 MOTORWAY
NOCTORUM WAY
TOWNFIELD LANE
TALBOT ROAD
HOLM LANE
HOLMLANDS DRIVE
PRESTBURY AVENUE
PRENTON ROAD
WATERPARK
PRENTON VILLAGE ROAD
Dairy
Prenton Jun. & Inf. Schs.
Lib.
Electricity Sub. Sta.
NORTH CHESHIRE TRADING ESTATE
86
Prenton Dell
Prenton
Rugby Football Ground
CH43
Cow Hey Covert
385
139
LANDICAN LANE
Storeton Grange

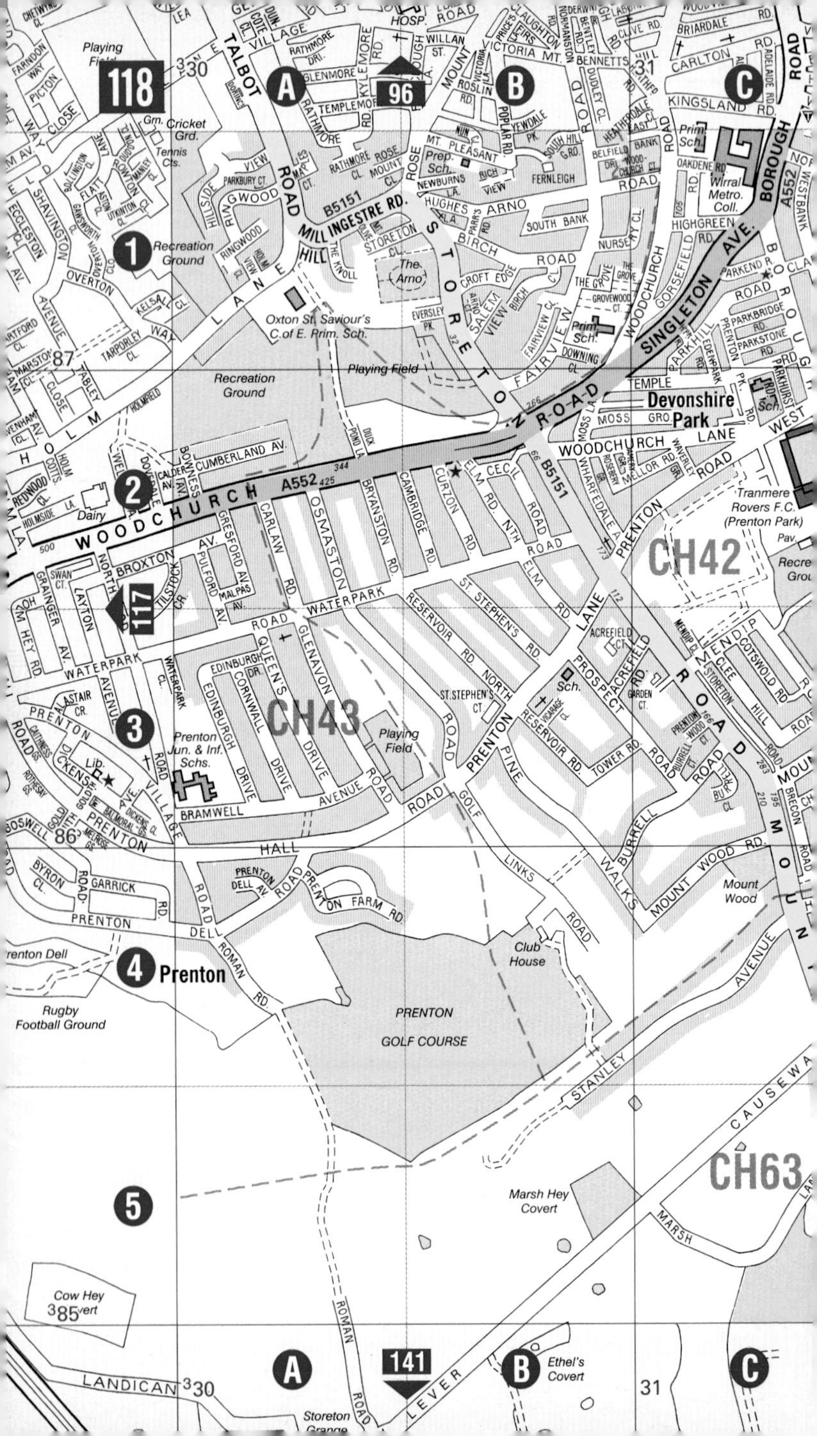
118
96
117
141
A
B
C
1
2
3
4
5
CH42
CH43
CH63
Prenton
Devonshire Park
WOODCHURCH A552
SINGLETON AVE.
STORETON ROAD
B5151
PRENTON GOLF COURSE
Tranmere Rovers F.C. (Prenton Park)
Recreation Ground
Playing Field
Oxton St. Saviour's C.of E. Prim. Sch.
Prenton Jun. & Inf. Schs.
Wirral Metro. Coll.
Rugby Football Ground
Marsh Hey Covert
Ethel's Covert
Club House
Mount Wood
LANDICAN
STANLEY
CAUSEWAY
LEVER
ROMAN ROAD

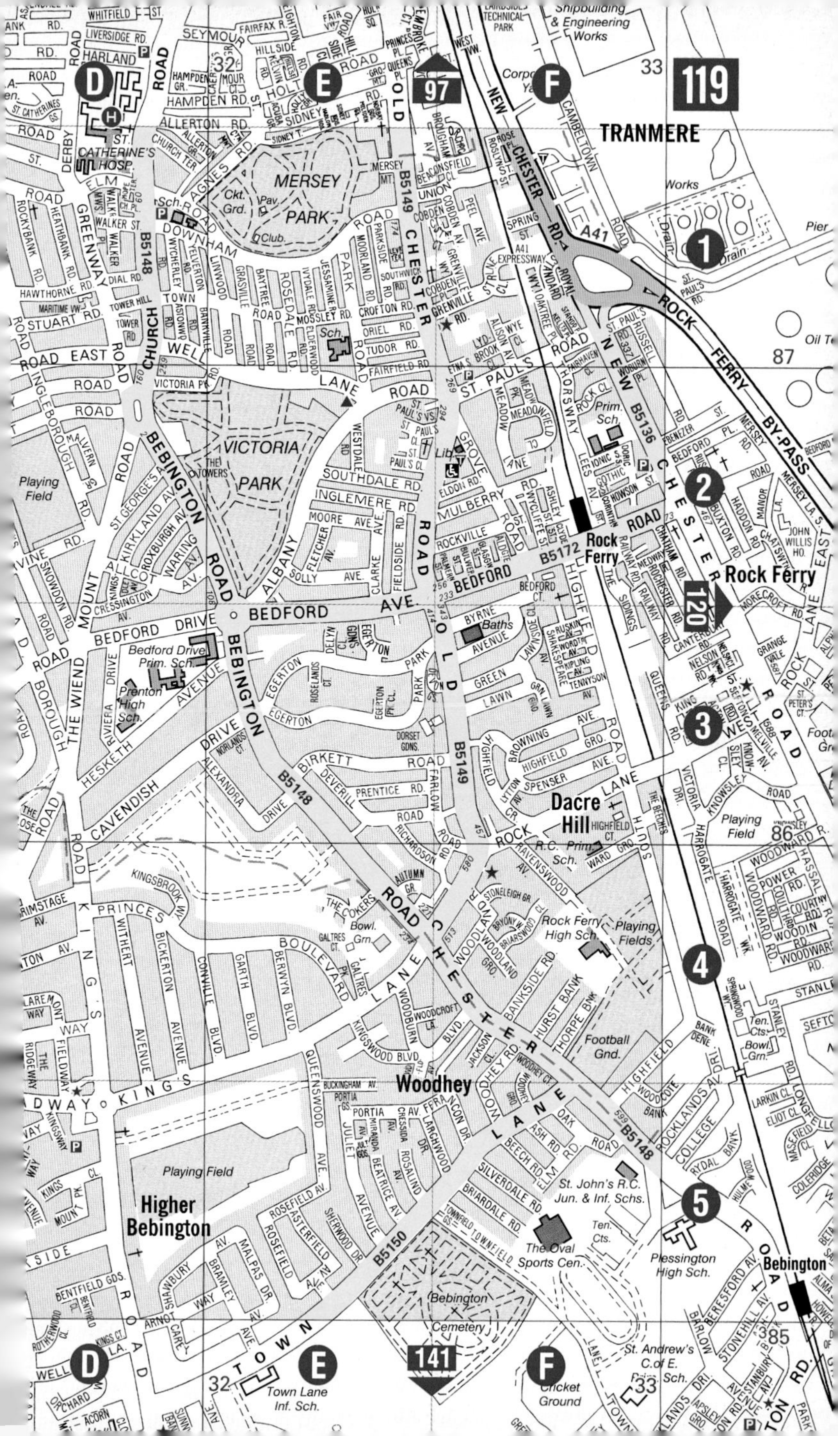
119
TRANMERE
Shipbuilding & Engineering Works
Works
MERSEY PARK
VICTORIA PARK
Rock Ferry
Dacre Hill
Woodhey
Higher Bebington
Bebington
97
120
141
D
E
F
1
2
3
4
5
NEW CHESTER RD.
A41
ROCK FERRY BY-PASS
B5149
B5148
B5136
B5172
B5150
OLD CHESTER ROAD
BEBINGTON ROAD
CHURCH ROAD
BEDFORD AVE.
BEDFORD ROAD
BEDFORD DRIVE
KINGS ROAD
TOWN LANE
WOODHEY RD.
HIGHFIELD ROAD
ST. PAUL'S ROAD
ST. CATHERINE'S HOSP.
Bedford Drive Prim. Sch.
Prenton High Sch.
Byrne Baths
Rock Ferry High Sch.
Playing Fields
Football Gnd.
Playing Field
St. John's R.C. Jun. & Inf. Schs.
The Oval Sports Cen.
Plessington High Sch.
Bebington Cemetery
Town Lane Inf. Sch.
Cricket Ground
St. Andrew's C.of E. Prim. Sch.
R.C. Prim. Sch.
Bowl. Grn.
Ten. Cts.
Pier
Oil Tanks
Lib.

TRANMERE
Shipbuilding & Engineering Works
Corporation Yard
Floating Stage
Works
Pier
Oil Terminal
Rock Ferry Pier
Slipway
RIVER
ROCK–A41–FERRY–BY–PASS
Rock Ferry
CH42
CH62
CH63
Dacre Hill
NEW CHESTER ROAD
CHESTER B5148
Rock Ferry High Sch.
Playing Fields
Football Gnd.
Playing Field
Football Grd.
Bus Depot
Spts. Club
Ckt. Gnd.
New Ferry Park
St. John's R.C. Jun. & Inf. Sch.
The Oval Sports Cen.
Plessington High Sch.
Bebington
BEBINGTON BOUNDARY RD.
NEW FERRY
St. Andrew's C.of E. Prim. Sch.
Cricket Ground
Art Gallery
Training

98
119
142

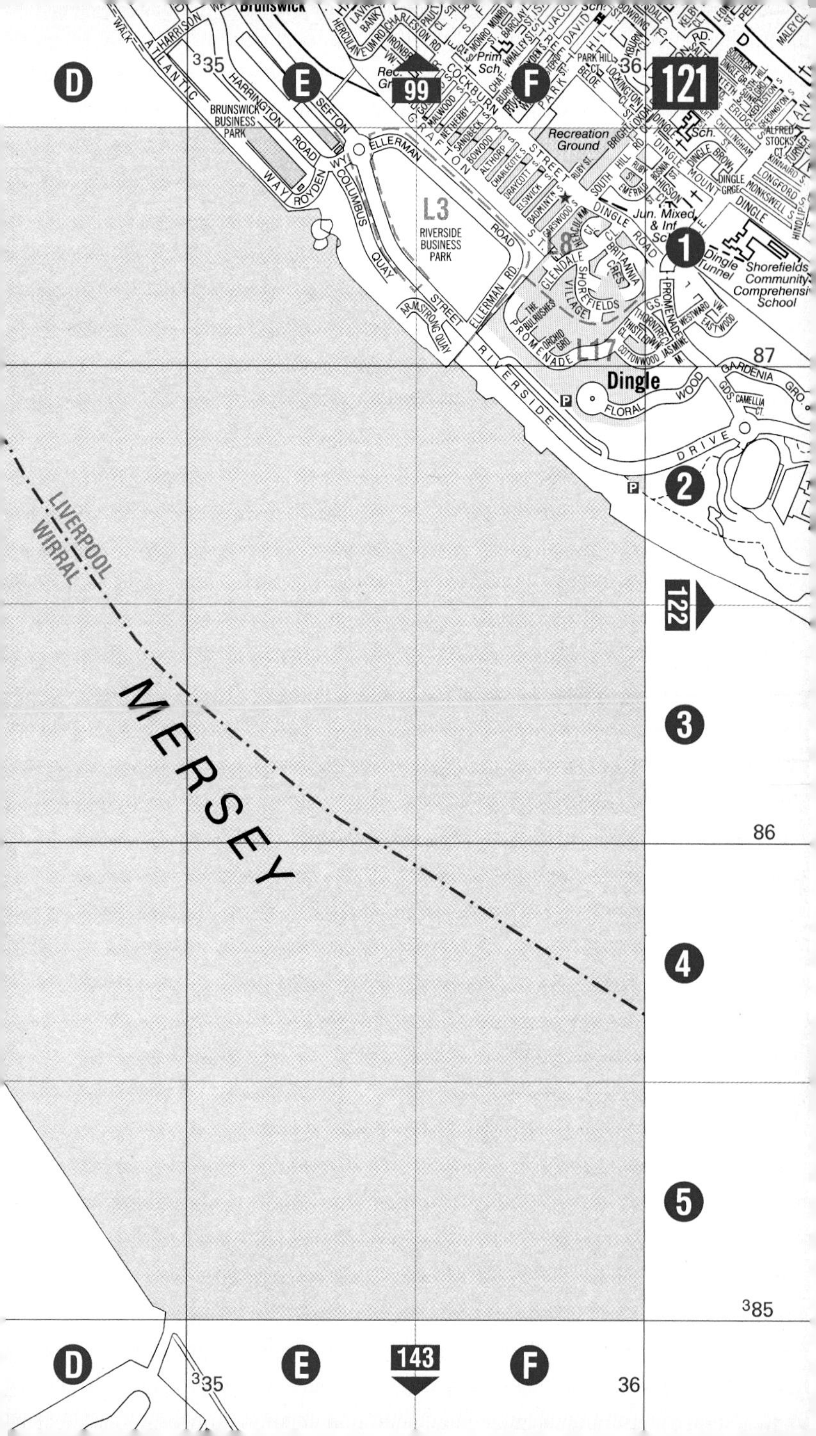
D
E
F
121
99
122
143
1
2
3
4
5
335
36
87
86
385
Brunswick
BRUNSWICK BUSINESS PARK
HARRINGTON ROAD
HARRISON
ATLANTIC
WALK
WAY
ROYDEN
SEFTON
ELLERMAN
COLUMBUS
QUAY
L3
RIVERSIDE BUSINESS PARK
ROAD
ELLERMAN RD.
ARMSTRONG QUAY
STREET
GRAFTON
COCKBURN
Recreation Ground
Prim Sch.
PARK HILL
DINGLE
Jun. Mixed & Inf Sch.
Dingle Tunnel
Shorefields Community Comprehensive School
L8
GLENDALE
SHOREFIELDS
VILLAGE
BRITANNIA CRES.
THE BULRUSHES
PROMENADE
ORCHID GRO.
L17
Dingle
RIVERSIDE
FLORAL WOOD
GARDENIA GRO.
CAMELLIA CT.
DRIVE
LIVERPOOL
WIRRAL
MERSEY

Recreation Ground
Dingle
Shorefields Community Comprehensive School
Dingle Tunnel
Playing Field
Rec. Grd.
Cricket Ground
St. Michael's
St. Michael's Hamlet
Priory Wood
Theatre
Liverpool Hope Univ. Coll.
St. Charles' R.C. Prim. School
Playing Field
T.A. Centre
Otterspo
RIVER MERSEY
LIVERPOOL
WIRRAL
AIGBURTH ROAD A561
RIVERSIDE DRIVE
100
121

123
101
124
D
E
F
1
2
3
4
5
38
39
87
86
385
L18
L19
17
Sefton Park
Mossley Hill
Aigburth Vale
Aigburth
Grassendale
Grassendale Pk.
Wood End Park
Queens Dr.
Ibbotson's Lane
Mossley Drive
Hill
Mossley Hill Drive
Park Avenue
Aigburth Vale
Victoria A5058 Rd.
Ashfield Rd.
Carnatic Road
Elmswood Road
Rose Lane
Mossley Hill Road
North Mossley Hill Road
Elmsley Road
Sudley Road
North Sudley Road
Sudley Road
Rosemont Road
Hillview
Barkhill Road
Aigburth Road
A561
A5058
Mersey Road
Riversdale Road
Promenade
Mersey Drive
The Promenade
Otterspool
Lane
Jericho Cl.
Cooper Av.
Cooper Av. North
Brodie Av.
Holmefield Rd.
South Sudley Rd.
Hall Road
Aigburth Hall Road
Darby Road
Beechwood Road
North Road
South Rd.
Liverpool College (Lwr. Sch.)
Playing Field
St. Anthony of Padua R.C. Jun. & Inf. Sch.
Mossley Hill Hospital
Nursing Home
Sports Grd.
Parkside Halls of Residence
Carnatic Halls (Halls of Residence)
Palm House
Lake
Dale Hall
Tennis Cts.
Tennis Courts
Sports Grd.
Holt Recreation Ground
Kelton Grange
Sudley Art Gallery
Sports Ground
Pavilion
Sudley Inf. Sch.
Sudley Jun. Sch.
Liverpool John Moores University
John Moores University, I.M. Marsh Campus
St. Margaret's C. of E. High Sch.
Mersey View School
Playing Fields
Otterspool Park
The Cottage
Recreation Ground
Liverpool Community College (Riversdale Cen.)
Liverpool Cricket Club
Liverpool Cricket & Football Ground
Greenways Sch.
Athletic Ground
Sports Ground
Bowl. Grn.
Pav.
Sub.

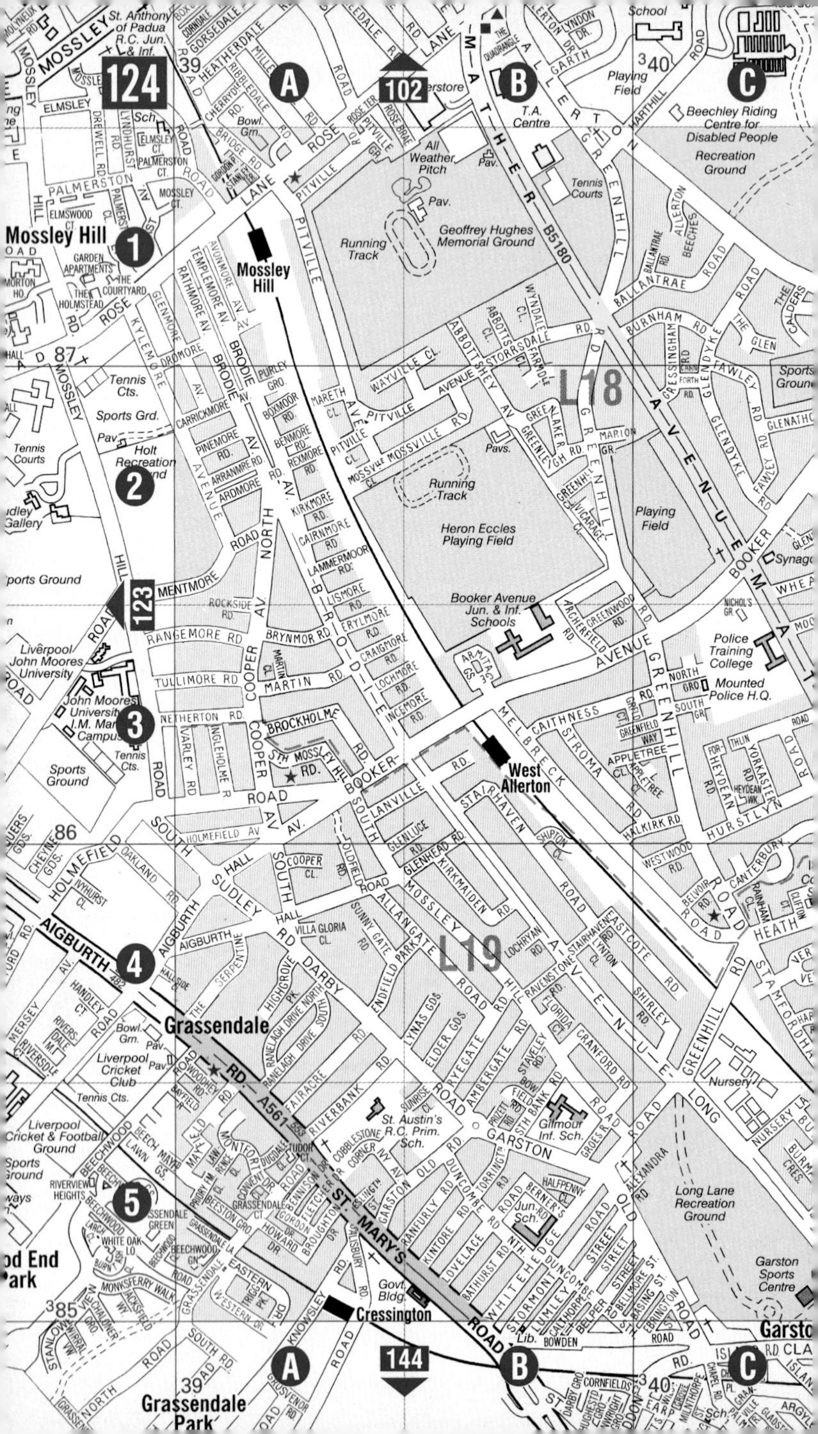

A
B
C
102
123
144
1
2
3
4
5
39
340
87
86
385
L18
L19
Mossley Hill
Mossley Hill
West Allerton
Grassendale
Cressington
Grassendale Park
Garston
St. Anthony of Padua R.C. Jun. & Inf.
Sch
Bowl. Grn.
All Weather Pitch
Pav.
T.A. Centre
Playing Field
School
Beechley Riding Centre for Disabled People
Recreation Ground
Tennis Courts
Running Track
Geoffrey Hughes Memorial Ground
B5180
Sports Ground
Tennis Cts.
Sports Grd.
Holt Recreation Ground
Tennis Courts
Sudley Gallery
Pavs.
Running Track
Heron Eccles Playing Field
Playing Field
Booker Avenue Jun. & Inf. Schools
Synagogue
Police Training College
Mounted Police H.Q.
Liverpool John Moores University
John Moores University I.M. Marsh Campus
Tennis Cts.
Sports Ground
Bowl. Grn.
Liverpool Cricket Club
Tennis Cts.
Liverpool Cricket & Football Ground
Sports Ground
St. Austin's R.C. Prim. Sch.
Gilmour Inf. Sch.
Jun. Sch.
Nursery
Long Lane Recreation Ground
Garston Sports Centre
Govt. Bldg.
Lib.
A561
MOSSLEY HILL
ROSE LANE
PITVILLE AVENUE
MATHER AVENUE
ALLERTON ROAD
GREENHILL ROAD
BOOKER AVENUE
BRODIE AVENUE
NORTH MOSSLEY HILL ROAD
MENTMORE ROAD
COOPER AV.
BROCKHOLME RD.
SOUTH MOSSLEY HILL RD.
ELMSLEY
PALMERSTON
GARDEN APARTMENTS
THE COURTYARD
THE HOLMSTEAD
KYLEMORE
GLENMORE
DROMORE
CARRICKMORE
PINEMORE RD.
ARRANMORE RD.
ARDMORE
RANGEMORE RD.
TULLIMORE RD
NETHERTON RD.
MARTIN
BRYNMOR RD.
ROCKSIDE RD.
ABBOTSHEY AV.
STORRSDALE RD.
WAYVILLE CL.
MOSSVILLE RD.
BALLANTRAE ROAD
BURNHAM RD.
GRESSINGHAM
GLENDYKE
FAWLEY RD.
CAITHNESS
STROMA
MELBRECK
STAIRHAVEN ROAD
HALKIRK RD.
HURSTLYN
YORKASTER RD.
CANTERBURY
AIGBURTH RD.
SUDLEY
HOLMEFIELD
DARBY RD.
ALLANGATE
MOSSLEY HILL
KIRKMAIDEN RD.
MOSSLEY AVENUE
RYEGATE ROAD
GARSTON OLD RD.
ST. MARY'S ROAD
LONG LANE
GREENHILL ROAD
ALEXANDRA RD.
BEECHWOOD
EASTERN DR.
KNOWSLEY ROAD
STAMFORDHAM

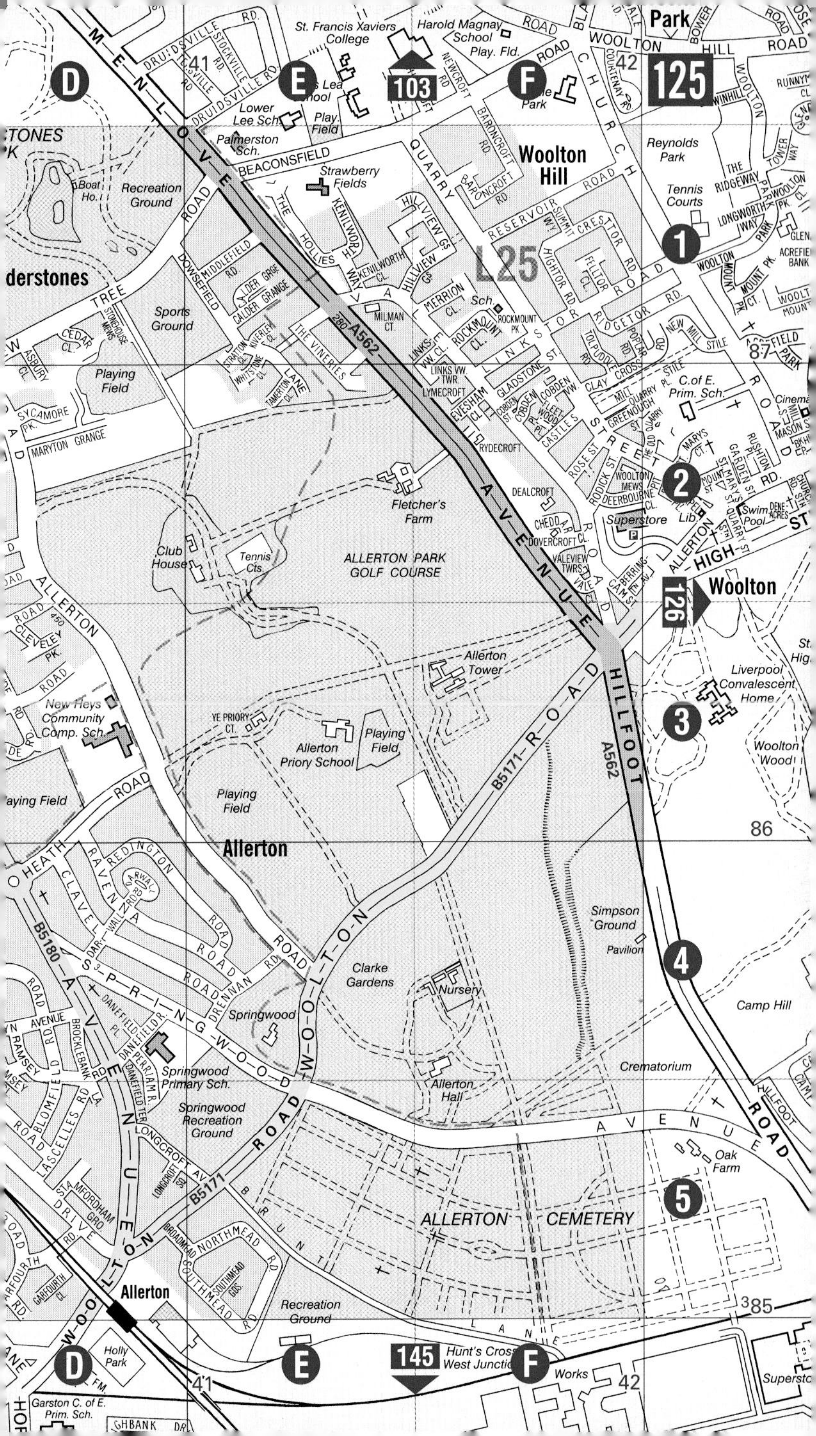
125
103
126
145
Woolton Hill
Woolton
Allerton
L25
ALLERTON PARK GOLF COURSE
ALLERTON CEMETERY
MENLOVE AVENUE
HILLFOOT ROAD
HILLFOOT AVENUE
WOOLTON ROAD
ALLERTON ROAD
SPRINGWOOD AVENUE
Fletcher's Farm
Allerton Tower
Allerton Priory School
Allerton Hall
Clarke Gardens
Springwood
Springwood Primary Sch.
Springwood Recreation Ground
Liverpool Convalescent Home
Woolton Wood
Camp Hill
Crematorium
Oak Farm
Simpson Ground
Strawberry Fields
Reynolds Park
Calderstones
New Heys Community Comp. Sch.
Recreation Ground
Sports Ground
Playing Field
Holly Park
Hunt's Cross West Junction
Works
Garston C. of E. Prim. Sch.

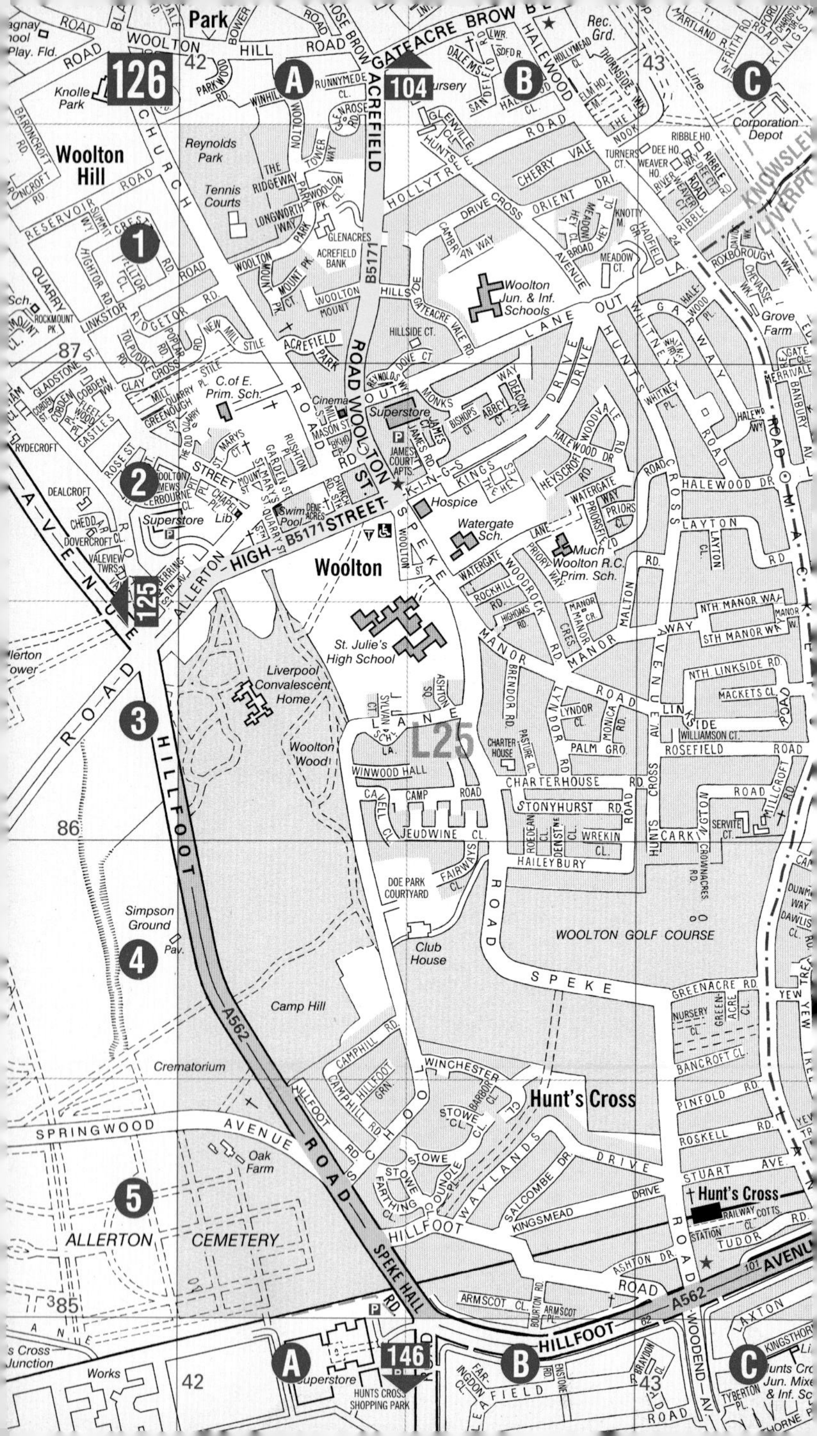
126
104
125
146
A
B
C
1
2
3
4
5
42
43
87
86
85
Woolton Hill
Woolton
Hunt's Cross
L25
Knolle Park
Reynolds Park
Tennis Courts
Rec. Grd.
Corporation Depot
Grove Farm
Woolton Jun. & Inf. Schools
C.of E. Prim. Sch.
Cinema
Superstore
Hospice
Watergate Sch.
Much Woolton R.C. Prim. Sch.
Swim Pool
Lib.
St. Julie's High School
Liverpool Convalescent Home
Woolton Wood
Club House
Camp Hill
Crematorium
Simpson Ground
Pav.
Oak Farm
ALLERTON CEMETERY
WOOLTON GOLF COURSE
Hunt's Cross
Works
HUNTS CROSS SHOPPING PARK
Hunts Cross Jun. Mixed & Inf. Sch.
Allerton Tower
Hunts Cross Junction
GATEACRE BROW
ACREFIELD
B5171
HIGH STREET
ALLERTON ROAD
WOOLTON ROAD
CHURCH ROAD
LANE OUT
KINGS DRIVE
HUNTS CROSS AVENUE
SPEKE ROAD
HILLFOOT ROAD
A562
SPEKE HALL RD.
HILLFOOT AVENUE
SPRINGWOOD AVENUE
MACKETS LANE
HALEWOOD DR.
MANOR ROAD
CHARTERHOUSE RD.
CAMP ROAD
WOOLTON HILL ROAD
HOLLYTREE ROAD
CHERRY VALE
ORIENT DRIVE
GARWAY
WAYLANDS DRIVE
KINGSMEAD DRIVE
ROSEFIELD ROAD
STUART AVE.
WOODEND AV.

127
105
128
147
D
E
F
1
2
3
4
5
44
345
87
86
385
COURSE
Cross Farm Junior Mixed & Infant School
Works
North End Cottages
North End
Nursery
Weston House
Halewood Farm
Foxhill Ho.
Foxhill Farm
Bridgefield
Halewood Green
L26
Sports Ground
Bowling Green
Holy Family R.C. Prim. Sch.
Hilton Grace Recreation Ground
Halewood C.of E Prim. Sch.
Comm. Cen.
Plantation Prim. Sch.
Halewood
HALEWOOD
St. Mark's R.C. Prim. Sch.
Halewood Triangle Country Park
Running Track
Tennis Courts
Playing Fields
Halewood Community Comp. School
Roseheath Primary School
Roseheath Ho.
Elsinore Heights
Lib.
St. Andrew's R.C. Prim. Sch.
Playing Field
New Hutte Prim. Sch.
Bowling
A562
GERRARDS LANE
FOXHILL LANE
NORTH END LANE
CHURCH ROAD
OKELL DRIVE
WINSTER DRIVE
CARTBRIDGE LANE
ROAD
HOLLIES ROAD
BAILEY'S LANE
WOOD ROAD
LEATHERS LANE
BLAKEACRE DRIVE
CHURCH AVENUE
COURT AV.
RONALDSWAY
WENSLEY AV.
HELMSLEY RD.
CATTERICK CL.
PENMANN CRES.
BEECHWOOD AVENUE
WOODLAND
OAKWOOD
DUNACRE WAY
HILLINGDEN AV.
ANTONS ROAD
ROSEHEATH DRIVE
KEMPSELL WALK
TRISPEN
BODMIN WAY
PENZANCE CLOSE
TORCROSS
CLIFTON AV.
SUTTONS
TURNSTONE DRIVE
FOXGLOVE AV.
FIRETHORNE RD.
HONEYSUCKLE DR.
DRIVE
STANFORD CRES.
ARNCLIFFE ROAD
PEMBREY WY.
SHERBORNE AVENUE
ABBERLEY ROAD
BLACKBURNE DR.
TORRINGTON DR.
HONEY HALL ROAD
BOUNDARY
Liverpool Loop Line

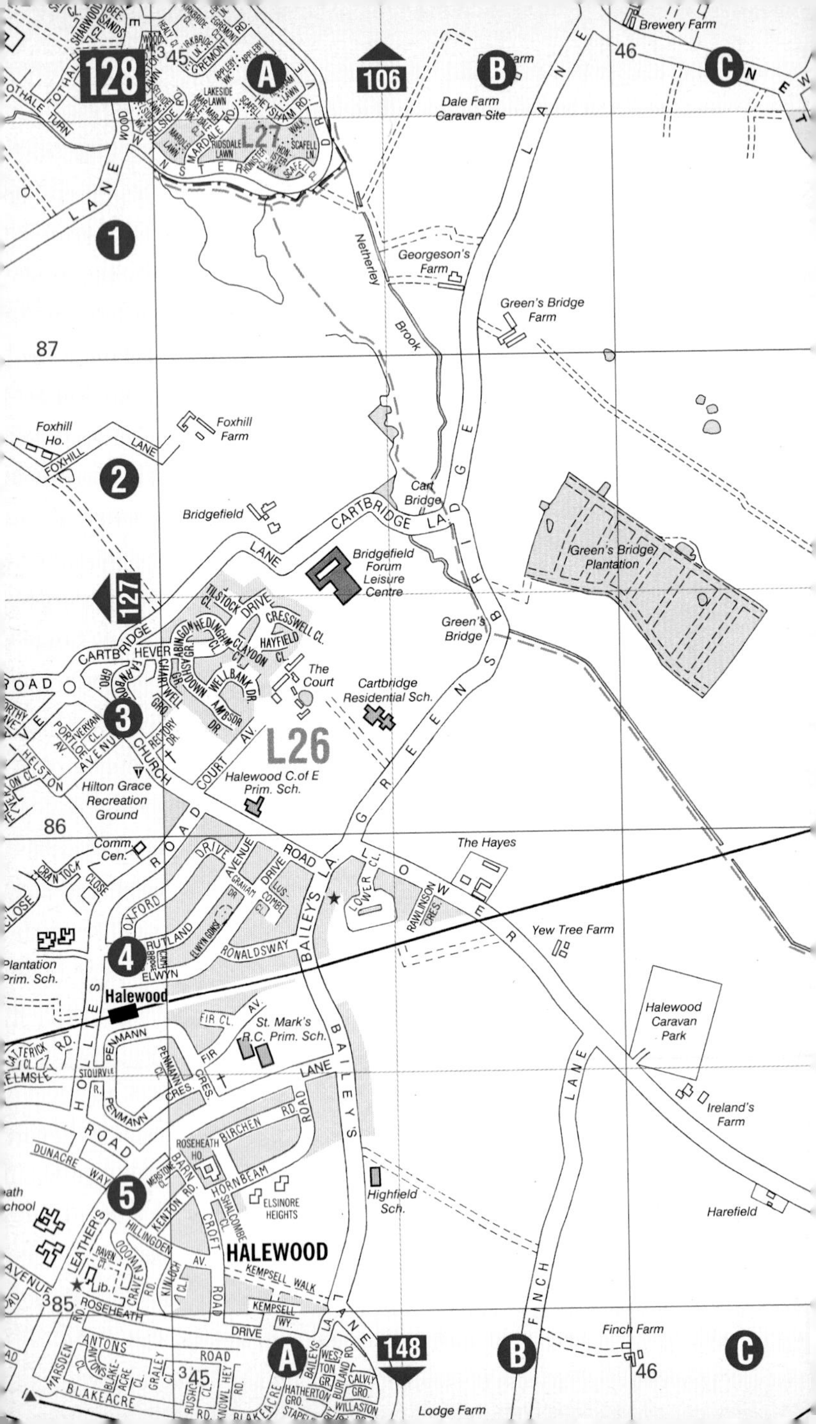
128
106
127
148
A
B
C
1
2
3
4
5
L27
L26
Brewery Farm
Dale Farm
Dale Farm Caravan Site
Georgeson's Farm
Green's Bridge Farm
Netherley Brook
Foxhill Ho.
Foxhill Farm
FOXHILL LANE
Bridgefield
Cart Bridge
CARTBRIDGE LANE
Bridgefield Forum Leisure Centre
Green's Bridge Plantation
Green's Bridge
GREENSBRIDGE LANE
The Court
Cartbridge Residential Sch.
Halewood C.of E Prim. Sch.
Hilton Grace Recreation Ground
Comm. Cen.
The Hayes
Yew Tree Farm
Halewood Caravan Park
Ireland's Farm
Harefield
Plantation Prim. Sch.
Halewood
St. Mark's R.C. Prim. Sch.
Highfield Sch.
ELSINORE HEIGHTS
HALEWOOD
Lib.
Finch Farm
FINCH LANE
Lodge Farm
BAILEY'S LANE
CHURCH ROAD
LOWER ROAD
TILSTOCK DRIVE
CRESSWELL CL.
HAYFIELD CL.
CLAYDON CT.
WELLBANK DR.
AMBSDR DR.
COURT AV.
RONALDSWAY
OXFORD DRIVE
RUTLAND AVENUE
ELWYN
PENNMANN
HOLLIES ROAD
KEMPSELL WALK
KEMPSELL WY.
ROSEHEATH DRIVE
ANTONS ROAD
BLAKEACRE
HORNBEAM
BIRCHEN RD.
LEATHER'S
HILLINGDEN
DUNACRE WAY
WINSTER DRIVE
HEYSHAM RD.
MARDALE RD.
WOOD LANE
TOTHALE TURN
87
86
45
46
345
385

129
107
130
149
D
E
F
1
2
3
4
5
47
48
87
86
385
ck Green
Markslands
STOCKSWELL
ROAD
Stock's House
A5300
CROSS HILLOCKS LANE
Dye House Farm
od Lane Farm
B5178
Cross Hillocks Farm
LANE
L35
Plumpton's Farm
St. Basils R.C. Prim. Sch.
LANCASTER AV.
VINE T.
ARDEN
PLUMLEY GDS.
GARNETTS
Spring Farm
Ditton C. of E. Prim. Sch.
HALL
SPINNEY AV.
BROADWAY
SANDIWAY
BRIARFIELD
WA8
Springfield Farm
ASH LANE
Tray Ashes Farm
New Farm
DALE CL.
CLINCTON CL.
SPRINGFIELD RD.
WOODVIEW RD.
Play. Field
Our Lady of Perpetual Succour R.C. Jun. Sch.
OAKFIELD
LAKESIDE
Clincton Wood
Ditton Brook
KNOWSLEY
HALTON
A562
Brook House Farm
SPEKE ROAD
Lovel's Hall (Site of)
Works

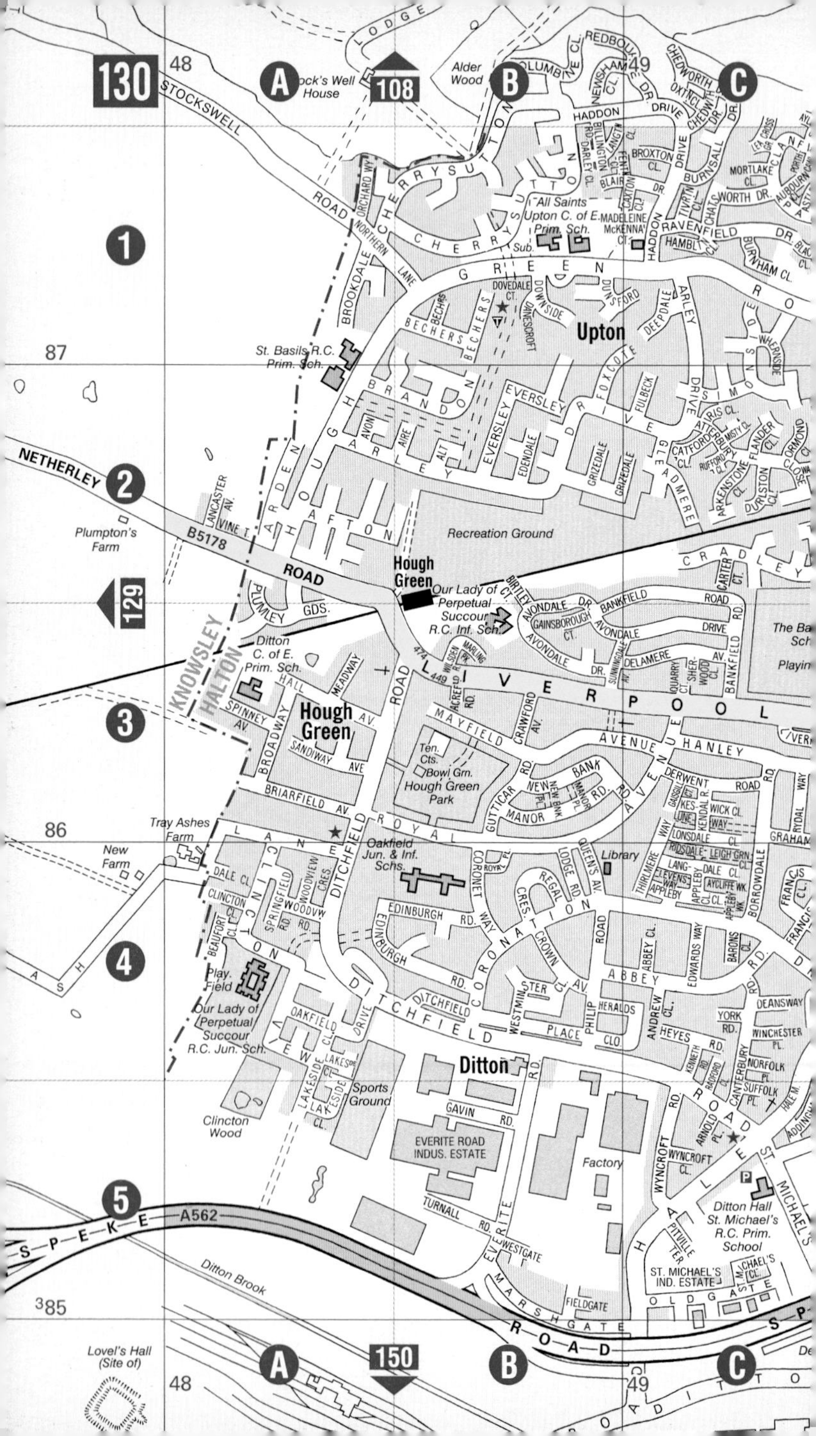
130
48
49
A
B
C
1
2
3
4
5
108
129
150
87
86
385
Stock's Well House
Alder Wood
LODGE
STOCKSWELL ROAD
COLUMBINE CL.
REDBOURNE
NEWSHAM CL.
CHEDWORTH DR.
OXTON CL.
HADDON DRIVE
BILLINGTON RD.
DARLEY CL.
LANGTON CL.
FENTON CL.
BROXTON CL.
BURNSALL DR.
MORTLAKE CL.
CHATSWORTH DR.
BLAIR
CAXTON CL.
TIVERTON CL.
RAVENFIELD DR.
HAMBLETON CL.
BURNHAM CL.
CHERRY SUTTON
ORCHARD WY.
NORTHERN LANE
BROOKDALE
All Saints Upton C. of E. Prim. Sch.
MADELEINE McKENNA CT.
Sub.
GREEN
DOVEDALE CT.
BECHERS
DANESCROFT
DOWNSIDE
DUNSFORD
DEEPDALE
ARLEY
Upton
St. Basils R.C. Prim. Sch.
BRANDON
HOUGH
FOXCOTE
FULBECK
EVERSLEY
DRIVE
SIMONSWOOD
WHERNSIDE
IRIS CL.
ATTERBURY
MISTY CL.
FLANDER CL.
ORMOND
CATFORD CL.
RUFFORD CL.
ARKENSTONE CL.
DURLSTON CL.
CLOSE
AVON
AIRE
ALT
ARLEY
EDENDALE
GRIZEDALE
GLEADMERE
NETHERLEY
Plumpton's Farm
LANCASTER AV.
VINE T.
ARDEN
HAFTON
Recreation Ground
B5178
ROAD
Hough Green
Our Lady of Perpetual Succour R.C. Inf. Sch.
BIRTLEY CT.
AVONDALE DR.
GAINSBOROUGH CT.
BANKFIELD ROAD
CRADLEY
CARTER CT.
AVONDALE
DRIVE
PLUMLEY GDS.
KNOWSLEY
HALTON
Ditton C. of E. Prim. Sch.
MEADWAY
HALL
WILSDEN RD.
MARLING PK.
ACREFIELD RD.
DELAMERE AV.
SUNNINGDALE AV.
QUARRY CT.
SHERWOOD CL.
BANKFIELD
The Ba Sch
Playin
LIVERPOOL
SPINNEY AV.
BROADWAY
Hough Green
SANDIWAY AVE
MAYFIELD
CRAWFORD AV.
AVENUE
HANLEY
Ten. Cts.
Bowl Grn.
Hough Green Park
BRIARFIELD AV.
GUTTICAR RD.
NEW BANK PL.
MANOR RD.
DERWENT ROAD
KESWICK CL.
KENDAL R.
LONSDALE CL.
RIDSDALE
LEIGH GRN.
LANGDALE CL.
LEVENS WAY
AYCLIFFE WK.
APPLEBY
THIRLMERE
BORROWDALE
GRAHAM
RYDAL WAY
Tray Ashes Farm
New Farm
ROYAL
LANE
CLINCTON
DITCHFIELD
Oakfield Jun. & Inf. Schs.
CORONET WAY
ROYAL PL.
LODGE RD.
QUEEN'S AV.
Library
REGAL CRES.
DALE CL.
SPRINGFIELD RD.
WOODVIEW CRES.
WOODVW RD.
EDINBURGH RD.
CORONATION
CROWN
ROAD
ABBEY CL.
EDWARDS WAY
BARONS CL.
FRANCIS
BEAUFORT CL.
Play. Field
Our Lady of Perpetual Succour R.C. Jun. Sch.
ASH
OAKFIELD CL.
VIEW
DRIVE
DITCHFIELD
WESTMINSTER CL.
ABBEY AV.
PHILIP
HERALDS CLO.
ANDREW CL.
HEYES RD.
DEANSWAY
YORK RD.
WINCHESTER PL.
NORFOLK PL.
SUFFOLK PL.
CANTERBURY
KENNETH RD.
RADFORD CL.
PLACE
LAKESIDE CL.
Sports Ground
Ditton
Clincton Wood
GAVIN RD.
EVERITE ROAD INDUS. ESTATE
Factory
WYNCROFT CL.
ARNOLD PL.
ST. MICHAEL'S
Ditton Hall
St. Michael's R.C. Prim. School
SPEKE
A562
TURNALL RD.
EVERITE
WESTGATE
PITVILLE TER.
HALE
ST. MICHAEL'S IND. ESTATE
Ditton Brook
MARSHGATE
FIELDGATE
OLDGATE
ROAD
Lovel's Hall (Site of)
DITTON

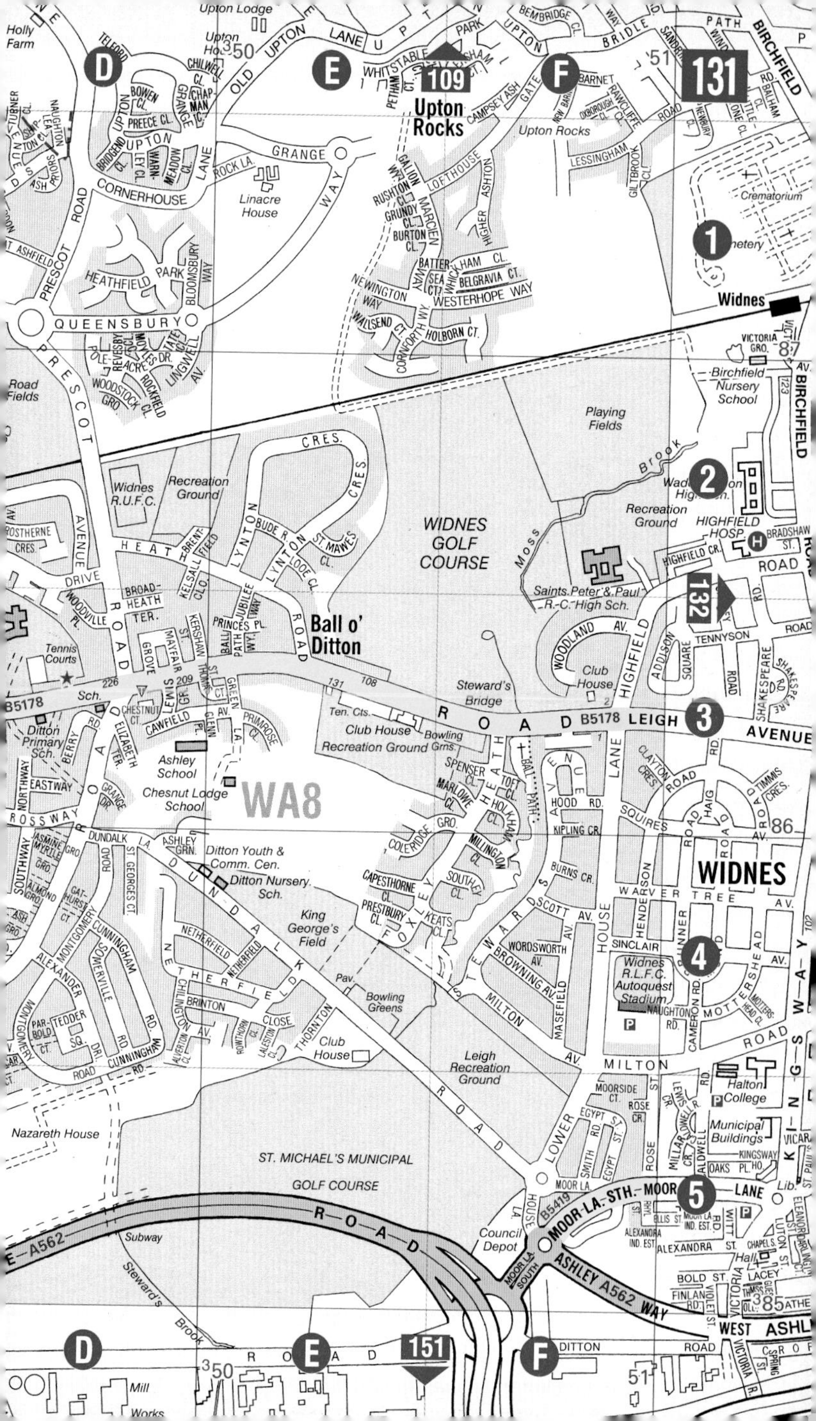
131
109
132
151
Upton Lodge
Holly Farm
Upton Ho.
Upton Rocks
Linacre House
Widnes
Crematorium
Cemetery
Victoria Gro.
Birchfield Nursery School
Playing Fields
Wade Deacon High Sch.
Recreation Ground
Highfield Hosp.
Widnes R.U.F.C.
Recreation Ground
WIDNES GOLF COURSE
Saints Peter & Paul R.C. High Sch.
Ball o' Ditton
Tennis Courts
Club House
Steward's Bridge
Ten. Cts.
Club House
Bowling Grns.
Recreation Ground
Ditton Primary Sch.
Ashley School
Chesnut Lodge School
WA8
Ditton Youth & Comm. Cen.
Ditton Nursery Sch.
King George's Field
WIDNES
Widnes R.L.F.C. Autoquest Stadium
Pav.
Bowling Greens
Club House
Leigh Recreation Ground
Halton College
Municipal Buildings
Nazareth House
ST. MICHAEL'S MUNICIPAL GOLF COURSE
Council Depot
Subway
Steward's Brook
Mill Works
Moss Brook
OLD UPTON LANE
UPTON BRIDLE PATH
BIRCHFIELD ROAD
PRESCOT ROAD
QUEENSBURY WAY
CORNERHOUSE LANE
GRANGE WAY
HEATH ROAD
LYNTON CRES.
B5178 LEIGH AVENUE
HIGHFIELD ROAD
DITTON ROAD
DUNDALK ROAD
NETHERFIELD
STEWARDS AV.
MILTON AV.
MILTON ROAD
LOWER HOUSE LANE
B5419 MOOR LA. STH.
MOOR LANE
ASHLEY A562 WAY
A562 ROAD
KINGSWAY
WARRINGTON ROAD
DITTON ROAD
WEST ASHLEY
ALEXANDRA ST.
BOLD ST.
VICTORIA RD.
CUNNINGHAM RD.
ALEXANDER DRIVE
ROSSWAY
SOUTHWAY
NORTHWAY
EASTWAY
HEATHFIELD PARK
BLOOMSBURY WAY
WESTERHOPE WAY
NEWINGTON WAY
D
E
F
1
2
3
4
5
350
51
86
87
85

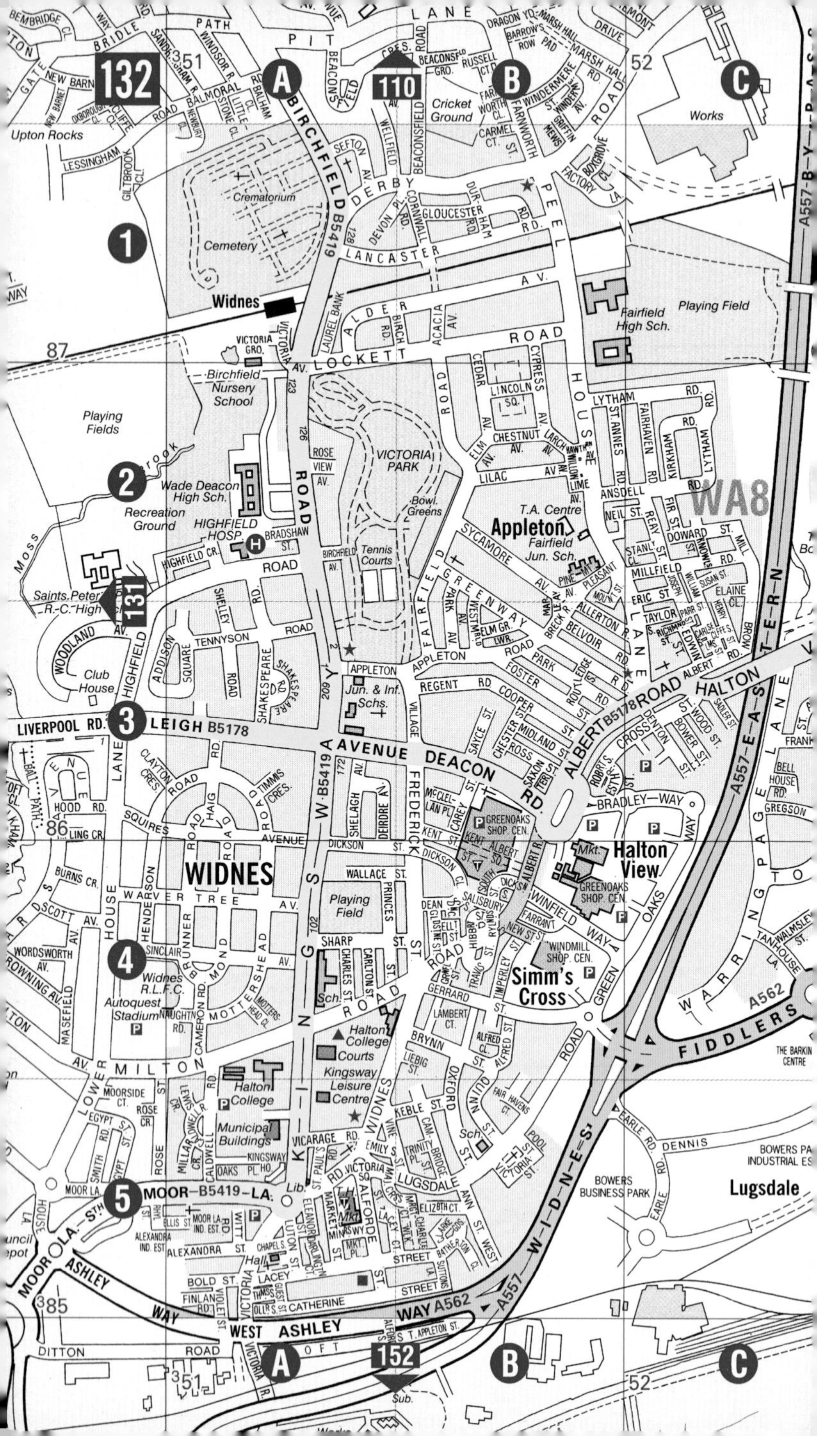

132
110
131
152
A
B
C
1
2
3
4
5
51
52
87
86
385
WA8
WIDNES
Widnes
Appleton
Halton View
Simm's Cross
Lugsdale
Upton Rocks
Crematorium
Cemetery
Cricket Ground
Works
Playing Field
Fairfield High Sch.
Playing Fields
Birchfield Nursery School
Wade Deacon High Sch.
Recreation Ground
HIGHFIELD HOSP.
Saints Peter & Paul R.C. High Sch.
Club House
VICTORIA PARK
Bowl. Greens
Tennis Courts
T.A. Centre
Fairfield Jun. Sch.
Jun. & Inf. Schs.
GREENOAKS SHOP. CEN.
WINDMILL SHOP. CEN.
Mkt.
Playing Field
Sch.
Widnes R.L.F.C.
Autoquest Stadium
Halton College
Courts
Kingsway Leisure Centre
Halton College
Municipal Buildings
Lib.
Hall
BOWERS BUSINESS PARK
BOWERS PARK INDUSTRIAL ESTATE
THE BARKIN CENTRE
ALEXANDRA IND. EST.
MOOR LA. IND. EST.
Sub.
BIRCHFIELD ROAD B5419
KINGSWAY B5419
LEIGH AVENUE B5178
LIVERPOOL RD.
DEACON RD.
ALBERT ROAD B5178
HALTON VIEW ROAD
A557 EASTERN BY-PASS
A557 WIDNES EASTERN BY-PASS
WIDNES EASTERN BY-PASS A557
FIDDLERS FERRY ROAD A562
WEST ASHLEY WAY A562
ASHLEY WAY
MOOR-B5419-LA.
MOOR LA.
DITTON ROAD
LOCKETT ROAD
LANCASTER RD.
DERBY RD.
PEEL HOUSE LANE
ALDER AV.
APPLETON VILLAGE
FREDERICK ST.
GREENWAY ROAD
WARRINGTON ROAD
PAGE LANE
MILTON AV.
LOWER HOUSE LANE
HIGHFIELD ROAD
VICTORIA RD.
GREEN OAKS WAY
WINFIELD WAY
GERRARD ST.
LUGSDALE RD.
DENNIS RD.
EARLE RD.
PIT LANE
MARSH HALL RD.
FARNWORTH ST.
WINDERMERE ST.
BEACONSFIELD RD.
SEFTON AV.
GLOUCESTER RD.
DURHAM RD.
CORNWALL RD.
DEVON PL.
LAUREL BANK
BIRCH RD.
ACACIA AV.
CEDAR RD.
CYPRESS AV.
LINCOLN SQ.
CHESTNUT AV.
LILAC AV.
SYCAMORE AV.
FAIRFIELD RD.
LYTHAM RD.
ST. ANNES RD.
FAIRHAVEN RD.
KIRKHAM RD.
ANSDELL RD.
NEIL ST.
DOWARD ST.
MILLFIELD RD.
ERIC ST.
TAYLOR ST.
ALLERTON RD.
BELVOIR RD.
FOSTER ST.
PARK ST.
ROUTLEDGE ST.
COOPER ST.
REGENT RD.
MIDLAND ST.
ROSS ST.
SAXON TER.
CHESTER ST.
SAYCE ST.
CROSS ST.
DENTON ST.
BOWER ST.
WOOD ST.
BRADLEY WAY
GREGSON RD.
BELL HOUSE RD.
TANHOUSE LA.
WALMSLEY ST.
SHELAGH AV.
DEIRDRE AV.
DICKSON ST.
WALLACE ST.
PRINCES ST.
SHARP ST.
CHARLES ST.
CARLTON ST.
KENT ST.
CAREY ST.
SALISBURY ST.
FARRANT ST.
NEW ST.
TIMPERLEY ST.
BRYNN ST.
LAMBERT CT.
ALFRED ST.
OXFORD ST.
QUINN ST.
KEBLE ST.
CAMBRIDGE ST.
VICARAGE RD.
VICTORIA SQ.
ALFORDE ST.
MARKET ST.
LACEY ST.
CATHERINE ST.
BOLD ST.
ALEXANDRA ST.
MOTTERSHEAD RD.
CAMERON RD.
MOND RD.
BRUNNER RD.
SINCLAIR AV.
WARVER TREE AV.
HENDERSON RD.
SQUIRES AVENUE
HAIG RD.
TIMMIS CRES.
CLAYTON CRES.
HOOD RD.
BURNS CR.
SCOTT AV.
WORDSWORTH AV.
BROWNING AV.
MASEFIELD AV.
MOORSIDE CT.
EGYPT ST.
SMITH RD.
ROSE ST.
LEWIS CR.
CALDWELL RD.
KINGSWAY HO.
OAKS PL.
SHAKESPEARE RD.
TENNYSON RD.
ADDISON SQUARE
SHELLEY RD.
WOODLAND AV.
BRADSHAW ST.
VICTORIA GRO.
ROSE VIEW AV.
BIRCHFIELD AV.
APPLETON ST.
BALMORAL RD.
LESSINGHAM RD.
GILTBROOK CL.
BEMBRIDGE CL.
NEW BARN AV.
BRIDLE PATH

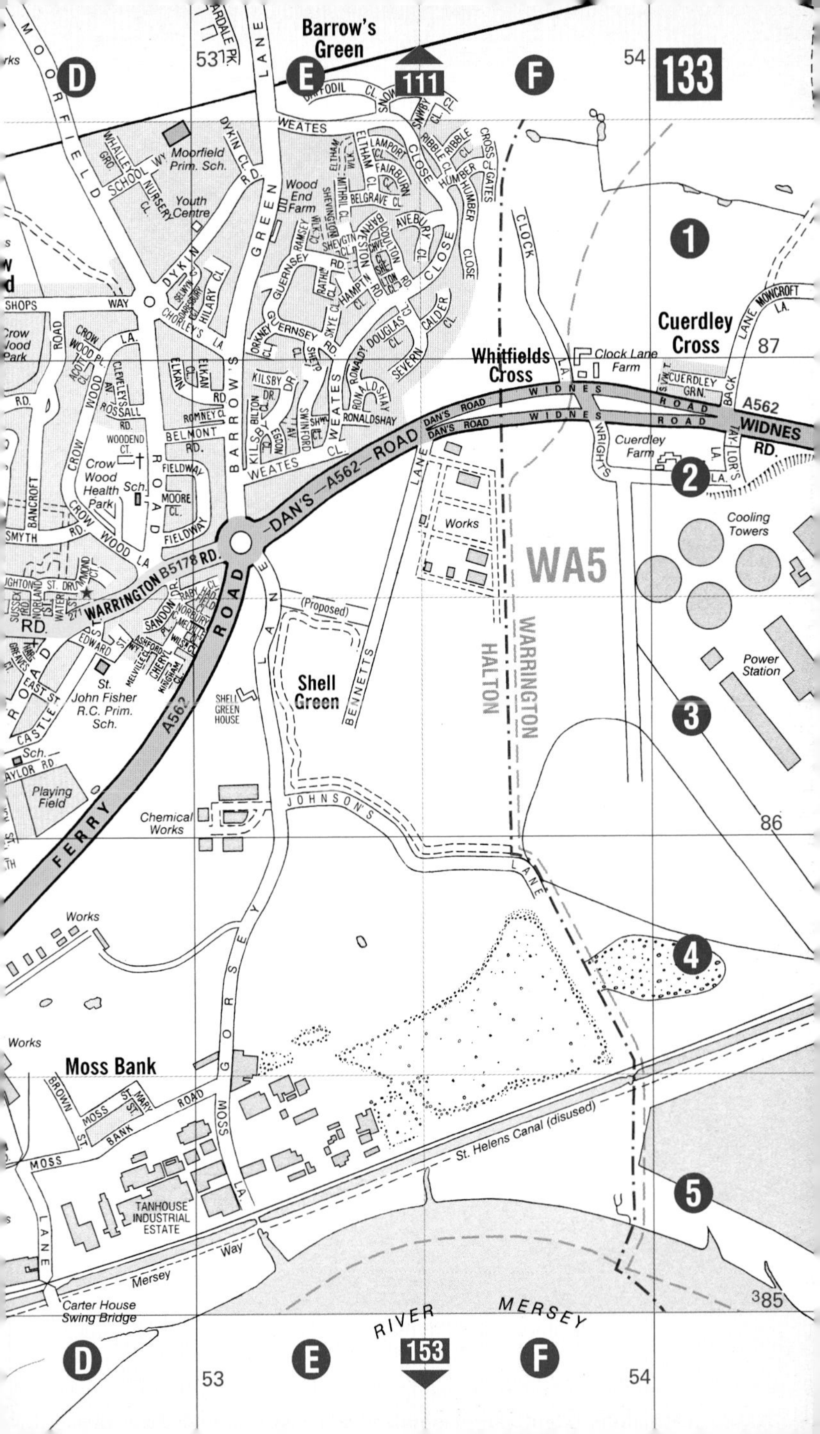
Barrow's Green
111
Moorfield Prim. Sch.
Youth Centre
Wood End Farm
Crow Wood Health Park
Crow Wood Park
Whitfields Cross
Clock Lane Farm
Cuerdley Cross
Cuerdley Farm
Cooling Towers
Power Station
WA5
WARRINGTON
HALTON
Works
Shell Green
SHELL GREEN HOUSE
(Proposed)
Chemical Works
St. John Fisher R.C. Prim. Sch.
Playing Field
Moss Bank
TANHOUSE INDUSTRIAL ESTATE
St. Helens Canal (disused)
Mersey Way
Carter House Swing Bridge
RIVER MERSEY
A562
WIDNES RD.
DAN'S ROAD
FERRY ROAD
WARRINGTON B5178 RD.
153
53
54
86
87
385

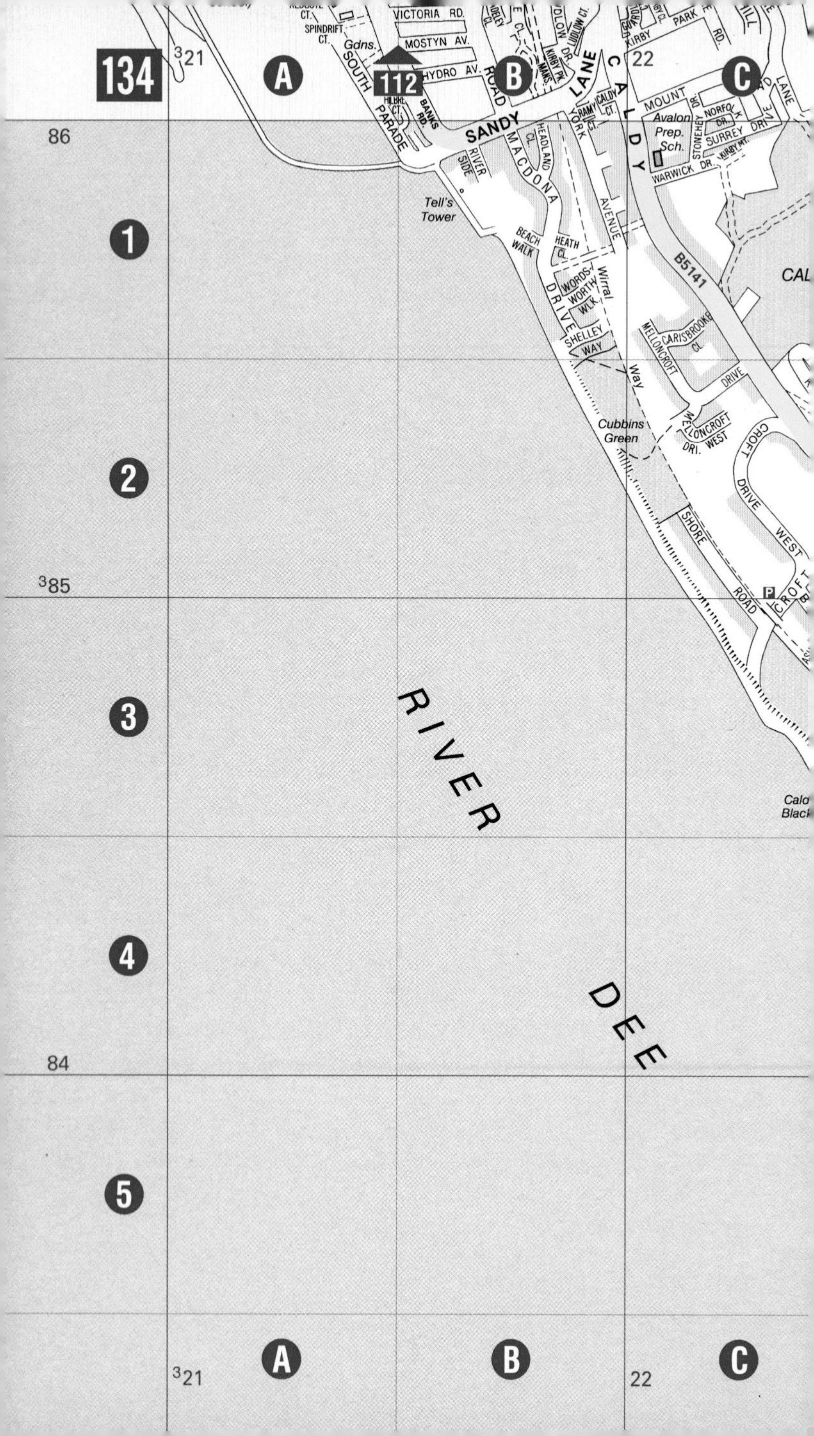

321
A
B
C
22
112
VICTORIA RD.
SPINDRIFT CT.
Gdns.
MOSTYN AV.
HYDRO AV.
SOUTH PARADE
HILBRE CT.
BANKS RD.
ROAD
SANDY LANE
KIRBY PK.
LUDLOW DR.
LUDLOW CT.
CALDY
KIRBY PARK RD.
MOUNT
Avalon Prep. Sch.
NORFOLK DR.
SURREY DRIVE
STONEHEY DR.
WARWICK DR.
KIRBY MT.
LANE
YORK AVENUE
CALDY CT.
HEADLAND CL.
MACDONA
RIVER SIDE
Tell's Tower
BEACH WALK
HEATH CL.
WORDSWORTH WLK.
DRIVE
SHELLEY WAY
Wirral Way
B5141
CAL
MELLONCROFT
CARISBROOKE CL.
DRIVE
MELLONCROFT DRI. WEST
Cubbins Green
CROFT DRIVE WEST
SHORE ROAD
CROFT
P
86
1
2
385
3
RIVER
DEE
4
84
5
Cald Black

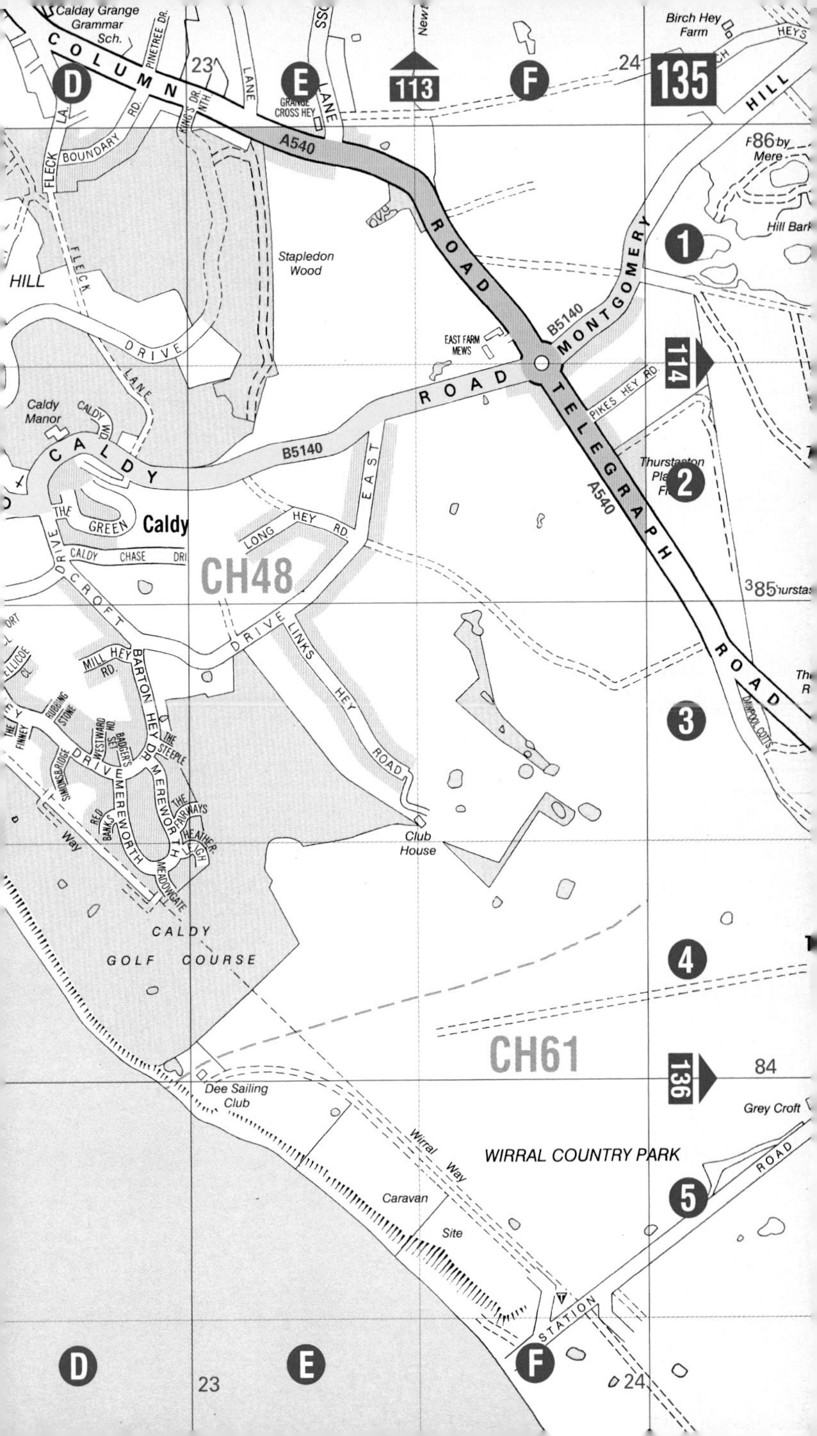

Calday Grange Grammar Sch.
COLUMN
PINETREE DR.
LANE
LANE
GRANGE CROSS HEY
113
Birch Hey Farm
HEYS
HILL
A540
BOUNDARY
RD.
FLECK LA.
KING'S DR. NTH.
Stapledon Wood
Hill Bark
MONTGOMERY
B5140
EAST FARM MEWS
114
ROAD
PIKES HEY RD.
TELEGRAPH
A540
Thurstaston
HILL
FLECK
DRIVE
LANE
Caldy Manor
CALDY WD.
CALDY
B5140
EAST
LONG HEY RD.
THE GREEN
Caldy
CALDY CHASE
DRIVE
CROFT
CH48
DRIVE
LINKS HEY ROAD
MILL HEY RD.
BARTON HEY DR.
ELLICOE CL.
RUBBING STONE
THE FINNEY
WESTWARD HO
SUNSET
BADGER'S
THE STEEPLE
SIMONSBRIDGE
MEREWORTH
THE FAIRWAYS
HEATHER-LEIGH
RED BANK
MEADOWGATE
Way
Club House
ROAD
DAWPOOL COTTS.
CALDY GOLF COURSE
CH61
136
84
Dee Sailing Club
Grey Croft
Wirral Way
WIRRAL COUNTRY PARK
ROAD
Caravan Site
STATION
D
E
F
1
2
3
4
5
23
24
85
86

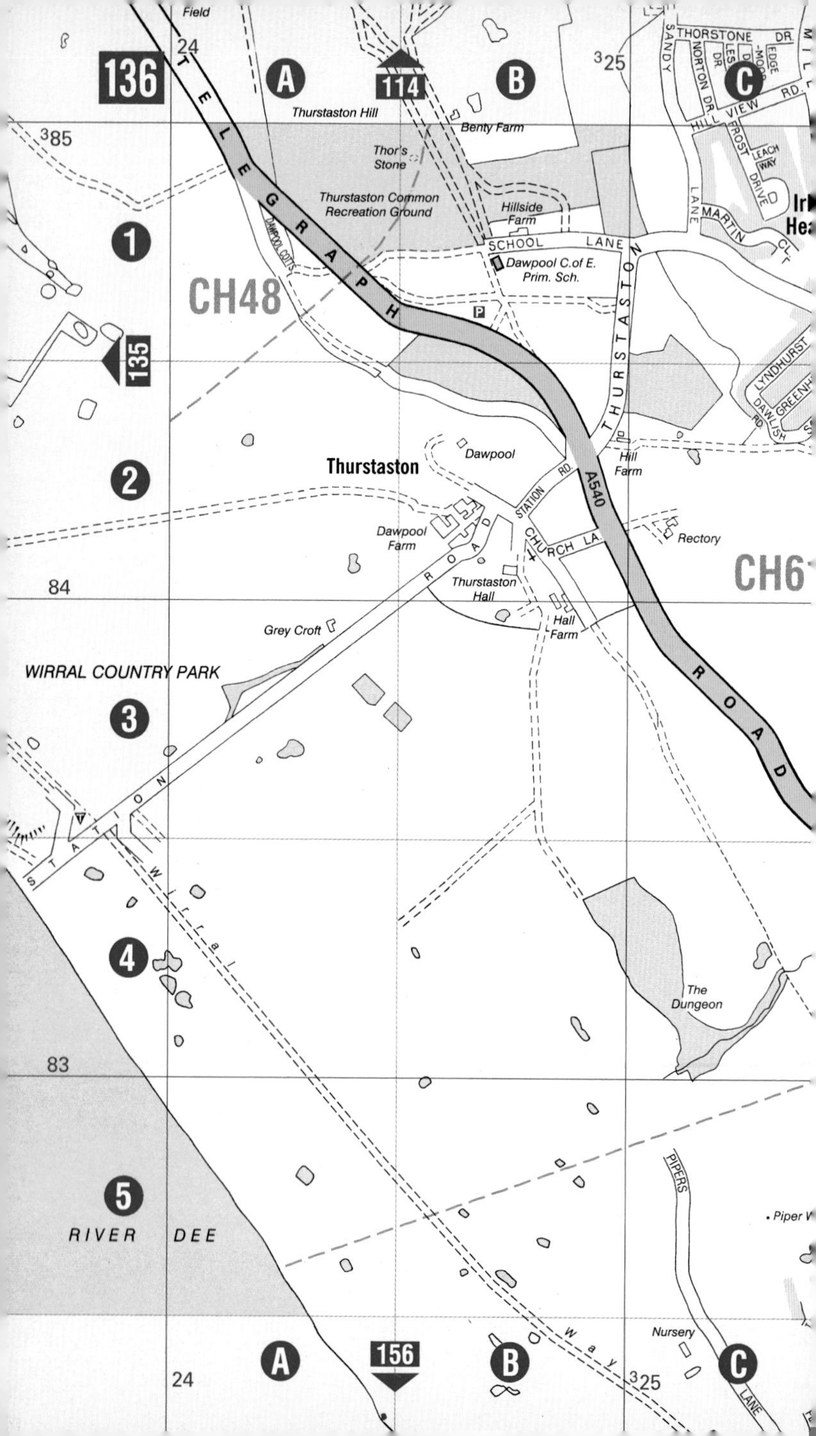
Field
24
A
114
B
325
C
THORSTONE DR.
SANDY
NORTON DR.
EDGE
MOOR
HILL VIEW RD.
Thurstaston Hill
Benty Farm
385
Thor's Stone
TELEGRAPH
FROST DRIVE
LEACH WAY
LANE
MARTIN CL.
Thurstaston Common Recreation Ground
Hillside Farm
1
SCHOOL LANE
DAWPOOL COTTS
Dawpool C.of E. Prim. Sch.
CH48
THURSTASTON
135
LYNDHURST
DAWLISH RD.
GREENHILL
Dawpool
Thurstaston
2
STATION RD.
A540
Hill Farm
Dawpool Farm
CHURCH LA.
Rectory
CH61
84
ROAD
Thurstaston Hall
Hall Farm
Grey Croft
WIRRAL COUNTRY PARK
3
ROAD
STATION
Wirral Way
4
The Dungeon
83
PIPERS LANE
5
RIVER DEE
Piper V
Nursery
A
156
B
24
325
C

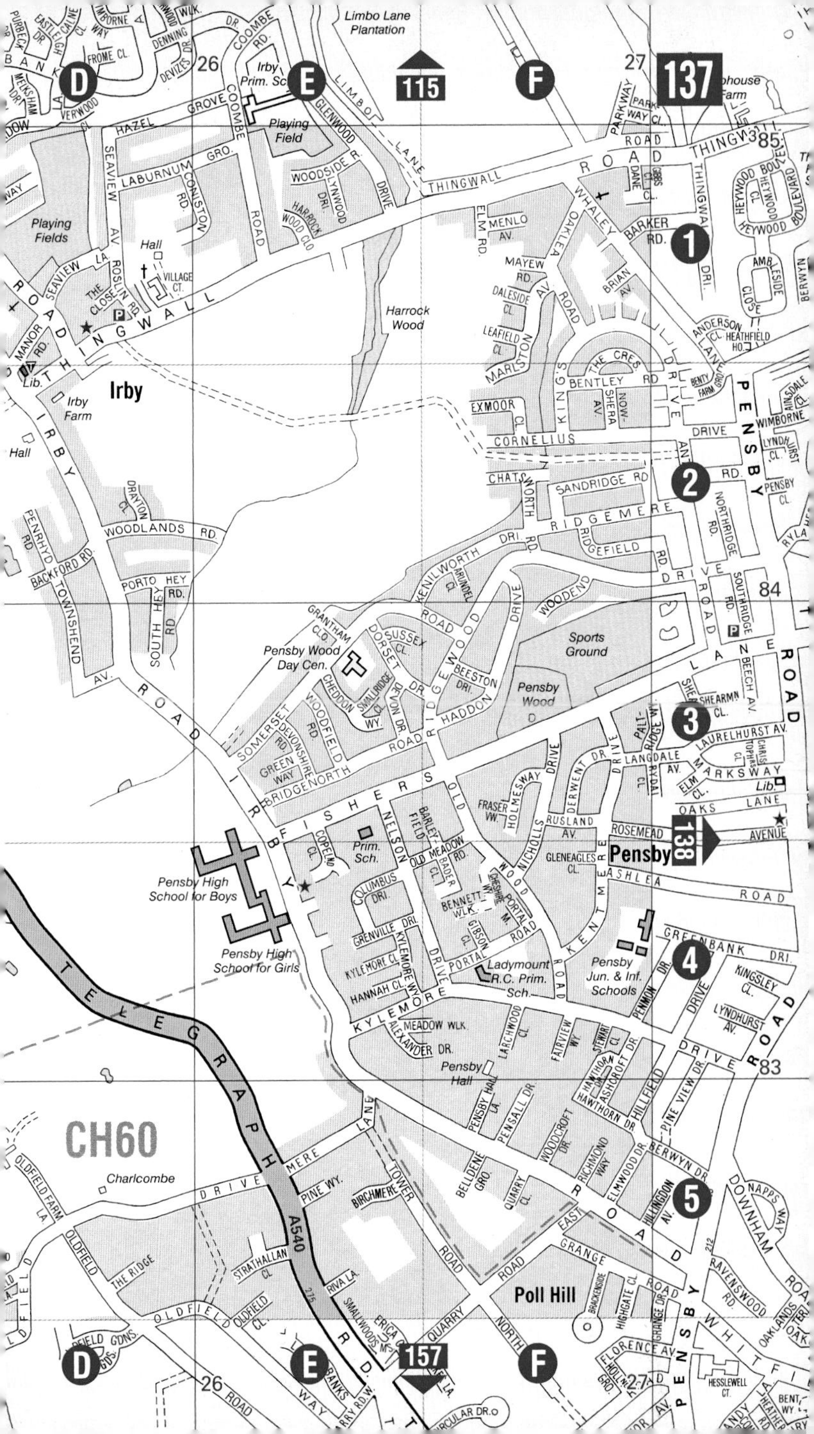
137
115
157
138
D
E
F
1
2
3
4
5
26
27
85
84
83
Irby
Pensby
Poll Hill
CH60
Limbo Lane Plantation
Harrock Wood
Playing Fields
Playing Field
Irby Prim. Sch.
Irby Farm
Hall
Lib.
Pensby Wood Day Cen.
Sports Ground
Pensby Wood
Prim. Sch.
Pensby High School for Boys
Pensby High School for Girls
Ladymount R.C. Prim. Sch.
Pensby Jun. & Inf. Schools
Pensby Hall
Charlcombe
THINGWALL ROAD
IRBY ROAD
TELEGRAPH RD.
A540
PENSBY ROAD
FISHERS LANE
KYLEMORE DRIVE
GREENBANK DRI.
ASHLEA ROAD
ROSEMEAD AVENUE
OAKS LANE
CORNELIUS DRIVE
RIDGEMERE RD.
WOODLANDS RD.
MERE DRIVE
GRANGE ROAD
WHITFIELD LANE

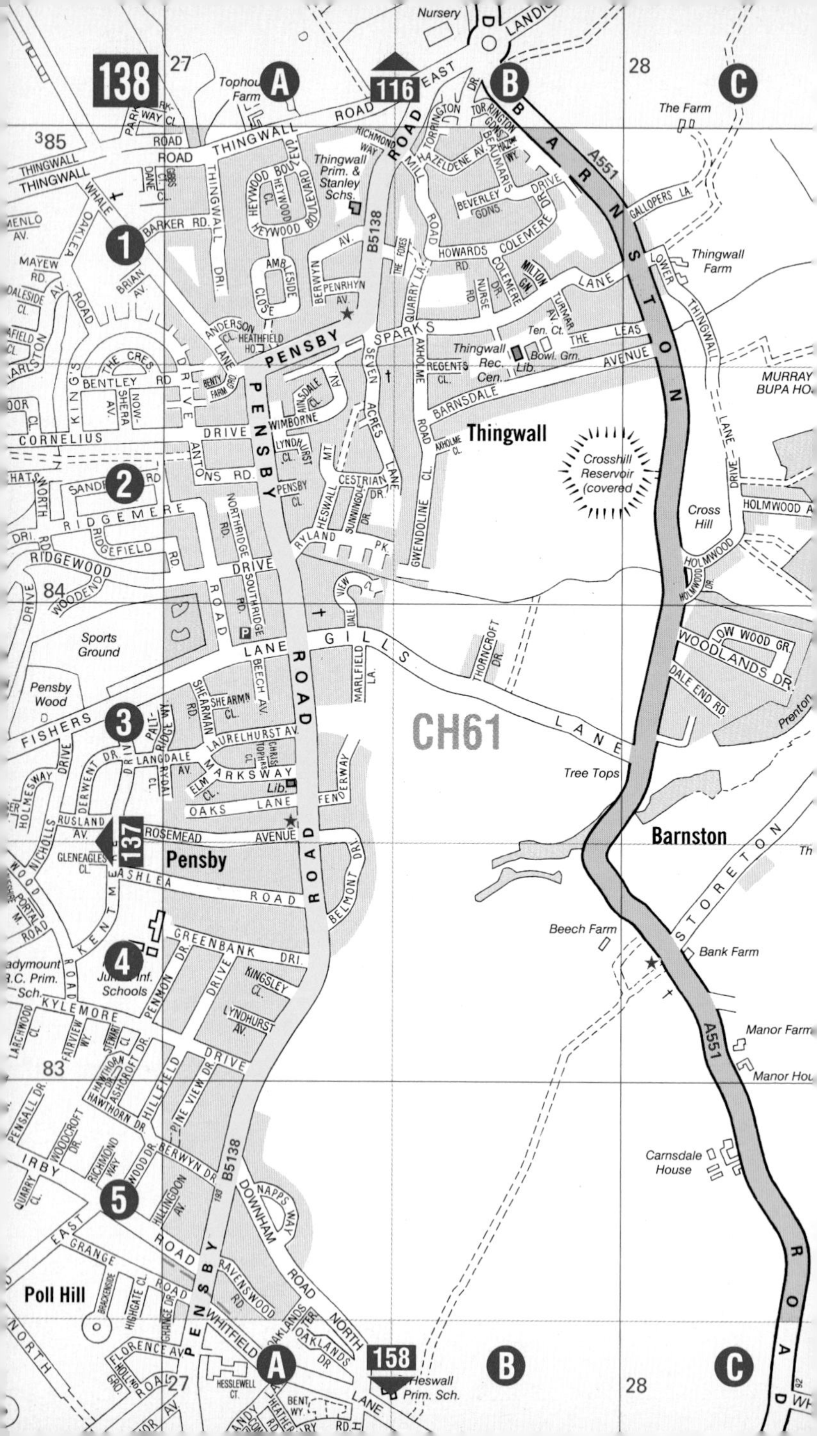
116
137
158
CH61
Thingwall
Pensby
Barnston
Poll Hill
Crosshill Reservoir (covered)
Sports Ground
Pensby Wood
PENSBY ROAD
B5138
BARNSTON ROAD
A551
THINGWALL ROAD
GILLS LANE
FISHERS LANE
STORETON LANE
The Farm
Thingwall Farm
Tree Tops
Beech Farm
Bank Farm
Manor Farm
Carnsdale House
Heswall Prim. Sch.
Thingwall Prim. & Stanley Schs.
Thingwall Rec. Cen.

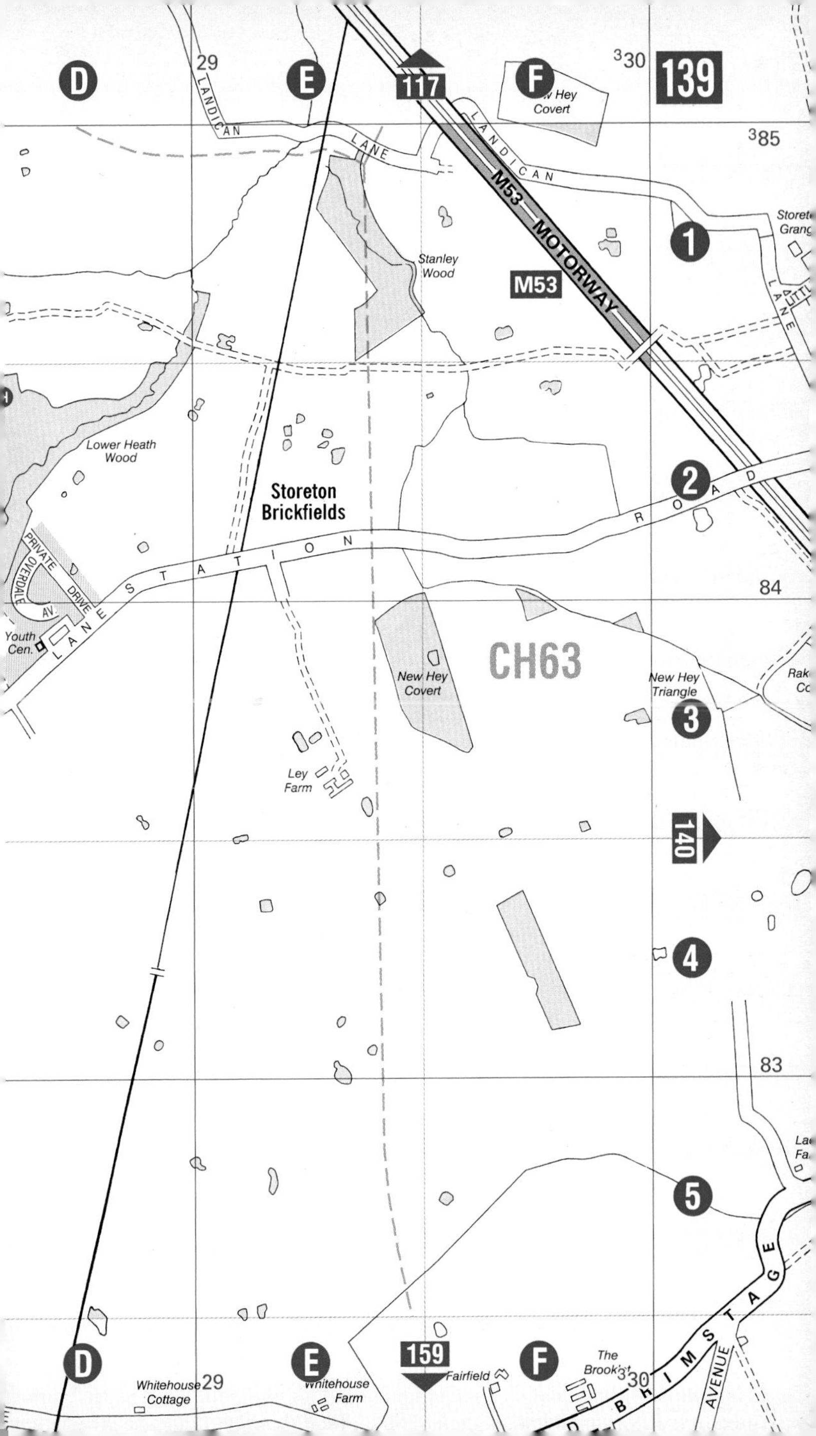
D
E
F
29
330
385
117
New Hey
Covert
LANDICAN LANE
LANDICAN
M53 MOTORWAY
M53
Stanley
Wood
Storeton
Grange
LITTLE LANE
1
2
3
4
5
Lower Heath
Wood
Storeton
Brickfields
STATION ROAD
STATION LANE
PRIVATE DRIVE
OVERDALE AV.
Youth
Cen.
84
New Hey
Covert
CH63
New Hey
Triangle
Ley
Farm
140
83
159
Whitehouse
Cottage
Whitehouse
Farm
Fairfield
The
Brook
BRIMSTAGE
AVENUE
D
E
F
29
330

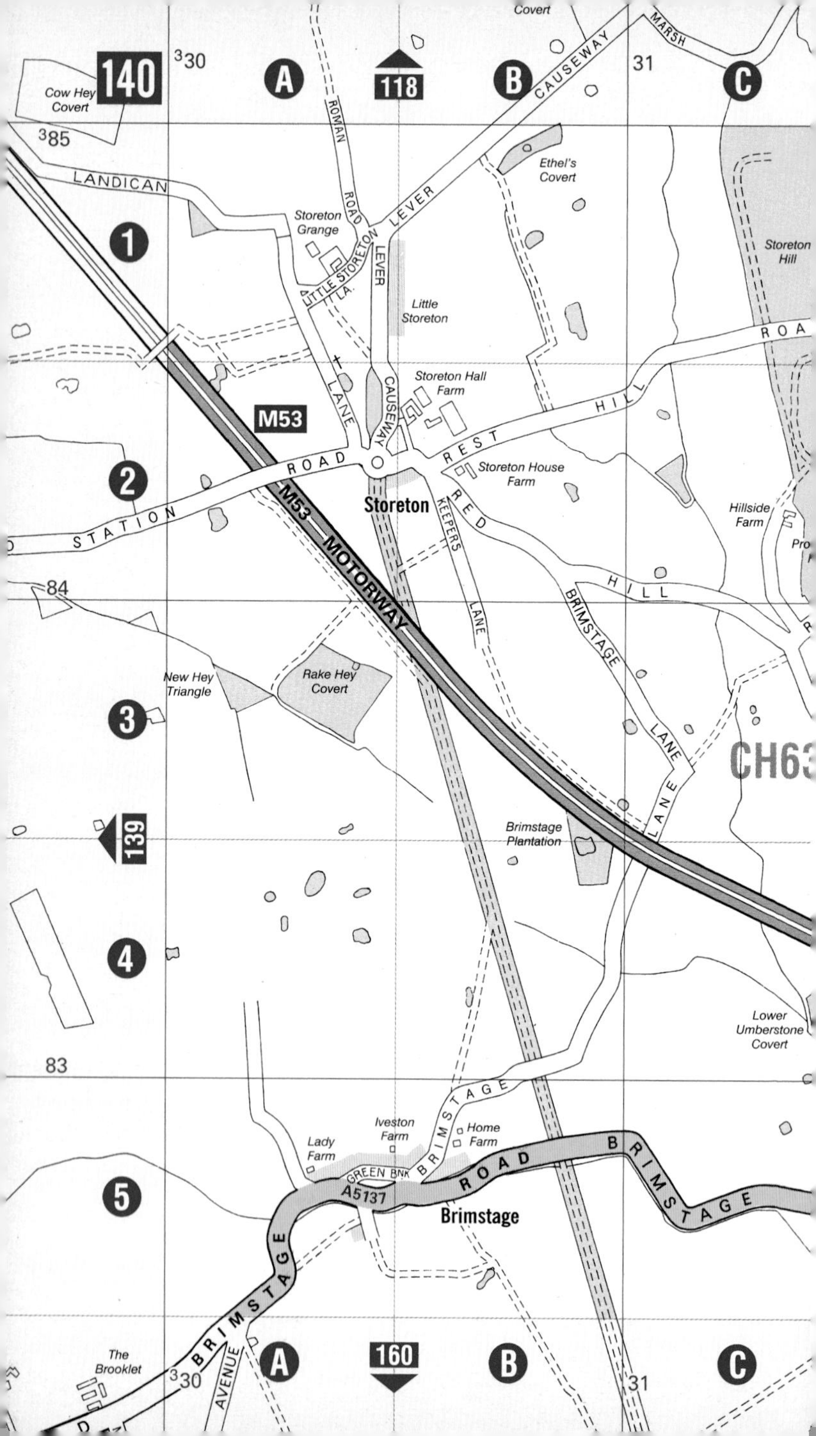

140
118
139
160
A
B
C
1
2
3
4
5
Cow Hey Covert
Covert
MARSH
CAUSEWAY
LANDICAN
ROMAN ROAD
Storeton Grange
LITTLE STORETON LA.
LEVER
LEVER CAUSEWAY
Ethel's Covert
Storeton Hill
Little Storeton
ROAD
LANE
CAUSEWAY
Storeton Hall Farm
HILL
M53
REST
ROAD
Storeton House Farm
Storeton
STATION
KEEPERS LANE
RED
Hillside Farm
M53 MOTORWAY
HILL
BRIMSTAGE LANE
New Hey Triangle
Rake Hey Covert
CH63
LANE
Brimstage Plantation
Lower Umberstone Covert
BRIMSTAGE
Iveston Farm
Home Farm
Lady Farm
GREEN BNK
A5137
ROAD
BRIMSTAGE
Brimstage
BRIMSTAGE
The Brooklet
AVENUE
330
31
385
84
83

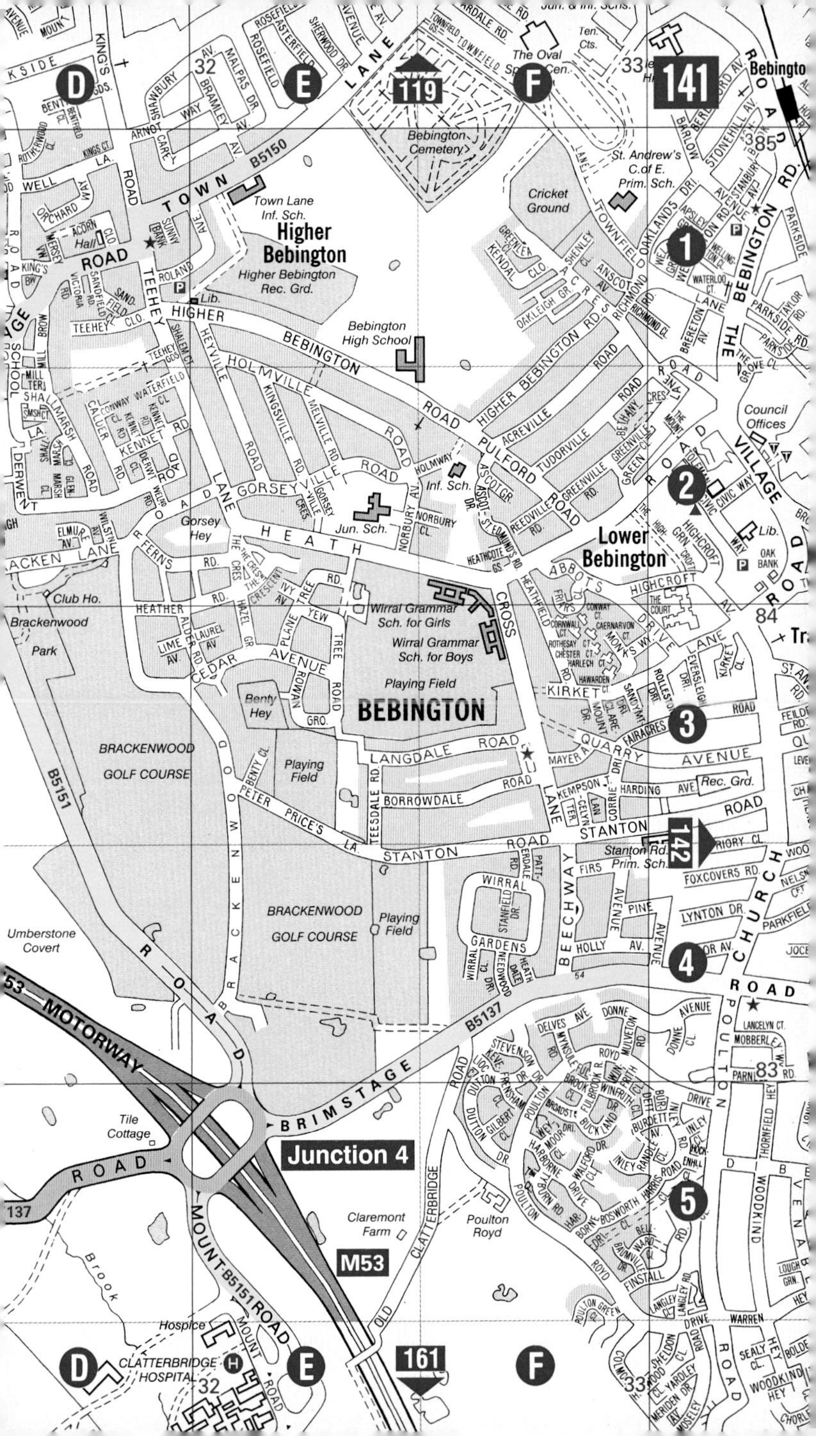
141
119
142
161
D
E
F
1
2
3
4
5
32
33
84
83
Higher Bebington
Lower Bebington
BEBINGTON
Bebington Cemetery
The Oval Sports Cen.
Cricket Ground
St. Andrew's C.of E. Prim. Sch.
Town Lane Inf. Sch.
Higher Bebington Rec. Grd.
Bebington High School
Council Offices
Wirral Grammar Sch. for Girls
Wirral Grammar Sch. for Boys
Playing Field
BRACKENWOOD GOLF COURSE
Brackenwood Park
Club Ho.
Gorsey Hey
Benty Hey
Stanton Rd. Prim. Sch.
Rec. Grd.
Umberstone Covert
Tile Cottage
Junction 4
M53
M53 MOTORWAY
Claremont Farm
Poulton Royd
Hospice
CLATTERBRIDGE HOSPITAL
TOWN LANE
B5150
HIGHER BEBINGTON ROAD
HEATH ROAD
BRACKENWOOD ROAD
B5151
BRIMSTAGE ROAD
B5137
STANTON ROAD
QUARRY AVENUE
CHURCH ROAD
POULTON ROAD
MOUNT ROAD
CLATTERBRIDGE ROAD
OLD CLATTERBRIDGE ROAD
PULFORD ROAD
VILLAGE ROAD
THE VILLAGE
BEBINGTON RD.
TEEHEY LANE
CROSS LANE
BEECHWAY
WIRRAL GARDENS
PETER PRICE'S LA.
LANGDALE ROAD
BORROWDALE ROAD
CEDAR AVENUE
HOLMVILLE ROAD
GORSEYVILLE ROAD
Bebington
Jun. Sch.
Inf. Sch.
Lib.

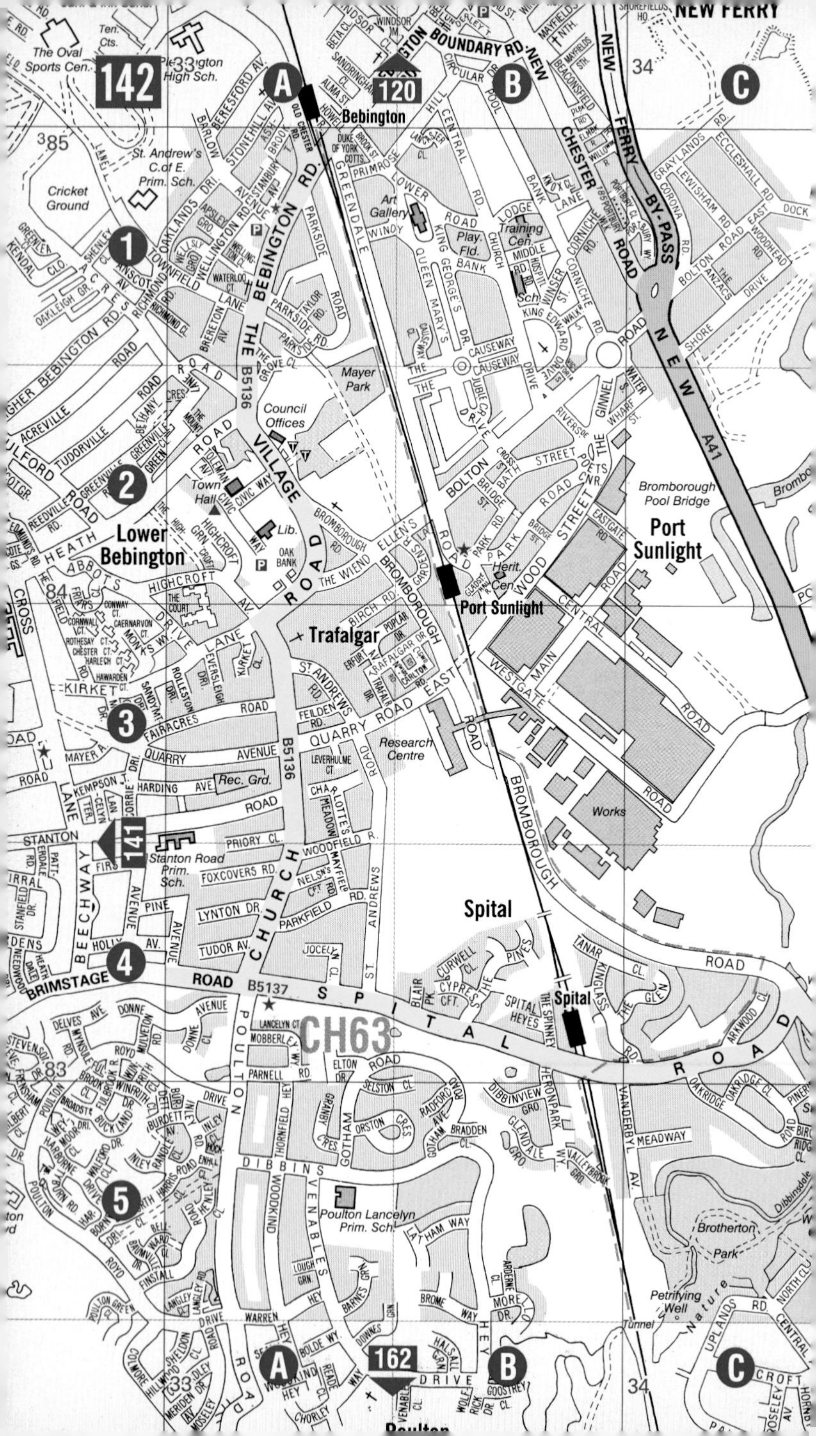

142
120
141
162
A
B
C
1
2
3
4
5
Bebington
Port Sunlight
Spital
Lower Bebington
Trafalgar
Port Sunlight
Spital
NEW FERRY
CH63
Mayer Park
Council Offices
Town Hall
Bromborough Pool Bridge
Research Centre
Works
Brotherton Park
Petrifying Well
Cricket Ground
The Oval Sports Cen.
St. Andrew's C.of E. Prim. Sch.
Stanton Road Prim. Sch.
Poulton Lancelyn Prim. Sch.
Art Gallery
Training Cen.
Rec. Grd.

RIVER MERSEY
Bromborough Dock
Depot
Cricket Gnd.
Works
YORK STREET
MANOR PLACE
SOUTH VIEW
THE GREEN
Sch.
Bowl. Grn.
Ten. Cts.
SOUTH ROAD
DOCK ROAD
CH62
SOUTH RD.
THERMAL ROAD
Factories
PORT CAUSEWAY
FAIRWAY CRES.
CROSSWAYS
WESTERN AV.
EASTERN AV.
NORTH WAYS
GREEN WAY
RINGWAYS
NORTH
TERMINUS ROAD
CORONATION DR.
MAGAZINE RD.
CROFT GRN.
FAIRWAY SOUTH
Bromborough Port
GEORGIA AV.
STADIUM ROAD
WIRRAL LEISURE PARK
SOUTH WIRRAL RETAIL PARK
Oil Storage Depot
COMMERCIAL RD.
Power Station
Superstore
WELTON RD.
WELTON ROAD
CARROCK RD.
DINSDALE RD.
MOSEDALE RD.
BASSENDALE RD.
CROFT BUSINESS CEN.
CALDBECK ROAD
THURSBY
SKIDDAW RD.
MARTINDALE RD.
HAWKSHEAD RD.
Slack Wood
PLANTATION ROAD
POWER ROAD
RIVERVIEW RD.
HALL
B5137
A41
CROFT AV. E.
HEATH FIELD
SUMMERFIELD
Sports Gnd.
AVENUE
STANHOPE DRIVE
STANHOPE DR.
RAKE
Rectory
NEW CHESTER ROAD
DENE
LANE
D E F
1 2 3 4 5
335 36 385 84 83
121
163

144
124
A
B
C
1
2
3
4
5
39
340
385
84
83
Grassendale Park
Cressington Park
Cressington
L19
A561
Garston Sands
Depot
Dock
Jetty
Works
Garston Channel
RIVER MERSEY
LIVERPOOL
WIRRAL
Recreation Ground
Garston Sports Centre
WEAVER INDUSTRIAL ESTATE
GRASSENDALE ESPLANADE
CRESSINGTON ESPLANADE
NORTH ROAD
SOUTH RD.
KNOWSLEY ROAD
EATON ROAD
SALISBURY ROAD
GROSVENOR RD
BEECHWOOD
GRASSENDALE GREEN
ST. MARY'S RD.
GARSTON
DOCK ROAD
ISLAND RD.
BOWDEN ROAD
CHURCH RD.
BLACKBURNE
WINDOW LA.
YORK
KING
VULCAN
SAUNBY
CAMPANIA
LUCANIA
BRUNSWICK ST.
Lib.
Sch.

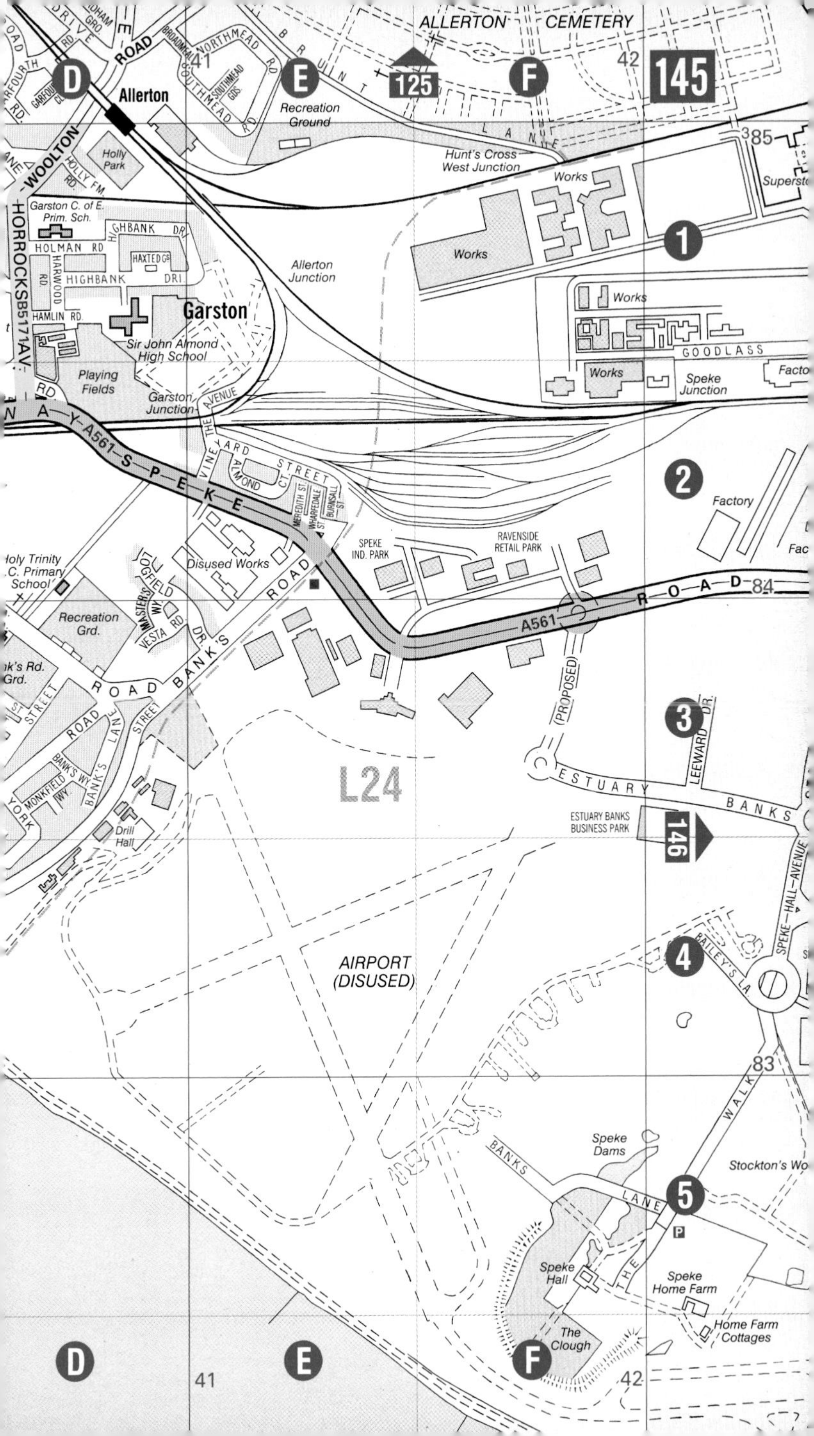
145
ALLERTON CEMETERY
125
146
Allerton
Garston
Recreation Ground
Hunt's Cross West Junction
Works
Superstore
Holly Park
Garston C. of E. Prim. Sch.
HIGHBANK DRI.
HOLMAN RD
HARWOOD RD.
HIGHBANK DRI.
HAXTED GDS
HAMLIN RD.
Sir John Almond High School
Playing Fields
Garston Junction
Allerton Junction
Speke Junction
GOODLASS
Factory
WOOLTON ROAD
HORROCKS AV.
B5171
A561 SPEKE ROAD
THE AVENUE
VINEYARD STREET
ALMOND CT.
MEREDITH ST.
WHARFEDALE ST.
BURNSALL ST.
SPEKE IND. PARK
RAVENSIDE RETAIL PARK
Disused Works
Holy Trinity C. Primary School
Recreation Grd.
LOGFIELD DR.
MASTER'S WY.
VESTA RD.
BANK'S ROAD
BANK'S LANE
BANK'S WY.
MONKFIELD WY.
YORK STREET
Drill Hall
(PROPOSED)
ESTUARY BANKS
LEEWARD DR.
ESTUARY BANKS BUSINESS PARK
L24
AIRPORT (DISUSED)
BAILEY'S LA.
SPEKE HALL AVENUE
WALK
Speke Dams
BANKS LANE
Stockton's Wood
Speke Hall
Speke Home Farm
Home Farm Cottages
The Clough
D
E
F
1
2
3
4
5
41
42
83
84
385

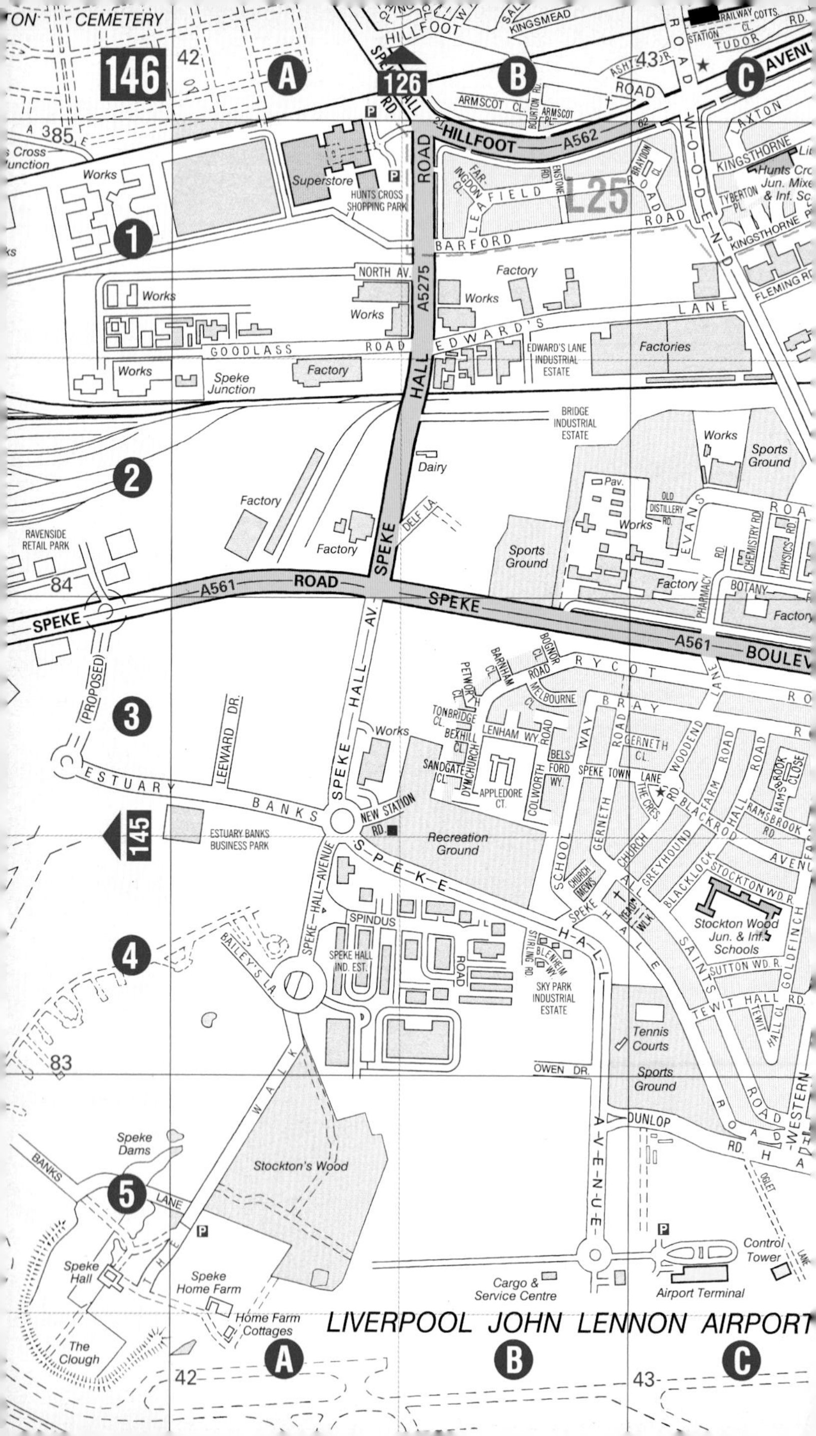
CEMETERY
HILLFOOT
KINGSMEAD
RAILWAY COTTS.
STATION
TUDOR
AVENUE
126
ARMSCOT CL.
ARMSCOT PL.
ROAD
HILLFOOT
A562
A 385
Hunts Cross Junction
Works
Superstore
HUNTS CROSS SHOPPING PARK
LAXTON
KINGSTHORNE
Hunts Cross Jun. Mixed & Inf. Sch.
TYBERTON PL.
KINGSTHORNE
L25
LEAFIELD
FARINGDON CL.
ENSTONE
BRAYDON CL.
WOODEND
BARFORD
NORTH AV.
Factory
Works
FLEMING
A5275
LANE
EDWARD'S
GOODLASS
ROAD
Factories
EDWARD'S LANE INDUSTRIAL ESTATE
Works
Factory
Speke Junction
HALL
BRIDGE INDUSTRIAL ESTATE
Works
Sports Ground
Dairy
Pav.
OLD DISTILLERY RD.
EVANS
CHEMISTRY RD.
PHYSICS
Factory
RAVENSIDE RETAIL PARK
DELF LA.
Factory
Sports Ground
Works
84
A561
ROAD
SPEKE
PHARMACY
BOTANY
Factory
SPEKE
SPEKE
A561
BOULEVARD
(PROPOSED)
BOGNOR CL.
BARNHAM CL.
PETWORTH CL.
RYCOT ROAD
MELBOURNE
BRAY
TONBRIDGE CL.
BEXHILL CL.
LENHAM WY.
GERNETH CL.
Works
LEEWARD DR.
SANDGATE CL.
DYMCHURCH
APPLEDORE CT.
COLWORTH
BELSFORD WY.
SPEKE TOWN LANE
THE CRES.
WOODEND
FARM
ROAD
HALL
RAMSBROOK CLOSE
RAMSBROOK RD.
ESTUARY
BANKS
NEW STATION RD.
Recreation Ground
SCHOOL
GERNETH
CHURCH
CHURCH MEWS
BLACKROD
GREYHOUND
BLACKLOCK
AVENUE
STOCKTON WD. R.
145
ESTUARY BANKS BUSINESS PARK
SPEKE
SPEKE HALL AVENUE
SPINDUS
SPEKE HALL IND. EST.
ROAD
STIRLING RD.
BLENHEIM WY.
SKY PARK INDUSTRIAL ESTATE
HALL
ALL SAINTS
MEADE WLK.
Stockton Wood Jun. & Inf. Schools
SUTTON WD. R.
GOLDFINCH
TEWIT HALL RD.
TEWIT HALL CL.
BAILEY'S LA.
Tennis Courts
Sports Ground
83
OWEN DR.
WESTERN
DUNLOP RD.
HALE
ROAD
AVENUE
OGLET
WALK
Stockton's Wood
Speke Dams
BANKS
LANE
THE
Speke Hall
Speke Home Farm
Home Farm Cottages
The Clough
Cargo & Service Centre
Control Tower
Airport Terminal
LANE
LIVERPOOL JOHN LENNON AIRPORT
42
43
A
B
C
1
2
3
4
5

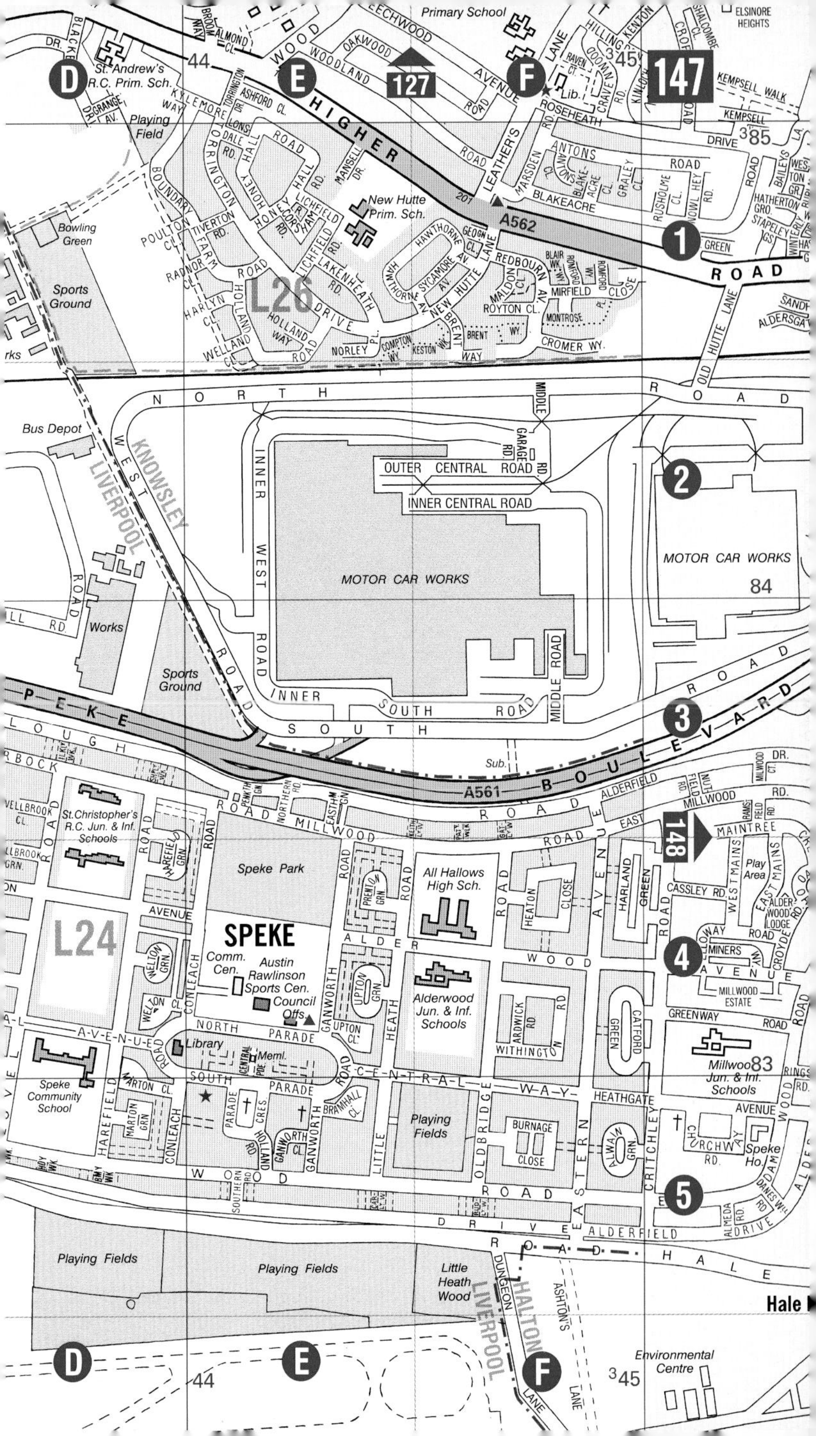

147
127
148
SPEKE
L24
L26
A562
A561
HIGHER ROAD
SPEKE BOULEVARD
NORTH ROAD
MOTOR CAR WORKS
St. Andrew's R.C. Prim. Sch.
New Hutte Prim. Sch.
St.Christopher's R.C. Jun. & Inf. Schools
All Hallows High Sch.
Alderwood Jun. & Inf. Schools
Millwood Jun. & Inf. Schools
Speke Community School
Speke Park
Comm. Cen.
Austin Rawlinson Sports Cen.
Council Offs.
Library
Playing Fields
Little Heath Wood
Environmental Centre
Sports Ground
Bus Depot
Works
Hale

128
147
A
B
C
1
2
3
4
5
L26
L24
45
46
85
84
83
Highfield Sch.
ELSINORE HEIGHTS
Harefield
Finch Farm
Lodge Farm
HIGHER ROAD
A562
FINCH LANE
SPEKE BOULEVARD
SA561P
A561
HIGHER ROAD
RAMSBROOK LANE
Ramsbrook Farm
Ramsbrook Bridge
MOTOR CAR WORKS
NORTH ROAD
EAST ROAD
SOUTH ROAD
MIDDLE ROAD
GARAGE RD.
OLD HUTTE LANE
BAILEY'S LANE
ACRE GREEN
BLAKEACRE RD.
ANTONS ROAD
ROSEHEATH DRIVE
KEMPSELL WY.
MIRFIELD CLOSE
ROYTON CL.
CROMER WY.
SANDHURST RD.
ALDERSGATE DR.
Hop Yard Wood
MILL WOOD
ALDERFIELD DRIVE
MILL WOOD
MAINTREE
Play Area
WESTMAINS
EAST MAINS
CASSLEY RD.
ELLOWAY ROAD
MINERS WY.
ALDERWOOD AVENUE
MILLWOOD ESTATE
GREENWAY ROAD
Millwood Jun. & Inf. Schools
St. Ambrose R.C. Jun. Mixed & Inf. School
HEATHGATE AVENUE
CHURCHWAY RD.
Speke Ho.
EASTERN AVENUE
HEATON CLOSE
HARLAND GREEN
CATFORD GREEN
ALWAIN GRN.
BURNAGE CLOSE
ARDWICK RD.
WITHINGTON RD.
CRITCHLEY WAY
HALE ROAD
LIVERPOOL
HALTON
Hale Heath
Brook Farm
Environmental Centre
DUNGEON LANE
ASHTON'S LANE
BAILEY'S LANE
OLD PLANTATION
LANGFORD
PHEASANT
LADYPOOL

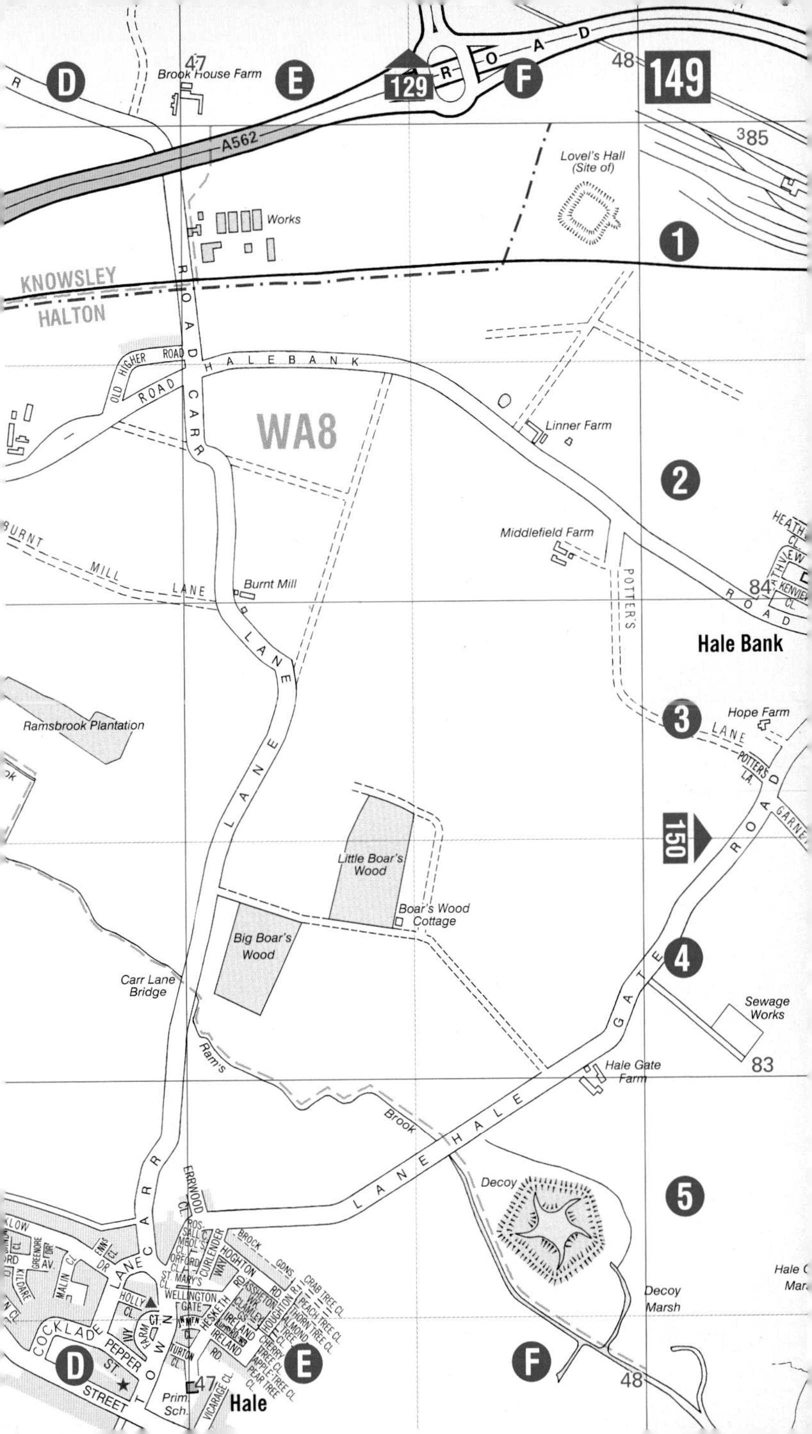
Brook House Farm
A562
ROAD
Lovel's Hall (Site of)
Works
KNOWSLEY
HALTON
HALEBANK
OLD HIGHER ROAD
CARR
WA8
Linner Farm
Middlefield Farm
BURNT MILL LANE
Burnt Mill
LANE
POTTER'S
Hale Bank
Ramsbrook Plantation
Hope Farm
POTTERS LA.
Little Boar's Wood
Boar's Wood Cottage
Big Boar's Wood
Carr Lane Bridge
Sewage Works
Hale Gate Farm
HALE GATE ROAD
Ram's Brook
LANE
Decoy
Decoy Marsh
COCKLADE STREET
PEPPER ST.
HOLLY CL.
IVY FARM CT.
TOWN LANE
WELLINGTON GATE
HESKETH RD
IRELAND RD
TURTON CL.
VICARAGE CL.
Prim. Sch.
Hale
ERRWOOD CL.
CURLENDER WAY
HOGHTON RD
BROCK GDNS.
CRAB TREE CL.
PEACH TREE CL.
THORN TREE CL.
ALMOND TREE CL.
CHERRY TREE CL.
APPLE TREE CL.
PEAR TREE CL.
MALIN CL.
KILDARE
GREENORE AV.
ST. MARY'S CL.

129
150

150
130
149
164
A
B
C
1
2
3
4
5
48
49
385
84
83
WA8
SPEKE ROAD A562
TURNALL RD.
EVERITE RD.
WESTGATE
MARSHGATE
FIELDGATE
OLDGATE
HALE RD.
PITVILLE TER.
Ditton Hall
St. Michael's R.C. Prim. School
ST. MICHAEL'S IND. ESTATE
DITTON ROAD
Lovel's Hall (Site of)
Ditton Brook
HARRISON ST.
LOVEL TER.
CLAPGATE CRES.
STAPLETON WAY
HOLLINS WAY
GOLDEN TRIANGLE INDUSTRIAL ESTATE
Superstore
Playing Field
BLACKBURNE AV.
BAGULEY AVENUE
CHURCH MEADOW W.
HEATHVIEW RD.
HEATHVIEW CL.
KENVIEW CL.
Halebank Prim. Sch.
FOUNDRY LA.
BROUGHTON WAY
PICKERINGS ROAD
HALE ROAD IND. EST.
Works
Ditton
Mersey Way
Linner Farm
HALEBANK ROAD
Middlefield Farm
POTTER'S LANE
POTTERS LA.
HALE CT.
HALE BNK. T.
FREDERICK TER.
Bank End Farm
COCK LANE ENDS
MERSEY VIEW RD.
Hale Bank
Hope Farm
Shore House
Pickering's Pasture Local Nature Reserve
GARNETT'S LA.
HALE GATE ROAD
Sewage Works
Hale Gate Farm
Decoy
Decoy Marsh
Hale Gate Marsh
RIVER

151
131
152
165
WIDNES
RUNCORN
MERSEY
WA7
The Marsh
West Bank
Runcorn Gap
Silver Jubilee Bridge
QUEENSWAY
A533
A557
WIDNES EASTERN BY-PASS
WESTON POINT EXPRESSWAY
MANCHESTER SHIP CANAL
St. Michael's Municipal Golf Course
Ditton Marsh
Steward's Brook
Mill
Works
West Bank Dock Estate
Eddarbridge Estate
West Bank Rec. Grd.
Spike Island Visitors Centre
Public Open Space
Bridgewater House
Custom House
The Pier
Pier
Bridgewater Lock
Alfred Pier
Warehouse
Runcorn
Westfield Prim. Sch.
Industrial Estate
Doctor's Bridge
Council Depot
Subway

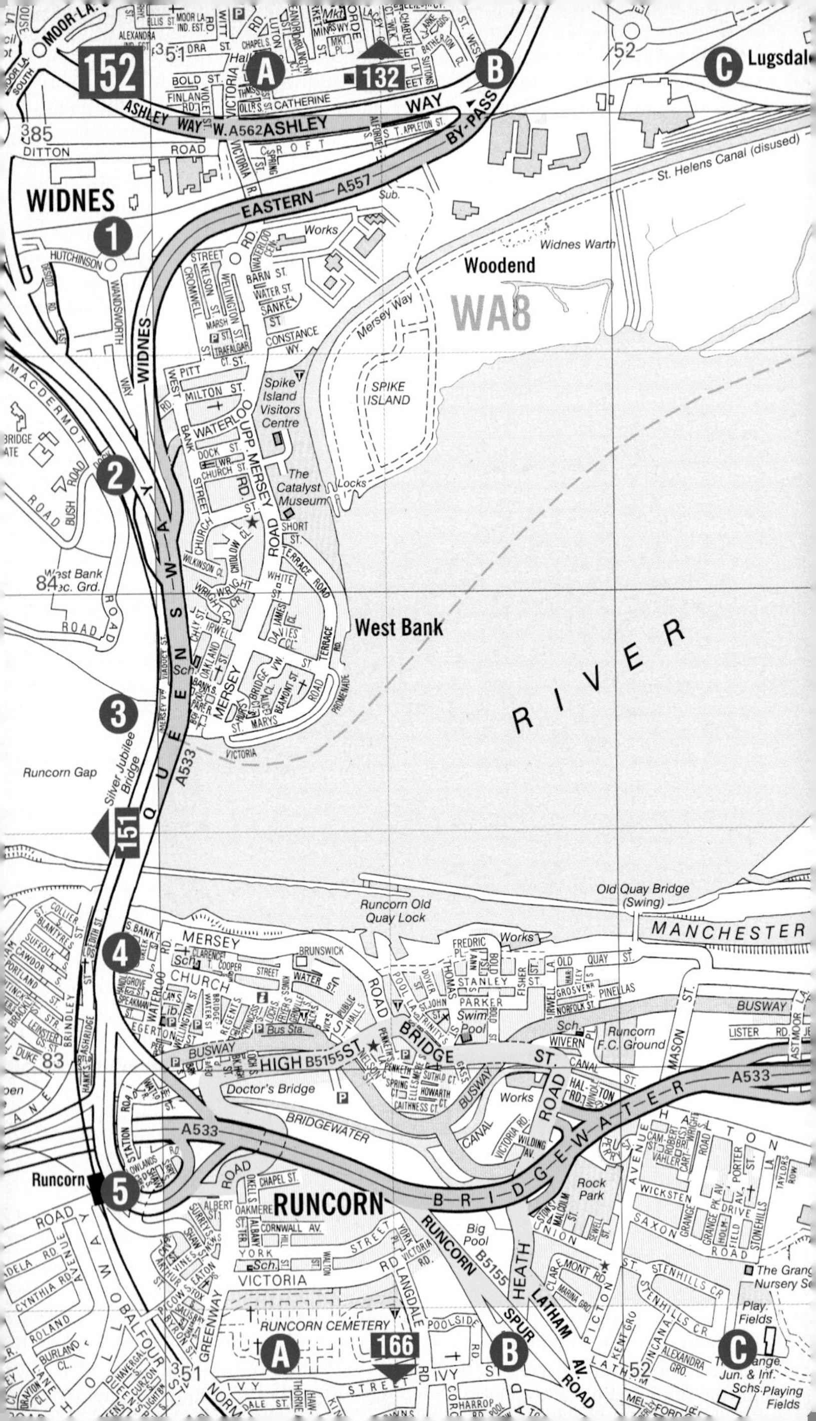

152
132
151
166
A
B
C
A
B
C
1
2
3
4
5
51
52
85
84
83
WIDNES
Lugsdale
ASHLEY WAY
W. A562 ASHLEY
WAY
BY-PASS
EASTERN A557
DITTON ROAD
CROFT
SPRING ST.
VICTORIA RD.
BOLD ST.
CATHERINE
ALFORDE ST.
T. APPLETON ST.
MOOR LA.
ALEXANDRA IND. EST.
MOOR LA. IND. EST.
St. Helens Canal (disused)
Sub.
Works
Widnes Warth
Woodend
WA8
HUTCHINSON
WANDSWORTH WAY
DESOTO RD. EAST
WIDNES
STREET
NELSON ST.
CROMWELL ST.
WELLINGTON ST.
WATERLOO CEN.
BARN ST.
WATER ST.
SANKEY ST.
MARSH ST.
TRAFALGAR CT.
CONSTANCE WY.
Mersey Way
SPIKE ISLAND
Spike Island Visitors Centre
PITT
WEST BANK
MILTON ST.
WATERLOO
UPP. MERSEY
DOCK ST.
CHURCH ST.
RD.
ROAD
The Catalyst Museum
Locks
SHORT ST.
TERRACE ROAD
WHITE ST.
WILKINSON CL.
WRIGHT CR.
IRWELL
DAVIES CL.
JAMES CL.
West Bank
MACDERMOTT ROAD
BUSH ROAD
West Bank Rec. Grd.
ROAD
QUEENSWAY
OAKLAND ST.
MERSEY
BRIDGE
BEAMONT ST.
MARYS
VICTORIA
PROMENADE
A533
Runcorn Gap
Silver Jubilee Bridge
RIVER
Runcorn Old Quay Lock
Old Quay Bridge (Swing)
MANCHESTER
MERSEY
CHURCH
STREET
BRUNSWICK
WATER ST.
Works
FREDRIC PL.
BOLD ST.
OLD QUAY ST.
STANLEY
PARKER
FISHER ST.
GROSVENOR
PINELLAS
NORFOLK ST.
Swim Pool
Sch.
Runcorn F.C. Ground
BUSWAY
LISTER RD.
MASON ST.
ASTMOOR LA.
Bus Sta.
HIGH B5155 ST.
BRIDGE
WIVERN PL.
CANAL
BUSWAY
HALTON RD.
WATERLOO
EGERTON
SPEAKMAN
Doctor's Bridge
NELSON ST.
PENKETH
SPRING CT.
HOWARTH CT.
CAITHNESS CT.
Works
CANAL
BRIDGEWATER
A533
VICTORIA RD.
WILDING AV.
B-R-I-D-G-E-W-A-T-E-R
HALTON
STATION ROAD
ROAD
CHAPEL ST.
Runcorn
RUNCORN
OAKMERE
ALBERT ST.
CORNWALL AV.
YORK
STREET
Sch.
VICTORIA
Big Pool
RUNCORN B5155
HEATH
SPUR
LATHAM AV.
ROAD
Rock Park
WICKSTEN
SAXON
GRANGE
DRIVE
ROAD
STONEHILLS
PORTER
TAYLORS ROW
UNION
MALCOLM ST.
CLAREMONT RD.
MARINA GRO.
PICTON
STENHILLS CR.
DUNCAN AV.
ALEXANDRA GRO.
KENT GRO.
LATHAM
The Grange Nursery Sch.
Play Fields
The Grange Jun. & Inf. Schs.
Playing Fields
RUNCORN CEMETERY
POOLSIDE RD.
LANGDALE
GREENWAY
HOLLOWAY
BALFOUR ST.
IVY STREET
NORMAN
DALE ST.
HARROP
MELFORD
ROAD
AVENUE
CYNTHIA RD.
ROLAND
BURLAND CL.
LANE
ST. COLLIER
BLANTYRE
SUFFOLK
CAWDOR
PORTLAND
LEINSTER
DUKE
BRINDLEY
ASHRIDGE
EDITH ST.

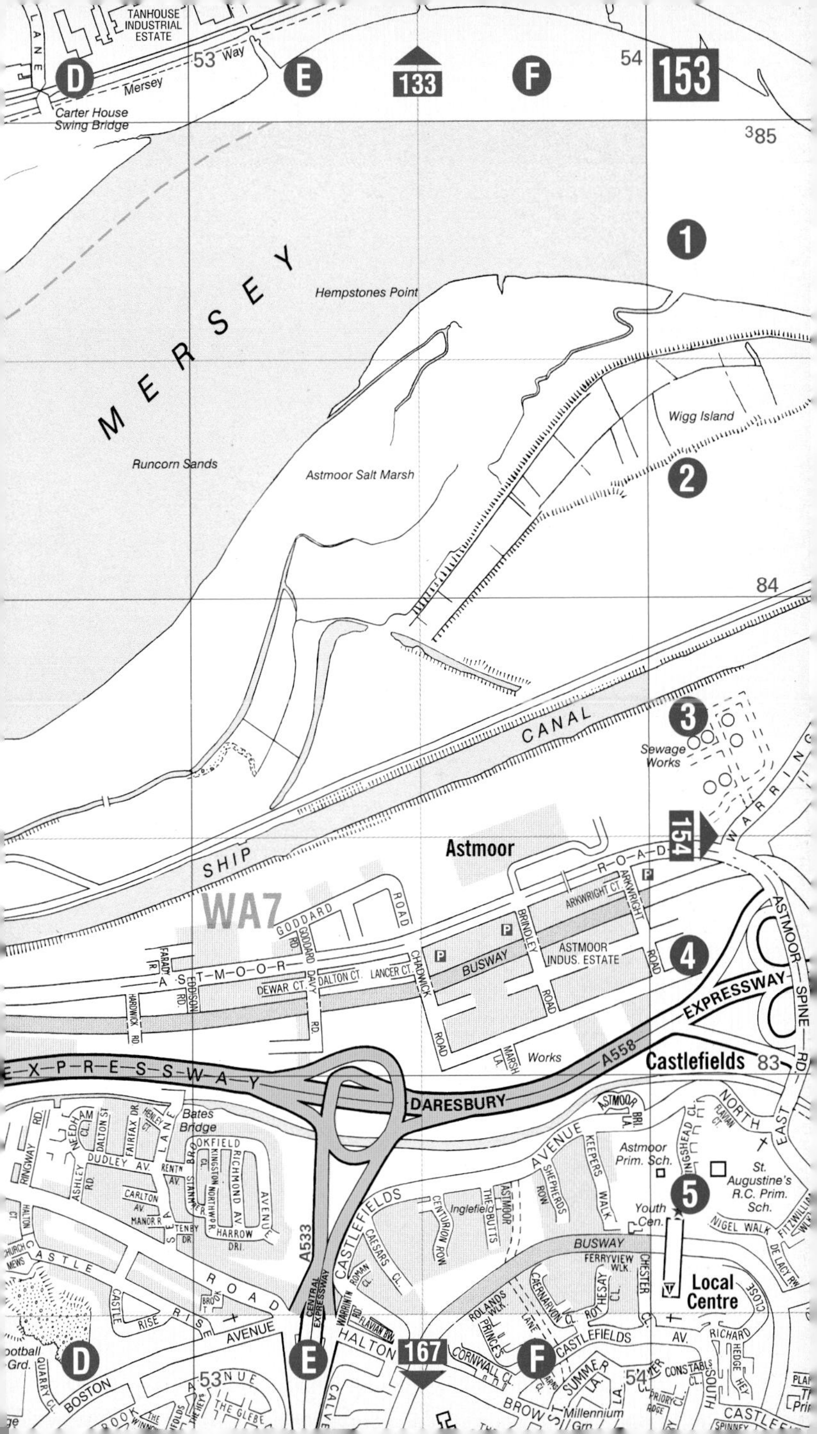
TANHOUSE INDUSTRIAL ESTATE
LANE
D
E
133
F
54
53
Way
Mersey
Carter House Swing Bridge
385
1
MERSEY
Hempstones Point
Wigg Island
Runcorn Sands
Astmoor Salt Marsh
2
84
3
Sewage Works
CANAL
SHIP
154
WARRING
Astmoor
ROAD
WA7
GODDARD
GODDARD RD.
ROAD
ARKWRIGHT CT.
ARKWRIGHT
BRINDLEY
ASTMOOR INDUS. ESTATE
BUSWAY
4
FARADAY R.
ASTMOOR R
EDISON RD.
DEWAR CT.
DAVY
DALTON CT.
LANCER CT.
CHADWICK
ROAD
HARDWICK RD.
RD.
ROAD
MARSH LA.
Works
ASTMOOR
SPINE
RD.
EXPRESSWAY
A558
Castlefields
83
EXPRESSWAY
DARESBURY
Bates Bridge
RINGWAY
NEEDHAM CL.
DALTON ST.
FAIRFAX DR.
HENLEY CT.
LANE
BROOKFIELD
KINGSTON CL.
RICHMOND AV.
NORTHWR.
AVENUE
ASHLEY RD.
DUDLEY AV.
RENTN AV.
STANIER
CARLTON AV.
MANOR R.
TENBY DR.
HARROW DRI.
SEA
ASTMOOR BRI. LA.
NORTH
EAST
FLAVIAN CT.
AVENUE
KEEPERS
WALK
SHEPHERDS ROW
Astmoor Prim. Sch.
St. Augustine's R.C. Prim. Sch.
5
Youth Cen.
CASTLEFIELDS
CENTURION ROW
Inglefield
THE BUTTS
ASTMOOR
NIGEL WALK
FITZWILLIAM WLK
DE LACY RW
HALTON CT.
CHURCH MEWS
CASTLE
ROAD
A533
CAESARS CL.
ROMAN CL.
BUSWAY
FERRYVIEW WLK.
CAERNARVON CL.
ROTHESAY CL.
CHESTER CL.
Local Centre
CLOSE
CASTLE
RISE
RISE
BROOK T
CENTRAL EXPRESSWAY
WARRINTN RD
FLAVIAN RW.
ROLANDS WLK.
PRINCES
LANE
CASTLEFIELDS
AV.
RICHARD
HEDGE HEY
SOUTH
Football Grd.
D
AVENUE
BOSTON
QUARRY CL.
E
HALTON
167
CORNWALL CL.
F
ARMS CL.
SUMMER LA.
LA.
54
CONSTABLES CL.
PRIORY CL.
BROW
53
NUE
THE WINNOW
THE HEYS
THE GLEBE
CALVE
Millennium Grn.
SPINNEY
CASTLEF
Prim.

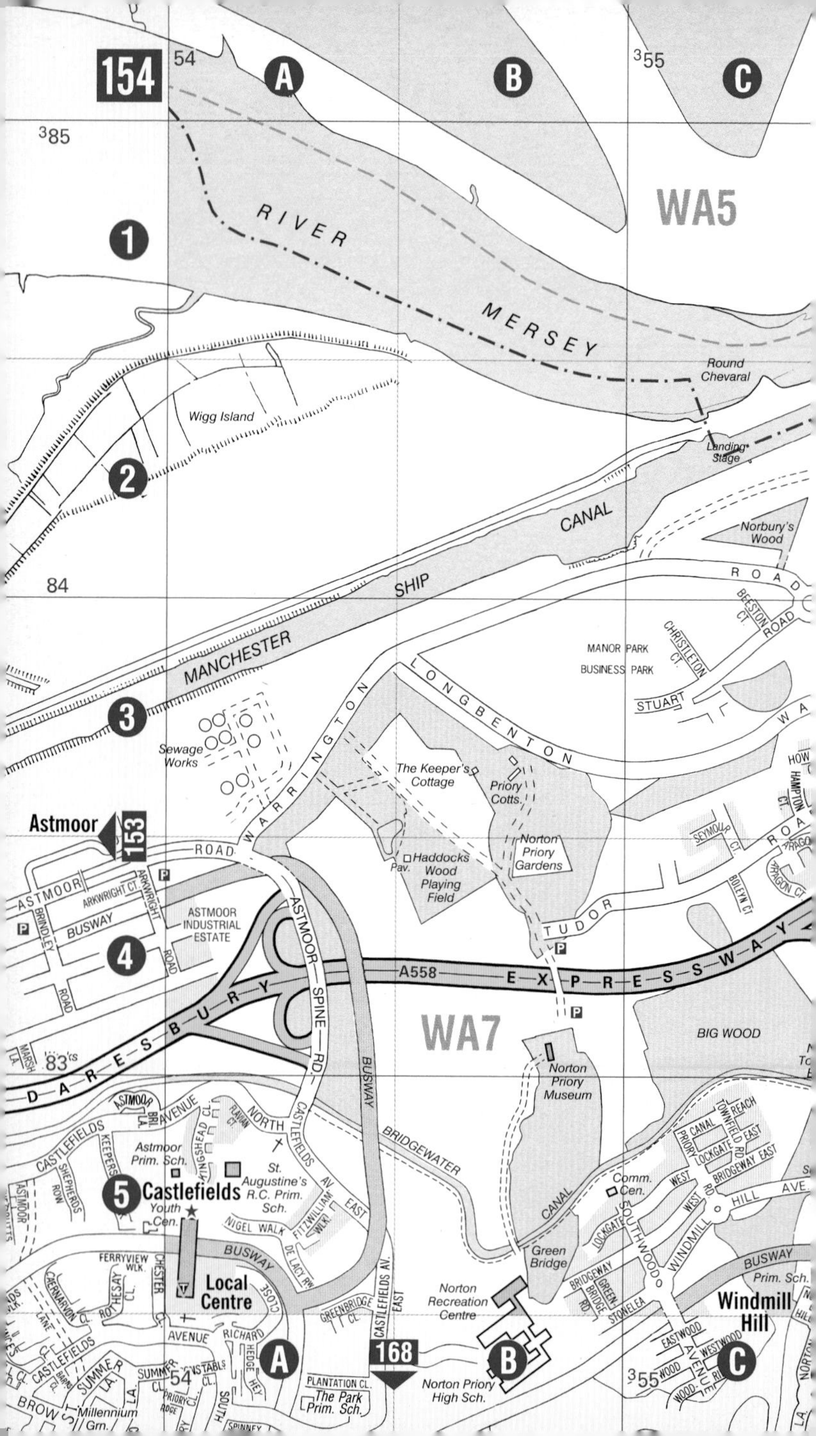

RIVER MERSEY
WA5
Round Chevaral
Wigg Island
Landing Stage
MANCHESTER SHIP CANAL
Norbury's Wood
ROAD
BEESTON CT.
ROAD
CHRISTLETON CT.
MANOR PARK
BUSINESS PARK
STUART
LONGBENTON
WARRINGTON ROAD
Sewage Works
The Keeper's Cottage
Priory Cotts.
Norton Priory Gardens
Haddocks Wood Playing Field
Pav.
Astmoor
153
ASTMOOR
ARKWRIGHT CT.
ARKWRIGHT ROAD
BRINDLEY ROAD
BUSWAY
ASTMOOR INDUSTRIAL ESTATE
SEYMOUR CT.
BOLEYN CT.
TUDOR
A558 EXPRESSWAY
DARESBURY
ASTMOOR SPINE RD.
BUSWAY
WA7
BIG WOOD
Norton Priory Museum
MARSH LA.
ASTMOOR BRI. LA.
AVENUE
NORTH
CASTLEFIELDS
KINGSHEAD CL.
BRIDGEWATER
CANAL
Astmoor Prim. Sch.
St. Augustine's R.C. Prim. Sch.
CASTLEFIELDS AV. EAST
KEEPERS
SHEPHERDS ROW
Castlefields
Youth Cen.
NIGEL WALK
FITZWILLIAM WLK.
DE LACY RW.
BUSWAY
FERRYVIEW WLK.
HESAY CL.
CHESTER CL.
CAERNARVON CL.
Local Centre
CLOSE
RICHARD
AVENUE
HEDGE HEY
CASTLEFIELDS
SUMMER LA.
CONSTABLES CL.
PRIORY CL.
SOUTH
GREENBRIDGE CL.
CASTLEFIELDS AV. EAST
168
PLANTATION CL.
The Park Prim. Sch.
Norton Recreation Centre
Norton Priory High Sch.
Green Bridge
Comm. Cen.
LOCKGATE
SOUTHWOOD
WEST
WINDMILL
HILL AVE.
PRIORY
CANAL
LOCKGATE
TOWNFIELD RD.
REACH
EAST
BRIDGEWAY EAST
BRIDGEWAY
BRIDGE RD.
GREEN-
STONELEA
BUSWAY
Prim. Sch.
Windmill Hill
EASTWOOD
WESTWOOD
AVENUE
WOOD
Millennium Grn.
BROW
ST.
A
B
C
1
2
3
4
5
54
355
385
84
83

Norton Marsh
Upper Moss-side Farm
Moss Side
MOSS SIDE
Bob's LA. Bridge
LAPWING LA.
Canal Cottages
Runcorn and Latchford Canal (Disused)
Jetties
MANCHESTER SHIP CANAL
WARRINGTON
HALTON
HALTON MOSS
WA4
SIX ACRE LANE
Moore
RUNCORN ROAD
Keckwick
Oxmoor Wood
Brook
GREEN WOOD
ROKEBY CT.
EASTGATE WY.
COURT
BERKELEY
Lodge Plantation
Manor Farm
FARM ROAD
ROAD
KINGS CT.
LANE
EVENWOOD CL.
BLACKHEATH LA.
GREEN WOOD DR.
Pitts Heath
EASTERN EXPRESSWAY
A558
Brook Plantation
BAYSWATER CL.
SUNNISIDE LA.
CALMINGTON LA.
LANE
RUNCORN RD.
WOODTHORN CL.
KECKWICK
New Farm
Keckwick
WATER
CHASE WAY
HERONS WAY
SELBY
FURNESS CT.
NEWMOORE LANE
STEVENTON
GODSTOW
HEATH
WALTHAM CT.
WHARFORD
BUCKFAST CT.
GLASTON CL.
BURY
SHERBORNE CL.
DELPH LANE
Village Farm
SANDYMOOR LANE
SEATON PARK
Sandymoor Wood
PARK
DORCHESTER
DORCHESTER PARK
RUDHEATH
PITTS
Brook
Poplar Farm
SANDYMOOR LA.
PILGRIMS WAY
BISHAM PARK
WALSINGHAM
MALMESBURY PARK
SHERIDAN WY.
HAYWOOD CR.
WINDMILL HILL
ADLINGTN RD.
ASHBURY CL.
ADLINGTON RD.
SWINDON CL.
HARVARD CL.
CHATTERIS PARK
ELY PARK
VILLAGE ST.
Norton Bridge
DRIVE
Keckwick
Bog Wood
Keckwick Hill Bridge
LANE
George Gleave's Bridge
Crow's Nest
FARNLEY CL.
NEWBURY CL.
CURL CL.
ALDERSEY CL.
CHORLTON CL.
AVENUE EAST
EALING CL.
LEDSTON CL.
ELMORE
D
E
F
1
2
3
4
5
56
57
85
84
83
169

24
A
136
B
325
C
Piper
PIPERS
Nursery
1
82
BROAD
DEESIDE
TARGET
ROAD
Play
RIVER
2
Sewage
Works
Carav
Parl
THE
Sailin
Club
3
DEE
81
4
5
380
A
B
C
24
325

Poll Hill
The Dales
Heswall Dales
Dales Farm
The Cave
Dellside
CH60
HESWALL
The Beacons
Puddy Dale
Lower Village
Gayton Hole
HESWALL GOLF COURSE
Club House
Gayton Grange
Gayton Prim. Sch.
Crest View
Wall End
Syringa
TELEGRAPH RD.
A540
THURSTASTON ROAD
DELAVOR ROAD
PENSBY ROAD
DAWSTONE RD.
GAYTON ROAD
STATION RD.
RIVERBANK RD.
COTTAGE LANE
MOUNT AV
ROCKY LA. STH
Lib.
Heswall Hall
Council Offs.
Bus. Sta.
Prim. Sch.
Bowl. Grn.
137
158
26
27
82
81
80

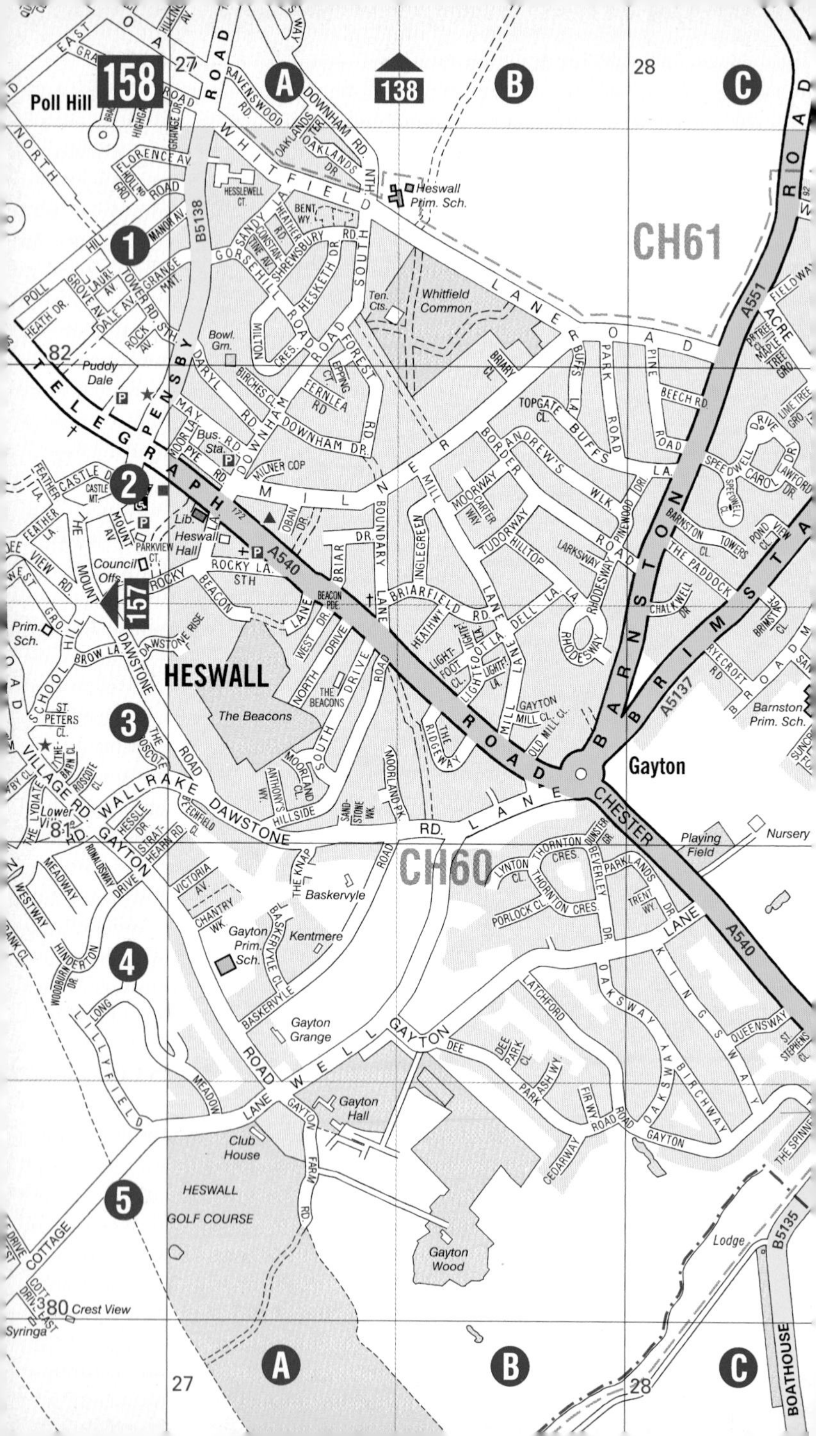
158
138
157
Poll Hill
HESWALL
Gayton
CH61
CH60
Whitfield Common
The Beacons
HESWALL GOLF COURSE
Gayton Wood
Gayton Hall
Gayton Grange
Baskervyle
Kentmere
Club House
Heswall Prim. Sch.
Gayton Prim. Sch.
Barnston Prim. Sch.
Heswall Hall
Council Offs.
Bus. Sta.
Lib.
Puddy Dale
Playing Field
Nursery
Lodge
Crest View
Syringa
TELEGRAPH ROAD
CHESTER ROAD
PENSBY ROAD
BARNSTON ROAD
BRIMSTAGE ROAD
WHITFIELD LANE
MILNER ROAD
DAWSTONE ROAD
GAYTON ROAD
GAYTON LANE
WELL LANE
COTTAGE LANE
BOATHOUSE LA.
A540
A551
A5137
B5138
B5135
27
28
82
81
80
A
B
C
1
2
3
4
5

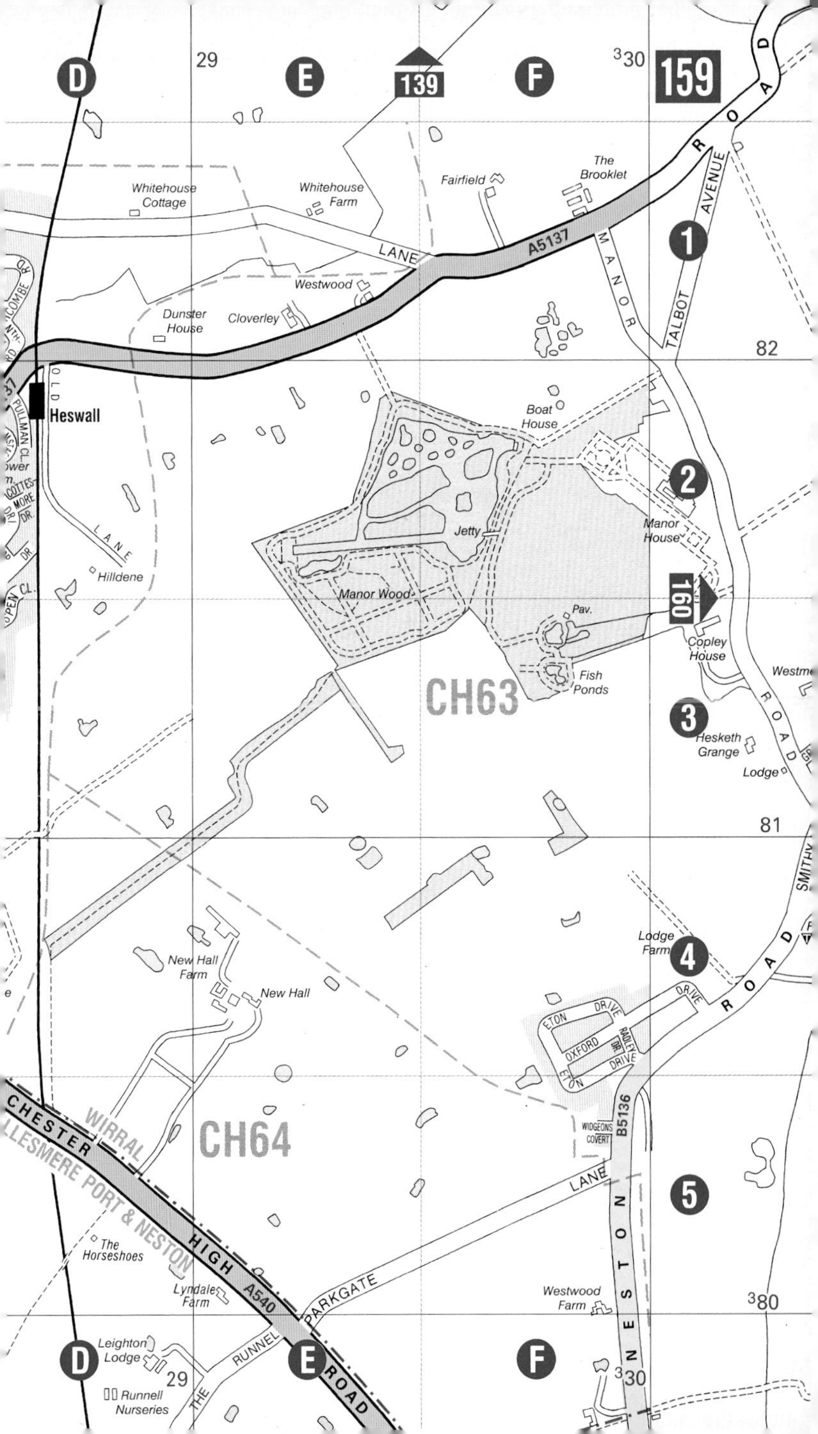

D
E
F
29
330
139
Whitehouse Cottage
Whitehouse Farm
Fairfield
The Brooklet
ROAD
TALBOT AVENUE
MANOR
A5137
LANE
Westwood
Dunster House
Cloverley
82
OLD LANE
Heswall
PULLMAN CL.
Hilldene
Boat House
Jetty
Manor House
Manor Wood
160
Pav.
Copley House
Fish Ponds
CH63
Westm
ROAD
Hesketh Grange
Lodge
81
SMITHY
Lodge Farm
ROAD
DRIVE
ETON DRIVE
OXFORD DRIVE
RADLEY DR.
New Hall Farm
New Hall
WIDGEONS COVERT
B5136
CH64
CHESTER
WIRRAL
ELLESMERE PORT & NESTON
HIGH
A540
LANE
NESTON
The Horseshoes
Lyndale Farm
PARKGATE
Westwood Farm
380
Leighton Lodge
RUNNEL
THE
Runnell Nurseries
ROAD
1
2
3
4
5

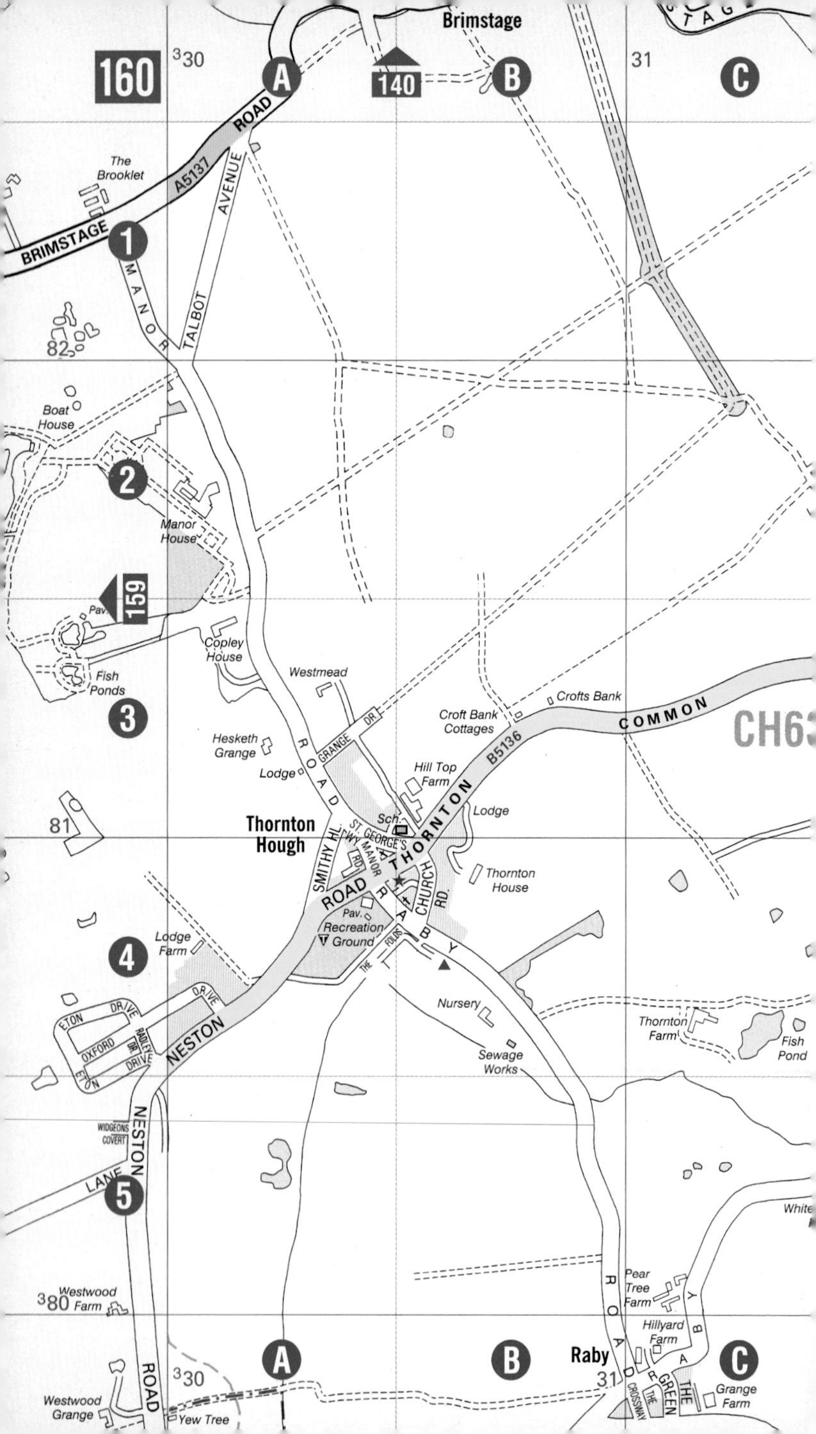
Brimstage
140
159
A
B
C
1
2
3
4
5
330
31
82
81
380
BRIMSTAGE
ROAD
A5137
The Brooklet
TALBOT
AVENUE
MANOR
ROAD
Boat House
Manor House
Pav.
Copley House
Fish Ponds
Westmead
GRANGE DR.
Hesketh Grange
Lodge
Thornton Hough
SMITHY HL.
ST. GEORGE'S WY
MANOR RD
Sch.
THORNTON
ROAD
RABY
CHURCH RD.
Pav.
Recreation Ground
THE FOLDS
Croft Bank Cottages
Crofts Bank
B5136
COMMON
CH63
Hill Top Farm
Lodge
Thornton House
Lodge Farm
ETON
DRIVE
OXFORD
RADLEY DR.
NESTON
Nursery
Sewage Works
Thornton Farm
Fish Pond
WIDGEONS COVERT
LANE
White
Westwood Farm
Pear Tree Farm
Hillyard Farm
Raby
CROSSWAY
THE GREEN
Grange Farm
Westwood Grange
Yew Tree

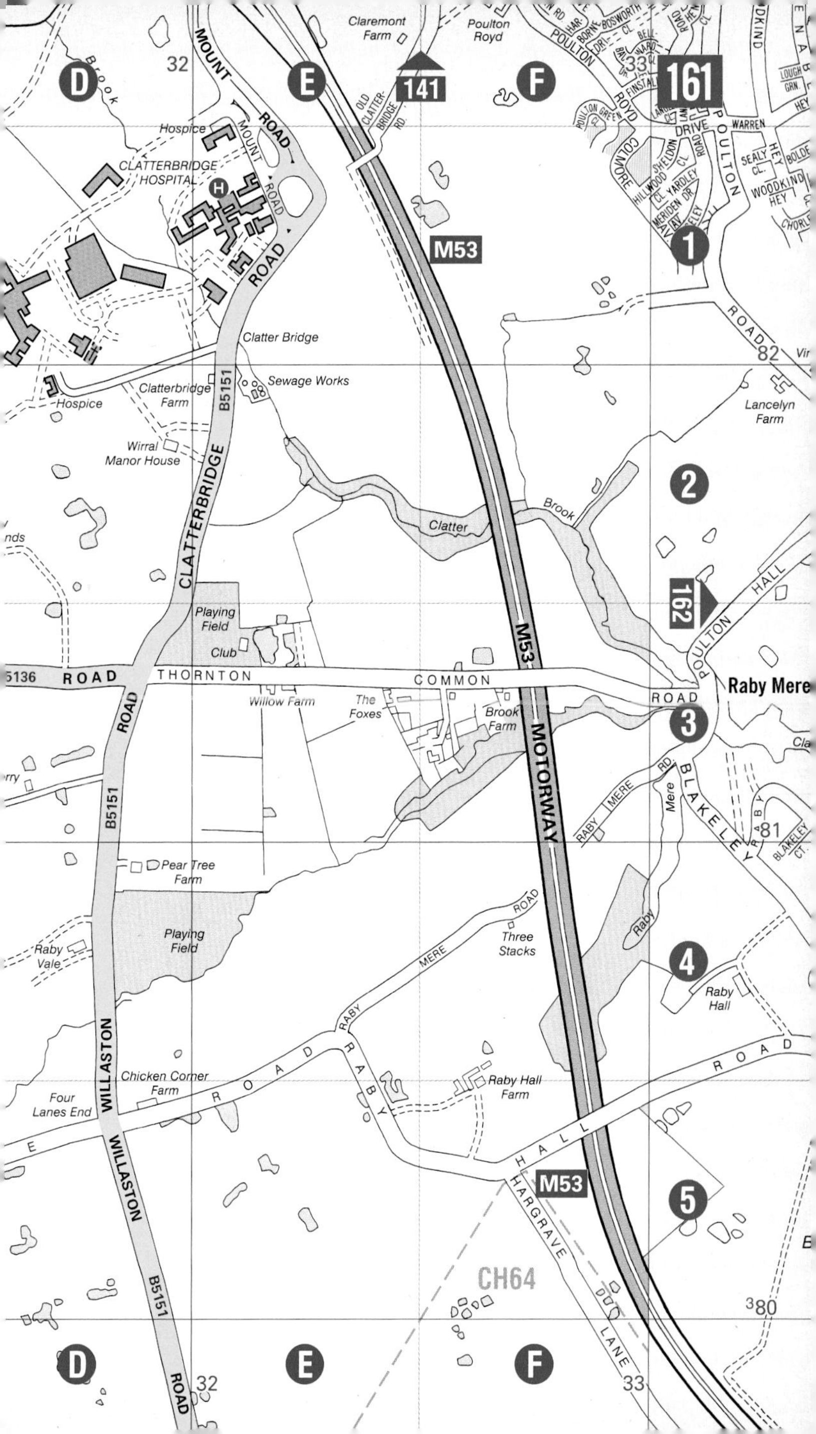
Claremont Farm
Poulton Royd
141
D
E
F
32
33
Brook
MOUNT ROAD
Hospice
CLATTERBRIDGE HOSPITAL
OLD CLATTERBRIDGE RD.
POULTON ROYD
COLMORE
DRIVE
WARREN
POULTON
SEALY CL.
WOODKIND HEY
M53
1
ROAD
82
Clatter Bridge
Sewage Works
Clatterbridge Farm
B5151
Hospice
Lancelyn Farm
Wirral Manor House
CLATTERBRIDGE
2
Clatter
Brook
162
POULTON HALL
Playing Field
Club
ROAD
THORNTON
COMMON
ROAD
Raby Mere
Willow Farm
The Foxes
Brook Farm
3
MOTORWAY
RABY MERE RD.
BLAKELEY
Mere
81
BLAKELEY CT.
Pear Tree Farm
Playing Field
Raby Vale
ROAD
Three Stacks
MERE
RABY
Raby
4
Raby Hall
WILLASTON
Chicken Corner Farm
ROAD
RABY
Raby Hall Farm
Four Lanes End
HALL
ROAD
M53
HARGRAVE
5
CH64
LANE
380
ROAD
32
33

Poulton Lancelyn Prim. Sch.
142
Brotherton Park
Petrifying Well
Tunnel
Poulton
Poulton Lancelyn
Local Nature Reserve
The Vineyard Farm
Lancelyn Farm
Bromborough Rake
BROMBOROUGH
Dibbinsdale
Poulton Hall
Poulton Bridge
161
CH63
Raby Mere
THORNTON COMMON RD.
Brook Farm
Clatter Brook
Little Hey
Three Stacks
Raby Hall
Raby Hall Farm
Club House
Plymyard Dale
Brookhurst Prim. Sch.
Brookhurst
BROMBOROUGH GOLF COURSE
M53
Dibbinsdale Brook
170
POULTON ROAD
RABY MERE RD.
BLAKELEY ROAD
DIBBINSDALE ROAD
PORT ROAD
RABY HALL ROAD
HARGRAVE ROAD
BROOKHURST AVENUE
CUNNINGHAM DRIVE

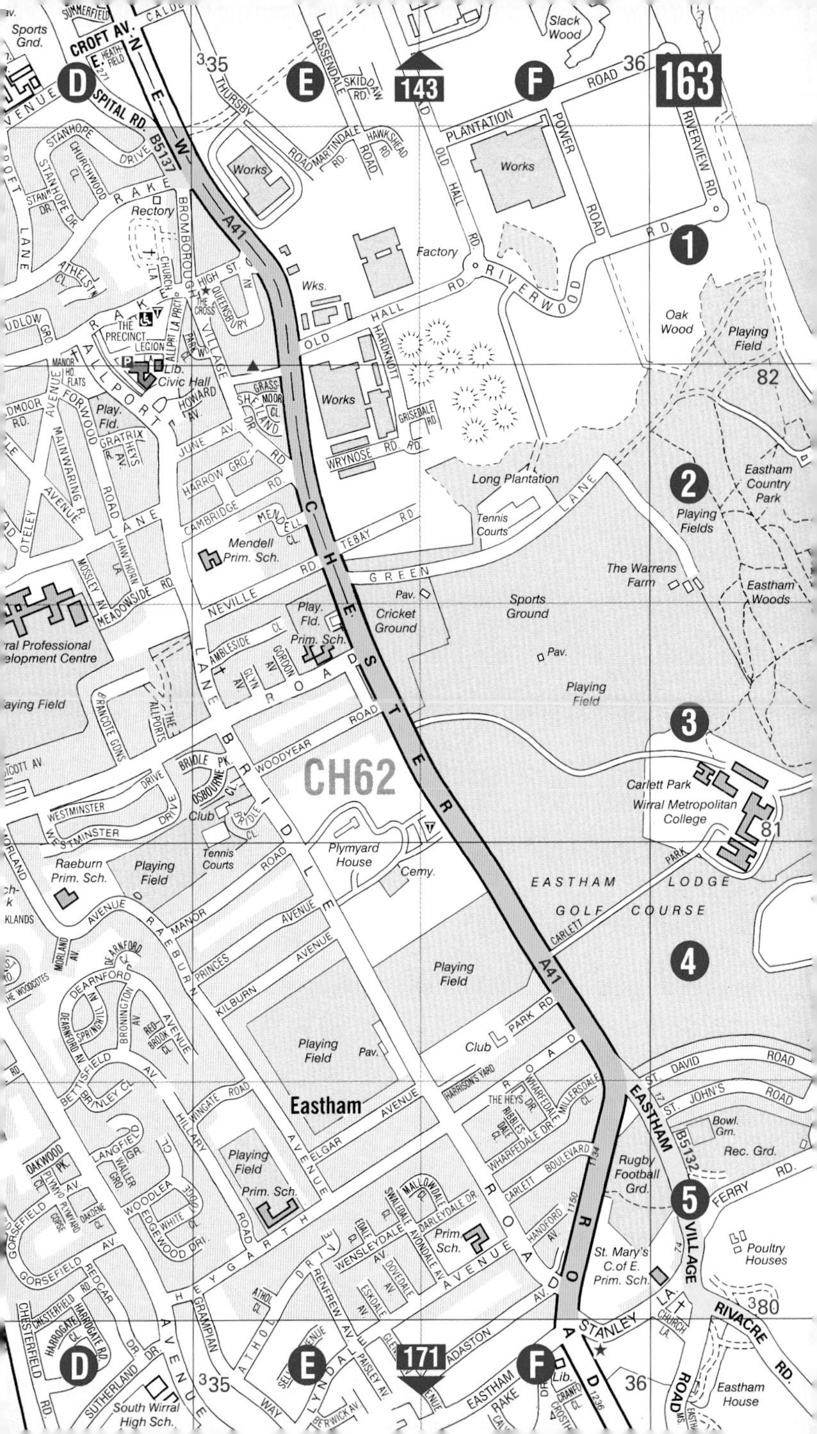
143
171
CH62
Eastham
A41
CHESTER ROAD
B5137
B5132
EASTHAM VILLAGE ROAD
Works
Factory
Wks.
Long Plantation
Oak Wood
Slack Wood
Playing Field
Playing Fields
Eastham Country Park
Eastham Woods
The Warrens Farm
Sports Ground
Cricket Ground
Tennis Courts
Mendell Prim. Sch.
Civic Hall
Rectory
The Precinct
Carlett Park
Wirral Metropolitan College
EASTHAM LODGE GOLF COURSE
Plymyard House
Cemy.
Raeburn Prim. Sch.
Rugby Football Grd.
St. Mary's C.of E. Prim. Sch.
Poultry Houses
Eastham House
South Wirral High Sch.
Bowl. Grn.
Rec. Grd.
Wirral Professional Development Centre
RIVERWOOD RD.
PLANTATION ROAD
POWER ROAD
RIVERVIEW RD.
OLD HALL RD.
BRIDLE ROAD
ALLPORT LANE
HEYGARTH ROAD
ST. DAVID ROAD
ST. JOHN'S ROAD
FERRY RD.
RIVACRE RD.
STANLEY LA.
EASTHAM RAKE
CARLETT BOULEVARD
SPITAL RD.
CROFT AV.

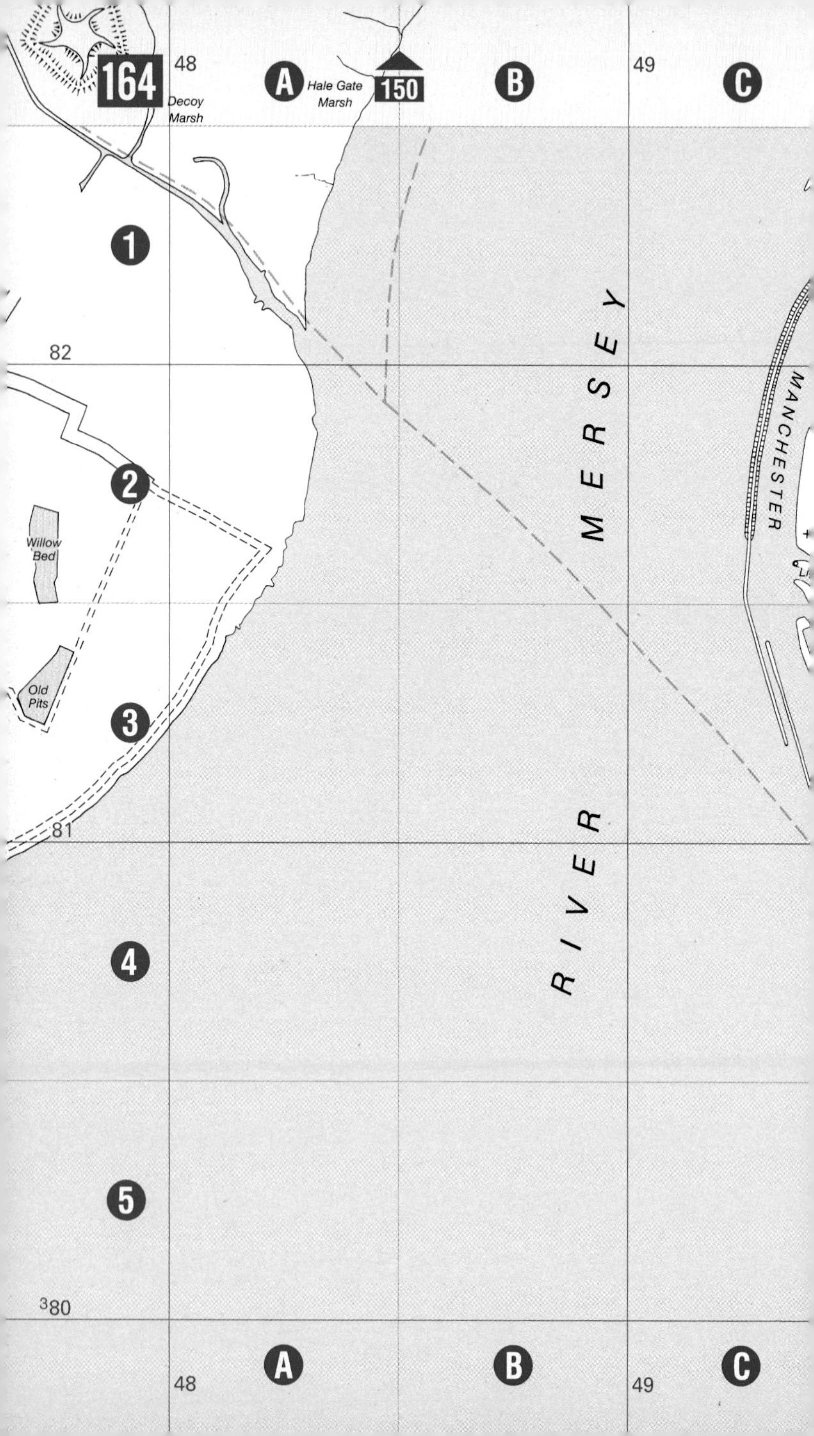
164
48
A
Hale Gate Marsh
150
B
49
C
Decoy Marsh
1
RIVER MERSEY
82
MANCHESTER
2
Willow Bed
Old Pits
3
81
4
5
380
A
48
B
49
C

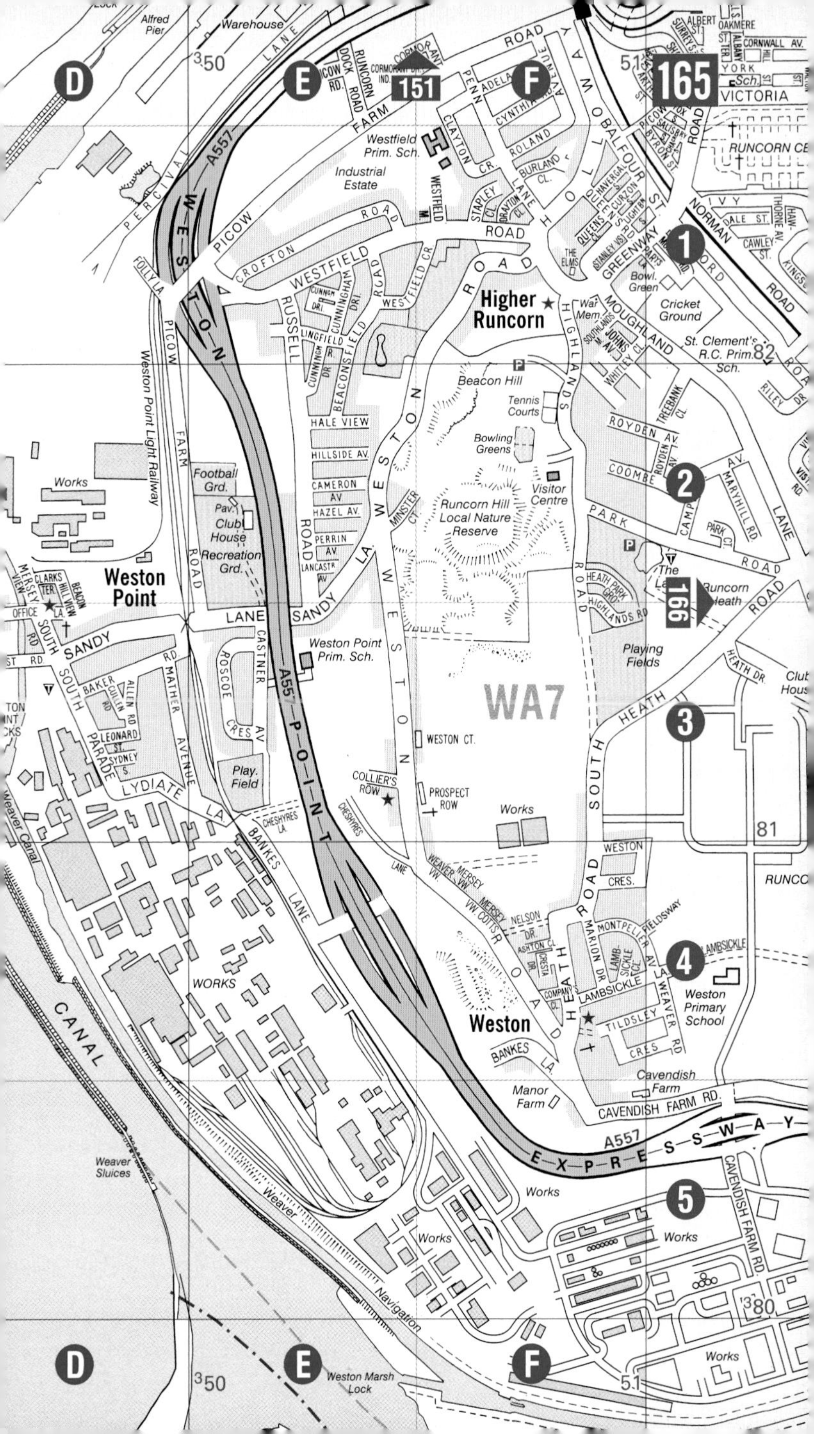
D
E
F
151
165
166
1
2
3
4
5
Alfred Pier
Warehouse
350
51
82
81
80
PERCIVAL LANE
A557
WESTON POINT EXPRESSWAY
A557 EXPRESSWAY
DOCK RD.
RUNCORN ROAD
PICOW FARM ROAD
CORMORANT IND.
Westfield Prim. Sch.
Industrial Estate
PENN
ADELA
CYNTHIA
CLAYTON CR.
ROLAND
BURLAND CL.
LANE
STAPLEY CL.
DRAYTON CL.
WESTFIELD M
HOLLOWAY
BALFOUR ST.
QUEENS CL.
CURZON
GREENWAY
THE ELMS
ALBERT ST.
OAKMERE
CORNWALL AV.
YORK
Sch.
VICTORIA
ROAD
PICOW
SALISBURY
BYRON
RUNCORN CEMETERY
IVY
NORMAN
DALE ST.
THORNE AV.
HAWKINGS
CAWLEY ST.
Bowl. Green
Cricket Ground
St. Clement's R.C. Prim. Sch.
RILEY DR.
FOLLY LA.
CROFTON
WESTFIELD ROAD
CUNNINGHAM DRI.
WESTFIELD CR.
RUSSELL
LINGFIELD
BEACONSFIELD
Higher Runcorn
War Mem.
HIGHLANDS ROAD
SOUTHLANDS M.
JOHNS AV.
WHITLEY CL.
MOUGHLAND
Beacon Hill
Tennis Courts
Bowling Greens
Visitor Centre
Runcorn Hill Local Nature Reserve
TREEBANK CL.
ROYDEN AV.
COOMBE
CAMPDEN
MARYHILL RD.
PARK CT.
PARK ROAD
LANE
HALE VIEW
HILLSIDE AV.
CAMERON AV.
HAZEL AV.
PERRIN AV.
LANCASTER AV.
MINSTER CT.
WESTON ROAD
Weston Point Light Railway
Works
FARM ROAD
Football Grd.
Pav.
Club House
Recreation Grd.
Weston Point
MERSEY VIEW
CLARKS TER.
HILL VIEW
BEACON LA.
OFFICE
SOUTH RD.
SANDY LANE
SANDY LA.
CASTNER AV
ROSCOE CRES
Weston Point Prim. Sch.
HEATH PARK GRO.
HIGHLANDS RD
The Runcorn Heath
Playing Fields
HEATH DR.
Club House
WA7
SOUTH HEATH
BAKER
GULLEN RD
ALLEN RD
MATHER AVENUE
LEONARD ST.
SYDNEY S.
SOUTH PARADE
LYDIATE LA.
Play. Field
WESTON CT.
COLLIER'S ROW
PROSPECT ROW
CHESHYRES LA.
BANKES LANE
Works
Weaver Canal
WESTON CRES.
HEATH ROAD
RUNCORN
FIELDSWAY
MONTPELIER AV.
MARION DR.
LAMBSICKLE CL.
LAMBSICKLE LA.
WEAVER RD
Weston Primary School
MERSEY VW.
WEAVER VW.
MERSEY VW. COTTS.
NELSON DR.
ASHTON CL.
CRESTA
COMPANY'S CL.
TILDSLEY CRES
Weston
BANKES LA.
WORKS
CANAL
Manor Farm
Cavendish Farm
CAVENDISH FARM RD.
CAVENDISH FARM RD
Works
Weaver Sluices
Weaver Navigation
Weston Marsh Lock

152
A
B
C
RUNCORN CEMETERY
Big Pool
LATHAM AV.
B5155
The Grange Nursery
Play. Fields
The Grange Jun. & Inf. Schs.
Playing Fields
Higher Runcorn
Cricket Ground
Bowl. Green
War Mem.
St. Clement's R.C. Prim. Sch.
Town Hall
PARK
1
2
3
4
5
82
Tennis Courts
Visitor Centre
The Lake
Runcorn Heath
165
Playing Fields
Club House
Pewithall Primary School
WA7
The Heath Comprehensive School
Public Open Space
Comm. Centre
Halton Junction
RUNCORN GOLF COURSE
Works
81
Weston
Weston Primary School
Cavendish Farm
Manor Farm
Cavendish School
A557 POINT
WESTON
EXPRESSWAY
BUSWAY
Clifton Hall
Equestrian Centre
Works
380
51
52
172
NORMAN ROAD
RUNCORN ROAD
HEATH ROAD
CLIFTON LANE
SOUTH HEATH ROAD
HIGHLANDS ROAD
MOUGHLAND LANE
PARK ROAD
BOSTON AV.
LINKWAY
MALPAS ROAD
ASCOT AVENUE
CAVENDISH FARM RD.
COW HEY

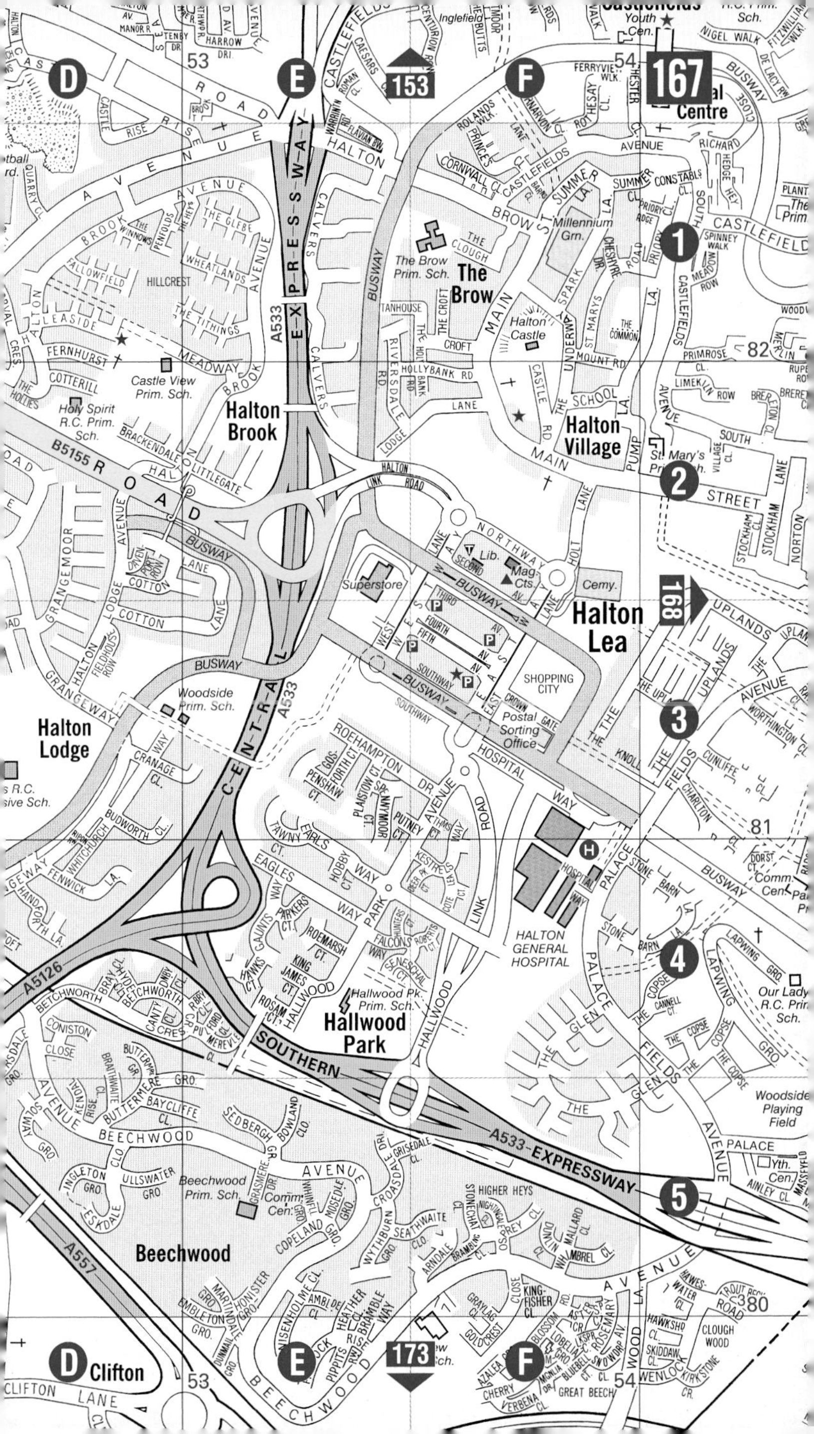

153
168
173
D
E
F
1
2
3
4
5
53
54
82
81
380
Castlefields
Youth Cen.
Halton Brook
Hillcrest
Castle View Prim. Sch.
Holy Spirit R.C. Prim. Sch.
The Brow Prim. Sch.
The Brow
Halton Castle
Millennium Grn.
Halton Village
St. Mary's Prim. Sch.
Halton Lea
Superstore
Lib.
Mag. Cts.
Cemy.
Shopping City
Postal Sorting Office
Halton Lodge
Woodside Prim. Sch.
Halton General Hospital
Hallwood Pk. Prim. Sch.
Hallwood Park
Our Lady R.C. Prim. Sch.
Woodside Playing Field
Yth. Cen.
Comm. Cen.
Beechwood Prim. Sch.
Beechwood
Clifton
Clough Wood
A533
EXPRESSWAY
CENTRAL
SOUTHERN
A533 EXPRESSWAY
B5155 ROAD
A5126
A557
BUSWAY
HALTON ROAD
HALTON BROOK AVENUE
HALTON LINK ROAD
MAIN ST.
HOSPITAL WAY
PALACE FIELDS AVENUE
BEECHWOOD AVENUE
CLIFTON LANE
WOOD LANE

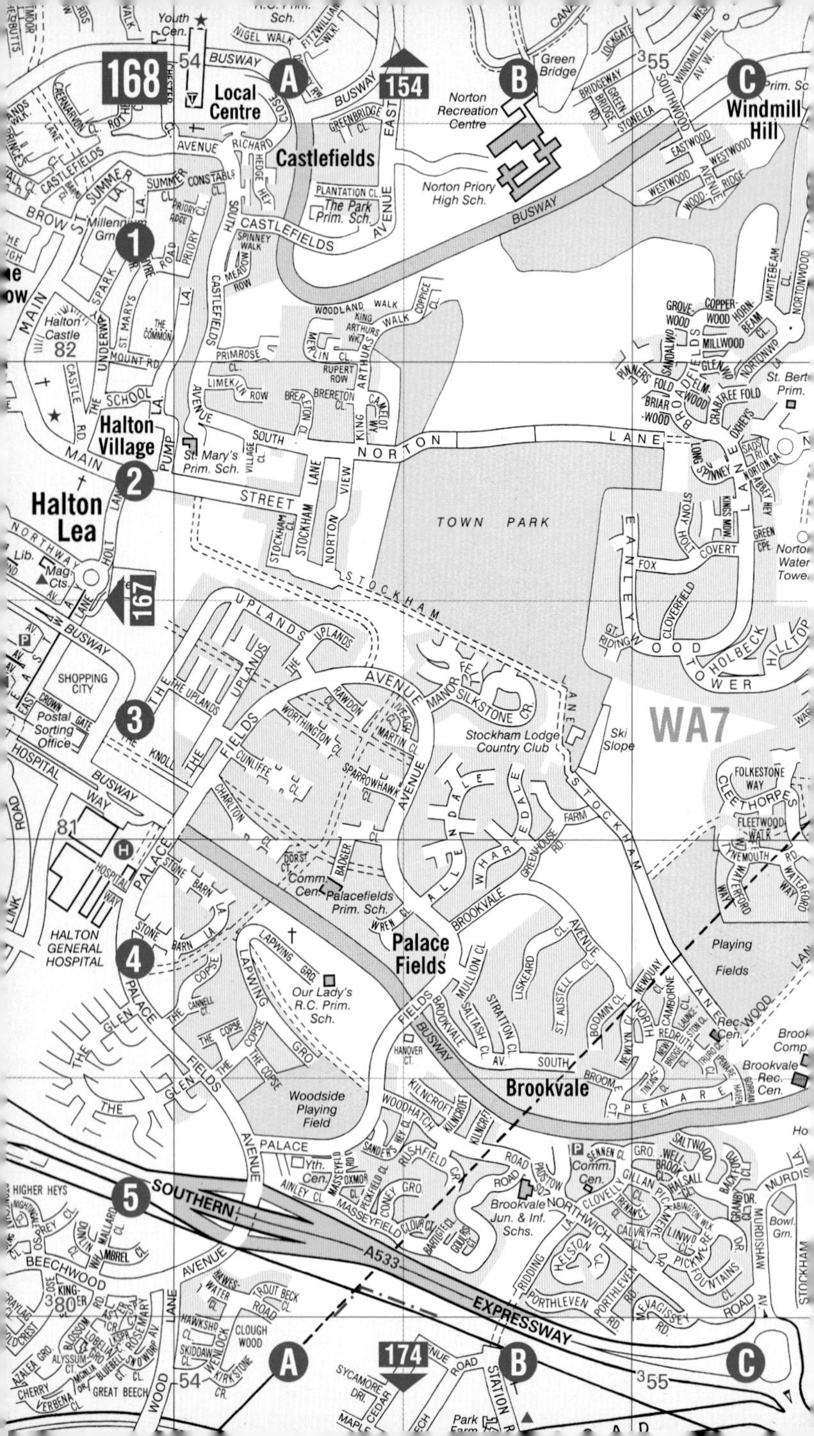

168
154
167
174
A
B
C
1
2
3
4
5
54
55
80
81
82
Youth Cen.
Local Centre
Castlefields
Norton Recreation Centre
Norton Priory High Sch.
Green Bridge
Windmill Hill
The Park Prim. Sch.
Halton Castle
Millennium Grn
Halton Village
Halton Lea
St. Mary's Prim. Sch.
TOWN PARK
Lib.
Mag. Cts.
SHOPPING CITY
Postal Sorting Office
HALTON GENERAL HOSPITAL
Stockham Lodge Country Club
Ski Slope
WA7
Comm. Cen.
Palacefields Prim. Sch.
Palace Fields
Our Lady's R.C. Prim. Sch.
Woodside Playing Field
Playing Fields
Rec. Cen.
Brookvale Rec. Cen.
Brookvale
Brookvale Jun. & Inf. Schs.
Yth. Cen.
Bowl. Grn.
Norton Water Tower
BUSWAY
NORTON LANE
MAIN STREET
STOCKHAM LANE
NORTON VIEW
CASTLEFIELDS AVENUE
PALACE FIELDS AVENUE
SOUTHERN EXPRESSWAY
A533
HOSPITAL WAY
HOLT LANE
NORTHWAY
UPLANDS
THE UPLANDS
THE FIELDS
BROOKVALE AVENUE
NORTHWICH ROAD
MURDISHAW AVENUE
BEECHWOOD AVENUE
WOOD LANE
EANLEY WOOD
TOWER
HOLBECK
FOX COVERT
STONY HOLT
BROADFIELDS
WESTWOOD
EASTWOOD
SOUTHWOOD
PENARE
PORTHLEVEN RD.
MEVAGISSEY RD.
STATION RD.
SYCAMORE DRI.
CEDAR

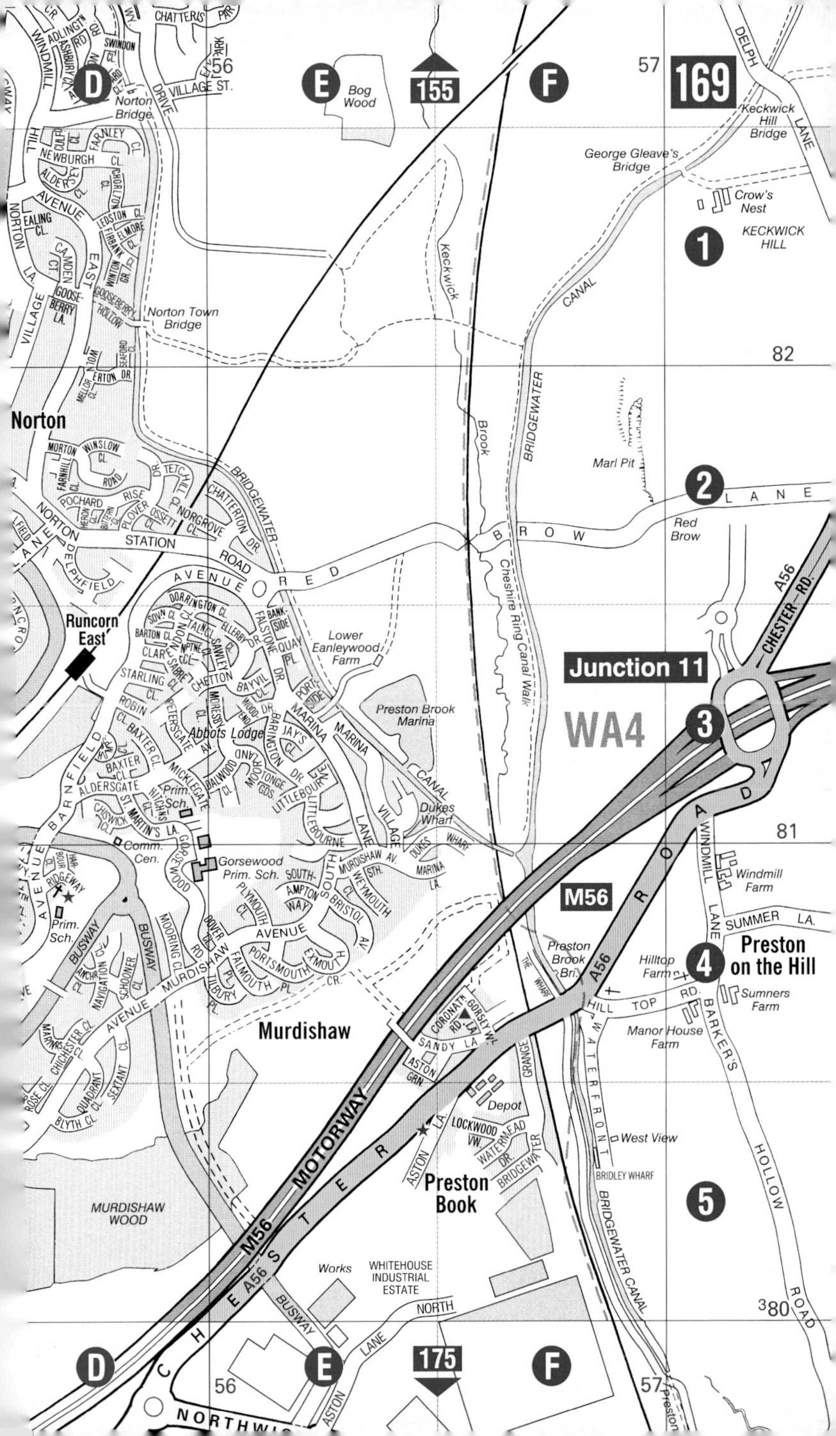

169
155
175
D
E
F
56
57
82
81
380
1
2
3
4
5
Bog Wood
Keckwick Hill Bridge
George Gleave's Bridge
Crow's Nest
KECKWICK HILL
DELPH LANE
Norton Bridge
VILLAGE ST.
DRIVE
CHATTERIS PARK
SWINDON CL.
WINDMILL HILL
ADLINGTON RD.
ASHBURY CL.
NEWBURGH CL.
FARNLEY CL.
ALDERSEY CL.
CHORLTON CL.
AVENUE
NORTON LA.
EALING CL.
CAMDEN CT.
EAST
LEDSTON CL.
ELMORE CL.
FIRBANK CL.
WINTON GR.
GOOSEBERRY LA.
GOOSEBERRY HOLLOW
VILLAGE
Norton Town Bridge
SEAFORD CL.
MELLOR CL.
ERTON DR.
Norton
Keckwick
Brook
CANAL
BRIDGEWATER
Marl Pit
MORTON
WINSLOW CL.
FARNHILL CL.
ROAD
RISE
POCHARD
HERON CL.
BITTERN CL.
PLOVER CL.
OSSETT CL.
TETCHILL CL.
NORGROVE CL.
CHATTERTON DR.
BRIDGEWATER
NORTON
STATION
ROAD
LANE
DELPHFIELD
RED BROW LANE
Red Brow
Cheshire Ring Canal Walk
AVENUE
DORRINGTON CL.
ELLERBY CL.
FALSTONE DR.
BANKSIDE
QUAY PL.
Lower Eanleywood Farm
A56
CHESTER RD.
Junction 11
WA4
Runcorn East
BARTON CL.
CLARENDON CL.
SAWLEY CL.
STARLING CL.
CHETTON
BAYVIL CL.
PORTSIDE
MARINA
ROBIN CL.
MORESBY CL.
PETERSGATE
Abbots Lodge
BARINGTON DR.
JAY'S CL.
Preston Brook Marina
BARNFIELD
BAXTER CL.
BALWOOD CL.
MOORLAND
TONGE GDS.
LITTLEBOURNE
CANAL
ALDERSGATE
MICKLEGATE
Prim. Sch.
ST. MARTIN'S LA.
HITCHINS CL.
CHISWICK CL.
Comm. Cen.
LANE
VILLAGE
Dukes Wharf
DUKES WHARF
MARINA LA.
WINDMILL LANE
Windmill Farm
SUMMER LA.
Gorsewood Prim. Sch.
GORSEWOOD
MURDISHAW AV.
WEYMOUTH CL.
SOUTHAMPTON WAY
SOUTH BRISTOL CL.
PLYMOUTH CL.
RIDGEWAY
HARBOUR CL.
Prim. Sch.
AVENUE
BUSWAY
MOORING CL.
DOVER CL.
AVENUE
EXMOUTH AV.
PORTSMOUTH CR.
FALMOUTH PL.
TILBURY PL.
MURDISHAW
M56
ROAD
Preston Brook Bri.
Preston on the Hill
Hilltop Farm
Sumners Farm
HILL TOP RD.
BARKER'S
Manor House Farm
ANCHOR CL.
NAVIGATION CL.
SCHOONER CL.
Murdishaw
CORONATION RD.
GORSEY LA.
SANDY LA.
ASTON GRN.
WATERFRONT
THE WHARF
GRANGE
MARINERS CL.
CHICHESTER CL.
ROSE CL.
QUADRANT CL.
SEXTANT CL.
BLYTH CL.
MOTORWAY
Depot
CHESTER
ASTON LA.
LOCKWOOD VW.
WATERMEAD DR.
BRIDGEWATER
West View
BRIDLEY WHARF
HOLLOW
ROAD
BRIDGEWATER CANAL
Preston Book
MURDISHAW WOOD
Works
WHITEHOUSE INDUSTRIAL ESTATE
NORTH
LANE
BUSWAY
ASTON
NORTHWI
Preston

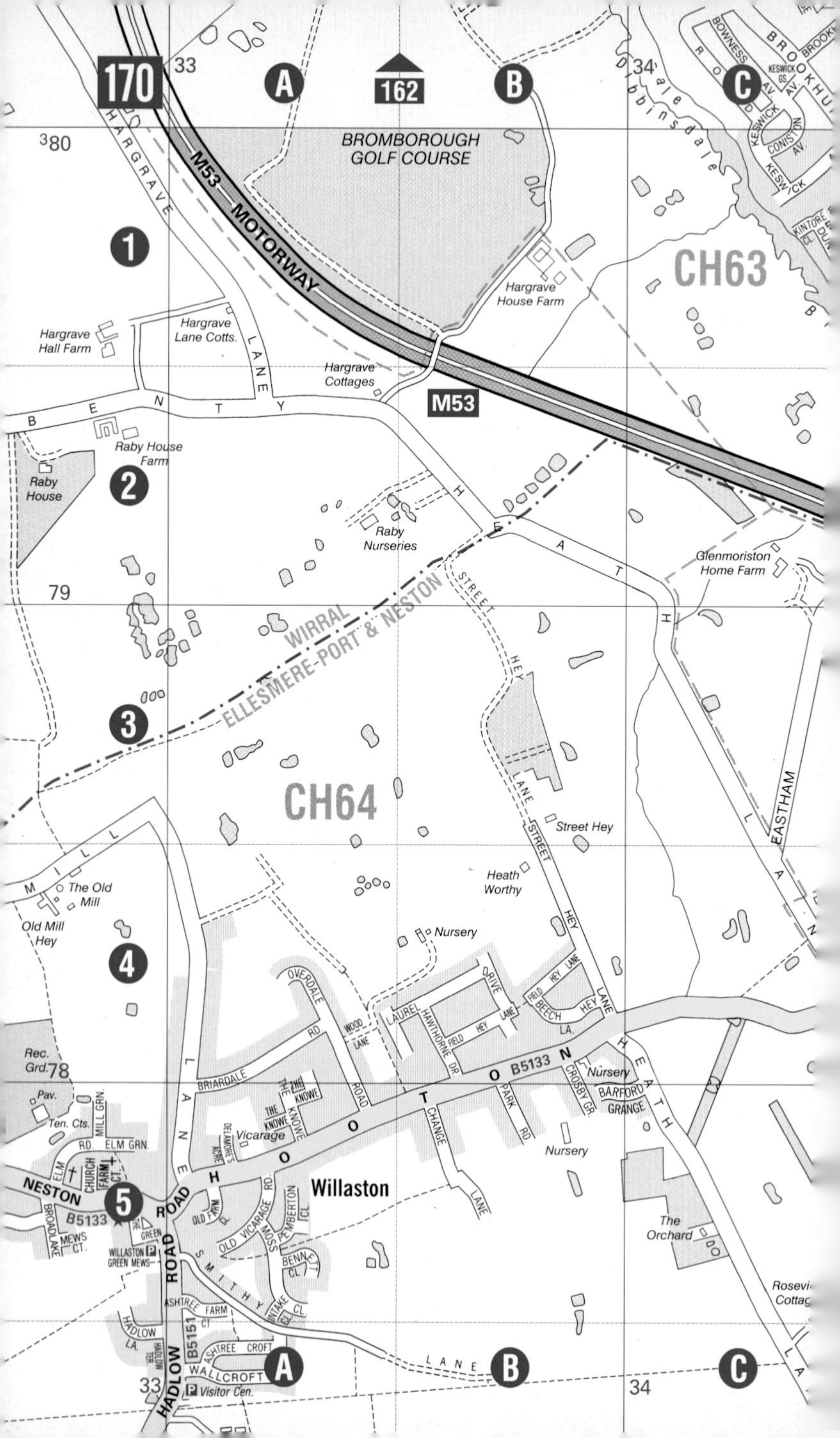
170
162
33
34
A
B
C
380
79
78
1
2
3
4
5
BROMBOROUGH GOLF COURSE
M53 MOTORWAY
M53
HARGRAVE LANE
BENTY HEATH
Hargrave Hall Farm
Hargrave Lane Cotts.
Hargrave Cottages
Hargrave House Farm
Raby House Farm
Raby House
Raby Nurseries
Dibbinsdale
CH63
CH64
WIRRAL
ELLESMERE PORT & NESTON
STREET HEY
STREET HEY LANE
Street Hey
Heath Worthy
Glenmoriston Home Farm
EASTHAM
HEATH LANE
MILL LANE
The Old Mill
Old Mill Hey
Nursery
Rec. Grd.
Pav.
Ten. Cts.
MILL GRN.
ELM GRN.
ELM RD.
CHURCH FARM CT.
NESTON ROAD
B5133
BROADLAKE
MEWS CT.
THE GREEN
WILLASTON GREEN MEWS
HOOTON ROAD
B5133
Willaston
OVERDALE RD.
BRIARDALE
THE KNOWE
Vicarage
DELAMORE'S ACRE
WOOD LANE
LAUREL
HAWTHORNE DR.
FIELD HEY LANE
DRIVE
BEECH LA.
HEY LANE
FIELD HEY LANE
CHANGE LANE
PARK RD.
CROSBY GR.
BARFORD GRANGE
Nursery
The Orchard
OLD FARM CL.
OLD VICARAGE RD.
MOSS
PEMBERTON CL.
BENNETT CL.
INTAKE CL.
SMITHY LANE
ASHTREE FARM CT.
ASHTREE CROFT
WALLCROFT
HADLOW LA.
HADLOW TER.
HADLOW ROAD
B5151
Visitor Cen.
BROWNESS AV.
BROOKHU
KESWICK GS.
KESWICK AV.
CONISTON AV.
KINTORE CL.

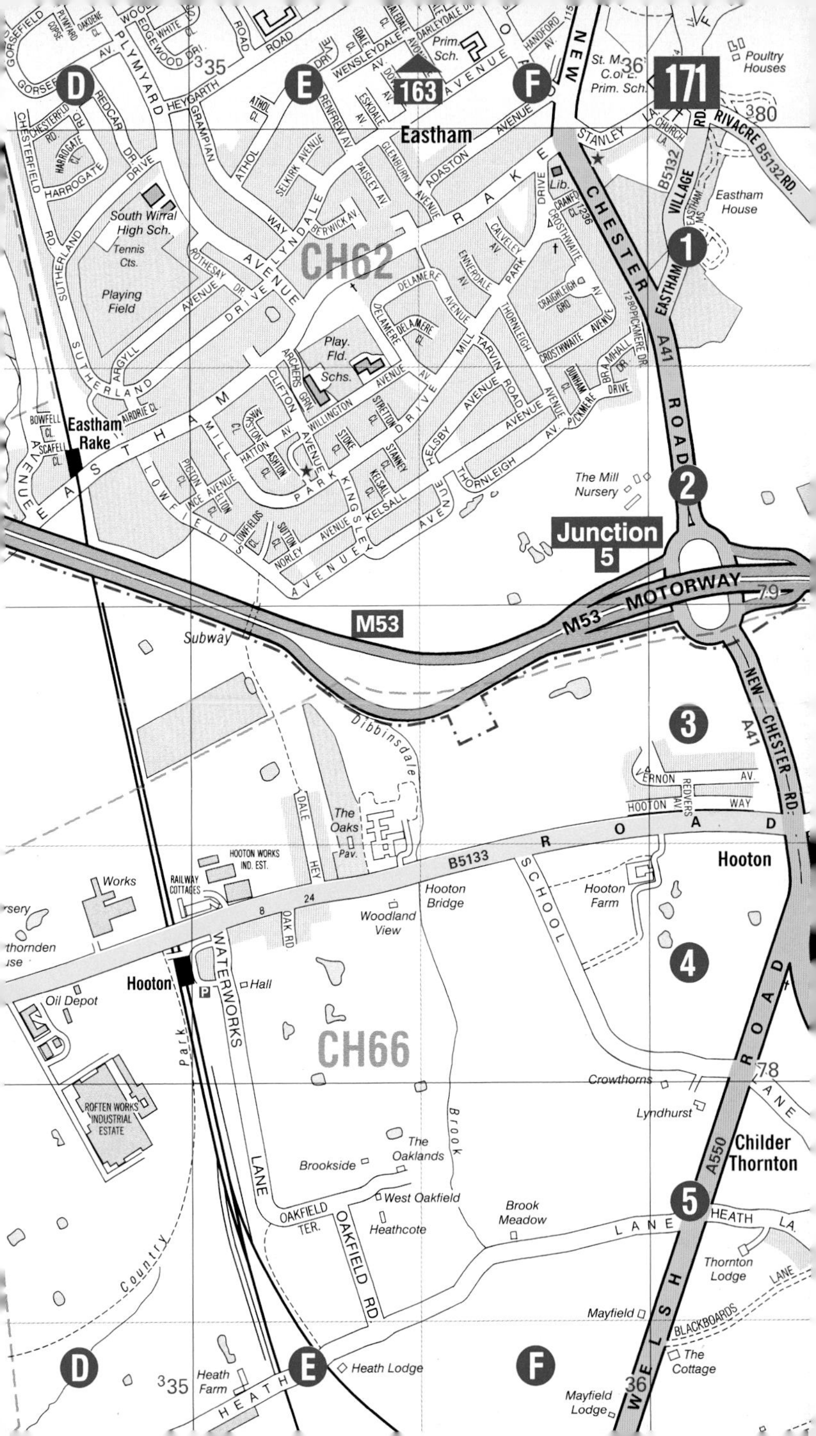
171
163
D
E
F
1
2
3
4
5
Eastham
CH62
CH66
Eastham Rake
Junction 5
M53
M53 MOTORWAY
Hooton
Childer Thornton
South Wirral High Sch.
Tennis Cts.
Playing Field
Play. Fld.
Schs.
Prim. Sch.
St. M. C. of E. Prim. Sch.
Lib.
Poultry Houses
Eastham House
The Mill Nursery
Subway
Dibbinsdale
The Oaks
Pav.
HOOTON WORKS IND. EST.
Works
RAILWAY COTTAGES
Oil Depot
ROFTEN WORKS INDUSTRIAL ESTATE
Hall
Hooton Bridge
Woodland View
Hooton Farm
Crowthorns
Lyndhurst
The Oaklands
Brookside
West Oakfield
Heathcote
Brook Meadow
Thornton Lodge
Mayfield
The Cottage
Mayfield Lodge
Heath Lodge
Heath Farm
Country Park
Brook
CHESTER ROAD
NEW CHESTER RD.
EASTHAM VILLAGE RD.
RIVACRE B5132 RD.
B5132
A41
A550
B5133
WELSH ROAD
HOOTON ROAD
SCHOOL LANE
WATERWORKS LANE
OAKFIELD RD.
OAKFIELD TER.
HEATH LANE
HEATH LA.
BLACKBOARDS LANE
OAK RD
DALE HEY
VERNON AV.
HOOTON WAY
REDVERS AV.
RAKE LANE
EASTHAM RAKE
MILL PARK DRIVE
MILL PARK AVENUE
KINGSLEY AVENUE
KELSALL AVENUE
THORNLEIGH AVENUE
THORNLEIGH AV.
TARVIN ROAD
HELSBY AVENUE
WILLINGTON AVENUE
STRETTON CL.
STANNEY CL.
KELSALL CL.
STOKE CL.
ASHTON CL.
HATTON AV.
MARSTON CL.
CLIFTON AVENUE
ARCHERS GRN.
LOWFIELDS AVENUE
LOWFIELDS CL.
PIGEON CL.
INCE AVENUE
ELTON CL.
SUTTON CL.
NORLEY AVENUE
SUTHERLAND RD.
SUTHERLAND AVENUE
ARGYLL AVENUE
AIRDRIE CL.
ROTHESAY DR.
LYNDALE AVENUE
ATHOL WAY
ATHOL CL.
GRAMPIAN WAY
SELKIRK AVENUE
BERWICK AV.
PAISLEY AV.
GLENBURN AVENUE
ADASTON AVENUE
RENFREW AV.
HEYGARTH RD.
PLYMYARD AV.
REDCAR DR.
HARROGATE DRIVE
HARROGATE CL.
CHESTERFIELD RD.
CHESTERFIELD CL.
BOWFELL CL.
SCAFELL CL.
DELAMERE AVENUE
DELAMERE CL.
ENNERDALE AV.
CALVELEY AV.
CROSTHWAITE AVENUE
CROSTHWAITE AV.
CRAIGLEIGH GRO.
PICKMERE DR.
PICKMERE DRIVE
BRAMHALL DR.
DUNHAM CL.
CRANFORD CL.
STANLEY LA.
CHURCH LA.
EASTHAM MS.
HANDFORD AV.
WENSLEYDALE AV.
DARLEYDALE DR.
ESKDALE AV.
EDALE CL.
GORSEFIELD AV.
PLYMYARD COPSE
OAKDENE CL.
EDGEWOOD DR.
WHITE LO. CL.
335
336
380
379
378
24
8

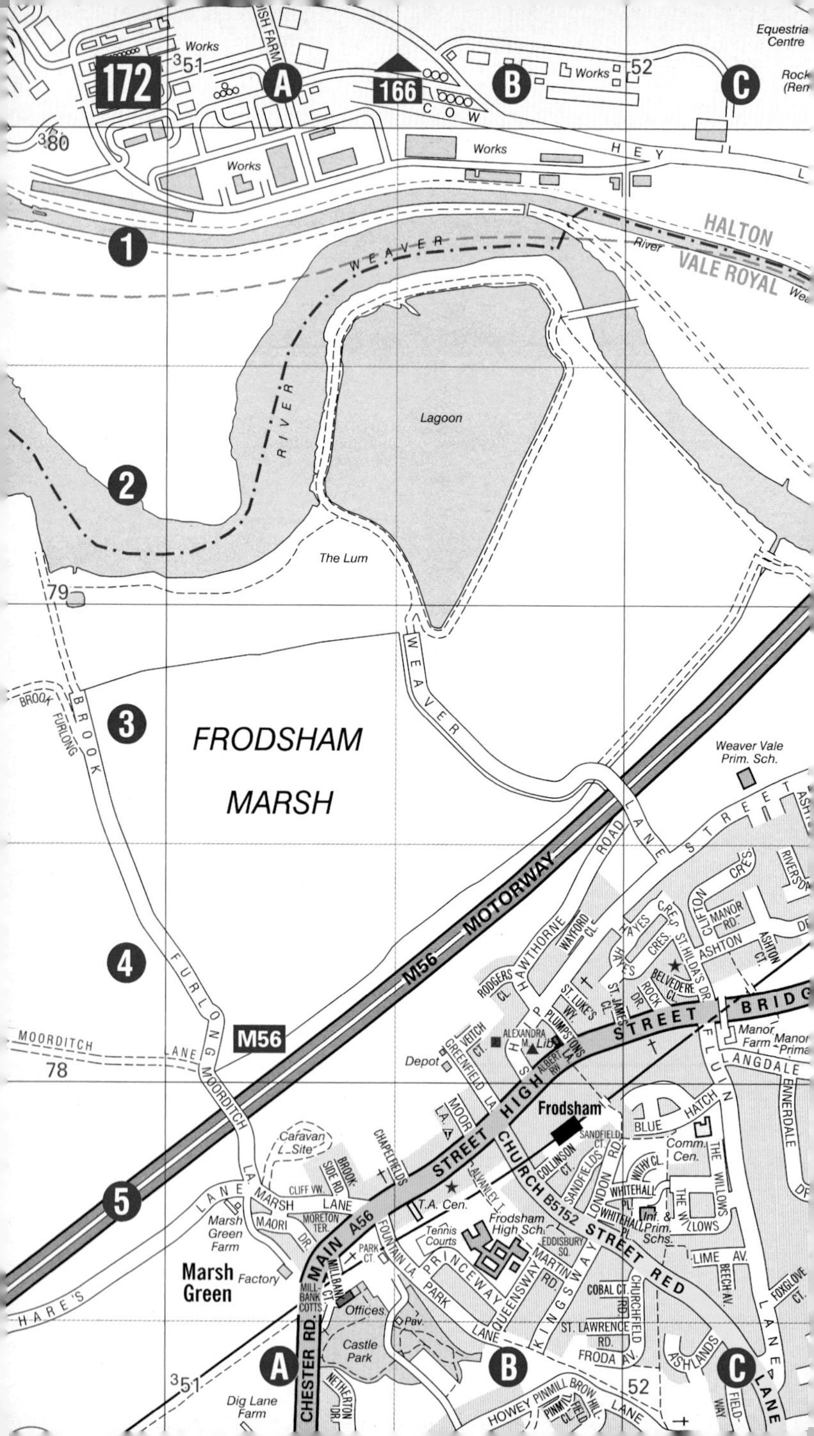
172
166
Works
Works
Works
Works
COW HEY LANE
Equestrian Centre
HALTON
VALE ROYAL
RIVER WEAVER
Lagoon
The Lum
FRODSHAM MARSH
BROOK FURLONG
WEAVER
M56 MOTORWAY
M56
MOORDITCH LANE
Weaver Vale Prim. Sch.
Frodsham
HIGH STREET
CHURCH STREET
B5152
MAIN STREET
A56
CHESTER RD.
MARSH LANE
Marsh Green Farm
Marsh Green
Factory
HARE'S LANE
Caravan Site
Castle Park
Offices
Frodsham High Sch.
Tennis Courts
T.A. Cen.
Depot
Comm. Cen.
Inf. & Prim. Schs.
Manor Farm
BLUE HATCH
LANGDALE
ENNERDALE
PRINCEWAY
QUEENSWAY
KINGSWAY
PARK LANE
FOUNTAIN LA.
ST. LAWRENCE RD.
FRODA AV.
CHURCHFIELD RD.
COBAL CT.
LIME AV.
BEECH AV.
FOXGLOVE CT.
THE WILLOWS
WHITEHALL PL.
HAWTHORNE
ROCK DR.
ASHTON
ST. HILDA'S DR.
Dig Lane Farm
HOWEY LANE
PINMILL BROW
52
51
78
79
80

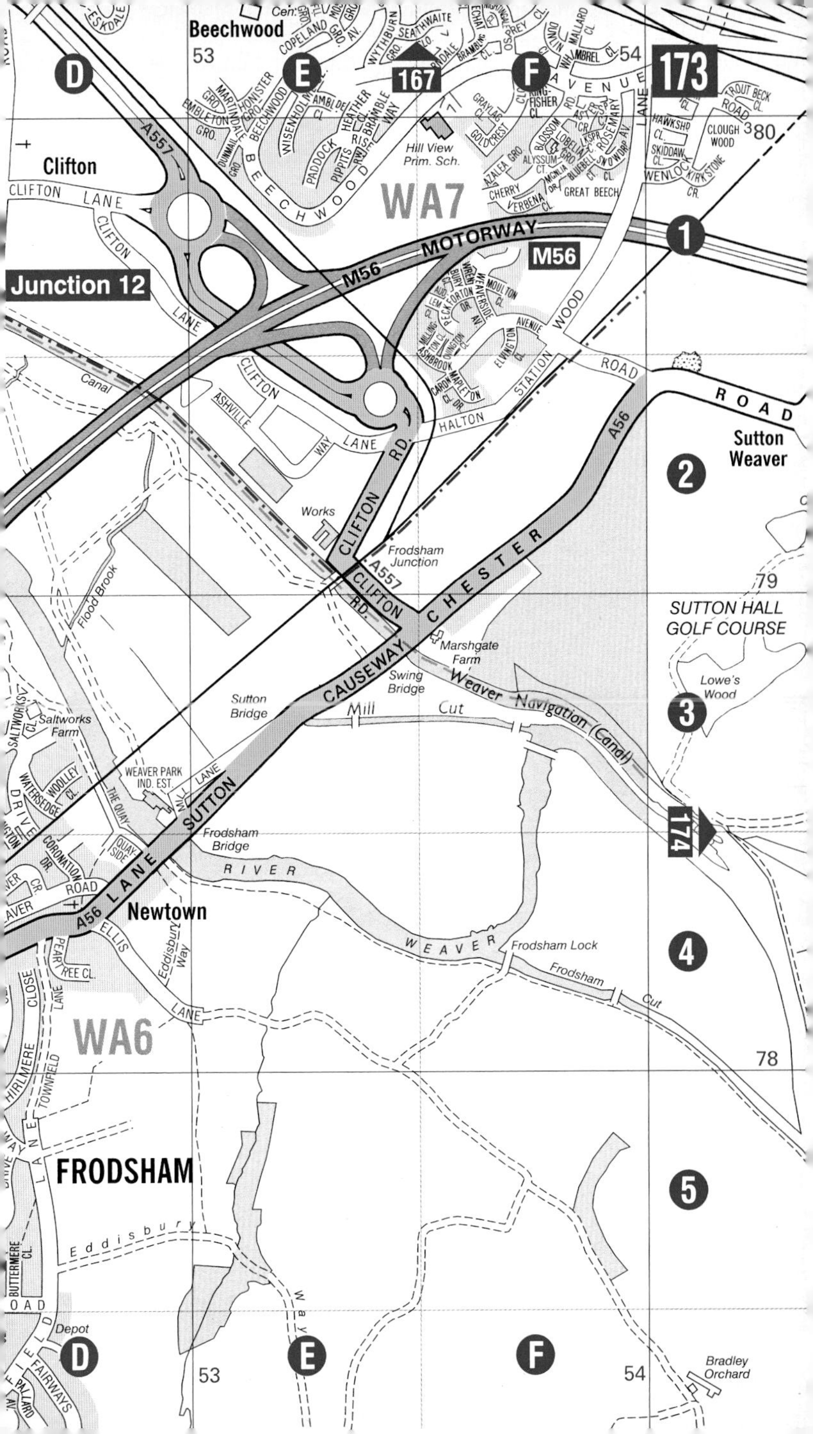
173
167
174
Beechwood
Clifton
Junction 12
Sutton Weaver
Newtown
FRODSHAM
WA7
WA6
MOTORWAY
M56
A557
A56
CLIFTON LANE
BEECHWOOD AVENUE
HALTON STATION ROAD
CLIFTON RD.
CHESTER ROAD
CAUSEWAY
SUTTON LANE
WOOD LANE
ELLIS LANE
Hill View Prim. Sch.
GREAT BEECH
SUTTON HALL GOLF COURSE
Lowe's Wood
Frodsham Junction
Works
Marshgate Farm
Swing Bridge
Sutton Bridge
Weaver Navigation (Canal)
Mill Cut
WEAVER PARK IND. EST.
Saltworks Farm
Frodsham Bridge
RIVER WEAVER
Frodsham Lock
Frodsham Cut
Flood Brook
Canal
Eddisbury Way
Depot
Bradley Orchard
Clough Wood
53
54
78
79
80
D
E
F
1
2
3
4
5

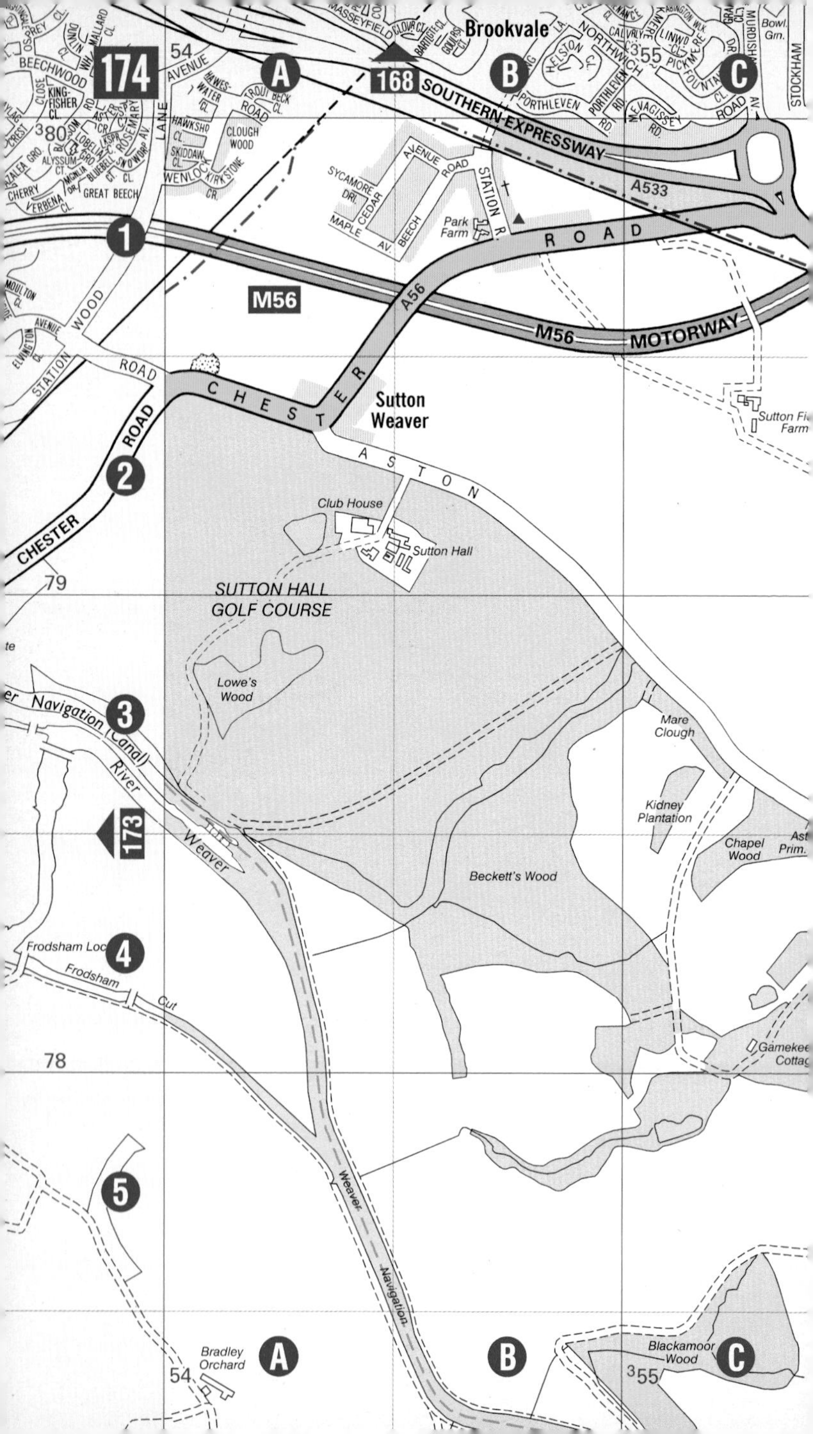

174
168
173
Brookvale
SOUTHERN EXPRESSWAY
A533
M56
M56 MOTORWAY
A56
CHESTER ROAD
ROAD
ASTON
Sutton Weaver
Club House
Sutton Hall
SUTTON HALL GOLF COURSE
Lowe's Wood
Mare Clough
Kidney Plantation
Chapel Wood
Beckett's Wood
Weaver Navigation (Canal)
River Weaver
Weaver Navigation
Frodsham Cut
Frodsham Loc
Bradley Orchard
Blackamoor Wood
Park Farm
Sutton Fi Farm
Gamekee Cottag
STATION R.
SYCAMORE DRI.
CEDAR AVENUE
MAPLE AV.
BEECH
WOOD AVENUE
STATION ROAD
LANE
PORTHLEVEN RD.
MEVAGISSEY RD.
NORTHWICH RD.
HELSTON CL.
PICKMERE
FOUNTAIN
STOCKHAM
MURDISHAW AV.
Bowl. Grn.
BEECHWOOD
OSPREY CL.
KINGFISHER CL.
HAWKSHD CL.
SKIDDAW CL.
WENLOCK
KIRKSTONE CR.
CLOUGH WOOD
TROUTBECK CL.
ROSEMARY
GREAT BEECH
CHERRY
VERBENA CL.
ALYSSUM
MOULTON CL.
ELVINGTON CL.
MASSEYFIELD
A B C
1 2 3 4 5
54 55
80 79 78

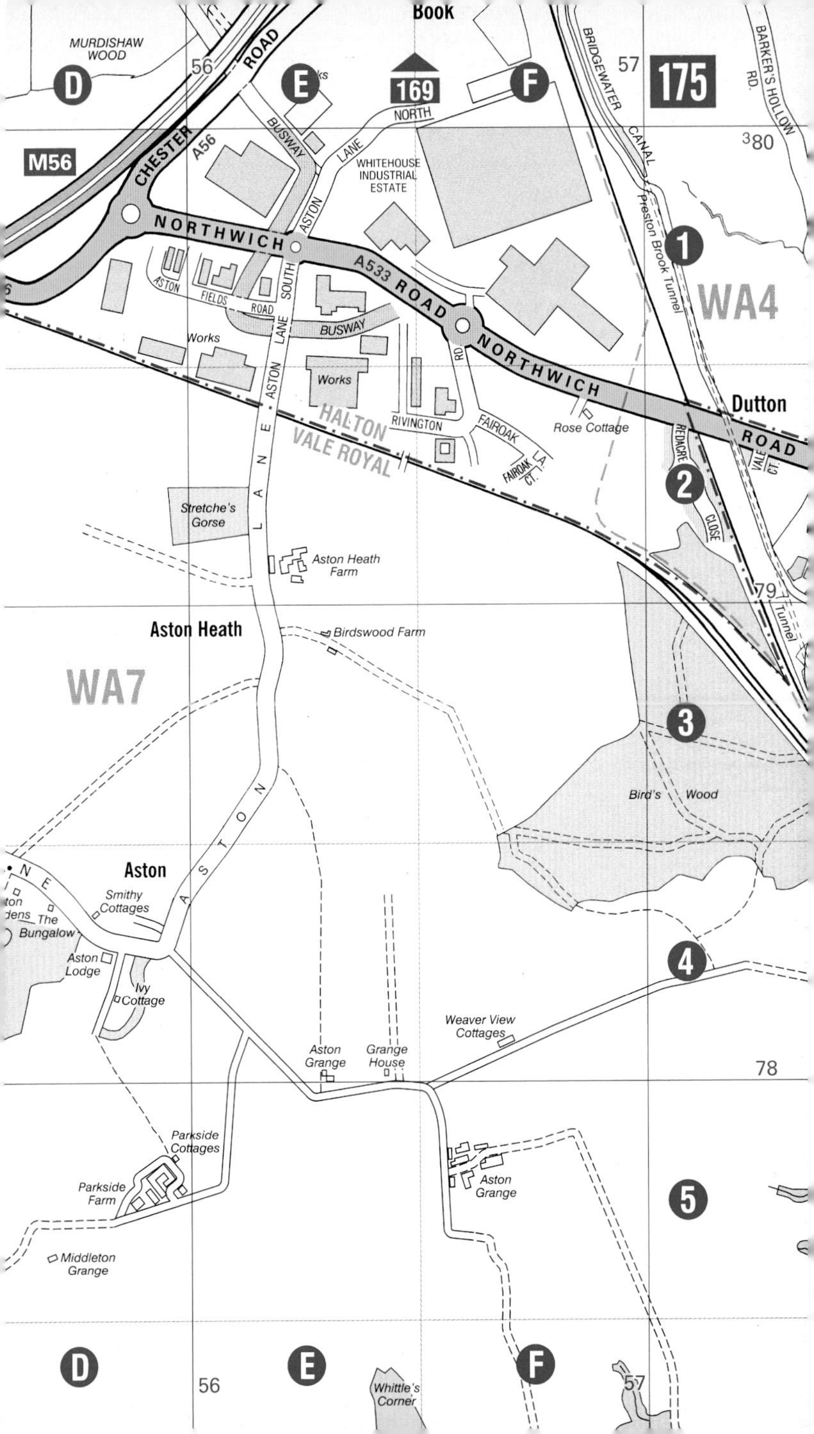
Book
169
175
MURDISHAW WOOD
56
57
380
79
78
D
E
F
M56
CHESTER ROAD
A56
NORTHWICH ROAD
A533 ROAD
NORTHWICH ROAD
NORTH LANE
ASTON LANE
WHITEHOUSE INDUSTRIAL ESTATE
BUSWAY
ASTON FIELDS ROAD
SOUTH ASTON LANE
Works
HALTON
VALE ROYAL
RIVINGTON RD.
FAIROAK LA.
FAIROAK CT.
Rose Cottage
BRIDGEWATER CANAL
Preston Brook Tunnel
BARKER'S HOLLOW RD.
WA4
Dutton
REDACRE CLOSE
VALE CT.
Tunnel
1
2
3
4
5
Stretche's Gorse
Aston Heath Farm
Aston Heath
Birdswood Farm
WA7
Bird's Wood
ASTON LANE
Aston
Smithy Cottages
The Bungalow
Aston Lodge
Ivy Cottage
Weaver View Cottages
Aston Grange
Grange House
Parkside Cottages
Parkside Farm
Middleton Grange
Whittle's Corner

INDEX

Including Streets, Places & Areas, Industrial Estates, Selected Subsidiary Addresses and Selected Places of Interest.

HOW TO USE THIS INDEX

1. Each street name is followed by its Posttown or Postal Locality and then by its map reference; e.g. Abberley Rd. *L25* —5C **126** is in the Liverpool 25 Postal District and is to be found in square 5C on page **126**. The page number being shown in bold type.
   A strict alphabetical order is followed in which Av., Rd., St., etc. (though abbreviated) are read in full and as part of the street name; e.g. Adamson St. appears after Adam Clo. but before Adam St.

2. Streets and a selection of Subsidiary names not shown on the Maps, appear in the index in *Italics* with the thoroughfare to which it is connected shown in brackets; e.g. *Alexander Way. L8 —5F **99** (off Pk. Hill Rd.)*

3. The page references shown in brackets indicate those streets that appear on the large scale map pages **4-5**; e.g. Addison St. *L3* —3D **77** (2E **4**) appears in square 3D on page **77** also appears in the enlarged section in square 2E on page **4**.

3. Places and areas are shown in the index in **bold type**, the map reference referring to the actual map square in which the town or area is located and not to the place name; e.g. **Aigburth. —4E 123**

4. An example of a selected place of interest is ***Academy, The. —3A 24 (Liverpool F.C.)***

GENERAL ABBREVIATIONS

All : Alley
App : Approach
Arc : Arcade
Av : Avenue
Bk : Back
Boulevd : Boulevard
Bri : Bridge
B'way : Broadway
Bldgs : Buildings
Bus : Business
Cvn : Caravan
Cen : Centre
Chu : Church
Chyd : Churchyard
Circ : Circle
Cir : Circus
Clo : Close
Comn : Common
Cotts : Cottages
Ct : Court
Cres : Crescent
Cft : Croft
Dri : Drive
E : East
Embkmt : Embankment
Est : Estate
Fld : Field
Gdns : Gardens
Gth : Garth
Ga : Gate
Gt : Great
Grn : Green
Gro : Grove
Ho : House
Ind : Industrial
Info : Information
Junct : Junction
La : Lane
Lit : Little
Lwr : Lower
Mc : Mac
Mnr : Manor
Mans : Mansions
Mkt : Market
Mdw : Meadow
M : Mews
Mt : Mount
Mus : Museum
N : North
Pal : Palace
Pde : Parade
Pk : Park
Pas : Passage
Pl : Place
Quad : Quadrant
Res : Residential
Ri : Rise
Rd : Road
Shop : Shopping
S : South
Sq : Square
Sta : Station
St : Street
Ter : Terrace
Trad : Trading
Up : Upper
Va : Vale
Vw : View
Vs : Villas
Vis : Visitors
Wlk : Walk
W : West
Yd : Yard

POSTTOWN AND POSTAL LOCALITY ABBREVIATIONS

Aig : Aigburth
Ain : Aintree
Ain R : Aintree Racecourse Retail & Bus. Pk.
Aller : Allerton
Anf : Anfield
Ash M : Ashton-in-Makerfield
Ast : Astmoor
Ast I : Astmoor Ind. Est.
Aston : Aston
Augh : Aughton
Beb : Bebington
Beech : Beechwood
B Vale : Belle Vale
Bic : Bickerstaffe
Bil : Billinge
Birk : Birkenhead
Bold : Bold
Bold H : Bold Heath
Boot : Bootle
Bow P : Bowring Park
Brim : Brimstage
B'grn : Broadgreen
Brom : Bromborough
Brom P : Bromborough Pool
Brook : Brookvale
Brun B : Brunswick Bus. Pk.
Burt : Burton
Btnwd : Burtonwood
Cald : Caldy
Cas : Castlefields
Chil T : Childer Thornton
Child : Childwall
Clftn : Clifton
Clo F : Clock Face
Club : Clubmoor
C Grn : Collins Green
Crank : Crank
Cress : Cressington
Croft B : Croft Bus. Pk.
Cron : Cronton
Cros : Crosby
Crox : Croxteth
Cuer : Cuerdley
Dar : Daresbury
Dent G : Dentons Green
Ding : Dingle
Dove : Dovecot
Down : Downholland
Dut : Dutton
East : Eastham
Ecc : Eccleston
Ecc L : Eccleston Lane Ends
Ecc P : Eccleston Park
Edg H : Edge Hill
Ersk : Erskine Ind. Est.
Eve : Everton
Fair : Fairfield
Faz : Fazakerley
Ford : Ford
Form : Formby
Fran : Frankby
Frod : Frodsham

Posttown and Postal Locality Abbreviations

Gars : Garston
Gate : Gateacre
Gil I : Gilmoss Ind. Est.
Grass P : Grassendale Park
Grea : Greasby
Gt Cro : Great Crosby
Haleb : Halebank
Hale V : Hale Village
Halew : Halewood
Hall P : Hallwood Park
Hals P : Halsnead Park
Halt : Halton
Halt B : Halton Brook
Halt L : Halton Lodge
Hay : Haydock
Hay I : Haydock Ind. Est.
Hel : Helsby
Hes : Heswall
High B : Higher Bebington
High : Hightown
Hoot : Hooton
Hoy : Hoylake
Hunts X : Hunts Cross
Huy : Huyton
Ince B : Ince Blundell
Irby : Irby
Kens : Kensington
K'ley : Kingsley
Kirkby : Kirkby
Kirk : Kirkdale
K Ash : Knotty Ash
Know : Knowsley
Know B : Knowsley Bus. Pk.
Know I : Knowsley Ind. Pk.
Know N : Knowsley Ind. Pk. N.
Know P : Knowsley Park
Laird T : Lairdside Technology Pk.
Lith : Litherland
L Cro : Little Crosby Village
L Sut : Little Sutton
Liv A : Liverpool John Lennon Airport
Low H : Low Hill
Lyd : Lydiate
Mag : Maghull
Mnr P : Manor Park
Mell : Melling
Meol : Meols
Mil B : Millers Bridge Ind. Est.
Moore : Moore
More : Moreton
Moss H : Mossley Hill
Murd : Murdishaw
Nest : Neston
N'ley : Netherley
N'ton : Netherton
New F : New Ferry
Newt W : Newton-le-Willows
Norl : Norley
Nor G : Norris Green
Nor C : North Cheshire Trad. Est.
Nort : Norton
Old I : Old Hall Ind. Est.
Old R : Old Roan
Old S : Old Swan
Orr P : Orrell Park
Padd M : Paddock Moor
Page M : Page Moss
Pal : Palacefields
Park : Parkgate
Parr : Parr
Parr I : Parr Ind. Est.
Penk : Penketh
Pens : Pensby
Port S : Port Sunlight
Pren : Prenton
Pres B : Preston Brook
Pres H : Preston on the Hill
Prin P : Princes Park
Prsct : Prescot
Raby M : Raby Mere
Rain : Rainhill
Rainf : Rainford
Reg I : Reginald Road Ind. Est.
Roby : Roby
Run : Runcorn
St H : St Helens
Sand P : Sandfield Park
S'frth : Seaforth
Seft : Sefton
Seft P : Sefton Park
Sher I : Sherdley Road Ind. Est.
Sim : Simonswood
Speke : Speke
Spit : Spital
Stan : Stanley
Stock V : Stockbridge Village
Ston : Stoneycroft
Sut L : Sutton Leach
Sut M : Sutton Manor
Sut W : Sutton Weaver
Tarb : Tarbock
Tarb G : Tarbock Green
Tarr I : Tarran Ind. Est.
That H : Thatto Heath
Thing : Thingwall
Thor : Thornton
Thor H : Thornton Hough
Thur : Thurstaston
Tox : Toxteth
Tran : Tranmere
Tue : Tuebrook
Upt : Upton
Wall : Wallasey
Walt : Walton
Wat : Waterloo
W'tree : Wavertree
W Der : West Derby
W Kir : West Kirby
West : Weston
West P : Weston Point
Whis : Whiston
White I : Whitehouse Ind. Est.
Wid : Widnes
Will : Willaston
Wind : Windle
Wind H : Windmill Hill
Wir : Wirral
W'chu : Woodchurch
Wltn : Woolton

INDEX

A41 Expressway. *Birk* —1F **119**
Abacus Rd. *L13* —2A **80**
Abberley Clo. *St H* —5F **45**
Abberley Rd. *L25* —5C **126**
(in two parts)
Abberton Pk. *Boot* —5A **12**
Abbey Clo. *Kirkby* —3F **23**
Abbey Clo. *Birk* —4F **97**
Abbey Clo. *Wid* —4C **130**
Abbey Ct. *L25* —2B **126**
Abbeyfield Dri. *L12* —4D **39**
Abbey Hey. *Nort* —2C **168**
Abbey Rd. *L6* —5B **56**
Abbey Rd. *Dent G* —1D **45**
Abbey Rd. *Hay* —1E **49**
Abbey Rd. *Wid* —4C **130**
Abbey Rd. *Wir* —4B **112**
Abbeystead Av. *Boot* —4A **20**
Abbeystead Rd. *L15* —1B **102**
Abbey St. *Birk* —4F **97**
Abbeyvale Dri. *L25* —3C **104**
Abbey Vw. *L16* —2E **103**
Abbeyway N. *Hay* —1F **49**
Abbeyway S. *Hay* —1F **49**
Abbeywood Gro. *Whis* —4F **85**
Abbot Clo. *Pren* —3C **94**
Abbotsbury Way. *L12* —5E **39**
Abbots Dri. *Wir* —2F **141**
Abbotsfield Rd. *Reg I* —5E **67**
(in two parts)
Abbotsford Ct. *Cros* —2C **16**
Abbotsford Gdns. *L23* —2C **16**
Abbotsford Rd. *Cros* —2C **16**
Abbotsford Rd. *Nor G* —1E **57**
Abbotsford St. *Wall* —4E **75**
Abbots Hall Av. *Clo F* —3D **89**
Abbots Way. *Bil* —2D **31**
Abbots Way. *W Kir* —3C **112**
Abbott Dri. *Boot* —3E **35**
Abbotts Clo. *L18* —1B **124**
Abbotts Clo. *Run* —2A **166**
Abbottshey Av. *L18* —1B **124**
Abdale Rd. *L11* —5F **37**
Abercrombie Rd. *Know I* —1B **40**
Abercromby Sq. *L7* —5F **77**
Aberdale Rd. *L13* —3B **80**
Aberdeen St. *Birk* —2C **96**
Aberford Av. *Wall* —1E **73**
Abergele Rd. *L13* —4F **79**
Aber St. *L6* —3A **78**
Abingdon Gro. *Walt* —1C **56**
Abingdon Gro. *Halew* —3A **128**
Abingdon Rd. *L4* —1C **56**
Abingdon Rd. *Wir* —1B **114**
Abington Wlk. *Brook* —5C **168**
Abney Clo. *L7* —1B **100**
Aboyne Clo. *L9* —4A **36**
Abram St. *L5* —1E **77**
Abyssinia Clo. *L15* —2E **101**
Acacia Av. *L36* —5D **83**
Acacia Av. *Wid* —1B **132**
Acacia Clo. *Wir* —3C **114**
Acacia Gro. *Ecc* —4A **44**
Acacia Gro. *L9* —2B **36**
Acacia Gro. *Run* —2C **166**
Acacia Gro. *Wall* —4E **75**
Acacia Gro. *Wir* —4A **112**
Acacia St. *Newt W* —4F **49**
Academy, The. —3A 24
(Liverpool F.C.)
Acanthus Rd. *L13* —2A **80**
Access Rd. *L12* —4D **59**
Acer Leigh. *L17* —2D **123**
Acheson Rd. *L13* —5E **57**
Ackers Hall. *L14* —1F **81**
Ackers Hall Av. *L14* —2F **81**
Ackers Hall Clo. *L14* —1F **81**
Ackers La. *Cros* —3C **8**
Ackers La. *Ecc* —4C **44**
Ackers Rd. *W'chu* —2C **116**
Ackers St. *Prsct* —5D **63**
Acland Rd. *Wall* —2B **74**
Aconbury Clo. *L11* —5F **37**
Aconbury Pl. *L11* —5F **37**
Acorn Clo. *Clo F* —2C **88**
Acorn Clo. *Wir* —1D **141**
Acorn Ct. *L8* —3E **99**
Acornfield Clo. *L33* —5C **24**
Acornfield Rd. *Know I* —4D **25**
Acorn Way. *Boot* —3D **35**
Acrefield Bank. *L25* —1A **126**
Acrefield Ct. *Birk* —3B **118**
Acrefield Pk. *L25* —1A **126**

Acrefield Rd. *L25* —5A **104**
Acrefield Rd. *Birk* —3B **118**
Acrefield Rd. *Wid* —3B **130**
Acre Grn. *L26* —1A **148**
Acre La. *Brom* —3C **162**
(in two parts)
Acre La. *Hes* —1C **158**
Acres Clo. *L25* —2A **104**
Acresfield. *L13* —4B **80**
Acresgate Ct. *L25* —3A **104**
Acres La. *L38 & L31* —1A **6**
Acres Rd. *Beb* —1F **141**
Acres Rd. *Meol* —4F **91**
Acreville Rd. *Wir* —2F **141**
Acton Clo. *Hay* —2C **48**
Acton Gro. *L6* —5C **56**
Acton La. *Wir* —2C **92**
Acton Rake. *Boot* —5D **11**
Acton Rd. *L32* —3C **22**
Acton Rd. *Birk* —3A **120**
Acton Rd. *Btnwd* —5E **69**
Acton Way. *L7* —1C **100**
Acuba Gro. *Birk* —5E **97**
Acuba Rd. *L15* —5C **80**
Adair Pl. *L13* —4E **57**
Adair Rd. *L13* —4E **57**
Adam Clo. *L19* —2C **144**
Adamson St. *L7* —4D **79**
Adam St. *L5* —5F **55**
Adaston Av. *Wir* —1F **171**
Adcote Clo. *L14* —3F **81**
Adcote Rd. *L14* —3F **81**
Adderley Clo. *Run* —1C **166**
Adderley St. *L7* —4B **78**
Addingham Av. *Wid* —5C **130**
Addingham Rd. *L18* —4B **102**
Addington St. *Wall* —3D **75**
Addison Sq. *Wid* —3F **131**
Addison St. *Boot* —3A **34**
Addison St. *L3* —3D **77** (2E **4**)
Addison Way. *L3* —3D **77** (2E **4**)
Adelaide Av. *That H* —4E **65**
Adelaide Pl. *L5* —2E **77**
Adelaide Rd. *S'frth* —1F **33**
Adelaide Rd. *Birk* —5C **96**
Adelaide Rd. *Kens* —4A **78**
Adelaide St. *Wall* —3B **74**
Adelaide Ter. *L22* —4C **16**
Adela Rd. *Run* —5F **151**
Adele Thompson Dri. *L8* —2A **100**
Adelphi St. *Birk* —3E **97**
Adkins St. *L5* —5A **56**
Adlam Cres. *L9* —1E **37**
Adlam Rd. *L9 & L10* —1E **37**
Adlington Ho. *L3* —3D **77** (2E **4**)
Adlington Rd. *Wind H* —5D **155**
Adlington St. *L3* —3D **77** (2E **4**)
Admin Rd. *Know I* —5C **24**
Admiral Gro. *L8* —4A **100**
Admiral St. *L8* —4F **99**
Adrian's Way. *L32* —3E **23**
Adshead Rd. *L13* —4E **57**
Adstone Rd. *L25* —4C **104**
Adswood Rd. *L36* —3E **83**
Africander Rd. *St H* —5A **30**
Afton. *Wid* —2A **130**
Agar Rd. *L11* —4F **57**
Agate St. *L5* —1A **78**
Agincourt Rd. *L12* —1C **80**
Agnes Gro. *Wall* —1C **74**
Agnes Rd. *L23* —2C **16**
Agnes Rd. *Birk* —1D **119**
Agnes St. *Clo F* —3C **88**
Agnes Way. *L7* —5B **78**
Aiden Long Gro. *Know P* —5E **61**
Aigburth. —4E 123
Aigburth Dri. *L8* —4C **100**
Aigburth Gro. *Wir* —1D **93**
Aigburth Hall Av. *L19* —4F **123**
Aigburth Hall Rd. *L19* —4A **124**
Aigburth Ho. *L17* —1E **123**
Aigburth Rd. *L17 & L19* —5B **100**
Aigburth St. *L7* —1B **100**
Aigburth Vale. —2D 123
Aigburth Va. *L17* —2D **123**
(in two parts)
Ailsa Rd. *Wall* —1A **74**
Ainley Clo. *Brook* —5A **168**
Ainsdale Clo. *L10* —5F **21**
Ainsdale Clo. *Brom* —5C **162**
Ainsdale Clo. *Thing* —2A **138**
Ainsdale Rd. *Boot* —2D **35**
Ainsworth Av. *Wir* —3C **92**
Ainsworth La. *Know B* —2B **40**
Ainsworth Rd. *Dent G* —3D **45**
Ainsworth St. *L3* —5E **77** (5H **5**)
Aintree. —2C 20
Aintree Clo. *Wir* —3F **71**
Aintree Ct. *L10* —2C **20**
Aintree La. *Faz* —4F **21**
Aintree La. *L10* —2C **20**
Aintree Racecourse. —4C 20
Aintree Racecourse Retail Pk. *Ain R* —4B **20**
Aintree Rd. *Boot* —4D **35**
Aintree Rd. *Faz* —2D **37**
Aintree Way. *Ain R* —3C **20**
Airdale Clo. *Pren* —3C **94**
Airdale Rd. *L15* —3E **101**
Airdrie Clo. *Wir* —2D **171**
Aire. *Wid* —2B **130**
Airegate. *L31* —5B **6**
Airlie Gro. *L13* —5D **57**
Airlie Rd. *Wir* —5B **90**
Aisthorpe Gro. *L31* —3D **13**
Akbar, The. *Wir* —1C **156**
Akenside Ct. *Boot* —2A **34**
Akenside St. *Boot* —2A **34**
Alabama Way. *Birk* —3F **97**
Alamein Rd. *L36* —2D **83**
Alan's Way. *L33* —1E **23**
Alastair Cres. *Pren* —3F **117**
Alban Rd. *L16* —1D **103**
Albany Av. *Ecc P* —4F **63**
Albany Rd. *Walt* —1B **36**
Albany Rd. *Birk* —2E **119**
Albany Rd. *Kens* —4A **78**
Albany Rd. *Old S* —2A **80**
Albany Rd. *Prsct* —5E **63**
Albany Ter. *Run* —5A **152**
Albemarle Rd. *Wall* —3D **75**
Alberta Gro. *Prsct* —1F **83**
Albert Dock. —1C 98 (7C 4)
Albert Dri. *L9* —2F **35**
Albert Edward Rd. *L7* —4A **78**
Albert Gro. *Cros* —1D **17**
Albert Gro. *W'tree* —1A **102**
Albert Pk. *L17* —4B **100**
Albert Rd. *Wat* —4D **17**
Albert Rd. *Birk* —5C **96**
Albert Rd. *Hoy* —5B **90**
Albert Rd. *Tue* —5D **57**
Albert Rd. *W Kir* —5A **112**
Albert Rd. *Wid* —4B **132**
Albert Row. *Frod* —4B **172**
Albert Schweitzer Av. *Boot* —2F **19**
Albert Sq. *Wid* —4B **132**
Albert St. *L7* —5A **78**
Albert St. *St H* —3A **46**
Albert St. *Run* —5A **152**
Albert St. *Wall* —2C **52**
Albert Ter. *C Grn* —2E **69**
Albion Pl. *Wall* —3B **52**
Albion St. *L5* —5E **55**
Albion St. *St H* —5E **45**
(in two parts)
Albion St. *Birk* —3F **97**
(in two parts)
Albion St. *Wall* —3A **52**
Albourne Rd. *L32* —5A **24**
Albury Clo. *L12* —1F **59**
Albury Clo. *Hay* —1C **48**
Albury Rd. *L32* —1F **39**
Alcester Rd. *L12* —5C **58**
Alcock St. *Run* —4A **152**
Aldams Gro. *L4* —2E **55**
Aldbourne Av. *L25* —4E **103**
Aldbourne Clo. *L25* —5E **103**
Alder Av. *L36* —1A **106**
Alder Av. *Wid* —1A **132**
Alder Clo. *Prsct* —5F **63**
Alder Cres. *L32* —2D **23**
Alderfield Dri. *L24* —3F **147**
Alder Gro. *L22* —3D **17**
Alder Hey Rd. *St H* —5C **44**
Alder La. *Crank* —1F **29**
Alder La. *Know* —1B **60**
(in two parts)
Alder La. *Btnwd* —4F **69**
Alder La. *Wid* —5F **107**
Alderley Av. *Birk* —2F **95**
Alderley Clo. *Bil* —1E **31**
Alderley Rd. *Wall* —3B **74**
Alderley Rd. *Wir* —4B **90**
Alderley Rd. N. *Wir* —4B **90**
Alderney Rd. *L5* —1C **76**
Alder Rd. *L12* —2B **80**
Alder Rd. *Prsct* —5F **63**
Alder Rd. *Wir* —3D **141**
Aldersey Clo. *Wind H* —1D **169**
Aldersgate. *Birk* —2F **119**
Aldersgate Av. *Murd* —3D **169**
Aldersgate Dri. *L26* —1A **148**
Aldersley St. *L3* —3D **77** (1F **5**)
Alderson Rd. *L15* —2D **101**
Alderville Rd. *L4* —1C **56**
Alder Wood Av. *L24* —4E **147**
Alderwood Lodge. *L24* —4A **148**
Aldford Clo. *Pren* —2E **117**
Aldford Clo. *Wir* —4B **162**
Aldford Rd. *L32* —1E **39**
Aldridge Clo. *L12* —5E **39**
Aldridge Dri. *Btnwd* —4F **69**
Aldrins La. *Boot* —1F **19**
Aldwark Rd. *L14* —2A **82**
Aldwych Rd. *L12* —5C **58**
Aldykes. *L31* —2E **13**
Alexander Dri. *L31* —4D **7**
Alexander Dri. *Wid* —4D **131**
Alexander Dri. *Wir* —4E **137**
Alexander Fleming Av. *Boot* —1F **19**
Alexander Grn. *L36* —2E **83**
Alexander Ho. *S'frth* —1F **33**
Alexander Wlk. *L4* —3F **55**
Alexander Way. L8 —5F ***99***
(off Pk. Hill Rd.)
Alexandra Clo. *L6* —3B **78**
Alexandra Ct. *That H* —3D **65**
Alexandra Ct. *Wall* —3A **52**
Alexandra Dri. *Boot* —2E **35**
Alexandra Dri. *L17* —5B **100**
Alexandra Dri. *St H* —2D **65**
Alexandra Dri. *Birk* —3E **119**
Alexandra Grn. *L17* —5B **100**
Alexandra Gro. *Run* —1C **166**
Alexandra Ho. *L17* —5B **100**
Alexandra Ind. Est. *Wid* —5F **131**
Alexandra M. *Frod* —4B **172**
Alexandra Mt. *L21* —5B **18**
Alexandra Pk. *L17* —1B **122**
Alexandra Rd. *Cros* —1D **17**
Alexandra Rd. *Wat* —5E **17**
Alexandra Rd. *Edg H* —1C **100**
Alexandra Rd. *Gars* —5C **124**
Alexandra Rd. *Old S* —4A **80**
Alexandra Rd. *Pren* —4B **96**
Alexandra Rd. *Wall* —3A **52**

Alexandra Rd. *Wir* —5A **112**
Alexandra St. *St H* —2D **65**
Alexandra St. *Wid* —5A **132**
Alexandra Vs. *L21* —5B **18**
Alex Clo. *L8* —3F **99**
Alfonso Rd. *L4* —3D **55**
Alford Av. *Sut M* —2B **88**
Alforde St. *Wid* —5A **132**
(in two parts)
Alford St. *L7* —4D **79**
Alfred Clo. *Wid* —4B **132**
Alfred M. *L1* —2E **99**
Alfred Pl. *L8* —5A **100**
Alfred Rd. *Hay* —1F **49**
Alfred Rd. *Pren* —4C **96**
Alfred Rd. *Wall* —5E **75**
Alfred Stocks Ct. *L8* —1A **122**
Alfred St. *L15* —1D **101**
Alfred St. *St H* —4B **46**
Alfred St. *Wid* —4B **132**
Alfriston Rd. *L12* —5C **58**
Algernon St. *Run* —4F **151**
Alice Ct. *Wid* —3A **152**
Alice St. *St H* —3E **67**
Alicia Wlk. *L10* —1B **38**
Alison Av. *Birk* —1F **119**
Alison Pl. *L13* —4E **57**
Alison Rd. *L13* —4E **57**
Alistair Dri. *Wir* —5C **162**
Allangate Clo. *Wir* —2C **114**
Allangate Rd. *L19* —4A **124**
Allan Rd. *St H* —1C **46**
Allanson St. *St H* —1D **67**
Allcot Av. *Birk* —2D **119**
Allenby Av. *L23* —3F **17**
Allenby Sq. *L13* —4F **79**
Allendale. *Run* —4B **168**
Allendale Av. *L9* —1B **36**
Allendale Av. *Rain* —3D **87**
Allen Ga. *L23* —5E **9**
Allen Rd. *West P* —3D **165**
Allerford Rd. *L12* —4C **58**
Allerton. —4E 125
Allerton Beeches. *L18* —1C **124**
Allerton Dri. *L18* —5B **102**
Allerton Gro. *Birk* —1D **119**
Allerton Pk. Golf Course. —2E 125
Allerton Rd. *Aller & Moss H* —4A **102**
Allerton Rd. *Birk* —5D **97**
Allerton Rd. *Wall* —5A **52**
Allerton Rd. *Wid* —3B **132**
Allerton Rd. *Wltn* —2A **126**
Allesley Rd. *L14* —1F **81**
Alleyne Rd. *L4* —3D **57**
Allington St. *L17* —1B **122**
Allonby Clo. *Pren* —5E **95**
Allport La. *Wir* —2D **163**
Allport La. Precinct. *Wir* —1D **163**
Allport Rd. *Wir* —4C **162**
Allports, The. *Wir* —3D **163**
All Saints Clo. *Boot* —2E **19**
All Saints Rd. *L24* —4C **146**
Allysum Ct. *Beech* —1F **173**
Alma Clo. *L10* —1B **38**
Almacs Clo. *L23* —2B **16**
Alma Dale Ter. *Boot* —5B **34**
Alman Ct. *L17* —1B **122**
Alma Pl. *St H* —1C **66**
Alma Rd. *L17* —4E **123**
Alma St. *St H* —1C **66**
Alma St. *Birk* —3E **97**
Alma St. *Wir* —5A **120**
Alma Ter. *L15* —1F **101**
Almeda Rd. *L24* —5A **148**
Almond Av. *Boot* —2C **18**
Almond Av. *Run* —2C **166**
Almond Clo. *L26* —5E **127**
Almond Clo. *Hay* —3F **47**
Almond Ct. *L19* —2E **145**
Almond Dri. *Btnwd* —5F **69**
Almond Gro. *Wid* —4D **131**
Almond Pl. *Wir* —1F **93**
Almond's Grn. *L12* —3A **58**
Almond's Gro. *L12* —4A **58**
Almond's Pk. *W Der* —3A **58**
Almonds Turn. *Boot* —1D **19**
Almond Tree Clo. *Hale V* —5E **149**
Almond Way. *Wir* —2C **114**
Alness Dri. *Rain* —4D **87**
Alnwick Dri. *Wir* —1B **92**
Aloeswood Clo. *L6* —1B **78**
Alpass Rd. *L17* —1B **122**
Alpha Dri. *Birk* —3A **120**
Alpha St. *L21* —3B **34**
Alpine Clo. *St H* —4C **44**
Alpine St. *Newt W* —5F **49**
Alresford Rd. *L19* —4F **123**
Alroy Rd. *L4* —4A **56**
Alscot Av. *L10* —1A **38**
Alscot Clo. *L31* —2D **13**
Alston Clo. *Wir* —1C **162**
Alstonfield Rd. *L14* —2A **82**
Alston Rd. *L17* —4E **123**
Alt. *Wid* —2B **130**
Alt Av. *L31* —3C **12**
Altbridge Pk. *L11* —4A **38**
(in two parts)
Altbridge Rd. *L36* —2D **83**
Altcar Av. *L15* —2C **100**
Altcar Dri. *Wir* —2D **93**
Altcar La. *Lyd* —2A **6**
Altcar Rd. *Boot* —3C **34**
Alt Ct. *L33* —5E **15**
Altcross Rd. *L11* —4C **38**
Altcross Way. *L11* —4C **38**
Altfield Rd. *L14* —4F **59**
Altfield Way. *L14* —4F **59**
Altfinch Clo. *L14* —4A **60**
Altham Rd. *L11* —4F **57**
Althorp St. *L8* —1F **121**
Altmoor Rd. *L36* —1D **83**
Alton Av. *L21* —4A **18**
Alton Rd. *L6* —1D **79**
Alton Rd. *Pren* —4A **96**
Alt Pk. —1D 83
Alt Rd. *Boot* —3C **34**
Alt Rd. *Huy* —3E **83**
Altside Ct. *L10* —1B **38**
Alt St. *L8* —2B **100**
Altway. *L10* —2C **20**
*Altway Ct. L10 —2C **20***
(off Altway)
Alundale Ct. *Boot* —5C **34**
Alundale Rd. *L12* —1E **81**
Alvanley Grn. *L32* —3C **22**
Alvanley Pl. *Pren* —3C **96**
Alvanley Rd. *Kirkby* —3C **22**
Alvanley Rd. *W Der* —1C **80**
Alvanley Ter. *Frod* —5B **172**
Alva Rd. *Rain* —4D **87**
Alvega Clo. *Wir* —5C **120**
Alverstone Av. *Birk* —2F **95**
Alverstone Rd. *L18* —4F **101**
Alverstone Rd. *Wall* —3D **75**
Alverton Clo. *Wid* —4D **131**
Alvina La. *Kirk* —4E **55**
Alvina La. *Kirkby* —5F **15**
Alwain Grn. *L24* —5F **147**
Alwen St. *Birk* —5F **73**
Alwyn Av. *L21* —4B **18**
Alwyn Clo. *L17* —1B **122**
Alwyn Gdns. *Wir* —1F **93**
Alwyn St. *L17* —1B **122**
Amanda Rd. *L10* —1B **38**
Amanda Rd. *Rain* —1B **86**
Amanda Way. *L31* —1B **22**
Amaury Clo. *L23* —5B **10**
Amaury Rd. *L23* —5B **10**
Ambassador Dri. *L26* —3A **128**
Ambergate Clo. *St H* —4D **67**
Ambergate Rd. *L19* —5B **124**
Amberley Av. *Wir* —2C **92**
Amberley Clo. *L6* —4D **57**
Amberley Clo. *Wir* —2C **92**
Amberley St. *L8* —2A **100**
Amber Way. *L14* —4A **60**
Ambleside Av. *Wir* —1D **93**
Ambleside Clo. *Beech* —5E **167**
Ambleside Clo. *Brom* —3E **163**
Ambleside Clo. *Thing* —1A **138**
Ambleside Pl. *St H* —4B **30**
Ambleside Rd. *Mag* —5D **7**
Ambleside Rd. *Aller* —3D **125**
Amelia Clo. *L6* —3F **77**
Amelia Clo. *Wid* —5B **110**
Amersham Rd. *L4* —1C **56**
(in two parts)
Amery Gro. *Birk* —2B **118**
Amethyst Clo. *L21* —5C **18**
Amethyst Clo. *Eve* —2B **78**
Amherst Rd. *L17* —2C **122**
Amity St. *L8* —4F **99**
Amos Av. *L21* —5C **18**
Ampleforth Clo. *L32* —4C **22**
Ampthill Rd. *L17* —2C **122**
Ampulla Rd. *L11* —5C **38**
Amusement Pk. —2B 52
(New Brighton)
Amy Wlk. *L10* —1B **38**
Ancaster Rd. *L17* —2C **122**
Ancholme Clo. *Whis* —5A **64**
Anchorage La. *L18* —1E **123**
Anchorage, The. *L3* —3D **99**
Anchor Clo. *Murd* —4D **169**
Ancient Meadows. *L9* —1B **36**
Ancroft Rd. *L14* —3A **82**
Ancrum Rd. *L33* —4D **15**
Anders Dri. *L33* —5F **15**
Anderson Av. *Boot* —3A **34**
Anderson Clo. *Rain* —5D **87**
Anderson Clo. *Wir* —1A **138**
Anderson Ct. *Brom* —4D **163**
Anderson Rd. *L21* —4D **19**
Anderson St. *L5* —5E **55**
(in two parts)
Anderson Way. *L21* —4D **19**
Anderton Ter. *L36* —4C **82**
Andover Way. *L25* —5D **127**
Andrew Av. *L31* —2A **22**
Andrew Clo. *Wid* —4C **130**
Andrew St. *L4* —2F **55**
Andrew's Wlk. *Wir* —2B **158**
Andromeda Way. *St H* —4A **68**
Anemone Way. *St H* —4A **68**
Anfield. —4A 56
Anfield. —4A 56
Anfield Rd. *L4* —4F **55**
Angela St. *L7* —1B **100**
Angers La. *L31* —4B **14**
Anglesea Rd. *L9* —5F **35**
Anglesea Way. *L8* —5F **99**
Anglesey Rd. *Wall* —1B **74**
Anglesey Rd. *Wir* —3A **112**
Anglezark Clo. *L7* —4B **78**
Anglican Ct. *L8* —2E **99**
Anglo Clo. *L9* —5C **20**
Angus Rd. *L11* —3F **57**
Angus Rd. *Wir* —4C **162**
Annandale Clo. *L33* —4D **15**
Anne Gro. *St H* —4C **66**
Annesley Rd. *L17* —2C **122**
Annesley Rd. *Wall* —3C **74**
Anne St. *Clo F* —3D **89**
Annie Rd. *Boot* —2D **35**
Ann St. *Run* —4B **152**
Ann St. W. *Wid* —5B **132**
Anscot Av. *Wir* —1F **141**

Ansdell Dri. *Ecc* —3B **44**
Ansdell Rd. *Wid* —2B **132**
Ansdell Vs. Rd. *Rain* —2C **86**
Anson Pl. *L3* —4F **77** (4J **5**)
Anson St. *L3* —4E **77** (4J **5**)
Anson Ter. *L3* —4F **77** (4J **5**)
Anstey Clo. *Wir* —5B **70**
Anstey Rd. *L13* —3B **80**
Ansty Clo. *St H* —2D **47**
Anthony's Way. *Wir* —3A **158**
Anthorn Clo. *Pren* —5D **95**
Antonio St. *Boot* —2D **55**
Antons Clo. *L26* —1F **147**
Antons Rd. *L26* —1F **147**
Antons Rd. *Wir* —2A **138**
Antrim Clo. *Hay* —2C **48**
Antrim St. *L13* —4E **57**
Anvil Clo. *Boot* —4B **34**
Anzacs, The. *Wir* —1C **142**
Anzio Rd. *L36* —2D **83**
Apollo Cres. *L33* —1E **23**
Apollo Way. *Boot* —1F **19**
Apostles Way. *Kirkby* —5D **15**
Appin Rd. *Birk* —4E **97**
Appleby Clo. *Wid* —4C **130**
Appleby Dri. *Boot* —2C **18**
Appleby Grn. *L12* —5D **59**
Appleby Gro. *Wir* —4D **163**
Appleby Lawn. *L27* —5A **106**
Appleby Rd. *L27* —5A **106**
Appleby Rd. *L33* —1D **23**
Appleby Rd. *Wid* —4C **130**
Appleby Wlk. *L27* —5A **106**
Appleby Wlk. *Wid* —4C **130**
Applecorn Clo. *Sut L* —5D **67**
Apple Ct. L6 —3B ***78***
(off Coleridge St.)
Appledore Ct. *L24* —3B **146**
Appledore Gro. *Sut L* —1C **88**
Apple Gth. *Wir* —3C **92**
Appleton. —3B 132
Appleton Dri. *Wir* —1E **115**
Appleton Rd. *Lith* —4A **18**
Appleton Rd. *St H* —2C **66**
Appleton Rd. *Walt* —2A **56**
Appleton Rd. *Wid* —3B **132**
Appleton St. *Wid* —1B **152**
Appleton Village. *Wid* —3A **132**
Appletree Clo. *Aller* —3B **124**
Apple Tree Clo. *Hale V* —5E **149**
Apple Tree Clo. *Stock V* —3B **60**
April Gro. *L6* —1D **79**
April Ri. *Boot* —2E **19**
Apsley Av. *Wall* —5B **52**
Apsley Brow. *L31* —1B **12**
Apsley Gro. *Wir* —1A **142**
Apsley Rd. *L12* —5C **58**
Apsley Rd. *Wir* —4B **120**
Aquarius Clo. *L14* —2A **82**
Arabis Gdns. *St H* —4B **68**
Aragon Clo. *L31* —4E **7**
Aragon Ct. *Mnr P* —4C **154**
Aran Clo. *Hale V* —5D **149**
Arborn Dri. *Wir* —3A **94**
Arbour La. *L33* —4A **24**
Arbury Av. *St H* —2D **47**
Arcadia Av. *L31* —4D **7**
Archbishop Warlock Ct. *L3* —2C **76**
Archer Clo. *L4* —4E **55**
Archerfield Rd. *L18* —3B **124**
Archer Gro. *St H* —4E **47**
Archers Ct. *Wir* —2A **116**
Archers Grn. *Wir* —1E **171**
Archer St. *L4* —4E **55**
Archers Way. *Upt* —2A **116**
Arch La. *Ash M* —2F **31**
Archway Rd. *L36* —4D **83**
Arctic Rd. *Boot* —5A **34**
Arden. *Wid* —2A **130**
Ardennes Rd. *L36* —3E **83**
(in two parts)
Arderne Clo. *Wir* —5B **142**
Ardleigh Clo. *L13* —4F **79**
Ardleigh Gro. *L13* —4F **79**
Ardleigh Pl. *L13* —4E **79**
Ardleigh Rd. *L13* —4E **79**
Ardmore Rd. *L18* —2A **124**
Ardrossan Rd. *L4* —3C **56**
Ardville Rd. *L11* —5D **37**
Ardwick Rd. *L24* —4F **147**
Ardwick St. *St H* —5C **46**
Argo Rd. *L22* —4D **17**
Argos Pl. *L20* —2D **55**
Argos Rd. *L20* —2D **55**
Argyle Rd. *Anf* —5B **56**
Argyle Rd. *Gars* —1C **144**
Argyle St. *L1* —1D **99** (7E **4**)
Argyle St. *St H* —3F **45**
Argyle St. *Birk* —3E **97**
Argyle St. S. *Birk* —4D **97**
Argyll Av. *Wir* —1D **171**
Ariel Pde. *Gars* —2C **144**
Aries Clo. *L14* —1A **82**
Ariss Gro. *Whis* —1A **86**
Arkenstone Clo. *Wid* —2C **130**
Arkle Rd. *Pren* —1F **95**
Arkles La. *L4* —4A **56**
Arkles Rd. *L4* —5A **56**
Arklow Dri. *Hale V* —5D **149**
Ark Royal Way. *Laird T* —5F **97**
Arkwood Clo. *Wir* —4C **142**
Arkwright Ct. *Ast I* —4F **153**
Arkwright Rd. *Ast I* —4F **153**
Arlescourt Rd. *L12* —1C **80**
Arley Clo. *Pren* —3C **94**
Arley Dri. *Wid* —2A **130**
Arley St. *L3* —2C **76** (1D **4**)
Arlington Av. *L18* —4E **101**
Arlington Ct. *Pren* —4F **95**
Arlington Rd. *Wall* —5E **51**
Armill Rd. *L11* —5C **38**
Armitage Gdns. *L18* —3B **124**
Armley Rd. *L4* —4B **56**
Armour Gro. *L13* —4A **80**
Armour Ho. *L1* —5D **4**
Armoury, The. *L12* —4B **58**
Armscot Clo. *L25* —5B **126**
Armscot Pl. *L25* —5B **126**
Armstrong Quay. *L3* —1E **121**
Arncliffe Dri. *Btnwd* —5F **69**
Arncliffe Rd. *L25* —4C **126**
Arndale. *Padd M* —5F **167**
Arnhem Rd. *L36* —2E **83**
Arno Ct. *Pren* —1B **118**
Arnold Av. *Dent G* —3D **45**
Arnold Clo. *St H* —2C **66**
Arnold Gro. *L15* —1A **102**
Arnold Pl. *Wid* —5C **130**
Arnold St. *L8* —3F **99**
Arnold St. *Wall* —1B **74**
Arno Rd. *Pren* —1B **118**
Arnot Clo. *St H* —3F **45**
Arnot St. *L4* —2F **55**
Arnot Way. *Wir* —1D **141**
Arnside. *L21* —5D **19**
Arnside Av. *Hay* —2B **48**
Arnside Av. *Rain* —2A **86**
Arnside Rd. *Edg H* —5C **78**
Arnside Rd. *Huy* —4B **82**
Arnside Rd. *Pren* —5A **96**
Arnside Rd. *Wall* —1B **74**
Arrad St. *L7* —1F **99** (7J **5**)
Arran Clo. *St H* —2E **47**
Arranmore Rd. *L18* —2A **124**
Arrowe Av. *Wir* —2D **93**
Arrowe Brook La. *Wir* —3D **115**
Arrowe Brook Rd. *Wir* —2F **115**
Arrowe Country Pk. —3A 116
Arrowe Ct. Wir —2A ***116***
(off Childwall Grn.)
Arrowe Hill. —1F 115
Arrowe Pk. Golf Course. —5A 116
Arrowe Pk. Rd. *Wir* —4A **94**
Arrowe Rd. *Wir* —1D **115**
Arrowe Side. *Wir* —5E **93**
Arrowsmith Rd. *Hay* —1F **49**
Arthur St. *L9* —5F **35**
Arthur St. *Birk* —2C **96**
(in two parts)
Arthur St. *Gars* —2D **145**
Arthur St. *Run* —5F **151**
Arundel Av. *L17* —3C **100**
Arundel Av. *Wall* —5F **51**
Arundel Clo. *Wir* —2F **137**
Arundell Clo. *Btnwd* —5F **69**
Arundel St. *Walt* —2E **55**
Arundel St. *Prin P* —3A **100**
Arvon St. *Boot* —2D **35**
Asbridge St. *L8* —2B **100**
Asbury Clo. *L18* —1D **125**
Asbury Rd. *Wall* —5D **51**
Ascot Av. *L21* —5A **18**
Ascot Av. *Run* —4B **166**
Ascot Dri. *L33* —5E **15**
Ascot Dri. *Beb* —2F **141**
Ascot Gro. *Beb* —2F **141**
Ascot Pk. *L23* —1F **17**
Ashbank Rd. *L11* —1A **58**
Ashbourne Av. *Boot* —2E **19**
Ashbourne Av. *L23* —1C **16**
Ashbourne Av. *Run* —4B **166**
Ashbourne Cres. *L36* —4B **82**
Ashbourne Rd. *L17* —2C **122**
Ashbrook Av. *Sut W* —2F **173**
Ashbrook Dri. *L9* —2C **36**
Ashbrook Ter. *Wir* —1A **142**
Ashburn Av. *L33* —1E **23**
Ashburton Av. *Pren* —3F **95**
Ashburton Rd. *Pren* —3F **95**
Ashburton Rd. *Wall* —2B **74**
Ashburton Rd. *Wir* —3B **112**
Ashbury Clo. *Wind H* —5D **155**
Ashbury Dri. *Hay* —1C **48**
Ashbury Rd. *L14* —5B **60**
Ashby Clo. *Wir* —5B **70**
Ash Clo. *L15* —1E **101**
Ashcombe Rd. *L14* —3B **80**
Ash Cres. *L36* —1E **105**
Ashcroft Dri. *Wir* —5F **137**
Ashcroft Rd. *Ain* —5B **20**
Ashcroft Rd. *Know I* —2B **24**
Ashcroft St. *Boot* —5B **34**
Ashcroft St. *St H* —5C **46**
Ashdale. *L36* —4D **83**
Ashdale Pk. *Wir* —5B **92**
Ashdale Rd. *Walt* —4A **36**
Ashdale Rd. *Wat* —3D **17**
Ashdale Rd. *Moss H* —4A **102**
Ashdown Cres. *Clo F* —2C **88**
Ashdown Dri. *Wir* —2C **114**
Ashdown Gro. *L26* —3A **128**
Ashfarm Ct. *L14* —3F **81**
Ashfield. *L15* —1D **101**
Ashfield. *Rain* —3D **87**
Ashfield Cres. *Bil* —1E **31**
Ashfield Cres. *Wir* —2D **163**
Ashfield Rd. *L17* —2D **123**
Ashfield Rd. *Brom* —2C **162**
Ashfield St. *L5* —1C **76**
Ashford Clo. *L26* —5E **127**
Ashford Rd. *Birk* —5C **96**
Ashford Rd. *Wir* —3C **90**
Ashford Way. *Wid* —3D **133**
Ash Grange. *K Ash* —3D **81**
Ash Gro. *Clo F* —2C **88**
Ash Gro. *L4* —3F **55**
Ash Gro. *S'frth* —2A **34**

Ash Gro. *Prsct* —2E **85**
Ash Gro. *Run* —2C **166**
Ash Gro. *Wall* —4C **52**
Ash Gro. *W'tree* —1D **101**
Ash Gro. *Wid* —4D **131**
Ashlands. *Frod* —5C **172**
Ash La. *Wid* —3E **129**
Ashlar Gro. *L17* —1E **123**
Ashlar Rd. *Wat* —3E **17**
Ashlar Rd. *Aig* —1E **123**
Ashlea Rd. *Wir* —4F **137**
Ashleigh Rd. *L31* —3F **13**
Ashley Av. *Wir* —2F **91**
Ashley Clo. *L33* —5E **15**
Ashley Clo. *Rain* —4D **87**
Ashley Grn. *Wid* —4D **131**
Ashley Rd. *Run* —5D **153**
Ashley St. *Birk* —2F **119**
Ashley Way. *Wid* —1A **152**
Ashley Way W. *Wid* —5F **131**
Ashmore Clo. *Wir* —3C **134**
Ashmuir Hey. *L32* —4F **23**
Ashover Av. *L14* —2A **82**
Ash Priors. *Wid* —1D **131**
Ashridge St. *Run* —4F **151**
Ash Rd. *L21* —1A **34**
Ash Rd. *Birk* —5C **96**
Ash Rd. *Hay* —1E **49**
Ash Rd. *Wir* —5F **119**
Ash St. *Boot* —4C **34**
Ashton Av. *Rain* —5C **86**
Ashton Clo. *Frod* —4C **172**
Ashton Clo. *West* —4F **165**
Ashton Clo. *Wir* —2E **171**
Ashton Ct. *Frod* —4C **172**
Ashton Dri. *L25* —5B **126**
Ashton Dri. *Frod* —4C **172**
Ashton Dri. *Wir* —4A **112**
Ashton Pk. *L25* —4D **127**
Ashton's Green. —4A 48
Ashtons Grn. Dri. *St H* —1F **67**
Ashton's La. *Hale V* —5F **147**
Ashton Sq. *L25* —3B **126**
Ashton St. *L3* —4F **77**
Ashton St. *L13* —3A **80**
Ashtree Cft. *Will* —5A **170**
Ashtree Farm Ct. *Will* —5A **170**
Ashtree Gro. *L12* —4E **39**
Ashurst Clo. *L25* —5B **104**
Ashurst Clo. *St H* —2E **47**
Ashurst Dri. *St H* —2D **47**
Ash Va. *L15* —1D **101**
Ash Vs. *Wall* —4C **74**
Ashville Rd. *Pren & Birk* —3A **96**
Ashville Rd. *Wall* —3C **74**
Ashville Way. *Sut W* —2E **173**
Ashwater Rd. *L12* —1C **58**
Ash Way. *Wir* —4B **158**
Ashwell St. *L8* —2E **99**
Ashwood Clo. *Kirkby* —5E **15**
Ashwood Clo. *N'ley* —4E **105**
Ashwood Ct. *Pren* —5C **72**
Ashwood Dri. *L12* —5D **39**
Askern Rd. *L32* —5F **23**
Askett Clo. *Hay* —1D **49**
Askew Clo. *Wall* —2D **75**
Askew St. *L4* —2F **55**
Askham Clo. *L8* —2B **100**
Aspen Clo. *Kirkby* —4F **15**
Aspen Clo. *Wir* —3D **159**
Aspendale Rd. *Birk* —5D **97**
Aspen Gdns. *St H* —5C **64**
Aspen Gro. *Tox* —3B **100**
Aspes Rd. *L12* —4E **59**
Aspinall Pl. *St H* —3D **65**
Aspinall St. *L5* —4D **55**
Aspinall St. *Birk* —2C **96**
Aspinall St. *Prsct* —5D **63**
Aspley Ho. *Wat* —4E **17**
Asquith Av. *Birk* —2B **96**
Asser Rd. *L11* —3E **57**
Assheton Wlk. *Hale V* —5E **149**
Assissian Cres. *Boot* —1E **19**
Aster Cres. *Beech* —5F **167**
Aster Dri. *L33* —5D **15**
Asterfield Av. *Wir* —5E **119**
Aster Rd. *Hay* —1F **49**
Astley Clo. *Wid* —1C **130**
Astley Rd. *L36* —5E **61**
Astmoor. —4F 153
Astmoor Bri. La. *Cas* —5F **153**
Astmoor Ind. Est. *Ast I* —4F **153**
Astmoor La. *Cas* —5F **153**
Astmoor La. *Halt* —4C **152**
Astmoor Rd. *Ast I* —4E **153**
Astmoor Spine Rd. *Ast I* —4A **154**
Aston Clo. *Pren* —1F **117**
Aston Fields Rd. *White I* —1D **175**
Aston Gardens. —4D 175
Aston Grn. *Pres B* —4E **169**
Aston Heath. —3E 175
Aston La. *Pres B* —5E **169**
Aston La. *Sut W & Aston* —2A **174**
Aston La. N. *Run & Pres B* —1E **175**
Aston La. N. *White I* —1E **175**
Aston La. S. *White I* —2E **175**
Aston St. *L19* —2C **144**
Astonwood Rd. *Birk* —1D **119**
Astor St. *L4* —1F **55**
Atheldene Rd. *L4* —1C **56**
Athelstan Clo. *Wir* —1D **163**
Atherton Clo. *L5* —1E **77**
Atherton Ct. *Wall* —3A **52**
Atherton Dri. *Wir* —1A **116**
Atherton Rake. *Boot* —1D **19**
Atherton Rd. *L9* —2C **36**
Atherton St. *St H* —3F **45**
Atherton St. *Prsct* —5D **63**
Atherton St. *Wall* —2A **52**
Athol Clo. *Newt W* —4F **49**
Athol Clo. *Wir* —5E **163**
Athol Dri. *Wir* —1E **171**
Atholl Cres. *L10* —3D **21**
Athol St. *L5* —1B **76**
(Gt. Howard St.)
Athol St. *L5* —1C **76**
(Vauxhall Rd.)
Athol St. *Birk* —2E **97**
Atkinson Gro. *L36* —2F **83**
Atlanta Ct. *L33* —3D **15**
Atlantic Pavilion. *L3* —1C **98** (7C **4**)
Atlantic Rd. *Boot* —5B **34**
Atlantic Way. *Boot* —5E **19**
Atlantic Way. *Brun B* —4D **99**
Atlas Bus. Complex. *Boot* —4A **34**
Atlas Ct. *St H* —5B **46**
Atlas Rd. *Boot* —4B **34**
Atlas St. *St H* —5B **46**
Atterbury Clo. *Wid* —2C **130**
Atterbury St. *L8* —4D **99**
Attlee Rd. *L36* —3A **84**
Attwood St. *L4* —4F **55**
Atwell St. *L6* —2A **78**
Atworth Ter. Will —5A 170
(off Neston Rd.)
Aubourn Clo. *Wid* —1C **130**
Aubrey Ct. *L6* —2A **78**
Aubrey St. *L6* —2F **77**
Auburn Rd. *L13* —5E **57**
Auburn Rd. *Wall* —4A **52**
Aubynes, The. *Wall* —4E **51**
Auckland Gro. *St H* —4D **65**
Auckland Rd. *L18* —4A **102**
Audlem Av. *Pren* —1F **117**
Audlem Clo. *Sut W* —1F **173**
Audley St. *L3* —4E **77** (3H **5**)
Audrey Wlk. *L10* —1B **38**
Aughton Clo. *Bil* —1E **31**
Aughton Ct. *Upt* —4A **94**
Aughton Rd. *Boot* —3D **35**
Augusta Clo. *L13* —4A **80**
August Rd. *L6* —1C **78**
August St. *Boot* —3C **34**
Aurorean Clo. *L27* —3D **105**
Austell Clo. *St H* —1D **47**
Austin Av. *St H* —3C **64**
Austin Clo. *L32* —2D **23**
Austin Rawlinson Sports Cen. —4E 147
Austin St. *Wall* —4A **74**
Autoquest Stadium. —4F 131
Autumn Gro. *Birk* —4E **119**
Autumn Way. *Clo F* —3C **88**
Avalon Ter. *Boot* —4B **34**
Avebury Clo. *Wid* —1E **133**
Avelon Clo. *L31* —2B **6**
Avelon Clo. *Pren* —4D **95**
Avenue, The. *Ecc* —5A **44**
Avenue, The. *L9* —5F **35**
Avenue, The. *Gars* —2E **145**
Avenue, The. *Halew* —5E **127**
Avenue, The. *Huy* —3E **83**
Avenue, The. *Wir* —2C **162**
Avery Ct. *L9* —2F **35**
Avery Cres. *Hay* —1C **48**
Avery Rd. *Hay* —1C **48**
Avery Sq. *Hay* —1C **48**
Aviemore Rd. *L13* —3F **79**
Avis Wlk. *L10* —1B **38**
Avolon Rd. *L12* —1D **81**
Avon. *Wid* —2A **130**
Avon Clo. *Kirk* —3E **55**
Avon Clo. *Kirkby* —4F **15**
Avon Ct. *L23* —5E **9**
Avondale Av. *L31* —2C **12**
Avondale Av. *East* —5E **163**
Avondale Av. *More* —5F **71**
Avondale Dri. *Wid* —3B **130**
Avondale Rd. *L15* —3E **101**
Avondale Rd. *Hay* —1C **48**
Avondale Rd. *Wir* —4B **90**
Avonmore Av. *L18* —1A **124**
Avon Rd. *Bil* —2D **31**
Avon St. *L6* —1B **78**
Avon St. *Birk* —5F **73**
Awelon Clo. *L12* —3B **58**
Axbridge Av. *Sut L* —1D **89**
Axholme Clo. *Wir* —2B **138**
Axholme Rd. *Wir* —1B **138**
Ayala Clo. *L9* —1F **35**
Aycliffe Rd. *St H* —5D **65**
Aycliffe Wlk. *Wid* —4C **130**
Aylesbury Av. *Pren* —2E **117**
Aylesbury Rd. *Wall* —4C **52**
Aylesford Rd. *L13* —3A **80**
Aylsham Clo. *Wid* —5C **108**
Aylsham Dri. *Wir* —2A **94**
Aylton Rd. *L36* —2B **82**
Aylward Pl. *Boot* —4B **34**
Aynsley Ct. *St H* —5B **64**
Ayr Rd. *L4* —1A **56**
Ayrshire Gdns. *St H* —1E **65**
Ayrshire Rd. *L4* —3C **56**
Aysgarth Av. *L12* —5C **58**
Aysgarth Rd. *Wall* —5F **51**
Azalea Gro. *L26* —2D **127**
Azalea Gro. *Beech* —1F **173**

Babbacombe Rd. *L16* —3E **103**
Bk. Barlow La. *L4* —3E **55**
Bk. Beau St. *L5* —2E **77** (1G **5**)
Bk. Bedford St. *L7* —1F **99**
Bk. Belmont Rd. *L6* —1B **78**
Bk. Berry St. *L1* —1E **99** (7G **5**)
Bk. Blackfield Ter. *L4* —4D **55**
Bk. Bold St. *L1* —5E **77** (6F **5**)
Bk. Boundary Clo. *L5* —5D **55**

Bk. Bridport St. *L3* —4G **5**
Back Broadway. *L11* —2E **57**
Bk. Canning St. *L8* —1E **99**
Bk. Catharine St. *L8* —1F **99**
Bk. Chadwick Mt. *L5* —4E **55**
Bk. Chatham Pl. *L7* —5A **78**
Bk. Colquitt St. *L1* —1D **99** (7G **5**)
Bk. Commutation Row. *L3* —4E **77** (3G **5**)
Bk. Egerton St. N. *L8* —2F **99**
Bk. Egerton St. S. *L8* —2F **99**
Bk. Falkner St. S. *L8* —1F **99**
Backford Clo. *Brook* —5C **168**
Backford Clo. *Pren* —1E **117**
Backford Rd. *Wir* —2D **137**
Bk. Gillmoss La. *L11* —2C **38**
Bk. Granton Rd. *L5* —5A **56**
Bk. Guilford St. *L6* —2F **77**
Bk. Hadfield Pl. L25 —2A ***126***
(off Church Rd.)
Bk. High St. *Run* —4A **152**
Bk. Holland Pl. *L7* —5B **78**
Bk. Hope Pl. *L1* —1E **99** (7H **5**)
Bk. Huskisson St. *L8* —2F **99**
Bk. Irvine St. *L7* —5A **78**
Bk. Kelvin Gro. *L8* —3A **100**
Bk. Knight St. *L1* —1E **99** (7G **5**)
Back La. *Augh* —1E **7**
Back La. *Cros* —2E **9**
Back La. *Cuer* —2F **133**
Back La. *Thor* —3B **10**
Back La. *Btnwd* —3D **69**
Bk. Langham St. *L4* —3F **55**
Bk. Leeds St. *L3* —3B **76** (2B **4**)
Bk. Legh St. *Newt W* —5F **49**
Bk. Lime St. *L1* —5F **5**
Bk. Lit. Canning St. *L8* —2F **99**
Bk. Lord St. *L1* —5C **76** (6D **4**)
Bk. Market St. *Newt W* —4F **49**
Bk. Maryland St. *L1* —1E **99** (7H **5**)
Bk. Menai St. *Birk* —3C **96**
Bk. Mersey Vw. *L22* —3C **16**
Bk. Mount St. *Wat* —4D **17**
Bk. Mt. Vernon Vw. *L7* —4A **78**
Bk. Mulberry St. *L7* —1F **99** (7J **5**)
Bk. Oliver St. *Birk* —3E **97**
Bk. Orford St. *L15* —1F **101**
Bk. Penny La. *C Grn* —2D **69**
Bk. Percy St. *L8* —2F **99**
Bk. Pickop St. *L3* —3C **76** (3D **4**)
Bk. Price St. *Birk* —2D **97**
Bk. Renshaw St. *L1* —5E **77** (6G **5**)
Bk. Rockfield Rd. *L4* —4F **55**
Bk. St Bride St. *L8* —1F **99**
Bk. Sandon St. *L8* —2F **99**
Bk. Sandown La. *L15* —1F **101**
Bk. Sea Vw. *Wir* —4B **90**
Bk. Seel St. *L1* —1D **99** (7F **5**)
Bk. Sir Howard St. *L8* —1F **99**
Bk. South Rd. *L22* —4E **17**
Bk. Stanley Rd. *Boot* —5C **34**
Bk. Towerlands St. *L7* —5B **78**
Bk. Wellesley Rd. *L8* —5A **100**
Bk. Westminster Rd. *L4* —3E **55**
Bk. Windsor Vw. *L8* —2B **100**
Bk. Winstanley Rd. *L22* —3E **17**
Bk. York Ter. *L5* —5E **55**
Badbury Clo. *Hay* —1D **49**
Badby Wood. *L33* —1F **23**
Baden Rd. *L13* —3B **80**
Bader Clo. *Wir* —4F **137**
Badger Clo. *Pal* —4A **168**
Badger's Set. *Wir* —3D **135**
Badger Way. *Pren* —4E **117**
Badminton St. *L8* —1F **121**
Baffin Clo. *Wir* —2A **72**
Bagnall St. *L4* —4F **55**
Bagot St. *L15* —2D **101**
Baguley Av. *Wid* —2A **150**
Bahama Clo. *Hay* —1D **49**
Bahama Rd. *Hay* —1D **49**
Bailey Ct. *Boot* —1E **35**
Bailey Dri. *Boot* —2E **35**
Baileys Clo. *Wid* —4A **110**
Bailey's La. *Hale V* —5A **148**
Bailey's La. *Halew* —4A **128**
(in two parts)
Bailey's La. *Speke* —4A **146**
Bailey St. *L1* —1D **99**
Bainton Clo. *L32* —1A **40**
Bainton Rd. *L32* —1A **40**
Baird Av. *Boot* —3A **34**
Baker Rd. *West P* —3D **165**
Bakers Grn. Rd. *L36* —2E **83**
Baker St. *L6* —3A **78**
Baker St. *L36* —4A **84**
Baker St. *St H* —5C **46**
Baker Way. *L6* —3A **78**
Bakewell Gro. *L9* —1B **36**
Bakewell Rd. *Btnwd* —4F **69**
Bala Gro. *Wall* —3A **74**
Bala St. *L4* —5B **56**
Balcarres Av. *L18* —4F **101**
Baldwin Av. *L16* —1E **103**
Baldwin St. *St H* —4A **46**
Bales, The. *Boot* —1A **20**
Balfe St. *L21* —2A **34**
Balfour Av. *Boot* —3B **34**
Balfour Rd. *Boot* —3B **34**
Balfour Rd. *Pren* —4B **96**
Balfour Rd. *Wall* —3A **74**
Balfour St. *L4* —4F **55**
Balfour St. *St H* —5D **45**
Balfour St. *Run* —1F **165**
Balham Clo. *Wid* —5A **110**
Balharry Av. *Hay* —1F **49**
Balker Dri. *St H* —3F **45**
Ballantrae Rd. *L18* —1B **124**
Ballantyne Dri. *Pren* —5C **72**
Ballantyne Gro. *Boot* —2E **35**
Ballantyne Gro. *L13* —4E **57**
Ballantyne Pl. *L13* —5E **57**
Ballantyne Rd. *L13* —5E **57**
Ballantyne Wlk. *Pren* —5C **72**
Ballard Rd. *Wir* —3F **113**
Ball Av. *Wall* —3A **52**
Balliol Clo. *Pren* —5C **72**
Balliol Ct. *Boot* —1C **54**
Balliol Gro. *L23* —3B **16**
Balliol Rd. *Boot* —1C **54**
Balliol Rd. E. *Boot* —1D **55**
Ball o' Ditton. —3D 131
Ball Path. *Wid* —3F **131**
Ball Path Way. *Wid* —3E **131**
Ball's Rd. *Pren* —5B **96**
Balls Rd. E. *Birk* —4C **96**
Ball St. *St H* —4D **47**
Balmer St. *That H* —3D **65**
Balmoral Av. *L23* —2E **17**
Balmoral Av. *St H* —4C **66**
Balmoral Clo. *L33* —5E **15**
Balmoral Ct. *L13* —1E **79**
Balmoral Gdns. *Pren* —3F **117**
Balmoral Rd. *Walt* —2A **36**
Balmoral Rd. *Fair* —2C **78**
Balmoral Rd. *Wall* —2B **52**
Balmoral Rd. *Wid* —5A **110**
Balm St. *L7* —4B **78**
Balniel St. *Clo F* —3D **89**
Balsham Clo. *L25* —5C **126**
Baltic Rd. *Boot* —5B **34**
Baltic St. *L4* —4F **55**
Baltimore St. *L1* —1E **99** (7H **5**)
Bamboo Clo. *L27* —3E **105**
Bamford Clo. *Run* —3C **166**
Bampton Av. *St H* —4B **30**
Bampton Rd. *L16* —1D **103**
Banbury Av. *L25* —2C **126**
Banbury Way. *Pren* —2E **117**
Bancroft Clo. *L25* —4C **126**
Bancroft Rd. *Wid* —2D **133**
Bandon Clo. *Hale V* —5D **149**
Banff Av. *Wir* —5D **163**
Bangor Rd. *Wall* —5D **51**
Bangor St. *L5* —1C **76**
Bankburn Rd. *L13* —5E **57**
Bank Dene. *Birk* —4A **120**
Bankes La. *West & West P* —4E **165**
(in two parts)
Bankfield Ct. *L13* —1F **79**
Bankfield Rd. *L13* —5F **57**
Bankfield Rd. *Wid* —3B **130**
Bankfield St. *L20* —3B **54**
Bankhall La. *L20* —3C **54**
Bankhall St. *L20* —3C **54**
Bankland Rd. *L13* —1F **79**
Bank La. *Mell & L33* —3C **14**
Bank Rd. *Boot* —5B **34**
Bank's Av. *Wir* —3D **91**
Bankside. *Pres B* —3E **169**
Bankside Rd. *Birk* —4F **119**
Bank's La. *Gars* —3D **145**
Banks La. *Speke* —5F **145**
Bank's Rd. *L19* —2C **144**
Banks Rd. *Hes* —3D **157**
Banks Rd. *W Kir* —4A **112**
Banks, The. *Wall* —4E **51**
Bank St. *Newt W* —5F **49**
Bank St. *St H* —5E **45**
Bank St. *Birk* —3E **97**
Bank St. *Wid* —3A **152**
Bank's Way. *L19* —3D **145**
Bankville Rd. *Birk* —1D **119**
Banner Hey. *Whis* —5D **85**
Bannerman St. *L7* —1C **100**
Banner St. *L15* —2D **101**
Banner St. *St H* —5F **45**
Banner Wlk. St H —5E ***45***
(off Banner St.)
Banning Clo. *Birk* —2D **97**
Banstead Gro. *L15* —2B **102**
Barbara Av. *L10* —1A **38**
Barbara St. *Clo F* —3E **89**
Barberry Clo. *Wir* —1B **92**
Barberry Cres. *Boot* —1A **20**
Barber St. *St H* —4C **46**
Barbour Dri. *Boot* —2E **35**
Barbrook Way. *L9* —5B **36**
Barchester Dri. *L17* —3C **122**
Barclay St. *L8* —5F **99**
Barcombe Rd. *Wir* —1D **159**
Bardley Cres. *Tarb G* —2A **106**
Bardon Clo. *L25* —4C **104**
Bardsay Rd. *L4* —2F **55**
Barford Clo. *Pren* —3B **94**
Barford Grange. *Will* —5B **170**
Barford Rd. *Hunts X* —1B **146**
Barford Rd. *Huy* —5F **61**
Barington Dri. *Murd* —3E **169**
Barkbeth Rd. *L36* —1C **82**
Barkbeth Wlk. *L36* —1C **82**
Barkeley Dri. *L21* —2F **33**
Barker Clo. *L36* —1F **105**
Barker La. *Wir* —2C **114**
(in three parts)
Barker Rd. *Wir* —1F **137**
Barker's Hollow Rd. *Dut & Pres H* —4F **169**
Barkerville Clo. *L13* —4D **57**
Barker Way. *L6* —1B **78**
Barkhill Rd. *L17* —3F **123**
Barkin Cen., The. *Wid* —4C **132**
Barkis Clo. *L8* —4F **99**
Bark Rd. *L21* —4C **18**
Barleyfield. *Wir* —3F **137**
Barlow Av. *Wir* —1A **142**
Barlow Gro. *St H* —1A **68**

Barlow La. *L4*—3E **55**
Barlow's Clo. *L9*—5D **21**
Barlow's La. *L9*—5D **21**
Barlow St. *L4*—3E **55**
Barmouth Rd. *Wall*—5D **51**
Barmouth Way. *L5*—5C **54**
Barnacre La. *Wir*—3C **92**
Barnard Rd. *Pren*—4B **96**
Barn Clo. *Boot*—1A **20**
Barncroft. *Nort*—2D **169**
Barncroft Pl. *L23*—4E **9**
Barn Cft. Rd. *L26*—5A **128**
Barncroft, The. *Wir*—5D **93**
Barndale Rd. *L18*—5F **101**
Barnes Clo. *Wid*—2D **133**
Barnes Dri. *L31*—3C **6**
Barnes Grn. *Wir*—5A **142**
Barnes Rd. *Wid*—2C **132**
Barnes St. *L6*—1A **78**
Barneston Rd. *Wid*—1E **133**
Barnet Clo. *L7*—1C **100**
Barnett Av. *Newt W*—5E **49**
Barnfield Av. *Murd*—5C **168**
Barnfield Clo. *Boot*—3E **19**
Barnfield Clo. *L12*—5B **58**
Barnfield Clo. *Wir*—2E **91**
Barnfield Dri. *L12*—5B **58**
Barnham Clo. *L24*—3B **146**
Barnham Dri. *L16*—2E **103**
Barn Hey. *Wir*—1A **112**
Barn Hey Cres. *Wir*—3F **91**
Barn Hey Grn. *L12*—5B **58**
Barn Hey Rd. *L33*—3A **24**
Barnhill Rd. *L15*—3A **102**
Barnhurst Clo. *L16*—2E **103**
Barnhurst Rd. *L16*—2E **103**
Barn La. *Btnwd*—5F **69**
Barnmeadow Rd. *L25*—4A **104**
Barnsbury Rd. *L4*—1B **56**
Barnsdale Av. *Wir*—2B **138**
Barnside Ct. *L16*—2E **103**
Barnston. —3C 138
Barnston La. *Wir*—5E **71**
Barnston Rd. *L9*—1A **36**
Barnston Rd. *Hes & Thing*—5B **116**
Barnston Towers Clo. *Wir*—2C **158**
Barnstream Clo. *L27*—3C **104**
Barn St. *Wid*—1A **152**
Barnwell Av. *Wall*—1B **74**
Barnwood Rd. *L36*—2B **82**
Baroncroft Rd. *L25*—5F **103**
Barons Clo. *Cas*—1F **167**
Barons Clo. *Wid*—4C **130**
Barons Hey. *L28*—3F **59**
Barren Gro. *Pren*—5B **96**
Barrington Rd. *L15*—3E **101**
Barrington Rd. *Wall*—3C **74**
Barrow Clo. *L12*—2C **58**
Barrowfield Rd. *Ecc*—3A **44**
Barrows Cotts. *Whis*—3E **85**
Barrow's Green. —5E 111
Barrows Grn. La. *Wid*—2E **133**
Barrow's Row. *Wid*—5B **110**
Barrow St. *St H*—5A **46**
Barr St. *L20*—3C **54**
Barrymore Rd. *L13*—3F **79**
Barrymore Rd. *Run*—3B **166**
Barrymore Way. *Wir*—4B **162**
Bartholomew Clo. *Rain*—5E **87**
Bartlegate Clo. *Brook*—5B **168**
Bartlett St. *L15*—2D **101**
Barton Clo. *L21*—3A **18**
Barton Clo. *St H*—4F **45**
Barton Clo. *Murd*—3D **169**
Barton Clo. *Wir*—5A **90**
Barton Clough. *Bil*—1E **31**
Barton Hey Dri. *Wir*—3C **134**
Barton Rd. *L9*—4F **35**
Barton Rd. *Wir*—5A **90**
Barwell Av. *St H*—2C **46**
Basil Clo. *L16*—1D **103**
Basildon Clo. *St H*—4E **65**
Basil Rd. *L16*—1D **103**
Basing St. *L19*—5C **124**
Baskervyle Clo. *Wir*—4A **158**
Baskervyle Rd. *Wir*—4A **158**
Basnett St. *L1*—5D **77** (5E **5**)
Bassendale Rd. *Croft B*—5E **143**
Bassenthwaite Av. *L33*—1D **23**
Bassenthwaite Av. *St H*—5A **30**
Bassenthwaite Av. *Pren*—4D **95**
Batchelor St. *L2*—4C **76** (4D **4**)
Bates Cres. *St H*—3D **65**
Batey Av. *Rain*—2B **86**
Batherton Clo. *Wid*—5B **132**
Bathgate Way. *L33*—4D **15**
Bath St. *L3*—4B **76** (2A **4**)
Bath St. *St H*—5F **45**
Bath St. *Wat*—5D **17**
Bath St. *Wir*—2B **142**
Bathurst Rd. *L19*—5B **124**
Batley St. *L13*—3A **80**
Battenberg St. *L7*—4A **78**
Battersea Ct. *Wid*—1E **131**
Battery Clo. *L17*—2C **122**
Baucher Dri. *Boot*—1E **35**
Baumville Dri. *Wir*—5F **141**
Baxter Clo. *Murd*—3D **169**
(in two parts)
Baxters La. *St H*—3D **67**
Baxters La. Ind. Est. *St H*—3D **67**
Baycliffe Clo. *Beech*—5D **167**
Baycliff Rd. *L12*—3E **59**
Bayfield Rd. *L19*—5A **124**
Bayhorse La. *L3*—4F **77** (3J **5**)
Baysdale Clo. *L8*—5F **99**
Bayswater Clo. *Run*—3F **155**
Bayswater Ct. *Wall*—5D **51**
Bayswater Gdns. *Wall*—4D **51**
Bayswater Rd. *Wall*—5D **51**
Baythorne Rd. *L4*—1C **56**
Baytree Rd. *Birk*—1E **119**
Baytree Rd. *Wir*—4F **113**
Bay Vw. Dri. *Wall*—4D **51**
Bayvil Clo. *Murd*—3E **169**
Beach Bank. *L22*—3C **16**
Beachcroft Rd. *Wir*—2E **91**
Beach Gro. *Wall*—4C **52**
Beach Lawn. *L22*—4C **16**
Beach Rd. *L21*—5A **18**
(in two parts)
Beach Rd. *Wir*—5A **90**
Beach Wlk. *Wir*—1B **134**
Beacon Ct. *L5*—5F **55**
Beacon Dri. *Wir*—4C **112**
Beacon Gro. *St H*—2D **47**
Beacon Hill Vw. *West P*—2D **165**
Beacon Ho. *L5*—2E **77**
Beacon La. *L5*—5F **55**
Beacon La. *Wir*—2A **158**
Beacon Pde. *Wir*—2A **158**
Beaconsfield. *Prsct*—5D **63**
Beaconsfield Clo. *Birk*—1E **119**
Beaconsfield Cres. *Wid*—5A **110**
Beaconsfield Gro. *Wid*—5B **110**
Beaconsfield Rd. *S'frth*—1F **33**
Beaconsfield Rd. *Dent G*—3C **44**
Beaconsfield Rd. *Run*—2E **165**
Beaconsfield Rd. *Wid*—1B **132**
Beaconsfield Rd. *Wir*—5B **120**
Beaconsfield Rd. *Wltn*—1E **125**
Beaconsfield St. *L8*—3A **100**
Beacons, The. *Wir*—3A **158**
Beames Clo. *L7*—5C **78**
Beamont St. *Wid*—3A **152**
Beatles Story, The. —1C 98
Beatrice Av. *Wir*—5E **119**
Beatrice St. *Boot*—2D **55**
Beattock Clo. *L33*—4D **15**
Beatty Clo. *Whis*—4D **85**
Beatty Clo. *Wir*—3C **134**
Beatty Rd. *L13*—3A **80**
Beauclair Dri. *L15*—2B **102**
Beaufort Clo. *Run*—3B **166**
Beaufort Clo. *Wid*—4A **130**
Beaufort Dri. *Wall*—1E **73**
Beaufort Rd. *Birk*—5F **73**
Beaufort St. *L8*—3E **99**
(Hill St.)
Beaufort St. *L8*—4E **99**
(Northumberland St.)
Beaufort St. *L8*—3E **99**
(Stanhope St.)
Beaufort St. *St H*—2C **66**
Beau La. *L3*—2E **77** (1G **5**)
Beaumaris Ct. *Pren*—4B **96**
Beaumaris Dri. *Hes*—1B **138**
Beaumaris Rd. *Wall*—5D **51**
Beaumaris St. *L20*—3B **54**
(in two parts)
Beaumont Av. *St H*—4C **44**
Beaumont Dri. *L10*—4E **21**
Beaumont St. *L8*—2B **100**
Beau St. *L3*—2E **77** (1G **5**)
Beauworth Av. *Wir*—1C **114**
Beaver Gro. *L9*—2A **36**
Bebington. —5B 120
Bebington Rd. *Beb*—1A **142**
Bebington Rd. *Birk*—2D **119**
Bebington Rd. *New F & Port S*
(in two parts) —5A **120**
Bechers. *Wid*—1B **130**
Bechers Dri. *Ain R*—3B **20**
Bechers Row. *L9*—2F **35**
Beck Clo. *L10*—1B **38**
Beckenham Av. *L18*—4F **101**
Beckenham Rd. *Wall*—2B **52**
Becket St. *L4*—3D **55**
(in two parts)
Beckett Clo. *L33*—5C **24**
Beckett Gro. *Wir*—5D **119**
Beck Gro. *St H*—5B **30**
Beck Rd. *Boot*—3C **34**
Beckwith St. *L1*—1C **98** (7E **4**)
Beckwith St. *Birk*—1B **96**
Beckwith St. E. *Birk*—2D **97**
Becky St. *L6*—1B **78**
Becontree Rd. *L12*—2D **81**
Bective St. *L7*—1C **100**
Bedale Wlk. *L33*—1F **23**
Bedburn Dri. *L36*—3A **82**
Bede Clo. *L33*—4E **15**
Bedford Av. *L31*—4E **13**
Bedford Av. *Birk*—3E **119**
Bedford Clo. *Edg H*—1F **99**
Bedford Clo. *Huy*—3A **84**
Bedford Ct. *Birk*—2F **119**
Bedford Dri. *Birk*—3D **119**
Bedford Pl. *Boot*—2B **54**
Bedford Pl. *L21*—1F **33**
Bedford Pl. *Birk*—2A **120**
Bedford Rd. *Boot & L4*—2C **54**
Bedford Rd. *Birk*—2F **119**
Bedford Rd. *Wall*—5B **52**
Bedford Rd. E. *Birk*—2A **120**
Bedford St. *Parr I & St H*—1D **67**
Bedford St. N. *L7*—5F **77**
Bedford St. S. *L7*—1F **99**
(in two parts)
Bedford Wlk. *L7*—1F **99**
Beecham Clo. *L36*—5D **83**
Beech Av. *Clo F*—2C **88**
Beech Av. *Cros*—4A **10**
Beech Av. *Ecc P*—4F **63**
Beech Av. *Mell*—2A **22**
Beech Av. *Aig*—2A **122**
Beech Av. *Frod*—5C **172**

Beech Av. *Hay* —1F **49**
Beech Av. *Hes* —3A **138**
Beech Av. *Upt* —3D **93**
Beechbank Rd. *L18* —4E **101**
Beechburn Cres. *L36* —3B **82**
Beechburn Rd. *L36* —3A **82**
Beech Clo. *Kirkby* —2C **22**
Beech Clo. *W Der* —5D **39**
Beech Ct. *L18* —1C **124**
Beech Ct. *Birk* —5D **97**
Beechcroft. *L31* —1C **12**
Beechcroft Rd. *Wall* —4C **74**
Beechdale Rd. *L18* —5A **102**
Beechdene Rd. *L4* —4B **56**
Beeches, The. *L18* —4D **103**
Beeches, The. *Birk* —3F **119**
Beeches, The. *Wir* —3E **71**
Beechfield. *L31* —1E **13**
Beechfield Clo. *Wir* —3A **158**
Beechfield Rd. *L18* —5D **103**
Beech Grn. *L12* —3A **58**
Beech Gro. *Boot* —3A **20**
Beech Gro. *S'frth* —2F **33**
Beech Gro. *Walt* —2B **36**
Beech Hey La. *Will* —4B **170**
Beechill Clo. *L25* —5C **104**
Beech La. *L18* —4C **102**
Beech Lawn. *L19* —5F **123**
Beech Lodge. *Pren* —4D **95**
Beech Meadows. *Prsct* —1A **84**
Beech Mt. *L7* —4C **78**
Beech Pk. *Cros* —4F **9**
Beech Pk. *W Der* —5A **58**
Beech Rd. *Walt* —1A **56**
Beech Rd. *Beb* —5F **119**
Beech Rd. *Birk* —5C **96**
Beech Rd. *Hes* —2C **158**
Beech Rd. *Huy* —5E **83**
Beech Rd. *Run* —2C **166**
Beech Rd. *Sut W* —1B **174**
Beech St. *Boot* —4C **34**
Beech St. *L7* —4C **78**
Beech St. *St H* —3D **65**
Beech Ter. *L7* —4C **78**
Beech Ter. *Wid* —3A **152**
Beechtree Rd. *L15* —5B **80**
Beechurst Clo. *L25* —4B **104**
Beechurst Rd. *L25* —4B **104**
Beechwalk, The. *L14* —2B **80**
Beechway. *L31* —1B **14**
Beechway. *Wir* —4F **141**
Beechway Av. *L31* —1B **14**
Beechwood. —5D 167
(Runcorn)
Beechwood. —1C 94
(Wallasey)
Beechwood Av. *L26* —5E **127**
Beechwood Av. *Beech* —4C **166**
Beechwood Av. *Wall* —1E **73**
Beechwood Clo. *Clo F* —2C **88**
Beechwood Clo. *L19* —5F **123**
Beechwood Ct. *L31* —1E **13**
Beechwood Ct. *Wir* —3B **116**
Beechwood Dri. *Pren* —2C **94**
Beechwood Gdns. *L19* —5F **123**
Beechwood Grn. *L19* —5A **124**
Beechwood Gro. *Prsct* —2E **85**
Beechwood Rd. *Lith* —2B **34**
Beechwood Rd. *Cress* —5F **123**
Beechwood Rd. *Wir* —2C **162**
Beesands Clo. *L27* —5F **105**
Beesley Rd. *Prsct* —5C **62**
Beeston Clo. *Pren* —3C **94**
Beeston Ct. *Mnr P* —3C **154**
Beeston Dri. *Boot* —5B **12**
Beeston Dri. *Wir* —3F **137**
Beeston Gro. *L19* —5A **124**
Beeston St. *L4* —2E **55**
Begonia Gdns. *St H* —4A **68**
Beilby Rd. *Hay* —1F **49**
Beldale Pk. *L32* —1B **22**
Beldon Cres. *L36* —3B **82**
Belem Clo. *L17* —4C **100**
Belem Tower. *L17* —4B **100**
Belfast Rd. *L13* —3B **80**
Belfield Cres. *L36* —5E **83**
Belfield Dri. *Pren* —1B **118**
Belford Dri. *Wir* —1B **92**
Belfort Rd. *L25* —5B **104**
Belfry Clo. *L12* —5E **59**
Belfry Clo. *Wir* —5B **70**
Belgrave Av. *Wall* —2C **74**
Belgrave Clo. *Wid* —1E **133**
Belgrave Rd. *S'frth* —1F **33**
Belgrave Rd. *Aig* —1B **122**
Belgrave St. *Wall* —1B **74**
Belgravia Ct. *Wid* —1F **131**
Belhaven Rd. *L18* —4F **101**
Bellair Av. *L23* —1A **18**
Bellairs Rd. *L11* —3E **57**
Bellamy Rd. *L4* —1E **55**
Bell Clo. *L36* —1F **105**
Belldene Gro. *Wir* —5F **137**
Bellefield Av. *L12* —5B **58**
Belle Va. Rd. *L25* —5B **104**
Belle Va. Shop. Cen. *L25* —3B **104**
Belle Vale Swimming Pool. —4C 104
Belle Vw. Rd. *Wall* —4D **75**
Belle Vue Rd. *L25* —5B **104**
Bellew Rd. *L11* —4F **57**
Bellfield Cres. *Wall* —3A **52**
Bellgreen Rd. *L11* —1A **58**
Bell Ho. Rd. *Wid* —3C **132**
Bellingham Dri. *Run* —2A **166**
Bellini Clo. *L21* —2A **34**
Bellis Gro. *L33* —5D **15**
Bell La. *Rain & Sut M* —4A **88**
Bellmore St. *L19* —5B **124**
Bell Rd. *Wall* —3D **75**
Bell's Clo. *L31* —3B **6**
Bells La. *L31* —4A **6**
Bell St. *L13* —3A **80**
Bellward Clo. *Wir* —5F **141**
Belmont. *Birk* —4C **96**
Belmont Av. *Wir* —1C **162**
Belmont Dri. *L6* —1C **78**
Belmont Dri. *Wir* —4A **138**
Belmont Gro. *L6* —1B **78**
Belmont Gro. *Pren* —4C **96**
Belmont Pl. *L19* —1C **144**
Belmont Rd. *L6* —1B **78**
Belmont Rd. *Wall* —2B **52**
Belmont Rd. *Wid* —2D **133**
Belmont Rd. *Wir* —3B **112**
Belmont St. *St H* —5D **45**
Belmont Vw. L6 —1C 78
(off Bk. Belmont Rd.)
Beloe St. *L8* —5F **99**
Belper St. *L19* —1B **144**
Belsford Way. *L24* —3B **146**
Belston Rd. *L16* —1C **102**
Belton Rd. *L36* —5D **61**
(in two parts)
Belvedere Av. *Sut L* —5D **67**
Belvedere Clo. *Frod* —4C **172**
Belvedere Clo. *Prsct* —4E **63**
Belvedere Ct. Wir —3A 116
(off Childwall Grn.)
Belvidere Pk. *L23* —2E **17**
Belvidere Rd. *Cros* —2D **17**
Belvidere Rd. *Prin P* —4A **100**
Belvidere Rd. *Wall* —5F **51**
Belvoir Rd. *L18* —4C **124**
Belvoir Rd. *Wid* —3B **132**
Bembridge Clo. *Wid* —5F **109**
Bempton Rd. *L17* —2B **122**
Benbow St. *Boot* —1B **54**
Benedict Ct. *Boot* —2D **55**
Benedict St. *Boot* —2D **55**
Bengel St. *L7* —4A **78**
Benledi St. *L5* —1D **77**
Benmore Rd. *L18* —2A **124**
Bennet's La. *Wir* —1E **91**
Bennett Clo. *Will* —5A **170**
Bennetts Hill. *Pren* —5B **96**
Bennetts La. *Wid* —3E **133**
Bennett St. *L19* —1C **144**
Bennett Wlk. *Wir* —4F **137**
Ben Nevis Rd. *Birk* —2D **119**
Bennison Dri. *L19* —5A **124**
Benson Clo. *Wir* —5F **93**
Benson St. *L1* —5E **77** (6G **5**)
Bentfield. *L17* —4E **123**
Bentfield Clo. *Wir* —5D **119**
Bentfield Gdns. *Wir* —5D **119**
Bentham Clo. *Pren* —1E **117**
Bentham Dri. *L16* —1D **103**
Bentinck Clo. *Birk* —3C **96**
Bentinck Pl. *Birk* —3C **96**
Bentinck St. *L5* —1B **76**
Bentinck St. *St H* —2D **67**
Bentinck St. *Birk* —3C **96**
Bentinck St. *Run* —4F **151**
Bentley Rd. *L8* —3B **100**
Bentley Rd. *Pren* —5B **96**
Bentley Rd. *Wir* —2F **137**
Bentley St. *Clo F* —2C **88**
Benton Clo. *L5* —5D **55**
Bent Way. *Wir* —1A **158**
Benty Clo. *Wir* —3E **141**
Benty Farm Gro. *Wir* —2A **138**
Benty Heath La. *Will* —2A **170**
Benwick Rd. *L32* —3B **22**
Berbice Rd. *L18* —3A **102**
Beresford Av. *Wir* —5A **120**
Beresford Clo. *Pren* —4A **96**
Beresford Rd. *L8* —5F **99**
Beresford Rd. *Pren* —4F **95**
Beresford Rd. *Wall* —4F **51**
Beresford St. *Boot* —2B **54**
Beresford St. *L5* —2E **77** (1H **5**)
Beresford St. *St H* —4E **65**
Bergen Clo. *Boot* —1E **55**
Berkeley Av. *Pren* —3F **117**
Berkeley Ct. *Mnr P* —3D **155**
Berkeley Ct. Wir —3A 116
(off Childwall Grn.)
Berkeley Dri. *Wall* —4C **52**
Berkeley Rd. *Cros* —5C **8**
Berkeswell Rd. *L11* —2A **58**
Berkley Av. *W Der* —3D **59**
Berkley St. *L8* —2F **99**
Berkshire Gdns. *St H* —1E **65**
Bermuda Rd. *Wir* —5C **70**
Bernard Av. *Wall* —4C **52**
Berner's Rd. *L19* —5B **124**
Berner St. *Birk* —1D **97**
Berrington Av. *L25* —2F **125**
Berringtons La. *Rainf* —3B **28**
Berry Hill Av. *Know* —5C **40**
Berrylands Clo. *Wir* —5D **71**
Berrylands Rd. *Wir* —4D **71**
Berry Rd. *Wid* —3D **131**
Berrys La. *St H* —2F **67**
Berry St. *Boot* —5B **34**
Berry St. *L1* —1E **99** (7G **5**)
Berry St. Ind. Est. *Boot* —5B **34**
Berrywood Dri. *Whis* —4F **85**
Bertha Gdns. *Birk* —1F **95**
Bertha St. *Birk* —1F **95**
Bertram Dri. *Wir* —3C **90**
Bertram Dri. N. *Wir* —3D **91**
Bertram Rd. *L17* —5C **100**
Bertram St. *Newt W* —5F **49**
Berwick Av. *Wir* —1E **171**
Berwick Clo. *L6* —2B **78**
Berwick Clo. *Pren* —3C **94**

Berwick Clo. Wir —1B 92
Berwick Dri. L23 —5C 8
Berwick St. L6 —2B 78
Berwyn Av. Hoy —4C 90
Berwyn Av. Thing —1A 138
Berwyn Boulevd. Wir —4E 119
Berwyn Dri. Wir —5A 138
Berwyn Gro. St H —5F 47
Berwyn Rd. L4 —3C 56
Berwyn Rd. Wall —1C 74
Beryl Rd. Pren —4C 94
Beryl St. L13 —5A 80
Beryl Wlk. L10 —1B 38
Besford Ho. L25 —4B 104
Besford Rd. L25 —4B 104
Bessborough Rd. Pren —5B 96
Bessbrook Rd. L17 —2D 123
Bessemer St. L8 —5F 99
Beta Clo. Wir —5A 120
Betchworth Cres. Beech —4D 167
Bethany Clo. Hay —1A 48
Bethany Cres. Wir —2F 141
Betjeman Gro. L16 —1E 103
Betony Clo. L26 —3E 127
Bettisfield Av. Wir —5D 163
Betula Clo. L9 —4B 36
Beulah Av. Bil —1D 31
Bevan Clo. That H —5D 65
Bevan's La. L12 —4C 58
Beverley Dri. Wir —4B 158
Beverley Gdns. Wir —1B 138
Beverley Rd. L15 —3A 102
Beverley Rd. Wall —5F 51
Beverley Rd. Wir —4B 120
Beversbrook Rd. L11 —1B 58
Bevington Bush. L3 —3D 77 (1E 5)
Bevington Hill. L3 —2D 77
Bevington St. L3 —2D 77
Bewey Clo. L8 —5E 99
Bewley Dri. L32 —4D 23
Bewsey St. St H —2D 65
Bexhill Clo. Speke —3B 146
Bianca St. Boot —2C 54
Bibbys La. Boot —3A 34
Bibby St. L13 —3F 79
Bickerstaffe St. L3 —3E 77 (1H 5)
Bickerstaffe St. St H —5A 46
Bickerton Av. Wir —4D 119
Bickerton St. L17 —1C 122
Bickley Clo. Run —1C 166
Bidder St. L3 —3E 77 (1H 5)
Bideford Av. Sut L —1C 88
Bidston. —1D 95
Bidston Av. St H —3D 47
Bidston Av. Birk —2F 95
Bidston Av. Wall —5E 51
Bidston By-Pass. Wir —5B 72
Bidston Ct. Pren —2E 95
Bidston Golf Course. —3C 72
Bidston Grn. Ct. Pren —1C 94
Bidston Grn. Dri. Pren —1C 94
Bidston Ind. Est. Wall —3D 73
Bidston Link Rd. Pren —4D 73
Bidston Moss. Wall —3D 73
Bidston Moss Nature Reserve. —3C 72
Bidston Observatory. —1D 95
Bidston Rd. L4 —3B 56
Bidston Rd. Pren —3E 95
Bidston Sta. App. Pren —4C 72
Bidston Vw. Pren —5C 72
Bidston Village Rd. Pren —5B 72
Bidston Way. St H —3D 47
Bigdale Dri. L33 —2F 23
Bigham Rd. L6 —3C 78
Biglands Dri. L36 —1F 105
Big Mdw. Rd. Wir —5A 94
Billinge Cres. St H —2D 47
Billingham Rd. St H —4D 65
Billings Clo. L5 —5C 54
Billington Rd. Wid —1B 130
Bilston Rd. L17 —4E 123
Bilton Clo. Wid —2E 133
Bingley Rd. L4 —4B 56
Binns Rd. L7 & L13 —4E 79
Binns Rd. Ind. Est. L13 —5F 79
Binns Way. L13 —5F 79
Binsey Clo. Wir —4D 93
Birbeck Rd. L33 —2A 24
Birbeck Wlk. L33 —2A 24
Birchall St. L20 —4C 54
Birch Av. L9 —2B 36
Birch Av. St H —2F 45
Birch Av. Wir —3D 93
Birch Clo. Mag —1F 13
Birch Clo. Pren —1B 118
Birch Clo. Whis —2E 85
Birch Ct. L8 —5A 100
(off Weller Way)
Birch Cres. Newt W —4F 49
Birchdale Clo. Wir —4D 93
Birchdale Rd. Walt —4A 36
Birchdale Rd. Wat —3D 17
Birchen Rd. L26 —5A 128
Birches Clo. Wir —2A 158
Birches, The. Stock V —4A 60
Birches, The. Wall —4E 75
Birchfield. Wir —2C 92
Birchfield Av. Wid —2A 132
Birchfield Clo. L7 —4E 79
Birchfield Clo. Wir —2C 92
Birchfield Rd. Walt —1A 56
Birchfield Rd. Edg H —4E 79
Birchfield Rd. Wid —4A 110
Birchfield St. L3 —3E 77 (2H 5)
Birchfield St. That H —4D 65
Birchfield Way. L31 —2B 6
Birch Gdns. St H —2F 45
Birch Gro. Huy —4D 83
Birch Gro. Prsct —2E 85
Birch Gro. Wall —4C 52
Birch Gro. W'tree —5A 80
Birch Heys. Wir —3A 114
Birchill Rd. Know I —3C 24
Birchley Av. Bil —2C 30
Birchley Rd. Bil —2B 30
Birchley St. St H —4A 46
Birchley Vw. St H —3B 30
Birchmere. Wir —5E 137
Birchmuir Hey. L32 —4F 23
Birchridge Clo. Wir —5C 142
Birch Rd. L36 —5E 83
Birch Rd. Beb —3A 142
Birch Rd. Hay —1E 49
Birch Rd. Meol —3E 91
Birch Rd. Pren —1B 118
Birch Rd. Run —2B 166
Birch Rd. Wid —1B 132
Birch St. L5 —1B 76
Birch Tree Av. St H —5F 29
Birch Tree Ct. L12 —4A 58
Birchtree Rd. L17 —1E 123
Birchview Way. Pren —4D 95
Birchway. Hes —5C 158
Birchwood Av. Birk —2D 97
Birchwood Clo. Birk —2D 97
Birchwood Way. L33 —5F 15
Birdcage Cotts. Hay —1E 49
(off Church Rd.)
Bird St. L7 —2C 100
Birdwood Rd. L11 —3F 57
Birkdale Av. Wir —4C 162
Birkdale Clo. Anf —5D 57
Birkdale Clo. Huy —5C 82
Birkdale Rd. Wid —4B 110
Birkenhead. —3F 97
Birkenhead Pk. —2A 96
Birkenhead Pk. Cricket Club Ground. —3B 96
Birkenhead Pk. R.F.C. Ground. —2A 96
Birkenhead Priory Mus. —3F 97
Birkenhead Rd. Hoy & Meol —3C 90
Birkenhead Rd. Wall —5E 75
Birkenhead Town Hall. —3F 97
Birkenshaw Av. L23 —5B 8
Birket Av. Wir —3F 71
Birket Clo. Wir —3A 72
Birket Ho. Birk —2D 97
Birket Sq. Wir —3A 72
Birkett Rd. Birk —3E 119
Birkett Rd. Wir —2B 112
Birkett St. L3 —3E 77 (1G 5)
Birkin Clo. L32 —5A 24
Birkin Rd. L32 —5A 24
Birkin Wlk. L32 —5A 24
Birley Ct. L8 —2F 99
Birnam Dri. Rain —4D 87
Birnam Rd. Wall —3D 75
Birstall Av. St H —3C 46
Birstall Ct. Run —3D 167
Birstall Rd. L6 —3B 78
Birt Clo. L8 —2A 100
Birtley Ct. Wid —2B 130
Bisham Pk. Run —5D 155
Bishopdale Dri. Rain —3D 87
Bishop Dri. Whis —5C 84
Bishopgate St. L15 —1D 101
Bishop Reeves Rd. Hay —1E 49
Bishop Rd. L6 —4C 56
Bishop Rd. St H —3E 45
Bishop Rd. Wall —4B 74
Bishops Ct. Wltn —2B 126
Bishop Sheppard Ct. L3 —2C 76
Bishops Way. Wid —1D 133
Bisley St. L15 —2E 101
Bisley St. Wall —1B 74
Bispham Dri. Wir —4E 91
Bispham Ho. L3 —3D 77 (2E 5)
Bispham St. L3 —3D 77 (2E 4)
Bittern Clo. Nort —2D 169
Bixteth St. L3 —4C 76 (3C 4)
Blackberry Gro. L26 —2D 127
Blackboards La. Chil T —5F 171
Blackbrook. —2F 47
Blackbrook Clo. L9 —5A 36
Blackbrook Clo. Wid —1C 130
Blackbrook Rd. St H —3E 47
Blackburne Av. Wid —2B 150
Blackburne Dri. L25 —5D 127
Blackburne Pl. L8 —1F 99
Blackburne St. L19 —3C 144
Blackburne Ter. L8 —1F 99
Black Denton's Pl. Wid —3C 132
Blackdown Gro. St H —1F 67
Blackfield St. L5 —5D 55
Blackheath Dri. Wir —3F 71
Blackheath La. Mnr P —3E 155
Black Horse Clo. Wir —3C 112
Black Horse Hill. Wir —4C 112
Black Horse La. L13 —2B 80
Black Horse Pl. L13 —3B 80
Blackhorse St. St H —4D 47
Blackhouse Wlk. L9 —5E 35
Blackhurst Rd. L31 —2C 6
Blackley Gro. L33 —5F 15
(off Carl's Way)
Blackleyhurst Av. Bil —1E 31
Blacklock Hall Rd. L24 —4C 146
Blacklow Brow. L36 —4D 83
Blackmoor Dri. L12 —5C 58
Blackpool St. Birk —4E 97
Blackrod Av. L24 —3C 146
Blackstock Ct. Boot —1D 19
Blackstock St. L3 —3C 76 (1D 4)
Blackstone Av. St H —3D 47
Blackstone St. L5 —5B 54
Blackthorn Cres. L28 —3B 60

Blackthorne Clo. *Wir* —2F **93**
Blackthorne Rd. *L9* —4B **36**
Blackwater Rd. *L11* —4D **39**
Blackwood Av. *L25* —5F **103**
Blair Dri. *Wid* —1B **130**
Blair Ind. Est. *L23* —2F **17**
Blair Pk. *Wir* —4B **142**
Blair St. *L8* —2E **99**
Blair Wlk. *L26* —1F **147**
Blaisdon Clo. *L11* —2A **58**
Blakeacre Clo. *L26* —1F **147**
Blakeacre Rd. *L26* —1F **147**
Blake Ct. *L19* —2C **144**
Blakefield Rd. *L23* —4C **10**
Blakeley Brow. *Wir* —4A **162**
Blakeley Ct. *Wir* —4A **162**
Blakeley Dell. *Raby M* —4B **162**
Blakeley Dene. *Wir* —3B **162**
Blakeley Rd. *Wir* —3A **162**
Blakeney Clo. *Wir* —2A **94**
Blakenhall Way. *Wir* —3D **93**
Blaking Dri. *Know* —4D **41**
Blantyre Rd. *L15* —3D **101**
Blantyre St. *Run* —4F **151**
Blay Clo. *L25* —4D **127**
Blaydon Clo. *Boot* —4F **19**
Blaydon Gro. *That H* —4D **65**
Blaydon Wlk. *Pren* —3E **95**
Bleak Hill Clo. *Wind* —1C **44**
Bleak Hill Rd. *St H & Wind* —3B **44**
Bleasdale Av. *L10* —3E **21**
Bleasdale Clo. *Wir* —3E **93**
Bleasdale Rd. *L18* —5A **102**
Bleasdale Way. *L21* —1B **18**
Blenheim Av. *L21* —5C **18**
Blenheim Dri. *Prsct* —1A **84**
Blenheim Rd. *L18* —4F **101**
Blenheim Rd. *Wall* —1D **75**
Blenheim St. *L5* —1C **76**
Blenheim Way. *L24* —4B **146**
Blenheim Way. *St H* —2B **46**
Blessington Rd. *L4* —4F **55**
Bletchley Av. *Wall* —2F **73**
Bligh St. *L15* —2D **101**
Blindfoot Rd. *Rainf & Wind* —1D **43**
Blisworth St. *L21* —2B **34**
Blomfield Rd. *L19* —5D **125**
Bloomfield Grn. *L17* —5C **100**
Bloomsbury Way. *Wid* —1D **131**
Blossom Gro. *L32* —1F **39**
Blossom St. *Boot* —3C **34**
Blucher St. *L22* —4C **16**
Bluebell Av. *Birk* —1F **95**
Bluebell Av. *Hay* —1E **49**
Bluebell Clo. *L22* —4E **17**
Bluebell Ct. *Beech* —1F **173**
Blue Bell La. *L36* —2E **83**
Blueberry Fields. *L10* —2F **37**
Bluecoat Chambers. *L1* —5D **77** (6E **5**)
***Bluecoat Chambers Art Gallery.* —5D 77 (6E 5)**
Bluefields St. *L8* —2F **99**
Blue Hatch. *Frod* —5C **172**
Blue Jay Clo. *L27* —4E **105**
Bluestone La. *L31* —1E **13**
Bluewood Dri. *Birk* —5D **73**
Blundell Rd. *Wid* —4C **130**
Blundellsands. —1C 16
Blundellsands Rd. E. *L23* —1C **16**
Blundellsands Rd. W. *L23* —2B **16**
Blundells Dri. *Wir* —5F **71**
Blundell's Hill. —4B 86
Blundells Hill Golf Course. —5A 86
Blundell's La. *Rain* —5A **86**
Blundell St. *L1* —2D **99**
Blyth Clo. *Murd* —5D **169**
Blythe Av. *Wid* —5B **110**
Blyth Hey. *Boot* —1D **19**
Blyth Rd. *Wir* —3C **162**
Blythswood St. *L17* —1A **122**
Boaler St. *L6* —3A **78**
Boaler St. Ind. Est. *L6* —2B **78**
Boardmans La. *St H* —4E **47**
Boathouse La. *Park* —5C **158**
Bobbies La. *Ecc* —4A **44**
(in two parts)
Bodden St. *Clo F* —2D **89**
Bodley St. *L4* —4F **55**
Bodmin Clo. *Brook* —4B **168**
Bodmin Gro. *St H* —1D **47**
Bodmin Rd. *L4* —2F **55**
Bodmin Way. *L26* —4E **127**
Bognor Clo. *L24* —3B **146**
Bolan St. *L13* —3F **79**
Bold. —5B 68
Bolde Way. *Wir* —1A **162**
Bold Heath. —2E 111
Bold Ind. Est. *Wid* —4C **110**
Bold Ind. Pk. *Bold* —5B **68**
Bold La. *St H & C Grn* —4B **68**
Bold Pl. *L1* —1E **99** (7G **5**)
Bold Rd. *St H* —4F **67**
Bold St. *L1* —5D **77** (6F **5**)
Bold St. *St H* —5F **45**
Bold St. *Run* —4B **152**
(in two parts)
Bold St. *Wid* —5A **132**
Boleyn Ct. *Mnr P* —4C **154**
Boleyn, The. *L31* —4E **7**
Bollington Clo. *Pren* —1F **117**
Bolton Av. *L32* —3C **22**
Bolton Rd. *Wir* —2B **142**
Bolton Rd. E. *Wir* —1C **142**
Bolton St. *L3* —5D **77** (5G **5**)
Bolton St. *St H* —4C **46**
(in two parts)
Bolton Wlk. *L32* —3C **22**
Bonchurch Dri. *L15* —5F **79**
Bond St. *L3* —2D **77**
Bond St. *Prsct* —5D **63**
Bonnington Av. *L23* —5C **8**
Bonsall Rd. *L12* —5B **58**
Boode Cft. *L28* —2B **60**
Booker Av. *L18* —3A **124**
Booth St. *L13* —3A **80**
Booth St. *St H* —4D **65**
Boothwood Clo. *L7* —1B **100**
Bootle. —4C 34
Bootle Municipal Golf Course. —3E 19
Bootle Stadium Sports Cen. —4E 35
Borax St. *L13* —4A **80**
Border Rd. *Wir* —2B **158**
Borella Rd. *L13* —5F **57**
Borough Pavement. *Birk* —3D **97**
Borough Pl. *Birk* —3E **97**
Borough Rd. *St H* —1E **65**
Borough Rd. *Birk* —1C **118**
Borough Rd. *Wall* —3D **75**
(in two parts)
Borough Rd. E. *Birk* —3E **97**
(in two parts)
Borough Way. *Wall* —4E **75**
Borrowdale Clo. *Frod* —5D **173**
Borrowdale Rd. *L15* —3E **101**
Borrowdale Rd. *St H* —3C **64**
Borrowdale Rd. *Beb* —3E **141**
Borrowdale Rd. *More* —1D **93**
Borrowdale Rd. *Wid* —4C **130**
Boscow Cres. *St H* —4D **67**
Bosnia St. *L8* —1A **122**
Bossom Ct. *L22* —5D **17**
Bostock St. *L5* —1D **77**
Boston Av. *Run* —2B **166**
Boswell Rd. *Pren* —3F **117**
Boswell St. *Boot* —3A **34**
Boswell St. *L8* —2B **100**
Bosworth Clo. *Wir* —5F **141**
Bosworth Rd. *St H* —2C **46**
Botanic Gro. *L7* —5C **78**
Botanic Pl. *L7* —4C **78**
Botanic Rd. *L7* —4C **78**
Botany Rd. *L24* —2C **146**
Botley Clo. *Wir* —4D **93**
Boulevard. *L6* —2C **78**
Boulevard, The. *L8* —3A **100**
Boulevard, The. *L12* —3B **58**
Boulton Av. *New F* —4B **120**
Boulton Av. *W Kir* —2B **112**
Boundary Dri. *Cros* —4D **9**
Boundary Dri. *Hunts X* —5D **127**
Boundary Farm Rd. *L26* —1D **147**
Boundary La. *Kirkby* —3E **25**
Boundary La. *Eve* —2A **78**
Boundary La. *Wir* —2A **158**
Boundary Rd. *Lith* —3D **19**
(in two parts)
Boundary Rd. *St H* —5E **45**
Boundary Rd. *Huy* —1A **106**
Boundary Rd. *Port S* —5B **120**
Boundary Rd. *Pren* —5D **73**
Boundary Rd. *W Kir* —1D **135**
Boundary St. *L5* —5B **54**
Boundary St. E. *L5* —5D **55**
Boundary Wlk. *L36* —1A **106**
Bourne Gdns. *St H* —2C **66**
Bournemouth Clo. *Murd* —4D **169**
Bourne St. *L6* —3B **78**
Bourton Rd. *L25* —5B **126**
Bousfield St. *L4* —4E **55**
Bowden Clo. *L12* —1E **59**
Bowden Rd. *L19* —1B **144**
Bowden St. *L21* —2B **34**
Bowdon Clo. *Ecc* —1B **64**
Bowdon Rd. *Wall* —5A **52**
Bowen Clo. *Wid* —5D **109**
Bower Gro. *L21* —1F **33**
Bower Ho. *Wir* —2F **93**
Bower Rd. *Huy* —2E **83**
Bower Rd. *Wir* —3C **158**
Bower Rd. *Wltn* —5A **104**
Bowers Bus. Pk. *Wid* —5B **132**
Bowers Pk. Ind. Est. *Wid* —5C **132**
Bower St. *Wid* —3C **132**
Bowfell Clo. *Wir* —2D **171**
Bowfield Rd. *L19* —5B **124**
Bowgreen Clo. *Pren* —2C **94**
Bowland Av. *L16* —5D **81**
Bowland Av. *Sut M* —3B **88**
Bowland Clo. *Beech* —5E **167**
Bowland Clo. *Wir* —1C **162**
Bowland Dri. *L21* —1B **18**
Bowles St. *Boot* —2A **34**
Bowley Rd. *L13* —1F **79**
Bowness Av. *St H* —5B **30**
Bowness Av. *Pren* —2A **118**
Bowness Av. *Wir* —5C **162**
Bowood St. *L8* —1F **121**
Bowring Golf Course. —5B 82
Bowring Park. —5A 82
Bowring Pk. Av. *L16* —5A **82**
Bowring Pk. Rd. *L14* —5E **81**
Bowring St. *L8* —5F **99**
Bowscale Clo. *Wir* —4E **93**
Bowscale Rd. *L11* —2A **58**
Boxdale Ct. *L18* —5A **102**
Boxdale Rd. *L18* —5A **102**
Boxgrove Clo. *Wid* —1B **132**
Boxmoor Rd. *L18* —2A **124**
Boxtree Clo. *L12* —4F **39**
Boxwood Clo. *L36* —4C **82**
Boycott St. *L5* —5A **56**
Boyd Clo. *Wir* —3B **72**
Boydell Clo. *L28* —4B **60**
Boyer Av. *L31* —3D **13**
Boyes Brow. *L33* —1D **23**
Boyton Ct. *L7* —1C **100**

Brabant Rd. *L17* —3E **123**
Braby Rd. *L21* —2C **34**
Bracewell Clo. *St H* —5C **66**
Bracken Ct. *Clo F* —2C **88**
Brackendale. *Halt B* —2D **167**
Brackendale. *Wir* —1C **116**
Brackendale Av. *L9* —1B **36**
Bracken Dri. *Wir* —4E **113**
Brackenhurst Dri. *Wall* —4C **52**
Brackenhurst Grn. *L33* —3E **23**
Bracken La. *Wir* —2D **141**
Brackenside. *Wir* —5F **137**
Bracken Way. *W Der* —1A **80**
Bracken Wood. *L12* —4E **39**
Brackenwood Golf Course. —3D 141
Brackenwood Gro. *Whis* —3F **85**
Brackenwood Rd. *Wir* —4E **141**
Brackley Av. *Boot* —4B **34**
Brackley Clo. *Boot* —4B **34**
Brackley Clo. *Run* —4F **151**
Brackley Clo. *Wall* —3A **74**
Brackley St. *Run* —4F **151**
Bracknell Av. *L32* —4D **23**
Bracknell Clo. *L32* —4D **23**
Bradbourne Clo. *L12* —5E **39**
Bradda Clo. *Wir* —2F **93**
Braddan Av. *L13* —1E **79**
Bradden Clo. *Wir* —5B **142**
Bradewell Clo. *L4* —3E **55**
Bradewell St. *L4* —3E **55**
Bradfield Av. *L10* —2C **20**
Bradfield St. *L7* —4C **78**
Bradgate Clo. *Wir* —5B **70**
Bradkirk Ct. *Boot* —5D **11**
Bradley Fold. *L36* —1B **106**
Bradley La. *Newt W* —1F **69**
Bradley Rd. *L21* —4B **18**
Bradley Way. *Wid* —3B **132**
Bradman Rd. *Know I* —2C **24**
Bradman Rd. *Wir* —5C **70**
Bradmoor Rd. *Wir* —2D **163**
Bradshaw Clo. *St H* —4D **45**
Bradshaw Pl. *L6* —3A **78**
Bradshaw St. *Wid* —2A **132**
Bradshaw Wlk. *Boot* —4B **34**
Bradstone Clo. *L10* —2B **38**
Bradville Rd. *L9* —1C **36**
Bradwell Clo. *Wir* —4D **113**
Braehaven Rd. *Wall* —4C **52**
Braemar Clo. *Whis* —3F **85**
Braemar St. *L20* —2D **55**
Braemore Rd. *Wall* —2F **73**
Braeside Cres. *Bil* —1D **31**
Braeside Gdns. *Wir* —4F **93**
Brae St. *L7* —4B **78**
Brahms Clo. *L8* —3B **100**
Braid St. *Birk* —1D **97**
Brainerd St. *L13* —1E **79**
Braithwaite Clo. *Beech* —4D **167**
Braithwaite Clo. *Rain* —3C **86**
Bramberton Pl. *L4* —2C **56**
Bramberton Rd. *L4* —2C **56**
Bramble Av. *Birk* —1F **95**
Bramble Way. *Padd M* —1E **173**
Bramble Way. *Wir* —4D **71**
Bramblewood Clo. *N'ley* —4E **105**
Bramblewood Clo. *Pren* —5D **95**
Brambling Clo. *Beech* —5F **167**
Brambling Pk. *L26* —3E **127**
Bramcote Av. *St H* —2C **46**
Bramcote Clo. *L33* —1A **24**
Bramcote Rd. *L33* —1F **23**
Bramcote Wlk. *L33* —1F **23**
Bramerton Ct. *Wir* —3A **112**
Bramford Clo. *Wir* —4E **93**
Bramhall Clo. *Wir* —5D **113**
Bramhall Dri. *Wir* —2F **171**
Bramhall Rd. *L22* —5E **17**
Bramhill Clo. *L24* —5E **147**
Bramley Av. *Wir* —5E **119**
Bramley Clo. *L27* —4D **105**
Bramleys, The. *L31* —3C **12**
Bramley Wlk. *L24* —5D **147**
Bramley Way. *L32* —2C **22**
Brampton Ct. *St H* —5B **48**
Brampton Dri. *L8* —1A **100**
Bramwell Av. *Pren* —3A **118**
Bramwell St. *St H* —4E **47**
Branch Way. *Hay* —2D **49**
Brancker Av. *Rain* —2B **86**
Brancote Ct. *Pren* —3E **95**
Brancote Gdns. *Wir* —3D **163**
Brancote Mt. *Pren* —3F **95**
Brancote Rd. *Pren* —3F **95**
Brandearth Hey. *L28* —4B **60**
Brandon. *Wid* —2A **130**
Brandon St. *Birk* —3F **97**
Brandreth Clo. *Rain* —3C **86**
Branfield Clo. *L12* —4E **39**
Branstree Av. *L11* —1F **57**
Bran St. *L8* —4E **99**
Branthwaite Clo. *L11* —2A **58**
Branthwaite Cres. *L11* —1A **58**
Branthwaite Gro. *L11* —2A **58**
Brasenose Rd. *Boot* —1B **54**
Brassey St. *L8* —3E **99**
Brassey St. *Birk* —1A **96**
Brattan Rd. *Birk* —5C **96**
Braunton Rd. *L17* —3E **123**
Braunton Rd. *Wall* —5A **52**
Braybrooke Rd. *L11* —5F **37**
Bray Clo. *Beech* —4D **167**
Braydon Clo. *L25* —1C **146**
Brayfield Rd. *L4* —2D **57**
Bray Rd. *L24* —3B **146**
Bray St. *Birk* —1B **96**
Brechin Rd. *L33* —3F **23**
Breckfield Pl. *L5* —1F **77**
Breckfield Rd. N. *L5* —5F **55**
Breckfield Rd. S. *L6* —1A **78**
Breck Pl. *Wall* —3A **74**
Breck Rd. *Eve & Anf* —2F **77**
Breck Rd. *Wall* —2F **73**
Breck Rd. *Wid* —3B **132**
Breckside Av. *Wall* —2E **73**
Breckside Pk. *L6* —5C **56**
Brecon Av. *Boot* —4F **19**
Brecon Rd. *Birk* —3C **118**
Brecon Wlk. *Boot* —4A **20**
Breeze Clo. *L9* —5F **35**
Breeze Hill. *Boot & L9* —5D **35**
Breeze La. *L9* —5F **35**
Brelade Rd. *L13* —2F **79**
Bremhill Rd. *L11* —5F **37**
Bremner Clo. *L7* —5C **78**
Brenda Cres. *Thor* —3A **10**
Brendale Av. *L31* —2C **12**
Brendan's Way. *Boot* —2E **19**
Brendon Av. *L21* —4A **18**
Brendon Gro. *St H* —4A **48**
Brendor Rd. *L25* —3B **126**
Brenig St. *Birk* —5F **73**
Brenka Av. *L9* —4B **20**
Brentfield. *Wid* —2D **131**
Brent Way. *L26* —1F **147**
(in two parts)
Brentwood Av. *Cros* —5F **9**
Brentwood Av. *Aig* —1C **122**
Brentwood Clo. *Ecc* —5B **44**
Brentwood Ct. Wir —2A 116
(off Childwall Grn.)
Brentwood St. *Wall* —3C **74**
Brereton Av. *L15* —2A **102**
Brereton Av. *Wir* —1A **142**
Brereton Clo. *Cas* —2A **168**
(in two parts)
Bretherton Pl. *Rain* —2C **86**
Bretherton Rd. *Prsct* —5E **63**
Bretlands Rd. *L23* —4B **10**
Brett St. *Birk* —1B **96**
Brewery La. *Mell* —1E **21**
Brewster St. *L4 & Boot* —2E **55**
Brian Av. *Wir* —1F **137**
Brian Cummings Ct. *L21* —2B **34**
Briardale Rd. *L18* —4F **101**
Briardale Rd. *Beb* —5F **119**
Briardale Rd. *Birk* —5C **96**
Briardale Rd. *Wall* —4E **75**
Briardale Rd. *Will* —4A **170**
Briar Dri. *L36* —4D **83**
Briar Dri. *Wir* —2A **158**
Briarfield Av. *Wid* —3A **130**
Briarfield Rd. *Hes* —2B **158**
Briars Clo. *Rain* —5D **87**
Briars Grn. *St H* —3F **45**
Briars La. *L31* —1E **13**
Briar St. *L4* —4D **55**
Briarswood Clo. *Birk* —4F **119**
Briarswood Clo. *Whis* —3F **85**
Briarwood. *Nort* —2C **168**
Briarwood Rd. *L17* —1E **123**
Briary Clo. *Wir* —1B **158**
Brickfields. *L36* —5A **84**
Brick St. *L1* —2D **99**
Brick St. *Newt W* —5F **49**
Brickwall Grn. *L29* —3F **11**
Brickwall La. *L29* —5D **11**
Bride St. *L4* —1F **55**
Bridge Ct. *Boot* —1D **19**
Bridge Ct. *Wir* —3A **112**
Bridge Cft. *L21* —2C **18**
Bridgecroft Rd. *Wall* —5B **52**
Bridge Farm Clo. *Wir* —5B **94**
Bridge Farm Dri. *L31* —5F **7**
Bridgefield Clo. *L25* —2B **104**
Bridgefield Forum Leisure Cen. —2A 128
Bridgeford Av. *L12* —4A **58**
Bridge Gdns. *L12* —3F **59**
Bridge Ind. Est. *L24* —2B **146**
Bridge La. *Boot* —2E **19**
Bridge La. *Frod* —4C **172**
Bridgeman St. *St H* —5D **45**
(in two parts)
Bridgend Clo. *Wid* —1D **131**
Bridgenorth Rd. *Wir* —3E **137**
Bridge Rd. *Clo F* —4D **89**
Bridge Rd. *Cros* —2C **16**
Bridge Rd. *Lith* —1B **34**
Bridge Rd. *Mag* —3D **13**
Bridge Rd. *Edg H* —1C **100**
Bridge Rd. *Huy* —4C **82**
Bridge Rd. *Moss H* —1A **124**
Bridge Rd. *Prsct* —1D **85**
Bridge Rd. *Wir* —3A **112**
Bridges La. *L29* —3F **11**
Bridge St. *Boot* —1B **54**
Bridge St. *St H* —5A **46**
Bridge St. *Birk* —2E **97**
(in two parts)
Bridge St. *Port S* —2B **142**
(in two parts)
Bridge St. *Run* —4B **152**
Bridge Vw. Clo. *Wid* —3A **152**
Bridgeview Dri. *L33* —1F **23**
Bridgewater Clo. *L21* —3A **18**
Bridgewater Expressway. *Run* —5B **152**
Bri. Water Grange. *Pres B* —5F **169**
Bridgewater St. *L1* —2D **99**
Bridgewater St. *Run* —4A **152**
Bridgewater Way. *L36* —1A **106**
Bridgeway. *L11* —2E **57**
Bridgeway E. *Wind H* —5C **154**
Bridgeway W. *Wind H* —5B **154**
Bridle Av. *Wall* —4E **75**
Bridle Clo. *Pren* —3B **94**
Bridle Clo. *Wir* —3E **163**

Bridle Ct. *St H* —3C **66**
Bridle Pk. *Brom* —3D **163**
Bridle Rd. *Boot* —5E **19**
Bridle Rd. *Brom & East* —3E **163**
Bridle Rd. *Wall* —4E **75**
Bridle Rd. Ind. Est. *Boot* —5F **19**
Bridle Way. *Boot* —5F **19**
Bridley Wharf. *Pres H* —5F **169**
Bridport St. *L3* —4E **77** (4G **5**)
Brierfield Rd. *L15* —3F **101**
Brierley Clo. *Boot* —1B **20**
Briery Hey Av. *L33* —3F **23**
Brightgate Clo. *L7* —1B **100**
Brighton le Sands. —3B 16
Brighton Rd. *Wat* —4D **17**
Brighton Rd. *Huy* —3B **84**
Brighton St. *Wall* —2D **75**
Brighton Va. *L22* —3C **16**
Bright St. *L6* —3F **77**
Bright St. *Birk* —3C **96**
(in two parts)
Bright Ter. *L8* —1F **121**
Brightwell Clo. *Wir* —5F **93**
Brill St. *Birk* —1B **96**
Brimstage. —5B 140
Brimstage Av. *Wir* —4D **119**
Brimstage Clo. *Wir* —3C **158**
Brimstage Grn. *Wir* —2D **159**
Brimstage La. *Wir* —3B **140**
Brimstage Rd. *L4* —1E **55**
Brimstage Rd. *Beb & High B* —5E **141**
Brimstage Rd. *Hes & Brim* —3C **158**
(in two parts)
Brimstage St. *Birk* —4C **96**
Brindley Clo. *L21* —3A **18**
Brindley Rd. *L32* —3C **22**
Brindley Rd. *Reg I* —5E **67**
Brindley Rd. *Ast I* —4F **153**
Brindley St. *L8* —3D **99**
Brindley St. *Run* —4F **151**
Brinley Clo. *Wir* —5D **163**
Brinton Clo. *Wid* —4D **131**
Brisbane Av. *Wall* —3A **52**
Brisbane St. *That H* —4D **65**
Briscoe Av. *Wir* —2E **93**
Briscoe Dri. *Wir* —2E **93**
Bristol Av. *Murd* —4E **169**
Bristol Av. *Wall* —2C **74**
Bristol Rd. *L15* —3A **102**
Britannia Av. *L15* —2C **100**
Britannia Cres. *L8* —1F **121**
Britannia Pavilion. *L3* —1C **98**
Britannia Rd. *Wall* —1A **74**
Britonside Av. *L32* —5F **23**
Brittarge Brow. *L27* —5E **105**
Britten Clo. *L8* —3B **100**
Broadacre Clo. *L18* —4C **102**
Broadbelt St. *L4* —1F **55**
Broadbent Ho. L31 —3D 13
(off Boyer Av.)
Broadfield Av. *Pren* —2C **94**
Broadfield Clo. *Pren* —2C **94**
Broadfields. *Run* —2C **168**
Broadgate Av. *St H* —3C **66**
Broad Green. —5D 81
Broad Grn. Rd. *L13* —3A **80**
Broadheath Av. *Pren* —2C **94**
Broadheath Ter. *Wid* —3D **131**
Broad Hey. *Boot* —2D **19**
Broad Hey Clo. *L25* —1B **126**
Broadhurst St. *L17* —1B **122**
Broadlake. *Will* —5A **170**
Broadlands. *Prsct* —1E **85**
Broad La. *Kirkby* —5F **23**
Broad La. *Nor G* —2D **57**
Broad La. *St H* —3B **30**
Broad La. *Thor* —1C **10**
Broad La. *Btnwd & C Grn* —2B **68**
Broad La. *Hes* —1C **156**
Broad La. Precinct. *L11* —2F **57**
Broadmead. *L19* —5D **125**
Broadmead. *Wir* —3C **158**
Broad Oak. —5E 47
Broad Oak Av. *Hay* —2B **48**
Broadoak Rd. *L14* —3F **81**
Broadoak Rd. *L31* —1E **13**
Broad Oak Rd. *St H* —5E **47**
Broad Pl. *L11* —3F **57**
Broad Sq. *L11* —3F **57**
Broadstone Dri. *Wir* —5F **141**
Broad Vw. *L11* —3F **57**
Broadway. *Ecc* —4A **44**
Broadway. *Faz* —1E **37**
Broadway. *L11* —2E **57**
Broadway. *St H* —3C **64**
Broadway. *Beb* —5D **119**
Broadway. *Grea* —4E **93**
Broadway. *Wall* —1F **73**
Broadway. *Wid* —3A **130**
Broadway Av. *Wall* —1F **73**
Broadway Community Leisure Cen. —3C 64
Broadway Mkt. *L11* —2E **57**
Broadwood Av. *L31* —3C **12**
Broadwood St. *L15* —2E **101**
Brock Av. *L31* —5E **7**
Brockenhurst Rd. *L9* —3A **36**
Brock Gdns. *Hale V* —5E **149**
Brock Hall Clo. *Clo F* —2C **88**
Brockhall Clo. *Whis* —5A **64**
Brockholme Rd. *L18* —3A **124**
Brocklebank La. *L19* —4D **125**
Brockley Av. *Wall* —2B **52**
Brockmoor Tower. *L4* —3D **55**
Brock St. *L4* —3E **55**
Brodie Av. *L18 & L19* —1A **124**
Bromborough. —1E 163
Bromborough Dock Est. *Wir* —1C **142**
Bromborough Golf Course. —5A 162
Bromborough Pool. —2D 143
Bromborough Port. —3F 143
Bromborough Rd. *Wir* —2A **142**
Bromborough Village Rd. *Wir* —1D **163**
Brome Way. *Wir* —5B **142**
Bromilow Rd. *St H* —1F **67**
Bromley Av. *L18* —4F **101**
Bromley Clo. *Wir* —3E **157**
Bromley Rd. *Wall* —4A **52**
Brompton Av. *Cros* —2C **16**
Brompton Av. *Kirkby* —5F **15**
Brompton Av. *Seft P* —3C **100**
Brompton Av. *Wall* —2C **74**
Brompton Ho. *L17* —4C **100**
Bromsgrove Rd. *Wir* —5C **92**
Bromyard Clo. *Boot* —4B **34**
Bronington Av. *Wir* —4D **163**
Bronshill Ct. *L23* —1A **16**
Bronte Clo. *L23* —1B **16**
Bronte St. *L3* —4E **77** (4H **5**)
Bronte St. *St H* —4D **45**
Brookbank Ct. *L10* —1B **38**
Brookbridge Rd. *L13* —5E **57**
Brook Clo. *Wall* —1C **74**
Brook Clo. *Wid* —3C **108**
Brookdale. *Wid* —1A **130**
Brookdale Av. N. *Wir* —5E **93**
Brookdale Av. S. *Wir* —5E **93**
Brookdale Clo. *Wir* —5E **93**
Brookdale Rd. *L15* —3E **101**
Brook End. *St H* —2A **68**
Brooke Rd. E. *L22* —3D **17**
Brooke Rd. W. *L22* —3C **16**
Brookfield Av. *Cros* —2D **17**
Brookfield Av. *Wat* —5F **17**
Brookfield Av. *Rain* —1C **86**
Brookfield Av. *Run* —5D **153**
Brookfield Dri. *L9* —3C **36**
Brookfield Gdns. *Wir* —4B **112**
Brookfield La. *Augh* —3F **7**
Brookfield Rd. *Wir* —4B **112**
Brookfields Green. —2F 7
Brook Furlong. *Frod* —3A **172**
Brook Hey Dri. *L33* —1F **23**
Brook Hey Wlk. *L33* —2A **24**
Brookhill Clo. *Boot* —5D **35**
Brookhill Rd. *Boot* —4D **35**
Brookhouse Gro. *Ecc* —5F **43**
Brookhurst. —5C 162
Brookhurst Av. *Wir* —4C **162**
Brookhurst Clo. *Wir* —5C **162**
Brookhurst Rd. *Wir* —4C **162**
Brookland La. *St H* —1A **68**
Brookland Rd. *Birk* —4D **97**
Brookland Rd. E. *L13* —3A **80**
Brookland Rd. W. *L13* —3A **80**
Brooklands. *Birk* —2D **97**
Brooklands Av. *L22* —5E **17**
Brooklands Dri. *L31* —2D **13**
Brooklands Rd. *Ecc* —4A **44**
Brooklands, The. *L36* —5E **83**
Brook Lea Ho. *L21* —2C **18**
Brooklet Rd. *Wir* —2C **158**
Brook Mdw. *Wir* —5E **115**
Brook Pk. *L31* —3C **12**
Brook Rd. *Boot* —5B **34**
Brook Rd. *L31* —2E **13**
Brook Rd. *Thor* —4A **10**
Brook Rd. *Walt* —4A **36**
Brooks All. *L1* —5D **77** (6E **5**)
Brookside. *Mag* —1E **13**
Brookside. *W Der* —3F **59**
Brookside. *K Ash* —2D **81**
Brookside Av. *Ecc* —3B **44**
Brookside Av. *Wat* —5F **17**
Brookside Av. *K Ash* —3D **81**
Brookside Clo. *Bil* —1E **31**
Brookside Clo. *Hay* —1B **48**
Brookside Clo. *Prsct* —2E **85**
Brookside Ct. *L23* —1E **17**
Brookside Cres. *Wir* —4D **93**
Brookside Dri. *Wir* —4E **93**
Brookside Rd. *Frod* —5A **172**
Brookside Rd. *Prsct* —2E **85**
Brookside Vw. *Hay* —1B **48**
Brookside Way. *Hay* —1B **48**
Brooks, The. *St H* —1A **46**
Brook St. *L3* —4B **76** (3B **4**)
Brook St. *St H* —5A **46**
Brook St. *Birk* —1C **96**
Brook St. *Run* —4A **152**
Brook St. *Whis* —1F **85**
Brook St. *Wir* —1A **142**
Brook St. E. *Birk* —2E **97**
Brook Ter. *Run* —5E **153**
Brook Ter. *Wir* —4B **112**
Brookthorpe Clo. *Wall* —5B **52**
Brookvale. —4B 168
Brook Va. *L22* —5F **17**
Brookvale Av. N. *Run* —4B **168**
Brookvale Av. S. *Brook* —4B **168**
Brookvale Clo. *Btnwd* —5F **69**
Brookvale Recreation Cen. —5C 168
Brook Wlk. *Wir* —5D **115**
Brookway. *Nor C* —3E **117**
Brookway. *Wall* —1A **74**
Brookway. *Wir* —4E **93**
Brookway La. *St H* —2F **67**
Brookwood Rd. *L36* —2E **83**
Broom Clo. *Ecc P* —5F **63**
Broome Ct. *Brook* —4B **168**
Broomfield Clo. *Wir* —1D **157**
Broomfield Gdns. *L9* —3F **35**
Broomfield Rd. *L9* —3F **35**
Broom Hill. *Pren* —2F **95**
Broomhill Clo. *L27* —3C **104**
Broomlands. *Wir* —2F **157**
Broomleigh Clo. *Wir* —2D **141**

Broom Rd. *St H*—3B **64**
Brooms Gro. *L10*—3E **21**
Broom Way. *L26*—5E **127**
Broseley Av. *Wir*—1C **162**
Broster Av. *Wir*—1C **92**
Broster Clo. *Wir*—1C **92**
Brosters La. *Wir*—2E **91**
Brotherton Clo. *Wir*—1C **162**
***Brotherton Pk.*—5C 142**
Brotherton Rd. *Wall*—4E **75**
Brougham Av. *Birk*—5F **97**
Brougham Rd. *Wall*—3D **75**
Brougham Ter. *L6*—3A **78**
Broughton Av. *Wir*—3A **112**
Broughton Dri. *L19*—5A **124**
Broughton Hall Rd. *L12*—1E **81**
Broughton Rd. *Wall*—3B **74**
Broughton Way. *Wid*—2B **150**
Brow La. *Wir*—3F **157**
Brownbill Bank. *L27*—4E **105**
Brown Edge. —4D 65
Brownheath Av. *Bil*—2D **31**
Browning Av. *Birk*—3F **119**
Browning Av. *Wid*—4F **131**
Browning Clo. *L36*—5F **83**
Browning Rd. *W Der*—5F **57**
Browning Rd. *Wat*—3D **17**
Browning Rd. *Wall*—1D **73**
Browning St. *Boot*—4A **34**
Brownlow Arc. *St H*—5A **46**
Brownlow Hill. *L3*—5E **77** (5G **5**)
Brownlow Rd. *Wir*—5B **120**
Brownlow St. *L3*—5F **77** (5J **5**)
Brownmoor Clo. *L23*—1A **18**
Brownmoor La. *L23*—2F **17**
Brownmoor Pk. *L23*—2F **17**
Brown's La. *Boot*—2F **19**
Brown St. *Wid*—5D **133**
Brownville Rd. *L13*—4D **57**
Brow Rd. *Pren*—5D **73**
Brow Side. *L5*—2F **77**
Brow, The. —1F 167
Broxholme Way. *L31*—3D **13**
Broxton Av. *Pren*—2F **117**
Broxton Av. *Wir*—3C **112**
Broxton Clo. *Wid*—1C **130**
Broxton Rd. *Wall*—5F **51**
Broxton St. *L15*—1E **101**
Bruce Cres. *Wir*—4C **162**
Bruce St. *L8*—4A **100**
Bruce St. *St H*—4E **45**
Bruen Clo. *L27*—3D **105**
Brunel Dri. *L21*—3A **18**
Brunner Rd. *Wid*—4A **132**
Brunsborough Clo. *Wir*—4C **162**
Brunsfield Clo. *Wir*—2C **92**
Brunstath Clo. *Wir*—1C **158**
Brunswick. *Run*—4A **152**
Brunswick Bus. Pk. *Brun B*—5E **99**
Brunswick Clo. *L4*—3E **55**
Brunswick M. *L22*—5E **17**
Brunswick M. *Birk*—2E **97**
Brunswick Pde. *L22*—5D **17**
Brunswick Pl. *L20*—3B **54**
Brunswick Rd. *L6*—3F **77** (2J **5**)
Brunswick Rd. *Newt W*—4F **49**
Brunswick St. *L3*—5B **76** (6B **4**)
Brunswick St. *St H*—5A **48**
Brunswick St. *Gars*—4C **144**
Brunswick Way. *Brun B*—4D **99**
Brunt La. *L19*—5E **125**
Brushford Clo. *L12*—1B **58**
Bruton Rd. *L36*—5D **61**
Bryanston Rd. *L17*—1B **122**
Bryanston Rd. *Birk*—2A **118**
Bryant Rd. *L21*—2B **34**
Bryceway, The. *L12*—2D **81**
Brydges St. *L7*—5A **78**
Bryer Rd. *Prsct*—2D **85**
Bryn Bank. *Wall*—2C **74**
Brynmor Rd. *L18*—3A **124**
Brynmoss Av. *Wall*—2F **73**
Brynn St. *St H*—4A **46**
Brynn St. *Wid*—4B **132**
Bryony Way. *Birk*—4F **119**
Brythen St. *L1*—5D **77** (5F **5**)
Buccleuch St. *Birk*—5F **73**
Buccleuch Way. *Birk*—5F **73**
Buchanan Rd. *L9*—5F **35**
Buchanan Rd. *Wall*—3D **75**
Buckfast Av. *Hay*—1F **49**
Buckfast Clo. *Boot*—1F **19**
Buckfast Ct. *Run*—4E **155**
Buckingham Av. *L17*—3D **101**
Buckingham Av. *Pren*—2F **95**
Buckingham Av. *Wid*—5A **110**
Buckingham Av. *Wir*—5E **119**
Buckingham Clo. *Boot*—2C **18**
Buckingham Clo. *St H*—1E **65**
Buckingham Ct. *L33*—1F **23**
Buckingham Dri. *St H*—1A **46**
Buckingham Ho. *L17*—4D **101**
Buckingham Rd. *Mag*—1C **12**
Buckingham Rd. *Walt*—2A **36**
Buckingham Rd. *Tue*—5D **57**
Buckingham Rd. *Wall*—2F **73**
Buckingham St. *L5*—1E **77**
Buckland Clo. *Wid*—5C **130**
Buckland Dri. *Wir*—5F **141**
Buckland St. *L17*—1B **122**
Buckley Hill La. *L29*—1D **19**
Buckley Wlk. *L24*—5D **147**
Buckley Way. *Boot*—5D **11**
Buckthorn Clo. *L28*—4B **60**
Buckthorn Gdns. *St H*—5C **64**
Bude Clo. *Pren*—3C **94**
Bude Rd. *Wid*—2E **131**
Budworth Av. *Sut M*—3B **88**
Budworth Av. *Wid*—2D **131**
Budworth Clo. *Halt L*—3D **167**
Budworth Clo. *Pren*—5E **95**
Budworth Ct. *Pren*—4F **95**
Budworth Dri. *L25*—2C **126**
Budworth Rd. *Pren*—5E **95**
Buerton Clo. *Pren*—5E **95**
Buffs La. *Wir*—1B **158**
Bulford Rd. *L9*—4D **37**
Bulkeley Rd. *Wall*—3D **75**
Bull Bri. La. *L10*—3E **21**
Bullens Rd. *Kirkby*—4F **23**
Bullens Rd. *Walt*—3F **55**
Bullfinch Ct. *L26*—3E **127**
Bull La. *L9*—1A **36**
(Caldy Rd.)
Bull La. *L9*—2F **35**
(Orrell La.)
Bullrush Dri. *Wir*—4A **72**
Bulrushes, The. *L17*—1F **121**
Bulwer St. *Boot*—3A **34**
Bulwer St. *L5*—1A **78**
Bulwer St. *Birk*—2F **119**
Bunbury Dri. *Run*—4C **166**
Bundoran Rd. *L17*—2D **123**
Bungalows, The. Thor H—*4B* ***160***
(off Raby Rd.)
Bunter Rd. *L32*—1F **39**
Bunting Ct. *L26*—2D **127**
Burbo Bank Rd. *L23*—1A **16**
Burbo Bank Rd. N. *L23*—5A **8**
Burbo Bank Rd. S. *L23*—2B **16**
Burbo Cres. *L23*—2B **16**
Burbo Mans. *L23*—2B **16**
Burbo Way. *Wall*—3E **51**
Burden Rd. *Wir*—1C **92**
Burdett Av. *Wir*—5F **141**
Burdett Clo. *Wir*—5A **142**
Burdett Rd. *L22*—3D **17**
Burdett Rd. *Wall*—1D **73**
Burdett St. *L17*—1B **122**
Burdon Clo. *Wid*—1D **131**
Burford Av. *Wall*—3F **73**
Burford Rd. *L16*—5C **80**
Burgess Gdns. *L31*—5C **6**
Burgess St. *L3*—4E **77** (3H **5**)
Burghill Rd. *L12*—4F **39**
Burgundy Clo. *L17*—2C **122**
Burland Clo. *Run*—1F **165**
Burland Rd. *L26*—1A **148**
Burleigh M. *L5*—4F **55**
Burleigh Rd. N. *L5*—4F **55**
Burleigh Rd. S. *L5*—5F **55**
Burley Clo. *L32*—4F **23**
Burlingham Av. *Wir*—5D **113**
Burlington Rd. *Wall*—2B **52**
Burlington St. *L3*—2C **76**
Burlington St. *Birk*—3E **97**
Burman Cres. *L19*—5C **124**
Burman Rd. *L19*—5C **124**
Burnage Av. *Clo F*—2C **88**
Burnage Clo. *L24*—5F **147**
Burnand St. *L4*—4F **55**
Burnard Clo. *L33*—3F **23**
Burnard Cres. *L33*—3F **23**
Burnard Wlk. *L33*—3F **23**
Burnell Clo. *St H*—4F **45**
Burnham Clo. *Wid*—1C **130**
Burnham Rd. *L18*—1C **124**
Burnie Av. *Boot*—3E **35**
Burnley Av. *Wir*—1F **93**
Burnley Clo. *L6*—2A **78**
Burnley Rd. *Wir*—5F **71**
Burnsall Dri. *Wid*—1C **130**
Burnsall St. *L19*—2E **145**
Burns Av. *Wall*—1A **74**
Burns Clo. *L16*—1F **103**
Burns Clo. *Whis*—3E **85**
Burns Cres. *Wid*—4F **131**
Burns Gro. *L36*—5A **84**
Burnside Av. *Wall*—4B **74**
Burnside Rd. *Wall*—4B **74**
Burns Rd. *Sut M*—3A **88**
Burns St. *Boot*—3A **34**
Burnt Ash Clo. *L19*—5F **123**
Burnthwaite Rd. *L14*—3C **80**
Burnt Mill La. *Wid*—2D **149**
Burrell Clo. *Birk*—3C **118**
Burrell Ct. *Birk*—3C **118**
Burrell Dri. *Wir*—2D **93**
Burrell Rd. *Birk*—4B **118**
Burrell St. *L4*—3F **55**
Burroughs Gdns. *L3*—2D **77**
Burrow's Av. *Hay*—3F **47**
Burrows Ct. *L3*—1C **76**
Burrows Ct. *St H*—5E **47**
Burrow's La. *Ecc L*—4E **63**
Burrows St. *Hay*—2A **48**
Burton Av. *Rain*—2A **86**
Burton Av. *Wall*—1E **73**
Burton Clo. *L1*—1D **99**
Burton Clo. *Rain*—2A **86**
Burton Clo. *Wid*—1E **131**
Burtonhead Rd. *St H*—1F **65**
Burton St. *L5*—5B **54**
Burtons Way. *L32*—5C **22**
Burtonwood. —5E 69
Burtonwood Ind. Est. *Btnwd*—4F **69**
Burtree Rd. *L14*—5A **60**
Burwell Clo. *L33*—2A **24**
Burwell Wlk. *L33*—2A **24**
Burwen Dri. *L9*—2F **35**
Busby's Cotts. *Wall*—3B **52**
Bushel's Dri. *Clo F*—3E **89**
Bushey Rd. *L4*—1C **56**
Bushley Clo. *Boot*—4B **34**
Bush Rd. *Wid*—2F **151**
Bush Way. *Wir*—2E **157**
Butcher's La. *Augh*—2F **7**

Bute St. *L5* —2E **77** (1G **5**)
(in two parts)
Butleigh Rd. *L36* —1D **83**
Butler Cres. *L6* —3B **78**
Butler St. *L6* —2B **78**
(in two parts)
Buttercup Clo. *L22* —4F **17**
Buttercup Clo. *Wir* —4A **72**
Buttercup Way. *L9* —4B **36**
Butterfield St. *L4* —4F **55**
Buttermere Av. *St H* —5A **30**
Buttermere Av. *Pren* —3C **94**
Buttermere Clo. *Kirkby* —1D **23**
Buttermere Clo. *Mag* —1E **13**
Buttermere Clo. *Frod* —5D **173**
*Buttermere Ct. Birk —4C **96***
(off Penrith St.)
Buttermere Gdns. *L23* —3F **17**
Buttermere Gro. *Beech* —5D **167**
Buttermere Rd. *L16* —5A **82**
Buttermere St. *L8* —2B **100**
Butterton Av. *Wir* —3D **93**
Butterwick Dri. *L12* —5E **39**
Button St. *L2* —5C **76** (5E **4**)
Butts, The. *Cas* —5F **153**
Buxted Rd. *L32* —5A **24**
Buxted Wlk. *L32* —5A **24**
Buxton La. *Wall* —1E **73**
Buxton Rd. *Birk* —2A **120**
Byerley St. *Wall* —4D **75**
Byland Clo. *Wid* —4C **110**
Byles St. *L8* —5A **100**
Byng Pl. *L4* —3D **57**
Byng Rd. *L4* —3D **57**
Byng St. *Mil B* —1B **54**
By-Pass, The. *Cros* —1E **17**
Byrne Av. *Birk* —3F **119**
Byrom St. *L3* —3D **77** (3F **5**)
Byrom Way. *L3* —3D **77** (2F **5**)
Byron Av. *L12* —4A **58**
Byron Av. *Whis* —3F **85**
Byron Clo. *St H* —3A **46**
Byron Clo. *Huy* —5A **84**
Byron Clo. *Pren* —4F **117**
Byron Rd. *Cros* —1C **16**
Byron Rd. *Mag* —4D **7**
Byron St. *Boot* —3A **34**
Byron St. *L19* —2C **144**
Byron St. *Run* —1A **166**
Byron Ter. *L23* —1C **16**
Byton Wlk. *L33* —1A **24**
Byway, The. *L23* —5E **9**

Cabbage Hall. —5C 56
Cabes Clo. *L14* —4A **60**
Cable Rd. *Whis* —1F **85**
Cable Rd. *Wir* —4B **90**
Cable Rd. S. *Wir* —5B **90**
Cable St. *L1* —5C **76** (6D **4**)
Cabot Grn. *L25* —4E **103**
Cadbury Clo. *L12* —1B **58**
Caddick Rd. *Know B* —3B **40**
Cadmus Wlk. *L6* —2F **77**
Cadnam Rd. *L25* —4D **105**
Cadogan St. *L15* —1D **101**
Cadwell Rd. *L31* —2B **6**
Caernarvon Clo. *Cas* —5F **153**
Caernarvon Clo. *Wir* —3A **94**
Caernarvon Ct. *Wir* —3F **141**
Caerwys Gro. *Birk* —5E **97**
Caesars Clo. *Cas* —5E **153**
Cains Brewery. —2D 99
Caird St. *L6* —3A **78**
Cairn Ct. *That H* —3D **65**
Cairnmore Rd. *L18* —2A **124**
Cairns St. *L8* —3A **100**
Cairo St. *L4* —2E **55**
Cairo St. *St H* —2D **65**

Caithness Ct. *Run* —5B **152**
Caithness Dri. *L23* —2F **17**
Caithness Dri. *Wall* —5C **52**
Caithness Gdns. *Pren* —3F **117**
Caithness Rd. *L18* —3B **124**
Calcott Rake. *Boot* —1E **19**
Calday Grange Clo. *Wir* —5D **113**
Caldbeck Gro. *St H* —4C **30**
Caldbeck Rd. *Croft B* —5D **143**
Calder Av. *Pren* —2F **117**
Calder Clo. *L33* —4F **15**
Calder Clo. *Wid* —1F **133**
Calder Dri. *Mag* —5E **7**
Calder Dri. *Moss H* —4C **102**
Calder Dri. *Rain* —3B **86**
Calderfield Rd. *L18* —4D **103**
Calder Grange. *L18* —1E **125**
Calderhurst Dri. *Wind* —2B **44**
Calder Rd. *L5* —5F **55**
Calder Rd. *Wir* —2D **141**
Calders, The. *L18* —1C **124**
Calderstones. —1C 124
Calderstones Av. *L18* —4B **102**
Calderstones Pk. —1D 125
Calderstones Rd. *L18* —5B **102**
Calder St. *L5* —5E **55**
Caldicott Av. *Wir* —3D **163**
Caldway Dri. *L27* —3D **105**
Caldwell Clo. *L33* —1F **23**
Caldwell Dri. *Wir* —2B **116**
Caldwell Rd. *L19* —4C **124**
Caldwell Rd. *Wid* —5A **132**
Caldwell St. *St H* —5D **47**
Caldy. —2D 135
Caldy Chase Dri. *Wir* —2D **135**
Caldy Ct. *Wir* —5B **112**
Caldy Golf Course. —4D 135
Caldy Gro. *St H* —3D **47**
Caldy Gro. *Hay* —1A **48**
Caldy Rd. *L9* —1A **36**
Caldy Rd. *Wall* —1B **74**
Caldy Rd. *Wir* —5B **112**
Caldy Wood. *Wir* —2D **135**
Caldywood Dri. *Whis* —3E **85**
Caledonia St. *L7* —1F **99** (7J **5**)
Calgarth Rd. *L36* —1C **82**
California Rd. *L13* —4D **57**
Callaghan Clo. *L5* —1D **77**
Callander Rd. *L6* —3D **79**
Callard Clo. *L27* —3C **104**
Callestock Clo. *L11* —3C **38**
Callington Clo. *L14* —5A **60**
Callon Av. *St H* —3E **47**
Callow Rd. *L15* —2D **101**
Calmet Clo. *L5* —5E **55**
Calmington La. *Run* —3F **155**
Calne Clo. *Wir* —5D **115**
Calthorpe St. *L19* —1B **144**
Calthorpe Way. *Pren* —3D **95**
Calvados Clo. *L17* —3C **122**
Calveley Av. *Wir* —1F **171**
Calveley Clo. *Pren* —1F **117**
Calveley Gro. *L26* —1A **148**
Calverley Clo. *Brook* —5B **168**
Calvers. *Run* —1E **167**
Camberley Dri. *L25* —4C **126**
Camborne Av. *L25* —3C **126**
Camborne Clo. *Brook* —4C **168**
Cambourne Av. *St H* —1D **47**
Cambourne Rd. *Btnwd* —5F **69**
Cambrian Clo. *Wir* —2C **92**
Cambrian Rd. *Wir* —2C **92**
Cambrian Way. *L25* —1B **126**
Cambria St. *L6* —3B **78**
Cambridge Av. *Cros* —5D **9**
Cambridge Av. *Lith* —5B **18**
Cambridge Ct. *L7* —1F **99** (7J **5**)
Cambridge Dri. *Cros* —5C **8**
Cambridge Dri. *Halew* —4F **127**

Cambridge Rd. *Boot* —1D **55**
Cambridge Rd. *Cros* —5C **8**
Cambridge Rd. *St H* —4E **45**
Cambridge Rd. *Walt* —5B **20**
Cambridge Rd. *Wat & S'frth* —1E **33**
Cambridge Rd. *Birk* —2B **118**
Cambridge Rd. *Brom* —2E **163**
Cambridge Rd. *Wall* —4B **52**
Cambridge St. *L7* —5F **77** (6J **5**)
(in three parts)
Cambridge St. *L15* —1D **101**
(in two parts)
Cambridge St. *Prsct* —5D **63**
Cambridge St. *Run* —5C **152**
Cambridge St. *Wid* —5B **132**
Camdale Clo. *L28* —4B **60**
Camden Ct. *Nort* —1D **169**
Camden St. *L3* —4E **77** (3G **5**)
Camden St. *Birk* —2E **97**
Camelford Rd. *L11* —3C **38**
Camellia Ct. *L17* —2A **122**
Camellia Gdns. *St H* —4B **68**
Camelot Clo. *Newt W* —4F **49**
*Camelot Ter. Boot —4B **34***
(off Tennyson St.)
Camelot Way. *Cas* —2A **168**
Cameo Clo. *L6* —2B **78**
Cameron Av. *Run* —2E **165**
Cameron Rd. *Wid* —4A **132**
Cameron Rd. *Wir* —3B **72**
Cameron St. *L7* —4C **78**
Cammell Ct. *Pren* —3B **96**
Campania St. *L19* —3C **144**
Campbell Av. *Run* —2A **166**
Campbell Dri. *L14* —3E **81**
Campbell St. *Boot* —5A **34**
Campbell St. *L1* —1D **99** (7E **5**)
Campbell St. *St H* —4E **45**
Campbeltown Rd. *Birk* —4F **97**
Camperdown St. *Birk* —3F **97**
Camphill Rd. *L25* —4A **126**
Campion Clo. *St H* —1B **46**
Campion Way. *L36* —2F **105**
Camp Rd. *L25* —3B **126**
Campsey Ash. *Wid* —5F **109**
Camrose Clo. *Run* —4C **166**
Cam St. *Wltn* —2F **125**
Canada Boulevd. *L3* —5B **76** (5B **4**)
Canal Reach. *Wind H* —5C **154**
Canalside. *West P* —3D **165**
Canalside Gro. *L5* —1C **76**
Canal St. *Boot* —5B **34**
(in two parts)
Canal St. *Newt W* —5F **49**
Canal St. *St H* —1F **65**
Canal St. *Run* —4B **152**
Canal Vw. *Mell* —2A **22**
Canberra Av. *That H* —4E **65**
Canberra La. *Gil I* —3C **38**
Candia Towers. *L5* —5E **55**
Cannell Ct. *Pal* —4A **168**
Canning Pl. *L1* —5C **76** (7D **4**)
Canning St. *L8* —1F **99**
Canning St. *Wat* —4D **17**
Canning St. *Birk* —2E **97**
Cannington Rd. *St H* —1B **66**
Canniswood Rd. *Hay* —2A **48**
Cannock Grn. *L31* —1B **12**
Cannon Hill. *Pren* —3B **96**
Cannon Mt. *Pren* —3B **96**
Cannon St. *Clo F* —3C **88**
Canon Rd. *L6* —4C **56**
Canon St. *Run* —4A **152**
Canon Wilson Clo. *Hay* —2D **49**
Canrow La. *Know* —3D **41**
Cansfield St. *St H* —4A **46**
Canterbury Av. *L22* —2D **17**
Canterbury Clo. *Ain* —3E **21**
Canterbury Clo. *Prsct* —4E **63**

Canterbury Pk. *L18* —4C **124**
Canterbury Rd. *Birk* —3A **120**
Canterbury Rd. *Wall* —3C **74**
Canterbury Rd. *Wid* —5C **130**
Canterbury St. *L3* —3E **77** (2H **5**)
Canterbury St. *St H* —3E **45**
Canterbury St. *Gars* —3C **144**
Canterbury Way. *Boot* —1F **19**
Canterbury Way. *L3* —3E **77** (2J **5**)
Canter Clo. *L9* —5D **21**
Cantley Clo. *Beech* —4D **167**
Cantsfield St. *L7* —2C **100**
Canvey Clo. *L15* —2B **102**
Cape Rd. *L9* —2C **36**
Capesthorne Clo. *Wid* —4E **131**
Capper Gro. *L36* —3E **83**
Capricorn Cres. *L14* —1F **81**
Capricorn Way. *Boot* —4B **34**
Capstick Cres. *L25* —3B **104**
Captains Clo. *Boot* —5D **19**
Captains Grn. *Boot* —5D **19**
Captains La. *Boot* —5E **19**
Caradoc Rd. *L21* —2A **34**
Caraway Clo. *L23* —5B **10**
Caraway Gro. *St H* —4D **45**
Carbis Clo. *L10* —2A **38**
Carden Clo. *L4* —4E **55**
Cardeston Clo. *Sut W* —2F **173**
Cardigan Av. *Birk* —3D **97**
Cardigan Clo. *St H* —1F **65**
Cardigan Rd. *Wall* —4B **52**
Cardigan St. *L15* —1D **101**
Cardigan Way. *Boot* —1B **20**
Cardigan Way. *L6* —2B **78**
Cardus Clo. *Wir* —1B **92**
Cardwell Rd. *L19* —1C **144**
Cardwell St. *L7* —1A **100**
Carey Av. *Wir* —1D **141**
Carey St. *Wid* —3B **132**
Carfax Rd. *L33* —1A **24**
Cargill Gro. *Birk* —4B **120**
Carham Rd. *Hoy* —5C **90**
Carisbrooke Clo. *Wir* —1C **134**
Carisbrooke Rd. *Boot & L4* —1E **55**
Carkington Rd. *L25* —3C **126**
Carland Clo. *L10* —2B **38**
Carlaw Rd. *Birk* —2A **118**
Carleen Clo. *L17* —2B **122**
Carlett Boulevd. *Wir* —5F **163**
Carlett Pk. *Wir* —4F **163**
Carley Wlk. *L24* —5E **147**
Carlile Way. *L33* —4F **15**
Carlingford Clo. *L8* —2A **100**
Carlisle Av. *Boot* —4F **19**
Carlisle Clo. *L4* —3D **57**
Carlisle Clo. *Pren* —4C **96**
Carlisle M. *Pren* —4C **96**
Carlisle St. *Wid* —3C **132**
Carlis Rd. *L32* —5F **23**
Carlow Clo. *Hale V* —5D **149**
Carlow St. *St H* —2D **65**
Carl's Way. *L33* —4F **15**
Carlton Av. *L18* —4A **102**
Carlton Av. *Run* —5D **153**
Carlton La. *L13* —2A **80**
Carlton La. *Wir* —3C **90**
Carlton Mt. *Birk* —1E **119**
Carlton Rd. *Birk* —5C **96**
Carlton Rd. *Wall* —3B **52**
Carlton Rd. *Wir* —3B **142**
Carlton St. *L3* —2B **76**
Carlton St. *St H* —5E **45**
Carlton St. *Prsct* —4E **63**
Carlton St. *Wid* —4A **132**
Carlton Ter. *Cros* —1D **17**
Carlton Ter. *Wir* —3C **90**
Carlyon Way. *L26* —3E **127**
Carmarthen Cres. *L8* —3D **99**
Carmel Clo. *Wall* —3B **52**
Carmel Ct. *Wid* —1B **132**
Carmelite Cres. *Ecc* —3A **44**
Carmel St. *L5* —5E **55**
Carmichael Av. *Wir* —2D **115**
Carnaby Clo. *L36* —1A **106**
Carnarvon Ct. *L9* —5F **35**
Carnarvon Rd. *L9* —5F **35**
Carnarvon St. *That H* —4D **65**
Carnatic Clo. *L18* —1E **123**
Carnatic Rd. *L18* —1E **123**
Carnation Rd. *L9* —4B **36**
Carnegie Av. *L23* —2D **17**
Carnegie Cres. *St H* —3E **67**
Carnegie Rd. *L13* —2E **79**
Carnegie Wlk. *St H* —3F **67**
Carnforth Av. *L32* —4F **23**
Carnforth Clo. *L12* —2B **58**
Carnforth Clo. *Birk* —4C **96**
Carnforth Rd. *L18* —2C **124**
Carno St. *L15* —1E **101**
Carnoustie Clo. *L12* —5F **59**
Carnoustie Clo. *Wir* —5B **70**
Carnoustie Gro. *Hay* —3B **48**
Carnsdale Rd. *Wir* —1F **93**
Carol Dri. *Wir* —2C **158**
Carole Clo. *Sut L* —5E **67**
Carolina St. *Boot* —5B **34**
Caroline Pl. *Pren* —4B **96**
Caronia St. *L19* —3C **144**
Carpathia St. *L19* —3C **144**
Carpenter's La. *Wir* —4B **112**
Carpenters Row. *L1* —1C **98**
Carraway Rd. *Gil I* —2B **38**
Carr Bri. Rd. *Wir* —5B **94**
Carr Clo. *L11* —1B **58**
Carr Cft. *L21* —2B **18**
Carrfield Av. *L23* —2A **18**
Carrfield Wlk. *L11* —5B **38**
Carr Ga. *Wir* —2B **92**
Carr Hey. *Wir* —1B **92**
Carr Hey Clo. *Wir* —2C **116**
Carr Ho. La. *Wir* —1B **92**
Carrick Ct. *L23* —2A **18**
Carrickmore Av. *L18* —2A **124**
Carrington Rd. *Wall* —5B **52**
Carrington St. *Birk* —1A **96**
Carr La. *Mag* —2A **6**
Carr La. *W Der* —1F **57**
Carr La. *Hoy* —5B **90**
Carr La. *Huy* —4C **82**
Carr La. *Meol & More* —5A **70**
Carr La. *Prsct* —1B **84**
Carr La. *W Kir* —1D **113**
Carr La. *Wid & Hale V* —2E **149**
Carr La. E. *L11* —1B **58**
Carr La. Ind. Est. *Hoy* —5C **90**
Carr Mdw. Hey. *Boot* —3C **18**
Carr Mill. —5C 30
Carr Mill Cres. *Bil* —1E **31**
Carr Mill Rd. *St H* —1C **46**
Carr Mill Rd. *Bil* —1D **31**
(in two parts)
Carrock Rd. *Croft B* —5E **143**
Carrow Clo. *Wir* —2B **92**
Carr Rd. *Boot* —1D **35**
Carrs Ter. *Whis* —3D **85**
Carr St. *Dent G* —3D **45**
Carruthers St. *L3* —3C **76** (1C **4**)
Carrville Way. *L12* —1A **60**
Carrwood Clo. *Hay* —2A **48**
Carsdale Rd. *L18* —4A **102**
Carsgoe Rd. *Hoy* —5C **90**
Carsington Rd. *L11* —1A **58**
Carstairs Rd. *L6* —2C **78**
Carsthorne Rd. *Hoy* —5C **90**
Cartbridge La. *L26* —3F **127**
Carter Av. *Rainf* —1A **28**
Carters, The. *Boot* —1A **20**
Carters, The. *Wir* —5C **92**
Carter St. *L8* —2F **99**
Carterton Rd. *Hoy* —5C **90**
Cartmel Av. *L31* —5E **7**
Cartmel Av. *St H* —1E **45**
Cartmel Clo. *Birk* —4C **96**
Cartmel Dri. *W Der* —2C **58**
Cartmel Dri. *Rain* —2A **86**
Cartmel Dri. *Wir* —2E **93**
Cartmell Clo. *Run* —4B **166**
Cartmel Rd. *L36* —1C **82**
Cartmel Ter. *L11* —5B **38**
Cartmel Way. *L36* —2C **82**
Cartwright St. *Run* —5C **152**
Carver St. *L3* —3F **77** (2J **5**)
Caryl Gro. *L8* —5E **99**
Caryl St. *L8* —4E **99**
(Park St.)
Caryl St. *L8* —3D **99**
(Stanhope St.)
Caryl St. *L8* —4D **99**
(Warwick St.)
Case Gro. *Prsct* —1E **85**
Case Rd. *Hay* —2D **49**
Cases St. *L1* —5D **77** (5F **5**)
Cashel Rd. *Birk* —4B **74**
Caspian Pl. *Boot* —5C **34**
Caspian Rd. *L4* —1C **56**
Cassia Clo. *L9* —4B **36**
Cassino Rd. *L36* —3D **83**
Cassio St. *Boot* —1E **55**
Cassley Rd. *L24* —4A **148**
Cassville Rd. *L18* —3A **102**
Castell Gro. *St H* —5F **45**
Castle Av. *St H* —5E **47**
Castle Clo. *Wir* —3A **72**
Castle Dri. *Hes* —2F **157**
Castlefield Clo. *L12* —4A **58**
Castlefield Rd. *L12* —4A **58**
Castlefields. —5A 154
Castlefields Av. E. *Cas & Run* —1A **168**
Castlefields Av. N. *Cas* —5E **153**
Castlefields Av. S. *Cas* —1F **167**
Castle Fields Est. *Wir* —2F **71**
Castleford Ri. *Wir* —3E **71**
Castleford St. *L15* —2A **102**
Castlegate Gro. *L12* —4A **58**
Castlegrange Clo. *Wir* —2E **71**
Castleheath Clo. *Wir* —3E **71**
Castle Hill. *L2* —5C **4**
Castle Keep. *L12* —4B **58**
Castle Mt. *Hes* —2F **157**
Castle Pk. —5A 172
Castle Ri. *Run* —5D **153**
Castle Rd. *Halt* —2F **167**
Castle Rd. *Wall* —5A **52**
Castlesite Rd. *L12* —4B **58**
Castle St. *L2* —5C **76** (5C **4**)
Castle St. *Birk* —3F **97**
Castle St. *Wid* —3D **133**
Castle St. *Wltn* —2F **125**
Castleton Dri. *Boot* —1B **20**
Castletown Clo. *L16* —1E **103**
Castleview Rd. *L12* —4B **58**
Castleway N. *Wir* —2A **72**
Castleway S. *Wir* —3A **72**
Castlewell. *Whis* —2F **85**
Castlewood Rd. *L6* —1B **78**
Castner Av. *West P* —3E **165**
Castor St. *L6* —1B **78**
Catalyst Mus., The. —2A 152
Catchdale Moss La. *St H* —4E **43**
Catford Clo. *Wid* —2C **130**
Catford Grn. *L24* —4F **147**
Catharine St. *L8* —2F **99** (7J **5**)
Cathcart St. *Birk* —2D **97**
Cathedral Clo. *L1* —2E **99**
Cathedral Ga. *L1* —1E **99**
Cathedral Rd. *L6* —5C **56**
Cathedral Wlk. *L3* —5E **77** (6H **5**)

Catherine Ct. L21 —2B 34
(off Linacre Rd.)
Catherine St. L21 —2B 34
Catherine St. Birk —3D 97
Catherine St. Wid —5A 132
Catherine Way. Hay —2F 47
Catkin Rd. L26 —2D 127
Catonfield Rd. L18 —4D 103
Catterall Av. St H —5D 67
Catterick Clo. L26 —4F 127
Caulfield Dri. Wir —1E 115
Caunce Av. Hay —2B 48
Causeway Clo. Wir —1B 142
Causeway, The. L12 —2D 81
Causeway, The. Wir —2B 142
(in two parts)
Cavan Rd. L11 —3E 57
Cavell Clo. L25 —3A 126
Cavendish Ct. L4 —2E 55
Cavendish Ct. L18 —1C 124
Cavendish Dri. L9 —5A 36
Cavendish Dri. Birk —3D 119
Cavendish Farm Rd. West —5F 165
Cavendish Gdns. L8 —4A 100
Cavendish Rd. Cros —2C 16
Cavendish Rd. Birk —2B 96
Cavendish Rd. Wall —2B 52
Cavendish St. Birk —1B 96
Cavendish St. Run —5F 151
(in two parts)
Cavern Ct. L6 —3B 78
(off Coleridge St.)
Cavern Quarter. —5C 76 (5D 4)
Cavern Walks. L2 —5C 76 (5D 4)
Cawdor St. L8 —3A 100
Cawdor St. Run —4F 151
Cawfield Av. Wid —3D 131
Cawley St. Run —1A 166
Cawthorne Av. L32 —5E 23
Cawthorne Clo. L32 —5E 23
Cawthorne Wlk. L32 —5E 23
Caxton Clo. Pren —3C 94
Caxton Clo. Wid —1C 130
Caxton Rd. Rain —5E 87
Cazneau St. L3 —2D 77 (1F 5)
Cearns Rd. Pren —4A 96
Cecil Dri. Ecc —3A 44
Cecil Rd. L21 —2F 33
Cecil Rd. Birk —2B 118
Cecil Rd. Wall —2A 74
Cecil Rd. Wir —4B 120
Cecil St. L15 —1D 101
Cecil St. St H —4F 67
Cedar Av. Beb —3E 141
Cedar Av. Run —3C 166
Cedar Av. Sut W —1A 174
Cedar Av. Wid —2B 132
Cedar Clo. L18 —1D 125
Cedar Clo. Whis —2E 85
Cedar Cres. L36 —5D 83
Cedar Dale Pk. Wid —5E 111
Cedardale Rd. L9 —4A 36
Cedar Gro. Mag —4D 13
Cedar Gro. Wat —3D 17
Cedar Gro. Hay —1E 49
Cedar Gro. Tox —3B 100
Cedar Rd. L9 —2B 36
Cedar Rd. Whis —3D 85
Cedars, The. L12 —5F 39
Cedars, The. Wir —2C 92
Cedar St. Boot —4C 34
Cedar St. St H —1D 65
Cedar St. Birk —4D 97
Cedar Ter. L8 —3B 100
Cedar Towers. L33 —2F 23
Cedarway. Wir —5B 158
Cedarwood Clo. Wir —5C 92
Cedarwood Ct. L36 —1E 105
Celandine Way. St H —4B 68
Celebration Dri. L6 —1C 78
Celendine Clo. L15 —1E 101
Celia St. L20 —2D 55
Celtic Rd. Wir —2E 91
Celtic St. L8 —3A 100
Celt St. L6 —2B 78
Cemeas Clo. L5 —1C 76
Centenary Clo. L4 —3C 56
Centenary Ho. Run —2C 166
Central Av. Ecc P —4F 63
Central Av. L24 —4C 146
Central Av. Prsct —5C 62
Central Av. Wir —1C 162
Central Dri. L12 —1B 80
Central Dri. Hay —2B 48
Central Dri. Sand P —1A 80
Central Expressway. Halt L —3E 167
Central Library. —4D 77 (3F 5)
Central Pde. L24 —4E 147
Central Pk. —3B 74
Central Pk. Av. Wall —2C 74
Central Rd. Port S —3B 142
Central Rd. Wir —5B 120
Central Shop. Cen. L1 —5D 77 (6F 5)
Central Sq. L31 —5D 7
Central St. St H —4A 46
Central Way. L24 —4E 147
Centreville Rd. L18 —3A 102
Centre Way. Huy —4E 83
Centurion Clo. Wir —2E 91
Centurion Dri. Wir —2E 91
Centurion Row. Cas —5F 153
Century Rd. L23 —1D 17
Ceres Ct. Pren —2C 94
Ceres St. L20 —2C 54
Cestrian Dri. Wir —2A 138
Chadlow Rd. L32 —1F 39
Chadwell Rd. L33 —1F 23
Chadwick Green. —2D 31
Chadwick Rd. St H —1C 46
Chadwick Rd. Ast I —4E 153
Chadwick St. L3 —2B 76 (1B 4)
Chadwick St. Wir —1E 93
Chaffinch Clo. L12 —2F 59
Chaffinch Glade. L26 —3E 127
Chainhurst Clo. L27 —4D 105
Chain La. St H —1D 47
Chain Wlk. Ecc —5C 44
Chalfont Rd. L18 —3D 125
Chalfont Way. L28 —4B 60
Chalgrave Clo. Wid —1E 133
Chalkwell Dri. Wir —3C 158
Challis St. Birk —5E 73
Challoner Clo. L36 —1F 105
Chaloner Gro. L19 —5F 123
Chaloner St. L3 —2D 99
Chalon Way. St H —5A 46
Chalon Way W. St H —5F 45
Chamberlain Dri. L33 —5F 15
Chamberlain St. St H —5D 45
Chamberlain St. Birk —5E 97
Chamberlain St. Wall —4A 74
Chancellor Rd. Mnr P —2D 155
Chancel St. L4 —4D 55
Chancery La. St H —5E 47
Chandos St. L7 —5B 78
Change La. Will —5B 170
Changford Grn. L33 —2A 24
Changford Rd. L33 —2A 24
Channell Rd. Fair —3C 78
Channel Reach. L23 —2B 16
Channel Rd. Cros —2B 16
Channel, The. Wall —4E 51
Chantrell Rd. Wir —4E 113
Chantry Clo. Pren —3C 94
Chantry Wlk. Wir —4A 158
Chapel Av. L9 —2A 36
Chapel Ct. St H —2D 65
Chapelfields. Frod —5A 172
Chapel Gdns. L5 —1D 77
Chapelhill Rd. Wir —1F 93
Chapel La. Boot —5F 11
Chapel La. Ecc —4B 44
Chapel La. Mell —1A 22
Chapel La. Btnwd —5E 69
Chapel La. Cron & Wid —4C 108
Chapel La. Rain —5E 87
Chapel Pl. L25 —2A 126
Chapel Pl. Gars —1C 144
Chapel Rd. Anf —5C 56
Chapel Rd. Gars —1C 144
Chapel Rd. Wir —3C 90
Chapel St. L3 —4B 76 (4B 4)
Chapel St. St H —3F 45
Chapel St. Hay —2E 49
Chapel St. Prsct —5D 63
Chapel St. Run —5A 152
Chapel St. Wid —5A 132
Chapel Ter. Boot —5B 34
Chapel Vw. Crank —1F 29
Chapel Walks. L3 —4B 4
Chapman Clo. L8 —4E 99
Chapman Clo. Wid —5D 109
Chapman Gro. Prsct —4E 63
Chardstock Dri. L25 —5C 104
Charing Cross. Birk —3C 96
Charlcombe St. Birk —5D 97
Charlecote St. L8 —1F 121
Charles Berrington Rd. L15 —3A 102
Charles Best Grn. Boot —1F 19
Charles Rd. Hoy —5B 90
Charles St. St H —4A 46
Charles St. Birk —2D 97
Charles St. Wid —4A 132
Charleston Rd. L8 —5E 99
Charlesville. Pren —4B 96
Charlesville Ct. Pren —4B 96
Charles Wlk. L14 —3F 81
Charlesworth Clo. L31 —2B 6
Charleywood Rd. Know I —4B 24
Charlock Clo. Boot —1A 20
Charlotte Rd. Wall —1C 74
Charlotte's Mdw. Wir —3A 142
Charlotte Wlk. Wid —5B 132
Charlotte Way. L1 —5F 5
Charlton Clo. Pal —3A 168
Charlton Ct. Pren —3F 95
Charlton Pl. L13 —5A 80
Charlton Rd. L13 —5A 80
Charlwood Av. L36 —5D 83
Charlwood Clo. Pren —3C 94
Charmalue Av. L23 —1F 17
Charmouth Clo. L12 —4E 39
Charnock Av. Newt W —5F 49
Charnock Rd. L9 —5C 36
Charnwood Rd. L36 —3B 82
Charnwood St. St H —4E 47
Charterhouse. L25 —3B 126
Charter Ho. Wall —2D 75
Charterhouse Dri. L10 —3E 21
Charterhouse Rd. L25 —3B 126
Chartmount Way. L25 —5B 104
Chartwell Gro. L26 —3A 128
Chaser Clo. L9 —5C 20
Chase, The. L36 —1F 105
Chase, The. Wir —5C 162
Chasewater. Run —3F 155
Chase Way. L5 —2E 77
Chatburn Wlk. L8 —5F 99
Chater Clo. Whis —5A 64
Chatham Clo. L21 —1F 33
Chatham Ct. Wat —5E 17
Chatham Pl. L7 —5B 78
Chatham Rd. Birk —2A 120
Chatham St. L8 —1F 99
Chatsworth Av. L9 —2F 35
Chatsworth Av. Wall —2C 74
Chatsworth Dri. L7 —1B 100

Chatsworth Dri. *Wid* —1C **130**
Chatsworth Rd. *Birk* —2A **120**
Chatsworth Rd. *Rain* —2B **86**
Chatsworth Rd. *Wir* —2F **137**
Chatteris Pk. *Run* —5D **155**
Chatterton Dri. *Murd* —2E **169**
Chatterton Rd. *L14* —2B **80**
Chaucer Dri. *L12* —1E **59**
Chaucer Rd. *Dent G* —2D **45**
Chaucer St. *Boot* —4A **34**
Chaucer St. *L3* —3D **77** (1F **5**)
Chaucer St. *Run* —1A **166**
Chavasse Pk. —5C 76
Cheadle Av. *L13* —3F **79**
Cheapside. *L2* —4C **76** (3D **4**)
Cheapside All. *L2* —4D **4**
Cheddar Clo. *L25* —2F **125**
Cheddar Gro. *L32* —1E **39**
Cheddar Gro. *Btnwd* —4F **69**
Cheddon Way. *Wir* —3E **137**
Chedworth Dri. *Wid* —5C **108**
Chedworth Rd. *L14* —2E **81**
Cheldon Rd. *L12* —1C **58**
Chelford Clo. *Pren* —2C **94**
Chellow Dene. *L23* —4A **10**
Chelmsford Clo. *L4* —4D **55**
Chelsea Ct. *L12* —3E **59**
Chelsea Rd. *Lith* —2B **34**
Chelsea Rd. *Walt* —2A **36**
Cheltenham Av. *L17* —3D **101**
Cheltenham Clo. *L10* —4E **21**
Cheltenham Cres. *L36* —5C **82**
Cheltenham Cres. *Run* —4B **166**
Cheltenham Cres. *Wir* —3E **71**
Cheltenham Rd. *Wall* —5E **51**
Chelwood Av. *L16* —5E **81**
Chemistry Rd. *L24* —2C **146**
Chenotrie Gdns. *Pren* —4D **95**
Chepstow Av. *Wall* —2C **74**
Chepstow St. *L4* —2E **55**
Chequers Gdns. *L19* —4F **123**
Cheriton Av. *Wir* —4D **113**
Cheriton Clo. *L26* —4E **127**
Chermside Rd. *L17* —3E **123**
Cherry Av. *L4* —2B **56**
Cherrybank. *Wall* —4B **74**
Cherry Blossom Rd. *Beech* —1F **173**
*Cherry Brow Ter. Will —5A **170***
(off Hadlow Rd.)
Cherry Clo. *L4* —2B **56**
Cherry Clo. *Newt W* —4F **49**
Cherrydale Rd. *L18* —5A **102**
Cherryfield Cres. *L32* —3E **23**
Cherryfield Dri. *L32* —3D **23**
Cherry Gdns. *L32* —1F **39**
Cherry La. *L4* —2A **56**
Cherry Sq. *Wall* —2B **74**
Cherrysutton. *Wid* —1A **130**
Cherry Tree Av. *Run* —2C **166**
Cherry Tree Clo. *Hale V* —5E **149**
Cherry Tree Clo. *Hay* —3A **48**
Cherry Tree Clo. *Whis* —3D **85**
Cherry Tree Dri. *St H* —1A **68**
Cherry Tree La. *St H* —3A **30**
Cherry Tree Rd. *L36* —1E **105**
Cherry Tree Rd. *Wir* —2F **93**
Cherry Va. *L25* —1B **126**
Cherry Vw. *L33* —5F **15**
Cheryl Dri. *Wid* —3D **133**
Cheshire Acre. *Wir* —2A **116**
Cheshire Av. *L10* —1B **38**
Cheshire Gdns. *St H* —1E **65**
Cheshire Gro. *Wir* —2E **93**
Cheshire Way. *Wir* —4F **137**
Cheshyre Dri. *Halt* —1F **167**
Cheshyres La. *West* —3E **165**
(in two parts)
Chesnell Gro. *L33* —5F **15**
Chesney Clo. *L8* —3E **99**
Chesnut Gro. *Birk* —5D **97**
Chesnut Rd. *L21* —5F **17**
Chester Av. *Boot* —4F **19**
Chester Clo. *L23* —1B **18**
Chester Clo. *Cas* —5F **153**
Chester Ct. *Wir* —3F **141**
Chesterfield Dri. *L33* —5E **15**
Chesterfield Rd. *L23* —5A **10**
Chesterfield Rd. *Wir* —1D **171**
Chesterfield St. *L8* —2E **99**
Chester High Rd. *Burt & Nest* —5D **159**
Chester La. *St H & Sut M* —2B **88**
Chester Rd. *Anf* —1D **79**
Chester Rd. *Dar* —3F **169**
Chester Rd. *Hel & Frod* —5A **172**
Chester Rd. *Hes* —3B **158**
Chester Rd. *Huy* —2A **84**
Chester Rd. *Sut W & Pres B* —3F **173**
Chester St. *L8* —2E **99**
Chester St. *Birk* —4F **97**
Chester St. *Prsct* —5D **63**
Chester St. *Wall* —3A **74**
Chester St. *Wid* —3B **132**
Chesterton St. *L19* —3C **144**
Chester Wlk. *L36* —2A **84**
Chestnut Av. *Cros* —4F **9**
Chestnut Av. *Hay* —3F **47**
Chestnut Av. *Huy* —1D **105**
Chestnut Av. *Wid* —2B **132**
Chestnut Clo. *Whis* —2E **85**
Chestnut Clo. *Wir* —3C **114**
Chestnut Ct. *Boot* —4B **34**
Chestnut Ct. *Wid* —3D **131**
Chestnut Gro. *Boot* —3B **34**
(Balfour Rd.)
Chestnut Gro. *Boot* —4B **34**
(Marsh La.)
Chestnut Gro. *St H* —1D **47**
Chestnut Gro. *Brom* —2C **162**
Chestnut Gro. *W'tree* —1F **101**
Chestnut Ho. *Boot* —4B **34**
Chestnut Rd. *Walt* —5B **36**
Chestnut St. *L7* —5F **77** (6J **5**)
Cheswood Clo. *Whis* —4E **85**
*Cheswood Ct. Wir —3A **116***
(off Childwall Grn.)
Chetton Dri. *Murd* —3D **169**
Chetwood Av. *L23* —5F **9**
Chetwood Dri. *Wid* —4F **109**
Chetwynd Clo. *Pren* —5F **95**
Chetwynd Rd. *Pren* —4A **96**
Chetwynd St. *L17* —1B **122**
Chevasse Wlk. *L25* —1C **126**
Cheverton Clo. *Wir* —1B **116**
Chevin Rd. *L9* —3A **36**
Cheviot Av. *St H* —5F **47**
Cheviot Clo. *Birk* —3D **119**
Cheviot Rd. *L7* —4E **79**
Cheviot Rd. *Birk* —3C **118**
Cheviot Way. *L33* —4F **15**
Cheyne Clo. *L23* —2A **16**
Cheyne Gdns. *L19* —4F **123**
Cheyne Wlk. *St H* —5F **65**
Chichester Clo. *L15* —1D **101**
Chichester Clo. *Murd* —4D **169**
Chidden Clo. *Wir* —1C **114**
Chidlow Clo. *Wid* —2A **152**
Chigwell Clo. *L12* —5E **39**
Chilcott Rd. *L14* —3C **80**
Childers St. *L13* —3F **79**
Childer Thornton. —5F 171
Childwall. —2D 103
Childwall Abbey Rd. *L16* —2D **103**
Childwall Av. *L15* —2C **100**
Childwall Av. *Wir* —2D **93**
Childwall Bank Rd. *L16* —2D **103**
Childwall Clo. *Wir* —2D **93**
Childwall Cres. *L16* —2D **103**
Childwall Fiveways. *L15* —2C **102**
Childwall Golf Course. —2E 105
Childwall Grn. *Wir* —2A **116**
Childwall Heights. *L25* —2F **103**
Childwall La. *Bow P* —4A **82**
Childwall La. *Child* —3F **103**
Childwall Mt. Rd. *L16* —2D **103**
Childwall Pde. *L14* —3A **82**
Childwall Pk. Av. *L16* —3D **103**
Childwall Priory Rd. *L16* —2C **102**
Childwall Rd. *L15* —2A **102**
Childwall Valley Rd. *L16 & L25* —2D **103**
Childwall Valley Rd. *L25 & L27* —3B **104**
Chilhem Clo. *L8* —5F **99**
Chilington Av. *Wid* —4D **131**
Chillerton Rd. *L12* —3D **59**
Chillingham St. *L8* —5A **100**
Chiltern Clo. *Kirkby* —1C **22**
Chiltern Clo. *W Der* —1F **59**
Chiltern Dri. *L32* —1C **22**
Chiltern Rd. *St H* —5F **47**
Chiltern Rd. *Birk* —3C **118**
Chilton Clo. *L31* —1D **13**
Chilton M. *L31* —1D **13**
Chilwell Clo. *Wid* —5D **109**
China Farm La. *Wir* —2E **113**
Chippenham Av. *Wir* —5C **92**
Chirkdale St. *L4* —2E **55**
Chirk Way. *Wir* —2F **93**
Chirton Clo. *Hay* —1D **49**
Chisenhale St. *L3* —2C **76** (1C **4**)
Chisledon Clo. *Hay* —1D **49**
Chislehurst Av. *L25* —3A **104**
Chislet Ct. *Wid* —5E **109**
Chisnall Av. *St H* —4C **44**
Chiswell St. *L7* —4C **78**
Chiswick Clo. *Murd* —3D **169**
Cholmondeley Rd. *Clftn* —1D **173**
Cholmondeley Rd. *W Kir* —4B **112**
Cholmondeley St. *Wid* —3A **152**
Cholsey Clo. *Wir* —5F **93**
Chorley Rd. *Prsct* —5B **62**
Chorley's La. *Wid* —1D **133**
Chorley St. *St H* —4F **45**
Chorley Way. *Wir* —1A **162**
Chorlton Clo. *L16* —1F **103**
Chorlton Clo. *Wind H* —1D **169**
Chorlton Gro. *Wall* —1D **73**
Christchurch Rd. *Pren* —5B **96**
Christian St. *L3* —3D **77** (2F **5**)
Christie St. *Wid* —3D **133**
Christleton Clo. *Pren* —2D **117**
Christleton Ct. *Mnr P* —3C **154**
Christmas St. *L20* —2C **54**
(Brasenose Rd.)
Christmas St. *L20* —2D **55**
(Stanley Rd.)
Christopher Clo. *L16* —1D **103**
Christophers Clo. *Wir* —3A **138**
Christopher St. *L4* —3F **55**
Christopher Taylor Ho. *Mag* —3D **13**
Christopher Way. *L16* —1D **103**
Christowe Wlk. *L11* —3C **38**
Chrisward Clo. *L7* —5C **78**
Chudleigh Clo. *L26* —3E **127**
Chudleigh Rd. *L13* —3E **79**
Church All. *L1* —5D **77** (6E **5**)
Church Av. *L9* —1B **36**
Church Clo. *Wall* —2D **75**
Church Cotts. *L25* —4C **104**
Church Cres. *Wall* —4E **75**
Churchdown Clo. *L14* —2F **81**
Churchdown Gro. *L14* —2E **81**
Churchdown Rd. *L14* —2E **81**
Church Dri. *Wir* —1B **142**
Church Farm Ct. *Will* —5A **170**
Church Farm Ct. *Wir* —3F **157**
Churchfield Rd. *L25* —4C **104**

Churchfield Rd. *Frod* —5C **172**
Churchfields. *Clo F* —2C **88**
Churchfields. *Wid* —4B **110**
Church Flats. *L4* —1F **55**
Church Gdns. *Boot* —5B **34**
Church Gdns. *Wall* —2D **75**
Church Grn. *Kirkby* —2E **23**
Church Grn. *Child* —2F **103**
Church Gro. *L21* —2F **33**
Church Hill. *Wall* —1F **73**
Churchill Av. *Birk* —2B **96**
Churchill Gdns. *St H* —5C **64**
Churchill Gro. *Wall* —1C **74**
Churchill Ho. *S'frth* —1F **33**
Churchill Ind. Est. *L9* —5C **20**
Churchill Way N. *L3* —4D **77** (3E **4**)
Churchill Way S. *L2* —4D **77** (4E **5**)
Churchlands. Wall —4E ***75***
(off Bridle Rd.)
Church La. *Augh* —1F **7**
Church La. *Ecc* —5A **44**
Church La. *Know* —4C **40**
Church La. *Walt* —1F **55**
Church La. *Aig* —3E **123**
Church La. *East* —5F **163**
Church La. *Thur* —2B **136**
Church La. *Upt* —2B **116**
Church La. *Wall* —2D **75**
(in two parts)
Church La. *Wir* —1D **163**
Churchmeadow Clo. *Wall* —2D **75**
Church Mdw. La. *Wir* —3E **157**
Church Mdw. Wlk. *Wid* —2B **150**
Church M. *L24* —4B **146**
Church Mt. *L7* —5B **78**
Church Pl. *Birk* —1D **119**
Church Rd. *Boot* —2D **35**
Church Rd. *Cros* —1E **17**
Church Rd. *Lith* —1B **34**
(in two parts)
Church Rd. *Mag* —3D **13**
Church Rd. *Rainf* —1A **28**
Church Rd. *S'frth* —2F **33**
Church Rd. *Walt* —1A **56**
Church Rd. *Wat* —4D **17**
Church Rd. *Beb* —4A **142**
Church Rd. *Birk* —1D **119**
Church Rd. *Gars* —2C **144**
Church Rd. *Halew* —2E **127**
Church Rd. *Hay* —2E **49**
Church Rd. *Stan* —4F **79**
Church Rd. *Thor H* —4B **160**
Church Rd. *Upt* —4A **94**
Church Rd. *Wall* —4E **75**
Church Rd. *W'tree* —3A **102**
Church Rd. *W Kir* —5A **112**
Church Rd. *Wltn* —5F **103**
Church Rd. N. *L15* —2A **102**
Church Rd. Roby. *Roby* —4C **82**
Church Rd. S. *L25* —2A **126**
Church Rd. W. *L4* —1F **55**
Church Sq. *St H* —5A **46**
Church St. *Boot* —5A **34**
Church St. *L1* —5D **77** (5E **4**)
Church St. *St H* —5A **46**
Church St. *Birk* —3F **97**
(in two parts)
Church St. *Frod* —5B **172**
Church St. *Prsct* —5D **63**
Church St. *Run* —4A **152**
Church St. *Wall* —2D **75**
Church St. *Wid* —2A **152**
Church Ter. *Birk* —1D **119**
Church Vw. *Boot* —5B **34**
Churchview Rd. *Birk* —1B **96**
Church Wlk. *Boot* —5B **34**
Church Wlk. *Ecc* —4A **44**
Church Wlk. *Wir* —5B **112**
Church Way. *Boot* —1D **19**
Church Way. *Kirkby* —2E **23**
Churchway Rd. *L24* —5A **148**
Churchwood Clo. *Wir* —1D **163**
Churchwood Ct. *Wir* —3B **116**
Churnet St. *L4* —3E **55**
Churn Way. *Wir* —5D **93**
Churston Rd. *L16* —4E **103**
Churton Av. *Pren* —1F **117**
Churton Ct. *L6* —3F **77**
Ciaran Clo. *L12* —3D **59**
Cicely St. *L7* —5B **78**
Cinder La. *Boot* —1D **35**
Cinder La. *L18* —4C **102**
Circular Dri. *Grea* —1D **115**
Circular Dri. *Hes* —1F **157**
Circular Dri. *Port S* —5B **120**
Circular Rd. *Birk* —4D **97**
Circular Rd. E. *L11* —3F **57**
Circular Rd. W. *L11* —3F **57**
Cirencester Av. *Wir* —5C **92**
Citrine Rd. *Wall* —4D **75**
Citron Clo. *L9* —4B **36**
City Gdns. *St H* —1F **45**
City Rd. *L4* —2F **55**
City Rd. *St H* —2F **45**
City Vw. *St H* —4A **30**
Civic Way. *L36* —4E **83**
Civic Way. *Beb* —2A **142**
Clairville Clo. *Boot* —5C **34**
Clairville Ct. *Boot* —5C **34**
Clairville Way. *L13* —1E **79**
Clamley Ct. *L24* —4A **148**
Clamley Gdns. *Hale V* —5E **149**
Clandon Rd. *L18* —3C **124**
Clanfield Av. *Wid* —1C **130**
Clanfield Rd. *L11* —1A **58**
Clapgate Cres. *Wid* —2B **150**
Clapham Rd. *L4* —5B **56**
Clare Clo. *St H* —4E **65**
Clare Cres. *Wall* —1F **73**
Claremont Av. *L31* —2B **12**
Claremont Av. *Wid* —5C **110**
Claremont Clo. *S'frth* —1F **33**
Claremont Dri. *Wid* —5B **110**
Claremont Rd. *Cros* —1E **17**
Claremont Rd. *S'frth* —1F **33**
Claremont Rd. *Run* —5B **152**
Claremont Rd. *W'tree* —3E **101**
Claremont Rd. *Wir* —3B **112**
Claremont Way. *Wir* —4D **119**
Claremount Dri. *Wir* —3F **141**
Claremount Rd. *Wall* —4F **51**
Clarence Av. *Wid* —5A **110**
Clarence Clo. *St H* —1C **66**
Clarence Rd. *Birk* —1C **118**
Clarence Rd. *Wall* —4D **75**
Clarence St. *L3* —5E **77** (5H **5**)
Clarence St. *Newt W* —4F **49**
Clarence St. *Run* —4F **151**
Clarence Ter. *Run* —4A **152**
Clarendon Clo. *Murd* —3D **169**
Clarendon Clo. *Pren* —4C **96**
Clarendon Gro. *L31* —2C **6**
Clarendon Rd. *S'frth* —2F **33**
Clarendon Rd. *Anf* —5C **56**
Clarendon Rd. *Gars* —1C **144**
Clarendon Rd. *Wall* —3D **75**
Clare Rd. *Boot* —1D **55**
Claret Clo. *L17* —3C **122**
Clare Wlk. *L10* —1B **38**
Clare Way. *Wall* —1F **73**
Claribel St. *L8* —3A **100**
Clarke Av. *Birk* —2E **119**
Clarke Gdns. *Wid* —5B **132**
Clarke's Cres. *Ecc* —4B **44**
Clarks Ter. *West P* —2D **165**
Classic Rd. *L13* —2A **80**
Clatterbridge Rd. *Wir* —2D **161**
(in two parts)
Claude Rd. *L6* —5C **56**
Claughton Clo. *L7* —5C **78**
Claughton Dri. *Wall* —3B **74**
Claughton Firs. *Pren* —5B **96**
Claughton Grn. *Pren* —4A **96**
Claughton Pl. *Birk* —3C **96**
Claughton Rd. *Birk* —3C **96**
Claughton St. *St H* —4A **46**
Clavell Rd. *L19* —4D **125**
Claverton Clo. *Run* —4B **166**
Clay Cross Rd. *L25* —2F **125**
Claydon Ct. *L26* —3A **128**
Clayfield Clo. *Boot* —5D **35**
Clayford Cres. *L14* —2B **80**
Clayford Pl. *L14* —2B **80**
Clayford Rd. *L14* —2B **80**
Clayford Way. *L14* —2C **80**
Clay La. *St H* —5D **43**
Clay La. *Btnwd* —5E **69**
Claypole Clo. *L7* —1C **100**
Clay St. *L3* —2B **76**
Clayton Cres. *Run* —1F **165**
Clayton Cres. *Wid* —3F **131**
Clayton La. *Wall* —4A **74**
Clayton Pl. *Birk* —4C **96**
Clayton Sq. *L1* —5D **77** (5F **5**)
Clayton St. *Birk* —4C **96**
Cleadon Clo. *L32* —1A **40**
Cleadon Rd. *L32* —1F **39**
Clearwater Clo. *L7* —4B **78**
Cleary St. *Boot* —4B **34**
Clee Hill Rd. *Birk* —3C **118**
Cleethorpes Rd. *Murd* —3C **168**
Clegg St. *L5* —2E **77**
Clematis Rd. *L27* —3E **105**
Clement Gdns. *L3* —2C **76**
Clementina Rd. *L23* —1B **16**
Clemmey Dri. *Boot* —2E **35**
Clent Av. *L31* —4C **6**
Clent Gdns. *L31* —4C **6**
Clent Rd. *L31* —4C **6**
Cleopas St. *L8* —5F **99**
Clevedon St. *L8* —4A **100**
Cleveland Clo. *L32* —1C **22**
Cleveland Sq. *L1* —1D **99** (7E **4**)
Cleveland St. *St H* —2C **66**
Cleveland St. *Birk* —1B **96**
Cleveley Pk. *L18* —3D **125**
Cleveley Rd. *L18* —3C **124**
Cleveley Rd. *Wir* —3E **91**
Cleveleys Av. *Wid* —2D **133**
Cleves, The. *L31* —4E **7**
Clieves Rd. *L32* —4F **23**
Cliff Dri. *Wall* —1D **75**
Cliffe St. *Wid* —3C **132**
Clifford Rd. *Wall* —3B **74**
Clifford St. *L3* —4E **77** (3H **5**)
Clifford St. *Birk* —1A **96**
Cliff Rd. *Wall* —3F **73**
Cliff St. *L7* —4C **78**
Cliff, The. *Wall* —2F **51**
Cliff Vw. *Frod* —5A **172**
Clifton. —1D 173
Clifton Av. *L26* —3E **127**
Clifton Av. *Wir* —2E **171**
Clifton Ct. *L19* —4C **124**
Clifton Ct. *Birk* —4D **97**
Clifton Cres. *St H* —1D **65**
Clifton Cres. *Birk* —3E **97**
Clifton Cres. *Frod* —4C **172**
Clifton Dri. *L10* —3D **21**
Clifton Gro. *L5* —2E **77**
Clifton Gro. *Wall* —2C **74**
Clifton La. *Clftn* —1D **173**
Clifton Rd. *Anf* —1D **79**
Clifton Rd. *Bil* —1D **31**
Clifton Rd. *Birk* —4D **97**
Clifton Rd. *Run* —3A **166**
Clifton Rd. *Sut W* —2E **173**

Clifton Rd. E. *L6* —1D **79**
Clifton St. *L19* —1C **144**
Clifton St. *St H* —4A **46**
Clifton Ter. *St H* —1D **65**
Cliftonville Rd. *Prsct* —5E **63**
Clincton Clo. *Wid* —4A **130**
Clincton Vw. *Wid* —4A **130**
Clinkham Wood. —5A 30
Clinton Pl. *L12* —4F **57**
Clinton Rd. *L12* —4F **57**
Clint Rd. *L7* —5C **78**
(in two parts)
Clint Way. *L7* —5C **78**
Clipper Vw. *Wir* —4B **120**
Clipsley Brook Vw. *Hay* —2F **47**
Clipsley Cres. *Hay* —1A **48**
Clipsley La. *Hay* —2B **48**
Clive Rd. *Pren* —5B **96**
Clock Face. —3D 89
Clock Face Rd. *Clo F & Wid* —1C **88**
Clock La. *Wid* —1F **133**
Cloisters, The. *Cros* —2D **17**
Cloisters, The. *Ecc* —4B **44**
Clorain Clo. *L33* —2A **24**
Clorain Rd. *L33* —2A **24**
Closeburn Av. *Wir* —4E **157**
Close St. *St H* —4E **65**
Close, The. *Cros* —2D **17**
Close, The. *Ecc* —3A **44**
Close, The. *L28* —4C **60**
Close, The. *Walt* —4F **35**
Close, The. *Beb* —3D **119**
Close, The. *Grea* —2D **115**
Close, The. *Hay* —3F **47**
Close, The. *Irby* —1D **137**
Cloudberry Clo. *L27* —3E **105**
Clough Rd. *L24* —3D **147**
Clough, The. *Halt* —1F **167**
Clough Wood. *Beech* —1A **174**
Clovelly Av. *St H* —5D **67**
Clovelly Gro. *Brook* —5B **168**
Clovelly Rd. *L4* —5B **56**
Clover Av. *L26* —2D **127**
Clover Ct. *Brook* —5B **168**
Cloverdale Rd. *L25* —2A **104**
Clover Dri. *Birk* —5E **73**
Cloverfield. *Nort* —3C **168**
Clover Hey. *St H* —1B **46**
Clubmoor. —4E 57
Club St. *St H* —4A **30**
Clwyd Gro. *L12* —3B **58**
Clwyd St. *Birk* —3D **97**
(in two parts)
Clwyd St. *Wall* —4A **52**
Clyde Rd. *L7* —4E **79**
Clydesdale Rd. *Wall* —1D **75**
Clydesdale Rd. *Wir* —3B **90**
Clyde St. *Boot* —3C **54**
Clyde St. *Birk* —2F **119**
Coach Ho. Ct. *Seft* —4E **11**
Coachmans Dri. *L12* —2E **59**
Coach Rd. *L33* —1B **42**
Coach Rd. *Bic & Rainf* —1B **26**
Coalgate La. *Whis* —4C **84**
Coalport Wlk. *St H* —5C **64**
Coal St. *L1* —4E **77** (4G **5**)
Coalville Rd. *St H* —2D **47**
Coastal Dri. *Wall* —3D **51**
Cobal Ct. *Frod* —5B **172**
Cobb Av. *L21* —2B **34**
Cobbles, The. *L26* —2D **127**
Cobblestone Corner. *L19* —5A **124**
Cobden Av. *Birk* —1F **119**
Cobden Ct. *Birk* —1E **119**
Cobden Pl. *L25* —2F **125**
Cobden Pl. *Birk* —1F **119**
Cobden St. *L6* —3F **77**
Cobden St. *Wltn* —2F **125**
Cobden Vw. *L25* —2F **125**
Cobham Av. *L9* —2F **35**
Cobham Rd. *Wir* —2D **93**
Cobham Wlk. *Boot* —1D **19**
Coburg Dock Marina. —3D 99
Coburg St. *Birk* —3D **97**
Coburg Wharf. *L3* —3C **98**
Cochrane St. *L5* —1F **77**
Cockburn St. *L8* —5F **99**
Cockerell Clo. *L4* —4F **55**
Cockerham Way. *L11* —3B **38**
Cock Glade. *Hals P* —5D **85**
(in two parts)
Cocklade La. *Hale V* —5D **149**
Cock La. Ends. *Wid* —3B **150**
Cockshead Rd. *L25* —3B **104**
Cockshead Way. *L25* —3B **104**
Cockspur St. *L3* —4C **76** (3D **4**)
Cockspur St. W. *L3* —4C **76** (3C **4**)
Coerton Rd. *L9* —1B **36**
Cokers, The. *Birk* —4E **119**
Colbern Clo. *L31* —1E **13**
Colby Clo. *L16* —1E **103**
Colebrooke Rd. *L17* —1A **122**
Coleman Dri. *Wir* —1C **114**
Colemere Dri. *Wir* —1B **138**
Coleridge Av. *Dent G* —4D **45**
Coleridge Dri. *Wir* —5A **120**
Coleridge Gro. *Wid* —4E **131**
Coleridge St. *Boot* —4A **34**
Coleridge St. *L6* —3B **78**
Colesborne Rd. *L11* —1A **58**
Coles Cres. *L23* —4B **10**
Coleshill Rd. *L11* —5E **37**
Cole St. *Pren* —3C **96**
Colette Rd. *L10* —1B **38**
Coleus Clo. *L9* —4B **36**
Colin Clo. *L36* —4C **82**
Colindale Rd. *L16* —2E **103**
Colin Dri. *L3* —1C **76**
Colinton St. *L15* —1E **101**
College Av. *Cros* —2D **17**
College Clo. *Pren* —3B **94**
College Clo. *Wall* —5E **51**
College Ct. *L12* —1A **80**
College Dri. *Wir* —5A **120**
College Fields. *L36* —5E **83**
College Grn. Flats. *L23* —2D **17**
College La. *L1* —5D **77** (6E **4**)
College Rd. *L23* —1C **16**
College Rd. N. *L23* —5C **8**
College St. *St H* —4A **46**
(in two parts)
College St. N. *L6* —3F **77** (2J **5**)
College St. S. *L6* —3F **77** (2J **5**)
College Vw. *Boot* —1C **54**
College Vw. *L36* —4E **83**
Collier's Row. *Run* —3E **165**
Collier St. *Run* —4F **151**
Collingwood Rd. *Wir* —3B **142**
Collin Rd. *Pren* —1E **95**
Collins Clo. *Boot* —3A **34**
Collins Green. —2D 69
Collins Grn. La. *C Grn* —2E **69**
Collins Ind. Est. *St H* —3C **46**
Collinson Ct. *Frod* —5B **172**
Colmoor Clo. *L33* —4F **15**
Colmore Av. *Wir* —1F **161**
Colmore Rd. *L11* —1E **57**
Colne Dri. *St H* —4D **67**
Colne Rd. *Btnwd* —5F **69**
Colquitt St. *L1* —1E **99** (7G **5**)
Coltart Rd. *L8* —3B **100**
Colton Rd. *L25* —2F **103**
Colton Wlk. *L25* —2F **103**
Columban Clo. *Boot* —2E **19**
Columbia La. *Pren* —5B **96**
Columbia Rd. *L4* —1A **56**
Columbia Rd. *Pren* —5B **96**
Columbia Rd. *Prsct* —5E **63**
Columbine Clo. *Wid* —5B **108**
Columbine Way. *St H* —4B **68**
Columbus Dri. *Wir* —4E **137**
Columbus Quay. *L3* —1E **121**
Columbus Way. *L21* —1B **34**
Column Rd. *Wir* —4C **112**
Colville Rd. *Wall* —2A **74**
Colville St. *L15* —1E **101**
Colwall Clo. *L33* —3A **24**
Colwall Rd. *L33* —3A **24**
Colwall Wlk. *L33* —3A **24**
Colwell Clo. *L14* —4A **60**
Colwell Ct. *L14* —4A **60**
Colwell Rd. *L14* —5A **60**
Colworth Rd. *L24* —3B **146**
Colwyn Rd. *L13* —4F **79**
Colwyn St. *Birk* —1A **96**
Colyton Av. *Sut L* —1D **89**
Combermere St. *L8* —3E **99**
Combermere St. *L15* —1D **101**
Comely Av. *Wall* —2C **74**
Comely Bank Rd. *Wall* —2D **75**
Comer Gdns. *L31* —4C **6**
Comfrey Gro. *L26* —2E **127**
Commercial Rd. *L5* —5C **54**
Commercial Rd. *Wir* —4E **143**
Common Fld. Rd. *Wir* —3B **116**
Common Rd. *Newt W* —1E **69**
Common St. *Newt W* —5E **49**
Common St. *St H* —4D **65**
Common, The. *Halt* —1F **167**
Commonwealth Pavilion. *L3* —1C **98** (7C **4**)
Commutation Row. *L1* —4D **77** (3G **5**)
Company's Clo. *West* —4F **165**
Compass Clo. *Murd* —5D **169**
Compass Ct. *Wall* —3F **51**
Compton Clo. *Hay* —1C **48**
Compton Rd. *L6* —2A **78**
Compton Rd. *Birk* —5D **73**
Compton Wlk. *Boot* —4B **34**
Compton Way. *Wltn* —1E **147**
Comus St. *L3* —3D **77** (1F **5**)
Concert Sq. *L1* —6F **5**
Concert St. *L1* —5D **77** (7F **5**)
Concordia Av. *Wir* —4A **94**
Concourse Ho. *L1* —4D **77** (4G **5**)
Concourse, The. *Wir* —3A **112**
Concourse Way. *St H* —1F **67**
Condor Clo. *L19* —1C **144**
Condron Rd. N. *L21* —4C **18**
Condron Rd. S. *L21* —4C **18**
Coney Cres. *Cros* —5B **10**
Coney Gro. *Brook* —5A **168**
Coney La. *Tarb G* —2F **105**
Coney Wlk. *Wir* —3D **93**
Conifer Clo. *Kirkby* —5E **15**
Conifer Clo. *Walt* —4B **36**
Conifers, The. *L31* —4C **6**
Coningsby Dri. *Wall* —2A **74**
Coningsby Rd. *L4* —4A **56**
Coniston Av. *Pren* —4C **94**
Coniston Av. *Prsct* —5F **63**
Coniston Av. *Wall* —4E **51**
Coniston Av. *Wir* —1C **170**
Coniston Clo. *Kirkby* —1D **23**
Coniston Clo. *Walt* —1B **36**
Coniston Clo. *Beech* —4D **167**
Coniston Dri. *Frod* —5C **172**
Coniston Gro. *St H* —1A **46**
Coniston Rd. *Mag* —5D **7**
Coniston Rd. *Irby* —1D **137**
Coniston St. *L5* —5A **56**
Conleach Rd. *L24* —5D **147**
Connaught Clo. *Birk* —1A **96**
Connaught Rd. *L7* —4A **78**
Connaught Way. *Birk* —1F **95**
Connolly Av. *Boot* —3E **35**

Conservation Cen., The.
—4D 77 (4E 5)
Consett Rd. *St H*—5D **65**
Constables Clo. *Cas*—1A **168**
Constance St. *L3*—4F **77** (3J **5**)
Constance St. *St H*—1D **65**
Constance Way. *Wid*—1A **152**
Constantine Av. *Wir*—1A **158**
Convent Clo. *L19*—5A **124**
Convent Clo. *Birk*—5D **97**
Conville Boulevd. *Wir*—4D **119**
Conway Clo. *L33*—5D **15**
Conway Clo. *Wir*—2D **141**
Conway Ct. *Beb*—3F **141**
Conway Pl. *Birk*—3D **97**
Conway St. *L5*—1E **77**
Conway St. *St H*—1D **65**
Conway St. *Birk*—2C **96**
(in two parts)
Conwy Dri. *L6*—1B **78**
Cook Av. *Hay*—1E **49**
Cook Rd. *Wir*—2B **72**
Cookson Rd. *L21*—2A **34**
Cookson St. *L1*—2E **99**
Cooks Rd. *L23*—5D **9**
Cook St. *L2*—5C **76** (5D **4**)
Cook St. *Birk*—4C **96**
Cook St. *Prsct*—5D **63**
Cook St. *Whis*—2F **85**
Coombe Dri. *Run*—2F **165**
Coombe Rd. *Wir*—5E **115**
Cooperage Clo. *L8*—5E **99**
Cooper Av. *Newt W*—5F **49**
Cooper Av. N. *L18*—3A **124**
Cooper Av. S. *L19*—3A **124**
Cooper Clo. *L19*—4A **124**
Cooper La. *Hay*—3B **48**
Cooper's La. *Know I*—2D **41**
Coopers Row. *Wat*—5E **17**
Cooper St. *St H*—4F **45**
Cooper St. *Run*—4A **152**
Cooper St. *Wid*—3B **132**
Copeland Clo. *Wir*—3E **137**
Copeland Gro. *Beech*—5E **167**
Copperas Hill. *L3*—5E **77** (5G **5**)
Copperas St. *St H*—5F **45**
Copperfield Clo. *L8*—4F **99**
Copperwood. *Run*—1C **168**
Copperwood Dri. *Whis*—4E **85**
Coppice Clo. *Cas*—1B **168**
Coppice Clo. *Pren*—3B **94**
Coppice Cres. *L36*—2F **83**
Coppice Grange. *Wir*—2C **92**
Coppice Gro. *Wir*—2C **114**
Coppice La. *Tarb G*—2B **106**
Coppice, The. *Know*—5D **41**
Coppice, The. *L4*—5C **56**
Coppice, The. *Wall*—4A **52**
Copple Ho. La. *L10*—1A **38**
Coppull Rd. *L31*—3C **6**
Copse Gro. *Wir*—5E **115**
Copse, The. *L18*—4D **103**
Copse, The. *Pal*—4A **168**
(in two parts)
Copthorne Rd. *L32*—3B **22**
Copthorne Wlk. *L32*—3B **22**
Copy Clo. *Boot*—5F **11**
Copy La. *Boot*—5F **11**
Copy Way. *Boot*—5F **11**
Coral Av. *L36*—3D **83**
Coral Av. *That H*—4F **65**
Coral Dri. *Boot*—5C **34**
Coral Ridge. *Pren*—3D **95**
Coral St. *L13*—5A **80**
Corbet Clo. *L32*—3C **22**
Corbet Wlk. *L32*—3C **22**
Corbridge Rd. *L16*—2C **102**
Corbyn St. *Wall*—4E **75**
Corfu St. *Birk*—3C **96**
Corinthian Av. *L13*—2A **80**
Corinthian St. *L21*—1F **33**
Corinthian St. *Birk*—2F **119**
Corinth Tower. *L5*—5E **55**
Corinto St. *L8*—2E **99**
Cormorant Ct. *Wall*—3E **51**
Cormorant Dri. *Run*—5E **151**
Cormorant Ind. Est. *Run*—5E **151**
Corncroft Rd. *Know*—5D **41**
Corndale Rd. *L18*—5A **102**
Cornelius Dri. *Wir*—2F **137**
Cornel Way. *L36*—1F **105**
Corner Brook. *L28*—4F **59**
Cornerhouse La. *Wid*—1D **131**
Cornett Rd. *L9*—1B **36**
Corney St. *L7*—2C **100**
Cornfields Clo. *L19*—1B **144**
Cornflower Way. *Wir*—4A **72**
Cornforth Way. *Wid*—2E **131**
Corn Hill. *L1*—1C **98**
Cornice Rd. *L13*—2A **80**
Corniche Rd. *Wir*—1B **142**
Cornmill Lodge. *L31*—5C **6**
Corn St. *L8*—4E **99**
Cornubia Rd. *Wid*—5C **132**
Cornwall Av. *Run*—5A **152**
Cornwall Clo. *Cas*—1F **167**
Cornwall Clo. *Wir*—4B **120**
Cornwall Ct. *Wir*—3F **141**
Cornwall Dri. *Pren*—3A **118**
Cornwallis St. *L1*—1D **99** (7G **5**)
(in two parts)
Cornwall Rd. *Wid*—1B **132**
Cornwall St. *Parr I*—1D **67**
Cornwood Clo. *L25*—2B **104**
Corona Av. *L31*—2C **6**
Corona Rd. *Wat*—4D **17**
Corona Rd. *Old S*—2A **80**
Corona Rd. *Wir*—1C **142**
Coronation Av. *K Ash*—3E **81**
Coronation Av. *Wall*—4B **52**
Coronation Bldgs. *Wall*—2A **74**
Coronation Bldgs. *Wir*—2C **112**
Coronation Ct. L9—4F 37
(off Ternhall Rd.)
Coronation Dri. *Cros*—2D **17**
Coronation Dri. *Frod*—4D **173**
Coronation Dri. *Hay*—1F **49**
Coronation Dri. *K Ash*—3E **81**
Coronation Dri. *Prsct*—2C **84**
Coronation Dri. *Wid*—4B **130**
Coronation Dri. *Wir*—4D **143**
Coronation Ho. *Run*—2C **166**
Coronation Rd. *Cros*—2D **17**
Coronation Rd. *Wind*—2C **44**
Coronation Rd. *Hoy*—5A **90**
Coronation Rd. *Lyd*—4C **6**
Coronation Rd. *Pres B*—4F **169**
Coronation Rd. *Run*—1B **166**
Coronation Wlk. *Bil*—1D **31**
Coroner's La. *Wid*—4A **110**
Coronet Rd. *L11*—5C **38**
Coronet Way. *Wid*—4B **130**
Corporation Rd. *Birk*—1F **95**
Corporation St. *St H*—4A **46**
(in two parts)
Corrie Dri. *Wir*—3F **141**
Corsewall St. *L7*—1D **101**
Corsham Rd. *L26*—1E **147**
Corsican Gdns. *St H*—5C **64**
Cortsway. *Wir*—4E **93**
Cortsway W. *Wir*—4D **93**
Corwen Clo. *Pren*—3B **94**
Corwen Clo. *Wir*—2F **93**
Corwen Cres. *L14*—4F **81**
Corwen Dri. *Boot*—1A **20**
Corwen Rd. *L4*—3C **56**
Corwen Rd. *Wir*—4C **90**
Cosgrove Clo. *L6*—4D **57**
Costain St. *L20*—3C **54**
Cote Lea Ct. *Hall P*—4F **167**
Cotham St. *St H*—5A **46**
Coton Way. *L32*—2C **22**
Cotsford Clo. *L36*—2C **82**
Cotsford Pl. *L36*—2C **82**
Cotsford Rd. *L36*—2C **82**
Cotsford Way. *L36*—2C **82**
Cotswold Gro. *St H*—5A **48**
Cotswold Rd. *Birk*—3C **118**
Cotswolds Cres. *L26*—5E **127**
Cotswold St. *L7*—4B **78**
Cottage Clo. *L32*—1E **39**
Cottage Clo. *Brom*—5C **162**
Cottage Dri. E. *Wir*—5F **157**
Cottage Dri. W. *Wir*—5F **157**
Cottage La. *Wir*—5F **157**
Cottage Pl. *Clo F*—2C **88**
Cottage St. *Birk*—2D **97**
Cottenham St. *L6*—3B **78**
Cotterdale Clo. *St H*—5C **66**
Cotterill. *Halt B*—2D **167**
Cottesbrook Clo. *L11*—5F **37**
Cottesbrook Pl. *L11*—5F **37**
Cottesbrook Rd. *L11*—5F **37**
Cottesmore Dri. *Wir*—2D **159**
Cotton La. *Halt L*—2D **167**
Cotton St. *L3*—2B **76**
Cottonwood. *L17*—1F **121**
Cottrell Clo. *L19*—3C **144**
Coulport Clo. *L14*—1A **82**
Coulsdon Pl. *L8*—5A **100**
Coulthard Rd. *Birk*—4A **120**
Coulton Rd. *Wid*—1E **133**
Council St. *Rain*—1A **86**
Countess Pk. *L12*—1C **58**
Countisbury Dri. *L16*—3E **103**
County Dri. *St H*—1E **65**
County Rd. *Kirkby*—1E **23**
County Rd. *Walt*—2F **55**
Court Av. *L26*—3A **128**
Courtenay Av. *L22*—3C **16**
Courtenay Rd. *Wat*—3C **16**
Courtenay Rd. *Wir*—4A **90**
Courtenay Rd. *Wltn*—5F **103**
Court Hey. —5F 81
Court Hey. *Mag*—1E **13**
Ct. Hey Av. *L36*—4A **82**
Ct. Hey Dri. *L16*—5F **81**
Court Hey Pk. —5F 81
Ct. Hey Rd. *L16*—5F **81**
Courthope Rd. *L4*—1B **56**
Courtland Rd. *L18*—4B **102**
Courtney Av. *Wall*—3A **74**
Courtney Rd. *Birk*—4A **120**
Court, The. *L28*—4C **60**
Court, The. *Wir*—2A **142**
Courtyard, The. *L18*—1F **123**
Covent Garden. *L2*—4B **76** (4C **4**)
Coventry Av. *Boot*—4F **19**
Coventry Rd. *L15*—3A **102**
Coventry St. *Birk*—3D **97**
Coverdale Av. *Rain*—3D **87**
Covertside. *Wir*—4D **113**
Cowan Dri. *L6*—2A **78**
Cowan Way. *Wid*—5F **109**
Cowdrey Av. *Pren*—5C **72**
Cow Hey La. *Run*—5A **166**
Cowley Clo. *Wir*—4D **93**
Cowley Hill. —3F 45
Cowley Hill La. *St H*—3E **45**
Cowley Rd. *L4*—2F **55**
Cowley St. *St H*—3A **46**
Cowper Rd. *L13*—3B **80**
Cowper St. *Boot*—3A **34**
Cowper St. *St H*—2C **66**
Cowper Way. *L36*—5A **84**
Coylton Av. *Rain*—4D **87**
Crab St. *St H*—4F **45**

Crab Tree Clo. *Hale V* —5E **149**
Crabtree Clo. *N'ley* —4D **105**
Crabtree Fold. *Nort* —2C **168**
Cradley. *Wid* —2C **130**
Crag Gro. *St H* —4B **30**
Craigburn Rd. *L13* —5E **57**
Craighurst Rd. *L25* —2A **104**
Craigleigh Gro. *Wir* —1F **171**
Craigmore Rd. *L18* —3A **124**
Craigside Av. *L12* —4A **58**
Craigs Rd. *L13* —5E **57**
Craigwood Way. *L36* —3B **82**
Craine Clo. *L4* —3B **56**
Cramond Av. *L18* —4F **101**
Cranage Clo. *Halt L* —3D **167**
Cranberry Clo. *L27* —3E **105**
Cranberry Clo. *St H* —3F **45**
Cranborne Av. *Wir* —2E **91**
Cranborne Rd. *L15* —2C **100**
Cranbourne Av. *Birk* —2A **96**
Cranbourne Av. *More* —2D **93**
Cranbrook St. *St H* —1B **66**
Crane Av. *St H* —5D **67**
Cranehurst Rd. *L4* —1B **56**
Cranfield Rd. *L23* —5A **10**
Cranford Clo. *Clo F* —3E **89**
Cranford Clo. *Wir* —1F **171**
Cranford Rd. *L19* —4B **124**
Cranford St. *Wall* —4C **74**
Crank. —1E 29
Crank Hill. *Crank* —1E **29**
Crank Rd. *Wind* —1C **44**
Cranleigh Gdns. *L23* —1D **17**
Cranleigh Pl. *L25* —3A **104**
Cranleigh Rd. *L25* —3A **104**
Cranmer St. *L5* —1C **76**
Cranmore Av. *L23* —3E **17**
Cranshaw Av. *Clo F* —3D **89**
Cranshaw La. *Wid* —4B **110**
Cranstock Gro. *Wind* —2C **44**
Cranston Clo. *St H* —3C **44**
Cranston Rd. *Know I* —3C **24**
Crantock Clo. *W Der* —4C **38**
Crantock Clo. *Halew* —4F **127**
Cranwell Clo. *L10* —3C **20**
Cranwell Rd. *L25* —2A **104**
Cranwell Rd. *Wir* —1B **114**
Cranwell Wlk. *L25* —2A **104**
Crask Wlk. *L33* —1F **23**
Craven Clo. *Birk* —3D **97**
Craven Lea. *L12* —5E **39**
Craven Pl. *Birk* —2C **96**
Craven Rd. *L12* —5C **58**
Craven Rd. *Rain* —3C **86**
Craven St. *L3* —4E **77** (3H **5**)
Craven St. *Birk* —3C **96**
Cravenwood Rd. *L26* —5F **127**
Crawford Av. *Mag* —4B **6**
Crawford Av. *Moss H* —4F **101**
Crawford Av. *Wid* —3B **130**
Crawford Clo. *Clo F* —2D **89**
Crawford Clo. *L12* —4D **59**
Crawford Dri. *L15* —5A **80**
Crawford Pk. *L18* —1F **123**
Crawford Pl. *Run* —4B **166**
Crawford St. *Clo F* —2E **89**
Crawford Way. *L7* —4E **79**
Crawley Clo. *L25* —4D **127**
Crawshaw Ct. *L36* —2B **82**
Crediton Clo. *L11* —3C **38**
Creek, The. *Wall* —3E **51**
Creer St. *L5* —2E **77**
Cremona Corner. *L22* —4E **17**
Cremorne Hey. *L28* —4B **60**
Crescent Ct. *L21* —2A **34**
Crescent Rd. *Cros* —5B **8**
Crescent Rd. *S'frth* —2A **34**
Crescent Rd. *Walt* —4B **36**
Crescent Rd. *Wall* —2C **74**
Crescents, The. *Rain* —2A **86**
Crescent, The. *Boot* —2E **35**
Crescent, The. *Mag* —3C **12**
Crescent, The. *Thor* —4A **10**
Crescent, The. *Wat* —4E **17**
Crescent, The. *Beb* —2E **141**
Crescent, The. *Grea* —1D **115**
Crescent, The. *Huy* —4A **84**
Crescent, The. *Pens* —1F **137**
Crescent, The. *Speke* —3C **146**
Crescent, The. *W Kir* —4A **112**
Crescent, The. *Whis* —2F **85**
Cressida Av. *Wir* —5E **119**
Cressingham Rd. *Wall* —3B **52**
Cressington Av. *Birk* —3D **119**
Cressington Esplanade. *L19* —1A **144**
Cressington Park. —1A 144
Cresson Ct. *Pren* —4F **95**
Cresswell Clo. *L26* —3A **128**
Cresswell St. *L6* —2F **77**
Cresta Dri. *West* —4F **165**
Cresttor Rd. *L25* —1F **125**
Creswell St. *St H* —5E **45**
Cretan Rd. *L15* —2D **101**
Crete Towers. *L5* —5E **55**
Crewe Grn. *Wir* —2A **116**
Cricklade Clo. *Boot* —4B **34**
Cringles Dri. *Tarb G* —2A **106**
Crispin Rd. *L27* —4E **105**
Crispin St. *St H* —5E **45**
Critchley Rd. *L24* —5A **148**
Critchley Way. *L33* —1F **23**
Croasdale Dri. *Beech* —5E **167**
Crockett's Wlk. *Ecc* —3B **44**
Crocus Av. *Birk* —1F **95**
Crocus Gdns. *St H* —4A **68**
Crocus St. *L5* —4D **55**
Croft Av. *Wir* —1C **162**
Croft Av. E. *Wir* —5D **143**
Croft Bus. Cen. *Croft B* —5D **143**
Croft Clo. *Pren* —5E **95**
Croft Dri. *Cald* —2C **134**
Croft Dri. *More* —2F **93**
Croft Dri. E. *Wir* —2D **135**
Croft Dri. W. *Wir* —2C **134**
Croft Edge. *Pren* —1B **118**
Croft End. *St H* —2F **67**
Crofters La. *L33* —5F **15**
Crofters, The. *Wir* —5D **93**
Croftfield. *L31* —1E **13**
Croft Grn. *Wir* —4D **143**
Croft La. *L9* —1D **37**
Croft La. *Wir* —1D **163**
Crofton Cres. *L13* —3B **80**
Crofton Rd. *L13* —3B **80**
Crofton Rd. *Birk* —1E **119**
Crofton Rd. *Run* —1E **165**
Croft Shop. Cen., The. *Stock V* —3A **60**
Croft St. *Wid* —1A **152**
Croftsway. *Wir* —2D **157**
Croft, The. *Kirkby* —1F **39**
Croft, The. *Mag* —2B **6**
Croft, The. *W Der* —4B **58**
Croft, The. *Halt* —1F **167**
Croft, The. *Wir* —2D **115**
Croft Way. *L23* —4B **10**
Croftwood Gro. *Whis* —4E **85**
Cromarty Rd. *L13* —4F **79**
Cromarty Rd. *Wall* —2F **73**
Cromdale Gro. *St H* —1E **67**
Cromer Dri. *Wall* —1A **74**
Cromer Rd. *L17* —3E **123**
Cromer Rd. *Wir* —4A **90**
Cromer Way. *L26* —1F **147**
Cromford Rd. *L36* —1E **83**
Crompton Ct. *Moss H* —4D **103**
Crompton Dri. *L12* —5E **39**
Cromptons La. *L18* —5C **102**
Crompton St. *L5* —1D **77**
Cromwell Rd. *L4* —1E **55**
Cromwell St. *Wid* —1A **152**
Crondall Gro. *L15* —2B **102**
Cronton. —4C 108
Cronton Av. *Whis* —5C **84**
Cronton Av. *Wir* —3F **71**
Cronton La. *Cron* —5B **86**
Cronton La. *Wid* —4E **109**
Cronton Pk. Av. *Wid* —3C **108**
Cronton Pk. Clo. *Wid* —3C **108**
Cronton Rd. *L15* —4A **102**
Cronton Rd. *Tarb* —2B **106**
Cronton Rd. *Wid* —4B **108**
Croome Dri. *Wir* —4C **112**
Croppers Hill Ct. *St H* —5E **45**
Cropper St. *L1* —5D **77** (6G **5**)
Crosby Clo. *Wir* —3F **93**
Crosby Grn. *L12* —4A **58**
Crosby Gro. *St H* —2D **65**
Crosby Gro. *Will* —4B **170**
Crosby Rd. N. *L22* —3E **17**
Crosby Rd. S. *L22 & L21* —5E **17**
Crosender Rd. *L23* —2C **16**
Crosfield Clo. *L7* —5C **78**
Crosfield Rd. *L7* —5C **78**
Crosfield Rd. *Prsct* —2F **85**
Crosfield Rd. *Wall* —3C **74**
Crosfield Wlk. *L7* —5C **78**
Crosgrove Rd. *L4* —2B **56**
Crosland Rd. *L32* —4A **24**
Cross Acre Rd. *L25* —2B **104**
Crossdale Rd. *L23* —2C **16**
Crossdale Rd. *Wir* —4D **163**
Crossdale Way. *St H* —4B **30**
Cross Farm Rd. *St H* —2C **66**
Crossfield St. *St H* —5B **46**
Crossford Rd. *L14* —5A **60**
Cross Gates. *Wid* —1F **133**
Crosshall St. *L1* —4D **77** (4E **4**)
Cross Hey. *Ford* —3B **18**
Cross Hey. *L31* —3E **13**
Cross Hey Av. *Pren* —4D **95**
Cross Hillocks La. *Wid* —2E **129**
Cross La. *Prsct & Whis* —2D **85**
Cross La. *Wall* —1D **73**
Cross La. *Wir* —3F **141**
Crossley Dri. *L15* —1A **102**
Crossley Dri. *Wir* —2D **157**
Crossley Rd. *St H* —3D **65**
Cross Mdw. Ct. St H —2C 66
(off Appleton Rd.)
Cross St. *L22* —4D **17**
Cross St. *St H* —5F **45**
Cross St. *Birk* —3F **97**
Cross St. *Port S* —2B **142**
Cross St. *Prsct* —4D **63**
Cross St. *Run* —4A **152**
Cross St. *Wid* —3C **132**
Cross, The. *Brom* —1E **163**
Crossvale Rd. *L36* —5E **83**
Crossway. *Pren* —1E **95**
Crossway. *Wid* —3D **131**
Crossways. *L25* —3F **103**
Crossways. *Wir* —4D **143**
Crossway, The. *Wir* —5C **160**
Crosswood Cres. *L36* —3C **82**
Crosthwaite Av. *Wir* —1F **171**
Croston Av. *Rain* —1B **86**
Croston Clo. *Wid* —1C **130**
Croston Ct. *L2* —4C **76** (4D **4**)
Crouch St. *L5* —5A **56**
Crouch St. *St H* —3D **67**
Crow La. W. *Newt W* —4F **49**
Crowmarsh Clo. *Wir* —5F **93**
Crownacres Rd. *L25* —4C **126**
Crown Av. *Wid* —4B **130**
Crown Ga. *Run* —3F **167**
Crown Rd. *L12* —4C **58**

Crown St. L7—4F 77
(in two parts)
Crown St. Newt W—5F 49
Crown St. That H—4D 65
Crownway. L36—2D 83
Crow St. L8—3D 99
Crowther St. St H—5D 45
Crow Wood. —2D 133
Crow Wood La. Wid—2D 133
Crow Wood Pl. Wid—1D 133
Croxdale Rd. L14—4A 60
Croxdale Rd. W. L14—4F 59
Croxeth Ga. L17—4C 100
Croxteth. —3D 39
Croxteth Av. L21—1A 34
Croxteth Av. Wall—2B 74
Croxteth Clo. L31—4E 7
Croxteth Country Pk. —2C 58
Croxteth Dri. L17—4C 100
Croxteth Gro. L8—3B 100
Croxteth Hall. —2D 59
Croxteth Hall La. Crox & W Der—5C 38
Croxteth La. Know—2B 60
Croxteth Park. —5A 40
Croxteth Rd. Boot—3B 34
Croxteth Rd. L8—3B 100
Croxteth Sports Cen. —4C 38
Croxteth Vw. L32—1F 39
(in two parts)
Croyde Pl. Sut L—2C 88
Croyde Rd. L24—4A 148
Croydon Av. L18—4F 101
Croylands St. L4—3E 55
Crucian Way. L12—5D 39
Crump St. L1—2E 99
Crutchley Av. Birk—1B 96
Cubbin Cres. L5—5D 55
Cubert Rd. L11—4C 38
Cuckoo Clo. L25—5A 104
Cuckoo La. L25—4A 104
Cuckoo Way. L25—5A 104
Cuerden St. L3—4D 77 (3F 5)
Cuerdley Cross. —2F 133
Cuerdley Grn. Cuer—2F 133
Culford Clo. Wind H—1D 169
Cullen Av. Boot—3D 35
Cullen Clo. Wir—1C 170
Cullen Rd. West P—3D 165
Cullen St. L8—2C 100
Culme Rd. L12—4F 57
Culzean Clo. L12—5E 39
Cumberland Av. Boot—2C 18
Cumberland Av. L17—3D 101
Cumberland Av. St H—3B 64
Cumberland Av. Pren—2A 118
Cumberland Clo. L6—5D 57
Cumberland Cres. Hay—2A 48
Cumberland Ga. Boot—1A 20
Cumberland Rd. Wall—4C 52
Cumberland St. L2—4C 76 (4D 4)
Cumber La. Whis—2F 85
Cumbria Way. L12—2C 58
Cummings St. L1—1E 99 (7G 5)
Cumpsty Rd. L21—4C 18
Cunard Av. Wall—1D 75
Cunard Building. —5B 76 (5B 4)
Cunard Clo. Pren—3C 94
Cunard Rd. L21—1B 34
Cunliffe Clo. Pal—3A 168
Cunliffe St. L2—4C 76 (3D 4)
Cunningham Clo. Pren—4E 117
Cunningham Clo. Wir—3C 134
Cunningham Dri. Run—2E 165
Cunningham Dri. Wir—2C 162
Cunningham Rd. L13—4A 80
Cunningham Rd. Wid—4D 131
Cuper Cres. L36—2D 83
Curate Rd. L6—4C 56
Curlender Clo. Birk—5E 73
Curlender Way. Hale V—5E 149
Curlew Av. Upt—3D 93
Curlew Clo. Upt—3D 93
Curlew Ct. Wir—5C 70
Curlew Gro. L26—3E 127
Curlew Way. Wir—5C 70
Curtana Cres. L11—5C 38
Curtis Rd. L4—2C 56
Curwell Clo. Wir—4B 142
Curzon Av. Birk—2B 96
Curzon Av. Wall—3B 52
Curzon Rd. L22—4E 17
Curzon Rd. Birk—2B 118
Curzon Rd. Wir—4A 90
Curzon St. Run—1F 165
Cusson Rd. Know I—5C 24
(Gale Rd.)
Cusson Rd. Know I—4B 24
(Lees Rd.)
Custley Hey. L28—3B 60
Custom Ho. La. L1—5C 76 (6D 4)
Cut La. L33—1E 41
Cygnet Ct. L33—3A 24
Cynthia Rd. Run—5F 151
Cypress Av. Wid—1B 132
Cypress Clo. L31—2A 22
Cypress Cft. Wir—4B 142
Cypress Gdns. St H—5C 64
Cypress Gro. Run—3C 166
Cypress Rd. L36—1D 105
Cyprian's Way. Boot—2E 19
Cyprus Gro. L8—5A 100
Cyprus St. Prsct—5D 63
Cyprus Ter. Wall—4B 52
Cyril Gro. L17—2E 123

Dacre Hill. —3F 119
Dacres Bri. La. Tarb G—2C 106
Dacre's Bri. La. Tarb G—2D 107
Dacre St. Boot—2B 54
Dacre St. Birk—3E 97
Dacy Rd. L5—5A 56
Daffodil Clo. Wid—5E 111
Daffodil Gdns. St H—4A 68
Daffodil Rd. L15—2B 102
Daffodil Rd. Birk—2F 95
Dagnall Rd. L32—4C 22
Dahlia Clo. L9—4B 36
Dahlia Clo. St H—4A 68
Daisy Gro. L7—5B 78
Daisy Mt. L31—2E 13
Daisy St. L5—4D 55
Dakin Wlk. L33—3F 23
Dalby Clo. St H—3C 46
Dale Acre Dri. Boot—2C 18
Dale Av. Brom—2D 163
Dale Av. Hes—1F 157
Dalebrook Clo. L25—2B 104
Dale Clo. L31—5C 6
Dale Clo. Wid—4A 130
Dale Cres. St H—5D 67
Dale End Rd. Wir—3C 138
Dale Gdns. Wir—1D 157
Dalegarth Av. L12—2F 59
Dale Hall. L18—2F 123
Dalehead Pl. St H—4B 30
Dale Hey. Hoot—3E 171
Dale Hey. Wall—3B 74
Dalehurst Clo. Wall—2D 75
Dale La. L33—5F 15
Dalemeadow Rd. L14—3D 81
Dale M. L25—5B 104
Dale Rd. Wir—4D 163
Daleside Clo. Wir—1F 137
Daleside Rd. L33—2F 23
Daleside Wlk. L33—2F 23
Dales Row. Whis—4B 84
Dales, The. —2E 157
Dale St. L2—4C 76 (5C 4)
Dale St. Gars—2C 144
Dale St. Run—1A 166
Dalesway. Wir—2E 157
Dale Vw. Clo. Hes—3A 138
Dalewood. W Der—5E 39
Dalewood Gdns. Whis—4F 85
Daley Pl. Boot—1E 35
Daley Rd. L21—4C 18
Dallas Gro. L9—2A 36
Dallinton Ct. L13—4B 80
Dalmeny St. L17—1B 122
Dalmorton Rd. Wall—3B 52
Dalry Cres. L32—1F 39
Dalrymple St. L5—1D 77
Dalry Wlk. L32—1F 39
Dalston Dri. St H—4B 30
Dalton Clo. L12—1C 58
Dalton Ct. Ast I—4E 153
Dalton Rd. Wall—4C 52
Dalton St. Run—5D 153
Daltry Clo. L12—4A 58
Dalwood Clo. Murd—3E 169
Damerham Cft. L25—2A 104
Damerham M. L25—2A 104
Damfield La. L31—1D 13
Dam Row. St H—1E 65
Damson Rd. L27—3E 105
Dam Wood Rd. L24—5C 146
Danby Clo. L5—1F 77
Danby Clo. Beech—4D 167
Danby Fold. Rain—3B 86
Dane Clo. Wir—1F 137
Dane Ct. Rain—3C 86
Danefield Pl. L19—4D 125
Danefield Rd. L19—4D 125
Danefield Rd. Wir—2C 114
Danefield Ter. L19—4D 125
Danehurst Rd. L9—1B 36
Danehurst Rd. Wall—4F 51
Danesbury Clo. Bil—1E 31
Danescourt Rd. L12—1C 80
Danescourt Rd. Birk—1A 96
Danescroft. Wid—1B 130
Dane St. L4—2F 55
Daneswell Dri. Wir—5F 71
Danes Well Rd. L24—5A 148
Daneville Rd. L4—1D 57
Danger La. Wir—4F 71
Daniel Clo. Boot—2A 34
Daniel Davies Dri. L8—2A 100
Daniel Ho. Boot—1C 54
Dannette Hey. L28—5C 60
Dansie St. L3—4E 77 (5J 5)
Dan's Rd. Wid—2E 133
Dante Clo. L9—5C 20
Danube St. L8—2B 100
Daphne Clo. L10—1B 38
Darby Gro. L19—1B 144
Darby Rd. L19—4A 124
D'Arcy Cotts. Wir—4B 160
(off Raby Rd.)
Darent Rd. Hay—1B 48
Daresbury Clo. L32—3C 22
Daresbury Ct. Wid—1D 133
Daresbury Expressway. Cas—5F 153
Daresbury Rd. Ecc—4B 44
Daresbury Rd. Wall—2A 74
Dark Entry. Know P—2E 61
Dark La. L31—1D 13
Darley Clo. Wid—1B 130
Darleydale Dri. Wir—5F 163
Darley Dri. L12—5C 58
Darlington Clo. Wall—2D 75
Darlington Ct. Wid—5A 132
Darlington St. Wall—2D 75
Darmond Rd. L33—2A 24
Darmond's Grn. Wir—3B 112
Darmonds Grn. Av. L6—4C 56

Darnley St. L8 —4E 99
Darrel Dri. L7 —2C 100
Darsefield Rd. L16 —2D 103
Dartington Rd. L16 —1C 102
Dartmouth Av. L10 —3C 20
Dartmouth Dri. Boot —1C 18
Darwall Rd. L19 —4D 125
Darwen St. L5 —1B 76
Darwick Dri. L36 —1F 105
Darwin Gro. That H —4E 65
Daryl Rd. Wir —1A 158
Daulby St. L3 —4F 77 (4J 5)
Dauntsey Brow. L25 —2B 104
Dauntsey M. L25 —2B 104
Davenham Av. Pren —1F 117
Davenham Clo. Pren —2F 117
Davenhill Pk. L10 —3C 20
Davenport Clo. Wir —3D 135
Davenport Gro. L33 —1E 23
Davenport Rd. Wir —3E 157
Davenport Row. Halt L —2D 167
Daventree Rd. Wall —1B 74
Daventry Rd. L17 —2E 123
Davidson Rd. L13 —3F 79
David St. L8 —5F 99
Davids Wlk. L25 —1C 126
Davies Clo. Wid —3A 152
Davies St. Boot —4D 35
Davies St. L2 —4C 76 (4D 4)
Davies St. St H —4C 46
Davis Rd. Wir —3B 72
Davy Clo. Ecc —3B 44
Davy Rd. Ast I —4E 153
Davy St. L5 —5A 56
Dawber Clo. L6 —2A 78
Dawlish Clo. L25 —4C 126
Dawlish Rd. Wall —2F 73
Dawlish Rd. Wir —2C 136
Dawn Clo. St H —4E 65
Dawn Wlk. L10 —1B 38
Dawpool Cotts. Wir —1A 136
Dawpool Dri. Brom —3C 162
Dawpool Dri. More —1E 93
Dawson Av. St H —4D 67
Dawson Av. Birk —1B 96
Dawson Gdns. L31 —5C 6
Dawson St. L1 —4D 77 (5E 5)
Dawson Way. L1 —5F 5
Dawstone Ri. Wir —3F 157
Dawstone Rd. Wir —3F 157
Days Mdw. Wir —1C 114
Day St. L13 —3F 79
Deacon Clo. L22 —5D 17
Deacon Ct. Wat —5D 17
Deacon Ct. Wltn —2B 126
Deacon Ind. Est. Newt W —1F 69
Deacon Rd. Wid —3B 132
Deakin St. Birk —1F 95
Dealcroft. L25 —2F 125
Dean Av. Wall —5E 51
Dean Clo. Bil —2D 31
Dean Clo. Wid —4B 132
Dean Dillistone Ct. L1 —2E 99
Deane Rd. L7 —4C 78
Dean Patey Ct. L1 —1E 99
Deansburn Rd. L13 —5E 57
Deanscales Rd. L11 —1F 57
Dean St. L22 —5D 17
Dean St. Wid —4B 132
Deans Way. Birk —1F 95
Deansway. Wid —4C 130
Dean Way. Sut M —4B 88
Deanwood Clo. Whis —4F 85
Dearham Av. St H —1A 46
Dearne Clo. L12 —1E 81
Dearnford Av. Wir —4D 163
Dearnford Clo. Wir —4D 163
Dearnley Av. St H —3E 47
Deauville Rd. L9 —1C 36
Debra Clo. L31 —1B 22
Dee Clo. L33 —4F 15
Dee Ct. L25 —1C 126
Dee Ho. L25 —1C 126
Deelands Pk. Wir —5C 70
Dee La. Wir —4A 112
Deeley Clo. L7 —5C 78
Dee Pk. Clo. Wir —4B 158
Dee Pk. Rd. Wir —4B 158
Deepdale. Wid —1C 130
Deepdale Av. Boot —3A 34
Deepdale Av. St H —4C 30
Deepdale Clo. Pren —3C 94
Deepdale Dri. Rain —3D 87
Deepdale Rd. L25 —2A 104
Deepfield Dri. L36 —1F 105
Deepfield Rd. L15 —3F 101
Deepwood Gro. Whis —4E 85
Deerbarn Dri. Boot —1B 20
Deerbolt Clo. L32 —2C 22
Deerbolt Cres. L32 —2C 22
Deerbolt Way. L32 —2C 22
Deerbourne Clo. L25 —2F 125
Dee Rd. Rain —3B 86
Deer Pk. Ct. Hall P —4F 167
Deeside. Hes —2C 156
Deeside Clo. Pren —3B 94
Dee Vw. Rd. Wir —2F 157
De Grouchy St. Wir —3B 112
Deirdre Av. Wid —3A 132
Delabole Rd. L11 —3D 39
De Lacy Row. Cas —5A 154
Delagoa Rd. L10 —2F 37
Delamain Rd. L13 —5E 57
Delamere Av. East —1E 171
Delamere Av. Sut M —3A 88
Delamere Av. Wid —3C 130
Delamere Clo. L12 —5D 39
Delamere Clo. Pren —3C 94
Delamere Clo. Wir —1E 171
Delamere Gro. Wall —3E 75
Delamore Pl. L4 —2E 55
Delamore's Acre. Will —5A 170
Delamore St. L4 —2E 55
Delavor Clo. Wir —2E 157
Delavor Rd. Wir —2E 157
Delaware Cres. L32 —2C 22
Delfby Cres. L32 —4A 24
Delf La. L24 —2B 146
Delf La. Walt —1A 56
Dell Clo. Wir —4B 162
Dell Ct. Pren —3F 117
Dellfield La. L31 —1E 13
Dell Gro. Birk —4A 120
Dell La. Wir —3B 158
Dellside Gro. St H —3C 66
Dell St. L7 —4C 78
Dell, The. L12 —3E 59
Dell, The. Birk —3A 120
Delph Ct. L21 —5A 18
Delphfield. Nort —2D 169
Delph La. Dar —4F 155
Delph La. Whis —1F 85
Delph Mdw. Gdns. Bil —1C 30
Delph Rd. L23 —2D 9
Delphwood Dri. Sher I —2B 66
Delta Dri. L12 —3E 59
Delta Rd. L21 —1B 34
Delta Rd. St H —4F 47
Delta Rd. E. Birk —3B 120
Delta Rd. W. Birk —3B 120
Deltic Way. Kirkby —5B 24
Deltic Way. N'ton —5B 20
Delves Av. Wir —4F 141
Delyn Clo. Birk —3E 119
Demesne St. Wall —3E 75
Denbigh Av. St H —4C 66
Denbigh Rd. L9 —5F 35
Denbigh Rd. Wall —3C 74
Denbigh St. L5 —1B 76
Dencourt Rd. L11 —2B 58
Deneacres. L25 —2A 126
Dene Av. Newt W —4F 49
Denebank Rd. L4 —4B 56
Denecliff. L28 —3C 60
Deneshey Rd. Wir —3C 90
Denes Way. L28 —4A 60
Denford Rd. L14 —1F 81
Denham Clo. L12 —5F 39
Denise Rd. L10 —1B 38
Denison Gro. That H —4E 65
Denman Dri. L6 —2C 78
Denman Gro. Wall —3E 75
Denman Rd. L6 —2C 78
Denman St. L6 —3B 78
Denmark St. L22 —4D 17
Dennett Clo. L31 —3D 13
Dennett Rd. Prsct —2C 84
Denning Dri. Wir —5D 115
Dennis Av. St H —4C 64
Dennis Rd. Wid —5C 132
Denny Clo. Wir —5F 93
Denston Clo. Pren —2B 94
Denstone Av. L10 —3D 21
Denstone Clo. L14 —2B 82
Denstone Clo. L25 —4B 126
Dentdale Dri. L5 —2E 77
Denton Dri. Wall —5C 52
Denton Gro. L6 —1C 78
Denton's Green. —3D 45
Dentons Grn. La. Dent G —3D 45
Denton St. L8 —5F 99
Denton St. Wid —3C 132
Dentwood St. L8 —5A 100
Denver Rd. L32 —4C 22
Depot Rd. L33 —1C 24
Derby & Rathbone Hall. L17 —5E 101
Derby Bldgs. L7 —5A 78
Derby Dri. Rainf —1B 28
Derby Gro. Mag —4D 13
Derby La. L13 —2A 80
Derby Rd. Boot & Kirk —5B 34
Derby Rd. L20 —5B 54
Derby Rd. Birk —1D 119
Derby Rd. Huy —3E 83
Derby Rd. Wall —5A 52
Derby Rd. Wid —1A 132
Derbyshire Hill. —1F 67
Derbyshire Hill Rd. St H —5F 47
Derby Sq. L2 —5C 76 (6C 4)
Derby Sq. Prsct —5E 63
Derby St. Gars —3C 144
Derby St. Huy —4A 84
Derby St. Prsct —5C 62
Derby Ter. L36 —3E 83
Dereham Av. Wir —2A 94
Dereham Cres. L10 —1F 37
Derna Rd. L36 —2D 83
Derringstone Clo. St H —2D 65
Derwent Av. Prsct —5F 63
Derwent Clo. Kirkby —1D 23
Derwent Clo. Mag —5F 7
Derwent Clo. Rain —3B 86
Derwent Clo. Wir —2D 141
Derwent Ct. L18 —4D 103
Derwent Dri. L21 —5D 19
Derwent Dri. Hes —3F 137
Derwent Dri. Wall —5A 52
Derwent Rd. Cros —2F 17
Derwent Rd. St H —1B 46
Derwent Rd. Beb —2D 141
Derwent Rd. Meol —3E 91
Derwent Rd. Pren —5B 96
Derwent Rd. Wid —3C 130
Derwent Rd. E. L13 —2A 80
Derwent Rd. W. L13 —2F 79
Derwent Sq. L13 —2F 79
Desborough Cres. L12 —4A 58

Desford Av. *St H*—2D **47**
Desford Clo. *Wir*—5B **70**
Desford Rd. *L19*—4E **123**
De Silva St. *L36*—4A **84**
Desmond Clo. *Pren*—2C **94**
Desmond Gro. *L23*—2F **17**
Desoto Rd. *Wid*—2D **151**
Desoto Rd. E. *Wid*—1F **151**
(in two parts)
Desoto Rd. W. *Wid*—1F **151**
Deva Clo. *L33*—3E **15**
Deva Rd. *Wir*—4A **112**
Deveraux Dri. *Wall*—3B **74**
Deverell Gro. *L15*—5B **80**
Deverell Rd. *L15*—1A **102**
Deverill Rd. *Birk*—3E **119**
Devilla Clo. *L14*—5A **60**
De Villiers Av. *L23*—5E **9**
Devisdale Gro. *Pren*—2C **94**
Devizes Dri. *Wir*—5D **115**
Devoke Av. *St H*—4A **30**
Devon Av. *Wall*—1C **74**
Devon Clo. *L23*—2A **16**
Devon Ct. *L5*—1A **78**
Devondale Rd. *L18*—4A **102**
Devon Dri. *Wir*—3E **137**
Devonfield Rd. *L9*—3F **35**
Devon Gdns. *L16*—4E **103**
Devon Gdns. *Birk*—3E **119**
Devon Pl. *Wid*—1A **132**
Devonport St. *L8*—4F **99**
Devonshire Clo. *Pren*—4B **96**
Devonshire Pl. *L5*—5E **55**
(in two parts)
Devonshire Pl. *Pren*—4A **96**
Devonshire Pl. *Run*—4A **152**
Devonshire Rd. *L8 & Prin P*—4A **100**
Devonshire Rd. *Wat*—3C **16**
Devonshire Rd. *Dent G*—3D **45**
Devonshire Rd. *Hes*—3E **137**
Devonshire Rd. *Pren*—4B **96**
Devonshire Rd. *Upt*—4E **93**
Devonshire Rd. *Wall*—2B **74**
Devonshire Rd. *W Kir*—5C **112**
Devonshire Rd. W. *L8*—4A **100**
Devon St. *L3*—4E **77** (3H **5**)
Devon St. *St H*—4D **45**
Devonwall Gdns. *L8*—4B **100**
Devon Way. *Child*—3E **103**
Devon Way. *Huy*—2A **84**
(in two parts)
Dewar Ct. *Ast I*—4E **153**
Dewberry Clo. *Birk*—5D **97**
Dewey Av. *L9*—5B **20**
Dewlands Rd. *L21*—5F **17**
Dewsbury Rd. *L4*—5B **56**
Dexter St. *L8*—3E **99**
Deycroft Av. *L33*—1F **23**
Deycroft Wlk. *L33*—1A **24**
Deyes End. *L31*—1D **13**
Deyes La. *L31*—1D **13**
Deysbrook La. *L12*—5C **58**
(in two parts)
Deysbrook Side. *L12*—5C **58**
Deysbrook Way. *L12*—3D **59**
Dial Rd. *Birk*—1D **119**
Dial St. *L7*—4C **78**
Diamond St. *L5*—2D **77**
Diana Rd. *Boot*—1D **35**
Diana St. *L4*—3F **55**
***Dibbinsdale Local Nature Reserve.* —2B 162**
Dibbinsdale Rd. *Wir*—2B **162**
Dibbins Grn. *Wir*—3B **162**
Dibbins Hey. *Wir*—5A **142**
Dibbinview Gro. *Wir*—5B **142**
Dibb La. *Cros*—3C **8**
Dicconson St. *St H*—4A **46**
Dickens Av. *Pren*—3F **117**
Dickens Clo. *Pren*—3F **117**
Dickensons St. L1—1D 99
(off Up. Frederick St.)
Dickens Rd. *St H*—3C **64**
Dickens St. *L8*—3F **99**
Dickinson Clo. *Hay*—2A **48**
Dickson Clo. *Wid*—4B **132**
Dickson St. *L3*—2B **76**
Dickson St. *Wid*—4A **132**
(in two parts)
Didcot Clo. *L25*—4D **127**
Didsbury Clo. *L33*—3F **23**
Digg La. *Wir*—5D **71**
Digmoor Rd. *L32*—1F **39**
Digmoor Wlk. *L32*—1F **39**
Dignum Mead. *L27*—4E **105**
Dilloway St. *St H*—4D **45**
Dinas La. *L36*—2A **82**
Dinas La. Pde. *L14*—2A **82**
Dinesen Rd. *L19*—5C **124**
Dingle. —1A 122
Dingle Av. *Newt W*—1F **69**
Dingle Brow. *L8*—1A **122**
Dingle Grange. *L8*—1A **122**
Dingle Gro. *L8*—5A **100**
Dingle La. *L8*—1A **122**
Dingle Mt. *L8*—1A **122**
Dingle Rd. *L8*—1F **121**
Dingle Rd. *Birk*—5C **96**
Dingle Ter. *L8*—5A **100**
Dingle Va. *L8*—1A **122**
Dingley Av. *L9*—2F **35**
Dingwall Dri. *Wir*—1E **115**
Dinmore Rd. *Wall*—2B **74**
Dinorben Av. *St H*—4C **66**
Dinorwic Rd. *L4*—5A **56**
Dinsdale Rd. *Croft B*—5E **143**
Ditchfield Pl. *Wid*—4B **130**
Ditchfield Rd. *Wid*—4A **130**
Ditton. —4B 130
Ditton La. *Wir*—3D **71**
Ditton Rd. *Wid*—1C **150**
Dixon Rd. *Know I*—5B **24**
Dobsons La. *St H*—3F **65**
Dobson St. *L6*—2F **77**
Dobson Wlk. *L6*—2A **78**
Dock Rd. *L19*—2B **144**
Dock Rd. *Birk*—4A **74**
Dock Rd. *Wid*—2F **151**
Dock Rd. N. *Wir*—1C **142**
Dock Rd. S. *Wir*—3D **143**
Docks Link. *Wall*—3F **73**
Dock St. *Wid*—2A **152**
Dodd Av. *St H*—4C **44**
Dodd Av. *Wir*—1D **115**
Doddridge Rd. *L8*—4E **99**
Dodds La. *L31*—5C **6**
Dodleston Clo. *Pren*—5D **95**
Dodman Rd. *L11*—3D **39**
Doe Pk. Courtyard. *L25*—4A **126**
Doe's Mdw. Rd. *Wir*—3B **162**
Dog & Gun. —5B 38
Domar Clo. *L32*—4E **23**
Dombey Pl. *L8*—3F **99**
Dombey St. *L8*—3F **99**
Domingo Dri. *L33*—5D **15**
Dominic Clo. *L16*—1E **103**
Dominic Rd. *L16*—1E **103**
Dominion St. *L6*—1C **78**
Domville. *Whis*—4E **85**
Domville Dri. *Wir*—1A **116**
Domville Rd. *L13*—5A **80**
Donaldson Ct. *L5*—5A **56**
Donaldson St. *L5*—5A **56**
Donalds Way. *L17*—3E **123**
Doncaster Dri. *Wir*—3F **93**
Donegal Rd. *L13*—3B **80**
Donne Av. *Wir*—4F **141**
Donne Clo. *Wir*—4A **142**
Donnington Clo. *L36*—1D **105**
Donsby Rd. *L9*—2B **36**
Dooley Dri. *Boot*—1B **20**
Doon Clo. *L4*—3E **55**
Dorans La. *L2*—5C **76** (5D **4**)
Dorbett Dri. *L23*—3F **17**
Dorchester Clo. *Wir*—5F **93**
Dorchester Dri. *L33*—5F **15**
Dorchester Pk. *Run*—4D **155**
Dorchester Rd. *L25*—3B **104**
Dorchester Way. *Btnwd*—5F **69**
Doreen Av. *Wir*—1D **93**
Dorgan Clo. *Rain*—2B **86**
Doric Rd. *L13*—2A **80**
Doric St. *L21*—1F **33**
Doric St. *Birk*—2F **119**
Dorien Rd. *L13*—4F **79**
Dorin Ct. *Pren*—5A **96**
Dorking Gro. *L15*—3B **102**
Dorothy St. *L7*—5B **78**
Dorothy St. *St H & That H*—4E **65**
Dorrington Clo. *Murd*—2D **169**
Dorrit St. *L8*—3F **99**
Dorset Av. *L15*—2C **100**
Dorset Clo. *Boot*—5D **35**
Dorset Ct. *L25*—3B **104**
Dorset Ct. *Pal*—4A **168**
Dorset Dri. *Wir*—3E **137**
Dorset Gdns. *Birk*—3E **119**
Dorset Rd. *St H*—2D **65**
Dorset Rd. *Anf*—5D **57**
Dorset Rd. *Huy*—3A **84**
Dorset Rd. *Wall*—4A **52**
Dorset Rd. *Wir*—3C **112**
Douglas Arc. Birk—3E 97
(off Douglas St.)
Douglas Av. *Bold*—5B **68**
Douglas Av. *Bil*—2D **31**
Douglas Clo. *L13*—2F **79**
Douglas Clo. *Wid*—1E **133**
Douglas Dri. *L31*—5F **7**
Douglas Dri. *Wir*—1D **93**
Douglas Pl. *Boot*—1B **54**
Douglas Rd. *L4*—5B **56**
Douglas Rd. *Wir*—3D **113**
Douglas St. *St H*—5D **45**
Douglas St. *Birk*—3E **97**
Douglas Way. *L33*—4F **15**
Doulton Clo. *Pren*—2B **94**
Doulton Pl. *Whis*—3C **84**
Doulton St. *St H*—5D **45**
Douro Pl. *L13*—4F **79**
Douro St. *L5*—2E **77** (1G **5**)
Dovecot. —3A 82
Dovecot Av. *L14*—3F **81**
Dovecot Pl. *L14*—2F **81**
Dove Ct. *L25*—1A **126**
Dovedale Av. *L31*—5C **6**
Dovedale Av. *Wir*—5E **163**
Dovedale Clo. *Pren*—2F **117**
Dovedale Ct. *Wid*—1B **130**
Dovedale Rd. *L18*—4F **101**
Dovedale Rd. *Wall*—4A **52**
Dovedale Rd. *Wir*—3B **90**
Dovepoint Rd. *Wir*—2E **91**
Dovercliffe Rd. *L13*—3B **80**
Dover Clo. *Birk*—2D **97**
Dover Clo. *Murd*—4E **169**
Dovercroft. *L25*—2F **125**
Dover Gro. *L16*—1F **103**
Dove Rd. *L9*—2F **35**
Dover Rd. *L31*—4C **12**
Dover St. *Run*—4B **152**
Dovesmead Rd. *Wir*—3D **159**
Dovestone Clo. *L7*—1B **100**
Dove St. *L8*—2B **100**
Dovey St. *L8*—4F **99**
Doward St. *Wid*—2C **132**
Dowhills Dri. *L23*—5B **8**

Dowhills Pk. *L23* —4B **8**
Dowhills Rd. *L23* —4B **8**
Downes Grn. *Wir* —1A **162**
Downham Clo. *L25* —4F **103**
Downham Dri. *Wir* —2A **158**
Downham Grn. *L25* —4F **103**
Downham Rd. *Birk* —1D **119**
Downham Rd. N. *Wir* —5A **138**
Downham Rd. S. *Wir* —2A **158**
Downham Way. *L25* —4F **103**
Downing Clo. *Pren* —1B **118**
Downing Rd. *Boot* —1D **55**
Downing St. *L5* —1A **78**
Downland Way. *St H* —2F **67**
Downside. *Wid* —1B **130**
Downside Clo. *Boot* —1E **19**
Downside Dri. *L10* —4F **21**
Downs Rd. *St H* —1D **65**
Downs Rd. *Run* —1A **166**
Downs, The. *L23* —2B **16**
Downway La. *St H* —2A **68**
Dowsefield La. *L18* —1E **125**
Dragon Clo. *L11* —4C **38**
Dragon Cres. *Whis* —2F **85**
Dragon Dri. *Whis* —3E **85**
Dragon La. *Whis* —4D **85**
Dragon Wlk. *L11* —4C **38**
Dragon Yd. *Wid* —5B **110**
Drake Clo. *L10* —1A **38**
Drake Clo. *Whis* —4E **85**
Drake Cres. *L10* —1F **37**
Drakefield Rd. *L11* —5D **37**
Drake Gdns. *St H* —5E **65**
Drake Pl. *L10* —1F **37**
Drake Rd. *L10* —1F **37**
Drake Rd. *More* —2B **72**
Drake St. *St H* —4D **45**
Drake Way. *L10* —1A **38**
Draw Well Rd. *Know I* —3D **25**
Draycott St. *L8* —1F **121**
Drayton Clo. *Run* —1F **165**
Drayton Clo. *Wir* —2D **137**
Drayton Cres. *St H* —2D **47**
Drayton Rd. *L4* —1A **56**
Drayton Rd. *Wall* —3C **74**
Drayton St. *St H* —5A **48**
Drennan Rd. *L19* —4E **125**
Drewell Rd. *L18* —5F **101**
Driffield Rd. *Prsct* —5C **62**
Drinkwater Gdns. *L3* —3E **77** (1G **5**)
Drive, The. *L12* —1B **80**
Driveway. *Whis* —4F **85**
(Cumber La.)
Driveway. *Whis* —4E **85**
(Lickers La.)
Droitwich Av. *Wir* —5C **92**
Dromore Av. *L18* —1F **123**
Dronfield Way. *L25* —2F **103**
(in two parts)
Druids' Cross Gdns. *L18* —5D **103**
Druids' Cross Rd. *L18* —5D **103**
Druids Pk. *L18* —5E **103**
Druidsville Rd. *L18* —5D **103**
Druids Way. *Wir* —2A **116**
Drum Clo. *L14* —1A **82**
Drummond Ct. *Wid* —2D **133**
Drummond Rd. *Cros* —5B **10**
Drummond Rd. *Walt* —2C **56**
Drummond Rd. *Wir* —1A **112**
Drummoyne Ct. *L23* —5A **8**
Drury La. *L2* —5C **76** (5C **4**)
Drybeck Gro. *St H* —5D **67**
Dryburgh Way. *L4* —3E **55**
Dryden Clo. *Pren* —2C **94**
Dryden Clo. *Whis* —3E **85**
Dryden Gro. *L36* —5F **83**
Dryden Rd. *L7* —5E **79**
Dryden St. *Boot* —3A **34**
Dryden St. *L5* —2D **77**
Dryfield Clo. *Wir* —5D **93**
Dublin St. *L3* —2B **76**
Duchess Way. *L13* —3E **79**
Ducie St. *L8* —3A **100**
Duckinfield St. *L3* —5F **77** (5J **5**)
Duck Pond La. *Birk* —2A **118**
Duddingston Av. *Cros* —3E **17**
Duddingston Av. *Moss H* —4F **101**
Duddon Av. *L31* —5F **7**
Duddon Clo. *Pren* —1F **117**
Dudley Av. *Run* —5D **153**
Dudley Clo. *Pren* —5B **96**
Dudley Gro. *L23* —3E **17**
Dudley Pl. *St H* —5C **46**
Dudley Rd. *L18* —4F **101**
Dudley Rd. *Wall* —3A **52**
Dudley St. *St H* —5C **46**
Dudlow Ct. *L18* —4C **102**
Dudlow Dri. *L18* —4C **102**
Dudlow Gdns. *L18* —3C **102**
Dudlow La. *L18* —3B **102**
Dudlow Nook Rd. *L18* —3C **102**
Dugdale Clo. *L19* —5A **124**
Duke Clo. *Run* —4F **151**
Duke of York Cotts. *Wir* —1A **142**
Dukes Rd. *L5* —5E **55**
Duke St. *L1* —1D **99** (7E **4**)
Duke St. *St H* —4F **45**
Duke St. *Wat* —5D **17**
Duke St. *Birk* —5C **74**
Duke St. *Gars* —1C **144**
Duke St. *Prsct* —4D **63**
Duke St. *Wall* —3B **52**
Duke St. Bri. *Birk* —5C **74**
Duke St. La. *L1* —1D **99** (7E **4**)
Dukes Wharf. *Pres B* —4E **169**
Dulas Grn. *L32* —4A **24**
Dulas Rd. *Kirkby* —4A **24**
Dulas Rd. *W'tree* —3B **102**
Dulverton Rd. *L17* —4E **123**
Dumbarton St. *L4* —2E **55**
Dumbrees Gdns. *L12* —3E **59**
Dumbrees Rd. *L12* —3E **59**
Dumbreeze Gro. *Know* —3D **41**
Dumfries Way. *L33* —4D **15**
Dunacre Way. *L26* —5F **127**
Dunbabin Rd. *L15 & L16* —3B **102**
Dunbar St. *L4* —1F **55**
Dunbeath Av. *Prsct & Rain* —5D **87**
Dunbeath Clo. *Rain* —5D **87**
Duncan Av. *Run* —1C **166**
Duncan Clo. *St H* —1E **65**
Duncan Dri. *Wir* —5D **93**
Duncansby Dri. *Wir* —1C **170**
Duncan St. *L1* —2E **99**
Duncan St. *St H* —5E **45**
Duncan St. *Birk* —3F **97**
Dunchurch Rd. *L14* —1F **81**
Duncombe Rd. N. *L19* —5B **124**
Duncombe Rd. S. *L19* —5B **124**
Duncote Clo. *Pren* —5A **96**
Duncote Clo. *Whis* —1A **86**
Dundale Rd. *L13* —3B **80**
Dundalk La. *Wid* —4D **131**
Dundalk Rd. *Wid* —4D **131**
Dundas St. *Boot* —2B **54**
Dundee Gro. *Wall* —3A **74**
Dundonald Rd. *L17* —3E **123**
Dundonald St. *Birk* —1A **96**
Dunedin St. *That H* —4E **65**
Dunfold Clo. *L32* —4F **23**
Dungeon La. *Hale V* —5F **147**
Dunham Clo. *Wir* —2F **171**
Dunham Rd. *L15* —5A **80**
Dunkeld Clo. *L6* —3A **78**
Dunkeld St. *L6* —3A **78**
Dunkerron Clo. *L27* —2C **104**
Dunlin Clo. *L27* —5E **105**
Dunlin Clo. *Beech* —5F **167**
Dunlin Ct. *L25* —4A **104**
Dunlins Ct. *Wall* —3E **51**
Dunlop Dri. *L31* —1B **22**
Dunlop Rd. *L24* —5C **146**
Dunluce St. *L4* —2E **55**
Dunmail Av. *St H* —4C **30**
Dunmail Gro. *Beech* —1E **173**
Dunmore Rd. *L13* —3E **79**
Dunmow Way. *L25* —4C **126**
Dunnerdale Rd. *L11* —1A **58**
Dunnett St. *L20* —2B **54**
Dunning Clo. *Wir* —4E **93**
Dunnings Bri. Rd. *Boot* —4E **19**
Dunnings Wlk. *Boot* —1A **20**
Dunnock Clo. *L25* —4A **104**
Dunraven Rd. *W Kir* —4A **112**
Dunriding La. *St H* —5D **45**
Dunscroft. *St H* —4D **67**
Dunsdon Clo. *L25* —5E **103**
Dunsdon Rd. *L25* —4E **103**
Dunsford. *Wid* —1B **130**
Dunsmore Clo. *Hay* —1C **48**
Dunsop Av. *Clo F* —2D **89**
Dunstall Clo. *Wir* —3E **71**
Dunstan La. *L7* —1C **100**
Dunstan St. *L15* —1E **101**
Dunster Gro. *Sut L* —2D **89**
Dunster Gro. *Wir* —3B **158**
Durants Cotts. *L31* —3E **13**
Durban Av. *L23* —5E **9**
Durban Rd. *L13* —4B **80**
Durban Rd. *Wall* —5B **52**
Durden St. *L7* —2C **100**
Durham Av. *Boot* —4F **19**
Durham M. E. *Boot* —4A **20**
Durham M. W. *Boot* —4F **19**
Durham Rd. *L21* —1E **33**
Durham Rd. *Wid* —1B **132**
Durham St. *L19* —3D **145**
Durham Way. *Boot* —4A **20**
Durham Way. *L36* —3A **84**
Durley Dri. *Pren* —3E **117**
Durley Rd. *L9* —2B **36**
Durlston Clo. *Wid* —2C **130**
Durning Rd. *L7* —5B **78**
Durrant Rd. *L11* —3E **57**
Dursley. *Whis* —4F **85**
Durston Rd. *L16* —1D **103**
Dutton. —2F **175**
Dutton Dri. *Wir* —5F **141**
Duxbury Clo. *L31* —4E **7**
Dwerryhouse La. *L11* —1B **58**
Dwerryhouse St. *L8* —3D **99**
Dyke St. *L6* —2A **78**
Dykin Clo. *Wid* —1E **133**
Dykin Rd. *Wid* —1D **133**
Dymchurch Rd. *L24* —3B **146**
Dymoke Rd. *L11* —5C **38**
Dymoke Wlk. *L11* —5C **38**
Dyson Hall Dri. *L9* —3D **37**
Dyson St. *L4* —2F **55**

Eagle Dene. *L10* —2A **38**
Eaglehall Rd. *L9* —4F **37**
Eaglehurst Rd. *L25* —5B **104**
Eagles Ct. *L32* —3E **23**
Eaglesfield Clo. *St H* —4D **67**
Eagles Way. *Hall P* —4E **167**
Ealing Clo. *Nort* —1D **169**
Ealing Rd. *L9* —1B **36**
Eanleywood La. *Nort* —2'
Eardisley Rd. *L18* —3A
Earle Clo. *Newt W* —5F
Earle Ho. *Wir* —4B **12**
Earle Rd. *L7* —1C **10**
Earle Rd. *Wid* —5C
Earle St. *L3* —4C 7
(in two parts)

Earle St. *Newt W* —1F **69**
Earl Rd. *Boot* —4D **35**
Earl's Clo. *L23* —2D **17**
Earlsfield Rd. *L15* —3F **101**
Earlston Rd. *Wall* —5A **52**
Earl St. *St H* —4C **46**
Earl St. *Wir* —4B **120**
Earls Way. *Hall P* —3E **167**
Earlswood Clo. *Wir* —1B **92**
Earlwood Gdns. *Whis* —4E **85**
Earp St. *L19* —1C **144**
Easby Rd. *L4* —4D **55**
(in two parts)
Easby Wlk. *L4* —4D **55**
Easedale Wlk. *L33* —1D **23**
Easenhall Clo. *Wid* —5B **110**
Easington Rd. *St H* —5D **65**
E. Albert Rd. *L17* —5B **100**
East Bank. *Birk* —1C **118**
Eastbourne M. *L9* —1B **36**
Eastbourne Rd. *Walt* —1B **36**
Eastbourne Rd. *Wat* —3B **16**
Eastbourne Rd. *Birk* —3C **96**
Eastbourne Wlk. *L6* —2F **77** (1J **5**)
E. Brook St. *L5* —5A **56**
Eastbury Clo. *Wid* —4C **110**
Eastcliffe Rd. *L13* —3B **80**
East Clo. *Ecc P* —4A **64**
Eastcote Rd. *L19* —4B **124**
Eastcott Clo. *Wir* —1C **114**
Eastcroft Rd. *Wall* —3C **74**
Eastdale Rd. *L15* —1F **101**
E. Dam Wood Rd. *L24* —5A **148**
Eastern Av. *L24* —5F **147**
Eastern Av. *Wir* —3D **143**
Eastern Dri. *L19* —5A **124**
Eastern Expressway. *Run* —3F **155**
E. Farm M. *Cald* —1F **135**
Eastfield Dri. *L17* —1C **122**
Eastfield Wlk. *L32* —4B **22**
East Front. *Hals P* —5E **85**
Eastgate Rd. *Port S* —2B **142**
Eastgate Way. *Mnr P* —3D **155**
Eastham. —5F 163
Eastham Clo. *L16* —5F **81**
Eastham Cres. *Clo F* —2B **88**
Eastham Grn. *L24* —3E **147**
Eastham Lodge Golf Course.
—4F 163
Eastham M. *East* —1F **171**
Eastham Rake. *Wir* —3C **170**
Eastham Village Rd. *Wir* —5F **163**
Eastlake Av. *L5* —1F **77**
E. Lancashire Rd. *Know* —2F **39**
E. Lancashire Rd. *L11* —5E **37**
E. Lancashire Rd. *St H & Wind*
—1E **43**
E. Lancashire Rd. *Hay* —1A **48**
East La. *L29* —1B **10**
East La. *Run* —3F **167**
Eastleigh Dri. *Wir* —5D **115**
East Mains. *L24* —4A **148**
Eastman Rd. *L13* —4E **57**
East Meade. *L31* —5C **6**
E. Millwood Rd. *L24* —3F **147**
Easton Rd. *L36* —3A **82**
Easton Rd. *Wir* —4B **120**
E. Orchard La. *L9* —1D **37**
Eastpark Ct. *Wall* —3E **75**
E. Prescot Rd. *L14* —3C **80**
East Rd. *L14* —4C **80**
East Rd. *L24* —2A **148**
East Rd. *L31* —1F **13**
East Side. *St H* —1C **66**
Eastside Ind. Est. *St H* —1C **66**
East St. *L3* —4B **76** (3C **4**)
East St. *Wat* —4D **17**
t St. *Birk* —4E **75**
Wid —3D **133**
Eastview Clo. *Pren* —5D **95**
Eastway. *L31* —5D **7**
(in three parts)
Eastway. *Grea* —5E **93**
East Way. *More* —5E **71**
Eastway. *Run* —3F **167**
Eastway. *Wid* —3D **131**
Eastwood. *L17* —1A **122**
Eastwood. *Wind H* —1C **168**
Eastwood Rd. *Btnwd* —4F **69**
Eaton Av. *Boot* —2D **35**
Eaton Av. *L21* —1B **34**
Eaton Av. *Wall* —2C **74**
Eaton Clo. *W Der* —4A **58**
Eaton Clo. *Huy* —4C **82**
Eaton Gdns. *L12* —2D **81**
Eaton Grange. *L12* —1C **80**
Eaton Rd. *Mag* —4D **13**
Eaton Rd. *W Der* —4B **58**
(in two parts)
Eaton Rd. *Cress* —1A **144**
Eaton Rd. *Dent G* —2D **45**
Eaton Rd. *Pren* —4B **96**
Eaton Rd. *Wir* —5A **112**
Eaton Rd. N. *L12* —4F **57**
Eaton St. *L3* —3C **76** (1C **4**)
Eaton St. *Prsct* —4D **63**
Eaton St. *Run* —5A **152**
Eaton St. *Wall* —1B **74**
Eaves La. *St H* —5B **66**
Ebenezer Howard Rd. *L21* —3C **18**
Ebenezer Rd. *L7* —4C **78**
Ebenezer St. *Birk* —2A **120**
Ebenezer St. *Hay* —2F **47**
Eberle St. *L2* —4C **76** (4D **4**)
Ebony Clo. *Wir* —1B **92**
Ebony Way. *L33* —5E **15**
Ebor La. *L5* —2E **77**
Ebrington St. *L19* —5C **124**
Ecclesall Av. *L21* —5D **19**
Eccles Dri. *L25* —2B **104**
Ecclesfield Rd. *Ecc* —2A **44**
Eccles Gro. *Clo F* —3E **89**
Eccleshall Rd. *Wir* —1C **142**
Eccleshill Rd. *L13* —1A **80**
Eccleston. —3B 44
Eccleston Av. *Brom* —1C **162**
Eccleston Clo. *Pren* —1F **117**
Eccleston Dri. *Run* —1C **166**
Eccleston Gdns. *St H* —2A **64**
(in two parts)
Eccleston Park. —5A 64
Eccleston Pk. Trad. Cen. *Ecc* —3B **64**
Eccleston Rd. *L9* —2F **35**
Eccleston St. *St H* —5E **45**
Eccleston St. *Prsct* —5D **63**
Echo La. *Wir* —5C **112**
Edale Clo. *Wir* —5E **163**
Edale Rd. *L18* —5A **102**
Eddarbridge Est. *Wid* —2F **151**
Eddisbury Rd. *Wall* —1C **74**
Eddisbury Rd. *W Kir* —2A **112**
Eddisbury Sq. *Frod* —5B **172**
Eddisbury Way. *L12* —4A **58**
Eddison Rd. *Ast I* —4D **153**
Eden Clo. *L33* —4F **15**
Eden Clo. *Rain* —4B **86**
Edendale. *Wid* —2B **130**
Eden Dri. N. *L23* —1A **18**
Eden Dri. S. *L23* —2A **18**
Edenfield Cres. *L36* —2F **83**
Edenfield Rd. *L15* —3F **101**
Edenhall Dri. *L25* —1C **126**
Edenhurst Av. *L16* —1A **104**
Edenhurst Av. *Wall* —1C **74**
Edenpark Rd. *Birk* —1C **118**
Eden St. *L8* —2B **100**
Eden Va. *Boot* —1E **19**
Edgar Ct. *Birk* —2D **97**
Edgar St. *L3* —3D **77** (1E **5**)
Edgar St. *Birk* —2D **97**
Edgbaston Clo. *L36* —5C **82**
Edgbaston Way. *Pren* —1C **94**
Edgefield Clo. *Pren* —5D **95**
Edgefold Rd. *L32* —4F **23**
Edge Gro. *L7* —4D **79**
Edge Hill. —5B 78
Edgehill Rd. *Wir* —1C **92**
Edge La. *Cros & Thor* —4A **10**
Edge La. *Edg H & Fair* —5B **78**
Edge La. *Old S* —4E **79**
Edge La. Dri. *L13* —4A **80**
Edge La. Retail Pk. *L13* —4F **79**
(in two parts)
Edgeley Gdns. *L9* —2F **35**
Edgemoor Clo. *Cros* —5B **10**
Edgemoor Clo. *W Der* —1D **81**
Edgemoor Clo. *Pren* —2B **94**
Edgemoor Dri. *Cros* —4A **10**
Edgemoor Dri. *Faz* —1A **38**
Edgemoor Dri. *Wir* —5C **114**
Edgemoor Rd. *L12* —1D **81**
Edge St. *St H* —5C **64**
Edgewood Dri. *Wir* —5D **163**
Edgewood Rd. *Meol* —2D **91**
Edgewood Rd. *Upt* —3F **93**
Edgeworth Clo. *St H* —3E **67**
Edgeworth St. *St H* —4E **67**
Edgworth Rd. *L4* —5B **56**
Edinburgh Clo. *Boot* —5A **20**
Edinburgh Dri. *L36* —5A **84**
Edinburgh Dri. *Pren* —3A **118**
Edinburgh Rd. *Kens* —4A **78**
Edinburgh Rd. *Wall* —1B **74**
Edinburgh Rd. *Wid* —4A **130**
Edinburgh Tower. *L5* —1E **77**
Edington St. *L15* —1E **101**
Edith Rd. *Boot* —2D **35**
Edith Rd. *L4* —5A **56**
Edith Rd. *Wall* —3D **75**
Edith St. *St H* —4F **67**
Edith St. *Run* —4F **151**
Edmondson St. *St H* —5F **47**
Edmonton Clo. *L5* —5D **55**
Edmund St. *L3* —4B **76** (4C **4**)
Edna Av. *L10* —1A **38**
Edrich Av. *Pren* —1C **94**
Edward Jenner Av. *Boot* —2F **19**
Edward Pavilion. *L3* —1C **98** (7C **4**)
Edward Rd. *Whis* —1F **85**
Edward Rd. *Wir* —5C **90**
Edward's La. *L24* —1B **146**
Edward's La. Ind. Est. *L24* —1B **146**
Edward St. *L3* —5E **77** (5H **5**)
Edward St. *St H* —2D **67**
Edward St. *Hay* —2A **48**
Edward St. *Wid* —3D **133**
Edwards Way. *Wid* —4C **130**
Edwin St. *Wid* —3C **132**
Effingham St. *Boot* —1B **54**
Egan Rd. *Pren* —1E **95**
Egbert Rd. *Wir* —3C **90**
Egdon Clo. *Wid* —2E **133**
Egerton Dri. *Wir* —4B **112**
Egerton Gdns. *Birk* —3E **119**
Egerton Gro. *Wall* —1B **74**
Egerton Pk. *Birk* —3E **119**
Egerton Pk. Clo. *Birk* —3E **119**
Egerton Rd. *L15* —2D **101**
Egerton Rd. *Pren* —3A **96**
Egerton Rd. *Prsct* —4C **62**
Egerton Rd. *Wir* —5B **120**
Egerton St. *L8* —2F **99**
Egerton St. *St H* —2D **67**
Egerton St. *Run* —4F **151**
Egerton St. *Wall* —3B **52**
Egerton Wharf. *Birk* —2E **97**
Eglington Av. *Whis* —3D **85**

Egremont. —1D 75
Egremont Clo. *L27* —5A **106**
Egremont Lawn. *L27* —5A **106**
Egremont Promenade. *Wall* —5D **53**
Egremont Rd. *L27* —5A **106**
Egypt St. *Wid* —5F **131**
Eighth Av. *Faz* —1D **37**
Eilian Gro. *L14* —4D **81**
Elaine Clo. *Wid* —2C **132**
Elaine St. *L8* —3F **99**
Elderberry Clo. *L11* —1C **58**
Elderdale Rd. *L4* —4B **56**
Elder Gdns. *L19* —4B **124**
Elder Gro. *Wir* —4B **112**
Eldersfield Rd. *L11* —1B **58**
Elderswood. *Rain* —2C **86**
Elderwood Rd. *Birk* —1E **119**
Eldon Clo. *St H* —1E **65**
Eldon Gro. *L3* —2D **77**
Eldonian Way. *L3* —2C **76**
Eldon Pl. *L3* —2C **76**
Eldon Pl. *Birk* —3D **97**
Eldon Rd. *Birk* —2F **119**
Eldon Rd. *Wall* —2B **74**
Eldon St. *L3* —2C **76**
Eldon St. *St H* —1E **65**
Eldred Rd. *L16* —3C **102**
Eleanor Rd. *Boot* —2D **35**
Eleanor Rd. *Pren* —5D **73**
Eleanor Rd. *Wir* —5D **71**
Eleanor St. *L20* —2B **54**
Eleanor St. *Wid* —5A **132**
Elephant La. *St H & That H* —4D **65**
Elfet St. *Birk* —1F **95**
Elgar Av. *Wir* —5E **163**
Elgar Rd. *L14* —1F **81**
Elgin Dri. *Wall* —5C **52**
Elgin Way. *Birk* —2E **97**
Eliot Clo. *Wir* —5A **120**
Eliot St. *Boot* —3B **34**
Elizabeth Ct. *Wid* —5B **132**
Elizabeth Rd. *Boot* —2D **35**
Elizabeth Rd. *Faz* —1B **38**
Elizabeth Rd. *Hay* —1E **49**
Elizabeth Rd. *Huy* —1F **105**
Elizabeth St. *Clo F* —3E **89**
Elizabeth St. *L3* —4F **77**
Elizabeth St. *St H* —3E **67**
Elizabeth Ter. *Wid* —3D **131**
Eliza St. *St H* —4F **67**
Elkan Clo. *Wid* —2E **133**
Elkan Rd. *Wid* —2D **133**
Elkstone Rd. *L11* —2B **58**
Ellaby Rd. *Rain* —2C **86**
Ellams Bri. Rd. *St H* —3E **67**
Ellel Gro. *L6* —1C **78**
Ellen Gdns. *St H* —4E **67**
Ellens Clo. *L6* —4A **78**
Ellen's La. *Wir* —2A **142**
Ellen St. *St H* —4E **67**
Elleray Pk. Rd. *Wall* —4A **52**
Ellerby Clo. *Murd* —3E **169**
Ellergreen Rd. *L11* —1F **57**
Ellerman Rd. *L3* —1E **121**
Ellerslie Av. *Rain* —1C **86**
Ellerslie Rd. *L13* —5D **57**
Ellerton Clo. *Wid* —1C **130**
Ellerton Way. *L12* —5E **39**
Ellesmere Dri. *L10* —3C **20**
Ellesmere Gro. *Wall* —5B **52**
Ellesmere St. *Run* —5B **152**
Elliot St. *L1* —5D **77** (5F **5**)
Elliot St. *St H* —5E **45**
Elliot St. *Wid* —4B **132**
Ellis Ashton St. *L36* —4A **84**
(in two parts)
Ellis La. *Frod* —4D **173**
Ellison Dri. *St H* —4C **44**
Ellison Gro. *L36* —4E **83**
Ellison St. *L13* —2F **79**
Ellison Tower. *L5* —1E **77**
Ellis Pl. *L8* —4F **99**
Ellis Rd. *Bil* —1D **31**
Ellis St. *Wid* —5A **132**
Ellon Av. *Rain* —4D **87**
Elloway Rd. *L24* —4A **148**
Elmar Rd. *L17* —2E **123**
(in two parts)
Elm Av. *L23* —5F **9**
Elm Av. *Wid* —2B **132**
Elm Av. *Wir* —3D **93**
Elm Bank. *L4* —4F **55**
Elmbank Rd. *L18* —4E **101**
Elmbank Rd. *Wir* —1B **142**
Elmbank St. *Wall* —3C **74**
Elm Clo. *L12* —5F **39**
Elm Clo. *Wir* —3A **138**
Elm Ct. *L23* —1C **16**
Elmcroft Clo. *L9* —2D **37**
Elmdale Rd. *L9* —4A **36**
Elmdene Ct. *Wir* —2C **114**
Elm Dri. *S'frth* —2F **33**
Elm Dri. *Wir* —1C **114**
Elmfield Clo. *That H* —3E **65**
Elmfield Rd. *L9* —3A **36**
*Elm Gdns. L21 —2A **34***
(off Elm Rd.)
Elm Grn. *Will* —5A **170**
Elm Gro. *Ecc P* —4F **63**
Elm Gro. *L7* —5A **78**
Elm Gro. *Birk* —5D **97**
Elm Gro. *Hoy* —4C **90**
Elm Gro. *Wid* —3B **132**
Elm Hall Dri. *L18* —4A **102**
Elmham Cres. *L10* —1F **37**
Elm Ho. *Prsct* —5C **62**
Elm Ho. M. *L25* —5B **104**
Elmhurst Rd. *L25* —2A **104**
Elmore Clo. *L5* —1F **77**
Elmore Clo. *Wind H* —1D **169**
Elm Park. —3C 78
Elm Pk. Rd. *Wall* —4A **52**
Elm Rd. *Kirkby* —2D **23**
Elm Rd. *S'frth* —2F **33**
Elm Rd. *St H* —3D **65**
Elm Rd. *Walt* —1A **56**
Elm Rd. *Beb* —5F **119**
Elm Rd. *Birk* —1D **119**
(Derby Rd.)
Elm Rd. *Birk* —2B **118**
(Waterpark Rd.)
Elm Rd. *Hay* —1E **49**
Elm Rd. *Irby* —1F **137**
Elm Rd. *Run* —2C **166**
Elm Rd. *Will* —5A **170**
Elm Rd. N. *Birk* —2B **118**
Elmsdale Rd. *L18* —4A **102**
Elmsfield Clo. *L25* —4A **104**
Elmsfield Pk. *Augh* —1F **7**
Elmsfield Rd. *L23* —4B **10**
Elms Ho. Rd. *L13* —3F **79**
Elmsley Ct. *L18* —1F **123**
Elmsley Rd. *L18* —5F **101**
Elms Rd. *L31* —4C **12**
Elms, The. *Ding* —5A **100**
Elms, The. *Lyd* —4D **7**
Elms, The. *Run* —1F **165**
Elm St. *L36* —4A **84**
Elm St. *Birk* —3D **97**
Elmswood Av. *Rain* —4D **87**
Elmswood Ct. *L18* —1F **123**
Elmswood Gro. *L36* —3B **82**
Elmswood Rd. *L17* —2D **123**
Elmswood Rd. *Birk* —5C **96**
Elmswood Rd. *Wall* —2D **75**
Elm Ter. *L7* —4C **78**
Elm Ter. *Wir* —4C **90**
Elmtree Clo. *L12* —4C **58**
Elmtree Gro. *Pren* —1E **95**
Elmure Av. *Wir* —2D **141**
Elm Va. *L6* —2D **79**
Elmwood. *Nort* —2C **168**
Elmwood Av. *L23* —5F **9**
Elmwood Dri. *Wir* —5F **137**
Elmworth Av. *Wid* —4A **110**
Elphin Gro. *L4* —2A **56**
Elric Wlk. *L33* —2A **24**
Elsbeck Gro. *St H* —5D **67**
Elsie Rd. *L4* —5A **56**
Elsinore Heights. *L26* —5A **128**
Elsmere Av. *L17* —1C **122**
Elstead Rd. *Kirkby* —4C **22**
Elstead Rd. *Walt* —4E **37**
Elstow St. *L5* —4D **55**
Elstree Rd. *L6* —3D **79**
Elswick St. *L8* —1F **121**
Eltham Av. *L21* —4B **18**
Eltham Clo. *Wid* —1E **133**
Eltham Clo. *Wir* —2B **116**
Eltham Grn. *Wir* —2B **116**
Eltham St. *L7* —4D **79**
Eltham Wlk. *Wid* —1E **133**
Elton Av. *Boot* —2E **19**
Elton Av. *L23* —1C **16**
Elton Clo. *Wir* —2E **171**
Elton Dri. *Wir* —4A **142**
Elton Head Rd. *St H* —1C **86**
Elton St. *L4* —1F **55**
Elvington Clo. *Sut W* —2F **173**
Elvington Rd. *L38* —1A **8**
Elwick Dri. *L12* —1C **58**
Elwood Clo. *L33* —4E **15**
Elworthy Av. *L26* —3F **127**
Elwyn Dri. *L26* —4F **127**
Elwyn Gdns. *Halew* —4A **128**
Elwyn Rd. *Wir* —2E **91**
Elwy St. *L8* —4A **100**
Ely Av. *Wir* —1C **92**
Ely Clo. *Boot* —4F **19**
Ely Pk. *Run* —5E **155**
Ember Cres. *L6* —2F **77**
Embledon St. *L8* —2B **100**
(in two parts)
Embleton Gro. *Beech* —5E **167**
Emerald Clo. *Boot* —2B **20**
Emerald St. *L8* —1F **121**
Emerson St. *L8* —2F **99**
Emery St. *L4* —2F **55**
Emily St. *St H* —4C **64**
Emily St. *Wid* —5A **132**
Emmett St. *St H* —2C **66**
*Empire Bri. L3 —4B **76** (4B **4**)*
(off Union St.)
Empire Rd. *L21* —2B **34**
Empress Clo. *L31* —1B **12**
Empress Rd. *Anf* —5C **56**
Empress Rd. *Kens* —4A **78**
Empress Rd. *Wall* —2C **74**
Emstry Wlk. *L32* —3C **22**
Endborne Rd. *L9* —2A **36**
Endbutt La. *L23* —1E **17**
Enderby Av. *St H* —2C **46**
Endfield Pk. *L19* —4A **124**
Endmoor Rd. *L36* —1D **83**
Endsleigh Rd. *Wat* —3B **16**
Endsleigh Rd. *Old S* —3E **79**
Enerby Clo. *Pren* —2C **94**
Enfield Av. *L23* —1E **17**
Enfield Rd. *L13* —4B **80**
Enfield St. *St H* —1E **65**
Enfield Ter. *Pren* —4B **96**
Enford Dri. *St H* —4D **67**
Enid St. *L8* —3F **99**
Ennerdale Av. *L31* —5E **7**
Ennerdale Av. *St H* —5B **30**
Ennerdale Av. *Wir* —1F **171**
Ennerdale Clo. *Kirkby* —5D **15**

Ennerdale Dri. *L21* —5D **19**
Ennerdale Dri. *Frod* —5C **172**
Ennerdale Nursing Home. *L9* —2D **37**
Ennerdale Rd. *L9* —2D **37**
Ennerdale Rd. *Pren* —3E **117**
Ennerdale Rd. *Wall* —3F **51**
Ennerdale St. *L3* —2D **77**
Ennis Clo. *Hale V* —5D **149**
Ennisdale Dri. *Wir* —3D **113**
Ennismore Rd. *Cros* —5C **8**
Ennismore Rd. *Old S* —3F **79**
Ennis Rd. *L12* —5E **59**
Ensor St. *L20* —2B **54**
Enstone Av. *L21* —4A **18**
Enstone Rd. *L25* —1B **146**
Ensworth Rd. *L18* —4B **102**
Epping Av. *Sut M* —3B **88**
Epping Clo. *Rain* —4D **87**
Epping Ct. *Wir* —2A **158**
Epping Gro. *L15* —3B **102**
Epsom Clo. *L10* —4E **21**
Epsom Dri. *Wir* —3F **71**
Epsom Gro. *L33* —5F **15**
Epsom Rd. *Wir* —3F **71**
Epsom St. *St H* —4E **47**
Epsom Way. *L5* —1D **77**
Epstein Ct. L6 —3B 78
(off Coleridge St.)
Epworth Clo. *Btnwd* —5F **69**
Epworth Grange. *Pren* —3A **96**
Epworth St. *L6* —4F **77** (3J **5**)
Eremon Clo. *L9* —5D **21**
Erfurt Av. *Wir* —3A **142**
Erica Ct. *Wir* —1E **157**
Eric Gro. *Wall* —2A **74**
Eric Rd. *Wall* —2A **74**
Eric St. *Wid* —2C **132**
Eridge St. *L8* —5A **100**
Erin Clo. *L8* —3E **99**
Erl St. *L9* —2A **36**
Ermine Cres. *L5* —1F **77**
Errington Ct. *L17* —4E **123**
Errington St. *L5* —5B **54**
Errol St. *L17* —1B **122**
Errwood Clo. *Hale V* —5E **149**
Erskine Clo. *St H* —2E **47**
Erskine Ind. Est. *L6* —3F **77**
Erskine Rd. *Wall* —3C **74**
Erskine St. *L6* —3F **77** (3J **5**)
Erylmore Rd. *L18* —3A **124**
Escolme Dri. *Wir* —1D **115**
Escor Rd. *L25* —3F **103**
Eshelby Clo. *L22* —4E **17**
Esher Clo. *Pren* —2C **94**
Esher Clo. *Wir* —4B **120**
Eshe Rd. *L23* —1C **16**
Eshe Rd. N. *L23* —5B **8**
Esher Rd. *L6* —3C **78**
Esher Rd. *Wir* —4B **120**
Eskburn Rd. *L13* —5E **57**
Eskdale Av. *St H* —5B **30**
Eskdale Av. *East* —5E **163**
Eskdale Av. *More* —5C **70**
Eskdale Clo. *Beech* —5D **167**
Eskdale Dri. *Mag* —5E **7**
Eskdale Rd. *L9* —2A **36**
Esk St. *L20* —3B **54**
Eslington St. *L19* —5A **124**
Esmond St. *L6* —1B **78**
Esonwood Rd. *Whis* —3D **85**
Espin St. *L4* —2F **55**
Esplanade. *Birk* —2A **120**
Esplanade, The. *Boot* —5C **34**
Esplanade, The. *Wat* —5D **17**
Esplanade, The. *Wir* —3B **120**
Esplen Av. *L23* —5F **9**
Essex Rd. *L36* —2A **84**
Essex Rd. *Wir* —3C **112**
Essex St. *L8* —4E **99**
Essex Way. *Boot* —4D **35**
Esther St. *Wid* —3B **132**
Esthwaite Av. *St H* —5C **30**
Estuary Banks. *Speke* —3F **145**
Estuary Banks Bus. Pk. *Speke* —3A **146**
Etal Clo. *L11* —2B **58**
Ethelbert Rd. *Wir* —3C **90**
Ethel Rd. *Wall* —3D **75**
Etna St. *L13* —3F **79**
Etna St. *Birk* —2F **119**
Eton Ct. *L18* —4D **103**
Eton Dri. *L10* —3C **20**
Eton Dri. *Wir* —4F **159**
Etonhall Dri. *St H* —4C **66**
Eton St. *L4* —2F **55**
Etruria St. *L19* —3C **144**
Etruscan Rd. *L13* —2A **80**
Ettington Rd. *L4* —4B **56**
Ettrick Clo. *L33* —4D **15**
Eurolink. *St H* —2F **87**
Europa Boulevd. *Birk* —3E **97**
Europa Pools Swimming Cen. —3D 97
Europa Sq. *Birk* —3D **97**
Euston Gro. *Pren* —4B **96**
Euston St. *L4* —1F **55**
Evans Clo. *Hay* —1F **49**
Evans Rd. *L24* —2C **146**
Evans Rd. *Wir* —4B **90**
Evans St. *Prsct* —4D **63**
Evellynne Clo. *L32* —3C **22**
Evelyn Av. *St H* —5E **47**
Evelyn Av. *Prsct* —5E **63**
Evelyn Rd. *Wall* —3C **74**
Evelyn St. *L5* —5D **55**
Evelyn St. *St H* —5E **47**
Evenwood. *St H* —5C **66**
Evenwood Clo. *Mnr P & Run* —3E **155**
Everdon Wood. *L33* —2F **23**
Evered Av. *L9* —4A **36**
Everest Rd. *L23* —1E **17**
Everest Rd. *Birk* —2D **119**
Evergreen Clo. *L27* —3E **105**
Evergreen Clo. *Wir* —3E **93**
Everite Rd. *Wid* —5B **130**
Everite Rd. Ind. Est. *Wid* —5B **130**
Everleigh Clo. *Pren* —2C **94**
Eversleigh Dri. *Wir* —3A **142**
Eversley. *Wid* —2B **130**
Eversley Pk. *Pren* —1B **118**
Eversley St. *L8* —3A **100**
(in two parts)
Everton. —2F 77
Everton Brow. *L3* —3E **77** (1H **5**)
Everton F.C. —2F 55
Everton Gro. *St H* —3D **47**
Everton Pk. Sports Cen. —1E 77
Everton Rd. *L6* —2F **77**
Everton Valley. *L4* —4E **55**
Everton Vw. *Boot* —1B **54**
Every St. *L6* —2B **78**
Evesham Clo. *L25* —2F **125**
Evesham Rd. *L4* —2D **57**
Evesham Rd. *Wall* —5F **51**
Ewanville. *L36* —5E **83**
Ewart Rd. *S'frth* —1F **33**
Ewart Rd. *St H* —2B **46**
Ewart Rd. *B'grn* —1A **104**
Ewden Clo. *L16* —2E **103**
Exchange Pas. E. *L2* —4C **76** (4C **4**)
Exchange Pas. W. *L2* —4C **76** (4C **4**)
Exchange Pl. *Rain* —3C **86**
Exchange St. *St H* —5A **46**
Exchange St. E. *L2* —4C **76** (4C **4**)
Exchange St. W. *L2* —4C **76** (5C **4**)
Exeley. *Whis* —4E **85**
Exeter Clo. *L10* —4E **21**
Exeter Rd. *Boot* —1C **54**
Exeter Rd. *Wall* —1C **74**
Exeter St. *St H* —4D **45**
Exford Rd. *L12* —3D **59**
Exmoor Clo. *Wir* —2F **137**
Exmouth Clo. *Birk* —3D **97**
Exmouth Cres. *Murd* —4E **169**
Exmouth Gdns. *Birk* —3D **97**
Exmouth St. *Birk* —3D **97**
Exmouth Way. *Birk* —3D **97**
Exmouth Way. *Btnwd* —5F **69**
Expressway. *Run* —3D **155**
Extension Vw. *St H* —3D **67**
Exwood Gro. *Whis* —4F **85**

Factory La. *Wid* —1B **132**
Factory Row. *St H* —2E **65**
Fairacre Rd. *L19* —5A **124**
Fairacres Rd. *Wir* —3F **141**
Fairbairn Rd. *L22* —4E **17**
Fairbank St. *L15* —2E **101**
Fairbeech Ct. *Pren* —2C **94**
Fairbeech M. *Pren* —2C **94**
Fairbrook Dri. *Birk* —5E **73**
Fairburn Clo. *Wid* —1E **133**
Fairburn Rd. *L13* —5E **57**
Fairclough Clo. *Prsct* —3B **86**
Fairclough Cres. *Hay* —2A **48**
Fairclough La. *Pren* —5B **96**
Fairclough Rd. *L36* —5C **60**
Fairclough Rd. *St H* —4C **44**
Fairclough Rd. *Rain* —3B **86**
Fairclough St. *L1* —5D **77** (6F **5**)
Fairclough St. *Btnwd* —5E **69**
Fairfax Dri. *Run* —5D **153**
Fairfax Pl. *L11* —1D **57**
Fairfax Rd. *L11* —1D **57**
Fairfax Rd. *Birk* —5E **97**
Fairfield. —3D 79
Fairfield. *L23* —1E **17**
(in two parts)
Fairfield Av. *L36* —4A **82**
Fairfield Clo. *L36* —4A **82**
Fairfield Cres. *Fair* —3D **79**
Fairfield Cres. *Huy* —4A **82**
Fairfield Cres. *Wir* —1D **93**
Fairfield Dri. *Wir* —3E **113**
Fairfield Gdns. *Crank* —3E **29**
(in two parts)
Fairfield Rd. *Birk* —2E **119**
Fairfield Rd. *Dent G* —3C **44**
Fairfield Rd. *Wid* —3B **132**
Fairfield St. *L7* —3E **79**
Fairford Cres. *L14* —2B **80**
Fairford Rd. *L14* —2B **80**
Fairhaven. *L33* —5E **15**
Fairhaven Clo. *Birk* —2F **119**
Fairhaven Dri. *Wir* —5C **162**
Fairhaven Rd. *Wid* —2C **132**
Fair Havens Ct. *Wid* —5B **132**
Fairholme Av. *Ecc P* —5F **63**
Fairholme Clo. *L12* —3A **58**
Fairholme M. *L23* —1E **17**
Fairholme Rd. *L23* —1E **17**
Fairhurst Ter. *Prsct* —5E **63**
Fairlawn Clo. *Wir* —4A **162**
Fairlawn Ct. *Pren* —4F **95**
Fairlawne Clo. *L33* —5E **15**
Fairlie Cres. *Boot* —1D **35**
Fairlie Dri. *Rain* —4D **87**
Fairmead Rd. *L11* —1E **57**
Fairmead Rd. *Wir* —5E **71**
Fairoak Clo. *Pren* —2C **94**
Fairoak Ct. *White I* —2F **175**
Fairoak La. *White I* —2F **175**
Fairoak M. *Pren* —2C **94**
Fairthorn Wlk. *L33* —2A **24**
Fair Vw. *Bil* —1D **31**
Fair Vw. *Birk* —5E **97**
Fair Vw. Av. *Bil* —1D **31**
Fairview Av. *Wall* —1A **74**

Fairview Clo. *Pren* —1B **118**
Fair Vw. Pl. *L8* —4A **100**
Fairview Rd. *Pren* —2B **118**
Fairview Way. *Wir* —4F **137**
Fair Way. *Wind* —3C **44**
Fairway. *Huy* —2A **84**
Fairway Cres. *Wir* —3D **143**
Fairway N. *Wir* —3D **143**
Fairways. *Cros* —5D **9**
Fairways. *Frod* —5D **173**
Fairways Clo. *L25* —4B **126**
Fairway S. *Wir* —4D **143**
Fairways, The. *Wir* —3D **135**
Fairways, The. *Wltn* —4D **127**
Fairway, The. *K Ash* —2D **81**
Falcon Cres. *L27* —5F **105**
Falconer St. *Boot* —2A **34**
Falcongate Ind. Est. Wall —5C 74
(off Old Gorsey La.)
Falconhall Rd. *L9* —4F **37**
Falcon Hey. *L10* —2A **38**
Falcon Rd. *Birk* —5C **96**
Falcons Way. *Hall P* —4E **167**
Falkland Rd. *Wall* —2D **75**
Falklands App. *L11* —1E **57**
Falkland St. *L3* —4F **77** (3J **5**)
(in two parts)
Falkland St. *Birk* —1A **96**
Falkner Sq. *L8* —1F **99**
Falkner St. *L8* —1F **99** (7J **5**)
(in two parts)
Fallbrook Dri. *L12* —3B **58**
(in two parts)
Fallow Clo. *Clo F* —2C **88**
Fallowfield. *L33* —1E **23**
Fallowfield. *Halt B* —1D **167**
Fallowfield Rd. *L15* —3F **101**
Fallowfield Rd. *Wir* —1A **94**
Fallows Way. *Whis* —5C **84**
Falls La. *L26* —2E **127**
Falmouth Pl. *Murd* —4E **169**
Falmouth Rd. *L11* —3C **38**
Falstaff St. *Boot* —2C **54**
Falstone Dri. *Pres B* —3E **169**
Faraday Rd. *Know I* —1B **40**
Faraday Rd. *Ast I* —4D **153**
Faraday Rd. *W'tree* —5E **79**
Faraday St. *L5* —1A **78**
Fareham Clo. *Wir* —3E **93**
Fareham Rd. *L7* —4C **78**
Faringdon Clo. *L25* —1B **146**
Farley Av. *Wir* —1C **162**
Farlow Rd. *Birk* —3F **119**
Farmbrook Rd. *L25* —2B **104**
Farm Clo. *Clo F* —3D **89**
Farm Clo. *Wir* —5C **92**
Farmdale Clo. *L18* —1B **124**
Farmdale Dri. *L31* —1E **13**
Far Mdw. La. *Wir* —1C **136**
Farmer Pl. *Boot* —1E **35**
Farmer's La. *Btnwd* —5F **69**
Farmfield Dri. *Pren* —2C **94**
Far Moss Rd. *L23* —4B **8**
Farm Rd. *Clo F* —3D **89**
Farmside. *Wir* —3F **71**
Farm Vw. *L21* —3B **18**
Farmview Clo. *L27* —2C **104**
Farnborough Gro. *L26* —3F **127**
Farndale. *Wid* —4A **110**
Farndon Av. *Sut M* —2B **88**
Farndon Av. *Wall* —5E **51**
Farndon Dri. *Wir* —3E **113**
Farndon Way. *Pren* —5F **95**
Farnhill Clo. *Wind H* —2D **169**
Farnley Clo. *Wind H* —1D **169**
Farnworth Av. *Wir* —2F **71**
Farnworth Clo. *Wid* —5B **110**
Farnworth Gro. *L33* —5E **15**
Farnworth Rd. *Penk* —5E **111**
Farnworth St. *L6* —3B **78**
Farnworth St. *St H* —4C **46**
Farnworth St. *Wid* —5B **110**
Farrant St. *Wid* —4B **132**
Farrar St. *L13* —4D **57**
Farrell Clo. *L31* —1B **22**
Farr Hall Dri. *Wir* —3E **157**
Farr Hall Rd. *Wir* —2E **157**
Farrier Rd. *L33* —3A **24**
Farriers Wlk. *Clo F* —2C **88**
Farriers Way. *Boot* —5F **19**
Farriers Way. *Wir* —2B **114**
Farringdon Clo. *St H* —1F **87**
Farthing Clo. *L25* —5A **126**
Farthingstone Clo. *Whis* —5A **64**
Fatherside Dri. *Boot* —2C **18**
Faversham Rd. *L11* —5E **37**
Fawcett Rd. *L31* —4D **7**
Fawley Rd. *L18* —2C **124**
Fawley Rd. *Rain* —5E **87**
Fazakerley. —4D 37
Fazakerley Bri. L3 —4B 76 (4B 4)
(off Fazakerley St.)
Fazakerley Clo. *L9* —4A **36**
Fazakerley Rd. *L9* —4A **36**
Fazakerley Rd. *Prsct* —2E **85**
Fazakerley Sports Cen. —5F 21
Fazakerley St. *L3* —4B **76** (4B **4**)
Fearnley Hall. *Birk* —4D **97**
Fearnley Rd. *Birk* —4D **97**
Fearnside St. *L7* —1C **100**
Feather La. *Wir* —2F **157**
(in two parts)
Feeny St. *Sut M* —4B **88**
Feilden Rd. *Wir* —3A **142**
Felicity Gro. *Wir* —5D **71**
Fell Gro. *St H* —5A **30**
Fell St. *L7* —4B **78**
Fell St. *Wall* —4E **75**
Felltor Clo. *L25* —1F **125**
Fellwood Gro. *Whis* —3E **85**
Felmersham Av. *L11* —5E **37**
Felspar Rd. *L32* —1E **39**
Felsted Av. *L25* —2C **126**
Felsted Dri. *L10* —4E **21**
Felthorpe Clo. *Upt* —2B **94**
Felton Clo. *Wir* —1C **92**
Felton Gro. *L13* —2F **79**
Feltree Ho. *Pren* —2C **94**
Feltwell Rd. *L4* —5B **56**
Feltwood Clo. *L12* —4F **59**
Feltwood Mnr. *L12* —4F **59**
Feltwood Rd. *L12* —3F **59**
Feltwood Wlk. *L12* —4F **59**
Fender Ct. *Wir* —3D **117**
Fender La. *Wir* —5A **72**
Fenderside Rd. *Pren* —1C **94**
Fender Vw. Rd. *Wir* —1A **94**
Fender Way. *Pren* —2B **94**
(in two parts)
Fenderway. *Wir* —3A **138**
Fenton Clo. *Boot* —5B **20**
Fenton Clo. *L24* —4D **147**
Fenton Clo. *St H* —4F **45**
Fenton Clo. *Wid* —1B **130**
Fenton Grn. *L24* —5D **147**
Fenwick La. *Halt L* —4D **167**
Fenwick St. *L2* —5C **76** (5C **4**)
Ferguson Av. *Wir* —1D **115**
Ferguson Rd. *Lith* —4C **18**
Ferguson Rd. *W Der* —3E **57**
Fern Bank. *L31* —1D **13**
Fernbank Av. *L36* —4D **83**
Fernbank Dri. *Boot* —1A **20**
Fernbank La. *Wir* —2F **93**
Fern Clo. *L27* —5E **105**
Ferndale Av. *Wall* —2C **74**
Ferndale Av. *Wir* —3B **114**
Ferndale Clo. *L9* —1A **36**
Ferndale Clo. *Wid* —2E **111**
Ferndale Rd. *Wat* —3D **17**
Ferndale Rd. *W'tree* —3E **101**
Ferndale Rd. *Wir* —4B **90**
Fern Gdns. *Ecc L* —4F **63**
Fern Gro. *Boot* —4C **34**
Fern Gro. *L8* —3B **100**
Fern Gro. *Pren* —4D **95**
Fern Hey. *L23* —5B **10**
Fernhill. *Wall* —3B **52**
Fernhill Av. *Boot* —5E **35**
Fernhill Clo. *Boot* —5E **35**
Fernhill Dri. *L8* —3A **100**
Fernhill Gdns. *Boot* —5E **35**
Fernhill M. E. *Boot* —5E **35**
Fernhill M. W. *Boot* —5E **35**
Fernhill Rd. *Boot* —2D **35**
Fernhill Sports Cen. —2D 35
Fernhill Wlk. *Clo F* —2C **88**
Fernhill Way. *Boot* —5E **35**
Fernhurst. *Halt B* —1D **167**
Fernhurst Rd. *L32* —4C **22**
Fernie Cres. *L8* —4E **99**
Fernlea Av. *That H* —4D **65**
Fernlea M. *Pren* —1C **94**
Fernlea Rd. *Wir* —2A **158**
Fernleigh. *Pren* —1B **118**
Fernleigh Rd. *L13* —3B **80**
Fern Lodge. *L8* —3B **100**
Ferns Clo. *Wir* —1C **156**
Ferns Rd. *Wir* —2D **141**
Fernwood Dri. *L26* —4E **127**
Fernwood Rd. *L17* —1E **123**
Ferny Brow Rd. *Wir* —1B **116**
Ferrey Rd. *L10* —1A **38**
Ferries Clo. *Birk* —4A **120**
Ferry Rd. *Wir* —5F **163**
Ferryside. *Wall* —4E **75**
Ferry Vw. Rd. *Wall* —4E **75**
Ferryview Wlk. *Cas* —5F **153**
Festival Ct. *L11* —5B **38**
Festival Way. *Run* —2C **166**
Ffrancon Dri. *Wir* —5F **119**
Fiddlers Ferry Rd. *Wid* —4C **132**
Fidler St. *St H* —2D **65**
Field Av. *L21* —5A **18**
Field Clo. *Clo F* —3D **89**
Field Clo. *Wir* —4B **120**
Fieldfare Clo. *L25* —4A **104**
Fieldgate. *Wid* —5B **130**
Field Hey La. *Will* —4B **170**
(in two parts)
Fieldhouse Row. *Halt L* —3D **167**
Fieldings, The. *L31* —3B **6**
Fielding St. *L6* —3A **78**
Field La. *Faz* —2A **38**
Field La. *Lith* —4A **18**
Field Rd. *Clo F* —3D **89**
Field Rd. *Wall* —4B **52**
Fields End. *L36* —1E **105**
Fieldsend Clo. *L27* —5E **105**
Fieldside Rd. *Birk* —2E **119**
Field St. *L3* —3E **77** (1H **5**)
(in two parts)
Fieldsway. *West* —4A **166**
Fieldton Rd. *L11* —1B **58**
Field Vw. *L21* —4A **18**
Field Wlk. *L23* —5B **10**
Fieldway. *Mag* —3D **13**
Fieldway. *Beb* —4D **119**
Fieldway. *Frod* —5C **172**
Fieldway. *Hes* —1C **158**
Fieldway. *Huy* —1F **105**
Fieldway. *Meol* —4F **91**
Field Way. *Rain* —1C **86**
Fieldway. *Wall* —1A **74**
Fieldway. *W'tree* —1C **102**
Fieldway. *Wid* —2D **133**
Fieldway Ct. *Birk* —1C **96**

Fifth Av. *Faz* —1E **37**
Fifth Av. *L9* —1D **37**
Fifth Av. *Pren* —2B **94**
Fifth Av. *Run* —3F **167**
Filbert Clo. *L33* —4F **15**
Filton Rd. *L14* —1B **82**
Finborough Rd. *L4* —1C **56**
Fincham. —1B 82
Fincham Clo. *L14* —1B **82**
Fincham Grn. *L14* —1B **82**
Fincham Rd. *L14* —1A **82**
Fincham Sq. *L14* —1A **82**
Finch Clo. *Clo F* —3D **89**
Finch Clo. *L14* —5F **59**
Finch Ct. *Birk* —2D **97**
Finchdean Clo. *Wir* —1C **114**
Finch Dene. *L14* —5F **59**
Finch La. *Halew* —1B **148**
Finch La. *K Ash* —5F **59**
Finch Lea Dri. *L14* —1A **82**
Finchley Dri. *St H* —1C **46**
Finchley Rd. *L4* —4B **56**
Finch Mdw. Clo. *L9* —4F **37**
Finch Pl. *L3* —4F **77** (3J **5**)
Finch Rd. *L14* —5A **60**
Finch Way. *L14* —1F **81**
Findley Dri. *Wir* —3F **71**
Findon Rd. *L32* —5F **23**
Fingall Rd. *L15* —3A **102**
Finger Ho. La. *Wid* —5D **89**
Fingland Rd. *L15* —2E **101**
Finlan Rd. *Wid* —5A **132**
Finlay Ct. *Boot* —1F **19**
Finlay St. *L6* —3C **78**
Finney Gro. *Hay* —2E **49**
Finney, The. *Cald* —3D **135**
Finsbury Pk. *Wid* —4C **110**
Finstall Rd. *Wir* —5F **141**
Finvoy Rd. *L13* —4E **57**
Fiona Wlk. *L10* —1C **38**
Fir Av. *L26* —4A **128**
Firbank Clo. *Wind H* —1D **169**
Firbrook Ct. *Pren* —5C **72**
Fir Clo. *L26* —4A **128**
Fir Cotes. *L31* —1E **13**
Firdale Rd. *L9* —4A **36**
Firdene Cres. *Pren* —5E **95**
Fire Sta. Rd. *Whis* —1F **85**
Firethorne Rd. *L26* —2D **127**
Fir Gro. *Walt* —5C **20**
Fir La. *L15* —2A **102**
Fir Rd. *L22* —3E **17**
Firs Av. *Wir* —4F **141**
Firscraig. *L28* —4C **60**
Firshaw Rd. *Wir* —2C **90**
First Av. *Cros* —1D **17**
First Av. *Faz* —2E **37**
First Av. *L9* —1C **36**
First Av. *Pren* —3C **94**
First Av. *Rain* —2B **86**
Firs, The. *Pren* —1E **95**
Firstone Gro. *L32* —5E **23**
Fir St. *St H* —3D **65**
Fir St. *Wid* —2C **132**
Firthland Way. *St H* —1F **67**
Fir Tree Dri. N. *L12* —5D **39**
Fir Tree Dri. S. *L12* —5D **39**
Fir Tree La. *Btnwd* —4F **69**
Fir Way. *Wir* —5B **158**
Fisher Av. *Whis* —4D **85**
Fisher Pl. *Whis* —4D **85**
Fishers La. *Wir* —3E **137**
Fisher St. *L8* —3D **99**
Fisher St. *St H* —3E **67**
Fisher St. *Run* —4B **152**
Fishguard Clo. *L6* —2F **77**
Fishwicks Ind. Est. *St H* —3C **66**
Fistral Clo. *L10* —2B **38**
Fistral Dri. *Wind* —2B **44**
Fitzclarence Wlk. *L6* —2F **77**
Fitzclarence Way. *L6* —2F **77**
Fitzgerald Rd. *L13* —3A **80**
Fitzpatrick Ct. *L3* —2C **76**
Fitzroy Way. *L6* —3A **78**
Fitzwilliam Wlk. *Cas* —5A **154**
Fiveways. *Ecc* —4A **44**
Flail Clo. *Wir* —5D **93**
Flambards. *Wir* —1C **116**
Flander Clo. *Wid* —2C **130**
Flatfield Way. *L31* —1E **13**
Flatt La. *Pren* —1F **117**
Flavian Brow. *Cas* —1E **167**
Flavian Ct. *Run* —5A **154**
Flawn Rd. *L11* —3E **57**
Flaxhill. *Wir* —5D **71**
Flaxman St. *L7* —4C **78**
Flaybrick Clo. *Pren* —1E **95**
Fleck La. *Wir* —5D **113**
Fleet Cft. Rd. *Wir* —2A **116**
Fleet La. *St H* —5E **47**
Fleet St. *L1* —5D **77** (6F **5**)
Fleetwood Gdns. *L33* —5F **15**
(in two parts)
Fleetwood Pl. *L25* —2F **125**
Fleetwoods La. *Boot* —1D **19**
Fleetwood Wlk. *Murd* —3C **168**
Fleming Ct. *L3* —2C **76**
Fleming Rd. *L24* —1C **146**
Flemington Av. *L4* —2D **57**
Fletcher Av. *Birk* —2E **119**
Fletcher Av. *Prsct* —4E **63**
Fletcher Clo. *Wir* —2A **116**
Fletcher Dri. *L19* —5A **124**
Flint Dri. *L12* —2D **59**
Flintshire Gdns. *St H* —1E **65**
Flint St. *L1* —2D **99**
Floral Pavillion Theatre. —2C 52
Floral Wood. *L17* —2F **121**
Florence Av. *Wir* —1F **157**
Florence Clo. *L9* —5F **35**
Florence Nightingale Clo. *Boot* —1F **19**
Florence Rd. *Wall* —3E **75**
Florence St. *L4* —3F **55**
Florence St. *St H* —4C **64**
Florence St. *Birk* —3D **97**
Florentine Rd. *L13* —2A **80**
Florida Ct. *L19* —4B **124**
Flowermead Clo. *Wir* —2F **91**
Fluin La. *Frod* —4C **172**
Fluker's Brook La. *Know* —2B **60**
Foinavon Clo. *L9* —1F **35**
Folds La. *St H* —1A **46**
Folds Rd. *Hay* —2F **47**
Folds, The. *Wir* —4A **160**
Foley Clo. *L4* —4E **55**
Foley St. *L4* —4E **55**
(in two parts)
Folkestone Way. *Murd* —3C **168**
Folly La. *Run* —1D **165**
Folly La. *Wall* —1E **73**
Fontenoy St. *L3* —4D **77** (2E **5**)
Fonthill Clo. *L4* —4D **55**
Fonthill Rd. *L4* —3D **55**
Ford. —4B 94
(Birkenhead)
Ford. —3B 18
(Litherland)
Ford Clo. *Boot* —1E **35**
Ford Clo. *L21* —3B **18**
Ford Clo. *Wir* —5B **94**
Fordcombe Rd. *L25* —5C **104**
Ford Dri. *Wir* —4B **94**
Fordham St. *L4* —3E **55**
Fordhill Vw. *Wir* —1A **94**
Ford La. *L21* —3B **18**
Ford La. *Wir* —4B **94**
Fordlea Rd. *L12* —3A **58**
Fordlea Way. *L12* —3A **58**
Ford Rd. *Prsct* —5F **63**
Ford Rd. *Wir* —4A **94**
Ford St. *L3* —3C **76** (1D **4**)
Ford Vw. *L21* —2B **18**
Ford Way. *Wir* —5A **94**
Fordway M. *Wir* —5A **94**
Forefield La. *L23* —5F **9**
Forest Clo. *Ecc P* —4F **63**
Forest Clo. *Wir* —2D **91**
Forest Ct. *Pren* —3F **95**
Forest Dri. *L36* —3C **82**
Forest Grn. *L12* —3A **58**
Forest Gro. *Ecc P* —4F **63**
Forest Lawn. *L12* —3B **58**
Forest Mead. *Ecc* —5A **44**
Forest Rd. *Hes* —1A **158**
Forest Rd. *Meol* —2D **91**
Forest Rd. *Pren* —2A **96**
Forest Rd. *Sut M* —3A **88**
Forfar Rd. *L13* —5D **57**
Forge Clo. *Wid* —4C **108**
Forge Cotts. *L17* —5C **100**
Forge St. *Boot* —3C **54**
Formby Av. *St H* —2D **65**
Formosa Dri. *L10* —1F **37**
Formosa Rd. *L10* —1F **37**
Formosa Way. *L10* —1F **37**
Fornals Grn. La. *Wir* —4E **91**
Forrester Av. *St H* —4C **64**
Forrest St. *L1* —1D **99** (7E **4**)
Forshaw Av. *St H* —3C **64**
Forshaw's La. *Btnwd* —3E **69**
Forsythia Clo. *L9* —5C **36**
Forthlin Rd. *L18* —3C **124**
(in two parts)
Forth St. *L20* —2B **54**
*Forton Lodge Flats. L23 —1C **16***
(off Blundellsands Rd. E.)
Fort St. *Wall* —4C **52**
Forwood Rd. *Wir* —2D **163**
Foscote Rd. *L33* —1A **24**
Foster Clo. *Whis* —1A **86**
Fosters Gro. *Hay* —2F **47**
Fosters Rd. *Hay* —2F **47**
Foster St. *L20* —4C **54**
Foster St. *Wid* —3B **132**
Foundry La. *Wid* —2B **150**
Foundry St. *St H* —5A **46**
Fountain Ct. *Cros* —5A **8**
Fountain La. *Frod* —5A **172**
Fountain Rd. *Know* —5D **41**
Fountain Rd. *Wall* —4B **52**
Fountains Av. *Hay* —1F **49**
Fountains Clo. *L4* —4F **55**
Fountains Clo. *Brook* —5C **168**
Fountains Ct. *Kirk* —4D **55**
Fountains Rd. *L4* —4D **55**
(in two parts)
Fountain St. *St H* —5C **64**
Fountain St. *Birk* —1C **118**
Four Acre Dri. *L21* —2B **18**
Four Acre La. *Clo F* —2B **88**
Fouracres. *L31* —3B **12**
Four Bridges. *Wall* —5E **75**
Fourth Av. *Faz* —1E **37**
Fourth Av. *L9* —1D **37**
Fourth Av. *Pren* —2B **94**
Fourth Av. *Run* —3F **167**
Fowell Rd. *Wall* —3B **52**
Fowler Clo. *L7* —5C **78**
Fowler St. *L5* —1A **78**
Foxcote. *Wid* —2B **130**
Foxcover Rd. *Hes* —3C **158**
Foxcovers Rd. *Beb* —4A **142**
Fox Covert. *Run* —2C **168**
Foxdale Clo. *Pren* —4A **96**
Foxdale Rd. *L15* —3E **101**
Foxdell Clo. *L13* —4A **80**
Foxes, The. *Wir* —1B **138**

Foxfield Rd. *Wir* —3D **91**
Foxglove Av. *L26* —3E **127**
Foxglove Clo. *L9* —4F **37**
Foxglove Ct. *Frod* —5C **172**
Foxglove Rd. *Birk* —2F **95**
Fox Hey Rd. *Wall* —2F **73**
Foxhill Clo. *Tox* —3A **100**
Foxhill La. *L26* —2E **127**
Foxhouse La. *L31* —2E **13**
Foxhunter Dri. *L9* —5C **20**
Foxleigh. *L26* —3D **127**
Foxleigh Grange. *Birk* —5F **73**
Foxley Heath. *Wid* —4E **131**
Fox Pl. *St H* —4A **46**
Fox's Bank La. *Whis* —1F **107**
Foxshaw Clo. *Whis* —5D **85**
Fox St. *L3* —2E **77** (1G **5**)
Fox St. *Birk* —3C **96**
Fox St. *Run* —5A **152**
Foxton Clo. *St H* —3D **47**
Foxton Clo. *Wir* —5B **70**
Foxwood. *L12* —3E **59**
Foxwood. *St H* —5C **64**
Foxwood Clo. *Wir* —3E **113**
Frampton Rd. *L4* —1D **57**
Franceys St. *L3* —5E **77** (5H **5**)
Francine Clo. *L3* —1C **76**
Francis Av. *Pren* —3B **96**
Francis Av. *Wir* —1D **93**
Francis Clo. *Rain* —2C **86**
Francis Clo. *Wid* —4C **130**
Francis Rd. *Frod* —4C **172**
Francis St. *St H* —4F **67**
Francis Way. *L16* —1D **103**
Frankby. —2B 114
Frankby Av. *Wall* —2A **74**
Frankby Clo. *Wir* —1B **114**
Frankby Grn. *Wir* —2B **114**
Frankby Gro. *Wir* —4F **93**
Frankby Rd. *L4* —3B **56**
Frankby Rd. *Grea & Wir* —1B **114**
Frankby Rd. *Meol* —3D **91**
Frankby Rd. *W Kir & Fran* —3D **113**
Franklin Gro. *L33* —4E **15**
Franklin Pl. *L6* —1B **78**
Franklin Rd. *Wir* —2A **72**
Frank St. *L8* —4E **99**
Frank St. *Wid* —3C **132**
Franton Wlk. *L32* —3C **22**
Fraser St. *L3* —4E **77** (3G **5**)
Freckleton Dri. *L33* —5F **15**
Freckleton Rd. *St H* —2B **64**
Freda Av. *St H* —5C **66**
Frederick Banting Clo. *Boot* —1F **19**
Frederick Gro. *L15* —1A **102**
Frederick Lunt Av. *Know* —5C **40**
Frederick St. *St H* —3F **67**
Frederick St. *Wid* —3B **132**
Frederick Ter. *Wid* —3A **150**
Fredric Pl. *Run* —4B **152**
Freedom Clo. *L7* —1A **100**
Freehold St. *L7* —3D **79**
Freeland St. *L4* —4E **55**
Freeman St. *L7* —1C **100**
Freeman St. *Birk* —2E **97**
Freemantle Av. *That H* —4E **65**
Freemasons Row. *L3* —3C **76** (2D **4**)
Freemont Rd. *L12* —4A **58**
Freeport Gro. *L9* —1B **36**
Freesia Av. *L9* —4B **36**
Freme Clo. *L11* —5B **38**
Frenchfield St. *Clo F* —3D **89**
French St. *St H* —2D **65**
French St. *Wid* —3D **133**
Frensham Clo. *Wir* —5F **141**
Frensham Way. *L25* —4D **127**
Freshfield Clo. *L36* —3C **82**
Freshfield Rd. *W'tree* —3F **101**
Freshford. *St H* —5D **67**
Friars Clo. *Wir* —2F **141**
Friarsgate Clo. *L18* —4C **102**
Friar St. *St H* —2F **45**
Frinstead Rd. *L11* —2A **58**
Frobisher Rd. *More* —2A **72**
Froda Av. *Frod* —5B **172**
Frodsham. —5B 172
Frodsham Dri. *St H* —3D **47**
Frodsham St. *L4* —2F **55**
Frodsham St. *Birk* —5E **97**
(in two parts)
Frogmore Rd. *L13* —3E **79**
Frome Clo. *Wir* —5D **115**
Frome Way. *L25* —4D **127**
Frontfield Ct. St H —1C 66
(off Appleton Rd.)
Frost Dri. *Wir* —1C **136**
Frost St. *L7* —4C **78**
Fryer St. *Run* —4A **152**
Fry St. *St H* —5E **47**
(in two parts)
Fuchsia Wlk. *Wir* —2C **114**
Fulbeck. *Wid* —2C **130**
Fulbrook Clo. *Wir* —4F **141**
Fulbrook Rd. *Wir* —5F **141**
Fulford Clo. *L12* —5F **59**
Fullerton Gro. *L36* —2E **83**
Fulmar Clo. *L27* —4E **105**
Fulmar Clo. *St H* —2B **46**
Fulmar Gro. *L12* —5E **39**
Fulshaw Clo. *L27* —3D **105**
Fulton Av. *Wir* —3E **113**
Fulton St. *L5* —1B **76**
Fulwood Clo. *L17* —2D **123**
Fulwood Dri. *L17* —2C **122**
Fulwood Pk. *L17* —3C **122**
Fulwood Rd. *L17* —2C **122**
Fulwood Way. *L21* —1C **18**
Furlong Clo. *L9* —5C **20**
Furness Av. *St H* —1E **45**
Furness Av. *W Der* —2C **58**
Furness Clo. *Wir* —3E **93**
Furness Ct. *Run* —3F **155**
Furness St. *L4* —4E **55**
Furze Way. *Wir* —5E **71**

Gable Ct. *L11* —5E **37**
Gables, The. *Mag* —3E **13**
Gables, The. *Prsct* —5F **63**
Gable Vw. *L11* —5E **37**
Gabriel Clo. *Wir* —1F **93**
Gainford Clo. *L14* —5A **60**
Gainford Clo. *Wid* —1C **130**
Gainford Rd. *L14* —5A **60**
Gainsborough Av. *L31* —2B **12**
Gainsborough Clo. *L12* —1E **81**
Gainsborough Ct. *Wid* —3B **130**
Gainsborough Rd. *L15* —3D **101**
Gainsborough Rd. *Wall* —1E **73**
Gainsborough Rd. *Wir* —3F **93**
Gaisgill Ct. *Wid* —3C **130**
Galemeade. *L11* —5B **38**
Gale Rd. *Know I* —5C **24**
Gale Rd. *Lith* —4C **18**
Galion Way. *Wid* —1E **131**
Gallagher Ind. Est. *Birk* —5B **74**
Gallopers La. *Wir* —1C **138**
Galloway Rd. *L22* —3E **17**
Galloway St. *L7* —1D **101**
Galston Av. *Rain* —4D **87**
Galston Clo. *L33* —4D **15**
Galsworthy Av. *Boot* —5D **19**
Galsworthy Pl. *Boot* —5E **19**
Galsworthy Wlk. *Boot* —1E **35**
Galton St. *L3* —3B **76** (2A **4**)
Galtres Ct. *Wir* —4E **119**
Galtres Pk. *Wir* —4E **119**
Gambier Ter. *L1* —2E **99**
Gamble Av. *St H* —2E **45**
Gamlin St. *Birk* —1F **95**
Gamston Wood. *L32* —4C **22**
Ganney's Mdw. Rd. *Wir* —2C **116**
Gannock St. *L7* —4C **78**
Ganton Clo. *Wid* —5B **110**
Ganworth Clo. *L24* —5E **147**
Ganworth Rd. *L24* —5E **147**
Garage Rd. *L24* —2F **147**
Garden Apartments. *L18* —1F **123**
Garden Cotts. *L12* —2D **81**
Garden Ct. *Birk* —3C **118**
Gardeners Vw. *L33* —4F **15**
Gardeners Way. *Rain* —1C **86**
Garden Hey Rd. *Meol* —3C **90**
Garden Hey Rd. *More* —2B **92**
Gardenia Gro. *L17* —2A **122**
Garden La. *L3* —2E **77**
Garden La. *L9* —5D **21**
Garden La. *Wir* —5E **71**
Garden Lodge Gro. *L27* —4D **105**
Gardenside. *Wir* —2B **72**
Gardenside St. *L6* —3F **77**
Gardens Rd. *Wir* —2B **142**
Garden St. *L25* —2A **126**
Garden Vw. *L12* —1D **81**
Garden Wlk. *Prsct* —1D **85**
Gardiner Av. *Hay* —2C **48**
Gardner Av. *Boot* —1D **35**
Gardner Rd. *Old S* —1E **79**
Gardners Dri. *L6* —2C **78**
Gardner's Row. *L3* —3D **77** (1E **5**)
Gareth Av. *St H* —2B **46**
Garfield Ter. *Wir* —4A **94**
Garfourth Clo. *L19* —5D **125**
Garfourth Rd. *L19* —5D **125**
Garmoyle Clo. *L15* —2D **101**
Garmoyle Rd. *L15* —2E **101**
Garnet St. *L13* —5F **79**
Garnet St. *St H* —4D **67**
Garnett Av. *L4* —3D **55**
Garnetts La. *Tarb G* —3D **129**
Garnett's La. *Wid* —3A **150**
Garrick Av. *Wir* —1C **92**
Garrick Rd. *Pren* —4F **117**
Garrick St. *L7* —2C **100**
Garrigill Clo. *Wid* —4B **110**
Garrowby Dri. *L36* —3C **82**
Garsdale Av. *Rain* —4D **87**
Garsfield Rd. *L4* —2D **57**
Garston. —1D 145
Garston Ind. Est. *L19* —3C **144**
Garston Old Rd. *L19* —5A **124**
Garston Recreation Cen. & Swimming Pool. —1C 144
Garston Sports Cen. —5C 124
Garston Way. *L19* —1B **144**
Garswood Clo. *L31* —4E **7**
Garswood Clo. *Wir* —2F **71**
Garswood Cres. *Bil* —1E **31**
Garswood Old Rd. *St H & Ash M* —5C **30**
Garswood Rd. *Bil* —1E **31**
Garswood St. *L8* —1F **121**
Garswood St. *St H* —4A **46**
Garter Clo. *L11* —5C **38**
Garth Boulevd. *Wir* —4E **119**
Garth Ct. *L22* —4E **17**
Garthdale Rd. *L18* —5A **102**
Garth Dri. *L18* —5B **102**
Garthowen Rd. *L7* —4D **79**
Garth Rd. *L32* —5A **24**
Garth, The. *L36* —3E **83**
Garth Wlk. *L32* —5A **24**
Gartons La. *Clo F & Sut M* —3B **88**
Garway. *L25* —1C **126**
Gascoyne St. *L3* —3C **76** (2C **4**)
Gaskell Ct. *St H* —5F **47**
Gaskell Pk. —5E 47

Gaskell Rake. *Boot* —5D **11**
Gaskell St. *St H* —2C **66**
Gaskill Rd. *L24* —3D **147**
Gas St. *Run* —5B **152**
Gatclif Rd. *L13* —3E **57**
Gateacre. —4B 104
Gateacre Brow. *L25* —5A **104**
Gateacre Pk. Dri. *L25* —2F **103**
Gateacre Ri. *L25* —5A **104**
Gateacre Shop. Cen. *Gate* —3A **104**
Gateacre Va. Rd. *L25* —1B **126**
Gateside Clo. *L27* —4E **105**
Gates La. *L29* —2B **10**
Gathurst Ct. *Wid* —4D **131**
Gatley Dri. *L31* —3E **13**
Gatley Wlk. *L24* —3F **147**
Gaunts Way. *Hall P* —4E **167**
Gautby Rd. *Birk* —5E **73**
Gavin Rd. *Wid* —5B **130**
Gawsworth Clo. *Ecc* —5B **44**
Gawsworth Clo. *Pren* —1F **117**
Gayhurst Cres. *L11* —1A **58**
Gaynor Av. *Hay* —1F **49**
Gayton. —3B 158
Gayton Av. *Wall* —3B **52**
Gayton Av. *Wir* —4C **118**
Gayton Farm Rd. *Wir* —5A **158**
Gayton La. *Wir* —4B **158**
Gayton Mill Clo. *Wir* —3B **158**
Gayton Parkway. *Wir* —5C **158**
Gayton Rd. *Hes* —4F **157**
Gaytree Ct. *Pren* —2C **94**
Gaywood Av. *L32* —5F **23**
Gaywood Clo. *L32* —5F **23**
Gaywood Clo. *Pren* —2C **94**
Gaywood Grn. *L32* —5F **23**
Gellings Rd. *Know B* —3A **40**
Gelling St. *L8* —4E **99**
Gemini Clo. *Boot* —4B **34**
Gemini Dri. *L14* —2F **81**
Geneva Clo. *L36* —2D **83**
Geneva Rd. *L6* —3C **78**
Geneva Rd. *Wall* —4D **75**
Genoa Clo. *L25* —2B **104**
Gentwood Pde. *L36* —2D **83**
Gentwood Rd. *L36* —2C **82**
George Hale Av. *Know P* —5E **61**
George Harrison Clo. *L6* —3B **78**
George Moore Ct. *L23* —4C **10**
George Rd. *Wir* —5C **90**
George's Dock Gates. *L3* —4B **76** (5B **4**)
Georges Dockway. *L3* —5B **76** (6B **4**)
George's Rd. *L6* —1B **78**
George St. *L3* —4C **76** (4C **4**)
George St. *St H* —5A **46**
George St. *Birk* —2E **97**
Georgia Av. *L33* —4D **15**
Georgia Av. *Wir* —4E **143**
Georgian Clo. *L26* —1F **147**
Georgian Clo. *Prsct* —5A **64**
Geraint St. *L8* —3F **99**
Gerald Rd. *Pren* —5A **96**
Gerard Av. *Wall* —4A **52**
Gerard Rd. *Wall* —5F **51**
Gerard Rd. *Wir* —3B **112**
Gerard's Bridge. —3A 46
Gerards Ct. *St H* —5C **30**
Gerards La. *St H & Sut L* —4D **67**
Gerard St. *L3* —3D **77** (3F **5**)
Germander Clo. *L26* —3E **127**
Gerneth Clo. *L24* —3C **146**
Gerneth Rd. *L24* —3B **146**
Gerrard Rd. *Bil* —1E **31**
Gerrard's La. *L26* —2E **127**
Gerrard St. *Wid* —4B **132**
Gertrude Rd. *L4* —5A **56**
Gertrude St. *St H* —4C **64**
Gertrude St. *Birk* —3F **97**
Geves Gdns. *L22* —4E **17**
Ghyll Gro. *St H* —4B **30**
Gibbons Av. *St H* —5C **44**
Gibbs Ct. *Wir* —1A **138**
Gibraltar Row. *L3* —4B **76** (3B **4**)
Gibson Clo. *Wir* —4F **137**
Gibson St. *L8* —2F **99**
Giddygate La. *L31* —1B **14**
Gidlow Rd. *L13* —3F **79**
Gidlow Rd. S. *L13* —4F **79**
Gilbert Clo. *Wir* —5F **141**
Gilbert Rd. *Whis* —1F **85**
Gilbert St. *L1* —1D **99** (7E **5**)
Gildarts Gdns. *L3* —2C **76**
Gildart St. *L3* —4E **77** (3J **5**)
Gilead St. *L7* —4B **78**
Gilescroft Av. *L33* —1A **24**
Gilescroft Wlk. *L33* —1A **24**
Gillan Clo. *Brook* —5C **168**
Gillar's Green. —1E 63
Gillars Grn. Dri. *Ecc* —5F **43**
Gillar's La. *St H* —3D **43**
(in two parts)
*Gillbrook Sq. Birk —1F **95***
(off Vaughan St., in two parts)
Gilleney Gro. *Whis* —1A **86**
Gillmoss. —3C 38
Gillmoss Clo. *L11* —4C **38**
Gillmoss La. *L11* —3C **38**
Gillmoss La. Ind. Est. *L10* —2B **38**
Gills La. *Wir* —3A **138**
Gill St. *L3* —4E **77** (4J **5**)
(in two parts)
Gilman St. *L4* —4A **56**
Gilmour Mt. *Pren* —5B **96**
Gilpin Av. *L31* —5E **7**
***Gilroy Nature Pk. —2C** 112*
Gilroy Rd. *L6* —3B **78**
Gilroy Rd. *Wir* —3C **112**
Giltbrook Clo. *Wid* —1F **131**
Gilwell Av. *Wir* —2E **93**
Gilwell Clo. *Wir* —2E **93**
Ginnel, The. *Wir* —2B **142**
Gipsy Gro. *L18* —4E **103**
Gipsy La. *L18* —4E **103**
Girton Av. *Boot* —1E **55**
Girtrell Clo. *Wir* —4D **93**
Girtrell Rd. *Wir* —4D **93**
Givenchy Clo. *L16* —1E **103**
Glade Rd. *L36* —2E **83**
Gladeswood Rd. *Know N* —3B **24**
Glade, The. *Wir* —2D **91**
Gladeville Rd. *L17* —1E **123**
Gladica Clo. *L36* —4B **84**
Gladstone Av. *L16* —1A **104**
Gladstone Av. *L21* —1A **34**
Gladstone Clo. *Birk* —3C **96**
*Gladstone Ct. L21 —2A **34***
(off Elm Rd.)
Gladstone Hall Rd. *Wir* —2B **142**
Gladstone Rd. *S'frth* —1F **33**
Gladstone Rd. *Walt* —5F **35**
Gladstone Rd. *Edg H* —5B **78**
Gladstone Rd. *Gars* —1C **144**
Gladstone Rd. *Wall* —3D **75**
Gladstone St. *L3* —3C **76** (2D **4**)
Gladstone St. *St H* —5D **45**
Gladstone St. *Birk* —3C **96**
Gladstone St. *Wid* —4B **132**
Gladstone St. *Wltn* —2F **125**
*Gladstone Ter. Will —5A **170***
(off Neston Rd.)
Glaisher St. *L5* —5A **56**
Glamis Gro. *St H* —4C **66**
Glamis Rd. *L13* —5D **57**
Glamorgan Clo. *St H* —1F **65**
Glanaber Pk. *L12* —3E **59**
Glasgow St. *Birk* —2F **119**
Glasier Rd. *Wir* —5C **70**
Glaslyn Way. *L9* —5A **36**
Glassonby Cres. *L11* —2A **58**
Glassonby Way. *L11* —2A **58**
Glastonbury Clo. *L6* —4D **57**
Glastonbury Clo. *Run* —4F **155**
Glasven Rd. *L33* —2F **23**
Gleadmere. *Wid* —2C **130**
Gleaston Clo. *Wir* —1C **162**
Gleave Clo. *Btnwd* —5F **69**
Gleave Cres. *L6* —2F **77**
Gleave St. *St H* —4A **46**
Glebe Clo. *L31* —1B **12**
Glebe End. *L29* —3E **11**
Glebe Hey. *L27* —4E **105**
Glebe Hey Rd. *Wir* —1A **116**
Glebelands Rd. *Wir* —1E **93**
Glebe La. *Wid* —4A **110**
Glebe Rd. *Wall* —5A **52**
Glebe, The. *Halt B* —1E **167**
Gleggside. *Wir* —4C **112**
Glegg St. *L3* —2B **76**
Glegside Rd. *L33* —3A **24**
Glenacres. *L25* —1A **126**
Glenalmond Rd. *Wall* —2D **75**
Glenathol Rd. *L18* —2C **124**
Glenavon Rd. *L16* —5C **80**
Glenavon Rd. *Pren* —3A **118**
Glenbank. *L22* —3C **16**
Glenbank Clo. *L9* —3A **36**
Glenburn Av. *Wir* —1E **171**
Glenburn Rd. *Wall* —3D **75**
Glenby Av. *L23* —3F **17**
Glencairn Rd. *L13* —3F **79**
Glencoe Rd. *Wall* —5B **52**
Glenconner Rd. *L16* —5E **81**
Glencourse Rd. *Wid* —4A **110**
Glencroft Clo. *L36* —1C **82**
Glendale Clo. *L8* —1F **121**
*Glendale Gro. L33 —5F **15***
(off Dorchester Dri.)
Glendale Gro. *Wir* —5B **142**
Glendale Rd. *St H* —1A **46**
Glendevon Rd. *Child* —5C **80**
Glendevon Rd. *Huy* —5E **83**
Glendower Rd. *L22* —4E **17**
Glendower St. *Boot* —2C **54**
Glendyke Rd. *L18* —2C **124**
Gleneagles Clo. *L33* —4D **15**
Gleneagles Clo. *Wir* —4F **137**
Gleneagles Dri. *Hay* —3A **48**
Gleneagles Dri. *Wid* —4A **110**
Gleneagles Rd. *L14* —5D **81**
Glenfield Clo. *Pren* —1C **94**
Glenfield Clo. *Wir* —5B **70**
Glenfield Rd. *L15* —3F **101**
Glengariff St. *L13* —4D **57**
Glenham Clo. *Wir* —3E **91**
Glenhead Rd. *L19* —4B **124**
Glenholm Rd. *L31* —3C **12**
Glenista Clo. *L9* —5A **36**
Glenluce Rd. *L19* —3A **124**
Glenlyon Rd. *L16* —1C **102**
Glenmarsh Clo. *L12* —5C **58**
Glenmarsh Clo. *Wir* —2D **141**
Glenmaye Clo. *L12* —1E **59**
Glenmore Av. *L18* —1F **123**
Glenmore Rd. *Pren* —5A **96**
Glenn Pl. *Wid* —3E **131**
Glen Pk. Rd. *Wall* —4A **52**
Glen Rd. *L13* —4B **80**
Glen Ronald Dri. *Wir* —4D **93**
Glenrose Rd. *L25* —5A **104**
Glenside. *L18* —2C **124**
Glen, The. *L18* —1C **124**
Glen, The. *Pal* —4F **167**
Glen, The. *Wir* —4C **142**
Glentree Clo. *Wir* —4D **93**
Glentrees Rd. *L12* —3B **58**
Glentworth Clo. *L31* —2D **13**
Glenville Clo. *L25* —5B **104**

Glenville Clo. *Run* —4B **166**
Glen Vine Clo. *L16* —1E **103**
Glen Way. *L33* —4F **15**
Glenway Clo. *L12* —4F **39**
Glenwood. *Run* —2C **168**
Glenwood Clo. *Whis* —4F **85**
Glenwood Dri. *Wir* —5E **115**
Glenwyllin Rd. *L22* —3E **17**
Globe Rd. *Boot* —4B **34**
Globe St. *L4* —4E **55**
Gloucester Ct. *L6* —3A **78**
Gloucester Pl. *L6* —3A **78**
Gloucester Rd. *Boot* —4D **35**
Gloucester Rd. *Anf* —1D **79**
Gloucester Rd. *Huy* —3A **84**
Gloucester Rd. *Wall* —5E **51**
Gloucester Rd. *Wid* —1B **132**
Gloucester Rd. N. *L6* —5D **57**
Gloucester St. *L1* —4D **77** (4F **5**)
Gloucester St. *St H* —1D **67**
Glover Pl. *Boot* —4B **34**
Glover's Brow. *L32* —1C **22**
Glover's La. *Boot* —1E **19**
Glover St. *L8* —3D **99**
Glover St. *St H* —1F **65**
Glover St. *Birk* —5C **96**
Glyn Av. *Brom* —3E **163**
Glynne Gro. *L16* —1A **104**
Glynne St. *Boot* —2D **35**
Glynn St. *L15* —2F **101**
Glyn Rd. *Wall* —1B **74**
Goddard Rd. *Ast I* —4E **153**
Godetia Clo. *L9* —4F **37**
Godstow. *Run* —3E **155**
Goldcrest Clo. *L12* —4F **39**
Goldcrest Clo. *Beech* —1F **173**
Goldcrest M. *L26* —3E **127**
Golden Gro. *L4* —2A **56**
Golden Triangle Ind. Est. *Wid* —2B **150**
Goldfinch Clo. *L26* —3E **127**
Goldfinch Farm Rd. *L24* —4C **146**
Goldie St. *L4* —4F **55**
Goldsmith Rd. *Pren* —3F **117**
Goldsmith St. *Boot* —4A **34**
Goldsmith St. *L6* —3B **78**
Goldsmith Way. *Pren* —3F **117**
Goldsworth Fold. *Rain* —3B **86**
Golf Links Rd. *Birk* —3B **118**
Gondover Av. *L9* —2F **35**
Gonville Rd. *Boot* —1D **55**
Goodacre Rd. *L9* —1B **36**
*Goodakers Ct. Wir —2A **116***
(off Goodakers Mdw.)
Goodakers Mdw. *Wir* —2A **116**
Goodall Pl. *L4* —2E **55**
Goodall St. *L4* —2E **55**
Goodban St. *St H* —3E **67**
Goodison Av. *L4* —3F **55**
Goodison Pk. —2F 55
Goodison Pl. *L4* —2F **55**
Goodison Rd. *L4* —2F **55**
Goodlass Rd. *L24* —1A **146**
Goodleigh Pl. *Sut L* —1C **88**
Good Shepherd Clo. *L11* —1B **58**
Goodwood Clo. *L36* —5D **83**
Goodwood Ct. *St H* —5D **65**
Goodwood Dri. *Wir* —3F **71**
Goodwood St. *L5* —1D **77**
Gooseberry Hollow. *Wind H* —1D **169**
Gooseberry La. *Nort* —1D **169**
Goose Grn., The. *Wir* —2D **91**
Goostrey Clo. *Wir* —1B **162**
Gordon Av. *Mag* —4C **6**
Gordon Av. *Wat* —3C **16**
Gordon Av. *Brom* —3E **163**
Gordon Av. *Grea* —1E **115**
Gordon Av. *Hay* —1F **49**
Gordon Ct. *Wir* —1E **115**
Gordon Dri. *Aig* —5A **124**
Gordon Dri. *Dove* —3E **81**
Gordon Pl. *L18* —1A **124**
Gordon Rd. *L21* —2F **33**
Gordon Rd. *Wall* —4B **52**
Gordon St. *Birk* —3C **96**
Gordon St. *W'tree* —2E **101**
*Gordon Ter. Will —5A **170***
(off Neston Rd.)
Goree. *L2* —5B **76** (5B **4**)
Gore's La. *Crank* —1A **30**
Gores Rd. *Know I* —4B **24**
Gore St. *L8* —3E **99**
Gorran Haven. *Brook* —5C **168**
Gorse Av. *L12* —2B **58**
Gorsebank Rd. *L18* —4E **101**
Gorsebank St. *Wall* —3C **74**
Gorseburn Rd. *L13* —5E **57**
Gorse Cres. *Wall* —4C **74**
Gorsedale Pk. *Wall* —4D **75**
Gorsedale Rd. *L18* —5A **102**
Gorsedale Rd. *Wall* —4B **74**
Gorsefield. *St H* —4D **65**
Gorsefield Av. *L23* —5B **10**
Gorsefield Av. *Wir* —5D **163**
Gorsefield Clo. *Wir* —5D **163**
Gorsefield Rd. *Birk* —1C **118**
Gorse Hey Ct. *L13* —1A **80**
Gorsehill Rd. *Wall* —4A **52**
Gorsehill Rd. *Wir* —1A **158**
Gorseland Ct. *L17* —2D **123**
Gorse La. *Wir* —5E **113**
Gorse Rd. *Wir* —3D **91**
Gorsewood Clo. *L25* —4C **104**
Gorsewood Gro. *L25* —4B **104**
Gorsewood Rd. *L25* —4B **104**
Gorsewood Rd. *Murd* —4D **169**
Gorsey Av. *Boot* —2C **18**
Gorsey Brow. *Bil* —1D **31**
Gorsey Cop Rd. *L25* —3A **104**
Gorsey Cop Way. *L25* —3A **104**
Gorsey Cft. *Ecc P* —4F **63**
Gorsey La. *Clo F & Bold* —3D **89**
Gorsey La. *Ford & Boot* —3B **18**
Gorsey La. *Btnwd* —5B **68**
Gorsey La. *High* —1A **8**
Gorsey La. *Wall* —3B **74**
Gorsey La. *Wid* —4E **133**
Gorseyville Cres. *Wir* —2E **141**
Gorseyville Rd. *Wir* —2E **141**
Gorsey Well La. *Pres B* —4F **169**
Gorst St. *L4* —4F **55**
Gorton Rd. *L13* —4B **80**
Gort Rd. *L36* —3E **83**
Goschen St. *Eve* —4F **55**
Goschen St. *Old S* —3F **79**
Goschen St. *Pren* —1F **95**
Gosford St. *L8* —5F **99**
Gosforth Ct. *Run* —3E **167**
Goswell St. *L15* —1E **101**
Gotham Rd. *Wir* —5A **142**
Gothic St. *Birk* —2F **119**
Gough Rd. *L13* —4E **57**
Goulders Ct. *Brook* —5B **168**
Gourley Rd. *L13* —5A **80**
Gourleys La. *Wir* —5D **113**
Government Rd. *Wir* —4B **90**
Govett Rd. *St H* —4C **64**
Gower St. *Boot* —3A **34**
Gower St. *L3* —1C **98** (7D **4**)
Gower St. *St H* —2D **67**
Gowrie Gro. *L21* —1B **34**
Goyt Hey Av. *Bil* —1E **31**
Grace Av. *L10* —1A **38**
Grace Rd. *L9* —2A **36**
Grace St. *L8* —5F **99**
Grace St. *St H* —3C **66**
Gradwell St. *L1* —5D **77** (6E **5**)
Grafton Cres. *L8* —3D **99**
Grafton Dri. *Wir* —5B **94**
Grafton Gro. *L8* —5E **99**
Grafton Rd. *Wall* —4B **52**
Grafton St. *L8* —1F **121**
(Beresford Rd.)
Grafton St. *L8* —3D **99**
(Grafton Cres.)
Grafton St. *L8* —4E **99**
(Park St.)
Grafton St. *L8* —3D **99**
(Parliament St.)
Grafton St. *St H* —5D **45**
Grafton St. *Pren* —4B **96**
Grafton Wlk. *Wir* —4C **112**
Graham Clo. *Wid* —3C **130**
Graham Dri. *L26* —4A **128**
Graham Rd. *Wid* —3C **130**
Graham Rd. *Wir* —3A **112**
Graham's Rd. *L36* —4F **83**
Graham St. *St H* —5C **46**
Grainger Av. *Pren* —2F **117**
Grainger Av. *Wir* —2B **112**
Grain Ind. Est. *L8* —5E **99**
Grain St. *L8* —5E **99**
Graley Clo. *L26* —1F **147**
Grammar School La. *Wir* —5D **113**
Grampian Av. *Wir* —1F **93**
Grampian Rd. *L7* —4E **79**
Grampian Way. *East* —5E **163**
Grampian Way. *More* —1E **93**
Granans Cft. *Boot* —1D **19**
Granard Rd. *L15* —3A **102**
Granary Way. *L3* —3D **99**
Granborne Chase. *L32* —2B **22**
Granby Clo. *Brook* —5C **168**
Granby Cres. *Wir* —5A **142**
Granby St. *L8* —2A **100**
Grandison Rd. *L4* —2B **56**
Grange. —4D 113
Grange Av. *W Der* —1E **81**
Grange Av. *Wall* —5B **52**
Grange Av. *Wltn* —5D **127**
Grange Av. N. *W Der* —1E **81**
Grange Ct. *L15* —2F **101**
Grange Cross Clo. *Wir* —5E **113**
Grange Cross Hey. *Wir* —5E **113**
Grange Cross La. *Wir* —5E **113**
Grange Dri. *St H* —3B **64**
Grange Dri. *Hes* —1A **158**
Grange Dri. *Thor H* —3A **160**
Grange Dri. *Wid* —3D **131**
Grange Farm Cres. *Wir* —3E **113**
Grangehurst Ct. *Gate* —5B **104**
Grange La. *Gate* —4A **104**
Grangemeadow Rd. *L25* —4A **104**
Grangemoor. *Run* —3D **167**
Grange Mt. *Hes* —1F **157**
Grange Mt. *Pren* —4C **96**
Grange Mt. *W Kir* —4D **113**
Grange Old Rd. *Wir* —4C **112**
Grange Park. —3B 64
Grange Pk. *L31* —3E **13**
Grange Pk. Av. *Run* —5C **152**
Grange Pk. Golf Course. —1B 64
Grange Pk. Rd. *St H* —2C **64**
Grange Pavement. *Birk* —3E **97**
Grange Pl. *Birk* —3C **96**
Grange Precinct. *Birk* —3D **97**
Granger Av. *Boot* —2E **35**
Grange Rd. *Boot* —3B **20**
Grange Rd. *Birk* —3D **97**
Grange Rd. *Hay* —2D **49**
(in two parts)
Grange Rd. *Hes* —5F **137**
Grange Rd. *Run* —5C **152**
Grange Rd. *W Kir* —4A **112**
Grange Rd. E. *Birk* —3E **97**
Grange Rd. W. *Pren & Birk* —3B **96**
Grange Rd. W. Sports Cen. —3B 96
Grangeside. *L25* —4A **104**

Grange St. *L6* —1C 78
Grange Ter. *L15* —2F 101
Grange, The. *Wall* —2C 74
Grange Va. *Birk* —3A 120
Grange Valley. *Hay* —2D 49
Grange Vw. *Pren* —4C 96
Grange Way. *L25* —4A 104
Grangeway. *Halt L & Run* —2C 166
Grangeway Ct. *Run* —2C 166
Grange Weint. *L25* —5A 104
Grangewood. *L16* —5F 81
Granite Ter. *L36* —4A 84
Grant Av. *L15* —3F 101
Grant Clo. *L14* —3A 82
Grant Clo. *St H* —4E 45
Grant Ct. *Boot* —5C 34
Grantham Clo. *Wir* —3E 137
Grantham Cres. *St H* —3C 46
Grantham Rd. *L33* —5E 15
Grantham St. *L6* —3B 78
Grantham Way. *Boot* —1B 20
Grantley Rd. *L15* —3A 102
Granton Rd. *L5* —5F 55
Grant Rd. *L14* —3F 81
Grant Rd. *Wir* —2B 72
Granville Av. *L31* —5C 6
Granville Clo. *Wall* —5E 51
Granville Rd. *Gars* —1C 144
Granville Rd. *W'tree* —2D 101
Granville St. *St H* —5D 47
Granville St. *Run* —4A 152
Grappenhall Way. *Pren* —2C 94
Grasmere Av. *St H* —1B 46
Grasmere Av. *Pren* —4C 94
Grasmere Av. *Prsct* —5F 63
Grasmere Clo. *L33* —1D 23
Grasmere Clo. *St H* —1B 46
Grasmere Ct. *St H* —1A 46
Grasmere Ct. Birk —4C 96
(off Penrith St.)
Grasmere Dri. *L21* —4E 19
Grasmere Dri. *Beech* —5E 167
Grasmere Dri. *Wall* —5A 52
Grasmere Fold. *St H* —1B 46
Grasmere Gdns. *L23* —2F 17
Grasmere Rd. *Mag* —5D 7
Grasmere Rd. *Frod* —5C 172
Grasmere St. *L5* —5A 56
Grassendale. —5A 124
Grassendale Ct. *L19* —5A 124
Grassendale Esplanade. *L19* —1A 144
Grassendale Grn. *L19* —5F 123
Grassendale La. *L19* —5A 124
Grassendale Park. —5F 123
Grassendale Rd. *L19* —5A 124
Grassington Cres. *L25* —2C 126
Grassmoor Clo. *Wir* —2E 163
Grass Wood Rd. *Wir* —2B 116
Grasville Rd. *Birk* —1E 119
Gratrix Rd. *Wir* —2D 163
Gray Av. *Hay* —2D 49
Gray Gro. *L36* —1F 105
Graylag Clo. *Beech* —5F 167
Graylands Pl. *L4* —2C 56
Graylands Rd. *L4* —2B 56
Graylands Rd. *Wir* —1C 142
Graylaw Ind. Est. *L9* —2C 36
Grayling Dri. *L12* —5D 39
Gray's Av. *Prsct* —5F 63
Grayson St. *L1* —1C 98
Grayston Av. *St H* —5D 67
Gray St. *Boot* —3A 34
Greasby. —1D 115
Greasby Coronation Pk. —1E 115
Greasby Hill Rd. *Wir* —5C 112
Greasby Rd. *Grea* —1C 114
Greasby Rd. *Wall* —2A 74
Gt. Ashfield. *Wid* —1D 131
Great Beech. *Beech* —1F 173
Gt. Charlotte St. *L1* —5D 77 (5F 5)
(in two parts)
Great Crosby. —1E 17
Gt. Crosshall St. *L3* —4C 76 (3D 4)
Gt. Delph. *Hay* —1D 49
Gt. George Pl. *L1* —2E 99
Gt. George Sq. *L1* —1D 99
Gt. George's Rd. *L22* —5D 17
Gt. George St. *L1* —2E 99
Great Hey. *Boot* —5D 11
Gt. Homer St. *L5* —5D 55
Gt. Homer St. Shop. Cen. *L5* —1E 77
Gt. Howard St. *L3 & L5* —3B 76 (1B 4)
Great Meols. —2F 91
Gt. Mersey St. *L5* —5C 54
(in two parts)
Gt. Nelson St. *L3* —2D 77
Gt. Newton St. *L3* —4F 77 (4J 5)
Gt. Orford St. *L3* —5F 77 (6J 5)
Gt. Richmond St. *L3* —3D 77 (1F 5)
Great Riding. *Nort* —3B 168
Gt. Western Ho. *Birk* —2F 97
Greaves St. *L8* —4F 99
Grebe Av. *St H* —4B 64
Grecian St. *L21* —5F 17
Grecian Ter. *L5* —5E 55
Gredington St. *L8* —5A 100
Greek St. *L3* —4E 77 (4H 5)
Greek St. *Run* —4F 151
Greenacre Clo. *L25* —4C 126
Greenacre Dri. *Wir* —3C 162
Greenacre Rd. *L25* —4C 126
Greenacres Clo. *Pren* —1C 94
Greenacres Ct. *Pren* —1C 94
Green Acres Est. *Wir* —2C 114
Greenall Ct. *Prsct* —5D 63
Greenall St. *St H* —4D 45
Green Av. *Wall* —3B 52
Green Bank. —1E 65
Greenbank. *L22* —5E 17
Green Bank. *Wir* —5A 140
Greenbank Av. *L31* —4C 6
Greenbank Av. *Wall* —4B 52
Greenbank Cres. *St H* —5F 45
Greenbank Dri. *Faz* —1B 38
Greenbank Dri. *Seft P* —4E 101
Greenbank Dri. *Wir* —4A 138
Greenbank La. *L17* —5E 101
Greenbank Rd. *L18* —4E 101
Greenbank Rd. *Birk* —1C 118
Greenbank Rd. *Wir* —2B 112
Greenbridge Clo. *Cas* —5A 154
Greenbridge Rd. *Wind H* —5B 154
Greenburn Av. *St H* —4C 30
Green Coppice. *Nort* —2C 168
Green Cft. *L23* —5B 10
Greencroft Rd. *Wall* —3C 74
Greendale Rd. *L25* —5F 103
Greendale Rd. *Wir* —1A 142
Grn. End La. *St H* —3B 66
Grn. End Pk. *L12* —4A 58
Greenes Rd. *Whis* —4D 85
Greenfield Ct. *L18* —3B 124
Greenfield Dri. *L36* —5F 83
Greenfield Gro. *L36* —5F 83
Greenfield La. *L21* —4A 18
Greenfield La. *Frod* —4B 172
Greenfield La. *Wir* —5D 137
Greenfield Rd. *L13* —3A 80
Greenfield Rd. *Dent G* —3D 45
Greenfields. —1C 94
Greenfields Av. *Wir* —3C 162
Greenfields Cres. *Wir* —3C 162
Greenfield Vw. *Bil* —1D 31
Greenfield Wlk. *L36* —5F 83
Greenfield Way. *L18* —3B 124
Greenfield Way. *Wall* —2B 74
Greenfinch Clo. *L12* —5F 39
Greenfinch Gro. *L26* —3E 127
Greengables Clo. *L8* —4A 100
Greengate. *St H* —3A 66
Green Gates. *L36* —5E 61
Greenham Av. *L33* —4F 15
Green Haven. *Pren* —4D 95
Greenhaven Clo. *L10* —1F 37
Greenheath Way. *Wir* —3F 71
Greenhey Clo. *Pren* —5E 117
Greenhey Dri. *Boot* —3C 18
Green Heys Dri. *L31* —1F 13
Greenheys Gdns. *L8* —3B 100
Greenheys Rd. *L8* —3B 100
Greenheys Rd. *Wall* —2B 74
Greenheys Rd. *Wir* —2C 136
Greenhill Av. *L18* —4C 102
Greenhill Clo. *L18* —2B 124
Greenhill Pl. *L36* —5E 83
Greenhill Rd. *Aller & Moss H* —1B 124
Greenhill Rd. *Gars* —4C 124
Greenholme Clo. *L11* —5A 38
Greenhouse Farm Rd. *Run* —4B 168
Greenhow Av. *Wir* —3B 112
Green Jones Brow. *Btnwd* —5F 69
Greenlake Rd. *L18* —2B 124
Greenlands. *L36* —5E 83
Greenland St. *L1* —2D 99
Green La. *Cros* —4B 10
Green La. *Ecc* —2E 43
Green La. *Ford* —3B 18
Green La. *L3* —5E 77 (6H 5)
Green La. *L31* —5A 6
Green La. *Mag* —1C 12
Green La. *S'frth* —1A 34
(in two parts)
Green La. *Wat* —3B 16
Green La. *Beb* —2F 141
Green La. *Birk* —5E 97
Green La. *Brom & East* —2E 163
Green La. *Btnwd* —4E 69
Green La. *Moss H* —5B 102
(in two parts)
Green La. *Old S & Ston* —1E 79
Green La. *Wall* —1B 72
(in two parts)
Green La. *Wid* —3E 131
Green La. N. *L16* —3C 102
Green Lawn. *L36* —2A 84
Green Lawn. *Birk* —3F 119
Green Lawn Gro. *Birk* —3F 119
Green Leach. —1A 46
Green Leach Av. *St H* —1B 46
Green Leach Ct. *St H* —1B 46
Green Leach La. *St H* —1B 46
Greenlea Clo. *Beb* —1F 141
Greenleaf St. *L8* —2C 100
Greenleas Rd. *Wall* —5D 51
Greenleigh Rd. *L18* —2B 124
Green Link. *L31* —5B 6
Green Mt. *Wir* —4A 94
Grn. Oaks Path. *Wid* —4C 132
Greenoaks Shop. Cen. *Wid* —3B 132
(in two parts)
Grn. Oaks Way. *Wid* —4B 132
Greenock St. *L3* —3B 76 (2A 4)
Greenodd Av. *L12* —2C 58
Greenore Dri. *Hale V* —5D 149
Greenough Av. *Rain* —1C 86
Greenough St. *L25* —2F 125
Green Pk. *Boot* —5F 11
Green Pk. Dri. *L31* —1B 12
Green Rd. *Prsct* —4C 62
Greensbridge La. *Tarb G* —3A 128
Greenside. *L6* —3F 77
Greenside Av. *Ain* —3D 21
Greenside Av. *W'tree* —2A 102
Greenside Clo. *L33* —4F 15
Green St. *L5* —2C 76
Greens Wlk. *L17* —1E 123
Green, The. *Cros* —1D 17

Green, The. *Ecc P* —4E **63**
Green, The. *L13* —4B **80**
Green, The. *Brom P* —2D **143**
Green, The. *Cald* —2D **135**
Green, The. *Will* —5A **170**
Green, The. *Wir* —5C **160**
Greenville Clo. *Wir* —2F **141**
Greenville Dri. *L31* —1C **12**
Greenville Rd. *Wir* —2F **141**
Greenway. *Cros* —5A **10**
Greenway. *Brom* —4D **143**
Greenway. *Grea* —5E **93**
Green Way. *Hes* —3E **137**
Greenway. *Huy* —2B **82**
Greenway Clo. *L36* —2B **82**
Greenway Rd. *L24* —4A **148**
Greenway Rd. *Birk* —1D **119**
Greenway Rd. *Run* —1F **165**
Greenway Rd. *Wid* —2B **132**
Greenway Sq. *Huy* —2B **82**
Greenway, The. *K Ash* —2D **81**
Greenwell Rd. *Hay* —2C **48**
Greenwich Ct. *L9* —5B **20**
Greenwich Rd. *L9* —5B **20**
Greenwood Clo. *Prsct* —5E **63**
Greenwood Ct. *Clo F* —2C **88**
Grn. Wood Dri. *Run* —3F **155**
Greenwood La. *Wall* —1C **74**
Greenwood Rd. *L18* —3B **124**
Greenwood Rd. *Meol* —3E **91**
Greenwood Rd. *Upt* —1B **116**
Greetham St. *L1* —1D **99** (7E **5**)
Gregory Clo. *L16* —1D **103**
Gregory Way. *L16* —1D **103**
Gregson Ct. *Wall* —3C **52**
Gregson Ho. *St H* —4A **46**
Gregson Rd. *L14* —3C **80**
Gregson Rd. *Prsct* —1D **85**
Gregson Rd. *Wid* —3C **132**
Gregson St. *L6* —3F **77**
Grenfell Rd. *L13* —3E **57**
Grenfell St. *Wid* —4B **132**
Grennan Ct. *Wall* —3B **52**
Grennan, The. *Wall* —3B **52**
Grenville Cres. *Wir* —3C **162**
Grenville Dri. *Wir* —4E **137**
Grenville Rd. *Birk* —1F **119**
Grenville St. S. *L1* —1D **99**
Grenville Way. *Birk* —1F **119**
Gresford Av. *L17* —3D **101**
Gresford Av. *Pren* —2A **118**
Gresford Av. *Wir* —3C **112**
Gresford Clo. *Whis* —3F **85**
Gresham St. *L7* —4D **79**
Gresley Clo. *L7* —5C **78**
Gressingham Rd. *L18* —2C **124**
Gretton Rd. *L14* —1B **82**
Greyhound Farm Rd. *L24* —4C **146**
Grey Rd. *L9* —4F **35**
Greystoke Clo. *Wir* —5F **93**
Greystone Cres. *L14* —4E **81**
Greystone Pl. *L10* —1E **37**
Greystone Rd. *Faz* —1E **37**
Greystone Rd. *B'grn* —3E **81**
(in two parts)
Grey St. *L8* —2F **99**
(in two parts)
Gribble Rd. *L10* —1A **38**
Grierson St. *L8* —2B **100**
Grieve Rd. *L10* —1A **38**
Griffin Av. *Wir* —1E **93**
Griffin Clo. *Ecc* —4F **43**
Griffin Clo. *L11* —4C **38**
Griffin Clo. *Btnwd* —5E **69**
Griffin M. *Wid* —1B **132**
Griffin St. *St H* —4E **67**
Griffin Wlk. *L11* —4C **38**
Griffiths Clo. *Wir* —1C **114**
Griffiths Rd. *L36* —4E **83**
Griffiths St. *L1* —1E **99**
Grimley Av. *Boot* —4A **34**
Grimshaw St. *St H* —5C **66**
Grinfield St. *L7* —5A **78**
Grinshill Clo. *L8* —3A **100**
Grinton Cres. *L36* —4D **83**
Grisedale Clo. *Beech* —5E **167**
Grisedale Rd. *Old I* —2E **163**
Grizedale. *Wid* —2B **130**
(in two parts)
Grizedale Av. *St H* —5B **30**
Grizedale Rd. *L5* —5F **55**
Groes Rd. *L19* —5B **124**
Grogan Sq. *Boot* —2D **35**
Gronow Pl. *Boot* —2E **35**
Grosmont Rd. *L32* —5F **23**
Grosvenor Av. *L23* —3E **17**
Grosvenor Av. *Wir* —4B **112**
Grosvenor Clo. *Boot* —2F **19**
Grosvenor Ct. *L15* —2C **102**
Grosvenor Ct. *Pren* —4B **96**
Grosvenor Dri. *Wall* —3B **52**
Grosvenor Pl. *Pren* —4A **96**
Grosvenor Rd. *Mag* —4C **12**
Grosvenor Rd. *St H* —1C **64**
Grosvenor Rd. *Walt* —1E **55**
Grosvenor Rd. *Aig* —1A **144**
Grosvenor Rd. *Hay* —1B **48**
Grosvenor Rd. *Pren* —3A **96**
Grosvenor Rd. *Prsct* —5D **63**
Grosvenor Rd. *Wall* —3B **52**
Grosvenor Rd. *W'tree* —1D **101**
Grosvenor Rd. *Wid* —4B **110**
Grosvenor Rd. *Wir* —5B **90**
Grosvenor St. *L3* —2D **77** (1F **5**)
Grosvenor St. *Run* —4B **152**
Grosvenor St. *Wall* —1B **74**
Grove Av. *Wir* —1F **157**
Grovedale Rd. *L18* —4F **101**
Grovehurst Av. *L14* —2F **81**
Groveland Av. *Wall* —5D **51**
Groveland Av. *Wir* —4B **90**
Groveland Rd. *Wall* —4D **51**
Grovelands. L7 —1F 99
(off Groveside)
Grove Mead. *L31* —1F **13**
Grove Mt. *Birk* —5E **97**
Grove Pk. *L8* —3B **100**
Grove Pk. Av. *W Der* —3B **58**
Grove Pl. *L4* —4E **55**
Grove Pl. *St H* —1F **65**
Grove Pl. *Wir* —4B **90**
Grove Rd. *L6* —3D **79**
Grove Rd. *Birk* —2F **119**
Grove Rd. *Wall* —5E **51**
Grove Rd. *Wir* —4B **90**
Grove Side. *L7* —1F **99**
Groveside. *Wir* —4A **112**
Grove Sq. *Wir* —5A **120**
Groves, The. *Kirkby* —1E **39**
Groves, The. *L8* —2A **100**
Groves, The. *Pren* —4A **96**
Grove St. *Boot* —4A **34**
Grove St. *St H* —5F **45**
Grove St. *Edg H* —1A **100**
Grove St. *Run* —4F **151**
Grove St. *W'tree* —1F **101**
Grove St. *Wir* —5B **120**
Grove Ter. *Wir* —4B **90**
Grove, The. *L28* —4C **60**
Grove, The. *Wind* —3C **44**
Grove, The. *Old S* —1F **79**
Grove, The. *Pren* —1B **118**
Grove, The. *Wall* —3C **74**
Grove, The. *Wir* —1A **142**
Grove Way. *L7* —1A **100**
Grovewood. *Run* —1C **168**
Grovewood Ct. *Pren* —1B **118**
Grovewood Gdns. *Whis* —3E **85**
Grundy Clo. *Wid* —1E **131**
Grundy St. *L5* —5B **54**
Guardian Ct. *Wir* —5C **112**
Guelph Pl. *L7* —4A **78**
Guelph St. *L7* —4A **78**
Guernsey Rd. *L13* —2F **79**
Guernsey Rd. *Wid* —1E **133**
Guest St. *Wid* —5A **132**
Guffitts Clo. *Wir* —2E **91**
Guffitt's Rake. *Wir* —2E **91**
Guildford Av. *Boot* —4F **19**
Guildford St. *Wall* —2D **75**
Guildhall Rd. *L9* —2A **36**
Guild Hey. *Know* —4D **41**
Guillemot Way. *L26* —3E **127**
Guilsted Rd. *L11* —1A **58**
Guinea Gap. *Wall* —3E **75**
Guinea Gap Baths & Recreation Cen. —3E 75
Guion Rd. *L21* —1B **34**
Guion St. *L6* —2B **78**
Gulls Way. *Wir* —2D **157**
Gunning Av. *Ecc* —3B **44**
Gunning Clo. *Ecc* —3B **44**
Gurnall St. *L4* —4F **55**
Gutticar Rd. *Wid* —3B **130**
Gwendoline Clo. *Wir* —2B **138**
Gwendoline St. *L8* —3F **99**
Gwenfron Rd. *L6* —3B **78**
Gwent Clo. *L6* —1B **78**
Gwent St. *L8* —3A **100**
Gwladys St. *L4* —2F **55**
Gwydir St. *L8* —4A **100**
Gwydrin Rd. *L18* —4C **102**

Hackett Av. *Boot* —2D **35**
Hackett Pl. *Boot* —2D **35**
(in two parts)
Hackins Hey. *L2* —4C **76** (4C **4**)
Hackthorpe St. *L5* —4E **55**
Hadassah Gro. *L17* —5C **100**
Hadden Clo. *Rain* —2A **86**
Haddock St. *L20* —2B **54**
Haddon Av. *L9* —2F **35**
Haddon Dri. *Wid* —5B **108**
Haddon Dri. *Wir* —3F **137**
Haddon Rd. *Birk* —2A **120**
Haddon Wlk. *L12* —5E **39**
Hadfield Av. *Wir* —4C **90**
Hadfield Clo. *Wid* —2E **133**
Hadfield Gro. *L25* —1C **126**
Hadleigh Rd. *L32* —4F **23**
Hadley Av. *Wir* —1C **162**
Hadlow Gdns. *Birk* —5E **97**
Hadlow La. *Will* —5A **170**
Hadlow Rd. *Will* —5A **170**
Hadlow Ter. *Will* —5A **170**
Hadwens Bldgs. *L3* —4C **76** (3D **4**)
Haggerston Rd. *L4* —1A **56**
Hahneman Rd. *L4* —1E **55**
Haig Av. *Wir* —1F **93**
Haigh Cres. *L31* —3C **6**
Haigh Rd. *L22* —4E **17**
Haigh St. *L3* —2F **77** (1J **5**)
(in two parts)
Haig Rd. *Wid* —3A **132**
Haileybury Av. *L10* —3D **21**
Haileybury Rd. *L25* —4B **126**
Hailsham Rd. *L19* —4E **123**
Halby Rd. *L9* —2B **36**
Halcombe Rd. *L12* —4D **59**
Halcyon Rd. *Birk* —5C **96**
Haldane Av. *Birk* —2F **95**
Haldane Rd. *L4* —1A **56**
Hale. —5D 149
Hale Bank. —3A 150
Halebank Rd. *Wid* —1E **149**
Halebank Ter. *Wid* —3A **150**

Hale Ct. *Wid*—3A **150**
Hale Dri. *L24*—5C **146**
Halefield St. *St H*—4F **45**
Hale Ga. Rd. *Wid*—5F **149**
Hale Heath. —5A 148
Hale M. *Wid*—5C **130**
Hale Rd. *L24*—4B **146**
Hale Rd. *Walt*—2E **55**
Hale Rd. *Haleb*—3B **150**
Hale Rd. *Hale V*—5C **146**
Hale Rd. *Wall*—5C **52**
Hale Rd. *Wid*—5C **130**
Hale Rd. Ind. Est. *Wid*—2B **150**
Hale St. *L2*—4C **76** (4D **4**)
Hale Vw. *Run*—2E **165**
Hale Vw. Rd. *L36*—4A **84**
Halewood. —4F 127
Halewood Clo. *L25*—5B **104**
Halewood Dri. *L25*—2C **126**
(Hunts Cross Av.)
Halewood Dri. *L25*—2B **126**
(Kings Dri.)
Halewood Green. —2E 127
Halewood Pl. *L25*—1C **126**
Halewood Rd. *L25*—5B **104**
Halewood Triangle Country Pk. —4D 127
Halewood Way. *L25*—2C **126**
Haley Rd. N. *Btnwd*—5D **69**
Haley Rd. S. *Btnwd*—5E **69**
Half Crown St. *L5*—5C **54**
Halfpenny Clo. *L19*—5B **124**
Halidon Ct. *Boot*—4A **34**
Halifax Cres. *L23*—4B **10**
Halkirk Rd. *L18*—3C **124**
Halkyn Av. *L17*—3D **101**
Halkyn Dri. *L5*—1A **78**
Hallam Wlk. *L7*—5C **78**
Hall Av. *Wid*—3A **130**
Hallbrook Ho. *L12*—3D **59**
Hall Dri. *L32*—2E **23**
Hall Dri. *Wir*—1D **115**
Hall La. *Bold*—3F **89**
Hall La. *L31*—2C **12**
Hall La. *L32*—3D **23**
Hall La. *Sim*—3F **15**
Hall La. *Walt*—1B **36**
Hall La. *Btnwd*—4F **69**
Hall La. *Cron & Wid*—2C **108**
Hall La. *Huy*—4F **83**
Hall La. *Kens*—4A **78**
Hall La. *Prsct*—1D **85**
Hall La. *Rain*—5C **86**
Hall Rd. *Hay*—1E **49**
Hall Rd. E. *L23*—4B **8**
Hall Rd. W. *L23*—4A **8**
Hallsands Rd. *L32*—5E **23**
Hallside Clo. *L19*—4F **123**
Hall St. *Clo F*—3D **89**
Hall St. *St H*—5A **46**
Halltine Clo. *L23*—4A **8**
Hallville Rd. *L18*—4A **102**
Hallville Rd. *Wall*—3C **74**
Hallwood Clo. *Run*—4B **166**
Hallwood Link Rd. *Run*—4F **167**
Hallwood Park. —4E 167
Hallwood Pk. Av. *Hall P*—4E **167**
Halsall Clo. *L23*—5E **9**
Halsall Clo. *Brook*—5C **168**
Halsall Grn. *Wir*—1B **162**
Halsall Rd. *Boot*—3C **34**
Halsall St. *Prsct*—4D **63**
Halsbury Rd. *L6*—3C **78**
Halsbury Rd. *Wall*—5B **52**
Halsey Av. *L12*—4F **57**
Halsey Cres. *L12*—4F **57**
Halsnead Av. *Whis*—5C **84**
Halsnead Cvn. Est. *Hals P*—5E **85**
Halsnead Pk. —1E 107
Halstead Rd. *L9*—2F **35**
Halstead Rd. *Wall*—3C **74**
Halstead Wlk. *L32*—4C **22**
Halton Brook. —2E 167
Halton Brook Av. *Halt B*—1D **167**
Halton Brow. *Halt*—1E **167**
Halton Ct. *Run*—5D **153**
Halton Cres. *Grea*—1B **114**
Halton Hey. *Whis*—5D **85**
Halton Lea. —3F 167
Halton Link Rd. *Halt*—2E **167**
Halton Lodge. —3D 167
Halton Lodge Av. *Halt L*—3D **167**
Halton Rd. *L31*—4D **7**
Halton Rd. *Run*—5B **152**
Halton Rd. *Wall*—5A **52**
Halton Sports Cen. —5C 168
Halton Sta. Rd. *Sut W*—2F **173**
Halton St. *Hay*—2E **49**
Halton View. —4C 132
Halton Vw. Rd. *Wid*—3C **132**
Halton Village. —2F 167
Halton Wlk. *L25*—3A **104**
Halton Wood. *L32*—2B **22**
Hambledon Dri. *Wir*—5C **92**
Hambleton Clo. *L11*—4B **38**
Hambleton Clo. *Wid*—1C **130**
Hamblett Cres. *St H*—2B **46**
Hamer St. *St H*—4F **45**
(Duke St.)
Hamer St. *St H*—5F **45**
(N. John St.)
Hamil Clo. *Wir*—2E **91**
Hamilton Ct. *L23*—1B **16**
Hamilton La. *Birk*—2E **97**
Hamilton Rd. *L5*—1F **77**
Hamilton Rd. *Wind*—2B **44**
Hamilton Rd. *Wall*—3A **52**
Hamilton Sq. *Birk*—2E **97**
Hamilton St. *Birk*—3E **97**
(in two parts)
Hamlet Rd. *Wall*—5F **51**
Hamlin Rd. *L19*—1D **145**
Hammersley Av. *Clo F*—3C **88**
Hammersley St. *Clo F*—3C **88**
Hammill St. *Dent G*—3D **45**
(in two parts)
Hammond Rd. *Know I*—2C **24**
Hammond St. *St H*—1D **67**
Hamnett Rd. *Prsct*—4E **63**
Hampden Gro. *Birk*—5D **97**
Hampden Rd. *Birk*—5D **97**
Hampden St. *L4*—1F **55**
Hampshire Av. *Boot*—2C **18**
Hampshire Gdns. *St H*—1F **65**
Hampson St. *L6*—1C **78**
Hampstead Rd. *L6*—3C **78**
Hampstead Rd. *Wall*—3C **74**
Hampton Clo. *Wid*—1E **133**
Hampton Ct. *Mnr P*—3C **154**
Hampton Ct. Rd. *L12*—1C **80**
Hampton Dri. *Wid*—4C **108**
Hampton Pl. *St H*—2B **46**
Hampton St. *L8*—2F **99**
Hanbury Rd. *L4*—3D **57**
Handel Ct. *L8*—3B **100**
Handel Rd. *L27*—3C **104**
Handfield Pl. *L5*—1A **78**
Handfield Rd. *L22*—4D **17**
Handfield St. *L5*—1A **78**
Handford Av. *Wir*—5F **163**
Handforth La. *Halt L*—4D **167**
Handley Ct. *L19*—4F **123**
Handley St. *Run*—4F **151**
Hands St. *L21*—2B **34**
Hanford Av. *L9*—2F **35**
Hankey Dri. *Boot*—3E **35**
Hankey St. *Run*—5F **151**
Hankinson St. *L13*—5F **79**
Hankin St. *L5*—5D **55**
Hanley Clo. *Wid*—3C **130**
Hanley Rd. *Wid*—3C **130**
Hanlon Av. *Boot*—2D **35**
Hanmer Rd. *L32*—3B **22**
Hannah Clo. *Wir*—4E **137**
Hannan Rd. *L6*—3B **78**
Hanover Clo. *Pren*—3F **95**
Hanover Ct. *Brook*—4B **168**
Hanover St. *L1*—5C **76** (7E **4**)
Hanson Pk. *Pren*—4E **95**
Hanson Rd. *L9*—3C **36**
Hans Rd. *L4*—2A **56**
Hanwell St. *L6*—5B **56**
Hanworth Clo. *L12*—5E **39**
Hapsford Rd. *L21*—2B **34**
Hapton St. *L5*—5E **55**
Harbern Clo. *L12*—5C **58**
Harbord Rd. *L22*—4C **16**
Harbord St. *L7*—5B **78**
Harbord Ter. *L22*—4C **16**
Harborne Dri. *Wir*—5F **141**
Harbour Clo. *Murd*—4D **169**
Harcourt Av. *Wall*—3E **75**
Harcourt St. *L4*—4D **55**
Harcourt St. *Birk*—2C **96**
Hardie Av. *Wir*—5C **70**
Hardie Clo. *Sut M*—3A **88**
Hardie Rd. *L36*—3A **84**
Harding Av. *Wir*—3F **141**
Harding Clo. *L5*—1A **78**
Hardinge Rd. *L19*—4C **124**
Harding St. *L8*—2B **100**
Hardknott Rd. *Old I*—1E **163**
Hard La. *Dent G & St H*—2D **45**
Hardman St. *L1*—1E **99** (7H **5**)
Hardshaw Cen., The. *St H*—5A **46**
Hardshaw St. *St H*—5A **46**
Hardwick Rd. *Ast I*—4D **153**
Hardy St. *L1*—2D **99**
(in two parts)
Hardy St. *Gars*—3C **144**
Harebell St. *L5*—4D **55**
Hare Cft. *L28*—3F **59**
Harefield Grn. *L24*—4D **147**
Harefield Rd. *L24*—5D **147**
Haresfinch. —2B 46
Haresfinch Rd. *St H*—2B **46**
Haresfinch Vw. *St H*—2B **46**
Hare's La. *Frod*—5A **172**
Harewell Rd. *L11*—2A **58**
Harewood Clo. *L36*—3E **83**
Harewood Rd. *Wall*—4A **52**
Harewood St. *L6*—2A **78**
Hargate Rd. *L33*—3F **23**
Hargate Wlk. *L33*—3F **23**
Hargrave Av. *Pren*—1E **117**
Hargrave Clo. *Pren*—1E **117**
Hargrave La. *Will*—5F **161**
Hargreaves Ct. *Wid*—3D **133**
Hargreaves Rd. *L17*—1C **122**
Hargreaves St. *St H*—4E **47**
Harker St. *L3*—3E **77** (2G **5**)
Harke St. *L7*—1B **100**
Harland Grn. *L24*—4F **147**
Harland Rd. *Birk*—5D **97**
Harlech Ct. *Wir*—3F **141**
Harlech Rd. *L23*—2C **16**
Harlech St. *L4*—2E **55**
Harlech St. *Wall*—4E **75**
Harleston Rd. *L33*—2A **24**
Harleston Wlk. *L33*—2A **24**
Harley Av. *Wir*—4C **118**
Harley St. *L9*—2A **36**
Harlian Av. *Wir*—2D **93**
Harlow Clo. *St H*—4F **65**
Harlow St. *L8*—5E **99**
Harlyn Clo. *L26*—1E **147**
Harmony Way. *L13*—5A **80**

Haroldene Gro. *Prsct* —1F **83**
Harold Rd. *Hay* —1F **49**
Harper Rd. *L9* —4A **36**
Harper St. *L6* —4A **78**
Harps Cft. *Boot* —2C **18**
Harptree Clo. *Whis* —3E **85**
Harradon Rd. *L9* —1B **36**
Harrier Dri. *L26* —3E **127**
Harringay Av. *L18* —4F **101**
Harrington Av. *Wir* —4C **90**
Harrington Rd. *Cros* —1D **17**
Harrington Rd. *Lith* —4D **19**
Harrington Rd. *Brun B* —5E **99**
Harrington Rd. *Huy* —2B **82**
Harrington St. *L2* —5C **76** (5D **4**)
Harrington Vw. *Wall* —1D **75**
Harris Clo. *Wir* —5A **142**
Harris Dri. *Boot* —2C **34**
Harris Gdns. *St H* —2B **66**
Harrismith Rd. *L10* —1E **37**
Harrison Dri. *Boot* —5E **35**
Harrison Dri. *Hay* —2A **48**
Harrison Dri. *Wall* —4D **51**
Harrison Hey. *L36* —5E **83**
Harrison Pk. —4E 51
Harrison St. *St H* —4D **67**
Harrison St. *Wid* —1B **150**
Harrison's Yd. *Wir* —5F **163**
Harrison Way. *Brun B* —5D **99**
Harris St. *St H* —4E **45**
Harris St. *Wid* —3C **132**
Harrocks Clo. *Boot* —5D **11**
Harrock Wood Clo. *Wir* —1E **137**
Harrogate Clo. *Wir* —1D **171**
Harrogate Dri. *L5* —1F **77**
Harrogate Rd. *Birk* —3A **120**
Harrogate Rd. *Wir* —1D **171**
Harrogate Wlk. *Birk* —4A **120**
Harrop Rd. *Run* —1B **166**
Harrops Cft. *Boot* —1E **19**
Harrowby Clo. *L8* —2A **100**
Harrowby Rd. *L21* —1F **33**
Harrowby Rd. *Birk* —5C **96**
Harrowby Rd. *Wall* —2D **75**
Harrowby Rd. S. *Birk* —5C **96**
Harrowby St. *L8* —2A **100**
(Granby St.)
Harrowby St. *L8* —2F **99**
(Park Way)
Harrow Clo. *Boot* —2F **19**
Harrow Clo. *Wall* —1F **73**
Harrow Dri. *L10* —3D **21**
Harrow Dri. *Run* —5E **153**
Harrow Gro. *Wir* —2E **163**
Harrow Rd. *L4* —5B **56**
Harrow Rd. *Wall* —1F **73**
Hartdale Rd. *Thor* —4A **10**
Hartdale Rd. *Moss H* —5A **102**
Hartford Clo. *Pren* —1F **117**
Harthill Av. *L18* —5B **102**
Harthill M. *Pren* —5C **72**
Harthill Rd. *L18* —4C **102**
Hartington Av. *Birk* —2B **96**
Hartington Rd. *W Der* —5B **58**
Hartington Rd. *Dent G* —3C **44**
Hartington Rd. *Gars* —1C **144**
Hartington Rd. *Tox* —3C **100**
Hartington Rd. *Wall* —2B **74**
Hartismere Rd. *Wall* —3D **75**
Hartland Clo. *Wid* —4A **110**
Hartland Gdns. *St H* —5D **65**
Hartland Rd. *L11* —1E **57**
Hartley Av. *L9* —3B **36**
Hartley Clo. *L4* —4F **55**
Hartley Gro. *L33* —5F **15**
Hartley Gro. *St H* —3C **64**
Hartley Quay. *L3* —1B **98** (7C **4**)
Hartley St. *Run* —4B **152**
Hartley's Village. —3B 36
Hartnup St. *L5* —5F **55**
(in two parts)
Hartopp Rd. *L25* —2A **104**
Hartopp Wlk. *L25* —2A **104**
Hartsbourne Av. *L25* —1F **103**
(in two parts)
Hartsbourne Clo. *L25* —2F **103**
Hart St. *L3* —4E **77** (4H **5**)
Hartwell St. *L21* —2B **34**
Hartwood Clo. *L32* —1F **39**
Hartwood Rd. *L32* —1F **39**
Hartwood Sq. *L32* —1F **39**
Harty Rd. *Hay* —3F **47**
Harvard Clo. *Wind H* —5D **155**
Harvard Gro. *Prsct* —4E **63**
Harvester Way. *Boot* —1A **20**
Harvester Way. *Wir* —5C **92**
Harvest La. *Wir* —5D **71**
Harvest Way. *Clo F* —2C **88**
Harvey Av. *Newt W* —5F **49**
Harvey Av. *Wir* —1D **115**
Harvey Rd. *Wall* —5A **52**
Harwich Gro. *L16* —1F **103**
Harwood Rd. *L19* —1D **145**
Haselbeech Clo. *L11* —5F **37**
Haselbeech Cres. *L11* —5F **37**
Hasfield Rd. *L11* —1B **58**
Haslemere. *Whis* —3F **85**
Haslemere Rd. *L25* —3A **104**
Haslemere Way. *L25* —3A **104**
Haslingden Clo. *L13* —4B **80**
Haslington Gro. *L26* —1A **148**
Hassal Rd. *Birk* —4A **120**
Hastings Dri. *L36* —1A **106**
Hastings Rd. *L22* —3B **16**
Haswell Dri. *L28* —3A **60**
Haswell St. *St H* —4F **45**
Hatchmere Clo. *Pren* —1F **117**
Hatfield Clo. *L12* —5F **39**
Hatfield Clo. *St H* —4F **65**
Hatfield Gdns. *L36* —5F **83**
Hatfield Rd. *Boot* —5E **35**
Hathaway. *L31* —3B **12**
Hathaway Clo. *L25* —3A **104**
Hathaway Rd. *L25* —3A **104**
Hatherley Av. *L23* —3E **17**
Hatherley Clo. *L8* —2A **100**
(in two parts)
Hatherley St. *L8* —2A **100**
Hatherley St. *Wall* —4E **75**
Hathersage Rd. *L36* —1E **83**
Hatherton Gro. *L26* —1A **148**
Hatton Av. *Wir* —2E **171**
Hatton Clo. *Wir* —1D **157**
Hatton Garden. *L3* —4C **76** (3D **4**)
Hatton Garden Ind. Est. L3
(off Johnson St.) —4C ***76*** *(3D* ***4****)*
Hatton Hill Rd. *L21* —4A **18**
Hatton's La. *L16* —3C **102**
Hauxwell Gro. *St H* —2B **46**
Havannah La. *St H* —5B **48**
Havelock Clo. *St H* —5F **45**
Haven Rd. *L10* —5F **21**
Haven Wlk. *L31* —3C **6**
Havergal St. *Run* —1F **165**
Haverstock Rd. *L6* —3D **79**
Haverton Wlk. *L12* —5E **39**
Hawarden Av. *L17* —3D **101**
Hawarden Av. *Pren* —3B **96**
Hawarden Av. *Wall* —2C **74**
Hawarden Ct. *Wir* —3F **141**
Hawarden Gro. *L21* —2A **34**
Hawdon Ct. *L7* —1C **100**
Hawes Av. *St H* —5C **30**
Haweswater Av. *Hay* —2A **48**
Haweswater Clo. *L33* —5D **15**
Haweswater Clo. *Beech* —5A **168**
Haweswater Gro. *L31* —5F **7**
Hawgreen Rd. *L32* —4B **22**
Hawick Clo. *L33* —4D **15**
Hawke Grn. *Tarb G* —2A **106**
Hawke St. *L3* —5E **77** (5G **5**)
Hawkesworth St. *L4* —5A **56**
Hawkhurst Clo. *L8* —5F **99**
Hawkins St. *L6* —3B **78**
Hawks Ct. *Hall P* —4E **167**
Hawkshead Av. *L12* —2C **58**
Hawkshead Clo. *L31* —5E **7**
Hawkshead Clo. *Beech* —1A **174**
Hawkshead Dri. *L21* —5D **19**
Hawkshead Rd. *Btnwd* —5E **69**
Hawkshead Rd. *Croft B* —1E **163**
Hawksmoor Clo. *L10* —1A **38**
Hawksmoor Rd. *L10* —2F **37**
Hawksmore Clo. *Wir* —3D **93**
Hawkstone St. *L8* —4A **100**
(Clevedon St.)
Hawkstone St. *L8* —5A **100**
(Peel St.)
Hawkstone Wlk. *L8* —5A **100**
Hawks Way. *Wir* —2E **157**
Haworth Dri. *Boot* —1D **35**
Hawthorn Av. *Run* —1A **166**
Hawthorn Av. *Wid* —2B **132**
Hawthorn Clo. *Bil* —1D **31**
Hawthorn Clo. *Hay* —3A **48**
Hawthorn Dri. *Ecc* —4B **44**
Hawthorn Dri. *Hes* —5F **137**
Hawthorn Dri. *W Kir* —4E **113**
Hawthorne Av. *L26* —1E **147**
Hawthorne Ct. *L21* —5B **18**
Hawthorne Dri. *Will* —4B **170**
Hawthorne Gro. *Wall* —4E **75**
Hawthorne Rd. *Lith & Boot* —5B **18**
Hawthorne Rd. *Birk* —1D **119**
Hawthorne Rd. *Frod* —4B **172**
Hawthorne Rd. *Sut L* —5D **67**
Hawthorn Gro. *L7* —5B **78**
Hawthorn Gro. *W Der* —5B **58**
Hawthorn La. *Wir* —2D **163**
Hawthorn Rd. *Huy* —4C **82**
Hawthorn Rd. *Prsct* —5E **63**
Haxted Gdns. *L19* —1D **145**
Haydn Rd. *L14* —5F **59**
Haydock. —2C 48
Haydock Community Leisure Cen. —2B 48
Haydock La. *Hay* —2C **48**
Haydock La. *Hay I* —1D **49**
Haydock Pk. Rd. *L10* —2E **21**
Haydock Rd. *Wall* —4C **52**
Haydock St. *Newt W* —4F **49**
Haydock St. *St H* —5A **46**
Hayes Av. *Prsct* —1E **85**
Hayes Cres. *Frod* —4C **172**
Hayes Dri. *L31* —2A **22**
Hayes St. *St H* —3C **64**
Hayfield Clo. *L26* —3A **128**
Hayfield Pl. *Wir* —1A **94**
Hayfield St. *L4* —4F **55**
Hayfield Way. *Clo F* —2C **88**
Hayles Clo. *L25* —3A **104**
Hayles Grn. *L25* —3A **104**
Hayles Gro. *L25* —3A **104**
Haylock Clo. *L8* —5F **99**
Hayman's Clo. *L12* —4A **58**
Haymans Grn. *Mag* —1E **13**
Hayman's Grn. *W Der* —4A **58**
Hayman's Gro. *L12* —4A **58**
Haywood Cres. *Wind H* —5D **155**
Haywood Gdns. *St H* —1D **65**
Hazel Av. *L32* —2C **22**
Hazel Av. *Run* —2E **165**
Hazel Av. *Whis* —3E **85**
Hazel Ct. L8 —5A ***100***
(off Byles St.)
Hazeldale Rd. *L9* —4A **36**
Hazeldene Av. *Wall* —1A **74**

Hazeldene Av. *Wir* —1B **138**
Hazeldene Way. *Wir* —1B **138**
Hazelfield Ct. *Clo F* —2C **88**
Hazel Gro. *Cros* —2F **17**
Hazel Gro. *St H* —5C **44**
Hazel Gro. *Walt* —2B **36**
Hazel Gro. *Beb* —3E **141**
Hazel Gro. *Irby* —5D **115**
Hazelhurst Rd. *L4* —4B **56**
Hazel M. *L31* —2B **22**
Hazel Rd. *L36* —1F **83**
Hazel Rd. *Birk* —4D **97**
Hazel Rd. *Wir* —4C **90**
Hazelslack Rd. *L11* —1A **58**
Hazelwood. *Wir* —4D **93**
Hazelwood Clo. *Sut M* —3B **88**
Hazelwood Gro. *L26* —2D **127**
Hazleton Rd. *L14* —3C **80**
Headbolt La. *Kirkby* —1E **23**
Headbourne Clo. *L25* —2F **103**
Headingley Clo. *L36* —5C **82**
Headingley Clo. *St H* —5C **66**
Headington Rd. *Wir* —4D **93**
Headland Clo. *Wir* —1B **134**
Headley Clo. *St H* —5F **45**
Head St. *L8* —3E **99**
Heald St. *L19* —1C **144**
Heald St. *Newt W* —5F **49**
Healy Clo. *L27* —5A **106**
Hearne Rd. *St H* —4D **45**
Heartwood Clo. *L9* —1A **36**
Heathbank Av. *Wall* —3A **74**
Heathbank Av. *Wir* —5C **114**
Heathbank Rd. *Birk* —1D **119**
Heathcliff Ho. *L4* —2B **56**
Heath Clo. *Ecc P* —4F **63**
Heath Clo. *L25* —4F **103**
Heath Clo. *Wir* —1B **134**
Heathcote Clo. *L7* —1B **100**
Heathcote Gdns. *Wir* —2F **141**
Heathcote Rd. *L4* —1F **55**
Heath Dale. *Wir* —4F **141**
Heath Dri. *Hes* —1F **157**
Heath Dri. *Upt* —4A **94**
Heath Dri. *West* —3A **166**
Heather Bank. *Wir* —1D **141**
Heather Brae. *Newt W* —4F **49**
Heather Brae. *Prsct* —1A **84**
Heather Brow. *Pren* —2F **95**
Heather Clo. *Kirk* —3F **55**
Heather Clo. *Kirkby* —1E **23**
Heather Clo. *Padd M* —5E **167**
Heather Ct. *L4* —3F **55**
Heatherdale Clo. *Birk* —1B **118**
Heatherdale Rd. *L18* —5A **102**
Heather Dene. *Wir* —4D **143**
Heatherdene Rd. *Wir* —3B **112**
Heatherland. *Wir* —5B **94**
Heatherleigh. *St H* —5D **65**
Heatherleigh. *Wir* —3E **135**
Heatherleigh Clo. *L9* —1A **36**
Heather Rd. *Beb* —3D **141**
Heather Rd. *Hes* —1A **158**
Heathers Cft. *Boot* —2E **19**
Heather Way. *L23* —4C **10**
Heathfield. *Wir* —5D **143**
Heathfield Av. *St H* —3E **65**
Heathfield Clo. *Lith* —2C **34**
Heathfield Dri. *L33* —1E **23**
Heathfield Ho. *Wir* —1A **138**
Heathfield Pk. *Wid* —1D **131**
Heathfield Rd. *Mag* —3F **13**
Heathfield Rd. *Wat* —3C **16**
Heathfield Rd. *Beb* —2F **141**
Heathfield Rd. *Pren* —5C **96**
Heathfield Rd. *W'tree* —3A **102**
Heathfield St. *L1* —5E **77** (6G **5**)
Heathgate Av. *L24* —5F **147**
Heath Hey. *L25* —4F **103**
Heathland Rd. *Clo F* —2C **88**
Heathlands, The. *Wir* —3E **71**
Heath La. *Will* —4C **170**
Heath Moor Rd. *Wir* —5D **71**
Heath Pk. Gro. *Run* —2F **165**
Heath Rd. *L19* —4C **124**
Heath Rd. *L36* —1B **82**
Heath Rd. *Run* —3F **165**
Heath Rd. *Wid* —2D **131**
Heath Rd. *Wir* —2E **141**
Heath Rd. Cres. *Run* —2B **166**
Heath Rd. S. *West* —4F **165**
Heathside. *Wir* —1D **157**
Heath St. *St H* —4D **65**
Heath Vw. *L21* —2B **18**
Heathview Clo. *Wid* —2A **150**
Heathview Rd. *Wid* —2A **150**
Heathwaite Cres. *L11* —2A **58**
Heathway. *Wir* —3B **158**
Heathwood. *L12* —1B **80**
Heatley Clo. *Pren* —2C **94**
Heaton Clo. *L24* —4F **147**
Heatwaves Leisure Cen. —3B 60 (Stockbridge)
Hebburn Way. *L12* —5A **40**
Hebden Pde. *L11* —5C **38**
Hebden Rd. *L11* —5B **38**
Hector Pl. *L20* —2D **55**
Hedgebank Clo. *L9* —5D **21**
Hedgecote. *L32* —1E **39**
Hedgecroft. *L23* —4C **10**
Hedgefield Rd. *L25* —3B **104**
Hedge Hey. *Cas* —1A **168**
Hedges Cres. *L13* —4E **57**
Hedingham Clo. *L26* —3A **128**
Hedworth Gdns. *St H* —5D **65**
Helena Rd. *St H* —4F **67**
Helena St. *L7* —5B **78**
Helena St. *Walt* —5F **35**
Helena St. *Birk* —4E **97**
Helford Clo. *Whis* —5A **64**
Helford Rd. *L11* —3D **39**
Heliers Rd. *L13* —4B **80**
Helmdon Clo. *L11* —2A **58**
Helmingham Gro. *Birk* —5E **97**
Helmsley Rd. *L26* —5F **127**
Helsby Av. *Wir* —2F **171**
Helsby Rd. *L9* —1B **36**
Helsby St. *L7* —5A **78**
Helsby St. *St H* —2D **67**
Helston Av. *L26* —3F **127**
Helston Av. *St H* —1D **47**
Helston Clo. *Brook* —5B **168**
Helston Grn. *L36* —3B **84**
Helston Rd. *L11* —3D **39**
Helton Clo. *Pren* —1E **117**
Hemans St. *Boot* —4A **34**
Hemer Ter. *Boot* —3A **34**
Hemingford St. *Birk* —3D **97**
Hemlock Clo. *L12* —5D **39**
Hempstead Clo. *St H* —4F **65**
Henbury Pl. *Run* —4B **166**
Henderson Clo. *Wir* —3D **93**
Henderson Rd. *L36* —3A **84**
Henderson Rd. *Wid* —4F **131**
Hendon Rd. *L6* —2D **79**
Hendon Wlk. *Wir* —1C **114**
Hengest Clo. *L33* —4E **15**
Henglers Clo. *L6* —3F **77**
Henley Av. *L21* —5A **18**
Henley Clo. *Wir* —5A **142**
Henley Ct. *St H* —2D **65**
Henley Ct. *Run* —5D **153**
Henley Rd. *L18* —4B **102**
Henllan Gdns. *St H* —4F **67**
Henlow Av. *L32* —5F **23**
Hennawood Clo. *L6* —1B **78**
Henry Edward St. *L3* —3D **77** (2E **4**)
Henry Hickman Clo. *Boot* —1F **19**
Henry St. *L1* —1D **99** (7E **5**)
Henry St. *L13* —4E **79**
Henry St. *St H* —4F **45**
Henry St. *Birk* —3E **97**
Henry St. *Wid* —3C **132**
Henthorne Rd. *Wir* —4B **120**
Henthorne St. *Pren* —4C **96**
Herald Clo. *L11* —5C **38**
Heralds Clo. *Wid* —4B **130**
Herbarth Clo. *L9* —5F **35**
Herberts La. *Wir* —3F **157**
Herbert St. *St H* —4E **67**
Herbert St. *Btnwd* —5E **69**
Herbert Taylor Clo. *L6* —1C **78**
Herculaneum Ct. *L8* —1F **121**
Herculaneum Rd. *L8* —5E **99**
Herdman Clo. *L25* —4B **104**
Hereford Av. *Wir* —3F **93**
Hereford Clo. *St H* —1F **65**
Hereford Dri. *Boot* —4F **19**
Hereford Rd. *S'frth* —1E **33**
Hereford Rd. *W'tree* —3A **102**
Heriot St. *L5* —5D **55**
Heriot Wlk. *L5* —5D **55**
Hermes Clo. *Boot* —5E **19**
Hermes Rd. *Gil I* —2B **38**
Hermitage Gro. *Boot* —1D **35**
Herm Rd. *L5* —1C **76**
Heron Clo. *Nort* —2D **169**
Heron Ct. *L26* —3E **127**
Herondale Rd. *L18* —5F **101**
Heronhall Rd. *L9* —4F **37**
Heronpark Way. *Wir* —5B **142**
Heron Rd. *Meol & W Kir* —4F **91**
Herons Ct. *L31* —3B **6**
Herons Way. *Run* —3F **155**
Hero St. *Boot* —1D **55**
Herrick St. *L13* —3F **79**
Herschell St. *L5* —5F **55**
Hertford Clo. *L26* —5F **127**
Hertford Dri. *Wall* —5C **52**
Hertford Rd. *Boot* —1C **54**
Hertford St. *St H* —1D **67**
Hesketh Av. *Birk* —3D **119**
Hesketh Dri. *L31* —1F **13**
Hesketh Dri. *Wir* —1A **158**
Hesketh Rd. *Hale V* —5E **149**
Hesketh St. *L17* —5C **100**
Heskin Clo. *Kirkby* —1E **39**
Heskin Clo. *Lyd* —3D **7**
Heskin Clo. *Rain* —3B **86**
Heskin Rd. *L32* —1E **39**
Heskin Wlk. *L32* —1E **39**
Hessle Dri. *Wir* —3F **157**
Hesslewell Ct. *Wir* —1A **158**
Heswall. —2F 157
Heswall Av. *Clo F* —2B **88**
Heswall Av. *Wir* —4C **118**
Heswall Golf Course. —5A 158
Heswall Mt. *Wir* —2A **138**
Heswall Rd. *L9* —1B **36**
Hetherlow Towers. *L4* —5A **36**
Hever Dri. *L26* —3F **127**
Heward Av. *St H* —5C **66**
Hewitson Av. *L13* —5F **57**
Hewitson Rd. *L13* —5F **57**
Hewitt Av. *St H* —4C **44**
Hewitt's La. *Know & L33* —2D **41**
Hewitts Pl. *L2* —4C **76** (4D **4**)
Hexagon, The. *Boot* —5C **34**
Hexham Clo. *St H* —5D **65**
Heyburn Rd. *L13* —5E **57**
Heydale Rd. *L18* —5A **102**
Heydean Rd. *L18* —3C **124**
Heydean Wlk. *L18* —3C **124**
Heyes Dri. *Wall* —2C **72**
Heyes Mt. *Rain* —4C **86**
Heyes Rd. *Wid* —4C **130**
Heyes St. *L5* —1A **78**

Heyes, The. *L25* —2B **126**
Heyes, The. *Halt B* —1E **167**
Heygarth Dri. *Wir* —5D **93**
Heygarth Rd. *Wir* —5E **163**
Hey Grn. Rd. *L15* —1E **101**
Hey Pk. *L36* —4F **83**
Hey Rd. *L36* —4F **83**
Heys Av. *Wir* —2D **163**
Heyscroft Rd. *L25* —2B **126**
Heysham Clo. *Murd* —4C **168**
Heysham Lawn. *L27* —5A **106**
Heysham Rd. *Boot* —3A **20**
Heysham Rd. *L27* —5A **106**
Heysmoor Heights. *L8* —3B **100**
Heysome Clo. *Crank* —1E **29**
Heys, The. *Wir* —5F **163**
Heythrop Dri. *Wir* —2D **159**
Heyville Rd. *Wir* —1E **141**
Heywood Boulevd. *Wir* —1A **138**
Heywood Clo. *Wir* —1A **138**
Heywood Ct. *L15* —5C **80**
Heywood Gdns. *Whis* —4E **85**
Heywood Rd. *L15* —1C **102**
Heyworth St. *L5* —1F **77**
Hibbert St. *Wid* —4B **132**
Hickmans Rd. *Birk* —5B **74**
Hickory Gro. *L31* —3A **22**
Hickson Av. *L31* —4C **6**
Hicks Rd. *S'frth* —1A **34**
Hicks Rd. *Wat* —3E **17**
Highacre Rd. *Wall* —4A **52**
Higham Av. *Ecc* —5F **43**
Higham Sq. *L5* —2E **77**
High Bank Clo. *Pren* —4D **95**
Highbank Dri. *L19* —1D **145**
Highbanks. *L31* —4C **6**
High Beeches. *L16* —5F **81**
High Carrs. *L36* —4B **82**
High Clere Cres. *L36* —1E **83**
Highcroft Av. *Wir* —2F **141**
Highcroft Grn. *Wir* —2A **142**
Highcroft, The. *Wir* —2F **141**
Higher Ashton. *Wid* —1F **131**
Higher Bebington Rd. *Wir* —1D **141**
Higher End Pk. *Boot* —5E **11**
Higher Heys. *Beech* —5F **167**
Higher La. *Crank & Rainf* —1C **28**
Higher La. *L9* —1C **36**
Higher Parr St. *St H* —5C **46**
Higher Rd. *L25 & L26* —5D **127**
Higher Rd. *Halew & Wid* —1B **148**
Higher Runcorn. —1F 165
Highfield. *L33* —4F **15**
Highfield Clo. *Wall* —2A **74**
Highfield Ct. *Birk* —3F **119**
Highfield Cres. *Birk* —3F **119**
Highfield Cres. *Wid* —2A **132**
Highfield Dri. *Crank* —1E **29**
Highfield Dri. *Wir* —5D **93**
Highfield Gro. *L23* —5F **9**
Highfield Gro. *Birk* —3F **119**
Highfield Pk. *L31* —1F **13**
Highfield Pl. *Prsct* —5D **63**
Highfield Rd. *Lith* —5A **18**
Highfield Rd. *Walt* —4F **35**
Highfield Rd. *Birk* —2F **119**
Highfield Rd. *Old S* —2A **80**
Highfield Rd. *Wid* —3F **131**
Highfields. *Hes* —1F **157**
Highfields. *Prsct* —5C **62**
Highfield S. *Birk* —4F **119**
Highfield Sq. *L13* —2F **79**
Highfield St. *L3* —3C **76** (2C **4**)
(in two parts)
Highfield St. *St H* —3D **67**
Highfield Vw. *L13* —2F **79**
Highgate Clo. *Nort* —1D **169**
Highgate Clo. *Wir* —5F **137**
Highgate Ct. *L7* —5A **78**
Highgate Rd. *L31* —4D **7**
Highgate St. *L7* —5A **78**
Highgreen Rd. *Birk* —1C **118**
Highgrove Pk. *L19* —4A **124**
Highlands Rd. *Run* —1F **165**
Highoaks Rd. *L25* —3B **126**
Highpark Rd. *Birk* —1C **118**
High Pk. St. *L8* —4F **99**
Highsted Gro. *L33* —5F **15**
High St. *L2* —4C **76** (4C **4**)
High St. *Brom* —1E **163**
High St. *Frod & Norl* —5B **172**
High St. *Hale V* —5D **149**
High St. *Prsct* —5D **63**
High St. *Run* —5A **152**
High St. *W'tree* —1F **101**
High St. *Wltn* —2A **126**
Hightor Rd. *L25* —1F **125**
Highville Rd. *L16* —3D **103**
Highwood Ct. *L33* —1F **23**
Hignett Av. *St H* —1A **68**
Higson Ct. *L8* —1A **122**
Hilary Av. *L14* —4E **81**
Hilary Clo. *L4* —3C **56**
Hilary Clo. *Prsct* —4E **63**
Hilary Clo. *Wid* —1E **133**
Hilary Dri. *Wir* —3A **94**
Hilary Rd. *L4* —3C **56**
Hilberry Av. *L13* —1E **79**
Hilbre Av. *Wall* —2A **74**
Hilbre Av. *Wir* —4E **157**
Hilbre Ct. *Wir* —5A **112**
Hilbre Rd. *Wir* —5B **112**
Hilbre St. *L3* —5E **77** (5G **5**)
Hilbre St. *Birk* —1D **97**
Hilbre Vw. *Wir* —4C **112**
Hilcrest Rd. *L4* —2D **57**
Hilda Rd. *L12* —1D **81**
Hildebrand Clo. *L4* —3C **56**
Hildebrand Rd. *L4* —3C **56**
Hillaby Clo. *L8* —3F **99**
Hillam Rd. *Wall* —5D **51**
Hillary Cres. *L31* —1D **13**
Hillary Dri. *L23* —1A **18**
Hillary Rd. *Wir* —5D **163**
Hillary Wlk. *L23* —1A **18**
Hill Bark Rd. *Wir* —2B **114**
Hillbrae Av. *St H* —5A **30**
Hillburn Dri. *Birk* —5E **73**
Hill Crest. *Boot* —1E **55**
Hillcrest. *L31* —2F **13**
Hillcrest. *Halt B* —1D **167**
Hillcrest Av. *L36* —4A **84**
Hillcrest Dri. *Upt* —1C **114**
Hillcrest Pde. *L36* —4A **84**
Hillcrest Rd. *Cros* —1A **18**
Hillcroft Rd. *L25* —5F **103**
Hillcroft Rd. *Wall* —3C **74**
Hillerton Clo. *L12* —1B **58**
Hillfield. *Frod* —5B **172**
Hillfield. *Nort* —2D **169**
Hillfield Dri. *Wir* —5F **137**
Hillfoot Av. *L25* —1B **146**
Hillfoot Clo. *Pren* —1C **94**
Hillfoot Grn. *L25* —5A **126**
Hillfoot Rd. *L25* —3F **125**
Hill Gro. *Wir* —2E **93**
Hillhead Rd. *Boot* —1E **55**
Hillingden Av. *L26* —5F **127**
Hillingdon Av. *Wir* —5A **138**
Hillingdon Rd. *L15* —3A **102**
Hill Ridge. *Pren* —4D **95**
Hill Rd. *Pren* —2E **95**
Hill School Rd. *St H* —3A **64**
Hillside. *L25* —5A **104**
Hillside Av. *L36* —5C **60**
Hillside Av. *Newt W* —1F **69**
Hillside Av. *St H* —2E **45**
Hillside Av. *Run* —2E **165**
Hillside Clo. *Boot* —1E **55**
Hillside Clo. *Bil* —1D **31**
Hillside Clo. *Birk* —5E **97**
Hillside Ct. *L25* —1A **126**
Hillside Ct. *Birk* —5E **97**
Hillside Cres. *L36* —5C **60**
Hillside Dri. *L25* —1A **126**
Hillside Rd. *Birk* —5E **97**
Hillside Rd. *Hes* —3A **158**
Hillside Rd. *Huy* —1E **83**
Hillside Rd. *Moss H* —4B **102**
Hillside Rd. *Pren* —1D **95**
Hillside Rd. *Wall* —2F **73**
Hillside Rd. *W Kir* —4D **113**
Hillside St. *L6* —3F **77**
Hillside Vw. *Pren* —1A **118**
Hills Moss Rd. *St H* —4F **67**
Hills Pl. *L15* —2A **102**
Hill St. *L8* —3D **99**
(in two parts)
Hill St. *St H* —3A **46**
Hill St. *Prsct* —5D **63**
Hill St. *Run* —5A **152**
*Hill St. Bus. Cen. L8 —3D **99***
(off Hill St.)
Hilltop. *Nort* —3C **168**
Hilltop La. *Hes* —2B **158**
Hilltop Rd. *L16* —2C **102**
Hill Top Rd. *Rainf* —3B **28**
Hill Top Rd. *Dut* —4F **169**
Hillview. *L17* —2E **123**
Hill Vw. *Wid* —4F **109**
Hillview Av. *Wir* —3B **112**
Hillview Ct. *Pren* —1C **94**
Hill Vw. Dri. *Wir* —3A **94**
Hillview Gdns. *L25* —1E **125**
*Hillview Mans. Wir —3B **112***
(off Lang La.)
Hill Vw. Rd. *Wir* —5C **114**
Hillwood Clo. *Wir* —1F **161**
Hilton Clo. *Birk* —3C **96**
Hilton Ct. *Boot* —1D **19**
Hilton Gro. *Wir* —3A **112**
Hinchley Grn. *L31* —1B **12**
Hinckley Rd. *St H* —3C **46**
Hindburn Av. *L31* —5F **7**
Hinderton Clo. *Birk* —5E **97**
Hinderton Dri. *Hes* —4F **157**
Hinderton Dri. *W Kir* —5E **113**
Hinderton Rd. *Birk* —4E **97**
Hindley Beech. *L31* —5C **6**
Hindley Wlk. *L24* —5D **147**
Hindlip St. *L8* —1A **122**
Hind St. *Birk* —4E **97**
Hinson St. *Birk* —3E **97**
Hinton Rd. *Run* —1A **166**
Hinton St. *Lith* —2B **34**
Hinton St. *Fair* —3C **78**
Historic Warships. —5D 75
Hitchens Clo. *Murd* —3D **169**
Hitchin Ct. *Gars* —1C **144**
H.M. Customs & Excise Mus. —1C 98 (7C 4)
Hobart Dri. *L33* —4E **15**
Hobart St. *That H* —3E **65**
Hobby Ct. *Hall P* —4E **167**
Hobhouse Ct. *Pren* —3B **96**
Hob La. Wlk. *L32* —3B **22**
Hoblyn Rd. *Pren* —1E **95**
Hockenhall All. *L2* —4C **76** (4D **4**)
Hockenhull Clo. *Wir* —5A **142**
Hodder Av. *L31* —5F **7**
Hodder Clo. *St H* —1B **46**
Hodder Pl. *L5* —5F **55**
Hodder Rd. *L5* —5F **55**
Hodder St. *L5* —5E **55**
Hodson Pl. *L6* —2F **77**
Hogarth St. *L21* —2A **34**
Hogarth Wlk. *L4* —3D **55**

Hoghton Clo. *St H*—3F **67**
Hoghton Rd. *St H*—3F **67**
Hoghton Rd. *Hale V*—5E **149**
Holbeck. *Nort*—3C **168**
Holbeck St. *L4*—5B **56**
Holborn Ct. *Wid*—1E **131**
Holborn Hill. *Birk*—5E **97**
Holborn Sq. *Birk*—5E **97**
Holborn St. *L6*—4A **78**
Holbrook Clo. *St H*—5C **66**
Holcombe Clo. *Wir*—5D **93**
Holden Gro. *L22*—3C **16**
Holden Rd. *L22*—3B **16**
Holden Rd. *Prsct*—2C **84**
Holden Rd. E. *L22*—3C **16**
Holden St. *L8*—1A **100**
Holden Ter. *L22*—3C **16**
Holdsworth St. *L7*—4B **78**
Holgate. *L23*—3B **10**
Holgate Pk. *L23*—3B **10**
Holin Ct. *Pren*—2F **95**
Holingsworth Ct. *St H*—4B **46**
Holkham Clo. *Wid*—3F **131**
Holkham Gdns. *St H*—5D **65**
Holland Ct. *Boot*—1D **19**
Holland Gro. *Wir*—1F **157**
Holland Pl. *L7*—5B **78**
Holland Rd. *Halew*—1E **147**
Holland Rd. *Speke*—5E **147**
Holland Rd. *Wall*—4C **52**
Holland St. *L7*—3D **79**
Holland Way. *L26*—1E **147**
Holley Ct. *Rain*—3C **86**
Holliers Clo. *L31*—1D **13**
Hollies Rd. *L26*—5F **127**
Hollies, The. *L25*—1E **125**
Hollies, The. *Halt B*—2D **167**
Hollingbourne Pl. *L11*—5A **38**
Hollingbourne Rd. *L11*—5A **38**
Hollinghurst Rd. *L33*—5F **15**
Hollingworth Clo. *L9*—5A **36**
Hollinhey Clo. *Boot*—5A **12**
Hollin Hey Clo. *Bil*—2D **31**
Hollins Clo. *L15*—1A **102**
Hollins Way. *Wid*—2B **150**
Hollocombe Rd. *L12*—1B **58**
Holloway. *Run*—1F **165**
Hollow Cft. *L28*—2A **60**
Holly Av. *Wir*—4F **141**
Hollybank Ct. *Birk*—4D **97**
Holly Bank Gro. *St H*—4C **46**
Hollybank Rd. *L18*—4E **101**
Hollybank Rd. *Birk*—4D **97**
Hollybank Rd. *Halt*—1F **167**
Holly Bank St. *St H*—4C **46**
Holly Clo. *Ecc*—4B **44**
Holly Clo. *Hale V*—5D **149**
Holly Ct. *Boot*—3B **34**
Holly Ct. *L5*—5A **56**
Hollydale Rd. *L18*—4A **102**
Holly Farm Rd. *L19*—1D **145**
Hollyfield Rd. *L9*—3F **35**
Holly Gro. *S'frth*—2F **33**
Holly Gro. *Birk*—5E **97**
Holly Gro. *Huy*—4B **82**
Holly Hey. *Whis*—5D **85**
Hollymead Clo. *L25*—5B **104**
Holly Mt. *W Der*—5A **58**
Holly Pl. *Wir*—2F **93**
Holly Rd. *L7*—4C **78**
Holly Rd. *Hay*—3F **47**
Hollyrood. *Prsct*—1A **84**
Holly St. *Boot*—4C **34**
Hollytree Rd. *L25*—1A **126**
Hollywood Rd. *L17*—1E **123**
Holman Rd. *L19*—1D **145**
Holm Cotts. *Pren*—2F **117**
Holme Clo. *Ecc P*—4A **64**
Holmefield Av. *L19*—3A **124**
Holmefield Rd. *L19*—4F **123**
Holme Rd. *Ecc*—1B **64**
Holmes La. L21—1A 34
(off Seaforth Rd.)
Holmes St. *L8*—2C **100**
Holme St. *L5*—4B **54**
Holmesway. *Wir*—3F **137**
Holmfield. *Pren*—2F **117**
Holmfield Av. *Run*—5C **152**
Holmfield Gro. *L36*—1F **105**
Holm Hey Rd. *Pren*—2F **117**
Holm Hill. *Wir*—5C **112**
Holmlands Cres. *Pren*—2E **117**
Holmlands Dri. *Pren*—2E **117**
Holmlands Way. *Pren*—2F **117**
Holm La. *Pren*—2F **117**
Holmleigh Rd. *L25*—3A **104**
Holmrook Rd. *L11*—1F **57**
Holmside Clo. *Wir*—1F **93**
Holmside La. *Pren*—2F **117**
Holmstead, The. *L18*—1F **123**
Holm Vw. Clo. *Pren*—1A **118**
Holmville Rd. *Wir*—1E **141**
Holmway. *Wir*—2F **141**
Holmwood Av. *Wir*—2C **138**
Holmwood Dri. *Hes*—2C **138**
Holt. —2A 86
Holt Av. *Bil*—1D **31**
Holt Av. *Wir*—1E **93**
Holt Coppice. *Augh*—1F **7**
Holt Cres. *Bil*—1D **31**
Holt Hill. *Birk*—5E **97**
Holt Hill Ter. *Birk*—4D **97**
Holt La. *L27*—3D **105**
(in two parts)
Holt La. *Halt*—2F **167**
Holt La. *Rain*—2A **86**
Holt Rd. *L7*—4B **78**
Holt Rd. *Birk*—5E **97**
Holt Way. *L32*—3D **23**
Holy Cross Clo. *L3*—3D **77** (2E **5**)
Holyrood. *Cros*—1A **16**
Holyrood Av. *Wid*—5A **110**
Holywell Clo. *St H*—5D **67**
Home Farm Clo. *Wir*—2C **116**
Home Farm Rd. *Know*—1C **60**
Home Farm Rd. *Wir*—2B **116**
Homefield Gro. *L31*—1C **12**
Homer Green. —1C 10
Homer Rd. *Know*—5C **40**
Homerton Rd. *L6*—3D **79**
Homestall Rd. *L11*—1A **58**
Homestead Av. *Boot*—2B **20**
Homestead Av. *Hay*—1E **49**
Homestead Clo. *L36*—3A **84**
Homestead M. *Wir*—3B **112**
Honeybourne Dri. *Whis*—5A **64**
Honey Hall Rd. *L26*—1E **147**
Honeys Grn. Clo. *L12*—1D **81**
Honey's Grn. La. *L12*—1D **81**
Honeys Grn. Precinct. *L12*—1D **81**
Honey St. *St H*—4C **64**
Honeysuckle Clo. *L26*—2D **127**
Honeysuckle Clo. *Wid*—5B **110**
Honeysuckle Dri. *L9*—5B **36**
Honister Av. *St H*—5C **30**
Honister Clo. *L27*—1A **128**
Honister Gro. *Beech*—5E **167**
Honister Wlk. *L27*—1A **128**
Honiston Av. *Rain*—2B **86**
Honiton Rd. *L17*—3E **123**
Hood Rd. *Wid*—3F **131**
Hood St. *Wall*—3D **75**
Hoole Rd. *Wir*—1B **116**
Hoose Ct. *Wir*—4C **90**
Hooton Rd. *L9*—1B **36**
Hooton Rd. *Will & Hoot*—5A **170**
Hooton Way. *Hoot*—3F **171**
Hooton Works Ind. Est. *Hoot*—4E **171**
Hope Clo. *St H*—4E **45**
Hope Pl. *L1*—1E **99** (7H **5**)
Hope St. *L1*—2E **99** (7J **5**)
Hope St. *Birk*—2D **97**
Hope St. *Prsct*—5D **63**
Hope St. *Wall*—3B **52**
Hope Ter. *Birk*—1D **119**
Hope Way. *L8*—1F **99**
Hopfield Rd. *Wir*—1F **93**
Hopkins Clo. *St H*—4D **45**
Hopwood Cres. *Rainf*—1A **28**
Hopwood St. *L5*—1C **76**
(in two parts)
Horace St. *St H*—4D **45**
Horatio St. *Birk*—3D **97**
Hornbeam Clo. *Hay*—2F **47**
Hornbeam Clo. *Wind H*—1C **168**
Hornbeam Clo. *Wir*—1B **92**
Hornbeam Rd. *Walt*—5C **36**
Hornbeam Rd. *Halew*—5A **128**
Hornby Av. *Boot*—3B **34**
Hornby Av. *Wir*—1C **162**
Hornby Boulevd. *L21 & Boot*—2B **34**
Hornby Chase. *L31*—3D **13**
Hornby Clo. *L9*—4F **35**
Hornby Ct. *Wir*—1C **162**
Hornby Cres. *Clo F*—2D **89**
Hornby Flats. *L21*—2B **34**
Hornby La. *L18*—4D **103**
Hornby Pk. *L18*—4D **103**
Hornby Pl. *L9*—3A **36**
Hornby Rd. *Boot*—3B **34**
(Knowsley Rd.)
Hornby Rd. *Boot*—4C **34**
(Stanley Rd.)
Hornby Rd. *L9*—4F **35**
Hornby Rd. *Wir*—1C **162**
Hornby St. *Cros*—1E **17**
Hornby St. *L5*—2D **77**
Hornby St. *S'frth*—2A **34**
Hornby St. *Birk*—3F **97**
Hornby Wlk. *L5*—2C **76**
Horne St. *L6*—2B **78**
Hornet Clo. *L6*—1A **78**
Hornhouse La. *Know I*—5B **24**
Hornsey Rd. *L4*—4B **56**
Hornspit La. *L12*—3A **58**
Horringford Rd. *L19*—4F **123**
Horrocks Av. *L19*—1D **145**
Horrocks Clo. *L36*—2D **83**
Horrocks Rd. *L36*—3D **83**
Horseman Pl. *Wall*—4E **75**
Horseshoe Dri. *L10*—1B **38**
Horsfall Gro. *L8*—5E **99**
Horsfall St. *L8*—5E **99**
Horwood Av. *Rain*—2B **86**
Horwood Clo. *L12*—1C **58**
Hoscar Ct. *Wid*—5D **131**
Hoscote Pk. *Wir*—4A **112**
Hose Side Rd. *Wall*—4F **51**
Hospital Rd. *Wir*—1B **142**
Hospital St. *St H*—4A **46**
Hospital Way. *Run*—3F **167**
(in two parts)
Hosta Clo. *L33*—5D **15**
Hostock Clo. *Whis*—4D **85**
Hotham St. *L3*—4E **77** (4G **5**)
Hothfield Rd. *Wall*—3D **75**
Hotspur St. *Boot*—2C **54**
Hough Green. —3A 130
Hough Green Pk. —3B 130
Hough Grn. Rd. *Wid*—2A **130**
Houghton Clo. *Wid*—2C **132**
Houghton Cft. *Wid*—4C **108**
Houghton La. *L1*—5D **77** (5F **5**)
Houghton Rd. *Hale V*—5E **149**
Houghton Rd. *Wir*—5B **94**
Houghton's La. *Ecc & St H*—1F **43**
Houghton St. *L1*—5D **77** (5F **5**)

Houghton St. *Prsct* —5D **63**
Houghton St. *Rain* —3C **86**
Houghton St. *Wid* —2D **133**
Houghton Way. *L1* —5F **5**
Hougoumont Av. *L22* —4E **17**
Hougoumont Gro. *L22* —4E **17**
Houlding St. *L4* —5A **56**
Houlgrave Rd. *L5* —1C **76**
Houlston Rd. *L32* —3B **22**
Houlston Wlk. *L32* —3B **22**
Houlton St. *L7* —4B **78**
House La. *Wid* —5F **131**
Hove, The. *Murd* —4D **169**
(in two parts)
Howard Av. *Wir* —2D **163**
Howard Clo. *Mag* —1F **13**
Howard Clo. *S'frth* —3C **18**
Howard Ct. *Mnr P* —3C **154**
Howard Dri. *L19* —5A **124**
Howard Florey Av. *Boot* —1F **19**
Howard's La. *Ecc & St H* —4E **43**
Howards Rd. *Wir* —1B **138**
Howard St. *St H* —3C **64**
Howarth Ct. *Run* —5B **152**
Howbeck Clo. *Pren* —3F **95**
Howbeck Ct. *Pren* —4F **95**
Howbeck Dri. *Pren* —3F **95**
Howbeck Rd. *Pren* —4F **95**
Howden Dri. *L36* —3A **82**
Howell Dri. *Wir* —2D **115**
Howell Rd. *Wir* —5A **120**
Howells Clo. *L31* —5D **7**
Howe St. *Boot* —2B **54**
Howey La. *Frod* —5B **172**
(in two parts)
Howson St. *Birk* —2F **119**
Hoylake. —5B 90
Hoylake Clo. *Murd* —3C **168**
(in two parts)
Hoylake Gro. *Clo F* —2C **88**
Hoylake Municipal Golf Course. —1B 112
Hoylake Rd. *Birk* —4D **73**
Hoylake Rd. *Wir* —2B **92**
Hoyle Rd. *Wir* —3B **90**
Huddleston Clo. *Wir* —1C **116**
Hudleston Rd. *L15* —5B **80**
Hudson Rd. *L31* —3D **13**
Hudson Rd. *Wir* —2A **72**
Hudson St. *St H* —5C **46**
Hudswell Clo. *Boot* —4B **20**
Hughenden Rd. *L13* —1F **79**
Hughes Av. *Prsct* —2D **85**
Hughes Clo. *L7* —5C **78**
Hughes Dri. *Boot* —2E **35**
Hughes La. *Pren* —1B **118**
Hughes St. *St H* —3D **67**
Hughes St. *Eve* —2A **78**
(in two parts)
Hughes St. *Gars* —2C **144**
Hughestead Gro. *L19* —1B **144**
Hughson St. *L8* —4E **99**
Hulmewood. *Wir* —5A **120**
Hulton Av. *Whis* —2F **85**
Humber Clo. *L4* —3E **55**
Humber Clo. *Wid* —1F **133**
Humber Cres. *St H* —5C **66**
Humber St. *Birk* —5F **73**
Hume Ct. *Wir* —3C **90**
Humphrey's Clo. *Murd* —3D **169**
Humphreys Hey. *L23* —5B **10**
Humphrey St. *Boot* —2D **35**
Huncote Av. *St H* —2D **47**
Hunslet Rd. *L9* —2B **36**
Hunstanton Clo. *Wir* —2A **94**
Hunter Ct. *Prsct* —5E **63**
Hunters Ct. *Hall P* —4E **167**
Hunters La. *L15* —2A **102**
Hunter St. *L3* —4D **77** (3F **5**)
Hunter St. *St H* —1C **66**
Huntingdon Clo. *Wir* —1B **92**
Huntingdon Gro. *L31* —3C **6**
Huntley Av. *St H* —4C **66**
Huntley Gro. *St H* —4C **66**
Huntly Rd. *L6* —3C **78**
Hunt Rd. *L31* —5D **7**
Hunt Rd. *Hay* —2E **49**
Hunt's Cross. —5C 126
Hunts Cross Av. *L25* —1B **126**
(in two parts)
Hunts Cross Shop. Pk. *L24* —1A **146**
Huntsman Wood. *L12* —3E **59**
Hurlingham Rd. *L4* —1C **56**
Hurrell Rd. *Birk* —5D **73**
Hursley Rd. *L9* —4E **37**
Hurst Bank. *Birk* —4F **119**
Hurst Gdns. *L13* —4A **80**
Hurstlyn Rd. *L18* —3C **124**
Hurst Pk. Clo. *L36* —2A **84**
Hurst Pk. Dri. *L36* —2A **84**
Hurst Rd. *L31* —3E **13**
Hurst St. *L1* —1C **98** (7D **4**)
(in two parts)
Hurst St. *L13* —4A **80**
Hurst St. *Wid* —3A **152**
Huskisson St. *L8* —2F **99**
Hutchinson St. *L6* —3A **78**
Hutchinson St. *Wid* —1F **151**
Hutchinson Wlk. *L6* —3A **78**
Huxley Clo. *Wir* —1B **92**
Huxley St. *L13* —4D **57**
Huyton. —4E 83
Huyton & Prescot Golf Course. —2B 84
Huyton Av. *St H* —2E **45**
Huyton Brook. *L36* —1F **105**
Huyton Bus. Pk. *Huy* —5A **84**
Huyton Chu. Rd. *L36* —4E **83**
Huyton Hall Cres. *L36* —4E **83**
Huyton Hey Rd. *L36* —4E **83**
Huyton Ho. Clo. *L36* —2B **82**
Huyton Ho. Rd. *L36* —2B **82**
Huyton La. *L36 & Prsct* —3E **83**
Huyton Leisure Cen. —5D 83
Huyton-with-Roby. —3C 82
Hyacinth Av. *L33* —5D **15**
Hyacinth Clo. *Hay* —2F **49**
Hyacinth Gro. *Wir* —4B **72**
Hyde Clo. *Beech* —4D **167**
Hyde Rd. *L22* —4D **17**
Hydrangea Way. *St H* —4A **68**
Hydro Av. *Wir* —5B **112**
Hygeia St. *L6* —2A **78**
Hylton Av. *Wall* —2A **74**
Hylton Rd. *L19* —4D **125**
Hyslop St. *L8* —3E **99**
Hythe Av. *L21* —5C **18**
Hythedale Clo. *L17* —2C **122**

Ibbotson's La. *L17* —5E **101**
Iberis Gdns. *St H* —4A **68**
Ibstock Rd. *Boot* —3B **34**
Iffley Clo. *Wir* —4D **93**
Ikin Clo. *Pren* —5C **72**
Ilchester Rd. *L16* —5E **81**
Ilchester Rd. *Birk* —5F **73**
Ilchester Rd. *Wall* —3D **75**
Ilford Av. *L23* —5D **9**
Ilford Av. *Wall* —3B **74**
Ilford St. *L3* —4E **77** (3J **5**)
Ilfracombe Rd. *Sut L* —1C **88**
Iliad St. *L5* —2E **77**
Ilkley Wlk. *L24* —3D **147**
Ilsley Clo. *Wir* —5F **93**
Imber Rd. *L32* —5F **23**
Imison St. *L9* —5E **35**
Imison Way. *L9* —5E **35**
Imperial Av. *Wall* —5C **52**
Imperial Bldgs. *L2* —4C **4**
Imrie St. *L4* —1F **55**
Ince Av. *Cros* —5C **8**
Ince Av. *Lith* —1B **34**
Ince Av. *Anf* —3B **56**
Ince Av. *Wir* —2E **171**
Ince Blundell Pk. —1A 10
Ince Clo. *Pren* —5F **95**
Ince Gro. *Pren* —1F **117**
Ince La. *L23* —1F **9**
Incemore Rd. *L18* —3A **124**
Ince Rd. *L23* —3A **10**
Inchcape Rd. *L16* —5E **81**
Inchcape Rd. *Wall* —1D **73**
Index St. *L4* —2F **55**
Ingestre Rd. *Pren* —1A **118**
Ingham Rd. *Wid* —5F **109**
Ingleborough Rd. *Birk* —2D **119**
Ingleby Rd. *Wall* —3A **74**
Ingleby Rd. *Wir* —4B **120**
Ingledene Rd. *L18* —4D **103**
Ingle Grn. *L23* —5A **8**
Inglegreen. *Wir* —2B **158**
Ingleholme Gdns. *Ecc P* —4A **64**
Ingleholme Rd. *L19* —3A **124**
Inglemere Rd. *Birk* —2E **119**
Inglemoss Dri. *Rainf* —4B **28**
Ingleside Ct. *Cros* —2C **16**
Ingleton Clo. *Wir* —5D **93**
Ingleton Dri. *St H* —4B **30**
Ingleton Grn. *L32* —5F **23**
Ingleton Gro. *Beech* —5D **167**
Ingleton Rd. *Kirkby* —5F **23**
Ingleton Rd. *Moss H* —4F **101**
Inglewood. *L12* —5A **40**
Inglewood. *Wir* —2D **93**
Inglewood Av. *Wir* —2D **93**
Inglewood Rd. *Rainf* —4C **28**
Inglis Rd. *L9* —1B **36**
Ingoe Clo. *L32* —4B **22**
Ingoe La. *L32* —5B **22**
Ingrave Rd. *L4* —1C **56**
Ingrow Rd. *L6* —3B **78**
Inigo Rd. *L13* —2A **80**
Inley Clo. *Wir* —5A **142**
Inley Rd. *Wir* —5F **141**
Inman Av. *St H* —1B **68**
Inman Rd. *L21* —1B **34**
Inman Rd. *Wir* —3E **93**
Inner Central Rd. *L24* —2F **147**
Inner Forum. *L11* —1E **57**
Inner S. Rd. *L24* —3E **147**
Inner W. Rd. *L24* —2E **147**
Insall Rd. *L13* —5B **80**
Intake Clo. *Will* —5A **170**
Interchange Motorway Ind. Est. *L36* —5A **84**
Inveresk Ct. *Pren* —3E **95**
Invincible Clo. *Boot* —5E **19**
Invincible Way. *Gil I* —2C **38**
Inwood Rd. *L19* —5C **124**
Iona Clo. *L12* —5A **40**
Ionic Rd. *L13* —2A **80**
Ionic St. *L21* —1F **33**
Ionic St. *Birk* —2F **119**
Irby. —1D 137
Irby Av. *Wall* —2A **74**
Irby Cricket Club Ground. —4C 114
Irby Heath. —1C 136
Irby Hill. —4C 114
Irbymill Hill. —3C 114
Irby Rd. *L4* —3B **56**
Irby Rd. *Wir* —2D **137**
Irbyside Rd. *Wir* —3B **114**
Ireland Rd. *Hale V* —5E **149**
Ireland Rd. *Hay* —2C **48**
Ireland St. *Wid* —2D **133**
Irene Av. *St H* —1C **46**

Irene Rd. *L16*—3C **102**
Ireton St. *L4*—1F **55**
Iris Av. *Birk*—1F **95**
Iris Clo. *Wid*—2C **130**
Iris Gro. *L33*—5D **15**
Irlam Dri. *L32*—3E **23**
Irlam Pl. *Boot*—4B **34**
Irlam Rd. *Boot*—4B **34**
Ironbridge Vw. *L8*—5E **99**
Ironside Rd. *L36*—2D **83**
Irvine Rd. *Birk*—2D **119**
Irvine St. *L7*—5A **78**
Irvine Ter. *Wir*—4B **120**
Irving Clo. *L9*—5C **20**
Irwell Chambers. *L3*—4C **4**
Irwell Clo. *L17*—1E **123**
Irwell Ho. *L17*—1E **123**
Irwell La. *L17*—1E **123**
Irwell La. *Run*—4B **152**
Irwell St. *L3*—5B **76** (6C **4**)
Irwell St. *Wid*—3A **152**
Irwin Rd. *St H*—4C **66**
Isaac St. *L8*—5F **99**
Isabel Gro. *L13*—4E **57**
Island Pl. *L19*—1C **144**
Island Rd. *L19*—1C **144**
Island Rd. S. *L19*—1D **145**
Islands Brow. *St H*—2B **46**
Isleham Clo. *L19*—4C **124**
Islington. *Cros*—5D **9**
Islington. *L3*—4E **77** (3G **5**)
Islington Sq. *L3*—3F **77** (3J **5**)
Islip Clo. *Wir*—5D **115**
Ismay Dri. *Wall*—1D **75**
Ismay Rd. *L21*—1B **34**
Ismay St. *L4*—2F **55**
Ivanhoe Rd. *Cros*—1C **16**
Ivanhoe Rd. *Aig*—5C **100**
Ivanhoe St. *Boot*—5B **34**
Iveagh Clo. *Pal*—3A **168**
Iver Clo. *Cron*—3C **108**
Ivernia Rd. *L4*—1B **56**
Ivor Rd. *Wall*—1C **74**
Ivory Dri. *L33*—5E **15**
Ivy Av. *L19*—5A **124**
Ivy Av. *Whis*—2A **86**
Ivy Av. *Wir*—2E **141**
Ivychurch M. *Run*—5D **153**
Ivydale Rd. *L18*—5F **101**
Ivydale Rd. *Walt*—4B **36**
Ivydale Rd. *Birk*—1E **119**
Ivy Farm Ct. *Hale V*—5D **149**
Ivyfarm Rd. *Rain*—2B **86**
Ivyhurst Clo. *L19*—4F **123**
Ivy La. *Wir*—4E **71**
Ivy Leigh. *L13*—1E **79**
Ivy St. *Birk*—3F **97**
Ivy St. *Run*—1A **166**

Jack McBain Ct. *L3*—2C **76**
Jack's Brow. *Know P*—1E **61**
Jacksfield Way. *L19*—5F **123**
Jackson Clo. *Rain*—5D **87**
Jackson Clo. *Wir*—4F **119**
Jacksons Pond Dri. *L25*—2F **103**
Jackson St. *L19*—1C **144**
Jackson St. *St H*—5C **46**
Jackson St. *Birk*—4E **97**
Jackson St. *Btnwd*—5E **69**
Jackson St. *Hay*—1A **48**
Jacobs Clo. *L21*—2B **34**
Jacob St. *L8*—5F **99**
Jacqueline Ct. *L36*—4C **82**
Jacqueline Dri. *L36*—2A **84**
Jade Clo. *L33*—2F **23**
Jade Rd. *L6*—2B **78**
Jamaica St. *L1*—2D **99**
Jamesbrook Clo. *Birk*—1A **96**
James Clarke St. *L5*—2C **76**
James Clo. *Wid*—3A **152**
James Ct. *L25*—2B **126**
James Ct. Apartments. *L25*—2A **126**
James Gro. *St H*—1E **65**
James Holt Av. *L32*—4C **22**
James Hopkins Way. *L4*—4D **55**
James Horrigan Ct. *Boot*—2C **18**
James Larkin Way. *L4*—4D **55**
James Rd. *L25*—2B **126**
James Rd. *Hay*—1F **49**
James Simpson Way. *Boot*—1F **19**
James St. *Clo F*—3D **89**
James St. *L2*—5C **76** (6C **4**)
James St. *Gars*—1C **144**
James St. *Pren*—5C **96**
James St. *Wall*—4E **75**
Jamieson Av. *L23*—1A **18**
Jamieson Rd. *L15*—2E **101**
Jane St. *St H*—4F **67**
Janet St. *L7*—5B **78**
Japonica Gdns. *St H*—4A **68**
Jarrett Rd. *L33*—1A **24**
Jarrett Wlk. *L33*—1A **24**
Jarrow Clo. *Pren*—5B **96**
Jasmine Clo. *L5*—1F **77**
Jasmine Clo. *Wir*—2D **93**
Jasmine Ct. *L36*—1F **83**
Jasmine Gdns. *St H*—4A **68**
Jasmine Gro. *Wid*—4D **131**
Jasmine M. *L17*—1A **122**
Jason St. *L5*—5E **55**
Jason Wlk. *L5*—5E **55**
Java Rd. *L4*—1D **57**
Jay's Clo. *Murd*—3E **169**
Jean Wlk. *L10*—2B **38**
Jedburgh Dri. *L33*—4D **15**
Jeffereys Cres. *L36*—4B **82**
Jeffreys Dri. *L36*—3A **82**
Jeffreys Dri. *Wir*—4D **93**
Jellicoe Clo. *Wir*—3D **135**
Jenkinson St. *L3*—3E **77** (1H **5**)
Jensen Ct. *Ast I*—4C **152**
Jericho Clo. *L17*—2D **123**
Jericho Ct. *L17*—2D **123**
Jericho Farm Clo. *L17*—3D **123**
Jericho Farm Wlk. *L17*—3D **123**
Jericho La. *L17*—3D **123**
Jermyn St. *L8*—3A **100**
Jerningham Rd. *L11*—5D **37**
Jersey Av. *L21*—4B **18**
Jersey Clo. *Boot*—5C **34**
Jersey St. *Boot*—5C **34**
Jersey St. *Clo F*—3C **88**
Jesmond St. *L15*—1D **101**
Jessamine Rd. *Birk*—1E **119**
Jessica Ho. *L20*—2D **55**
Jet Clo. *L6*—2B **78**
Jeudwine Clo. *L25*—3B **126**
Joan Av. *Grea*—5E **93**
Joan Av. *More*—1D **93**
Jocelyn Clo. *Wir*—4A **142**
John Bagot Clo. *L5*—1E **77**
John F. Kennedy Heights. *L3* —2E **77** (1H **5**)
John Hunter Way. *Boot*—2F **19**
John Lennon Dri. *L6*—3B **78**
John Middleton Clo. *Hale V*—5D **149**
John Moores Clo. *L7*—1A **100**
Johns Av. *Hay*—1E **49**
Johns Av. *Run*—1F **165**
Johnson Av. *Prsct*—2D **85**
Johnson Gro. *L12*—1E **81**
Johnson Rd. *Pren*—3F **117**
Johnson's La. *Wid*—3E **133**
Johnson St. *L3*—4C **76** (3E **4**)
Johnson St. *St H*—4C **46**
Johnson Wlk. L7—5C 78
(off Deeley Clo.)
Johnston Av. *Boot*—2E **35**
John St. *L3*—3E **77** (1H **5**)
John St. *Birk*—2F **97**
John Willis Ho. *Birk*—2A **120**
Jones Farm Rd. *L25*—4C **104**
Jones St. *L3*—5E **77** (5H **5**)
Jonville Rd. *L9*—1C **36**
Jordan St. *L1*—2D **99**
Joseph Gardner Way. *Boot*—3B **34**
Joseph Lister Clo. *Boot*—2F **19**
Joseph Morgan Heights. *L10*—5A **22**
Joseph St. *St H*—4E **67**
Joseph St. *Wid*—2C **132**
Joshua Clo. *L5*—5E **55**
Joyce Wlk. *L10*—1C **38**
Joy La. *Clo F*—4E **89**
Joy Wlk. *Clo F*—3E **89**
Jubilee Av. *L14*—5D **81**
Jubilee Ct. *Hay*—1B **48**
Jubilee Cres. *Hay*—1F **49**
Jubilee Cres. *Wir*—2B **142**
Jubilee Dri. *Boot*—4A **20**
Jubilee Dri. *L7*—4B **78**
Jubilee Dri. *Whis*—4D **85**
Jubilee Dri. *Wir*—2B **112**
Jubilee Ho. *Run*—2C **166**
Jubilee Pk. —2C 82
Jubilee Rd. *Cros*—2C **16**
Jubilee Rd. *L21*—1B **34**
Jubilee Way. *Wid*—3E **131**
Jubits La. *Sut M*—1A **110**
Juddfield St. *Hay*—2A **48**
Judges Dri. *L6*—2C **78**
Judges Way. *L6*—2C **78**
Julian Way. *Wid*—5F **109**
Julie Gro. *L12*—1E **81**
Juliet Av. *Wir*—5E **119**
Juliet Gdns. *Wir*—5E **119**
July Rd. *L6*—1C **78**
July St. *Boot*—3C **34**
Junction La. *Newt W*—1F **69**
Junction La. *St H*—4E **67**
Junct. One Retail Pk. *Wall*—3D **73**
June Av. *Wir*—2E **163**
June Rd. *L6*—1D **79**
June St. *Boot*—4C **34**
Juniper Clo. *L28*—3B **60**
Juniper Clo. *St H*—4D **45**
Juniper Clo. *Wir*—2C **114**
Juniper Cres. *L12*—2F **59**
Juniper Gdns. *L23*—4B **10**
Juniper St. *L20*—3C **54**
Justan Way. *Rain*—1B **86**
Juvenal Pl. *L3*—2E **77** (1G **5**)
Juvenal St. *L3*—2D **77** (1F **5**)

Kaigh Av. *L23*—5D **9**
Kale Clo. *Wir*—5B **112**
Kale Gro. *L33*—5F **15**
Kara Clo. *Boot*—5C **34**
Karan Way. *L31*—2A **22**
Karen Clo. *Btnwd*—5F **69**
Karonga Rd. *L10*—1E **37**
Karonga Way. *L10*—1F **37**
Karslake Rd. *L18*—4F **101**
Karslake Rd. *Wall*—3D **75**
Katherine Wlk. *L10*—1C **38**
Kearsley Clo. *L4*—4E **55**
Kearsley St. *L4*—4E **55**
Keats Av. *Whis*—3F **85**
Keats Clo. *Wid*—4F **131**
Keats Gro. *L36*—5F **83**
Keats St. *St H*—3F **67**
Keble Dri. *L10*—2C **20**
Keble Dri. *Wall*—5D **51**
Keble Rd. *Boot*—2C **54**
Keble St. *L6*—3A **78**
Keble St. *Wid*—5B **132**

Keckwick. —3F 155
Keckwick La. *Dar* —3F **155**
Kedleston St. *L8* —5A **100**
Keegan Dri. *Wall* —4E **75**
Keele Clo. *Pren* —4C **72**
Keenan Dri. *Boot* —3E **35**
Keene Ct. *Boot* —1D **19**
Keepers La. *Wir* —2B **140**
Keepers Wlk. *Cas* —5F **153**
Keighley Av. *Wall* —1E **73**
Keightley St. *Birk* —2C **96**
Keir Hardie Av. *Boot* —3E **35**
Keith Av. *L4* —2F **55**
Keith Dri. *Wir* —5C **162**
Keithley Wlk. *L24* —3E **147**
Kelbrook Clo. *St H* —5D **67**
Kelby Clo. *L8* —5A **100**
Kelday Clo. *L33* —3E **23**
Kelkbeck Clo. *L31* —5F **7**
Kellet's Pl. *Birk* —1F **119**
Kellett Rd. *Wir* —3B **72**
Kellitt Rd. *L15* —2E **101**
Kelly Dri. *Boot* —3E **35**
Kelly St. *Prsct* —5E **63**
Kelmscott Dri. *Wall* —2E **73**
Kelsall Av. *Sut M* —2B **88**
Kelsall Av. *Wir* —2E **171**
Kelsall Clo. *Pren* —1F **117**
Kelsall Clo. *Wid* —2D **131**
Kelsall Clo. *Wir* —2E **171**
Kelsey Clo. *St H* —4D **45**
Kelso Clo. *L33* —4D **15**
Kelso Rd. *L6* —3C **78**
Kelton Gro. *L17* —2E **123**
Kelvin Gro. *L8* —3A **100**
Kelvin Pk. *Wall* —5D **75**
Kelvin Rd. *Birk* —5E **97**
Kelvin Rd. *Wall* —5E **75**
Kelvinside. *L23* —3F **17**
Kelvinside. *Wall* —5D **75**
Kemberton Dri. *Wid* —4A **110**
Kemble St. *L6* —3B **78**
Kemble St. *Prsct* —5D **63**
Kempsell Wlk. *L26* —5A **128**
Kempsell Way. *L26* —5A **128**
Kempsey Gro. *That H* —4E **65**
Kempson Ter. *Wir* —3F **141**
Kempston St. *L3* —4E **77** (3H **5**)
Kempton Clo. *L36* —5C **82**
Kempton Clo. *Run* —4C **166**
Kempton Pk. Rd. *L10* —2E **21**
Kempton Rd. *L15* —1D **101**
Kempton Rd. *Wir* —4B **120**
Kemsley Rd. *L14* —3F **81**
Kenbury Clo. *L33* —1A **24**
Kenbury Rd. *L33* —1A **24**
Kendal Clo. *Beb* —1F **141**
Kendal Dri. *L31* —5D **7**
Kendal Dri. *St H* —5B **30**
Kendal Dri. *Rain* —2A **86**
Kendal Pk. *L12* —5D **59**
Kendal Ri. *Beech* —5D **167**
Kendal Rd. *L16* —2E **103**
Kendal Rd. *Wall* —4A **74**
Kendal Rd. *Wid* —3C **130**
Kendal St. *Birk* —3E **97**
Kendricks Fold. *Rain* —3B **86**
Kenilworth Av. *Run* —2B **166**
Kenilworth Clo. *L25* —1E **125**
Kenilworth Dri. *Wir* —2F **137**
Kenilworth Gdns. *Wir* —3E **93**
Kenilworth Rd. *Cros* —1C **16**
Kenilworth Rd. *Child* —2D **103**
Kenilworth Rd. *Wall* —3D **75**
Kenilworth St. *Boot* —5B **34**
Kenilworth Way. *L25* —1E **125**
Kenley Av. *Wid* —4D **109**
Kenmare Rd. *L15* —3E **101**
Kenmay Wlk. *L33* —2A **24**
Kenmore Rd. *Pren* —3E **117**
Kennelwood Av. *L33* —2F **23**
Kennessee Clo. *L31* —2E **13**
Kennesse Green. —2D 13
Kenneth Clo. *Boot* —2E **19**
Kenneth Rd. *Wid* —4C **130**
Kennet Rd. *Hay* —2C **48**
Kennet Rd. *Wir* —2D **141**
Kennford Rd. *L11* —3C **38**
Kensington. —4B 78
Kensington. *L7* —4A **78**
Kensington Av. *St H* —4C **66**
Kensington Dri. *Prsct* —1A **84**
Kensington Gdns. *Wir* —1F **93**
Kensington St. *L6* —3A **78**
Kent Av. *Lith* —5C **18**
Kent Clo. *Boot* —4D **35**
Kent Clo. *Wir* —2B **162**
Kent Gdns. *L1* —1D **99** (7F **5**)
Kent Gro. *Run* —1B **166**
Kentmere Av. *St H* —5C **30**
Kentmere Dri. *Wir* —4F **137**
Kent M. *Pren* —5A **96**
Kenton Clo. *B Vale* —2B **104**
Kenton Rd. *L26* —5F **127**
Kent Pl. *Birk* —3D **97**
Kent Rd. *St H* —3C **66**
Kent Rd. *Wall* —3A **74**
Kents Bank. *L12* —2C **58**
Kent St. *L1* —1D **99** (7F **5**)
(in two parts)
Kent St. *Pren* —5A **96**
Kent St. *Wid* —3B **132**
Kenview Clo. *Wid* —2A **150**
Kenwood Clo. *L27* —4F **105**
Kenwright Cres. *St H* —3C **66**
Kenwyn Rd. *Wall* —1B **74**
Kenyon Clo. *L33* —4F **15**
Kenyon Rd. *L15* —4A **102**
Kenyons La. *Lyd & Mag* —3D **7**
Kenyons La. N. *Hay* —1F **49**
Kenyons La. S. *Hay* —1F **49**
Kenyon's Lodge. *L31* —4E **7**
Kenyon Ter. *Pren* —4B **96**
Kepler St. *L21* —2A **34**
Keppel St. *Boot* —2B **54**
Kerr Gro. *St H* —5E **47**
Kerris Clo. *L17* —2B **122**
Kerrysdale Clo. *St H* —4D **67**
Kersey Rd. *L32* —5F **23**
Kersey Wlk. *L32* —5F **23**
Kershaw Av. *L23* —2F **17**
Kershaw St. *Wid* —3D **131**
Kerswell Clo. *St H* —5D **67**
Keston Wlk. *L26* —1F **147**
Kestrel Av. *Wir* —3D **93**
Kestrel Clo. *St H* —2B **46**
Kestrel Clo. *Wir* —3D **93**
Kestrel Dene. *L10* —2A **38**
Kestrel Gro. *L26* —3D **127**
Kestrel Rd. *Hes* —3C **158**
Kestrel Rd. *More* —1C **92**
Kestrels Way. *Hall P* —4F **167**
Keswick Av. *Wir* —1C **170**
Keswick Clo. *L31* —5E **7**
Keswick Clo. *Wid* —3C **130**
Keswick Dri. *L21* —5D **19**
Keswick Dri. *Frod* —5C **172**
Keswick Gdns. *Wir* —5C **162**
Keswick Pl. *Pren* —5D **73**
Keswick Rd. *L18* —2C **124**
Keswick Rd. *St H* —3E **45**
Keswick Rd. *Wall* —4F **51**
Keswick Way. *L16* —1A **104**
Kevelioc Clo. *Wir* —4F **141**
Kew St. *L5* —1D **77**
Keybank Rd. *L12* —3A **58**
Kiddman St. *L9* —5F **35**
Kidstone Clo. *St H* —4D **67**
Kilburn Av. *Wir* —4E **163**
Kilburn Gro. *St H* —4E **65**
Kilburn St. *L21* —2B **34**
Kildale Clo. *L31* —5C **6**
Kildare Clo. *Hale V* —5D **149**
Kildonan Rd. *L17* —2D **123**
Kilgraston Gdns. *L17* —3E **123**
Killarney Gro. *Wall* —3A **74**
Killarney Rd. *L13* —3A **80**
Killester Rd. *L25* —5B **104**
Killington Way. *L4* —3E **55**
Kilmalcolm Clo. *Pren* —5F **95**
Kilmore Clo. *L9* —5C **20**
Kilmory Av. *L25* —2C **126**
Kiln Clo. *Ecc* —3C **44**
Kilncroft. *Brook* —5B **168**
(in two parts)
Kiln La. *Dent G & Ecc* —3B **44**
Kiln Rd. *Wir* —1A **116**
Kilnyard Rd. *L23* —1D **17**
Kilrea Clo. *L11* —3F **57**
Kilrea Rd. *L11* —3E **57**
(Ferguson Rd.)
Kilrea Rd. *L11* —3F **57**
(Muirhead Av.)
Kilsail Rd. *L32* —1A **40**
Kilsby Dri. *Wid* —2E **133**
Kilshaw Rd. *Btnwd* —5F **69**
Kilshaw St. *L6* —2A **78**
(in two parts)
Kimberley Av. *L23* —2D **17**
Kimberley Av. *That H* —4E **65**
Kimberley Clo. *L8* —2A **100**
Kimberley Dri. *L23* —1D **17**
Kimberley Rd. *Wall* —5B **52**
Kimberley St. *Pren* —1F **95**
Kindale Rd. *Pren* —3E **117**
Kinder St. *L6* —3F **77**
King Arthurs Wlk. *Cas* —2A **168**
King Av. *Boot* —2E **35**
King Edward Clo. *Rain* —2B **86**
King Edward Dri. *Wir* —1B **142**
King Edward Rd. *Dent G* —2D **45**
King Edward Rd. *Rain* —2B **86**
King Edward St. *L3* —4B **76** (3B **4**)
Kingfield Rd. *L9* —3F **35**
Kingfisher Bus. Pk. *Boot* —1C **34**
Kingfisher Clo. *Kirkby* —3E **15**
Kingfisher Clo. *Beech* —5F **167**
Kingfisher Clo. *N'ley* —4F **105**
Kingfisher Dri. *St H* —2B **46**
Kingfisher Gro. *L12* —2F **59**
Kingfisher Way. *Wir* —3D **93**
King George Dri. *Wall* —5C **52**
King George Rd. *Hay* —1F **49**
King George's Dri. *Wir* —1B **142**
King George's Way. *Pren* —2E **95**
Kingham Clo. *L25* —2C **126**
Kingham Clo. *Wid* —3D **133**
King James Ct. *Hall P* —4E **167**
Kinglake Rd. *Wall* —1D **75**
Kinglake St. *L7* —5A **78**
Kinglass Rd. *Wir* —4B **142**
King's Av. *Wir* —3D **91**
Kingsbrook Way. *Wir* —4D **119**
King's Brow. *Wir* —1D **141**
Kingsbury. *Wir* —4D **113**
Kings Clo. *Aig* —1C **122**
Kings Clo. *Wir* —5D **119**
Kings Ct. *S'frth* —1F **33**
Kings Ct. *Hoy* —4A **90**
Kings Ct. *Run* —3D **155**
Kings Ct. *Wir* —1D **141**
Kingscourt Rd. *L12* —1C **80**
Kingsdale Av. *Birk* —2D **119**
Kingsdale Av. *Rain* —3D **87**
Kingsdale Rd. *L18* —4A **102**
Kings Dock Rd. *L1* —2D **99**
Kingsdown Rd. *L11* —2A **58**

Kingsdown St. *Birk* —5E **97**
Kings Dri. *L25* —5C **104**
King's Dri. *Cald* —2C **134**
King's Dri. *Thing* —2F **137**
Kings Dri. *Wltn* —2B **126**
King's Dri. N. *Wir* —5E **113**
Kingsfield Rd. *L31* —3C **12**
King's Gap, The. *Wir* —4A **90**
Kingshead Clo. *Cas* —5A **154**
Kingsheath Av. *L14* —2E **81**
Kingsland Cres. *L11* —5E **37**
Kingsland Rd. *L11* —5D **37**
Kingsland Rd. *Birk* —5C **96**
King's La. *Wir* —5D **119**
Kingsley Av. *Wir* —2E **171**
Kingsley Clo. *L31* —2C **6**
Kingsley Clo. *Wir* —4A **138**
Kingsley Cres. *Run* —1A **166**
Kingsley Rd. *L8* —2A **100**
Kingsley Rd. *Dent G* —2D **45**
Kingsley Rd. *Run* —1A **166**
Kingsley Rd. *Wall* —3B **74**
Kingsley St. *Birk* —1A **96**
Kingsmead Dri. *L25* —5B **126**
Kingsmead Gro. *Pren* —4F **95**
Kings Mdw. *Nort* —2C **168**
Kingsmead Rd. *Pren* —4F **95**
Kingsmead Rd. *Wir* —4F **71**
Kingsmead Rd. N. *Pren* —4F **95**
Kingsmead Rd. S. *Pren* —4F **95**
Kings Mt. *Pren* —5B **96**
Kingsnorth. *Whis* —4F **85**
Kings Pde. *L3* —1C **98**
King's Pde. *Wall* —3D **51**
Kings Pk. *L21* —1F **33**
King's Rd. *Boot* —1C **54**
Kings Rd. *Cros* —1D **17**
Kings Rd. *St H* —1C **64**
King's Rd. *Beb* —4D **119**
Kings Sq. *Birk* —3E **97**
Kings Ter. *Boot* —2C **54**
Kingsthorne Pk. *L25* —1C **146**
Kingsthorne Rd. *L25* —1C **146**
Kingston Clo. *L12* —1E **81**
Kingston Clo. *Run* —5E **153**
Kingston Clo. *Wir* —1E **93**
King St. *St H* —5F **45**
King St. *Wat* —4D **17**
King St. *Birk* —3A **120**
King St. *Gars* —3C **144**
King St. *Prsct* —5D **63**
King St. *Run* —4A **152**
King St. *Wall* —1D **75**
Kingsville Rd. *Wir* —2E **141**
Kings Wlk. *Birk* —3A **120**
Kings Wlk. *Wir* —4C **112**
Kingsway. *St H* —5A **30**
Kingsway. *Wat* —3E **17**
Kingsway. *Beb* —5D **119**
Kingsway. *Frod* —5B **172**
Kingsway. *Hes* —4C **158**
Kingsway. *Huy* —2D **83**
Kingsway. *Prsct* —1D **85**
Kingsway. *Wall* —5A **52**
(Belvidere Rd.)
Kingsway. *Wall* —3F **75** (1A **4**)
(Seacombe Promenade)
Kingsway. *Wid* —5A **132**
Kingsway Ho. *Wid* —5A **132**
Kingsway Leisure Cen. —5A 132
Kingsway Pde. *L36* —2C **82**
Kingsway Pk. *L3* —2D **77** (1F **5**)
Kingsway Tunnel App. *Wall* —2E **73**
Kingswell Clo. *L7* —1B **100**
Kings Wharf. *Birk* —5E **75**
Kingswood Av. *Walt* —1B **36**
Kingswood Av. *Wat* —3F **17**
Kingswood Boulevd. *Wir* —4E **119**
Kingswood Bus. Pk. *Prsct* —1A **84**
Kingswood Ct. *L33* —1F **23**
Kingswood Dri. *L23* —2D **17**
Kingswood Rd. *Wall* —1C **74**
Kington Rd. *Wir* —3A **112**
Kinley Gdns. *Boot* —3E **35**
Kinloch Clo. *L26* —5F **127**
Kinloss Rd. *Wir* —1C **114**
Kinmel Clo. *L4* —3D **57**
Kinmel Clo. *Birk* —2D **97**
Kinmel St. *L8* —4A **100**
Kinmel St. *St H* —3C **66**
Kinnaird Rd. *Wall* —5A **52**
Kinnaird St. *L8* —1A **122**
Kinnerton Clo. *Wir* —1B **92**
Kinnock Pk. *Btnwd* —5E **69**
Kinross Rd. *Faz* —1E **37**
Kinross Rd. *Wat* —5E **17**
Kinross Rd. *Wall* —5D **51**
Kintore Clo. *Wir* —1C **170**
Kintore Rd. *L19* —5B **124**
Kipling Av. *L36* —5A **84**
Kipling Av. *Birk* —3F **119**
Kipling Cres. *Wid* —3F **131**
Kipling Gro. *Sut M* —3A **88**
Kipling St. *Boot* —2A **34**
Kirby Clo. *Wir* —5C **112**
Kirby Mt. *Wir* —1C **134**
Kirby Pk. *Wir* —5C **112**
Kirby Pk. Mans. *Wir* —5B **112**
Kirby Rd. *Boot* —2D **35**
Kirkbride Clo. *L27* —5A **106**
Kirkbride Lawn. *L27* —5A **106**
*Kirkbride Wlk. L27 —5A **106***
(off Kirkbride Clo.)
Kirkburn Clo. *L8* —5F **99**
Kirkby. —2C 22
Kirkby Bank Rd. *Know I* —3B **24**
Kirkby Park. —2C 22
Kirkby Pool. —3E 23
Kirkby Rank La. *Kirkby* —4E **25**
Kirkby Row. *L32* —2C **22**
Kirkby Sports Cen. —5C 22
Kirkby Stadium. —4C 22
Kirk Cotts. *Wall* —4B **52**
Kirkdale. —3E 55
Kirkdale Rd. *L5* —5D **55**
Kirkdale Va. *L4* —4E **55**
Kirket Clo. *Wir* —3A **142**
Kirket La. *Wir* —3F **141**
Kirkfield Gro. *Birk* —3A **120**
Kirkham Rd. *Wid* —2C **132**
Kirkland Av. *Birk* —2D **119**
Kirkland Clo. *L9* —1F **35**
Kirkland Rd. *Wall* —3C **52**
Kirklands, The. *Wir* —5C **112**
Kirkland St. *St H* —4E **45**
Kirkmaiden Rd. *L19* —4B **124**
Kirkman Fold. *Rain* —3B **86**
Kirkmore Rd. *L18* —2A **124**
Kirkmount. *Wir* —4A **94**
Kirk Rd. *L21* —2C **34**
Kirkside Clo. *L12* —5D **39**
Kirkstone Av. *St H* —5C **30**
Kirkstone Cres. *Beech* —1A **174**
Kirkstone Rd. N. *L21* —4C **18**
Kirkstone Rd. S. *L21* —5D **19**
Kirkstone Rd. W. *L21* —3B **18**
Kirkston Rd. N. *L21* —3C **18**
Kirk St. *L5* —5E **55**
Kirkway. *Beb* —5D **119**
Kirkway. *Grea* —5E **93**
Kirkway. *Wall* —4B **52**
Kirkway. *Wir* —4F **93**
Kirstead Wlk. *L31* —2B **22**
Kitchener Dri. *L9* —2F **35**
Kitchener St. *St H* —4D **45**
Kitchen St. *L1* —2D **99**
Kitling Rd. *Know B* —3B **40**
Kiverley Clo. *L18* —1E **125**
Knap, The. *Wir* —4A **158**
Knaresborough Rd. *Wall* —2F **73**
Knightbridge Wlk. *L33* —3D **15**
Knighton Rd. *L4* —2D **57**
Knight Rd. *Btnwd* —5F **69**
Knight St. *L1* —1E **99** (7G **5**)
Knightsway. *L22* —3F **17**
Knoclaid Rd. *L13* —4E **57**
Knoll, The. *Pal* —3F **167**
Knoll, The. *Pren* —1A **118**
Knotty Ash. —3C 80
Knotty M. *L25* —1B **126**
Knowe, The. *Will* —5A **170**
Knowle Clo. *L12* —1C **58**
Knowles Ho. Av. *Ecc* —5F **43**
Knowles St. *Birk* —2C **96**
Knowles St. *Wid* —2C **132**
Knowl Hey Rd. *L26* —1A **148**
Knowsley. —4C 40
Knowsley Bus. Pk. *Know B* —2B **40**
Knowsley Clo. *Birk* —3A **120**
Knowsley Ct. *Birk* —3A **120**
Knowsley Heights. *L36* —1E **83**
Knowsley Ind. Pk. *Know I* —5B **24**
(Abercrombie Rd.)
Knowsley Ind. Pk. *Know I* —3B **24**
(Kirkby Bank Rd.)
Knowsley La. *Know & Know P* —2C **60**
Knowsley Outdoor Education Cen. & Watersports. —1F 61
Knowsley Park. —3F 41
Knowsley Pk. La. *Prsct* —4C **62**
Knowsley Rd. *Boot* —3A **34**
Knowsley Rd. *Ecc & St H* —5C **44**
Knowsley Rd. *L19* —1A **144**
Knowsley Rd. *Birk* —3A **120**
Knowsley Rd. *Rain* —4D **87**
Knowsley Rd. *Wall* —5A **52**
Knowsley Safari Pk. —2C 62
Knowsley Sports Club. —5B 22
Knowsley St. *L4* —1F **55**
Knowsley United F.C. —1D 83
Knox Clo. *Wir* —1B **142**
Knox St. *Birk* —3F **97**
Knutsford Clo. *Ecc* —1B **64**
Knutsford Grn. *Wir* —5F **71**
Knutsford Rd. *Wir* —5E **71**
Knutsford Wlk. *L31* —3D **7**
Kramar Wlk. *L33* —3F **23**
Kremlin Dri. *L13* —1F **79**
Kylemore Av. *L18* —1F **123**
Kylemore Clo. *Wir* —4E **137**
Kylemore Dri. *Wir* —4E **137**
Kylemore Rd. *Pren* —5A **96**
Kylemore Way. *L26* —5E **127**
Kylemore Way. *Wir* —4E **137**
Kynance Rd. *L11* —3D **39**

Laburnum Av. *L36* —1E **105**
Laburnum Av. *St H* —1D **47**
*Laburnum Ct. L8 —5A **100***
(off Weller Way)
Laburnum Cres. *L32* —2D **23**
Laburnum Gro. *Mag* —1E **13**
Laburnum Gro. *Irby* —1D **137**
Laburnum Gro. *Run* —2B **166**
Laburnum Gro. *W'tree* —1A **102**
Laburnum Pl. *Boot* —5D **35**
Laburnum Rd. *L7* —3D **79**
Laburnum Rd. *Pren* —5B **96**
Laburnum Rd. *Wall* —4B **52**
Lace St. *L3* —3D **77** (3E **4**)
Lacey Ct. *Wid* —5A **132**
Lacey Rd. *Prsct* —5E **63**
Lacey St. *St H* —3D **65**
Lacey St. *Wid* —5A **132**
Lad La. *L3* —4B **76** (3B **4**)
Ladybower Clo. *L7* —1B **100**

Lady Chapel Clo. *L1* —2E **99**
Ladyewood Rd. *Wall* —3C **74**
Ladyfield. *Pren* —2C **94**
Ladyfields. *L12* —1B **80**
***Lady Lever Art Gallery.* —*1A* 142**
Lady Mountford Ho. *L18* —1F **123**
Ladypool. *Hale V* —5C **148**
Ladysmith Rd. *L10* —1F **37**
Laffak. —1D 47
Laffak Rd. *St H* —5C **30**
Laggan St. *L7* —4B **78**
Lagrange Arc. *St H* —5A **46**
Laird Clo. *Birk* —1F **95**
Lairdside Technical Pk. *Birk* —5F **97**
Lairds Pl. *L3* —2D **77**
Laird St. *Birk* —1F **95**
Laithwaite Clo. *Sut M* —3B **88**
Lakeland Clo. *L1* —1D **99** (7E **4**)
Lakemoor Clo. *St H* —4D **67**
Lakenheath Rd. *L26* —1E **147**
Lake Pl. *Wir* —4B **90**
Lake Rd. *L15* —2A **102**
Lake Rd. *Wir* —4B **90**
Lakeside Clo. *Wid* —4A **130**
Lakeside Ct. *Wall* —3C **52**
Lakeside Lawn. *L27* —5A **106**
Lakeside Vw. *L22* —5D **17**
Lakes Rd. *Faz* —1D **37**
Lake St. *L4* —4A **56**
Lake Vw. *Hals P* —1E **107**
Laleston Clo. *Wid* —4E **131**
Lambert Ct. *Wid* —4B **132**
Lambert St. *L3* —3H **5**
Lambert Way. *L3* —4E **77** (3H **5**)
Lambeth Rd. *L5 & L4* —4D **55**
Lambeth Wlk. *L4* —4D **55**
Lambourn Av. *Wid* —4C **108**
Lambourne Gro. *St H* —5A **48**
Lambourne Rd. *L4* —2D **57**
Lambshear La. *L31* —3C **6**
Lambsickle Clo. *West* —4F **165**
Lambsickle La. *West* —4F **165**
Lambton Rd. *L17* —1A **122**
Lammermoor Rd. *L18* —2A **124**
Lampeter Rd. *L6* —5C **56**
Lamport Clo. *Wid* —1E **133**
Lamport St. *L8* —3E **99**
Lanark Clo. *St H* —1F **65**
Lancashire Gdns. *St H* —1F **65**
Lancaster Av. *Cros* —2D **17**
Lancaster Av. *Run* —2E **165**
Lancaster Av. *Seft P* —3C **100**
Lancaster Av. *Wall* —1B **74**
Lancaster Av. *Whis* —3D **85**
Lancaster Av. *Wid* —2A **130**
Lancaster Clo. *Kirk* —5D **55**
Lancaster Clo. *Mag* —1F **13**
Lancaster Clo. *Newt W* —4F **49**
Lancaster Clo. *Wir* —1B **142**
Lancaster Rd. *Huy* —2A **84**
Lancaster Rd. *Wid* —1A **132**
Lancaster St. *Kirk* —5D **55**
Lancaster St. *Walt* —5F **35**
Lancaster Wlk. *Kirk* —5D **55**
Lancaster Wlk. *Huy* —2A **84**
Lance Clo. *L5* —1F **77**
Lancefield Rd. *L9* —3F **35**
Lance Gro. *L15* —2A **102**
Lance La. *L15* —2A **102**
Lancelots Hey. *L3* —4B **76** (4B **4**)
Lancelyn Ct. *Wir* —4A **142**
Lancelyn Precinct. Wir —*4A* ***142***
(off Spital Rd.)
Lancelyn Ter. *Wir* —3F **141**
Lancer Ct. *Ast I* —4E **153**
Lancing Clo. *L25* —3D **127**
(in two parts)
Lancing Dri. *L10* —3D **21**
Lancing Rd. *L25* —3D **127**
Lancing Way. *L25* —3D **127**
Lancots La. *St H* —3D **67**
Lander Rd. *L21* —2B **34**
Landford Av. *L9* —4E **37**
Landford Pl. *L9* —4E **37**
Landican. —4C 116
Landican La. *Upt & High B* —3C **116**
Landican Rd. *Wir* —5B **116**
Landmark, The. *L5* —1E **77**
Landor Clo. *L5* —1C **76**
Landseer Rd. *L5* —1F **77**
Lanfranc Clo. *L16* —1E **103**
Lanfranc Way. *L16* —1E **103**
Langbar. *Whis* —4E **85**
Langdale Av. *Wir* —3F **137**
Langdale Clo. *Kirkby* —4F **23**
Langdale Clo. *Wid* —4C **130**
Langdale Dri. *L31* —5E **7**
Langdale Gro. *St H* —1B **46**
Langdale Rd. *L15* —3E **101**
Langdale Rd. *Run* —5B **152**
Langdale Rd. *Wall* —4F **51**
Langdale Rd. *Wir* —3E **141**
Langdale St. *Boot* —5D **35**
Langdale Way. *Frod* —4C **172**
Langfield Gro. *Wir* —5D **163**
Langford. *Hale V* —5C **148**
Langford Rd. *L19* —4F **123**
Langham Av. *L17* —1C **122**
Langham Ct. *L4* —3F **55**
Langham St. *L4* —3F **55**
Langholme Heights. *L11* —4F **37**
Langland Clo. *L4* —3D **57**
Lang La. *Wir* —3B **112**
Lang La. S. *Wir* —4C **112**
Langley Clo. *W Der* —5F **39**
Langley Clo. *Wir* —5A **142**
Langley Clo. Shop. Cen. *W Der* —5F **39**
Langley Rd. *Wir* —5A **142**
Langley St. *L8* —3E **99**
Langrove St. *L5* —1E **77**
Langsdale St. *L3* —3E **77** (2H **5**)
(in two parts)
Langshaw Lea. *L27* —5F **105**
Langstone Av. *Wir* —2C **114**
Langton Clo. *Wid* —1B **130**
Langton Rd. *Kirkby* —5F **15**
Langton Rd. *W'tree* —2D **101**
Langtree St. *St H* —5C **46**
Langtry Clo. *L4* —2D **55**
Langtry Rd. *L4* —3D **55**
Lansbury Av. *St H* —1E **67**
Lansbury Rd. *L36* —4A **84**
Lansdowne. *L12* —5A **58**
Lansdowne Clo. *Birk* —1A **96**
Lansdowne Ct. *Pren* —1F **95**
Lansdowne Pl. *L5* —5F **55**
Lansdowne Pl. *Pren* —1F **95**
Lansdowne Rd. *Pren & Birk* —1F **95**
Lansdowne Rd. *Wall* —4F **51**
Lansdowne Way. *L36* —4E **83**
Lanville Rd. *L19* —3A **124**
Lanyork Rd. *L3* —3B **76** (2B **4**)
Lapford Cres. *L33* —1A **24**
Lapford Wlk. *L33* —1A **24**
Lapwing Clo. *L12* —2F **59**
Lapwing Ct. *L26* —3E **127**
Lapwing Gro. *Pal* —4A **168**
Lapwing La. *Moore* —1F **155**
Lapworth Clo. *Wir* —1B **92**
Lapworth St. *L5* —5D **55**
Larch Av. *Wid* —2B **132**
Larch Clo. *Cress* —5F **123**
Larch Clo. *Run* —3C **166**
Larch Ct. L8 —*5A* ***100***
(off Weller Way)
Larchdale Gro. *L9* —4A **36**
Larchfield Rd. *L23* —5B **10**
Larch Gro. *L15* —5A **80**
Larch Gro. *Pren* —1E **95**
Larch Lea. *L5* —1B **78**
(in two parts)
Larch Rd. *L36* —4C **82**
Larch Rd. *Birk* —4C **96**
Larch Rd. *Hay* —1E **49**
Larch Rd. *Run* —3C **166**
Larch Towers. *L33* —2F **23**
Larchwood Av. *L31* —3C **12**
Larchwood Clo. *L25* —4B **104**
Larchwood Clo. *Wir* —4F **137**
Larchwood Dri. *Wir* —5E **119**
Larcombe Av. *Wir* —4F **93**
Larkfield Clo. *L17* —2C **122**
Larkfield Gro. *L17* —2C **122**
Larkfield Rd. *L17* —2C **122**
Larkfield Vw. *L15* —1E **101**
Larkhill Av. *Wir* —2A **94**
Larkhill Clo. *L13* —4E **57**
Larkhill La. *Club* —4E **57**
Larkhill Pl. *L13* —4E **57**
Larkhill Vw. *L13* —4F **57**
Larkhill Way. *Wir* —2A **94**
Larkin Clo. *Wir* —5A **120**
Lark La. *L17* —1B **122**
Larkspur Clo. *Beech* —1F **173**
Larksway. *Wir* —2B **158**
Lark Way. *L17* —1B **122**
Larton Rd. *Wir* —3E **113**
Lascelles Rd. *L19* —5D **125**
Lascelles St. *St H* —5C **46**
Latchford Rd. *Wir* —4B **158**
Late Moffatt Rd. W. *L9* —1B **36**
Latham Av. *Run* —5B **152**
Latham St. *L5* —5D **55**
(in two parts)
Latham St. *St H* —4D **47**
Latham St. *Wid* —3C **132**
Latham Way. *Wir* —5B **142**
Lathbury La. *L17* —4E **101**
Lathom Av. *L21* —2F **33**
Lathom Av. *Wall* —2B **74**
Lathom Clo. *L21* —2F **33**
Lathom Dri. *L31* —4E **7**
Lathom Rd. *Boot* —3C **34**
Lathom Rd. *L36* —3E **83**
Lathum Clo. *Prsct* —1E **85**
Latimer St. *L5* —5D **55**
Latrigg Rd. *L17* —2E **123**
Lauder Clo. *L33* —4D **15**
Launceston Clo. *Brook* —4C **168**
Laund, The. *Wall* —1F **73**
Laurel Av. *Beb* —3E **141**
Laurel Av. *Hes* —1F **157**
Laurel Bank. *Wid* —1A **132**
Laurelbanks. *Wir* —1E **157**
Laurel Ct. *St H* —1B **46**
Laurel Dri. *Ecc* —4F **43**
Laurel Dri. *Will* —4B **170**
Laurel Gro. *Wat* —3D **17**
Laurel Gro. *Huy* —1E **105**
Laurel Gro. *Tox* —3C **100**
Laurelhurst Av. *Wir* —3A **138**
Laurel Rd. *L7* —3D **79**
Laurel Rd. *St H* —1D **65**
Laurel Rd. *Birk* —5D **97**
Laurel Rd. *Hay* —3F **47**
Laurel Rd. *Prsct* —5E **63**
Laurels, The. *Wir* —3E **71**
Laurence Deacon Ct. *Birk* —2C **96**
Lauren Clo. *L36* —4B **84**
Lauriston Rd. *L4* —2C **56**
Laurus Clo. *L27* —4F **105**
Lavan Clo. *L6* —3A **78**
Lavan St. *L6* —3A **78**
Lavan St. *St H* —4E **65**
Lavender Clo. *Run* —1C **166**
Lavender Cres. *Prsct* —5E **63**
Lavender Gdns. *L23* —4B **10**

Lavender Gdns. *St H* —4A **68**
Lavender Way. *L9* —4B **36**
Lavrock Bank. *L8* —5E **99**
Lawford Dri. *Wir* —2C **158**
Lawler Gro. *Prsct* —4E **63**
Lawler St. *L21* —2B **34**
Lawns Av. *Wir* —4B **162**
Lawnside Clo. *Birk* —3F **119**
Lawns, The. *Pren* —2D **95**
Lawrence Clo. *L19* —5A **124**
Lawrence Gro. *L15* —2E **101**
Lawrence Rd. *L15* —2D **101**
Lawrence Rd. *Wind* —2C **44**
Lawrenson St. *St H* —5E **45**
Lawson Wlk. *L12* —5D **39**
Lawton Av. *Boot* —3E **35**
Lawton Rd. *Wat* —3D **17**
Lawton Rd. *Huy* —4C **82**
Lawton Rd. *Rain* —4D **87**
Lawton St. *L1* —5D **77** (6G **5**)
Laxey St. *L8* —3E **99**
Laxton Rd. *L25* —5C **126**
Layford Clo. *L36* —5D **61**
Layford Rd. *L36* —1D **83**
Layton Av. *Pren* —2F **117**
Layton Clo. *L25* —2C **126**
Layton Rd. *L25* —2C **126**
Leach Cft. *Stock V* —4A **60**
Leach La. *Sut L* —2D **89**
Leach St. *St H* —4F **45**
Leach Way. *Wir* —1C **136**
Lea Clo. *Pren* —5E **95**
Lea Cross Gro. *Wid* —1C **130**
Leadenhall Clo. *L5* —5F **55**
Leadenhall St. *L5* —5F **55**
Leafield Clo. *Wir* —1F **137**
Leafield Rd. *L25* —1B **146**
Leagate. *L10* —5F **21**
Lea Green. —1F 87
Lea Grn. Ind. Est. *St H* —3A **88**
Lea Grn. Rd. *Sut M* —3F **87**
Lea Gro. *L17* —5C **100**
Leamington Gdns. *Wir* —5B **94**
Leamington Rd. *L11* —1D **57**
Leander Rd. *Wall* —1A **74**
Lea Rd. *Wall* —1C **74**
Leaside. *Halt B* —1D **167**
Leasowe. —2A 72
Leasowe Av. *Wall* —5E **51**
Leasowe Gdns. *Wir* —3E **71**
Leasowe Golf Course. —1A 72
Leasowe Recreation Cen. —3A 72
Leasowe Rd. *L9* —1B **36**
Leasowe Rd. *Wir & Wall* —3D **71**
Leasoweside. *Wir* —2B **72**
Leas, The. *Wall* —4E **51**
Leas, The. *Wir* —1B **138**
Leatherbarrows La. *L31* —3F **13**
Leather La. *L2* —4C **76** (4D **4**)
Leather's La. *L26* —1F **147**
Leathwood. *L31* —1E **13**
Leaway. *Wir* —5D **93**
Leawood Gro. *Wir* —1F **93**
Leckwith Rd. *Boot* —3B **20**
Ledbury Clo. *Ecc* —5B **44**
Ledbury Clo. *L12* —4F **39**
Ledbury Clo. *Pren* —2E **117**
Ledger Rd. *Hay* —3A **48**
Ledsham Clo. *Pren* —5E **95**
Ledsham Rd. *L32* —3C **22**
Ledsham Wlk. *L32* —3C **22**
Ledson Pk. *L33* —4F **15**
Ledston Clo. *Wind H* —1D **169**
Leece St. *L1* —1E **99** (7H **5**)
Lee Clo. *Rain* —5D **87**
Leecourt Clo. *L12* —1D **81**
Leeds St. *L3* —3B **76** (2B **4**)
Lee Hall Rd. *L25* —4C **104**
Lee Manor Sports Cen. —4D 105
Leeming Clo. *L19* —2C **144**
Lee Pk. Av. *L25* —4C **104**
Lee Pk. Golf Course. —5D 105
Lee Rd. *Wir* —4C **90**
Lees Av. *Birk* —2F **119**
Leeside Av. *L32* —5E **23**
Leeside Clo. *L32* —4F **23**
Lees La. *L12* —4D **59**
Lees Rd. *Know I* —4B **24**
Lee St. *St H* —3E **67**
Leeswood. *L22* —4E **17**
Leeswood Rd. *Wir* —1A **116**
Lee Va. Rd. *L25* —5C **104**
Leeward Dri. *Speke* —3A **146**
Legh Rd. *Hay* —2A **48**
Legh Rd. *Wir* —5B **120**
Legh St. *Newt W* —5F **49**
Legion La. *Wir* —1D **163**
Legion Rd. *St H* —3D **65**
Leicester Av. *L22* —2D **17**
Leicester Rd. *Boot* —4D **35**
Leicester St. *That H* —3D **65**
Leigh Av. *Wid* —3F **131**
Leigh Bri. Way. *L5* —1C **76**
Leigh Grn. Clo. *Wid* —4C **130**
Leigh Pl. *L1* —5D **77** (5F **5**)
Leigh Rd. *Wir* —3B **112**
Leighs Hey Cres. *L32* —4F **23**
Leigh St. *L1* —5D **77** (5E **4**)
(in three parts)
Leigh St. *Edg H* —5C **78**
Leighton Av. *L31* —5D **7**
Leighton Av. *Wir* —3E **91**
Leighton Rd. *Birk* —5E **97**
Leighton St. *L4* —2E **55**
Leinster Gdns. *Run* —4F **151**
Leinster Rd. *L13* —3B **80**
Leinster St. *Run* —4F **151**
Leison St. *L4* —4D **55**
(in two parts)
Leiston Clo. *Wir* —5E **115**
Lemon Clo. *L7* —5C **78**
Lemon Gro. *L8* —3C **100**
Lemon St. *L5* —5D **55**
Lemon Tree Wlk. *St H* —2D **65**
Lenfield Dri. *Hay* —2F **47**
Lenham Way. *L24* —3B **146**
Lennox Av. *Wall* —4B **52**
Lennox La. *Pren* —5C **72**
Lenthall St. *L4* —1F **55**
Lenton Rd. *L25* —4C **104**
Leo Clo. *L14* —2F **81**
Leominster Rd. *Wall* —2B **74**
Leonard Cheshire Dri. *Boot* —2F **19**
Leonard Ho. *Wall* —5F **75**
Leonards Clo. *L36* —5D **61**
Leonard St. *St H* —4F **67**
Leonard St. *West P* —3D **165**
Leonora St. *L8* —5A **100**
Leopold Gro. *St H* —1C **88**
Leopold Rd. *Wat* —3C **16**
Leopold Rd. *Kens* —4B **78**
Leopold St. *Wall* —3E **75**
Leslie Av. *Wir* —1D **115**
Leslie Rd. *St H* —3C **64**
Lesseps Rd. *L8* —2C **100**
Lessingham Rd. *Wid* —1F **131**
Lester Clo. *L4* —4E **55**
Lester Dri. *Ecc* —3A **44**
Lester Dri. *Wir* —5C **114**
Lester Gro. *L36* —2F **83**
Lestock St. *L8* —2E **99**
Leta St. *L4* —2F **55**
(in two parts)
Letchworth St. *L6* —1B **78**
Lethbridge Clo. *L5* —5C **54**
Letitia St. *L8* —4F **99**
Letterstone Clo. *L6* —2F **77**
Letterstone Wlk. *L6* —2F **77**
Levens Hey. *Wir* —1D **93**
Leven St. *L4* —3E **55**
Levens Way. *Wid* —4C **130**
Lever Av. *Wall* —4E **75**
Lever Causeway. *Wir* —2A **140**
Leveret Rd. *L24* —4A **148**
Leverhulme Ct. *Wir* —3A **142**
Lever St. *Clo F* —3D **89**
Lever Ter. *Birk* —1E **119**
Leveson Rd. *L13* —5B **80**
Lewis Cres. *Wid* —5A **132**
Lewis Gro. *Wid* —3D **131**
Lewisham Rd. *L11* —1F **57**
Lewisham Rd. *Wir* —1C **142**
Lewis St. *St H* —4E **45**
Lexham Rd. *L14* —3B **80**
Lexington Way. *L33* —4E **15**
Leybourne Clo. *L25* —3A **104**
Leybourne Grn. *L25* —3A **104**
Leybourne Gro. *L25* —4A **104**
Leybourne Rd. *L25* —3A **104**
Leyburn Clo. *L32* —1E **39**
(in two parts)
Leyburn Rd. *Wall* —5F **51**
Ley Clo. *Clo F* —2C **88**
Leyfield Clo. *L12* —5D **59**
Leyfield Ct. *L12* —5D **59**
Leyfield Rd. *L12* —5C **58**
Leyfield Wlk. *L12* —5D **59**
Leyland Gro. *Hay* —2B **48**
Leyland St. *Prsct* —5D **63**
Leyton Clo. *Run* —4B **166**
Liberton Ct. *L5* —5F **55**
Liberty St. *L15* —2E **101**
Libra Clo. *L14* —1A **82**
Librex Rd. *Boot* —2C **34**
Lichfield Av. *L22* —2D **17**
Lichfield Clo. *Boot* —4A **20**
Lichfield Rd. *Halew* —1E **147**
Lichfield Rd. *W'tree* —3A **102**
Lichfield St. *Wall* —4C **52**
Lickers La. *Whis* —4D **85**
Liddell Av. *L31* —1A **22**
Liddell Ct. *Wall* —1D **73**
Liddell Rd. *L12* —4F **57**
Lidderdale Rd. *L15* —3E **101**
Lidgate Clo. *L33* —5F **15**
Liebig St. *Wid* —4B **132**
Liffey St. *L8* —2B **100**
Lifton Rd. *L33* —3F **23**
Lightbody St. *L5* —1B **76**
Lightburn St. *Run* —1F **165**
Lightfoot Clo. *Wir* —3B **158**
Lightfoot La. *Wir* —3B **158**
Lighthouse Rd. *Wir* —5B **90**
Lightwood Dri. *L7* —1C **100**
Lightwood St. *L7* —1C **100**
Lilac Av. *Wid* —2B **132**
Lilac Cres. *Run* —2C **166**
Lilac Gro. *L36* —1D **105**
Lilac Gro. *Bil* —1D **31**
Lilac Gro. *Hay* —3F **47**
Lilford Av. *L9* —2F **35**
Lilley Rd. *L7* —3D **79**
Lillian Rd. *L4* —5B **56**
Lillie Clo. *Pren* —1C **94**
Lillyfield. *Wir* —4F **157**
Lilly Grn. *L4* —2B **56**
Lilly Gro. *L4* —2B **56**
(in two parts)
Lilly Va. *L7* —3D **79**
Lily Gro. *L7* —5B **78**
Lily Rd. *L21* —2B **34**
Limbo La. *Wir* —4D **115**
Lime Av. *Frod* —5C **172**
Lime Av. *Wid* —2B **132**
Lime Av. *Wir* —3D **141**
Lime Clo. *L13* —2A **80**
Lime Ct. *L33* —5E **15**

Limedale Rd. L18—4A 102
Lime Gro. S'frth—2A 34
Lime Gro. Run—2C 166
Lime Gro. Tox—3B 100
Limehurst Gro. Wir—4D 163
Limekiln Ct. L5—1D 77
Limekiln La. L5 & L3—1D 77 (1E 5)
Limekiln La. Wall—4A 74
Limekiln Row. Cas—2A 168
Limes, The. Wir—4F 93
Lime St. L1—4D 77 (5F 5)
Limetree Clo. L9—4B 36
Lime Tree Gro. Wir—2C 158
Lime Va. Rd. Bil—2C 30
Linacre Ct. Boot—1C 54
Linacre La. Boot—3C 34
Linacre Rd. L21—1B 34
Linbridge Rd. L14—5F 59
Lincoln Clo. Anf—2B 78
Lincoln Clo. Huy—3B 84
Lincoln Clo. Run—4C 166
Lincoln Cres. St H—2B 46
Lincoln Dri. L10—2D 21
Lincoln Dri. Wall—5C 52
Lincoln Gdns. Birk—5A 74
Lincoln Grn. L31—2B 12
Lincoln Ho. St H—4A 46
Lincoln Rd. St H—1D 65
Lincoln Sq. Wid—2B 132
Lincoln St. L19—3C 144
Lincoln St. Birk—5A 74
Lincoln Way. L36—3B 84
Lincoln Way. Rain—5D 87
Lincombe Rd. L36—2B 82
Lindale Dri. Clo F—2C 88
Lindale Rd. L7—3E 79
Lindby Clo. L32—5A 24
Lindby Rd. L32—5A 24
Linden Av. Boot—3F 19
Linden Av. L23—1C 16
Linden Ct. Wid—5F 109
Linden Dri. L36—5E 83
Linden Dri. Pren—3E 117
Linden Gro. Bil—2C 30
Linden Gro. Wall—4B 52
Linden Rd. L27—4E 105
Lindens, The. L31—3C 12
Lindens, The. Pren—4C 96
Linden Way. Ecc—4B 44
Linden Way. Wid—5F 109
Lindenwood. L32—5F 23
Lindeth Av. Wall—3B 74
Lindfield Clo. L8—5E 99
Lindisfarne Dri. L12—5F 39
Lindley Clo. L7—1C 100
Lindley St. L7—1C 100
Lindrick Clo. Rain—2A 86
Lindsay Rd. L4—3D 57
Lindsay St. Clo F—3D 89
Lind St. L4—2F 55
Lindwall Clo. Pren—5C 72
Linear Pk. Wir—5C 70
Lineside Clo. L25—4B 104
Linford Gro. St H—3C 46
Lingdale Av. Pren—3F 95
Lingdale Ct. Pren—2F 95
Lingdale Rd. Pren—2F 95
Lingdale Rd. Wir—3A 112
Lingdale Rd. N. Birk—2F 95
Lingfield Clo. L36—5C 82
Lingfield Gro. L14—4C 80
Lingfield Rd. L14—4C 80
Lingfield Rd. Run—1E 165
Lingford Clo. L27—5F 105
Lingham Clo. Wir—5D 71
Lingham La. Wir—3C 70
Lingham Pk. —1C 92
Lingholme Rd. St H—4E 45
Lingmell Av. St H—4B 30
Lingmell Rd. L12—3B 58
Ling St. L7—4B 78
Lingtree Rd. L32—3B 22
Lingwell Av. Wid—2D 131
Linhope Way. L17—1B 122
Link Av. L23—5A 10
Link Av. St H—2E 47
Linkfield Clo. L27—3C 104
Link Rd. Huy—5B 84
Links Clo. Wall—4F 51
Links Clo. Wir—4B 162
Links Hey Rd. Wir—3E 135
Linkside. Wir—5D 119
Linkside Ct. L23—5A 8
Linkside Rd. L25—3C 126
Links Rd. Kirkby—4A 24
Linkstor Rd. L25—1F 125
Links Vw. Pren—4E 95
Links Vw. Wall—3F 51
Linksview Clo. L25—1F 125
Links Vw. Tower. L25—2F 125
Linksway. Wall—4F 51
Link Way. St H—2B 44
Linkway. Run—2C 166
Linkway E. St H—1B 66
Linkway W. St H—5F 45
Linner Rd. L24—5C 146
Linnet Clo. L17—4C 100
Linnet Ho. L17—4B 100
Linnet La. L17—4B 100
Linnets Way. Wir—2E 157
Linnet Way. L33—3E 15
Linslade Clo. L33—1F 23
Linslade Cres. L33—1F 23
Linton St. L4—2F 55
Linum Gdns. St H—4B 68
Linville Av. L23—1B 16
Linwood Clo. Brook—5C 168
Linwood Gro. Whis—4E 85
Linwood Rd. Birk—1E 119
Lionel St. St H—4F 67
Lions Clo. Pren—3F 95
Lipton Clo. Boot—1B 54
Lisburn La. L13—4E 57
Lisburn La. Tue—5E 57
Lisburn Rd. L17—2D 123
Liscard. —1B 74
Liscard Cres. Wall—1B 74
Liscard Gro. Wall—2A 74
Liscard Ho. Wall—2B 74
Liscard Rd. L15—2D 101
Liscard Rd. Wall—2B 74
Liscard Village. Wall—1B 74
Liscard Way. Wall—2B 74
Liskeard Clo. Brook—4B 168
Lisleholme Clo. L12—5C 58
Lisleholme Cres. L12—5C 58
Lisleholme Rd. L12—5C 58
Lismore Ct. Cros—1C 16
Lismore Rd. L18—2A 124
Lister Cres. L7—4C 78
Lister Dri. L13—2E 79
Lister Rd. L7—3C 78
Lister Rd. Ast—4C 152
Liston St. L4—1F 55
Litcham Clo. Wir—2B 94
Litchborough Gro. Whis—5A 64
Litherland. —1B 34
Litherland Av. Wir—5D 71
Litherland Cres. St H—1C 46
Litherland Pk. L21—5B 18
Litherland Rd. Boot—2C 34
Lithou Clo. L5—1C 76
Little Acre. L31—2E 13
Lit. Barn Hey. Boot—5D 11
Little Bongs. —2D 81
Little Bongs. L14—2D 81
Littlebourne. Murd—3E 169
Lit. Brook La. L32—5D 23
Lit. Canning St. L8—2F 99
Lit. Catharine St. L8—2F 99
Littlecote Clo. Clo F—2C 88
Little Ct. L3—2C 76
Little Cft. Whis—3D 85
Little Crosby. —2D 9
Lit. Crosby Rd. Cros & L Cro—2D 9
Littledale. L14—3D 81
Littledale Rd. Wall—3D 75
Little Delph. Hay—1C 48
Littlegate. Halt B—2E 167
Lit. Hardman St. L1—1E 99 (7H 5)
Lit. Heath Rd. L24—5E 147
Lit. Heyes St. L5—5A 56
Lit. Heys La. L23—2F 9
Lit. Howard St. L3—2B 76 (1B 4)
Lit. Huskisson St. L8—2F 99
Littlemore Clo. Wir—4D 93
Lit. Moss Hey. L28—4B 60
Lit. Parkfield Rd. L17—5B 100
Littler Rd. Hay—3F 47
Lit. St Bride St. L8—1F 99
Littlestone Clo. Wid—5A 110
Lit. Storeton La. Wir—1A 140
Little St. St H—2E 67
Littleton Clo. Pren—5E 95
Littlewood Clo. Whis—3E 85
Lit. Woolton St. L7—5F 77
Littondale Av. Rain—4D 87
Liver Ind. Est. L9—4C 36
Livermore Ct. L8—3C 100
Liverpool. —4D 77
Liverpool John Lennon Airport. —5C 146
Liverpool Anglican Cathedral. —2E 99
Liverpool Cricket Club Ground. —4F 123
Liverpool Empire Theatre. —4E 77 (4G 5)
Liverpool F.C. —4A 56
Liverpool F.C. Visitor Cen. & Mus. (off Anfield Ground) —4A 56
Liverpool Institute for the Performing Arts. —1E 99
Liverpool Metropolitan R.C. Cathedral. —5F 77 (6J 5)
Liverpool Municipal Golf Course. —4A 22
Liverpool Mus. —4D 77 (3F 5)
Liverpool Parish Church. —5B 76 (5B 4)
Liverpool Pl. Wid—3C 130
Liverpool Rd. Cros & Gt Cro—5D 9
Liverpool Rd. St H—5F 45
Liverpool Rd. Hay—1A 48
Liverpool Rd. Huy & Page M—2B 82
Liverpool Rd. Lyd—4C 6
Liverpool Rd. Prsct—5B 62
Liverpool Rd. Wid—3B 130
Liverpool Rd. N. L31—4C 6
Liverpool Rd. S. L31—1C 12
Liverpool St. St H—5F 45
Liverpool Town Hall. —5C 76 (5C 4)
Liverpool Watersports Cen. —2D 99
Liverpool Way, The. L33—4A 24
Liversidge Rd. Birk—5D 97
Liver St. L1—1C 98 (7D 4)
Livingston Av. L17—5C 100
Livingston Ct. L17—5C 100
Livingston Dri. L17—1C 122
Livingston Dri. N. L17—1C 122
Livingston Dri. S. L17—1C 122
Livingstone Gdns. Birk—2C 96
Livingstone Rd. Wir—2A 72
Livingstone St. Birk—2C 96
Llanrwst Clo. L8—4E 99
Lloyd Av. Birk—2B 96
Lloyd Clo. L6—2F 77

Lloyd Cres. *Newt W*—5F **49**
Lloyd Dri. *Wir*—1C **114**
Lloyd Rd. *Prsct*—4E **63**
Lloyd St. *Hay*—2F **47**
Lobelia Av. *L9*—4B **36**
Lobelia Gro. *Beech*—1F **173**
Local Cen. *Run*—5A **154**
Lochinvar St. *L9*—5F **35**
Lochmore Rd. *L18*—3A **124**
Lochryan Rd. *L19*—4B **124**
Loch St. *Run*—4A **152**
(in two parts)
Lockerby Rd. *L7*—3D **79**
Locker Pk. *Wir*—5C **92**
Locke St. *Gars*—3C **144**
Lockett Rd. *Wid*—1A **132**
Lockfields Vw. *L3*—1C **76**
Lockgate E. *Wind H*—5C **154**
Lockgate W. *Wind H*—5B **154**
Lockington Clo. *L8*—5F **99**
Lock St. *St H*—3C **46**
Lockton Rd. *Know*—3B **40**
Lockwood Vw. *Pres B*—5F **169**
Loddon Clo. *Wir*—2B **94**
Lodge La. *L8*—2B **100**
Lodge La. *Halt*—2E **167**
Lodge La. *Wid*—5A **108**
Lodge La. *Wir*—1B **142**
Lodge Rd. *Wid*—4B **130**
Lodwick St. *L20*—2B **54**
Lofthouse Ga. *Wid*—1E **131**
Logan Rd. *Birk*—5B **74**
Logan Towers. *L5*—1C **76**
Logfield Dri. *L19*—2D **145**
Lognor Rd. *L32*—3C **22**
Lognor Wlk. *L32*—3C **22**
Logwood Rd. *L36*—1A **106**
Lois Ct. *Wall*—5C **52**
Lombard Rd. *Wir*—4F **71**
Lombardy Av. *Wir*—2B **114**
Lomond Gro. *Wir*—1F **93**
Lomond Rd. *L7*—4E **79**
Londonderry Rd. *L13*—4D **57**
London Rd. *L3*—4E **77** (4G **5**)
(in two parts)
London Rd. *Frod*—5B **172**
Longacre Clo. *Wall*—1D **73**
Long Acres. *Wir*—4D **93**
Long Av. *L9*—2B **36**
Longbenton Way. *Mnr P*—3B **154**
Longborough Rd. *Know*—5C **40**
Longcroft Av. *L19*—5D **125**
Longcroft Sq. *L19*—5D **125**
Longdale La. *L29*—3D **11**
Longdown Rd. *L10*—2A **38**
Longfellow Dri. *Wir*—5A **120**
Longfellow St. *Boot*—3A **34**
Longfellow St. *L8*—2B **100**
Longfield Av. *L23*—4E **9**
Longfield Clo. *Wir*—5D **93**
Longfield Pk. *Clo F*—2D **89**
Longfield Rd. *L21*—2B **34**
Longfield Wlk. *L23*—4E **9**
Longfold. *L31*—1E **13**
Longford St. *L8*—1A **122**
Long Hey. *Whis*—4D **85**
Long Hey Rd. *Wir*—2E **135**
Longland Rd. *Wall*—5B **52**
Long La. *Thor*—2A **10**
Long La. *Walt*—2B **36**
Long La. *Gars*—5C **124**
Long La. *W'tree*—1E **101**
Long Mdw. *Ecc*—4B **44**
Long Mdw. *Wir*—4F **157**
Longmeadow Rd. *Know*—4D **41**
Longmoor Clo. *L10*—1E **37**
Longmoor Gro. *L9*—2B **36**
Longmoor La. *L9 & L10*—2B **36**
Long Moss. *Boot*—3C **18**
Longreach Rd. *L14*—2F **81**
Longridge Av. *St H*—3D **47**
Longridge Av. *Wir*—3E **93**
Longridge Wlk. *L4*—3E **55**
Longsight Clo. *Pren*—5E **117**
Long Spinney. *Nort*—2C **168**
Longstone Wlk. *L7*—1B **100**
Longton La. *Rain*—1A **86**
Longview. —1F 83
Long Vw. Av. *Rain*—2A **86**
Longview Av. *Wall*—1A **74**
Longview Cres. *L36*—3F **83**
Longview Dri. *L36*—2F **83**
Longview La. *L36*—1F **83**
Longview Rd. *L36*—2F **83**
Long Vw. Rd. *Rain*—2A **86**
Longville St. *L8*—4E **99**
Longwood Clo. *Rainf*—4B **28**
Longworth Way. *L25*—1A **126**
Lonie Gro. *St H*—3C **64**
Lonsborough Rd. *Wall*—3C **74**
Lonsdale Av. *St H*—4B **64**
Lonsdale Av. *Wall*—5A **52**
Lonsdale Clo. *Ford*—3B **18**
Lonsdale Clo. *Wid*—3C **130**
Lonsdale M. *Ford*—3B **18**
Lonsdale Rd. *Ford*—3B **18**
Lonsdale Rd. *Halew*—1E **147**
Looe Clo. *Wid*—2E **131**
Looe Rd. *L11*—3D **39**
Loomsway. *Wir*—1D **137**
Loraine St. *L5*—5F **55**
Lordens Clo. *L14*—1A **82**
Lordens Rd. *L14*—1A **82**
Lord Nelson St. *L1 & L3*—4D **77** (4G **5**)
Lords Av. *Pren*—1C **94**
Lord St. *L2*—5C **76** (5D **4**)
Lord St. *St H*—3F **45**
(in two parts)
Lord St. *Birk*—2E **97**
Lord St. *Gars*—2C **144**
Lord St. *Run*—4F **151**
Loreburn Rd. *L15*—3A **102**
Lorenzo Dri. *L11*—2E **57**
Loretto Dri. *Wir*—3A **94**
Loretto Rd. *Wall*—1F **73**
Lorne Ct. *Pren*—5B **96**
Lorne Rd. *L22*—4D **17**
Lorne Rd. *Pren*—5A **96**
Lorne St. *L7*—3E **79**
Lorn St. *Birk*—3E **97**
Lorton Av. *St H*—4A **30**
Lorton St. *L8*—2B **100**
Lostock Clo. *Bil*—1E **31**
Lothair Rd. *L4*—4A **56**
Lothian St. *L8*—3A **100**
Lotus Gdns. *St H*—4A **68**
Loudon Gro. *L8*—3A **100**
Lough Grn. *Wir*—5A **142**
Loughlin Dri. *L33*—5F **15**
Loughrigg Av. *St H*—4B **30**
Louis Braille Clo. *Boot*—1F **19**
Louis Pasteur Av. *Boot*—1F **19**
Lovelace Rd. *L19*—5B **124**
Love La. *L3*—2B **76** (1B **4**)
Love La. *Wall*—3A **74**
Lovel Rd. *L24*—5D **147**
Lovel Ter. *Wid*—2B **150**
Lovel Way. *L24*—4D **147**
Lovett Dri. *Prsct*—1E **85**
Lowden Av. *L21*—3B **18**
Lowell St. *L4*—2F **55**
Lwr. Appleton Rd. *Wid*—3B **132**
Lwr. Bank Vw. *L20*—2B **54**
Lower Bebington. —2A 142
Lwr. Breck Rd. *L6*—5C **56**
Lwr. Castle St. *L2*—5C **76** (5C **4**)
Lwr. Church St. *Wid*—2A **152**
Lower Clo. *L26*—4A **128**
Lwr. Farm Rd. *L25*—2F **103**
Lwr. Flaybrick Rd. *Pren*—1E **95**
Lower Grn. *Wir*—1A **116**
Lower Hey. *L23*—5B **10**
Lwr. House La. *L11*—4F **37**
Lwr. House La. *Wid*—5F **131**
Lower La. *L9*—1E **37**
Lwr. Mersey Vw. *L20*—2B **54**
Lwr. Milk St. *L3*—4C **76** (3D **4**)
Lower Rd. *L26 & Wid*—4B **128**
Lower Rd. *Wir*—1B **142**
Lwr. Sandfield Rd. *L25*—5B **104**
Lowerson Cres. *L11*—3E **57**
Lowerson Rd. *L11*—3E **57**
Lwr. Thingwall La. *Wir*—1C **138**
Lowe St. *St H*—4F **45**
Lowe St. S. *St H*—5F **45**
Loweswater. *Hay*—2A **48**
Loweswater Cres. *Hay*—2A **48**
Loweswater Way. *L33*—1D **23**
Lowfield La. *St H*—5F **65**
Lowfield Rd. *L14*—3C **80**
Lowfield Rd. Ind. Est. *St H*—1E **87**
Lowfields Av. *Wir*—2D **171**
Lowfields Clo. *Wir*—2E **171**
Low Hill. *L6*—3A **78**
Lowlands Rd. *Run*—5F **151**
Lowndes Rd. *L6*—5D **57**
Lowry Bank. *Wall*—3E **75**
Lowther Av. *Ain*—3D **21**
Lowther Av. *Mag*—5E **7**
Lowther Cres. *St H*—3B **64**
Lowther Dri. *Rain*—3B **86**
Lowther St. *L8*—2A **100**
Lowwood Gro. *Birk*—4D **97**
Low Wood Gro. *Wir*—3C **138**
Lowwood Rd. *Birk*—4D **97**
Low Wood St. *L6*—3A **78**
Loxdale Clo. *L8*—5F **99**
Loxwood Clo. *L25*—2B **104**
Loyola Hey. *Rain*—1E **109**
Lucania St. *L19*—2C **144**
Lucan Rd. *L17*—2D **123**
Lucerne Rd. *Wall*—4D **75**
Lucerne St. *L17*—1C **122**
Lucius Clo. *L9*—1F **35**
Luck St. *L17*—5C **100**
Ludlow Ct. *Wir*—5B **112**
Ludlow Cres. *Run*—2B **166**
Ludlow Dri. *W Kir*—5B **112**
Ludlow Gro. *Wir*—1D **163**
Ludlow St. *L4*—2F **55**
Ludwig Rd. *L4*—5B **56**
Lugard Rd. *L17*—2E **123**
Lugsdale. —5C 132
Lugsdale Rd. *Wid*—5B **132**
Lugsmore La. *St H*—2C **64**
Luke St. *L8*—3F **99**
Luke St. *Wall*—4E **75**
Lully St. *L7*—1A **100**
Lulworth Av. *L22*—3C **16**
Lulworth Rd. *L25*—4C **104**
Lumber La. *Btnwd*—3E **69**
Lumby Av. *Huy*—3E **83**
Lumley Rd. *Wall*—3D **75**
Lumley St. *L19*—5B **124**
Lumley Wlk. *Hale V*—5E **149**
Lunar Dri. *Boot*—5F **11**
Lunar Rd. *L9*—2B **36**
Lune Av. *L31*—5E **7**
Lunesdale Av. *L9*—1B **36**
Lune St. *L23*—1E **17**
Luneway. *Wid*—3C **130**
Lunsford Rd. *L14*—2F **81**
Lunt. —2D 11
Lunt Av. *Boot*—3A **20**
Lunt Av. *Whis*—3E **85**
Lunt La. *L29*—2D **11**
Lunt Rd. *Boot*—2C **34**

Lunt Rd. L29 —1C 10
Lunts Heath. —5B 110
Lunt's Heath Rd. Wid —4A 110
Lupin Dri. Hay —2F 49
Lupin Way. L14 —1A 82
Lupton Dri. L23 —1A 18
Luscombe Clo. L26 —4A 128
Lusitania Rd. L4 —1A 56
Luther Gro. St H —1B 68
Luton Gro. L4 —3E 55
Luton St. L5 —5B 54
Luton St. Wid —5A 132
Lutyens Clo. L4 —3F 55
Luxmore Rd. L4 —2A 56
Lycett Rd. L4 —4B 56
Lycett Rd. Wall —1E 73
Lyceum Pl. L1 —5D 77 (6F 5)
Lycroft Clo. Run —4B 166
Lydbrook Clo. Birk —1F 119
Lydbury Cres. L32 —5F 23
Lydford Rd. L12 —3B 58
Lydia Ann St. L1 —1D 99 (7E 5)
Lydiate. —2B 6
Lydiate La. Thor —4B 10
Lydiate La. West P —3D 165
Lydiate La. Wltn & Halew —2C 126
Lydiate Pk. L23 —4B 10
Lydiate Rd. Boot —3C 34
Lydiate, The. Wir —3F 157
Lydia Wlk. L10 —1B 38
Lydieth Lea. L27 —3E 105
Lydney Rd. L36 —2B 82
Lyelake Clo. L32 —4F 23
Lyelake Rd. L32 —4F 23
Lyle St. L5 —1C 76
Lyme Clo. L36 —5F 61
Lymecroft. L25 —2F 125
Lyme Cross Rd. L36 —5E 61
Lyme Gro. L36 —1F 83
Lyme Rd. St H —2C 64
Lyme St. Newt W —4E 49
Lyme St. Hay —2E 49
Lyme Tree Ct. Wid —3C 108
Lymewood Ct. Hay —1D 49
Lymington Gro. Boot —2F 19
Lymington Rd. Wall —2F 73
Lymm Rd. Pren —2C 94
Lynas Gdns. L19 —4B 124
Lynas St. Birk —1D 97
Lyncot Rd. L9 —5B 20
Lyncroft Rd. Wall —4C 74
Lyndale Av. Wir —1E 171
Lyndene Rd. L25 —2A 104
Lyndhurst. L31 —1D 13
Lyndhurst. Wir —3A 112
Lyndhurst Av. L18 —1F 123
Lyndhurst Av. Wir —4A 138
Lyndhurst Clo. Wir —2A 138
Lyndhurst Rd. Cros —1A 18
Lyndhurst Rd. Hes —2C 136
Lyndhurst Rd. Hoy —2F 91
Lyndhurst Rd. Moss H —5F 101
Lyndhurst Rd. Wall —5F 51
Lyndon Dri. L18 —5B 102
Lyndon Gro. Run —2B 166
Lyndor Clo. L25 —3B 126
Lyndor Rd. L25 —3B 126
Lyneham. Whis —4F 85
Lynholme Rd. L4 —4B 56
Lynmouth Rd. L17 —4E 123
Lynnbank. Pren —5B 96
Lynnbank Rd. L18 —4D 103
Lynn Clo. St H —4C 44
Lynn Clo. Run —3C 166
Lynscot Pl. L16 —1D 103
Lynsted Rd. L14 —3F 81
Lynton Clo. L19 —4B 124
Lynton Clo. Wir —4B 158
Lynton Ct. L23 —1B 16
Lynton Cres. Wid —2E 131
Lynton Dri. Wir —4A 142
Lynton Grn. L25 —5F 103
Lynton Gro. Sut L —1C 88
Lynton Rd. L36 —3B 84
Lynton Rd. Wall —5E 51
Lynton Way. Wind —2B 44
Lynwood Av. Wall —3A 74
Lynwood Dri. Wir —1E 137
Lynwood Gdns. L9 —3F 35
Lynwood Rd. L9 —3F 35
Lynxway, The. L12 —2D 81
Lyon Clo. St H —5F 45
Lyon Rd. L4 —5B 56
Lyons Clo. Wir —5E 71
Lyons Rd. Wir —5E 71
Lyon St. L19 —3C 144
Lyon St. St H —5E 45
Lyra Rd. L22 —4D 17
Lyster Rd. Boot —5A 34
Lytham Clo. L10 —4F 21
Lytham Clo. L12 —5E 59
Lytham Ct. L32 —1C 22
Lytham Rd. Wid —2B 132
Lyttelton Rd. L17 —2E 123
Lytton Av. Birk —3F 119
Lytton Gro. L21 —2A 34
Lytton St. L6 —3F 77

Mab La. L12 —3F 59
MacAlpine Clo. Wir —3A 94
Macbeth St. L20 —2C 54
McBride St. L19 —1C 144
McClellan Pl. Wid —3B 132
McCormack Av. St H —4E 47
McCulloch St. St H —5C 46
Macdermot Rd. Wid —2F 151
MacDona Dri. Wir —1B 134
Macdonald Av. St H —3E 47
Macdonald Dri. Wir —1D 115
Macdonald Rd. Wir —1C 92
MacDonald St. L15 —1E 101
Mace Rd. L11 —5C 38
McFarlane Av. St H —4C 44
Macfarren St. L13 —3A 80
McGoldrick Pk. —5F 83
McGough Clo. Sut M —3A 88
McGregor St. L5 —1E 77
MacKenzie Rd. Wir —3B 72
McKeown Clo. L5 —1D 77
Mackets Clo. L25 —3C 126
Macket's La. L25 —2C 126
Mack Gro. Boot —3D 19
McMinnis Av. St H —1A 68
McNair Hall. L18 —1F 123
MacQueen St. L13 —4A 80
McVinnie Rd. Prsct —5F 63
Maddock Rd. Wall —1D 75
Maddocks St. L13 —4A 80
Maddock St. Birk —1C 96
Maddrell St. L3 —2B 76
Madeira Dri. L25 —3B 104
Madelaine St. L8 —3A 100
Madeleine McKenna Ct. Wid —1B 130
Madeley Clo. Wir —5B 112
Madeley Dri. Wir —5B 112
Madeley St. L6 —2C 78
Madryn Av. L33 —3A 24
Madryn St. L8 —4A 100
Maelor Clo. Wir —4C 162
Mafeking Clo. L15 —1F 101
Magazine Av. Wall —4B 52
Magazine Brow. Wall —4C 52
Magazine La. Wall —4B 52
Magazine Rd. Wir —4D 143
Magazines Promenade. Wall —3C 52
Magdala St. L8 —2B 100
Magdalen Ho. Boot —1C 54
Magdalen Sq. Boot —1F 19
Maghull. —5D 7
Maghull La. L31 —1B 14
(in two parts)
Maghull Smallholdings Est. L31 —4F 7
Maghull St. L1 —7D 4
Magnolia Clo. L26 —2D 127
Magnolia Clo. Hay —3F 47
Magnolia Dri. Beech —1F 173
Magnolia Wlk. Wir —2C 114
Magnum St. L5 —1F 77
Maguire Av. Boot —4E 35
Mahon Av. Boot —2D 35
Mahon Ct. L8 —2F 99
Maiden La. L13 —4D 57
Maidford Rd. L14 —1E 81
Main Av. St H —3C 64
Main Clo. Hay —2A 48
Main Dri. Hals P —5D 85
Main Front. Hals P —5E 85
Main Rd. Wir —3B 142
Mainside Rd. L32 —4F 23
Main St. Bil —1D 31
Main St. Frod —5A 172
Main St. Halt —1F 167
Maintree Cres. L24 —3A 148
Mainwaring Rd. Wall —3D 75
Mainwaring Rd. Wir —2D 163
Maitland Clo. L8 —2B 100
Maitland Rd. Wall —3C 52
Maitland St. L8 —2B 100
Major Cross St. Wid —5A 132
Major St. L5 —5D 55
Makepeace Wlk. L8 —3F 99
Makin St. L4 —1F 55
Malcolm Cres. Wir —4C 162
Malcolm Gro. L20 —2D 55
Malcolm Pl. L15 —5F 79
Malcolm St. Run —5B 152
Malden Rd. L6 —3B 78
Maldon Clo. L26 —1F 147
Maldwyn Rd. Wall —1B 74
Maley Clo. L8 —5A 100
Malhamdale Av. Rain —4D 87
Malin Clo. Hale V —5D 149
Mallaby St. Birk —1A 96
Mallard Clo. W Der —5F 39
Mallard Clo. Beech —5F 167
Mallard Clo. Halew —3E 127
Mallard Gdns. St H —5E 65
Mallard Ho. L31 —3B 6
Mallard Way. St H —2B 46
Mallard Way. Wir —5C 70
Malleson Rd. L13 —4E 57
Mallins Clo. L8 —5A 100
Mallory Av. L31 —3B 6
Mallory Gro. St H —2D 47
Mallory Rd. Birk —2C 118
Mallowdale Clo. Wir —5E 163
Mallow Rd. L6 —3C 78
Mallow Way. L36 —1F 105
Mall, The. L5 —1A 78
Malmesbury Clo. Wir —5C 92
Malmesbury Pk. Run —5D 155
Malmesbury Rd. L11 —1D 57
Malpas Av. Pren —2A 118
Malpas Dri. Wir —5E 119
Malpas Gro. Wall —5A 52
Malpas Rd. L11 —3D 39
Malpas Rd. Run —3B 166
Malpas Rd. Wall —5F 51
Malta Clo. L36 —3D 83
Malta St. L8 —4F 99
Malta Wlk. L8 —4F 99
Malt Ho. Ct. Wind —2C 44
Malton Clo. Wid —4C 108
Malton Rd. L25 —3B 126
Malt St. L7 —1B 100
Malvern Av. L14 —4F 81

Malvern Clo. *Kirkby* —1C **22**
Malvern Clo. *L6* —4D **57**
Malvern Cres. *L14* —4F **81**
Malvern Gro. *L10* —3C **20**
Malvern Gro. *Birk* —2D **119**
Malvern Rd. *Boot* —3C **34**
Malvern Rd. *L6* —3C **78**
Malvern Rd. *St H* —5F **47**
Malvern Rd. *Wall* —1D **73**
Malwood St. *L8* —5F **99**
Manchester Rd. *Prsct* —5C **62**
Manchester St. *L1* —4D **77** (4E **5**)
Mandela Ct. *L8* —4B **100**
Mandeville St. *L4* —1F **55**
Manesty's La. *L1* —5D **77** (6E **4**)
Manfred St. *Ersk* —4F **77**
Manhattan Sq. *L9* —5B **20**
Manica Cres. *L10* —1F **37**
Manion Av. *L31* —2B **6**
Manion Clo. *L31* —2B **6**
Manley Clo. *Pren* —1F **117**
Manley Pl. *St H* —4E **65**
Manley Rd. *Wat* —3C **16**
Manley Rd. *Huy* —1A **106**
Mannering Ct. *L17* —5C **100**
Mannering Rd. *L17* —5B **100**
Manners La. *Wir* —4E **157**
Manningham Rd. *L4* —5B **56**
Manning St. *St H* —5F **45**
Mannington Clo. *Wir* —3E **91**
Mann Island. *L3* —5B **76** (6B **4**)
Mann St. *L8* —3D **99**
Manor Av. *L23* —5D **9**
Manor Av. *Newt W* —4F **49**
Manor Av. *Rain* —4C **86**
Manorbier Cres. *L9* —5A **36**
Manor Clo. *Boot* —1E **55**
Manor Clo. *L12* —5D **39**
Manor Ct. *Sut L* —2D **89**
Manor Cres. *L25* —3B **126**
Manor Dri. *Boot* —2B **20**
Manor Dri. *L23* —5D **9**
Manor Dri. *Wir* —2F **93**
Mnr. Farm Rd. *L36* —5F **83**
Mnr. Farm Rd. *Run* —3D **155**
Manor Fell. *Run* —3B **168**
Manor Green. —2C 94
Manor Gro. *L32* —3B **22**
Manor Hill. *Pren* —3A **96**
Manor Ho. *L17* —1B **122**
Manor Ho. Clo. *L31* —1C **12**
Manor Ho. Clo. *St H* —4A **30**
Manor Ho. Flats. *Wir* —1D **163**
Manor Ho., The. *Wir* —2F **93**
Manor La. *Birk* —2A **120**
Manor La. *Wall* —1C **74**
Manor M. *Wall* —1C **74**
Mnr. Park Av. *Mnr P* —3C **154**
Manor Pk. Bus. Pk. *Mnr P* —3B **154**
Manor Pl. *Wid* —3B **130**
Manor Pl. *Wir* —2D **143**
Manor Rd. *Cros* —4C **8**
Manor Rd. *East* —4D **163**
Manor Rd. *Frod* —4C **172**
Manor Rd. *Hay* —1F **49**
Manor Rd. *Hoy* —3C **90**
Manor Rd. *Irby* —1D **137**
Manor Rd. *Run* —5D **153**
Manor Rd. *Thor H* —1F **159**
Manor Rd. *Wall* —1B **74**
Manor Rd. *Wid* —3B **130**
Manor Rd. *Wltn* —3B **126**
Manorside Clo. *Wir* —3F **93**
Manor St. *St H* —1C **66**
Manor Vw. *L12* —2F **59**
Manor Way. *L25* —3B **126**
Manor Way. *Pren* —2C **94**
Manorwood Dri. *Whis* —4E **85**
Mansell Clo. *Wid* —4B **110**
Mansell Dri. *L26* —1E **147**
Mansell Rd. *L6* —3B **78**
Mansfield St. *L3* —3E **77** (2G **5**)
Mansion Dri. *L11* —4B **38**
Manton Rd. *L6* —3C **78**
Manvers Rd. *L16* —1E **103**
Manville Rd. *Wall* —4B **52**
Manville St. *St H* —2C **66**
Maori Dri. *Frod* —5A **172**
Maple Av. *Hay* —1B **48**
Maple Av. *Run* —2C **166**
Maple Av. *Sut W* —1A **174**
Maple Av. *Wid* —3B **132**
Maple Clo. *S'frth* —2A **34**
Maple Clo. *W Der* —5D **39**
Maple Clo. *Whis* —3E **85**
Maple Cres. *L36* —4D **83**
Mapledale Rd. *L18* —4A **102**
Maple Gro. *L8* —3C **100**
Maple Gro. *St H* —5C **44**
Maple Gro. *Brom* —2C **162**
Maple Gro. *Prsct* —1E **85**
Maples Ct. *Pren* —1A **118**
Maple St. *Birk* —4D **97**
Mapleton Clo. *Pren* —3E **117**
Mapleton Dri. *Sut W* —2F **173**
Maple Towers. *L33* —2F **23**
Maple Tree Gro. *Wir* —1C **158**
Maplewood. *L32* —5F **23**
Maplewood Clo. *N'ley* —4E **105**
Maplewood Gro. *Pren* —1E **95**
Marathon Clo. *L6* —2F **77**
Marble Clo. *Boot* —1C **54**
Marbury Rd. *L32* —3C **22**
Marc Av. *L31* —1B **22**
Marcham Way. *L11* —2B **58**
Marchfield Rd. *L9* —3F **35**
March Rd. *L6* —1D **79**
Marchwood Way. *L25* —2A **104**
Marcien Way. *Wid* —1E **131**
Marcot Rd. *L6* —2D **79**
Marcus Ct. *L36* —2A **84**
Marcus St. *Birk* —2D **97**
Mardale Av. *St H* —5B **30**
Mardale Clo. *L27* —5A **106**
Mardale Lawn. *L27* —1A **128**
Mardale Rd. *L27* —1A **128**
Mardale Rd. *Huy* —1C **82**
Mardale Wlk. *Huy* —1C **82**
Mardale Wlk. *N'ley* —5A **106**
Mareth Clo. *L18* —2A **124**
Marford Rd. *L12* —4B **58**
Marfords Av. *Wir* —3C **162**
Margaret Av. *Boot* —2C **34**
Margaret Av. *St H* —4C **66**
Margaret Ct. *St H* —2D **65**
Margaret Ct. *Wid* —5B **132**
Margaret Rd. *Cros* —5A **8**
Margaret Rd. *Walt* —1E **55**
Margaret St. *Clo F* —3E **89**
Margaret St. *L6* —2A **78**
Margery Rd. *St H* —2C **64**
Marian Av. *Newt W* —5F **49**
Marian Clo. *Rain* —4C **86**
Marian Clo., The. *Boot* —1E **19**
Marian Dri. *Rain* —4B **86**
Marian Dri. *Wir* —1E **93**
Marian Rd. *Hay* —1E **49**
Marian Sq. *Boot* —2F **19**
Marian Way, The. *Boot* —1E **19**
Maria Rd. *L9* —5F **35**
Marie Curie Av. *Boot* —1F **19**
(in two parts)
Marigold Way. *St H* —4A **68**
Marina. —5C 16
Marina Av. *L21* —1B **34**
Marina Av. *St H* —4C **66**
Marina Cres. *Boot* —4A **20**
Marina Cres. *L36* —5D **83**
Marina Gro. *Run* —5B **152**
Marina La. *Pres B* —3E **169**
(in two parts)
Marina Village. *Pres B* —3E **169**
Marine Cres. *L22* —4D **17**
Marine Dri. *Wir* —3D **157**
Marine Lake. —2B 52
Marine Pk. *Wir* —2B **112**
Marine Pk. Mans. *Wall* —2B **52**
Marine Promenade. *Wall* —2B **52**
Marine Rd. *Wir* —4A **90**
Mariners Clo. *Murd* —4D **169**
Mariners Pde. *L1* —5C **76** (7D **4**)
Mariners Pk. Wall —1D 75
(off Cunard Av.)
Mariners Rd. *L23* —3B **16**
Mariners Rd. *Wall* —4C **52**
Mariners Wharf. *L3* —3C **98**
Marines Way. *Boot* —4C **34**
Marine Ter. *L22* —5D **17**
Marine Ter. *Wall* —4C **52**
Marion Dri. *West* —4F **165**
Marion Gro. *L18* —2B **124**
Marion Rd. *Boot* —2D **35**
Marion St. *Birk* —3E **97**
Maritime Ct. *Boot* —5F **11**
Maritime Ct. *L12* —3A **58**
Maritime Ct. *Wir* —3B **116**
Maritime Enterprise Cen. *Boot* —4B **34**
Maritime Grange. *Wall* —4E **75**
Maritime Gro. *Pren* —4B **96**
Maritime Pk. *Pren* —4C **96**
Maritime Pl. *L3* —3E **77** (2H **5**)
Maritime Vw. *Birk* —1D **119**
Maritime Way. *L1* —1D **99** (7E **4**)
Marius Clo. *L4* —3F **55**
Market Pl. *Prsct* —5D **63**
Market Pl. *Wid* —5A **132**
Market Pl. S. *Birk* —3E **97**
Market Sq. *L1* —5F **5**
Market Sq. L32 —3E 23
(off St Chads Pde.)
Market St. *Newt W* —4F **49**
Market St. *St H* —5A **46**
Market St. *Birk* —3E **97**
Market St. *Wid* —5A **132**
Market St. *Wir* —5B **90**
Market Way. *L1* —5F **5**
Markfield Cres. *L25* —3C **126**
Markfield Cres. *St H* —3C **46**
Markfield Rd. *Boot* —3B **34**
Mark Rake. *Brom & Wir* —1D **163**
Mark St. *L5* —4E **55**
Mark St. *Wall* —4E **75**
Marksway. *Wir* —3A **138**
Marlborough Av. *Boot* —3A **20**
Marlborough Av. *L31* —4D **7**
Marlborough Cres. *Wid* —4A **110**
Marlborough Gro. *Pren* —5B **96**
Marlborough Pl. *L3* —3C **76** (2D **4**)
Marlborough Rd. *Cros* —2D **17**
Marlborough Rd. *Wat* —5E **17**
Marlborough Rd. *Prsct* —4E **63**
Marlborough Rd. *Tue* —5D **57**
Marlborough Rd. *Wall* —4B **52**
Marlborough St. *L3* —3C **76** (2D **4**)
Marlbrook Rd. *L25* —3B **104**
Marldon Av. *L23* —3E **17**
Marldon Rd. *L12* —3A **58**
Marled Hey. *L28* —3A **60**
Marley Clo. *Rain* —5E **87**
Marlfield La. *Wir* —3A **138**
Marlfield Rd. *L12* —5B **58**
Marline Av. *Wir* —3C **162**
Marling Pk. *Wid* —3B **130**
Marlowe Clo. *L19* —2C **144**
Marlowe Clo. *Wid* —3F **131**
Marlowe Dri. *L12* —5F **57**
Marlowe Rd. *Wall* —2A **74**

Marl Rd. *Boot* —2B **20**
Marl Rd. *Know I* —2C **24**
Marlsford St. *L6* —3C **78**
Marlston Av. *Wir* —2F **137**
Marlston Pl. *Run* —4B **166**
Marlwood Av. *Wall* —1E **73**
Marmaduke St. *L7* —5B **78**
Marmion Av. *Boot* —1E **35**
Marmion Rd. *L17* —5B **100**
Marmion Rd. *Wir* —4B **90**
Marmonde St. *L4* —3E **55**
Marnwood Rd. *L32* —4C **22**
Marnwood Wlk. *L32* —4C **22**
Marple Clo. *Pren* —1E **117**
Marquis Ho. *Wir* —4B **120**
Marquis St. *L3* —4E **77** (4H **5**)
Marquis St. *Birk* —5E **97**
Marquis St. *Wir* —4B **120**
Marram Clo. *Wir* —5A **72**
Marsden Av. *St H* —4C **44**
Marsden Clo. *Wall* —1D **75**
Marsden Rd. *L26* —1F **147**
Marsden St. *L6* —3A **78**
Marsden Way. *L6* —3A **78**
Marshall Av. *St H* —3C **66**
Marshall Clo. *Kirkby* —5F **15**
Marshall Pl. *L3* —2C **76** (1E **4**)
Marshall's Clo. *Lyd* —3C **6**
Marshall's Cross. —5B 66
Marshall's Cross Rd. *St H* —5B **66**
Marshall St. *Birk* —1C **96**
Marsham Clo. *Wir* —2A **94**
Marsham Rd. *L25* —4C **104**
Marsh Av. *Boot* —2E **35**
Marshfield Clo. *L36* —3F **83**
Marshfield Ct. *Wir* —3E **71**
Marshfield Rd. *L11* —2B **58**
Marshgate. *Wid* —5B **130**
Marshgate Pl. *Frod* —3C **172**
Marshgate Rd. *L12* —1B **58**
Marsh Green. —5A 172
Marsh Hall Pad. *Wid* —5B **110**
Marsh Hall Rd. *Wid* —5B **110**
Marshlands Rd. *Wall* —5E **51**
Marsh La. *Boot* —4A **34**
Marsh La. *Ast* —4F **153**
Marsh La. *Frod* —5A **172**
Marsh La. *Wir* —5C **118**
Marshside Clo. *L8* —4F **99**
Marsh St. *Kirk* —2D **55**
Marsh St. *St H* —4C **46**
Marsh St. *Wid* —1A **152**
Marsh, The. —2E 151
Marsland Gro. *St H* —3E **67**
Marston Clo. *Pren* —1F **117**
Marston Clo. *Wir* —2E **171**
Marston Cres. *L38* —1A **8**
Marten Av. *Wir* —3C **162**
Martensen St. *L7* —5B **78**
Martin Av. *St H* —2F **45**
Martin Clo. *L18* —3A **124**
Martin Clo. *Pal* —3A **168**
Martin Clo. *Rain* —2A **86**
Martin Clo. *Wir* —1C **136**
Martindale Gro. *Beech* —5E **167**
Martindale Rd. *L18* —4D **103**
Martindale Rd. *St H* —3B **30**
Martindale Rd. *Croft B* —1E **163**
Martine Clo. *L31* —1B **22**
Martin Gro. *Prsct* —1E **85**
Martinhall Rd. *L9* —4F **37**
Martin Rd. *L18* —3A **124**
Martin Rd. *Frod* —5B **172**
Martin's La. *Wall* —2C **74**
Martland Av. *L10* —2E **21**
Martland Rd. *L25* —5C **104**
Martlesham Cres. *Wir* —1B **114**
Martlett Rd. *L12* —1D **81**
Martock. *Whis* —4F **85**
Marton Clo. *L24* —5D **147**
Marton Grn. *L24* —5D **147**
Marton Rd. *L36* —5E **61**
Marvin St. *L6* —3A **78**
Marwood Tower. *L5* —5D **55**
Marybone. *L3* —3C **76** (3D **4**)
Maryfields. *L23* —1E **17**
Maryhill Rd. *Run* —2A **166**
Maryland La. *Wir* —5D **71**
Maryland St. *L1* —1E **99** (7H **5**)
(in two parts)
Marylebone Av. *St H* —5F **65**
Mary Rd. *Boot* —2D **35**
Mary St. *Clo F* —3E **89**
Mary St. *Wid* —5D **133**
Maryton Grange. *L18* —2D **125**
Maryville Rd. *Prsct* —5E **63**
Marywell Clo. *St H* —4D **67**
Masefield Av. *Wid* —4F **131**
Masefield Clo. *Wir* —5A **120**
Masefield Cres. *Boot* —5D **19**
Masefield Gro. *L16* —1E **103**
Masefield Gro. *Dent G* —3D **45**
Masefield Pl. *Boot* —5D **19**
Masefield Rd. *L23* —4C **10**
Maskell Rd. *L13* —3F **79**
Mason Av. *Wid* —5A **110**
Mason St. *Wat* —4D **17**
Mason St. *Edg H* —5A **78**
Mason St. *Run* —4C **152**
Mason St. *Wall* —3B **52**
Mason St. *Wltn* —2A **126**
Masseyfield Rd. *Brook* —5A **168**
Massey Pk. *Wall* —1A **74**
Massey St. *St H* —3C **66**
Massey St. *Birk* —1D **97**
Master's Way. *L19* —3D **145**
Mather Av. *L18 & L19* —5B **102**
Mather Av. *St H* —5E **47**
Mather Av. *West P* —3D **165**
Mather Rd. *Pren* —4B **96**
Mathew St. *L2* —5C **76** (5D **4**)
Mathieson Rd. *Wid* —2E **151**
Matlock Av. *L9* —2A **36**
Matterdale Clo. *Frod* —5D **173**
Matthew Clo. *Wall* —4E **75**
Matthew St. *Wall* —4E **75**
Maud St. *L8* —3F **99**
Maunders Ct. *L23* —5A **10**
Maureen Wlk. *L10* —1B **38**
Mauretania Rd. *L4* —1A **56**
Maurice Jones Ct. *Wir* —5E **71**
Mavis Dri. *Wir* —1A **116**
Max Rd. *L14* —1F **81**
Maxton Rd. *L6* —3C **78**
Maxwell Clo. *Wir* —3A **94**
Maxwell Pl. *L13* —5F **57**
Maxwell Rd. *L13* —5F **57**
Maxwell St. *St H* —5E **45**
May Av. *Wall* —3D **75**
Maybank Gro. *L17* —3F **123**
Maybank Rd. *Birk* —5D **97**
Maybury Way. *L17* —2C **122**
May Clo. *L21* —2B **34**
Mayer Av. *Wir* —3F **141**
Mayew Rd. *Wir* —1F **137**
Mayfair Av. *Cros* —5E **9**
Mayfair Av. *Bow P* —3F **81**
Mayfair Clo. *Form* —1A **8**
Mayfair Clo. *Anf* —2B **78**
Mayfair Gro. *Wid* —3D **131**
Mayfayre Av. *L31* —2C **6**
Mayfield Av. *St H* —3E **65**
Mayfield Av. *Wid* —3B **130**
Mayfield Clo. *L12* —5C **58**
Mayfield Gdns. *L19* —5F **123**
Mayfield Rd. *L19* —5A **124**
Mayfield Rd. *Wall* —1F **73**
Mayfield Rd. *Wir* —4A **142**
Mayfields. *L4* —3E **55**
Mayfields Ho. *Wir* —5B **120**
Mayfields N. *Wir* —5B **120**
Mayfields S. *Wir* —5B **120**
Mayford Clo. *L25* —3B **104**
Maynard St. *L8* —2B **100**
May Pl. *L3* —5E **77** (6H **5**)
Maypole Ct. *Boot* —5D **11**
May Rd. *Wir* —2A **158**
May St. *Boot* —3C **34**
May St. *L3* —5E **77** (6H **5**)
Maytree Clo. *L27* —2C **104**
Mayville Rd. *L18* —4A **102**
Mazenod Ct. *L3* —3C **76** (2D **4**)
Mazzini Clo. *L5* —1E **77**
Mead Av. *L21* —5C **18**
Meade Clo. *Rain* —5D **87**
Meade Rd. *L13* —5E **57**
Meadfoot Rd. *Wir* —5D **71**
Meadow Av. *Clo F* —3D **89**
Meadow Bank. *L31* —5B **6**
(Airegate)
Meadow Bank. *L31* —1B **22**
(Beldale Pk.)
Meadowbank Clo. *L12* —1E **81**
Mdw. Brook Clo. *L10* —1B **38**
Meadowbrook Rd. *Wir* —2D **93**
Meadow Clo. *Newt W* —5F **49**
Meadow Clo. *Wid* —1D **131**
Meadow Ct. *L25* —1B **126**
Meadow Cres. *Wir* —2B **116**
Meadowcroft. *St H* —5C **66**
Meadow Cft. *Hes* —1C **158**
Meadowcroft Pk. *L12* —2D **81**
Meadowcroft Rd. *Wir* —2E **91**
Meadow Dri. *L36* —1F **105**
Meadowfield Clo. *L9* —1A **36**
Meadowfield Clo. *Birk* —2F **119**
Meadowgate. *Wir* —4D **135**
Meadow Hey. *Boot* —3A **34**
Mdw. Hey Clo. *L25* —1B **126**
Meadow La. *Mag* —1E **13**
Meadow La. *St H* —1F **67**
Meadow La. *W Der* —2B **58**
Meadow La. *Birk* —2F **119**
Mdw. Oak Dri. *L25* —4A **104**
Meadow Pk. *Birk* —2F **119**
Meadow Rd. *Wir* —4F **113**
Meadow Row. *Cas* —1A **168**
Meadowside. *Wir* —2B **72**
Meadowside Dri. *L33* —5F **15**
Meadowside Rd. *Wir* —3D **163**
Meadows, The. *Rain* —3C **86**
Meadow St. *Wall* —3A **52**
Meadow, The. *Wir* —2B **116**
(in two parts)
Meadow Vw. *L21* —2B **18**
Meadow Wlk. *Wir* —4E **137**
Meadow Way. *L12* —2B **58**
Meadway. *Boot* —3F **19**
Meadway. *Mag* —3B **12**
Meadway. *Halt B* —1E **167**
Meadway. *Hes* —4F **157**
Meadway. *Spit* —5C **142**
Meadway. *Upt* —3B **94**
Meadway. *Wall* —1A **74**
Meadway. *W'tree* —1C **102**
Meadway. *Whis* —2F **85**
Meadway. *Wid* —3A **130**
Meander, The. *L12* —2E **59**
Measham Clo. *St H* —3C **46**
Measham Way. *L12* —4E **39**
Medbourne Cres. *L32* —5F **23**
Meddowcroft Rd. *Wall* —5F **51**
Medea Clo. *L5* —5E **55**
Medea Towers. *L5* —5E **55**
Medlock St. *L4* —3E **55**
Medway. *Boot* —4C **34**
Medway Rd. *Birk* —2F **119**

Melbourne Clo. *L24* —3B **146**
Melbourne St. *That H* —4E **65**
Melbourne St. *Wall* —3A **52**
Melbreck Rd. *L18* —3B **124**
Melbury Rd. *L14* —5B **60**
Melda Clo. *L6* —3F **77**
Meldon Clo. *L12* —1C **58**
Meldrum Rd. *L15* —3B **102**
Melford Dri. *Pren* —3E **117**
Melford Dri. *Run* —1C **166**
Melford Gro. *L6* —5C **56**
Meliden Gdns. *St H* —4F **67**
Meliden Gdns. *Birk* —5E **97**
Melksham Dri. *Wir* —5D **115**
Melling. —5F 13
Melling Av. *L9* —1B **36**
Melling Dri. *L32* —2E **23**
Melling La. *L31* —3E **13**
Melling Mount. —3C 14
Melling Rd. *Boot* —3C **34**
Melling Rd. *L9* —5B **20**
Melling Rd. *Wall* —4C **52**
Melling Way. *L32* —2E **23**
Melloncroft Dri. *Wir* —1C **134**
Melloncroft Dri. W. *Wir* —2C **134**
Mellor Clo. *Tarb G* —2A **106**
Mellor Clo. *Wind H* —2D **169**
Mellor Rd. *Birk* —2C **118**
Melly Rd. *L17* —1B **122**
Melrose. *Wir* —1A **94**
Melrose Av. *Ecc* —3B **44**
Melrose Av. *L23* —2E **17**
Melrose Av. *Btnwd* —4F **69**
Melrose Av. *Wir* —4B **90**
Melrose Gdns. *Pren* —3F **117**
Melrose Rd. *Kirk* —3D **55**
Melrose Rd. *Kirkby* —4D **15**
Melrose Rd. *Wat* —5E **17**
Melton Clo. *Wir* —4E **93**
Melton Rd. *Run* —3B **166**
Melverley Rd. *L32* —3B **22**
Melville Av. *Birk* —3A **120**
Melville Clo. *St H* —4C **44**
Melville Clo. *Wid* —3D **133**
(in two parts)
Melville Pl. *L7* —1A **100**
Melville Rd. *Boot* —1C **34**
Melville Rd. *Wir* —2E **141**
Melville St. *L8* —4F **99**
Melwood. —4C 58
(Liverpool F.C. Sports Ground)
Melwood Dri. *L12* —4C **58**
Menai Rd. *Boot* —2D **35**
Menai St. *Birk* —3C **96**
Mendell Clo. *Wir* —2E **163**
Mendip Clo. *L26* —5E **127**
Mendip Clo. *Birk* —3C **118**
Mendip Gro. *St H* —5F **47**
Mendip Rd. *L15* —3A **102**
Mendip Rd. *Birk* —3C **118**
Menlo Av. *Wir* —1F **137**
Menlo Clo. *Pren* —5F **95**
Menlove Av. *L18 & L25* —4A **102**
Menlove Ct. *L18* —4B **102**
Menlove Gdns. N. *L18* —4B **102**
Menlove Gdns. S. *L18* —4B **102**
Menlove Gdns. W. *L18* —4B **102**
Menlove Mans. *L18* —3C **102**
Menstone Rd. *L13* —2F **79**
Mentmore Cres. *L11* —2B **58**
Mentmore Rd. *L18* —2F **123**
Meols. —3E 91
Meol's Clo. *Hale V* —5E **149**
Meols Dri. *W Kir & Hoy* —2A **112**
Meols Pde. *Wir* —3C **90**
Mercer Av. *L32* —3C **22**
*Mercer Ct. Boot —5C **34***
(off Clairville Clo.)
Mercer Ct. *W Der* —5E **59**
Mercer Dri. *L4* —4E **55**
Mercer Heights. *L32* —4C **22**
Mercer Rd. *Hay* —2C **48**
Mercer Rd. *Pren* —1E **95**
Mercer St. *L19* —2C **144**
Mercer St. *Btnwd* —5E **69**
Merchant Clo. *Boot* —5B **20**
Merchants Ho. *L1* —6D **4**
Mere Av. *Wir* —4B **162**
Mere Bank. *L17* —4E **101**
Merebank. *Pren* —5E **95**
Merebrook Gro. *L33* —5F **15**
Merecliff. *L28* —3C **60**
Merecroft Av. *Wall* —4C **74**
Meredale Rd. *L18* —5A **102**
Meredith St. *L19* —2E **145**
Mere Farm Gro. *Pren* —5F **95**
Mere Farm Rd. *Pren* —5E **95**
Mere Grn. *L4* —2A **56**
Mere Gro. *St H* —4B **30**
Mereheath. *Wir* —3E **71**
*Mereheath Gdns. Wir —3E **71***
(off Mereheath)
Mere Hey. *Ecc* —5A **44**
Mereland Way. *St H* —1F **67**
Mere La. *L5* —5F **55**
Mere La. *Wall* —4E **51**
Mere La. *Wir* —5E **137**
Mere Pk. *Cros* —1D **17**
Mere Pk. Rd. *Wir* —1C **114**
Meres Rd. *Faz* —1E **37**
Merevale Clo. *Beech* —4E **167**
Mereview Cres. *L12* —5D **39**
Merewood. *L32* —5F **23**
Mereworth. *Wir* —3D **135**
Meribel Clo. *L23* —5A **10**
Meriden Av. *Wir* —1A **162**
Meriden Clo. *St H* —2D **47**
Meriden Rd. *L25* —3B **104**
Merlin Av. *Wir* —3D **93**
Merlin Clo. *St H* —2B **46**
Merlin Clo. *Cas* —1A **168**
Merlin Clo. *Wir* —3D **93**
Merlin Ct. *L26* —3D **127**
Merlin St. *L8* —3F **99**
Merriford Grn. *L4* —2B **56**
Merrills La. *Wir* —4B **94**
Merrilocks Grn. *L23* —5A **8**
Merrilocks Rd. *L23* —5A **8**
Merrilox Av. *L31* —4D **7**
Merrion Clo. *L25* —1F **125**
Merritt Av. *Birk* —1B **96**
Merrivale Rd. *L25* —2C **126**
Merriwood. *L23* —4B **8**
Mersey Av. *Mag* —5F **7**
Mersey Av. *Aig* —4F **123**
*Merseybank Ho. Wir —4B **120***
(off New Ferry Rd.)
Merseybank Rd. *Wir* —4B **120**
Mersey Ct. *L23* —2C **16**
*Mersey Ct. Wall —4E **75***
(off Borough Rd. E.)
Mersey Ho. *Boot* —4B **34**
Mersey La. S. *Birk* —2A **120**
Mersey Mt. *Birk* —1E **119**
Mersey Pk. —1E 119
Mersey Rd. *Cros* —2C **16**
Mersey Rd. *Aig* —4E **123**
Mersey Rd. *Birk* —2A **120**
Mersey Rd. *Run* —4A **152**
Mersey Rd. *Wid* —3A **152**
Merseyside Ho. *L1* —5D **4**
Merseyside Maritime Mus. —1C 98 (7C 4)
Merseyside Welcome Cen. —5D 77
(off Clayton Sq.)
Merseyside Young Peoples Theatre. —5F 77 (6J 5)
Mersey St. *St H* —5A **48**
Mersey St. *Wall* —4E **75**
Mersey Tunnel. *L3* —3A **76** (1A **4**)
Mersey Valley Golf Course. —2F 111
Mersey Vw. *L19* —1C **144**
Mersey Vw. *Wat* —3C **16**
Mersey Vw. *West* —4F **165**
Mersey Vw. *West P* —2D **165**
Mersey Vw. *Wid* —3A **152**
Mersey Vw. *Wir* —1D **141**
Mersey Vw. Cotts. *West* —4F **165**
Mersey Vw. Rd. *Wid* —3B **150**
Mersham Ct. *Wid* —5F **109**
Merstone Clo. *L26* —5F **127**
Merthyr Gro. *L16* —5E **81**
Merton Bank Rd. *St H* —3C **46**
Merton Clo. *L36* —4B **82**
Merton Cres. *L36* —4B **82**
Merton Dri. *L36* —4A **82**
Merton Dri. *Wir* —1A **116**
Merton Gro. *Boot* —5C **34**
Merton Gro. *L23* —2C **16**
Merton Ho. *Boot* —5C **34**
Merton Pl. *Pren* —3C **96**
Merton Rd. *Boot* —5C **34**
Merton Rd. *Wall* —1A **74**
Merton St. *St H* —3C **46**
Merton Towers. *Boot* —5D **35**
Mesham Clo. *Wir* —4E **93**
Methuen St. *L15* —1E **101**
Methuen St. *Birk* —1A **96**
Mevagissey Rd. *Brook* —5C **168**
Mews Ct. *L28* —3B **60**
Mews Ct. *Will* —5A **170**
Mews, The. *L28* —4C **60**
Mews, The. *Aig* —3F **123**
Meyrick Rd. *L11* —1E **57**
Micawber Clo. *L8* —4F **99**
Michael Dragonette Ct. *L3* —2C **76**
Micklefield Rd. *L15* —3F **101**
Micklegate. *Murd* —3D **169**
Micklehead Green. —3A 88
Middlefield Rd. *L18* —1E **125**
Middleham Clo. *L32* —4C **22**
Middlehey Av. *Know* —4D **41**
Middlehurst Av. *St H* —4F **45**
Middlehurst Clo. *Ecc P* —4A **64**
Middlemass Hey. *L27* —4E **105**
Middle Rd. *L24* —2F **147**
(in two parts)
Middle Rd. *Wir* —1B **142**
Middlesex Rd. *Boot* —4D **35**
Middleton Rd. *Wat* —3F **17**
Middleton Rd. *Fair* —4E **79**
Middle Way. *L11* —4D **39**
Middlewood. *L32* —5F **23**
Midghall St. *L3* —3C **76** (2D **4**)
Midhurst Rd. *L12* —5F **39**
Midland St. *Pren* —4C **96**
Midland St. *Wid* —3B **132**
Midland Ter. *L22* —4D **17**
Midlothian Dri. *L23* —1C **16**
Midway Rd. *L36* —2E **83**
Milbrook Cres. *L32* —2E **23**
Milbrook Dri. *L32* —2E **23**
Milbrook Wlk. *L32* —2E **23**
Mildenhall Rd. *L25* —3A **104**
Mildenhall Way. *L25* —2A **104**
Mildmay Rd. *Boot* —3B **34**
Mildmay Rd. *L11* —1E **57**
Mile End. *L5* —2D **77**
Miles Clo. *Wir* —2C **114**
Miles La. *Wir* —2C **114**
Miles St. *L8* —4A **100**
Milestone Hey. *L28* —3B **60**
Milford Dri. *L12* —5E **39**
Milford St. *L5* —5B **54**
Milk St. *St H* —5A **46**
Millachip Ct. *L6* —1B **78**
Milland Clo. *L11* —5C **38**

Millar Cres. *Wid* —5A **132**
Mill Bank. *L13* —5F **57**
Millbank Cotts. *L31* —4E **7**
Millbank Cotts. *Frod* —5A **172**
Millbank Ct. *L9* —5D **21**
Millbank Ct. *Frod* —5A **172**
Millbank La. *L31* —4F **7**
Mill Bank Rd. *Wall* —3A **74**
Millbeck Gro. *St H* —3B **30**
Millbrook Bus. Pk. *Rainf* —2C **28**
Millbrook La. *Ecc* —4B **44**
Mill Brow. *Ecc* —4B **44**
Mill Brow. *St H* —1D **89**
Mill Brow. *Wid* —2C **132**
Mill Brow. *Wir* —1D **141**
Mill Brow Clo. *St H* —1D **89**
Millburn Heights. *L5* —1E **77**
Millbutt Clo. *Wir* —1D **141**
Mill Clo. *L23* —4E **9**
Mill Clo. *Birk* —5D **97**
Mill Ct. *Boot* —5D **11**
Millcroft. *L23* —5A **10**
Millcroft Rd. *L25* —3C **126**
Miller Av. *L23* —5D **9**
Millers Bri. *Boot* —1B **54**
Millers Bri. Ind. Est. *Mil B* —1B **54**
Millers Clo. *Wir* —1B **92**
Millerscroft. *L32* —2C **22**
Millersdale. *Clo F* —2C **88**
Millersdale Av. *L9* —1B **36**
Millersdale Clo. *Wir* —5F **163**
Millersdale Gro. *Beech* —4D **167**
Millersdale Rd. *L18* —5A **102**
Millers Fold. *Ecc* —4B **44**
Millers Way. *Wir* —1C **92**
Millfield Clo. *L13* —1A **80**
Millfield Clo. *Wir* —2D **141**
Millfield Rd. *Wid* —2C **132**
Millfields. *Ecc* —5A **44**
Mill Grn. *Will* —5A **170**
Millgreen Clo. *L12* —5E **39**
Mill Grn. La. *Wid* —4D **111**
Mill Gro. *L21* —5B **18**
Mill Hey. *Rain* —5E **87**
Mill Hey Rd. *Wir* —3D **135**
Mill Hill. *Pren* —1A **118**
Mill Hill Rd. *Wir* —4C **114**
Millhouse Clo. *Wir* —5B **70**
Millhouse La. *Wir* —5B **70**
Millington Clo. *Pren* —3E **117**
Millington Clo. *Sut W* —1F **173**
Millington Clo. *Wid* —4F **131**
Mill La. *Boot* —5D **35**
Mill La. *Kirkby* —2C **22**
Mill La. *Know* —3D **41**
Mill La. *L3* —4D **77** (3F **5**)
(in two parts)
Mill La. *Rainf* —2B **28**
Mill La. *St H* —1C **88**
Mill La. *W Der* —5A **58**
Mill La. *Cron* —4D **109**
Mill La. *Frod & K'ley* —3D **173**
Mill La. *Grea* —1C **114**
Mill La. *Hes* —2B **158**
Mill La. *Old S & W'tree* —4A **80**
Mill La. *Rain* —4C **86**
Mill La. *Wall* —3A **74**
Mill La. *Wid* —5C **110**
Mill La. *Will* —4A **170**
Millom Av. *Rain* —2B **86**
Millom Gro. *L12* —2C **58**
Millom Gro. *St H* —3C **64**
Mill Pk. Dri. *Wir* —2E **171**
Mill Rd. *L6* —2F **77**
(in two parts)
Mill Rd. *Brom* —4D **143**
Mill Rd. *High B* —5D **119**
Mill Rd. *Thing* —1B **138**
Mill Spring Ct. *Boot* —5D **35**
Mill Sq. *L10* —3E **21**
Millstead Rd. *L15* —1A **102**
Millstead Wlk. *L15* —1A **102**
Mill Stile. *L25* —2F **125**
Mill St. *L8* —3E **99**
Mill St. *L25* —2A **126**
Mill St. *St H* —4F **45**
Mill St. *Birk* —5D **97**
Mill St. *Prsct* —5D **63**
Mill Ter. *Wir* —2D **141**
Millthwaite Ct. *Wall* —2F **73**
Millthwaite Rd. *Wall* —2F **73**
Millvale St. *L6* —3B **78**
Mill Vw. *Kirkby* —1C **22**
Mill Vw. *L8* —4E **99**
Mill Vw. Dri. *Wir* —1C **140**
Millway Rd. *L24* —3A **148**
Millwood. *Run* —1C **168**
Millwood. *Wir* —1D **141**
Millwood Av. *Ecc* —5F **43**
Millwood Est. *L24* —4A **148**
Millwood Gdns. *Whis* —4F **85**
Millwood Rd. *L24* —3E **147**
Mill Yard. —1D 81
Milman Clo. *Wir* —4F **93**
Milman Ct. *L25* —1E **125**
Milman Rd. *L4* —2F **55**
Milner Cop. *Wir* —2A **158**
Milne Rd. *L13* —3E **57**
Milner Rd. *L17* —3E **123**
Milner Rd. *Wir* —2A **158**
Milner St. *L8* —1B **100**
Milner St. *Birk* —1A **96**
Milnthorpe Clo. *L4* —3E **55**
Milnthorpe Rd. *Btnwd* —5E **69**
Milnthorpe St. *L19* —1C **144**
Milroy St. *L7* —5B **78**
Milton Av. *L14* —4F **81**
Milton Av. *Whis* —3E **85**
Milton Av. *Wid* —4F **131**
Milton Clo. *Whis* —3E **85**
Milton Cres. *Wir* —1A **158**
Milton Grn. *Wir* —1B **138**
Milton Pavement. *Birk* —3D **97**
Milton Rd. *L7* —4E **79**
Milton Rd. *Walt* —1E **55**
Milton Rd. *Wat* —3E **17**
Milton Rd. *Birk* —5C **96**
Milton Rd. *W Kir* —3A **112**
Milton Rd. *Wid* —4F **131**
Milton Rd. E. *Birk* —5D **97**
Milton St. *Boot* —4B **34**
Milton St. *Sut M* —4A **88**
Milton St. *Wid* —2A **152**
Milton Way. *L31* —5B **6**
Milverney Way. *St H* —1A **66**
Milverton St. *L6* —2C **78**
Milwood Ct. *L24* —3A **148**
Mimosa Rd. *L15* —2A **102**
Mindale Rd. *L15* —1F **101**
Minehead Gro. *Sut L* —1D **89**
Minehead Rd. *L17* —3E **123**
Miners Way. *L24* —4A **148**
Miners Way. *Wid* —5A **132**
Mines Av. *L17* —5F **123**
Mine's Av. *Prsct* —5E **63**
Mine Way. *Hay* —1F **49**
Minshull St. *L7* —5A **78**
Minstead Av. *L33* —3F **23**
Minster Ct. *L7* —1A **100**
Minster Ct. *Run* —2E **165**
Minto Clo. *L7* —4B **78**
Minton Clo. *L12* —5F **39**
Minton Way. *Wid* —4B **110**
Mintor Rd. *L33* —3A **24**
Minto St. *L7* —4B **78**
Minver Rd. *L12* —4D **59**
Miranda Av. *Wir* —5E **119**
Miranda Pl. *L20* —2D **55**
Miranda Rd. *L20* —1D **55**
Mirfield Clo. *L26* —1F **147**
Mirfield St. *L6* —3B **78**
Miriam Pl. *Birk* —1F **95**
Miriam Rd. *L4* —5A **56**
Miskelly St. *L20* —3C **54**
Missouri Rd. *L13* —4D **57**
Mistle Thrush Way. *L12* —4F **39**
Miston St. *L20* —3C **54**
Misty Clo. *Wid* —2C **130**
Mitchell Av. *Btnwd* —5E **69**
Mitchell Cres. *L21* —4B **18**
Mitchell Rd. *St H* —2C **64**
Mitchell Rd. *Bil* —1E **31**
Mitchell Rd. *Prsct* —5C **62**
Mithril Clo. *Wid* —1E **133**
Mitre Clo. *Whis* —5D **85**
Mitylene St. *L5* —5E **55**
Mobberley Way. *Wir* —4A **142**
Mockbeggar Dri. *Wall* —4E **51**
Mockbeggar Wharf. *Wall* —4E **51**
Modred St. *L8* —4F **99**
Moel Famau Vw. *L17* —2B **122**
Moffatdale Rd. *L4* —3C **56**
Moffatt Rd. *L9* —1B **36**
Moira St. *L6* —4F **77**
Molesworth Gro. *L16* —5E **81**
Molineux Av. *L14* —5D **81**
Molland Clo. *L12* —3D **59**
Mollington Av. *L11* —1F **57**
Mollington Rd. *L32* —3C **22**
Mollington Rd. *Wall* —3C **74**
Mollington St. *Birk* —4E **97**
Molly's La. *Know* —1D **41**
Molton Rd. *L16* —1C **102**
Molyneux Clo. *L36* —4F **83**
Molyneux Clo. *Prsct* —2D **85**
Molyneux Clo. *Wir* —4F **93**
Molyneux Ct. *L11* —5B **38**
Molyneux Ct. *B'grn* —5D **81**
Molyneux Dri. *Prsct* —2D **85**
Molyneux Dri. *Wall* —3B **52**
Molyneux Rd. *Mag* —3F **13**
Molyneux Rd. *Wat* —3E **17**
Molyneux Rd. *Kens* —3B **78**
Molyneux Rd. *Moss H* —5F **101**
Molyneux Way. *L10* —2C **20**
Monaghan Clo. *L9* —1A **36**
Monash Clo. *L33* —4E **15**
Monash Rd. *L11* —3E **57**
Monastery La. *St H* —4D **67**
Monastery Rd. *L6* —5C **56**
Monastery Rd. *St H* —4E **67**
Mona St. *Boot* —2D **35**
Mona St. *St H* —5D **45**
Mona St. *Birk* —2F **95**
Mond Rd. *L10* —1F **37**
Mond Rd. *Wid* —4A **132**
Monfa Rd. *Boot* —2D **35**
Monica Dri. *Wid* —4A **110**
Monica Rd. *L25* —3B **126**
Monkfield Way. *L19* —3D **145**
Monk Rd. *Wall* —2B **74**
Monksdown Rd. *L11* —2A **58**
Monks Ferry. *Birk* —3F **97**
Monksferry Wlk. *L19* —5F **123**
Monk St. *L5* —5F **55**
Monk St. *Birk* —3F **97**
Monks Way. *L25* —2B **126**
Monks Way. *Beb* —3F **141**
Monks Way. *W Kir* —4C **112**
Monkswell Dri. *L15* —1A **102**
Monkswell St. *L8* —1A **122**
Monmouth Dri. *L10* —4F **21**
Monmouth Gro. *St H* —1D **67**
Monmouth Rd. *Wall* —2F **73**
Monro Clo. *L8* —5F **99**
Monro St. *L8* —5F **99**
Mons Sq. *Boot* —5C **34**

Montague Rd. *Old S* —4A **80**
Montclair Dri. *L18* —3B **102**
Monterey Rd. *L13* —4B **80**
Montfort Dri. *L19* —5A **124**
Montgomery Clo. *Whis* —4D **85**
Montgomery Hill. *Wir* —1F **135**
Montgomery Rd. *Walt* —1A **36**
Montgomery Rd. *Huy* —2D **83**
Montgomery Rd. *Wid* —4D **131**
Montgomery Way. *L6* —2B **78**
Montpelier Av. *West* —4F **165**
Montpellier Cres. *Wall* —3A **52**
Montpellier Ho. *Wall* —3A **52**
Montrose Av. *Wall* —5E **75**
Montrose Bus. Pk. *L7* —4E **79**
Montrose Ct. *L12* —4F **59**
Montrose Ct. *Wir* —5B **90**
Montrose Pl. *L26* —1F **147**
Montrose Rd. *L13* —5D **57**
Montrose Way. *L13* —4F **79**
Montrovia Cres. *L10* —1F **37**
Monument Pl. *L3* —4E **77** (4H **5**)
Monville Rd. *L9* —1C **36**
Moorbridge Clo. *Boot* —1A **20**
Moor Clo. *L23* —5F **9**
Moor Coppice. *L23* —5F **9**
Moor Ct. *L10* —1A **38**
Moorcroft Rd. *L18* —3C **124**
Moorcroft Rd. *Wall* —1D **73**
Moorditch La. *Frod* —4A **172**
Moor Dri. *L23* —5E **9**
Moore Av. *St H* —5A **48**
Moore Av. *Birk* —2E **119**
Moore Clo. *Wid* —2D **133**
Moore Dri. *Hay* —1F **49**
Moore St. *Boot* —3B **34**
Mooreway. *Rain* —5E **87**
Moorfield. *L33* —5F **15**
Moorfield Rd. *L23* —5A **10**
Moorfield Rd. *Dent G* —3C **44**
Moorfield Rd. *Wid* —5D **111**
Moorfields. *L2* —4C **76** (4D **4**)
Moorfields Av. *Pren* —5D **95**
Moorfield Shop. Cen. *L33* —4F **15**
Moorfoot Rd. *St H* —5F **47**
Moorfoot Rd. Ind. Est. *St H* —4F **47**
Moorfoot Way. *L33* —4D **15**
Moorgate Av. *L23* —2F **17**
Moorgate La. *L32* —5A **24**
Moorgate Rd. *Know I* —2F **39**
Moorgate Rd. S. *Know* —2F **39**
Moorgate St. *L7* —5B **78**
Moorhey Rd. *L31* —4C **12**
Moor Ho. *L23* —5E **9**
Mooring Clo. *Murd* —4D **169**
Moorings, The. *L31* —3B **6**
Moorings, The. *Birk* —4D **97**
Moorings, The. *Wir* —2C **156**
Moorland Av. *L23* —5E **9**
Moorland Clo. *Wir* —3A **158**
Moorland Dri. *Murd* —3E **169**
Moorland Pk. *Wir* —3A **158**
Moorland Rd. *L31* —4C **12**
Moorland Rd. *Birk* —1E **119**
Moorlands Rd. *L23* —4B **10**
Moor La. *Cros* —5E **9**
Moor La. *Faz* —5B **22**
Moor La. *Ince B* —1F **9**
Moor La. *L29* —2D **11**
Moor La. *Walt* —5F **35**
Moor La. *Frod* —5B **172**
Moor La. *Wid* —5F **131**
(in two parts)
Moor La. *Wir* —2A **158**
Moor La. Ind. Est. *Wid* —5A **132**
Moor La. S. *Wid* —5F **131**
Moor Park. —4E 9
Moor Pl. *L3* —4E **77** (4H **5**)
Moorside Clo. *L23* —1F **17**
Moorside Ct. *Wid* —5F **131**
Moorside Rd. *L23* —1F **17**
Moor St. *L2* —5C **76** (6C **4**)
Moorway. *Wir* —2B **158**
Moorwood Cres. *Clo F* —2C **88**
Moray Clo. *St H* —3E **45**
Morcroft Rd. *L36* —1E **83**
Morden St. *L6* —2C **78**
Morecambe St. *L6* —1C **78**
Morecroft Rd. *Birk* —2A **120**
Morella Rd. *L4* —3C **56**
Morello Clo. *St H* —3F **45**
Morello Dri. *Wir* —5B **142**
Moresby Clo. *Murd* —3E **169**
Moret Clo. *L23* —5A **10**
Moreton. —5D 71
Moreton Av. *Clo F* —2C **88**
Moreton Common. —2D 71
Moreton Gro. *Wall* —5E **51**
Moreton Rd. *Wir* —2F **93**
Moreton Ter. *Frod* —5A **172**
Morgan M. *Boot* —2D **19**
Morgan St. *St H* —1D **67**
Morland Av. *Brom* —4D **163**
Morley Av. *Birk* —1B **96**
Morley Ct. *L14* —2E **81**
Morley La. *L4* —4E **55**
Morley Rd. *Run* —1A **166**
Morley Rd. *Wall* —3A **74**
Morley St. *L4* —4E **55**
Morley St. *St H* —3F **45**
(in two parts)
Morley Way. *St H* —4F **45**
Morningside. *L23* —2F **17**
Morningside Pl. *L11* —2F **57**
Morningside Rd. *L11* —2E **57**
Morningside Vw. *L11* —3F **57**
Morningside Way. *L11* —3F **57**
Mornington Av. *L23* —3E **17**
Mornington Rd. *Wall* —4B **52**
Mornington St. *L8* —4E **99**
Morpeth Clo. *Wir* —1B **92**
Morpeth Rd. *Wir* —1A **112**
Morpeth St. *L8* —2F **99**
Morpeth Wharf. *Birk* —1E **97**
Morris Clo. *Hay* —3F **47**
Morris Ct. *Pren* —4F **95**
Morrissey Clo. *St H* —4D **45**
Morris St. *St H* —2E **67**
Morston Av. *L32* —5E **23**
Morston Cres. *L32* —5E **23**
Morston Wlk. *L32* —5E **23**
Mortimer St. *Birk* —2F **97**
Mortlake Clo. *Wid* —1C **130**
Morton Ho. *L18* —1F **123**
Morton Rd. *Wind H* —2D **169**
Morton St. *L8* —4F **99**
(in two parts)
Mortuary Rd. *Wall* —5B **52**
Morvah Clo. *L12* —1C **58**
Morval Cres. *L4* —1E **55**
Morval Cres. *Run* —1D **167**
Moscow Dri. *L13* —1F **79**
Mosedale Av. *St H* —4B **30**
Mosedale Gro. *Beech* —5E **167**
Mosedale Rd. *L9* —3A **36**
Mosedale Rd. *Croft B* —5E **143**
Moseley Av. *Wall* —2A **74**
Moseley Rd. *Wir* —1A **162**
Moses St. *L8* —5F **99**
Moss Bank. —4A 30
(St Helens)
Moss Bank. —5D 133
(Widnes)
Moss Bank Pk. *L21* —5A **18**
Moss Bank Rd. *St H* —5F **29**
Moss Bank Rd. *Wid* —5D **133**
Mossborough Hall La. *Rainf* —3B **26**
Mossborough Rd. *Rainf* —3D **27**
Mossbrow Rd. *L36* —1E **83**
Moss Clo. *Will* —5A **170**
Mosscraig. *L28* —4C **60**
Mosscroft Clo. *L36* —2A **84**
Mossdale Dri. *Rain* —3D **87**
Mossdale Rd. *L33* —5F **15**
Mossdene Rd. *Wall* —2F **73**
Moss End Way. *Know* —2D **25**
Mossfield Rd. *L9* —2F **35**
Moss Ga. Gro. *L14* —3A **82**
Moss Ga. Rd. *L14* —3A **82**
Moss Grn. Way. *St H* —2A **68**
Moss Gro. *L8* —3B **100**
Moss Gro. *Birk* —2B **118**
Mosshill Clo. *L31* —4C **6**
Mosslands. *Ecc* —4A **44**
Mosslands Dri. *Wall* —1E **73**
Moss La. *Boot & Orr P* —2E **35**
Moss La. *Crank* —1E **29**
Moss La. *Kirkby* —2B **24**
Moss La. *Lith* —5B **18**
Moss La. *Mag* —5E **7**
Moss La. *Sim* —2F **15**
(in two parts)
Moss La. *St H* —2A **68**
Moss La. *Wind* —5F **27**
Moss La. *Birk* —2B **118**
Moss La. *High & Cros* —1C **8**
Moss La. *Lyd* —2B **6**
Moss La. *Wid* —5E **133**
Mosslawn Rd. *L32* —4A **24**
Mosslea Pk. *L18* —5F **101**
Mossley Av. *L18* —4E **101**
Mossley Av. *Wir* —2D **163**
Mossley Ct. *L18* —1F **123**
Mossley Hill. —1F 123
Mossley Hill Dri. *L17* —4D **101**
Mossley Hill Rd. *L18 & L19* —2F **123**
Mossley Rd. *Birk* —1E **119**
Moss Nook. —2F 67
Moss Nook La. *L31* —2A **14**
Moss Nook La. *Rainf* —1F **27**
(in two parts)
Moss Pits Clo. *L10* —1E **37**
Moss Pits La. *Faz* —1E **37**
Moss Pits La. *W'tree* —3B **102**
Moss Side. —5E 7
Moss Side. *K Ash* —3A **82**
Moss Side La. *Moore* —1E **155**
Moss St. *Gars* —1C **144**
Moss St. *Low H* —4F **77** (3J **5**)
Moss St. *Prsct* —4D **63**
Moss St. *Wid* —5D **133**
Moss Vw. *Lith* —5C **18**
Moss Vw. *Mag* —1F **13**
Mossville Clo. *L18* —2A **124**
Mossville Rd. *L18* —2A **124**
Moss Way. *L11* —3C **38**
Mossy Bank Rd. *Wall* —2D **75**
Mostyn Av. *Old R* —2C **20**
Mostyn Av. *Gars* —4D **125**
Mostyn Av. *Hes* —2D **157**
Mostyn Av. *W Kir* —5B **112**
Mostyn Clo. *L4* —4E **55**
Mostyn St. *Wall* —3B **74**
Mottershead Clo. *Wid* —4A **132**
Mottershead Rd. *Wid* —4A **132**
Mottram Clo. *L33* —3F **23**
Moughland La. *Run* —1F **165**
Mould St. *L5* —5D **55**
Moulton Clo. *Sut W* —1F **173**
Mounsey Rd. *Birk* —4D **97**
Mount Av. *Boot* —1D **35**
Mount Av. *Beb* —5D **119**
Mount Av. *Hes* —2F **157**
Mount Clo. *L32* —1C **22**
Mount Ct. *Wall* —3A **52**
Mount Cres. *L32* —1B **22**
Mount Dri. *Wir* —5D **119**

Mount Gro. Birk —4C 96
Mt. Grove Pl. Birk —4C 96
Mt. Haven Clo. Wir —4A 94
Mount Merrion. L25 —5A 104
Mount Olive. Pren —1A 118
Mount Pk. L25 —1A 126
Mount Pk. Wir —5D 119
Mount Pk. Ct. L25 —1A 126
Mount Pleasant. L3 —5E 77 (6G 5)
Mount Pleasant. Wat —4D 17
Mount Pleasant. Pren —1B 118
Mount Pleasant. Wid —2B 132
Mt. Pleasant Av. St H —1A 68
Mt. Pleasant Rd. Wall —5A 52
Mount Rd. L32 —2B 22
(in two parts)
Mount Rd. Beb & High B —5E 141
Mount Rd. Birk & Wir —3C 118
Mount Rd. Halt —1F 167
Mount Rd. Upt —4A 94
Mount Rd. Wall —3A 52
Mount Rd. W Kir —5C 112
Mount St. L1 —1E 99 (7H 5)
Mount St. Wat —4D 17
Mount St. Wid —2B 132
Mount St. Wltn —2A 126
Mount, The. Hes —2F 157
Mount, The. Wall —2C 74
Mount, The. Wir —2A 142
Mount Vernon. L7 —5A 78
Mt. Vernon Grn. L7 —4A 78
Mt. Vernon Rd. L7 —4A 78
Mt. Vernon St. L7 —4F 77
Mt. Vernon Vw. L7 —4A 78
Mountview Clo. L8 —4A 100
Mountway. Wir —5D 119
Mt. Wood Rd. Birk —4C 118
Mowbray Av. St H —3C 46
Mowbray Ct. L20 —2C 54
Mowbray Gro. L13 —5A 80
Mowcroft La. Cuer —1F 133
Moxon St. St H —1C 64
Moyles Clo. Wid —1D 131
Moyles Ct. Wid —2D 131
(off Moyles Clo.)
Mozart Clo. L8 —3B 100
Muirfield Clo. L12 —5E 59
Muirfield Rd. L36 —5C 82
Muirhead Av. L6 —2C 78
Muirhead Av. L13 —5E 57
Muirhead Av. E. L11 —3A 58
Mulberry Av. St H —5C 44
Mulberry Clo. L33 —4F 15
Mulberry Gro. Wall —3D 75
Mulberry Pl. L7 —1F 99 (7J 5)
Mulberry Rd. Birk —2F 119
Mulberry St. L7 —1F 99 (7J 5)
(in two parts)
Mulcrow Clo. Parr & St H —4D 47
Mulgrave St. L8 —2A 100
Mulliner St. L7 —2C 100
Mullion Clo. L26 —3E 127
Mullion Clo. Brook —4B 168
Mullion Rd. L11 —3C 38
Mullion Wlk. L11 —3C 38
Mullrea Clo. L27 —3C 104
Mulveton Rd. Wir —4F 141
Mulwood Clo. L12 —5F 39
Mumfords Gro. Wir —2E 91
Mumfords La. Wir —2D 91
Muncaster Clo. Wir —1D 163
Munster Rd. L13 —3B 80
Murat Gro. L22 —4C 16
Murat St. L22 —4C 16
Murcote Rd. L14 —1F 81
Murdishaw. —4E 169
Murdishaw Av. Murd —5C 168
Murdishaw Av. S. Murd —4D 169
Muriel St. L4 —3F 55
Murphy Gro. St H —4E 47
Murrayfield Dri. Wir —2F 71
Murrayfield Rd. L25 —3A 104
Murrayfield Wlk. L25 —3A 104
Murray Gro. Wir —3A 112
Museum of Liverpool Life. —1B 98 (7B 4)
Musker Dri. Boot —2C 18
Musker Gdns. L23 —2F 17
Musker St. L23 —2F 17
Muspratt Rd. L21 —2A 34
Muttocks Rake. Boot —5D 11
Myers Av. Whis —1A 86
Myerscough Av. Boot —3E 35
Myers Rd. E. L23 —2E 17
Myers Rd. W. Cros —2D 17
Mynsule Rd. Wir —4F 141
Myrtle Av. Hay —1B 48
Myrtle Gro. L22 —3D 17
Myrtle Gro. Bil —1D 31
Myrtle Gro. Wall —3D 75
Myrtle Gro. Wid —4D 131
Myrtle Pde. L7 —1F 99
Myrtle St. L7 —1F 99 (7J 5)

Nairn Clo. Wir —1D 171
Nansen Gro. L4 —2A 56
Nant Pk. Ct. Wall —3C 52
Nantwich Clo. Wir —2A 116
Napier Clo. St H —5E 45
Napier Dri. Wir —1F 93
Napier Rd. Wir —4B 120
Napier St. St H —5E 45
Naples Rd. Wall —3D 75
Napps Clo. L25 —2F 103
Napps Wlk. L25 —2F 103
(off Napps Clo.)
Napps Way. L25 —1F 103
Napps Way. Wir —5A 138
Naseby Clo. Pren —5C 94
Naseby St. L4 —1F 55
Nash Gro. L3 —3D 77 (1F 5)
Natal Rd. L9 —2B 36
Nathan Dri. Hay —2E 49
Nathan Gro. L33 —1F 23
National Wildflower Cen. —1F 103
Naughton Lea. Wid —1D 131
Naughton Rd. Wid —4A 132
Navigation Clo. Boot —1A 20
Navigation Clo. Murd —4D 169
Navigation Wharf. L3 —3D 99
Naylor Rd. Pren —1E 95
Naylor Rd. Wid —3D 133
Naylorsfield Dri. L27 & L25 —2C 104
Naylor's Rd. L27 —2D 105
Naylor St. L3 —3C 76 (2D 4)
Nazeby Av. L23 —2F 17
Neale Dri. Wir —1E 115
Neasham Clo. L26 —4F 127
Nedens Gro. L31 —4C 6
Nedens La. L31 —4C 6
Needham Clo. Run —5D 153
Needham Cres. Pren —5D 95
Needham Rd. L7 —4C 78
Needwood Dri. Wir —4F 141
Neills Rd. Bold —5B 68
Neilson Rd. L17 —1B 122
Neil St. Wid —2B 132
Nell's La. Augh —2F 7
Nelson Av. Whis —4E 85
Nelson Ct. Birk —3A 120
Nelson Dri. West —4F 165
Nelson Dri. Wir —3E 137
Nelson Pl. Whis —4E 85
Nelson Rd. L7 —5B 78
Nelson Rd. L21 —1B 34
Nelson Rd. Birk —3A 120
Nelson's Cft. Wir —4A 142
Nelson St. Boot —1B 54
Nelson St. L1 —2D 99
Nelson St. Newt W —5F 49
(in two parts)
Nelson St. St H —4D 67
Nelson St. Run —4A 152
Nelson St. Wall —4C 52
Nelson St. W'tree —2E 101
Nelson St. Wid —1A 152
Nelville Rd. L9 —1C 36
Neptune Clo. Murd —3D 169
Neptune St. Birk —1D 97
Neptune Theatre. —5D 77 (6F 5)
Ness Gro. L32 —3C 22
Neston Av. Clo F —2B 88
Neston Rd. Thor H & Nest —5F 159
Neston Rd. Will —5A 170
Neston St. L4 —2F 55
Netherby St. L8 —1F 121
Netherfield. Wid —4D 131
Netherfield Clo. Pren —5C 94
Netherfield Rd. N. L5 —5E 55
Netherfield Rd. S. L5 —2E 77
Netherley Rd. L27 & Tarb G —4F 105
Netherley Rd. Wid —2E 129
Netherton. —5F 11
Netherton Dri. Frod —5A 172
Netherton Grange. Boot —2B 20
Netherton Grn. Boot —5F 11
Netherton Ind. Est. Boot —4F 19
Netherton La. Boot —5E 11
(in two parts)
Netherton Pk. Rd. L21 —5D 19
Netherton Rd. Boot —2D 35
Netherton Rd. L18 —3F 123
Netherton Rd. Wir —1E 93
Netherton Way. Boot —4E 19
(in two parts)
Netherwood Rd. L11 —1E 57
Netley St. L4 —3E 55
Nettlestead Rd. L11 —3A 58
Neva Av. Wir —1D 93
Neville Av. St H —1B 68
Neville Clo. Pren —5C 94
Neville Rd. L22 —4E 17
Neville Rd. Wall —2A 74
Neville Rd. Wir —3E 163
Neville St. Newt W —4F 49
Nevin St. L6 —3A 78
Nevison St. L7 —5B 78
Nevitte Clo. L28 —3A 60
New Acres Clo. Pren —1C 94
New Albert Ter. Run —4B 152
(off Bold St.)
Newark Clo. Boot —5B 12
Newark Clo. L36 —5D 61
Newark Clo. Pren —5C 94
Newark St. L4 —2E 55
New Bank Pl. Wid —3B 130
New Bank Rd. Wid —3B 130
New Barnet. Wid —5F 109
New Bird St. L1 —2D 99
Newbold Cres. Wir —3E 113
Newbold Gro. L12 —1F 59
Newborough Av. Cros —1A 18
Newborough Av. Moss H —4F 101
New Boston. —1F 49
Newbridge Clo. Brook —4C 168
Newbridge Clo. Wir —1B 116
New Brighton. —2B 52
New Brighton Cricket & Bowling Club Ground. —5B 52
Newburgh Clo. Wind H —1D 169
Newburn. Pren —4B 96
Newburns La. Pren —1B 118
Newburn St. L4 —1F 55
Newbury Clo. L36 —5D 83
Newbury Clo. Wid —5A 110
Newbury Way. L12 —1E 81

Newbury Way. *Wir* —3F **71**
Newby Av. *Rain* —2A **86**
Newby Dri. *L36* —3C **82**
Newby Gro. *L12* —1C **58**
Newby Pl. *St H* —5A **30**
Newby St. *L4* —3F **55**
Newcastle Rd. *L15* —3A **102**
New Chester Rd. *Birk & Wir* —4F **97**
New Chester Rd. *Hoot* —3F **171**
New Chester Rd. *Wir & Hoot* —1F **171**
Newcombe St. *L6* —1B **78**
Newcroft Rd. *L25* —5F **103**
New Cross St. *St H* —4F **45**
(Duke St.)
New Cross St. *St H* —5F **45**
(Westfield St.)
New Cross St. *Prsct* —4D **63**
New Cut La. *L33* —1A **42**
Newdales Clo. *Pren* —1C **94**
Newdown Rd. *L11* —3C **38**
Newdown Wlk. *L11* —3D **39**
Newell Rd. *Wall* —1B **74**
Newenham Cres. *L14* —2E **81**
New Ferry. —4B 120
New Ferry By-Pass. *Wir* —4B **120**
New Ferry Rd. *Wir* —5B **120**
Newfield Clo. *L23* —4C **10**
Newfields. *St H* —4C **44**
Newfort Way. *Boot* —2A **34**
New Glade Hill. *St H* —2E **47**
New Grey Rock Clo. *L6* —2B **78**
New Hall. *L10* —5F **21**
New Hall La. *L11* —3E **57**
New Hall La. *Wir* —5B **90**
Newhall St. *L1* —2D **99**
Newhall Swimming Pool. —5F 21
Newhaven Rd. *Wall* —4C **52**
New Hedley Gro. *L5* —1C **76**
New Henderson St. *L8* —3E **99**
New Hey. *Sand P* —1A **80**
New Hey Rd. *Wir* —5B **94**
Newholme Clo. *L12* —5E **39**
Newhope Rd. *Birk* —2C **96**
Newhouse Rd. *L15* —2D **101**
New Hutte La. *L26* —1F **147**
Newick Rd. *L32* —4C **22**
Newington. *L1* —5D **77** (6G **5**)
Newington Way. *Wid* —1E **131**
New Islington. *L3* —3E **77** (3G **5**)
Newland Clo. *Wid* —1C **130**
Newland Ct. *L17* —1C **122**
Newland Dri. *Wall* —2A **74**
Newlands Rd. *St H* —1C **46**
Newlands Rd. *Wir* —3B **142**
Newling St. *Birk* —2C **96**
Newlyn Av. *Lith* —4A **18**
Newlyn Av. *Mag* —1E **13**
Newlyn Clo. *Brook* —4B **168**
Newlyn Clo. *Wir* —1E **91**
Newlyn Gro. *St H* —1D **47**
Newlyn Rd. *L11* —3C **38**
Newlyn Rd. *Wir* —2E **91**
Newman St. *L4* —3D **55**
New Mill Stile. *L25* —1A **126**
Newmoore La. *Run* —4E **155**
Newmorn Ct. *L17* —2C **122**
Newport Av. *Wall* —4D **51**
Newport Clo. *Pren* —5C **94**
Newport Ct. *L5* —5C **54**
New Quay. *L3* —4B **76** (4B **4**)
Newquay Clo. *Brook* —4C **168**
Newquay Ter. *L3* —4B **76** (4B **4**)
New Red Rock Vw. *L6* —2B **78**
New Rd. *Ecc L* —4E **63**
New Rd. *Old S & Tue* —1D **79**
New Rd. Ct. *L13* —1E **79**
Newsham Clo. *Wid* —5B **108**
Newsham Dri. *L6* —2C **78**
Newsham Pk. —2D 79
Newsham Rd. *L36* —1B **106**
Newsham St. *L5* —1D **77**
New Sta. Rd. *L24* —3A **146**
Newstead Av. *L23* —2B **16**
Newstead Rd. *L8* —2B **100**
Newstet Rd. *Know I* —3B **24**
New St. *St H* —1C **88**
New St. *Run* —5A **152**
New St. *Wall* —4E **75**
New St. *Wid* —4B **132**
Newton. —4E 113
Newton Clo. *L12* —3B **58**
Newton Common. —5E 49
Newton Ct. *L13* —5E **79**
Newton Cross La. *Wir* —4E **113**
Newton Dri. *Wir* —4E **113**
Newton Pk. Rd. *Wir* —4E **113**
Newton Rd. *L13* —3E **79**
Newton Rd. *St H* —5A **48**
Newton Rd. *Hoy* —4C **90**
Newton Rd. *Wall* —2A **74**
Newton St. *Birk* —2C **96**
Newton Wlk. *Boot* —4B **34**
Newton Way. *L3* —5F **77** (5J **5**)
Newton Way. *Wir* —4F **93**
New Tower Ct. *Wall* —3C **52**
Newtown. —4D 173
Newtown Gdns. *L32* —3E **23**
New Way. *L14* —1A **82**
New Way Bus. Cen. *Wall* —4D **75**
Nicander Rd. *L18* —4F **101**
Nicholas Rd. *L23* —1B **16**
Nicholas Rd. *Wid* —4C **130**
Nicholas St. *L3* —3D **77** (1E **5**)
Nicholl Rd. *Ecc* —2A **44**
Nicholls Dri. *Wir* —4F **137**
Nichol's Gro. *L18* —2C **124**
Nicholson St. *L5* —5E **55**
Nicholson St. *St H* —4E **47**
Nickleby Clo. *L8* —4F **99**
Nickleby St. *L8* —3F **99**
Nicola Ct. *Wall* —5C **52**
Nidderdale Av. *Rain* —3D **87**
Nigel Rd. *Wir* —2C **158**
Nigel Wlk. *Cas* —5A **154**
Nightingale Clo. *Kirkby* —2B **22**
Nightingale Clo. *Beech* —5F **167**
Nightingale Clo. *N'ley* —4F **105**
Nightingale Rd. *L12* —5F **39**
Nimrod St. *L4* —2F **55**
Ninth Av. *Faz* —1D **37**
Nithsdale Rd. *L15* —3E **101**
Nixon St. *L4* —1F **55**
Noctorum. —5D 95
Noctorum Av. *Pren* —4C **94**
Noctorum Dell. *Pren* —5D **95**
Noctorum La. *Pren* —3D **95**
Noctorum Rd. *Pren* —4D **95**
Noctorum Way. *Pren* —5D **95**
Noel St. *L8* —2B **100**
Nook La. *St H* —2F **67**
Nook Ri. *L15* —1B **102**
Nook, The. *L25* —1B **126**
Nook, The. *Wind* —2B **44**
Nook, The. *Pren* —4B **96**
Nook, The. *Wir* —2B **114**
Norbreck Av. *L14* —4E **81**
Norbury Av. *L18* —4F **101**
Norbury Av. *Wir* —2E **141**
Norbury Clo. *L32* —3D **23**
Norbury Clo. *Wid* —3D **133**
Norbury Clo. *Wir* —2F **141**
Norbury Fold. *Rain* —5E **87**
Norbury Gdns. *Birk* —5E **97**
Norbury Rd. *L32* —3D **23**
Norbury Wlk. *L32* —3D **23**
Norcliffe Rd. *Rain* —2B **86**
Norcott Dri. *Btnwd* —5F **69**
Norfolk Clo. *Boot* —4D **35**
Norfolk Clo. *Pren* —5C **94**
Norfolk Dri. *Wir* —5C **112**
Norfolk Pl. *L21* —1A **34**
Norfolk Pl. *Wid* —4C **130**
Norfolk Rd. *L31* —3C **12**
Norfolk Rd. *St H* —2D **65**
Norfolk St. *L1* —2D **99**
Norfolk St. *Run* —4B **152**
Norgate St. *L4* —4F **55**
Norgrove Clo. *Murd* —2D **169**
Norlands Ct. *Birk* —3E **119**
Norland's La. *Rain* —1E **109**
Norland's La. *Wid* —1E **109**
Norlands, The. *Wid* —3F **109**
Norland St. *Wid* —3D **133**
Norleane Cres. *Run* —2B **166**
Norley Av. *East* —2E **171**
Norley Dri. *Ecc* —5A **44**
Norley Pl. *L26* —1E **147**
Norman Av. *Hay* —1F **49**
Normandale Rd. *L4* —2D **57**
Normandy Rd. *L36* —3D **83**
Norman Rd. *Boot* —1C **34**
Norman Rd. *L23* —2D **17**
Norman Rd. *Run* —1A **166**
Norman Rd. *Wall* —4E **75**
Norman Salisbury Ct. *St H* —4F **45**
Normans Rd. *St H* —4F **67**
Normanston Clo. *Pren* —5B **96**
Normanston Rd. *Pren* —5B **96**
Norman St. *L3* —4F **77** (4J **5**)
Norman St. *Birk* —1F **95**
Normanton Av. *L17* —1C **122**
Norma Rd. *L22* —4E **17**
Normington Clo. *L31* —3C **6**
Norris Clo. *Pren* —5C **94**
Norris Green. —1F 57
Norris Grn. Cres. *L11* —2F **57**
Norris Grn. Rd. *L12* —5B **58**
Norris Grn. Way. *L11* —2A **58**
Norris Rd. *Prsct* —5C **62**
Norseman Clo. *L12* —3B **58**
N. Atlantic Clo. *L36* —2D **83**
North Av. *Ain* —3E **21**
North Av. *L24* —1A **146**
N. Barcombe Rd. *L16* —2D **103**
Northbrook Clo. *L8* —2A **100**
Northbrooke Way. *Wir* —1A **116**
Northbrook Rd. *Wall* —3D **75**
Northbrook St. *L8* —2A **100**
(Granby St.)
Northbrook St. *L8* —2F **99**
(Park Way)
N. Cantril Av. *L12* —3E **59**
(in two parts)
N. Cheshire Trad. Est. *Nor C* —4E **117**
North Clo. *Wir* —5C **142**
Northcote Clo. *L5* —2F **77**
Northcote Rd. *Wall* —5D **51**
Northdale Rd. *L15* —1F **101**
N. Dingle. *L4* —3D **55**
North Dri. *Sand P* —1A **80**
North Dri. *Wall* —3F **51**
North Dri. *W'tree* —1F **101**
North Dri. *Wir* —3A **158**
North End. —1E 127
N. End La. *Halew* —1E **127**
Northern La. *Wid* —1A **130**
Northern Perimeter Rd. *Boot* —5E **11**
Northern Rd. *L24* —3E **147**
Northern Rd., The. *L23* —5E **9**
Northfield Clo. *Clo F* —3D **89**
Northfield Clo. *L33* —1A **24**
Northfield Rd. *Boot & L9* —2E **35**
N. Florida Rd. *Hay* —1D **49**
North Front. *Hals P* —5E **85**
Northgate Rd. *L13* —1F **79**
North Gro. *L18* —3C **124**
N. Hill St. *L8* —4F **99**

N. John St. *L2* —4C **76** (4D **4**)
N. John St. *St H* —5F **45**
N. Linkside Rd. *L25* —3C **126**
N. Manor Way. *L25* —3C **126**
North Meade. *L31* —5B **6**
Northmead Rd. *L19* —5E **125**
N. Mersey Bus. Cen. *Know I* —1C **24**
N. Mossley Hill Rd. *L18* —5F **101**
N. Mount Rd. *L32* —1B **22**
Northop Rd. *Wall* —5F **51**
North Pde. *Kirkby* —3E **23**
North Pde. *L24* —4E **147**
North Pde. *Hoy* —4A **90**
N. Park Ct. *Wall* —3E **75**
N. Park Rd. *L32* —1B **22**
N. Parkside Wlk. *L12* —3A **58**
N. Perimeter Rd. *L33* —1C **24**
Northridge Rd. *Wir* —2A **138**
North Rd. *L14* —4C **80**
North Rd. *L24* —2D **147**
North Rd. *St H* —3F **45**
North Rd. *Birk* —1C **118**
North Rd. *Grass P* —5F **123**
North Rd. *W Kir* —4A **112**
North St. *L3* —4D **77** (3E **4**)
North St. *Hay* —2E **49**
N. Sudley Rd. *L17* —2E **123**
North Ter. *Wir* —2E **91**
Northumberland Gro. *L8* —4D **99**
Northumberland St. *L8* —4D **99**
Northumberland Ter. *L5* —5E **55**
Northumberland Way. *Boot* —2C **18**
North Vw. *Edg H* —5A **78**
North Vw. *Huy* —4A **84**
N. Wallasey App. *Wall* —1C **72**
Northway. *Mag & Augh* —3C **12**
(in three parts)
Northway. *Run* —2F **167**
Northway. *W'tree* —5B **80**
Northway. *Wid* —3D **131**
Northway. *Wir* —1D **159**
Northways. *Wir* —4D **143**
Northwich Clo. *L23* —4B **10**
Northwich Rd. *Brook* —5B **168**
Northwich Rd. *White I* —1D **175**
N. William St. *Wall* —4E **75**
Northwood. —2F 23
Northwood Rd. *L36* —2F **83**
Northwood Rd. *Pren* —2F **117**
Northwood Rd. *Run* —5E **153**
Norton. —2D 169
Norton Dri. *Wir* —5C **114**
Norton Ga. *Nort* —2C **168**
Norton Gro. *L31* —4D **13**
Norton Gro. *That H* —4D **65**
Norton Hill. *Wind H* —1C **168**
Norton La. *Halt* —2A **168**
(in two parts)
Norton La. *Nort* —1D **169**
Norton Priory Mus. & Gardens. —4B 154
Norton Recreation Cen. —5B 154
Norton Rd. *Wir* —3A **112**
Norton Sta. Rd. *Nort* —2D **169**
Norton St. *Boot* —3B **34**
Norton St. *L3* —4E **77** (3G **5**)
Norton Vw. *Halt* —2A **168**
Norton Village. *Nort* —2D **169**
Nortonwood La. *Wind H* —2C **168**
Norville Rd. *L14* —4C **80**
Norwich Dri. *Wir* —2A **94**
Norwich Rd. *L15* —3A **102**
Norwich Way. *Kirkby* —3E **23**
Norwood Av. *L21* —4B **18**
Norwood Ct. *Wir* —1D **115**
Norwood Gro. *L6* —2B **78**
Norwood Rd. *Wall* —4B **74**
Norwood Rd. *Wir* —5E **93**
Norwyn Rd. *L11* —1E **57**
Nottingham Clo. *Rain* —1C **86**
Nottingham Rd. *L36* —5C **82**
Nowshera Av. *Wir* —2F **137**
Nuffield Clo. *Wir* —5F **93**
Nun Clo. *Pren* —1B **118**
Nunn St. *St H* —5D **47**
Nunsford Clo. *L21* —3D **19**
Nunthorpe Av. *Know* —3B **40**
Nurse Rd. *Wir* —1B **138**
Nursery Clo. *L25* —4C **126**
Nursery Clo. *Pren* —1B **118**
Nursery Clo. *Wid* —1D **133**
Nursery La. *L19* —5C **124**
Nursery Rd. *L31* —3C **6**
Nursery Rd. *St H* —4D **65**
Nursery St. *L5* —5D **55**
Nutfield Rd. *L24* —3A **148**
Nutgrove. —5C 64
Nutgrove Av. *St H* —4D **65**
Nutgrove Hall Dri. *St H* —4D **65**
Nutgrove Rd. *St H* —5C **64**
Nut St. *That H* —4D **65**
Nuttall St. *L7* —5B **78**
Nuttall St. *St H* —2F **65**
Nyland Rd. *L36* —1D **83**

Oak Av. *L9* —2B **36**
Oak Av. *Hay* —1E **49**
Oak Av. *Wir* —3D **93**
Oak Bank. *Birk* —4C **96**
Oak Bank. *Wir* —2A **142**
Oakbank Rd. *L18* —4E **101**
Oakbank St. *Wall* —3C **74**
Oakbourne Clo. *L17* —2C **122**
Oak Clo. *L12* —2F **59**
Oak Clo. *Whis* —3E **85**
Oak Clo. *Wir* —2D **93**
Oak Ct. L8 —5A 100
(off Weller Way)
Oakdale Av. *Wall* —4D **75**
Oakdale Dri. *Wir* —2C **114**
Oakdale Rd. *Wat* —3D **17**
Oakdale Rd. *Moss H* —4A **102**
Oakdale Rd. *Wall* —4D **75**
Oakdene Clo. *Wir* —5D **163**
Oakdene Ct. *Rain* —4C **86**
Oakdene Rd. *L4* —4B **56**
Oakdene Rd. *Birk* —1C **118**
Oak Dri. *Run* —3C **166**
Oakenholt Rd. *Wir* —5E **71**
Oakes St. *L3* —4F **77** (4J **5**)
Oakfield. *L4* —5B **56**
Oakfield Av. *L25* —5A **104**
Oakfield Clo. *That H* —4D **65**
Oakfield Dri. *Huy* —1F **105**
Oakfield Dri. *Wid* —4A **130**
Oakfield Gro. *L36* —5F **83**
Oakfield Rd. *Walt* —5A **56**
Oakfield Rd. *Brom* —2C **162**
Oakfield Rd. *Chil T* —5E **171**
Oakfield Ter. *Chil T* —5E **171**
Oakham Dri. *L10* —4F **21**
Oakham Dri. *Wir* —5B **70**
Oakham St. *L8* —3D **99**
Oakhill Clo. *Mag* —5D **7**
Oakhill Clo. *W Der* —5D **39**
Oakhill Cottage La. *L31* —3D **7**
Oakhill Dri. *L31* —3D **7**
Oak Hill Park. —4B 80
Oakhill Pk. *L13* —4B **80**
Oakhill Rd. *Mag* —5D **7**
Oakhill Rd. *Old S* —4B **80**
Oakhurst Clo. *L25* —4B **104**
Oakland Clo. *L21* —2C **34**
Oakland Dri. *Wir* —3A **94**
Oakland Rd. *L19* —4F **123**
Oaklands. *Rain* —4C **86**
Oaklands. *Wir* —4D **163**
Oaklands Av. *L23* —4D **9**
Oaklands Ct. *Clo F* —2C **88**
Oaklands Dri. *Beb* —1F **141**
Oaklands Dri. *Hes* —1A **158**
Oaklands Ter. *Wir* —1A **158**
Oakland St. *Wid* —3A **152**
Oakland Va. *Wall* —3C **52**
Oak La. *L12* —2B **58**
Oakleaf M. *Pren* —4D **95**
Oaklea Rd. *Wir* —1F **137**
Oaklee Gro. *L33* —1A **24**
Oak Leigh. *L13* —1E **79**
Oakleigh Gro. *Wir* —1F **141**
Oakley Clo. *L12* —5E **39**
Oak Meadows. *Rain* —5E **87**
Oakmere Clo. *L9* —1A **36**
Oakmere Clo. *Wir* —3E **71**
Oakmere Dri. *Wir* —5C **92**
Oakmere St. *Run* —5A **152**
Oakridge Clo. *Wir* —5C **142**
Oakridge Rd. *Wir* —5C **142**
Oak Rd. *L36* —5D **83**
Oak Rd. *Beb* —5F **119**
Oak Rd. *Hoot* —4E **171**
Oak Rd. *Whis* —3E **85**
Oaks Clo. *Clo F* —3D **89**
Oaks La. *Wir* —3A **138**
Oaksmeade Clo. *L12* —1F **59**
Oaks Pl. *Wid* —5A **132**
Oaks, The. *L12* —5F **39**
Oaks, The. *St H* —2D **89**
Oaks, The. *Wir* —2C **162**
Oakston Av. *Rain* —4D **87**
Oak St. *Boot* —4C **34**
Oak St. *St H* —3E **67**
Oaksway. *Hes* —4B **158**
Oak Ter. *L7* —4C **78**
Oakthorn Gro. *Hay* —2C **48**
Oak Towers. *L33* —2F **23**
Oaktree Pl. *Birk* —1F **119**
Oaktree Rd. *Ecc* —3A **44**
Oak Va. *L13* —4B **80**
Oak Vale Park. —4B 80
Oak Vw. *L24* —4A **148**
Oakwood Clo. *B Vale* —4B **104**
Oakwood Dri. *L36* —5F **83**
Oakwood Dri. *Pren* —1E **95**
Oakwood Pk. *Wir* —5D **163**
Oakwood Rd. *L26* —5E **127**
Oakworth Clo. *L33* —1E **23**
Oakworth Dri. *Tarb G* —2A **106**
Oakworth Dri. *Wir* —5C **120**
Oarside Dri. *Wall* —5A **52**
Oatfield La. *L21* —3B **18**
Oatlands Rd. *L32* —3C **22**
Oatlands, The. *Wir* —5C **112**
Oban Dri. *Wir* —2A **158**
Oban Rd. *L4* —5B **56**
Oberon St. *L20* —2C **54**
O'Brien Gro. *St H* —4E **47**
Observatory Rd. *Pren* —1E **95**
Oceanic Rd. *L13* —4F **79**
Ocean Rd. *L21* —1B **34**
O'Connell Clo. *St H* —2C **48**
O'Connell Rd. *L3* —2D **77**
Octavia Ct. *Huy* —5F **83**
Octavia Hill Rd. *L21* —4C **18**
Odsey St. *L7* —4C **78**
Odyssey Cen. *Birk* —1C **96**
Ogden Clo. *L13* —3F **57**
Ogle Clo. *Prsct* —1E **85**
Oglet La. *L24* —5C **146**
Oil St. *L3* —2B **76** (1A **4**)
O'Keefe Rd. *St H* —4C **46**
Okehampton Rd. *L16* —1D **103**
Okell Dri. *L26* —2D **127**
Okell St. *Run* —5A **152**
Old Albert Ter. Run —4B 152
(off Thomas St.)

Old Barn Rd. *L4* —5B **56**
Old Barn Rd. *Wall* —3A **74**
Old Bidston Rd. *Birk* —1B **96**
Oldbridge Rd. *L24* —5F **147**
Old Chester Rd. *Birk & Beb* —5E **97**
Old Church Yd. *L2* —4B **76** (5C **4**)
Old Clatterbridge Rd. *Wir* —5E **141**
Old Colliery Rd. *Whis* —3D **85**
Old Distillery Rd. *L24* —2C **146**
Old Dover Rd. *L36* —1C **104**
Old Eccleston La. *St H* —5C **44**
Old Farm Clo. *Will* —5A **170**
Old Farm Rd. *Cros* —5F **9**
Old Farm Rd. *Kirkby* —2F **39**
Old Field. *Whis* —2F **85**
Oldfield Clo. *Wir* —5E **137**
Oldfield Cotts. *Wir* —5D **137**
Oldfield Dri. *Hes* —1D **157**
Oldfield Farm La. *Hes* —5D **137**
Oldfield Gdns. *Wir* —1D **157**
Oldfield La. *Wir* —5A **92**
Oldfield Rd. *L19* —4A **124**
Oldfield Rd. *Hes* —5D **137**
Oldfield Rd. *Wall* —5F **51**
Oldfield St. *St H* —3F **45**
Oldfield Way. *Wir* —5D **137**
Oldgate. *Wid* —5C **130**
Old Gorsey La. *Wall* —4B **74**
Old Greasby Rd. *Wir* —4F **93**
Old Hall Clo. *L31* —3D **13**
Old Hall La. *L32* —3D **23**
Old Hall Rd. *L31* —3D **13**
Old Hall Rd. *Brom* —1E **163**
Old Hall St. *L3* —4B **76** (3B **4**)
Oldham Pl. *L1* —5E **77** (6H **5**)
Oldham St. *L1* —5E **77** (7G **5**)
Old Haymarket. *L1* —4D **77** (4F **5**)
Old Higher Rd. *Wid* —2D **149**
Old Hute La. *L24* —2A **148**
Old Kennel Clo. *L12* —3F **59**
Old La. *Ecc P* —4E **63**
Old La. *L31* —3E **7**
Old La. *Hes* —2D **159**
Old La. *Rain* —3B **86**
Old Leeds St. *L3* —4B **76** (3B **4**)
Old Marylands La. *Wir* —5E **71**
Old Mdw. *Know* —4D **41**
Old Mdw. Rd. *Wir* —4E **137**
Old Mill Av. *St H* —1D **89**
Old Mill Clo. *L15* —1A **102**
Old Mill Clo. *Wir* —3B **158**
Old Mill La. *Know* —4E **41**
Old Mill La. *W'tree* —1A **102**
Old Nook La. *St H* —2E **47**
Old Orchard. *Hals P* —5E **85**
Old Post Office Pl. *L1* —6E **5**
Old Pump La. *Wir* —1C **114**
Old Quarry, The. *L25* —2A **126**
Old Quay St. *Run* —4B **152**
Old Racecourse Rd. *L31* —2B **12**
Old Rectory Grn. *Augh* —1F **7**
Old Rectory Grn. *L29* —3E **11**
Old Riding. *L14* —1F **81**
Old Rockerrians R.F.C. Ground. *—4F 117*
Old Ropery. *L2* —5C **76** (5C **4**)
Old Rough La. *L33* —2E **23**
Old School Way. *Birk* —2E **95**
Old Swan. —3A 80
Old Thomas La. *L14* —5D **81**
Old Upton La. *Wid* —5E **109**
Old Vicarage Rd. *Will* —5A **170**
Old Whint Rd. *Hay* —2A **48**
Old Wood La. *L27* —5F **105**
Old Wood Rd. *Wir* —3F **137**
Oleander Dri. *St H* —4C **44**
Olga Rd. *St H* —4C **66**
Olinda St. *Wir* —5B **120**
Olive Clo. *L31* —3A **22**
Olive Cres. *Birk* —5E **97**
Olivedale Rd. *L18* —4F **101**
Olive Gro. *Boot* —4A **20**
Olive Gro. *Huy* —4D **83**
Olive Gro. *W'tree* —5A **80**
Olive La. *L15* —5A **80**
Olive Mt. *Birk* —5E **97**
Olive Mt. Heights. *L15* —1B **102**
Olive Mt. Rd. *L15* —1A **102**
Olive Mt. Vs. *L15* —5A **80**
Olive Mt. Wlk. *L15* —1A **102**
Oliver Lyme Ho. *Prsct* —5E **63**
Oliver Lyme Rd. *Prsct* —5E **63**
Olive Rd. *L22* —5E **17**
Oliver Rd. *St H* —2C **64**
Oliver St. *Birk* —3D **97**
Oliver St. E. *Birk* —3E **97**
Olivetree Rd. *L15* —5B **80**
Olive Va. *L15* —1F **101**
Olivia Clo. *Pren* —5C **94**
Olivia M. *Pren* —5C **94**
Olivia St. *Boot* —2D **55**
Ollerton Clo. *Pren* —5C **94**
Ollery Grn. *Boot* —1B **20**
Ollier St. *Wid* —5A **132**
Olney St. *L4* —1F **55**
Olton St. *L15* —1E **101**
Olympia St. *L6* —3A **78**
Olympic Way. *Boot* —5B **20**
O' Neill St. *Boot* —4B **34**
(in two parts)
Onslow Rd. *L6* —3C **78**
Onslow Rd. *Wall* —3B **52**
Onslow Rd. *Wir* —3B **120**
Opal Clo. *L21* —5C **18**
Opal Clo. *Eve* —2B **78**
Open Eye Gallery. —5D 77 (6F 5)
Openfields Clo. *L26* —2E **127**
Oppenheim Av. *St H* —3C **64**
Orange Gro. *L8* —3B **100**
Orange Tree Clo. *L28* —3B **60**
Oran Way. *L36* —3D **83**
Orb Clo. *L11* —4C **38**
Orb Wlk. *L11* —5C **38**
Orchard Av. *L14* —5D **81**
Orchard Clo. *Ecc P* —4A **64**
Orchard Clo. *St H* —1D **47**
Orchard Clo. *Hals P* —5E **85**
Orchard Ct. *L31* —1E **13**
Orchard Ct. *Birk* —1F **119**
Orchard Dale. *L23* —1F **17**
Orchard Dene. *Rain* —3C **86**
Orchard Gdns. *Hals P* —1E **107**
Orchard Grange. *Wir* —2C **92**
Orchard Hey. *Boot* —1B **20**
Orchard Hey. *Ecc* —5A **44**
Orchard Hey. *L31* —2E **13**
Orchard Rd. *Wir* —5E **71**
Orchard, The. *L17* —3F **123**
Orchard, The. *Huy* —4E **83**
Orchard, The. *Rain* —1C **86**
Orchard, The. *Wall* —4A **52**
Orchard Way. *Wid* —1A **130**
Orchard Way. *Wir* —1D **141**
Orchid Gro. *L17* —1F **121**
Orchid Way. *St H* —4B **68**
O'Reilly Ct. *L3* —2C **76**
Orford Clo. *Hale V* —5D **149**
Orford St. *L15* —1F **101**
Oriel Clo. *L2* —5B **76** (5C **4**)
Oriel Clo. *Old R* —2D **21**
Oriel Cres. *L20* —2C **54**
Oriel Dri. *L10* —2C **20**
Oriel Lodge. *Boot* —1C **54**
Oriel Rd. *Boot* —5B **34**
Oriel Rd. *L20* —2C **54**
Oriel Rd. *Birk* —1E **119**
Oriel St. *L3* —3C **76** (1D **4**)
Orient Dri. *L25* —1B **126**
Origen Rd. *L16* —5D **81**
Oriole Clo. *St H* —4B **64**
Orith Av. *Ecc* —5F **43**
Orkney Clo. *St H* —1D **47**
Orkney Clo. *Wid* —1E **133**
Orlando Clo. *Pren* —5C **94**
Orlando St. *Boot* —2C **54**
Orleans Rd. *L13* —3A **80**
Ormande St. *Sher I* —2B **66**
Ormesby Gro. *Wir* —4B **162**
Ormiston Rd. *Wall* —4B **52**
Ormond Clo. *Wid* —2C **130**
Ormonde Av. *L31* —3C **12**
Ormonde Cres. *L33* —3A **24**
Ormonde Dri. *L31* —2C **12**
Ormond M. *Pren* —5C **94**
Ormond St. *L3* —4C **76** (4C **4**)
Ormond St. *Wall* —1B **74**
Ormond Way. *Pren* —5C **94**
Ormsby St. *L15* —2E **101**
Ormside Gro. *St H* —4D **67**
Ormskirk Rd. *Know* —2D **41**
Ormskirk Rd. *L9 & L10* —5B **20**
Ormskirk St. *St H* —4F **45**
Orphan Dri. *L6* —1D **79**
Orphan St. *L7* —1A **100**
Orrell. —2D 35
Orrell Hey. *Boot* —1D **35**
Orrell La. *Boot & L9* —1E **35**
Orrell Mt. *Boot* —1C **34**
Orrell Mt. Ind. Est. *Boot* —1C **34**
Orrell Rd. *L21 & Boot* —5C **18**
Orrell Rd. *Wall* —4C **52**
Orrell St. *St H* —5C **46**
Orret's Mdw. Rd. *Wir* —1B **116**
Orrysdale Rd. *Wir* —3A **112**
Orry St. *L5* —1D **77**
Orsett Rd. *L32* —5F **23**
Orston Cres. *Wir* —5A **142**
Ortega Clo. *Wir* —5C **120**
Orthes St. *L3* —5F **77** (6J **5**)
Orton Rd. *L16* —1C **102**
Orville St. *St H* —4E **67**
Orwell Clo. *Sut M* —3A **88**
Orwell Rd. *L4* —3D **55**
Osbert Rd. *L23* —1B **16**
Osborne Av. *Wall* —4B **52**
Osborne Gro. *Prsct* —1A **84**
Osborne Gro. *Wall* —5B **52**
Osborne Rd. *Ecc* —3A **44**
Osborne Rd. *Lith* —4C **18**
Osborne Rd. *Pren* —4B **96**
Osborne Rd. *Tue* —5E **57**
Osborne Rd. *Wall* —4C **52**
Osborne Va. *Wall* —4B **52**
Osborne Wood. *L17* —3C **122**
Osbourne Clo. *Wir* —3E **163**
Osmaston Rd. *Birk* —2A **118**
Osprey Clo. *L27* —4F **105**
Osprey Clo. *Beech* —5F **167**
Ossett Clo. *Nort* —2D **169**
Ossett Clo. *Pren* —5C **94**
Osterley Gdns. *L9* —2F **35**
O'Sullivan Cres. *St H* —3E **47**
Oswald Clo. *L33* —4E **15**
Oteley Av. *Wir* —2D **163**
Othello Clo. *L20* —2C **54**
Otterburn Clo. *Wir* —1B **92**
Otterspool. —3C 122
Otterspool Dri. *L17* —4D **123**
Otterspool Rd. *L17* —3D **123**
Otterton Rd. *L11* —3C **38**
Ottley St. *L6* —3C **78**
Otway St. *L19* —3C **144**
Oulton Clo. *L31* —3B **6**
Oulton Clo. *Pren* —1E **117**
Oulton La. *L36* —1D **105**
Oulton Rd. *L16* —3D **103**
Oulton Way. *Pren* —2E **117**

Oundle Dri. *L10*—2C **20**
Oundle Pl. *L25*—5B **126**
Oundle Rd. *Wir*—5E **71**
Outer Central Rd. *L24*—2E **147**
Outer Forum. *L11*—1E **57**
Out La. *L25*—2A **126**
Outlet La. *L31 & Bic*—1E **15**
Oval Sports Cen., The. ***—5F*** *119*
Oval, The. *Wall*—5F **51**
Overbrook La. *Know B*—3C **40**
Overbury St. *L7*—1B **100**
Overchurch Rd. *Wir*—3E **93**
Overdale Av. *Wir*—2D **139**
Overdale Rd. *Will*—4A **170**
Overdene Wlk. *L32*—4F **23**
Overgreen Gro. *Wir*—5D **71**
Overton Av. *L21*—4B **18**
Overton Clo. *L32*—4D **23**
Overton Clo. *Pren*—1F **117**
Overton Grn. *L32*—4D **23**
Overton Rd. *Wall*—2B **74**
Overton St. *L7*—5B **78**
Overton Way. *Pren*—1F **117**
Ovington Clo. *Sut W*—1F **173**
Ovolo Rd. *L13*—2A **80**
Owdale Rd. *L9*—4A **36**
Owen Clo. *St H*—2D **65**
Owen Dri. *L24*—4B **146**
Owen Rd. *Kirk*—3D **55**
Owen Rd. *Know I*—1C **40**
Owen Rd. *Rain*—4C **86**
Owen St. *St H*—2C **64**
Oxborough Clo. *Wid*—5F **109**
Oxbow Rd. *L12*—3E **59**
Oxendale Clo. *L8*—2B **100**
Oxenholme Cres. *L11*—2A **58**
Oxford Av. *Boot*—5D **35**
Oxford Av. *L21*—5B **18**
Oxford Clo. *L17*—2C **122**
Oxford Dri. *Wat*—3C **16**
Oxford Dri. *Halew*—4F **127**
Oxford Dri. *Wir*—4F **159**
Oxford Ho. Boot —5E ***35***
(off Fernhill Rd.)
Oxford Rd. *Boot*—5D **35**
Oxford Rd. *Walt*—5B **20**
Oxford Rd. *Wat*—3C **16**
Oxford Rd. *Huy*—2A **84**
Oxford Rd. *Run*—1A **166**
Oxford Rd. *Wall*—2C **74**
Oxford St. *L7*—5F **77** (6J **5**)
(in two parts)
Oxford St. *St H*—4F **45**
(Cooper St.)
Oxford St. *St H*—3F **45**
(Rutland St.)
Oxford St. *Wid*—5B **132**
Oxford St. E. *L7*—5A **78**
Oxheys. *Nort*—2C **168**
Ox La. *Tarb G*—2C **106**
Oxley Av. *Wir*—3B **72**
Oxley St. *St H*—4D **67**
Oxmoor Clo. *Brook*—5A **168**
Oxton. —5F 95
Oxton Clo. *Kirkby*—5B **22**
Oxton Clo. *Aig*—2C **122**
Oxton Clo. *Wid*—5C **108**
Oxton Cricket Club Ground. —5F 95
Oxton Rd. *Birk*—4C **96**
Oxton Rd. *Wall*—3B **74**
Oxton St. *L4*—3F **55**

Pacific Rd. *Boot*—5B **34**
(Atlantic Rd.)
Pacific Rd. *Boot*—4B **34**
(Sea Vw. Rd.)
Pacific Rd. *Birk*—2F **97**
Packenham Rd. *L13*—5F **57**
Paddington. *L7*—5A **78**
(in two parts)
Paddock Clo. *L23*—4B **8**
Paddock Gro. *Clo F*—3D **89**
Paddock Ri. *Padd M*—1E **173**
Paddock Rd. *Know P*—5A **62**
Paddock, The. *Kirkby*—1D **39**
Paddock, The. *Hes*—2C **158**
Paddock, The. *More*—2C **92**
Paddock, The. *Prsct*—4A **64**
Paddock, The. *Upt*—4B **94**
Paddock, The. *Wltn*—5B **104**
Padeswood Clo. *St H*—5C **66**
Padstow Clo. *L26*—3E **127**
Padstow Dri. *Wind*—2B **44**
Padstow Rd. *L16*—1D **103**
Padstow Rd. *Wir*—1C **114**
Padstow Sq. *Brook*—5B **168**
Pagebank Rd. *L14*—3A **82**
Pagefield Rd. *L15*—3F **101**
Page Grn. *L36*—3C **82**
Page La. *Wid*—3C **132**
Page Moss. —4B 82
Page Moss Av. *L36*—2B **82**
Page Moss La. *L14*—3A **82**
Page Moss Pde. *L36*—2B **82**
Page Wlk. *L3*—3E **77** (2H **5**)
Pagewood Clo. *Pren*—5D **95**
Paignton Clo. *L36*—3B **84**
Paignton Rd. *L16*—1D **103**
Paignton Rd. *Wall*—5F **51**
Paisley Av. *St H*—1D **47**
Paisley Av. *Wir*—1E **171**
Paisley Ct. *L14*—2F **81**
Paisley St. *L3*—3B **76** (2A **4**)
Palace Fields. —4B 168
Palace Fields Av. *Brook & Pal*—4F **167**
Palace Rd. *L9*—2A **36**
Palatine Arc. *St H*—5A **46**
Palatine Rd. *Wall*—4D **75**
Palatine Rd. *Wir*—1C **162**
Palatine, The. *Boot*—5C **34**
Palermo Clo. *Wall*—4D **75**
Paley Clo. *L4*—4F **55**
Palladio Rd. *L13*—2A **80**
Pallard Av. *Frod*—5D **173**
Pall Mall. *L3*—3B **76** (1C **4**)
Pall Mall Cen. *L3*—3B **76** (2C **4**)
Palm Clo. *L9*—5C **36**
Palm Ct. L8 —5A ***100***
(off Weller Way)
Palmer Clo. *St H*—4F **45**
Palmerston Av. *L21*—1A **34**
Palmerston Clo. *L18*—1F **123**
Palmerston Ct. *L18*—1F **123**
Palmerston Dri. *L21*—1B **34**
Palmerston Rd. *Gars*—1C **144**
Palmerston Rd. *Moss H*—1F **123**
Palmerston Rd. *Wall*—2F **73**
Palmerston St. *Birk*—2F **119**
Palm Gro. *L25*—3B **126**
Palm Gro. *Pren*—3A **96**
Palm Hill. *Pren*—5B **96**
Palmwood Av. *Rain*—4D **87**
Palmwood Clo. *Pren*—3E **117**
Paltridge Way. *Wir*—3F **137**
Pamela Clo. *L10*—1B **38**
Pampas Gro. *L9*—4B **36**
Pankhurst Rd. *L21*—3C **18**
Pansy St. *L5*—4D **55**
Parade. *L3*—1B **98** (7C **4**)
Parade Cres. *L24*—5E **147**
Parade St. *St H*—4A **46**
Parade, The. *W'tree*—5B **80**
Paradise Gdns. *L15*—2F **101**
Paradise La. *Whis*—4D **85**
Paradise St. *L1*—1C **98** (6E **4**)
Paragon Clo. *Wid*—4B **110**
Parbold Av. *St H*—3D **47**
Parbold Ct. *Wid*—4D **131**
Parbrook Clo. *L36*—5D **61**
Parbrook Rd. *L36*—5D **61**
Park Av. *Cros*—5E **9**
Park Av. *Ecc P*—4F **63**
Park Av. *Faz*—1C **36**
Park Av. *Hay*—2A **48**
Park Av. *Lyd*—4D **7**
Park Av. *Moss H*—1E **123**
Park Av. *Rain*—2C **86**
Park Av. *Wall*—3D **75**
Park Av. *Wid*—2B **132**
Parkbourn Dri. *L31*—5F **7**
Parkbourn Sq. *L31*—5F **7**
Parkbridge Rd. *Birk*—1C **118**
Pk. Brow Dri. *L32*—5F **23**
Parkbury Ct. *Pren*—1A **118**
Park Clo. *Kirkby*—1B **22**
Park Clo. *Birk*—3C **96**
Park Ct. *Kirkby*—2C **22**
Park Ct. *L22*—5E **17**
Park Ct. *Frod*—5A **172**
Park Ct. *Run*—2A **166**
Parkdale Av. *L9*—1A **36**
Park Dri. *Cros*—5A **8**
Park Dri. *Thor*—3A **10**
Park Dri. *Pren*—2A **96**
Parkend Rd. *Birk*—1C **118**
Parker Av. *L21*—1F **33**
Parker Clo. *Boot*—4B **20**
Parkers Ct. *Hall P*—4E **167**
Parker St. *L1*—5D **77** (5F **5**)
Parker St. *Run*—4B **152**
Parkfield Av. *Boot*—5A **20**
Parkfield Av. *Birk*—3D **97**
Parkfield Dri. *Wall*—2B **74**
Parkfield Gro. *L31*—1C **12**
Parkfield Pl. *Birk*—3D **97**
Parkfield Rd. *Wat*—3E **17**
Parkfield Rd. *Aig*—5B **100**
Parkfield Rd. *Wir*—4A **142**
Parkgate La. *Nest*—5E **159**
Parkgate Way. *Murd*—4C **168**
Park Gro. *Birk*—4D **97**
Pk. Hill Ct. *L8*—5F **99**
Pk. Hill Rd. *L8*—5F **99**
Parkhill Rd. *Birk*—1C **118**
Parkholme. *L22*—4E **17**
Park Ho. St. *St H*—4C **46**
Parkhurst Rd. *L11*—2F **57**
Parkhurst Rd. *Birk*—2C **118**
Parkinson Rd. *L9*—4A **36**
Parkland Clo. *L8*—4F **99**
Parkland Ct. *Pren*—1C **94**
Parklands. *Know*—5D **41**
Parklands. *Wid*—1C **130**
Parklands Ct. Wir —2A ***116***
(off Childwall Grn.)
Parklands Dri. *Wir*—4B **158**
Parklands Way. *L22*—4E **17**
Park La. *Boot*—1E **35**
(L20)
Park La. *Boot*—3F **19**
(L30)
Park La. *L1*—1C **98** (7D **4**)
Park La. *Mag*—4F **7**
Park La. *Frod*—5B **172**
Park La. *Wir*—5A **70**
Park La. W. *Boot*—2F **19**
Park Pl. *Boot*—5C **34**
Park Pl. *L8*—3E **99**
Park Rd. *Kirkby*—2B **22**
Park Rd. *St H*—4C **46**
Park Rd. *Wat*—4E **17**
Park Rd. *Birk*—1E **119**
Park Rd. *East*—4F **163**
Park Rd. *Hes*—1B **158**
Park Rd. *Meol*—2E **91**
Park Rd. *Port S*—2B **142**

Park Rd. *Prsct* —4C **62**
Park Rd. *Run* —2F **165**
Park Rd. *Tox* —4F **99**
Park Rd. *Wall* —3C **74**
Park Rd. *W Kir* —4A **112**
Park Rd. *Wid* —3B **132**
Park Rd. *Will* —5B **170**
Park Rd. E. *Birk* —3C **96**
Park Rd. N. *Birk* —2F **95**
Park Rd. S. *Pren* —3B **96**
Park Rd. Sports Cen. —4F 99
Park Rd. W. *Pren* —2F **95**
Parkside. *Boot* —4C **34**
Parkside. *Wall* —3C **74**
Parkside Av. *Sut M* —3B **88**
Parkside Clo. *L27* —5E **105**
Parkside Clo. *Wir* —1A **142**
Parkside Dri. *L12* —3A **58**
Parkside Rd. *Birk* —1E **119**
Parkside Rd. *Wir* —1A **142**
Parkside St. *L6* —3F **77**
Parkstile La. *L11* —4C **38**
Parkstone Rd. *Birk* —1C **118**
Park St. *Boot* —5C **34**
Park St. *L8* —4D **99**
Park St. *St H* —4C **46**
Park St. *Birk* —2D **97**
(in two parts)
Park St. *Hay* —2F **47**
Park St. *Wall* —2C **74**
Park Ter. *L22* —5E **17**
Park, The. *L36* —5E **83**
Parkvale Av. *Nor C* —4E **117**
Pk. Vale Rd. *L9* —2A **36**
Park Vw. *L6* —1D **79**
Park Vw. *L21* —5A **18**
Park Vw. *Thor* —3B **10**
Park Vw. *Walt* —4A **36**
Park Vw. *Wat* —3D **17**
Park Vw. *Huy* —2C **82**
Park Vw. *Wir* —2C **162**
Parkview Clo. *Birk* —2C **96**
Parkview Ct. *Hes* —2F **157**
Parkview Dri. *L27* —5E **105**
Parkview Rd. *L11* —2D **39**
Pk. Wall Rd. *L29* —1A **10**
Parkway. *Boot* —5F **11**
Parkway. *Cros* —3F **17**
Park Way. *Huy* —4D **61**
Parkway. *Irby* —5F **115**
Park Way. *Meol* —3E **91**
Park Way. *Tox* —2F **99**
(in two parts)
Parkway. *Wall* —4E **51**
Parkway Clo. *Wir* —5F **115**
Parkway E. *L32* —2B **22**
Parkway W. *L32* —2B **22**
Park W. *Wir* —3D **157**
Parkwood Clo. *Wir* —1D **163**
Parkwood Rd. *L25* —5A **104**
Parkwood Rd. *Whis* —4E **85**
Parlane St. *St H* —4C **46**
(in two parts)
Parliament Clo. *L1* —2E **99**
Parliament Pl. *L8* —2F **99**
Parliament St. *L8* —2D **99**
Parliament St. *That H* —4D **65**
Parlington Clo. *Wid* —5C **130**
Parlow Rd. *L11* —3E **57**
Parnell Rd. *Wir* —4A **142**
Parr. —5D 47
Parr Community Swimming Pool. —5C 46
Parren Av. *Whis* —5C **84**
Parr Gro. *Hay* —2A **48**
Parr Gro. *Wir* —5C **92**
Parr Ind. Est. *St H* —1E **67**
Parr Mt. Ct. *St H* —5C **46**
Parr Mt. St. *St H* —5C **46**
Parr's Rd. *Pren* —1B **118**
Parr Stocks. —1D 67
Parr Stocks Rd. *Parr & St H* —5D **47**
Parr St. *L1* —1D **99** (7F **5**)
Parr St. *L21* —4B **18**
Parr St. *St H* —5B **46**
Parr St. *Wid* —3C **132**
Parry's La. *Run* —1A **166**
Parry St. *Wall* —4D **75**
Parsonage Rd. *Wid* —3A **152**
Parthenon Dri. *L11* —5D **37**
Partington Av. *Boot* —4E **35**
Parton St. *L6* —3C **78**
Partridge Clo. *L12* —5F **39**
Partridge Rd. *Cros* —1B **16**
Partridge Rd. *Kirkby* —2B **22**
Passport Office. —5C 76 (5C 4) (off Water St.)
Passway. *St H* —5C **30**
Pasture Av. *Wir* —4E **71**
Pasture Clo. *Clo F* —2C **88**
Pasture Clo. *L25* —3B **126**
Pasture Cres. *Wir* —5E **71**
Pasture La. *Rainf* —1A **28**
Pasture Rd. *Wir* —3D **71**
Pastures, The. *St H* —4A **68**
Pastures, The. *Wir* —4F **113**
Pateley Clo. *L32* —4C **22**
Pateley Wlk. *L24* —3F **147**
Paterson St. *Birk* —3C **96**
Patmos Clo. *L5* —5E **55**
Paton Clo. *Wir* —3D **113**
Patricia Av. *Birk* —5F **73**
Patricia Gro. *Boot* —2D **35**
Patrick Av. *Boot* —1D **35**
Pattens Clo. *Boot* —1D **19**
Patten St. *Birk* —1A **96**
Patten's Wlk. *Know* —3D **41**
Patterdale Cres. *L31* —5E **7**
Patterdale Dri. *St H* —3B **64**
Patterdale Rd. *L15* —3E **101**
Patterdale Rd. *Wir* —4F **141**
Pauldings La. *L21* —5A **18**
Pauline Wlk. *L10* —1B **38**
Paul McCartney Way. *L6* —3B **78**
Paul Orr Ct. *L3* —2C **76**
Paulsfield Dri. *Wir* —2E **93**
Paul St. *L3* —3C **76** (1D **4**)
Paulton Clo. *L8* —5F **99**
Paverley Bank. *L27* —3D **105**
Pavilion Clo. *L8* —2B **100**
Pavilion Sports Cen. —5A 58
Paxton Rd. *L36* —2E **83**
Peacehaven Clo. *L16* —1F **103**
Peach Gro. *L31* —1B **22**
Peach Gro. *Hay* —1E **49**
Peach St. *L7* —5F **77**
Peach Tree Clo. *Hale V* —5E **149**
Pearce Clo. *L25* —3F **103**
Pear Gro. *L6* —3B **78**
Pearl Way. *L6* —2B **78**
Pearson Dri. *Boot* —1E **35**
Pearson Rd. *Birk* —5E **97**
Pearson St. *L15* —2F **101**
Pear Tree Av. *L12* —2F **59**
Pear Tree Av. *Run* —3C **166**
Peartree Clo. *Frod* —4D **173**
Pear Tree Clo. *Hale V* —5E **149**
Pear Tree Clo. *Wir* —1C **158**
Pear Tree Rd. *L36* —1E **105**
Peasefield Rd. *L14* —2A **82**
Peasley Cross. —2C 66
Peasley Cross La. *St H* —5B **46**
Peatwood Av. *L32* —1F **39**
Peckers Hill Rd. *St H* —4E **67**
Peckfield Clo. *Brook* —5A **168**
Peckforton Dri. *Sut W* —1F **173**
Peckmill Grn. *L27* —5F **105**
Pecksniff Clo. *L8* —4F **99**
Peebles Av. *St H* —1D **47**
Peebles Clo. *L33* —4D **15**
Peel Av. *Birk* —1F **119**
Peel Clo. *Whis* —3E **85**
Peel Cottage. *L31* —5B **6**
Peel Ho. La. *Wid* —1B **132**
Peel Pl. *L8* —2F **99**
Peel Pl. *St H* —3A **46**
Peel Rd. *Boot* —3A **34**
Peel St. *L8* —5A **100**
Peel St. *Run* —4F **151**
Peel Wlk. *L31* —5B **6**
Peet Av. *Ecc* —4C **44**
Peet St. *L7* —5B **78**
Pelham Gro. *L17* —5C **100**
Pelham Rd. *Wall* —3A **74**
Pemberton Clo. *Will* —5A **170**
Pemberton Rd. *L13* —3A **80**
Pemberton Rd. *Wir* —1B **116**
Pemberton St. *St H* —5E **45**
Pembrey Way. *L25* —4D **127**
Pembroke Av. *Wir* —2E **93**
Pembroke Clo. *St H* —1E **65**
Pembroke Ct. *Birk* —5E **97**
Pembroke Ct. *Mnr P* —2C **154**
Pembroke Gdns. *L3* —4F **77** (4J **5**)
Pembroke Pl. *L3* —4E **77** (4J **5**)
Pembroke Rd. *Boot* —5C **34**
Pembroke St. *L3* —4F **77** (4J **5**)
Pembury Clo. *L12* —5E **39**
Penare. *Brook* —5C **168**
Penarth Clo. *L7* —1B **100**
Pencombe Rd. *L36* —2B **82**
Penda Dri. *L33* —4E **15**
Pendennis Rd. *Wall* —3C **74**
Pendennis St. *L6* —1B **78**
Pendine Clo. *L6* —2C **78**
Pendle Av. *St H* —3D **47**
Pendlebury St. *Clo F* —2C **88**
Pendle Clo. *Wir* —3E **93**
Pendle Dri. *L21* —1C **18**
Pendleton Grn. *L26* —5E **127**
(in two parts)
Pendleton Rd. *L4* —1A **56**
Pendle Vw. *L21* —1C **18**
Pendle Vs. *L21* —2C **18**
Penfold. *L31* —1E **13**
Penfold Clo. *L18* —4D **103**
Penfolds. *Halt B* —1D **167**
Pengwern Gro. *L15* —1D **101**
Pengwern St. *L8* —4A **100**
Pengwern Ter. *Wall* —4C **52**
Penhale Clo. *L17* —2B **122**
Peninsula Clo. *Wall* —3E **51**
Penketh Ct. *Run* —4B **152**
Penketh Grn. *L24* —3E **147**
Penketh's La. *Run* —4A **152**
Penkett Ct. *Wall* —5C **52**
Penkett Gdns. *Wall* —5C **52**
Penkett Gro. *Wall* —5C **52**
Penkett Rd. *Wall* —5B **52**
Penkford La. *C Grn* —2D **69**
Penkford St. *Newt W* —5E **49**
Penlake Ind. Est. *St H* —4E **67**
Penlake La. *St H* —4E **67**
Penley Cres. *L32* —3B **22**
Penlinken Dri. *L6* —2B **78**
Penmann Clo. *L26* —4F **127**
Penmann Cres. *L26* —4F **127**
Penmon Dri. *Wir* —4F **137**
Pennant Av. *L12* —2C **58**
Pennard Av. *L36* —5D **61**
Pennine Clo. *St H* —5E **47**
Pennine Dri. *St H* —5F **47**
Pennine Rd. *Birk* —3C **118**
Pennine Rd. *Wall* —2F **73**
Pennine Way. *L32* —1C **22**
Pennington Av. *Boot* —1E **35**
Pennington Clo. *Frod* —3D **173**

Pennington La. *St H* —5B **48**
Pennington Rd. *L21* —2C **34**
Pennington St. *L4* —1F **55**
Penn La. *Run* —5F **151**
Pennsylvania Rd. *L13* —4D **57**
Penny La. *L18* —5F **101**
Penny La. *C Grn* —3D **69**
Penny La. *Hay* —1F **49**
Penny La. *Wid* —2F **107**
Penny La. Neighbourhood Cen. *L15* —3F **101**
Pennystone Clo. *Wir* —3D **93**
Penpoll Ind. Est. *Boot* —2C **34**
Penrhos Rd. *Wir* —5A **90**
Penrhyd Rd. *Wir* —2D **137**
Penrhyn Av. *L21* —1B **34**
Penrhyn Av. *Wir* —1A **138**
Penrhyn Cres. *Run* —3A **166**
Penrhyn Rd. *Know B* —3B **40**
Penrhyn St. *L5* —1D **77**
Penrith Clo. *Frod* —4D **173**
Penrith Cres. *L31* —5E **7**
Penrith Rd. *St H* —3B **64**
Penrith St. *Birk* —4C **96**
Penrose Av. E. *L14* —4E **81**
Penrose Av. W. *L14* —4E **81**
Penrose St. *L5* —5E **55**
Penryn Av. *St H* —1D **47**
Pensall Dri. *Wir* —5F **137**
Pensarn Rd. *L13* —4F **79**
Pensby. —3A 138
Pensby Clo. *Wir* —2A **138**
Pensby Hall La. *Wir* —5F **137**
Pensby Rd. *Hes* —2F **157**
Pensby Rd. *Thing* —2A **138**
Pensby St. *Birk* —1B **96**
Penshaw Ct. *Run* —3E **167**
Pentire Av. *Wind* —2B **44**
Pentire Clo. *L10* —2B **36**
Pentland Av. *L4* —2A **56**
Pentland Av. *St H* —5F **47**
Pentland Rd. *L33* —1A **24**
Penuel Rd. *L4* —1F **55**
Penvalley Cres. *L6* —2C **78**
Peony Gdns. *St H* —4B **68**
Peover St. *L3* —3D **77** (1F **5**)
Peploe Rd. *Walt* —1D **57**
Peplow Rd. *Kirkby* —3B **22**
Pepper St. *Hale V* —5D **149**
Pera Clo. *L6* —3A **78**
Perch Rock Fort. —1B 52
Percival La. *Run* —5E **151**
Percival Way. *St H* —3C **44**
Percy Rd. *Wall* —4D **75**
Percy St. *Boot* —3B **34**
Percy St. *L8* —2F **99**
Percy St. *St H* —4F **67**
Peregrine Way. *L26* —3E **127**
Perimeter Rd. *L33* —5D **25**
Perriam Rd. *L19* —4D **125**
Perrin Av. *Run* —2E **165**
Perrin Rd. *Wall* —1E **73**
Perrins Rd. *Btnwd* —5F **69**
Perrygate Clo. *L7* —1B **100**
Perry St. *L8* —3D **99**
Perry St. *Run* —5B **152**
Pershore Rd. *L32* —5E **23**
Perth Av. *That H* —4E **65**
Perth Clo. *L33* —4D **15**
Perth St. *L6* —3A **78**
Peterborough Dri. *Boot* —1E **19**
Peterborough Rd. *L15* —3A **102**
Peterlee Clo. *St H* —4F **65**
Peterlee Way. *Boot* —4A **20**
Peter Lloyd Leisure Cen. —1F 79
Peter Mahon Way. *Boot* —4B **34**
Peter Price's La. *Wir* —3E **141**
Peter Rd. *L4* —1E **55**
(in two parts)
Petersfield Clo. *Boot* —4A **20**
Petersgate. *Murd* —3D **169**
Peter's La. *L1* —5D **77** (6E **5**)
Peter St. *L1* —4D **77** (4E **4**)
Peter St. *St H* —4E **45**
Peter St. *Wall* —4E **75**
Peterwood. *Birk* —3A **120**
Petham Ct. *Wid* —5E **109**
Petherick Rd. *L11* —3C **38**
Petton St. *L5* —5F **55**
Petunia Clo. *L14* —2A **82**
Petunia Clo. *St H* —4A **68**
Petworth Clo. *L24* —3B **146**
Peveril St. *L9* —5F **35**
Pex Hill Country Pk. & Vis. Cen. —3E 109
Pharmacy Rd. *L24* —3C **146**
Pheasant Fields. *Hale V* —5C **148**
Pheasant Gro. *L26* —3E **127**
Philbeach Rd. *L4 & L11* —1D **57**
Philharmonic Hall. —1F 99 (7J 5)
Philip Gro. *St H* —4C **66**
Philip Rd. *Wid* —4B **130**
Phillimore Rd. *L6* —3C **78**
Phillip Gro. *L12* —1E **81**
Phillips Clo. *Thor* —4B **10**
Phillips St. *L3* —3C **76** (2D **4**)
Phillips Way. *Wir* —2E **157**
Phipps' La. *Btnwd* —3E **69**
Phoenix Dri. *L14* —2A **82**
Physics Rd. *L24* —2C **146**
Phythian Clo. *L6* —3A **78**
Phythian St. *L6* —3A **78**
Phythian St. *Hay* —2F **47**
Picadilly. *Bil* —1E **31**
Pickerill Rd. *Wir* —1D **115**
Pickering Rake. *Boot* —5D **11**
Pickering Rd. *Wall* —3B **52**
Pickerings Clo. *Run* —4C **166**
Pickering's Pasture Local Nature Reserve. —3B 150
Pickerings Rd. *Haleb* —2B **150**
Pickering St. *L6* —1A **78**
Pickmere Dri. *Brook* —5C **168**
Pickmere Dri. *Wir* —2F **171**
(in two parts)
Pickop St. *L3* —3C **76** (2D **4**)
Pickwick St. *L8* —3F **99**
Pickworth Way. *L31* —3B **22**
Picow Farm Rd. *Run* —1E **165**
Picow Rd. *Run* —5E **151**
Picow St. *Run* —5A **152**
Picton Av. *Run* —1B **166**
Picton Clo. *Pren* —5F **95**
Picton Clo. *Wir* —2D **171**
Picton Cres. *L15* —1E **101**
Picton Gro. *L15* —1D **101**
Picton Rd. *Wat* —4D **17**
Picton Rd. *W'tree* —1D **101**
Picton Sports Cen. —1F 101
Piele Rd. *Hay* —1D **49**
Pighue La. *L7 & L13* —5E **79**
Pigot St. *St H* —5E **45**
Pigott's Rake. *Boot* —5D **11**
Pike Ho. Rd. *Ecc* —3A **44**
Pike Pl. *Ecc* —4B **44**
Pikes Bri. Fold. *Ecc* —4A **44**
Pikes Hey Rd. *Wir* —2F **135**
Pilchbank Rd. *L14* —2E **81**
Pilch La. *L14* —2E **81**
Pilch La. E. *L36* —4A **82**
Pilgrim St. *L1* —1E **99** (7H **5**)
Pilgrim St. *Birk* —3F **97**
Pilgrims Way. *Run* —4D **155**
Pilkington Glass Mus. —1B 64
Pilling La. *L31* —2A **6**
Pilot Gro. *L15* —1D **101**
Pimblett Rd. *Hay* —1E **49**
Pimbley Gro. E. *L31* —4C **12**
Pimbley Gro. W. *L31* —4C **12**
Pimhill Clo. *L8* —3A **100**
Pimpernel Way. *St H* —4A **68**
Pincroft Way. *L4* —4D **55**
Pine Av. *St H* —2F **45**
Pine Av. *Wid* —2B **132**
Pine Av. *Wir* —4F **141**
Pine Clo. *Kirkby* —2C **22**
Pine Clo. *Hay* —2C **48**
Pine Clo. *Huy* —2D **83**
Pine Clo. *Whis* —3E **85**
*Pine Ct. L8 —5A **100***
(off Byles St.)
*Pine Ct. Birk —3D **97***
(off Byles St.)
Pinedale Clo. *Pren* —5D **95**
Pine Gro. *Boot* —4D **35**
Pine Gro. *Wat* —3D **17**
Pinehurst Av. *Wat* —2C **16**
Pinehurst Av. *Anf* —4B **56**
Pinehurst Rd. *L4* —4B **56**
Pinellas. *Run* —4B **152**
Pinemore Rd. *L18* —2A **124**
Pineridge Clo. *Wir* —5C **142**
Pine Rd. *Run* —3C **166**
Pine Rd. *Wir* —1C **158**
Pines, The. *L12* —4F **39**
Pines, The. *Wir* —4B **142**
Pinetop Clo. *L6* —2B **78**
Pinetree Av. *Pren* —5C **94**
Pinetree Clo. *Boot* —2F **19**
Pine Tree Clo. *Wir* —1F **93**
Pinetree Ct. *Wall* —1F **73**
Pinetree Dri. *Wir* —5D **113**
Pine Tree Gro. *Wir* —1F **93**
Pinetree Rd. *L36* —5D **83**
Pine Vw. Dri. *Wir* —5A **138**
Pine Views. *L1* —2E **99**
Pine Walks. *Birk* —3B **118**
Pine Way. *Wir* —5E **137**
Pinewood Av. *W Der* —5D **39**
Pinewood Clo. *N'ley* —3E **105**
Pinewood Dri. *Wir* —2B **158**
Pinewood Gdns. *L33* —5E **15**
Pinewood Rd. *Btnwd* —4F **69**
Pinfold Clo. *Boot* —5E **11**
Pinfold Ct. *Cros* —5D **9**
Pinfold Ct. *Wir* —2A **112**
Pinfold Cres. *L32* —5A **24**
Pinfold Dri. *Ecc* —5A **44**
Pinfold La. *Know* —5B **40**
Pinfold La. *Wir* —2A **112**
Pinfold Rd. *L25* —5C **126**
Pingwood La. *L33* —4F **15**
Pinmill Brow. *Frod* —5B **172**
Pinmill Clo. *Frod* —5B **172**
Pinners Fold. *Nort* —2B **168**
Pinnington Pl. *L36* —4D **83**
Pinnington Rd. *Whis* —3E **85**
Pintail Clo. *St H* —2B **46**
Piper's Clo. *Wir* —2D **157**
Piper's End. *Wir* —2D **157**
Pipers La. *Hes* —5C **136**
(in two parts)
Pipit Clo. *L26* —2E **127**
Pippits Row. *Padd M* —1E **173**
Pirrie Rd. *L9* —5D **37**
Pitch Clo. *Wir* —5D **93**
Pit La. *Wid* —5A **110**
Pit Pl. *L25* —2A **126**
Pitsmead Rd. *L32* —4E **23**
Pitts Heath La. *Run* —4D **155**
Pitt St. *L1* —1D **99**
Pitt St. *St H* —5C **46**
Pitt St. *Wid* —2A **152**
Pitville Av. *L18* —1A **124**
Pitville Clo. *L18* —2A **124**
Pitville Gro. *L18* —1A **124**
Pitville Rd. *L18* —1A **124**

Pitville Ter. *Wid* —5C **130**
Plaistow Ct. *Run* —3E **167**
Plane Clo. *L9* —5B **36**
Plane Tree Gro. *Hay* —1F **49**
Planetree Rd. *L12* —4E **59**
Plane Tree Rd. *Wir* —3E **141**
Plantation Clo. *Cas* —1A **168**
Plantation Rd. *Brom* —1F **163**
Planters, The. *Boot* —1B **20**
Planters, The. *Wir* —5C **92**
Platt Gro. *Birk* —4A **120**
Platts St. *Hay* —2A **48**
Plattsville Rd. *L18* —4A **102**
Playfield Rd. *L12* —4F **59**
Playfield Wlk. *L12* —4F **59**
Playhouse Theatre. —5D 77 (5F 5)
Pleasant Hill St. *L8* —3D **99**
Pleasant St. *Boot* —1B **54**
Pleasant St. *L3* —5E **77** (6H **5**)
Pleasant St. *Wall* —4B **52**
Pleasant Vw. *Boot* —1B **54**
Pleasant Vw. *L7* —4E **79**
Pleasington Clo. *Pren* —5E **95**
Pleasington Dri. *Pren* —5E **95**
Plemont Rd. *L13* —1F **79**
Plimsoll St. *L7* —5B **78**
Plover Dri. *Nort* —2D **169**
Pluckington Rd. *L36* —3B **84**
Plumbers Way. *L36* —4F **83**
Plumer St. *L15* —2E **101**
Plumer St. *Birk* —1A **96**
Plumley Gdns. *Wid* —2A **130**
Plumpstons La. *Frod* —4B **172**
Plumpton St. *L6* —2F **77**
Plum Tree Clo. *Prsct* —5A **64**
Plum Tree Clo. *Stock V* —3B **60**
Plymouth Clo. *Murd* —4E **169**
Plymyard Av. *Brom & East* —4C **162**
Plymyard Clo. *Wir* —5D **163**
Plymyard Copse. *Wir* —5D **163**
Pochard Ri. *Nort* —2D **169**
Pocket Nook. —4C 46
Pocket Nook St. *St H* —4B **46**
Podium Rd. *L13* —2A **80**
Poets Corner. *Wir* —2B **142**
Poets Grn. *Whis* —3F **85**
(in two parts)
Poleacre Dri. *Wid* —2D **131**
Pollard Rd. *L15* —5A **80**
Poll Hill. —1F 157
Poll Hill Rd. *Wir* —1F **157**
Pollitt Cres. *Clo F* —2C **88**
Pollitt Sq. *Wir* —4C **120**
Pollitt St. *Clo F* —3C **88**
Pomfret St. *L8* —3F **99**
Pomona St. *L3* —5E **77** (6H **5**)
Pond Clo. *L6* —2C **78**
Pond Grn. Way. *St H* —2F **67**
Pond Vw. Clo. *Wir* —2C **158**
Pond Wlk. *St H* —2A **68**
Ponsonby Rd. *Wall* —1E **73**
Ponsonby St. *L8* —3A **100**
Pool Bank. *Wir* —5B **120**
Poolbank Rd. *Wir* —5B **120**
Pool End. *St H* —1F **67**
Poole Rd. *Wall* —1D **75**
Poole Wlk. *L8* —5A **100**
Pool Hey. *L28* —3B **60**
(in two parts)
Pool Hollow. *Run* —1B **166**
Pool La. *Brom P* —2C **142**
Pool La. *Run* —4B **152**
Pool La. *Upt* —2A **116**
Poolside Rd. *Run* —1B **166**
Pool St. *Birk* —2D **97**
Pool St. *Wid* —5B **132**
Poolwood Rd. *Wir* —5B **94**
Pope St. *Boot* —3A **34**
Poplar Av. *Ecc* —4A **44**
Poplar Av. *L23* —5F **9**
Poplar Av. *Run* —3C **166**
Poplar Av. *Wir* —4F **93**
Poplar Bank. *L36* —4E **83**
Poplar Clo. *Run* —3C **166**
*Poplar Ct. L8 —5A **100***
(off Weller Way)
Poplar Dri. *Kirkby* —2C **22**
Poplar Dri. *Eve* —1A **78**
Poplar Dri. *Wir* —3A **142**
Poplar Farm Clo. *Wir* —3C **92**
Poplar Gro. *L21* —2F **33**
Poplar Gro. *St H* —5C **44**
Poplar Gro. *Birk* —5D **97**
Poplar Gro. *Hay* —2C **48**
Poplar Gro. *Prsct* —1E **85**
Poplar Rd. *L25* —1F **125**
Poplar Rd. *Hay* —2C **48**
Poplar Rd. *Pren* —5B **96**
Poplar Ter. *Wall* —4B **52**
Poplar Way. *L4* —3D **55**
Poppleford Clo. *L25* —4C **104**
Poppy Clo. *Wir* —4A **72**
Porchester Rd. *L11* —2F **57**
Porchfield Clo. *L11* —5B **38**
Porlock Av. *L16* —4E **103**
Porlock Av. *Sut L* —1C **88**
Porlock Clo. *Wir* —4B **158**
Portal M. *Wir* —4F **137**
Portal Rd. *Wir* —4F **137**
Portbury Clo. *Wir* —1B **142**
Portbury Wlk. *Wir* —1B **142**
Portbury Way. *Wir* —1C **142**
Port Causeway. *Wir* —3C **142**
Portelet Rd. *L13* —2F **79**
Porter Clo. *Rain* —5E **87**
Porter St. *L3* —2B **76**
Porter St. *Run* —5C **152**
Portgate Clo. *L12* —1C **58**
Porthcawl Clo. *Wid* —1C **130**
Porthleven Rd. *Brook* —5B **168**
Portia Av. *Wir* —5E **119**
Portia Gdns. *Wir* —5E **119**
Portia St. *Boot* —2C **54**
Portico. —4B 64
Portico Av. *Prsct* —5A **64**
Portico Ct. *Prsct* —5A **64**
Portico La. *Prsct* —5F **63**
Portland Av. *L22* —3C **16**
Portland Ct. *Wall* —2A **52**
Portland Gdns. *L5* —2C **76**
Portland Pl. *L5* —2E **77**
Portland St. *L5* —2C **76**
Portland St. *Newt W* —4F **49**
Portland St. *Birk* —1A **96**
Portland St. *Run* —4F **151**
Portland St. *Wall* —2A **52**
Portland Way. *St H* —2F **67**
Portlemouth Rd. *L11* —3C **38**
Portloe Av. *L26* —3F **127**
Portman Rd. *L15* —2D **101**
Port of Liverpool Building. —5B 76 (6B 4)
Porto Hey Rd. *Wir* —2D **137**
Porton Rd. *L32* —4C **22**
Portreath Way. *Wind* —2B **44**
Portree Av. *Wir* —5D **163**
Portree Clo. *L9* —4F **35**
Portrush St. *L13* —5E **57**
Portside. *Pres B* —3E **169**
Portsmouth Pl. *Murd* —4E **169**
Port Sunlight. —2B 142
Port Sunlight Heritage Cen. —2B 142
Portway. *L25* —5C **126**
Portwood Clo. *L7* —1B **100**
Post Office La. *West P* —3D **165**
Potter's La. *Wid* —2F **149**
(in two parts)
Pottery Clo. *Whis* —3C **84**
Pottery Fields. *Prsct* —5E **63**
Pottery La. *Whis & Huy* —3B **84**
Poulsom Dri. *Boot* —3C **18**
Poulter Rd. *L9* —1B **36**
Poulton. —1B 162
(Bebington)
Poulton. —3A 74
(Wallasey)
Poulton Bri. Rd. *Birk* —4A **74**
Poulton Clo. *L26* —1D **147**
Poulton Dri. *Wid* —4C **130**
Poulton Grn. Clo. *Wir* —5F **141**
Poulton Hall Rd. *Raby M* —3A **162**
Poulton Hall Rd. *Wall* —3A **74**
Poulton Rd. *Wall* —3A **74**
Poulton Rd. *Wir* —4A **142**
Poulton Royd Dri. *Wir* —5F **141**
Poulton Va. *Wall* —4A **74**
Poverty La. *L31* —2E **13**
Powell Dri. *Bil* —2D **31**
Powell St. *St H* —4E **67**
Powell St. *Pren* —1F **95**
Power Rd. *Birk* —4A **120**
Power Rd. *Brom* —1F **163**
Powis St. *L8* —4A **100**
Pownall Sq. *L3* —4C **76** (3D **4**)
Pownall St. *L1* —1C **98** (7D **4**)
Poynter St. *St H* —4E **65**
Pratt Rd. *Prsct* —5C **62**
Precincts, The. *L23* —1E **17**
Precinct, The. *Wir* —1D **163**
Preece Clo. *Wid* —1D **131**
Preesall Way. *L11* —3C **38**
(in two parts)
Premier St. *L5* —1F **77**
Prentice Rd. *Birk* —3E **119**
Prenton. —4F 117
Prenton Av. *Clo F* —2B **88**
Prenton Dell Av. *Pren* —4A **118**
Prenton Dell Rd. *Pren* —3E **117**
Prenton Farm Rd. *Pren* —4A **118**
Prenton Golf Course. —4B 118
Prenton Grn. *L24* —4E **147**
Prenton Hall Rd. *Pren* —3F **117**
Prenton La. *Birk* —3B **118**
Prenton Pk. —2C 118
Prenton Pk. Rd. *Birk* —1C **118**
Prenton Rd. E. *Birk* —2C **118**
Prenton Rd. W. *Birk* —2B **118**
Prenton Village Rd. *Pren* —3F **117**
Prenton Way. *Nor C* —3D **117**
Prentonwood Ct. *Birk* —3C **118**
Prescot. —5D 63
Prescot By-Pass. *Prsct* —5B **62**
Prescot Cen. *Prsct* —5D **63**
Prescot Dri. *L6* —3D **79**
Prescot F.C. Ground. —4C 84
Prescot Leisure Cen. —1E 85
Prescot Mus. —5C 62
Prescot Rd. *Mag & Mell* —1C **22**
Prescot Rd. *St H* —3B **64**
Prescot Rd. *Cron* —5F **107**
Prescot Rd. *Fair & Old S* —3C **78**
Prescot Rd. *Wid* —1D **131**
Prescot St. *L7* —4F **77** (3J **5**)
Prescot St. *Wall* —3A **52**
Preseland Rd. *L23* —2E **17**
Prestbury Av. *Pren* —2E **117**
Prestbury Clo. *Pren* —2E **117**
Prestbury Clo. *Wid* —4E **131**
Prestbury Dri. *Ecc* —1B **64**
Prestbury Rd. *L11* —4F **37**
Preston Av. *Prsct* —1C **84**
Preston Book. —5F 169
Preston Brook Marina. —3E 169
Preston Gro. *L6* —1C **78**
Preston on the Hill. —4F 169
Preston St. *L1* —4D **77** (4E **4**)
Preston St. *Sut M* —4A **88**

Preston Way. L23 —1A 18
Prestwick Dri. L23 —4C 8
Prestwood Cres. L14 —2F 81
Prestwood Rd. L14 —2F 81
Pretoria Rd. L9 —2B 36
Price Gro. St H —1A 68
Price's La. Pren —5B 96
Price St. L1 —1C 98 (7E 4)
Price St. Birk —1B 96
Primrose Clo. Cas —1A 168
Primrose Clo. Wid —3E 131
Primrose Ct. Wall —3B 52
Primrose Dri. L36 —1E 83
Primrose Gro. Hay —1E 49
Primrose Gro. Wall —4E 75
Primrose Hill. L3 —4D 77 (3E 4)
Primrose Hill. Wir —1A 142
Primrose Rd. L18 —4C 102
Primrose Rd. Birk —2F 95
Primrose St. L4 —3D 55
Primula Clo. St H —4A 68
Primula Dri. L9 —4B 36
Prince Albert M. L1 —2D 99
Prince Alfred Rd. L15 —2F 101
Prince Andrew's Gro. Wind —2C 44
Prince Edward St. Birk —2C 96
Prince Edwin St. L5 —2E 77
Princes Av. Cros —1D 17
Princes Av. East —4E 163
Princes Av. Prin P —2F 99
Princes Av. W Kir —4B 112
Princes Boulevd. Wir —4D 119
Prince's Clo. Cas —1F 167
Princes Gdns. L3 —3C 76 (2C 4)
(in two parts)
Princes Ga. E. L8 —3B 100
Princes Ga. W. L8 —3A 100
Princes Pde. L3 —4A 76 (3A 4)
Princes Park. —3B 100
Princes Pk. —4B 100
Princes Pk. Mans. L8 —4B 100
Princes Pavement. Birk —3E 97
Princes Pl. Birk —5E 97
Princes Pl. Wid —3E 131
Princes Rd. L8 —2F 99
Princes Rd. St H —2C 64
Princess Av. St H —3E 45
Princess Av. Hay —1F 49
Princess Dri. L12 & L14 —3E 59
Princess Rd. Wall —4B 52
Princess St. Run —4A 152
Princess Ter. Pren —4C 96
Princes St. Boot —2B 54
Princes St. L2 —4C 76 (4D 4)
Princes St. Wid —4A 132
Princess Way. S'frth —2F 33
Prince St. L22 —5E 17
Princes Way. St H —5A 30
Princesway. Wall —5A 52
Princeway. Frod —5B 172
Prince William St. L8 —3E 99
Priors Clo. L25 —2B 126
Priorsfield. Wir —1E 93
Priorsfield Rd. L25 —2B 126
Prior St. Boot —2A 34
Priory Clo. Aig —2B 122
Priory Clo. Halt —1A 168
Priory Clo. Whis —5C 84
Priory Clo. Wir —4A 142
Priory Ct. L36 —4D 83
Priory Farm Clo. L19 —5A 124
Priory Gdns. St H —1F 45
Priory Ridge. Cas —1A 168
Priory Rd. L4 —3A 56
Priory Rd. Wall —3E 75
Priory Rd. Wind H —5C 154
Priory Rd. Wir —4C 112
Priory St. L19 —3D 145
Priory St. Birk —3F 97
Priory, The. Rain —3C 86
Priory Way. L25 —2B 126
Priory Wharf. Birk —3F 97
Pritchard Av. L21 —1F 33
Pritt St. L3 —3E 77 (1G 5)
Private Dri. Wir —2D 139
Prizett Rd. L19 —5B 124
Probyn Rd. Wall —1E 73
Procter Rd. Birk —3A 120
Proctor Ct. Boot —1D 19
Proctor Rd. Wir —5C 90
Proctors Clo. Wid —2C 132
Progress Pl. L1 —4D 4
Promenade. Wir —3B 90
Promenade Gdns. L17 —1F 121
Promenade, The. L17 —4C 122
Prophet Wlk. L8 —4E 99
Prospect Ct. L6 —2D 79
Prospect Rd. St H —4D 47
Prospect Rd. Birk —3B 118
Prospect Row. Run —3F 165
Prospect St. Ersk —4F 77
Prospect Va. L6 —2D 79
Prospect Va. Wall —1F 73
Prospect Way. Boot —2B 20
Providence Cres. L8 —3E 99
Provident St. St H —5A 48
Province Pl. Boot —2D 35
Province Rd. Boot —2D 35
Prussia St. L3 —3C 4
(Old Hall St.)
Prussia St. L3 —3C 4
(Pall Mall)
Public Hall St. Run —4A 152
Pudsey St. L1 —4E 77 (4G 5)
Pugin St. L4 —4E 55
Pulford Av. Pren —2A 118
Pulford Clo. Beech —4E 167
Pulford Rd. Beb —2F 141
Pulford St. L4 —4F 55
Pullman Clo. Wir —2D 159
Pumpfields Rd. L3 —3C 76 (1C 4)
Pump House Mus. —2F 97
Pump La. Halt —2F 167
Pump La. Wir —4B 92
Pump Rd. Birk —1E 97
Punnell's La. L31 —2A 6
Purbeck Dri. Wir —5D 115
Purley Gro. L18 —2A 124
Purley Rd. L22 —3C 16
Purser Gro. L15 —1D 101
Putney Ct. Run —3E 167
Pye Rd. Wir —2A 158
Pyes Gdns. St H —1B 46
Pyes La. L28 —4C 60
Pye St. L15 —2F 101
Pye St. St H —4F 67
Pygon's Hill La. L31 —1D 7
Pym St. L4 —1F 55
Pyramids Shop. Cen., The. Birk —3D 97

Quadrangle, The. L18 —5B 102
Quadrant Clo. Murd —5D 169
Quadrant, The. Wir —5B 90
(off Station Rd.)
Quaker La. Wir —1F 157
Quakers All. L2 —4C 76 (4D 4)
Quakers Mdw. Know —4D 41
Quarry Av. Wir —3F 141
Quarry Bank. L33 —2F 23
Quarry Bank. Birk —4D 97
Quarrybank Pl. Birk —4C 96
Quarrybank St. Birk —4C 96
Quarry Clo. Kirkby —2F 23
Quarry Clo. Old S —1F 79
Quarry Clo. Run —1D 167
Quarry Clo. Wir —5F 137
Quarry Ct. Wid —3C 130
Quarry Dale. L33 —2F 23
Quarry Grn. L33 —2F 23
Quarry Grn. Flats. L33 —2F 23
Quarry Hey. L33 —2F 23
Quarry La. Wir —1B 138
Quarry Pk. Rain —5D 87
Quarry Pl. L25 —2F 125
Quarry Rd. Boot —1D 55
Quarry Rd. Thor —4A 10
Quarry Rd. Old S —1F 79
Quarry Rd. E. Beb —3A 142
Quarry Rd. E. Hes —1E 157
Quarry Rd. W. Wir —1E 157
Quarryside Dri. L33 —2A 24
Quarry St. L25 —1F 125
Quarry St. S. L25 —2A 126
Quartz Way. L21 —5C 18
Quayle Clo. Hay —2B 48
Quay Pl. Pres B —3E 169
Quayside. Frod —4D 173
Quay, The. Frod —3D 173
Queen Anne St. L3 —3E 77 (2G 5)
Queen Av. L2 —4C 76 (5D 4)
Queen Av. Shop. Arc. L2 —5C 4
Queen Elizabeth Ct. L21 —5A 18
Queen Mary's Dri. Wir —1B 142
Queen's Av. Meol —3D 91
Queen's Av. Wid —4B 130
Queensbury. Wir —3D 113
Queensbury Av. Wir —1E 163
Queensbury St. L8 —4F 99
Queensbury Way. Wid —1D 131
Queens Clo. L19 —1C 144
Queens Clo. Run —1F 165
Queens Ct. Eve —1A 78
Queens Ct. W'tree —5C 80
Queenscourt Rd. L12 —1C 80
Queensdale Rd. L18 —4A 102
Queens Dock Commercial Cen. L1 —2D 99
Queen's Dri. Wind —2C 44
Queen's Dri. Pren —3A 118
Queens Dri. Wir —2E 157
Queens Dri. Flyover. L13 —4C 80
Queens Dri. Mossley Hill. Moss H —5E 101
Queens Drive Public Baths & Recreation Cen. —1F 55
Queens Dri. Stoneycroft. L13 —1A 80
Queens Dri. Walton. Walt —1A 56
Queens Dri. Wavertree. W'tree —1C 102
Queens Dri. W. Derby. L13 —3E 57
Queensland Av. That H —4E 65
Queensland Pl. That H —4E 65
Queensland St. L7 —1A 100
Queens M. L6 —1A 78
Queens Pk. —3B 74
(Hoylake)
Queens Pk. Community Leisure Cen. —4E 45
Queens Pl. Birk —5E 97
Queen Sq. L1 —4D 77 (4E 5)
(in two parts)
Queen's Rd. Boot —1C 54
Queens Rd. Cros —1E 17
Queens Rd. St H —2C 64
Queens Rd. Birk —3F 119
Queens Rd. Eve —1A 78
Queens Rd. Hay —1F 49
Queen's Rd. Hoy —4A 90
Queens Rd. Prsct —5E 63
Queen's Rd. Run —1F 165
Queens Rd. Wall —2E 75
Queen St. L22 —5D 17
Queen St. St H —3F 45
Queen St. Birk —5E 97
Queen St. Gars —2C 144
Queen St. Run —4A 152

Queen St. *Wall* —1B **74**
Queens Wlk. *L1* —2E **99**
Queensway. *L22* —3F **17**
Queensway. *St H* —5A **30**
Queensway. *Birk* —1A **98** (7A **4**)
Queensway. *Frod* —5B **172**
Queensway. *Wall* —5A **52**
Queensway. *Wid* —1F **151**
Queensway. *Wir* —4C **158**
Queens Wharf. *L3* —2C **98**
Queenswood Av. *Wir* —4E **119**
Quernmore Rd. *L33* —2A **24**
Quernmore Wlk. *L33* —2A **24**
Quickswood Clo. *L25* —4F **103**
Quickswood Dri. *L25* —4F **103**
Quickswood Grn. *L25* —4F **103**
Quickthorn Cres. *L28* —4B **60**
Quigley Av. *Boot* —4A **20**
Quigley St. *Birk* —5E **97**
Quinesway. *Wir* —4A **94**
Quinn St. *Wid* —5B **132**
Quintbridge Clo. *L26* —4E **127**
Quorn St. *L7* —4B **78**

Raby. —5C 160
Raby Av. *Wir* —4B **162**
Raby Clo. *Brom* —3A **162**
Raby Clo. *Hes* —3F **157**
Raby Clo. *Wid* —2D **133**
Raby Dell. *Raby M* —4B **162**
Raby Dri. *More* —2D **93**
Raby Dri. *Raby M* —3A **162**
Raby Gro. *Wir* —4D **119**
Raby Hall Rd. *Wir* —5E **161**
Raby Mere. —3A 162
Raby Mere Rd. *Wir* —5C **160**
(in two parts)
Raby Rd. *Thor H* —4B **160**
Rachel St. *L5* —2D **77**
Radburn Clo. *L23* —5B **10**
Radburn Rd. *L23* —5B **10**
Radford Av. *Wir* —5B **142**
Radford Clo. *Wid* —5C **130**
Radley Dri. *L10* —2C **20**
Radley Dri. *Wir* —4F **159**
Radley Rd. *Wall* —1F **73**
Radleys Ct. *L8* —3F **99**
Radley St. *St H* —4E **65**
Radmore Rd. *L14* —3C **80**
Radnor Av. *Wir* —1F **157**
Radnor Clo. *L26* —1D **147**
Radnor Dri. *Boot* —4E **35**
Radnor Dri. *Wall* —5C **52**
Radnor Dri. *Wid* —2C **130**
Radnor Pl. *L6* —1D **79**
Radnor Pl. *Pren* —3C **96**
Radshaw Ct. *L33* —5F **15**
Radstock Gro. *Sut L* —1D **89**
Radstock Rd. *L6* —3C **78**
Radstock Rd. *Wall* —1E **73**
Radway Rd. *L36* —1F **83**
Raeburn Av. *East* —4D **163**
Raeburn Av. *W Kir* —3C **112**
Raffles Rd. *Birk* —4C **96**
Raffles St. *L1* —2E **99**
Rafter Av. *Boot* —1E **35**
Raglan St. *L19* —2C **144**
Raglan Wlk. *L19* —2C **144**
Railside Ct. *L5* —1C **76**
Railton Av. *Rain* —4D **87**
Railton Clo. *Rain* —5D **87**
Railton Rd. *L11* —1E **57**
Railway Cotts. *L25* —5C **126**
Railway Cotts. *Hoot* —4D **171**
Railway Rd. *Birk* —2F **119**
(in two parts)
Railway St. *L19* —2C **144**
Railway St. *St H* —4B **46**

Railway Ter. *St H* —4E **67**
Railway Vw. *L32* —2C **22**
Railway Vw. *C Grn* —2D **69**
Rainbow Clo. *Wid* —1C **130**
Rainbow Dri. *Mell* —1B **22**
Rainbow Dri. *Halew* —4E **127**
Raines Clo. *Wir* —5E **93**
Rainford Av. *Boot* —3E **35**
Rainford By-Pass. *Rainf* —1F **27**
Rainford Gdns. *L2* —5C **76** (5E **4**)
Rainford Hall Cotts. *Crank* —3E **29**
Rainford Ind. Est. *Rainf* —1C **28**
Rainford Rd. *Wind & Dent G* —1C **44**
Rainford Rd. *Bil* —1B **30**
Rainford Sq. *L2* —5C **76** (5D **4**)
Rainham Clo. *L19* —4C **124**
Rainhill. —3C 86
Rainhill Pk. —3D 87
Rainhill Rd. *Rain & St H* —3C **86**
Rainhill Stoops. —5E 87
Rake Clo. *Wir* —5A **94**
Rake Hey. *Wir* —1B **92**
Rake Hey Clo. *Wir* —1C **92**
Rake La. *Wall* —1B **74**
Rake La. *Wir* —5A **94**
Rake M. *Wir* —5A **94**
Rakersfield Ct. *Wall* —3C **52**
Rakersfield Rd. *Wall* —3C **52**
Rakes La. *L23* —4C **10**
Rake, The. *Brom* —2C **162**
Raleigh Av. *Whis* —4D **85**
Raleigh Rd. *Wir* —2A **72**
Raleigh St. *Boot* —2B **54**
Rame Clo. *L10* —2B **38**
Ramford St. *St H* —1D **67**
Ramilies Rd. *Moss H* —4F **101**
Ramleh Clo. *L23* —2B **16**
Rampit Clo. *Hay* —1F **49**
Ramsbrook Clo. *L24* —3C **146**
Ramsbrook La. *Wid & Hale V* —2C **148**
Ramsbrook Rd. *L24* —3C **146**
Ramsey Clo. *L19* —4D **125**
Ramsey Clo. *Whis* —3E **85**
Ramsey Clo. *Wid* —1E **133**
Ramsey Ct. *Wir* —5B **112**
Ramsey Rd. *L19* —4D **125**
Ramsfield Rd. *L24* —3A **148**
Ramsons Clo. *L26* —3E **127**
Randall Dri. *Boot* —2C **18**
Randle Clo. *Wir* —5F **141**
Randle Heights. *L11* —3E **39**
Randles Rd. *Know B* —3A **40**
Randolph St. *L4* —4F **55**
Randon Gro. *St H* —4F **45**
Ranelagh Av. *L21* —5A **18**
Ranelagh Dri. N. *L19* —4A **124**
Ranelagh Dri. S. *L19* —4A **124**
Ranelagh Pl. *L3* —5E **77** (5G **5**)
Ranelagh St. *L1* —5D **77** (6F **5**)
Ranfurly Rd. *L19* —5B **124**
Rangemore Rd. *L18* —3F **123**
Rankin Hall. *L18* —2E **123**
Rankin St. *Wall* —4A **74**
Ranworth Clo. *L11* —5E **37**
Ranworth Pl. *L11* —5E **37**
Ranworth Sq. *L11* —5E **37**
Ranworth Way. *L11* —5F **37**
Rappart Rd. *Wall* —3D **75**
Rashid Mufti Ct. *L8* —3A **100**
Ratcliffe Pl. *Rain* —2B **86**
Rathbone Rd. *W'tree* —1F **101**
Rathlin Clo. *Wid* —1E **133**
Rathmore Av. *L18* —1A **124**
Rathmore Clo. *Pren* —1A **118**
Rathmore Dri. *Pren* —5A **96**
Rathmore Rd. *Pren* —5A **96**
Raven Clo. *L6* —3A **78**
Raven Ct. *L26* —5F **127**
Ravendale Clo. *Pren* —5D **95**

Ravenfield Clo. *L26* —4E **127**
Ravenfield Dri. *Wid* —1C **130**
Ravenglass Av. *L31* —5D **7**
Ravenhead. —2E 65
Ravenhead Av. *L32* —1E **39**
Ravenhead Retail Pk. *St H* —2A **66**
Ravenhead Rd. *St H* —2E **65**
Ravenhill Cres. *Wir* —2F **71**
Ravenhurst Way. *Whis* —5D **85**
Ravenna Rd. *L19* —4D **125**
Ravenscroft Rd. *Pren* —4C **96**
Ravenside Retail Pk. *L24* —2F **145**
Ravensthorpe Grn. *L11* —5F **37**
Ravenstone Clo. *Wir* —2E **93**
Ravenstone Dri. *St H* —4C **66**
Ravenstone Rd. *L19* —4B **124**
Ravenswood Av. *Birk* —4F **119**
Ravenswood Rd. *L13* —3A **80**
Ravenswood Rd. *Wir* —5A **138**
Raven Way. *Boot* —5C **34**
Rawcliffe Clo. *Wid* —5F **109**
Rawcliffe Rd. *L9* —4F **35**
Rawcliffe Rd. *Birk* —4D **97**
Rawdon Clo. *Pal* —3A **168**
Rawlinson Cres. *L26* —4B **128**
Rawlinson Rd. *L13* —4A **80**
Rawlins St. *L7* —3D **79**
Rawson Clo. *L21* —1F **33**
Rawson Rd. *L21* —5F **17**
(in two parts)
Raydale Clo. *L9* —5A **36**
Raymond Av. *Boot* —4A **20**
Raymond Pl. *L5* —2D **77**
Raymond Rd. *Wall* —3C **74**
Raynham Rd. *L13* —4F **79**
Reade Clo. *Wir* —1A **162**
Reading Clo. *L5* —4D **55**
Reading St. *L5* —4D **55**
Reads Ct. *L9* —1F **35**
Reapers Way. *Boot* —1A **20**
Rear Comn. Pas. *L6* —3D **79**
Reay Ct. *Wall* —3E **75**
Reay St. *Wid* —2C **132**
Rebecca Gdns. *St H* —4C **66**
Recreation St. *St H* —5C **46**
Rector Rd. *L6* —4C **56**
Rectory Clo. *Birk* —5D **97**
Rectory Clo. *Wir* —3F **157**
Rectory Dri. *L26* —3F **127**
Rectory Gdns. *St H* —5C **66**
Rectory La. *Hes* —3E **157**
Rectory Rd. *Wir* —5B **112**
Redacre Clo. *Dut* —2F **175**
Red Banks. *Wir* —3D **135**
Redbourn Av. *L26* —1F **147**
Redbourne Dri. *Wid* —5B **108**
Redbourn St. *L6* —5C **56**
Redbrook Clo. *Wir* —4D **163**
Redbrook St. *L6* —5B **56**
Red Brow La. *Pres B* —2E **169**
Redbrow Way. *L33* —1E **23**
Redburn Clo. *L8* —5A **100**
Redcap Clo. *Wall* —3E **51**
Redcar Dri. *Wir* —5D **163**
Redcar M. *L6* —5B **56**
Redcar Rd. *Wall* —5D **51**
Redcar St. *L6* —5B **56**
Red Cat La. *Crank* —1E **29**
Redcote Ct. *W Kir* —5A **112**
Redcroft. *Wir* —1C **114**
Red Cross St. *L1* —5C **76** (6C **4**)
Red Cut La. *L33* —5E **25**
Redditch Clo. *Wir* —5C **92**
Redfern St. *L20* —3C **54**
Redfield Clo. *Wall* —2D **75**
Redford Clo. *Wir* —5C **92**
Redford St. *L6* —5C **56**
Redgate Av. *L23* —1A **18**
Redgate Dri. *St H* —5D **47**

Redgrave St. *L7* —4C **78**
Redhill Av. *L32* —5F **23**
Red Hill Rd. *Wir* —2B **140**
Redhouse Bank. *Wir* —3A **112**
Redhouse La. *Wir* —3A **112**
Redington Rd. *L19* —4D **125**
Redland Rd. *L9* —5B **20**
Red La. *Frod* —5C **172**
Red Lion Clo. *L31* —1C **12**
Red Lomes. *Boot* —5D **11**
Redmain Way. *L12* —1F **59**
Redmere Dri. *Wir* —2D **159**
Redmires Clo. *L7* —1B **100**
Redmont St. *Birk* —5E **97**
Redmoor Cres. *L33* —5E **15**
Redpoll Gro. *L26* —2E **127**
Red Rock St. *L6* —2B **78**
Red Rum Clo. *L9* —5D **21**
Redruth Av. *St H* —1D **47**
Redruth Clo. *Brook* —4C **168**
Redruth Rd. *L11* —3D **39**
Redstone Clo. *Wir* —3D **91**
Redstone Dri. *Wir* —1C **156**
Redstone Pk. *Wall* —3F **51**
Redstone Ri. *Pren* —3D **95**
Redvers Av. *Hoot* —3F **171**
Redvers Dri. *L9* —2F **35**
Redwald Clo. *L33* —4F **15**
Redwing La. *L25* —4F **103**
Redwing Way. *L26* —2D **127**
Redwood Av. *L31* —4C **6**
Redwood Clo. *L25* —4B **104**
Redwood Clo. *Pren* —2F **117**
*Redwood Ct. L8 —5A **100***
(off Byles St.)
Redwood Dri. *Hay* —3F **47**
Redwood Gro. *Boot* —4C **34**
Redwood Rd. *L25* —4B **104**
Redwood Way. *L33* —4E **15**
Reedale Clo. *L18* —5A **102**
Reedale Rd. *L18* —5A **102**
Reeds Av. E. *Wir* —3F **71**
Reeds Av. W. *Wir* —3F **71**
Reed's La. *Rainf* —2E **27**
Reeds La. *Wir* —2F **71**
Reeds Rd. *L36* —2E **83**
Reedville. *Pren* —4B **96**
Reedville Gro. *Wir* —4F **71**
Reedville Rd. *Wir* —2F **141**
Reeves Av. *Boot* —3E **35**
Reeves St. *St H* —5E **47**
Regal Cres. *Wid* —4B **130**
Regal Dri. *Wind* —3C **44**
Regal Rd. *L11* —5C **38**
Regal Tower. *L11* —5C **38**
Regal Wlk. *L4* —4E **55**
Regent Av. *Boot* —2F **19**
Regent Av. *L14* —4E **81**
Regent Av. *Hay* —1B **48**
Regent Rd. *Boot & Kirk* —3F **33**
Regent Rd. *Cros* —1D **17**
Regent Rd. *L3* —2B **54**
Regent Rd. *Wall* —5D **51**
Regent Rd. *Wid* —3B **132**
Regents Clo. *Wir* —2B **138**
Regents Rd. *St H* —1C **64**
Regent St. *L3* —2B **76**
Regent St. *Newt W* —5F **49**
Regent St. *Run* —4A **152**
Regents Way. *Wir* —4D **119**
Regina Av. *L22* —3C **16**
Reginald Rd. *St H* —5E **67**
Reginald Rd. Ind. Est. *Reg I* —5F **67**
Regina Rd. *L9* —2A **36**
Reigate Clo. *L25* —1C **126**
Rendal Clo. *L5* —1A **78**
Rendcombe Grn. *L11* —5F **37**
Rendelsham Clo. *Wir* —4E **93**
Rendel St. *Birk* —2D **97**
Renfrew Av. *St H* —1D **47**
Renfrew Av. *Wir* —5E **163**
Renfrew St. *L7* —4A **78**
Rennell Rd. *L14* —3C **80**
Rennie Av. *St H* —4C **44**
Renshaw St. *L1* —5E **77** (6G **5**)
Renton Av. *Run* —5D **153**
Renville Rd. *L14* —4C **80**
Renwick Av. *Rain* —2A **86**
Renwick Rd. *L9* —3A **36**
Repton Gro. *L10* —3C **20**
Repton Rd. *L16* —1C **102**
Reservoir Rd. *L25* —1F **125**
Reservoir Rd. *Birk* —3B **118**
Reservoir Rd. N. *Birk* —3B **118**
Reservoir St. *L6* —2A **78**
Reservoir St. *St H* —4C **64**
Rest Hill Rd. *Wir* —2B **140**
Retford Rd. *L33* —3F **23**
Retford Wlk. *L33* —3F **23**
Reva Rd. *L14* —3E **81**
Revesby Clo. *Wid* —2D **131**
Rex Cohen Ct. *L17* —4E **101**
Rexmore Rd. *L18* —2A **124**
Rexmore Way. *L15* —2E **101**
Reynolds Av. *St H* —1B **68**
Reynolds Clo. *L6* —2A **78**
Reynolds Way. *L25* —2A **126**
Rhiwlas St. *L8* —4A **100**
Rhodesia Rd. *L9* —2B **36**
Rhodesway. *Wir* —3B **158**
Rhona Clo. *Wir* —1C **170**
Rhosesmor Clo. *L32* —1F **39**
Rhosesmor Rd. *L32* —2F **39**
Rhyl St. *L8* —4E **99**
Rhyl St. *Wid* —5F **131**
Rialto Clo. *L8* —2F **99**
Ribble Av. *L31* —5E **7**
Ribble Av. *Rain* —3C **86**
Ribble Clo. *Wid* —1F **133**
Ribble Cres. *Bil* —2C **30**
Ribbledale Rd. *L18* —5A **102**
Ribble Ho. *L25* —1C **126**
Ribble Rd. *L25* —1C **126**
Ribbler's Ct. *L32* —2F **39**
Ribbler's La. *Know* —2F **39**
Ribbler's La. *L32* —1D **39**
Ribblesdale Av. *L9* —1B **36**
Ribblesdale Clo. *Wir* —5F **163**
Ribble St. *Birk* —5F **73**
Ribchester Way. *Tarb G* —2A **106**
Rice Hey Rd. *Wall* —1C **74**
Rice La. *L9* —5F **35**
Rice La. *Wall* —1C **74**
Rice St. *L1* —1E **99** (7H **5**)
Richard Allen Way. *L5* —2E **77**
Richard Chubb Dri. *Wall* —5D **53**
Richard Clo. *Cas* —1A **168**
Richard Gro. *L12* —1E **81**
Richard Hesketh Dri. *L32* —3C **22**
Richard Kelly Clo. *L4* —3D **57**
Richard Kelly Dri. *L4* —1D **57**
Richard Kelly Pl. *L4* —3D **57**
Richard Martin Rd. *L21* —4C **18**
Richard Rd. *L23* —4A **8**
Richards Gro. *St H* —4E **47**
Richardson Rd. *Birk* —3E **119**
Richardson St. *L7* —2C **100**
Richland Rd. *L13* —1F **79**
Richmond Av. *L21* —5A **18**
Richmond Av. *Hay* —1B **48**
Richmond Av. *Run* —5E **153**
Richmond Clo. *Ecc* —4A **44**
Richmond Clo. *Wir* —1F **141**
Richmond Ct. *Lith* —1B **34**
Richmond Cres. *Boot* —2F **19**
Richmond Gro. *L31* —4E **7**
Richmond Ho. *L3* —4B **76** (4B **4**)
Richmond Pde. *L3* —4B **4**
Richmond Pk. *L6* —5B **56**
Richmond Rd. *L23* —5E **9**
Richmond Rd. *Wir* —1F **141**
Richmond Row. *L3* —3E **77** (1G **5**)
Richmond St. *L1* —5D **77** (5E **5**)
Richmond St. *Wall* —2B **52**
Richmond St. *Wid* —3C **132**
Richmond Ter. *L6* —1A **78**
Richmond Way. *Hes* —5F **137**
Richmond Way. *Tarb G* —2A **106**
Richmond Way. *Thing* —1A **138**
Rich Vw. *Pren* —1B **118**
Rickaby Clo. *Wir* —2C **162**
Rickman St. *L4* —3D **55**
Rickman Way. *L36* —1F **105**
Ridding La. *Run* —5B **168**
Riddock Rd. *L21* —3B **34**
Ridgefield Rd. *Wir* —2F **137**
Ridgemere Rd. *Wir* —2F **137**
Ridge, The. *Wir* —5D **137**
Ridgetor Rd. *L25* —1F **125**
Ridgeview Rd. *Pren* —4D **95**
Ridgeway. *Murd* —4D **169**
Ridgeway Dri. *L31* —3D **7**
Ridgeway, The. *L25* —1A **126**
Ridgeway, The. *Beb* —4D **119**
Ridgeway, The. *Cron* —3C **108**
Ridgeway, The. *Hes* —3B **158**
Ridgeway, The. *Meol* —4E **91**
Ridgewood Dri. *St H* —5C **66**
Ridgewood Dri. *Wir* —3F **137**
Ridgewood Way. *L9* —1A **36**
Ridgmont Av. *L11* —1F **57**
Riding Clo. *Clo F* —2C **88**
Ridingfold. *L26* —2D **127**
Riding Hill Rd. *Know* —1D **61**
Riding Hill Wlk. *Know* —1D **61**
Ridings Hey. *Pren* —5D **95**
Ridings, The. *Pren* —4D **95**
Riding St. *L3* —4E **77** (4J **5**)
Ridley Gro. *Wir* —3A **112**
Ridley La. *L31* —1D **13**
Ridley Rd. *L6* —3C **78**
Ridley St. *Pren* —4C **96**
Ridsdale. *Wid* —4C **130**
Ridsdale Lawn. *L27* —1A **128**
Riesling Dri. *L33* —5D **15**
Rigby Dri. *Wir* —2D **115**
Rigby Rd. *L31* —4B **6**
Rigby St. *L3* —4B **76** (3B **4**)
Rigby St. *St H* —4F **45**
(Duke St.)
Rigby St. *St H* —5F **45**
(N. John St.)
Riley Av. *Boot* —3D **35**
Riley Dri. *Run* —2A **166**
Rimmer Av. *L16* —5A **82**
Rimmerbrook Rd. *L25* —2B **104**
Rimmer Clo. *L21* —1B **34**
Rimmer Gro. *St H* —5E **47**
Rimmer St. *L3* —4E **77** (3H **5**)
Rimmington Rd. *L17* —2E **123**
Rimrose Rd. *Boot* —3A **34**
Rimrose Valley Rd. *L23* —2A **18**
Rindlebrook La. *Prsct* —1C **84**
Ringcroft Rd. *L13* —3B **80**
Ringo Starr Dri. *L6* —3B **78**
Ringsfield Rd. *L24* —4A **148**
Ringway Rd. *L25* —5C **104**
Ringway Rd. *Run* —5D **153**
Ringways. *Wir* —4D **143**
Ringwood. *Pren* —1A **118**
Ringwood Av. *L14* —4F **81**
Ripley Av. *L21* —4B **18**
Ripley Clo. *L31* —1E **13**
Ripon Clo. *Boot* —4F **19**
Ripon Clo. *L36* —3A **84**
Ripon Rd. *Wall* —5E **51**
Ripon Row. *Halt L* —3D **167**

Ripon St. *L4* —2F **55**
Ripon St. *Birk* —5E **97**
Risbury Rd. *L11* —1F **57**
Rishton Clo. *L5* —1F **77**
Rishton St. *L5* —1A **78**
Ritchie Av. *L9* —2C **36**
Ritherup La. *Rain* —2C **86**
Ritson St. *L8* —3B **100**
Rivacre Rd. *East & Hoot* —5F **163**
Riva La. *Wir* —5E **137**
River Avon St. *L8* —2B **100**
Riverbank Clo. *Wir* —4F **157**
Riverbank Rd. *L19* —5A **124**
Riverbank Rd. *Wir* —4F **157**
River Gro. *Wir* —4B **120**
Riversdale. *Frod* —4C **172**
Riversdale Clo. *L33* —1E **23**
Riversdale Ct. *L19* —4F **123**
Riversdale M. *L19* —4F **123**
Riversdale Rd. *S'frth* —1F **33**
Riversdale Rd. *Aig* —5F **123**
Riversdale Rd. *Halt* —1E **167**
Riversdale Rd. *Wall* —2D **75**
Riversdale Rd. *Wir* —4A **112**
Riverside. *W Der* —2E **59**
Riverside. *Port S* —2B **142**
River Side. *W Kir* —1B **134**
Riverside Bus. Pk. *L3* —1F **121**
Riverside Clo. *Boot* —3A **34**
Riverside Dri. *L17* —2F **121**
Riverside Gro. *St H* —4D **67**
Riverside Ho. *Wall* —5E **75**
Riverside Vw. *Aig* —3C **122**
Riverside Wlk. *L3* —1B **98** (7B **4**)
Riverslea Rd. *L23* —3B **16**
River Vw. *L22* —3C **16**
River Vw. *Wir* —4C **120**
Riverview Heights. *L19* —5F **123**
Riverview Rd. *Wall* —3E **75**
Riverview Rd. *Wir* —5F **143**
Riverview Wlk. *L8* —5F **99**
River Way. *L25* —1C **126**
Riverwood Rd. *Brom* —1F **163**
Riviera Dri. *Birk* —3D **119**
Rivington Av. *St H* —2E **45**
Rivington Av. *Pren* —5E **95**
Rivington Rd. *Dent G & St H* —5D **45**
Rivington Rd. *Wall* —3C **74**
Rivington Rd. *White I* —2E **175**
Rivington St. *St H* —1D **65**
Roadwater Clo. *L25* —2B **104**
Robarts Rd. *L4* —5A **56**
Robeck Rd. *L13* —5B **80**
Robert Dri. *Wir* —1E **115**
Robert Gro. *L12* —1E **81**
Roberts Av. *Hay* —3F **47**
Roberts Ct. *L21* —5A **18**
Roberts Ct. *Hall P* —4F **167**
Roberts Dri. *Boot* —1E **35**
Robertson St. *L8* —4E **99**
Roberts St. *L3* —3B **76** (2A **4**)
Robert St. *Birk* —2D **97**
Robert St. *Run* —5C **152**
Robert St. *Wid* —3B **132**
Robina Rd. *St H* —3D **67**
Robin Clo. *Murd* —3D **169**
Robins La. *St H* —3C **66**
Robinson M. Birk —3F 97
(off Gertrude St.)
Robinson Pl. *St H* —5C **46**
Robinson Rd. *L21* —4C **18**
Robinson St. *St H* —5D **47**
Robin Way. *Wir* —2B **116**
Robsart St. *L5* —1E **77**
Robson St. *Eve* —4F **55**
Robson St. *Old S* —5F **79**
Roby. —4C 82
Roby Clo. *Rain* —2C **86**
Roby Mt. Av. *L36* —4D **83**
Roby Rd. *Bow P & Huy* —5F **81**
(in two parts)
Roby St. *Boot* —4C **34**
Roby St. *L15* —2E **101**
Roby St. *St H* —2D **65**
Roby Well Way. *Bil* —1D **31**
Rocastle Clo. *L6* —3A **78**
Rochester Av. *Boot* —4F **19**
Rochester Gdns. *St H* —2D **65**
Rochester Rd. *Birk* —2F **119**
Rock Av. *Wir* —1F **157**
Rock Bank. *Wir* —4A **94**
Rockbank Rd. *L13* —1E **79**
Rockbourne Av. *L25* —4F **103**
Rockbourne Grn. *L25* —4F **103**
Rockbourne Way. *L25* —4F **103**
Rock Clo. *Birk* —2F **119**
Rock Ct. *L13* —3A **80**
Rock Dri. *Frod* —4C **172**
Rocket Trad. Cen. *L14* —5C **80**
Rock Ferry. —2A 120
Rock Ferry By-Pass. *Birk* —1A **120**
Rockfield Clo. *Wid* —2D **131**
Rockfield Gdns. *L31* —5C **6**
Rockfield Rd. *L4* —4F **55**
Rockford Av. *L32* —1E **39**
Rockford Clo. *L32* —1E **39**
Rockford Wlk. *L32* —1E **39**
Rock Gro. *L13* —3F **79**
Rockhill Rd. *L25* —2B **126**
Rockhouse St. *L6* —1C **78**
Rockingham Ct. *L33* —1F **23**
Rockland Rd. *L22* —3E **17**
Rockland Rd. *Wall* —4F **51**
Rocklands Av. *Wir* —5A **120**
Rocklands La. *Wir* —3C **160**
Rock La. *L31* —4F **13**
Rock La. *Wid* —1E **131**
Rock La. E. *Birk* —3A **120**
(in two parts)
Rock La. W. *Birk* —3F **119**
Rockley St. *L4* —3E **55**
(in two parts)
Rockmount Clo. *L25* —1F **125**
Rockmount Pk. *L25* —1F **125**
Rockmount Rd. *L17* —3F **123**
Rock Pk. *Birk* —2A **120**
(in two parts)
Rock Pk. Rd. *Birk* —3B **120**
Rockpoint Av. *Wall* —4C **52**
Rockside Rd. *L18* —2A **124**
Rock St. *L13* —3A **80**
Rock St. *St H* —3C **64**
Rock Vw. *L5* —5E **55**
Rock Vw. *Mag* —1A **22**
Rockville Rd. *L14* —5C **80**
Rockville St. *Birk* —2F **119**
Rockwell Clo. *L12* —3D **59**
Rockwell Rd. *L12* —3D **59**
Rockybank Rd. *Birk* —1D **119**
Rocky La. *Anf* —1C **78**
Rocky La. *Child* —1C **102**
Rocky La. *Wir* —2F **157**
Rocky La. S. *Wir* —2A **158**
Roderick Rd. *L4* —1A **56**
Roderick St. *L3* —3E **77** (2H **5**)
Rodgers Clo. *Frod* —4B **172**
Rodick St. *L25* —2F **125**
Rodmell Rd. *L9* —2B **36**
Rodney St. *Boot* —1B **54**
Rodney St. *L1* —1E **99** (7H **5**)
Rodney St. *St H* —5E **45**
Rodney St. *Birk* —4D **97**
Roe All. *L1* —5D **77** (6F **5**)
Roedean Clo. *Mag* —5D **7**
Roedean Clo. *Wltn* —3B **126**
Roehampton Dri. *L23* —4C **8**
Roehampton Dri. *Run* —3E **167**
Roemarsh Clo. *L12* —1B **58**
Roemarsh Ct. *Hall P* —4E **167**
Roe St. *L1* —4D **77** (5F **5**)
Roften Works Ind. Est. *Hoot* —5D **171**
Rogers Av. *Boot* —3E **35**
Rogersons Grn. *L26* —2E **127**
Rokeby Clo. *L3* —2E **77** (1H **5**)
Rokeby Ct. *Mnr P* —2D **155**
Rokeby St. *L3* —3E **77** (1H **5**)
Roker Av. *Wall* —3A **74**
Rokesmith Av. *L7* —1C **100**
Roland Av. *St H* —1C **46**
Roland Av. *Run* —1F **165**
Roland Av. *Wir* —1D **141**
Rolands Wlk. *Cas* —5F **153**
Roleton Clo. *Boot* —1B **20**
Rolleston Dri. *Beb* —3A **142**
Rolleston Dri. *Wall* —4F **51**
Rolling Mill La. *St H* —3F **67**
Rollo St. *L4* —4D **55**
Roman Clo. *Cas* —5E **153**
Roman Rd. *Meol* —2D **91**
Roman Rd. *Pren* —4A **118**
(in two parts)
Rome Clo. *L36* —3D **83**
Romer Rd. *L6* —3C **78**
Romford Way. *L26* —1F **147**
(in two parts)
Romilly St. *L6* —3A **78**
Romilly St. *Birk* —3D **97**
Romley St. *L4* —1F **55**
Romney Clo. *Wid* —2E **133**
Romulus St. *L7* —4D **79**
Ronald Clo. *L22* —4F **17**
Ronald Rd. *L22* —4F **17**
Ronald Ross Av. *Boot* —2F **19**
Ronaldshay. *Wid* —2E **133**
Ronald St. *L13* —3F **79**
Ronaldsway. *Cros* —4A **10**
Ronaldsway. *Faz* —1A **38**
Ronaldsway. *Halew* —4A **128**
Ronaldsway. *Hes* —4F **157**
Ronaldsway. *Upt* —3F **93**
Ronan Clo. *Boot* —4A **34**
Ronan Rd. *Wid* —2D **151**
Rone Clo. *Wir* —1D **93**
Rookery La. *Rainf* —1A **28**
Rooks Way. *Wir* —2E **157**
Rooley, The. *L36* —5D **83**
Roosevelt Dri. *L9* —5B **20**
Roper's Bri. Clo. *Whis* —3D **85**
Roper St. *L8* —4F **99**
Roper St. *St H* —4C **46**
Rosalind Av. *Wir* —5E **119**
Rosalind Way. *L20* —2D **55**
Rosam Ct. *Hall P* —4E **167**
Rosclare Dri. *Wall* —5F **51**
Roscoe & Gladstone Hall. *L17* —5E **101**
Roscoe Clo. *Tarb G* —2A **106**
Roscoe Cres. *West P* —3E **165**
Roscoe La. *L1* —1E **99** (7G **5**)
Roscoe Pl. *L1* —5E **77** (7G **5**)
Roscoe St. *L1* —1E **99** (7H **5**)
Roscoe St. *St H* —1D **65**
Roscommon St. *L5* —2E **77**
(in two parts)
Roscote Clo. *Wir* —3F **157**
Roscote, The. *Wir* —3F **157**
Roseacre. *Wir* —3A **112**
Roseate Ct. *Wall* —3E **51**
Rose Av. *Boot* —1C **34**
Rose Av. *St H* —4C **66**
Rose Av. *Hay* —2E **49**
Rose Bank Rd. *Child* —2D **103**
Rosebank Rd. *Huy* —5C **60**
Rosebank Way. *L36* —1C **82**
Roseberry Av. *Wall* —2C **74**
Rosebery Av. *L22* —3C **16**
Rosebery Gro. *Birk* —2B **118**
Rosebery Rd. *Dent G* —3D **45**

Rosebery St. *L8* —2A **100**
Rosebourne Clo. *L17* —2B **122**
Rose Brae. *L18* —5A **102**
Rosebrae Ct. *Birk* —2F **97**
Rose Brow. *L25* —5A **104**
Rose Clo. *Murd* —5D **169**
Rose Ct. *L15* —2E **101**
Rose Ct. *Birk* —3D **97**
Rose Cres. *Wid* —5F **131**
Rosecroft. *Wir* —4C **162**
Rosecroft Ct. *Wir* —5A **90**
Rosedale Av. *L23* —1E **17**
Rosedale Clo. *L9* —4B **36**
Rosedale Rd. *L18* —4A **102**
Rosedale Rd. *Birk* —1E **119**
Rose Dri. *Rainf* —1A **28**
Rosefield Av. *Wir* —5E **119**
Rosefield Rd. *L25* —3C **126**
Rosegarth Grn. *L13* —2B **80**
Roseheath Dri. *L26* —5F **127**
Roseheath Ho. *L26* —5A **128**
Rose Hill. *L3* —3D **77** (1F **5**)
Rosehill Av. *Bold* —5B **68**
Rosehill Ct. *L25* —5A **104**
Roseland Clo. *L31* —3B **6**
Roselands Ct. *Birk* —3E **119**
Rose La. *L18* —1F **123**
Rose Lea Clo. *Wid* —4A **110**
Rosemary Av. *Beech* —1F **173**
Rosemary Clo. *L7* —1A **100**
Rosemary Clo. *Pren* —1E **95**
Rosemead Av. *Wir* —3F **137**
Rosemont Rd. *L17* —2E **123**
Rosemoor Dri. *L23* —5A **10**
Rose Mt. *Pren* —1B **118**
Rose Mt. Clo. *Pren* —1A **118**
Rose Mt. Dri. *Wall* —5A **52**
Rose Pl. *L3* —3D **77** (1F **5**)
(in two parts)
Rose Pl. *Rainf* —1A **28**
Rose Pl. *Birk* —1F **119**
(New Chester Rd.)
Rose Pl. *Birk* —5D **97**
(Victoria Rd.)
Roseside Dri. *L27* —4F **105**
Rose St. *L1* —4F **5**
Rose St. *L25* —2F **125**
Rose St. *Wid* —5F **131**
Rose Ter. *L18* —5A **102**
Rose Va. *L5* —1E **77**
(Gt. Homer St., in two parts)
Rose Va. *L5* —1E **77**
(Netherfield Rd. N.)
Rose Vw. Av. *Wid* —2A **132**
Rose Vs. *L15* —2F **101**
Rosewarne Clo. *L17* —2B **122**
Rosewood Clo. *N'ley* —4E **105**
Rosewood Clo. *Stock V* —4B **60**
Rosewood Dri. *Wir* —1B **92**
Rosewood Gdns. *L11* —2B **58**
Roseworth Av. *L9* —1A **36**
Roskell Rd. *L25* —5C **126**
Roslin Rd. *Pren* —5B **96**
Roslin Rd. *Wir* —1D **137**
Roslyn St. *Birk* —1F **119**
Rossall Av. *L10* —2D **21**
Rossall Clo. *Hale V* —5E **149**
Rossall Rd. *L13* —4B **80**
Rossall Rd. *Wid* —2D **133**
Rossall Rd. *Wir* —5F **71**
Ross Av. *Wir* —2C **72**
Ross Clo. *Know* —5D **41**
Rossendale Clo. *Pren* —5D **95**
Rossett Av. *L17* —3D **101**
Rossett Rd. *L23* —2C **16**
Rossett St. *L6* —1C **78**
Rossini St. *L21* —2A **34**
Rosslyn Av. *L31* —2B **12**
Rosslyn Cres. *Wir* —1E **93**
Rosslyn Dri. *Wir* —1E **93**
Rosslyn Pk. *Wir* —2E **93**
Rosslyn St. *L17* —1B **122**
Rossmore Gdns. *L4* —3B **56**
Ross St. *St H* —4C **46**
Ross St. *Wid* —3B **132**
Ross Tower Ct. *Wall* —3C **52**
Rostherne Av. *Wall* —3A **74**
Rostherne Cres. *Wid* —2D **131**
Rosthwaite Gro. *St H* —4B **30**
Rosthwaite Rd. *L12* —5B **58**
Roswell Ct. *L28* —5B **60**
Rothbury Clo. *Beech* —4E **167**
Rothbury Clo. *Wir* —1C **92**
Rothbury Ct. *Sut M* —4B **88**
Rothbury Rd. *L14* —5F **59**
Rotherham Clo. *L36* —2E **83**
Rotherwood Clo. *Wir* —1D **141**
Rothesay Clo. *St H* —1E **47**
Rothesay Clo. *Cas* —5F **153**
Rothesay Ct. *Wir* —3F **141**
Rothesay Dri. *L23* —2E **17**
Rothesay Dri. *Wir* —1E **171**
Rothesay Gdns. *Pren* —3F **117**
Rothsay Clo. *L5* —2E **77**
Rothwells La. *L23* —3B **10**
Rothwell St. *L6* —2A **78**
Rotunda St. *L5* —1D **77**
Roughdale Av. *L32* —1F **39**
Roughdale Av. *Sut M* —2B **88**
Roughdale Clo. *L32* —1F **39**
Roughwood Dri. *L33* —2F **23**
Roundabout, The. *Wid* —3D **109**
Round Hey. *L28* —3A **60**
Round Meade, The. *L31* —5B **6**
Roundwood Dri. *Sher I* —2B **66**
Routledge St. *Wid* —3B **132**
Rowan Av. *L12* —2F **59**
Rowan Clo. *St H* —1D **47**
Rowan Clo. *Hay* —3F **47**
Rowan Clo. *Run* —3C **166**
Rowan Ct. *L17* —2E **123**
Rowan Ct. *Wir* —2B **114**
Rowan Dri. *L32* —2C **22**
Rowan Gro. *L36* —1D **105**
Rowan Gro. *Wir* —3E **141**
Rowan Tree Clo. *Wir* —1C **114**
Rowena Clo. *L23* —5F **9**
Rowsley Gro. *L9* —1B **36**
Rowson St. *Prsct* —4D **63**
Rowson St. *Wall* —2B **52**
Rowthorn Clo. *Wid* —4E **131**
Rowton Clo. *Pren* —1F **117**
Roxborough Clo. *Btnwd* —5F **69**
Roxborough Wlk. *L25* —1C **126**
Roxburgh Av. *L17* —1C **122**
Roxburgh Av. *Birk* —2D **119**
Roxburgh St. *Boot & L4* —1E **55**
Royal Av. *Wid* —3B **130**
Royal Court Theatre. —4D 77 (4F 5)
Royal Cft. *L12* —2B **80**
Royal Gro. *St H* —2D **65**
Royal Liver Building. —5B 76 (5B 4)
Royal Liverpool Golf Course. —1A 112
Royal Mail St. *L3* —5E **77** (5G **5**)
Royal Pl. *Wid* —4B **130**
Royal Standard Way. *Birk* —1F **119**
Royal St. *L4* —4E **55**
Royden Av. *Run* —2F **165**
Royden Av. *Wall* —1D **75**
Royden Pk. —4A 114
Royden Rd. *Wir* —3E **93**
(in two parts)
Royden St. *L8* —5F **99**
Royden Way. *L3* —1E **121**
Roysten Gdns. *St H* —1D **67**
Royston Av. *Wall* —2D **75**
Royston St. *L7* —5B **78**
Royton Clo. *L26* —1F **147**
Royton Rd. *L22* —3F **17**
Rubbing Stone. *Wir* —3D **135**
Ruby St. *L8* —1F **121**
(in two parts)
Rudd Av. *St H* —1A **68**
Rudd St. *Wir* —4B **90**
Rudgate. *Whis* —4E **85**
Rudgrave M. *Wall* —1D **75**
Rudgrave Pl. *Wall* —1D **75**
Rudgrave Sq. *Wall* —1D **75**
Rudheath La. *Run* —4D **155**
Rudley Wlk. *L24* —5F **147**
Rudston Rd. *L16* —1C **102**
Rudyard Clo. *L14* —3C **80**
Rudyard Rd. *L14* —3C **80**
Rufford Av. *L31* —4E **7**
Rufford Clo. *L10* —5F **21**
Rufford Clo. *Prsct* —1F **85**
Rufford Clo. *Wid* —2C **130**
Rufford Rd. *Boot* —3C **34**
Rufford Rd. *L6* —3C **78**
Rufford Rd. *Wall* —3B **74**
Rufford Wlk. *St H* —2E **47**
Rugby Dri. *L10* —4E **21**
Rugby Rd. *L9* —5B **20**
Rugby Rd. *Wall* —1F **73**
Ruislip Clo. *L25* —2C **126**
Rullerton Rd. *Wall* —2A **74**
Rumford Pl. *L3* —4B **76** (4B **4**)
Rumford St. *L2* —4C **76** (4C **4**)
Rumney Pl. *L4* —3D **55**
Rumney Rd. *L4* —3E **55**
Rumney Rd. W. *L4* —3D **55**
Runcorn. —4A 152
Runcorn Dock Rd. *Run* —5E **151**
Runcorn F.C. Ground. —4B 152
Runcorn Golf Course. —4A 166
Runcorn Hill Local Nature Reserve & Vis. Cen. —2F 165
Runcorn Rd. *Nort & Moore* —3F **155**
Runcorn Spur Rd. *Run* —5B **152**
Runcorn Swimming Pool. —4B 152
Rundle Rd. *L17* —2E **123**
Rundle St. *Birk* —1A **96**
Runic St. *L13* —4F **79**
Runnel's La. *L23* —5C **10**
Runnel, The. *Nest* —5E **159**
Runnymead Wlk. Wid —2C 132
(off William St.)
Runnymede. *L36* —2D **83**
Runnymede Clo. *L25* —5A **104**
Runnymede Dri. *Hay* —2A **48**
Runton Rd. *L25* —4C **104**
Rupert Dri. *L6* —3A **78**
Rupert Rd. *L36* —3C **82**
Rupert Row. *Cas* —2A **168**
Ruscar Clo. *L26* —2E **127**
Ruscombe Rd. *L14* —1F **81**
Rushden Rd. *L32* —4A **24**
Rushey Hey Rd. *L32* —3E **23**
Rushfield Cres. *Brook* —5B **168**
Rushgreen Clo. *Pren* —2C **94**
Rushlake Dri. *L27* —4D **105**
Rushmere Rd. *L11* —1F **57**
Rusholme Clo. *L26* —1A **148**
Rushton Clo. *Wid* —1E **131**
Rushton Pl. *L25* —2A **126**
Rushton's Wlk. *Boot* —1D **19**
Rushy Vw. *Newt W* —4F **49**
Ruskin Av. *Birk* —3F **119**
Ruskin Av. *Wall* —3A **74**
Ruskin Clo. *Boot* —5C **34**
Ruskin Dri. *Dent G* —4D **45**
Ruskin St. *L4* —2E **55**
Ruskin Way. *L36* —5D **83**
Rusland Av. *Wir* —3F **137**
Rusland Rd. *L32* —5E **23**
Russell Ct. *Wid* —5B **110**

Russell Pl. *L3* —5E **77** (5H **5**)
Russell Pl. *Gars* —1C **144**
Russell Rd. *Birk* —1F **119**
(in two parts)
Russell Rd. *Gars* —1C **144**
Russell Rd. *Huy* —4B **84**
Russell Rd. *Moss H* —4F **101**
Russell Rd. *Run* —1E **165**
Russell Rd. *Wall* —1E **73**
Russell St. *L3* —4E **77** (4H **5**)
Russell St. *Birk* —2E **97**
Russet Clo. *L27* —4E **105**
Russet Clo. *St H* —3F **45**
Russian Av. *L13* —1F **79**
Russian Dri. *L13* —1F **79**
Rutherford Clo. *L13* —5E **79**
Rutherford Rd. *Mag* —3E **13**
Rutherford Rd. *Wind* —2C **44**
Rutherford Rd. *Moss H* —3A **102**
Rutherglen Av. *L23* —3F **17**
Ruth Evans Ct. *Rain* —2A **86**
Ruthven Rd. *Lith* —1A **34**
Ruthven Rd. *Old S* —5B **80**
Rutland Av. *Halew* —4F **127**
Rutland Av. *Seft P* —3D **101**
Rutland Clo. *L5* —1F **77**
Rutland Ho. *L17* —4D **101**
Rutland St. *Boot* —4D **35**
Rutland St. *St H* —3F **45**
Rutland St. *Run* —4F **151**
Rutland Way. *L36* —3B **84**
Rutter St. *L8* —4E **99**
Rycot Rd. *L24* —3B **146**
Rycroft Rd. *L10* —1E **37**
Rycroft Rd. *Meol* —3E **91**
Rycroft Rd. *Wall* —3C **74**
Rydal Av. *Cros* —3F **17**
Rydal Av. *Pren* —4C **94**
Rydal Av. *Prsct* —5F **63**
Rydal Bank. *Wall* —2C **74**
Rydal Bank. *Wir* —5A **120**
Rydal Clo. *Ain* —3F **21**
Rydal Clo. *Kirkby* —1D **23**
Rydal Clo. *Hes* —3A **138**
Rydal Gro. *St H* —1A **46**
Rydal Gro. *Run* —2B **166**
Rydal Rd. *L36* —5E **83**
Rydal St. *L5* —5A **56**
Rydal Way. *Wid* —3C **130**
Rydecroft. *L25* —2F **125**
Ryder Clo. *Rain* —2A **86**
Ryder Rd. *Wid* —5B **110**
Rye Clo. *Clo F* —2C **88**
Ryecote. *L32* —1E **39**
Rye Ct. *L12* —5E **59**
Rye Cft. *L21* —2B **18**
Ryecroft Rd. *Hes* —3C **158**
Ryedale Clo. *L8* —2B **100**
Ryefield La. *L21* —2B **18**
Ryegate Rd. *L19* —4B **124**
Rye Gro. *L12* —5E **59**
Rye Hey Rd. *L32* —3E **23**
Ryland Pk. *Wir* —2A **138**
Rylands Hey. *Wir* —5D **93**
Rylands St. *Wid* —4B **132**
Ryleys Gdns. *L2* —4D **4**
Rymer Gro. *L4* —2A **56**
Ryton Rd. *L32* —4D **23**

Sabre Clo. *Murd* —3D **169**
Sackville Rd. *Wind* —2C **44**
Saddle Clo. *L9* —5D **21**
Saddlers Ri. *Nort* —2C **168**
Sadler's La. *St H* —1E **43**
Sadler St. *Wid* —3C **132**
Saffron Gdns. *St H* —1D **67**
Saffron M. *L23* —4B **10**
St Agnes Rd. *Kirk* —3D **55**
St Agnes Rd. *Huy* —4E **83**
St Aidan's Ct. *Pren* —3F **95**
St Aidan's Gro. *L36* —4C **60**
St Aidans Ter. L5 —5D 55
(off Latham St.)
St Aidan's Ter. *Pren* —3F **95**
St Aidan's Way. *Boot* —2E **19**
St Albans. *L6* —1A **78**
St Albans Clo. *Hay* —1F **49**
St Albans Ct. *L5* —1C **76**
St Alban's Rd. *Boot* —5C **34**
St Albans Rd. *Pren* —2A **96**
St Albans Rd. *Wall* —2B **74**
St Alban's Sq. *Boot* —1C **54**
St Ambrose Cft. *Boot* —1E **19**
St Ambrose Gro. *L4* —5B **56**
St Ambrose Rd. *Wid* —3C **132**
St Ambrose Way. *L5* —2E **77** (1H **5**)
St Andrew Rd. *L4* —5B **56**
St Andrews Av. *L12* —5E **59**
St Andrew's Ct. *L22* —5E **17**
St Andrews Dri. *Cros* —4B **8**
St Andrew's Dri. *Huy* —4C **60**
St Andrews Gdns. *L3* —4E **77** (4H **5**)
St Andrew's Gro. *Boot* —2C **18**
St Andrews Gro. *St H* —2B **46**
St Andrews Pl. *L17* —1C **122**
St Andrews Rd. *Boot* —2C **34**
St Andrew's Rd. *L23* —4B **8**
St Andrews Rd. *Beb* —3A **142**
St Andrew's Rd. *Pren* —3B **96**
St Andrew St. *L3* —5E **77** (5J **5**)
St Andrews Vw. *L33* —4E **15**
St Annes Clo. *Birk* —2D **97**
St Anne's Cotts. *L14* —2C **80**
St Anne's Ct. *L13* —3F **79**
St Anne's Ct. *L17* —3E **123**
St Annes Gdns. *L17* —3E **123**
St Annes Gro. *L17* —3E **123**
St Annes Gro. *Birk* —1C **96**
St Anne's Ho. *Boot* —1C **54**
St Annes Pl. *Birk* —1C **96**
St Anne's Rd. *Aig* —3E **123**
St Anne's Rd. *Huy* —5E **83**
St Annes Rd. *Wid* —2B **132**
St Annes Ter. *Birk* —2C **96**
St Anne St. *L3* —3E **77** (1G **5**)
St Anne St. *Birk* —1C **96**
(in three parts)
St Annes Way. *Birk* —2D **97**
St Ann Pl. *Rain* —2C **86**
St Anns. —5C 44
St Ann's Rd. *St H* —5C **44**
St Anthony's Clo. *Huy* —4C **60**
St Anthony's Gro. *Boot* —2D **19**
St Anthony's Pl. *L5* —1D **77**
St Anthony's Rd. *L23* —5B **8**
St Anthony's Shop. Cen. *L5* —1D **77**
St Asaph Gro. *Boot* —4F **19**
St Augustine St. *L5* —1D **77**
St Augustine's Way. *Boot* —1D **19**
St Austell Clo. *Brook* —4B **168**
St Austell Clo. *Wir* —5B **70**
St Austells Rd. *L4* —1E **55**
St Bartholomews Ct. *Huy* —3C **82**
St Benedict's Gro. *L36* —4C **60**
St Benet's Way. *Boot* —2E **19**
St Bernard's Clo. *Boot* —2D **19**
St Bernards Clo. *L8* —2A **100**
St Bernard's Dri. *Boot* —2D **19**
St Brendan's Clo. *L36* —4C **60**
St Bride's Rd. *Wall* —1D **75**
St Bride St. *L8* —1F **99**
St Bridget's Gro. *Boot* —2D **19**
St Bridget's La. *Wir* —5B **112**
St Brigids Cres. *L5* —1C **76**
St Catherine's Clo. *L36* —5E **83**
St Catherines Gdns. *Birk* —5D **97**
St Catherine's Rd. *Boot* —5C **34**
St Chad's Dri. *L32* —3E **23**
St Chads Pde. *L32* —3E **23**
St Christoper's Dri. *L36* —4C **60**
St Christopher's Av. *Boot* —1D **19**
St Clare Rd. *L15* —2E **101**
St Columbas Clo. *Wall* —1D **75**
St Cuthberts Clo. *L12* —5E **39**
St Cyrils Clo. *L27* —3C **104**
St Damian's Cft. *Boot* —2E **19**
St David Rd. *Pren* —3A **96**
St David Rd. *Wir* —4F **163**
St David's Clo. *Rain* —2C **86**
St David's Gro. *Boot* —3D **19**
St Davids La. *Pren* —4D **95**
St Davids Rd. *Anf* —5B **56**
St David's Rd. *Huy* —1B **82**
St Domingo Gro. *L5* —5F **55**
St Domingo Rd. *L5* —4E **55**
St Domingo Va. *L5* —5F **55**
St Dunstan's Gro. *Boot* —2D **19**
St Edmond's Rd. *Boot* —1C **54**
St Edmund's Rd. *Wir* —2F **141**
St Edwards Clo. *Birk* —1B **96**
St Elmo Rd. *Wall* —1D **75**
St Gabriel's Av. *L36* —4A **84**
St George's Av. *Wind* —3C **44**
St George's Av. *Birk* —2D **119**
St Georges Ct. *Wall* —1E **73**
St Georges Ct. *Wid* —4D **131**
St George's Gro. *Boot* —3D **19**
St George's Gro. *Wir* —1D **93**
St George's Hall. —4D 77 (4F 5)
St George's Heights. *L5* —1E **77**
St George's Hill. *L5* —1E **77**
St George's Mt. *Wall* —3B **52**
St George's Pk. *Wall* —3B **52**
St George's Pl. *L1* —4D **77** (4F **5**)
St Georges Rd. *St H* —1D **65**
St George's Rd. *Huy* —1E **83**
St George's Rd. *Wall* —5E **51**
St George's Way. *L1* —5F **5**
St George's Way. *Wir* —3A **160**
St Gerard Clo. *L5* —5D **55**
St Gregory's Cft. *Boot* —1E **19**
St Helens. —5A 46
St Helen's Clo. *Pren* —3B **96**
St Helens Cricket Club Ground. —3E 45
St Helens Football Ground. —4F 67
St Helens Linkway. *St H* —1A **66**
St Helens Retail Pk. *St H* —1B **66**
St Helens R.L.F.C. Ground. —5C 44
St Helens Rd. *Ecc P & Prsct* —4D **63**
St Helens Rd. *Rainf* —3B **28**
St Helens R.U.F.C. Ground. —1A 44
St Helens Transport Mus. —4B 46
St Hilary Brow. *Wall* —2F **73**
St Hilary Dri. *Wall* —1F **73**
St Hilda's Dri. *Frod* —4C **172**
St Hugh's Clo. *Pren* —3B **96**
St Hugh's Ho. *Boot* —5C **34**
St Ives Ct. *Pren* —2A **96**
St Ives Gro. *L13* —3F **79**
St Ives Rd. *Pren* —3A **96**
St Ives Way. *L26* —4F **127**
St James' Clo. *L12* —5A **58**
St James Clo. *Frod* —4B **172**
St James Clo. *Grea* —5D **93**
St James Ct. *Wall* —3B **52**
St James Dri. *Boot* —4B **34**
St James Mt. *Rain* —4C **86**
St James Pl. *L8* —2E **99**
St James' Rd. *Ecc P & Prsct* —5E **63**
St James Rd. *L1* —2E **99**
St James Rd. *Birk* —1F **95**
St James Rd. *Huy* —5E **83**
St James Rd. *Rain* —4C **86**
St James Rd. *Wall* —3B **52**
St James St. *L1* —2D **99**

St James Way. *Boot* —1D **19**
St Jerome's Way. *Boot* —1E **19**
St Johns Av. *L9* —3A **36**
St Johns Brow. *Run* —4B **152**
St John's Cen. *L1* —5D **77** (5F **5**)
St John's Clo. *Wir* —3D **91**
St John's Ct. *Wat* —4D **17**
St John's Ho. *Boot* —5C **34**
St John's La. *L1* —4D **77** (4F **5**)
St John's Pavement. *Birk* —3D **97**
St John's Pl. *L22* —4D **17**
St John's Rd. *Boot & Kirk* —1B **54**
St John's Rd. *Wat* —4D **17**
St John's Rd. *Huy* —5F **83**
St John's Rd. *Wall* —1E **73**
St John's Rd. *Wir* —5F **163**
St John's Sq. *L1* —5F **5**
St John's Sq. *Birk* —3D **97**
St John's Ter. *Boot* —1B **54**
St John St. *Newt W* —5F **49**
St John St. *St H* —3D **65**
St John St. *Birk* —3D **97**
St John St. *Run* —4B **152**
St Johns Way. *L1* —5D **77** (5F **5**)
St Joseph's Clo. *L36* —4C **60**
St Josephs Clo. *St H* —2C **66**
St Josephs Cres. *L3* —3D **77** (2G **5**)
St Jude's Clo. *L36* —4C **60**
St Kilda's Rd. *Wir* —2E **93**
St Laurence Clo. *Birk* —2D **97**
St Laurence Dri. *Birk* —2D **97**
St Laurence Gro. *L32* —5F **23**
St Lawrence Clo. *L8* —5A **100**
St Lawrence Rd. *Frod* —5B **172**
St Leonard's Clo. *Boot* —1D **19**
St Lucia Rd. *Wall* —1D **75**
St Lukes Clo. *L14* —5F **59**
St Luke's Ct. *L4* —1A **56**
St Lukes Cres. *Wid* —5B **110**
St Luke's Gro. *Boot* —1D **19**
St Lukes Pl. *L1* —1E **99** (7G **5**)
St Luke's Rd. *L23* —1D **17**
St Luke's Rd. *St H* —5D **45**
St Luke's Way. *L36* —4C **60**
St Luke's Way. *Frod* —4B **172**
St Margaret's Gro. *Boot* —2C **18**
St Margaret's Rd. *Wir* —5A **90**
St Mark's Gro. *Boot* —1C **18**
St Mark's Rd. *L36* —5F **83**
St Mark's St. *Hay* —2A **48**
St Martins Gro. *L32* —1F **39**
St Martin's Ho. *Boot* —5C **34**
St Martin's La. *Murd* —3D **169**
St Martin's Mkt. *L5* —1E **77**
St Martins M. *L5* —2E **77**
*St Mary's Arc. St H —5A **46***
(off St Mary's Mkt.)
St Mary's Av. *L4* —1A **56**
St Mary's Av. *Bil* —1C **30**
St Mary's Av. *Wall* —2B **74**
St Mary's Church Tower. —3F 97
(off Priory St.)
St Mary's Clo. *Hale V* —5D **149**
St Mary's Clo. *Old S* —5F **79**
St Marys Ct. *L25* —2A **126**
St Mary's Ct. *Wir* —5A **94**
St Mary's Ga. *Birk* —3F **97**
St Mary's Gro. *Boot* —2C **18**
St Mary's Gro. *L4* —1A **56**
St Mary's La. *L4* —1A **56**
St Mary's Mkt. *St H* —5A **46**
St Mary's Pl. *L4* —1A **56**
St Mary's Rd. *Wat* —4F **17**
St Mary's Rd. *Gars* —5A **124**
St Marys Rd. *Halt* —1F **167**
St Mary's Rd. *Huy* —4E **83**
St Marys Rd. *Wid* —3A **152**
St Mary's St. *L25* —2A **126**
St Mary's St. *Wall* —2B **74**
St Mathews Clo. *L4* —1D **57**
St Mathews Clo. *Huy* —3F **83**
St Matthew's Av. *L21* —5C **18**
St Matthews Gro. *St H* —3C **64**
St Mawes Clo. *Wid* —2E **131**
St Mawes Way. *Wind* —2B **44**
St Michael Rd. *Augh* —1F **7**
St Michael's Chu. Rd. *L17* —1B **122**
St Michaels Clo. *L17* —2C **122**
St Michael's Clo. *Wid* —5C **130**
St Michaels Ct. *L36* —3E **83**
St Michael's Gro. *Boot* —2C **18**
St Michaels Gro. *L6* —2B **78**
St Michael's Gro. *Wir* —1D **93**
St Michael's Hamlet. —2B 122
St Michael's Ind. Est. *Wid* —5C **130**
St Michael's Municipal Golf Course. —5E 131
St Michael's Rd. *Cros* —5B **8**
St Michaels Rd. *St H* —3A **88**
St Michael's Rd. *Aig* —2B **122**
St Michael's Rd. *Wid* —5C **130**
St Monica's Dri. *Boot* —1D **19**
St Nicholas' Dri. *Boot* —1D **19**
St Nicholas Gro. *St H* —4D **67**
St Nicholas Pl. *L3* —5B **76** (5A **4**)
(in two parts)
St Nicholas' Rd. *Wall* —1D **73**
St Nicholas Rd. *Whis* —5D **85**
St Oswald Gdns. *L13* —3A **80**
St Oswald's Av. *Pren* —1C **94**
St Oswald's Ct. *Boot* —2F **19**
St Oswald's La. *Boot* —2F **19**
St Oswald's M. *Pren* —5C **72**
St Oswald's St. *L13* —4A **80**
St Paschal Baylon Boulevd. *L16* —1F **103**
St Patrick's Clo. *L33* —5E **15**
St Patrick's Dri. *Boot* —1D **19**
St Paul's Av. *Wall* —4E **75**
St Pauls Clo. *L33* —5D **15**
St Paul's Clo. *Birk* —2E **119**
St Pauls Pl. *Boot* —1D **55**
St Paul's Rd. *Birk* —2F **119**
(in two parts)
St Paul's Rd. *Wall* —4D **75**
St Paul's Rd. *Wid* —5A **132**
St Paul's Sq. *L3* —4B **76** (3C **4**)
St Paul St. *St H* —5E **45**
St Paul's Vs. *Birk* —2E **119**
St Peters Clo. *Kirkby* —5D **15**
St Peters Clo. *Wir* —3F **157**
St Peter's Ct. *L17* —5B **100**
St Peter's Ct. *Birk* —3A **120**
St Peter's Ho. *Boot* —1D **55**
St Peter's M. *Birk* —3A **120**
St Peter's Rd. *L9* —2C **36**
St Peter's Rd. *Birk* —3A **120**
St Peters Row. *L31* —4D **13**
St Peter's Way. *Pren* —5C **94**
St Philip's Av. *L21* —5C **18**
St Richards Clo. *L20* —2D **55**
St Seiriol Gro. *Pren* —3A **96**
St Stephens Clo. *L25* —4C **104**
St Stephens Clo. *Wir* —4C **158**
St Stephen's Ct. *Birk* —3B **118**
St Stephen's Gro. *Boot* —2D **19**
St Stephen's Pl. *L3* —3D **77** (2E **5**)
St Stephen's Rd. *Birk* —2B **118**
St Teresa's Rd. *St H* —4D **45**
St Thomas Ct. *Wid* —3D **131**
St Thomas's Dri. *Boot* —2D **19**
St Thomas Sq. *St H* —5F **45**
St Vincent Rd. *Pren* —3A **96**
St Vincent Rd. *Wall* —1D **75**
St Vincents Clo. *L12* —5E **59**
St Vincent St. *L3* —4E **77** (4H **5**)
St Vincent Way. *L3* —4E **77** (4H **5**)
St Werburghs Sq. *Birk* —3D **97**
St William Rd. *L23* —5B **10**
St William Wlk. *L23* —5B **10**
St Winifred Rd. *Rain* —1B **86**
St Winifred Rd. *Wall* —4B **52**
Saker St. *L4* —4F **55**
Salacre Clo. *Wir* —5B **94**
Salacre Cres. *Wir* —5A **94**
Salacre La. *Wir* —4A **94**
Salacre Ter. *Wir* —4A **94**
Salcombe Dri. *L25* —5B **126**
Salem Vw. *Pren* —1B **118**
Salerno Dri. *L36* —2D **83**
(in two parts)
Sales Wood Av. *Ecc* —5A **44**
Saline Clo. *L14* —5A **60**
Salisbury Av. *Boot* —4A **20**
Salisbury Av. *Wir* —4A **112**
Salisbury Dri. *Wir* —5B **120**
Salisbury Hall. *L18* —2E **123**
Salisbury Ho. *Boot* —4B **34**
Salisbury Pk. *L16* —4D **103**
Salisbury Rd. *Boot* —4B **34**
(in two parts)
Salisbury Rd. *L9* —5A **36**
Salisbury Rd. *Anf* —5F **55**
Salisbury Rd. *Gars* —5A **124**
Salisbury Rd. *Wall* —3A **52**
Salisbury Rd. *W'tree* —2D **101**
Salisbury St. *L3* —2E **77** (1H **5**)
(in two parts)
Salisbury St. *Birk* —4D **97**
Salisbury St. *Prsct* —4D **63**
Salisbury St. *Run* —1A **166**
Salisbury St. *Wid* —4B **132**
Salisbury Ter. *L15* —1F **101**
Salop St. *L4* —3F **55**
Saltash Clo. *L26* —3E **127**
Saltash Clo. *Brook* —4B **168**
Saltburn Rd. *Wall* —1D **73**
(in two parts)
Saltergate Rd. *L8* —5A **100**
Salthouse Quay. *L3* —1C **98** (7C **4**)
Saltney St. *L3* —1B **76**
Saltpit La. *L31* —1E **13**
Saltwood Dri. *Brook* —5C **168**
Saltworks Clo. *Frod* —3D **173**
Salvia Way. *L33* —5D **15**
Samaria Av. *Wir* —5C **120**
Samphire Gdns. *St H* —4B **68**
Samuel St. *St H* —4D **65**
Sanbec Gdns. *Wid* —4D **109**
Sandalwood. *Run* —1C **168**
Sandalwood Clo. *L6* —1B **78**
Sandalwood Dri. *Pren* —5D **95**
Sandalwood Gdns. *St H* —4C **66**
Sandbeck St. *L8* —1F **121**
Sandbourne. *Wir* —1A **94**
Sandbrook Ct. *Wir* —1E **93**
Sandbrook La. *Wir* —1E **93**
Sandbrook Rd. *L25* —1A **104**
Sandcliffe Rd. *Wall* —3E **51**
Sandeman Rd. *L4* —3D **57**
Sanderling Rd. *L33* —2A **24**
Sanders Hey Clo. *Brook* —5A **168**
Sandfield. *L36* —4D **83**
Sandfield Av. *Wir* —2D **91**
Sandfield Clo. *L12* —1C **80**
Sandfield Clo. *Wir* —1D **141**
Sandfield Ct. *Frod* —5B **172**
Sandfield Cres. *St H* —5F **45**
Sandfield Park. —1B 80
Sandfield Pk. *Wir* —2D **157**
Sandfield Pk. E. *L12* —5C **58**
Sandfield Pl. *Boot* —4B **34**
Sandfield Rd. *Boot* —5D **35**
Sandfield Rd. *Ecc* —3A **44**
Sandfield Rd. *L25* —5B **104**
Sandfield Rd. *Beb* —1D **141**
Sandfield Rd. *Upt* —3B **116**

Sandfield Rd. *Wall* —4B **52**
Sandfields. *Frod* —5B **172**
Sandfield Ter. *Wall* —4B **52**
Sandfield Wlk. *L13* —2B **80**
Sandford Dri. *L31* —5D **7**
Sandford St. *Birk* —2E **97**
Sandforth Clo. *L12* —5A **58**
Sandforth Ct. *L13* —1A **80**
Sandforth Rd. *L12* —5A **58**
Sandgate Clo. *L24* —3B **146**
Sandham Gro. *Wir* —2C **158**
Sandham Rd. *L24* —3A **148**
Sandhead St. *L7* —1D **101**
Sandhey Rd. *Wir* —3C **90**
Sandheys Av. *L22* —4C **16**
Sandheys Clo. *L4* —4E **55**
Sandheys Gro. *L22* —3C **16**
Sandheys Rd. *Wall* —4B **52**
Sandheys Ter. *L22* —4C **16**
Sandhills Bus. Pk. *L5* —4C **54**
Sandhills La. *L5* —4B **54**
Sandhills, The. *Wir* —3E **71**
Sandhills Vw. *Wall* —1D **73**
Sandhurst. *L23* —1C **16**
Sandhurst Clo. *S'frth* —1F **33**
Sandhurst Dri. *L10* —3D **21**
Sandhurst Rd. *L26* —1A **148**
Sandhurst Rd. *Rain* —1A **86**
Sandhurst St. *L17* —1A **122**
Sandhurst Way. *L31* —2B **6**
Sandicroft Rd. *L12* —1F **59**
Sandino St. *L8* —3E **99**
Sandiway. *Brom* —4C **162**
Sandiway. *Huy* —5F **83**
Sandiway. *Meol* —2D **91**
Sandiway. *Whis* —4D **85**
Sandiway Av. *Wid* —3A **130**
Sandiways. *Mag* —1E **13**
Sandiways Av. *Boot* —3A **20**
Sandiways Rd. *Wall* —5E **51**
Sandlea Pk. *Wir* —4A **112**
Sandlewood Gro. *L33* —1F **23**
Sandon Clo. *Rain* —2B **86**
Sandon Ind. Est. *L5* —5B **54**
Sandon Pl. *Wid* —3D **133**
Sandon Promenade. *Wall* —2D **75**
(in two parts)
Sandon Rd. *Wall* —2D **75**
Sandon St. *St H* —3D **65**
Sandon St. *Wat* —4D **17**
Sandon St. *Tox* —1F **99**
Sandon Way. *L5* —5B **54**
Sandown Clo. *Run* —4B **166**
Sandown Ct. *L15* —1F **101**
Sandown La. *L15* —1F **101**
Sandown Park. —5F 79
Sandown Pk. Rd. *L10* —2E **21**
Sandown Rd. *S'frth* —1F **33**
Sandown Rd. *W'tree* —5F **79**
Sandpiper Clo. *Wir* —3D **93**
Sandpiper Gro. *L26* —3E **127**
Sandpipers Ct. *Wir* —4A **90**
Sandridge Rd. *Wall* —4B **52**
Sandridge Rd. *Wir* —2F **137**
Sandringham Av. *L22* —5E **17**
Sandringham Av. *Wir* —3C **90**
Sandringham Clo. *L33* —5E **15**
Sandringham Clo. *Hoy* —3C **90**
Sandringham Clo. *New F* —5A **120**
Sandringham Dri. *L17* —5B **100**
Sandringham Dri. *St H* —5C **66**
Sandringham Dri. *Wall* —3A **52**
Sandringham Rd. *L31* —2C **12**
Sandringham Rd. *Wat* —5E **17**
Sandringham Rd. *Tue* —5D **57**
Sandringham Rd. *Wid* —5F **109**
Sandrock Rd. *Wall* —4B **52**
Sands Rd. *L18* —5F **101**
Sandstone. *Wall* —1C **74**
Sandstone Clo. *Rain* —5C **86**
Sandstone Dri. *Whis* —1A **86**
Sandstone Dri. *Wir* —4E **113**
Sandstone Rd. E. *L13* —2F **79**
Sandstone Rd. W. *L13* —2F **79**
Sandstone Wlk. *Wir* —3A **158**
Sandwash Clo. *Rainf* —1B **28**
Sandway Cres. *L11* —1A **58**
Sandy Brow La. *L33* —1E **41**
Sandy Grn. *L9* —2C **36**
Sandy Gro. *L13* —5F **57**
Sandy Knowle. *L15* —1A **102**
Sandy La. *Crank & St H* —4E **29**
Sandy La. *Mell* —5A **14**
Sandy La. *Walt* —2B **36**
Sandy La. *Cron* —4D **109**
Sandy La. *Hes* —1A **158**
Sandy La. *Irby* —5C **114**
Sandy La. *Lyd* —1B **6**
Sandy La. *Old S* —5F **57**
Sandy La. *Pres B* —4E **169**
Sandy La. *Wall* —5E **51**
Sandy La. *W Kir* —1B **134**
Sandy La. *West P* —3D **165**
Sandy La. *Wid* —3F **111**
Sandy La. N. *Wir* —5C **114**
Sandymoor La. *Run* —4D **155**
Sandy Moor La. *Run* —5D **155**
Sandymount Dri. *Wall* —4A **52**
Sandymount Dri. *Wir* —3F **141**
Sandy Rd. *L21* —5F **17**
Sandyville Gro. *L4* —3E **57**
Sandyville Rd. *L4* —3D **57**
Sandy Way. *Pren* —4A **96**
Sankey Rd. *L31* —3D **13**
Sankey Rd. *Hay* —3F **47**
Sankey St. *L1* —1E **99**
Sankey St. *Newt W* —5F **49**
Sankey St. *St H* —1D **67**
Sankey St. *Wid* —1A **152**
Sankey Valley Ind. Est. *Newt W* —1F **69**
Sankey Valley Pk. *Newt W* —1F **69**
Santon Av. *L13* —1E **79**
Sapphire Dri. *L33* —5E **15**
Sapphire St. *L13* —5F **79**
Sarah's Cft. *Boot* —2E **19**
Sark Rd. *L13* —2F **79**
Sartfield Clo. *L16* —1E **103**
Sarum Rd. *L25* —2A **104**
Satinwood Cres. *L31* —2A **22**
Saughall Massie. —3C 92
Saughall Massie La. *Wir* —4E **93**
Saughall Massie Rd. *Upt* —3C **92**
Saughall Massie Rd. *W Kir* —3D **113**
Saughall Rd. *Wir* —2C **92**
Saunby St. *L19* —3C **144**
Saunders Av. *Prsct* —2D **85**
Saunderton Clo. *Hay* —1C **48**
Saville Rd. *L31* —4C **6**
Saville Rd. *Old S* —4B **80**
Savoy Ct. *L22* —5D **17**
Savoylands Clo. *L17* —2C **122**
Sawley Clo. *Murd* —3E **169**
Sawpit La. *Huy* —4F **83**
Saxby Rd. *L14* —1A **82**
Saxon Clo. *L6* —1B **78**
Saxon Ct. *St H* —3E **45**
Saxonia Rd. *L4* —1A **56**
Saxon Rd. *L23* —2D **17**
Saxon Rd. *Hoy* —3C **90**
Saxon Rd. *More* —5F **71**
Saxon Rd. *Run* —5C **152**
Saxon Ter. *Wid* —3B **132**
Saxon Way. *L33* —4E **15**
Saxony Rd. *L7* —4A **78**
Sayce St. *Wid* —3B **132**
Scafell Clo. *L27* —1A **128**
Scafell Clo. *Wir* —2D **171**
Scafell Lawn. *L27* —1A **128**
Scafell Rd. *St H* —5A **30**
Scafell Wlk. *L27* —5A **106**
Scape La. *L23* —5E **9**
Scargreen Av. *L11* —5F **37**
Scarisbrick Av. *L21* —1B **34**
Scarisbrick Clo. *L31* —4E **7**
Scarisbrick Cres. *L11* —5D **37**
Scarisbrick Dri. *L11* —5D **37**
Scarisbrick Pl. *L11* —1D **57**
Scarisbrick Rd. *L11* —5D **37**
Scarsdale Rd. *L11* —2F **57**
Sceptre Clo. *Newt W* —5F **49**
Sceptre Rd. *L11* —4C **38**
Sceptre Tower. *L11* —5C **38**
Sceptre Wlk. *L11* —5C **38**
Scholar St. *L7* —2C **100**
Scholes La. *St H* —4A **64**
Scholes Pk. *St H* —4B **64**
Schomberg St. *L6* —3A **78**
School Clo. *L27* —2C **104**
School Clo. *Wir* —4F **71**
Schoolfield Clo. *Wir* —2B **116**
Schoolfield Rd. *Wir* —2B **116**
School Hill. *Wir* —3F **157**
School La. *Ain* —3D **21**
School La. *Know & Know B* —2A **40**
School La. *L1* —5D **77** (6E **4**)
School La. *Lith* —5B **18**
School La. *Mag* —5F **7**
School La. *Mell* —5A **14**
School La. *S'frth* —1A **34**
School La. *Chil T* —4F **171**
School La. *Halt* —2F **167**
School La. *High B* —1D **141**
School La. *Hoy* —4B **90**
(in two parts)
School La. *Huy* —4A **84**
School La. *Meol* —2D **91**
School La. *New F* —5B **120**
School La. *Pren* —5C **72**
School La. *Rain* —5E **87**
(in two parts)
School La. *Thur* —1B **136**
School La. *Wall* —2E **73**
(in two parts)
School La. *Wid* —2E **111**
School La. *Wltn* —5A **126**
School Pl. *Birk* —2D **97**
School St. *Hay* —2F **47**
School Way. *L24* —4B **146**
School Way. *Wid* —1D **133**
Schooner Clo. *Murd* —4D **169**
Science Rd. *L24* —3C **146**
Scone Clo. *L11* —5C **38**
Scorecross. *St H* —3B **66**
Score La. *L16* —5C **80**
Scoresby Rd. *Wir* —3C **72**
Score, The. *St H* —5A **66**
(in two parts)
Scorpio Clo. *L14* —1A **82**
Scorton St. *L6* —1C **78**
Scotchbarn La. *Prsct* —5E **63**
Scotchbarn Pool. —5E 63
Scoter Rd. *L33* —3F **23**
Scotia Av. *Wir* —5C **120**
Scotia Rd. *L13* —2A **80**
Scotland Rd. *L3 & L5* —3D **77** (2F **5**)
Scots Pl. *Birk* —2F **95**
Scott Av. *L36* —5A **84**
Scott Av. *Sut M* —3A **88**
Scott Av. *Whis* —3F **85**
Scott Av. *Wid* —4F **131**
Scott Clo. *Kirk* —4F **55**
Scott Clo. *Mag* —1D **13**
Scotts Quays. *Birk* —5E **75**
Scott St. *Boot* —3B **34**
Scott St. *Wall* —1B **74**
Scythes, The. *Boot* —1B **20**
Scythes, The. *Wir* —5C **92**

Scythia Clo. Wir —4C 120
Seabank Av. Wall —1C 74
Seabank Cotts. Wir —1F 91
Seabank Rd. Wall —3B 52
Seabank Rd. Wir —4E 157
Sea Brow. L1 —5C 76 (6C 4)
Seacombe Promenade. Wall —2E 75
Seacombe Tower. L5 —5E 55
Seacombe Vw. Wall —4E 75
Sea Ct. Flats. Wall —4F 51
Seacroft Clo. L14 —5A 60
Seacroft Rd. L14 —5A 60
Seafield Av. L23 —2E 17
Seafield Av. Wir —4E 157
Seafield Dri. Wall —4F 51
Seafield Rd. Boot —4B 34
Seafield Rd. L9 —3F 35
Seafield Rd. Wir —4B 120
Seaford Clo. Wind H —1D 169
Seafore Clo. L31 —3B 6
Seaforth. —1E 33
Seaforth Dri. Wir —2E 93
Seaforth Nature Reserve. —1D 33
Seaforth Rd. L21 —3A 34
Seaforth Va. N. L21 —1A 34
Seaforth Va. W. L21 —2A 34
Seagram Clo. L9 —5C 20
Sea La. Run —5D 153
Sealy Clo. Wir —1A 162
Seaman Rd. L15 —2E 101
Seaport Rd. L8 —3A 100
Sea Rd. Wall —3F 51
Seascale Av. St H —3B 64
Seath Av. St H —4E 47
Seathwaite Clo. L23 —2B 16
Seathwaite Clo. Beech —5E 167
Seathwaite Cres. L33 —1D 23
Seaton Clo. L12 —5A 40
Seaton Gro. St H —5D 65
Seaton Pk. Run —4E 155
Seaton Rd. Birk —5C 96
Seaton Rd. Wall —5A 52
Sea Vw. Wir —4B 90
Seaview Av. Irby —1D 137
Seaview Av. Wall —1A 74
Seaview La. Wir —1D 137
Sea Vw. Rd. Boot —4A 34
Seaview Rd. Wall —5A 52
Seaview Ter. L22 —4C 16
Seawood Gro. Wir —2D 93
Second Av. Cros —1D 17
Second Av. Faz —2E 37
Second Av. L9 —1C 36
Second Av. Pren —3B 94
Second Av. Rain —2B 86
Second Av. Run —2F 167
Sedbergh Av. L10 —2C 20
Sedbergh Gro. Beech —5E 167
Sedbergh Rd. Wall —1F 73
Sedburgh Gro. L36 —3B 82
Sedburn Rd. L32 —1A 40
Seddon Clo. Ecc —5F 43
Seddon Rd. L19 —1B 144
Seddon Rd. St H —2B 64
Seddons Ct. Ecc L —4D 63
Seddon St. L1 —1D 99 (7E 4)
Seddon St. St H —1F 45
Sedgefield Clo. Wir —1A 94
Sedgefield Rd. Wir —1A 94
Sedgeley Wlk. L36 —1F 83
Sedgemoor Rd. L11 —5E 37
Sedgewick Cres. Btnwd —5E 69
Sedley St. L6 —5B 56
Sedum Gro. L33 —5D 15
Seeds La. L9 —5C 20
Seeley Av. Birk —2A 96
Seel Rd. L36 —4F 83
Seel St. L1 —5D 77 (6E 5)
Sefton. —3F 11
Sefton Av. L21 —1B 34
Sefton Av. Wid —1A 132
Sefton Bus. Pk. Boot —5A 20
Sefton Clo. L32 —2B 22
(in three parts)
Sefton Cricket Club Ground. —4D 101
Sefton Dri. Ain —3D 21
Sefton Dri. Kirkby —2C 22
Sefton Dri. Mag —2B 12
Sefton Dri. Thor —3A 10
Sefton Dri. Seft P —4B 100
Sefton Fold Dri. Bil —1D 31
Sefton Fold Gdns. Bil —1D 31
Sefton Gro. L17 —5C 100
Sefton La. L31 —2A 12
Sefton La. Ind. Est. L31 —2A 12
Sefton Mill Ct. L29 —3F 11
Sefton Mill La. L29 —3F 11
Sefton Moss La. Boot —2D 19
Sefton Moss Vs. L21 —5B 18
Sefton Park. —5D 101
Sefton Pk. —5D 101
Sefton Pk. Rd. L8 —3B 100
Sefton Retail Pk. Boot —2A 20
Sefton Rd. Boot —3D 35
Sefton Rd. Faz —1D 37
Sefton Rd. Lith —5B 18
Sefton Rd. Walt —3A 36
Sefton Rd. Birk —3A 120
Sefton Rd. Wall —4B 52
Sefton Rd. Wir —4A 120
Sefton R.U.F.C. Ground. —5D 59
Sefton St. L8 & L3 —3D 99
Sefton St. Lith —5B 18
(in two parts)
Sefton St. Newt W —5F 49
Sefton St. Brun B —5E 99
Sefton Town. —5D 11
Sefton Vw. Cros —1A 18
Sefton Vw. S'frth —5B 18
Selborne. Whis —4F 85
Selborne Clo. L8 —2A 100
Selborne St. L8 —2F 99
Selbourne Clo. Wir —1C 116
Selby Clo. St H —1D 65
Selby Clo. Run —3F 155
Selby Gro. L36 —3B 84
Selby Rd. L9 —2A 36
Selby St. Wall —1B 74
Seldon St. L6 —3A 78
Selina Rd. L4 —1E 55
Selkirk Av. Wir —1E 171
Selkirk Dri. Ecc —3B 44
Selkirk Rd. L13 —4F 79
Sellar St. L4 —4E 55
Selsdon Rd. L22 —3C 16
Selsey Clo. L7 —1B 100
Selside Lawn. L27 —5A 106
Selside Rd. L27 —1A 128
Selside Wlk. L27 —5F 105
Selston Clo. Wir —5A 142
Selworthy Grn. L16 —3D 103
Selwyn Clo. Wid —1D 133
Selwyn St. L4 —2E 55
Seneschal Ct. Hall P —4E 167
Sennen Clo. Brook —5B 168
Sennen Rd. L32 —5F 23
Sentinel Way. Boot —5B 20
September Rd. L6 —1C 78
Serenade Rd. L33 —4F 15
Sergrim Rd. L36 —3C 82
Serpentine N., The. L23 —5A 8
Serpentine Rd. Wall —1C 74
Serpentine S., The. L23 —1B 16
Serpentine, The. Cros —5A 8
Serpentine, The. Gars —4A 124
Servia Rd. L21 —1B 34
Servite Clo. L22 —3C 16
Servite Ct. L25 —3C 126
Servite Ho. L17 —5B 100
Sessions Rd. L4 —3D 55
Seth Powell Way. L36 —5C 60
Settrington Rd. L11 —2F 57
Seven Acre Rd. L23 —5B 10
Seven Acres La. Wir —2A 138
Sevenoaks Clo. L5 —1E 77
Seventh Av. Faz —1D 37
Seventh Av. L9 —1D 37
Severn Clo. St H —5C 66
Severn Clo. Bil —2D 31
Severn Clo. Wid —2E 133
Severn Rd. L33 —4F 15
Severn Rd. Rain —3B 86
Severn St. L5 —5F 55
Severn St. Birk —5A 74
Severs St. L6 —2A 78
Sewell St. Prsct —5D 63
Sewell St. Run —5B 152
Sextant Clo. Murd —5D 169
Sexton Av. St H —1B 68
Sexton Way. L14 —4E 81
Seymour Ct. Birk —5E 97
Seymour Ct. Mnr P & Run —3C 154
Seymour Dri. L31 —4E 7
Seymour Pl. E. Wall —3B 52
Seymour Pl. W. Wall —3B 52
Seymour Rd. L21 —1B 34
Seymour Rd. B'grn —4D 81
Seymour St. L3 —4E 77 (4H 5)
Seymour St. Mil B —1B 54
Seymour St. St H —4D 67
Seymour St. Birk —5D 97
Seymour St. Wall —3B 52
Shacklady Rd. L33 —1A 24
Shackleton Rd. Wir —2B 72
Shadwell Clo. L5 —5B 54
Shadwell St. L5 —1B 76
Shaftesbury Rd. Cros —1D 17
Shaftesbury St. L8 —3E 99
Shaftesbury Ter. L13 —3A 80
Shaftesbury Way. Btnwd —4F 69
Shaftsbury Av. L33 —5E 15
Shaftway Clo. Hay —1F 49
Shakespeare Av. Birk —3F 119
Shakespeare Clo. L6 —2A 78
Shakespeare Rd. Sut M —4A 88
Shakespeare Rd. Wall —4D 75
Shakespeare Rd. Wid —3A 132
Shakespeare St. Boot —3A 34
Shakespeare St. L19 —2C 144
(in two parts)
Shalcombe Clo. L26 —5A 128
Shaldon Clo. L32 —5A 24
Shaldon Gro. L32 —5A 24
Shaldon Rd. L32 —1A 40
Shaldon Wlk. L32 —5A 24
Shalem Ct. Wir —1D 141
Shalford Gro. Wir —4D 113
Shallcross Ct. L6 —2A 78
Shallcross Pl. L6 —2A 78
Shallmarsh Clo. Wir —2D 141
Shallmarsh Ct. Wir —2D 141
Shallmarsh Rd. Wir —2D 141
Shalom Ct. L17 —4E 101
Shamrock Rd. Birk —2F 95
Shand St. L19 —3C 144
Shanklin Rd. L15 —5F 79
Shannon St. Birk —5F 73
Shard Clo. L11 —3B 38
Shard St. St H —4E 67
Sharpeville Clo. L4 —4D 55
Sharples Cres. L23 —2F 17
Sharp St. Wid —4A 132
Sharwood Rd. L27 —5F 105
Shavington Av. Pren —1F 117
Shawbury Av. Wir —5D 119
Shawell Ct. Wid —2E 133

Shaw Entry. *Prsct* —1F **107**
Shaw Gdns. *St H* —5E **65**
Shaw Hill St. *L1* —4D **77** (4E **5**)
Shaw La. *Prsct & Whis* —2D **85**
Shaw La. *Wir* —2C **114**
Shaw Rd. *L24* —2C **146**
Shaws All. *L1* —1C **98** (7D **4**)
(in two parts)
Shaws Dri. *Wir* —3D **91**
Shaw St. *L6* —2F **77** (1J **5**)
Shaw St. *St H* —5B **46**
Shaw St. *Birk* —4C **96**
Shaw St. *Hay* —2E **49**
Shaw St. *Run* —5F **151**
(in two parts)
Shaw St. *Wall* —3E **75**
Shaw St. *Wir* —4B **90**
Shawton Rd. *L16* —1C **102**
Shearman Clo. *Wir* —3A **138**
Shearman Rd. *Wir* —3A **138**
Shearwater Clo. *L27* —5F **105**
Sheehan Heights. *L5* —5C **54**
Sheen Rd. *Wall* —5C **52**
Sheila Wlk. *L10* —2B **38**
Sheil Pl. *L6* —3C **78**
Sheil Rd. *L6* —2C **78**
Shelagh Av. *Wid* —3A **132**
Sheldon Clo. *Wir* —1A **162**
Sheldon Rd. *L12* —3D **59**
Shelley Clo. *L36* —5F **83**
Shelley Gro. *L19* —2C **144**
Shelley Pl. *Whis* —3F **85**
Shelley Rd. *Wid* —3A **132**
Shelley St. *Boot* —4B **34**
(in two parts)
Shelley St. *Sut M* —4B **88**
Shelley Way. *Wir* —1B **134**
Shell Green. —3E 133
Shell Grn. Ho. *Wid* —3E **133**
Shellingford Rd. *L14* —2A **82**
Shelmore Dri. *L8* —5E **99**
Shelton Clo. *L13* —4A **80**
Shelton Clo. *Wid* —1E **133**
Shelton Rd. *Wall* —5A **52**
Shenley Clo. *Wir* —1F **141**
Shenley Rd. *L15* —1C **102**
Shenstone St. *L7* —5B **78**
Shenton Av. *St H* —2D **47**
Shepherd Clo. *Wir* —5C **92**
Shepherds Row. *Cas* —5F **153**
Shepherd St. *L6* —4F **77**
Sheppard Av. *L16* —1A **104**
Shepston Av. *L4* —2A **56**
Shepton Rd. *L36* —5D **61**
Sherborne Av. *Boot* —1E **19**
Sherborne Av. *L25* —4D **127**
Sherborne Clo. *Run* —4F **155**
Sherborne Rd. *Wall* —1F **73**
Sherborne Sq. *L36* —4E **83**
Sherbourne Way. *Btnwd* —5F **69**
Sherbrooke Clo. *L14* —2E **81**
Sherburn Clo. *L9* —5D **21**
Sherdley Ct. *Rain* —2C **86**
Sherdley Pk. —4B 66
Sherdley Pk. Dri. *St H* —5C **66**
Sherdley Pk. Golf Course. —4A 66
Sherdley Rd. *Sher I* —2B **66**
Sherdley Rd. *St H* —5F **65**
(in two parts)
Sherford Clo. *L27* —5F **105**
Sheridan Way. *Run* —5D **155**
Sheriff Clo. *L5* —2E **77**
Sheringham Clo. *St H* —5D **47**
Sheringham Clo. *Wir* —2A **94**
Sherlock Av. *Hay* —1E **49**
Sherlock La. *Wall* —4A **74**
Sherlock St. *L5* —4F **55**
Sherman Dri. *Rain* —5D **87**
Sherry Ct. *L17* —4D **101**
Sherry La. *Wir* —2A **116**
Sherwell Clo. *L15* —5A **80**
Sherwood Av. *L23* —5D **9**
Sherwood Av. *Wir* —1D **137**
Sherwood Clo. *Rain* —1C **86**
Sherwood Clo. *Wid* —3C **130**
Sherwood Ct. *W Der* —5F **39**
Sherwood Ct. *Huy* —4F **83**
Sherwood Cres. *Btnwd* —5E **69**
Sherwood Dri. *Wir* —5E **119**
Sherwood Gro. *Wir* —3F **91**
Sherwood Rd. *Cros* —5C **8**
Sherwood Rd. *Wall* —3C **74**
Sherwood Rd. *Wir* —4F **91**
Sherwood's La. *L10* —5F **21**
Sherwood St. *L3* —1B **76**
Sherwyn Rd. *L4* —3C **56**
Shetland Clo. *Wid* —1E **133**
Shetland Dri. *Wir* —2E **163**
Shevington Clo. *St H* —4C **66**
Shevington Clo. *Wid* —1E **133**
Shevington's La. *L33* —5D **15**
Shevington Wlk. *Wid* —1E **133**
Shewell Clo. *Birk* —5D **97**
Shiel Rd. *Wall* —4B **52**
Shimmin St. *L7* —5A **78**
Shipley Wlk. *L24* —3D **147**
Ship St. *Frod* —4B **172**
Shipton Clo. *L19* —3B **124**
Shipton Clo. *Pren* —3E **117**
Shipton Clo. *Wid* —1D **131**
Shirdley Av. *L32* —1F **39**
Shirdley Wlk. *L32* —1F **39**
Shirebourne Av. *St H* —1B **46**
Shiregreen. *St H* —5C **66**
Shires, The. *St H* —1E **65**
Shirley Rd. *L19* —4C **124**
Shirley St. *Wall* —3E **75**
Shirwell Gro. *Sut L* —2C **88**
Shobdon Clo. *L12* —4F **39**
Shop La. *L31* —1C **12**
Shop Rd. *Know* —4C **40**
Shore Bank. *Wir* —4C **120**
Shore Dri. *Wir* —1C **142**
Shorefields. *Wir* —4B **120**
Shorefields Ho. *Wir* —5C **120**
Shorefields Village. *L8* —1F **121**
Shore La. *Wir* —2C **134**
Shore Rd. *Boot* —3F **33**
Shore Rd. *Birk* —2E **97**
Shore Rd. *Cald* —2C **134**
Short Clo. *Newt W* —5E **49**
Shortfield Rd. *Wir* —5A **94**
Shortfield Way. *Wir* —5A **94**
Short St. *Newt W* —5E **49**
Short St. *Hay* —2E **49**
Short St. *Wid* —2A **152**
Shortwood Rd. *L14* —3F **81**
Shottesbrook Grn. *L11* —5F **37**
Shrewsbury Av. *Old R* —2C **20**
Shrewsbury Av. *Wat* —2D **17**
Shrewsbury Clo. *Pren* —3F **95**
Shrewsbury Dri. *Wir* —3A **94**
Shrewsbury Pl. *L19* —1C **144**
Shrewsbury Rd. *L19* —1C **144**
Shrewsbury Rd. *Hes* —1A **158**
Shrewsbury Rd. *Pren* —2F **95**
Shrewsbury Rd. *Wall* —1F **73**
Shrewsbury Rd. *W Kir* —5A **112**
Shrewton Rd. *L25* —2A **104**
Shropshire Clo. *Boot* —1A **20**
Shropshire Gdns. *St H* —1F **65**
Shuttleworth Clo. *Wir* —3E **93**
Sibford Rd. *L12* —1D **81**
Siddall St. *St H* —1F **45**
Siddeley Dri. *Newt W* —5F **49**
Siddeley St. *L17* —1C **122**
Sidewell St. *Gars* —2C **144**
Sidgreave St. *St H* —5E **45**
Sidings, The. *Birk* —2F **119**
Sidlaw Av. *St H* —5F **47**
Sidney Av. *Wall* —3A **52**
Sidney Gdns. *Birk* —5E **97**
Sidney Pl. *L7* —1A **100**
Sidney Powell Av. *L32* —3C **22**
Sidney Rd. *Boot* —1D **55**
Sidney Rd. *Birk* —5E **97**
Sidney St. *St H* —4D **45**
Sidney St. *Birk* —2E **97**
Sidney Ter. *Birk* —1E **119**
Sienna Clo. *L25* —3C **104**
Signal Works Rd. *L9* —5E **21**
Silcroft Rd. *L32* —5E **23**
Silkhouse La. *L2* —4C **76** (4C **4**)
Silkstone Clo. *L7* —1B **100**
Silkstone Clo. *St H* —5D **45**
Silkstone Cres. *Pal* —3B **168**
Silkstone St. *St H* —5D **45**
(in two parts)
Silver Av. *Hay* —3A **48**
Silverbeech Av. *L18* —5B **102**
Silverbeech Rd. *Wall* —3C **74**
Silverbirch Gdns. *Wall* —1E **73**
Silver Birch Way. *L31* —2B **6**
Silverbrook Rd. *L27* —3C **104**
Silverburn Av. *Wir* —5E **71**
Silverdale Av. *L13* —1E **79**
Silverdale Clo. *L36* —1E **105**
Silverdale Clo. *Frod* —5C **172**
Silverdale Dri. *L21* —5D **19**
Silverdale Gro. *St H* —5A **30**
Silverdale Rd. *Pren* —5A **96**
Silverdale Rd. *Wir* —5F **119**
Silverlea Av. *Wall* —1A **74**
Silver Leigh. *L17* —3D **123**
Silverlime Gdns. *St H* —4C **64**
Silverstone Dri. *L36* —1D **105**
Silverstone Gro. *L31* —2B **6**
Silverton Rd. *L17* —4E **123**
Silverwell Rd. *L11* —3D **39**
Silverwell Wlk. *L11* —3D **39**
Silvester St. *L5* —1C **76**
Simms Av. *St H* —5E **47**
Simm's Cross. —4B 132
Simm's Rd. *L6* —5D **57**
Simnel Clo. *L25* —3B **104**
Simon Ct. *L33* —5E **15**
Simonsbridge. *Wir* —3D **135**
Simons Clo. *Whis* —1D **107**
Simon's Cft. *Boot* —2C **18**
Simonside. *Wid* —2C **130**
Simonstone Gro. *St H* —4D **67**
Simonswood La. *L33* —4A **24**
Simonswood Wlk. *L33* —3A **24**
Simpson St. *L1* —2D **99**
Simpson St. *Birk* —3D **97**
Sim St. *L3* —3E **77** (2H **5**)
Sinclair Av. *Prsct* —1F **85**
Sinclair Av. *Wid* —4F **131**
Sinclair Clo. *Prsct* —5F **63**
Sinclair Dri. *L18* —3B **102**
Sinclair St. *L19* —2C **144**
Singleton Av. *St H* —3D **47**
Singleton Av. *Birk* —1C **118**
Singleton Dri. *Know* —5D **41**
Sirdar Clo. *L7* —1B **100**
Sir Howard St. *L7* —1F **99**
Sir Howard Way. *L8* —1F **99**
Sir Thomas St. *L1* —4C **76** (4D **4**)
Siskin Grn. *L25* —4A **104**
Sisters Way. *Birk* —3D **97**
Six Acre La. *Moore* —2F **155**
Sixth Av. *Faz* —1D **37**
Sixth Av. *L9* —1D **37**
Skeffington. *Whis* —4E **85**
Skellington Fold. *L27* —4E **105**
Skelthorne St. *L3* —5D **77** (5G **5**)
Skelton Clo. *St H* —1A **46**

Skerries Rd. *L4* —4A **56**
Skiddaw Clo. *Beech* —1A **174**
Skiddaw Rd. *Wir* —5E **143**
Skipton Rd. *Anf* —4B **56**
Skipton Rd. *Huy* —3B **84**
Skirving Pl. *L5* —5D **55**
Skirving St. *L5* —5D **55**
Skye Clo. *Wid* —1E **133**
Sky Pk. Ind. Est. *L24* —4B **146**
Slag La. *Hay* —1B **48**
(in two parts)
Slater Pl. *L1* —1D **99** (7F **5**)
Slater St. *L1* —1D **99** (7F **5**)
Slatey Rd. *Pren* —3B **96**
Sleaford Rd. *L14* —1B **82**
Sleepers Hill. *L4* —4F **55**
Slessor Av. *Wir* —3D **113**
Slim Rd. *L36* —2E **83**
Slingsby Dri. *Wir* —5A **94**
Smallridge Clo. *Wir* —3E **137**
Smallwoods M. *Wir* —5E **137**
Smeaton St. *L4* —2E **55**
(in two parts)
Smeaton St. S. *L4* —2E **55**
Smethick Wlk. *Boot* —1A **20**
Smilie Av. *Wir* —5C **70**
Smith Av. *Birk* —1B **96**
Smithdown Gro. *L7* —1A **100**
Smithdown La. *L7* —5A **78**
(in two parts)
Smithdown Pl. *L15* —4A **102**
Smithdown Rd. *L7 & L15* —2B **100**
Smith Dri. *Boot* —3E **35**
Smithfield St. *L3* —4C **76** (3D **4**)
Smithfield St. *St H* —1D **67**
Smith Pl. *L5* —5D **55**
Smith Rd. *Wid* —5F **131**
Smith St. *L5* —4D **55**
Smith St. *St H* —4E **67**
Smith St. *Prsct* —5E **63**
Smithy Clo. *Wid* —4C **108**
Smithy Hey. *Wir* —4C **112**
Smithy Hill. *Wir* —4A **160**
Smithy La. *Augh* —1F **7**
Smithy La. *L4* —1F **55**
Smithy La. *Cron* —3C **108**
Smithy La. *Will* —5A **170**
Smollett St. *Boot* —2A **34**
Smollett St. *L6* —3B **78**
Smugglers Way. *Wall* —3E **51**
Smyth Rd. *Wid* —2D **133**
Snaefell Av. *L13* —1E **79**
Snaefell Gro. *L13* —1E **79**
Snave Clo. *L21* —2B **34**
Snowberry Clo. *Wid* —5E **111**
Snowberry Rd. *L14* —4A **60**
Snowden Rd. *Wir* —1C **92**
Snowdon Gro. *St H* —4C **66**
Snowdon La. *L5* —1C **76**
Snowdon Rd. *Birk* —2D **119**
Snowdrop Av. *Birk* —1F **95**
Snowdrop Clo. *Beech* —1F **173**
Snowdrop St. *L5* —4D **55**
Soho Pl. *L3* —3E **77** (2H **5**)
Soho Sq. *L3* —3E **77** (2H **5**)
Soho St. *L3* —3E **77** (1H **5**)
(in two parts)
Solar Rd. *L9* —2B **36**
Solly Av. *Birk* —2E **119**
Solomon St. *L7* —4B **78**
Solway Gro. *Beech* —5D **167**
Solway St. *L8* —2B **100**
(in two parts)
Solway St. *Birk* —5A **74**
Solway St. W. *L8* —2B **100**
(in two parts)
Soma Av. *L21* —5C **18**
Somerford Ho. *L23* —2B **16**
Somerford Rd. *L14* —2F **81**
Somerford Wlk. Wid —1E 133
(off Barneston Rd.)
Somerset Pl. *L6* —1D **79**
Somerset Rd. *Boot* —4D **35**
Somerset Rd. *L22* —3C **16**
Somerset Rd. *Hes* —3E **137**
Somerset Rd. *Wall* —1E **73**
Somerset Rd. *W Kir* —3C **112**
Somerset St. *St H* —1D **67**
Somerton St. *L15* —1E **101**
Somerville Clo. *Brom* —4B **162**
Somerville Gro. *L22* —3D **17**
Somerville Rd. *L22* —3D **17**
Somerville Rd. *Wid* —4D **131**
Somerville St. Clo. *L5* —5E **55**
Sommer Av. *L12* —4A **58**
Sonning Av. *L21* —4A **18**
Sonning Rd. *L4* —1D **57**
Sorany Clo. *L23* —4A **10**
Sorogold St. *St H* —5C **46**
Sorrel Clo. *Pren* —4D **95**
S. Albert Rd. *L17* —5B **100**
Southampton Way. *Murd* —4E **169**
South Av. *Prsct* —5B **62**
South Bank. *Pren* —1B **118**
S. Bank Rd. *Edg H* —4D **79**
S. Bank Rd. *Gars* —5B **124**
S. Bank Ter. *Run* —4F **151**
S. Barcombe Rd. *L16* —2E **103**
S. Boundary Rd. *Know I* —5B **24**
Southbourne Rd. *Wall* —1D **73**
Southbrook Rd. *L27* —3C **104**
Southbrook Way. *L27* —3C **104**
S. Cantril Av. *L12* —4F **59**
S. Chester St. *L8* —3E **99**
Southcroft Rd. *Wall* —1D **73**
Southdale Rd. *L15* —1F **101**
Southdale Rd. *Birk* —2E **119**
Southdean Rd. *L14* —5B **60**
Southdene. —5A 24
South Dri. *Hes* —3A **158**
South Dri. *Irby* —2C **136**
South Dri. *Sand P* —1A **80**
South Dri. *Upt* —4A **94**
South Dri. *W'tree* —1F **101**
Southern Cres. *L8* —4D **99**
Southern Expressway. *Hall P* —4E **167**
Southern Rd. *L24* —5E **147**
Southey Clo. *Wid* —4F **131**
Southey Gro. *L31* —4D **13**
Southey Rd. *St H* —3C **64**
Southey St. *Boot* —4B **34**
(in two parts)
Southey St. *L15* —2D **101**
S. Ferry Quay. *L3* —3C **98**
Southfield Rd. *L9* —2E **35**
South Front. *Hals P* —1E **107**
Southgate Clo. *L12* —5E **39**
Southgate Rd. *L13* —3A **80**
South Gro. *Ding* —5A **100**
South Gro. *Moss H* —3C **124**
S. Hey Rd. *Wir* —3D **137**
S. Highville Rd. *L16* —3D **103**
S. Hill Gro. *L8* —5A **100**
S. Hill Gro. *Pren* —1B **118**
S. Hill Rd. *L8* —1F **121**
S. Hill Rd. *Pren* —5B **96**
S. Hunter St. *L1* —1E **99** (7J **5**)
S. John St. *L2 & L1* —5C **76** (5D **4**)
S. John St. *St H* —5C **46**
Southlands M. *Run* —1F **165**
South La. *Wid* —4E **111**
South La. Entry. *Wid* —5F **111**
S. Manor Way. *L25* —3C **126**
South Meade. *L31* —1B **12**
Southmead Gdns. *L19* —5E **125**
Southmead Rd. *L19* —5E **125**
S. Moor Dri. *L23* —1E **17**
S. Mossley Hill Rd. *L19* —3A **124**
Southney Clo. *L31* —3B **22**
South Pde. *Cros* —2F **17**
South Pde. *Kirkby* —3E **23**
South Pde. *Speke* —4E **147**
South Pde. *W Kir* —4A **112**
South Pde. *West P* —3D **165**
S. Park Ct. *L32* —2C **22**
S. Park Ct. *Wall* —3E **75**
S. Park Rd. *L32* —2B **22**
S. Parkside Dri. *L12* —4B **58**
S. Parkside Wlk. *L12* —3B **58**
S. Park Way. *Boot* —1D **55**
Southport Rd. *Boot* —2E **35**
Southport Rd. *Thor* —3A **10**
Southport Rd. *Lyd* —1A **6**
Southport St. *St H* —5A **48**
South Quay. *L3* —1C **98**
Southridge Rd. *Wir* —2A **138**
South Rd. *L9* —2D **37**
South Rd. *L14* —3C **80**
South Rd. *L24* —3E **147**
South Rd. *Wat* —5D **17**
South Rd. *Birk* —1C **118**
South Rd. *Grass P* —1A **144**
South Rd. *W Kir* —5B **112**
South Rd. *West P* —3D **165**
S. Sefton Bus. Cen. *Boot* —1B **54**
South Sta. Rd. *L25* —4B **104**
South St. *L8* —4A **100**
South St. *That H* —4D **65**
South St. *Wid* —4B **132**
S. Sudley Rd. *L19* —3F **123**
South Vw. *Wat* —5E **17**
South Vw. *Huy* —4B **84**
South Vw. *Wir* —2D **143**
S. View Ter. *Cuer* —2F **133**
South Vs. *Wall* —4B **52**
Southward Rd. *Hay* —1F **49**
Southwark Gro. *Boot* —4F **19**
South Way. *L15* —1B **102**
Southway. *Run* —3F **167**
(in two parts)
Southway. *Wid* —4D **131**
Southwell Pl. *L8* —4E **99**
Southwell St. *L8* —4E **99**
Southwick Rd. *Birk* —1E **119**
S. Wirral Retail Pk. *Wir* —4D **143**
Southwood Av. *Wind H* —5C **154**
Southwood Clo. *L32* —5A **24**
Southwood Rd. *L17* —2B **122**
Sovereign Clo. *Murd* —3D **169**
Sovereign Hey. *L11* —5C **38**
Sovereign Rd. *L11* —5C **38**
Sovereign Way. *L11* —5C **38**
Spark La. *Halt* —1F **167**
Sparks La. *Hes* —1B **138**
Sparling St. *L1* —2D **99**
(in two parts)
Sparrow Hall Clo. *L9* —4E **37**
Sparrow Hall Rd. *L9* —4E **37**
Sparrowhawk Clo. *L26* —3E **127**
Sparrowhawk Clo. *Pal* —3A **168**
Speakman Rd. *Dent G* —2D **45**
Speakman St. *Run* —4F **151**
Speedwell Clo. *Wir* —2C **158**
Speedwell Dri. *Wir* —2C **158**
Speedwell Rd. *Birk* —2F **95**
Speke. —4B 146
Speke Boulevd. *L24* —3B **146**
Speke Chu. Rd. *L24* —4B **146**
Speke Hall. —5F 145
Speke Hall Av. *L24* —4A **146**
Speke Hall Ind. Est. *L24* —4A **146**
Speke Hall Rd. *L25 & L24* —5A **126**
Speke Ind. Pk. *L24* —2E **145**
Spekeland Rd. *L7* —1C **100**
Speke Rd. *Gars & Speke* —2C **144**
(in two parts)
Speke Rd. *Halew & Wid* —2C **148**

Speke Rd. *Hunts X & Wltn* —2B **126**
Speke Town La. *L24* —3B **146**
Spellow La. *L4* —3F **55**
Spellow Pl. *L3* —4B **4**
Spence Av. *Boot* —3D **35**
Spencer Av. *Wir* —5A **72**
Spencer Clo. *L36* —1F **105**
Spencer Gdns. *St H* —3D **67**
Spencer Pl. *Boot* —1D **35**
Spencer's La. *L31* —3E **21**
Spencer St. *L6* —2F **77**
Spennymoor Ct. *Run* —3E **167**
Spenser Av. *Birk* —3F **119**
Spenser Clo. *Wid* —3F **131**
Spenser St. *Boot* —4B **34**
Spicer Gro. *L32* —3E **23**
Spice St. *L9* —2B **36**
Spike Islands Visitors Cen. —2A 152
Spindle Clo. *L6* —2F **77**
Spindrift Ct. *W Kir* —5A **112**
Spindus Rd. *L24* —4A **146**
Spinnaker Clo. *Murd* —4D **169**
Spinney Av. *Wid* —3A **130**
Spinney Clo. *Clo F* —2C **88**
Spinney Clo. *L33* —5C **24**
Spinney Cres. *L23* —4B **8**
Spinney Grn. *Ecc* —1A **64**
Spinney Rd. *L33* —5C **24**
Spinney, The. *Beb* —4B **142**
Spinney, The. *Hes* —5C **158**
Spinney, The. *Prsct* —4C **62**
Spinney, The. *Stock V* —4A **60**
Spinney, The. *W Kir* —4E **113**
Spinney, The. *Wir* —3A **94**
Spinney Vw. *L33* —5D **25**
Spinney Wlk. *Cas* —1A **168**
Spinney Way. *L36* —3C **82**
Spital. —4B 142
Spital Heyes. *Wir* —4B **142**
Spital Rd. *Wir* —4A **142**
Spofforth Rd. *L7* —1D **101**
Spooner Av. *L21* —5C **18**
Sprainger St. *L3* —2B **76**
Sprakeling Pl. *Boot* —1E **35**
Spray St. *St H* —4E **45**
Spreyton Clo. *L12* —1C **58**
Sprig Clo. *L9* —5D **21**
Springbank Clo. *Run* —4B **166**
Spring Bank Rd. *L4* —1B **78**
Springbourne Rd. *L17* —2B **122**
Springbrook Clo. *Ecc* —4A **44**
Spring Clo. *L33* —5F **15**
Spring Ct. *Run* —5B **152**
Springdale Clo. *L12* —5C **58**
Springfield. *L3* —3E **77** (2G **5**)
(in two parts)
Springfield Av. *L21* —5C **18**
Springfield Av. *Wir* —3E **113**
Springfield Clo. *St H* —3C **64**
Springfield Clo. *Wir* —2C **116**
Springfield La. *Ecc* —3A **44**
Springfield Pk. *Hay* —1C **48**
Springfield Rd. *Augh* —2F **7**
Springfield Rd. *St H* —3C **64**
Springfield Rd. *Wid* —4A **130**
Springfield Sq. *L4* —3F **55**
Springfield Way. *L12* —3E **59**
Spring Gdns. *L31* —2E **13**
Spring Gro. *L12* —5C **58**
Springhill Av. *Wir* —4D **163**
Springmeadow Rd. *L25* —4A **104**
Springpool. *St H* —4D **67**
Springs Clo. *Boot* —4D **35**
Spring St. *Birk* —1F **119**
Spring St. *Wid* —1A **152**
Spring Va. *Wall* —4E **51**
Springville Rd. *L9* —1C **36**
Springwell Rd. *Boot* —1D **35**
Springwood Av. *Gars & Wltn* —4D **125**
Springwood Ct. L19 —4D 125
(off Ramsey Rd.)
Springwood Gro. *L32* —1F **39**
Springwood Way. *Wir* —4A **120**
Spruce Clo. *Birk* —5D **97**
Spruce Gro. *L28* —4B **60**
(in two parts)
Sprucewood Clo. *L6* —1B **78**
Spur Clo. *L11* —5C **38**
Spurgeon Clo. *L5* —1F **77**
Spurling Rd. *Btnwd* —5F **69**
Spurriers La. *L31* —2C **14**
Spurstow Clo. *Pren* —1F **117**
Spur, The. *L23* —2D **17**
Squires Av. *Wid* —3F **131**
Squires Clo. *Hay* —2B **48**
Squires St. *L7* —1A **100**
Stable Clo. *Wir* —5D **93**
Stables, The. *L23* —5A **10**
Stackfield, The. *Wir* —3F **113**
Stadium Rd. *Wir* —4E **143**
Stadtmoers Pk. —4B 84
Stadtmoers Vis. Cen. —4C 84
Stafford Clo. *L36* —2A **84**
Stafford Moreton Way. *L31* —1C **12**
Stafford Rd. *St H* —2D **65**
Stafford St. *L3* —4E **77** (3H **5**)
Stag La. *Boot* —3B **20**
Stainburn Av. *L11* —5E **37**
Stainer Clo. *L14* —1F **81**
Stainton Clo. *L26* —4E **127**
Stainton Clo. *St H* —5B **30**
Stairhaven Rd. *L19* —3B **124**
Stakes, The. *Wir* —3E **71**
Stalbridge Av. *L18* —4F **101**
Staley Av. *L23* —2F **17**
Staley St. *Boot* —2C **34**
Stalisfield Av. *L11* —1A **58**
Stalisfield Gro. *L11* —1A **58**
Stalisfield Pl. *L11* —1A **58**
Stalmine Rd. *L9* —4A **36**
Stamford Ct. *Boot* —5D **35**
Stamfordham Dri. *L19* —4C **124**
Stamfordham Gro. *L19* —5D **125**
Stamfordham Pl. *L19* —5C **124**
Stamford St. *L7* —4C **78**
Stanbury Av. *Wir* —1A **142**
Standale Rd. *L15* —1F **101**
Standard Pl. *Birk* —1F **119**
Standard Rd. *L11* —4C **38**
Standen Clo. *St H* —4E **45**
Stand Farm Rd. *L12* —5E **39**
Standish Av. *Bil* —1E **31**
Standish Ct. *Wid* —4D **131**
Standish St. *L3* —3C **76** (3E **4**)
Standish St. *St H* —4A **46**
Stand Pk. Av. *Boot* —3F **19**
Stand Pk. Clo. *Boot* —3F **19**
Stand Pk. Rd. *L16* —3D **103**
Stand Pk. Way. *Boot* —2E **19**
Standring Gdns. *St H* —3B **64**
Stanfield Av. *L5* —1F **77**
Stanfield Dri. *Wir* —4F **141**
Stanford Av. *Wall* —4B **52**
Stanford Cres. *L25* —3D **127**
Stangate. *L31* —5B **6**
Stanhope Dri. *L36* —3C **82**
Stanhope Dri. *Wir* —1D **163**
Stanhope St. *L8* —3D **99**
(in two parts)
Stanhope St. *St H* —3F **45**
Stanier Way. *L7* —5C **78**
Staniforth Pl. *L16* —5D **81**
Stanley. —4E 79
Stanley Av. *Wall* —5D **51**
Stanley Av. *Wir* —4B **118**
Stanley Bank Rd. *St H* —1A **48**
Stanley Bungalows. *Know* —5C **40**
Stanley Clo. *L4* —4D **55**
Stanley Clo. *Wall* —4E **75**
Stanley Clo. *Wid* —2C **132**
Stanley Ct. *Birk* —1F **119**
Stanley Cres. *Prsct* —5C **62**
Stanley Gdns. *L9* —3F **35**
Stanley Ho. *Boot* —4B **34**
Stanley Ind. Est. *L13* —2E **79**
Stanley La. *Wir* —1F **171**
Stanley Park. —4B 18
Stanley Pk. —3A 56
Stanley Pk. *L21* —4A **18**
Stanley Pk. Av. N. *L4* —2B **56**
(in two parts)
Stanley Pk. Av. S. *L4* —3B **56**
Stanley Precinct. *Boot* —5D **35**
Stanley Rd. *Boot & Kirk* —2C **34**
Stanley Rd. *Mag* —4C **12**
Stanley Rd. *Wat* —5E **17**
Stanley Rd. *Birk* —5F **73**
Stanley Rd. *Hoy* —5A **90**
Stanley Rd. *Huy* —3E **83**
Stanley Rd. *New F* —4A **120**
Stanley St. *L1* —4C **76** (4D **4**)
Stanley St. *Fair* —3D **79**
Stanley St. *Gars* —3C **144**
Stanley St. *Run* —4B **152**
Stanley St. *Wall* —4E **75**
Stanley Ter. *L18* —1A **124**
Stanley Ter. *Wall* —4B **52**
Stanley Theatre. —5F 77
Stanley Vs. *Run* —1F **165**
Stanley Yd. *L9* —5A **36**
Stanlowe Vw. *L19* —5F **123**
Stanmore Pk. *Wir* —1B **114**
Stanmore Rd. *L15* —3B **102**
Stanmore Rd. *Run* —5D **153**
Stanney Clo. *East* —2E **171**
Stannyfield Clo. *L23* —4B **10**
Stannyfield Dri. *L23* —4B **10**
Stansfield Av. *L31* —1F **13**
Stanton Av. *L21* —4A **18**
Stanton Clo. *Boot* —5D **11**
Stanton Clo. *Hay* —2C **48**
Stanton Cres. *L32* —3C **22**
Stanton Rd. *L18* —4F **101**
Stanton Rd. *Wir* —4E **141**
Stanwood Clo. *Ecc* —5F **43**
Stanwood Gdns. *Whis* —3E **85**
Stapehill Clo. *L13* —4B **80**
Stapeley Gdns. *L26* —1A **148**
Staplands Rd. *L14* —4D **81**
Stapleford Rd. *L25* —3C **104**
Staplehurst Clo. *L12* —5E **39**
Stapleton Av. *L24* —4D **147**
Stapleton Av. *Rain* —2C **86**
Stapleton Av. *Wir* —5D **93**
Stapleton Clo. *L25* —2B **104**
Stapleton Clo. *Rain* —2C **86**
Stapleton Rd. *Rain* —1B **86**
Stapleton Way. *Wid* —2B **150**
Stapley Clo. *Run* —1F **165**
Star Inn Cotts. *Rainf* —1A **28**
Starling Clo. *Murd* —3D **169**
Starling Gro. *L12* —2F **59**
Star St. *L8* —3E **99**
Startham Av. *Bil* —2D **31**
Starworth Dri. *Wir* —5C **120**
Statham Rd. *Pren* —1C **94**
Station App. *Meol* —3E **91**
Station App. *Wir* —4E **71**
Station Clo. *L25* —5C **126**
Station M. *L32* —2C **22**
Station Rd. *Mag* —2E **13**
Station Rd. *Mell* —2A **22**
Station Rd. *St H* —4E **67**
Station Rd. *Birk* —5F **73**
Station Rd. *Hay* —2C **48**
Station Rd. *Hes* —4F **157**
Station Rd. *Hoy* —5B **90**

Station Rd. *Huy* —4C **82**
Station Rd. *Lyd* —1A **6**
Station Rd. *Prsct* —5D **63**
Station Rd. *Rain* —3C **86**
Station Rd. *Run* —5F **151**
Station Rd. *Sut W* —1B **174**
Station Rd. *Thur* —5F **135**
Station Rd. *Wall* —2A **74**
Station Rd. *Wid* —5C **110**
Station Rd. *Wir* —2D **139**
Station Rd. *Wltn* —4A **104**
Station St. *Rain* —3C **86**
Statton Rd. *L13* —5B **80**
Staveley Rd. *L19* —4B **124**
Stavert Clo. *L11* —5B **38**
Staverton Pk. *L32* —4C **22**
Stavordale Rd. *Wir* —5A **72**
Steble St. *L8* —4F **99**
Steel Av. *Wall* —5C **52**
Steel Ct. *L5* —5C **54**
Steeplechase Clo. *L9* —5C **20**
Steeple, The. *Wir* —3D **135**
Steeple Vw. *L33* —5E **15**
Steers Cft. *L28* —3F **59**
Steers St. *L6* —2F **77**
Steinberg Ct. *L3* —2C **76**
Stella Precinct. *L21* —2A **34**
Stenhills Cres. *Run* —5C **152**
Stepford St. *L8* —5F **99**
Stephens La. *L2* —4C **76** (4C **4**)
Stephenson Ct. L7 —5C 78
(off Crosfield Rd.)
Stephenson Ho. *L7* —1A **100**
Stephenson Rd. *L13* —4A **80**
Stephenson Way. *W'tree* —5E **79**
Stephen Way. *Rain* —1B **86**
Stepney Gro. *L4* —2A **56**
Sterling Way. *L5* —5D **55**
Sterndale Clo. *L7* —1B **100**
Sterrix Av. *Boot* —3C **18**
Sterrix Grn. *L21* —3C **18**
Sterrix La. *L21 & Boot* —3C **18**
Steve Biko Clo. *L8* —2B **100**
Stevenage Clo. *St H* —4F **65**
Stevenson Cres. *St H* —4D **45**
Stevenson Dri. *Wir* —4F **141**
Stevenson St. *L15* —1E **101**
Stevens Rd. *Wir* —3C **158**
Stevens St. *St H* —3D **65**
Steventon. *Run* —4D **155**
Steward Ct. *Prsct* —1F **85**
Stewards Av. *Wid* —4F **131**
Stewart Av. *Boot* —4E **35**
Stewart Clo. *Wir* —4F **137**
Stile Hey. *L23* —5B **10**
Stiles Rd. *L33* —4F **15**
Stillington Rd. *L8* —5A **100**
Stirling Av. *L23* —2E **17**
Stirling Cres. *St H* —5C **66**
Stirling Rd. *L24* —4B **146**
Stirling St. *Wall* —4B **74**
Stockbridge La. *L36* —1B **82**
Stockbridge Pl. *L5* —5A **56**
Stockbridge St. *L5* —1A **78**
Stockbridge Village. —3A 60
Stockdale Clo. *L3* —3C **76** (2D **4**)
Stockham Clo. *Halt* —2A **168**
Stockham La. *Brook* —5C **168**
Stockham La. *Halt* —2A **168**
(in three parts)
Stockmoor Rd. *L11* —5F **37**
Stockpit Rd. *Know I* —3C **24**
Stocks Av. *St H* —5E **47**
Stockswell Rd. *Cron & Wid* —5F **107**
Stockton Gro. *St H* —5D **65**
Stockton Wood Rd. *L24* —4C **146**
Stockville Rd. *L18* —5E **103**
Stoddart Rd. *L4* —1A **56**
Stoke Clo. *Wir* —2E **171**
Stokesay. *Pren* —3D **95**
Stokesley Av. *L32* —3C **22**
Stoke St. *Birk* —1B **96**
Stonebarn Dri. *L31* —4C **6**
Stone Barn La. *Pal* —4F **167**
Stonebridge La. *Walt & Crox* —2A **38**
Stoneby Dri. *Wall* —4A **52**
Stonechat Clo. *L27* —5E **105**
Stonechat Clo. *Beech* —5F **167**
Stonecrop. *L18* —4E **103**
Stonecrop Clo. *Beech* —5F **167**
Stonecross Dri. *Rain* —5D **87**
Stonedale Cres. *L11* —4A **38**
Stonefield Rd. *L14* —2F **81**
Stonegate Dri. *L8* —5F **99**
Stonehaven Clo. *L16* —1F **103**
Stone Hey. *Whis* —5D **85**
Stonehey Dri. *Wir* —1C **134**
Stonehey Rd. *L32* —5E **23**
Stone Hey Wlk. *L32* —5E **23**
Stonehill Av. *L4* —5B **56**
Stonehill Av. *Wir* —1A **142**
Stonehills La. *Run* —5C **152**
Stonehill St. *L4* —5B **56**
Stonehouse M. *Aller* —1D **125**
Stonehouse Rd. *Wall* —1E **73**
Stonelea. *Wind H* —1B **168**
Stoneleigh Gro. *Birk* —4F **119**
Stoneridge Ct. *Pren* —1C **94**
Stone Sq. *Boot* —3E **35**
Stone St. *L3* —2B **76**
Stone St. *Prsct* —5D **63**
Stoneville Rd. *L13* —2A **80**
Stoneycroft. —2A 80
Stoneycroft Clo. *L13* —1A **80**
Stoneycroft Cres. *L13* —1A **80**
Stoney Hey Rd. *Wall* —4A **52**
Stoneyhurst Av. *L10* —2C **20**
Stoney La. *Rain* —3A **86**
Stoney La. *Whis* —2F **85**
Stoney Vw. *Rain* —3B **86**
Stonham Clo. *Wir* —4E **93**
Stonyfield. *Boot* —5E **11**
Stony Holt. *Run* —2C **168**
Stonyhurst Clo. *St H* —1B **46**
Stonyhurst Rd. *L25* —3B **126**
Stopgate La. *Sim* —4F **15**
Stopgate La. *Walt* —4D **37**
Store St. *L20* —2D **55**
Storeton Brickfields. —2E 139
Storeton Clo. *Pren* —1A **118**
Storeton La. *Wir* —4C **138**
Storeton Rd. *Birk* —3C **118**
Storeton Rd. *Pren* —1B **118**
Stormont Rd. *L19* —5B **124**
Storrington Av. *L11* —5A **38**
Storrington Heys. *L11* —5B **38**
(in three parts)
Storrsdale Rd. *L18* —1B **124**
Stour Av. *Rain* —3C **86**
Stourcliffe Rd. *Wall* —2A **74**
Stourport Clo. *Wir* —5C **92**
Stourton Rd. *L32* —5E **23**
Stourton St. *Wall* —4C **74**
Stourvale Rd. *L26* —4F **127**
Stowe Av. *L10* —3E **21**
Stowe Clo. *L25* —5A **126**
Stowell St. *L7* —1F **99** (7J **5**)
Stowford Clo. *L12* —1C **58**
Strada Way. *L3* —3F **77** (2J **5**)
Stradbroke Rd. *L15* —3A **102**
Strafford Dri. *Boot* —4E **35**
Strand Rd. *Boot* —5A **34**
(in two parts)
Strand Rd. *Wir* —4B **90**
Strand Shop. Cen. *Boot* —4C **34**
Strand St. *L1* —5C **76** (6C **4**)
Strand, The. *L2* —5B **76** (5C **4**)
Stratford Rd. *L19* —4F **123**
Strathallan Clo. *Wir* —5E **137**
Strathcona Rd. *L15* —2E **101**
Strathcona Rd. *Wall* —5B **52**
Strathearn Rd. *Wir* —4F **157**
Strathlorne Clo. *Birk* —1F **119**
Strathmore Dri. *L23* —2E **17**
Strathmore Gro. *St H* —5C **66**
Strathmore Rd. *L6* —2C **78**
Stratton Clo. *L18* —1E **125**
Stratton Clo. *Brook* —4B **168**
Stratton Clo. *Wall* —5C **52**
Stratton Dri. *St H* —5D **65**
Stratton Pk. *Wid* —4F **109**
Stratton Rd. *L32* —4C **22**
Stratton Wlk. *L32* —4C **22**
Strauss Clo. *L8* —3B **100**
Strawberry Rd. *L11* —1E **57**
Streatham Av. *L18* —4F **101**
Street Hey La. *Will* —2B **170**
Stretford Clo. *L33* —5E **15**
Stretton Av. *St H* —5F **47**
Stretton Av. *Bil* —1E **31**
Stretton Av. *Wall* —2A **74**
Stretton Clo. *L12* —5A **40**
Stretton Clo. *Pren* —1E **117**
Stretton Clo. *Wir* —2E **171**
Stretton Way. *L36* —5B **84**
Strickland St. *St H* —4B **46**
Stringhey Rd. *Wall* —1C **74**
Stroma Rd. *L18* —3B **124**
Stroud Clo. *Wir* —1C **114**
Stuart Av. *L25* —5C **126**
Stuart Av. *Wir* —5F **71**
Stuart Clo. *Wir* —1A **94**
Stuart Dri. *L14* —3E **81**
Stuart Gro. *L20* —2D **55**
Stuart Rd. *Mell* —2B **22**
Stuart Rd. *Walt* —1E **55**
Stuart Rd. *Wat & Cros* —3E **17**
Stuart Rd. *Wind* —2C **44**
Stuart Rd. *Birk* —1D **119**
Stuart Rd. *Mnr P* —3C **154**
Stuart Rd. N. *Boot* —5E **35**
Studholme St. *L20* —4C **54**
Studland Rd. *L9* —4E **37**
Studley Rd. *Wall* —5E **51**
Sturdee Rd. *L13* —5B **80**
Sturgess St. *Newt W* —5F **49**
Suburban Rd. *L6* —5C **56**
Sudbury Clo. *L25* —2D **127**
Sudbury Rd. *L22* —3B **16**
Sudell Av. *L31* —5F **7**
Sudell La. *L31* —1D **7**
Sudley Art Gallery. —2F 123
Sudley Grange. *L17* —3E **123**
Sudworth Rd. *Wall* —4A **52**
Suffield Rd. *L4* —3D **55**
Suffolk Pl. *Wid* —5C **130**
Suffolk St. *Boot* —4D **35**
Suffolk St. *L1* —1D **99** (7F **5**)
Suffolk St. *Run* —4F **151**
Suffton Pk. *L32* —4C **22**
Sugar La. *Know* —5C **40**
Sugar St. *L9* —3B **36**
Sugnall St. *L7* —1F **99** (7J **5**)
(in two parts)
Sulby Av. *L13* —1E **79**
Sulgrave Clo. *L16* —5C **80**
Sullington Dri. *L27* —3E **105**
Sullivan Av. *Wir* —5F **93**
Sumley Clo. *St H* —3D **47**
Summer Clo. *Cas* —1F **167**
Summerfield. *Wir* —5D **143**
Summerfield Clo. *Ecc* —5F **43**
Summerhill Dri. *L31* —3F **13**
Summer La. *Halt* —1F **167**
Summer La. *Pres H* —4F **169**
Summers Av. *Boot* —4E **35**
Summer Seat. *Boot* —5A **34**

Summer Seat. *L3* —2D **77** (1E **4**)
Summers Rd. *Brun B* —4D **99**
Summertrees Av. *Wir* —5D **93**
Summertrees Clo. *Wir* —5D **93**
Summerwood. *Wir* —5D **115**
Summit, The. *Wall* —1C **74**
Summit Way. *L25* —1F **125**
Sumner Clo. *L5* —1C **76**
Sumner Clo. *Rain* —5D **87**
Sumner Gro. *L33* —5F **15**
Sumner Rd. *Pren* —1F **95**
Sumner St. *Hay* —2A **48**
Sunbeam Rd. *L13* —3A **80**
Sunbourne Rd. *L17* —2B **122**
Sunbury Rd. *L4* —4B **56**
Sunbury Rd. *Wall* —3C **74**
Sunbury St. *St H* —3C **64**
Suncroft Rd. *Wir* —3C **158**
Sundale Av. *Prsct* —5F **63**
Sundew Clo. *L9* —1F **35**
Sundridge St. *L8* —5A **100**
Sunfield Rd. *Wir* —4F **71**
Sunflower Clo. *St H* —4A **68**
Sunlight St. *L6* —1C **78**
Sunloch Clo. *L9* —5D **21**
Sunningdale. *Wir* —1F **93**
Sunningdale Av. *Wid* —3B **130**
Sunningdale Clo. *L36* —5C **82**
Sunningdale Clo. *Btnwd* —5F **69**
Sunningdale Dri. *L23* —4C **8**
Sunningdale Dri. *Brom* —4B **162**
Sunningdale Dri. *Hes* —2A **138**
Sunningdale Rd. *L15* —1F **101**
Sunningdale Rd. *Wall* —3F **51**
Sunniside La. *Run* —3E **155**
Sunny Bank. *Beb* —1D **141**
Sunnybank. *Upt* —3F **93**
Sunnybank Av. *Pren* —5D **95**
Sunny Bank Rd. *L16* —2D **103**
Sunnydale. *Rain* —3D **87**
Sunny Ga. Rd. *L19* —4A **124**
Sunnymede Dri. *L31* —4D **7**
Sunnyside. *Prin P* —4A **100**
Sunnyside. *Wir* —4D **71**
Sunnyside Rd. *L23* —2C **16**
Sunrise Clo. *L19* —5B **124**
Sunsdale Rd. *L18* —4A **102**
Sunset Clo. *L33* —5F **15**
Surby Clo. *L16* —1E **103**
Surrey Av. *Wir* —4F **93**
Surrey Dri. *Wir* —1C **134**
Surrey St. *Boot* —4D **35**
Surrey St. *L1* —1D **99** (7E **5**)
Surrey St. *St H* —5D **47**
Surrey St. *Run* —5A **152**
(in two parts)
Surrey St. *Wall* —3A **74**
Susan Gro. *Wir* —1D **93**
Susan St. *Wid* —2C **132**
Susan Wlk. *Prsct* —1F **85**
Sussex Clo. *Boot* —4D **35**
Sussex Clo. *Wir* —3E **137**
Sussex Gro. *St H* —1C **66**
Sussex Rd. *L31* —3D **13**
Sussex Rd. *Wid* —3D **133**
Sussex Rd. *Wir* —3C **112**
Sussex St. *Boot* —4D **35**
Sussex St. *L22* —3C **16**
Sutcliffe St. *L6* —3B **78**
Sutherland Ct. *Run* —5B **152**
Sutherland Dri. *Wir* —1D **171**
Sutherland Rd. *Prsct* —5E **63**
Sutton. —3F 67
Sutton Causeway. *Frod* —3E **173**
Sutton Clo. *Wir* —2E **171**
Sutton Community Leisure Cen. —5B 66
Sutton Cricket Club Ground. —4C 66
Sutton Hall Golf Course. —2A 174
Sutton Heath. —5E 65
Sutton Heath Rd. *St H* —5E **65**
Sutton Leach. —1D 89
Sutton Lodge Rd. *St H* —1B **66**
Sutton Manor. —4A 88
Sutton Moss Rd. *St H* —3F **67**
Sutton Oak Dri. *St H* —2D **67**
Sutton Pk. —4C 66
Sutton Pk. Dri. *St H* —4C **66**
Sutton Rd. *St H* —2C **66**
Sutton Rd. *Wall* —4B **52**
Suttons La. *Wid* —5B **132**
Sutton St. *L13* —1E **79**
Sutton St. *Run* —5B **152**
Suttons Way. *L26* —3E **127**
Sutton Weaver. —2A 174
Sutton Wood Rd. *L24* —4C **146**
Suzanne Boardman Ho. *L6* —1C **78**
Swainson Rd. *L10* —1E **37**
Swale Av. *Rain* —3C **86**
Swaledale Av. *Rain* —3D **87**
Swaledale Clo. *Wir* —5E **163**
Swalegate. *L31* —5C **6**
Swallow Clo. *Kirkby* —3E **15**
Swallow Clo. *W Der* —5F **39**
Swallow Clo. *N'ley* —4F **105**
Swallow Fields. *L9* —4E **37**
Swallowhurst Cres. *L11* —1A **58**
Swan Av. *St H* —1A **68**
Swan Ct. *Pren* —2F **117**
Swan Cres. *L15* —1A **102**
Swanhey. *L31* —3E **13**
Swan La. *Augh* —1E **7**
Swan Rd. *Newt W* —4D **49**
Swanside. —3E 81
Swanside Av. *L14* —3E **81**
Swanside Pde. *L14* —3E **81**
Swanside Rd. *L14* —3E **81**
Swanston Av. *L4* —2A **56**
Swan St. *L13* —3F **79**
Swan Wlk. *L31* —3E **13**
Sweden Gro. *L22* —4D **17**
Sweet Briar Ct. *Clo F* —4D **89**
Sweeting St. *L2* —5C **76** (5C **4**)
Swift Gro. *L12* —4F **39**
Swift's Clo. *Boot* —1D **19**
Swift's La. *Boot* —1D **19**
Swift St. *St H* —3A **46**
Swinbrook Grn. *L11* —5F **37**
Swinburne Clo. *L16* —1F **103**
Swinburne Rd. *Dent G* —3D **45**
Swindale Clo. *L8* —2B **100**
Swinderby Dri. *L31* —2B **22**
Swindon Clo. *L5* —4D **55**
Swindon Clo. *Wind H* —5D **155**
Swindon Clo. *Wir* —5C **92**
Swindon St. *L5* —4D **55**
Swinford Av. *Wid* —2E **133**
Swisspine Gdns. *St H* —4C **64**
Swiss Rd. *L6* —3C **78**
Switch Island. *Boot* —5B **12**
Sword Clo. *L11* —5C **38**
Sword Wlk. *L11* —5C **38**
Swynnerton Way. *Wid* —4B **110**
Sybil Rd. *L4* —4A **56**
Sycamore Av. *Cros* —4F **9**
Sycamore Av. *Halew* —1F **147**
Sycamore Av. *Hay* —3F **47**
Sycamore Av. *Wid* —2B **132**
Sycamore Av. *Wir* —2D **93**
Sycamore Clo. *Ecc* —4B **44**
Sycamore Clo. *Walt* —5C **36**
Sycamore Clo. *Wir* —2D **93**
Sycamore Ct. L8 —5A 100
(off Weller Way)
Sycamore Dri. *Sut W* —1A **174**
Sycamore Gdns. *St H* —2E **45**
Sycamore Pk. *L18* —2D **125**
Sycamore Ri. *Wir* —2C **114**
Sycamore Rd. *Wat* —3E **17**
Sycamore Rd. *Birk* —5D **97**
Sycamore Rd. *Huy* —1E **105**
Sycamore Rd. *Run* —2C **166**
Sydenham Av. *L17* —3C **100**
Sydenham Ho. *L17* —4C **100**
Syder's Gro. *Know* —5C **40**
Sydney St. *L9* —2A **36**
Sydney St. *West P* —3D **165**
Sylvan Ct. *L25* —3A **126**
Sylvandale Gro. *Wir* —4D **143**
Sylvania Rd. *L4* —1A **56**
Sylvia Clo. *L10* —2B **38**
Syren St. *L20* —3C **54**
Syston Av. *St H* —2C **46**

Tabley Av. *Wid* —2C **130**
Tabley Clo. *Pren* —2F **117**
Tabley Gdns. *St H* —5D **65**
Tabley Rd. *L15* —2D **101**
Tabley St. *L1* —1C **98**
Tace Clo. *L8* —2F **99**
Taggart Av. *L16* —3D **103**
Tagus Clo. *L8* —3B **100**
Tagus St. *L8* —2B **100**
Tailor's La. *L31* —2E **13**
Talbot Av. *Thor H* —1A **160**
Talbot Clo. *St H* —4F **45**
Talbot Ct. *L36* —5E **83**
Talbot Ct. *Pren* —5A **96**
Talbot Rd. *Pren* —5A **96**
Talbot St. *Boot* —4B **34**
Talbotville Rd. *L13* —5B **80**
Talgarth Way. *L25* —2A **104**
Taliesin St. *L5* —1D **77**
Talisman Clo. *Murd* —3D **169**
Talisman Way. *Boot* —4A **34**
Talland Clo. *L26* —3E **127**
Tallarn Rd. *L32* —3B **22**
Talton Rd. *L15* —2D **101**
Tamar Clo. *L6* —2A **78**
Tamarisk Gdns. *St H* —5C **64**
Tamar Rd. *Hay* —2C **48**
Tamerton Clo. *L18* —2E **125**
Tamworth St. *L8* —4E **99**
Tamworth St. *Newt W* —5F **49**
Tamworth St. *St H* —4E **45**
Tanar Clo. *Wir* —4B **142**
Tanat Dri. *L18* —5B **102**
Tancred Rd. *L4* —4F **55**
Tancred Rd. *Wall* —1A **74**
Tanhouse. *Halt* —1E **167**
Tanhouse Ind. Est. *Wid* —5D **133**
Tan Ho. La. *Btnwd* —5F **69**
Tanhouse La. *Wid* —4C **132**
Tanhouse Rd. *L23* —5B **10**
Tansley Clo. *Wir* —4E **113**
Tanworth Gro. *Wir* —5B **70**
Tapley Pl. *L13* —4F **79**
Taplow St. *L6* —5B **56**
Tarbock Green. —5D 107
Tarbock Rd. *Huy* —5D **83**
Tarbock Rd. *Speke* —3D **147**
Tarbot Hey. *Wir* —1C **92**
Tarbrock Ct. *Boot* —5D **11**
Target Rd. *Wir* —2C **156**
Tariff St. *L5* —1C **76**
Tarleton Clo. *L26* —5E **127**
Tarleton St. *L1* —5D **77** (5E **5**)
Tarlton Clo. *Rain* —1A **86**
Tarnbeck. *Nort* —2C **168**
Tarncliff. *L28* —3C **60**
Tarn Gro. *St H* —5B **30**
Tarporley Clo. *Pren* —1F **117**
Tarran Dri. *Tarr I* —4D **71**
Tarran Rd. *Tarr I* —4D **71**
Tarran Way E. *Tarr I* —3D **71**
Tarran Way Ind. Est. *Tarr I* —4D **71**

Tarran Way N. Tarr I —4D 71
Tarran Way S. Tarr I —4D 71
Tarran Way W. Tarr I —4D 71
Tarves Wlk. L33 —3F 23
Tarvin Clo. Run —4C 166
Tarvin Clo. Sut M —2B 88
Tarvin Rd. Wir —1F 171
Tasker Ter. Rain —2C 86
Tasman Gro. That H —4E 65
Tate Clo. Wid —1D 131
Tate Gallery. —1B 98 (7B 4)
Tate St. L4 —3F 55
Tatlock Clo. Bil —1E 31
Tatlock St. L5 —2C 76
(in two parts)
Tattersall Pl. Boot —1B 54
Tattersall Rd. L21 —1A 34
Tattersall Way. L7 —4E 79
Tatton Rd. L9 —2F 35
Tatton Rd. Birk —4D 97
Taunton Av. Sut L —1D 89
Taunton Dri. L10 —3E 21
Taunton Rd. L36 —4B 84
Taunton Rd. Wall —5E 51
Taunton St. L15 —1E 101
Taurus Rd. L14 —2A 82
Tavener Clo. Wir —5C 162
Tavistock Rd. Wall —5F 51
Tavy Rd. L6 —2A 78
Tawd St. L4 —3E 55
Tawny Ct. Hall P —3E 167
Taylor Clo. St H —3E 67
Taylor Pk. —1C 64
Taylor Rd. Hay —2E 49
Taylors Clo. L9 —5E 35
Taylor's La. Cuer —2F 133
(in two parts)
Taylors La. L9 —5E 35
Taylors Row. Run —5C 152
Taylor St. L5 —1D 77
Taylor St. St H —4E 67
Taylor St. Birk —2E 97
Taylor St. Wid —3C 132
Taylor St. Ind. Est. L5 —1D 77
(off Taylor St.)
Teakwood Clo. L6 —1A 78
Teal Clo. St H —2B 46
Teal Gro. L26 —3E 127
Teals Way. Wir —2E 157
Teasville Rd. L18 —5E 103
Tebay Clo. L31 —5F 7
Tebay Rd. Wir —2E 163
Teck St. L7 —4A 78
Tedburn Clo. L25 —5C 104
Tedbury Clo. L32 —5E 23
Tedbury Wlk. L32 —5E 23
Tedder Sq. Wid —4D 131
Teehey Clo. Wir —1D 141
Teehey Gdns. Wir —1D 141
Teehey La. Wir —1D 141
Tees Clo. L4 —2D 55
Teesdale Rd. Hay —1C 48
Teesdale Rd. Wir —3E 141
Teesdale Way. Rain —1C 86
Tees Pl. L4 —2E 55
Tees St. L4 —2D 55
Tees St. Birk —5F 73
Teign Clo. L6 —2A 78
Teilo St. L8 —4F 99
Telary Clo. L5 —1C 76
Telegraph La. Wall —1C 72
Telegraph Rd. Hes —4D 137
Telegraph Rd. W Kir & Thur —2F 135
Telegraph Way. L32 —3E 23
Telford Clo. Pren —5B 96
Telford Clo. Wid —5D 109
Tempest Hey. L2 —4C 76 (4C 4)
Temple Ct. L2 —5C 76 (5D 4)
Temple La. L2 —4C 76 (4D 4)
Templemore Av. L18 —1A 124
Templemore Rd. Pren —5A 96
Temple Rd. Birk —2C 118
Temple St. L2 —4C 76 (4D 4)
Templeton Cres. L12 —2B 58
Tenby Av. L21 —4A 18
Tenby Dri. Run —5D 153
Tenby Dri. Wir —1F 93
Tenby St. L5 —5A 56
Tennis St. Dent G —3D 45
Tennis St. N. Dent G & St H —3E 45
Tennyson Av. Birk —3F 119
Tennyson Rd. L36 —1A 106
Tennyson Rd. Wid —3A 132
Tennyson St. Boot —3B 34
Tennyson St. Sut M —4A 88
Tennyson Wlk. L8 —3F 99
Tensing Rd. L31 —1D 13
Tenterden St. L5 —2D 77
Tenth Av. Faz —1D 37
Terence Rd. L16 —3D 103
Terminus Rd. L36 —1C 82
Terminus Rd. Wir —4D 143
Tern Clo. L33 —3E 15
Tern Clo. Wid —5B 110
Ternhall Rd. L9 —4F 37
Ternhall Way. L9 —4F 37
Tern Way. St H —4A 64
Tern Way. Wir —5B 70
Terrace Rd. Wid —2A 152
Terret Cft. L28 —4B 60
Tetbury St. Birk —4C 96
Tetchill Clo. Nort —2D 169
Tetlow St. L4 —3F 55
Tetlow Way. L4 —3F 55
Teulon Clo. L4 —3F 55
Tewit Hall Clo. L24 —4C 146
Tewit Hall Rd. L24 —4C 146
Tewkesbury Clo. W Der —4F 39
Tewkesbury Clo. Wltn —3C 126
Teynham Av. Know —4D 41
Teynham Cres. L11 —1F 57
Thackeray Gdns. Boot —5D 19
Thackray Rd. St H —3D 65
Thames Rd. St H —5C 66
Thames St. L8 —3B 100
Thatcher's Mt. C Grn —2D 69
Thatto Heath. —3D 65
Thatto Heath Pk. —3D 65
Thatto Heath Rd. St H —3D 65
Thermal Rd. Wir —3D 143
Thermopylae Ct. Pren —3D 95
(off Vyner Rd. S.)
Thermopylae Pas. Pren —3C 94
(in two parts)
Thingwall. —1A 138
Thingwall Av. L14 —4D 81
Thingwall Dri. Wir —1A 138
Thingwall Hall Dri. L14 —4D 81
Thingwall La. L14 —3D 81
Thingwall Recreation Cen. —1B 138
Thingwall Rd. L15 —2B 102
Thingwall Rd. Wir —1D 137
Thingwall Rd. E. Wir —1A 138
Third Av. Cros —1D 17
Third Av. Faz —1E 37
Third Av. L9 —1D 37
Third Av. Pren —3B 94
Third Av. Run —2F 167
Thirlmere Av. Lith —5D 19
Thirlmere Av. St H —5A 30
Thirlmere Av. Pren —3C 94
Thirlmere Clo. L31 —5E 7
Thirlmere Clo. Frod —5D 173
Thirlmere Dri. L21 —5D 19
Thirlmere Dri. Wall —1B 74
Thirlmere Grn. L5 —1A 78
Thirlmere Rd. Eve —1A 78
Thirlmere Wlk. L33 —1D 23
Thirlmere Way. Wid —4C 130
Thirlstane St. L17 —1B 122
Thirsk Clo. Run —4C 166
Thistledown Clo. L17 —1F 121
Thistleton Av. Birk —1F 95
Thistlewood Rd. L7 —4E 79
Thistley Hey Rd. L32 —3F 23
Thomas Clo. L19 —2C 144
Thomas Ct. Hall P —3F 167
Thomas Dri. L14 —4C 80
Thomas Dri. Prsct —2C 84
Thomas La. L14 —2D 81
Thomas St. Birk —4E 97
(in two parts)
Thomas St. Run —4B 152
Thomas St. Wid —5A 132
Thomaston St. L5 —5E 55
(in two parts)
Thomas Winder Ct. L5 —5D 55
Thompson Rd. L21 —1F 33
(in two parts)
Thompson St. St H —2D 65
Thompson St. Birk —5E 97
Thomson St. L6 —2B 78
Thorburn Clo. Wir —4B 120
Thorburn Ct. Wir —3B 120
Thorburn Cres. Wir —4B 120
Thorburn Rd. Wir —4B 120
Thorburn St. L7 —5B 78
Thorley Clo. L15 —5A 80
Thornaby Gro. St H —5D 65
Thornbeck Clo. L12 —5E 39
Thornbridge Av. L21 —5D 19
Thornbrook Clo. L12 —4D 59
Thornbury Rd. L4 —4C 56
Thorncliffe Rd. Wall —3A 74
Thorn Clo. Run —3C 166
Thorncroft Dri. Wir —3B 138
Thorndale Rd. L22 —3D 17
Thorndale St. L5 —4E 55
Thorndyke Clo. Rain —5E 87
Thorne La. Wall —1F 73
Thornes Rd. L6 —3B 78
Thorness Clo. Wir —2C 114
Thorneycroft St. Birk —1A 96
Thornfield Hey. Wir —5A 142
Thornfield Rd. Cros —4A 10
Thornfield Rd. Walt —3F 35
Thornham Av. St H —3C 66
Thornham Clo. Wir —2A 94
Thornhead La. L12 —5D 59
Thornhill Rd. L15 —2A 102
Thornholme Cres. L11 —2F 57
Thornhurst. L32 —1E 39
Thornleigh Av. Wir —1F 171
Thornley Rd. Wir —2C 92
Thornridge. Wir —1A 94
Thorn Rd. St H —5C 44
Thorn Rd. Run —3C 166
Thorns Dri. Wir —2C 114
Thornside Wlk. L25 —5B 104
Thorns, The. L31 —5B 6
Thornton. —4B 10
Thornton. Wid —4E 131
Thornton Av. Boot —1D 35
Thornton Av. Wir —4D 119
Thornton Comn. Rd. Wir —4B 160
Thornton Cres. Wir —4B 158
Thornton Gro. L36 —3C 82
Thornton Gro. Wir —4D 119
Thornton Hough. —4B 160
Thornton Rd. Boot —3C 34
Thornton Rd. L16 —5E 81
Thornton Rd. Beb —4C 118
Thornton Rd. Wall —5A 52
Thornton St. L21 —2B 34
Thornton St. Birk —1A 96
Thorntree Clo. Aig —1F 121
Thorn Tree Clo. Hale V —5E 149

Thornwood Clo. *L6* —1B **78**
Thornycroft Rd. *L15* —2D **101**
Thorpe Bank. *Birk* —4F **119**
Thorstone Dri. *Wir* —5C **114**
Thorsway. *Birk* —2F **119**
Thorsway. *Wir* —1D **135**
Three Butt La. *L12* —5F **57**
Three Lanes End. —4B 92
Threlfall St. *L8* —5A **100**
Thresher Av. *Wir* —5C **92**
Threshers, The. *Boot* —1B **20**
Throne Rd. *L11* —5C **38**
Throne Wlk. *L11* —4C **38**
Thurne Way. *L25* —3A **104**
Thurnham St. *L6* —1C **78**
Thursby Clo. *L32* —5F **23**
Thursby Cres. *L32* —4F **23**
Thursby Rd. *Croft B* —5E **143**
Thursby Wlk. *L32* —5F **23**
Thurstaston. —2B 136
Thurstaston Rd. *Hes* —1E **157**
Thurstaston Rd. *Irby & Thur* —2B **136**
Thurston Rd. *L4* —5B **56**
Tibb's Cross La. *Wid* —2C **110**
Tichbourne Way. *L6* —3F **77**
Tickle Av. *St H* —5D **47**
Tideswell Clo. *L7* —1B **100**
Tideway. *Wall* —3E **51**
Tilbrook Dri. *St H* —4D **67**
Tilbury Pl. *Murd* —4E **169**
Tildsley Cres. *West* —4F **165**
Tillotson Clo. *L8* —4E **99**
Tilney St. *L9* —2A **36**
Tilstock Av. *Wir* —4B **120**
Tilstock Clo. *L26* —2A **128**
Tilstock Cres. *Pren* —3F **117**
Tilston Clo. *L9* —5D **37**
Tilston Rd. *Kirkby* —3C **22**
Tilston Rd. *Walt* —4D **37**
Tilston Rd. *Wall* —5A **52**
Time Pk. *Whis* —1F **85**
Timmis Cres. *Wid* —3A **132**
Timon Av. *Boot* —3E **35**
Timor Av. *That H* —3E **65**
Timperley St. *Wid* —4B **132**
Timpron St. *L7* —1B **100**
Timway Dri. *L12* —3E **59**
Tinas Way. *Wir* —4A **94**
Tinling Clo. *Prsct* —5E **63**
Tinsley Clo. *L26* —2E **127**
Tinsley St. *L4* —4A **56**
Tintagel Clo. *Brook* —5C **168**
Tintagel Rd. *L11* —3D **39**
Tintern Dri. *Wir* —1E **93**
Tiptree Clo. *L12* —4F **39**
Titchfield St. *L5 & L3* —2C **76**
Tithebarn Clo. *Wir* —3F **157**
Tithebarn Gro. *L15* —2A **102**
Tithe Barn La. *Kirkby* —4D **23**
Tithe Barn La. *L32* —5C **22**
Tithebarn La. *Mag* —5F **13**
Tithebarn Rd. *Know* —4D **41**
Tithebarn Rd. *L23* —1F **17**
Tithebarn St. *L2* —4C **76** (4C **4**)
Tithings, The. *Halt B* —1E **167**
Tiverton Av. *Wall* —2A **74**
Tiverton Clo. *L36* —3B **84**
Tiverton Clo. *Wid* —1C **130**
Tiverton Rd. *L26* —1E **147**
Tiverton St. *L15* —1E **101**
Tobermory Clo. *Hay* —3A **48**
Tobin Clo. *L5* —2C **76**
Tobin St. *Wall* —2D **75**
Tobruk Rd. *L36* —2D **83**
Todd Rd. *St H* —5B **46**
Toft Clo. *Wid* —3F **131**
Toft St. *L7* —4C **78**
Toftwood Av. *Rain* —5D **87**
Toftwood Gdns. *Rain* —5D **87**
Toleman Av. *Wir* —2A **142**
Tollemache Rd. *Birk & Pren* —2E **95**
Tollemache St. *Wall* —3B **52**
Tollerton Rd. *L12* —5F **57**
Tolpuddle Rd. *L25* —1F **125**
Tolpuddle Way. *L4* —3D **55**
Tolver St. *St H* —4A **46**
Tom Mann Clo. *L3* —3D **77** (3F **5**)
Tonbridge Clo. *L24* —3B **146**
Tonbridge Dri. *L10* —2D **21**
Tontine Mkt. *St H* —5A **46**
Topaz Clo. *L4* —1E **55**
Topcliffe Gro. *L12* —5A **40**
Topgate Clo. *Hes* —2B **158**
Topham Dri. *Ain R* —3B **20**
Topham Ter. *L9* —5B **20**
Topsham Clo. *L25* —5C **104**
Torcross Way. *Halew* —3E **127**
Torcross Way. *Wltn* —5C **104**
Tordelow Clo. *L6* —2A **78**
Toronto Clo. *L36* —4D **61**
Toronto St. *Wall* —3E **75**
Torrington Dri. *L26* —5E **127**
Torrington Dri. *Wir* —1B **138**
Torrington Gdns. *Wir* —5B **116**
Torrington Rd. *L19* —5B **124**
Torrington Rd. *Wall* —2A **74**
Torrisholme Rd. *L9* —5D **37**
Torr St. *L5* —5E **55**
(in two parts)
Torus Rd. *L13* —2A **80**
Torview. *L15* —3A **102**
Torwood. *Pren* —3D **95**
Tothale Turn. *L27* —5F **105**
Totnes Av. *L26* —3F **127**
Totnes Rd. *L11* —3C **38**
Tourist Info. Cen. —1C 98 (7C 4)
(Albert Dock)
Tourist Info. Cen. —2F 97
(Birkenhead)
Tourist Info. Cen. —2C 52
(New Brighton)
Tourist Info. Cen. —5D 77 (5F 5)
(Queen Sq.)
Tourist Info. Cen. —4A 152
(Runcorn)
Towcester St. *L21* —2B **34**
Tower Gdns. *L3* —5B **76** (5C **4**)
Tower Hill. —5F 15
Tower Hill. *Birk* —1D **119**
Towerlands St. *L7* —5A **78**
Tower La. *Nort* —3C **168**
Tower Promenade. *Wall* —2C **52**
Tower Quays. *Birk* —1E **97**
Tower Rd. *Birk* —1E **97**
Tower Rd. *Pren* —3B **118**
Tower Rd. *Tran* —1D **119**
Tower Rd. N. *Wir* —5E **137**
Tower Rd. S. *Wir* —1F **157**
Towers Av. *L31* —5C **6**
Tower's Rd. *L16* —3C **102**
Towers, The. *Birk* —2E **119**
Tower St. *Brun B* —4D **99**
Tower Way. *L25* —1A **126**
Tower Wharf. *Birk* —1E **97**
Town End. —3C 108
Townfield Clo. *Pren* —1E **117**
Townfield Gdns. *Wir* —5F **119**
Townfield La. *Frod* —5C **172**
Townfield La. *Pren* —1E **117**
Townfield La. *Wir* —5F **119**
Townfield Rd. *Wind H* —5C **154**
Townfield Rd. *Wir* —4B **112**
Town Fields. *Wall* —5E **51**
Townfield Vw. *Wind H* —5C **154**
Townfield Way. *Wall* —2B **74**
Town Hall Dri. *Run* —1B **166**
Town La. *Beb* —1D **141**
Town La. *Hale V* —5D **149**
*Townley Ct. Wir —4B **90***
(off Marmion Rd.)
Town Mdw. La. *Wir* —5B **70**
Town Pk. Info. Cen. —2B 168
Town Rd. *Birk* —1D **119**
Town Row. *L12* —4B **58**
Townsend Av. *Club & Nor G* —3E **57**
(in two parts)
Townsend La. *Anf & Club* —5C **56**
Townsend St. *L5* —5B **54**
Townsend St. *Birk* —5E **73**
Townsend Vw. *Ford* —3B **18**
Townsend Vw. *Nor G* —5E **37**
Townshend Av. *Wir* —2D **137**
Town Vw. *Pren* —4C **96**
Town Vw. M. *Pren* —4C **96**
Towson St. *L5* —5F **55**
(in two parts)
Toxteth. —4F 99
Toxteth Gro. *L8* —5A **100**
Toxteth Sports Cen. —3F 99
Toxteth St. *L8* —4E **99**
Trafalgar. —3A 142
Trafalgar Av. *Wall* —1D **75**
Trafalgar Ct. *Wid* —1A **152**
Trafalgar Dri. *Wir* —3A **142**
Trafalgar Rd. *Wall* —1C **74**
Trafalgar St. *Dent G* —4E **45**
Trafalgar Way. *Ersk* —3F **77**
Trafford Cres. *Run* —4C **166**
Tramway & Mus. —2F 97
Tramway Rd. *L17* —1C **122**
Tranmere. —5F 97
Tranmere Rovers F.C. —2C 118
Trapwood Clo. *Ecc* —5A **44**
Travanson Clo. *L10* —2B **38**
Travers' Entry. *St H* —4A **68**
Traverse St. *St H* —5C **46**
Travis Dri. *L33* —5F **15**
Travis St. *Wid* —4B **132**
Trawden Way. *L21* —1C **18**
Treborth St. *L8* —4A **100**
Trecastle Rd. *L33* —1A **24**
Treebank Clo. *Run* —2A **166**
Treetop Ct. *L6* —2B **78**
Treetops Dri. *Birk* —5D **73**
Tree Vw. Ct. *L31* —2E **13**
Treforris Rd. *Wall* —4F **51**
Trefula Pk. *L12* —5A **58**
Trelawney Clo. *L25* —3B **104**
Tremore Clo. *L12* —2B **58**
Trenance Clo. *Brook* —5B **168**
Trendeal Rd. *L11* —3D **39**
Trent Av. *Mag* —5F **7**
Trent Av. *Bow P* —3F **81**
Trent Clo. *L12* —5D **39**
Trent Clo. *St H* —1C **88**
Trent Clo. *Rain* —3B **86**
Trent Clo. *Wid* —5B **110**
Trentham Av. *L18* —4F **101**
Trentham Clo. *Wid* —5B **110**
Trentham Rd. *L32* —4C **22**
Trentham Rd. *Wall* —3C **74**
Trentham St. *Run* —4F **151**
Trentham Wlk. *L32* —4C **22**
Trent Pl. *Rain* —3B **86**
(in two parts)
Trent Rd. *Bil* —1C **30**
Trent Rd. *Rain* —3B **86**
Trent St. *L5* —5C **54**
Trent St. *Birk* —5F **73**
Trent Way. *Wir* —4C **158**
Tressel Dri. *Sut M* —3A **88**
Tressell St. *L9* —5F **35**
Trevelyan St. *L9* —5F **35**
Treviot Clo. *L33* —4D **15**
Trevor Dri. *L23* —1F **17**
Trevor Rd. *L9* —2A **36**
Triad, The. *Boot* —4C **34**

Trimley Clo. *Wir* —4E **93**
Tring Clo. *Wir* —2A **94**
Trinity Ct. *Wir* —4B **90**
Trinity Gro. *L23* —2B **16**
Trinity La. *Birk* —2E **97**
Trinity Pl. *Boot* —5D **35**
Trinity Pl. *Wid* —5B **132**
Trinity Rd. *Boot* —1C **54**
Trinity Rd. *Wall* —1B **74**
Trinity Rd. *Wir* —4B **90**
Trinity St. *St H* —4C **46**
Trinity St. *Birk* —2C **96**
Trinity St. *Run* —4B **152**
Trinity Wlk. *L3* —3E **77** (2H **5**)
Trispen Clo. *L26* —4E **127**
Trispen Rd. *L11* —4D **39**
Trispen Wlk. *L11* —4D **39**
Tristram's Cft. *Boot* —2D **19**
Troon Clo. *L12* —5E **59**
Troon Clo. *Hay* —3A **48**
Troon Clo. *Wir* —5C **162**
Trotwood Clo. *L9* —5D **21**
Troutbeck Av. *L31* —5E **7**
Troutbeck Av. *Newt W* —4E **49**
Trout Beck Clo. *Beech* —5A **168**
Troutbeck Clo. *Wir* —2A **116**
Troutbeck Gro. *St H* —3B **30**
Troutbeck Rd. *L18* —4D **103**
Trouville Rd. *L4* —4C **56**
Trowbridge St. *L3* —5E **77** (5H **5**)
Trueman Clo. *Pren* —1C **94**
Trueman St. *L3* —4D **77** (3E **4**)
Truro Av. *Boot* —1F **19**
Truro Clo. *St H* —1D **47**
Truro Clo. *Brook* —4C **168**
Truro Rd. *L15* —3A **102**
Tudor Av. *Wall* —4E **75**
Tudor Av. *Wir* —4A **142**
Tudor Clo. *L7* —5F **77** (6J **5**)
Tudor Ct. *L19* —5A **124**
Tudor Grange. *Wir* —1D **115**
Tudor Ho. *L27* —5F **105**
Tudor Rd. *Cros* —2D **17**
Tudor Rd. *Birk* —1E **119**
Tudor Rd. *Hunts X* —5C **126**
Tudor Rd. *Mnr P* —4B **154**
Tudor St. *L6* —3B **78**
Tudor Vw. *L33* —5E **15**
(in two parts)
Tudorville Rd. *Wir* —2F **141**
Tudorway. *Wir* —2B **158**
Tue Brook. —1E 79
Tue La. *Wid* —3B **108**
Tuffins Corner. *L27* —4D **105**
Tulip Av. *Birk* —1F **95**
Tulip Rd. *L15* —2A **102**
Tulip Rd. *Hay* —2F **49**
Tullimore Rd. *L18* —3F **123**
Tullis St. *St H* —1E **65**
Tulloch St. *L6* —3B **78**
Tully Av. *Newt W* —5E **49**
Tumilty Av. *Boot* —4E **35**
Tunnel Rd. *L7* —1B **100**
Tunnel Rd. *Birk* —4E **97**
Tunstall Clo. *Wir* —4E **93**
Tunstall St. *L7* —2C **100**
Tunstalls Way. *Clo F* —2D **89**
Tupelo Clo. *L12* —4F **39**
Tupman St. *L8* —4F **99**
Turmar Av. *Wir* —1B **138**
Turnacre. *K Ash* —3E **81**
Turnall Rd. *Wid* —5B **130**
Turnberry Clo. *W Der* —5F **59**
Turnberry Clo. *Huy* —5C **82**
Turnberry Clo. *Wir* —5B **70**
Turnbridge Rd. *L31* —4C **6**
Turner Av. *Boot* —1E **35**
Turner Clo. *L8* —1A **122**
Turner Clo. *Wid* —1D **131**
Turner Home, The. *L8* —5A **100**
Turners Ct. *L25* —1B **126**
Turner St. *Birk* —4C **96**
Turney Rd. *Wall* —2A **74**
Turnstone Clo. *L12* —5E **39**
Turnstone Dri. *L26* —3E **127**
Turret Rd. *Wall* —5A **52**
Turriff Dri. *Wir* —1C **170**
Turriff Rd. *L14* —2A **82**
Turton Clo. *Hale V* —5D **149**
Turton St. *L5* —5D **55**
Tuscan Clo. *Wid* —4B **110**
Tuson Dri. *Wid* —5F **109**
Tweed Clo. *L6* —2B **78**
Tweed St. *Birk* —5A **74**
Twickenham Dri. *L36* —5C **82**
Twickenham Dri. *Wir* —3F **71**
Twickenham St. *L6* —5B **56**
Twigden Clo. *L10* —5F **21**
Twig La. *L31* —1E **13**
Twig La. *L36* —3C **82**
Two Butt La. *Rain & Whis* —1A **86**
Twomey Clo. *L5* —2C **76**
Twyford Av. *L21* —4B **18**
Twyford Clo. *L31* —1E **13**
Twyford Clo. *Wid* —4B **110**
Twyford La. *Wid* —2C **110**
Twyford Pl. *St H* —5C **46**
Twyford St. *L6* —5B **56**
Tyberton Pl. *L25* —1C **146**
Tyburn Clo. *Wir* —5F **141**
Tyburn Rd. *Wir* —5F **141**
Tyndall Av. *L22* —5F **17**
Tyne Clo. *L4* —3E **55**
Tyne Clo. *That H* —5D **65**
Tynemouth Clo. *L5* —1A **78**
Tynemouth Rd. *Murd* —4C **168**
Tyne St. *Birk* —5F **73**
Tynron Gro. *Pren* —5D **95**
Tynville Rd. *L9* —1C **36**
Tynwald Clo. *L13* —1F **79**
Tynwald Cres. *Wid* —4F **109**
Tynwald Hill. *L13* —2F **79**
Tynwald Pl. *L13* —2F **79**
Tynwald Rd. *Wir* —4A **112**
Tyrer Gro. *Prsct* —4E **63**
Tyrers Av. *L31* —2B **6**
Tyrer St. *L1* —5D **77** (5F **5**)
Tyrer St. *Birk* —5F **73**

Uldale Clo. *L11* —1A **58**
Uldale Way. *L11* —1A **58**
Ullet Rd. *L8 & L17* —5B **100**
Ullet Wlk. *L17* —4D **101**
Ullswater Av. *St H* —5A **30**
Ullswater Av. *Pren* —3D **95**
Ullswater Clo. *L33* —1D **23**
Ullswater Gro. *Beech* —5D **167**
Ullswater St. *L5* —5A **56**
Ulster Rd. *L13* —3B **80**
Ultonia St. *L19* —3C **144**
Ulverscroft. *Pren* —5F **95**
Ulverston Clo. *L31* —5E **7**
Ulverston Clo. *Hay* —2A **48**
Ulverston Lawn. *L27* —5F **105**
Umbria St. *L19* —3C **144**
Undercliffe Rd. *L13* —2A **80**
Underhill Rd. *St H* —1D **65**
Underley St. *L7* —2C **100**
Underley Ter. *Wir* —5B **120**
Underway, The. *Halt* —2F **167**
Unicorn Rd. *L11* —4C **38**
Unicorn Way. *Birk* —4F **97**
Union Bank La. *Bold H & Wid* —5B **88**
Union Ct. *L2* —5C **76** (5D **4**)
Union St. *L3* —4B **76** (4B **4**)
Union St. *St H* —3A **46**
Union St. *Birk* —1E **119**
Union St. *Run* —5B **152**
Union St. *Wall* —2D **75**
Union Ter. *Wall* —2B **52**
Unity Gro. *Know B* —2A **40**
Unity Theatre. —1E 99 (7H 5)
University of Liverpool Art Gallery. —1F 99
University Rd. *Boot* —1D **55**
Upavon Av. *Wir* —1B **114**
Upchurch Clo. *L8* —5F **99**
Upland Clo. *St H* —3B **64**
Upland Rd. *St H* —3B **64**
Upland Rd. *Upt* —3F **93**
Uplands Rd. *Brom* —1C **162**
Uplands, The. *Pal* —3F **167**
Up. Baker St. *L6* —3A **78**
Up. Beau St. *L5* —2E **77** (1G **5**)
Up. Beckwith St. *Birk* —1B **96**
Upper Bidston Village. —5C 72
Up. Brassey St. *Birk* —1F **95**
Up. Bute St. *L5* —2E **77**
Up. Duke St. *L1* —1E **99** (7G **5**)
Up. Essex St. *L8* —4F **99**
Up. Flatbrick Rd. *Birk* —2E **95**
Up. Frederick St. *L1* —1D **99** (7E **5**)
(in two parts)
Up. Hampton St. *L8* —2F **99**
Up. Harrington St. *L8* —3E **99**
Up. Hill St. *L8* —3E **99**
(in three parts)
Up. Hope Pl. *L7* —1F **99** (7J **5**)
Up. Huskisson St. *L7* —2A **100**
Up. Mann St. *L8* —3E **99**
(in two parts)
Up. Mason St. *L7* —5A **78**
Up. Mersey Rd. *Wid* —2A **152**
Up. Newington. *L1* —5E **77** (6G **5**)
Up. Park St. *L8* —4F **99**
Up. Parliament St. *L8* —2E **99**
Up. Pitt St. *L1* —1D **99**
Up. Pownall St. *L1* —1D **99**
Up. Rice La. *Wall* —1C **74**
Up. Stanhope St. *L8* —2E **99**
(in two parts)
Up. Warwick St. *L8* —3F **99**
Up. William St. *L3* —2B **76**
Uppingham Av. *L10* —3E **21**
Uppingham Rd. *L13* —1F **79**
Uppingham Rd. *Wall* —1F **73**
Upton. —4A 94
(Birkenhead)
Upton. —1B 130
(Cronton)
Upton Barn. *L31* —5C **6**
Upton Bridle Path. *Wid* —5F **109**
Upton By-Pass. *Wir* —3E **93**
Upton Clo. *L24* —4E **147**
Upton Clo. *Wir* —4F **93**
Upton Ct. *Wir* —3A **94**
Upton Cricket Club Ground. —4F 93
Upton Grange. *Wid* —1D **131**
Upton Grn. *L24* —4E **147**
Upton La. *Wid* —5E **109**
Upton Pk. Dri. *Wir* —3A **94**
Upton Rd. *Pren* —4C **94**
Upton Rd. *Wir* —1E **93**
Upton Rocks. —5E 109
Urmson Rd. *Wall* —1B **74**
Ursula St. *Boot* —2D **55**
Utkinton Clo. *Pren* —1F **117**
Utting Av. *L4* —4B **56**
Utting Av. E. *L11* —2E **57**
UVECO Bus. Cen. *Birk* —4A **74**
Uxbridge St. *L7* —1B **100**
(in two parts)

Vahler Ter. *Run* —5C **152**
Vale Clo. *L25* —2F **125**

Vale Ct. *Dut*—2F **175**
Vale Dri. *Wall*—4C **52**
Vale Gro. *L32*—4A **24**
Vale Lodge. *L9*—4F **35**
Va. Lodge Clo. *L9*—5F **35**
Valencia Gro. *Ecc P*—4F **63**
Valencia Rd. *L15*—1A **102**
Valentia Rd. *Wir*—5A **90**
Valentine Gro. *L10*—4E **21**
Valentine Rd. *Newt W*—5F **49**
Valentines Way. *Ain R*—3C **20**
Valerian Rd. *Birk*—2F **95**
Valerie Clo. *L10*—2B **38**
Vale Rd. *Cros*—1D **17**
Vale Rd. *Wltn*—1E **125**
Valescourt Rd. *L12*—1C **80**
Valeview Towers. *L25*—2F **125**
Valiant Clo. *L12*—5A **40**
Valiant Way. *Laird T*—5F **97**
Valkyrie Rd. *Wall*—1A **74**
Vallance Rd. *L4*—4C **56**
Valleybrook Gro. *Wir*—5B **142**
Valley Clo. *Ain*—4F **21**
Valley Clo. *Cros*—1B **18**
Valley Rd. *Kirkby*—5A **22**
Valley Rd. *L4*—5A **56**
Valley Rd. *Birk*—4D **73**
Valley Rd. *Wir*—2D **163**
Valley Rd. Bus. Pk. *Birk*—4E **73**
Valley Views. L25—2A ***104***
(off Hartsbourne Av.)
Vanbrugh Cres. *L4*—4C **56**
Vanbrugh Rd. *L4*—3C **56**
Vanderbilt Av. *L9*—5B **20**
Vanderbyl Av. *Wir*—5C **142**
Vandries St. *L3*—2B **76** (1A **4**)
Vandyke St. *L8*—2B **100**
Vanguard St. *L5*—5F **55**
Vardon St. *Birk*—1C **96**
Varley Rd. *L19*—3A **124**
Varley Rd. *St H*—4C **46**
Varthen St. *L5*—4F **55**
Vatt Way. *L7*—5C **78**
Vaughan Rd. *Wall*—4B **52**
Vaughan St. *Birk*—1F **95**
Vaux Cres. *Boot*—3D **35**
Vauxhall. —1B 76
Vauxhall Rd. *L3 & L5*
—3C **76** (1D **4**)
Vaux Pl. *Boot*—3D **35**
Venables Clo. *Wir*—1B **162**
Venables Dri. *Wir*—5A **142**
Venice St. *L5*—5F **55**
Venmore St. *L5*—5F **55**
(in two parts)
Ventnor Rd. *L15*—1F **101**
Venture Ct. Birk—4E ***97***
(off Clifton Rd.)
Verbena Clo. *Beech*—1F **173**
Verdala Pk. *L18*—2C **124**
Verdi Av. *L21*—2A **34**
Verdi St. *L21*—2F **33**
Verdi Ter. *L21*—2F **33**
Vere St. *L8*—4E **99**
(in two parts)
Vermont Av. *L23*—1D **17**
Vermont Clo. *L33*—3D **15**
Vermont Rd. *L23*—1D **17**
Vermont Way. *Boot*—4C **34**
Verney Cres. *L19*—4C **124**
Verney Cres. S. *L19*—4C **124**
Vernon Av. *Hoot*—3F **171**
Vernon Av. *Wall*—4D **75**
Vernon Sangster Sports Cen. —4A 56
Vernon St. *L2*—4C **76** (3D **4**)
Vernon St. *St H*—4C **46**
Verona St. *L5*—5F **55**
Verulam Clo. *L8*—2A **100**
Verwood Clo. *Wir*—5D **115**
Verwood Dri. *L12*—5A **40**
Veryan Clo. *L26*—3F **127**
Vescock St. *L5*—1D **77**
Vesta Rd. *L19*—3D **145**
Vesuvius Pl. *L5*—5D **55**
Vesuvius St. *L5*—5D **55**
Vetch Hey. *L27*—4E **105**
Viaduct St. *Newt W*—5F **49**
Viaduct St. *Wid*—3A **152**
Vicarage Clo. *Birk*—3B **118**
Vicarage Clo. *Hale V*—5E **149**
Vicarage Clo. *Moss H*—2B **124**
Vicarage Dri. *Hay*—1A **48**
Vicarage Gro. *Wall*—1C **74**
Vicarage Lawn. *L25*—4C **104**
Vicarage Pl. *Prsct*—5C **62**
Vicarage Rd. *Hay*—1A **48**
Vicarage Rd. *Wid*—5A **132**
Vicar Rd. *L6*—4C **56**
Vicar St. *Run*—4A **152**
Viceroy St. *L5*—5F **55**
Vickers Rd. *Wid*—2E **151**
Victoria Av. *Cros*—1C **16**
Victoria Av. *L15*—1F **101**
Victoria Av. *St H*—5A **30**
Victoria Av. *B'grn*—4D **81**
Victoria Av. *Wid*—1A **132**
Victoria Av. *Wir*—4A **158**
Victoria Clo. *L17*—1E **123**
Victoria Ct. *L17*—5B **100**
Victoria Ct. *Birk*—2D **97**
Victoria Ct. *W'tree*—1F **101**
Victoria Dri. *L9*—2F **35**
Victoria Dri. *Birk*—3A **120**
Victoria Dri. *Wir*—4A **112**
Victoria Fields. *Birk*—5C **96**
Victoria Gdns. *Pren*—5B **96**
Victoria Gro. *Wid*—1A **132**
Victoria Ho. *Prsct*—5D **63**
Victoria La. *Pren*—5B **96**
Victoria Mt. *Pren*—5B **96**
Victoria Pde. *Wall*—2C **52**
Victoria Park. —1F 35
(Aintree)
Victoria Park. —1F 101
(Liverpool)
Victoria Pk. —3F 45
(St Helens)
Victoria Pk. —2E 119
(Tranmere)
Victoria Pk. —3D 17
(Waterloo)
Victoria Pk. —2B 132
(Widnes)
Victoria Pk. Rd. *Birk*—2D **119**
Victoria Pl. *Rain*—3C **86**
Victoria Pl. *Wall*—4E **75**
Victoria Promenade. *Wid*—3A **152**
Victoria Rd. *Cros*—1D **17**
Victoria Rd. *Wat*—5E **17**
Victoria Rd. *Aig*—1E **123**
Victoria Rd. *Beb*—1D **141**
Victoria Rd. *Birk*—5C **96**
Victoria Rd. *Huy*—4F **83**
Victoria Rd. *Run*—5A **152**
(in two parts)
Victoria Rd. *Tue*—5E **57**
Victoria Rd. *Wall*—3A **52**
(in two parts)
Victoria Rd. *W Kir*—5B **112**
Victoria Rd. *Wid*—5A **132**
Victoria Rd. W. *Cros*—1C **16**
Victoria Sq. *St H*—4A **46**
Victoria Sq. *Wid*—5A **132**
Victoria St. *L2 & L1*—5C **76** (5D **4**)
Victoria St. *St H*—3A **46**
Victoria St. *Rain*—3C **86**
Victoria St. *Wid*—5B **132**
Victoria St. *Wir*—2B **142**
Victoria Ter. *L15*—3A **102**
(in two parts)
Victoria Ter. *Rain*—3C **86**
Victor St. *L15*—1D **101**
Victory Clo. *Boot*—5E **19**
Vienna St. *L5*—5F **55**
Viennese Rd. *L25*—3B **104**
Viewpark Clo. *L16*—2F **103**
View Rd. *Rain*—4C **86**
Viking Clo. *L21*—1A **34**
Village Clo. *Cas*—2A **168**
Village Clo. *Wall*—5E **51**
Village Ct. *L17*—2C **122**
Village Ct. *Irby*—1D **137**
Village Courts. *Boot*—5F **11**
Village Grn. Ct. *Pren*—1C **94**
Village Nook. *Ain*—3E **21**
Village Rd. *Beb*—1D **141**
Village Rd. *Hes*—3F **157**
Village Rd. *Pren*—5A **96**
Village Rd. *W Kir*—4C **112**
Village St. *L6*—2F **77**
Village St. *Run*—5D **155**
Village, The. *Beb*—1A **142**
Village Way. *Wall*—5E **51**
Villa Gloria Clo. *L19*—4A **124**
Villas Rd. *L31*—1B **14**
Villiers Cres. *Ecc*—3F **43**
Villiers Rd. *Know B*—2B **40**
Vincent Ct. *L1*—1D **99** (7F **5**)
Vincent Naughton Ct. *Birk*—4E **97**
Vincent Rd. *L21*—4C **18**
Vincent Rd. *Rain*—2B **86**
Vincent St. *L13*—5F **79**
Vincent St. *St H*—4A **46**
Vincent St. *Birk*—3D **97**
Vineries, The. *L25*—1E **125**
Vineside Rd. *L12*—1D **81**
Vine St. *L7*—1F **99**
Vine St. *Birk*—2C **96**
Vine St. *Run*—5A **152**
Vine St. *Wid*—5A **132**
Vine Ter. *Wid*—2A **130**
Vineyard St. *L19*—2E **145**
Vining Rd. *Prsct*—5F **63**
Vining St. *L8*—3F **99**
Viola Clo. *L33*—5D **15**
Viola St. *Boot*—2C **54**
Violet Rd. *L21*—2B **34**
Violet Rd. *Birk*—2F **95**
Violet St. *Wid*—5A **132**
Virgil St. *L5*—2D **77**
Virgil St. *St H*—4E **45**
Virginia Av. *L31*—4C **6**
Virginia Gro. *L31*—4C **6**
Virginia Rd. *Wall*—2B **52**
Virginia St. *L3*—4B **76** (3B **4**)
Virgin's La. *L23*—3F **9**
Vista Rd. *Hay*—1F **49**
Vista Rd. *Run*—2A **166**
Vista Way. *Newt W*—4F **49**
Vittoria Clo. *Birk*—2D **97**
Vittoria St. *Birk*—2C **96**
Vivian Av. *Wall*—4E **75**
Voelas St. *L8*—3A **100**
Vogan Av. *L23*—2A **18**
Volunteer St. *St H*—4F **45**
Volunteer St. *Frod*—4D **173**
Vronhill Clo. *L8*—3A **100**
Vulcan Clo. *Birk*—1F **95**
Vulcan St. *Boot*—4A **34**
Vulcan St. *L3*—2B **76**
Vulcan St. *Birk*—1F **95**
Vulcan St. *Gars*—3C **144**
Vyner Clo. *Pren*—3E **95**
Vyner Ct. *Pren*—3E **95**
Vyner Rd. *Wall*—1F **73**
Vyner Rd. N. *L25*—4A **104**

Vyner Rd. N. *Pren* —2D **95**
Vyner Rd. S. *L25* —4A **104**
Vyner Rd. S. *Pren* —3D **95**
Vyrnwy St. *L5* —4F **55**

Waddicar. —1A 22
Waddicar La. *L31* —2A **22**
Wadebridge Rd. *L10* —2A **38**
Wadeson Rd. *L4* —1D **57**
Wadham Pk. *Boot* —1C **54**
Wadham Rd. *Boot* —2C **54**
Wagon La. *Hay* —4A **48**
(in two parts)
Waine Gro. *Whis* —1A **86**
Waine St. *St H* —4D **47**
Waine St. *Hay* —2F **47**
Wainwright Clo. *L7* —1B **100**
Wainwright Gro. *L19* —1B **144**
Wakefield Dri. *Wir* —2F **71**
Wakefield Rd. *Boot* —3A **20**
Wakefield St. *L3* —3E **77** (2G **5**)
Walby Clo. *Wid* —2C **130**
Walby Clo. *Wir* —2C **116**
Walden Rd. *L14* —3C **80**
Waldgrave Pl. *L15* —5B **80**
Waldgrave Rd. *L15* —5A **80**
Waldron Clo. *L3* —3C **76** (2D **4**)
Walford Clo. *Wir* —5F **141**
Walker Art Gallery. —4D 77 (3F 5)
Walker Av. *Sut M* —3B **88**
Walker Dri. *Boot* —1C **34**
Walker M. *Birk* —1D **119**
Walker Pl. *Birk* —1D **119**
Walker Rd. *L21* —1A **34**
Walker's Cft. *Wall* —1F **73**
Walkers La. *Sut M* —3A **88**
Walker St. *L6* —3A **78**
Walker St. *Birk* —1D **119**
Walker St. *Port S* —1B **142**
Walker St. *Wir* —4B **90**
Walker Way. *L9* —2F **35**
Walk, The. *L28* —4C **60**
Walk, The. *Speke* —5F **145**
Wallace Av. *L36* —2A **84**
Wallace Dri. *L36* —2F **83**
Wallace St. *L9* —2A **36**
Wallace St. *Wid* —4A **132**
Wallacre Rd. *Wall* —2E **73**
Wallasey. —2F 73
Wallasey Bri. Rd. *Birk* —5F **73**
Wallasey Cricket Club Ground. —5F 51
Wallasey Golf Course. —5C 50
Wallasey R.F.C. Ground. —2D 73
Wallasey Rd. *Wall* —2F **73**
Wallasey Village. *Wall* —5E **51**
Wallcroft. *Will* —5A **170**
Waller Clo. *L4* —4E **55**
Waller St. *Boot* —2A **34**
Wallgate Rd. *L25* —2F **103**
Wallgate Way. *L25* —3F **103**
Wallingford Rd. *Wir* —5F **93**
Wallrake. *Wir* —3F **157**
Wallsend Ct. *Wid* —1E **131**
Walmer Rd. *L22* —5E **17**
Walmesley Rd. *Ecc* —3A **44**
Walmsley St. *L5* —5C **54**
Walmsley St. *Wall* —1C **74**
Walmsley St. *Wid* —4C **132**
Walney Rd. *L12* —3A **58**
Walney Ter. *L12* —3A **58**
Walnut Av. *L9* —5C **36**
Walnut Gro. *L31* —2A **22**
Walnut St. *L7* —5F **77**
Walpole Av. *Whis* —3F **85**
Walpole Rd. *Run* —3B **166**
Walsh Clo. *L5* —2C **76**
Walsh Rd. *L14* —4C **80**
Walsingham Ct. Wall —3D 75
(off Liscard Rd.)
Walsingham Dri. *Run* —5D **155**
Walsingham Rd. *L16* —5E **81**
Walsingham Rd. *Wall* —3D **75**
Walter Beilin Ct. *L17* —4E **101**
Walter Gro. *St H* —4E **67**
Walter St. *L5* —1B **76**
Waltham Ct. *Run* —3E **155**
Waltham Rd. *L6* —5C **56**
Waltho Av. *L31* —1E **13**
Walton. —1F 55
Walton Breck Rd. *L4* —4F **55**
Walton Hall Av. *L4 & L11* —2A **56**
Walton Hall Pk. —5B 36
Walton La. *L4* —4F **55**
Walton Lodge Rd. *L9* —4F **35**
Walton Pk. *L9* —4A **36**
Walton Pk. Gdns. *L4* —1A **56**
Walton Rd. *L4* —4E **55**
Walton Rd. *Dent G* —2D **45**
Walton Sports Cen. —1B 56
Walton St. *Birk* —3E **97**
Walton St. *Run* —5A **152**
Walton Va. *L9* —2A **36**
Walton Village. *L4* —1F **55**
(in two parts)
Wambo La. *L25* —4B **104**
Wandsworth Rd. *L11* —2F **57**
Wandsworth Way. *Wid* —1F **151**
Wango La. *L10* —4E **21**
Wantage Vw. *L36* —5C **82**
Wapping. *L1* —1C **98** (7D **4**)
Wapping Quay. *L3* —2C **98**
Wapshare Rd. *L11* —2E **57**
Warbler Clo. *L26* —2D **127**
Warbreck Av. *L9* —1A **36**
Warbreck Moor. *L9* —1B **36**
Warbreck Park. —1A 36
Warbreck Rd. *L9* —2A **36**
Warburton Hey. *Rain* —2B **86**
Warden St. *L4* —3E **55**
Wardgate Av. *L12* —5E **39**
Ward Gro. *Birk* —4F **119**
Ward Rake. *Boot* —1D **19**
Ward Rd. *L23* —5A **8**
Ward St. *L3* —4E **77** (4G **5**)
Ward St. *St H* —4F **45**
(in two parts)
Ward St. *Prsct* —4D **63**
Wareing Rd. *L9* —2C **36**
Waresley Cres. *L9* —4E **37**
Warham Rd. *L4* —4C **56**
Waring Av. *St H* —1B **68**
Waring Av. *Birk* —2D **119**
Warkworth Clo. *L36* —1B **106**
Warkworth Clo. *Wid* —1C **130**
Warmington Rd. *L14* —3C **80**
Warner Dri. *L4* —3C **56**
Warnerville Rd. *L13* —5B **80**
Warnley Clo. *Wid* —1D **131**
Warren Cft. *Nort* —3C **168**
Warren Dri. *Pren* —3C **94**
Warren Dri. *Wall* —3F **51**
Warren Golf Course. —4F 51
Warren Hey. *Wir* —5A **142**
Warrenhouse Rd. *Kirkby* —1A **24**
Warrenhouse Rd. *Wat* —3B **16**
Warren Hurst. *Wall* —3A **52**
Warren Rd. *L23* —5A **8**
Warren Rd. *Wir* —4A **90**
Warren St. *L3* —5E **77** (5H **5**)
Warren, The. *Wir* —4B **94**
Warren Way. *Wir* —1D **157**
Warrington New Rd. *St H* —5B **46**
Warrington Old Rd. *St H* —1B **66**
Warrington Rd. *Ast I & Mnr P* —3A **154**
Warrington Rd. *Prsct & Whis* —5D **63**
Warrington Rd. *Rain & Bold H* —2B **86**
Warrington Rd. *Run* —5E **153**
Warrington Rd. *Wid* —4C **132**
Warrington St. *Birk* —5E **97**
Warton Clo. *L25* —2C **126**
Warton St. *Boot* —2A **34**
Warton Ter. *Boot* —2B **34**
Warwick Av. *L23* —2D **17**
Warwick Clo. *L36* —3A **84**
Warwick Clo. *Pren* —4C **96**
Warwick Ct. *L8* —3A **100**
Warwick Dri. *Wall* —5C **52**
Warwick Dri. *Wir* —1C **134**
Warwick Rd. *Boot* —4D **35**
Warwick Rd. *L36* —3A **84**
Warwick Rd. *Wir* —4E **93**
Warwick St. *L8* —3D **99**
Warwick St. *St H* —5D **45**
Wasdale Av. *L31* —5E **7**
Wasdale Av. *St H* —5B **30**
Wasdale Rd. *L9* —3A **36**
Washbrook Av. *Pren* —5C **72**
Washbrook Clo. *St H* —4B **44**
Washington Dri. *L33* —4D **15**
Washington Pde. *Boot* —4C **34**
Washway La. *St H* —1F **45**
Wastdale Ct. *Wir* —5C **70**
Wastdale Dri. *Wir* —5C **70**
Wastdale M. *Wir* —5C **70**
Wastle Bri. Rd. *L36* —1E **83**
Waterdale Cres. *St H* —4D **67**
Waterdale Pl. *St H* —4D **67**
Waterfield Clo. *Wir* —2D **141**
Waterford Rd. *L27* —3C **104**
Waterford Rd. *Pren* —4F **95**
Waterford Way. *Murd* —4C **168**
(in two parts)
Waterfront. *Pres H* —4F **169**
Watergate La. *L25* —2B **126**
Watergate Way. *L25* —2B **126**
Waterhouse Clo. *L6* —5B **56**
Waterland La. *St H* —1F **67**
Water La. *Tarb G* —5C **106**
Waterloo. —4E 17
Waterloo Cen. *Wid* —1A **152**
Waterloo Clo. *L22* —5D **17**
Waterloo Ct. *Beb* —1A **142**
Waterloo Park. —4F 17
Waterloo Pl. *Birk* —4E **97**
Waterloo Quay. *L3* —3A **76** (1A **4**)
Waterloo Rd. *L3* —2B **76** (1A **4**)
Waterloo Rd. *S'frth* —1F **33**
Waterloo Rd. *Wat* —5E **17**
Waterloo Rd. *Run* —5F **151**
(in two parts)
Waterloo Rd. *Wall* —2B **52**
Waterloo Rd. *Wid* —2A **152**
Waterloo St. *L15* —2A **102**
Waterloo St. *St H* —5F **45**
Watermead Dri. *Pres B* —5F **169**
Waterpark Clo. *Pren* —3F **117**
Waterpark Dri. *L28* —3F **59**
Waterpark Rd. *Pren & Birk* —3F **117**
Watersedge. *Frod* —3D **173**
Waterside. *Boot* —5E **11**
Waterside. *St H* —4B **46**
Waterside Ct. *St H* —4B **46**
Waterside Dri. *Frod* —3C **172**
Waterside Pk. *L36* —4D **83**
Water St. *Cros* —4B **10**
Water St. *L3 & L2* —5B **76** (5B **4**)
Water St. *St H* —5F **45**
Water St. *Wat* —5D **17**
Water St. *Birk* —3F **97**
Water St. *Run* —4A **152**
Water St. *Wall* —2D **75**
Water St. *Wid* —3D **133**
(Halton Vw. Rd.)
Water St. *Wid* —1A **152**
(Waterloo Rd.)

Water St. Wir—2C 142
Waterway Av. Boot—2B 20
Waterworks La. Hoot—4E 171
Waterworks St. Boot—4D 35
Watery La. Ecc—2B 44
Watery La. St H—3E 67
Watford Rd. L4—4A 56
Watkin Clo. Boot—4B 20
Watkins Av. Newt W—5F 49
Watkinson St. L1—2D 99
Watling Av. L21—4A 18
Watling Way. Whis—5A 64
Watmough St. L5—2E 77 (1H 5)
Watson St. Birk—2D 97
Watton Beck Clo. L31—5F 7
Watton Clo. L12—1A 60
Watts Clift Way. St H—5B 46
Watts Clo. L33—1A 24
Watts La. Boot—2E 35
Wauchope St. L15—1E 101
Wavell Av. Wid—4C 130
Wavell Rd. L36—2E 83
Waverley Dri. Prsct—1A 84
Waverley Gro. Birk—2C 118
Waverley Rd. Cros—1C 16
Waverley Rd. Seft P—5C 100
Waverley Rd. Wir—4C 90
Waverley St. Boot—5B 34
Waverton Av. Pren—2E 117
Wavertree. —1F 101
Wavertree Athletics Cen. —2F 101
Wavertree Av. L13—5E 79
Waver Tree Av. Wid—4F 131
Wavertree Boulevd. L7—5D 79
Wavertree Boulevd. S. L7—5D 79
Wavertree Cricket Club Ground. —1F 101
Wavertree Gdns. L15—2F 101
Wavertree Green. —2B 102
Wavertree Grn. L15—2A 102
Wavertree Nook Rd. L15—5B 80
Wavertree Pk. —5C 78
Wavertree Rd. L7—5B 78
Wavertree Shop. Cen. L7—5C 78
Wavertree Technology Pk. L7—4E 79
Wavertree Technology Pk. L13—5E 79
Wavertree Tennis Cen. —2E 101
Wavertree Trad. Est. L15—2E 101
Wavertree Va. L15—1D 101
Wayford Clo. Frod—4B 172
Waylands Dri. L25—5B 126
Wayville Clo. L18—2A 124
Weardale Rd. L15—3E 101
Weasdale Clo. St H—4D 67
Weates Clo. Wid—1E 133
Weatherby. Wir—5B 94
Weaver Av. L33—4F 15
Weaver Av. Rain—3B 86
Weaver Ct. L25—1C 126
Weaver Cres. Frod—4D 173
Weaver Gro. St H—5A 48
Weaver Ho. L25—1C 126
Weaver Ind. Est. L19—3C 144
Weaver La. Frod—3B 172
Weaver Pk. Ind. Est. Frod—3D 173
Weaver Rd. Frod—4D 173
Weaver Rd. West—4A 166
Weaverside Av. Sut W—1F 173
Weavers La. L31—4F 13
Weaver St. L9—5F 35
Weaver Vw. West—4F 165
Webb Clo. L7—5C 78
Webb Dri. Btnwd—5F 69
Webber Rd. Know I—4B 24
Webb St. L7—2C 100
Webb St. St H—2D 67
Webster Av. Boot—4E 35
Webster Av. Wall—1D 75
Webster Dri. L32—3E 23
Webster Rd. L7—2C 100
Websters Holt. Wir—3F 93
Webster St. L3—4D 77 (3E 5)
Webster St. Lith—1B 34
Wedge Av. Hay—3A 48
Wedgewood Gdns. St H—5B 64
Wedgewood St. L7—4B 78
Wedgwood Dri. Wid—4B 110
Weightman Gro. L9—2A 36
Weirside. St H—5D 67
Welbeck Av. L18—4F 101
Welbourne Rd. L16—5C 80
Weld Blundell Av. L31—2B 6
Weldon St. L4—1F 55
Weld Rd. L23—2C 16
Welfield Pl. L8—5A 100
Welford Av. Pren—2F 117
Welland Clo. L26—1E 147
Welland Rd. Wir—2D 141
Wellbank Dri. L26—3A 128
Wellbrae Clo. Wir—4D 93
Wellbrook Clo. L24—3D 147
Wellbrook Clo. Brook—5C 168
Wellbrook Grn. L24—4D 147
Wellbrow Rd. L4—1A 56
Wellcroft Rd. L36—2E 83
Weller St. L8—4F 99
Weller Way. L8—5A 100
Wellesbourne Pl. L11—1A 58
Wellesbourne Rd. L11—5A 38
Wellesley Gro. Wir—1A 142
Wellesley Rd. L8—5A 100
Wellesley Rd. Wall—2B 74
Wellesley Ter. L8—5A 100
Wellfield. Rainf—1A 28
Wellfield. Wid—1A 132
Wellfield Av. L32—4E 23
Wellfield Rd. L9—4A 36
Wellgreen Rd. L25—2F 103
Wellgreen Wlk. L25—2F 103
Wellington Av. L15—3D 101
Wellington Clo. L10—2C 20
Wellington Clo. Beb—1A 142
Wellington Fields. L15—3D 101
Wellington Gdns. L22—4D 17 (off Wellington St.)
Wellington Ga. Hale V—5D 149
Wellington Gro. L15—1E 101
Wellington Rd. L21—1A 34
Wellington Rd. Beb—1A 142
Wellington Rd. Pren—4A 96
Wellington Rd. Tox—5F 99
Wellington Rd. Wall—2A 52
Wellington Rd. W'tree—2E 101
Wellington St. L3—2D 77 (1E 5)
Wellington St. Wat—4D 17
Wellington St. Gars—1C 144
Wellington St. Run—4A 152
Wellington St. Wid—1A 152
Wellington St. Ind. Est. Wid—1A 152 (off Wellington St.)
Wellington Ter. L8—4A 100
Wellington Ter. St H—3A 46
Wellington Ter. Birk—4D 97
Well La. Boot—5D 35
Well La. L16 & L25—2F 103 (in two parts)
Well La. Beb—1D 141
Well La. Birk—1D 119
Well La. Grea—1C 114
Well La. Hes—4A 158
Well La. Gdns. Boot—5D 35
Wells St. L15—2F 101
Wellstead Clo. L15—1A 102
Wellstead Rd. L15—1A 102
Wellstead Wlk. L15—1A 102
Welsh Rd. L Sut & Chil T—5F 171
Welton Av. Wir—4F 93
Welton Clo. L24—4D 147
Welton Grn. L24—4D 147
Welton Rd. Croft B—5D 143
Welwyn Clo. St H—5F 65
Wembley Gdns. L9—2F 35
Wembley Rd. Cros—2F 17
Wembley Rd. Moss H—4B 102
Wendell St. L8—2C 100
Wendover Av. L17—1C 122
Wendover Clo. Hay—1D 49
Wendover Clo. Pren—5D 95
Wendron Rd. L11—3D 39
Wenger Rd. Wid—4B 110
Wenlock Dri. L26—5E 127
Wenlock Rd. L4—4B 56
Wenlock Rd. Beech—1A 174
Wenning Av. L31—5E 7
Wensley Av. L26—5F 127
Wensley Dale. L9—1A 36
Wensleydale Av. Wir—5E 163
Wensleydale Clo. L31—5B 6
Wensleydale Dri. Rain—3D 87
Wensley Rd. L9—1A 36
Wentworth Av. Wall—4B 52
Wentworth Clo. Pren—5D 95
Wentworth Clo. Wid—4A 110
Wentworth Dri. L5—2F 77
Wentworth Dri. Wir—5B 162
Wentworth Gro. L36—4B 82
Wernbrook Clo. Pren—5D 95
Wernbrook Rd. L4—4C 56
Wervin Clo. Pren—2E 117
Wervin Rd. L32—4D 23
Wervin Rd. Pren—2E 117
Wervin Way. L32—4C 22
Wesley Av. Hay—1E 49
Wesley Av. Wall—1C 74
Wesley Ct. L22—5D 17
Wesley Gro. Wall—3E 75
Wesley Hall Gdns. St H—5D 65
Wesley Pl. L15—1F 101
Wesley St. L22—5D 17
W. Albert Rd. L17—5B 100
West Bank. —2A 152
Westbank Av. Wall—4C 52
W. Bank Dock Est. Wid—2E 151
W. Bank Rd. L7—4E 79
Westbank Rd. Birk—1C 118
W. Bank St. Wid—2A 152
Westbourne Av. L23—4B 10
Westbourne Av. Wir—4B 112
Westbourne Gro. Wir—4B 112
Westbourne Rd. Pren—4C 96
Westbourne Rd. Wall—2F 73
Westbourne Rd. Wir—4A 112
Westbourne St. L6—3F 77
Westbrook Av. Prsct—5B 62
Westbrook Rd. L25—4C 104
Westbrook Rd. Wir—2C 92
Westbury Clo. L17—3C 122
Westbury St. Birk—5E 97
Westcliffe Rd. L12—4F 57
West Clo. Ecc P—4A 64
West Clo. Pren—4D 95
Westcombe Rd. L4—4C 56
Westcott Rd. L4—5B 56
Westcott Way. Pren—5D 95
Westdale Rd. L15—1F 101
Westdale Rd. Birk—2E 119
Westdale Vw. L15—1F 101
West Derby. —4D 59
West Derby Golf Course. —5D 59
W. Derby Rd. L6—3A 78 (Brunswick Rd.)
W. Derby Rd. L6 & L13—1D 79 (Rocky La.)
W. Derby St. L7—4F 77
West Derby Village. —4B 58
W. Derby Village. L12—4B 58
West Dri. Hes—3A 158

West Dri. *Upt* —4A **94**
W. End Gro. *Hay* —2F **47**
W. End Rd. *Hay* —2F **47**
Westerhope Way. *Wid* —1F **131**
***Western Approaches Mus.* —4C 76 (4C 4)**
Western Av. *Huy* —3A **82**
Western Av. *Speke* —5C **146**
Western Av. *Wir* —3D **143**
Western Dri. *L19* —5A **124**
Westerton Rd. *L12* —5E **59**
Westfield Av. *L14* —4E **81**
Westfield Cres. *Run* —1E **165**
Westfield Dri. *L12* —5E **39**
Westfield M. *Run* —1F **165**
Westfield Rd. *L9* —2E **35**
Westfield Rd. *Run* —1E **165**
Westfield Rd. *Wall* —5D **75**
Westfield St. *St H* —5F **45**
Westfield Wlk. *L32* —3B **22**
Westgate. *Wid* —5B **130**
Westgate Rd. *L15* —4A **102**
Westgate Rd. *Wir* —3B **142**
West Gro. *Wir* —2F **157**
Westhead Av. *L33* —3F **23**
Westhead Clo. *L33* —4A **24**
Westhead Wlk. *L33* —3F **23**
(in two parts)
Westhouse Clo. *Wir* —5C **162**
West Kirby. —3A 112
W. Kirby Concourse. *W Kir* —4A **112**
W. Kirby Rd. *Wir* —4B **92**
W. Knowe. *Pren* —5F **95**
***West Lancashire Golf Course.* —3A 8**
West La. *Run* —3E **167**
Westleigh Pl. *Sut L* —1C **88**
W. Lodge Dri. *Wir* —3A **112**
West Mains. *L24* —4A **148**
West Meade. *L31* —5B **6**
Westminster Av. *Boot* —1E **19**
Westminster Clo. *L4* —2E **55**
Westminster Clo. *Wid* —4B **130**
Westminster Ct. *Pren* —4F **95**
Westminster Dri. *Hay* —1F **49**
Westminster Dri. *Wir* —3D **163**
Westminster Gro. *Prsct* —1A **84**
Westminster Rd. *L4* —2D **55**
Westminster Rd. *Wall* —2B **74**
W. Moor Dri. *L23* —5E **9**
Westmoreland Rd. *Wall* —4C **52**
Westmorland Av. *Boot* —2C **18**
Westmorland Av. *Wid* —3B **132**
Westmorland Dri. *L3* —3C **76** (2D **4**)
Westmorland Pl. *L5* —1D **77**
Westmorland Rd. *L36* —4E **83**
W. Oakhill Pk. *L13* —4A **80**
Weston. —4F 165
Weston Ct. *L23* —2B **16**
Weston Ct. *Run* —3F **165**
Weston Cres. *West* —4F **165**
Weston Gro. *Mag* —4D **13**
Weston Gro. *Halew* —1A **148**
Weston Point. —3D 165
Weston Point Docks. *West P* —3D **165**
Weston Point Expressway. *West P* —1E **165**
Weston Rd. *Run & West* —2E **165**
W. Orchard La. *L9* —5D **21**
Westover Clo. *L31* —1C **12**
Westover Rd. *L31* —1C **12**
West Park. —1D 65
W. Park Gdns. *Pren* —1C **94**
West Pk. Rd. *St H* —1D **65**
West Rd. *L14* —4C **80**
West Rd. *L24* —2D **147**
West Rd. *Pren* —4D **95**
West Rd. *West P* —3D **165**
Westry Clo. *Wir* —1B **92**
West Side. *St H* —1C **66**
W. Side Av. *Hay* —2A **48**
West St. *St H* —2D **65**
West St. *Prsct* —5C **62**
West St. *Wall* —1B **74**
Westvale. —3C 22
West Vw. *L36* —4B **84**
West Vw. *Birk* —5F **97**
West Vw. *Wall* —3A **52**
West Vw. Av. *L36* —4B **84**
Westview Clo. *Pren* —5D **95**
Westward Ho. *Wir* —3D **135**
Westward Vw. *Wat* —3B **16**
Westward Vw. *Aig* —1A **122**
Westway. *Mag* —5C **6**
Westway. *Grea* —5E **93**
Westway. *Hes* —4F **157**
West Way. *More* —5E **71**
West Way. *Pren* —5D **95**
Westway. *Run* —3E **167**
Westway. *W'tree* —1B **102**
W. Way Sq. *Wir* —5E **71**
Westwick Pl. *L36* —3B **82**
Westwood. *Wind H* —1C **168**
Westwood Ct. *Pren* —4F **95**
Westwood Gro. *Wall* —2A **74**
Westwood Rd. *L18* —4C **124**
Westwood Rd. *Pren* —3C **94**
Wetherby Av. *Wall* —1E **73**
Wetherby Ct. *L36* —1C **82**
Wethersfield Rd. *Pren* —1E **117**
Wetstone La. *Wir* —5C **112**
Wexford Av. *Hale V* —5D **149**
Wexford Clo. *Pren* —5E **95**
Wexford Rd. *Pren* —5F **95**
Weybourne Clo. *Wir* —2A **94**
Weyman Av. *Whis* —3E **85**
Weymoor Clo. *Wir* —5F **141**
Weymouth Av. *St H* —2F **67**
Weymouth Clo. *L16* —1F **103**
Weymouth Clo. *Murd* —4E **169**
Weymouth Rd. *Btnwd* —5F **69**
Whaley La. *Wir* —1F **137**
Whalley Av. *St H* —1E **45**
Whalley Ct. *Boot* —1D **19**
Whalley Gro. *Wid* —1D **133**
Whalley Rd. *Birk* —4D **97**
Whalley St. *L8* —5F **99**
Wharfedale. *Run* —4B **168**
Wharfedale Av. *Birk* —2B **118**
Wharfedale Dri. *Rain* —3D **87**
Wharfedale Dri. *Wir* —5F **163**
Wharfedale Rd. *Wall* —5F **51**
Wharfedale St. *L19* —2E **145**
Wharford La. *Run* —4E **155**
Wharf Rd. *Newt W* —5E **49**
Wharf Rd. *Birk* —5F **73**
Wharf St. *Wir* —2B **142**
Wharf, The. *Pres B* —4F **169**
Wharmby Rd. *Hay* —2E **49**
Wharncliffe Rd. *L13* —3A **80**
Wharton Clo. *Wir* —3D **93**
Wharton St. *Sher I* —2B **66**
Whatcroft Clo. *Halt L* —4D **167**
Wheatcroft Rd. *L18* —2C **124**
Wheatear Clo. *L27* —5E **105**
Wheatfield Clo. *Boot* —2B **20**
Wheatfield Clo. *Wir* —2F **93**
Wheatfield Rd. *Wid* —4C **108**
Wheatfield Vw. *L21* —3B **18**
Wheat Hill Rd. *L36* —2E **105**
Wheathills Ind. Est. *L27* —3E **105**
Wheatland Bus. Pk. *Wall* —4D **75**
Wheatland Clo. *Clo F* —2C **88**
Wheatland La. *Wall* —3D **75**
Wheatland Rd. *Wir* —3C **158**
Wheatlands. *Halt B* —1E **167**
Wheatley Av. *Boot* —3E **35**
Wheatsheaf Av. *Sut L* —5D **67**
Wheeler Dri. *L31* —2B **22**
Whelan Gdns. *St H* —1E **87**
Whernside. *Wid* —1C **130**
Whetstone La. *Birk* —4D **97**
Whickham Clo. *Wid* —1F **131**
Whimbrel Clo. *Beech* —5F **167**
Whimbrel Pk. *L26* —3E **127**
Whinbury Ct. *Clo F* —2C **88**
Whincraig. *L28* —4C **60**
Whinfell Gro. *Beech* —5E **167**
Whinfell Rd. *L12* —1B **80**
Whinfield Rd. *Cros* —4A **10**
Whinfield Rd. *Walt* —2F **35**
Whinhowe Rd. *L11* —1A **58**
Whinmoor Clo. *Pren* —3D **95**
Whinmoor Rd. *W Der* —1C **80**
Whinmoor Rd. *Walt* —1A **38**
Whinney Gro. E. *L31* —4C **12**
Whinney Gro. W. *L31* —4C **12**
Whiston. —3E 85
Whiston Cross. —3D 85
Whiston La. *Huy* —2A **84**
Whiston Lane Ends. —4E 85
Whitburn Rd. *L33* —1A **24**
Whitby Av. *Wall* —1E **73**
Whitby Rd. *Run* —1A **166**
Whitby St. *L6* —5D **57**
Whitchurch Way. *Halt L* —4D **167**
Whitcroft Rd. *L6* —3D **79**
Whitebeam Clo. *L33* —4F **15**
Whitebeam Clo. *Wind H* —1C **168**
Whitebeam Dri. *L12* —5D **39**
Whitebeam Gdns. *St H* —5C **64**
Whitebeam Wlk. *Wir* —2B **114**
Whitechapel. *L1* —5D **77** (6E **4**)
Whitefield Av. *L4* —3E **55**
Whitefield Clo. *Wir* —1B **116**
Whitefield Dri. *L32* —3B **22**
Whitefield La. *Tarb G* —4A **106**
Whitefield Rd. *L6* —2A **78**
Whitefield Rd. *Dent G* —3D **45**
Whitefield Sq. *L32* —3C **22**
Whitefield Way. *L6* —2A **78**
Whitegate Clo. *Know* —4D **41**
Whitehall Clo. *L4* —2E **55**
Whitehall Pl. *Frod* —5B **172**
(in two parts)
Whitehart Clo. *L4* —2B **56**
Whiteheath Way. *Wir* —3F **71**
Whitehedge Rd. *L19* —5B **124**
White Ho. Clo. *Hay* —2B **48**
Whitehouse Ind. Est. *White I* —1E **175**
Whitehouse La. *Hes* —1C **158**
Whitehouse Rd. *L13* —4B **80**
Whitelands Mdw. *Wir* —4E **93**
White Lodge Av. *L36* —3D **83**
White Lodge Clo. *Wir* —5D **163**
Whitely Gro. *L33* —5F **15**
White Mdw. Dri. *L23* —4A **10**
White Oak Lodge. *L19* —5F **123**
White Rock Ct. *L6* —2B **78**
White Rock St. *L6* —2B **78**
Whiteside Av. *St H* —3E **47**
Whiteside Clo. *L5* —1D **77**
Whiteside Clo. *Wir* —5A **94**
Whiteside Rd. *Hay* —2B **48**
Whitestone Clo. *Know* —1C **60**
White St. *L1* —1D **99**
White St. *Wid* —2A **152**
Whitethorn Dri. *L28* —3B **60**
Whitewell Dri. *Wir* —3F **93**
Whitewood Pk. *L9* —2D **37**
Whitfield Ct. *Birk* —5D **97**
Whitfield Gro. *Hay* —2A **48**
Whitfield La. *Wir* —1A **158**
Whitfield Rd. *Walt* —3A **36**
Whitfields Cross. —2F 133
Whitfield St. *Birk* —5D **97**
(in two parts)
Whitford Rd. *Birk* —5C **96**

Whitham Av. *L23* —2F **17**
Whithorn St. *L7* —1D **101**
Whitland Rd. *L6* —2D **79**
Whitley Clo. *Run* —2F **165**
Whitley Dri. *Wall* —1C **74**
Whitley St. *L3* —2B **76**
Whitman St. *L15* —2E **101**
Whitmoor Clo. *Rain* —5E **87**
Whitney Pl. *L25* —2C **126**
Whitney Rd. *L25* —1C **126**
Whitstable Pk. *Wid* —5E **109**
Whitstone Clo. *L18* —2E **125**
Whittaker Clo. *L13* —5F **79**
Whittaker St. *St H* —2D **67**
Whittier St. *L8* —2C **100**
Whittle Av. *Hay* —3A **48**
Whittle Clo. *L5* —5E **55**
Whittle St. *L5* —5E **55**
Whittle St. *St H* —2D **65**
Whittlewood Ct. *L33* —1F **23**
Wicket Clo. *L11* —3D **39**
Wickham Clo. *Wall* —4D **75**
Wicksten Dri. *Run* —5C **152**
Widdale Av. *Rain* —3D **87**
Widgeons Covert. *Wir* —5F **159**
Widmore Rd. *L25* —5C **104**
Widnes. —4B 132
Widnes Cricket Club Ground. —5B 110
Widnes Eastern By-Pass. *Wid* —1F **109**
Widnes Golf Course. —2E 131
Widnes Rd. *Wid & Cuer* —2F **133**
Widnes Vikings R.L.F.C. —4F 131
Wiend, The. *Birk* —3D **119**
Wiend, The. *Wir* —2A **142**
Wightman St. *L6* —3B **78**
Wignall Clo. *L32* —1E **39**
Wignall Pk. —1F 39
Wilberforce Rd. *L4* —2B **56**
Wilbraham Pl. *L5* —1D **77**
Wilbraham St. *Clo F* —3E **89**
Wilbraham St. *L5* —1D **77**
Wilbraham St. *Birk* —3E **97**
Wilburn St. *L4* —2F **55**
Wilbur St. *St H* —4E **67**
Wilcock Clo. *L5* —1D **77**
Wilcote Clo. *Wid* —5C **110**
Wildbrook Dri. *Birk* —4D **73**
Wildcherry Gdns. *St H* —4C **64**
Wilde St. *L3* —4E **77** (3G **5**)
Wilding Av. *Run* —5B **152**
Wild Pl. *Boot* —1E **35**
Wilfer Clo. *L7* —1C **100**
Wilfred Owen Dri. *Birk* —2E **95**
Wilkes Av. *Wir* —3B **72**
Wilkie St. *L15* —2D **101**
Wilkinson Clo. *Wid* —2A **152**
Wilkinson Ct. *L15* —1D **101**
Wilkin St. *L4* —4E **55**
Willan St. *Pren* —5B **96**
Willard St. *Boot* —2D **35**
Willaston. —5A 170
Willaston Dri. *L26* —1A **148**
Willaston Grn. M. *Will* —5A **170**
Willaston Rd. *L4* —2B **56**
Willaston Rd. *More* —5D **71**
Willaston Rd. *Thor H* —5D **161**
Willedstan Av. *L23* —2E **17**
William Brown St. *L3* —4D **77** (3F **5**)
William Harvey Clo. *Boot* —2F **19**
William Henry St. *Boot* —1B **54**
William Henry St. *L3* —3E **77** (1H **5**)
William Morris Av. *Boot* —3E **35**
William Moult St. *L5* —1D **77**
William Rd. *Hay* —2F **47**
William Roberts Av. *L32* —3C **22**
William Roberts Recreation Cen. —2E 57
Williams Av. *Boot* —3E **35**
Williamson Art Gallery & Mus. —4B 96
Williamson Ct. *L25* —3C **126**
Williamson Sq. *L1* —5D **77** (5E **5**)
Williamson St. *L1* —5D **77** (5E **4**)
Williamson St. *St H* —4C **46**
Williamson Student Village. *L7* —5A **78**
Williams St. *Prsct* —5D **63**
William St. *St H* —4A **46**
William St. *Birk* —3E **97**
William St. *Wall* —4E **75**
William St. *Wid* —2C **132**
William Wall Rd. *L21* —3B **18**
Willingdon Rd. *L16* —5E **81**
Willington Av. *Wir* —2E **171**
Willink Rd. *St H* —1C **46**
Willis Clo. *Whis* —4D **85**
Willis La. *Whis* —4D **85**
Williton Rd. *L16* —4E **103**
Willmer Rd. *L4* —4B **56**
Willmer Rd. *Birk* —4C **96**
Willoughby Dri. *St H* —3B **64**
Willoughby Rd. *Wat* —4E **17**
Willoughby Rd. *B'grn* —4E **81**
Willoughby Rd. *Wall* —2F **73**
Willow Av. *Kirkby* —2C **22**
Willow Av. *Huy* —1E **105**
Willow Av. *Whis* —3E **85**
Willow Av. *Wid* —2B **132**
Willowbank Clo. *L36* —1C **82**
Willowbank Rd. *Birk* —1D **119**
Willowbank Rd. *Wir* —1B **142**
Willow Clo. *Run* —3B **166**
Willowcroft Rd. *Wall* —3C **74**
Willowdale Rd. *Walt* —4A **36**
Willowdale Rd. *Moss H* —4F **101**
Willow Dene. *L11* —2D **39**
Willow Grn. *L25* —5F **103**
Willow Gro. *Prsct* —1E **85**
Willow Gro. *W'tree* —1A **102**
Willow Gro. *Wir* —2D **93**
Willowherb Clo. *L26* —2D **127**
Willow Hey. *L31* —3E **13**
Willow Ho. *L21* —2A **34**
Willow Lea. *Pren* —5A **96**
Willowmeade. *L11* —5B **38**
Willow Moss Clo. *Wir* —4B **72**
Willow Pk. *Wir* —5C **92**
Willow Rd. *L15* —1D **101**
Willow Rd. *St H* —5C **44**
Willow Rd. *Hay* —1E **49**
Willows, The. *Clo F* —2C **88**
Willows, The. *Frod* —5C **172**
Willows, The. *Wall* —4E **51**
Willow Tree Av. *Clo F* —2D **89**
Willow Way. *Cros* —5E **9**
Willow Way. *Crox* —3D **39**
Wills Av. *L31* —5C **6**
Willsford Av. *L31* —2B **22**
Wilmere La. *Wid* —4A **110**
Wilne Rd. *Wall* —5A **52**
Wilsden Rd. *Wid* —3B **130**
Wilson Av. *Wall* —2E **75**
Wilson Bus. Cen. *L36* —5A **84**
Wilson Clo. *St H* —5E **45**
Wilson Clo. *Wid* —3D **133**
Wilson Gro. *L19* —1C **144**
Wilson Rd. *L36* —4F **83**
Wilson Rd. *Prsct* —2D **85**
Wilson Rd. *Wall* —2E **75**
Wilson's La. *L21* —5B **18**
Wilstan Av. *Wir* —2D **141**
Wilton Grange. *Wir* —2A **112**
Wilton Gro. *L13* —4A **80**
Wilton Rd. *L36* —5D **83**
Wilton Rd. *Birk* —3A **120**
Wilton's Dri. *Know* —5C **40**
Wilton St. *L3* —3E **77** (2H **5**)
Wilton St. *Wall* —2B **74**
Wiltshire Dri. *Boot* —2D **19**
Wiltshire Gdns. *St H* —1F **65**
Wimbledon St. *L15* —2E **101**
Wimbledon St. *Wall* —1B **74**
Wimborne Av. *Wir* —2A **138**
Wimborne Clo. *L14* —5B **60**
Wimborne Pl. *L14* —1B **82**
Wimborne Rd. *L14* —5A **60**
Wimborne Way. *Wir* —5D **115**
Wimbrick Clo. *Wir* —1F **93**
Wimbrick Hey. *Wir* —1F **93**
Wimpole St. *L7* —4B **78**
Winchester Av. *Ain* —2D **21**
Winchester Av. *L22* —3C **16**
Winchester Clo. *Wltn* —4B **126**
Winchester Dri. *Wall* —2F **73**
Winchester Pl. *Wid* —4C **130**
Winchester Rd. *L6* —5C **56**
Winchester Wlk. *Huy* —2A **84**
Winchfield Rd. *L15* —3F **101**
Windbourne Rd. *L17* —2B **122**
Windermere Av. *St H* —5A **30**
Windermere Av. *Wid* —5B **110**
Windermere Ct. Birk —4C 96
(off Penrith St.)
Windermere Dri. *Kirkby* —1D **23**
Windermere Dri. *L31* —5E **7**
Windermere Dri. *W Der* —2C **58**
Windermere Pl. *St H* —5A **30**
Windermere Rd. *Hay* —2B **48**
Windermere Rd. *Pren* —4C **94**
Windermere St. *L5* —5A **56**
Windermere St. *Wid* —5B **110**
Windermere Ter. *L8* —4B **100**
Windfield Clo. *L33* —4F **15**
Windfield Grn. *L19* —4C **144**
Windfield Rd. *L19* —4C **144**
Windle Ash. *L31* —5C **6**
Windle Av. *L23* —1A **18**
Windlebrook Cres. *Wind* —2B **44**
Windle City. *St H* —2F **45**
Windle Gro. *Wind* —2C **44**
Windle Hall Dri. *St H* —1E **45**
Windlehurst. —1F 45
Windlehurst Av. *St H* —2E **45**
Windle Pilkington Cen. *St H* —4F **45**
Windles Green. —5C 10
Windleshaw Rd. *Dent G* —3D **45**
Windle St. *St H* —3F **45**
Windle Va. *Dent G* —3E **45**
Windmill Av. *L23* —5F **9**
Windmill Clo. *L33* —5E **15**
Windmill Gdns. *St H* —4D **47**
Windmill Gdns. *Pren* —1C **94**
Windmill Hill. —5C 154
Windmill Hill Av. E. *Wind H* —5D **155**
Windmill Hill Av. N. *Run* —4D **155**
Windmill Hill Av. S. *Wind H* —1C **168**
Windmill Hill Av. W. *Wind H* —5C **154**
Windmill La. *Pres H* —4F **169**
Windmill Shop. Cen. *Wid* —4B **132**
Windmill St. *Run* —5B **152**
Window La. *L19* —3C **144**
Windsor Av. *L21* —5A **18**
Windsor Clo. *Boot* —5F **11**
Windsor Clo. *Grea* —1D **115**
Windsor Clo. *New F* —5A **120**
Windsor Ct. *Boot* —3E **35**
Windsor Dri. *Huy* —3A **82**
Windsor Gro. *Run* —2B **166**
Windsor M. *Wir* —5A **120**
Windsor Pk. Rd. *L10* —2E **21**
Windsor Rd. *Boot* —3E **35**
Windsor Rd. *Cros* —5D **9**
Windsor Rd. *Mag* —1C **12**
Windsor Rd. *St H* —5D **45**
Windsor Rd. *Walt* —2A **36**
Windsor Rd. *Huy* —4A **82**
Windsor Rd. *Prsct* —2F **85**
Windsor Rd. *Tue* —5D **57**

Windsor Rd. Wid —5A 110
Windsor St. L8 —2E 99
Windsor St. Pren —4C 96
Windsor St. Wall —2B 52
Windsor Vw. L8 —2B 100
Windus St. St H —5E 45
Windy Arbor. —1C 106
Windy Arbor Brow. Whis —1C 106
Windy Arbor Clo. Whis —5D 85
Windy Arbor Rd. Whis —4D 85
Windy Bank. Port S —1A 142
Wineva Gdns. L23 —2F 17
Winfield Way. Wid —4B 132
Winford St. Wall —3D 75
Winfrith Clo. Wir —4F 141
Winfrith Dri. Wir —5F 141
Winfrith Rd. L25 —5C 104
Wingate Av. St H —5D 65
Wingate Clo. Pren —5E 95
Wingate Rd. Kirkby —1F 23
Wingate Rd. Aig —2E 123
Wingate Rd. Wir —5E 163
Wingate Towers. L36 —2D 83
Wingate Wlk. L33 —2F 23
Wingfield Clo. L29 —2D 11
Wingrave Way. L11 —2B 58
Winhill. L25 —5A 104
Winifred Rd. L10 —1B 38
Winifred St. L7 —5B 78
Winkle St. L8 —4F 99
Winmoss Dri. L33 —5F 15
Winnington Rd. Wir —1A 112
Winnows, The. Halt B —1D 167
Winser St. Wir —1B 142
Winsford Clo. Hay —1F 49
Winsford Dri. Btnwd —4E 69
Winsford Rd. L13 —5E 57
Winsham Clo. L32 —5E 23
Winsham Rd. L32 —5E 23
Winskill Rd. L11 —2A 58
Winslade Ct. L4 —1B 56
Winslade Rd. L4 —2B 56
Winslow Clo. Wind H —2D 169
Winslow St. L4 —2F 55
Winstanley Ho. Wir —5B 120 (off Winstanley Rd.)
Winstanley Rd. L22 —3E 17
Winstanley Rd. Wir —5B 120
Winster Dri. L27 —5A 106
Winston Av. St H —1B 68
Winston Dri. Pren —4C 94
Winstone Rd. L14 —2A 82
Winston Gro. Wir —1E 93
Winterburn Cres. L12 —4C 58
Winterburn Heights. L12 —4D 59 (off Winterburn Cres.)
Winter Gdns., The. Wall —3A 52 (off Atherton St.)
Winter Gro. St H —5B 48
Winterhey Av. Wall —3B 74
Winterley Dri. L26 —1A 148
Winter St. L6 —3A 78
Winthrop Pk. Pren —4E 95
Winton Clo. Wall —3F 51
Winton Gro. Wind H —1D 169
Winwick Vw. C Grn —2D 69
Winwood Hall. L25 —3A 126
Wirral Bus. Cen. Birk —4C 74
Wirral Bus. Pk., The. Wir —1F 115
Wirral Clo. Wir —4F 141
Wirral Country Pk. —5F 135
Wirral Gdns. Wir —4F 141
Wirral Ladies Golf Course, The. —3E 95
Wirral Leisure Pk. Wir —4E 143
Wirral Mt. Wall —1F 73
Wirral Mt. Wir —4D 113
Wirral Tennis Cen. —4D 73
Wirral Vw. L19 —5F 123
Wirral Vs. Wall —5E 51
Wirral Way. Pren —4C 94
Wirral Way. Wir —2D 157
Wisenholme Clo. Beech —1E 173
Wisteria Way. St H —4A 68
Witham Clo. Boot —1A 20
Withburn Clo. Wir —4E 93
Withensfield. Wall —5B 52
Withens La. Wall —5B 52
Withens Rd. L31 —4D 7
Withens, The. L28 —4B 60
Withert Av. Wir —4D 119
Withington Rd. L24 —4F 147
Withington Rd. Wall —3C 74
Withins Rd. Hay —1E 49
Withnell Clo. L13 —4B 80
Withnell Rd. L13 —4B 80
Withy Clo. Frod —5C 172
Witley Av. Wir —5E 71
Witley Clo. Wir —5E 71
Witney Clo. Wir —1C 114
Wittenham Clo. Wir —5F 93
Wittering La. Wir —2D 157
Witton Rd. L13 —5D 57
Witt Rd. Wid —5A 132
Wivern Pl. Run —4B 152
Woburn Clo. L13 —1F 79
Woburn Clo. Hay —1F 49
Woburn Dri. Cron —3D 109
Woburn Grn. L13 —2F 79
Woburn Hill. L13 —2F 79
Woburn Pl. Birk —2F 119
Woburn Rd. Wall —5B 52
Wokefield Way. St H —4C 44
Wokingham Gro. L36 —1E 105
Wolfenden Av. Boot —3E 35
Wolfe Rd. St H —1E 67
Wolferton Clo. Upt —2B 94
Wolfe St. L8 —4E 99
Wolfrick Dri. Wir —1B 162
Wolseley Rd. St H —3F 45
Wolsey St. L20 —2C 54
Wolstenholme Sq. L1 —1D 99 (7F 5)
Wolverton Dri. Wind H —1D 169
Wolverton St. L6 —5B 56
Woodall Dri. Run —1B 166
Wood Av. Boot —3E 35
Woodbank Clo. L16 —1F 103
Woodbank Pk. Pren —5E 95
Woodberry Clo. L33 —4F 15
Woodberry Clo. Pren —5D 95
Woodbine St. L5 —4D 55
Woodbourne Rd. L14 —2D 81
Woodbridge Av. L26 —2D 127
Woodbrook Av. L9 —1F 35
Woodburn Boulevd. Wir —4E 119
Woodburn Dri. Wir —4F 157
Woodchurch. —2C 116
Woodchurch Ct. Birk —1C 118
Woodchurch La. Birk —2B 118
Woodchurch La. Upt —4C 116
Woodchurch Leisure Cen. —1C 116
Woodchurch Rd. L13 —2A 80
Woodchurch Rd. Birk —1C 118
Woodchurch Rd. Upt & Pren —3B 116
Wood Clo. L32 —3D 23
Wood Clo. Birk —2D 97
Woodcote Bank. Birk —5F 119
Woodcote Clo. L33 —1A 24
Woodcotes, The. Wir —4D 163
Woodcot La. Wir —1F 157
Woodcroft Dri. Wir —5F 137
Woodcroft La. Wir —4E 119
Woodcroft Rd. L15 —2D 101
Woodcroft Way. Clo F —2C 88
Woodend. —1B 152
Woodend. Hals P —1E 107
Woodend. Murd —3E 169
Woodend. Wir —2F 137
Woodend Av. Cros —4E 9
Woodend Av. Mag —3C 12
Woodend Av. Hunts X & Speke —1C 146
Woodend Ct. Wid —2D 133
Woodend La. L24 —3C 146
Wood End Park. —5F 123
Woodene Clo. L32 —1A 40
Woodfarm Hey. L28 —3A 60
Woodfield Av. Wir —4E 119
Woodfield Rd. Walt —3F 35
Woodfield Rd. Beb —4A 142
Woodfield Rd. Hes —3E 137
Woodfield Rd. Huy —4C 82
Woodford Clo. Run —4B 166
Woodford Rd. L14 —2E 81
Woodford Rd. Wind —2C 44
Woodford Rd. Wir —4B 120
Woodgate. L27 —3C 104
Woodger St. L19 —2C 144
Wood Grn. Pren —1C 94
Wood Grn. Prsct —5C 62
Woodgreen Rd. L13 —2A 80
Wood Gro. L13 —4F 79
Woodhall Av. Wall —2D 75
Woodhall Rd. L13 —3A 80
Woodhatch Rd. Brook —5A 168
Woodhead Rd. Wir —1C 142
Woodhead St. Wir —5B 120
Woodhey Ct. Wir —4F 119
Woodhey Gro. Wir —5F 119
Woodhey Rd. L19 —4A 124
Woodhey Rd. Wir —5F 119
Woodhill. Wir —5B 94
Woodhouse Clo. L4 —4E 55
Woodin Rd. Birk —4A 120
Woodkind Hey. Wir —5A 142
Woodland Av. Wid —3F 131
Woodland Av. Wir —2D 91
Woodland Dri. Wall —4C 52
Woodland Dri. Wir —1A 116
Woodland Gro. Birk —4F 119
Woodland Rd. Mell —1A 22
Woodland Rd. S'frth —1F 33
Woodland Rd. Walt —3C 56
Woodland Rd. Birk —4F 119
Woodland Rd. Halew —5E 127
Woodland Rd. Upt —1A 116
Woodland Rd. W Kir —4E 113
Woodlands Dri. Wir —3C 138
Woodlands Pk. L12 —1A 80
Woodlands Rd. Faz —1D 37
Woodlands Rd. St H —2B 46
Woodlands Rd. Aig —2E 123
Woodlands Rd. Huy —4B 82
Woodlands Rd. Irby —2D 137
Woodlands Sq. L27 —5F 105
Woodlands, The. Birk —4D 97
Woodlands, The. Prsct —4F 63
Woodlands, The. Wir —4F 93
Woodland Vw. L23 —3A 10
Woodland Wlk. Cas —1A 168
Woodland Wlk. Wir —1C 162
Wood La. Brook —4C 168
Wood La. Grea —4D 93
Wood La. Huy —4B 84
Wood La. N'ley —4F 105
Wood La. Prsct —1B 84
Wood La. Sut W —1F 173
Wood La. Wall —5E 51
Wood La. Will —4A 170
Wood Lea. L12 —5E 39
Woodlea Clo. Wir —5D 163
Woodlee Rd. L25 —5C 104
Woodleigh Clo. L31 —2B 6
Woodley Rd. L31 —4C 12
Woodpecker Clo. L12 —2F 59
Woodpecker Clo. Wir —4D 93
Woodpecker Dri. L26 —2E 127

Woodridge. *Wind H*—1C **168**
Wood Rd. *L26*—5E **127**
Woodrock Rd. *L25*—2B **126**
Woodruff St. *L8*—5F **99**
Woodside Av. *St H*—5F **29**
Woodside Av. *Wir*—2E **93**
Woodside Bus. Pk. *Birk*—2F **97**
Woodside Clo. *L12*—3B **58**
Woodside Ferry App. *Birk*—2F **97**
Woodside Rd. *Hay*—1E **49**
Woodside Rd. *Wir*—1E **137**
Woodside St. *L7*—5B **78**
Woodside Way. *L33*—5F **15**
Woodsorrel Rd. *L15*—2B **102**
Woodsorrel Rd. *Birk*—2F **95**
Woodstack St. *St H*—4E **67**
Woodstock Gro. *Wid*—2D **131**
Woodstock Rd. *Wall*—3A **74**
Woodstock St. *L5*—1D **77**
Wood St. *L1*—5D **77** (6F **5**)
Wood St. *S'frth*—1B **34**
Wood St. *St H*—4C **46**
Wood St. *Birk*—2D **97**
Wood St. *Gars*—1C **144**
Wood St. *Hoy*—4B **90**
Wood St. *Port S*—2B **142**
Wood St. *Prsct*—5D **63**
Wood St. *Wid*—3C **132**
Woodthorn Clo. *Dar*—3F **155**
Wood Va. *St H*—5E **65**
Woodvale Clo. *Pren*—1C **94**
Woodvale Ct. *Wir*—3A **116**
Woodvale Rd. *W Der*—5F **39**
Woodvale Rd. *Wltn*—2B **126**
Woodview. *Know*—5E **41**
Woodview Av. *Wall*—4D **75**
Woodview Cres. *Wid*—4A **130**
Wood Vw. Rd. *L25*—5F **103**
Woodview Rd. *Wid*—4A **130**
Woodville Av. *L23*—2D **17**
Woodville Pl. *Wid*—3D **131**
Woodville Rd. *Birk*—5C **96**
Woodville St. *St H*—4B **46**
(in two parts)
Woodville Ter. *L6*—1B **78**
Woodward Rd. *Know I*—1C **24**
Woodward Rd. *Birk*—4A **120**
Woodway. *Wir*—5E **93**
Woodyear Rd. *Wir*—3E **163**
Woolacombe Av. *Sut L*—1C **88**
Woolacombe Rd. *L16*—3D **103**
Wooler Clo. *Wir*—1C **92**
Woolfall Clo. *L36*—2B **82**
Woolfall Cres. *L36*—2B **82**
Woolfall Heath. —1C 82
Woolfall Heath Av. *L36*—1C **82**
Woolfall Heights. *L36*—1C **82**
Woolfall Ter. *L21*—2A **34**
Woolhope Rd. *L4*—1B **56**
Woolley Clo. *Frod*—3D **173**
Woolston Rd. *Hay*—1D **49**
Woolton. —2A 126
Woolton Golf Course. —4B 126
Woolton Hill. —5F 103
Woolton Hill Rd. *L25*—5E **103**
Woolton M. *L25*—2F **125**
Woolton Mt. *L25*—1A **126**
Woolton Park. —5A 104
Woolton Pk. *L25*—5A **104**
Woolton Pk. Clo. *L25*—1A **126**
Woolton Rd. *Gars & Aller*—1C **144**
Woolton Rd. *W'tree*—3B **102**
Woolton Rd. *Wltn*—4E **125**
Woolton St. *L25*—2A **126**
(in two parts)
Woolton Swimming Pool. —2A 126
Woolton Views. *L25*—4D **127**
Worcester Av. *Wat*—3C **16**
Worcester Av. *Old S*—4D **57**
Worcester Clo. *St H*—1F **65**
Worcester Ct. *Boot*—5D **35**
Worcester Dri. *L13*—4D **57**
Worcester Dri. N. *L13*—4D **57**
Worcester Rd. *Boot*—4D **35**
Worcester Rd. *Pren*—1D **95**
Wordsworth Av. *Birk*—3F **119**
Wordsworth Av. *Sut M*—3A **88**
Wordsworth Av. *Wid*—4F **131**
Wordsworth St. *Boot*—3A **34**
Wordsworth St. *L8*—2B **100**
Wordsworth Wlk. *Wir*—1B **134**
Wordsworth Way. *L36*—5F **83**
World of Glass Mus. —5A 46
Worrow Clo. *L11*—5B **38**
Worrow Rd. *L11*—5B **38**
Worsley Brow. —3E 67
Worsley Brow. *St H*—3E **67**
Worsley St. *Hay*—2F **47**
Worthing St. *L22*—3C **16**
Worthington Clo. *Pal*—3A **168**
Worthington St. *L8*—3D **99**
Wortley Rd. *L10*—1E **37**
Wray Av. *Clo F*—2D **89**
Wrayburn Clo. *L7*—1C **100**
Wrekin Clo. *L25*—3B **126**
Wrekin Dri. *L10*—3E **21**
Wrenbury Clo. *Pren*—2F **117**
Wrenbury Clo. *Sut W*—1F **173**
Wrenbury St. *L7*—4C **78**
Wren Clo. *Pal*—4A **168**
Wrenfield Gro. *L17*—2C **122**
Wren Gro. *L26*—3E **127**
Wright Cres. *Wid*—2A **152**
Wrights La. *Cuer*—2F **133**
Wrights Ter. *L15*—2A **102**
Wright St. *L5*—1D **77**
Wright St. *Wall*—2D **75**
Wrigley Rd. *Hay*—2E **49**
Wroxham Clo. *Wir*—5A **94**
Wroxham Ct. *Wir*—4A **94**
Wroxham Dri. *Wir*—5A **94**
Wroxham Way. *Wir*—5A **94**
Wryneck Clo. *St H*—4B **64**
Wrynose Rd. *Old I*—2E **163**
Wulstan St. *L4*—4D **55**
Wycherley Rd. *Birk*—1D **119**
Wycherley St. *Prsct*—5D **63**
Wycliffe Rd. *L4*—4C **56**
Wycliffe Rd. *Hay*—1E **49**
Wycliffe St. *Birk*—2F **119**
Wye Clo. *Birk*—1F **119**
Wyedale Rd. *Hay*—1C **48**
Wye St. *L5*—5F **55**
Wykeham St. *L4*—3D **55**
Wykeham Way. *L4*—4D **55**
Wyken Gro. *St H*—3C **46**
Wyke Rd. *Prsct*—1E **85**
Wyllin Rd. *L33*—3A **24**
Wylva Av. *L23*—2A **18**
Wylva Rd. *L4*—5A **56**
Wyncroft Clo. *Wid*—5C **130**
Wyncroft Rd. *Wid*—5C **130**
Wyncroft St. *L8*—5A **100**
Wyndale Clo. *L18*—1B **124**
Wyndcote Rd. *L18*—4B **102**
Wyndham Av. *L14*—4F **81**
Wyndham Rd. *Wall*—1D **73**
Wyndham St. *L4*—1F **55**
Wynne Rd. *St H*—3E **45**
Wynnstay Av. *L31*—4D **7**
Wynnstay St. *L8*—3A **100**
Wynstay Rd. *Wir*—3C **90**
Wynwood Pk. *L36*—4C **82**
Wyre Rd. *L5*—4F **55**
Wyrescourt Rd. *L12*—1D **81**
Wyresdale Av. *St H*—1E **45**
Wyresdale Rd. *L9*—1B **36**
Wysall Clo. *St H*—3D **47**
Wyswall Clo. *L26*—2E **127**
Wythburn Cres. *St H*—5B **30**
Wythburn Gro. *Beech*—5E **167**
Wyvern Rd. *Wir*—1F **93**

Yanwath St. *L8*—2B **100**
Yarcombe Clo. *L26*—3F **127**
Yardley Dri. *Wir*—1A **162**
Yardley Rd. *Know I*—4C **24**
Yarrow Av. *L31*—5F **7**
Yates Ct. *Prsct*—1D **85**
Yates St. *L8*—4E **99**
Yates Wlk. *L8*—4E **99**
Yeadon Wlk. *L24*—4B **146**
Yelverton Clo. *L26*—3F **127**
Yelverton Rd. *L4*—4C **56**
Yelverton Rd. *Birk*—1D **119**
Yeoman Cotts. *Wir*—5C **90**
Ye Priory Ct. *L25*—3E **125**
Yew Bank Rd. *L16*—2D **103**
Yewdale Av. *St H*—4B **30**
Yewdale Pk. *Pren*—5B **96**
Yewdale Rd. *L9*—4B **36**
Yew Tree Av. *Newt W*—4F **49**
Yew Tree Av. *St H*—5C **66**
Yew Tree Clo. *L12*—5E **59**
Yew Tree Clo. *Wir*—2A **116**
Yew Tree Grn. *L31*—1B **22**
Yew Tree La. *L12*—1E **81**
Yewtree La. *Wir*—3B **112**
Yew Tree Rd. *Walt*—4F **35**
Yew Tree Rd. *Aller*—1D **125**
Yew Tree Rd. *Beb*—3E **141**
Yew Tree Rd. *Hunts X*—4C **126**
Yew Tree Rd. *Huy*—5D **83**
Yew Tree Rd. *More*—4F **71**
Yew Way. *Wir*—5F **71**
Yorkaster Rd. *L18*—3C **124**
York Av. *Cros*—1D **17**
York Av. *L22*—5D **17**
York Av. *Seft P*—3D **101**
York Av. *Wall*—3D **75**
York Av. *Wir*—1B **134**
York Clo. *Boot*—5F **11**
York Clo. *St H*—4F **45**
(in two parts)
York Cotts. *L25*—5B **104**
York Ho. *L17*—4D **101**
York Pl. *L22*—5D **17**
York Pl. *Run*—5B **152**
York Rd. *Cros*—1E **17**
York Rd. *Mag*—3D **13**
York Rd. *Huy*—3A **84**
York Rd. *Wall*—4D **75**
York Rd. *Wid*—4C **130**
Yorkshire Gdns. *St H*—1F **65**
York St. *L1*—1D **99** (7E **5**)
York St. *Walt*—5F **35**
York St. *Wat*—5D **17**
York St. *Gars*—3C **144**
York St. *Run*—5A **152**
York St. *Wir*—2D **143**
York Ter. *L5*—5E **55**
York Way. *Gars*—3D **145**
York Way. *Huy*—3A **84**
Youatt Av. *Prsct*—2E **85**
Youens Way. *L14*—2E **81**

Zander Gro. *L12*—5F **39**
Zara Ct. *Hay*—1C **48**
Zetland Rd. *L18*—4F **101**
Zetland Rd. *Wall*—4F **51**
Zig Zag Rd. *L12*—1D **81**
Zig Zag Rd. *Wall*—5B **52**
Zircon Cres. *L21*—5C **18**

HOSPITALS and HOSPICES covered by this atlas

N.B. Where Hospitals and Hospices are not named on the map, the reference given is for the road in which they are situated.

ALDER HEY CHILDREN'S HOSPITAL —2C **80**
Eaton Rd.
West Derby
LIVERPOOL
L12 2AP
Tel: 0151 2284811

ARROWE PARK HOSPITAL —3A **116**
Arrowe Park Rd.
WIRRAL
Merseyside
CH49 5PE
Tel: 0151 6785111

ASHTON HOUSE HOSPITAL —5B **96**
26 Village Rd., Oxton
BIRKENHEAD
Merseyside
CH43 5SR
Tel: 0151 653 9660

BROADGREEN HOSPITAL —4C **80**
Thomas Dri.
LIVERPOOL
L14 3LB
Tel: 0151 7062000

CARDIOTHORACIC CENTRE (BROADGREEN HOSPITAL) —4C **80**
Thomas Dri.
LIVERPOOL
L14 3PE
Tel: 0151 2281616

CLAIRE HOUSE CHILDREN'S HOSPICE —1E **161**
Clatterbridge Rd.
WIRRAL
Merseyside
CH63 4JD
Tel: 0151 3344626

CLATTERBRIDGE HOSPITAL —1E **161**
Clatterbridge Rd.
WIRRAL
Merseyside
CH63 4JY
Tel: 0151 3344000

FAIRFIELD HOSPITAL —3E **29**
Crank Rd., Crank
ST HELENS
Merseyside
WA11 7RS
Tel: 01744 739311

HALTON GENERAL HOSPITAL —4F **167**
Hospital Way
RUNCORN
Cheshire
WA7 2DA
Tel: 01928 714567

HALTON HAVEN —5C **168**
Barnfield Av.
Murdishaw
RUNCORN
Cheshire
WA7 6EP
Tel: 01928 719454

HIGHFIELD HOSPITAL —2A **132**
Highfield Rd.
WIDNES
Cheshire
WA8 7DJ
Tel: 0151 4242103

HOYLAKE COTTAGE HOSPITAL —3C **90**
Birkenhead Rd., Meols
WIRRAL
Merseyside
CH47 5AQ
Tel: 0151 6323381

KEVIN WHITE UNIT —3D **101**
Smithdown Rd.
LIVERPOOL
L9 7JP
Tel: 0151 3308074

LIVERPOOL UNIVERSITY DENTAL HOSPITAL —4F **77** (4J **5**)
Pembroke Pl.
LIVERPOOL
L3 5PS
Tel: 0151 7062000

LIVERPOOL WOMEN'S HOSPITAL —1A **100**
Crown St.
LIVERPOOL
L8 7SS
Tel: 0151 708 9988

LOURDES HOSPITAL —4F **101**
57 Greenbank Rd.
LIVERPOOL
L18 1HQ
Tel: 0151 7337123

MARIE CURIE CENTRE, LIVERPOOL —2B **126**
Speke Rd., Woolton
LIVERPOOL
L25 8QA
Tel: 0151 4281395

MARTLEW DAY HOSPITAL —1C **86**
Elton Head Rd.
ST HELENS
Merseyside
WA9 5BZ
Tel: 0151 4263465

MOSSLEY HILL HOSPITAL —5E **101**
Park Av., Mossley Hill
LIVERPOOL
L18 8BU
Tel: 0151 2503000

MURRAYFIELD BUPA HOSPITAL —2D **139**
Holmwood Dri., Heswall
WIRRAL
Merseyside
CH61 1AU
Tel: 0151 6487000

PARK LODGE DAY HOSPITAL —1D **79**
Orphan Dri.
LIVERPOOL
L6 7UN
Tel: 0151 2876934

Hospitals & Hospices

RATHBONE HOSPITAL —4A **80**
Mill La.
Old Swan
LIVERPOOL
L13 4AW
Tel: 0151 2503000

ROYAL LIVERPOOL UNIVERSITY HOSPITAL —4F **77** (3J **5**)
Prescot St.
LIVERPOOL
L7 8XP
Tel: 0151 7062000

ST BARTHOLOMEW'S DAY HOSPITAL —4C **82**
Station Rd.
Huyton
LIVERPOOL
L36 4HU
Tel: 0151 4896241

ST CATHERINE'S HOSPITAL (BIRKENHEAD) —5D **97**
Church Rd.
BIRKENHEAD
Merseyside
CH42 0LQ
Tel: 0151 6787272

ST HELENS HOSPITAL (MERSEYSIDE) —2C **66**
Marshalls Cross Rd.
ST HELENS
Merseyside
WA9 3DA
Tel: 0151 4261600

ST JOHN'S HOSPICE IN WIRRAL —1E **161**
Mount Rd.
Higher Bebington
WIRRAL
Merseyside
CH63 6JE
Tel: 0151 3342778

ST JOSEPH'S HOSPICE. —3A **10**
Ince Rd.
LIVERPOOL
L23 4UE
Tel: 0151 9243812

SCOTT CLINIC —1C **86**
Rainhill Rd.
ST HELENS
Merseyside
WA9 5BD
Tel: 0151 4306300

SIR ALFRED JONES MEMORIAL HOSPITAL —1C **144**
Church Rd., Garston
LIVERPOOL
L19 2LP
Tel: 0151 2503000

UNIVERSITY HOSPITAL AINTREE —1E **37**
Longmoor La.
LIVERPOOL
L9 7AL
Tel: 0151 525 5980

VICTORIA CENTRAL HOSPITAL —2B **74**
Mill La.
WALLASEY
Merseyside
CH44 5UF
Tel: 0151 6785111

WALTON HOSPITAL DAY SURGICAL UNIT & OUTPATIENTS —5F **3**
Rice La.
LIVERPOOL
L9 1AE
Tel: 0151 529 4895

WATERLOO DAY HOSPITAL —4E **17**
Park Rd.
Waterloo
LIVERPOOL
L22 3XR
Tel: 0151 9287243

WHISTON HOSPITAL —2F **85**
Warrington Rd.
PRESCOT
Merseyside
L35 5DR
Tel: 0151 4261600

WILLOWBROOK HOSPICE —4A **64**
Portico La.
PRESCOT
Merseyside
L35 7JS
Tel: 0151 4308736

WILLOW HOUSE RESOURCE CENTRE FOR THE ELDERLY —3E **85**
168 Dragon La.
PRESCOT
Merseyside
L35 3QY
Tel: 0151 4306048

WOODLANDS DAY HOSPICE —2D **37**
Longmoor La.
LIVERPOOL
L9 7LA
Tel: 0151 5292299

ZOE'S PLACE - BABY HOSPICE —1E **81**
Yew Tree La.
LIVERPOOL
L12 9HH
Tel: 0151 2280353